TEACHER'S EXAMINATION GUIDE

ALGEBRA AND TRIGONOM-ETRY is a comprehensive course in second-year algebra, covering the standard scope-and-sequence topics.

The new and innovative full-color design, use of photographs, color bands, and tinted boxes, highlight the features of the text.

READY FOR (See page 379)
Exercises keyed to previous sections preview skills needed in the upcoming chapter.

CHAPTER OPENING
(See page 244)
An attractive full-color photograph begins each chapter.

LESSON DEVELOPMENT
(See pages 566–567)
Lessons are made up of single-concept components, each using the unique *Example/Try This* format. Important information, such as theorems, definitions, and problem-solving hints, are highlighted in tinted boxes.

EXERCISE SETS
(See pages 452–453)
Three levels of exercises make up each exercise set: *Exercises, Extension,* and *Challenge.*

REVIEWS AND TESTS
(See pages 377–378)
Each chapter ends with a *Chapter Review,* keyed to the sections of the chapter, and a *Chapter Test.* Five *Cumulative Reviews* are spaced throughout the text. These are truly cumulative, reviewing concepts back to Chapter 1.

CALCULATORS (See page 495)
Using a Calculator, with examples and practice problems, shows how to use calculators to solve algebra problems.

CAREERS (See page 496)
Attractive full-color pages show algebra in different careers. Applications problems are included.

CONSUMER APPLICATIONS
(See page 549)
Arithmetic and algebra skills are applied to consumer topics.

COMPUTER ACTIVITIES
(See pages 730–741)
Seven BASIC programming lessons show how to use computers to solve algebra problems.

SUPPLEMENTS
(See pages T82–T83)
Material for applications, practice, enrichment, computers and video cassette reviews provide a complete teacher support package.

Teacher's Edition

ALGEBRA
AND TRIGONOMETRY

MERVIN L. KEEDY
MARVIN L. BITTINGER
STANLEY A. SMITH
LUCY J. ORFAN

ADDISON-WESLEY PUBLISHING COMPANY

MENLO PARK, CALIFORNIA   READING, MASSACHUSETTS   LONDON
AMSTERDAM   DON MILLS, ONTARIO   SYDNEY

ABOUT THE PHOTOGRAPHS

The full-color photographs that appear on the cover and on the first page of each chapter serve to illustrate a variety of well-designed and manufactured objects in the physical world. As the students in your class learn algebraic skills and apply them in applications problems, the photographs will remind them of the many uses that mathematics has in today's world. The photographs illustrate applications in the following categories.

ARCHITECTURE AND ENGINEERING   The photograph on the cover is of a radio telescope. The first page of Chapter 1 shows the Franklin Avenue office complex in Garden City, New York; Chapter 5 begins with the Occidental Petroleum Building; Chapter 10, with a firehouse in Seattle, Washington; Chapter 12, with a barn in Massachusetts; and Chapter 16 with a church arch. Other examples of architecture are shown at the beginning of Chapters 4 and 9.

MANUFACTURE AND INDUSTRY   This category is represented by the logs at the beginning of Chapter 2, the storage tanks on the first page of Chapter 15, and the colored bins at the beginning of Chapter 6. The last are part of a paint plant in Ohio.

TRANSPORTATION   The first page of Chapter 3 is a United Airlines DC 10. Chapter 14 begins with a photograph of the wheel of a sports car.

ENERGY   Heating pipes are shown at the beginning of Chapter 7. The first page of Chapter 8 has a photograph of natural gas storage tanks.

RECREATION   The first page of Chapter 11 shows a ski lift tower in Jackson Hole, Wyoming. Chapter 13 begins with a photograph of benches at the State Fair in Salem, Oregon.

ISBN 0–201–20340–5

ABCDEFGHIJKL–VH–89876543

CONTENTS

Guide to the Student Edition and Supplements   **T4**

Tips for Teachers   **T12**

Objectives   **T16**

Quizzes   **T25**

Teaching Suggestions   **T43**

Computer Activities   **T68**

Assignment Guide   **T72**

References to Supplements   **T82**

Additional Answers   **T88**

ORGANIZATION

Full-color photographs appear at the beginning of each chapter. Each section title is in a large colored band.

EXAMPLES alternate with Try This Exercises in the unique Example/Try This format. The fully worked Examples show in detail how to work each exercise. Side comments explain what is being done in each step.

13—3 Geometric Sequences and Series

Geometric Sequences

The following sequence is not arithmetic.

$$3, 6, 12, 24, 48, 96, \ldots$$

If we multiply each term by 2 we get the next term. In other words, the ratio of any term and the preceding one is 2.

DEFINITION

A sequence in which a constant r can be multiplied by each term to get the next is called a *geometric sequence*. The constant r is called the *common ratio*.

The notation for geometric sequences is the same as the notation for arithmetic sequences; a_1 is the first term, a_2 is the second term, a_3 is the third term, and so on.

To find the common ratio, divide any term by the one before it.

EXAMPLES
Each of the following are geometric sequences. Identify the common ratio.

	Sequence	Common ratio
1.	$3, 6, 12, 24, \ldots$	2
2.	$3, -6, 12, -24, \ldots$	-2
3.	$1, \frac{1}{2}, \frac{1}{4}, \frac{1}{8}, \ldots$	$\frac{1}{2}$

TRY THIS Identify the common ratio of each geometric sequence.

1. $1, 5, 25, 125, \ldots$ 2. $3, -9, 27, -81, \ldots$

3. $48, -12, 3, \ldots$ 4. $54, 18, 6, \ldots$

The nth Term

If we let a_1 be the first term and r be the common ratio, then $a_1 r$ is the second term, $a_1 r^2$ is the third term, and so on. Generalizing, we have the following.

THEOREM 13-4

In a geometric sequence, the nth term is given by $a_n = a_1 r^{n-1}$.

Note that the exponent is one less than the number of the term.

EXAMPLE 4
Find the 11th term of the geometric sequence 64, -32, 16, -8, ... Note that the $a_1 = 64$, $n = 11$, and $r = \frac{-32}{64}$, or $-\frac{1}{2}$.

$$a_n = a_1 r^{n-1} \qquad \text{Theorem 13-4}$$
$$a_{11} = 64 \cdot \left(-\frac{1}{2}\right)^{11-1}$$
$$= 64 \cdot \left(-\frac{1}{2}\right)^{10}$$
$$= 2^6 \cdot \frac{1}{2^{10}} = 2^{-4}, \text{ or } \frac{1}{16}$$

TRY THIS

5. Find the 6th term of the geometric sequence 3, -15, 75, ...

Numbers $m_1, m_2, m_3, \ldots$ are called geometric means of the numbers a and b if $a, m_1, m_2, m_3, \ldots, b$ forms a geometric sequence. We can use the nth term to insert geometric means between two numbers. The two numbers and their geometric means are terms of a geometric sequence.

EXAMPLE 5
Insert two geometric means between 3 and 24.

3 is the 1st term and 24 is the 4th term.

$$24 = 3(r)^{4-1}$$
$$8 = r^3$$
$$2 = r$$

So we have 3, 6, 12, 24.

TRY THIS EXERCISES are like the Examples that precede them. They draw students into the development of the lesson and provide immediate reinforcement of the concept or skill being learned. Try This Exercises cover all course objectives. Try This Exercises can be used

- as oral exercises for *immediate response*.
- as boardwork.
- as independent paper-and-pencil work.
- as oral exercises to *summarize* each section.
- as additional *review* before each chapter test.

Important information, such as theorems, definitions, and problem-solving hints, are highlighted in attractively tinted boxes.

PRACTICE

There are abundant exercises, with many applications problems throughout.

Exercise Sets are in three levels of difficulty:

EXERCISES are carefully written to match the Examples and Try This Exercises. These cover all the objectives of the course.

Now we solve the system

$$2w + 2l = 204$$
$$lw = 2565$$

and get the solution (45, 57). Now check in the original problem: The perimeter is $2 \cdot 45 + 2 \cdot 57$, or 204. The area is $45 \cdot 57$, or 2565. The numbers check, so the answer is $l = 57$ m, $w = 45$ m.

TRY THIS

8. The difference of two numbers is 4 and the difference of their squares is 72. What are the numbers?

9. The perimeter of a rectangular field is 34 ft and the length of a diagonal is 13 ft. Find the dimensions of the field.

10-6

Exercises

Solve each system graphically. Then solve algebraically.

1. $x^2 + y^2 = 25$
   $y - x = 1$
2. $x^2 + y^2 = 100$
   $y - x = 2$
3. $y^2 - x^2 = 9$
   $2x - 3 = y$
4. $x + y = -6$
   $xy = -7$
5. $4x^2 + 9y^2 = 36$
   $3y + 2x = 6$
6. $9x^2 + 4y^2 = 36$
   $3x + 2y = 6$
7. $y^2 = x + 3$
   $2y = x + 4$
8. $y = x^2$
   $3x = y + 2$

Solve.

9. $x^2 + 4y^2 = 25$
   $x + 2y = 7$
10. $y^2 - x^2 = 16$
    $2x - y = 1$
11. $x^2 - xy + 3y^2 = 5$
    $x - y = 2$
12. $2y^2 + xy + x^2 = 7$
    $x - 2y = 5$
13. $3x + y = 7$
    $4x^2 + 5y = 24$
14. $2y^2 + xy = 5$
    $4y + x = 7$

15. The sum of two numbers is 14 and the sum of their squares is 106. What are the numbers?

16. The sum of two numbers is 15 and the difference of their squares is also 15. What are the numbers?

17. A rectangle has perimeter 28 cm and the length of a diagonal is 10 cm. What are its dimensions?

18. A rectangle has perimeter 6 m and the length of a diagonal $\sqrt{5}$ m. What are its dimensions?

19. A rectangle has area 20 in.^{2} and perimeter 18 in. Find its dimensions.

20. A rectangle has area 2 yd^2 and perimeter 6 yd. Find its dimensions.

Extension

Solve.

21. $x + 1 = y$
    $xy = 1$

22. $x^2 + y^2 = 1$
    $xy = 1$

Solve. Use a calculator.

23. $x^2 + y^2 = 19,380,510.36$
    $27,942.25x - 6.125y = 0$

24. $2x + 2y = 1660$
    $xy = 35,325$

Challenge

25. Given the area A and the perimeter P of a rectangle, show that the length L and the width W are given by these formulas.

$$L = \frac{1}{4}(P + \sqrt{P^2 - 16A})$$

$$W = \frac{1}{4}(P - \sqrt{P^2 - 16A})$$

26. Show that a hyperbola does not intersect its asymptotes. That is, solve the following system.

$$\frac{x^2}{a^2} - \frac{y^2}{b^2} = 1$$

$$y = \frac{b}{a}x \ \left(\text{or, } y = -\frac{b}{a}x\right)$$

27. Find an equation of a circle that passes through the points $(2, 4)$ and $(3, 3)$ and whose center is on the line $3x - y = 3$.

28. Find an equation of a circle that passes through the points $(7, 3)$ and $(5, 5)$ and whose center is on the line $y - 4x = 1$.

29. The area of a rectangle inscribed in a unit circle is 1. Find its length and width.

EXTENSION problems may be slightly more difficult, or integrate the lesson with previous lessons for continued review and added depth. Frequently they include problem solving and applications.

CHALLENGE provides more difficult problems or new ideas that are beyond the scope of a middle track course. These are often applications.

USING A CALCULATOR shows how to use calculators and apply problem-solving techniques in algebra.

USING A CALCULATOR/What's Stored in the Memory?

Try this problem with your calculator.

Enter: 1 ÷ 3 =

Display: 1   3 0.3333333

Does the calculator have an infinite string of three's stored in the memory? Without clearing the calculator, repeat the following steps until the display shows fewer than seven three's.

Enter: × 1000 − 333 =

Display: 1000 333.33333 333 0.3333333

How many three's does your calculator really

have in its answer to 1 ÷ 3? Try the problem again with 2 ÷ 3. Some calculators will give 7 as the final digit of the result.

The following "trick" works on some calculators. Can you explain why it works?

Enter: 1 ÷ 3 = × 3 =

Display: 1   3 0.3333333   3   1

Now press the x^2 key six or seven times. On some calculators, you will eventually get 0.9999999 as the square of 1!

10–6 Systems of Equations **453**

T 7

APPLICATIONS

Colorfully highlighted features throughout the text show the many applications of algebra.

CAREERS in boxed full-color pages show algebra being used in forestry, clothing manufacturing, railroad traffic control, ocean-ography, communications, astron-omy, engineering, stress analysis and aerial surveying. Applications problems are included.

CONSUMER APPLICATIONS apply arithmetic and algebra skills to topics such as buying a new car, understanding life insurance, financing a home, finding a job, and filing income tax returns.

COMPUTER ACTIVITIES intro-duce programming in BASIC. They contain programs for solving algebra problems.

CAREERS/Astronomy

Astronomers study celestial bodies using telescopes equipped with devices such as cameras, spectrometers (for measuring wave lengths of radiant en-ergy), and photometers (for measuring light intensity). In-struments carried into space in balloons, satellites, or space probes provide addi-tional information for astron-omers to use to determine sizes, brightnesses, shapes, motions, and positions of celestial bodies.

earth-launched satellites. To perform their calculations, astronomers first observe the motions and positions of the space vehicle. For instance, an orbiting solar observatory launched by the United States was found to have an apogee (point farthest from the earth) of 358 miles and a perigee (point closest to the earth) of 205 miles. Astrono-mers use the equation $\frac{x^2}{a^2} + \frac{y^2}{b^2} = 1$, which you learned in Section 10–3, to find vertices and foci of an elliptical orbit.

then used by astronomers re-searching subjects such as the statistical theory of motion of celestial bodies.

$$\frac{x^2}{a^2} + \frac{y^2}{b^2} = 1$$

Let $a = 358$ and $b = 205$.

$$\frac{x^2}{358^2} + \frac{y^2}{205^2} = 1$$

The vertices are $(-358, 0)$, $(358, 0)$, $(0, 205)$, and

Exercises
For each ellipse find the cen-ter, vertices, and foci. Then graph the ellipse.

1. $\frac{x^2}{49} + \frac{y^2}{16} = 1$
2. $\frac{(x-3)^2}{4} + \frac{(y-1)^2}{25} = 1$

CONSUMER APPLICATION/Finding a Job

Most people have jobs to earn the money they need for living expenses. One of the ways to find a job is to use the "Help-Wanted" advertisements found in newspapers. Here are some typical ads.

EXECUTIVE SECRETARY	JEWELRY SALES	CASHIER
Typing (50 wpm) and shorthand required. Excellent benefits, potential for advance-ment. Salary $13,500.	$15,000 or more! Leading firm seeks salesperson to sell to distributors. Sales experience required. 25% commission.	Quality department store. $6.25/hr. for 40-hour week, time and a half overtime. No experience necessary.

Note how earnings are calculated in different ways. To see how similar jobs differ in pay, we can compare them for the same time period.

COMPUTER ACTIVITIES

Expressions and Numbers in BASIC

In order to use a computer, we must use a computer language. One of the most common computer languages is called BASIC. There are different versions of BASIC, so minor changes may be necessary for a particular computer.

To represent numbers in BASIC we use signs and decimal points, but not commas. We do not use fractional notation.

$-125 \qquad 25.692 \qquad 49321 \qquad .333333334$

BASIC uses a type of exponential notation for very large or small numbers.

1.23456789E+05: The "E+05" means "times 10^5" so, 1.23456789E+05 means 123456.789

7.9872E−06: The "E−06" means "times 10^{-6}" so, 7.9872E−06 means .0000079872

To represent variables we use a single letter, or a single letter followed by a single digit.

$X \qquad T \qquad T5 \qquad N1 \qquad A2$

There are five arithmetic operations in BASIC. The order in which the computer performs these operations is the same as in algebra.

Operation	BASIC symbol	Example
Exponentiation	^	Y ^ 2 means Y^2
Multiplication	*	6 * T means 6T
Division	/	P/3 means P ÷ 3
Addition	+	R + S means R + S
Subtraction	−	5 − Q means 5 − Q

1. Operations within parentheses first.
2. Exponentiations in order from left to right.
3. Multiplication and division from left to right.
4. Addition and subtraction from left to right.

When $Y = 2$: Y ^ 3 + 3 * Y − 5 means $Y^3 + 3Y − 5$ or $2^3 + (3 \cdot 2) − 5$ or $8 + 6 − 5 = 9$

When $X = 5$: X ^ 2 + 2 * X − (X + 4)/3 means $X^2 + 2X − \frac{X+4}{3}$ or $5^2 + 2(5) − \frac{5+4}{3} = 25 + 10 − 3 = 32$

Computer Activities **731**

EVALUATION

Many opportunities for ongoing review and maintenance of skills are available throughout the text.

READY FOR exercises (keyed to sections of preceding chapters) provide a preview of skills from preceding lessons that will be needed in the following chapter.

CHAPTER REVIEWS at the end of each chapter are keyed to the sections of the chapter, and review all the important skills and concepts of the chapter.

CHAPTER TESTS follow the Chapter Reviews.

CUMULATIVE REVIEWS are each truly cumulative, reviewing skills and concepts back to Chapter 1.

This Teacher's Edition also provides Quizzes, at least two per chapter. The Teacher's Resource Book has two *Chapter Tests* per chapter, a *Mid-Year Test,* and an *End-Of-Year Test.*

Ready for Quadratic Functions?

3–2   Graph.

1. $2y = \frac{1}{3}x - 1$ 2. $y = -2x + 3$

3–3   Tell whether or not each graph is the graph of a function.

3.   4.

CHAPTER 8   Review

Review the material in the chapter. Then see how you have done by trying these review exercises. If you miss an exercise, restudy the indicated lesson.

CHAPTER 3   Test

1. Consider the set $\{-4, -2, 0, 2\}$. Find the set of ordered pairs determined by the relation ≤ (is less than or equal to).
2. List the domain and range of the relation $\{(-1, 4), (2, 3), (-2, -3), (1, -2)\}$.
3. Graph the relation which is the solution set of $y = 3x - 1$.
4. Graph the relation which is the solution set of $y = x^2 - 1$.

Which of the following are graphs of functions?

5.   6. $y = f(x)$

CHAPTERS 1–4   Cumulative Review

1–2   Evaluate each expression for $x = -1$ and $y = 4$.

1. $-(2x - y - 6)$ 2. $2|y - 8| - |x|$

1–5   Simplify.

3. $3x - 2(5y - 4x)$ 4. $8y - [2y - (5y - 7)]$

1–7

5. $(2x^2y)(-5x^{-5}y^6)$ 6. $\frac{-28x^{-1}y^2}{4x^3y^{-1}}$ 7. $(8x^3)^{-2}$

2–2   Solve.

8. $-7t + 23 = -33$ 9. $\frac{1}{8}x + \frac{3}{2} = \frac{1}{3} - \frac{1}{6}x$ 10. $(x - 7)(2x + 1) = 0$

2–5   Solve.

11. $3x - 8 > 2x - 1$ 12. $-\frac{2}{3}y \le 12$ 13. $-3 + 7x < 2x + 9$

2–6

14. The sum of three consecutive odd integers is greater than 30. What are the least possible values for the integers?

2–7   Solve.

15. $-3 < 4x + 1 < 6$ 16. $2x + 1 < -1$ or $x - 3 > 4$

2–8

17. $|x| < \frac{1}{2}$ 18. $|14 - y| < 10$

3–2   Graph.

19. $-x + 2y = 1$ 20. $2x - y = -4$

3–4   Graph using intercepts.

21. $5x - 3y = 15$ 22. $-2x + 7y = 14$

3–6   Find an equation of each line. Write in standard form.

23. Line with slope $-\frac{1}{2}$ and containing $(-8, 0)$
24. Line containing $(-2, -1)$ and $(-3, 7)$

204 CHAPTER 4 SYSTEMS OF EQUATIONS AND INEQUALITIES

TEACHER'S RESOURCE BOOK

The Teacher's Resource Book, a supplement unique to the Addison-Wesley Algebra program, contains 176 pages of teaching aids to help fit the course to the special needs of any class.

Packaged in a convenient three-ring binder, these blackline masters provide a range of handouts from testing to computer worksheets.

Contents
Teacher's Aids
Tests
    Chapter Tests (free response)
    Multiple-choice Chapter Tests
    Mid-Year Test
    End-of-Year Test
Skills Practice
Applications
    Career Applications
    Consumer Applications
    Problem Solving
    Calculator Problems
Computer Projects
Answers

Chapter Tests include two tests for each chapter. The free response chapter tests are like the chapter tests in the text. The multiple-choice chapter tests help prepare students for the PSAT and other standardized tests. Also included are a *Mid-Year Test* and an *End-of-Year Test.*

Skills Practice (two to four worksheets for each chapter) are like the first level of Exercises in the text, providing more practice with important algebra skills.

Applications (two to four worksheets for each chapter) complement the applications and special features of the text. These contain career and consumer applications, problem-solving refreshers, and calculator problems.

Computer Projects provide further opportunities to use the introduction to BASIC programming in the text.

TEACHER'S EDITION

The Teacher's Edition contains two parts:

128 pages at the front of the text with references, guides, and teaching suggestions; and the annotated Student Edition containing answers in blue for ready identification.

Material in the front of the text includes the following:

Tips for Teachers
This unique feature contains tips on computers and calculators. New teachers will find this material very practical and experienced teachers may also find additional ideas.

Objectives
Section objectives for the entire course are listed.

Quizzes
This section contains at least two quizzes for each chapter.

Teaching Suggestions
Numerous suggestions serve a variety of teacher needs. Their easy-to-locate format makes them helpful sources of teaching ideas.

Assignment Guide
Daily assignments are given for four levels of courses for each semester. Assignment days for review, testing, and supplemental materials are included.

Reference to Supplements
This chart lists supplementary features in the Student Edition, the Teacher's Edition, the Teacher's Resource Book, and other supplements. It also indicates where each of the features, such as Skills Practice, Applications, and Computer Projects, may be used.

Additional Answers
Answers for most exercises appear overprinted on student pages. Answers too long for the student pages are in the front part of this Teacher's Edition.

TIPS FOR TEACHERS

Computer Tips

Computer Programming

A one-semester course in computer programming is probably the fastest way to become familiar with how computers work and the types of problems they are used to solve. Most community colleges offer such a course. It may be called "Computer Programming in BASIC" or "Introduction to Computer Programming."

If you are unfamiliar with computers, invite a teacher from your school or district to teach a brief course in computer programming. Perhaps a two-week session in the spring would be a good time to arrange for your guest computer teacher to take over your class.

If you wish some or all of your students to have actual hands-on computer programming experience, you should have access to enough computers so that each student can have 2 hours of computer time per week. The computers should be equipped with a printer for students to be able to hand in assignments.

If you have access to only a limited number of computers, you might have students take turns during the school year. There are many software programs available that students may use independently to learn the rudiments of programming.

Computer Literacy

A course in computer literacy usually consists of a short history of computers, a description of the hardware—the parts of a computer and what they do, examples of applications of computers, and an introduction to systems analysis, the science of setting up problems so that they can be programmed into and solved by a computer. Some community colleges offer a course in computer literacy, although such courses may vary greatly in their content.

The basic elements of computer literacy can be self-taught by using books or magazine articles. One such book is *Computers and Data Processing* by Capron and Williams (Benjamin/Cummings, 1982). Your librarian may be able to suggest others.

To help your students become "computer literate" have each one be responsible for preparing a 20-minute report.

Testing and Record Keeping

Commercially-produced software management programs can be helpful to school administrators or anyone who wishes to monitor the progress of more than 50 students.

Keep in mind that these record keeping or management programs almost always require that you use multiple-choice form tests. If you prefer to use standard form, or free-response tests, you may wish to continue to use traditional testing materials.

A computer can be used to correct tests for you only if (1) you also have a card reader and (2) you use multiple-choice tests in which students fill in circles on separate answer cards. The Chatsworth card reader is probably the most commonly used at this time.

There are a few software programs available that include either randomly generated test items or test items pulled from a master test bank. A program of this type will help you construct tests for special purposes such as make-up tests or tests for students covering highly-individualized curriculums.

Interactive Practice and Problem Solving

There are an ever-increasing number of commercially produced software diskettes for your students to use along with their algebra textbooks and worksheets. As you begin to choose among the wide variety of diskettes, the following points may be helpful.

Check with other teachers in your school or district for recommended software. If a particular diskette has worked well for another teacher, it will probably work for you also.

If your school or district has a media or computer specialist, that person may be a good source for recommendations and evaluations.

Before deciding to purchase a diskette, check to see exactly how many diskettes you will need at one time. Companies do not allow copying diskettes, but may provide backup diskettes, review copies, and discounts on multiple purchases.

Many magazines now include reviews of software as well as textbooks. The Computing Teacher includes a Software Reviews section. Also, Purser's Magazine is a publication specifically designed to evaluate software.

REFERENCES:

Robert Taylor, Editor: *The Computer in the School: Tutor, Tool, Tutee,* Teachers College Press, 1980. This book contains three papers by Alfred Bork, four papers by Thomas Dwyer, four papers by Arthur Luehrmann, four papers by Seymour Papert, and four papers by Patrick Suppes.

Morsund, David, *Precollege Computer Literacy: A Personal Computing Approach,* International Council for Computers in Education (ICCE), c/o Dept. of Computer and Information Science, University of Oregon, Eugene, OR 94703, 1981.

Lathrop, Ann and Bobby Goodson, *Courseware in the Classroom: Selecting, Organizing, and Using Education Software.* Menlo Park, CA: Addison-Wesley, 1983.

The Computing Teacher, International Council for Computers in Education (ICCE), University of Oregon, Eugene, OR 97403.

The Mathematics Teacher, November 1981 issue on Microcomputers, National Council of Teachers of Mathematics (NCTM), Reston, VA 22091.

Purser's Magazine, P.O. Box 466, El Dorado, CA 95623.

Calculator Tips

Computation

Although your students will not be using calculators in every class period, each student should have access to a calculator with at least a memory and a square root key.

Most likely, your students will not all be using the same type of calculator. Near the beginning of the school year, set aside part of a class to discuss the different types of calculators. You might choose a problem from the previous day's class and have several different students explain how they would solve it on different calculators.

Whether or not you allow students to use calculators when they are taking quizzes and tests is, of course, an individual decision. Keep in mind that the tests available with this program, and most teacher-constructed tests, were designed to be worked without calculators. Their emphasis is, appropriately, on algebraic concepts and skills rather than on arithmetical proficiency.

If you begin to integrate student use of calculators into your curriculum, you may find you are spending less time on some topics. For example, working square roots by hand or using a table of logarithms are skills that the majority of algebra teachers spend less time on than in the past. Use this extra time to increase your emphasis on problem solving and applying algebraic skills to real-world situations.

Problem Solving

If each of your students has access to even a simple, four-function calculator, you can take advantage of this tool to more effectively teach problem solving. When students are encouraged to use calculators for tedious or lengthy computations, they are often more willing to tackle new or apparently difficult problems; they can begin to concentrate on solving problems rather than finding answers.

Consumer applications offer good opportunities to show students the advantages of mastering the use of a calculator. Problems in percent and compound interest are good examples.

Having calculators available in your classroom can give you opportunities to incorporate discovery learning into your instruction. Students can be encouraged to use "guess and check" or successive approximation methods as they approach new problems.

Calculators are also helpful in teaching students the rudiments of mathematical modeling. As they learn to translate ever more complex real-world problems into mathematical statements, they will also see more reasons for learning algebraic concepts and skills.

OBJECTIVES

Chapter 1 Objectives

One objective for each Section is listed.

(1–1) Identify natural numbers, whole numbers, integers, and rational and irrational numbers; convert between fractional and decimal notation for rational numbers; determine which of two numbers is greater; state the axioms for the real numbers. (1–2) Find the additive inverse and absolute value of any number; evaluate expressions involving additive inverses or absolute values. (1–3) Add and subtract real numbers; use the properties of real numbers to write equivalent expressions. (1–4) Multiply and divide real numbers; recognize divisions by 0 as impossible; use properties of real numbers to write equivalent expressions. (1–5) Use the distributive laws to multiply, factor, and collect like terms; write the inverse of a sum as a sum of the inverses; evaluate expressions that have parentheses within parentheses. (1–6) Rewrite expressions with and without exponents or negative exponents. (1–7) Use exponential notation in multiplication, division, and raising a power to a power; apply the order of operations. (1–8) Convert numbers to scientific notation; multiply and divide in scientific notation. (1–9) Use the axioms of the real numbers and properties of equality to justify equivalent expressions; write a sequence of equivalent statements to prove a theorem (optional).

Chapter 2 Objectives

(2–1) Solve equations using the addition and multiplication principles. (2–2) Solve equations containing fractions, decimals, or parentheses; use the principle of zero products to solve equations. (2–3) Solve problems by translating to equations. (2–4) Solve a formula for a specified letter. (2–5) Graph inequalities in one variable; solve inequalities using the addition and multiplication principles. (2–6) Solve problems using inequalities. (2–7) Solve and graph conjunctions and disjunctions of inequalities in one variable. (2–8) Find the distance between two coordinates using absolute value; solve equations and inequalities involving absolute value. (2–9) Write proofs of conditional statements; write and prove converses of conditionals; solve an equation or inequality by proving a statement and its converse; use the addition and multiplication principles to write equivalent statements (optional).

(3–1) Find Cartesian products, relations, and the domain and range of a relation; use set-builder notation. (3–2) Graph ordered pairs and equations; determine whether an ordered pair is a solution of an equation; describe the domain and the range of a relation given its graph. (3–3) Recognize a graph of a function; find the function value $f(x)$ given x; find the domain of a function; graph absolute value and greatest integer functions. (3–4) Identify, find the standard form of, and graph linear equations; find and use intercepts. (3–5) Find the slope of a line containing a given pair of points; use the Point-Slope Equation to find an equation of a line given a point on the line and its slope. (3–6) Use the Two-Point Equation to find an equation of a line given two points on the line; find the slope and y-intercept of a line given the Slope-Intercept Equation for the line; write an equation of a line given its slope and y-intercept. (3–7) Tell, without graphing, whether the graphs of two equations are parallel or perpendicular; write an equation of the line parallel or perpendicular to a given line through a given point. (3–8) Find a linear function that fits two data points and use the equation to make predictions.

Chapter 3 Objectives

(4–1) Determine whether an ordered pair is a solution of a system of equations; solve a system of two linear equations in two variables by graphing, the substitution method, or the addition method. (4–2) Solve problems by translating to systems of two equations and solving the system. (4–3)

Chapter 4 Objectives

Determine whether an ordered triple is a solution of a system of three equations in three variables; solve a system of equations in three variables. (4–4) Solve problems by translating to a system of three equations in three variables. (4–5) Determine whether a system of two or three equations is consistent or inconsistent and whether it is dependent or independent. (4–6) Solve systems of linear equations using matrices (optional). (4–7) Evaluate determinants of 2×2 and 3×3 matrices; solve systems of equations in two or three variables using Cramer's Rule (optional). (4–8) Graph linear inequalities and systems of linear inequalities in two variables in the plane, finding vertices, if they exist. (4–9) Solve problems using linear programming.

Chapter 5 Objectives

(5–1) Determine the degree of each term of a polynomial and the degree of the polynomial; add, subtract, and find additive inverses of polynomials. (5–2) Multiply any two polynomials; square and cube a binomial; multiply the sum and difference of the same two terms. (5–3) Factor polynomials which have a common factor, are the difference of squares, or are the squares of binomials. (5–4) Factor trinomials of the type $x^2 + ax + b$ and the type $ax^2 + bx + c$. (5–5) Factor a polynomial with more than two terms by grouping to find a common factor or a difference of two squares; factor trinomials by completing the square. (5–6) Factor polynomials that are the sums or differences of two cubes. (5–7) Factor polynomials using any of the methods learned previously. (5–8) Solve equations by factoring and using the principle of zero products. (5–9) Solve problems by translating to equations and solving the equations by factoring.

Chapter 6 Objectives

(6–1) Multiply and divide two fractional expressions; simplify a fractional expression by removing a factor of 1. (6–2) Find the least common multiple of algebraic expressions. (6–3) Add and subtract fractional expressions which have the same denominator or different denominators. (6–4) Simplify complex fractional expressions. (6–5) Divide a polynomial by a divisor that is a monomial or by a divisor that is not a monomial; express any remainder in two ways. (6–6) Solve fractional equations. (6–7) Solve work and motion problems. (6–8) Solve a formula containing fractional expressions for a given letter. (6–9) Find an equation of variation given a description of direct or inverse variation; solve problems involving direct or inverse variation.

(7–1) Find principal square roots and cube roots; simplify radical expressions. (7–2) Multiply and simplify radical expressions; approximate values for radical expressions using a square root table. (7–3) Simplify radical expressions with a quotient as a radicand; divide and simplify radical expressions. (7–4) Add or subtract radical expressions; simplify by collecting like radical terms; multiply radical expressions that contain more than one term; rationalize the denominator of a radical expression. (7–5) Evaluate $\sqrt[k]{a^m}$ two ways; write expressions with fractional exponents as radical expressions and vice versa; convert expressions with negative exponents to expressions without negative exponents; use fractional exponents to simplify radical expressions. (7–6) Solve radical equations with one or two radical terms. (7–7) Express a square root of a negative number as an imaginary number; multiply imaginary numbers; add and subtract complex numbers. (7–8) Solve equations like $3x + yi = 5x + 1 + 2i$ for x and y; multiply, divide, and find conjugates and reciprocals of complex numbers; multiply a complex number by its conjugate. (7–9) Determine whether a complex number is a solution of an equation; find an equation which has given complex numbers as solutions; solve first-degree equations which have complex numbers as solutions; verify that a given complex number is a square root of another complex number and find the other square root. (7–10) Graph complex numbers in a plane; find absolute values of complex numbers. (7–11) Find a polynomial in $\bar{z}$ that is the conjugate of a polynomial in z.

Chapter 7 Objectives

Chapter 8 Objectives

(8–1) Solve equations of the types $ax^2 + bx + c = 0$, $ax^2 + c = 0$, and $ax^2 + bx = 0$; translate problems to quadratic equations and solve. (8–2) Solve quadratic equations using the Quadratic Formula; find approximate values of solutions to quadratic equations using a square root table. (8–3) Determine the nature of the solutions of a quadratic equation with real coefficients without solving it; find, without solving, the sum and product of the solutions of a quadratic equation; find a quadratic equation given its solutions or the sum and product of the solutions. (8–4) Solve equations that are quadratic in form. (8–5) Solve a quadratic formula for a given letter; use quadratic equations to solve problems. (8–6) Find an equation of quadratic variation given direct, inverse, or joint variation; solve problems involving quadratic variation.

Chapter 9 Objectives

(9–1) Test the equation of a relation for symmetry with respect to the x-axis, the y-axis, or the origin; determine whether a function is even or odd. (9–2) Sketch a graph which is a vertical or horizontal translation of a given graph. (9–3) Sketch a graph which is a vertical or horizontal stretching or shrinking of a given graph. (9–4) Graph a function $f(x) = ax^2$ or $f(x) = a(x - h)^2$ and determine the vertex and line of symmetry. (9–5) Graph a function $f(x) = a(x - h)^2 + k$ and determine the vertex, line of symmetry, and minimum or maximum value; determine, without graphing, the vertex, line of symmetry, and minimum or maximum value of a function $f(x) = a(x - h)^2 + k$. (9–6) Express $f(x) = ax^2 + bx + c$ as $f(x) = a(x - h)^2 + k$ and find the vertex, line of symmetry, and maximum or minimum value; solve minimum and maximum problems involving quadratic functions. (9–7) Find the x-intercepts of the graph of a quadratic function, if they exist. (9–8) Fit a quadratic function to three data points; solve problems involving quadratic functions.

Chapter 10 Objectives

(10–1) Use the Distance Formula to find the distance between any two points in the plane; find the midpoint of a segment given the endpoints. (10–2) Find the equation of a circle given the center and radius of the circle; find the center and radius of a circle given its equation, by first completing the square if the equation is not in standard form, and then graph the circle. (10–3) Find the center, vertices and foci of an ellipse given its equation, by first completing the square if necessary, and then graph the ellipse. (10–4) Find the center, vertices, foci, and asymptotes of a hyperbola given its equation, by first completing the square if necessary, and then graph the hyperbola; graph a hyperbola which has an equation of the form $xy = c$. (10–5) Find the vertex, focus, and directrix of a parabola given its equation, by first completing the square if necessary, and then graph the parabola; find an equation of a parabola given the focus and directrix of the parabola. (10–6) Solve systems of a first-degree and a second-degree equation and problems involving them by graphing or the substitution method. (10–7) Solve systems of second-degree equations and problems involving them by graphing, the addition method, or the substitution method.

(11–1) Determine whether a number is a root of a polynomial; find the quotient and the remainder given a polynomial and a divisor; express $P(x)$ in the form $P(x) = d(x) \cdot Q(x) + R(x)$. (11–2) Use synthetic division to divide a polynomial by $x - r$; use the Remainder Theorem to find $P(r)$; determine whether a given number is a root of $P(x)$ and whether $x - r$ is a factor of $P(x)$. (11–3) Factor a polynomial to find its roots and their multiplicities; find a polynomial with specified roots; find all the roots of a polynomial given its degree and several roots; find the polynomial of lowest degree with rational coefficients that has given roots; find all the roots of a polynomial given one of its roots. (11–4) Find the rational roots and the other roots, if possible, of a polynomial with integer coefficients. (11–5) Use Descartes' Rule of Signs to find the number of positive or negative real roots of a polynomial with real coefficients; find the upper and lower bounds of the roots of a polynomial with real coefficients. (11–6) Graph polynomial functions; approximate roots of polynomial equations.

Chapter 11
Objectives

Chapter 12 Objectives

(12–1) Write an equation of the inverse of a relation given the equation of the relation; graph the inverse of a relation given the graph of the relation; determine whether the graph of a relation is symmetric with respect to the line $y = x$ given its equation; determine whether the inverse of a function is a function; if so, find a formula for the inverse. (12–2) Graph exponential and logarithmic functions. (12–3) Convert exponential equations to logarithmic equations and vice versa; solve logarithmic equations; simplify expressions like $a^{\log_a x}$ and $\log_a a^x$. (12–4) Use the basic properties of logarithms. (12–5) Use a table and scientific notation to find common logarithms and antilogarithms. (12–6) Use a table and linear interpolation to find logarithms and antilogarithms. (12–7) Solve exponential and logarithmic equations and problems involving them. (12–8) Graph the function $y = e^x$; use a calculator or a table to find natural logarithms; solve problems involving exponential and logarithmic functions; change logarithmic bases; find the logarithm of a number to any base.

Chapter 13 Objectives

(13–1) Find any term in a sequence given a formula for the general term of the sequence; find a rule for the general term of a sequence; recognize a series as a sum of terms of a sequence or a sequence of partial sums; find the sum of a sequence; convert between sigma notation and other notation for a series. (13–2) Identify the first term and the common difference of an arithmetic sequence; find the nth term of an arithmetic sequence; solve for any of the numbers a_n, a_1, n, or d, given the other three; construct an arithmetic sequence given two terms and their place in the sequence; find arithmetic means; find the sum of the first n terms of an arithmetic series. (13–3) Identify the first term and common ratio of a geometric sequence; find the nth term of a geometric sequence; find geometric means; find the sum of the first n terms of a geometric series. (13–4) Determine whether an infinite geometric series is convergent; find the sum of an infinite geometric series when $|r| < 1$. (13–5) Use the Fundamental Counting Principle to determine the total number of ways a compound event may occur; find the total number of permutations of a set of n objects; express a factorial as a product and evaluate. (13–6) Find the number of permutations of n objects taken r at a time with and without replacement. (13–7) Find the number of combinations of a set of n objects taken r at a time. (13–8) Find the rth term of the binomial expansion of $(a + b)^n$; use the Binomial Theorem to expand expressions like $(x^2 + 3y)^9$; determine the number of subsets of a finite set. (13–9) Compute the probability of a simple event.

Chapter 14 Objectives

(14–1) Find the dimensions of a matrix; add and subtract matrices of the same dimensions. (14–2) Multiply matrices when possible; write a matrix equation equivalent to a system of equations. (14–3) Show that the product of a square matrix and its inverse is the identity matrix; calculate the inverse of a square matrix, if it exists, and use it to solve a system of equations.

Chapter 15 Objectives

(15–1) Find sine, cosine, tangent, cotangent, secant, and cosecant function values for an angle of a right triangle, given the lengths of the sides of the triangle; find trigonometric function values for $45°$, $30°$, and $60°$; use trigonometric functions to find lengths of sides of right triangles; find the six trigonometric function values for an angle given one of the function values. (15–2) Find the quadrant of the terminal side of an angle; find trigonometric function values of an angle or rotation; find the reference angle of a rotation and use it to find trigonometric function values. (15–3) Convert from degree to radian measure and vice versa; use cofunction identities to find trigonometric function values; use a table and interpolation to find trigonometric function values. (15–4) Graph the six trigonometric functions and identify their domain and range; identify periodic functions from their graphs; find the amplitude of functions. (15–5) Derive identities from the quotient, the Pythagorean, and the cofunction identities. (15–6) Sketch graphs of $y = A \sin \theta$
$y = A \cos \theta$, $y = \sin B\theta$, $y = \cos B\theta$
$y = A \sin B\theta$, and $y = A \cos B\theta$;

determine the amplitude and period for transformations of the sine curve. (15–7) Compute with and simplify trigonometric expressions; solve equations containing trigonometric expressions.

Chapter 16 Objectives

(16–1) Use the cosine, sine, and tangent sum and difference identities to simplify trigonometric expressions and find function values of angles. (16–2) Use the double-angle and half-angle identities to find function values. (16–3) Prove trigonometric identities. (16–4) Find all values, by sketching graphs, of arcsin a, arccos a, and arctan a, in degrees and in radians; find principal values of the inverses of the trigonometric functions. (16–5) Solve simple trigonometric equations. (16–6) Solve triangles; solve problems involving triangles. (16–8) Use the law of sines to solve any triangle, given a side and two angles or two sides and an angle opposite one of them, recognizing when a solution does not exist; use the law of sines to find areas of triangles. (16–8) Use the law of cosines, with the law of sines, to solve any triangle, given two sides and the included angle or three sides. (16–9) Find the sum of two vectors; solve problems involving vectors. (16–10) Find two vectors whose sum is the given vector; add vectors, giving answers as ordered pairs; use properties of vectors. (16–11) Change from trigonometric notation to rectangular notation, and vice versa; use trigonometric notation to multiply or divide complex numbers; use DeMoivre's Theorem to find powers and roots of complex numbers.

QUIZZES

There are alternate Chapter Tests in the **Teacher's Resource Book.** This material includes two tests for each chapter, a Mid-Year Test, and an End-of-Year Test.

This section contains 43 quizzes. Most chapters have two or three quizzes, with emphasis on sections in the first half of each chapter.

Quizzes given in the first half of a chapter are an advantage to both students and teachers for two reasons: they highlight early difficulties within a limited range of concepts and they allow the student to demonstrate an understanding of skills and concepts.

QUIZ 1   Sections 1–1 to 1–3

1. Write in decimal notation: $\frac{4}{11}$

2. Write in fractional notation: 2.0007

3. Is 6.07077077707777 ... rational or irrational? Give the reason.

4. Evaluate, using $x = \frac{1}{2}$, $y = -7$: $9x - (-4y) + |2xy|$.

Calculate.

5. $-7.82 + (-3.39)$ **6.** $-7 - [-(-12)] - 1$

Complete.

7. $-3x + 4(-y) = -3x + (-y)4$ by the ____ law.

8. $-3x + (6a + 5c) = -3x + (5c + 6a)$ by the ____ law.

ANSWERS: **1.** $0.\overline{36}$ **2.** $2\frac{7}{10,000}$ **3.** Irrational; no fixed set of repeating decimals   **4.** $-16\frac{1}{2}$ **5.** -11.21

6. -20 **7.** Commutative law for multiplication

8. Commutative law for addition

Chapter 1
Quizzes

QUIZ 2   Section 1–4

Complete.

1. $-\frac{13}{2} \times 0 = 0$ by the ___ property of 0.

2. $\frac{5}{14}$ is the number which when multiplied by ___ = ___, according to the definition of division.
3. The product of 2 negative real numbers is ___ .
4. The quotient of 2 real numbers is negative if ___ .
5. Because $0.25 \times 4 = 1$, the numbers 0.25 and 4 are called ___ .
6. Zero divided by any nonzero number is ___ .
7. $6(x - 2)$ and $(2 - x)6$ (are or are not) equivalent expressions.
8. A negative number and its reciprocal have (different or the same) signs.

ANSWERS: **1.** Multiplicative   **2.** 14, 5
3. Positive   **4.** One only of the numbers is negative
5. Multiplicative inverses   **6.** Zero   **7.** Are not
8. The same

QUIZ 3   Sections 1–5 to 1–6

Simplify.

1. $10(a + 6)$ 2. $-\frac{1}{2}y\left(8y - 6w + \frac{1}{2}y\right)$

Factor.

3. $12x - 24y$ 4. $z - 9z$

Simplify.

5. $x + y(-x) - (x - xy)$ 6. $-\left(-7a + \frac{1}{2}c + 5a - \frac{3}{2}c\right)$
7. $[16(a - 5) + 4a] - \{5[3(a - 1)] + 10\}$

Evaluate.

8. -10^4 9. $(4^{-2} + 7 \cdot 8^{-1}) - [-8^0(16^{-1})]$

10. Write an equivalent expression without negative exponents:

$$\frac{x^2 y^{-3}}{z^{-2}}$$

ANSWERS: **1.** $10a + 60$ **2.** $-4\frac{1}{4}y^2 + 3yw$

3. $12(x - 2y)$ **4.** $-8z$ **5.** 0 **6.** $2a + c$

7. $5a - 75$ **8.** $10,000$ **9.** $\frac{7}{8}$ **10.** $\frac{x^2 \cdot z^2}{y^3}$

QUIZ 4   Sections 2–1 to 2–3

1. Solve $3x - 5 = 5x + 5 - 7x$.

2. To solve $3x = 9$, we multiply by $\frac{1}{3}$: $\frac{1}{3} \cdot 3x = \frac{1}{3} \cdot 9$.

This is an application of the ___ principle for ___.

3. Solve $4 - 2(2x - 1) - 5x = (3 - 4x) - (2x + 3)$.

4. Solve $(3x + 4)(2x - 5) = 0$.

Translate to an equation and solve.

5. Find three consecutive odd integers such that the sum of twice the first, 3 times the second and 4 times the third is 103.

ANSWERS: **1.** 2 **2.** Multiplication; equations

3. 2 **4.** $-\frac{4}{3}, \frac{5}{2}$ **5.** 9, 11, 13

QUIZ 5   Sections 2–4 to 2–6

1. Solve $D = r \cdot t$ for t (distance formula).

2. Solve $\frac{PV}{T} = k$ for V (physics formula).

3. When each side of an inequality is multiplied by a negative number, the inequality symbol ___.

4. When a negative number is added to each side of an inequality, the inequality symbol ___.

5. Find the solution set for $3 - 5x \le 2 - 2x + 4$.

6. Does the graph of $3x \le -5$ lie to the left or to the right of zero?

7. Translate to an inequality and solve.

A salesperson can be paid by Plan A $250/month and 20% of gross sales, or by Plan B $750/month and 25% of gross sales over $5000. Assuming that sales always exceed $5000, for what gross sales is Plan B better?

Chapter 2
Quizzes

ANSWERS: 1. $t = \frac{D}{r}$ 2. $V = \frac{kT}{P}$ 3. Is reversed
4. Stays the same 5. $x \geq -1$ 6. Left
7. More than $15,000

QUIZ 6 Sections 2–7 to 2–8

1. If two inequalities are joined by "or," the result is called a ____ (conjunction, disjunction), and the solution set is the ____ (union, intersection) of their individual solution sets.
2. Solve $-7 \leq x - 3 \leq 4$.
3. Solve $2x - 5 < 3$ or $2x - 3 > 9$.

Is 5 an element of each of the following solution sets?
4. $-2 < x \leq 7$ 5. $x < -2$ or $x \geq 7$
6. Find the distance along a number line between the points having the given coordinates -7 and 15.
7. Solve $|2x - 3| \leq 5$.

ANSWERS: 1. Disjunction, union 2. $-4 \leq x \leq 7$
3. $x < 4$ or $x > 6$ 4. Yes 5. No 6. 22
7. $-1 \leq x \leq 4$

Chapter 3
Quizzes

QUIZ 7 Sections 3–1 to 3–2

Consider the set $\{-4, -2, 0, 2\}$.
1. Find the set of ordered pairs determined by the relation $<$.
2. Find the set of ordered pairs determined by the relation $\geq$.
3. Given the set of ordered pairs $\{(a, b), (c, d), (e, f), (g, h)\}$, list the domain and the range.
4. Tell in which quadrant or on which axis each point lies. $(3, -5), (-2, -7), (3, 0), (-2, 1), (0, 5)$
5. Consider the equation $3x - 2y = 6$. Tell whether each given ordered pair is a solution.
   $(2, 0), (0, -3), \left(1, -\frac{3}{2}\right)$

ANSWERS: **1.** $\{(-4, -2)(-4, 0)(-4, 2)(-2, 0)$
$(-2, 2)(0, 2)\}$ **2.** $\{(2, 2), (2, 0), (2, -2),$
$(2, -4), (0, 0), (0, -2), (0, -4), (-2, -2),$
$(-2, -4), (-4, -4)\}$ **3.** Domain $\{a, c, e, g\}$;
range $\{b, d, f, h\}$ **4.** IV, III, x-axis, II, y-axis
5. Yes, yes, yes

QUIZ 8   Sections 3–3 to 3–5

1. Given $f(x) = 2x^2 + 3x - 5$, find $f(0), f(-2), f(3)$.
2. Find the domain of the function $f(x) = \dfrac{2x + 3}{x^2 - 4x + 3}$.
3. Find the intercepts of the graph of this equation.
   $2x - 3y = 12$
4. Find the slope of the line between these two points.
   $(3, 2), (0, -4)$
5. Find the slope, if it exists, of each of these lines.
   $y = -4, 2x = 3$
6. Find the equation of the line having a slope of 3 and
   containing the point $(1, -1)$. Write the equation in
   standard form.

ANSWERS: **1.** $-5, -3, 22$ **2.** $\{x \mid x \neq 1, x \neq 3\}$
3. $(0, -4), (6, 0)$ **4.** 2 **5.** 0, no slope
6. $3x - y - 4 = 0$

QUIZ 9   Sections 3–6 to 3–7

1. Find the equation of the line containing the points
   $(3, -2)$ and $(2, -4)$.
2. Find the slope and y-intercept of the line $3x - 2y = 8$.
3. Find the equation of the line having slope $\frac{2}{5}$ and
   y-intercept $(0, -1)$.
4. Write an equation of the line containing the point
   $(-2, -3)$ and parallel to the line whose equation
   is $2x + 3y = 6$.
5. What is the equation of the line containing $(3, 1)$
   which is perpendicular to the line $4x - 3y = 9$?

ANSWERS: **1.** $2x - y - 8 = 0$ **2.** $m = \frac{3}{2}, b = -4$

3. $y = \frac{2}{5}x - 1$ **4.** $2x + 3y + 13 = 0$ **5.** $3x + 4y = 13$

Chapter 4 Quizzes

QUIZ 10   Section 4–1

1. In which quadrant lies the point of intersection of the two lines whose equations are $3x - 2y = 6$ and $4x + 3y = -12$? (Hint: Decide by graphing.)

2. Solve using the substitution method.
$$2x - y = 2$$
$$3y - 2x = 6$$

3. Solve using the addition method.
$$4x + 2y = 18$$
$$3x - 4y = -14$$

ANSWERS: **1.** III   **2.** $(3, \ 4)$ **3.** $(2, \ 5)$

QUIZ 11   Sections 4–2 to 4–3

1. To raise funds, the sophomore class sold hats for $3.50 each and banners for $2.50. They sold 120 items and grossed $342. How many hats and how many banners did they sell?

2. Solve.
$$3x + 2y + z = -1$$
$$x + 3y - z = 0$$
$$2x - 2y + z = 2$$

ANSWERS: **1.** 42 hats and 78 banners
2. $(1, -1, -2)$

QUIZ 12   Sections 4–4 to 4–5

1. There are $3 worth of nickels, dimes and quarters in a jar, a total of 24 coins. The number of dimes is half the number of nickels and quarters combined. How many coins of each kind are in the jar?

2. Determine whether the following system of equations are dependent, independent, or inconsistent.

$$2x + 3y = 7 \qquad 2x - y = 1 \qquad 5x - 2y = 1$$
$$y = x - 2 \qquad 3y = 6x - 3 \qquad 4 + 2.5x = y$$

ANSWERS: **1.** 9, 8, 7   **2.** Independent, dependent, inconsistent

QUIZ 13   Sections 5-1 to 5-3

1. Determine the degree of each term and the degree of the polynomial. $y^2z - 2yz^4 + z^2 + y$
2. Add $3x^2 - 2x^3 + x - 5$ and $2x - 3x^4 + x^3 - x^2$.
3. Subtract $3x^2 + 4x^3 + 5x - 4$ from $3x - 2x^3 + 5x^2 - 1$.
4. Multiply $(x - y)^3$.
5. Factor $4x^2y^2 - 9$.
6. Factor $-36x + 12x^2 + 27$.

ANSWERS: 1. 3, 5, 2, 1; 5   2. $-3x^4 - x^3 + 2x^2 + 3x - 5$ 3. $-6x^3 + 2x^2 - 2x + 3$
4. $x^3 - 3x^2y + 3xy^2 - y^3$ 5. $(2xy + 3)(2xy - 3)$
6. $3(2x - 3)^2$

QUIZ 14   Sections 5-4 to 5-5

Factor completely.

1. $2x^2 - 6x - 20$ 2. $6x^2 - x - 15$
3. $2ax - ay - 4bx + 2by$ 4. $9x^2 + 12xy + 4y^2 - 25$
5. $2x^2 - 16x - 66$ (Use the completing the square method. Show work.)

ANSWERS: 1. $2(x - 5)(x + 2)$ 2. $(2x + 3)(3x - 5)$
3. $(a - 2b)(2x - y)$ 4. $(3x + 2y + 5)(3x + 2y - 5)$
5. $2(x - 11)(x + 3)$

QUIZ 15   Sections 5-6 to 5-8

Factor completely.

1. $27x^3 - 8y^3$ 2. $8x^3 - 18xy^2$
3. $10x^2 - 41xy - 18y^2$ 4. Solve $2x^2 - x - 6 = 0$.

ANSWERS: 1. $(3x - 2y)(9x^2 + 6xy + 4y^2)$
2. $2x(2x + 3y)(2x - 3y)$ 3. $(2x - 9y)(5x + 2y)$
4. $2, \dfrac{-3}{2}$

QUIZ 16   Sections 6-1 to 6-3

1. Multiply and simplify $\dfrac{2x^3 - 8x}{2x^2 + x - 3} \cdot \dfrac{2x + 3}{4x^2 + 8x}$.

2. Divide and simplify $\dfrac{4x^2 - 4x + 1}{2x^2 - 5x + 2} \div \dfrac{2x^2 - 3x + 1}{x^3 - 8}$.

3. Subtract and simplify $\dfrac{2a + b}{2a^2 - 5ab + 3b^2} - \dfrac{a - b}{3a(2a - 3b)}$.

ANSWERS: **1.** $\dfrac{x - 2}{2(x - 1)}$ **2.** $\dfrac{x^2 + 2x + 4}{x - 1}$

3. $\dfrac{5a^2 + 5ab - b^2}{3a(2a - 3b)(a - b)}$

QUIZ 17 Sections 6–4 to 6–5

1. Simplify $\dfrac{\dfrac{1}{ab} - 1}{\dfrac{1}{ab} - ab}$.

2. Simplify $\dfrac{2y^{-1} - 2x^{-1}}{2xy^{-1} + 1 - 3yx^{-1}}$.

3. Simplify $(x^3 - 4x + 3) \div (x - 1)$.

ANSWERS: **1.** $\dfrac{1}{1 + ab}$ **2.** $\dfrac{2}{2x + 3y}$ **3.** $x^2 + x - 3$

QUIZ 18 Sections 6–6 to 6–8

1. Solve $\dfrac{3a - 1}{a - 3} - \dfrac{a + 5}{a + 2} = 2$.

2. The numerator of a fractional number is 3 more than the denominator. If 8 is added to both the numerator and denominator, the result is $\frac{7}{6}$. What is the original fractional number?

3. Solve $I = \dfrac{2V}{R + 2r}$ for R.

ANSWERS: **1.** $a = -5$ **2.** $\dfrac{13}{10}$

3. $R = \dfrac{2V - 2rI}{I}$ or $\dfrac{2V}{I} - 2r$

Chapter 7 Quizzes

QUIZ 19 Sections 7–1 to 7–3

Assume that all variables under radical signs represent positive numbers.

1. Simplify $-\sqrt{\dfrac{196}{25}}, \; \sqrt{(x - 3)^2}, \; \sqrt[4]{81x^4}, \; \sqrt[3]{\dfrac{-x^6}{27}}$.

2. Simplify $\sqrt{48x^3y^4}$.

3. Multiply and simplify $\sqrt[3]{12} \cdot \sqrt[3]{18}$.

4. Multiply and simplify $\sqrt{3tw^3} \cdot \sqrt{6tw}$.

5. Divide and simplify $\sqrt{\dfrac{81x^4}{25y^2}}$.

6. Divide and simplify $\dfrac{\sqrt{27x^5}}{\sqrt{3x}}$.

ANSWERS: 1. $\dfrac{-14}{5}$, $|x - 3|$, $3x$, $\dfrac{-x^2}{3}$ 2. $4xy^2\sqrt{3x}$

3. 6 4. $3tw^2\sqrt{2}$ 5. $\dfrac{9x^2}{5y}$ 6. $3x^2$

QUIZ 20 Sections 7–4 to 7–5

Assume that all variables under radical signs represent positive numbers.

1. Add $5a\sqrt{3a} + \sqrt{12a^3}$.

2. Multiply $(2\sqrt{3} - 1)(3\sqrt{3} + 2)$.

3. Rationalize the denominator: $\sqrt{\dfrac{x^2}{y}}$, $\dfrac{\sqrt{a}}{\sqrt{b^3}}$.

4. Rationalize the denominator: $\dfrac{\sqrt{3} + 2\sqrt{5}}{2\sqrt{3} - \sqrt{5}}$.

5. Rewrite without fractional exponents and simplify $(x^3y^5)^{\frac{1}{2}}$.

6. Write as a single radical expression $x^{\frac{1}{2}} \cdot y^{\frac{2}{3}}$.

ANSWERS: 1. $7a\sqrt{3a}$ 2. $16 + \sqrt{3}$
3. $\dfrac{x}{y} \cdot \sqrt{y}$, $\dfrac{1}{b^2} \cdot \sqrt{ab}$ 4. $\dfrac{16 + 5\sqrt{15}}{7}$ 5. $xy^2\sqrt{xy}$
6. $\sqrt[6]{x^3y^4}$

QUIZ 21 Sections 7–6 to 7–7

Assume that all expressions under radical signs represent positive numbers.

1. Solve $\sqrt[3]{x + 2} = 2$.
2. Solve $\sqrt{x - 3} + \sqrt{8 - x} = 3$.
3. Multiply and simplify $\sqrt{-3} \cdot \sqrt{-18}$.
4. Multiply $(2 + 3i)(3 - 2i)$.

5. Divide $\dfrac{8 + i}{2 - 3i}$.

ANSWERS: 1. 6 2. 4, 7 3. $-3\sqrt{6}$
4. $12 + 5i$ 5. $1 + 2i$

QUIZ 22   Section 7–9

1. Are $1 - i$ and $1 + i$ solutions to the equation
   $x^2 - 2x + 2 = 0$?
2. Find an equation having $1 + 5i$ and $1 - 5i$ as solutions.
3. Solve $(3 - i)x + 3 - 2i = 3 - 2(2i - x)$.
4. The graph of $-4 + 3i$ is a point on the ____ quadrant.
5. Find $|5 + 12i|$.

ANSWERS: 1. Yes, yes   2. $x^2 - 2x + 26 = 0$
3. $1 - i$ 4. Second   5. 13

Chapter 8
Quizzes

QUIZ 23   Sections 8–1 to 8–2

1. Solve $6x^2 + x - 12 = 0$.
2. Solve $2x^2 - 6x = 0$.
3. The length of a rectangle is 6 cm more than 3 times the
   width. The area is 45 square cm. Find the dimensions.

4. Solve, using the quadratic formula.
   $4x^2 - 4x - 1 = 0$

ANSWERS: 1. $-\frac{3}{2}, \frac{4}{3}$ 2. 0, 3

3. Length 15, width 3   4. $\frac{1 \pm \sqrt{2}}{2}$

QUIZ 24   Sections 8–3 to 8–4

1. Use the discriminant to determine the nature of the
   roots of $x^2 - 2x + 2 = 0$.
2. What is the sum and what is the product of the roots
   of $3x^2 + 4x - 8 = 0$? Do not solve the equation.
3. Find a quadratic equation whose solutions are $3 + \sqrt{2}$
   and $3 - \sqrt{2}$.
4. Solve $(x^2 - 3x)^2 - 2(x^2 - 3x) - 8 = 0$.

ANSWERS: 1. Complex conjugates
2. Sum = $\frac{-4}{3}$, product = $\frac{-8}{3}$ 3. $x^2 - 6x + 7 = 0$
4. $-1, 1, 2, 4$

QUIZ 25   Sections 9–1 to 9–3

1. Tell whether the following functions are symmetric with respect to the x-axis, the y-axis and/or the origin.

$$y = 3x^2 + 2 \qquad 4x^2 - 9y^2 = 1 \qquad y^2 = x^2 + 3x - 2$$

2. Determine whether each function is even, odd, or neither.

$$f(x) = x^4 + 3x^2 \qquad f(x) = x^{\frac{3}{2}} \qquad f(x) = 2x - x^{-1}$$

3. Tell how the position of the graphs of these equations compares to the position of the graph of $y = x^2$. (Is the graph up or down from that of $y = x^2$ and by how much?)

$$y = x^2 + 3$$
$$y = x^2 - 2$$

4. Tell whether the graphs of the given equations have been stretched or shrunk in comparison to the graph of $y = x^2$.

$$y = 3x^2$$
$$y = \tfrac{1}{2}x^2$$

ANSWERS: 1. y-axis; x-axis, y-axis, origin; x-axis
2. Even, neither, odd   3. Up 3, down 2
4. Stretched, shrunk

QUIZ 26   Sections 9–4 to 9–5

Describe the graph of each of the following functions by answering these questions:

a. What is the name of the curve?
b. Where is the vertex?
c. What is the line of symmetry?
d. Does it open up or down?
e. Does it have a maximum or a minimum?
f. Is it stretched or shrunk with respect to $y = x^2$?
g. Has it been translated to the left or right with respect to $y = x^2$?

1. $f(x) = 3(x - 2)^2 + 5$

2. $f(x) = -\tfrac{1}{2}(x + 1)^2 + 2$

ANSWERS: 1. Parabola, $(2, 5)$, $x = 2$, up, minimum, stretched, right   2. Parabola, $(-1, 2)$, $x = -1$, down, maximum, shrunk, left

QUIZ 27   Sections 9–6 to 9–7

1. What is the maximum rectangular area that can be enclosed with 100 meters of fencing? What are the dimensions?

2. For the graph of each function, find the x-intercepts, the line of symmetry and the vertex. Tell whether the vertex is a maximum or a minimum.
$$f(x) = x^2 - 6x + 2 \qquad f(x) = -x^2 - 8x - 18$$

ANSWERS: 1. Area 625 square meters, 25 m × 25 m
2. $3 + \sqrt{7}$ and $3 - \sqrt{7}$, $x = 3$, $(3, -7)$, minimum; no intercepts, $x = -4$, $(-4, -2)$, maximum

Chapter 10 Quizzes

QUIZ 28   Sections 10–1 to 10–2

1. Find the distance between $(-2.5, -7)$ and $(-4.5, 6)$.
2. Find the midpoint of the segment having $(-c, -d)$ and (d, d) as endpoints.
3. Write each equation:
   a. A circle with center at the origin and radius 9.
   b. A circle with center at $(1, 1)$ and radius 7.
4. Find the center of this circle:
$$x^2 + y^2 + 4x - 6y + 12 = 0.$$

ANSWERS: 1. $\sqrt{173}$ 2. $\left(\frac{-c + d}{2}, 0\right)$
3a. $x^2 + y^2 = 81$ b. $(x - 1)^2 + (y - 1)^2 = 49$
4. $(-2, 3)$

QUIZ 29   Sections 10–3 to 10–4

1. Give the x- and y-intercepts of the graph of this equation:
$$\frac{x^2}{16} + \frac{y^2}{36} = 1.$$
2. What are the foci for the equation in question 1?
3. Write in standard form: $9x^2 + 12y^2 = 36$.
4. What are the vertices of $\frac{x^2}{16} - \frac{y^2}{100} = 1$?
5. Name the asymptotes of the equation in Exercise 4.

ANSWERS: **1.** $(4, 0)$, $(-4, 0)$, $(0, 6)$, $(0, -6)$

2. $(0, 2\sqrt{5})$, $(0, -2\sqrt{5})$ **3.** $\frac{x^2}{4} + \frac{y^2}{3} = 1$

4. $(4, 0)$, $(-4, 0)$ **5.** $y = \frac{5}{2}x$, $y = \frac{-5}{2}x$

QUIZ 30 Sections 10–5 to 10–6

1. Write the equation of the parabola $x = \frac{2}{9}y^2$ in the $y^2 = 4px$ form. Identify the focus, the directrix and the vertex.
2. Find the equation of a parabola with focus $(-2, 5)$ and directrix $y = 1$.
3. Solve by graphing. Estimate the solutions to the nearest integer.

$x^2 + y^2 = 9$
$y = x^2 + 2$

4. Solve by substitution $x - 2y = 1$ and $xy = 36$.

ANSWERS: **1.** $\left(0, +\frac{9}{8}\right)$, directrix: $y = -\frac{9}{8}$,
vertex $(0, 0)$ **2.** $(x + 2)^2 = 8(y - 3)$ **3.** $(1, 3)$,
$(-1, 3)$ **4.** $(9, 4)$, $\left(-8, -\frac{9}{2}\right)$

QUIZ 31 Sections 11–1 to 11–3

1. Find whether -2 is a root of $P(x) = 3x^4 - 5x^3 - 12x^2 + 15x - 10$.
2. Use synthetic division to find the remainder when $x + 2$ is divided into $3x^4 + 4x^3 + x^2 + 9x + 3$.
3. Complete the sentence: In a polynomial $P(x)$, the function value $P(a) = $ ____ .
4. For $P(x)$ $P(1) = 0$ and $P(0) = 6$. Give a factor of $P(x)$.
5. A polynomial of degree 5 with rational coefficients has roots $\sqrt{3}$, $2 + i$, and -3. What are its other roots?

ANSWERS: **1.** Yes **2.** 5 **3.** The remainder when $P(x)$ is divided by $x - a$. **4.** $x - 1$ **5.** $-\sqrt{3}$, $2 - i$.

Chapter 11
Quizzes

QUIZ 32   Sections 11–4 to 11–5

1. Let $P(x) = 2x^3 - 3x^2 + 4x - 8$. List the possible positive rational roots.
2. Find all rational roots of $2x^3 + x^2 + 10x + 5$.
3. What does Descartes' Rule of Signs tell about the number of positive real roots for the equation $3x^3 + 5x^2 - x + 4$?
4. Tell why 5 is an upper bound for the roots of $3x^4 - 11x^3 - 18x^2 + 10$.

ANSWERS: **1.** 1, 2, 4, 8, $\frac{1}{2}$ **2.** $-\frac{1}{2}$ **3.** Either 2 or 0   **4.** Synthetic division by 5 yields all positive coefficients.

Chapter 12
Quizzes

QUIZ 33   Sections 12–1 to 12–2

1. Write the equation of the inverse of the function $y = -3x + 5$. Express your answer in slope intercept form.
2. Find the inverse of the relation {(1, 1), (2, 2), (10, 2), (2, 10)}.
3. Complete these pairs from the function $y = \left(\frac{1}{2}\right)^x$.

   (0, ___)   (3, ___)   (___, 4)
4. If $y = \log_4 x$, then $x =$ ___.

5. Complete these pairs from the function $y = \log_{10} x$.

   (10, ___)   (1, ___)   (___, 10)

ANSWERS: **1.** $y = -\frac{1}{3}x + \frac{5}{3}$ **2.** {(1, 1), (2, 2), (2, 10), (10, 2)}   **3.** (0, 1), $\left(3, \frac{1}{8}\right)$, $(-2, 4)$ **4.** $x = 4^y$
5. (10, 1), (1, 0), $(10^{10}, 10)$.

QUIZ 34   Sections 12–3 to 12–4

1. $y = \log_a b$ implies that ___.
2. Simplify $\log_a a^5$.
3. Simplify $6^{\log_6 10}$.
4. Solve $\log_x 0.1 = -1$.

Complete, using theorems about logarithms. Assume all logs are base a.

5. $\log \frac{x}{y} = $ ____
6. $\log p^{10} = $ ____
7. $\log (6x) = $ ____
8. Express as a single logarithm $\log_a 10^2 - 2 \log_a \sqrt{10}$.

ANSWERS: **1.** $a^y = b$ **2.** 5 **3.** 10 **4.** 10
5. $\log x - \log y$ **6.** $10 \log p$ **7.** $\log 6 + \log x$
8. $\log_a 10$

QUIZ 35   Sections 12–5 to 12–6

1. If $\log 7.45 = 0.8722$, then $\log 7450 = $ ____ and $\log .0745 = $ ____ .
2. The table shows $\log 700 = 2.8451$. Find antilog $(0.8451 - 1)$.
3. Find $\log 0.3582$. (The entry for "358" in the table is 0.5539. The entry for "359" is 0.5551.)
4. Find antilog 5.4806. (In the table the entry for "302" is 0.4800, the entry for "303" is 0.4814, the entry for "548" is 0.7388, and the entry for "549" is 0.7396.)

ANSWERS: **1.** 3.8722, $0.8722 + (-2)$ **2.** 0.7
3. 0.5541 **4.** 302,400

QUIZ 36   Sections 13–1 to 13–2

1. Evaluate $\sum_{k=1}^{6} (-1)^k \cdot k$.
2. In a sequence where $a_n = (n)^{n-1}$, find the first term.
3. In an arithmetic sequence, 13 is the 4th term and 34 is the 7th term. Find the first term and the common difference.
4. Insert 5 arithmetic means between 100 and 145.
5. Find the sum of 100 consecutive integers beginning with 26.

ANSWERS: **1.** 3 **2.** 1
3. $a = -8, d = 7$ **4.** 107.5, 115, 122.5, 130, 137.5
5. 7550

Chapter 13
Quizzes

QUIZ 37   Sections 13–3 to 13–4

1. Find the tenth term of the geometric sequence
   $-8, -4, -2, \ldots$
2. Find the sum of the first 7 terms of 16, 24, 36, ...
3. Tell whether this infinite series has a sum:
   $10 + 15 + 22.5 + \ldots$
4. Find the sum: $24 + 2.4 + 0.24 + 0.024 + \ldots$

ANSWERS: 1. $-\frac{1}{64}$ 2. 514.75   3. No

4. $26\frac{2}{3}$

QUIZ 38   Sections 13–5 to 13–7

1. List all the permutations of the letters A, B, C, D,
   where A is always in the 4th place.
2. Evaluate 5!, 1!, and 0!.
3. How many 3-digit phone numbers can be made from
   the digits 4, 5, 6, 7, 8?
4. List all combinations of the letters A, B, C, D, taken
   3 at a time.

5. Evaluate $\binom{7}{3}$.

ANSWERS: 1. $BCDA, BDCA, CBDA, CDBA, DBCA,$
$DCBA$ 2. 120, 1, 1   3. 60   4. $ABC, ABD, ACD,$
BCD 5. 35

Chapter 14
Quizzes

QUIZ 39   Sections 14–1 to 14–2

Given $A = \begin{bmatrix} 2 & -1 \\ 4 & 0 \end{bmatrix}$ and $B = \begin{bmatrix} 1 & -1 \\ 0 & 5 \end{bmatrix}$:

1. Find $A - B$.   2. Find AB.   3. Find $6B$.

4. Write a matrix equation equivalent to
   $2x = 19$
   $3x - y = 2.$

ANSWERS: 1. $\begin{bmatrix} 1 & 0 \\ 4 & -5 \end{bmatrix}$ 2. $\begin{bmatrix} 2 & -7 \\ 4 & -4 \end{bmatrix}$

3. $\begin{bmatrix} 6 & -6 \\ 0 & 30 \end{bmatrix}$ 4. $\begin{bmatrix} 2 & 0 & 19 \\ 3 & -1 & 2 \end{bmatrix}$

QUIZ 40   Sections 15–1 to 15–3

1. The reference angle for 260° is ___.
2. The reference angle for 440° is ___.
3. If $\sin \theta = \frac{3}{10}$ and $\cos \theta = \frac{19}{20}$, then $\tan \theta =$ ___.
4. $\sin 30° = \cos$ ___°.
5. If $\sin \theta = \frac{-5}{13}$, then $\tan \theta =$ ___.
6. Convert 80 degrees to radian measure.
7. Convert $\frac{6\pi}{5}$ to degree measure ___.
8. If $\sin 30°40' = 0.5100$ and $\sin 30°50' = 0.5125$, then $\sin 30°44' =$ ___.

ANSWERS: 1. 80°   2. 80°   3. $\frac{6}{19}$ 4. 60°
5. $\frac{5}{12}, -\frac{5}{12}$ 6. $\frac{4\pi}{9}$ 7. 216°   8. 0.5110

QUIZ 41   Sections 15–4 to 15–6

1. The amplitude of the sine function is ___.
2. The period of the tangent function is ___.
3. The graph of ___ ($\sin x$ or $\cos x$) is symmetric with respect to the y-axis.
4. $\sin^2 65° + \cos^2$ ___ $= 1$
5. $1 + \tan^2 \theta =$ ___
6. $\cos \left(\theta - \frac{\pi}{2}\right) =$ ___
7. The period of the function $y = -\sin 2\theta$ is ___.
8. The amplitude of $y = -2 \cos \left(\frac{1}{3}\theta\right)$ is ___.

ANSWERS: 1. 1   2. π (or 180°)   3. $\cos x$
4. 65°   5. $\text{Sec}^2 \theta$ 6. $\text{Sin } \theta$ 7. π 8. 2

QUIZ 42   Sections 16–1 to 16–3

1. Complete $\cos (\alpha - \beta) =$ ___.
2. Derive a value for $\sin 120°$ using $\sin (90° + 30°)$.

Chapter 15
Quizzes

Chapter 16
Quizzes

3. Complete $\tan (\alpha - \beta) = $ ____ .

4. If $\cos \theta = -\frac{4}{5}$ and θ is in quadrant II, find $\cos 2\theta$.

5. $\sin \frac{\theta}{2} = $ ____ .

6. Prove this identity: $\tan x + \cot x = \sec x \csc x$.

ANSWERS: 1. $\cos \alpha \cos \beta + \sin \alpha \sin \beta$
2. $\sin 90° \cos 30° + \cos 90° \sin 30°$

3. $\frac{\tan \alpha - \tan \beta}{1 + \tan \alpha \tan \beta}$ 4. $\frac{7}{25}$ 5. $\pm \sqrt{\frac{1 - \cos \theta}{2}}$

6. $\tan x + \cot x = \frac{\sin x}{\cos x} + \frac{\cos x}{\sin x} = \frac{\sin^2 x + \cos^2 x}{\cos x \sin x}$

$= \frac{1}{\cos x \sin x} = \sec x \csc x$

QUIZ 43   Sections 16–4 to 16–6

1. For arcsin x, the domain is ____ and the range is ____ .

2. Find all values of $\cos^{-1} \frac{\sqrt{3}}{2}$.

3. Solve, finding all solutions from $0°$ to $360°$:
   $2 \sin^2 x - 5 \sin x = 3$.

4. Find the solution in terms of θ. Do not evaluate. From
   the top of a 2000-foot highrise apartment building
   at the beachfront, the angle of depression to a fishing
   boat is $10°$. How far is the boat from the base of
   the building?

ANSWERS: 1. Domain: $-1 \leq x \leq 1$, range $-\frac{\pi}{2} \leq y \leq \frac{\pi}{2}$

2. $30 + 360k$, $330 + 360k$, where k is an integer
3. $x = 210°, 330°$ 4. $d = 2000 \div \tan 10$

TEACHING SUGGESTIONS

BACKGROUND MATERIAL   In Axioms for the Real Numbers on page 5 we conclude by saying that any system in which these axioms hold is called a *field*. This is an important concept in algebra. While in elementary algebra we are chiefly concerned with using these axioms to manipulate expressions, more advanced students should be able to appreciate ideas about the structure of algebraic systems. There are other fields besides the real numbers. The rational numbers form a field, and so do the complex numbers.

BACKGROUND MATERIAL   The definition of division exactly parallels the definition of subtraction. Division is defined to be the operation opposite to multiplication, as subtraction is defined to be the operation opposite to addition. Similarly, Theorem 1–2 exactly parallels Theorem 1–1. This emphasizes that addition and multiplication are the two main operations of algebra.

Chapter 1
SECTION 1–1

SECTION 1–3

FOCUS ON STUDENT QUESTIONS
   Question: When I try to solve $x = x + 6$, I get $0 = 6$. What is the solution?
   Answer: Not all equations have solutions. Theorem 2–1 says that the original equation must be true. If we use the multiplication and addition principles and obtain a false equation such as $0 = 6$, we know the original equation has no solution. The equation $x = x + 6$ is not true for any value of x.

Chapter 2
SECTION 2–1

SECTION 2–2

PROBLEM SOLVING   Which of the following conditions satisfy the equation $3ax(bx - cy) = 0$?

1. $a = 0$ 2. $x = c$ and $y = b$ 3. $b = 0$
4. $y = 0$ and $x = 1$ 5. $x = 0$ 6. $b = 0$ and $cy = 0$
7. $x = \frac{cy}{b}$ 8. $b = -y$ and $c = -x$

Answer: 1, 2, 5, 6, 7, 8

SECTION 2–3

PROBLEM-SOLVING STRATEGY   It is important that students learn how to approach a word problem. The following points should be emphasized.

1. Read the problem carefully, more than once.
2. Make a list of the information given.
3. Draw a picture, if possible.
4. Write down what the variables represent. (Caution students that variables must stand for numbers. A student who lets x stand for Ruth and y stand for Anne in an age problem may be limited in seeing all aspects of a situation.)
5. Notice how *what* translates to a variable, *of* translates to a multiplication sign, and *is* translates to an equals sign.
6. When checking the answer to a problem, check the conditions of the problem itself to detect errors in translating as well as errors in solving an equation.

SECTION 2–5

TEACHING SUGGESTIONS   Remind students that to *solve* an equation or inequality means to find all of its solutions (its solution set). To *graph* an equation or inequality means to make a picture of its solution set.

CHALKBOARD EXAMPLE
Solve.

$$2x \le 5x - 1 + (-3x)$$
$$2x \le 5x - 1 - 3x$$
$$2x \le 2x - 1$$
$$0 \le -1$$

This is never true, so there is no solution.

SECTION 2–6

PROBLEM-SOLVING STRATEGY   Remind students that when translating problems to inequalities, they should use $\le$ for "at most" and $\ge$ for "at least."

CHALKBOARD EXAMPLE   Find all sets of four consecutive positive odd integers whose sum is less than 30.

To translate we use x to represent the smallest of four consecutive odd integers. The next three can then be represented as $x + 2$, $x + 4$, and $x + 6$.

The sum of the four integers must be less than 30, that is,

$$x + (x + 2) + (x + 4) + (x + 6) < 30$$
$$4x + 12 < 30$$
$$4x < 18$$
$$x < 4.5$$

The positive odd integers that are less than 4.5 are 1 and 3. Thus the possible sets of four consecutive odd integers are

$\{1, \ 3, \ 5, \ 7\}$ and $\{3, \ 5, \ 7, \ 9\}$.

For each set of four numbers, the sum is less than 30, so we have two answers to the problem.

TEACHING SUGGESTIONS   Remind students to use "and" and "or" carefully when constructing compound inequalities. (See Mathematical Language/The Inclusive Or on page 89.)

$|x| < a$ $|x| > a$
$x < $ and $x > -a$ $x > a$ or $x < -a$
$-a < x < a$

While the two statements of a conjunction can be combined, the two statements of a disjunction cannot. A common error is to try to construct a compound inequality without the word *or*.

TEACHING SUGGESTION   In forming Cartesian products, that is, pairs of $A \times B$, we take the first member from A and the second member from B. Also, when we find the domain and range, we are identifying *sets*.

TEACHING SUGGESTION   Students sometimes get confused in applying the vertical line test because it is stated in the negative. Given the graph of a relation, first try to show it is *not* a function by finding a vertical line that crosses the graph more than once. If this is not possible, then the graph is of a function.

SECTION 2–8

Chapter 3

SECTION 3–1

SECTION 3–3

SECTION 3-4

TEACHING SUGGESTION   Some equations with variables in denominators have graphs that come close to being lines. For example, consider

$$3 + \frac{2y}{x} + \frac{4}{x} = 0$$

If we multiply by x on both sides, we get

$3x + 2y + 4 = 0$

This is the standard form of a linear equation. The point $(0, -2)$, however, is not in the graph of the first equation because x cannot equal 0, so its graph is not an entire line.

COMPUTER SUPPLEMENTS   *Computer Graphing Experiments 1, Algebra One and Algebra Two,* by Lund and Andersen (Addison-Wesley 1982) provides a diskette and worksheets for graphing. The diskette has thirteen topics suitable for use in conjunction with Chapters 3 and 4. See also References to Supplements in this Teacher's Edition.

SECTION 3-6

FOCUS ON STUDENT QUESTIONS
   Question: In Theorem 3-6 there are several x's and y's. How do I distinguish between them?
   Answer: The letters with subscripts—x_1, x_2, y_1, and y_2—are not variables. They are the coordinates of the two given points. Only x and y are variables in this equation. Substitute the coordinates of one point for x_1 and y_1 and the coordinates of the other point for x_2 and y_2. Only x and y remain in the simplified equation.

CHALLENGE   The intercept form of a linear equation is given in the Exercise 4a. Teachers may want to show students how this form is derived.

$$ax + by = c \quad \frac{ax}{c} + \frac{by}{c} = 1 \quad \frac{x}{\left(\frac{c}{a}\right)} + \frac{y}{\left(\frac{c}{b}\right)} = 1$$

The intercepts are $\left(\frac{c}{a}, 0\right)$ and $\left(0, \frac{c}{b}\right)$.

SECTION 3-7

BACKGROUND MATERIAL   Theorem 3-9 is a good example of a theorem consisting of a statement and its converse. The first part of it tells us that the set of pairs of lines having -1 as a product of slopes is a subset of the set of perpendicular lines (no lines vertical). The second part tells us that the set of perpendicular lines is a subset of the set having -1 as product of slopes. Thus these are the same set.

Such theorems are often expressed more concisely using the words "if and only if," as follows: Two nonvertical lines are perpendicular *if and only if* the product of the slopes is -1.

PROBLEM SOLVING   Have students graph the function representing the price of any number of 30¢ stamps. The graph is not the graph of the linear function $f(s) = 0.30s$. There cannot be a nonintegral number of stamps or a negative number of stamps. The function is discontinuous and nonnegative, and the graph is represented by the points $(0, 0)$, $(1, 0.30)$, $(2, 0.60)$, etc.

Chapter 4

CHALKBOARD EXAMPLE
Solve.

$$5x + y = -2 \qquad ①$$
$$x + 7y = 3 \qquad ②$$

Multiply ② by -5 and add the result to ①.

$$\begin{array}{r} 5x + y = -2 \\ -5x - 35y = -15 \\ \hline -34y = -17 \end{array}$$

Now we solve for y. Then we substitute the result in the first equation to find x.

$$-34y = -17 \qquad x + 7\left(\tfrac{1}{2}\right) = 3$$
$$y = \tfrac{1}{2} \qquad\qquad x + \tfrac{7}{2} = 3$$
$$x = 3 - \tfrac{7}{2}, \text{ or } -\tfrac{1}{2}$$

The solution is $\left(-\tfrac{1}{2}, \tfrac{1}{2}\right)$.

CHALKBOARD EXAMPLE
An interest problem   Two investments are made totaling $4800. In the first year they yield $584 in simple interest. Part of the money is invested at 11% and the rest at 13%. Find the amount invested at each rate of interest.

Organizing information in a table will help in translating. The rows in the table come from the formula for simple interest: $I = Prt$.

	First Investment	Second Investment	Total
Principal	x	y	$4800
Rate of Interest	11%	13%	
Time	1 yr	1 yr	
Interest	11% x or 0.11x	13% y or 0.13y	$ 584

Notice that we have used x and y for the numbers of dollars invested. They total $4800, and this gives us one equation.

$x + y = 4800$

Look at the last column. The interest, or *yield,* totals $584. This gives us a second equation.

$0.11x + 0.13y = 584$, or $11x + 13y = 58,400$

We solve the system.

$$x + y = 4800$$
$$11x + 13y = 58,400$$

We find that $x = 2000$ and $y = 2800$. This checks in the problem, so $2000 is invested at 11% and $2800 at 13%.

SECTION 4–3

CHALKBOARD EXAMPLE
Solve.

$$x + y + z = 180 \quad ①$$
$$x \quad\quad - z = -70 \quad ②$$
$$2y - z = 0 \quad ③$$

Note that there is no y in equation ②. We begin by multiplying ① by -1 and adding it to ②.

$$x + y + z = 180$$
$$-y - 2z = -250$$
$$2y - z = 0$$

To eliminate y from the third equation we multiply ② by 2 and add it to ③.

$$x + y + z = 180$$
$$-y - 2z = -250$$
$$-5z = -500$$

Now we solve ③ for z.

$$x + y + z = 180$$
$$-y - 2z = -250$$
$$z = 100$$

Next we substitute 100 for z in ②, and solve for y.

$$-y - 2(100) = -250$$
$$-y - 200 = -250$$
$$-y = -50$$
$$y = 50$$

Finally, we substitute 50 for y and 100 for z in ①.
The solution is (30, 50, 100).

CHALKBOARD EXAMPLE   In professional hockey, a win counts as 2 points, a loss as 0 points, and a tie as 1 point. Find the number of losses, wins and ties for a team that has played 62 games, has 83 points, and has 7 more losses than ties.

$$W + L + T = 62$$
$$2W + T = 83$$
$$L - T = 7$$

We solve the system and find that $W = 37$, $L = 16$, and $T = 9$. These numbers check in the original problem, so we have a solution.

BACKGROUND MATERIAL   Linear programming is an example of mathematics developed recently. It was developed around the time of World War II. This is unusual, because most of the mathematics taught in high school is centuries old.

FOCUS ON STUDENT QUESTIONS
   Question: In $3x^3 + 2x^2 - x + 5$, what degree does the term 5 have?
   Answer: If a polynomial is a constant other than 0, it has degree 0. The polynomial 0 is not given a degree, because statements of certain theorems are simplified if the zero polynomial is not given a degree.

TEACHING SUGGESTION   Two polynomials can be multiplied without going through all the steps of Example 1.

Chapter 5

Students should learn to do this, proceeding mentally as much as possible. For $(p - 3)(p^3 + 4p^2 - 5)$, start by multiplying every term in the second polynomial by p: $p^4 + 4p^3 - 5p$. Then multiply every term in the second polynomial by -3: $-3p^3 - 12p^2 + 15$. Then collect like terms: $p^4 + p^3 - 12p^2 - 5p + 15$.

PREVENTING STUDENT ERRORS   A common error made by students is to multiply $(A + B)^2$ and get $A^2 + B^2$. If they memorize the rule on page 214, they will not make this mistake.

SECTION 5–5

CHALKBOARD EXAMPLE   Factor $x^2 - 6.2x + 8.61$ by completing the square. To complete the square we take half of -6.2, obtaining -3.1. $(-3.1)^2 = 9.61$. We then add 0, naming it $9.61 - 9.61$.

$$
\begin{aligned}
x^2 - 6.2x + 8.61 &= x^2 - 6.2x + 8.61 + 9.61 - 9.61 \\
&= (x^2 - 6.2x + 9.61) + 8.61 - 9.61 \\
&= (x - 3.1)^2 - 1 \\
&= (x - 3.1 + 1)(x - 3.1 - 1) \\
&= (x - 2.1)(x - 4.1)
\end{aligned}
$$

SECTION 5–6

TEACHING SUGGESTIONS   To learn factoring of sums or differences of cubes, the patterns given in this section must be learned.

An expression like $a^6 - b^6$ can be thought of as a difference of two squares or the difference of two cubes. The former factorization causes no difficulty. But the factorization as the difference of cubes creates the factor $a^4 + a^2b^2 + b^4$, which students will not recognize as being factorable. It factors as $(a^2 + ab + b^2)(a^2 - ab + b^2)$.

Chapter 6

INTRODUCTION   Most teachers agree that students' ability with fractions is an indicator of their general abilities. Adding fractional expressions is the most intricate of the standard algebraic techniques. Finding the LCM of algebraic expressions is much the same as for other numbers except that they are usually more complicated. Factoring skills are used in fractional addition, subtraction, and multiplication.

The idea of multiplying an expression by 1 is the key to understanding this chapter.

PROBLEM SOLVING   Consider the function

$$f(x) = \frac{x^2 - x - 2}{x^2 - 4}.$$

We can see that 2 is not a sensible replacement for x, because the denominator would be 0. What happens to the function values as x gets very close to 2? Have students find the function values for values of x close to 2: 1, 1.9, 1.99, 1.999, and 3, 2.1, 2.01, 2.001. It should be clear that as x approaches 2, $f(x)$ approaches $\frac{3}{4}$.

To find what happens another way, we begin by factoring the expression.

$$\frac{x^2 - x - 2}{x^2 - 4} = \frac{(x - 2)(x + 1)}{(x - 2)(x + 2)} = \frac{(x + 1)}{(x + 2)}$$

Evaluating this expression using 2 for x gives us $\frac{3}{4}$. Students should remember that 2 is *not* in the domain of $f(x)$. While the graph of the function approaches $\frac{3}{4}$ as x approaches 2, the curve is not continuous at this point.

PREVENTING STUDENT ERRORS   When subtracting fractional expressions, the use of parentheses in the numerator is very important.

Incorrect: $\dfrac{3x + 12}{x^2 + 4} - \dfrac{x - 8}{x^2 + 4} = \dfrac{3x + 12 - x - 8}{x^2 + 4}$

Correct: $\dfrac{3x + 12}{x^2 + 4} - \dfrac{x - 8}{x^2 + 4} = \dfrac{3x + 12 - (x - 8)}{x^2 + 4}$

BACKGROUND MATERIAL   We are careful to say in Theorem 7–1 that negative numbers do not have square roots in the *real number system*. In Section 7–7 we study the complex numbers where $i = \sqrt{-1}$. Also notice in Theorem 7–3 that while every nonzero real number has three cube roots in the system of complex numbers, only one of them is a real number.

Question: Is the absolute value sign needed for $\sqrt{x^3} = |x|\sqrt{x}$?

Answer: If x is negative, then x^3 is negative and $\sqrt{x^3}$ cannot be simplified in the real number system. If x is 0 or positive, the absolute value signs are not needed.

SECTION 7–2

BACKGROUND MATERIAL   Using absolute value notation to simplify radicals is essential unless we assume that radicands and variables in radicands are all nonnegative. The use of absolute value notation can become very cumbersome for students at this level. Therefore, we assume in the exercises for the rest of the chapter that all variables represent nonnegative real numbers.

TEACHING SUGGESTIONS   Be sure students realize the significance of the restriction in Theorem 7–5 that a and b are nonnegative. This is also important when the equation of the theorem is reversed as in Simplifying by Factoring on page 297.

Incorrect: $\sqrt{-4} \cdot \sqrt{-5} = \sqrt{(-4)(-5)} = \sqrt{20}$

Incorrect: $\sqrt{20} = \sqrt{(-4)(-5)} = \sqrt{-4} \cdot \sqrt{-5}$

The symbols $\sqrt{-4}$ and $\sqrt{-5}$ have no meaning in the system of real numbers. Therefore they cannot be multiplied together.

SECTION 7–3

BACKGROUND MATERIAL   Note that Theorem 7–6 is not true unless we assume that the radicand in the numerator is nonnegative and the radicand in the denominator is positive. In the exercises for this section we assume that expressions under radical signs represent positive numbers. Thus we do not need to be concerned about the possibility of 0 in the denominator.

SECTION 7–4

CHALKBOARD EXAMPLES
Multiply.

1. $\sqrt[3]{a^2}(\sqrt[3]{3a} - \sqrt[3]{2}) = \sqrt[3]{a^2} \cdot \sqrt[3]{3a} - \sqrt[3]{a^2} \cdot \sqrt[3]{2}$
$$= \sqrt[3]{3a^3} - \sqrt[3]{2a^2}$$
$$= a\sqrt[3]{3} - \sqrt[3]{2a^2}$$

2. $(\sqrt{a} + \sqrt{3})(\sqrt{b} + \sqrt{3}) = \sqrt{a}\sqrt{b} + \sqrt{a}\sqrt{3} + \sqrt{3}\sqrt{b} + \sqrt{3}\sqrt{3}$
$$= \sqrt{ab} + \sqrt{3a} + \sqrt{3b} + 3$$

3. $\dfrac{4}{\sqrt{3}+1} = \dfrac{4}{\sqrt{3}+1} \cdot \dfrac{\sqrt{3}-1}{\sqrt{3}-1} = \dfrac{4(\sqrt{3}-1)}{(\sqrt{3}+1)(\sqrt{3}-1)}$
$$= \dfrac{4(\sqrt{3}-1)}{(\sqrt{3})^2 - 1^2} = \dfrac{4(\sqrt{3}-1)}{3-1}$$
$$= \dfrac{4(\sqrt{3}-1)}{2} = 2(\sqrt{3}-1)$$

CHALKBOARD EXAMPLE
Solve.

$$\sqrt[3]{4x^2 + 1} = 5$$
$$(\sqrt[3]{(4x^2 + 1)})^3 = 5^3$$
$$4x^2 + 1 = 125$$
$$4x^2 = 124$$
$$x^2 = 31$$
$$x = \pm\sqrt{31}$$

Both $\sqrt{31}$ and $-\sqrt{31}$ check. These are solutions.

BACKGROUND MATERIAL It is important to remember that both real numbers and imaginary numbers are *subsets* of the set of complex numbers. Real numbers can be expressed $a + 0i$ and imaginary numbers as $0 + bi$. In what ways does this system differ from the system of real numbers?

- Multiplication is not repeated addition. Its definition makes it an operation separate from addition.
- The complex numbers are not ordered. That is, given two complex numbers, we cannot say $a + bi < c + di$.
- The graphs of the complex numbers fill up the plane, while the real numbers can be graphed on a single line.

TEACHING SUGGESTIONS Students may need to be reminded that $-\sqrt{-3}\sqrt{-7} \neq -\sqrt{(-3)(-7)}$. They should also be reminded that all imaginary numbers must be expressed in terms of i before simplifying.

CHALKBOARD EXAMPLE Sometimes we rationalize denominators to simplify answers.
Solve.

$$-5x^2 + 2 = 0$$
$$-5x^2 = -2$$
$$x^2 = \frac{2}{5}$$

$$x = \sqrt{\frac{2}{5}} \qquad \text{or} \qquad x = -\sqrt{\frac{2}{5}}$$
$$x = \sqrt{\frac{2}{5} \cdot \frac{5}{5}} \qquad \text{or} \qquad x = -\sqrt{\frac{2}{5} \cdot \frac{5}{5}}$$
$$x = \frac{\sqrt{10}}{5} \qquad \text{or} \qquad x = -\frac{\sqrt{10}}{5}$$

These numbers check, so the solutions are $\frac{\sqrt{10}}{5}$ and $-\frac{\sqrt{10}}{5}$.

FOCUS ON STUDENT QUESTIONS
Question: To solve $3x^2 + 5x = 0$, can I multiply both sides by $\frac{1}{3x}$?
Answer: This is another case that illustrates the need for the restriction in the multiplication principle. Multiplying by an expression with a variable may give us an equation with a different solution set. In this case, we lose the solution 0.

SECTION 8–4

TEACHING SUGGESTIONS   Once students have solved for u, don't let them forget to solve for x.

Teachers should also remind students to check solutions in the original equation. Reducing an equation to one quadratic in form can sometimes introduce numbers that are not solutions of the original equation.

SECTION 8–5

TEACHING SUGGESTIONS   Teachers should remind students that when solving formulas for a given variable, they should use the same principles used to solve any equation.

Teachers should point out to students that the Quadratic Formula gives two different solutions, one found by adding the radical quantity, the other by subtracting it. Although both are solutions to the equation, one may not be a solution to a given situation or formula.

Chapter 9

SECTION 9–1

BACKGROUND MATERIAL   The notions of symmetry are very helpful in graphing. Students should learn, in graphing any equation, to look for symmetries before beginning to plot points in order to save a great deal of time.

CHALKBOARD EXAMPLE
Text $x^2 + y^4 + 5 = 0$ for symmetry with respect to the axes.
   We replace x by $-x$.
$$(-x)^2 + y^4 + 5 = 0$$
$$x^2 + y^4 + 5 = 0$$
This is equivalent to the original equation, so the graph is symmetric with respect to the y-axis.

We replace y by $-y$.

$$x^2 + (-y)^4 + 5 = 0$$
$$x^2 + y^4 + 5 = 0$$

This is equivalent to the original equation, so the graph is symmetric with respect to the x-axis.

TEACHING SUGGESTIONS It is important for teachers to stress that when replacing a variable x by $x - a$, the replacement must be made everywhere the variable occurs.

Teachers should also remind students that if we *subtract* a *positive* constant from y, this translates in the *positive* direction. This is what should be remembered. Of course if we subtract a *negative* constant, this translates in the *negative* direction (downward in this case).

SECTION 9–2

BACKGROUND MATERIAL The stretching and shrinking transformations are important in graphing. The theorems will be stated in a way analogous to the translation theorems. For example, note that Theorem 9–7 is stated to be analogous to the translation theorems. Before, we subtracted; here we divide. Before, we talked about a positive constant; here we talk about a constant whose absolute value is greater than 1.

SECTION 9–3

TEACHING SUGGESTIONS Teachers should point out to students that when we say that we stretch both ways from the horizontal axis, this means that *each point* will be twice as far from that axis as it was before the stretching.

Students may also find it helpful to remember that any function of the form $f(x) = ax^2$ is an even function.

BACKGROUND MATERIAL The best way to study a specific quadratic function is to put it into the form $f(x) = a(x - h)^2 + k$. Students may think that there should be some way to analyze the function in its standard form. Unfortunately the bx term is difficult to analyze directly. When the methods of calculus are available, students will have other techniques for this kind of analysis.

SECTION 9–6

APPLICATIONS: MATHEMATICAL MODELS It should be pointed out that the data given in the table for pizza diameters and prices on page 410 is not sufficient to determine that a quadratic function is a good mathematical

SECTION 9–8

model. It is true that a quadratic function will fit the three data points, but more information is needed before we can conclude that a quadratic function will give correct answers.

The model rocket example is an example of a mathematical model derived from theoretical considerations. The assumption made in the derivation of this quadratic function is that there is no friction or air resistance. Since, in the real world, there is air resistance, this model will give only approximate answers.

Chapter 10

SECTION 10-2

TEACHING SUGGESTIONS   Point out to students that the formula for a circle with center at (h, k) is obtained by applying the translation theorems, Theorems 9–5 and 9–6, to Theorem 10–1. Thus $(x - h)^2 + (y - k)^2 = r^2$ has a graph congruent to, but translated h units to the right of and k units upward from the graph of $x^2 + y^2 = r^2$.

Can the stretching and shrinking theorems also be applied? Multiplying the x portion by $\frac{1}{2}$ stretches the graph vertically. If we multiply both elements by the same constant, we maintain the circular shape. Thus $\frac{1}{2}(x - h)^2 + \frac{1}{2}(y - k)^2 = r^2$ is the circle $(x - h)^2 + (y - k)^2 = r^2$ stretched in the vertical and horizontal dimensions. We see it is still the equation of a circle when after multiplying both sides by 2, we obtain an equation in the standard form for the equation of a circle.

COMPUTER SUPPLEMENTS   *Computer Graphing Experiments 3, Conic Sections,* by Lund and Andersen (Addison-Wesley 1982) provides a diskette and worksheets for graphing. The diskette has fifteen topics suitable for use in conjunction with Chapter 10. See also References to Supplements in this Teacher's Edition.

SECTION 10-3

TEACHING SUGGESTIONS   The theorems for translating, stretching, and shrinking learned in Chapter 9 can be applied to ellipses as they were for circles in the previous section. This analysis can lead to the consideration of *similar ellipses.* One ellipse is similar to another if the equation of one can be obtained from the equation of the other by dividing the x and y elements by the same constant, so that the proportions of vertical and horizontal dimensions of the graph are preserved.

This analysis can also be used to show that an ellipse is a stretched circle. Consider the unit circle $x^2 + y^2 = 1$. If we replace x by x/a and y by y/b, this stretches or shrinks the graph, according to Theorems 9–7 and 9–8. When we replace x by x/a and y by y/b we get the standard form for the equation of an ellipse. Therefore, an ellipse is a circle transformed by a stretch or shrink in the x-direction and a stretch or shrink in the y-direction.

TEACHING SUGGESTIONS   Students should be encouraged to apply the symmetry, translation, and shrinking and stretching theorems learned in Chapter 9 to hyperbolas. The equation $x^2 - y^2 = 1$ represents an *equilateral hyperbola* that has perpendicular asymptotes. By interchanging x and y we reflect across the line $y = x$. By multiplying x by $\frac{1}{a}$ and y by $\frac{1}{c}$ we get other hyperbolas by stretching or by shrinking.

SECTION 10–4

PREVENTING STUDENT ERRORS   In graphing hyperbolas with asymptotes along the coordinate axes, students often make the error of connecting points across the origin, getting an N-shaped or backwards N-shaped curve. Remind them that the graph of a hyperbola approaches but does not cross, its asymptotes.

BACKGROUND MATERIAL   The parabola is the quadratic curve most familiar to students. The equation $y = x^2$ has a simple graph that students should quickly recognize from earlier work. Yet the analytic definition, $x^2 = 4py$ seems awkward. The purpose of this section is to analyze the function. In this form of the equation certain properties of the function are more apparent.

SECTION 10–5

TEACHING SUGGESTIONS   Teachers should point out that although parabolas have shapes that seem similar to hyperbolas, the curves are different. For one thing, parabolas do not have asymptotes.

PROBLEM-SOLVING STRATEGY   Students should sketch a graph of each curve even when only an algebraic solution is requested. This will help them spot wrong answers,

SECTION 10–6

which are not uncommon when there is so much computation to be done. Also, knowing the probable number of solutions helps students avoid the error of finding only some of the solutions when there are several.

Chapter 11

SECTION 11–1

BACKGROUND MATERIAL   When we speak of "roots," or "zeroes," of polynomial $P(x)$, we are also speaking about "roots" or "solutions" of the polynomial equation $P(x) = 0$.

CHALKBOARD EXAMPLES
1. Determine whether the following numbers are roots of the polynomial $P(x) = x^2 + 1$.
   a. $1 + i$ $P(1 + i) = (1 + i)^2 + 1$
   $= 1 + 2i + i^2 + 1$
   No. $= 1 + 2i - 1 + 1 = 1 + 2i$
   b. $-i$ $P(-i) = (-i)^2 + 1$
   Yes. $= -1 + 1$

2. By division determine whether $x - 2$ is a factor of the polynomial $x^4 - 16$.

$$
\begin{array}{r}
x^3 + 2x^2 + 4x + 8 \\
\hline
x - 2 \overline{\smash{)}x^4 \qquad\qquad -16} \\
\underline{x^4 - 2x^3} \\
2x^3 \\
\underline{2x^3 - 4x^2} \\
4x^2 \\
\underline{4x^2 - 8x} \\
8x - 16 \\
\underline{8x - 16} \\
0
\end{array}
$$

Yes.

SECTION 11–2

BACKGROUND MATERIAL   Evaluating a polynomial by substituting a value for x can be a cumbersome process, especially when the polynomial includes large powers of x or when large or awkward values are substituted for x. Theorem 11–1 provides a new method for evaluating polynomials using synthetic division.

Theorem 11–2 follows closely from Theorem 11–1. If we find by synthetic division that $P(r) = 0$, then by definition we know that r is a root of $P(x)$. Thus, $(x - r)$ is a factor of $P(x)$.

CHALKBOARD EXAMPLE
$P(x) = x^3 + 5x^2 - 2x - 24$

a. Is $(x + 4)$ of a factor of $P(x)$?

$$
\begin{array}{r|rrrr}
-4 & 1 & 5 & -2 & -24 \\
   &   & -4 & -4 & 24 \\
\hline
   & 1 & 1 & -6 & 0 \\
\end{array}
$$

Yes.

b. Find another factor of $P(x)$.

$P(x) = (x + 4)(x^2 + x - 6)$

c. Complete the factorization of $P(x)$.

$P(x) = (x + 4)(x + 3)(x - 2)$

d. Solve the equation $P(x) = 0$.

$x + 4 = 0 \quad$ or $\quad x + 3 = 0 \quad$ or $\quad x - 2 = 0$

$x = -4 \quad$ or $\quad x = -3 \quad$ or $\quad x = 2$

The solutions are -4, -3, and 2.

BACKGROUND MATERIAL   The sequence of ideas in this section is as follows: We recall Theorem 7–10 that establishes the possibility of factoring a polynomial of degree n into n linear factors. Then Theorem 11–3 uses this idea to establish that every polynomial of degree n has at least one and at most n roots. Example 3 on page 476 shows that if a polynomial has a single complex root, it has complex numbers as coefficients. But Theorem 11–4 points out that if all the coefficients of the polynomial are real numbers, then complex roots occur in conjugate pairs. Theorem 11–5 further asserts that if all the coefficients of the polynomial are rational, then irrational roots occur in pairs as generated by the Quadratic Formula.

SECTION 11–3

PREVENTING STUDENT ERRORS   Finding the variations of signs in a polynomial is not a difficult task. However, occasionally students will look at only the plus and minus signs, forgetting to consider that the initial term has a positive sign.

SECTION 11–5

TEACHING SUGGESTION   In Example 6 on page 488 the upper bound was found immediately. Students, however, are unlikely to be so lucky in their initial choices for a. Encourage students to consider the problem before selecting values for a at random. For example, consider why we might have chosen 4 in Example 6. One reason is that we know that the first number in the second row must be at least 11, in order for the addition to give a nonnegative result.

SECTION 11–6

COMPUTER SUPPLEMENTS *Computer Graphing Experiments 1, Algebra One and Algebra Two,* by Lund and Andersen (Addison-Wesley 1982) provides a diskette and worksheets for graphing. The diskette has nine topics suitable for use in conjunction with Chapters 11 and 12. See also References to Supplements in this Teacher's Edition.

Chapter 12

SECTION 12–1

TEACHING SUGGESTIONS Teachers should emphasize that f^{-1} does not mean $\frac{1}{f}$. Examples 4 and 5 on pages 505–506 illustrate the idea that if we interchange variables and solve, we get an equation of a function that does the reverse of what the original function does. The new function is the *inverse* of the given function.

Theorem 12–2 is important. Students should get sufficient drill so that they can *immediately* simplify such expressions. While this is very easy, the drill and practice are still necessary.

SECTION 12–3

TEACHING SUGGESTION Teachers should emphasize to students the importance of being able to convert an exponential equation to a logarithmic equation and vice versa. Understanding the rest of the chapter depends on understanding the definition of logarithms in terms of exponents. The relationship between $\log_a b = c$ and $b = a^c$ must be immediately recognizable to students.

SECTION 12–5

TEACHING SUGGESTIONS Students may find it valuable to use the table of logarithms on page 524 to draw an accurate graph of the logarithm function.

SECTION 12–6

APPLICATIONS: INTERPOLATION The theory behind interpolation is much more valuable than knowing how to find exact values of logarithms. In fact, students who enter professions that require them to deal with data, and its analysis and presentation, will have to understand linear approximations of non-linear functions.

TEACHING SUGGESTION   Have students try interpolation on a familiar curve, such as $y = x^2$. For example, using the points $(0, 0)$ and $(1, 1)$ from the graph, and linear interpolation, what is the value of y when $x = 0.5$ or $x = 0.25$?

APPLICATIONS   The applications of exponential and logarithmic functions presented in this section illustrate the value of these functions in describing a variety of phenomena in everyday life. Students should not believe that working with exponential and logarithmic functions is an exercise limited to the classroom and their homework.

SECTION 12–7

TEACHING SUGGESTION   Since the functions e^x and $\ln x$ are inverses of each other, we can apply Theorem 12–2. Thus $e^{\ln x} = x$ and $\ln e^x = x$.

SECTION 12–8

TEACHING SUGGESTION   A sequence can also be defined as a function whose domain is the set of all natural numbers. If the sequence is finite there will be only a finite set of function values not zero.

Chapter 13

SECTION 13–1

BACKGROUND MATERIAL   The question, "What is the sum of the first ten positive integers?", is really an application of Theorem 13–2. The sum is $1 + 2 + \cdots + 10$, which is a series.

SECTION 13–2

Gauss, as a child, is known to have discovered this theorem on his own. He reasoned that the first and last numbers would have the same sum as the second and the second-to-last numbers. And that sum would be the same for the third and the third-to-last numbers. Since it takes two terms each time to form a sum, the number of such equal sums would be half the number of terms in the series. Thus he found the formula: $\left(\frac{n}{2}\right)(a_1 + a_n)$.

Another way to look at the formula is as follows: S_n is n multiplied by the average of the first and last terms. That is, $S_n = n\left(\frac{1}{2}\right)(a_1 + a_n)$.

GEOMETRY CONNECTION   It is interesting to recall the meaning of "geometric mean" from geometry. To find the

SECTION 13–3

geometric mean by construction, construct the two segments side by side on a straight line. Bisect this segment. Use this midpoint as the center of a circle that passes through the opposite ends of the two original segments. The length of a segment from, and perpendicular to, the line of the two segments to the circle is the geometric mean of the two segments.

SECTION 13-5

TEACHING SUGGESTIONS   It is important that students see that Theorem 13-9 is analogous to the Fundamental Counting Principle. When calculating the number of permutations, the number of objects left after each choice is one less than the preceding time.

SECTION 13-6

TEACHING SUGGESTIONS   The following device may be helpful to students in learning to compute $_nP_r$.

$$_7P_3 = 7 \cdot 6 \cdot 5$$

——This number indicates the first factor.

——This number indicates how many factors.

SECTION 13-8

TEACHING SUGGESTION   Students usually assume that permutations and combinations are not really mathematical until they come to the lesson on the Binomial Theorem. Then they see that combinations are related to multiplying polynomials. The relationship between these products and Pascal's Triangle should be emphasized since students are usually fascinated by the similarities coming from such varied sources.

SECTION 13-9

APPLICATIONS: PROBABILITY   A desire to calculate odds in games of chance gave rise to the theory of probability. Today the theory of probability and its closely related field, mathematical statistics, have many applications, most of them not related to games of chance. Opinion polls, with such uses as predicting elections, are a familiar example. Quality control, in which a prediction about the percentage of faulty items manufactured is made without testing them all, is an important application, among many, in business. Still other applications are in the areas of genetics, medicine, and the kinetic theory of gases.

BACKGROUND MATERIAL   A matrix is a mathematical element, which, like a polynomial or a complex number, can be combined with other like elements to form a system. For matrices, the elements in a system must have the same dimensions so that addition can be defined. As with any new system, we investigate ideas of commutativity and associativity, the existence of a zero element, and additive inverses. All theorems that are based on these ideas for real numbers have a counterpart in a theorem about matrices, since these properties are valid in any system of matrices with the same dimensions.

APPLICATIONS: MATRICES   Consider the matrices in Example 4 on page 607. Suppose that each column heading is a kind of vegetable purchased by a market: tomatoes, corn and cucumbers. Each row heading in the left matrix is a day of the week: Monday, Tuesday, Wednesday and Thursday. Thus the 4×3 matrix is a chart of the number of pounds of each vegetable received each day. Now look at the 1×3 matrix in this example. Suppose the three numbers represent the cost in dollars of one pound of tomatoes, one pound of corn, and one pound of cucumbers. The product of these two matrices is a 1×4 matrix that shows how much was spent each day on these vegetables. Matrices were invented to handle this kind of computation. They are very important in computer science, where large batches of data are manipulated.

TEACHING SUGGESTIONS   Relate the trigonometric functions to previous experiences with functions. The sine, cosine, and tangent functions consist of ordered pairs where the domain elements are angle measures and the range elements are numbers obtained from ratios of the sides of a right triangle.

Students should be required to memorize function values for $45°$, $30°$, and $60°$. They should also be required to memorize the approximate square roots of 2, 3, and 5. The square roots of 2 and 3 are especially important in finding decimal approximations for function values of $30°$, $45°$, and $60°$.

Chapter 14

SECTION 14–1

SECTION 14–2

Chapter 15

SECTION 15–1

SECTION 15-2

BACKGROUND MATERIAL   With the angle concept extended to include rotations, it is possible to extend the trigonometric functions to rotations. Once again, the input–output idea of a function should be stressed. Thus, for example, the sine function consists of all ordered pairs of the form $(\theta, \sin \theta)$ where θ is a measure of a rotation.

SECTION 15-3

BACKGROUND MATERIAL   Radian measure provides a convenient and consistent link between the measure of angles and the measure of length on the x- and y-axes. In effect, the circle is coordinatized in the same units used to measure a radius of the circle. Be sure to stress the importance of memorizing the relationships between radian and degree measure as shown on page 639.

TEACHING SUGGESTION   Be sure to relate the work on interpolation to that previously discussed in Chapter 12. Students can examine successive values of the sine function in the table and observe that it is approximately linear over short intervals. Hence, linear interpolation is appropriate.

SECTION 15-4

BACKGROUND MATERIAL   Many people use the trigonometric graphs to define their reference points. Thus, once the shape of the sine graph has been learned, it is easy to sketch it quickly and then to use it as a reference.

TEACHING SUGGESTIONS   The graphing of the trigonometric functions should be related to earlier experiences with graphing functions. In this case we plot the inputs (rotation sizes) on the first axis and the outputs (function values) on the second axis. As with any function, it is appropriate to consider the questions of domain and range, even or odd, and periodicity. Comparisons of the graphs of the tangent and cotangent functions, the cosine and secant functions, and the sine and cosecant functions should help to clarify the reciprocal relationship.

Just as students learned the relation between $f(x)$ and $f(x + c)$ in Chapter 9, they can see that $\sin\left(\theta + \frac{\pi}{2}\right)$ is the graph of $\sin \theta$ shifted to the left $\frac{\pi}{2}$. Clearly $\cos \theta = \sin\left(\theta + \frac{\pi}{2}\right)$.

SECTION 15-5

TEACHING SUGGESTION   The function analysis, relating $f(x)$ to $f(x \pm c)$, should be used to make Theorem 15-4 a summary of obvious facts rather than a collection of random phrases. Students should sketch these graphs.

1. $\sin \theta$
2. $-\sin \theta$
3. $\cos \theta$
4. $-\cos \theta$
5. $\sin \left(\theta + \frac{\pi}{2}\right)$
6. $\sin \left(\theta - \frac{\pi}{2}\right)$
7. $\cos \left(\theta + \frac{\pi}{2}\right)$
8. $\cos \left(\theta - \frac{\pi}{2}\right)$

Then we match these graphs to obtain four cofunction identities.

TEACHING SUGGESTIONS   It is important to stress in this section that the trigonometric functions behave as all functions with respect to transformations. It may be worthwhile to review the role of certain constants in stretching and shrinking learned in Chapter 9.

SECTION 15–6

COMPUTER SUPPLEMENTS   *Computer Graphing Experiments 2, Trigonometric Functions,* by Lund and Andersen (Addison-Wesley 1982) provides a diskette and worksheets for graphing. The diskette has fifteen topics suitable for use in conjuntion with Section 15–6. See also References to Supplements in this Teacher's Edition.

TEACHING SUGGESTION   It is important to point out that expressions containing trigonometric functions can be handled like algebraic expressions in computing and simplifying, but that we can sometimes do further simplification by using trigonometric identities.

SECTION 15–7

BACKGROUND MATERIAL   The derivations in this section put algebraic skills to work. In particular, the derivation of $\cos (\alpha - \beta)$ is considered by many teachers to be as important as deriving the Quadratic Formula. There are several accessible proofs of this theorem.

Chapter 16

SECTION 16–1

TEACHING SUGGESTIONS   Once the identity for a cosine of a difference is learned, students can then derive most of the others from it. The sum and difference identities in Theorem 16–1 are basic and important. Students should be required to memorize them.

SECTION 16–2

TEACHING SUGGESTIONS   In developing the half-angle identities, be sure students understand the relationship between θ and ϕ as illustrated on page 679. Since we know an identity in 2θ we may use it to derive an identity in θ or $\frac{\phi}{2}$.

Again, students should memorize the identities in Theorem 16–2.

ENRICHMENT   Students may appreciate the opportunity to consider the graphical significance of the identities in Theorem 16–2.

Here are three exercises that should be instructive.

1. Draw an accurate graph of $y = \sin x$. To obtain the graph of $y = \sin^2 x$, square each y-coordinate. So, for $x = \frac{\pi}{3}$, $\sin \frac{\pi}{3} = 0.5$, $\sin^2 \frac{\pi}{3} = 0.25$. The completed graph stays within the range from 0 to 1, since $\sin^2 x$ cannot be negative.

2. Start by drawing accurate graphs of $y = \sin x$ and $y = \cos x$ on the same axes. Then for each x-coordinate, find the product of the y-coordinates of each graph and double it. This will be the y-coordinate for the graph of $y = 2 \sin x \cos x$. Students should recognize this graph as the graph of $y = \sin 2x$ from Section 15–6.

3. Start by drawing the graphs of $y = \sin^2 x$ and $y = \cos^2 x$ by any method on the same axes. The sum of two y-coordinates for each x-coordinate will be 1 in every case. Thus the graph of $y = \sin^2 x + \cos^2 x$ is identical to the graph of $y = 1$, illustrating the identity $\sin^2 x + \cos^2 x \equiv 1$.

SECTION 16–4

TEACHING SUGGESTION   Teachers should relate inverses of trigonometric functions to previous experiences with inverses of relations. Remind students that while all functions have inverses, these inverses may or may not be functions. This will lead naturally to the need to distinguish between the inverse of the function and finding principal values by restricting ranges.

SECTION 16–5

TEACHING SUGGESTIONS   When finding multiple solutions to trigonometric equations, it is valuable to have a method. Some students may find the graphs of the trigonometric functions most helpful. Say $\cos x = \frac{1}{2}$. Visualizing the line $y = \frac{1}{2}$ cutting through the cosine curve indicates values for x between 0 and π, and between $\frac{3}{2}\pi$ and 2π.

Other students may prefer to think about the signs of the function values in the four quadrants. For $\cos \theta = \frac{1}{2}$, a positive number, they recall that cosine is positive in the first and fourth quadrants. Thus x must be between 0 and π or between $\frac{3}{2}\pi$ and 2π.

PREVENTING STUDENT ERRORS It is important in solving trigonometric equations to substitute possible answers into the original equation to make sure that they are actually solutions. It sometimes turns out that they are not.

BACKGROUND MATERIAL   It is interesting to note that the law of cosines does, in effect, extend the idea of the Pythagorean Theorem to any triangle.

SECTION 16–8

BACKGROUND MATERIAL   Trigonometric notation for complex numbers is very powerful, as shown by the incredible simplicity of Theorems 16–7 through 16–10. The concept of roots of complex numbers, too thorny to be treated until now, becomes easy to consider, making this topic an excellent culmination of the course.

SECTION 16–11

COMPUTER ACTIVITIES

Overview

The Computer Activities may be used with or without a computer. For classes without access to a computer, students follow the steps of the sample programs. Students should tell what the computer will do at each step, supply the value of appropriate variables, and find the output. The Exercises may also be worked without a computer. The Exercises emphasize writing and understanding BASIC expressions and programs. If individual students have access to home computers, they may run the programs at home and report their results.

For classes with access to a computer, type and save the sample programs before class, or ask a student to do so. List, discuss, and run the programs for each specific activity. If the system has a printer, program listings and printouts of output are valuable.

Some students may already be familiar with programming in BASIC. These students can be very helpful assisting other students, answering questions, or demonstrating programs.

ADDITIONAL PROGRAMS

1. A program to find the vertex, line of symmetry, and the maximum or minimum value of a quadratic function of the form $Y = AX^2 + BX + C$. The coordinates of the vertex are (X, Y), where $X = \frac{-B}{2A}$ and $Y = \frac{4AC - B^2}{4A}$, the equation of the line of symmetry is $X = \frac{-B}{2A}$, and the value of Y at the vertex is a minimum if A is positive, a maximum if A is negative.

```
10 REM LINE OF SYMMETRY,VERTEX, MAX OR MIN
20 READ A, B, C
30 IF A=0 THEN 160
40 LET X=-B/(2 * A)
50 PRINT "LINE OF SYMMETRY IS X= ";X
```

```
60 LET Y=(4 * A * C - B ^ 2) / (4 * A)
70 PRINT "VERTEX IS ("";X;"","";Y;")"
80 LET S = SGN(A)
90 IF S = +1 THEN 120
100 PRINT "MAXIMUM VALUE IS "; Y
110 GO TO 20
120 PRINT "MINIMUM VALUE IS "; Y
130 GO TO 20
140 DATA -2,10,-7,4,8,-3,-1,-4,3
150 DATA 0,0,0
160 END
```
Output:
```
LINE OF SYMMETRY IS X = 2.5
VERTEX IS (2.5, 5.5)
MAXIMUM VALUE IS 5.5
LINE OF SYMMETRY IS X = -1
VERTEX IS (-1, -7)
MINIMUM VALUE IS -7
LINE OF SYMMETRY IS X = -2
VERTEX IS (-2, 7)
MAXIMUM VALUE IS 7
```

2. A program to find some ordered pair solution to a system of two equations. This program uses nested loops to find integer values of X and Y (from -5 to 5) that are solutions of this system:

$$2X^2 + 5Y^2 = 22$$
$$3X^2 - Y^2 = -1$$

```
10 REM INTEGER SOLUTIONS
20 FOR X=-5 TO 5
30 FOR Y=-5 TO 5
40 IF 2 * X ^ 2 + 5 * Y ^ 2<>22 THEN 70
50 IF 3 * X ^ 2 - Y ^ 2 <> -1 THEN 70
60 PRINT "("";X;"","";Y;"") IS A SOLUTION"
70 NEXT Y
80 NEXT X
90 END
```
Output:
```
(-1, -2) IS A SOLUTION
(-1, 2) IS A SOLUTION
(1, -2) IS A SOLUTION
(1, 2) IS A SOLUTION
```

3. A program to compute missing angles or sides of a triangle using the Law of Sines:

$$\frac{A}{SIN\ A} = \frac{B}{SIN\ B} = \frac{C}{SIN\ C}$$

Here we use A1, B1, and C1 to denote the angles and A, B, and C to denote the sides opposite angles A1, B1, and C1 respectively. Given A1, C1, and A, we solve the triangle and find the area.

```
10 LET K = 3.14159/180
20 READ A1, C1, A
30 IF A1 = 0 THEN 200
40 REM COMPUTE THIRD ANGLE
50 LET B1 = 180 - (A1 + C1)
60 REM COMPUTE OTHER TWO SIDES
70 LET B = A * SIN(B1 * K)/SIN(A1 * K)
80 LET C = A * SIN(C1 * K)/SIN(A1 * K)
90 REM COMPUTE AREA
100 LET R = .5 * B * C * SIN(A1 * K)
110 PRINT "ANGLES: "A1;TAB(15);B1;
    TAB(28)C1
120 PRINT "SIDES: " A;TAB(15);B;TAB(28);C
130 PRINT "AREA: ";R
140 PRINT
150 GO TO 20
160 DATA 43,57,4.56
170 DATA 42,30,20
180 DATA 138,30,20
190 DATA 0,0,0
200 END
```

Output:

```
ANGLES: 43         80         57
SIDES:  4.56       6.58465729 5.60754765
AREA:   12.59097
ANGLES: 42         108        30
SIDES:  20         28.4266675 14.9447637
AREA:   142.133223
ANGLES: 138        12         30
SIDES:  20         6.21436372 14.9447197
AREA:   31.0717936
```

4. A program using an array to print the prime numbers from 2 to 150 with the Sieve of Eratosthenes. The program marks each multiple of 2, 3, 5 and so on with a 1, then prints those which have not been marked.

```
10 DIM Z(150)
20 FOR X = 2 TO 75
30 IF Z(X) = 1 THEN 70
40 FOR Y = 2*X TO 150 STEP X
50 LET Z(Y) = 1
60 NEXT Y
70 NEXT X
80 FOR P = 2 TO 150
90 IF Z(P) = 0 THEN 110
100 PRINT P,
110 NEXT P
120 END
```

Output:

```
2       3       5
7       11      13
17      19      23
29      31      37
41      43      47
53      59      61
67      71      73
79      83      89
97      101     103
107     109     113
127     131     137
139     149
```

ASSIGNMENT GUIDE

The following schedules of assignments are for regular, regular with trigonometry, advanced, and advanced with trigonometry courses. There is a total of 174 assignment days for each course, or 87 days per semester. Review and testing days for each chapter are included in the total. Optional assignment days for supplemental material are also included and have been marked with asterisks. *Even* or *odd* exercises are shown as e/o.

The regular course does not include Chapters 14, 15 and 16, or Sections 1–9, 2–9, 4–6, 4–7, 4–9, and 12–8.

The regular course with trigonometry does not include Chapters 13 and 14, or Sections 1–9, 2–9, 4–6, 4–7, 4–9, and 16–11.

The advanced course includes all chapters through Chapter 14. It does not include Chapters 15 and 16 on trigonometry.

The advanced course with trigonometry includes all sections except 12–8 and 13–9.

REGULAR COURSE

First Semester

Chapter	1	2	3	4	5	6	7	Supplements
Days	11	11	12	11	12	11	13	6*

Second Semester

Chapter	8	9	10	11	12	13	Supplements
Days	10	10	17	12	14	15	9*

REGULAR COURSE WITH TRIGONOMETRY

First Semester

Chapter	1	2	3	4	5	6	7	Supplements
Days	11	11	12	11	12	11	13	6*

Second Semester

Chapter	8	9	10	11	12	15	16	Supplements
Days	9	10	11	9	9	11	21	7*

ADVANCED COURSE

First Semester

Chapter	1	2	3	4	5	6	7	Supplements
Days	9	10	12	15	11	11	13	6*

Second Semester

Chapter	8	9	10	11	12	13	14	Supplements
Days	8	10	12	8	11	11	8	19*

ADVANCED COURSE WITH TRIGONOMETRY

First Semester

Chapter	1	2	3	4	5	6	7	8	Supplements
Days	7	8	9	14	8	11	13	8	9*

Second Semester

Chapter	9	10	11	12	13	14	15	16	Supplements
Days	10	9	8	9	10	8	9	19	5*

FIRST SEMESTER

Day	Regular Course	Regular Course with Trigonometry	Advanced Course	Advanced Course with Trigonometry
1	**1–1:** 1–42 e/o, 43	**1–1:** 1–42 e/o, 43	**1–1:** 1–42 e/o, 43–46	**1–1:** 1–42 mult. of 3, 43–46 **1–2:** 1–28 mult. of 3, 29–36
2	**1–2:** 1–34 e/o	**1–2:** 1–34 e/o	**1–2:** 1–34 e/o, 35, 36	**1–3:** 1–62 e/o, 63, 64 **1–4:** 1–56 mult. of 3, 57–68 e/o
3	**1–3:** 1–62 e/o	**1–3:** 1–62 e/o	**1–3:** 1–62 e/o, 63, 64 **1–4:** 1–64 e/o, 66–68	**1–5:** 1–98 mult. of 3
4	**1–4:** 1–61 e/o, 66–68	**1–4:** 1–61 e/o, 66–68	**1–5:** 1–98 mult. of 3 **1–6:** 1–52 e/o	**1–6:** 1–52 mult. of 3 **1–7:** 1–60 mult. of 3
5	**1–5:** 1–62 e/o	**1–5:** 1–62 e/o	**1–7:** 1–60 e/o	**1–8:** 1–36 mult. of 3 **1–9:** 1–25 e/o, 26
6	**1–5:** 63–98 e/o	**1–5:** 63–98 e/o	**1–8:** 1–36 e/o	Chapter 1 Review
7	**1–6:** 1–47 e/o	**1–6:** 1–47 e/o	**1–9:** 1–25 e/o, 26	Chapter 1 Test Ready for Ch. 2?
8	**1–7:** 1–52 e/o	**1–7:** 1–52 e/o	Chapter 1 Review	**2–1:** 1–57 mult. of 4 **2–2:** 1–44 mult. of 4
9	**1–8:** 1–30 e/o	**1–8:** 1–30 e/o	Chapter 1 Test Ready for Ch. 2?	**2–3:** 1–32 e/o **2–4:** 1–32 e/o
10	Chapter 1 Review	Chapter 1 Review	**2–1:** 1–57 e/o **2–2:** 1–44 e/o	**2–5:** 19–45 e/o **2–6:** 1–8 e/o
11	Chapter 1 Test Ready for Ch. 2?	Chapter 1 Test Ready for Ch. 2?	**2–3:** 1–32 e/o	**2–7:** 1–38 e/o
12	**2–1:** 1–47 e/o, 48, 49	**2–1:** 1–47 e/o 48, 49	**2–4:** 1–32 e/o	**2–8:** 1–58 e/o
13	**2–2:** 1–40 e/o	**2–2:** 1–40 e/o	**2–5:** 1–45 e/o	**2–9:** 1–33 mult. of 3
14	**2–3:** 1–22 odd	**2–3:** 1–22 odd	**2–6:** 1–8	Chapter 2 Review
15	**2–3:** 1–30 even	**2–3:** 1–30 even	**2–7:** 1–38 e/o	Chapter 2 Test Ready for Ch. 3?
16	**2–4:** 1–28 e/o	**2–4:** 1–28 e/o	**2–8:** 1–16 e/o 17–58 e/o	**3–1:** 1–32 e/o
17	**2–5:** 1–40 e/o	**2–5:** 1–40 e/o	**2–9:** 1–33 mult. of 3	**3–2:** 1–53 mult. of 3

FIRST SEMESTER

Day	Regular Course	Regular Course with Trigonometry	Advanced Course	Advanced Course with Trigonometry
18	2–6: 1–8	2–6: 1–8	Chapter 2 Review	3–3: 1–48 e/o
19	2–7: 1–30 e/o	2–7: 1–30 e/o	Chapter 2 Test Ready for Ch. 3?	3–4: 1–64 mult. of 3
20	2–8: 1–49 e/o	2–8: 1–49 e/o	3–1: 1–32 e/o	3–5: 1–54 e/o
21	Chapter 2 Review	Chapter 2 Review	3–2: 1–32 e/o	3–6: 1–46 e/o
22	Chapter 2 Test Ready for Ch. 3?	Chapter 2 Test Ready for Ch. 3?	3–2: 32–52 e/o	3–7: 1–28 e/o, 29, 30
23	3–1: 1–32 e/o	3–1: 1–32 e/o	3–3: 1–48 e/o	3–8: 1–14
24	3–2: 1–29 e/o	3–2: 1–29 e/o	3–4: 1–32 e/o	Computer Activities pp. 730–734*
25	3–2: 30–49 e/o	3–2: 30–49 e/o	3–4: 33–62 e/o, 63, 64	Computer Activities pp. 730–734*
26	3–3: 1–28 e/o, 29–39	3–3: 1–28 e/o, 29–39	3–5: 1–54 e/o	Chapter 3 Test Ready for Ch. 4?
27	3–4: 1–32 e/o	3–4: 1–32 e/o	3–6: 1–46 e/o	4–1: 1–20 e/o
28	3–4: 33–62 e/o	3–4: 33–62 e/o	3–7: 1–28 e/o, 29, 30	4–1: 21–55 e/o
29	Consumer Application, p. 151*	Consumer Application, p. 151*	3–8: 1–14	4–2: 1–20
30	3–5: 1–46 e/o	3–5: 1–46 e/o	Chapter 3 Review	4–2: 21–34
31	3–6: 1–36 e/o	3–6: 1–36 e/o	Chapter 3 Test Ready for Ch. 4?	4–3: 1–31 mult. of 3
32	3–7: 1–28 e/o	3–7: 1–28 e/o	4–1: 1–20 e/o	4–4: 1–20 e/o
33	3–8: 1–7	3–8: 1–7	4–1: 21–55 e/o	4–5: 1–30 e/o
34	Chapter 3 Review	Chapter 3 Review	4 2: 1–20	4–6: 1–14 e/o
35	Chapter 3 Test Ready for Ch. 4?	Chapter 3 Test Ready for Ch. 4?	4–2: 21–34	Computer Activities pp. 735–737*
36	4–1: 1–20 e/o	4–1: 1–20 e/o	4–3: 1,2,3–21 mult. of 3, 22–31 e/o	4–7: 1–38 e/o
37	4–1: 21–50 e/o	4–1: 21–50 e/o	4–4: 1–20 e/o	4–8: 1–49 mult. of 4
38	4–2: 1–26 odd	4–2: 1–26 odd	4–5: 1–30 e/o	4–9: 1–3
39	4–2: 1–26 even	4–2: 1–26 even	4–6: 1–14 e/o	4–9: 4–8
40	4–3: 1,2,3–21 mult. of 3, 23–28 e/o	4–3: 1,2,3–21 mult. of 3, 23–28 e/o	4–7: 1–38 e/o	Chapter 4 Review

FIRST SEMESTER

Day	Regular Course	Regular Course with Trigonometry	Advanced Course	Advanced Course with Trigonometry
41	4–4: 1–18 e/o	4–4: 1–18 e/o	4–8: 1–4, 5–25 e/o	Chapter 4 Test Ready for Ch. 5?
42	4–5: 1–26 e/o	4–5: 1–26 e/o	4–8: 26–49 mult. of 3	Cum. Rev. 1–4*
43	4–8: 1–4, 5–25 mult. of 3	4–8: 1–4, 5–25 mult. of 3	4–9: 1–3	5–1: 1–22 mult. of 3, 23–34 e/o 5–2: 1–51 mult. of 3, 52
44	4–8: 26–46 mult. of 3	4–8: 26–46 mult. of 3	4–9: 4–8	5–3: 1–66 mult. of 3 5–4: 1–77 mult. of 4
45	Chapter 4 Review	Chapter 4 Review	Chapter 4 Review	5–5: 1–51 e/o
46	Chapter 4 Test Ready for Ch. 5?	Chapter 4 Test Ready for Ch. 5?	Chapter 4 Test Ready for Ch. 5?	5–6: 1–21 mult. of 3, 22–35 e/o 5–7: 1–54 mult. of 3
47	Cum. Rev. 1–4*	Cum. Rev. 1–4*	Cum. Rev. 1–4*	Careers/Oceanography, p. 339*
48	5–1: 1–28 e/o	5–1: 1–28 e/o	5–1: 1–34 e/o	5–8: 1–20 e/o, 21, 22
49	5–2: 1–42 e/o	5–2: 1–42 e/o	5–2: 1–51 e/o, 52	5–9: 1–40 e/o
50	5–3: 1–57 e/o	5–3: 1–57 e/o	5–3: 1–66 e/o	Chapter 5 Review
51	5–4: 1–63 e/o	5–4: 1–63 e/o	5–4: 1–77 e/o	Chapter 5 Test Ready for Ch. 6?
52	5–5: 1–23	5–5: 1–23	5–5: 1–51 e/o	6–1: 1–59 e/o
53	5–5: 24–47 e/o	5–5: 24–47 e/o	5–6: 1–35 e/o	6–2: 1–34 e/o, 35, 36
54	5–6: 1–34 e/o	5–6: 1–34 e/o	5–7: 1–32 e/o	6–3: 1–44 e/o
55	5–7: 1–30 e/o	5–7: 1–30 e/o	5–8: 1–20 e/o, 21, 22	6–4: 1–33 e/o
56	5–8: 1–20 e/o, 21	5–8: 1–20 e/o, 21	5–9: 1–40 e/o	6–5: 1–36 mult. of 3, 37, 38
57	5–9: 1–32 e/o	5–9: 1–32 e/o	Chapter 5 Review	6–6: 1–35 e/o
58	Chapter 5 Review	Chapter 5 Review	Chapter 5 Test Ready for Ch. 6?	6–7: 1–32 e/o
59	Chapter 5 Test Ready for Ch. 6?	Chapter 5 Test Ready for Ch. 6?	6–1: 1–59 e/o	6–8: 1–20 e/o, 21, 22
60	6–1: 1–42 e/o	6–1: 1–42 e/o	6–2: 1–34 e/o, 35, 36	6–9: 1–40 e/o
61	6–2: 1–34 e/o	6–2: 1–34 e/o	6–3: 1–44 e/o	Chapter 6 Review

FIRST SEMESTER

Day	Regular Course	Regular Course with Trigonometry	Advanced Course	Advanced Course with Trigonometry
62	**6–3:** 1–37 e/o	**6–3:** 1–37 e/o	**6–4:** 1–33 e/o	Chapter 6 Test Ready for Ch. 7?
63	**6–4:** 1–26 e/o	**6–4:** 1–26 e/o	**6–5:** 1–36 e/o, 37, 38	**7–1:** 1–62 e/o
64	**6–5:** 1–36 e/o	**6–5:** 1–36 e/o	**6–6:** 1–35 e/o	**7–2:** 1–55 e/o
65	**6–6:** 1–34 e/o	**6–6:** 1–34 e/o	**6–7:** 1–32 e/o	**7–3:** 1–22 e/o, 23
66	**6–7:** 1–30 e/o	**6–7:** 1–30 e/o	**6–8:** 1–20 e/o, 21, 22	**7–4:** 1–102 mult. of 3
67	**6–8:** 1–20 e/o, 21	**6–8:** 1–20 e/o, 21	**6–9:** 1–40 e/o	**7–5:** 1–66 e/o, 67
68	**6–9:** 1–32 e/o	**6–9:** 1–32 e/o	Chapter 6 Review	**7–6:** 1–52 e/o, 53
69	Chapter 6 Review	Chapter 6 Review	Chapter 6 Test Ready for Ch. 7?	**7–7:** 1–54 e/o
70	Chapter 6 Test Ready for Ch. 7?	Chapter 6 Test Ready for Ch. 7?	**7–1:** 1–62 e/o	**7–8:** 1–52 e/o
71	**7–1:** 1–52 e/o	**7–1:** 1–52 e/o	**7–2:** 1–53 e/o	**7–9:** 1–30 e/o
72	**7–2:** 1–53 e/o	**7–2:** 1–53 e/o	**7–3:** 1–22 e/o, 23	**7–10:** 1–24 e/o
73	**7–3:** 1–22 e/o	**7–3:** 1–22 e/o	**7–4:** 1–102 mult. of 3	**7–11:** 1–17
74	**7–4:** 1–88 mult. of 3	**7–4:** 1–88 mult. of 3	**7–5:** 1–66 e/o, 67	Chapter 7 Review
75	**7–5:** 1–66 e/o	**7–5:** 1–66 e/o	**7–6:** 1–52 e/o	Chapter 7 Test Ready for Ch. 8?
76	**7–6:** 1–40 e/o	**7–6:** 1–40 e/o	**7–7:** 1–54 e/o	**8–1:** 1–64 e/o
77	**7–7:** 1–47 e/o	**7–7:** 1–47 e/o	**7–8:** 1–52 e/o	**8–2:** 1–54 e/o
78	**7–8:** 1–46 e/o	**7–8:** 1–46 e/o	**7–9:** 1–30 e/o	**8–3:** 1–71 e/o
79	**7–9:** 1–30 e/o	**7–9:** 1–30 e/o	**7–10:** 1–24 e/o	**8–4:** 1–29 e/o
80	**7–10:** 1–24 e/o	**7–10:** 1–24 e/o	**7–11:** 1–17	**8–5:** 1–40 e/o
81	**7–11:** 1–16	**7–11:** 1–16	Chapter 7 Review	**8–6:** 1–27 e/o, 28
82	Chapter 7 Review	Chapter 7 Review	Chapter 7 Test	Chapter 8 Review
83	Chapter 7 Test	Chapter 7 Test	Consumer Application, p. 285*	Chapter 8 Test
84	Cum. Rev. 1–7*	Cum. Rev. 1–7*	Cum. Rev. 1–7*	Cum. Rev. 1–7*
85	Cum. Rev. 1–7*	Cum. Rev. 1–7*	Cum. Rev. 1–7*	Cum. Rev. 1–7*
86	Review Ch. 1–7	Review Ch. 1–7	Review Ch. 1–7	Review Ch. 1–8
87	Mid-year Test Ready for Ch. 8?	Mid-year Test Ready for Ch. 8?	Mid-year Test Ready for Ch. 8?	Mid-year Test Ready for Ch. 9?

SECOND SEMESTER

Day	Regular Course	Regular Course with Trigonometry	Advanced Course	Advanced Course with Trigonometry
1	**8–1:** 1–56 e/o	**8–1:** 1–56 e/o	**8–1:** 1–64 e/o	**9–1:** 1–67 e/o
2	**8–2:** 1–34 e/o	**8–2:** 1–34 e/o	**8–2:** 1–54 e/o	**9–2:** 1–22 e/o
3	**8–2:** 35–51 e/o	**8–2:** 35–51 e/o **8–3:** 1–27 e/o	**8–3:** 1–71 e/o	**9–3:** 1–42 e/o
4	**8–3:** 1–27 e/o	**8–3:** 28–65 e/o	**8–4:** 1–29 e/o	**9–4:** 1–27 mult. of 3
5	**8–3:** 28–65 e/o	**8–4:** 1–18 e/o	Computer Activities pp. 738–739*	**9–5:** 1–27 e/o
6	**8–4:** 1–18 e/o	**8–5:** 1–29 e/o	Computer Activities pp. 738–739*	**9–6:** 1–30 e/o
7	**8–5:** 1–29 e/o	**8–6:** 1–19 e/o	**8–5:** 1–40 e/o	**9–7:** 1–29 e/o
8	**8–6:** 1–19 e/o	Chapter 8 Review	**8–6:** 1–27 e/o, 28	**9–8:** 1–15 e/o
9	Chapter 8 Review	Chapter 8 Test Ready for Ch. 9?	Chapter 8 Review	Chapter 9 Review
10	Chapter 8 Test Ready for Ch. 9?	**9–1:** 1–58 e/o	Chapter 8 Test Ready for Ch. 9?	Chapter 9 Test Ready for Ch. 10?
11	**9–1:** 1–58 e/o	**9–2:** 1–19 e/o	**9–1:** 1–67 e/o	**10–1:** 1–33 e/o
12	**9–2:** 1–19 e/o	**9–3:** 1–27 e/o	**9–2:** 1–22 e/o	**10–2:** 1–28 e/o, 29, 30
13	**9–3:** 1–27 e/o	**9–4:** 1–21 mult. of 3	**9–3:** 1–42 e/o	**10–3:** 1–33 mult. of 3
14	**9–4:** 1–21 mult. of 3	**9–5:** 1–25 e/o	**9–4:** 1–27 mult. of 3	**10–4:** 1–26 e/o
15	Careers/Communications, p. 415*	**9–6:** 1–24 e/o	Careers/Communications, p. 415*	**10–5:** 1–32 e/o
16	**9–5:** 1–25 e/o	**9–7:** 1–21 e/o	**9–5:** 1–27 e/o	**10–6:** 1–29 e/o
17	**9–6:** 1–24 e/o	**9–8:** 1–10 e/o	**9–6:** 1–30 e/o	**10–7:** 1–24 mult. of 3, 25–29 e/o
18	**9–7:** 1–21 e/o	Chapter 9 Review	**9–7:** 1–29 e/o	Chapter 10 Review
19	**9–8:** 1–10 e/o	Chapter 9 Test Ready for Ch. 10?	**9–8:** 1–15 e/o	Chapter 10 Test Ready for Ch. 11?
20	Chapter 9 Review	**10–1:** 1–31 e/o	Chapter 9 Review	**11–1:** 1–22 e/o
21	Chapter 9 Test Ready for Ch. 10?	**10–2:** 1–28 e/o	Chapter 9 Test Ready for Ch. 10?	**11–2:** 1–41 e/o, 42
22	**10–1:** 1–31 odd	**10–3:** 1–14 e/o	**10–1:** 1–33 e/o	**11–3:** 1–52 e/o
23	**10–1:** 1–31 even	**10–3:** 15–30 e/o	**10–2:** 1–28 e/o, 29, 30	**11–4:** 1–30 e/o

SECOND SEMESTER

Day	Regular Course	Regular Course with Trigonometry	Advanced Course	Advanced Course with Trigonometry
24	**10–2:** 1–28 odd	Consumer Application, p. 459*	**10–3:** 1–33 by 3's (1,4, …)	**11–5:** 1–30 e/o, 31
25	**10–2:** 1–28 even	**10–4:** 1–16 mult. of 3, 17–23 e/o	**10–3:** 1–33 by 3's (3,6, …)	**11–6:** 1–22 e/o
26	**10–3:** 1–30 by 3's (1,4, …)	**10–5:** 1–18 e/o	Consumer Application, p. 459*	Chapter 11 Review
27	**10–3:** 1–30 by 3's (2,5, …)	**10–5:** 19–31 e/o	**10–4:** 1–26 e/o	Chapter 11 Test Ready for Ch. 12?
28	**10–3:** 1–30 by 3's (3,6, …)	**10–6:** 1–20 e/o	**10–5:** 1–32 by 3's (1,4, …)	**12–1:** 1–59 e/o
29	**10–4:** 1–16 by 3's (1,4, …), 17–23 odd	**10–7:** 1–14 e/o	**10–5:** 1–32 by 3's (3,6, …)	**12–2:** 1–39 e/o
30	**10–4:** 1–16 by 3's (3,6, …), 17–23 even	Chapter 10 review	**10–6:** 1–29 odd	**12–3:** 1–45 e/o
31	**10–5:** 1–18 e/o	Chapter 10 Test Ready for Ch. 11?	**10–6:** 1–29 even	**12–4:** 1–53 e/o
32	**10–5:** 19–31 e/o	**11–1:** 1–18 e/o	**10–7:** 1–24 mult. of 3, 25–29 e/o	**12–5:** 1–61 mult. of 3
33	**10–6:** 1–20 odd	Careers/Astronomy p. 496*	Chapter 10 Review	**12–6:** 1–27 mult. of 3
34	**10–6:** 1–20 even	**11–2:** 1–26 e/o	Chapter 10 Test Ready for Ch. 11?	**12–7:** 1–61 mult. of 3
35	Consumer Application, p. 459*	**11–2:** 27–41 e/o	Computer Activities pp. 730–734*	Chapter 12 Review
36	**10–7:** 1–14 odd	**11–3:** 1–48 e/o	Computer Activities pp. 730–734*	Chapter 12 Test Ready for Ch. 13?
37	**10–7:** 1–14 even	**11–4:** 1–24 e/o	**11–1:** 1–22 e/o	**13–1:** 1–34 e/o
38	Chapter 10 Review	**11–5:** 1–28 e/o	**11–2:** 1–41 e/o, 42	**13–2:** 1–43 e/o, 44
39	Chapter 10 Test Ready for Ch. 11?	**11–6:** 1–16 e/o	**11–3:** 1–52 e/o	**13–3:** 1–33 e/o
40	**11–1:** 1–18 e/o	Chapter 11 Review	Identifying Conic Sections, p. 480*	**13–4:** 1–22 e/o, 23
41	Careers/Astronomy p. 496*	Chapter 11 Test Ready for Ch. 12?	**11–4:** 1–30 e/o	**13–5:** 1–28 e/o
42	**11–2:** 1–26 e/o	Cum. Rev. 1–11*	**11–5:** 1–30 e/o, 31	**13–6:** 1–24 e/o

SECOND SEMESTER

Day	Regular Course	Regular Course with Trigonometry	Advanced Course	Advanced Course with Trigonometry
43	**11–2:** 27–41 e/o	**12–1:** 1–51 e/o	**11–6:** 1–22 e/o	**13–7:** 1–18 e/o, 19
44	**11–3:** 1–48 odd	**12–2:** 1–24 e/o	Chapter 11 Review	**13–8:** 1–22 e/o
45	**11–3:** 1–48 even	**12–3:** 1–40 e/o	Chapter 11 Test Ready for Ch. 12?	Chapter 13 Review
46	**11–4:** 1–24 e/o	**12–4:** 1–42 e/o	Careers/Astronomy p. 496*	Chapter 13 Test Ready for Ch. 14?
47	**11–5:** 1–28 odd	**12–5:** 1–57 e/o	**12–1:** 1–59 e/o	**14–1:** 1–39 odd
48	**11–5:** 1–28 even	**12–6:** 1–27 e/o	**12–2:** 1–39 e/o	**14–1:** 1–39 even
49	**11–6:** 1–16 odd	**12–7:** 1–35 e/o	**12–3:** 1–45 e/o	**14–2:** 1–44 odd
50	**11–6:** 1–16 even	Chapter 12 Review	**12–4:** 1–53 e/o	**14–2:** 1–44 even
51	Chapter 11 Review	Chapter 12 Test Ready for Ch. 15?	**12–5:** 1–61 e/o	**14–3:** 1–24 odd
52	Chapter 11 Test Ready for Ch. 12?	**15–1:** 1–16 e/o, 17–19	**12–6:** 1–32 e/o	**14–3:** 1–24 even
53	Cum. Rev. 1–11*	**15–2:** 1–59 e/o	**12–7:** 1–61 mult. of 3	Chapter 14 Review
54	**12–1:** 1–51 e/o	**15–3:** 1–51 e/o	Careers/Engineering p. 596*	Chapter 14 Test Ready for Ch. 15?
55	**12–2:** 1–24 odd	**15–3:** 52–90 e/o	**12–8:** 1–28 e/o	**15–1:** 1–16 e/o, 17–23
56	**12–2:** 1–24 even	**15–4:** 1–26 e/o	**12–8:** 29–49 e/o	**15–2:** 1–67 e/o, 68
57	**12–3:** 1–40 odd	**15–5:** 1–20 e/o	Chapter 12 Review	**15–3:** 1–92 mult. of 3, 74
58	**12–3:** 1–40 even	**15–6:** 1–27 mult. of 3	Chapter 12 Test Ready for Ch. 13?	**15–4:** 1–26 e/o
59	**12–4:** 1–42 odd	**15–7:** 1–24 e/o	**13–1:** 1–34 e/o	**15–5:** 1–40 e/o
60	**12–4:** 1–42 even	**15–7:** 25–42 e/o	**13–2:** 1–43 e/o, 44	**15–6:** 1–33 mult. of 3
61	Consumer Application, p. 549*	Chapter 15 Review	**13–3:** 1–33 e/o	**15–7:** 1–46 e/o
62	**12–5:** 1–57 odd	Chapter 15 Test Ready for Ch. 16?	**13–4:** 1–22 e/o, 23	Chapter 15 Review
63	**12–5:** 1–57 even	**16–1:** 1–57 odd	**13–5:** 1–28 e/o	Chapter 15 Test Ready for Ch. 16?
64	**12–6:** 1–27 e/o	**16–1:** 1–57 even	**13–6:** 1–30 e/o	**16–1:** 1–57 odd
65	**12–7:** 1–35 odd	**16–2:** 1–34 odd	**13–7:** 1–24 e/o	**16–1:** 1–57 even

SECOND SEMESTER

Day	Regular Course	Regular Course with Trigonometry	Advanced Course	Advanced Course with Trigonometry
66	**12–7:** 1–35 even	**16–2:** 1–34 even	Consumer Application, p. 722*	**16–2:** 1–34 odd
67	Chapter 12 Review	**16–3:** 1–30 by 3's (1,4, . . .), 31	**13–8:** 1–25 e/o	**16–2:** 1–34 even
68	Chapter 12 Test Ready for Ch. 13?	**16–3:** 1–30 by 3's (3,6, . . .)	**13–9:** 1–22	**16–3:** 1–30 by 3's (1,4, . . .), 31
69	**13–1:** 1–28 odd	**16–4:** 1–60 odd	Chapter 13 Review	**16–3:** 1–30 by 3's (3,6, . . .)
70	**13–1:** 1–28 even	**16–4:** 1–60 even	Chapter 13 Test Ready for Ch. 14?	**16–4:** 1–60 odd
71	**13–2:** 1–36 odd	**16–5:** 1–44 e/o	Computer Activities pp. 740–741*	**16–4:** 1–60 even
72	**13–2:** 1–36 even	**16–6:** 1–41 odd	Computer Activities pp. 740–741*	**16–5:** 1–44 e/o
73	**13–3:** 1–30 odd	**16–6:** 1–41 even	**14–1:** 1–36 odd, 37–39	**16–6:** 1–41 e/o
74	**13–3:** 1–30 even	**16–7:** 1–20 e/o, 21	**14–1:** 1–36 even	**16–7:** 1–20 e/o, 21,22
75	**13–4:** 1–22 odd	**16–7:** 22, 23–33 e/o	**14–2:** 1–44 odd	**16–7:** 23–33 e/o **16–8:** 1–8 e/o
76	**13–4:** 1–22 even	**16–8:** 1–8 e/o	**14–2:** 1–44 even	**16–8:** 9–34 e/o
77	**13–5:** 1–26 e/o, 27	**16–8:** 9–34 e/o	**14–3:** 1–24 odd	Careers/Aerial Surveying, p. 666*
78	**13–6:** 1–24 e/o	**16–9:** 1–20 odd	**14–3:** 1–24 even	**16–9:** 1–20 e/o
79	**13–7:** 1–18 e/o, 19	**16–9:** 1–20 even	Careers/Stress Analysis, p. 618*	**16–10:** 1–27 e/o
80	**13–8:** 1–18 e/o	**16–10:** 1–27 odd	Chapter 14 Review	**16–11:** 1–38 e/o
81	**13–9:** 1–19	**16–10:** 1–27 even	Chapter 14 Test	**16–11:** 39–67 e/o
82	Chapter 13 Review	Chapter 16 Review	Computer Activities pp. 735–737*	Chapter 16 Review
83	Chapter 13 Test	Chapter 16 Test	Computer Activities pp. 735–737*	Chapter 16 Test
84	Cum. Rev. 1–14*	Cum. Rev. 1–16*	Cum. Rev. 1–14*	Cum. Rev. 1–16*
85	Cum. Rev. 1–14*	Cum. Rev. 1–16*	Cum. Rev. 1–14*	Cum. Rev. 1–16*
86	Review Ch. 1–13	Review Ch. 1–16	Review Ch. 1–14	Review Ch. 1–16
87	End of Year Test	End of Year Test	End of Year Test	End of Year Test

REFERENCES TO SUPPLEMENTS

APPLICATIONS
In the **Teacher's Resource Book** order code 20337, Applications 1–5 cover Career topics, Applications 6–12 cover Consumer topics, Applications 13–28 cover Problem Solving, and Applications 29–36 cover Calculator topics.

PRACTICE MASTERS
Making Practice Fun by Ray Chayo © 1978 Addison-Wesley order code 3856. A book of 89 blackline masters of activity-based practice. For remediation and reinforcement.

ENRICHMENT MASTERS
Math Motivators by Alfred S. Posamentier and Gordon Sheridan © 1983 Addison-Wesley order code 5582. A book of 38 blackline masters of Investigations in Algebra including one page of teacher resources for each investigation.

The investigations referenced in the following charts relate directly to the indicated sections of the student book and may be assigned for independent student work. Other investigations may also be assigned at the teacher's discretion.

COMPUTER GRAPHING EXPERIMENTS
Computer Graphing Experiments, Volumes 1, 2, and 3 by Charles Lund and Edwin Andersen © 1982 Addison-Wesley order code 23465 for Volume 1 Algebra One & Two, order code 23470 for Volume 2 Trigonometric Functions, order code 23475 for Volume 3 Conic Sections, and order code 23480 for Volumes 1–3. An interactive Apple II or Apple II Plus program. Each volume contains a diskette, backup diskette, blackline master worksheets, plus answers and teacher notes. No programming knowledge is required.

The experiments referenced in the following charts relate directly to the indicated sections of the student book and may be assigned for independent student work. Other experiments may be assigned at the teacher's discretion.

COMPUTERS: SUPPLEMENTARY READING
Using Computers in Mathematics by Gerald H. Elgarten, Alfred S. Posamentier, and Stephen E. Moresh © 1983 Addison-Wesley order code 10450. A textbook for an introductory computer course or a supplement to teach the BASIC language. All computer ideas are introduced in the context of mathematical concepts. The Instructor's Commentary, order code 10449, has 148 detailed lesson plans. The Solutions Manual, order code 10456, contains complete solutions.

The sections of this book referenced in the following charts relate directly to the indicated sections of the student book and are sources for supplementary computer programs. Other sections may also be helpful sources for the teacher.

VIDEO REVIEW
The *Addison-Wesley Video Cassette Reviews for Intermediate Algebra* by Keedy, Bittinger © 1983. This series of videotape films consists of televised review lessons for second-year Algebra. Each cassette contains a review of 2–4 specific objectives.

The videotaped lessons are taught by a classroom teacher, Professor John Jobe, and can be used for students who missed class presentations or who need review.

Student Textbook

	Chapter 1		Chapter 2		Chapter 3		Chapter 4	
Sections	Sec. 1–1 to 1–4	Sec. 1–5 to 1–9	Sec. 2–1 to 2–6	Sec. 2–7 to 2–10	Sec. 3–1 to 3–5	Sec. 3–6 to 3–8	Sec. 4–1 to 4–3	Sec. 4–4 to 4–9
Chapter Review and Test		pp. 50–53		pp. 99–101		pp. 152–155		pp. 202–203
Computer Activities		pp. 731–732		pp. 732–734		pp. 734–735		pp. 735–737

Teacher's Edition

Quizzes	1, 2	3	4, 5	6	7, 8	9	10, 11	12
Teaching Suggestions	p. T43		pp. T43-45	p. T45	pp. T45-46	pp. T46-47	pp. T47-49	p. T49

Teacher's Resource Book

Chapter Tests		1		2		3		4
Multiple Choice Chapter Tests		1		2		3		4
Mid-Year Test								
End-of-Year Test								
Skills Practice	1, 2	3, 4	5	6	7	8	9	10
Applications	7	13	8	14, 29	15	30, 31	9	16
Computer Projects			1	2	3	4, 5		6

Other Supplementary Materials

Practice Masters	2,3	1,36	4–6,15	16,17	7–9,29	10	11–14,73	72,74
Enrichment Masters	pp.9,57	p.11		pp.61,63		p.21	pp.39,49	pp.29,31, 71,73,75
Computer Graphing Experiments					Vol. 1, 1–3,9, 14–15	Vol. 1, 4,10–11	Vol. 1, 8	Vol. 1, 5–7
Using Computers in Mathematics		Sec. 1–2 to 1–4	Sec. 1–7		Sec. 2–1			Sec. 2–5

Student Textbook

	Chapter 5		Chapter 6		Chapter 7		Chapter 8	
Sections	Sec. 5–1 to 5–5	Sec. 5–6 to 5–9	Sec. 6–1 to 6–5	Sec. 6–6 to 6–9	Sec. 7–1 to 7–5	Sec. 7–6 to 7–11	Sec. 8–1 to 8–2	Sec. 8–3 to 8–6
Chapter Review and Test		pp. 241–243		pp. 286–289		pp. 340–342		pp. 377–378
Computer Activities		pp. 737–738						pp. 738–740

Teacher's Edition

Quizzes	13, 14	15	16, 17	18	19, 20	21, 22	23	24
Teaching Suggestions	pp. T49-50	p. T50	pp. T50-51		pp. T51-52	p. T53	pp. T53-54	p. T54

Teacher's Resource Book

Chapter Tests		5		6		7		8
Multiple Choice Chapter Tests		5		6		7		8
Mid-Year Test						Mid-Year Test		
End-of-Year Test								
Skills Practice	11	12	13, 14		15	16	17	18
Applications	17	32	18	33	19	34		20
Computer Projects	7	8	9	10	11	12	13	

Other Supplementary Materials

Practice Masters	18–24	25–27	31–34	35	37–43	44–46	47–49	50, 51, 53
Enrichment Masters	p.19	p.69	pp.47,51					
Computer Graphing Experiments				Vol. 1, 12–13				
Using Computers in Mathemtics	Sec. 2–6		Sec. 5–5		Sec. 2–4		Sec. 4–1	

Student Textbook

	Chapter 9		Chapter 10		Chapter 11		Chapter 12	
Sections	Sec. 9–1 to 9–3	Sec. 9–4 to 9–8	Sec. 10–1 to 10–4	Sec. 10–5 to 10–7	Sec. 11–1 to 11–3	Sec. 11–4 to 11–6	Sec. 12–1 to 12–4	Sec. 12–5 to 12–8
Chapter Review and Test		pp. 416–419		pp. 461–463		pp. 497–498		pp. 550–553
Computer Activities								

Teacher's Edition

Quizzes	25	26, 27	28, 29	30	31	32	33, 34	35
Teaching Suggestions	pp. T54-55	pp. T55-56	pp. T56-57	pp. T57-58	pp. T58-59	pp. T59-60	p. T60	pp. T60-61

Teacher's Resource Book

Chapter Tests		9		10		11		12
Multiple Choice Chapter Tests		9		10		11		12
Mid-Year Test								
End-of-Year Test								
Skills Practice	19	20	21	22	23	24	25	26
Applications	10	21	4	22	23		5	24, 35
Computer Projects	14		15, 16	17		18		

Other Supplementary Materials

Practice Masters	28	52	54–57	58	59–61	62	30, 63	64–66
Enrichment Masters	p. 25			p. 59				
Computer Graphing Experiments		Vol. 3, 1–4	Vol. 3, 7–17	Vol. 3, 5–6, 22, 23		Vol. 1, 20–24	Vol. 1, 16–17, 19	Vol. 1, 18
Using Computers in Mathematics		Sec. 3–6, 3–7						

Student Textbook

	Chapter 13		Chapter 14	Chapter 15		Chapter 16	
Sections	Sec. 13–1 to 13–4	Sec. 13–5 to 13–9	Sec. 14–1 to 14–3	Sec. 15–1 to 15–3	Sec. 15–4 to 15–7	Sec. 16–1 to 16–3	Sec. 16–4 to 16–11
Chapter Review and Test		pp. 597–599	pp. 619–620		pp. 667–669		pp. 723–725
Computer Activities		pp. 740–741					

Teacher's Edition

Quizzes	36, 37	38	39	40	41	42	43
Teaching Suggestions	pp. T61-62	p. T62	p. T63	pp. T63-64	pp. T64-65	pp. T65-66	pp. T66-67

Teacher's Resource Book

Chapter Tests		13	14		15		16
Multiple Choice Chapter Tests		13	14		15		16
Mid-Year Test							
End-of-Year Test							End-of-Year Test
Skills Practice	27	28	29,30	31	32	33	34
Applications	11	25	26	12	27, 36	6, 28	
Computer Projects	19		20				

Other Supplementary Materials

Practice Masters	67–71	76–79	75	80–82	83	83	86–89
Enrichment Masters	pp. 15, 17	pp. 33, 35					
Computer Graphing Experiments					Vol. 2, 1–14	Vol. 2, 1–14	
Using Computers in Mathematics	Sec. 4–3,	Sec. 6–1 to 6–5		Sec. 3–1 to 3–3			Sec. 3–5, 4–6

ADDITIONAL ANSWERS

CHAPTER 1 Pages 45–46
TRY THIS

1. Axiom 2 (Associative law) 2. None. We need a theorem. 3. Axiom 4 (Additive property of zero) 4. Axiom 7 (Property of reciprocals) 5. 1. Axiom 2 (Associative law of addition) 3. Axiom 4 (Additive property of zero)

Pages 47–48
EXERCISE SET 1–9

1. Axiom 3 2. Axiom 2 3. Axiom 5 4. Axiom 3 5. None 6. None 7. None 8. None 9. Symmetric property of equality 10. Reflective property of equality 11. Axiom 1 12. Axiom 2 13. None 14. Axiom 3 15. Axiom 1 16. Transitive property of equality 17. 1. Axiom 1 and Axiom 2, repeated use. 2. Axiom 5 3. Axiom 4 4. Axiom 5 18. 1. $(a + b)c = c(a + b)$, Axiom 1; 2. $c(a + b) = c \cdot a + c \cdot b$, Axiom 3; 3. $c \cdot a + c \cdot b = a \cdot c + b \cdot c$, Axiom 1 19. 1. Axiom 6 3. Axiom 5 6. Axiom 5 20. 5. Theorem 1–11 6. Axiom 2 7. Axiom 1 and Theorem 1–11 21. To prove Theorem 1–2, we use the definition of division. It says that $a \div b$ is that number which when multiplied by b gives a. We show that $a \cdot \left(\frac{1}{b}\right)$ works the same way. 1. $\left(a \cdot \frac{1}{b}\right) \cdot b$ = $a \cdot \left(\frac{1}{b} \cdot b\right)$, Axiom 2; 2. $a \cdot \left(\frac{1}{b} \cdot b\right)$ = $a\left(b \cdot \frac{1}{b}\right)$, Axiom 1; 3. $a\left(b \cdot \frac{1}{b}\right) = a \cdot 1$, Axiom 7; 4. $a \cdot 1 = 1 \cdot a$, Axiom 1; 5. $1 \cdot a = a$, Axiom 6; 6. $a \div b = a \cdot \frac{1}{b}$, Definition of division. 22. 1. $a(b - c)$

= $[b + (-c)]$, Theorem 1–1; 2. $a[b + (-c)] = a \cdot b + a \cdot (-c)$, Axiom 3; 3. $a \cdot b + a \cdot (-c) = a \cdot b + [-(ac)]$, Theorem 1–13; 4. $a \cdot b + [-(ac)] = ab - ac$, Theorem 1–1; 5. $a(b - c) = ab - ac$, Transitive property of equality, Statements 1–4 23. 1. $(-a)(-b) = (-1 \cdot a)(-1 \cdot b)$, Theorem 1–11; 2. $(-1 \cdot a)(-1 \cdot b) = (-1)(-1) \cdot a \cdot b$, Axioms 1 and 2; 3. $(-1)(-1) \cdot ab = 1 \cdot ab$, $(-1)(-1) = 1$; 4. $1 \cdot ab = ab$, Axiom 6; 5. $(-a)(-b) = ab$, Transitive property of equality, Statements 1–4 24. 1. $a - a = a + (-a)$, Theorem 1–1; 2. $a + (-a) = 0$, Axiom 5; 3. $a - a = 0$, Reflexive property of equality, Statements 1–2 25. $\frac{n}{n} = n \div n = 1$ by the definition of division 26. a. Yes; b. No; c. No; d. Yes; e. Yes

CHAPTER 2 Pages 74–75
TRY THIS

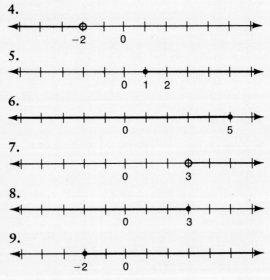

Page 77
EXERCISE SET 2–5

1.
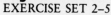
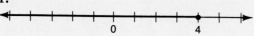

2.
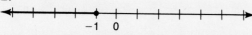

3.
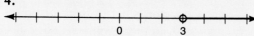

4.
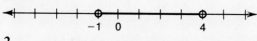

Pages 81–82
TRY THIS

1.
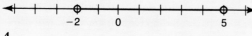

2.
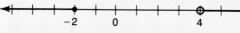

4.
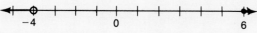

5.
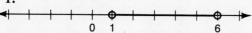

Page 83
EXERCISE SET 2–7

1.
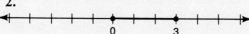

2.

3.
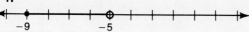

4.
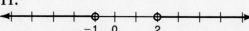

11.
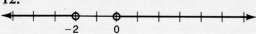

12.

13.
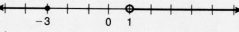

14.
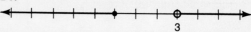

15.
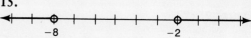

16.

Pages 86–87
TRY THIS

9.
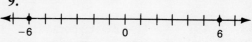

10.
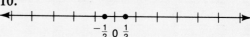

11.
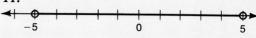

12.

13.
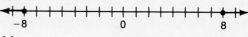

14.

Pages 91–94
TRY THIS

1. 1. $-3x + 8 > 23$, Hypothesis; 2. $-3x > 15$, Using the addition principle, adding -8 on both sides; 3. $x < -5$, Using the multiplication principle, multiplying on both sides by $-\frac{1}{3}$; 4. If $-3x + 8 > 23$, then $x < -5$, Statements 1–3.

4a. Prove the converse: If $x < -5$, then $-3x + 8 > 23$. 1. $x < -5$, Hypothesis; 2. $-3x > 15$, Using the multiplication principle, multiplying on both sides by $-\frac{1}{3}$; 3. $-3x + 8 > 23$, Using the addition principle, adding -8 on both sides; 4. If $x < -5$, then $-3x + 8 > 23$, statements 1–3.

4b. The antecedent and the consequent have the same solution set.

Pages 95–97
EXERCISE SET 2–9

1. 1. $7x - 12 = 37$, Hypothesis; 2. $7x = 49$, Addition principle, adding 12; 3. $x = 7$, Multiplication principle, multiplying by $\frac{1}{7}$; 4. If $7x - 12 = 37$, then, $x = 7$, Statements 1–3.

2. Proof is similar to proof of Exercise 1.

3. 1. $15x - 5 \geq 11 - 2x$, Hypothesis; 2. $17x \geq 16$, Addition principle twice, adding $2x$, then 5; 3. $x \geq \frac{16}{17}$, Multiplication principle, multiplying by $\frac{1}{17}$; 4. If $15x - 5 \geq 11 - 2x$, then $x \geq \frac{16}{17}$, Statements 1–3

4. Proof is similar to Exercise 3.

9. Proof is the reverse of Exercise 1.

10. Proof is the reverse of Exercise 2.

11. Proof is the reverse of Exercise 3.

12. Proof is the reverse of Exercise 4.

31. If $a = b$, then $a + c = b + c$. 1. If $a = b$, Hypothesis; 2. $a + c = x$, a unique number, Addition is an "operation"; 3. $b + c = x$, Substituting b for a in Statement 2; 4. $a + c = b + c$, Transitive property of equality

32. Proof is similar to proof of Exercise 31, except $c \neq 0$.

33. We must prove a statement and its converse. **a.** If $a = 0$ or $b = 0$, then $ab = 0$. Theorem 1–9; 1. $a = 0$, Hypothesis; 2. $ab = 0$, 3. $b = 0$, Hypothesis; 4. $ab = 0$, Theorem 1–9; 5. If $a = 0$ or $b = 0$, then $ab = 0$, Statements 1–4 **b.** If $ab = 0$, then $a = 0$ or $b = 0$.

We prove this by contradiction. 1. $ab = 0$, $a \neq 0$, Hypothesis; 2. a has reciprocal $\frac{1}{a}$, Axiom 7; 3. $\frac{1}{a}(ab) = \frac{1}{a} \cdot 0$, Statement 1 and Theorem 2–2; 4. $\frac{1}{a} \cdot 0 = 0$, Statement 3 and Theorem 1–9; 5. $\frac{1}{a}(ab) = \left(\frac{1}{a} \cdot a\right)b$, Statement 3 and Axiom 1; 6. $\left(\frac{1}{a} \cdot a\right)b = 1 \cdot b$, Axiom 7; 7. $1 \cdot b = b$, Axiom 6; 8. $b = 0$, Transitive property of equality, Statements 3–7 Finally, we conclude that if $ab = 0$ and one factor is not 0, then the other factor is 0. In other words, if $ab = 0$, then $a = 0$ or $b = 0$. That is what we were to show.

34. 1. $a < b$ and $b < c$, Hypothesis; 2. $b - a$ and $c - b$ are positive, Definition of $<$; 3. $(b - a) + (c - b)$ is positive, Axiom 8; 4. $(b - a) + (c - b) = c - a$, Axioms 1 and 2 and Theorem 1–1; 5. $a < c$, Definition of $<$; 6. If $a < b$ and $b < c$, then $a < c$, Statements 1–5

35. $a < b$, Hypothesis; 2. $b - a$ is positive, Definition of $<$; 3. $b - a = (b - a) + 0$, Axiom 4; 4. $(b - a) + 0 = (b - a) + (c - c)$, Axiom 5; 5. $(b - a) + (c - c) = (b + c) - (a + c)$, Axioms 1 and 2, and Theorem 1–1; 6. $b - a = (b + c) - (a + c)$ and $(b + c) - (a + c)$ is positive, Transitive property of equality, Statements 3–5; 7. $a + c < b + c$, Definition of $<$; 8. If $a < b$, then $a + c < b + c$, Statements 1–7

36. Proof is similar to proof of Exercise 35. Use two cases, $c > 0$ and $c < 0$.

37. We wish to prove that for any numbers a and b, $|ab| = |a| \cdot |b|$. According to Axiom 9, the numbers a and b are positive, zero, or their inverses are positive (they are negative). The proof therefore breaks down into four cases.

Case 1
1. a and b are positive, Hypothesis;
2. ab is positive, Axiom 8; 3. $|ab|$
$= ab$, $|a| = a$, $|b| = b$, Definition of
absolute value; 4. $|a| \cdot |b|$ is positive,
Axiom 8; 5. $|a| \cdot |b| = ab$, Statements 2
and 4; 6. $|ab| = |a| \cdot |b|$, Statements 3
and 5, Transitive property of equality
Case 2
1. a and b are negative, Hypothesis;
2. $|a| = -a$ and $|b| = -b$, Definition
of absolute value; 3. $|a| \cdot |b| = (-a)$
$(-b)$, Statement 2, substitution;
4. $(-a)(-b)$ is positive, Axiom 8;
5. $(-a)(-b) = ab$, so ab is positive,
Theorem 1–14; 6. $|a| \cdot |b| = ab$, State-
ment 3, Transitive property of equality
There are two other cases, which are
similarly proved: one or both of a and
b is 0; and one of a and b is positive,
the other negative.

38. The Proof is similar to the proof of
Exercise 37.
39. The proof breaks down into three
cases: $a > 0$, $a = 0$, and $a < 0$.
Case 1
1. $a > 0$, Hypothesis; 2. $|a| = a$,
Definition of absolute value; 3. $|a|^2$
$= a^2$, Multiplication principle for
equations
Case 2
1. $a = 0$, Hypothesis; 2. $|0|^2 = |0| \cdot |0|$
$= 0 \cdot 0 = 0$, Definition of absolute
value; 3. $0^2 = 0$, Arithmetic; 4. $|0|^2$
$= 0^2$, Transitive property of equality,
Statements 2–3; 5. $|a|^2 = a^2$, Statement
1, substitution
Case 3
1. $a < 0$, Hypothesis; 2. $|a| = -a$,
Definition of absolute value; 3. $|a|^2$
$= (-a)(-a)$, Statement 2, Multi-
plication principle for equations;
4. $(-a)(-a) = a^2$, Theorem 1–14;

5. $|a|^2 = a^2$, Transitive property of
equality, Statements 3–5
40. If x is an integer, then x is a rational
number. If x is a rational number, then
x is an integer
41. If x is a quitter, then x never wins. If
x never wins, then x is a quitter.
42. If a set of birds is of the same feather,
then they flock together. If a set of
birds flocks together, then they are of
the same feather.

CHAPTER 3   Pages 105–106
EXERCISE SET 3–1
1. $\{(0, a), (0, b), (0, c), (2, a), (2, b),$
$(2, c), (4, a), (4, b), (4, c), (5, a), (5, b),$
$(5, c)\}$ 2. $\{(1, d), (1, e), (1, f), (3, d),$
$(3, e), (3, f), (5, d), (5, e), (5, f), (9, d),$
$(9, e), (9, f)\}$ 3. $\{(x, 1), (x, 2), (y, 1)$
$(y, 2), (z, 1), (z, 2)\}$ 4. $\{(5, a), (5, z),$
$(7, a), (7, z), (10, a), (10, z)\}$ 5. $\{(5, 5),$
$(5, 6), (5, 7), (5, 8), (6, 5), (6, 6), (6, 7),$
$(6, 8), (7, 5), (7, 6), (7, 7), (7, 8), (8, 5),$
$(8, 6), (8, 7), (8, 8)\}$ 6. $\{(-2, -2),$
$(-2, 0), (-2, 2), (-2, 4), (0, -2), (0, 0),$
$(0, 2), (0, 4), (2, -2), (2, 0), (2, 2), (2, 4),$
$(4, -2), (4, 0), (4, 2), (4, -4)\}$
21a. $(-1, -1)$ $(0, -1)$ $(1, -1)$ $(2, -1)$
$(-1, 0)$ $(0, 0)$ $(1, 0)$ $(2, 0)$ $(-1, 1)$ $(0, 1)$
$(1, 1)$ $(2, 1)$ $(-1, 2)$ $(0, 2)$ $(1, 2)$ $(2, 2)$
22a. $(-1, -1)$ $(1, -1)$ $(3, -1)$ $(5, -1)$
$(-1, 1)$ $(1, 1)$ $(3, 1)$ $(5, 1)$ $(-1, 3)$ $(1, 3)$
$(3, 3)$ $(5, 3)$ $(-1, 5)$ $(1, 5)$ $(3, 5)$ $(5, 5)$

Pages 108–111
TRY THIS
1.

5.

6.

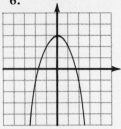

7.

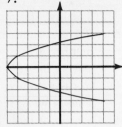

8.

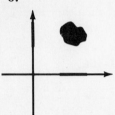

9.

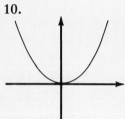

10.

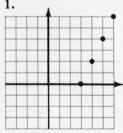

Pages 111–113
EXERCISE SET 3–2

1.

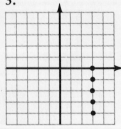

2.

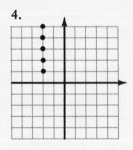

3.

4.

5.

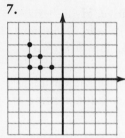

6.

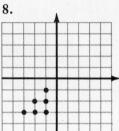

7.

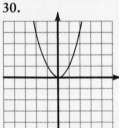

8.

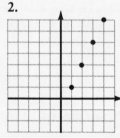

21. Line through $(1,\ 1)$ and $(-1,\ -1)$
22. Line through $(-1,\ -2)$ and $(1,\ 2)$
23. Line through $(-1,\ 2)$ and $(1,\ -2)$
24. Line through $(-2,\ 1)$ and $(2,\ -1)$
25. Line through $(0,\ 3)$ and $(-3,\ 0)$
26. Line through $(0,\ -2)$ and $(2,\ 0)$
27. Line through $(2,\ 4)$ and $(-1,\ -5)$
28. Line through $(-1,\ 5)$ and $(1,\ -3)$
29. Line through $(2,\ -1)$ and $(-1,\ 5)$

30.

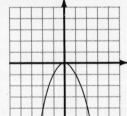

31.

30. Domain $= R$, Range: $\{y \mid y \geq 0\}$
31. Domain $= R$, Range: $\{y \mid y \leq 0\}$

32. 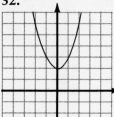 **33.**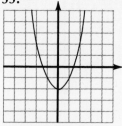

32. Domain = R, Range: $\{y \mid y \geq 2\}$
33. Domain = R, Range: $\{y \mid y \geq -2\}$

34. 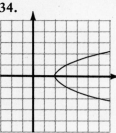 **35.**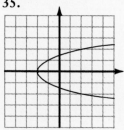

34. Domain: $\{x \mid x \geq 2\}$, Range = R
35. Domain: $\{x \mid x \geq -2\}$, Range = R
38. Horizontal line through $(0, 2)$
39. Vertical line through $(-3, 0)$
40. Line through $(0, 1)$ and $(-1, 0)$
41. Line through $(1, 0)$ and $(0, -1)$
42. Line through $(0, 0)$ and $(1, 2)$
43. Line through $(0, 0)$ and $(2, 1)$

44. 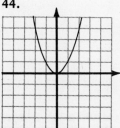 **45.**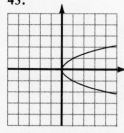

46. 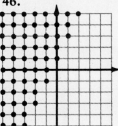 **47.**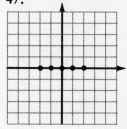

48. 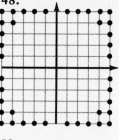 **49.**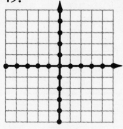

50. 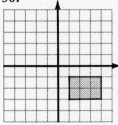 **51.**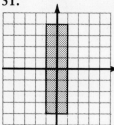

52. 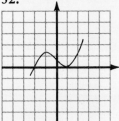 **53.**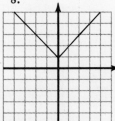

Page 119
TRY THIS

8. 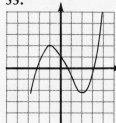 **9.**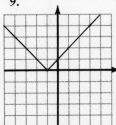

10. 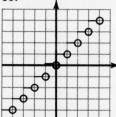 **11.**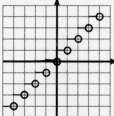

Page 121
EXERCISE SET 3–3

25.
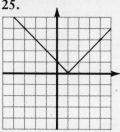

26.
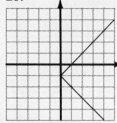

27.
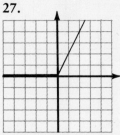

28.
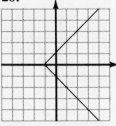

29.
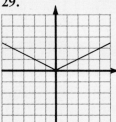

30.
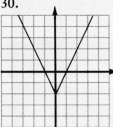

31.
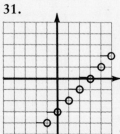

32.
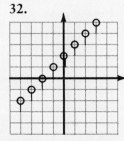

33.
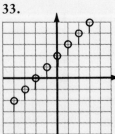

40.
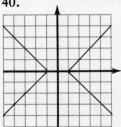

41.
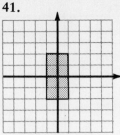

43.
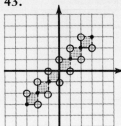

Pages 124–126
TRY THIS

9.
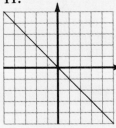

10.
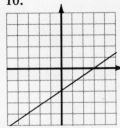

11.
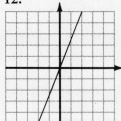

12.
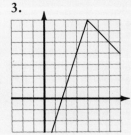

13. The graph of $y = 2x + 1$ is moved up 1 unit from the graph of $y = 2x$.

14. The graph of $y = 2x - 4$ is moved down 4 units from the graph of $y = 2x$.

15–17.
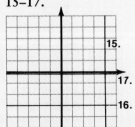

CHAPTER 4   Page 158
TRY THIS

3.

Page 192
EXERCISE SET 4–7

37. $\begin{vmatrix} 1 & x & x^2 \\ 1 & y & y^2 \\ 1 & z & z^2 \end{vmatrix}$

$= \begin{vmatrix} y & y^2 \\ z & z^2 \end{vmatrix} - \begin{vmatrix} x & x^2 \\ z & z^2 \end{vmatrix} + \begin{vmatrix} x & x^2 \\ y & y^2 \end{vmatrix}$

$= yz^2 - zy^2 - (xz^2 - zx^2) + (xy^2 - yx^2)$

$= yz^2 - zy^2 - xz^2 + zx^2 + xy^2 - yx^2$

$= (x - y)(y - z)(z - x)$

38. To solve for y, multiply the first equation by d, and the second equation by $-a$, to get $adx + bdy = cd$ and $-adx - aey = -af$. Adding, we get $aey - bdy = af - cd$, so $y = \frac{af - cd}{ae - bd}$. Solve for x in a similar manner.

Pages 194–196
TRY THIS

2.
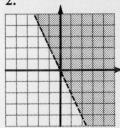

3.
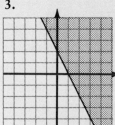

4.
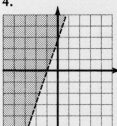

5.
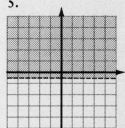

6.
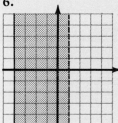

7.
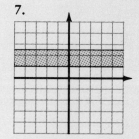

8.
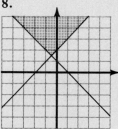

9.
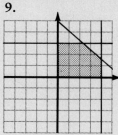

Pages 196–197
EXERCISE SET 4–8

5.
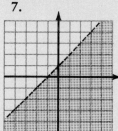

6.
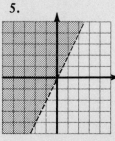

7.
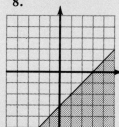

8.
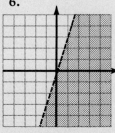

9.
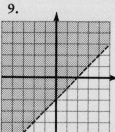

10.
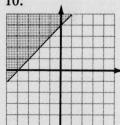

11.
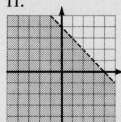

12.
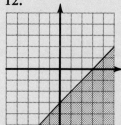

13.

14.

23.

24.

15.

16.

25.

26.

17.

18.

27.

28.

19.

20.

29.

30.

21.

22.

31.

32.

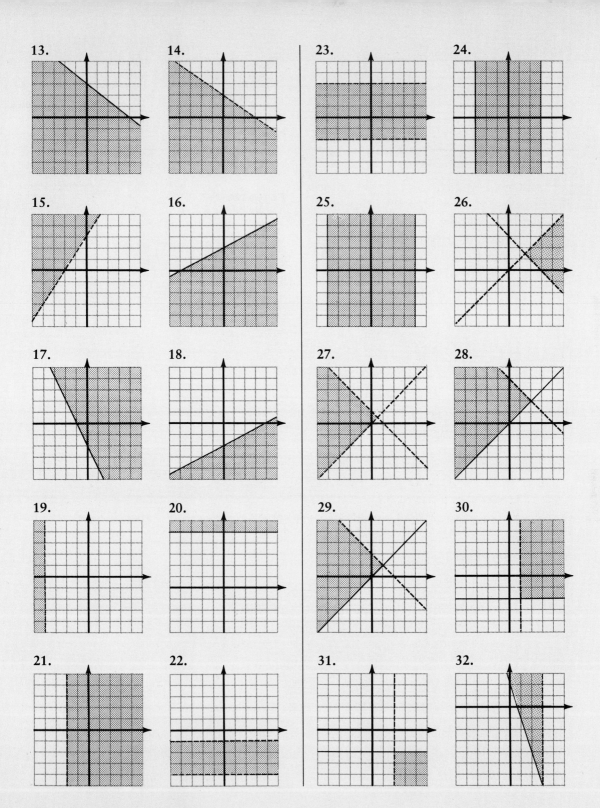

33.
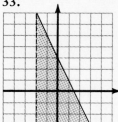

34.
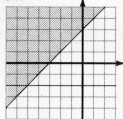

49.
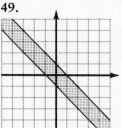

50.
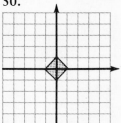

35.
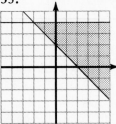

36.
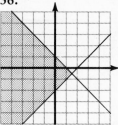

51.
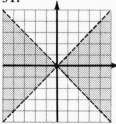

37.
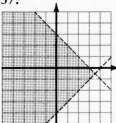

38.
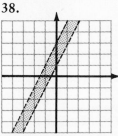

39.
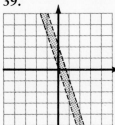

40.
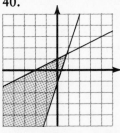

47.
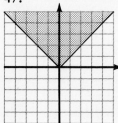

48.
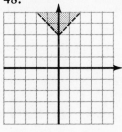

CHAPTER 5   Pages 211–212
EXERCISE SET 5-1

7. $3x^2y - 5xy^2 + 7xy + 2$ **8.** $2x^2y - 7xy^2 + 8xy + 5$ **9.** $3x + 2y - 2z - 3$ **10.** $7x^2 + 12xy - 2x - y - 9$ **11.** $9.46y^4 + 2.50y^3 - 11.8y - 3.1$ **12.** $\frac{1}{2}x^5 - \frac{3}{10}x^3 - \frac{1}{4}x^2 + \frac{2}{3}x - 19$ **25.** $55x^5 - 59x^4 + 14x^3 + 12x^2 + 18x + 175$ **26.** $-29x^5 + 15x^4 - 86x^3 + 68x^2 - 50x - 25$ **27.** $29x^5 - 15x^4 + 86x^3 - 68x^2 + 50x + 25$ **28.** $178x^5 - 199x^4 + 6x^3 + 76x^2 + 38x + 600$

Page 221
EXERCISE SET 5-3

1. $y(y - 5)$ **2.** $x(x + 9)$ **3.** $2a(2a + 1)$
4. $3y(2y + 1)$ **5.** $y^2(y + 9)$ **6.** $x^2(x + 8)$
7. $3(y^2 - y - 3)$ **8.** $5(x^2 - x + 3)$
9. $3x^2(2 - x^2)$ **10.** $4y^2(2 + y^2)$
11. $2a(2b - 3c + 6d)$
12. $2x(4y + 5z - 7w)$
13. $4xy(x - 3y)$ **14.** $5x^2y^2(y + 3x)$
15. $x^2(x^4 + x^3 - x + 1)$
16. $y(y^3 - y^2 + y + 1)$
17. $12x(2x^2 - 3x + 6)$
18. $5(2a^4 + 3a^2 - 5a - 6)$ **19.** $(x + 4)(x - 4)$ **20.** $(y + 3)(y - 3)$ **21.** $(3x + 5)(3x - 5)$ **22.** $(2a + 7)(2a - 7)$

23. $(2x + 5)(2x - 5)$ **24.** $(10y + 9)$
$(10y - 9)$ **25.** $6(x + y)(x - y)$
26. $8(x + y)(x - y)$ **27.** $3(x^4 + y^4)$
$(x^2 + y^2)(x + y)(x - y)$ **28.** $5(x^2 + y^2)$
$(x + y)(x - y)$ **29.** $4x(y^2 + z^2)(y + z)$
$(y - z)$ **30.** $a^2(3a + b)(3a - b)$
31. $(y - 3)^2$ **32.** $(x - 4)^2$ **33.** $(x + 7)^2$
34. $(x + 8)^2$ **35.** $(x + 1)^2$ **36.** $(x - 1)^2$
37. $(a + 2)^2$ **38.** $(a - 2)^2$ **39.** $(y - 6)^2$
40. $(y + 6)^2$ **41.** $y(y - 9)^2$ **42.** $a(a + 12)^2$
43. $3(2a + 3)^2$ **44.** $5(2y + 5)^2$
45. $2(x - 10)^2$ **46.** $2(4x + 3)^2$
47. $(1 - 4d)^2$ **48.** $(5y - 8)^2$
49. $\frac{1}{7}x(4x^5 - 6x^3 + x - 3)$ **50.** $\left(\frac{1}{5} + x\right)$
$\left(\frac{1}{5} - x\right)$ **51.** $(0.5 + y)(0.5 - y)$
52. $(0.2x + 0.3y)(0.2x - 0.3y)$
53. $(xy + 2)^2(xy - 2)^2$ **54.** $(4a - 3b)^2$
55. $(3y^4 + 2)^2$ **56.** $\left(\frac{1}{6}x^4 + \frac{2}{3}\right)^2$
57. $(0.5x + 0.3)^2$ **58.** $x(x - 6)$
59. $9x(x + 6)$ **60.** $(a^8 + 1)(a^4 + 1)(a^2 + 1)$
$(a + 1)(a - 1)$ **61.** $(y^{16} + 1)(y^8 + 1)(y^4 + 1)$
$(y^2 + 1)(y + 1)(y - 1)$ **62.** $(x^a - y)(x^a + y)$
63. $(x^{2a} - y^b)(x^{2a} + y^b)$ **64.** $y^a(y^a - 5)$
65. $(y^a - 3)(y^a - 3)$ **66.** $(y - a)(y - a)$

Pages 223–224
EXERCISE SET 5–4

1. $(x + 5)(x + 4)$ **2.** $(x + 5)(x + 3)$
3. $(y - 4)^2$ **4.** $(a - 5)^2$ **5.** $(x - 9)(x + 3)$
6. $(t - 5)(t + 3)$ **7.** $(m - 7)(m + 4)$
8. $(x - 4)(x + 2)$ **9.** $(x + 9)(x + 5)$
10. $(y + 8)(y + 4)$ **11.** $(y + 9)(y - 7)$
12. $(x + 8)(x - 5)$ **13.** $(t - 7)(t - 4)$
14. $(y - 5)(y - 9)$ **15.** $(x + 5)(x - 2)$
16. $(x + 3)(x - 2)$ **17.** $(x + 2)(x + 3)$
18. $(y + 7)(y + 1)$ **19.** $(8 - y)(4 + y)$
20. $(8 - x)(7 + x)$ **21.** $(t + 5)(t + 3)$
22. $(3b + 2)(b + 2)$ **23.** $(3x + 1)(3x + 4)$
24. $(3y - 2)(2y + 1)$ **25.** $(3a - 4)(a + 1)$
26. $(6a + 5)(a - 2)$ **27.** $(12z + 1)(z - 3)$
28. $(3a + 4)(3a - 2)$ **29.** $(2t + 5)(2t - 3)$
30. $(3x + 2)(x - 6)$ **31.** $(3x + 5)(2x - 5)$
32. $(3x - 5)(2x + 3)$ **33.** $(5y + 4)(2y - 3)$
34. $(3a - 4)(a - 2)$ **35.** $(4a - 1)(3a - 1)$

36. $(5y + 2)(7y + 4)$ **37.** $(3a + 2)(3a + 4)$
38. $(5t - 3)(t + 1)$ **39.** $(5x + 3)(3x - 1)$
40. $4(2x + 1)(x - 4)$ **41.** $6(3x - 4)(x + 1)$
42. $x(3x + 1)(x - 2)$ **43.** $y(6y - 5)(3y + 2)$
44. $(24x + 1)(x - 2)$ **45.** $(5y + 2)(3y - 5)$
46. $(7x + 3)(3x + 4)$ **47.** $(5y + 4)(2y + 3)$
48. $(5x + 4)(8x - 3)$ **49.** $(6y + 5)(4y - 3)$
50. $(4a - 3)(3a - 2)$ **51.** $(4a - 3)(5a - 2)$
52. $(x^2 + 16)(x^2 - 5)$ **53.** $(y^2 + 12)(y^2 - 7)$
54. $\left(x + \frac{4}{5}\right)\left(x - \frac{1}{5}\right)$ **55.** $\left(y + \frac{4}{7}\right)\left(y - \frac{2}{7}\right)$
56. $(y - 0.1)(y + 0.5)$ **57.** $(t + 0.9)(t - 0.3)$
58. $(2x - 3y)(x + 2y)$ **59.** $(2m + 5n)$
$(m - 2n)$ **60.** $(2x - 3y)(4x + 3y)$
61. $(2t + s)(t - 4s)$ **62.** $(7ab + 6)(ab + 1)$
63. $(9xy - 4)(xy + 1)$ **64.** $3(x - 11)(x + 15)$
65. $x(x - 15)(x + 15)$ **66.** $4y(y - 12)^2$
67. $3x(y - 25)^2$ **68.** $7(x - 25y)(x + 25y)$
69. $12(x - 3y)^2$ **70.** $15t(t - 7)(t + 3)$
71. $6x(x + 9)(x + 4)$ **72.** $(x^a + 8)(x^a - 3)$
73. $(x + a)(x + b)$ **74.** $(2x^a - 3)(2x^a + 1)$
75. $(bx + a)(dx + c)$ **76.** $\left(\frac{1}{2}p - \frac{2}{5}\right)^2$
77. $\frac{1}{3}\left(\frac{2}{3}r + \frac{1}{2}s\right)^2$

Page 233
EXERCISE SET 5–7

1. $(x + 12)(x - 12)$ **2.** $(2x + 3)(x + 4)$
3. $3(x^2 + 2)(x^2 - 2)$ **4.** $2x(y + 5)(y - 5)$
5. $(a + 5)^2$ **6.** $(p + 8)^2$ **7.** $2(x - 11)$
$(x + 6)$ **8.** $3(y - 12)(y + 7)$ **9.** $(3x + 5y)$
$(3x - 5y)$ **10.** $(4a + 9b)(4a - 9b)$
11. $(2c - d)^2$ **12.** $(10b + a)(7b - a)$
13. $(x^2 + 2)(2x - 7)$ **14.** $(3m^2 + 8)$
$(m + 3)$ **15.** $(4x - 15)(x - 3)$
16. $3(y + 7)(y - 2)$ **17.** $(m^3 + 10)(m^3 - 2)$
18. $(x + 6)(x - 6)(x + 1)(x - 1)$
19. $(c - b)(a + d)$ **20.** $(w + z)(x - y)$
21. $(m + 1)(m^2 - m + 1)(m - 1)$
$(m^2 + m + 1)$ **22.** $(2t + 1)(4t^2 - 2t + 1)$
$(2t - 1)(4t^2 + 2t + 1)$ **23.** $(x + y + 3)$
$(x - y + 3)$ **24.** $(t + p + 5)(t - p + 5)$
25. $(6y - 5)(6y + 7)$ **26.** $-2b(7a + 1)$
$(2a - 1)$ **27.** $(a^4 + b^4)(a^2 + b^2)(a + b)$
$(a - b)$ **28.** $2(x^2 + 4)(x + 2)(x - 2)$

29. $(2p + 3q)(4p^2 - 6pq + 9q^2)$
30. $(5x + 4y)(25x^2 - 20xy + 16y^2)$
31. $(4p - 1)(16p^2 + 4p + 1)$ 32. $(2y - 5)$
$(4y^2 + 10y + 25)$ 33. $ab(a + 4b)(a - 4b)$
34. $xy(x + 5y)(x - 5y)$ 35. $(4xy - 3)$
$(5xy - 2)$ 36. $(3ab + 4)(9ab + 2)$
37. $2(x + 2)(x - 2)(x + 3)$ 38. $3(x + 3)$
$(x - 3)(x + 2)$ 39. $2(5x - 4y)$
$(25x^2 + 20xy + 16y^2)$ 40. $(3a - 7b)$
$(9a^2 + 21ab + 49b^2)$ 41. $2(2x + 3y)$
$(4x^2 - 6xy + 9y^2)$ 42. $2(5a + 3b)$
$(25a^2 + 15ab + 9b^2)$ 43. $x(x - 2p)$
44. $(5x - 12)(6x - 5)$ 45. $5(c^{10} - 4d^{10})$
$(c^{10} + 4d^{10})$ 46. $3(a + b - c + d)$
$(a + b + c - d)$ 47. $8(a - 7)^2$
48. $(11 + y^2)(4 - y^2)$ 49. $(x - 1)^3$
$(x^2 + 1)(x + 1)$ 50. $4(3a^2 - 4)$
51. $y(y - 1)^2(y - 2)$ 52. $(3x^{2s} + 4y^t)$
$(9x^{4s} + 12x^{2s}y^t + 16y^{2t})$ 53. $c(c^w + 1)^2$
54. $6(2x^{2a} - 1)(2x^{2a} + 1)$

CHAPTER 6   Page 251
EXERCISE SET 6-1
56. $\frac{a}{b} \cdot \frac{c}{d} = (ab^{-1})(cd^{-1}) = (ac)(b^{-1}d^{-1})$
$= (ac)(bd)^{-1} = \frac{ac}{bd}$
57. $\frac{a}{b} \cdot \frac{b}{a} = \frac{a \cdot b}{b \cdot a} = \frac{a \cdot b}{a \cdot b} = 1$; thus the reciprocal of $\frac{a}{b}$ is $\frac{b}{a}$.
58. $\frac{a}{b} \div \frac{c}{d}$ is that number which when multiplied by $\frac{c}{d}$ gives $\frac{a}{b}$. We assert that
$\frac{a}{b} \cdot \frac{d}{c}$ is that number by multiplying it by
$\frac{c}{d} \cdot \left(\frac{a}{b} \cdot \frac{d}{c}\right) \cdot \frac{c}{d} = \frac{a}{b} \cdot \left(\frac{d}{c} \cdot \frac{c}{d}\right) = \frac{a}{b} \cdot 1 = \frac{a}{b}$
59. $(a^{-1}b^{-1})(ab) = (aa^{-1})(bb^{-1}) = 1 \cdot 1$
$= 1$, using associative and commutative
laws and property of multiplicative inverses. Thus, $(ab)^{-1} = a^{-1}b^{-1}$.

Page 259
EXERCISE SET Set 6-3
43. $\frac{a}{c} + \frac{b}{c} = ac^{-1} + bc^{-1} = (a + b)c^{-1}$
$= \frac{a + b}{c}$
44. $\frac{a}{c} - \frac{b}{c} = ac^{-1} - bc^{-1} = (a - b)c^{-1}$
$= \frac{a - b}{c}$

Page 284
EXERCISE SET 6-9
37. $\frac{\text{number of words in book}}{\text{number of pages in book}}$
$= \frac{\text{number of words on } n \text{ pages}}{n}$,
where n is some small number, say 1,
or 2, or 3

39. $P = kQ$, so $Q = \frac{1}{k}P$ and $\frac{1}{k}$ becomes the
constant of variation
40. $A = \frac{k}{B}$, so $B = \frac{k}{A}$, and $\frac{1}{A} = \frac{B}{k} = \frac{1}{k} \cdot B$

CHAPTER 7   Page 309
EXERCISE SET 7-4
83. $-\frac{\sqrt{15} + 20 - 6\sqrt{2} - 8\sqrt{30}}{77}$
84. $-\frac{3\sqrt{2} + 2\sqrt{42} - 3\sqrt{15} - 6\sqrt{35}}{25}$
85. $\frac{|x| - 2\sqrt{xy} + |y|}{|x| - |y|}$
86. $\frac{|a| + 2\sqrt{ab} + |b|}{|a| - |b|}$
87. $\frac{3\sqrt{6} + 4}{2}$ 88. $\frac{4\sqrt{6} + 9}{3}$ 89. $\frac{7}{\sqrt{21}}$
90. $\frac{2}{\sqrt{6}}$ 91. $\frac{52}{3\sqrt{91}}$ 92. $\frac{7}{\sqrt[3]{98}}$
93. $\frac{7|x|}{\sqrt{21xy}}$ 94. $\frac{5y^2}{x\sqrt[3]{150x^2y^2}}$ 95. $\frac{-11}{4(\sqrt{3} - 5)}$
96. $\frac{-22}{\sqrt{6} + 5\sqrt{2} + 5\sqrt{3} + 25}$ 97. $\frac{3}{\sqrt{10} + 2 + \sqrt{15} + \sqrt{6}}$

Page 320
EXERCISE SET 7-6
53. Suppose $a = b$. Then a and b are
names for the same number. Then, for
a natural number n, a^n and b^n are
unique and must be the names for the
same number.

Page 332
EXERCISE SET 7-9
7. $x^2 + 25$ 8. $x^2 + 49$ 9. $x^2 - 2x$
$+ 2$ 10. $x^2 - 4x + 5$ 11. $x^2 - 4x$
$+ 13$ 12. $x^2 - 8x + 25$ 13. $x^2 - ix$
$- 3x + 3i$ 14. $x^2 - ix - 5x + 5i$
15. $x^3 - x^2 + 9x - 9$ 16. $x^3 - x^2 + 4x - 4$
17. $x^3 - 2ix^2 - 3x^2 + 5ix + x - 2i + 2$
18. $x^3 - 2ix^2 + x - 2i$ 19. $\frac{2}{5} + \frac{6}{5}i$
20. $\frac{12}{5} - \frac{1}{5}i$ 21. $\frac{8}{5} - \frac{9}{5}i$ 22. $\frac{8}{29} + \frac{9}{29}i$
23. $2 - i$ 24. $-\frac{1}{5} + \frac{7}{5}i$ 25. $\frac{11}{25} + \frac{2}{25}i$
26. $\frac{4}{5} + \frac{3}{5}i$

TRY THIS
1.

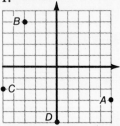

EXERCISE SET 7–10

The graphs for Exercises 1–6 have points on the real-imaginary grid that correspond to points with the following coordinates on the x–y coordinate grid:

1. $(3, 2), (-4, -2), (2, -5)$ **2.** $(-5, 3),$ $(-2, -3), (3, -4)$ **3.** $(-4, 2),$ $(-3, -4), (2, -3)$ **4.** $(-5, 5), (-5, 4),$ $(3, -2)$ **5.** $(-3, -4), (-2, -5), (5, 3)$

6. $(2, 2), (-3, -3), (2, -3)$

19. Let $z = a + bi$. $|z| = |a + bi|$
$= \sqrt{a^2 + b^2}$. Then $-z = -(a + bi)$
$= -a - bi$. $|-z| = |-a - bi|$
$= \sqrt{(-a)^2 + (-b)^2} = \sqrt{a^2 + b^2}$
$\therefore |z| = |-z|$

20. Let $z = a + bi$. $|z| = |a + bi|$
$= \sqrt{a^2 + b^2}$. The conjugate of z is
$a - bi$. $|a - bi| = \sqrt{a^2 + (-b)^2}$
$= \sqrt{a^2 + b^2}$. $\therefore |a + bi| = |a - bi|$

21. $(ac - bd) + (ad + bc)i$

22. $\frac{ac + bd}{c^2 + d^2} + \frac{bc - ad}{c^2 + d^2}i$

23. Let $z = a + bi$ and $w = c + di$. Then
$|z \cdot w| = |(ac - bd) + (ad + bc)i|$
$= \sqrt{(ac - bd)^2 + (ad + bc)^2}$
$= \sqrt{a^2c^2 + b^2d^2 + a^2d^2 + b^2c^2}$
$|z| \cdot |w| = \sqrt{a^2 + b^2}\ \sqrt{c^2 + d^2}$
$= \sqrt{a^2c^2 + a^2d^2 + b^2c^2 + b^2d^2}$.
$\therefore |z \cdot w| = |z| \cdot |w|$

24. $\left| \frac{z}{w} \right| = \frac{a + bi}{c + di} = \frac{ac + bd}{c^2 + d^2} + \frac{bc - ad}{c^2 + d^2}i$

$= \sqrt{\left(\frac{ac + bd}{c^2 + d^2}\right)^2 + \left(\frac{bc - ad}{c^2 + d^2}\right)^2}$

$= \frac{\sqrt{a^2b^2 + b^2d^2 + b^2c^2 + a^2d^2}}{c^2 + d^2}$

$\frac{|z|}{|w|} = \frac{\sqrt{a^2 + b^2}}{\sqrt{c^2 + d^2}} = \frac{\sqrt{a^2 + b^2}}{\sqrt{c^2 + d^2}} \cdot \frac{\sqrt{c^2 + d^2}}{\sqrt{c^2 + d^2}}$

$= \frac{\sqrt{a^2c^2 + a^2d^2 + b^2c^2 + b^2d^2}}{c^2 + d^2}$

$\therefore \left| \frac{z}{w} \right| = \frac{|z|}{|w|}$

EXERCISE SET 7–11

16. Let $z = a + bi$ and $w = c + di$. Then
$\overline{z \cdot w} = \overline{(a + bi)(c + di)} = \overline{(ac - bd)}$
$\overline{+ (bc + ad)i} = (ac - bd) - (bc + ad)i$.
Now $\bar{z} \cdot \bar{w} = \overline{(a + bi)} \cdot \overline{(c + di)}$
$= (a - bi)(c - di) = (ac - bd)$
$- (bc + ad)i$. Thus $\overline{z \cdot w} = \bar{z} \cdot \bar{w}$.

17. Theorem: If $P(z)$ is a polynomial with real coefficients in the complex number z, then $\overline{P(z)} = P(\bar{z})$. Proof: Let $P(z)$
$= a_n z^n + a_{n-1} z^{n-1} + \ldots + a_1 z + a_0$,
where the coefficients are real.

$\overline{P(z)} = \overline{a_n z^n + a_{n-1} z^{n-1} + \ldots + a_1 z + a_0}$
$= \overline{a_n z^n} + \overline{a_{n-1} z^{n-1}} + \ldots + \overline{a_1 z} + \overline{a_0}$
$= \overline{a_n} \cdot \overline{z^n} + \overline{a_{n-1}} \cdot \overline{z^{n-1}} + \ldots + \overline{a_1} \bar{z} + \overline{a_0}$
$= a_n \overline{z^n} + a_{n-1} \cdot \overline{z^{n-1}} + \ldots + a_1 \bar{z} + a_0$
$= a_n \bar{z}^n + a_{n-1} \bar{z}^{n-1} + \ldots + a_1 \bar{z} + a_0$
$= P(\bar{z})$

CAREERS EXERCISE

4. $k_c = \frac{k_b - K - k_b}{K}$ **5.** $B = R(V_m - A)$

12. $a = n(b_1 - b_2) - L$

14. $v_1 = \frac{V(m_1 + m_2) - m_2 v_2}{m_1}$ **15.** $a = \frac{b(m - P)}{P - m}$

18. $b = \frac{2P}{(h^3 - m^3)}$ **19.** $a_1 = \frac{a_2(1 - M)}{(M - W)}$

CHAPTER 8   Page 356
EXERCISE SET 8–2

54. The solutions of $cx^2 + bx + a = 0$ are $\frac{-b \pm \sqrt{b^2 - 4ac}}{2c}$. The reciprocals of these are $\frac{2c}{-b \pm \sqrt{b^2 - 4ac}}$. Multiply $\frac{2c}{-b + \sqrt{b^2 - 4ac}}$ by $\frac{-b - \sqrt{b^2 - 4ac}}{-b - \sqrt{b^2 - 4ac}}$ and multiply $\frac{2c}{-b - \sqrt{b^2 - 4ac}}$ by $\frac{-b + \sqrt{b^2 - 4ac}}{-b + \sqrt{b^2 - 4ac}}$
The results are $\frac{-b - \sqrt{b^2 - 4ac}}{2a}$ and $\frac{b + \sqrt{b^2 - 4ac}}{2a}$ which are the solutions to $ax^2 + bx + c = 0$.

EXERCISE SET 8-3

16. Sum $= -7$; product $= 8$ **17.** Sum $= 2$; product $= 10$ **18.** Sum $= 1$; product $= 1$ **19.** Sum $= -1$; product $= -1$ **20.** Sum $= 2$; product $= -4$ **21.** Sum $= -\frac{1}{2}$; product $= 2$ **22.** Sum $= 0$; product $= -25$ **23.** Sum $= 0$; product $= -49$ **24.** Sum $= -\frac{5}{9}$; product $= \frac{4}{9}$ **25.** Sum $= \frac{12}{25}$; product $= \frac{2}{25}$ **26.** Sum $= 54$; product $= 9$ **27.** Sum $= -4$; product $= -2$ **28.** $2x^2 + 10x + 1 = 0$ **29.** $4x^2 + 4\pi x + 1 = 0$ **30.** $x^2 - \sqrt{3}x + 8 = 0$ **31.** $x^2 - 5x - \sqrt{2} = 0$ **32.** $x^2 + 2x - 99 = 0$ **33.** $x^2 - 16 = 0$ **34.** $x^2 - 14x + 49 = 0$ **35.** $x^2 + 10x + 25 = 0$ **36.** $25x^2 - 20x - 12 = 0$ **37.** $8x^2 + 6x + 1 = 0$ **38.** $4x^2 - 2(c + d)x + cd = 0$ **39.** $12x^2 - (4k + 3m)x + km = 0$ **40.** $x^2 - 4\sqrt{2}x + 6 = 0$ **41.** $x^2 + \sqrt{3}x - 6 = 0$ **42.** $x^2 + \pi x - 2\pi^2 = 0$ **43.** $x^2 - \pi x - 12\pi^2 = 0$ **56.** a. $k < \frac{9}{4}$ b. $k = \frac{9}{4}$ c. $k > \frac{9}{4}$ **57.** a. $k < \frac{1}{4}$ b. $k = \frac{1}{4}$ c. $k > \frac{1}{4}$ **58.** a. $k < 4$ b. $k = 4$ c. $k > 4$ **59.** a. $k < 1$ b. $k = 1$ c. $k > 1$ **60.** a. $k < \frac{5}{4}$ b. $k = \frac{5}{4}$ c. $k > \frac{5}{4}$ **61.** a. $k > \frac{11}{3}$ b. $k = \frac{11}{3}$ c. $k < \frac{11}{3}$ **66.** Given $a^2x + bx + c = 0$, $a \neq 0$, a, b, $c \, \epsilon$ rationals, $b^2 - 4ac > 0$ and $b^2 - 4ac = d^2$ where $d \, \epsilon$ rationals. $\therefore x = \frac{-b \pm \sqrt{b^2 - 4ac}}{2a} = \frac{-b \pm d}{2a}$. By the closure properties in rationals both $\frac{-b + d}{2a}$ and $\frac{-b - d}{2a}$ are rational. **67.** a. Two rational solutions b. Two real (not rational) solutions **68.** Given $ax^2 + bx + c = 0$ with rational coefficients. Let $a = \frac{m}{n}$, $b = \frac{m'}{n'}$ and $c = \frac{m''}{n''}$ where m, n, m', n', m'', n'' are integers. $\therefore \frac{m}{n}x^2 + \frac{m'}{n'}x + \frac{m''}{n''} = 0$. Multiply this quadratic equation by $(nn'n'')$ the LCM of the denominators. The result is $n'n''mx^2 + nn''m'x + nn'm'' = 0$. Since integers are closed with respect to multiplication $n'n''m$, $nn''m'$, and $nn'm''$ represent integer coefficients **69.** 1. If $b^2 - 4ac = 0$, then $x = \frac{-b \pm \sqrt{b^2 - 4ac}}{2a} = \frac{-b \pm \sqrt{0}}{2a} = \frac{-b}{2a}$. Since both a

and b are real, $\frac{-b}{2a}$ is real by the closure properties and $ax^2 + bx + c = 0$ has one real solution. 2. If a, b, and $c \, \epsilon$ reals and $b^2 - 4ac > 0$, then $\sqrt{b^2 - 4ac}$ represents a positive real number (let $\sqrt{b^2 - 4ac} = d$). Thus $x = \frac{-b \pm \sqrt{b^2 - 4ac}}{2a} = \frac{-b \pm d}{2a}$. By the closure properties in the reals both $\frac{-b + d}{2a}$ and $\frac{-b - d}{2a}$ are real. Since $\frac{-b + d}{2a} \neq \frac{-b - d}{2a}$, there exists two real solutions. 3. If $b^2 - 4ac < 0$, then $\sqrt{b^2 - 4ac}$ represents an imaginary number. The two solutions, $x = \frac{-b \pm \sqrt{b^2 - 4ac}}{2a}$ are both complex and can be written as $-\frac{b}{2a} + \frac{1}{2a}\sqrt{b^2 - 4ac}$ and $-\frac{b}{2a} - \frac{1}{2a}\sqrt{b^2 - 4ac}$. By definition they are complex conjugates of each other. **70.** $h = -36$, $k = 15$ **71.** $\frac{-q(r - p)}{p(q - r)} - 2$ or $\frac{r(p - q)}{2p(q - r)}$

CHAPTER 9   Page 382
TRY THIS

1.

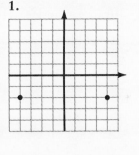

Page 385
TRY THIS
4.

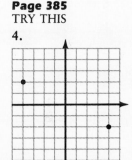

EXERCISE SET 9-1

7. Points $(3, -7)$, $(3, 7)$ **8.** Points $(-5, 2)$, $(-5, -2)$ **9.** Points $(-4, 3)$, $(4, 3)$ **10.** Points $(1, -6)$, $(-1, -6)$ **23.** Points $(2, -4)$, $(-2, 4)$ **24.** Points $(4, 3)$, $(-4, -3)$ **25.** Points $(-3, 6)$, $(3, -6)$ **26.** Points $(-4, -3)$, $(4, 3)$ **59.** Quadrilateral with vertices $(0, -4)$, $(4, -4)$, $(1, 2)$, $(-2, 2)$, and $(0, -4)$ **60.** Quadrilateral with vertices $(0, 4)$,

$(4, -4)$, $(-1, -2)$, $(2, -2)$, and $(0, 4)$ **61.** Quadrilateral with vertices $(0, -4)$, $(-4, -4)$, $(-1, 2)$, $(2, 2)$, and $(0, -4)$

Page 391
EXERCISE SET 9–2
1. Ray from $(0, 2)$ through $(2, 4)$; ray from $(0, 2)$ through $(-2, 4)$ **2.** Ray from $(0, 3)$ through $(2, 5)$; ray from $(0, 3)$ through $(-2, 5)$ **3.** Ray from $(0, -2)$ through $(2, 0)$; ray from $(0, -2)$ through $(-2, 0)$ **4.** Ray from $(0, -3)$ through $(3, 0)$; ray from $(0, -3)$ through $(-3, 0)$ **5.** Ray from $(0, 5)$ through $(2, 7)$; ray from $(0, 5)$ through $(-2, 7)$ **6.** Ray from $(0, 6)$ through $(2, 8)$; ray from $(0, 6)$ through $(-2, 8)$ **7.** Ray from $(0, -4)$ through $(4, 0)$; ray from $(0, -4)$ through $(-4, 0)$ **8.** Ray from $(0, -5)$ through $(5, 0)$; ray from $(0, -5)$ through $(-5, 0)$ **9.** Ray from $\left(0, \frac{1}{2}\right)$ through $\left(3, \frac{7}{2}\right)$; ray from $\left(0, \frac{1}{2}\right)$ through $\left(-3, \frac{7}{2}\right)$.   **10.** Ray from $\left(0, \frac{3}{4}\right)$ through $\left(2, \frac{11}{4}\right)$; ray from $\left(0, \frac{3}{4}\right)$ through $\left(-2, \frac{11}{4}\right)$

Pages 396–397
EXERCISE SET 9–3
1. Ray from $(0, 0)$ through $(2, 8)$; ray from $(0, 0)$ through $(-2, 8)$ **2.** Ray from $(0, 0)$ through $(2, 6)$; ray from $(0, 0)$ through $(-2, 6)$ **3.** Ray from $(0, 0)$ through $(2, 10)$; ray from $(0, 0)$ through $(-2, 10)$ **4.** Ray from $(0, 0)$ through $(2, 12)$; ray from $(0, 0)$ through $(-2, 12)$ **5.** Ray from $(0, 0)$ through $(4, 1)$; ray from $(0, 0)$ through $(-4, 1)$ **6.** Ray from $(0, 0)$ through $(3, 1)$; ray from $(0, 0)$ through $(-3, 1)$ **7.** Ray from $(0, 0)$ through $(2, -6)$; ray from $(0, 0)$ through $(-2, -6)$ **8.** Ray from $(0, 0)$ through $(2, -8)$; ray from $(0, 0)$ through $(-2, -8)$ **9.** Ray from $(0, 0)$ through $(4, -1)$; ray from $(0, 0)$ through $(-4, -1)$ **10.** Graph

consists of segments from $(-4, 0)$ to $(0, 12)$ to $(2, -12)$ to $(3, 0)$ **11.** Graph consists of segments from $(-4, 0)$ to $(0, 8)$ to $(2, -8)$ to $(3, 0)$ **12.** Graph consists of segments from $(-4, 0)$ to $(0, -8)$ to $(2, 8)$ to $(3, 0)$ **13.** Graph consists of segments from $(-4, 0)$ to $(0, -12)$ to $(2, 12)$ to $(3, 0)$ **14.** Graph consists of segments from $(-4, 0)$ to $(0, 16)$ to $(2, -16)$ to $(3, 0)$ **15.** Graph consists of segments from $(-4, 0)$ to $(0, 20)$ to $(2, -20)$ to $(3, 0)$ **16.** Graph consists of segments from $(-4, 0)$ to $(0, 2)$ to $(2, -2)$ to $(3, 0)$ **17.** Graph consists of segments from $(-4, 0)$ to $\left(0, \frac{4}{3}\right)$ to $\left(2, -\frac{4}{3}\right)$ to $(3, 0)$ **18.** Graph consists of segments from $(-4, 0)$ to $(0, -2)$ to $(2, 2)$ to $(3, 0)$ **19.** Ray from $(0, 0)$ through $(4, 8)$; ray from $(0, 0)$ through $(-4, 8)$ **20.** Ray from $(0, 0)$ through $(2, 6)$; ray from $(0, 0)$ through $(-2, 6)$ **21.** Ray from $(0, 0)$ through $(4, 2)$; ray from $(0, 0)$ through $(-4, 2)$ **22.** Graph consists of segments from $\left(-\frac{4}{3}, 0\right)$ to $(0, 4)$ to $\left(\frac{2}{3}, -4\right)$ to $(1, 0)$ **28.** Graph consists of segments from $(-4, 2)$ to $(0, 6)$ to $(2, -2)$ to $(3, 2)$ **29.** Graph consists of segments from $(-4, -1)$ to $(0, 3)$ to $(2, -5)$ to $(3, -1)$ **30.** Graph consists of segments from $(-3, 0)$ to $(1, 4)$ to $(3, -4)$ to $(4, 0)$ **31.** Graph consists of segments from $(-6, 0)$ to $(-2, 4)$ to $(0, -4)$ to $(1, 0)$ **32.** Graph consists of segments from $(-4, 0)$ to $(0, -8)$ to $(2, 8)$ to $(3, 0)$ **33.** Graph consists of segments from $(-4, 0)$ to $\left(0, \frac{4}{3}\right)$ to $\left(2, -\frac{4}{3}\right)$ to $(3, 0)$ **34.** Graph consists of segments from $(-4, 0)$ to $(0, 12)$ to $(2, -12)$ to $(3, 0)$ **35.** Graph consists of segments from $(-4, 0)$ to $(0, -2)$ to $(2, 2)$ to $(3, 0)$ **36.** Graph consists of segments from $(-2, 3)$ to $(2, 7)$ to $(4, -1)$ to $(5, 3)$ **37.** Graph consists of segments from

$(-2, 0)$ to $(2, -12)$ to $(4, 12)$ to $(5, 0)$
38. Graph consists of segments from $(-5, -2)$ to $(-1, 6)$ to $(1, -10)$ to $(2, -2)$ **39.** Graph consists of segments from $(-6, -1)$ to $(-2, 1)$ to $(0, -3)$ to $(1, -1)$

40.

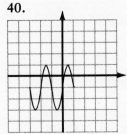

41.

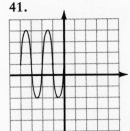

42.

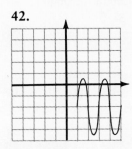

43.

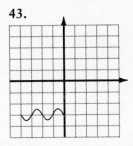

Page 400
EXERCISE SET 9–4
1. Parabola through $(-2, 4)$, $(0, 0)$, $(2, 4)$; $(0, 0)$; $x = 0$ **2.** Parabola through $(-2, -4)$, $(0, 0)$, $(2, -4)$; $(0, 0)$; $x = 0$
3. Parabola through $(-1, -4)$, $(0, 0)$, $(1 -4)$; $(0, 0)$; $x = 0$ **4.** Parabola through $(-1, 2)$, $(0, 0)$, $(1, 2)$; $(0, 0)$; $x = 0$
5. Parabola through $(1, 4)$, $(3, 0)$, $(5, 4)$; $(3, 0)$; $x = 3$ **6.** Parabola through $(5, 4)$, $(7, 0)$, $(9, 4)$; $(7, 0)$; $x = 7$ **7.** Parabola through $(-5, -1)$, $(-4, 0)$, $(-3, -1)$; $(-4, 0)$; $x = -4$ **8.** Parabola through $(1, -1)$, $(2, 0)$, $(3, -1)$; $(2, 0)$; $x = 2$
9. Parabola through $(2, 2)$, $(3, 0)$, $(4, 2)$; $(3, 0)$; $x = 3$ **10.** Parabola through $(6, -4)$, $(7, 0)$, $(8, -4)$; $(7, 0)$; $x = 7$
11. Parabola through $(-10, -2)$, $(-9, 0)$, $(-8. -2)$; $(-9, 0)$; $x = -9$ **12.** Parabola through $(-8, 2)$, $(-7, 0)$, $(-6, 2)$;

$(-7, 0)$; $x = -7$ **13.** Parabola through $(0, 3)$, $(1, 0)$, $(2, 3)$; $(1, 0)$; $x = 1$
14. Parabola through $(1, -4)$, $(2, 0)$, $(3, -4)$; $(2, 0)$; $x = 2$ **15.** Parabola through $\left(0, -\frac{3}{4}\right)$, $\left(\frac{1}{2}, 0\right)$, $\left(1, -\frac{3}{4}\right)$; $\left(\frac{1}{2}, 0\right)$; $.x = 0$
16. Parabola through $\left(-\frac{3}{2}, -2\right)$, $\left(-\frac{1}{2}, 0\right)$, $\left(\frac{1}{2}, -2\right)$; $\left(-\frac{1}{2}, 0\right)$; $x = -\frac{1}{2}$ **17.** Parabola through $\left(-2, \frac{1}{2}\right)$, $(-1, 0)$, $\left(0, \frac{1}{2}\right)$; $(-1, 0)$; $x = -1$ **18.** Parabola through $\left(1, \frac{1}{3}\right)$, $(2, 0)$, $\left(3, \frac{1}{3}\right)$; $(2, 0)$; $x = 2$ **19.** All points below, and including, parabola through $(-2, 4)$, $(0, 0)$, $(2, 4)$ **20.** All points above parabola through $(-2, 4)$, $(0, 0)$, $(2, 4)$ **21.** All points above parabola through $(-1, 2)$, $(0, 0)$, $(1, 2)$ **22.** All points below, and including, parabola through $(-1, 2)$, $(0, 0)$, $(1, 2)$ **23.** All points below parabola through $(-2, -4)$, $(0, 0)$, $(2, -4)$ **24.** All points above, and including, parabola through $(-2, -4)$, $(0, 0)$, $(2, -4)$ **25.** All points below parabola through $(-3, -3)$, $(0, 0)$, $(3, -3)$ **26.** All points above parabola through $(-2, -2)$, $(0, 0)$, $(2, -2)$
27. All points below, and including, parabola through $(-5, 3)$, $(4, 0)$, $(-3, 3)$

Page 401
TRY THIS
1.a. Parabola through $(1, 7)$, $(2, 4)$, $(3, 7)$ **b.** $(2, 4)$ **c.** $x = 2$ **d.** Yes, 4 **e.** No **2.a.** Parabola through $(-3, 4)$, $(-2, -1)$, $(-1, -4)$ **b.** $(-2, -1)$ **c.** $x = -2$ **d.** No **e.** Yes, 1

Pages 402–403
EXERCISE SET 9–5
1. Parabola through $(1, 5)$, $(3, 1)$, $(5, 5)$; $(3, 1)$; $x = 3$; min. $= 1$ **2.** Parabola through $(-4, 1)$, $(-2, -3)$, $(0, 1)$; $(-2, -3)$; $x = -2$; min. $= -3$
3. Parabola through $(-3, 2)$, $(-1, -2)$, $(1, 2)$; $(-1, -2)$; $x = -1$; min. $= -2$
4. Parabola through $(-1, 6)$, $(1, 2)$,

$(3, 6)$; $(1, 2)$; $x = 1$; min. = 2   5. Parabola
through $(0, -1)$, $(1, -3)$, $(2, -1)$;
$(1, -3)$; $x = 1$; min. = -3 6. Parabola
through $(-2, 6)$, $(-1, 4)$, $(0, 6)$;
$(-1, 4)$; $x = -1$; min. = 4   7. Parabola
through $(-5, -2)$, $(-4, 1)$, $(-3, -2)$;
$(-4, 1)$; $x = -4$; max. = 1; 8. Parabola
through $(4, -5)$, $(5, -3)$, $(6, -5)$;
$(5, -3)$; $x = 5$; max. = -3 9. $(9, 5)$;
$x = 9$; min. = 5   10. $(-5, -8)$; $x = -5$;
min. = -8 11. $\left(-\frac{1}{4}, -13\right)$; $x = -\frac{1}{4}$; min.
= -13 12. $\left(\frac{1}{4}, 19\right)$; $x = \frac{1}{4}$; min. = 19
13. $(10, -20)$; $x = 10$; max. = -20
14. $(-12, 23)$; $x = -12$; max. = 23
15. $(-4.58, 65\pi)$; $x = -4.58$; min. = 65π
16. $(38.2, -\sqrt{34})$; $x = 38.2$; min.
= $-\sqrt{34}$ 17. $f(x) = -2x^2 + 4$ 18. $f(x)$
= $2(x - 2)^2$ 19. $f(x) = 2(x - 6)^2$ 20. $f(x)$
= $-2x^2 + 3$ 21. $f(x) = -2(x - 3)^2 + 8$
22. $f(x) = 2(x + 2)^2 + 3$ 23. $f(x)$
= $2(x + 3)^2$ 24. $f(x) = -2(x + 4)^2 - 3$
25. $f(x) = 2(x - 2)^2 - 3$

Page 406
EXERCISE SET 9–6
6. $f(x) = \left(x + \frac{5}{2}\right)^2 - \frac{9}{4}$; $\left(-\frac{5}{2}, -\frac{9}{4}\right)$
$x = -\frac{5}{2}$, min. = $-\frac{9}{4}$ 7. $f(x) = \left(x - \frac{9}{2}\right)^2$
$-\frac{81}{4}$; $\left(\frac{9}{2}, -\frac{81}{4}\right)$, $x = \frac{9}{2}$, min. = $-\frac{81}{4}$ 8. $f(x)$
= $\left(x + \frac{1}{2}\right)^2 - \frac{1}{4}$, $\left(-\frac{1}{2}, -\frac{1}{4}\right)$, $x = -\frac{1}{2}$, min. =
$-\frac{1}{4}$ 9. $f(x) = 3(x - 4)^2 + 2$; $(4, 2)$, $x = 4$,
min. = 2   10. $f(x) = 4(x + 1)^2 - 7$;
$(-1, -7)$, $x = -1$, min. = -7 11. $f(x)$
= $\frac{3}{4}(x + 6)^2 - 27$; $(-6, -27)$, $x = -6$,
min. = -27 12. $f(x) = -2\left(x - \frac{1}{2}\right)^2 + \frac{3}{2}$;
$\left(\frac{1}{2}, \frac{3}{2}\right)$, $x = \frac{1}{2}$, max. = $\frac{3}{2}$

23.

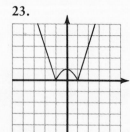

24.

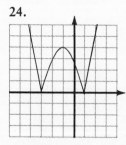

20.

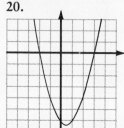

21.

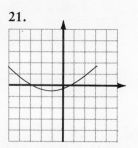

22. All points below parabola through
$(1, -4)$, $(2, -5)$, $(3, -4)$ 23. All points
above, and including, parabola through
$(-4, 0)$, $\left(-\frac{3}{2}, -\frac{25}{4}\right)$, $(1, 0)$ 24. All points
below, and including, parabola through
$(-2, 0)$, $\left(-\frac{5}{2}, -\frac{1}{4}\right)$, $(-3, 0)$

Pages 417–418
CHAPTER 9 REVIEW
30. Graph consists of segments from
$(-4, 2)$ to $(-3, 1)$ to $(-2, 1)$ to $(0, -2)$
to $(2, 1)$ to $(3, 1)$ to $(4, 2)$ 31. Graph
consists of segments from $(-3, 0)$ to
$(-2, -1)$ to $(-1, -1)$ to $(1, -4)$ to
$(3, -1)$ to $(4, -1)$ to $(5, 0)$ 32. Parabola
through $(-2, 8)$, $(0, 0)$, $(2, -8)$; $(0, 0)$;
$x = 0$ 33. Parabola through $(-2, 1)$,
$(0, 0)$, $(2, 1)$; $(0, 0)$; $x = 0$ 34. Parabola
through $(-3, 8)$, $(-1, 0)$, $(1, -8)$;
$(-1, 0)$; $x = -1$ 35. Parabola through
$(1, 3)$, $(2, 0)$, $(3, 3)$; $(2, 0)$; $x = 2$
36. Parabola through $(-2, 1)$, $(-1, 3)$,
$(0, 1)$; $(-1, 3)$; $x = -1$; max. = 3
37. Parabola through $\left(0, 5\frac{1}{2}\right)$, $(1, 5)$,
$\left(2, 5\frac{1}{2}\right)$; $(1, 5)$; $x = 1$; min. = 5
38. Parabola through $(-3, -2)$, $(-2, 1)$,
$(-1, -2)$; $(-2, 1)$; $x = -2$; max. = 1
39. $f(x) = (x - 4)^2 - 11$; $(4, -11)$; $x = 4$;
min. = -11 40. $f(x) = -\frac{1}{2}(x - 6)^2 + 2$;
$(6, 2)$; $x = 6$; $x = 6$; max. = 2   41. $f(x)$
= $-2(x + 1)^2 + 5$; $(-1, 5)$; $x = -1$;
max. = 5   44. $\left(\frac{-2 + \sqrt{10}}{2}, 0\right)$, $\left(\frac{-2 - \sqrt{10}}{2}, 0\right)$
45. $(1 + \sqrt{5}, 0)$, $(1 - \sqrt{5}, 0)$ 46. $(3, 0)$,
$(1, 0)$ 47. $f(x) = -2x^2 - 4x + 3$ 48. $f(x)$
= $3x^2 - 6x + 5$ 49. $f(x) = -x^2 + 8x - 8$

CHAPTER 9 TEST

3. y-axis   6. x-axis   7. Neither
13. Parabola through $(-2, 8)$, $(0, 0)$, $(2, 8)$; $(0, 0)$; $x = 0$ 14. Parabola through $(4, 2)$, $(5, 0)$, $(6, 2)$; $(5, 0)$; $x = 5$

CHAPTER 10   Page 423
EXERCISE SET 10–1

27. If two points are on a vertical line, they have coordinates (a, y_1) and (a, y_2). Thus, the distance from one to the other is $|y_2 - y_1|$. Now
$$\sqrt{(a-a)^2 + (y_2 - y_1)^2}$$
$$= \sqrt{0 + (y_2 - y_1)^2} = \sqrt{(y_2 - y_1)^2}$$
$= |y_2 - y_1|$. The proof for a horizontal line is similar.

28. Let $P_1(x_1, y_1)$ and $P_2(x_2, y_2)$ be the endpoints of a segment and M be the point $\left(\frac{x_1 + x_2}{2}, \frac{y_1 + y_2}{2}\right)$. If the $d(P_1M)$
$= d(MP_2) = \frac{1}{2}d(P_1P_2)$, then M is the midpoint of $\overline{P_1P_2}$. $d(P_1M)$
$$= \sqrt{\left(\frac{x_1 + x_2}{2} - x_1\right)^2 + \left(\frac{y_1 + y_2}{2} - y_1\right)^2}$$
$= \frac{1}{2}\sqrt{(x_2 - x_1)^2 + (y_2 - y_1)^2}$. $d(MP_2)$
$$= \sqrt{\left(x_2 - \frac{x_1 + x_2}{2}\right)^2 + \left(y_2 - \frac{y_1 + y_2}{2}\right)^2}$$
$= \frac{1}{2}\sqrt{(x_2 - x_1)^2 + (y_2 - y_1)^2}$. $d(P_1P_2)$
$= \sqrt{(x_2 - x_1)^2 + (y_2 - y_1)^2}$.
$\therefore M$ is the midpoint of $\overline{P_1P_2}$.

29. The midpoint of $\overline{DB}$ has coordinates $\left(\frac{a}{2}, \frac{b}{2}\right)$ which is the same as the midpoint of $\overline{AC}$.

32. The vertices are $O(0, 0)$, $H(0, h)$, and $B(b, 0)$. Then $P = \left(\frac{b}{2}, \frac{h}{2}\right)$. Use the distance formula to find the distances between P and H, P and B, and P and O.

33. The vertices are $O(0, 0)$, $A(a, b)$, $B(c, d)$, and $C(k, 0)$. The midpoints are $M_1\left(\frac{a}{2}, \frac{b}{2}\right)$, $M_2\left(\frac{a+c}{2}, \frac{b+d}{2}\right)$, M_3 $\left(\frac{c+k}{2}, \frac{d}{2}\right)$, and $M_4\left(\frac{k}{2}, 0\right)$. Find the slopes of $\overline{M_1M_2}$, $\overline{M_2M_3}$, $\overline{M_3M_4}$, $\overline{M_4M_1}$, and compare. Also, find the lengths of the segments and compare. The opposite sides of a parallelogram are parallel and have equal lengths.

Page 427
TRY THIS
4.

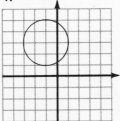

Page 428
EXERCISE SET 10–2
24.a. Center: $(0, 0)$ with radius of 2
c. Semicircle from $(-2, 0)$ through $(0, 2)$ to $(2, 0)$ d. Semicircle from $(-2, 0)$ through $(0, -2)$ to $(2, 0)$ 25. Yes
26. Yes   27. No   28. No   29. $a_1 = 20 - 10\sqrt{3}$ ft, $a_2 = 20 + 10\sqrt{3}$ ft   30. From the equation of a circle we have $b^2 + c^2 = a^2$; $c^2 = a^2 - b^2$; the slope of $\overline{AB}$ is $\frac{c}{b+a}$ and the slope of $\overline{BC}$ is $\frac{c}{b-a}$; since $\frac{c}{b+a} \cdot \frac{c}{b-a} = \frac{c^2}{b^2 - a^2} = \frac{a^2 - b^2}{b^2 - a^2} = -1$, $\overline{AB}$ and $\overline{BC}$ are perpendicular and angle ABC is a right angle.

Pages 430–432

1.

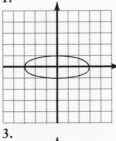

2.

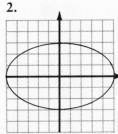

3.

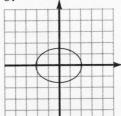

4.

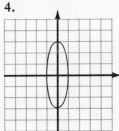

5.

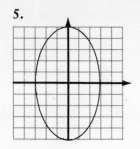

6.

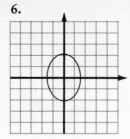

7.

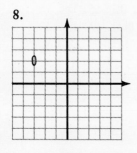

8.

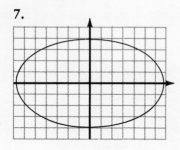

9.

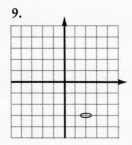

Pages 433–435
EXERCISE SET 10–3

1. Vertices: $(-2, 0)$, $(2, 0)$, $(0, -1)$, $(0, 1)$; Foci: $(-\sqrt{3}, 0)$, $(\sqrt{3}, 0)$ **2.** Vertices: $(-1, 0)$, $(1, 0)$, $(0, -2)$, $(0, 2)$; Foci: $(0, -\sqrt{3})$, $(0, \sqrt{3})$ **3.** Vertices: $(-3, 0)$, $(3, 0)$, $(0, -4)$, $(0, 4)$; Foci: $(0, -\sqrt{7})$, $(0, \sqrt{7})$ **4.** Vertices: $(-4, 0)$, $(4, 0)$, $(0, -3)$, $(0, 3)$; Foci: $(-\sqrt{7}, 0)$, $(\sqrt{7}, 0)$ **5.** Vertices: $(-\sqrt{3}, 0)$, $(\sqrt{3}, 0)$, $(0, -\sqrt{2})$, $(0, \sqrt{2})$; Foci: $(-1, 0)$, $(1, 0)$ **6.** Vertices: $(-\sqrt{7}, 0)$, $(\sqrt{7}, 0)$, $(0, -\sqrt{5})$, $(0, \sqrt{5})$; Foci: $(-\sqrt{2}, 0)$, $(\sqrt{2}, 0)$ **7.** Vertices: $\left(-\frac{1}{2}, 0\right)$, $\left(\frac{1}{2}, 0\right)$, $\left(0, -\frac{1}{3}\right)$, $\left(0, \frac{1}{3}\right)$; Foci: $\left(-\frac{\sqrt{5}}{6}, 0\right)$, $\left(\frac{\sqrt{5}}{6}, 0\right)$ **8.** Vertices: $\left(-\frac{1}{5}, 0\right)$, $\left(\frac{1}{5}, 0\right)$, $\left(0, -\frac{1}{4}\right)$, $\left(0, \frac{1}{4}\right)$; Foci: $\left(0, -\frac{3}{20}\right)$,

$\left(0, \frac{3}{20}\right)$ **9.** Center: $(1, 2)$; Vertices: $(-1, 2)$, $(3, 2)$, $(1, 1)$, $(1, 3)$; Foci: $(1 - \sqrt{3}, 2)$, $(1 + \sqrt{3}, 2)$ **10.** Center: $(1, 2)$; Vertices: $(0, 2)$, $(2, 2)$, $(1, 0)$, $(1, 4)$; Foci: $(1, 2 - \sqrt{3})$, $(1, 2 + \sqrt{3})$ **11.** Center: $(-3, 2)$; Vertices: $(-8, 2)$, $(2, 2)$, $(-3, -2)$, $(-3, 6)$; Foci: $(-6, 2)$, $(0, 2)$ **12.** Center: $(2, -3)$; Vertices: $(-3, -3)$, $(7, -3)$, $(2, -7)$, $(2, 1)$; Foci: $(-1, -3)$, $(5, -3)$ **13.** Center: $(-2, 1)$; Vertices: $(-10, 1)$, $(6, 1)$, $(-2, 1 - 4\sqrt{3})$, $(-2, 1 + 4\sqrt{3})$; Foci: $(-6, 1)$, $(2, 1)$ **14.** Center: $(5, 5)$; Vertices: $(5 - 4\sqrt{3}, 5)$, $(5 + 4\sqrt{3}, 5)$, $(5, 13)$, $(5, -3)$; Foci: $(5, 9)$, $(5, 1)$ **15.** Center: $(2, -1)$; Vertices: $(-1, -1)$, $(5, -1)$, $(2, -3)$, $(2, 1)$; Foci: $(2 - \sqrt{5}, -1)$, $(2 + \sqrt{5}, -1)$ **16.** Center: $(5, -2)$; Vertices: $(3, -2)$, $(7, -2)$, $(5, -2 - \sqrt{2})$, $(5, -2 + \sqrt{2})$; Foci: $(5 - \sqrt{2}, -2)$, $(5 + \sqrt{2}, -2)$ **17.** Center: $(1, 1)$; Vertices: $(0, 1)$, $(2, 1)$, $(1, -1)$, $(1, 3)$; Foci: $(1, 1 - \sqrt{3})$, $(1, 1 + \sqrt{3})$ **18.** Center: $(-3, 1)$; Vertices: $(-5, 1)$, $(-1, 1)$, $(-3, -2)$, $(-3, 4)$; Foci: $(-3, 1 - \sqrt{5})$, $(-3, 1 + \sqrt{5})$ **19.** Center: $(2.003125, -1.00513)$; Vertices: $(5.0234302, -1.00515)$, $(-1.0171802, -1.00515)$, $(2.003125, -3.0186868)$, $(2.003125, 1.0083868)$ **20.** Center: $(-3.0035, 1.002)$; Vertices: $(-3.0035, -1.97008)$, $(-3.0035, 3.97408)$, $(-1.02211, 1.002)$, $(-4.98489, 1.002)$ **21.** $\frac{x^2}{4} + \frac{y^2}{9} = 1$ **22.** $x^2 + \frac{y^2}{16} = 1$ **23.** $\frac{(x-3)^2}{4} + \frac{(y-1)^2}{25} = 1$ **24.** $\frac{(x+1)^2}{4} + \frac{(y-2)^2}{9} = 1$ **27a.** Center: $(0, 0)$; Vertices: $(1, 0)$, $(-1, 0)$, $(0, 3)$, $(0, -3)$; Foci: $(0, 2\sqrt{2})$, $(0, -2\sqrt{2})$ **c.** Semi-ellipse from $(-1, 0)$ through $(0, 3)$ to $(1, 0)$ **d.** Semi-ellipse from $(-1, 0)$ through $(0, -3)$ to $(1, 0)$ **31.** $F_1P + F_2P = 2a$; By the distance formula $\sqrt{(x+c)^2 + y^2} + \sqrt{(x-c)^2 + y^2} = 2a$; $\sqrt{(x+c)^2 + y^2} = 2a - \sqrt{(x-c)^2 + y^2}$; $x^2 + 2cx + c^2 + y^2 = 4a^2 - 4a\sqrt{(x-c)^2 + y^2}$

$+ x^2 - 2cx + c^2 + y^2; -4a^2 + 4cx$
$= -4a\sqrt{(x-c)^2 + y^2}; -a^2 + cx$
$= -a\sqrt{(x-c)^2 + y^2}; a^4 - 2a^2cx + c^2x^2$
$= a^2x^2 - 2a^2cx + a^2c^2 + a^2y^2; x^2(a^2 - c^2)$
$+ a^2y^2 = a^2(a^2 - c^2)$; It follows from when
P is at $(0, b)$ that $b^2 = a^2 - c^2$. Substituting
b^2 for $a^2 - c^2$ in the last equation, we have
the equation of the ellipse $b^2x^2 + a^2y^2$
$= a^2b^2$, or $\frac{x^2}{a^2} + \frac{y^2}{b^2} = 1$.

33.

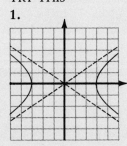

AB is a fixed distance, say 1. BC is fixed
but arbitrary, say 4, so that AC is 5. With
the B track as x-axis and the A track as
y-axis, four points on the path of C are
$(5, 0), (0, -4), (-5, 0)$, and $(0, 4)$. If the
path is an ellipse, then its equation would
be $\frac{x^2}{25} + \frac{y^2}{16} = 1$. Any other point we find for
a C position satisfies this equation.

Let A and B be in an arbitrary position
as shown. Then, by similar triangles, we
find the coordinates of C. We show that the
coordinates of C satisfy the equation.
$\frac{(\sqrt{1-p^2} + 4\sqrt{1-p^2})^2}{25} + \frac{(4p)^2}{16} = 1$;
$\frac{(1-p^2)(25)}{25} + \frac{16p^2}{16} = 1; 1 - p^2 + p^2 = 1$;
$1 = 1$

Pages 438–441
TRY THIS

1.

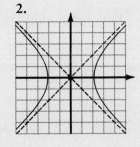

2.

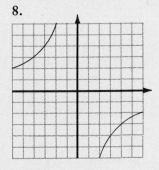

3.

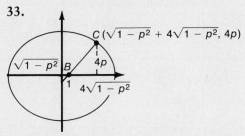

4.

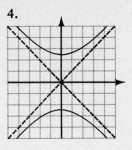

5.

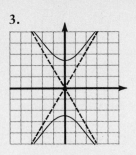

6.

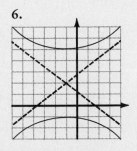

7.

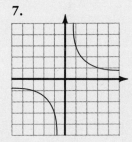

8.

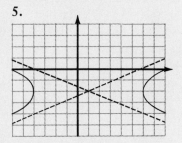

Pages 441–442
EXERCISE SET 10–4
1. Center: $(0, 0)$; Foci: $(-\sqrt{10}, 0)$,
$(\sqrt{10}, 0)$; Vertices: $(-3, 0), (3, 0)$; Asym:
$y = -\frac{1}{3}x, y = \frac{1}{3}x$ **2.** Center: $(0, 0)$;
Foci: $(-\sqrt{10}, 0), (\sqrt{10}, 0)$; Vertices:

$(-1, 0), (1, 0)$; Asym: $y = -3x$, $y = 3x$
3. Center: $(2, -5)$; Foci: $(2 - \sqrt{10}, -5)$, $(2 + \sqrt{10}, -5)$; Vertices: $(-1, -5)$, $(5, -5)$; Asym: $y + 5 = -\frac{1}{3}(x - 2)$, $y + 5 = \frac{1}{3}(x - 2)$ **4.** Center: $(2 - 5)$; Foci: $(2 - \sqrt{10}, -5)$, $(2 + \sqrt{10}, -5)$; Vertices: $(1, -5)$, $(3, -5)$; Asym: $y + 5 = 3(x - 2)$, $y + 5 = -3(x - 2)$ **5.** Center: $(-1, -3)$; Foci: $(-1, -3 - 2\sqrt{5})$, $(-1, -3 + 2\sqrt{5})$; Vertices: $(-1, -5)$, $(-1, -1)$; Asym: $y + 3 = -\frac{1}{2}(x + 1)$, $y + 3 = \frac{1}{2}(x + 1)$
6. Center: $(-1, -3)$; Foci: $(-1, -3 - \sqrt{41})$, $(-1, -3 + \sqrt{41})$; Vertices: $(-1, -8)$, $(-1, 2)$; Asym: $y + 3 = -\frac{5}{4}(x + 1)$, $y + 3 = \frac{5}{4}(x + 1)$ **7.** Center: $(0, 0)$; Foci: $(-\sqrt{5}, 0)$, $\sqrt{5}, 0)$; Vertices: $(-2, 0)$, $(2, 0)$; Asym: $y = -\frac{1}{2}x$, $y = \frac{1}{2}x$
8. Center: $(0, 0)$; Foci: $(-\sqrt{5}, 0)$, $(\sqrt{5}, 0)$; Vertices: $(-1, 0)$, $(1, 0)$; Asym: $y = -2x$, $y = 2x$ **9.** Center: $(0, 0)$; Foci: $(0, -\sqrt{5})$, $(0, \sqrt{5})$; Vertices: $(0, -1)$, $(0, 1)$; Asym. $y = -\frac{1}{2}x$, $y = \frac{1}{2}x$ **10.** Center: $(0, 0)$; Foci: $(0, -\sqrt{5})$, $(0, \sqrt{5})$; Vertices: $(0, -2)$, $(0, 2)$; Asym: $y = -2x$, $y = 2x$ **11.** Center: $(0, 0)$; Foci: $(-2, 0)$, $(2, 0)$; Vertices: $(-\sqrt{2}, 0)$, $(\sqrt{2}, 0)$; Asym: $y = -x$, $y = x$
12. Center: $(0, 0)$; Foci: $(-\sqrt{6}, 0)$, $(\sqrt{6}, 0)$; Vertices: $(-\sqrt{3}, 0)$, $(\sqrt{3}, 0)$; Asym: $y = -x$, $y = x$ **13.** Center: $(1, -2)$; Foci: $(1 - \sqrt{2}, -2)$, $(1 + \sqrt{2}, -2)$; Vertices: $(0, -2)$, $(2, -2)$; Asym: $y + 2 = -(x - 1)$, $y + 2 = (x - 1)$ **14.** Center: $(-1, -2)$; Foci: $(-1 - \sqrt{5}, -2)$, $(-1 + \sqrt{5}, -2)$; Vertices: $(-2, -2)$, $(0, -2)$; Asym: $y + 2 = -2(x + 1)$, $y + 2 = 2(x + 1)$ **15.** Center: $\left(\frac{1}{3}, 3\right)$; Foci: $\left(\frac{1}{3} - \sqrt{37}, 3\right)$, $\left(\frac{1}{3} + \sqrt{37}, 3\right)$; Vertices: $\left(-\frac{2}{3}, 3\right)$, $\left(\frac{4}{3}, 3\right)$; Asym: $y - 3 = -6\left(x - \frac{1}{3}\right)$, $y - 3 = 6\left(x - \frac{1}{3}\right)$ **16.** Center: $(-3, 1)$; Foci: $(-3 + \sqrt{13}, 1)$, $(-3 - \sqrt{13}, 1)$; Vertices: $(-5, 1)$, $(-1, 1)$; Asym: $y - 1 = -\frac{3}{2}(x + 3)$, $y - 1 = \frac{3}{2}(x + 3)$

17.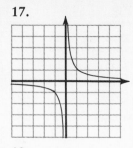

18.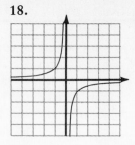

19.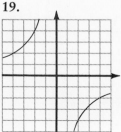

20.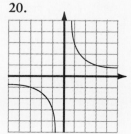

21. Center: $(1.023, -2.044)$; Vertices: $(2.07, -2.044)$, $(-0.024, -2.044)$; Asym: $y + 2.044 = -(x - 1.023)$, $y + 2.044 = x - 1.023$ **24.** $PF_1 - PF_2 = 2a$; By the distance formula: $\sqrt{(x + c)^2 + y^2} - \sqrt{(x - c)^2 + y^2} = 2a$; $\sqrt{(x + c)^2 + y^2} = 2a + \sqrt{(x - c)^2 + y^2}$; $x^2 + 2xc + c^2 + y^2 = 4a^2 + 4a\sqrt{(x - c)^2 + y^2} + x^2 - 2xc + c^2 + y^2$; $4cx - 4a^2 = 4a\sqrt{(x - c)^2 + y^2}$; $cx - a^2 = a\sqrt{(x - c)^2 + y^2}$; $c^2x^2 - 2a^2cx + a^4 = a^2x^2 - 2cxa^2 + a^2c^2 + a^2y^2$; $x^2(c^2 - a^2) - a^2y^2 = a^2(c^2 - a^2)$; In the triangle F_1PF_2, $PF_1 - PF_2 < F_1F_2$, or $2a < 2c$, so $a < c$, and $c^2 > a^2$, so $c^2 - a^2 > 0$. We represent $c^2 - a^2$ by b^2: $x^2b^2 - a^2y^2 = a^2b^2$, or $\frac{x^2}{a^2} - \frac{y^2}{b^2} = 1$.

Pages 444–447
TRY THIS
1.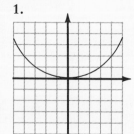

2.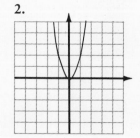

3.

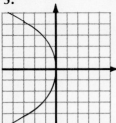

8.

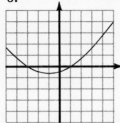

9.

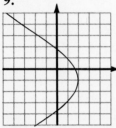

27.

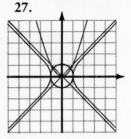

28.

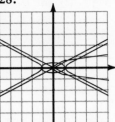

30a.

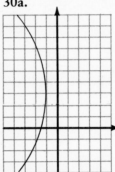

32.

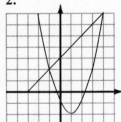

$$F_1 y = W \cdot \frac{x}{2} = kx \cdot \frac{x}{2};$$
$$y = \frac{k}{2F_1} x^2$$

Page 448
EXERCISE SET 10–5

15. Vertex: $(-2, 1)$; Focus: $\left(-2, -\frac{1}{2}\right)$; Directrix: $y = \frac{5}{2}$ **16.** Vertex: $(-2, 3)$; Focus: $(-7, 3)$; Directrix: $x = 3$
17. Vertex: $(-1, -3)$; Focus: $\left(-1, -\frac{7}{2}\right)$; Directrix: $y = -\frac{5}{2}$ **18.** Vertex: $(7, -3)$; Focus: $\left(\frac{29}{4}, -3\right)$; Directrix: $x = \frac{27}{4}$
19. Vertex: $(0, -2)$; Focus: $\left(0, -\frac{7}{4}\right)$; Directrix: $y = -\frac{9}{4}$ **20.** Vertex: $(2, -2)$; Focus: $\left(2, -\frac{3}{2}\right)$; Directrix: $y = -\frac{5}{2}$
21. Vertex: $(-2, -1)$; Focus: $\left(-2, -\frac{3}{4}\right)$; Directrix: $y = -\frac{5}{4}$ **22.** Vertex: $(-3, 1)$; Focus: $\left(-3, \frac{5}{4}\right)$; Directrix: $y = \frac{3}{4}$ **23.** Vertex: $\left(\frac{23}{4}, \frac{1}{2}\right)$; Focus: $\left(6, \frac{1}{2}\right)$; Directrix: $x = \frac{11}{2}$
24. Vertex: $\left(-\frac{17}{4}, -\frac{1}{2}\right)$; Focus: $\left(-4, -\frac{1}{2}\right)$; Directrix: $x = -\frac{9}{2}$ **25.** Vertex: $(0, 0)$; Focus: $(0, 2014.0625)$; Directrix: $y = -2014.0625$ **26.** Vertex: $(0, 0)$; Focus: $(-1911.47, 0)$; Directrix: $x = 1911.47$

Page 449
TRY THIS

1.

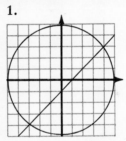

2.

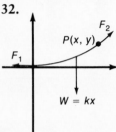

3.

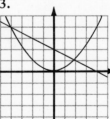

Pages 452–453
EXERCISE SET 10–6

1. $(-4, -3), (3, 4)$ **2.** $(-8, -6), (6, 8)$
3. $(4, 5), (0, -3)$ **4.** $(-7, 1), (1, -7)$

5. $(0, 2), (3, 0)$ 6. $(0, 3), (2, 0)$
7. $(-2, 1)$ 8. $(1, 1), (2, 4)$ 9. $(3, 2)$,
$(4, \frac{3}{2})$ 10. $(3, 5), (-\frac{5}{3}, -\frac{13}{3})$ 11. $(\frac{7}{3}, \frac{1}{3})$,
$(1, -1)$ 12. $(1, -2), (\frac{11}{4}, -\frac{9}{8})$
13. $(1, 4), (\frac{11}{4}, -\frac{5}{4})$ 14. $(-3, \frac{5}{2}), (3, 1)$
25. $WL = A$; $2(L + W) = P$; $L + W = \frac{P}{2}$;
$L = \frac{P}{2} - W$; $W(\frac{P}{2} - W) = A$; $W^2 - \frac{WP}{2} + A$

$= 0$; $W = \dfrac{\frac{P}{2} \pm \sqrt{(\frac{P}{2})^2 - 4A}}{2} = \frac{P}{4} \pm \frac{\sqrt{P^2 - 16A}}{4}$

$= \frac{1}{4}(P \pm \sqrt{P^2 - 16A})$

26. There is no number x such that $\frac{x^2}{a^2}$
$- \frac{(\frac{b}{a}x)^2}{b^2} = 1$, because the left side simplifies
to $\frac{x^2}{a^2} - \frac{x^2}{a^2}$ which is 0.

Page 454
TRY THIS

1.
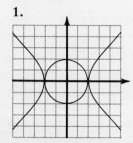

2.
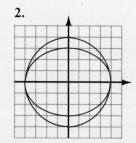

Pages 460–461
CHAPTER 10 REVIEW
14. Center $(2, -1)$; vertices $(-3, -1)$,
$(7, -1), (2, 3), (2, -5)$; foci $(-1, -1)$,
$(5, -1)$ 15. Center $(-2, 1)$; vertices
$(-6, 1), (2, 1), (-2, 4), (-2, -2)$; foci
$(-2 - \sqrt{7}, 1), (-2 + \sqrt{7}, 1)$ 16. Center
$(-2, \frac{1}{4})$; vertices $(0, \frac{1}{4}), (-4, \frac{1}{4})$; foci
$(-2 + \sqrt{6}, \frac{1}{4}), (-2 - \sqrt{6}, \frac{1}{4})$; asymptotes
$y - \frac{1}{4} = \frac{\sqrt{2}}{2}(x + 2)$, $y - \frac{1}{4} = -\frac{\sqrt{2}}{2}(x + 2)$
17. Center $(0, 0)$; vertices $(\sqrt{6}, 0)$,
$(-\sqrt{6}, 0)$; foci $(\sqrt{22}, 0), (-\sqrt{22}, 0)$;
asymptotes $y = \frac{\sqrt{6}}{3}x$, $y = -\frac{\sqrt{6}}{3}x$ 18. Vertex
$(0, 0)$; focus $(-3, 0)$; directrix $x = 3$
19. Vertex $(1, -1)$; focus $(1, \frac{3}{2})$; directrix
$y = \frac{1}{2}$ 20. Vertex $(3, -2)$; focus $(2, 3)$;
directrix $x = 4$

CHAPTER 11 Page 473
EXERCISE SET 11–2
1. $Q(x) = 2x^3 + x^2 - 3x + 10$, $R(x) = -42$
2. $Q(x) = x^2 - 5x + 3$, $R(x) = 9$ 3. $Q(x)$
$= x^2 - 4x + 8$, $R(x) = -24$ 4. $Q(x) = x^2$
$+ 2x + 1$, $R(x) = 12$ 5. $Q(x) = x^3 + x^2$
$+ x + 1$, $R(x) = 0$ 6. $Q(x) = x^4 - 2x^3$
$+ 4x^2 - 8x + 16$, $R(x) = 0$ 7. $Q(x)$
$= 2x^3 + x^2 + \frac{7}{2}x + \frac{7}{4}$, $R(x) = -\frac{1}{8}$ 8. $Q(x)$
$= 3x^3 + \frac{3}{4}x^2 - \frac{29}{16}x - \frac{29}{64}$, $R(x) = \frac{483}{256}$
9. $Q(x) = x^3 + x^2y + xy^2 + y^3$, $R(x) = 0$
10. $Q(x) = x^2 + 2ix + (2 - 4i)$, $R(x) = -6$
$- 2i$ 11. $P(1) = 0$; $P(-2) = -60$; $P(3)$
$= 0$ 12. $P(-3) = 69$; $P(-2) = 41$; $P(1)$
$= -7$ 13. $P(20) = 5,935,988$; $P(-3)$
$= -772$ 14. $P(-10) = -220,050$;
$P(5) = -750$ 35. $-5 < x < 1$ or
$x > 2$ 36. $-5 < x < 1$ or $2 < x < 3$

Pages 478–480
EXERCISE SET 11–3
1. -3(multiplicity 2); 1(multiplicity 1)
2. -2(multiplicity 1); π(multiplicity 5)
3. 3(multiplicity 2); -4(multiplicity 3);
0(multiplicity 4) 4. 0(multiplicity 3);
1(multiplicity 2); -4(multiplicity 1)
5. 2(multiplicity 2); 3(multiplicity 2)
6. 2(multiplicity 2); -1(multiplicity 2)
51. Let $P(x) = a_n x^n + a_{n-1} x^{n-1} + \ldots + a_1 x$
$+ a_0$, where the coefficients are real numbers. Suppose z is a complex root of $P(x)$.
Then $P(z) = 0$, or $a_n z^n + a_{n-1} z^{n-1}$
$+ \ldots + a_1 z + a_0 = 0$. Now let us find the
conjugate of each side of the equation. First
note that $\overline{0} = 0$, since 0 is a real number.
Then we have the following.
$$\begin{aligned}
0 = \overline{0} &= \overline{a_n z^n + a_{n-1} z^{n-1} + \ldots + a_1 z + a_0} \\
&= \overline{a_n z^n} + \overline{a_{n-1} z^{n-1}} + \ldots + \overline{a_1 z} + \overline{a_0} \\
&= \overline{a_n} \cdot \overline{z^n} + \overline{a_{n-1}} \cdot \overline{z^{n-1}} + \ldots + \overline{a_1} \cdot \overline{z} + \overline{a_0} \\
&= a_n \overline{z^n} + a_{n-1} \overline{z^{n-1}} + \ldots + a_1 \overline{z} + a_0 \\
&= a_n \overline{z}^n + a_{n-1} \overline{z}^{n-1} + \ldots + a_1 \overline{z} + a_0
\end{aligned}$$
52. Similar to the proof of Theorem 11–4

Page 480
TWO VARIABLE POLYNOMIALS

Identifying Conic Sections

5. Ellipse with center $(-3, 1)$ and vertices $(-5, 1), (-3, 5), (-1, 1), (-3, -3)$
6. Parabola with vertex $(7, -3)$; focus $(7\frac{1}{4}, -3)$; and directrix $x = 6\frac{3}{4}$; through points $(16, 0)$ and $(16, -6)$ **7.** Hyperbola with center $(-3, 1)$; foci $(-3 + \frac{2\sqrt{26}}{3}, 1)$ and $(-3 - \frac{2\sqrt{26}}{3}, 1)$; vertices $(-3 + \frac{4\sqrt{2}}{3}, 1)$ and $(-3 - \frac{4\sqrt{2}}{3}, 1)$; asymptotes $y - 1 = \frac{3}{2}(x + 3)$ and $y - 1 = -\frac{3}{2}(x + 3)$ **8.** Parabola with vertex $(-3, 1)$; focus $(-3, 1\frac{1}{4})$; and directrix $y = \frac{3}{4}$; through points $(0, 10)$ and $(-6, 10)$

Page 490
EXERCISE SET 11-5

31. Given a, b and c positive, let $P(x) = x^4 + ax^2 + bx - c$. There is one variation in sign, so just one positive root. $P(-x) = x^4 + ax^2 - bx - c$, hence $P(-x)$ has one variation of sign so there is just one negative root. 0 is not a root. Since the equation is of degree 4 it has 4 roots and therefore just 2 nonreal roots.

Pages 493-494
TRY THIS

1.

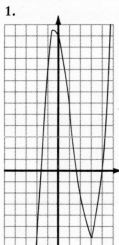

2a.

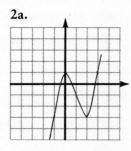

Pages 494-495
EXERCISE SET 11-6

1.

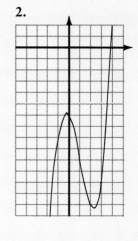

2.

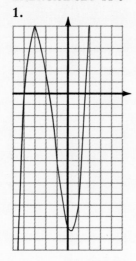

3.

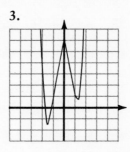

4.

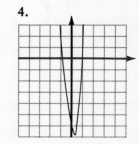

5.

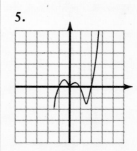

6.

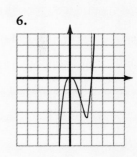

7.

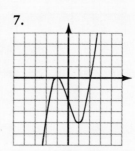

8.

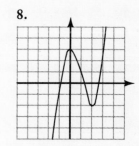

9.

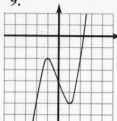

10.

11.

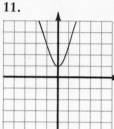

12.

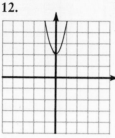

13.

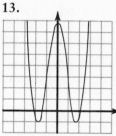

14.

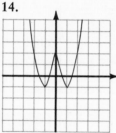

15.

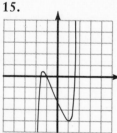

16.

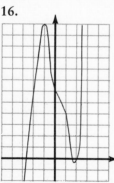

19.

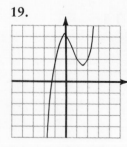

20.

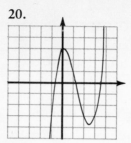

21.

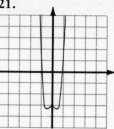

22. $P(x) = 3x^4 - 5x^3 + 4x^2 - 5$

Perform synthetic division using a as the divisor and 3, -5, 4, 0, and -5 as the coefficients to find $P(a)$
$= a[a(a(3a - 5) + 4)] - 5$. This expression is the same expression obtained by factoring to find nested form.

Page 496
CAREERS
1. Center: $(0, 0)$; Vertices: $(7, 0)$, $(-7, 0)$, $(0, 4)$, $(0, -4)$; Foci: $(\sqrt{33}, 0)$, $(-\sqrt{33}, 0)$ **2.** Center: $(3, 1)$; Vertices: $(5, 1)$, $(1, 1)$, $(3, 6)$, $(3, -4)$; Foci: $(3, \sqrt{21} + 1)$, $(3, -\sqrt{21} + 1)$ **3.** Center: $(0, 0)$; Vertices: $(4, 0)$, $(-4, 0)$, $(0, 2)$, $(0, -2)$; Foci: $(2\sqrt{3}, 0)$, $(-2\sqrt{3}, 0)$
4. Center: $(-2, 1)$; Vertices: $(\sqrt{3} - 2, 1)$, $(-\sqrt{3} - 2, 1)$, $(-2, \sqrt{2} + 1)$, $(-2, -\sqrt{2} + 1)$ Foci: $(\sqrt{5} - 2, 1)$, $(-\sqrt{5} - 2, 1)$ **5.** Center: $(-2, 1)$; Vertices: $(2, 1)$, $(-6, 1)$, $(-2, 4)$, $(-2, -2)$; Foci: $(\sqrt{7} - 2, 1)$, $(-\sqrt{7} - 2, 1)$
6. $(-700, 0)$, $(700, 0)$, $(0, 400)$, $(0, -400)$; $(-574.5, 0)$ $(574.5, 0)$

Page 497
CHAPTER 11 REVIEW
13. Cubic curve through $(-2, -6)$, $(-1, 0)$, $(-\frac{1}{2}, \frac{3}{8})$, $(0, 0)$, $(\frac{1}{2}, -\frac{3}{8})$, $(1, 0)$, $(2, 6)$

Page 498
CHAPTER 11 TEST
11. Cubic curve through $(-2, -13)$, $(-1, -1)$, $(0, 1)$, $(\frac{1}{3}, \frac{31}{27})$, $(1, 1)$, $(2, 3)$
12. Curve through $(-2, 31.2)$, $(-1, 0)$,

$(-0.5, -1.05)$, $(0, -0.8)$, $(0.5, -1.05)$, $(1, 0)$, $(2, 31.2)$

Pages 498–501
CHAPTERS 1–11 CUMULATIVE REVIEW
19. All points above dashed line through $(-1, -1)$, $(0, 0)$, $(1, 1)$ **20.** All points below dashed line through $(-1, -1)$, $(0, 0)$, $(1, 1)$ **21.** All points below dashed line through $(0, 1)$ and $(1, 0)$ **52.** $\frac{2}{3}a\sqrt{3}$

CHAPTER 12   Pages 507–508
EXERCISE SET 12–1
1. $\{(1, 0), (6, 5), (-4, -2)\}$
2. $\{(-2, -1), (0, 0), (1, 3)\}$
3. $\{(-1, -1), (-4, -3)\}$ **4.** $x = 4y - 5$
5. $x = 3y + 5$ **6.** $x = 3y^2 + 2$ **7.** $x = 5y^2 - 4$ **8.** $y^2 - 3x^2 = 3$ **9.** $2y^2 + 5x^2 = 4$
10. $y \cdot x = 7$ **11.** $y \cdot x = -5$ **12.** $yx^2 = 1$
13. No **14.** No **15.** Yes **16.** Yes
17. Yes **18.** Yes **19.** Yes **20.** Yes
21. Yes **22.** Yes **23.** No **24.** No
25. $f^{-1}(x) = x + 1$ **26.** $f^{-1}(x) = x + 2$
27. $f^{-1}(x) = x - 4$ **28.** $f^{-1}(x) = x - 3$
29. $f^{-1}(x) = x - 8$ **30.** $f^{-1}(x) = x - 7$
31. $f^{-1}(x) = \frac{x-5}{2}$ **32.** $f^{-1}(x) = \frac{x-2}{3}$
33. $f^{-1}(x) = \frac{x+1}{3}$ **34.** $f^{-1}(x) = \frac{x+3}{4}$
35. $f^{-1}(x) = 2(x - 2)$ **36.** $f^{-1}(x) = \frac{10(x-4)}{7}$
37. $f^{-1}(x) = x^2 + 1$ **38.** $f^{-1}(x) = x$
39. $f^{-1}(x) = x^2 - 2$ **44.** $f(x)$; parabola through $(-2, 5)$, $(0, 1)$, $(2, 5)$; $f^{-1}(x)$: parabola through $(5, 2)$, $(1, 0)$, $(5, -2)$
45. $f(x)$: parabola through $(-3, 6)$, $(0, -3)$, $(3, 6)$; $f^{-1}(x)$: parabola through $(6, -3)$, $(-3, 0)$, $(6, 3)$ **46.** $f(x)$: rays from $(0, 0)$ through $(5, 5)$ and from $(0, 0)$ through $(-5, 5)$; $f^{-1}(x)$: rays from $(0, 0)$ through $(5, -5)$ and from $(0, 0)$ through $(5, 5)$ **47.** $f(x)$: rays from $(0, 0)$ through $(5, 5)$ and from $(0, 0)$ through $(5, -5)$; $f^{-1}(x)$: rays from $(0, 0)$ through $(-5, 5)$ and from $(0, 0)$ through $(5, 5)$ **48.** x, x
49. x, x **50.** $2x^2 + 2$; $4x^2 + 1$ **51.** $x^2 + 6x + 9$; $x^2 + 3$ **52.** $2x - 5$; $2x - 1$

53. $12x^2 - 12x + 5$; $6x^2 + 3$ **54.** $\frac{16}{x^2} - 1$; $\frac{2}{4x^2 - 1}$ **55.** $x^4 - 2x^2$; $x^4 - 2x^2$ **56.** x-axis: no; y-axis: yes; origin: no; $y = x$: no
57. x-axis: yes; y-axis: yes; origin: yes; $y = x$: no **58.** x-axis: no; y-axis: no; origin: yes; $y = x$: no **59.** x-axis: no; y-axis: no; origin: yes; $y = x$: no

56.

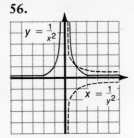

57.

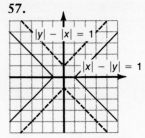

58.

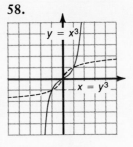

59.

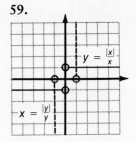

Pages 511–513
TRY THIS
2.

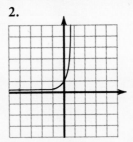

3.

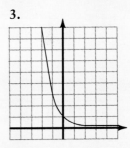

4.

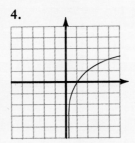

5.

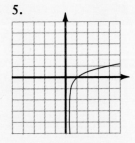

ADDITIONAL ANSWERS   T 113

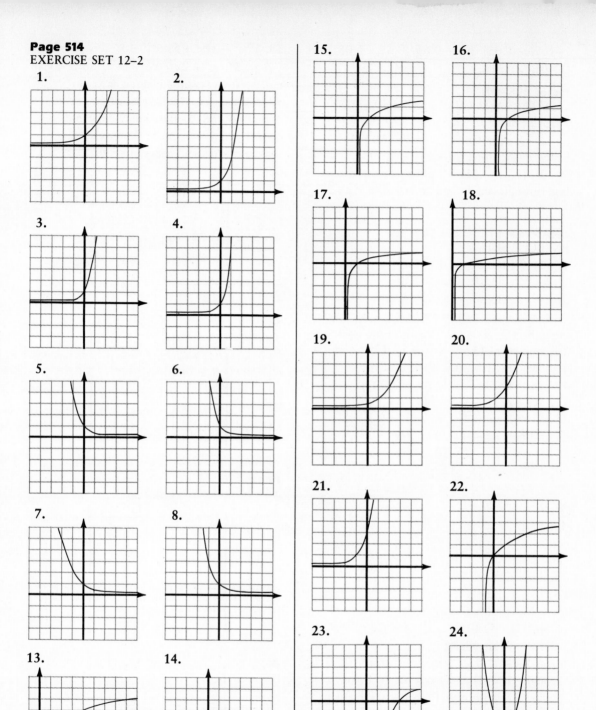

25.

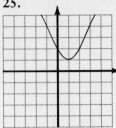

26.

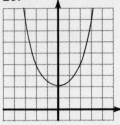

27.

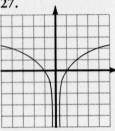

37.

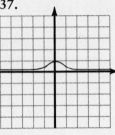

38.

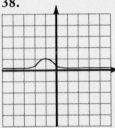

39.

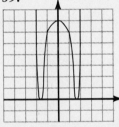

Page 523
EXERCISE SET 12–4

51. $\log_a \left(\frac{1}{x}\right) = \log_a 1 - \log_a x = 0 - \log_a x$
$= -\log_a x$ **52.** Let $\log_a \left(\frac{1}{x}\right) = M$. Then a^M
$= \frac{1}{x}$, so $a^{-M} = x$ or $\left(\frac{1}{a}\right) = x$. Thus $\log_{1/a} x$
$= \log_a \left(\frac{1}{x}\right)$.   **53.** $\log_a \left(\frac{x + \sqrt{x^2-5}}{5} \cdot \frac{x - \sqrt{x^2-5}}{x - \sqrt{x^2-5}}\right)$
$= \log_a \left(\frac{x^2 - (x^2-5)}{5(x - \sqrt{x^2-5})}\right) = \log_a \left(\frac{1}{x - \sqrt{x^2-5}}\right)$
$= -\log_a (x - \sqrt{x^2-5})$

Page 530
EXERCISE SET 12–5
22. 2.5403   **23.** 3.9405   **24.** 1.7202
25. 1.3139   **26.** 2.9212   **27.** 1.9657
28. 3.5877   **29.** 5.7952   **30.** 7.1271 − 10
31. 8.8463 − 10   **32.** 9.8062 − 10
33. 6.3345 − 10   **34.** 9.2380 − 10
35. 7.5403 − 10   **36.** 5.6064 − 10

37. 2330   **38.** 83,600   **39.** 18   **40.** 426
41. 0.613   **42.** 0.0973   **43.** 25.2
44. 346   **45.** 0.00973   **46.** 0.0346
47. 0.000613   **48.** 0.00000426   **49.** 6.34
50. 15,500   **51.** 0.613   **52.** 0.0951
53. 2.5378   **54.** 3.7536   **55.** 4.754264
56. −1.953321   **57.** −0.321371
58. 2.726465   **59.** 78,397,100
60. 0.000000027   **61.** 0.000583

Pages 540-541
EXERCISE SET 12–7
38. 1; 10,000   **39.** $\pm 2\sqrt{6}$ **40.** $\emptyset$
41. 25, $\frac{1}{25}$ **42.** −9; 9   **43.** 100, $\frac{1}{100}$
44. $\frac{7}{4}$ **45.** $-\frac{1}{2}$ **46.** $\log_x y - \log_x a$
47. $t = \frac{\log_b y - \log_b k}{a}$ **48.** $t = -\frac{1}{k} \log \left| \frac{T - T_0}{T_1 - T_0} \right|$
49. $n = \log_v c - \log_v P$, or $\log_v \frac{c}{P}$
50. $Q = a^b \cdot \sqrt[3]{y}$ **51.** $y = xa^{2x}$ **52.** 10, 100
53. 100, $\frac{1}{10}$ **54.** 5   **55.** $\{x \,|\, x \geq 1\}$ for bases
a such that $a > 1$ **56.** $\left\{x \,\middle|\, x < \frac{\log 0.8}{\log 0.5} \approx 0.3219\right\}$

57. 2^{10} **58.** $\left(\frac{\log 1125}{(\log 125)(\log 3)}, \frac{\log \frac{81}{125}}{(\log 125)(\log 3)}\right)$

59. 88   **60.** 1, 4   **61.** $\left(0, \frac{3}{2}\right)$

Page 542
TRY THIS
1.

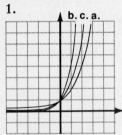

2.

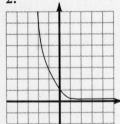

Page 547
EXERCISE SET 12–8
1.

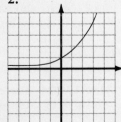

2.

3.

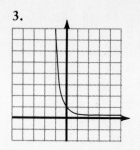

4.

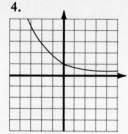

5.

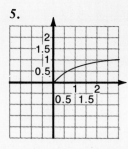

6.

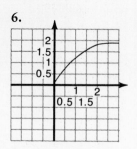

Page 548
EXERCISE SET 12–8
39. By Theorem 12–9, $\ln x = \frac{\log x}{\log e}$; $\approx \frac{\log x}{0.4343}$ by Table 2; $\approx 2.3026 \log x$, multiplying by $\frac{2.3026}{2.3026}$ **40.** By Theorem 12–9, $\log x = \frac{\ln x}{\ln 10}$; $\approx \frac{\ln x}{2.3026}$ by Table 2; $\approx 0.4343 \ln x$, multiplying by $\frac{0.4343}{0.4343}$
41. e^{π} **42.** $e^{\sqrt{\pi}}$ **43.** 2; 2.25; 2.48832; 2.593742; 2.704814; 2.716924 **44.** 4.0; 2.867972; 2.731999; 2.719642; 2.718418
45. $N = N_0 2 - \frac{t}{H}$ **46.** By Theorem 12–9, $\log_a b = \frac{\log_b b}{\log_b a} = \frac{1}{\log_b a}$ **47.** By Theorem 12–9, $a^{(\log_b M) - (\log_b a)} = a^{\log_a M} = M$, by Theorem 12–4. **48.** By Theorem 12–9, $\log_M a = \frac{\log_b a}{\log_b M}$, so $(\log_b M)(\log_M a) = \log_b a$. Then, by Theorem 12–6, $\log_M a^{\log_b M} = \log_b a$. Then, by definition of logarithms, $a^{\log_b M} = M^{\log_b a}$. Now raise both sides to the power, $\log_b a$, and the result follows.
49. $\log_a (\log_a x) = \log_a \left(\frac{\log_b x}{\log_b a}\right)$, by Theorem 12–9 $= \log_a (\log_b x) = \log_a (\log_b a)$, by Theorem 12–7.

CHAPTER 14 Page 604
EXERCISE SET 14–1
5. $\begin{bmatrix} -2 & -3 \\ 6 & -4 \end{bmatrix}$ **6.** $\begin{bmatrix} -2 & -6 \\ 1 & 0 \end{bmatrix}$ **7.** $\begin{bmatrix} 4 & 4 \\ 0 & 0 \end{bmatrix}$ **8.** $\begin{bmatrix} 4 & 6 \\ 1 & 5 \end{bmatrix}$

9. $\begin{bmatrix} -5 & 0 & 11 \\ 3 & 2 & 0 \end{bmatrix}$ **10.** $\begin{bmatrix} -3 & 3 & 4 \\ 8 & 2 & -1 \end{bmatrix}$ **11.** $\begin{bmatrix} 0 & -2 & 3 \\ 1 & -1 & 2 \\ 1 & -5 & 5 \end{bmatrix}$

12. $\begin{bmatrix} -5 & 3 & 3 \\ 2 & 0 & -5 \\ -4 & -6 & -4 \end{bmatrix}$ **13.** $\begin{bmatrix} 1 & 2 \\ 4 & -3 \end{bmatrix}$ **14.** $\begin{bmatrix} -3 & -5 \\ 2 & -1 \end{bmatrix}$

15. $\begin{bmatrix} 1 & -1 \\ -1 & 1 \end{bmatrix}$ **16.** $\begin{bmatrix} 1 & 1 \\ 1 & 1 \end{bmatrix}$ **17.** $\begin{bmatrix} 4 & 7 \\ 2 & -2 \end{bmatrix}$ **18.** $\begin{bmatrix} 4 & 4 \\ -3 & 2 \end{bmatrix}$

19. $\begin{bmatrix} 2 & -2 \\ -2 & -2 \end{bmatrix}$ **20.** $\begin{bmatrix} -2 & 0 \\ 3 & 7 \end{bmatrix}$ **21.** $\begin{bmatrix} 3 & -7 & 7 \\ 0 & 0 & 3 \\ 0 & 0 & 6 \end{bmatrix}$

22. $\begin{bmatrix} 2 & 2 & -7 \\ -1 & -1 & 4 \\ 5 & 1 & 3 \end{bmatrix}$ **23.** $\begin{bmatrix} -1 & -6 & 3 \\ -13 & 2 & 2 \end{bmatrix}$ **24.** $\begin{bmatrix} 2 & 3 & -7 \\ 5 & 0 & -1 \end{bmatrix}$

25. $\begin{bmatrix} -1 & -1 \\ -1 & -1 \end{bmatrix}$ **26.** $\begin{bmatrix} 3 & 3 & -7 \\ 5 & -2 & -1 \end{bmatrix}$ **27.** $\begin{bmatrix} -1 & -3 \\ -2 & -6 \end{bmatrix}$

28. $\begin{bmatrix} 4 & -5 & 2 \\ -1 & 0 & 4 \\ 2 & 3 & 5 \end{bmatrix}$ **29.** $\begin{bmatrix} 0 & 2 \\ 2 & 0 \end{bmatrix}$ **30.** $\begin{bmatrix} 0 & -4 \\ -3 & -5 \end{bmatrix}$

31. $\begin{bmatrix} -3 & 7 & -7 \\ 0 & 0 & -3 \\ 0 & 0 & -6 \end{bmatrix}$ **32.** $\begin{bmatrix} -2 & -2 & 7 \\ 1 & 1 & -4 \\ -5 & -1 & -3 \end{bmatrix}$

33. $\begin{bmatrix} 1 & 6 & -3 \\ 13 & -2 & -2 \end{bmatrix}$ **34.** $\begin{bmatrix} 1 & -3 & -4 \\ -8 & 2 & 1 \end{bmatrix}$

35. $\begin{bmatrix} -3 & -3 \\ 1 & 1 \end{bmatrix}$ **36.** $\begin{bmatrix} -1 & -2 \\ -4 & 3 \end{bmatrix}$

37. $(A + F) + C = A + (F + C) = \begin{bmatrix} 5 & 4 \\ 2 & -3 \end{bmatrix}$
38. $(G + H) + M = (M + G) + H = \begin{bmatrix} -4 & 3 & 1 \\ 2 & -1 & -2 \\ -1 & -8 & 0 \end{bmatrix}$ **39.** A and H do not have the same dimensions.

Pages 610–611
EXERCISE SET 14–2
1. $\begin{bmatrix} -2 & -4 \\ -8 & -6 \end{bmatrix}$ **2.** $\begin{bmatrix} 15 & -25 \\ -10 & 5 \end{bmatrix}$ **3.** $\begin{bmatrix} 14 & -14 \\ -14 & 14 \end{bmatrix}$

4. $\begin{bmatrix} 12 & 12 \\ 12 & 12 \end{bmatrix}$ **5.** $\begin{bmatrix} t & 3t \\ 2t & 6t \end{bmatrix}$ **6.** $\begin{bmatrix} 3p & 3p \\ -p & -p \end{bmatrix}$

7. $\begin{bmatrix} 2 & -9 & -6 \\ 3 & -3 & -4 \\ -2 & 2 & -1 \end{bmatrix}$ **8.** $\begin{bmatrix} 1 & 2 & -5 \\ -1 & 0 & 1 \\ -2 & 3 & -1 \end{bmatrix}$ **9.** $[-22]$

10. $[-36]$ **11.** $[-36]$ **12.** $[-9]$ **13.** $\begin{bmatrix} 1 & 3 \\ -6 & 17 \end{bmatrix}$

14. $\begin{bmatrix} -8 & 8 \\ 3 & -3 \end{bmatrix}$ **15.** $\begin{bmatrix} 0 & 0 \\ 0 & 0 \end{bmatrix}$ **16.** $\begin{bmatrix} 0 & 0 \\ 0 & 0 \end{bmatrix}$

17. $[-14 \ -11 \ -3]$ **18.** $[25 \ 25]$

19. $[-13 \ -1 \ -4]$ **20.** $\begin{bmatrix} -15 \\ 5 \end{bmatrix}$ **21.** $\begin{bmatrix} 3 & 3 \\ -1 & -1 \end{bmatrix}$

22. $\begin{bmatrix} -3 & 5 \\ 2 & -1 \end{bmatrix}$ **23.** $\begin{bmatrix} -5 & 4 & 3 \\ 5 & -9 & 4 \\ 7 & -18 & 17 \end{bmatrix}$

24. $\begin{bmatrix} 14 & 12 & 16 \\ -2 & -2 & -6 \\ 5 & 5 & -9 \end{bmatrix}$ **25.** $\begin{bmatrix} -7 \\ -18 \end{bmatrix}$ **26.** $[9 \ -9]$

27. Not possible **28.** Not possible

29. $\begin{bmatrix} 3 & -2 & 4 \\ 2 & 1 & -5 \end{bmatrix} \begin{bmatrix} x \\ y \\ z \end{bmatrix} = \begin{bmatrix} 17 \\ 13 \end{bmatrix}$

30. $\begin{bmatrix} 3 & 2 & 5 \\ 4 & -3 & 2 \end{bmatrix} \begin{bmatrix} x \\ y \\ z \end{bmatrix} = \begin{bmatrix} 9 \\ 10 \end{bmatrix}$

31. $\begin{bmatrix} 1 & -1 & 2 & -4 \\ 2 & -1 & -1 & 1 \\ 1 & 4 & -3 & -1 \\ 3 & 5 & -7 & 2 \end{bmatrix} \begin{bmatrix} x \\ y \\ z \\ w \end{bmatrix} = \begin{bmatrix} 12 \\ 0 \\ 1 \\ 9 \end{bmatrix}$

32. $\begin{bmatrix} 2 & 4 & -5 & 12 \\ 4 & -1 & 12 & -1 \\ -1 & 4 & 0 & 2 \\ 2 & 10 & 1 & 0 \end{bmatrix} \begin{bmatrix} x \\ y \\ z \\ w \end{bmatrix} = \begin{bmatrix} 2 \\ 5 \\ 13 \\ 5 \end{bmatrix}$

35. I is a multiplicative identity.

39. $A + B = \begin{bmatrix} a+e & c+g \\ b+f & d+h \end{bmatrix}$, $B + A$

$= \begin{bmatrix} a+e & c+g \\ b+f & d+h \end{bmatrix}$ 40. $(A + B) + C$

$= \begin{bmatrix} a+e & c+g \\ b+f & d+h \end{bmatrix} + \begin{bmatrix} p & r \\ q & s \end{bmatrix} = \begin{bmatrix} a+e+p & c+g+r \\ b+f+q & d+h+s \end{bmatrix}$,

$A + (B + C) = \begin{bmatrix} a & c \\ b & d \end{bmatrix} + \begin{bmatrix} e+p & g+r \\ f+q & h+s \end{bmatrix}$

$= \begin{bmatrix} a+e+p & c+g+r \\ b+f+q & d+h+s \end{bmatrix}$ 41. $A - B \begin{bmatrix} a & c \\ b & d \end{bmatrix}$

$- \begin{bmatrix} e & g \\ f & h \end{bmatrix} = \begin{bmatrix} a-e & c-g \\ b-f & d-h \end{bmatrix}$, $A + (-B) = \begin{bmatrix} a & c \\ b & d \end{bmatrix}$

$+ \begin{bmatrix} -e & -g \\ -f & -h \end{bmatrix} = \begin{bmatrix} a-e & c-g \\ b-f & d-h \end{bmatrix}$ 42. $(-1)A$

$= (-1) \begin{bmatrix} a & c \\ b & d \end{bmatrix} = \begin{bmatrix} -a & -c \\ -b & -d \end{bmatrix}$,

$-A = - \begin{bmatrix} a & c \\ b & d \end{bmatrix} = \begin{bmatrix} -a & -c \\ -b & -d \end{bmatrix}$

43. $k(A + B) = k \begin{bmatrix} a+e & c+g \\ b+f & d+h \end{bmatrix} = \begin{bmatrix} ka+ke & kc+kg \\ kb+kf & kd+kh \end{bmatrix}$,

$kA + kB = \begin{bmatrix} ka & kc \\ kb & kh \end{bmatrix} + \begin{bmatrix} ke & kg \\ kf & kd \end{bmatrix} = \begin{bmatrix} ka+ke & kc+kg \\ kb+kf & kd+kh \end{bmatrix}$

44. $(k + m)A = (k + m) \begin{bmatrix} a & c \\ b & d \end{bmatrix}$

$= \begin{bmatrix} (k+m)a & (k+m)c \\ (k+m)b & (k+m)d \end{bmatrix} = \begin{bmatrix} ka+ma & kc+mc \\ kb+mb & kd+md \end{bmatrix}$,

$kA + mA = k \begin{bmatrix} a & c \\ b & d \end{bmatrix} + m \begin{bmatrix} a & c \\ b & d \end{bmatrix} = \begin{bmatrix} ka & kc \\ kb & kd \end{bmatrix}$

$+ \begin{bmatrix} ma & mc \\ mb & md \end{bmatrix} \begin{bmatrix} ka+ma & kc+mc \\ kb+mb & kd+md \end{bmatrix}$

Pages 616–617
EXERCISE SET 14–3

1. $\begin{bmatrix} 1 & 2 \\ 3 & 4 \end{bmatrix} \begin{bmatrix} -2 & 1 \\ \frac{3}{2} & -\frac{1}{2} \end{bmatrix} = \begin{bmatrix} 1 & 0 \\ 0 & 1 \end{bmatrix}$ 2. $\begin{bmatrix} 3 & 4 \\ 2 & 6 \end{bmatrix} \begin{bmatrix} \frac{6}{10} & -\frac{4}{10} \\ -\frac{2}{10} & \frac{3}{10} \end{bmatrix}$

$= \begin{bmatrix} 1 & 0 \\ 0 & 1 \end{bmatrix}$ 3. $\begin{bmatrix} 7 & 4 \\ 3 & 2 \end{bmatrix} \begin{bmatrix} 1 & -2 \\ -\frac{3}{2} & \frac{7}{2} \end{bmatrix} = \begin{bmatrix} 1 & 0 \\ 0 & 1 \end{bmatrix}$

4. $\begin{bmatrix} 2 & 3 \\ 3 & 6 \end{bmatrix} \begin{bmatrix} 2 & -1 \\ -1 & \frac{2}{3} \end{bmatrix} = \begin{bmatrix} 1 & 0 \\ 0 & 1 \end{bmatrix}$

5. $A^{-1} = \begin{bmatrix} -3 & 2 \\ 5 & -3 \end{bmatrix}$ 6. $A^{-1} = \begin{bmatrix} 2 & -5 \\ -1 & 3 \end{bmatrix}$

7. $A^{-1} = \begin{bmatrix} 2 & -3 \\ -7 & 11 \end{bmatrix}$ 8. $A^{-1} = \begin{bmatrix} -3 & 5 \\ 5 & -8 \end{bmatrix}$

9. $A^{-1} = \begin{bmatrix} \frac{2}{11} & \frac{3}{11} \\ -\frac{1}{11} & \frac{4}{11} \end{bmatrix}$ 10. $A^{-1} = \begin{bmatrix} 0 & 1 \\ -1 & 0 \end{bmatrix}$

11. $A^{-1} = \begin{bmatrix} \frac{3}{8} & -\frac{1}{4} & \frac{1}{8} \\ -\frac{1}{8} & \frac{3}{4} & -\frac{3}{8} \\ -\frac{1}{4} & \frac{1}{2} & \frac{1}{4} \end{bmatrix}$ 12. $A^{-1} = \begin{bmatrix} -\frac{1}{2} & \frac{1}{2} & \frac{1}{2} \\ 1 & 0 & -1 \\ \frac{3}{2} & -\frac{1}{2} & -\frac{1}{2} \end{bmatrix}$

13. $A^{-1} = \begin{bmatrix} \frac{1}{3} & 0 & \frac{1}{3} \\ -\frac{2}{5} & \frac{2}{5} & \frac{1}{3} \\ \frac{2}{15} & \frac{1}{3} & -\frac{1}{15} \end{bmatrix}$

24a. Multiply A by what we assert to be A^{-1} to show $AA^{-1} = I$.

Page 618
CAREERS

1. $\begin{bmatrix} 1 \times 10^6 & 0 & -1 \times 10^6 & 0 \\ 0 & 0 & 0 & 0 \\ -1 \times 10^6 & 0 & 1 \times 10^6 & 0 \\ 0 & 0 & 0 & 0 \end{bmatrix}$

2. $\begin{bmatrix} 0.5 \times 10^6 & 0.5 \times 10^6 & -0.5 \times 10^6 & -0.5 \times 10^6 \\ 0.5 \times 10^6 & 0.5 \times 10^6 & -0.5 \times 10^6 & -0.5 \times 10^6 \\ -0.5 \times 10^6 & -0.5 \times 10^6 & 0.5 \times 10^6 & 0.5 \times 10^6 \\ -0.5 \times 10^6 & -0.5 \times 10^6 & 0.5 \times 10^6 & 0.5 \times 10^6 \end{bmatrix}$

3. $\begin{bmatrix} 10472 & 0 & -10472 & 0 \\ 0 & 0 & 0 & 0 \\ -10472 & 0 & 10472 & 0 \\ 0 & 0 & 0 & 0 \end{bmatrix}$

4. $F_H = 20,000$; $-20,000$ $F_V = 0$; 0

Page 619
CHAPTER 14 TEST

4. $\begin{bmatrix} 0 & 12 & 6 \\ -3 & 6 & 0 \\ 0 & 6 & 3 \end{bmatrix}$ 5. $\begin{bmatrix} -2 & -4 & 2 \\ -4 & 0 & -2 \\ 4 & -2 & 0 \end{bmatrix}$ 6. $\begin{bmatrix} -2 & 6 & 1 \\ 0 & 10 & 5 \\ -1 & -6 & -4 \end{bmatrix}$

Pages 620–623
CHAPTERS 1–14 CUMULATIVE REVIEW
16. All points inside, and including, triangle with vertices $(-2, -1)$, $(5, -1)$, $(5, 2\frac{1}{2})$
17. All points inside, and including, triangle with vertices $(0, 0)$, $(0, 5)$, $(5, 0)$ 18. All points inside, and including, triangle with vertices $(0, 0)$, $(6, 0)$, $(3, 3)$ 50. $f^{-1}(x)$ $= \frac{1}{3}x + \frac{4}{3}$ 51. $f^{-1}(x) = x^2 - 1$ 62. $\frac{1}{2}, \frac{1}{5}, \frac{1}{8}$, $\frac{1}{11}; \frac{1}{29}; \frac{1}{44}$ 63. $-2, 4, -8, 16; 1024; -32768$

Chapter 15   Page 626
TRY THIS
1. $\sin \theta = \frac{4}{5}$; $\cos \theta = \frac{3}{5}$; $\tan \theta = \frac{4}{3}$

Pages 629–630
EXERCISE SET 15–1
13. $\sin \theta = \frac{\sqrt{3}}{2}$ $\sec \theta = 2$; $\cos \theta = \frac{1}{2}$; $\csc \theta = \frac{2\sqrt{3}}{3}$ $\cot \theta = \frac{2\sqrt{3}}{3}$ 14. $\sin \theta = \frac{\sqrt{2}}{2}$; $\tan \theta = 1$; $\cot \theta = 1$; $\sec \theta = \sqrt{2}$; $\csc \theta = \sqrt{2}$ 15. $\cos \theta = \frac{\sqrt{3}}{2}$; $\tan \theta = \frac{\sqrt{3}}{3}$; $\cot$

$\theta = \sqrt{3}$; sec $\theta = \frac{2\sqrt{3}}{3}$; csc $\theta = 2$ **16.** sin $\theta = \frac{\sqrt{3}}{2}$; cos $\theta = \frac{1}{2}$; tan $\theta = \sqrt{3}$; cot $\theta = \frac{\sqrt{3}}{3}$; csc $\theta = \frac{2\sqrt{3}}{3}$ **17.** sin $\theta = \frac{1}{2}$; cos $\theta = \frac{\sqrt{3}}{2}$; tan $\theta = \frac{\sqrt{3}}{3}$; cot $\theta = \sqrt{3}$; sec $\theta = \frac{2\sqrt{3}}{3}$; csc $\theta = 2$ **18.** sin $\theta = \frac{\sqrt{3}}{2}$; cos $\theta = \frac{1}{2}$; tan $\theta = \sqrt{3}$; cot $\theta = \frac{\sqrt{3}}{3}$; sec $\theta = 2$; csc $\theta = \frac{2\sqrt{3}}{3}$

Pages 636–637
EXERCISE SET 15–2

13. sin $\theta = -\frac{3}{5}$; cos $\theta = -\frac{4}{5}$; tan $\theta = \frac{3}{4}$

14. sin $\theta = \frac{5}{13}$; cos $\theta = -\frac{12}{13}$; tan $\theta = -\frac{5}{12}$

15. sin $\theta = -\frac{3}{5}$; cos $\theta = \frac{4}{5}$; tan $\theta = -\frac{3}{4}$

16. sin $\theta = -\frac{\sqrt{2}}{2}$; cos $\theta = -\frac{\sqrt{2}}{2}$; tan $\theta = 1$

17. sin $\theta = \frac{\sqrt{3}}{2}$; cos $\theta = -\frac{1}{2}$; tan $\theta = -\sqrt{3}$

18. sin $\theta = -\frac{1}{2}$; cos $\theta = \frac{\sqrt{3}}{2}$; tan $\theta = -\frac{\sqrt{3}}{3}$

19. All function values are positive.   **20.** The cosine and secant function values are positive, the other four are negative.   **21.** Same as 20.   **22.** The tangent and cotangent function values are positive, the other four are negative.   **23.** All function values are positive.   **24.** The sine and cosecant function values are positive, the other four are negative.

25.

θ	cot θ	sec θ	csc θ
0°	—	1	—
90°	0	—	1
180°	—	−1	—
270°	0	—	−1

56. sin 30° = 0.500; cos 30° = 0.866; tan 30° = 0.577; csc 30° = 2.000; sec 30° = 1.155; cot 30° = 1.732
57. sin 60° = 0.866; cos 60° = 0.500; tan 60° = 1.732; csc 60° = 1.155; sec 60° = 2.000; cot 60° = 0.577
58. sin 120° = 0.866; cos 120° = −0.500; tan 120° = −1.732; csc 120° = 1.155; sec 120° = −2.000; cot 120° = −0.577
59. sin 225° = −0.707; cos 225° = −0.707; tan 225° = 1.000; csc 225° = −1.414; sec 225° = −1.414;

cot 225° = 1.000   **60.** sin $\theta = -\frac{8}{17}$; cos $\theta = -\frac{15}{17}$; tan $\theta = \frac{8}{15}$; csc $\theta = -\frac{17}{8}$; sec $\theta = -\frac{17}{15}$; cot $\theta = \frac{15}{8}$ **61.** sin $\theta = \frac{4}{7}$; cos $\theta = -\frac{\sqrt{33}}{7}$; tan $\theta = -\frac{4\sqrt{33}}{33}$; csc $\theta = \frac{7}{4}$; sec $\theta = -\frac{7\sqrt{33}}{33}$; cot $\theta = -\frac{\sqrt{33}}{4}$

62. sin $\theta = -\frac{5}{13}$; cos $\theta = \frac{12}{13}$; tan $\theta = -\frac{5}{12}$; csc $\theta = -\frac{13}{5}$; sec $\theta = \frac{13}{12}$; cot $\theta = -\frac{12}{5}$

Pages 651–653
EXERCISE SET 15–4

3. and **4.** Cosine curve, see page 647.
15. See page 649.   **17.** See page 650.
16.

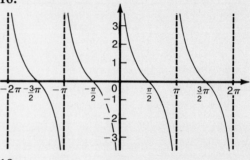

18.

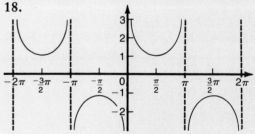

19. The set of all real numbers except πk, k an integer   **20.** The set of all real numbers   **21.** Yes, π **22.** odd   **23.** The set of all real numbers except $k\pi$, k an integer   **24.** $\{x \mid x \geq 1 \text{ and } x \leq -1\}$ **25.** Yes, 2π **26.** odd   **27.**   **a.** Sine curve, see page 647.   **b.** Curve through $(-\pi, 0)$, $\left(-\frac{\pi}{2}, 1\right)$, $(0, 0)$, $\left(\frac{\pi}{2}, -1\right)$, $(\pi, 0)$ **c.** Curve through points listed in 27b   **d.** They are the same.   **28.**   **a.** Cosine curve, see page 647.   **b.** Cosine curve, see page 647.   **c.** Curve through $(-\pi, 1)$, $\left(-\frac{\pi}{2}, 0\right)$, $(0, -1)$,

$\left(\frac{\pi}{2}, 0\right), (\pi, 1)$ **d.** They are the same.
29.   **a.** Sine curve, see page 647.   **b.** Curve through points listed in 27b, above   **c.** Curve through points listed in 27b, above   **d.** They are the same.   **30.**   **a.** Sine curve, see page 647.   **b.** Curve through points listed in 27b, above   **c.** Curve through points listed in 27b, above   **d.** They are the same.   **31.**   **a.** Cosine curve, see page 647.   **b.** Curve through points listed in 28c, above   **c.** Curve through points listed in 28c, above   **d.** They are the same   **32.**   **a.** Cosine curve, see page 647.   **b.** Curve through points listed in 28c, above   **c.** Curve through points listed in 28c, above   **d.** They are the same.
33.   **a.** $\left\{x \mid x = \frac{\pi}{2} + 2k\pi, k \text{ an integer}\right\}$
b. $\left\{x \mid x = \frac{3\pi}{2} + 2k\pi, k \text{ an integer}\right\}$
34.   **a.** $\{x \mid x = 2k\pi, k \text{ an integer}\}$
b. $\{x \mid x = \pi + 2k\pi, k \text{ an integer}\}$
35. $\left\{x \mid x = k\pi, k \text{ an integer}\right\}$
36. $\left\{x \mid x = \frac{\pi}{2} + k\pi, k \text{ an integer}\right\}$ **37.** If the graph of tan x were reflected across the y-axis and then translated to the right a distance of $\frac{\pi}{2}$, the graph of cot x could be obtained. There are other ways to describe the relation.   **38.** If the graph of sec x were translated to the right $\frac{\pi}{2}$ units, the graph of csc x would be obtained. There are other descriptions.   **39.** The sine and tangent functions; the cosine and cotangent functions.
40.

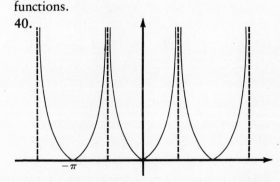

41. $\left\{x \mid -\frac{\pi}{2} + 2k\pi < x < \frac{\pi}{2} + 2\pi k, k \text{ an integer}\right\}$

42. $\left\{x \mid (2k+1)\pi < x < (2k+2)\pi, x \neq \frac{3\pi}{2} + 2\pi k, k \text{ an integer}\right\}$ **43–44.** See page 647 for graphs.

Pages 658–659
EXERCISE SET 15–5
9. $\sin\left(\frac{\pi}{4} - \frac{\pi}{2}\right) = \sin\left(-\frac{\pi}{4}\right) = -\frac{\sqrt{2}}{2} = -\cos\frac{\pi}{4}$
10. $\cos\left(0 - \frac{\pi}{2}\right) = \cos\left(-\frac{\pi}{2}\right) = 0 = \sin 0$
11. $\sin\left(\frac{\pi}{2} - \frac{5\pi}{4}\right) = \sin\left(-\frac{\pi}{4}\right) = -\frac{\sqrt{2}}{2} = \cos\frac{5\pi}{4}$
12. $\cos\left(\frac{\pi}{2} - \frac{\pi}{3}\right) = \cos\frac{\pi}{6} = \frac{\sqrt{3}}{2} = \sin\frac{\pi}{3}$
21. $\sin\theta \equiv \cos\left(\frac{\pi}{2} - \theta\right)$, $\cos\theta \equiv \sin\left(\frac{\pi}{2} - \theta\right)$, $\tan\theta \equiv \cot\left(\frac{\pi}{2} - \theta\right)$, $\cot\theta \equiv \tan\left(\frac{\pi}{2} - \theta\right)$, $\sec\theta \equiv \csc\left(\frac{\pi}{2} - \theta\right)$, $\csc\theta \equiv \sec\left(\frac{\pi}{2} - \theta\right)$
22. The function of an angle is equal to the cofunction of its complement.
Answers for Exercises 37–40 may vary.

37. $\theta = 30°$; $\frac{1 - \sin 30°}{\cos 30°} = \frac{\cos 30°}{1 + \sin 30°}$; $\frac{\frac{1}{2}}{\frac{\sqrt{3}}{2}} = \frac{\frac{\sqrt{3}}{2}}{\frac{3}{2}}$; $\frac{\sqrt{3}}{3} = \frac{\sqrt{3}}{3}$ **38.** $\theta = 60°$;
$\frac{1 - \cos 60°}{\sin 60°} = \frac{\sin 60°}{1 + \cos 60°}$; $\frac{\frac{1}{2}}{\frac{\sqrt{3}}{2}} = \frac{\frac{\sqrt{3}}{2}}{\frac{3}{2}}$; $\frac{\sqrt{3}}{3} = \frac{\sqrt{3}}{3}$
39. $x = \frac{\pi}{2}$; $\csc\frac{\pi}{2} - \cos\frac{\pi}{2}\cot\frac{\pi}{2} = \sin\frac{\pi}{2}$; $1 - 0 \cdot 0 = 1$; $1 = 1$ **40.** $x = \frac{\pi}{4}$; $\sec\frac{\pi}{4} - \sin\frac{\pi}{4}\tan\frac{\pi}{4} = \cos\frac{\pi}{4}$; $\sqrt{2} - \frac{\sqrt{2}}{2} \cdot 1 = \frac{\sqrt{2}}{2}$; $\frac{\sqrt{2}}{2} = \frac{\sqrt{2}}{2}$

Pages 660–662
TRY THIS
1.

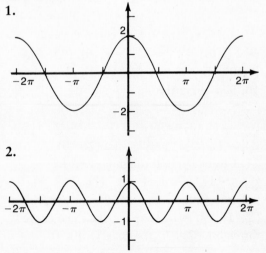

2.

3.

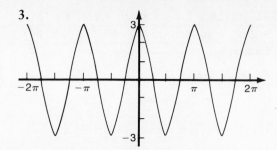

Page 662
EXERCISE SET 15–6

1. Sine curve through $(-2\pi, 0)$, $\left(\frac{-3\pi}{2}, \frac{1}{2}\right)$, $(-\pi, 0)$, $\left(\frac{-\pi}{2}, -\frac{1}{2}\right)$, $(0, 0)$, $\left(\frac{\pi}{2}, \frac{1}{2}\right)$, $(\pi, 0)$, $\left(\frac{3\pi}{2}, -\frac{1}{2}\right)$, $(2\pi, 0)$ **2.** Cosine curve through $\left(-2\pi, \frac{1}{2}\right)$, $\left(\frac{-3\pi}{2}, 0\right)$, $\left(-\pi, -\frac{1}{2}\right)$, $\left(\frac{3\pi}{2}, 0\right)$, $\left(2\pi, \frac{1}{2}\right)$ **3.** Sine curve through $(-2\pi, 0)$ $\left(\frac{-3\pi}{2}, 3\right)$, $(-\pi, 0)$, $\left(\frac{-\pi}{2}, -3\right)$, $(0, 0)$, $\left(\frac{\pi}{2}, 3\right)$, $(\pi, 0)$, $\left(\frac{3\pi}{2}, -3\right)$, $(2\pi, 0)$ **4.** Cosine curve through $(-2\pi, 3)$, $\left(\frac{-3\pi}{2}, 0\right)$, $(-\pi, -3)$, $\left(\frac{-\pi}{2}, 0\right)$, $(0, 3)$, $\left(\frac{\pi}{2}, 0\right)$, $(\pi, -3)$, $\left(\frac{3\pi}{2}, 0\right)$, $(2\pi, 3)$ **5.** Sine curve through $(-2\pi, 0)$, $\left(\frac{-3\pi}{2}, -\frac{1}{3}\right)$, $(-\pi, 0)$, $\left(\frac{-\pi}{2}, \frac{1}{3}\right)$, $(0, 0)$, $\left(\frac{\pi}{2}, -\frac{1}{3}\right)$, $(\pi, 0)$, $\left(\frac{3\pi}{2}, \frac{1}{3}\right)$, $(2\pi, 0)$ **6.** Cosine curve through $\left(-2\pi, -\frac{1}{3}\right)$, $\left(\frac{-3\pi}{2}, 0\right)$, $\left(-\pi, \frac{1}{3}\right)$, $\left(\frac{-\pi}{2}, 0\right)$, $\left(0, -\frac{1}{3}\right)$, $\left(\frac{\pi}{2}, 0\right)$, $\left(\pi, \frac{1}{3}\right)$, $\left(\frac{3\pi}{2}, 0\right)$, $\left(2\pi, -\frac{1}{3}\right)$ **7.** Sine curve through $(-2\pi, 0)$, $\left(\frac{-3\pi}{2}, 4\right)$, $(-\pi, 0)$, $\left(\frac{-\pi}{2}, -4\right)$, $(0, 0)$, $\left(\frac{\pi}{2}, 4\right)$, $(\pi, 0)$, $\left(\frac{3\pi}{2}, -4\right)$, $(2\pi, 0)$ **8.** Cosine curve through $(-2\pi, 4)$, $\left(\frac{-3\pi}{2}, 0\right)$, $(-\pi, -4)$, $\left(\frac{-\pi}{2}, 0\right)$, $(0, 4)$, $\left(\frac{\pi}{2}, 0\right)$, $(\pi, -4)$, $\left(\frac{3\pi}{2}, 0\right)$, $(2\pi, 4)$ **9.** Sine curve through $(-2\pi, 0)$, $\left(\frac{-3\pi}{2}, -2\right)$, $(-\pi, 0)$, $\left(\frac{-\pi}{2}, 2\right)$, $(0, 0)$, $\left(\frac{\pi}{2}, -2\right)$, $(\pi, 0)$, $\left(\frac{3\pi}{2}, 2\right)$, $(2\pi, 0)$ **10.** Sine curve through $(-2\pi, 0)$, $\left(\frac{-11\pi}{6}, 1\right)$, $\left(\frac{-3\pi}{2}, -1\right)$, $\left(\frac{-7\pi}{6}, 1\right)$, $\left(\frac{-5\pi}{6}, -1\right)$, $\left(\frac{-\pi}{2}, 1\right)$, $\left(\frac{-\pi}{6}, -1\right)$, $(0, 0)$, $\left(\frac{\pi}{6}, 1\right)$, $\left(\frac{\pi}{2}, -1\right)$, $\left(\frac{5\pi}{6}, 1\right)$, $\left(\frac{7\pi}{6}, -1\right)$, $\left(\frac{3\pi}{2}, 1\right)$, $\left(\frac{11\pi}{6}, -1\right)$, $(2\pi, 0)$ **11.** Cosine curve through $(-2\pi, 1)$ $\left(\frac{-5\pi}{3}, -1\right)$, $\left(\frac{-4\pi}{3}, 1\right)$, $(-\pi, -1)$, $\left(\frac{-2\pi}{3}, 1\right)$, $\left(\frac{-\pi}{3}, -1\right)$, $(0, 1)$, $\left(\frac{\pi}{3}, -1\right)$, $\left(\frac{2\pi}{3}, 1\right)$, $(\pi, -1)$, $\left(\frac{4\pi}{3}, 1\right)$, $\left(\frac{5\pi}{3}, -1\right)$, $(2\pi, 1)$ **12.** Sine curve through $(-2\pi, 0)$, $(-\pi, -1)$, $(0, 0)$,

$(\pi, 1)$, $(2\pi, 0)$ **13.** Cosine curve through $(-2\pi, -1)$, $(-\pi, 0)$, $(0, 1)$, $(\pi, 0)$, $(2\pi, -1)$ **14.** Sine curve through $(-3\pi, 0)$, $\left(\frac{-3\pi}{2}, 1\right)$, $(0, 0)$, $\left(\frac{3\pi}{2}, -1\right)$, $(3\pi, 0)$ **15.** Cosine curve through $(-3\pi, -1)$, $\left(\frac{-3\pi}{2}, 0\right)$, $(0, 1)$, $\left(\frac{3\pi}{2}, 0\right)$, $(3\pi, -1)$ **16.** Sine curve through $(-2\pi, 0)$, $\left(\frac{-7\pi}{4}, -1\right)$, $\left(\frac{-5\pi}{4}, 1\right)$, $\left(\frac{-3\pi}{4}, -1\right)$, $\left(\frac{-\pi}{4}, 1\right)$, $\left(\frac{\pi}{4}, -1\right)$, $\left(\frac{3\pi}{4}, 1\right)$, $\left(\frac{5\pi}{4}, -1\right)$, $\left(\frac{7\pi}{4}, 1\right)$, $(2\pi, 0)$ **17.** Cosine curve through $(-2\pi, 1)$, $\left(\frac{-3\pi}{2}, -1\right)$, $(-\pi, 1)$, $\left(\frac{-\pi}{2}, -1\right)$, $(0, 1)$, $\left(\frac{\pi}{2}, -1\right)$, $(\pi, 1)$, $\left(\frac{3\pi}{2}, -1\right)$, $(2\pi, 1)$ **18.** Sine curve through $(-2\pi, 0)$, $\left(\frac{-11\pi}{6}, -1\right)$, $\left(\frac{-3\pi}{2}, 1\right)$, $\left(\frac{-7\pi}{6}, -1\right)$, $\left(\frac{-5\pi}{6}, 1\right)$, $\left(\frac{-\pi}{2}, -1\right)$, $\left(\frac{-\pi}{6}, 1\right)$, $(0, 0)$, $\left(\frac{\pi}{6}, -1\right)$, $\left(\frac{\pi}{2}, 1\right)$, **19.** Sine curve through $(-2\pi, 0)$, $\left(\frac{-7\pi}{4}, 2\right)$, $\left(\frac{-5\pi}{4}, -2\right)$, $\left(\frac{-3\pi}{4}, 2\right)$, $\left(\frac{-\pi}{4}, -2\right)$, $(0, 0)$, $\left(\frac{\pi}{4}, 2\right)$, $\left(\frac{3\pi}{4}, -2\right)$, $\left(\frac{5\pi}{4}, 2\right)$, $\left(\frac{7\pi}{2}, -2\right)$, $(2\pi, 0)$ **20.** Cosine curve through $(-2\pi, 2)$, $\left(\frac{-7\pi}{4}, \frac{1}{2}\right)$, $\left(\frac{-5\pi}{4}, -\frac{1}{2}\right)$, $\left(\frac{-3\pi}{4}, \frac{1}{2}\right)$, $\left(\frac{-\pi}{4}, -\frac{1}{2}\right)$, $(0, 0)$, $\left(\frac{\pi}{4}, \frac{1}{2}\right)$, $\left(\frac{3\pi}{4}, -\frac{1}{2}\right)$, $(2\pi, 0)$ **21.** Sine curve through $(-2\pi, 0)$. $\left(\frac{-7\pi}{4}, \frac{1}{2}\right)$, $\left(\frac{-5\pi}{4}, -\frac{1}{2}\right)$, $\left(\frac{-3\pi}{4}, \frac{1}{2}\right)$, $\left(\frac{-\pi}{4}, -\frac{1}{2}\right)$, $(0, 0)$, $\left(\frac{\pi}{4}, \frac{1}{2}\right)$, $\left(\frac{3\pi}{4}, -\frac{1}{2}\right)$, $\left(\frac{5\pi}{4}, \frac{1}{2}\right)$, $\left(\frac{7\pi}{4}, -\frac{1}{2}\right)$, $(2\pi, 0)$ **22.** Cosine curve through $\left(-2\pi, \frac{1}{2}\right)$, $\left(\frac{-3\pi}{2}, -\frac{1}{2}\right)$, $\left(-\pi, \frac{1}{2}\right)$, $\left(-2\pi, \frac{1}{2}\right)$, $\left(0, \frac{1}{2}\right)$, $\left(\frac{\pi}{2}, -\frac{1}{2}\right)$, $\left(\pi, \frac{1}{2}\right)$, $\left(\frac{3\pi}{2}, -\frac{1}{2}\right)$, $\left(2\pi, \frac{1}{2}\right)$ **23.** Sine curve through $(-2\pi, 0)$, $(-\pi, 2)$, $(0, 0)$, $(\pi, -2)$, $(2\pi, 0)$ **24.** Cosine curve through $(-2\pi, 2)$, $(-\pi, 0)$, $(0, -2)$, $(\pi, 0)$, $(2\pi, 2)$ **25.** Sine curve through $(-2\pi, 0)$, $\left(\frac{-7\pi}{4}, -\frac{1}{2}\right)$, $\left(\frac{-5\pi}{4}, \frac{1}{2}\right)$, $\left(\frac{-3\pi}{4}, -\frac{1}{2}\right)$, $\left(\frac{-\pi}{4}, \frac{1}{2}\right)$, $(0, 0)$, $\left(\frac{\pi}{4}, -\frac{1}{2}\right)$, $\left(\frac{3\pi}{4}, \frac{1}{2}\right)$, $\left(\frac{5\pi}{4}, -\frac{1}{2}\right)$, $\left(\frac{7\pi}{4}, \frac{1}{2}\right)$, $(2\pi, 0)$ **26.** Cosine curve through $\left(-2\pi, \frac{1}{2}\right)$, $\left(\frac{-3\pi}{2}, -\frac{1}{2}\right)$, $\left(-\pi, \frac{1}{2}\right)$, $\left(\frac{-\pi}{2}, -\frac{1}{2}\right)$, $\left(0, \frac{1}{2}\right)$, $\left(\frac{\pi}{2}, -\frac{1}{2}\right)$, $\left(\pi, \frac{1}{2}\right)$, $\left(\frac{3\pi}{2}, -\frac{1}{2}\right)$, $\left(2\pi, \frac{1}{2}\right)$ **27.** Sine curve through $(-2\pi, 0)$, $\left(\frac{-7\pi}{4}, \frac{1}{2}\right)$, $\left(\frac{-5\pi}{4}, -\frac{1}{2}\right)$, $\left(\frac{-3\pi}{4}, \frac{1}{2}\right)$, $\left(\frac{-\pi}{4}, -\frac{1}{2}\right)$, $(0, 0)$, $\left(\frac{\pi}{4}, \frac{1}{2}\right)$, $\left(\frac{3\pi}{4}, -\frac{1}{2}\right)$, $\left(\frac{5\pi}{4}, \frac{1}{2}\right)$, $\left(\frac{7\pi}{4}, -\frac{1}{2}\right)$, $(2\pi, 0)$ **28.** Cosine curve through $(-2\pi, -1)$, $\left(\frac{-3\pi}{2}, 1\right)$, $(-\pi, -1)$, $\left(\frac{-\pi}{2}, 1\right)$, $(0, -1)$, $\left(\frac{\pi}{2}, 1\right)$, $(\pi, -1)$, $\left(\frac{3\pi}{2}, 1\right)$, $(2\pi, -1)$

29. Sine curve through $(-2\pi,\ 0)$, $\left(\frac{-7\pi}{4},\ -1\right), \left(\frac{-5\pi}{4},\ 1\right), \left(\frac{-3\pi}{4},\ -1\right), \left(\frac{-\pi}{4},\ 1\right)$, $(0,\ 0), \left(\frac{\pi}{4},\ -1\right), \left(\frac{3\pi}{4},\ 1\right), \left(\frac{5\pi}{4},\ -1\right), \left(\frac{7\pi}{4},\ 1\right)$, $(2\pi,\ 0)$ **30.** Sine curve through $(-2\pi,\ 2)$, $\left(\frac{-3\pi}{2},\ 3\right), (-\pi,\ 2), \left(\frac{-\pi}{2},\ 1\right), (0,\ 2), \left(\frac{\pi}{2},\ 3\right)$, $(\pi,\ 2), \left(\frac{3\pi}{2},\ 1\right), (2\pi,\ 2)$ **31.** Sine curve through $(0,\ 2), \left(\frac{\pi}{4},\ 0\right), \left(\frac{\pi}{2},\ 2\right), \left(\frac{3\pi}{4},\ 4\right), (\pi,\ 2)$ **32.** Sine curve through $(-2\pi,\ -3)$, $\left(-\pi,\ -2\frac{1}{2}\right), (0,\ -3), \left(\pi,\ -3\frac{1}{2}\right), (2\pi,\ -3)$

Page 665
EXERCISE SET 15–7

33. $\tan x = -7$ or $\tan x = 3$ **34.** $\sec\theta = 5$ or $\sec\theta = 2$ **35.** $\sin\theta = \frac{3}{4}$ or $\sin\theta = -\frac{1}{2}$
36. $\cos x = -\frac{1}{3}$ or $\cos x = -\frac{5}{2}$ **37.** $\cot x = -10$ or $\cot x = 1$ **38.** $\csc\theta = -5$ or $\csc\theta = 2$ **39.** $\sin\theta = 3$ or $\sin\theta = -2$
40. $\sin x = -\frac{1}{2}$ or $\sin x = 2$ **41.** $\tan\theta = 3 \pm \sqrt{13}$ **42.** $\csc x = \frac{3 \pm \sqrt{41}}{4}$
43. $\frac{1}{\sin\theta} - \cos\theta\,\frac{\cos\theta}{\sin\theta} = \frac{1 - \cos^2\theta}{\sin\theta} = \frac{\sin^2\theta}{\sin\theta}$ $= \sin\theta$ **44.** $\frac{1}{\cos\theta} - \sin\theta\,\frac{\sin\theta}{\cos\theta} = \frac{1 - \sin^2\theta}{\cos^2\theta}$ $= \frac{\cos^2}{\cos\theta} = \cos\theta$ **45.** $(1 - \sin\theta)(1 + \sin\theta)$ $= \cos^2\theta,\ 1 - \sin^2\theta = \cos^2\theta,\ \cos^2\theta = \cos^2\theta$
46. $(1 - \cos\theta)(1 + \cos\theta) = \sin^2\theta,\ 1 - \cos^2\theta$ $= \sin^2\theta,\ \sin^2\theta = \sin^2\theta$

Pages 667–668
CHAPTER 15 REVIEW

34. Cosine curve with amplitude 3 through $(-2\pi,\ 3), \left(-\frac{3}{2}\pi,\ 0\right), (-\pi,\ -3), \left(-\frac{\pi}{2},\ 0\right)$, $(0,\ 3), \left(\frac{\pi}{2},\ 0\right), (\pi,\ -3), \left(\frac{3}{2}\pi,\ 0\right), (2\pi,\ 3)$
35. Sine curve with period π through $(2\pi,\ 0), \left(-\frac{7}{4}\pi,\ 1\right), \left(-\frac{5}{4}\pi,\ -1\right), \left(-\frac{3}{4}\pi,\ -1\right)$, $\left(-\frac{\pi}{4},\ -1\right), (0,\ 0), \left(\frac{\pi}{4},\ 1\right), \left(\frac{3}{4}\pi,\ -1\right), \left(\frac{5}{4}\pi,\ 1\right)$, $\left(\frac{7}{4}\pi,\ -1\right), (2\pi,\ 0)$

Pages 668–669
CHAPTER 15 TEST

2. $\cos\theta = \frac{2}{\sqrt{5}}$, $\tan\theta = \frac{1}{2}$, $\cot\theta = 2$, $\sec\theta = \frac{\sqrt{5}}{2}$, $\csc\theta = \sqrt{5}$ **3.** $\sin\theta = \frac{-8}{17}$, $\cos\theta = \frac{15}{17}$, $\tan\theta = \frac{-8}{15}$, $\cot\theta = \frac{15}{-8}$, $\sec\theta = \frac{17}{15}$, $\csc\theta = \frac{17}{-8}$
10. $38° \ 45'$

Page 669
READY FOR CHAPTER 16?

3. $\frac{\sqrt[3]{100mn^2}}{5n}$ **5.** $f^{-1}(x) = \frac{x+2}{3}$ **7.** $\sqrt{a^2 + b^2}$

Chapter 16   Page 676
EXERCISE SET 16–1

47. $\sin\frac{\pi}{2}\cos x - \cos\frac{\pi}{2}\sin x = 1\cdot\cos x - 0\cdot\sin x = \cos x$ **48.** $-\cos x$
49. $\cos\frac{\pi}{2}\cos x + \sin\frac{\pi}{2}\sin x = 0 + \sin x = \sin x$ **50.** $-\sin x$ **55.** $\sin(\sin x)$ $\cos(\sin y) + \cos(\sin x)\sin(\sin y)$
56. $\cos(\cos x)\cos(\cos y) - \sin(\cos x)$ $\sin(\cos y)$ **57.** $\sin x\cos y\cos z + \cos x$ $\sin y\cos z + \cos x\cos y\sin z - \sin x\sin y$ $\cos z$

Page 684
EXERCISE SET 16–3

1. $\csc x - \cos x\cot x\ \ \sin x$

$$\begin{array}{c|c}
\dfrac{1}{\sin x} - \cos x\,\dfrac{\cos x}{\sin x} & \sin x \\[2mm]
\dfrac{1 - \cos^2 x}{\sin x} & \\[2mm]
\dfrac{\sin^2 x}{\sin x} & \\[2mm]
\sin x &
\end{array}$$

2. $\sec x - \sin x\tan x\ \ \cos x$

$$\begin{array}{c|c}
\dfrac{1}{\cos x} - \sin x\,\dfrac{\sin x}{\cos x} & \cos x \\[2mm]
\dfrac{1 - \sin^2 x}{\cos x} & \\[2mm]
\dfrac{\cos^2 x}{\cos x} & \\[2mm]
\cos x &
\end{array}$$

3. $\dfrac{1 + \cos\theta}{\sin\theta} + \dfrac{\sin\theta}{\cos\theta} \qquad \dfrac{\cos\theta + 1}{\sin\theta\cos\theta}$

$$\begin{array}{c|c}
\dfrac{1 + \cos\theta}{\sin\theta}\cdot\dfrac{\cos\theta}{\cos\theta} + \dfrac{\sin\theta}{\cos\theta}\cdot\dfrac{\sin\theta}{\sin\theta} & \dfrac{\cos\theta + 1}{\sin\theta\cos\theta} \\[2mm]
\dfrac{\cos\theta + \cos^2\theta + \sin^2\theta}{\sin\theta\cos\theta} & \\[2mm]
\dfrac{\cos\theta + 1}{\sin\theta\cos\theta} &
\end{array}$$

4. $\dfrac{1}{\sin\theta\cos\theta} - \dfrac{\cos\theta}{\sin\theta} \qquad \dfrac{\sin\theta\cos\theta}{1 - \sin^2\theta}$

$$\begin{array}{c|c}
\dfrac{1}{\sin\theta\cos\theta} - \dfrac{\cos\theta}{\sin\theta}\cdot\dfrac{\cos\theta}{\cos\theta} & \dfrac{\sin\theta\cos\theta}{\cos^2\theta} \\[2mm]
\dfrac{1 - \cos^2\theta}{\sin\theta\cos\theta} & \dfrac{\sin\theta}{\cos\theta} \\[2mm]
\dfrac{\sin^2\theta}{\sin\theta\cos\theta} & \\[2mm]
\dfrac{\sin\theta}{\cos\theta} &
\end{array}$$

5.

$$\frac{1-\sin x}{\cos x} \qquad\qquad \frac{\cos x}{1+\sin x}$$

$$\frac{1-\sin x}{\cos x}\cdot\frac{\cos x}{\cos x} \qquad \frac{\cos x}{1+\sin x}\cdot\frac{1-\sin x}{1-\sin x}$$

$$\frac{\cos x-\sin x\cos x}{\cos^2 x} \qquad \frac{\cos x-\cos x\sin x}{1-\sin^2 x}$$

$$\qquad\qquad\qquad \frac{\cos x-\sin x\cos x}{\cos^2 x}$$

6.

$$\frac{1-\cos x}{\sin x} \qquad\qquad \frac{\sin x}{1+\cos x}$$

$$\frac{1-\cos x}{\sin x}\cdot\frac{\sin x}{\sin x} \qquad \frac{\sin x}{1+\cos x}\cdot\frac{1-\cos x}{1-\cos x}$$

$$\frac{\sin x-\cos x\sin x}{\sin^2 x} \qquad \frac{\sin x-\sin x\cos x}{1-\cos^2 x}$$

$$\qquad\qquad\qquad \frac{\sin x-\cos x\sin x}{\sin^2 x}$$

7.

$$\frac{1+\tan\theta}{1+\cot\theta} \qquad \frac{\sec\theta}{\csc\theta}$$

$$\frac{1+\dfrac{\sin\theta}{\cos\theta}}{1+\dfrac{\cos\theta}{\sin\theta}} \qquad \frac{\dfrac{1}{\cos\theta}}{\dfrac{1}{\sin\theta}}$$

$$\frac{\dfrac{\cos\theta+\sin\theta}{\cos\theta}}{\dfrac{\sin\theta+\cos\theta}{\sin\theta}} \qquad \frac{\sin\theta}{\cos\theta}$$

$$\frac{\sin\theta}{\cos\theta}$$

8.

$$\frac{\cot\theta-1}{1-\tan\theta} \qquad \frac{\csc\theta}{\sec\theta}$$

$$\frac{\dfrac{\cos\theta}{\sin\theta}-1}{1-\dfrac{\sin\theta}{\cos\theta}} \qquad \frac{\dfrac{1}{\sin\theta}}{\dfrac{1}{\cos\theta}}$$

$$\frac{\dfrac{\cos\theta-\sin\theta}{\sin\theta}}{\dfrac{\cos\theta-\sin\theta}{\cos\theta}} \qquad \frac{\cos\theta}{\sin\theta}$$

9.

$$\frac{\sin x+\cos x}{\sec x+\csc x} \qquad \frac{\sin x}{\sec x}$$

$$\frac{\sin x+\cos x}{\dfrac{1}{\cos x}+\dfrac{1}{\sin x}} \qquad \frac{\sin x}{\dfrac{1}{\cos x}}$$

$$\frac{\sin x+\cos x}{\dfrac{\sin x+\cos x}{\cos x\sin x}} \qquad \cos x\sin x$$

$$\cos x\sin x$$

10.

$$\frac{\sin x-\cos x}{\sec x-\csc x} \qquad \frac{\cos x}{\csc x}$$

$$\frac{\sin x-\cos x}{\dfrac{1}{\cos x}+\dfrac{1}{\sin x}} \qquad \frac{\cos x}{\dfrac{1}{\sin x}}$$

$$\frac{\sin x-\cos x}{\dfrac{\sin x-\cos x}{\cos x\sin x}} \qquad \cos x\sin x$$

$$\cos x\sin x$$

11.

$$\frac{1+\tan\theta}{1-\tan\theta}+\frac{1+\cot\theta}{1-\cot\theta} \qquad 0$$

$$\frac{1+\dfrac{\sin\theta}{\cos\theta}}{1-\dfrac{\sin\theta}{\cos\theta}}+\frac{1+\dfrac{\cos\theta}{\sin\theta}}{1-\dfrac{\cos\theta}{\sin\theta}} \qquad 0$$

$$\frac{\dfrac{\cos\theta+\sin\theta}{\cos\theta}}{\dfrac{\cos\theta-\sin\theta}{\cos\theta}}+\frac{\dfrac{\sin\theta+\cos\theta}{\sin\theta}}{\dfrac{\sin\theta-\cos\theta}{\sin\theta}}$$

$$\frac{\cos\theta+\sin\theta}{\cos\theta-\sin\theta}+\frac{\sin\theta+\cos\theta}{\sin\theta-\cos\theta}$$

$$\frac{\cos\theta+\sin\theta}{\cos\theta-\sin\theta}-\frac{\cos\theta+\sin\theta}{\cos\theta-\sin\theta}$$

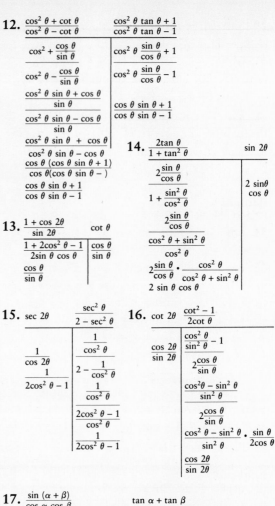

12.

$$\frac{\cos^2\theta+\cot\theta}{\cos^2\theta-\cot\theta} \qquad \frac{\cos^2\theta\tan\theta+1}{\cos^2\theta\tan\theta-1}$$

$$\frac{\cos^2+\dfrac{\cos\theta}{\sin\theta}}{\cos^2\theta-\dfrac{\cos\theta}{\sin\theta}} \qquad \frac{\cos^2\theta\dfrac{\sin\theta}{\cos\theta}+1}{\cos^2\theta\dfrac{\sin\theta}{\cos\theta}-1}$$

$$\frac{\dfrac{\cos^2\theta\sin\theta+\cos\theta}{\sin\theta}}{\dfrac{\cos^2\theta\sin\theta-\cos\theta}{\sin\theta}} \qquad \frac{\cos\theta\sin\theta+1}{\cos\theta\sin\theta-1}$$

$$\frac{\cos^2\theta\sin\theta+\cos\theta}{\cos^2\theta\sin\theta-\cos\theta}$$

$$\frac{\cos\theta(\cos\theta\sin\theta+1)}{\cos\theta(\cos\theta\sin\theta-)}$$

$$\frac{\cos\theta\sin\theta+1}{\cos\theta\sin\theta-1}$$

13.

$$\frac{1+\cos 2\theta}{\sin 2\theta} \qquad \cot\theta$$

$$\frac{1+2\cos^2\theta-1}{2\sin\theta\cos\theta} \qquad \frac{\cos\theta}{\sin\theta}$$

$$\frac{\cos\theta}{\sin\theta}$$

14.

$$\frac{2\tan\theta}{1+\tan^2\theta} \qquad\qquad \sin 2\theta$$

$$\frac{2\dfrac{\sin\theta}{\cos\theta}}{1+\dfrac{\sin^2\theta}{\cos^2\theta}} \qquad\qquad 2\sin\theta\cos\theta$$

$$\frac{2\dfrac{\sin\theta}{\cos\theta}}{\dfrac{\cos^2\theta+\sin^2\theta}{\cos^2\theta}}$$

$$2\frac{\sin\theta}{\cos\theta}\cdot\frac{\cos^2\theta}{\cos^2\theta+\sin^2\theta}$$

$$2\sin\theta\cos\theta$$

15.

$$\sec 2\theta \qquad \frac{\sec^2\theta}{2-\sec^2\theta}$$

$$\frac{1}{\cos 2\theta} \qquad \frac{\dfrac{1}{\cos^2\theta}}{2-\dfrac{1}{\cos^2\theta}}$$

$$\frac{1}{2\cos^2\theta-1} \qquad \frac{\dfrac{1}{\cos^2\theta}}{\dfrac{2\cos^2\theta-1}{\cos^2\theta}}$$

$$\frac{1}{2\cos^2\theta-1}$$

16.

$$\cot 2\theta \qquad \frac{\cot^2\theta-1}{2\cot\theta}$$

$$\frac{\cos 2\theta}{\sin 2\theta} \qquad \frac{\dfrac{\cos^2\theta}{\sin^2\theta}-1}{2\dfrac{\cos\theta}{\sin\theta}}$$

$$\frac{\dfrac{\cos^2\theta-\sin^2\theta}{\sin^2\theta}}{2\dfrac{\cos\theta}{\sin\theta}}$$

$$\frac{\cos^2\theta-\sin^2\theta}{\sin^2\theta}\cdot\frac{\sin\theta}{2\cos\theta}$$

$$\frac{\cos 2\theta}{\sin 2\theta}$$

17.

$$\frac{\sin(\alpha+\beta)}{\cos\alpha\cos\beta} \qquad\qquad \tan\alpha+\tan\beta$$

$$\frac{\sin\alpha\cos\beta+\cos\alpha\sin\beta}{\cos\alpha\cos\beta} \qquad \frac{\sin\alpha}{\cos\alpha}+\frac{\sin\beta}{\cos\beta}$$

$$\qquad\qquad\qquad \frac{\sin\alpha\cos\beta+\cos\alpha\sin\beta}{\cos\alpha\cos\beta}$$

18.

$$\frac{\cos(\alpha-\beta)}{\cos\alpha\sin\beta} \qquad\qquad \tan\alpha+\cot\beta$$

$$\frac{\cos\alpha\cos\beta+\sin\alpha\sin\beta}{\cos\alpha\sin\beta} \qquad \frac{\sin\alpha}{\cos\alpha}+\frac{\cos\beta}{\sin\beta}$$

$$\frac{\sin\alpha\sin\beta+\cos\alpha\cos\beta}{\cos\alpha\sin\beta} \qquad \frac{\sin\alpha\sin\beta+\cos\alpha\cos\beta}{\cos\alpha\sin\beta}$$

19.

$$1-\cos 5\theta\cos 3\theta-\sin 5\theta\sin 3\theta \qquad 2\sin^2\theta$$

$$1-(\cos 5\theta\cos 3\theta+\sin 5\theta\sin 3\theta) \qquad 2\cdot\frac{1-\cos 2\theta}{2}$$

$$1-\cos(5\theta-3\theta)$$

$$1-\cos 2\theta \qquad\qquad\qquad 1-\cos 2\theta$$

20.

$$2\sin\theta\cos^3\theta+2\sin^3\theta\cos\theta \qquad \sin 2\theta$$

$$2\sin\cos\theta(\cos^2\theta+\sin^2\theta) \qquad 2\sin\theta\cos\theta$$

$$2\sin\theta\cos\theta(1)$$

$$2\sin\theta\cos\theta$$

21.

$$\frac{\dfrac{\tan\theta + \sin\theta}{2\tan\theta}}{} \quad \left| \cos^2\dfrac{\theta}{2} \right.$$

$$\frac{\dfrac{\sin\theta}{\cos\theta} + \sin\theta}{2\dfrac{\sin\theta}{\cos\theta}} \quad \left| \dfrac{1 + \cos\theta}{2} \right.$$

$$\frac{\dfrac{\sin\theta + \sin\theta\cos\theta}{\cos\theta}}{2\dfrac{\sin\theta}{\cos\theta}}$$

$$\frac{\sin\theta + \sin\theta\cos\theta}{2\sin\theta}$$

$$\frac{1 + \cos\theta}{2}$$

22.

$$\frac{\dfrac{\tan\theta - \sin\theta}{2\tan\theta}}{} \quad \left| \sin^2\dfrac{\theta}{2} \right.$$

$$\frac{\dfrac{\sin\theta}{\cos\theta} - \sin\theta}{2\dfrac{\sin\theta}{\cos\theta}} \quad \left| \dfrac{1 - \cos\theta}{2} \right.$$

$$\frac{\dfrac{\sin\theta - \sin\theta\cos\theta}{\cos\theta}}{2\dfrac{\sin\theta}{\cos\theta}}$$

$$\frac{1 - \cos\theta}{2}$$

23.

$$\frac{\cos^4 x - \sin^4 x}{} \quad \left| \cos 2x \right.$$
$$(\cos^2 x - \sin^2 x)(\cos^2 x + \sin^2 x) \quad \left| \cos^2 x - \sin^2 x \right.$$
$$\cos^2 x - \sin^2 x$$

24.

$$\frac{\dfrac{\cos^4 x - \sin^4 x}{1 - \tan^4 x}}{} \quad \left| \cos^4 x \right.$$

$$\frac{\dfrac{\cos^4 x - \sin^4 x}{1 - \dfrac{\sin^4 x}{\cos^4 x}}}{} \quad \left| \cos^4 x \right.$$

$$\frac{\dfrac{\cos^4 x - \sin^4 x}{\dfrac{\cos^4 x - \sin^4 x}{\cos^4 x}}}{}$$

$$\cos^4 x$$

25.

$$\frac{\dfrac{\tan 3\theta - \tan\theta}{1 + \tan 3\theta\tan\theta}}{} \quad \left| \dfrac{2\tan\theta}{1 - \tan^2\theta} \right.$$

$$\tan(3\theta - \theta) \quad \left| \tan 2\theta \right.$$

$$\tan 2\theta$$

26.

$$\frac{\left(\dfrac{1 + \tan\theta}{1 - \tan\theta}\right)^2}{} \quad \left| \dfrac{1 + \sin 2\theta}{1 - \sin 2\theta} \right.$$

$$\frac{\left(\dfrac{\cos\theta + \sin\theta}{\cos\theta - \sin\theta}\right)^2}{} \quad \left| \dfrac{1 + \sin 2\theta}{1 - \sin 2\theta} \right.$$

$$\frac{\sin^2\theta + 2\sin\theta\cos\theta + \cos^2\theta}{\sin^2\theta - 2\sin\theta\cos\theta + \cos^2\theta}$$

$$\frac{1 + \sin 2\theta}{1 - \sin 2\theta}$$

27.

$$\frac{\sin(\alpha + \beta)\sin(\alpha - \beta)}{}$$
$$(\sin\alpha\cos\beta + \cos\alpha\sin\beta)(\sin\alpha\cos\beta - \cos\alpha\sin\beta)$$
$$\sin^2\alpha\cos^2\beta - \cos^2\alpha\sin^2\beta$$
$$\sin^2\alpha(1 - \sin^2\beta) - (1 - \sin^2\alpha)(\sin^2\beta)$$
$$\sin^2\alpha - \sin^2\alpha\sin^2\beta - \sin^2\beta + \sin^2\alpha\sin^2\beta$$
$$\sin^2\alpha - \sin^2\beta$$

28.

$$\frac{\cos(\alpha + \beta)\cos(\alpha - \beta)}{}$$
$$(\cos\alpha\cos\beta - \sin\alpha\sin\beta)(\cos\alpha\cos\beta + \sin\alpha\sin\beta)$$
$$\cos^2\alpha\cos^2\beta - \sin^2\alpha\sin^2\beta$$
$$\cos^2\alpha(1 - \sin^2\beta) - (1 - \cos^2\alpha)\sin^2\beta$$
$$\cos^2\alpha - \cos^2\alpha\sin^2\beta - \sin^2\beta + \cos^2\alpha\sin^2\beta$$
$$\cos^2\alpha - \sin^2\beta$$

29.

$$\frac{\cos(\alpha + \beta) + \cos(\alpha - \beta)}{}$$
$$(\cos\alpha\cos\beta - \sin\alpha\sin\beta) + (\cos\alpha\cos\beta + \sin\alpha\sin\beta)$$
$$2\cos\alpha\cos\beta$$

30.

$$\frac{\sin(\alpha + \beta) + \sin(\alpha - \beta)}{}$$
$$(\sin\alpha\cos\beta + \cos\alpha\sin\beta) + (\sin\alpha\cos\beta - \cos\alpha\sin\beta)$$
$$2\sin\alpha\cos\beta$$

31. $\begin{pmatrix} \cos x & \sin x \\ -\sin x & \cos x \end{pmatrix} = \cos^2 x + \sin^2 x = 1,$

$\begin{pmatrix} \cos x & -\sin x \\ \sin x & \cos x \end{pmatrix} = \cos^2 x + \sin^2 x = 1$

Page 685
TRY THIS

1.

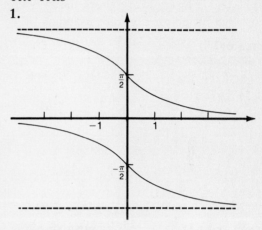

Pages 687-688
EXERCISE SET 16-4

1. $\frac{\pi}{4} + 2k\pi, \frac{3\pi}{4} + 2k\pi$ **2.** $\frac{\pi}{3} + 2k\pi,$
$\frac{2\pi}{3} + 2k\pi$ **3.** $\frac{\pi}{4} + 2k\pi, \frac{7\pi}{4} + 2k\pi$
4. $\frac{\pi}{6} + 2k\pi, \frac{11\pi}{6} + 2k\pi$ **5.** $\frac{\pi}{4} + k\pi$
6. $\frac{3\pi}{4} + k\pi$ **7.** $\frac{5\pi}{4} + 2k\pi, \frac{7\pi}{4} + 2k\pi$
8. $\frac{4\pi}{3} + 2k\pi, \frac{5\pi}{3} + 2k\pi$ **9.** $\frac{3\pi}{4} + 2k\pi,$
$\frac{5\pi}{4} + 2k\pi$ **10.** $\frac{5\pi}{6} + 2k\pi, \frac{7\pi}{6} + 2k\pi$
11. $\frac{\pi}{3} + k\pi$ **12.** $\frac{\pi}{6} + k\pi$ **13.** $\frac{\pi}{4} + k\pi$
14. $\frac{\pi}{6} + k\pi$ **15.** $\frac{5\pi}{6} + k\pi$ **16.** $\frac{2\pi}{3} + k\pi$
26. $23° + k360°, 157° + k360°$ **27.** $74°$
$+ k360°, 106° + k360°$ **28.** $39° + k360°,$
$141° + k360°$ **29.** $61° + k360°, 199°$
$+ k360°$ **30.** $36°58' + k360°, 323°02'$
$+ k360°$ **31.** $22°6' + k360°, 337°54'$
$+ k360°$ **32.** $21°25' + k360°, 338°35'$
$+ k360°$ **33.** $74°8' + k360°, 285°52'$
$+ k360°$ **34.** $20°10' + k180°$
35. $47°30' + k180°$ **36.** $38°20' + k180°$
37. $64°30' + k180°$ **38.** $31° + k360°,$

$329° + k360°$ **39.** $46° + k360°, 314°$
$+ k360°$ **40.** $9°10' + k360°, 170°50'$
$+ k360°$ **47.** The semicircle to the right of
the y-axis from (and including) $-\frac{\pi}{2}$ to (and
including) $\frac{\pi}{2}$ **48.** The semicircle above the
x-axis from (and including) to (and including)
π **49.** The semicircle to the right of the
y-axis from (not including) $-\frac{\pi}{2}$ to (not including) $\frac{\pi}{2}$ **50.** The semicircle above the x-axis
from (not including) 0 to (not including) π

Page 691
EXERCISE SET 16–5
1. $\frac{4\pi}{3}, \frac{5\pi}{3}$ **2.** $\frac{5\pi}{6}, \frac{11\pi}{6}$ **3.** $123°41', 303°41'$
4. $14°29', 165°31'$ **5.** $\frac{\pi}{6}, \frac{5\pi}{6}, \frac{7\pi}{6}, \frac{11\pi}{6}$
6. $\frac{\pi}{4}, \frac{3\pi}{4}, \frac{5\pi}{4}, \frac{7\pi}{4}$ **7.** $\frac{\pi}{6}, \frac{5\pi}{6}, \frac{3\pi}{2}$ **8.** $\frac{2\pi}{3}, \pi, \frac{4\pi}{3}$
9. 0   **10.** $\frac{3\pi}{2}$ **11.** $\frac{\pi}{6}, \frac{5\pi}{6}$ **12.** $\frac{\pi}{6}, \frac{5\pi}{6}$
13. $109°28', 120°, 240°, 250°32'$
14. $\frac{\pi}{6}, \frac{5\pi}{6}, \frac{3\pi}{2}$ **15.** $0, \frac{\pi}{2}, \pi, \frac{3\pi}{2}$ **16.** $\frac{\pi}{4}, \frac{\pi}{2}, \frac{5\pi}{4}, \frac{3\pi}{2}$
17. $0, \pi$ **18.** $0, \frac{2\pi}{3}, \pi, \frac{4\pi}{3}$ **19.** $\frac{3\pi}{2}, \frac{7\pi}{4}$
20. $\frac{\pi}{6}, \frac{\pi}{3}, \frac{5\pi}{6}, \frac{5\pi}{3}$ **21.** $\frac{\pi}{4}, \frac{\pi}{2}, \frac{3\pi}{4}, \frac{5\pi}{4}, \frac{3\pi}{2}, \frac{7\pi}{4}$
22. $0, \frac{\pi}{4}, \frac{3\pi}{4}, \pi, \frac{5\pi}{4}, \frac{7\pi}{4}$ **23.** $0, \frac{\pi}{2}, \pi, \frac{3\pi}{2}$
24. $0, \frac{\pi}{2}, \pi, \frac{3\pi}{2}$ **25.** 0   **26.** $0, \frac{\pi}{2}, \pi, \frac{3\pi}{2}$
27. $\frac{\pi}{6}, \frac{5\pi}{6}, \pi$ **28.** $\frac{2\pi}{3}, \frac{4\pi}{3}, \frac{3\pi}{2}$ **29.** $\frac{\pi}{6}, \frac{5\pi}{6}, \frac{7\pi}{6}, \frac{11\pi}{6}$
30. $\frac{\pi}{4}, \frac{3\pi}{4}, \frac{5\pi}{4}, \frac{7\pi}{4}$ **31.** $63°26', 243°26',$
$101°19', 281°19'$ **32.** $45°, 225°,$
$116°34', 296°34'$ **33.** $\frac{2\pi}{3}, \frac{4\pi}{3}$ **34.** $\frac{\pi}{6}, \frac{5\pi}{6}$
35. $\frac{\pi}{12}, \frac{5\pi}{12}$ **36.** $\frac{7\pi}{12}, \frac{23\pi}{12}$ **37.** $\frac{\pi}{6}, \frac{3\pi}{2}$ **38.** $\frac{7\pi}{4}$
39. $60°, 120°, 240°, 300°$ **40.** $60°,$
$120°, 240°, 300°$ **41.** $60°, 240°$
42. $3°35', 6°23', 173°37', 176°35'$
43. $30°$ **44.** 1

Pages 695–697
EXERCISE SET 16–6
1. $m\angle B = 53°50', b = 37.2, c = 46.1$
2. $m\angle B = 2°20', b = 0.40, c = 9.74$
3. $m\angle A = 77°20', a = 436.5, c = 447.4$
4. $m\angle A = 20°10', a = 46.6, c = 135.3$
5. $m\angle B = 72°40', a = 4.2, c = 14.2$
6. $m\angle B = 11°20', a = 6686, b = 6819$
7. $m\angle A = 66°50', b = 0.0148,$
$c = 0.0375$ **8.** $m\angle A = 20°40',$
$b = 0.0129, c = 0.0138$ **9.** $m\angle A$

$= 42°30', a = 35.6, b = 32.6$
10. $m\angle B = 1°10', a = 3949, b = 80.4$
11. $m\angle A = 7°40', a = 0.131, b = 0.973$
12. $m\angle A = 33°30', a = 0.0247,$
$b = 0.0373$ **13.** $c = 21.6, m\angle A = 33°40',$
$m\angle B = 56°20'$ **14.** $c = 22.4, m\angle A$
$= 22°30', m\angle B = 63°30'$ **15.** $b = 12.0,$
$m\angle A = 53°10', m\angle B = 36°50'$
16. $b = 42.4, m\angle A = 19°30', m\angle B$
$= 70°30'$ **17.** $a = 3.57, m\angle A = 63°20',$
$m\angle B = 26°40'$ **18.** $a = 439, m\angle A$
$= 77°10', m\angle B = 12°50'$ **37.** Area
$= \frac{1}{2}ab = \frac{1}{2}\frac{c^2}{c^2}ab = \frac{1}{2}c^2\frac{a}{c}\frac{b}{c} = \frac{1}{2}c^2 \sin A \cos A$
$= \frac{1}{4}c^2 2 \sin A \cos a = \frac{1}{4}c^2 \sin 2A$
38. Area $= \frac{ab}{2}, \frac{a}{c} = \sin A, a = c \sin A.$
Substituting, Area $= \frac{bc}{2} \sin A$ **40.** $d = 40\sqrt{5h},$
where d and h are in miles; 38.9 miles
41. $C = L - H; d^2 = L^2 - H^2$
$= (L + H)(L - H) = C(L + H); C = \frac{d^2}{L + H} \approx \frac{d^2}{2L}$

Page 702–703
EXERCISE SET 16–7
1. $m\angle C = 50°, a = 18.4, c = 16.3$
2. $m\angle C = 70°, a = 29.5, c = 37.3$
3. $m\angle C = 96°, b = 15.2, c = 20.3$
4. $m\angle C = 80°, a = 74.2, c = 114$
5. $m\angle C = 17°, a = 26.3, c = 10.5$
6. $m\angle A = 30°, b = 27.7, c = 16.0$
7. $m\angle A = 121°, a = 33.4, c = 14.0$
8. $m\angle B = 26°, a = 17.2, c = 8.91$
9. $m\angle B = 68°50', a = 32.3, b = 32.3$
10. $m\angle A = 16°, a = 13.2, c = 34.2$
11. $m\angle A = 12°20', m\angle C = 17°40',$
$c = 4.25$ **12.** $m\angle C = 48°40',$
$m\angle B = 101°20', b = 11.8$ or
$m\angle C = 131°20', m\angle B = 18°40',$
$b = 3.84$ **13.** $m\angle A = 20°20',$
$m\angle B = 99°40', b = 34.1$
14. $m\angle A = 38°40', m\angle C = 96°20',$
$c = 23.9$ **15.** $m\angle B = 56°20',$
$m\angle C = 87°40', c = 40.8$ or
$m\angle B = 123°40', m\angle C = 20°20',$
$c = 14.2$ **16.** $m\angle B = 41°10',$

$m\angle A = 95°50'$, $a = 40.8$
17. $m\angle C = 44°40'$, $m\angle B = 19°$,
$b = 6.25$ 18. $m\angle B = 28°30'$,
$m\angle C = 103°40'$, $c = 37.1$
19. $m\angle B = 44°20'$, $m\angle A = 74°30'$,
$a = 33.3$ 20. $m\angle A = 41°10'$,
$m\angle C = 80°10'$, $c = 37.6$ 31. Area $= bh$,
$h = a \sin \theta$, so Area $= ab \sin \theta$ 32. Area
$= \frac{1}{2}bd \sin \theta + \frac{1}{2}ac \sin \theta + \frac{1}{2}ad \sin (180° - \theta)$
$+ \frac{1}{2}bc \sin (180° - \theta) = \frac{1}{2}(bd + ac + ad + bc)$
$\sin \theta = \frac{1}{2}(a + b)(c + d) \sin \theta$ 33. Suppose
that objects at A and B are moving as
shown, with velocities v_a and v_b, and paths
intersecting at P. Let θ be the bearing from
A to B, assumed constant.

Pages 706–707
EXERCISE SET 16–8
1. $c = 12.0$, $m\angle A = 20°40'$,
$m\angle B = 24°20'$ 2. $a = 47.6$,
$m\angle B = 35°50'$, $m\angle C = 28°10'$
3. $a = 14.9$, $m\angle B = 23°40'$,
$m\angle C = 126°20'$ 4. $c = 11.4$,
$m\angle A = 22°20'$, $m\angle B = 37°40'$
5. $a = 24.8$, $m\angle B = 20°40'$,
$m\angle C = 26°20'$ 6. $c = 13.7$,
$m\angle A = 71°30'$, $m\angle B = 48°30'$
7. $b = 74.8$, $m\angle A = 95°30'$,
$m\angle C = 11°50'$ 8. $a = 55.6$,
$m\angle B = 149°30'$, $m\angle C = 6°$
9. $m\angle A = 29°$, $m\angle B = 46°30'$,
$m\angle C = 104°30'$ 10. $m\angle A = 42°50'$,
$m\angle B = 61°$, $m\angle C = 76°10'$
11. $m\angle A = 34°50'$,
$m\angle B = 58°50'$, $m\angle C = 86°20'$
12. $m\angle A = 44°$, $m\angle B = 52°40'$,
$m\angle C = 83°20'$ 13. $m\angle A = 36°10'$,
$m\angle B = 43°30'$, $m\angle C = 100°20'$
14. $m\angle A = 37°20'$, $m\angle B = 37°20'$,
$m\angle C = 105°20'$ 15. $m\angle A = 73°40'$,
$m\angle B = 51°50'$, $m\angle C = 54°30'$
16. $m\angle A = 24°10'$, $m\angle B = 30°40'$,
$m\angle C = 125°10'$ 17. $m\angle A = 25°40'$,
$m\angle B = 126°$, $m\angle C = 28°20'$

18. $m\angle A = 33°40'$, $m\angle B = 107°$,
$m\angle C = 39°20'$ 33. Add the three
equations in Theorem 16–6.   34. $\frac{\cos A}{a}$
$+ \frac{\cos B}{b} + \frac{\cos C}{c} = \frac{bc \cos A + ac \cos B + ab \cos C}{abc}$
$= \frac{2(bc \cos A + ac \cos B + ab \cos C)}{2abc} = \frac{a^2 + b^2 + c^2}{2abc}$

Page 720
TRY THIS
7. $\sqrt{2}$ cis $45°$ and $\sqrt{2}$ cis $225°$ or $1 + i$ and
$1 - i$

Page 721
EXERCISE SET 16–11
45. $-8 - 8i\sqrt{3}$ 46. $-8 + 8i\sqrt{3}$ 47. -8
$- 8i\sqrt{3}$ 48. -64 49. i 50. -1
51. 1 52. $\frac{1}{2} - \frac{\sqrt{3}}{2}i$ 53. $\sqrt{2}$ cis $60°$ and
$\sqrt{2}$ cis $240°$ or $\sqrt{2}$ cis$\frac{\pi}{3}$ and $\sqrt{2}$ cis$\frac{4\pi}{3}$
54. $\sqrt{2}$ cis $105°$ and $\sqrt{2}$ cis $285°$ or $\sqrt{2}$ cis
$\frac{7\pi}{12}$ and $\sqrt{2}$ cis$\frac{19\pi}{12}$ 55. cis $30°$, cis $150°$,
and cis $270°$ or cis$\frac{\pi}{6}$, cis$\frac{5\pi}{6}$, and cis$\frac{3\pi}{2}$
56. cis $90°$, cis $210°$, and cis $330°$ or cis$\frac{\pi}{2}$,
cis$\frac{7\pi}{6}$, and cis$\frac{11\pi}{6}$ 57. 2 cis $0°$, 2 cis $90°$,
2 cis $180°$, and 2 cis $270°$ or 2 cis 0, 2
cis$\frac{\pi}{2}$, 2 cis π, and 2 cis $\frac{3\pi}{2}$ 58. 2 cis $45°$,
2 cis $135°$, 2 cis $225°$, and 2 cis $315°$ or
2 cis$\frac{\pi}{4}$, 2 cis$\frac{3\pi}{4}$, 2 cis$\frac{5\pi}{4}$, and 2 cis$\frac{7\pi}{4}$
59. $(1 + 0i)^3 = (\text{cis } 0)^3 = \text{cis } 0 = 1$,
$\left(-\frac{1}{2} + \frac{\sqrt{3}}{2}i\right)^3 = (\text{cis } 120)^3 = \text{cis } 0 = 1$,
$\left(-\frac{1}{2} - \frac{\sqrt{3}}{2}i\right) = (\text{cis } 240)^3 = \text{cis } 0 = 1$
60. cis $60°$, cis $180°$, cis $300°$ or $\frac{1}{2} + \frac{\sqrt{3}}{2}i$,
-1, $\frac{1}{2} - \frac{\sqrt{3}}{2}i$ 61. cis $90°$, cis $180°$, cis
$270°$, cis 0, or ± 1, $\pm i$ 62. $|z \cdot w|$
$= |r_1 r_2 \text{ cis } (\theta_1 + \theta_2)| = |r_1 r_2 \cos (\theta_1 + \theta_2)$
$+ r_1 r_2 i \sin (\theta_1 + \theta_2)| =$
$\overline{\sqrt{r_1^2 r_2^2 \cos^2 (\theta_1 + \theta_2) + r_1^2 r_2^2 \sin^2 (\theta_1 + \theta_2)}}$
$= \sqrt{r_1^2 r_2^2} = r_1 r_2 \cdot |z| \cdot |w|$
$= |r_1 \text{ cis } \theta_1| \cdot |r_2 \text{ cis } \theta_2|$
$= |r_1 \cos \theta_1 + r_1 i \sin\theta_1| \cdot |r_2 \cos \theta_2 + r_2 i \sin \theta_2|$
$= \sqrt{r_1^2 \cos^2 \theta_1 + r_1^2 \sin^2 \theta_1}$
$\cdot \sqrt{r_2^2 \cos^2 \theta_2 + r_2^2 \sin^2 \theta_2}$
$= \sqrt{r_1^2} \cdot \sqrt{r_2^2} = r_1 r_2$
63. $\left|\frac{z}{w}\right| = \left|\frac{r_1}{r_2} \text{ cis } (\theta_1 - \theta_2)\right|$

$$= \left| \frac{r_1}{r_2} \cos (\theta_1 - \theta_2) - \frac{r_1}{r_2} i \sin (\theta_1 - \theta_2) \right|$$

$$= \sqrt{\frac{r_1}{r_2} \cos^2 (\theta_1 - \theta_2) + \frac{r_1^2}{r_2^2} \sin^2 (\theta_1 - \theta_2)}$$

$$= \sqrt{\frac{r_1^2}{r_2^2}} = \frac{r_1}{r_2} \cdot \left| \frac{z}{w} \right| = \left| \frac{r_1 \operatorname{cis} \theta_1}{r_2 \operatorname{cis} \theta_2} \right|$$

$$= \left| \frac{r_1 \cos \theta_1 + r_1 \, i \sin \theta_1}{r_2 \cos \theta_2 + r_2 \, i \sin \theta_2} \right|$$

$$= \frac{\sqrt{r_1^2 \cos^2 \theta_1 + r_1^2 \sin^2 \theta_1}}{\sqrt{r_2^2 \cos^2 \theta_2 + r_2^2 \sin^2 \theta_2}} = \frac{\sqrt{r_1^2}}{\sqrt{r_2^2}} = \frac{r_1}{r_2}$$

64. $\sqrt[3]{68.4321}$, $\sqrt[3]{68.4321}$ cis 120°, $\sqrt[3]{68.4321}$ cis 240° 65. $\sqrt[3]{456.86}$, $\sqrt[3]{456.86}$ cis 120°, $\sqrt[3]{456.86}$ cis 240°

Pages 726–729
CHAPTERS 1–16 CUMULATIVE REVIEW

21. $\left(\frac{1}{3} x^3 + 7y \right) \left(\frac{1}{3x^3} - 7y \right)$

22. $2(x + 2)(x - 2)(x + 3)$

Page 734
4. Output:
```
X = 1000
X ^ 2 = 1000000
X ^ 3 = 1E + 09
X ^ 4 = 1E + 12
```
5–6. Answers may vary.
5.
```
10 LET F = 77
20 LET C = 5/9*(F - 32)
30 PRINT C; "IS THE CELSIUS
      TEMPERATURE."
40 END
```
Output: 25 IS THE CELSIUS
      TEMPERATURE.

6.
```
10 LET P1 = 3.14159
20 LET R = 6
30 LET H = 10
40 LET V = (P1 * R ^ 2 * H)/3
50 PRINT V
60 END
```
Output: 376.9908

Page 735
   Output:
3. `30 IF X * Y<>12 THEN 60`
4. `30 IF Y<> -4 * X + 1 THEN 60`
5. `30 IF 2 * X - 3 * Y<>6 THEN 60`

6. Answers may vary.
```
10 PRINT "INPUT X"
20 INPUT X
30 REM Y = F(X)
40 LET Y = 2 * X + 1
50 REM G = G(X)
60 LET G = X ^ 2 + 2
70 REM H = H(X)
80 LET H = 2 * G + 1
90 PRINT H, " = F(G(X)) = H(X)"
100 END
```
Sample output:
```
-2
13 = F(G(X)) = H(X)
-1
7 = F(G(X)) = H(X)
0
5 = F(G(X)) = H(X)
1
7 = F(G(X)) = H(X)
2
13 = F(G(X)) = H(X)
3
23 = F(G(X)) = H(X)
```

Page 737
1. Output:
```
THE SOLUTION IS (3,-2)
THE SOLUTION IS (1.88235294,
    -.176470588)
THE SOLUTION IS (0,.5)
NO UNIQUE SOLUTION
```
2. Output:
```
GROSS PAY = $411.6
GROSS PAY = $360
GROSS PAY = $230.4
GROSS PAY = $217.5
```
3. Answers may vary.
```
10 READ P
20 LET R = .12
30 LET T = 2
40 LET I = P * R * T
50 PRINT "INTEREST AT .12 FOR
      2 YEARS IS $"; I
```

```
60 GO TO 10
70 DATA 600, 1000, 2500, 10000,
   50000
80 END
```
Output:
```
INTEREST AT .12 FOR 2 YEARS IS
   $144
   $240
   $600
   $2400
   $12000
```

Page 738

1. Output for first program:
```
$100 INVESTED FOR 5 YEARS GROWS TO
   $180.611124
```
Output for second program:
```
$100 INVESTED FOR 5 YEARS GROWS TO
   $180.611124
$101 INVESTED FOR 5 YEARS GROWS TO
   $182.417235
$102 INVESTED FOR 5 YEARS GROWS TO
   $184.223346
$103 INVESTED FOR 5 YEARS GROWS TO
   $186.029458
$104 INVESTED FOR 5 YEARS GROWS TO
   $187.835569
$105 INVESTED FOR 5 YEARS GROWS TO
   $189.64168
$106 INVESTED FOR 5 YEARS GROWS TO
   $191.447791
$107 INVESTED FOR 5 YEARS GROWS TO
   $193.253903
$108 INVESTED FOR 5 YEARS GROWS TO
   $195.060014
$109 INVESTED FOR 5 YEARS GROWS TO
   $196.866125
$110 INVESTED FOR 5 YEARS GROWS TO
   $198.672236
$111 INVESTED FOR 5 YEARS GROWS TO
   $200.478347
$112 INVESTED FOR 5 YEARS GROWS TO
   $202.284459
$113 INVESTED FOR 5 YEARS GROWS TO
   $204.09057
$114 INVESTED FOR 5 YEARS GROWS TO
   $205.896681
$115 INVESTED FOR 5 YEARS GROWS TO
   $207.702792
$116 INVESTED FOR 5 YEARS GROWS TO
   $209.508904
$117 INVESTED FOR 5 YEARS GROWS TO
   $211.315015
$118 INVESTED FOR 5 YEARS GROWS TO
   $213.121126
$119 INVESTED FOR 5 YEARS GROWS TO
   $214.927237
$120 INVESTED FOR 5 YEARS GROWS TO
   $216.733348
$121 INVESTED FOR 5 YEARS GROWS TO
   $218.53946
$122 INVESTED FOR 5 YEARS GROWS TO
   $220.345571
$123 INVESTED FOR 5 YEARS GROWS TO
   $222.151682
$124 INVESTED FOR 5 YEARS GROWS TO
   $223.957794
$125 INVESTED FOR 5 YEARS GROWS TO
   $225.763905
```

2–5. Answers may vary.

2a.
```
10 LET R = .15
20 LET N = 4
30 LET T = 10
40 FOR P
   = 10000 TO
     10025
   .
   .
   .
```
b.
```
10 LET R = .18
20 LET N = 12
30 LET T = 25
40 FOR P
   = 500 TO 515
   .
   .
   .
```

3.
```
10 FOR X = 1 TO 10
20 PRINT X, X ^ 2, X ^ 3
30 NEXT X
40 END
```

4.
```
10 FOR X = 1 TO 9
20 LET Y = 2 * X ^ 2 + 8 * X + 10
30 PRINT X, Y
40 NEXT X
50 END
```

5.
```
10 LET S = 0
20 FOR N = 1 TO 25
```

```
30 LET S = S + N
40 NEXT N
50 PRINT "THE SUM IS"; S
60 END
```

Pages 739–740

1. Output:
```
THE SOLUTIONS ARE -2 AND -3
THE ONE SOLUTION IS -.5
NO REAL NUMBER SOLUTIONS
```
2–5. Answers may vary.

2. `140 DATA 2,8,8,2,3,3,6,-1,-2`
   Output:
```
THE ONE SOLUTION IS -2
NO REAL NUMBER SOLUTIONS
THE SOLUTIONS ARE .66666667
  AND -.5
```

3.
```
10 PRINT "INPUT A AND B"
20 INPUT A,B
30 LET C = SQR(A ^ 2 + B ^ 2)
40 PRINT "C = "; C
50 END
```
   Output:
```
C = 1.41421356
C = 5
C = 29.6816442
C = 36.0555128
```

4.
```
10 REM NUMBERS, SIGNS, ABSOLUTE
     VALUES
20 FOR X = -10 TO 10
30 PRINT X, SGN(X), ABS(X)
40 NEXT X
50 END
```
   Output:
```
-10   -1   10
-9    -1    9
      .
      .
10     1   10
```

5.
```
10 REM DISTANCE (KM) YOU CAN SEE
20 FOR H = 1 TO 10
30 LET V = 3.5 * SQR(H)
40 PRINT "WHEN H = "; H;
     "  V = "; V
50 NEXT H
60 END
```

Output:
```
WHEN H = 1    V = 3.5
WHEN H = 2    V = 4.94974747
WHEN H = 3    V = 6.06217783
WHEN H = 4    V = 7
WHEN H = 5    V = 7.82623792
WHEN H = 6    V = 8.57321411
WHEN H = 7    V = 9.26012959
WHEN H = 8    V = 9.899219495
WHEN H = 9    V = 10.5
WHEN H = 10   V = 11.0079718
```

Page 741

1.
```
20 DIM S(40)
    .
    .
50 FOR X = 3 TO 40
    .
    .
90 FOR X = 1 TO 40
```
   Output will contain:
```
S(25)=75025   S(40)=102334155
```

2. Answers may vary. In line 50 any test
   scores may be used.
```
10 REM FIND AVERAGE
20 DIM Y(8)
30 FOR I = 1 TO 8
40 READ Y(I)
50 DATA 0,0,0,0,0,0,0,0
60 NEXT I
70 LET S = 0
80 FOR I = 1 TO 8
90 LET S = S + Y(I)
100 NEXT I
110 PRINT "THE AVERAGE IS"; S/8
120 END
```

3. Answers may vary.
```
10 REM SUM OF GEOMETRIC SERIES
20 PRINT "INPUT, A, R, N"
30 INPUT A, R, N
40 LET S = (A - A * R ^ N)/(1 - R)
50 PRINT "SUM IS "; S
60 END
```
   a. Output: SUM IS .484375
   b. Output: SUM IS 10.5
   c. Output: SUM IS 1275

ALGEBRA
AND TRIGONOMETRY

MERVIN L. KEEDY
MARVIN L. BITTINGER
STANLEY A. SMITH
LUCY J. ORFAN

ADDISON-WESLEY PUBLISHING COMPANY
MENLO PARK, CALIFORNIA   READING, MASSACHUSETTS   LONDON
AMSTERDAM   DON MILLS, ONTARIO   SYDNEY

PHOTOGRAPHS

Cover: © William James Warren

© Gary C. Benson / Aperture: 102 and 420
© Ira Block / The Image Bank West: 339
© Rene Burri / Magnum Photos: 496 (left)
Cameron Davidson / Bruce Coleman Inc.: 290
© 1980 Kristin Finnegan / Aperture: 554
© 1981/1980 Jay Freis: 156 and 380
© 1980 George Hall / Woodfin Camp & Associates: 600
© George Hall: 666 (right)
© Jerry Howard / Stock Boston: 502
© Richard Kalvar / Magnum Photos: 54
© 1981 John Madere / The Image Bank West: 618 (right)
© 1981 David Kent Madison / Bruce Coleman Inc.: 464
© Michael Melford / Peter Arnold Inc.: 14
© Michael Melford / The Image Bank West: 98
NASA / The Image Bank West: 496 (right)
© 1982 Chuck O'Rear / Woodfin Camp & Associates: 240 (left)
© 1978 Nick Pavloff: 415 (right)
R. Phillips / The Image Bank West: 206
© 1977 Sepp Seitz / Woodfin Camp & Associates: 244
© Glenn Short / After-Image: 415 (left)
© 1979 Frank Siteman / Stock Boston: 624
© 1979 Chad Slattery / Stock Boston: 618 (left)
© Tom Tracy: 49
A. Upitis / The Image Bank West: 596
© William James Warren: 240 (right)
© Baron Wolman: 346 and 666 (left)
© Jonathan T. Wright / Bruce Coleman Inc.: 670

ILLUSTRATION

Michel Allaire

TECHNICAL ILLUSTRATION

Sally Shimizu
Phyllis Rockne

DESIGN AND PRODUCTION

Design Office, San Francisco

ISBN 0–201–20339–1

ABCDEFGHIJK–VH–89876543

AUTHORS

MERVIN L. KEEDY

Mervin L. Keedy is Professor of Mathematics at Purdue University. He received his Ph.D. degree at the University of Nebraska and formerly taught at the University of Maryland. He has also taught mathematics and science in junior and senior high schools. Professor Keedy is the author of many books on mathematics. Most recently, he is co-author of *General Mathematics* (Addison-Wesley, 1983) and *Applying Mathematics* (Addison-Wesley, 1983).

MARVIN L. BITTINGER

Marvin L. Bittinger is Professor of Mathematics Education at Indiana University-Purdue University at Indianapolis. He earned his Ph.D. degree at Purdue University. He is the author of *Logic and Proof* (Addison-Wesley, 1980) and is co-author of *General Mathematics* (Addison-Wesley, 1983).

STANLEY A. SMITH

Stanley A. Smith is Coordinator, Office of Mathematics (K–12), for Baltimore County Public Schools, Maryland. He has taught junior high school mathematics and science and senior high school mathematics. He earned his M.A. degree at the University of Maryland. He is co-author of *General Mathematics* (Addison-Wesley, 1983) and *Applying Mathematics* (Addison-Wesley, 1983).

LUCY JAJOSKY ORFAN

Lucy Jajosky Orfan is Assistant Professor of Mathematics Education at Kean College of New Jersey. She earned her M.A. degree at New York University and her Ed.D. at Fairleigh Dickinson University. She currently teaches mathematics education courses at both the undergraduate and graduate level.

PREFACE

This text, *Algebra and Trigonometry,* is for students who are ready for their second course in algebra. The authors have also published *Algebra,* a first-year course. In both these books, skills are heavily emphasized, because without skills students cannot adequately cope with the concepts—the big ideas—that make algebra important.

Section Organization

Each section has alternating Examples and Try This exercises. Try This exercises are very much like the examples that precede them. They are carefully and strategically placed to draw students into an active development of the lesson. Immediate reinforcement of the concept or skill being learned is the goal. This kind of skill development builds success since the homework exercises grow directly from the Try This exercises.

Exercise Sets

Three levels of exercises are provided for each section. The first, labeled *Exercises,* provides problems that follow the same pattern as the Examples and Try This exercises. The second, labeled *Extension,* provides problems that combine single concepts presented in the Exercises into several-step problems. The third level, labeled *Challenge,* provides highly motivated students with problems that are related—sometimes in not so obvious ways—to the material of the lesson.

Applications

Much attention has been given to problems in which algebra is applied to situations arising from daily life. These appear not only in Exercise Sets for appropriate sections, but also in the *Career, Consumer Application,* and *Using a Calculator* features.

Computer Activities

This appendix contains a series of computer activities keyed to appropriate chapters. The activities provide an introduction to programming in the BASIC language.

On-Going Review

There are many opportunities for students to review previous concepts in order to maintain their skills at a high level. Before each of Chapters 2–16 there are *Ready For* exercises (keyed to preceding sections) providing review of skills needed in that chapter. In addition, each chapter has a *Chapter Review,* (keyed to sections) and *Chapter Test.* There are also five Cumulative Reviews, each reviewing skills beginning with Chapter 1.

TO THE STUDENTS

Why Study Algebra?

Most of you have studied beginning algebra and geometry by now. You know that you tend to be successful in dealing with mathematics courses. So you know that algebra is practical as you prepare for other courses in math, science, or engineering. You know that algebra is the basis for all these courses.

For some of you, algebra will open up new ways of seeing and thinking about the events that happen in the world—the first step in formulating interests that will turn into lifelong careers. For you who plan to be scientists or engineers this is obviously true. But remember, everyone must be aware that numbers are around us everywhere, and dealing with them is important in surprisingly many careers. You who will work in business, the social sciences, history, psychology or health fields will find that information about the past and present—so often presented as data—must be analyzed, compared, researched, summarized, or restated in ways in which a mathematical understanding of what you are doing will deepen your knowledge and extend the usefulness of what you are doing.

Computers will also affect many of you during your lives. One of the skills needed to use and understand computers is the effective use of variables. Learning how to deal with variables and seeing their role in formulating statements may be the most important result of studying algebra for all of you, regardless of your future careers.

There are many reasons to study algebra, and one of these is that algebra is interesting for its own sake, the way a game or puzzle can be interesting. Whatever your goals we hope this book will help you succeed in your studies, and will make this important year in your lives an interesting and enjoyable one.

The Authors

CONTENTS

CHAPTER 1 Real Numbers and Their Properties

1–1 The Set of Real Numbers **1**
1–2 Algebraic Expressions **7**
1–3 Addition and Subtraction **11**
1–4 Multiplication and Division **16**
1–5 The Distributive Law **23**
1–6 Exponential Notation **31**
1–7 Properties of Exponents **35**
1–8 Scientific Notation **41**
1–9 Proofs in Algebra **44**

CAREERS/Forestry **49**
COMPUTER ACTIVITY/Expressions and Numbers in BASIC **731**
CHAPTER 1 Review **50**
CHAPTER 1 Test **52**

CHAPTER 2 Solving Equations and Inequalities

Ready for Solving Equations and Inequalities? **53**
2–1 Solving Equations **55**
2–2 More on Solving Equations **60**
2–3 Solving Problems **64**
2–4 Solving Formulas **70**
2–5 Solving Inequalities **73**
2–6 Solving Problems with Inequalities **78**
2–7 Compound Inequalities **80**
2–8 Absolute Value **84**
2–9 Proofs **90**

Using a Calculator **69**
CAREERS/Clothing Manufacturing **98**
COMPUTER ACTIVITY/BASIC Programs **732**
CHAPTER 2 Review **99**
CHAPTER 2 Test **100**

CHAPTER 3 Graphs, Relations, and Functions

Ready for Graphs, Relations, and Functions? **101**
3–1 Relations and Ordered Pairs **103**
3–2 Graphs of Equations **107**
3–3 Functions **114**
3–4 Graphs of Linear Equations **122**
3–5 Slope **129**
3–6 More Equations of Lines **136**
3–7 Parallel and Perpendicular Lines **140**
3–8 Applications of Linear Functions **146**

Using a Calculator **139**
CONSUMER APPLICATION/Buying a New Car **151**
COMPUTER ACTIVITY/INPUT and IF...THEN Statements **734**
CHAPTER 3 Review **152**
CHAPTER 3 Test **154**

CHAPTER 4 Systems of Equations and Inequalities

Ready for Systems of Equations and Inequalities? **155**
4–1 Systems of Equations in Two Variables **157**
4–2 Solving Problems with Two Equations **164**
4–3 Systems of Equations in Three Variables **170**
4–4 Solving Problems with Three Equations **176**
4–5 Inconsistent and Dependent Equations **179**
4–6 Matrices and Systems **184**
4–7 Determinants and Cramer's Rule **187**
4–8 Systems of Inequalities **193**
4–9 Linear Programming **198**

COMPUTER ACTIVITY/READ and DATA Statements **735**
CHAPTER 4 Review **202**
CHAPTER 4 Test **203**
CHAPTERS 1–4 Cumulative Review **204**

CHAPTER 5 Polynomials and Factoring

Ready for Polynomials and Factoring? **205**
5–1 Addition and Subtraction of Polynomials **207**
5–2 Multiplication of Polynomials **213**
5–3 Factoring **218**
5–4 More Factoring **222**
5–5 Factoring by Grouping **225**
5–6 Sums or Differences of Two Cubes **229**
5–7 Factoring: A General Strategy **232**
5–8 Solving Equations by Factoring **234**
5–9 Solving Problems **237**

CAREERS/Railroad Traffic Control **240**
COMPUTER ACTIVITY/FOR . . . NEXT Statements **737**
CHAPTER 5 Review **241**
CHAPTER 5 Test **242**

CHAPTER 6 Fractional Expressions and Equations

Ready for Fractional Expressions and Equations? 243
6–1 Multiplying and Simplifying 245
6–2 Least Common Multiples 252
6–3 Addition and Subtraction 255
6–4 Complex Fractional Expressions 260
6–5 Division of Polynomials 263
6–6 Solving Fractional Equations 267
6–7 Solving Problems 271
6–8 Formulas 276
6–9 Variation 279

USING A CALCULATOR 251
CONSUMER APPLICATION/Understanding Life Insurance 285
CHAPTER 6 Review 286
CHAPTER 6 Test 288

CHAPTER 7 Powers, Roots, and Complex Numbers

Ready for Powers, Roots, and Complex Numbers? 289
7–1 Radical Expressions 291
7–2 Multiplying and Simplifying 297
7–3 Dividing and Simplifying 301
7–4 Operations with Radical Expressions 304
7–5 Rational Numbers as Exponents 310
7–6 Solving Radical Equations 317
7–7 Imaginary and Complex Numbers 321
7–8 More About Complex Numbers 325
7–9 Solutions of Equations 329
7–10 Graphical Representation 333
7–11 Conjugates of Polynomials 335

USING A CALCULATOR 296
CAREERS/Oceanography 339
CHAPTER 7 Review 340
CHAPTER 7 Test 341
CHAPTERS 1–7 Cumulative Review 342

CHAPTER 8   Quadratic Equations

Ready for Quadratic Equations? **345**
8–1 Introduction to Quadratic Equations **347**
8–2 The Quadratic Formula **353**
8–3 Solutions of Quadratic Equations **357**
8–4 Equations in Quadratic Form **362**
8–5 Formulas and Problems **365**
8–6 Quadratic Variation **370**

COMPUTER ACTIVITY/Programs for Solving Quadratic Equations **738**
CHAPTER 8 Review **377**
CHAPTER 8 Test **378**

CHAPTER 9   Quadratic Functions

Ready for Quadratic Functions? **379**
9–1 Symmetry **381**
9–2 Transformations **389**
9–3 Stretching and Shrinking **393**
9–4 Graphs of $f(x) = ax^2$ **398**
9–5 Graphs of $f(x) = a(x - h)^2 + k$ **401**
9–6 Standard Form for Quadratic Equations **404**
9–7 x-intercepts and Graphs **408**
9–8 Applications of Quadratic Functions **410**

CAREERS/Communications **415**
CHAPTER 9 Review **416**
CHAPTER 9 Test **418**

CHAPTER 10   Equations of Second Degree

Ready for Equations of Second Degree? **419**
10–1 Coordinate Geometry **421**
10–2 Conic Sections: Circles **424**
10–3 Ellipses **429**
10–4 Hyperbolas **436**
10–5 Parabolas **443**

10–6 Systems of Equations **449**
10–7 Systems of Second-Degree Equations **454**

USING A CALCULATOR **453**
CONSUMER APPLICATION/Financing a Home **459**
CHAPTER 10 Review **461**
CHAPTER 10 Test **462**

CHAPTER 11   Polynomial Functions

Ready for Polynomial Functions? **462**
11–1 Polynomials and Polynomial Functions **465**
11–2 The Remainder and Factor Theorems **469**
11–3 Theorems About Roots **475**
11–4 Rational Roots **481**
11–5 Descartes' Rule and Bounds on Roots **486**
11–6 Graphs of Polynomial Functions **491**

USING A CALCULATOR **495**
CAREERS/Astronomy **496**
CHAPTER 11 Review **497**
CHAPTER 11 Test **498**
CHAPTERS 1–11 Cumulative Review **498**

CHAPTER 12   Exponential and Logarithmic Functions

Ready for Exponential and Logarithmic Functions? **501**
12–1 Inverse Relations and Functions **503**
12–2 Exponential and Logarithmic Functions **509**
12–3 Exponential and Logarithmic Relationships **515**
12–4 Properties of Logarithmic Functions **518**
12–5 Common Logarithms **524**
12–6 Interpolation **531**
12–7 Exponential and Logarithmic Equations **535**
12–8 The Number e and Applications **542**

USING A CALCULATOR **508**
CONSUMER APPLICATION/Finding a Job **549**
CHAPTER 12 Review **550**
CHAPTER 12 Test **552**

CHAPTER 13 Sequences, Series, and Probability

Ready for Sequences, Series, and Probability? **553**
13–1 Sequences and Series **555**
13–2 Arithmetic Sequences and Series **559**
13–3 Geometric Sequences and Series **566**
13–4 Infinite Geometric Series **572**
13–5 Permutations **576**
13–6 Permutations of n Objects r at a Time **581**
13–7 Combinatorial Algebra: Combinations **585**
13–8 The Binomial Theorem **589**
13–9 Probability **593**

CAREERS/Engineering **596**
COMPUTER ACTIVITY/Programs for Sequences and Series **740**
CHAPTER 13 Review **597**
CHAPTER 13 Test **598**

CHAPTER 14 Matrices

Ready for Matrices? **599**
14–1 Addition and Subtraction of Matrices **601**
14–2 Multiplying Matrices and Numbers **605**
14–3 Inverses of Matrices **612**

CAREERS/Stress Analysis **618**
CHAPTER 14 Review **619**
CHAPTER 14 Test **619**
CHAPTERS 1–14 Cumulative Review **620**

CHAPTER 15 Trigonometric Functions

Ready for Trigonometric Functions? **623**
15–1 Trigonometric Functions in Triangles **625**
15–2 More on Trigonometric Functions **631**
15–3 Radians, Cofunctions, and Tables **638**
15–4 Graphs of Trigonometric Functions **646**

15–5 Trigonometric Function Relationships **654**
15–6 More Graphs **660**
15–7 Algebraic Manipulations **663**

CAREERS/Aerial Surveying **666**
CHAPTER 15 Review **667**
CHAPTER 15 Test **668**

CHAPTER 16 Trigonometric Identities and Equations

Ready for Trigonometric Identities and Equations **669**
16–1 Sum and Difference Identities **671**
16–2 Double-Angle and Half-Angle Identities **677**
16–3 Proving Identities **682**
16–4 Inverses of the Trigonometric Functions **685**
16–5 Trigonometric Equations **689**
16–6 Solving Right Triangles and Applications **692**
16–7 The Law of Sines **698**
16–8 The Law of Cosines **704**
16–9 Vectors **708**
16–10 Vectors and Coordinates **712**
16–11 Trigonometric Notation **716**

CONSUMER APPLICATION/Filing Income Tax Returns **722**
CHAPTER 16 Review **723**
CHAPTER 16 Test **724**
CHAPTERS 1–16 Cumulative Review **726**

COMPUTER APPENDIX 730

TABLES 1 Squares and Square Roots **742**
         2 Common Logarithms **743**
         3 Values of Trigonometric Functions **745**
         4 Function Values of e^x and e^{-x} **750**
         5 Natural Logarithms **751**
         6 Symbols **753**
Glossary **754**
Selected Answers **758**
Index **781**

1

CHAPTER ONE

Real Numbers and Their Properties

1–1 The Set of Real Numbers

Numbers are important in algebra as well as arithmetic. The most important set of numbers in ordinary algebra is the set of real numbers.

Some Subsets of the Real Numbers

There is exactly one real number for each point of a number line.

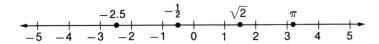

The positive numbers are usually pictured to the right of 0. The negative numbers are pictured to the left. Zero is neither positive nor negative.

There are several kinds of real numbers.

DEFINITION

The *natural numbers* are the numbers used for counting,

$$1, 2, 3, 4, 5, \text{ and so on.}$$

The *whole numbers* are the natural numbers and zero,

$$0, 1, 2, 3, 4, \text{ and so on.}$$

The *integers* consist of the natural numbers, zero and the additive inverses of the natural numbers. The integers are

$$0, 1, -1, 2, -2, 3, -3, \text{ and so on.}$$

TRY THIS Consider the following numbers.

$$\frac{2}{3}, -5, 0, 17, 5.3, -8.4, 12, 1$$

1. Which are natural numbers? 1, 12, 17
2. Which are whole numbers? 0, 1, 12, 17
3. Which are integers? −5, 0, 1, 12, 17

Another subset of the set of real numbers is the set of rational numbers.

> **DEFINITION**
>
> *The rational numbers* are the integers and quotients of integers, provided that the divisor is not equal to 0.

Rational numbers are those that can be named with fractional notation having integers for numerator and denominator. The following are rational numbers.

$$\frac{4}{5}, \frac{-4}{7}, -6, 9, 234, \frac{14}{-3}, 9.3, -4.1, -\frac{2}{3}$$

EXAMPLES
Show that each number is rational by naming it as a quotient of integers.

1. -13 We can name -13 as $\frac{-13}{1}$, or $\frac{26}{-2}$. There are many such names.

2. 3.5 We can name 3.5 as $\frac{35}{10}$ or $\frac{-35}{-10}$. There are many such names.

3. $-\frac{2}{3}$ We can name $-\frac{2}{3}$ as $\frac{-2}{3}$ or $\frac{2}{-3}$, and so on.

TRY THIS Show that each number is rational by naming it as a quotient of integers. Write at least two such names for each number. Answers may vary.

4. $-\frac{3}{7}$ 5. -13 6. 9.3 7. $-\frac{-4}{5}$ 4. $\frac{-3}{7}, \frac{3}{-7}$ 5. $\frac{-13}{1}, \frac{26}{-2}$ 6. $\frac{93}{10}, \frac{-93}{-10}$ 7. $\frac{4}{5}, \frac{-8}{-10}$

Decimal and Fractional Notation

Rational numbers can also be named using decimal notation.

EXAMPLES
Find decimal notation.

4. $\frac{5}{8}$ Since $\frac{5}{8}$ means $5 \div 8$, we divide. $8\overline{)5.000}$ = 0.625

5. $\frac{6}{11}$ We divide. $11\overline{)6.0000}$ = 0.5454...

Repeating decimal notation can be abbreviated by writing a bar over the repeating part. In Example 5, the answer can be written $0.\overline{54}$. When repeating decimals occur in problems we round them. Decimal notation for rational numbers either ends or repeats.

TRY THIS Find decimal notation.

8. $\frac{7}{8}$ 9. $\frac{7}{11}$ 10. $-\frac{17}{15}$ 8. 0.875   9. $0.\overline{63}$ 10. $-1.1\overline{3}$

If we know decimal notation for a rational number, we can find fractional notation.

EXAMPLES
Find fractional notation.

6. 4.9   The last decimal place is *tenths*, so we use a denominator of 10, obtaining $\frac{49}{10}$.

7. 0.725   The last decimal place is *thousandths*, so we can use a denominator of 1,000, obtaining $\frac{725}{1000}$.

TRY THIS Find fractional notation.

11. 5.3   12. -0.367 13. 1.9032   11. $\frac{53}{10}$ 12. $\frac{-367}{1000}$ 13. $\frac{19032}{10,000}$

Irrational Numbers

Every rational number can be named as a quotient of integers in the form $\frac{a}{b}$. If a number cannot be named that way, it is called irrational. We can prove that there is no rational number that is a square root of 2. That is, we cannot find integers a and b for which

$$\frac{a}{b} \cdot \frac{a}{b} = 2.$$

We can come close, but there is no rational number whose square root is *exactly* 2. Thus $\sqrt{2}$ is not a rational number. Therefore it is irrational. Unless a whole number is a perfect square, its square root is irrational.

The following numbers are irrational.

$$\sqrt{3}, \quad \sqrt{8}, \quad -\sqrt{45}, \quad \sqrt[3]{11}, \quad \pi$$

Decimal notation for rational numbers either ends or repeats. Decimal notation for irrational numbers never ends and never repeats.

EXAMPLES

Which of the following are rational? Which are irrational?

8. 8.974974974 . . . (numeral repeats)
   The number is rational, since the numeral repeats.

9. 3.12112111211112111112 . . . (numeral does not repeat)
   The number is irrational, since the numeral does not end and does not repeat.

10. 4.325   The number is rational since the numeral ends.

11. $\sqrt{17}$ Since 17 does not have a whole number square root, the number $\sqrt{17}$ is irrational.

TRY THIS Which of the following are rational? Which are irrational?

14. $\frac{59}{37}$ 15. 7.42   16. 0.476476476 . . . (numeral repeats)

17. 2.5734107656631 . . . (numeral does not repeat)

18. $\sqrt{49}$ 19. $-\sqrt{32}$

14. rational
15. rational
16. rational
17. irrational
18. rational
19. irrational

Order on the Real Number Line

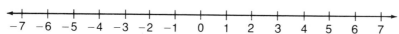

The number line shows the real numbers arranged in order. We say that one number is greater than another if it appears to the right of the other on the line. A number is less than another if it appears to the left of the other. The symbol $<$ means is less than. The symbol $>$ means is greater than.

EXAMPLES

Insert $<$ or $>$ to make true sentences.

12. -9 2 $-9 < 2$ because -9 is to the left of 2

13. 1.2 -1.2 $1.2 > -1.2$ because 1.2 is to the right of -1.2

14. -6 -8 $-6 > -8$ because -6 is to the right of -8

TRY THIS Insert $<$ or $>$ to make true sentences.

20. $-5 \; < \; -4$ 21. $-\frac{1}{4} \; < \; \frac{1}{2}$ 22. $-9.8 \; < \; -4.5$

Axioms for the Real Numbers

We use number properties in algebra to determine whether expressions are equivalent. We accept some of these properties without proof. These are called axioms. We will use axioms later to prove other properties, called theorems.

Axioms for Real Numbers

1. The Commutative Laws of Addition and Multiplication.
   For any numbers a and b, $a + b = b + a$ and $a \cdot b = b \cdot a$.

2. The Associative Laws of Addition and Multiplication.
   For any numbers a, b and c, $a + (b + c) = (a + b) + c$ and $a(bc) = (ab)c$.

3. The Distributive Law of Multiplication over Addition.
   For any numbers a, b and c, $a(b + c) = ab + ac$.

4. The Additive Property of Zero.
   For any number a, $a + 0 = a$.

5. Property of Additive Inverses.
   For each number a, there is one and only one additive inverse $-a$, for which $a + (-a) = 0$.

6. The Multiplicative Property of One.
   For any number a, $a \cdot 1 = a$.

7. Property of Multiplicative Inverses, or Reciprocals.
   For each nonzero number a, there is one and only one reciprocal $\frac{1}{a}$, for which $a \cdot \frac{1}{a} = 1$.

Any number system in which these axioms hold is called a field. Hence the axioms are known as the field axioms. So far, we are familiar with two fields, the rational numbers and the real numbers.

1–1

Exercises

Consider the following numbers. -5, 0, 2, $-\frac{1}{2}$, -3, $\frac{7}{8}$, 14, $-\frac{8}{3}$, 2.43, $7\frac{1}{2}$

1. Name the natural numbers. 2, 14
2. Name the whole numbers. 0, 2, 4
3. Name the rational numbers. All the numbers are rational.
4. Name the integers. -5, 0, 2, -3, 14

Show that each number is rational by naming it as a quotient of
two integers. Write at least two such names for each number. Answers may vary.

5. 14 $\frac{28}{2}, \frac{14}{1}$ **6.** $-\frac{9}{7}$ $\frac{-9}{7}, \frac{-18}{14}$ **7.** 2.6 $\frac{26}{10}, \frac{-26}{-10}$ **8.** -3.9 $\frac{-39}{10}, \frac{78}{-20}$

9. 8 $\frac{8}{1}, \frac{24}{3}$ **10.** -5 $\frac{-5}{1}, \frac{10}{-2}$ **11.** 4.15 $\frac{415}{100}, \frac{-830}{-200}$ **12.** $-\frac{6}{7}$ $\frac{-12}{14}, \frac{6}{-7}$

Find decimal notation.

13. $\frac{3}{8}$ 0.375   **14.** $\frac{7}{25}$ 0.28   **15.** $\frac{5}{3}$ 1.6̄   **16.** $\frac{7}{6}$ 1.16̄

17. $\frac{3}{7}$ 0.4285...   **18.** $-\frac{4}{7}$ −0.5714...   **19.** $\frac{9}{16}$ 0.5625   **20.** $-\frac{5}{12}$ −0.416̄

Find fractional notation.

21. 2.7   **22.** −13.91   **23.** −0.145   **24.** −0.0213

25. −0.23   **26.** −0.06704   **27.** 11.235   **28.** 56.39

21. $\frac{27}{10}$
22. $\frac{-1391}{100}$
23. $\frac{-145}{1000}$
24. $\frac{-213}{10,000}$
25. $\frac{-23}{100}$
26. $\frac{-6704}{100,000}$
27. $\frac{11235}{1000}$
28. $\frac{5639}{100}$

Consider the following numbers. $\frac{3}{17}$, $-\sqrt{25}$, $\sqrt{42}$, $-12.3333333 \ldots,$

4.1231234123451234561234567 . . . (numeral does not repeat)

29. Name the rational numbers.   **30.** Name the irrational numbers.
$\frac{3}{17}, -\sqrt{25}, -12.33 \ldots$ $\sqrt{42}, 4.1231234123451234561234567$

Insert $<$ or $>$ to make true sentences.

31. $55 > 40$ **32.** $31 < 94$ **33.** $2.3 < 3.2$ **34.** $4.7 < 47$

35. $-10 < -4$ **36.** $-6 > -20$ **37.** $-2.3 > -3.2$ **38.** $-16 < -13$

Extension

The number 3 can be named 3, III, $\sqrt{9}$, $\frac{36}{12}$, $(\sqrt{3})^2$, $\sqrt[3]{27}$ and so on.
Write five different names for each of the following. Answers may vary.

39. 2   **40.** 10   **41.** 0.5   **42.** −3

43. Find decimal notation for $\frac{1}{13}, \frac{2}{13}, \frac{3}{13}, \ldots, \frac{12}{13}$. Study the repeating portions. What pattern do you find?

39. $\frac{4}{2}, \sqrt{4}, \frac{39}{18}, \sqrt[3]{8}, (\sqrt{2})^2$
40. $\sqrt{100}, \sqrt[3]{1000}, \frac{20}{2}, \frac{50}{5}, \frac{-10}{-1}$
41. $\frac{5}{10}, \frac{50}{100}, \frac{10}{20}, \frac{2.5}{5}, \frac{-25}{-50}$
42. $\frac{-3}{1}, \frac{3}{-1}, \sqrt{9}, \sqrt[3]{27}, -\frac{18}{6}$
43. 0.076923, 0.153846, 0.230769,
. . . , 0.923076; The repeating portion of $\frac{2}{13}$ is two times the repeating portion of $\frac{1}{13}$ and the repeating portion of $\frac{3}{13}$ is three times the repeating portion of $\frac{1}{13}$ and so on.

Challenge

44. Suppose that $n = 0.88\bar{8}$. Find fractional notation for n. (Hint: Find $10n$ and then $10n − n$.) $\frac{8}{9}$

45. Write a name for an irrational number using only the digits 0 and 9. Answers may vary. Example: 0.909900999000...

46. A set of numbers is said to be *densely ordered* if between any two numbers there is another. Which of the following sets are densely ordered?
   a. natural numbers no   **b.** integers no   **c.** multiples of 10 no
   d. even integers no   **e.** rational numbers yes   **f.** real numbers yes

1–2 Algebraic Expressions

In algebra we use letters to represent numbers. For example, in the formula for the area of a circle,

$$A = \pi r^2$$

the letter A stands for the area and r stands for the radius. The Greek letter π stands for the ratio of circumference to diameter of a circle. The letters A and r can represent various numbers, so they are called variables. The letter π represents only one number, so it is called a constant.

Algebraic expressions are made up of numerals and letters, as well as other mathematical symbols, such as $+$, or $\sqrt{}$.

Evaluating Expressions

Expressions containing variables may represent various numbers. We sometimes substitute numbers for the variables and then find the resulting number named by the expression. We say that we are evaluating the expression.

EXAMPLE 1

Evaluate $2y + x$. Use $y = 5$ and $x = 3$.

$$
\begin{aligned}
2y + x &= 2 \cdot 5 + 3 \quad \text{Substituting 5 for } y \text{ and 3 for } x \\
&= 10 + 3 \\
&= 13
\end{aligned}
$$

The value of the expression is 13.

TRY THIS Evaluate the expression $5x - y$.

1. Use $y = 5$ and $x = 10$. 45 **2.** Use $y = 7$ and $x = 31$. 148

Additive Inverses

The additive inverse of a number is the number you add to it to get 0. The additive inverse is also the number opposite to it on the number line. The additive inverse (or simply inverse) of a number x is named $-x$. Additive inverses are sometimes called "opposites."

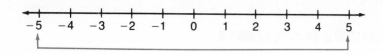

To find the additive inverse of 5 we reflect to the opposite side of 0. The inverse of 5 is -5. (We read -5 as "the inverse of 5" or "negative 5.")

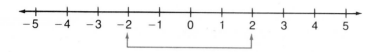

To find the additive inverse of -2 we reflect to the opposite side of 0. The inverse of -2 is 2. In symbols, $-(-2) = 2$. ("The inverse of the inverse of 2 is 2," or "the inverse of negative 2 is 2.")

EXAMPLES

2. Evaluate the expression $-y$ when $y = 4$ and $y = 0$.

When $y = 4$, $-y = -(4)$ Substituting 4 for y
$$= -4$$

When $y = 0$, $-y = -(0)$ Substituting 0 for y
$$= 0$$

3. Evaluate the expression $-(-x)$ when $x = 6$, and $x = -7$.

When $x = 6$, $-(x) = -(-(6))$ Substituting 6 for x
$$= 6$$

When $x = -7$, $-(-x) = -(-(-7))$ Substituting -7 for x
$$= -7$$

TRY THIS Evaluate the expressions $-x$ and $-(-x)$.

3. Use $x = 10$.   4. Use $x = 0$.   5. Use $x = -8$.

3. $-x = -10; -(-x) = 10$
4. $-x = -(-x) = 0$
5. $-x = 8; -(-x) = -8$

Taking the additive inverse of a number is sometimes called "changing its sign."

Absolute Value

The absolute value of a number is its distance from 0 on a number line. The absolute value of a number n is written $|n|$. Since 4 is 4 units from 0, $|4| = 4$ (the absolute value of 4 is 4). Since -7 is 7 units from 0, $|-7| = 7$ (the absolute value of -7 is 7). The absolute value of 0 is 0.

EXAMPLE 4

Evaluate the following expression. Use $x = 15$ and $y = -10$.

$$|x| + 2 \cdot |y| = |15| + 2 \cdot |-10| \quad \text{Substituting}$$
$$= 15 + 2 \cdot (10) \quad \text{Taking absolute values}$$
$$= 15 + 20$$
$$= 35$$

TRY THIS Evaluate the following expressions. Use $x = -16$ and $y = -4$.

6. $|x| - 2 \cdot |y|$ ₈ 7. $\dfrac{|x|}{|y|}$ ₄

The absolute value of a nonnegative real number is that number itself. The absolute value of a negative number is its additive inverse. We make our definition of absolute value as follows.

DEFINITION

For any real number x,
$\quad |x| = x$ if x is not negative, and
$\quad |x| = -x$ (the inverse of x) if x is negative.

1–2

Exercises

Evaluate each expression.

1. $3x + y$; Use $x = 16$ and $y = 6$. ₅₄
2. $5y - x$; Use $x = 8$ and $y = 11$. ₄₇
3. $2p + 3t$; Use $p = 20$ and $t = 17$. ₉₁
4. $5s - 3t$; Use $s = 14$ and $t = 13$. ₃₁
5. $3x + 5y + z$; Use $x = 18$, $y = 9$ and $z = 4$. ₁₀₃
6. $8x + 4y - 2z$; Use $x = 5$, $y = 17$ and $z = 8$. ₉₂

Evaluate each expression.

7. $-y$; Use $y = 4$. -4   8. $-y$; Use $y = -8$. 8
9. $-(-x)$; Use $x = -17$. -17 10. $-(-x)$; Use $x = 12$. 12
11. $-(y + 4)$; Use $y = 2$. -6   12. $-(y + 20)$; Use $y = 6$. -26
13. $-(x - 2)$; Use $x = 17$. -15 14. $-(x + 2)$; Use $x = 1$. -3

Find the following absolute values.

15. $|-4|$ 4   16. $|-23|$ 23   17. $|9|$ 9   18. $|11|$ 11
19. $\left|\frac{2}{3}\right|$ $\frac{2}{3}$ 20. $|-0.4|$ 0.4 21. $|13 + 2 - 15|$ 0   22. $|16 - 3 + 5|$ 18

Evaluate each expression.

23. $3|x + 2|$; Use $x = 4$. 18   26. $|p| - |q|$; Use $p = -31$ and $q = -12$. 19
24. $5|y|$; Use $y = -23$. 115   27. $|p + q|$; Use $p = 21$ and $q = -9$. 12
25. $|p| + |q|$; Use $p = 21$ and $q = -9$. 30 28. $|p - q|$; Use $p = 31$ and $q = 11$. 20

Extension

Write expressions for each of the following.

29. Five more than the absolute value of a number $5 + |x|$
30. The inverse of a number increased by its absolute value $-x + |x|$
31. The absolute value of the difference of two numbers $|x - y|$
32. The inverse of the absolute value of twice some number $-|2x|$
33. The absolute value of the sum of two numbers $|x + y|$
34. The sum of the absolute value of two numbers $|x| + |y|$

Express each of the following sentences in mathematical notation.

35. The absolute value of the difference of x and y is greater than 5. $|x - y| > 5$
36. The number x has an absolute value of 7. $|x| = 7$
37. Three times the absolute value of a number is 8. $3|x| = 8$
38. The absolute value of the sum of two numbers is less than the square root of 2. $|x + y| = \sqrt{2}$

Challenge

39. Compare the sum of the absolute values of two numbers with the absolute value of their sum. State a generalization.

40. Compare the product of the absolute values of two numbers with the absolute value of their product. State a generalization.

39. The sum of the absolute value of two numbers is equal to the absolute value of their sum when the two numbers have the same sign or one of them is zero.

40. The product of the absolute value of two numbers is equal to the absolute value of their product for all numbers.

1-3 Addition and Subtraction

Addition of Real Numbers

For review, we summarize the rules of signs for adding.

Rules for Addition of Real Numbers

1. The sum of two positive numbers is positive.
2. The sum of two negative numbers is negative. We add the absolute values and take the additive inverse of the result.
3. The sum of a number and its additive inverse is 0. (Inverses have the same absolute value).
4. To add a positive and a negative number with different absolute values, find the difference of the absolute values. If the negative number has the greater absolute value, the sum is negative. If the positive number has the greater absolute value, the sum is positive.

EXAMPLES
Add.

1. $-5 + (-9)$
We are adding two negative numbers. We add the absolute values.
$5 + 9 = 14$
Then we make the answer negative. $-5 + (-9) = -14$

2. $23 + (-11)$
The positive addend has the greater absolute value, so the answer is positive. $23 + (-11) = 12$

3. $-9.2 + 3.1 = -6.1$

4. $-\frac{5}{4} + \frac{1}{7} = -\frac{35}{28} + \frac{4}{28} = -\frac{31}{28}$

TRY THIS Add.

1. $-8 + (-9)$ ₋17
2. $-8.9 + (-9.7)$ ₋18.6
3. $-\frac{6}{5} + \left(-\frac{23}{10}\right)$ $-\frac{35}{10} = -\frac{7}{2}$

4. $14 + (-28)$ ₋14
5. $-4.5 + (7.8)$ 3.3
6. $\frac{3}{8} + \left(-\frac{5}{6}\right)$ $-\frac{11}{24}$

Subtraction of Real Numbers

Subtraction is defined in terms of addition. Subtraction and addition are opposite operations.

DEFINITION

Definition of Subtraction

The difference $m - n$ is that number which when added to n gives m.

We can always subtract by adding an inverse. That fact can be proved, and we shall prove it later. If a statement can be proved, we call it a theorem.

THEOREM 1—1

The Subtraction Theorem

For any real numbers m and n, $m - n = m + (-n)$.
(To subtract, we can add an inverse.)

The number being subtracted is called the subtrahend. To subtract, we can change the sign of the subtrahend and then add the result to the other number.

EXAMPLES
Subtract by adding an inverse.

5. $5 - (-4) = 5 + 4$ Adding the inverse of the subtrahend,
$\qquad\qquad = 9$ or changing the sign and adding

6. $-19.4 - 5.6 = -19.4 + (-5.6) = -25$

7. $-\dfrac{4}{3} - \left(-\dfrac{2}{5}\right) = -\dfrac{4}{3} + \dfrac{2}{5} = -\dfrac{20}{15} + \dfrac{6}{15} = -\dfrac{14}{15}$

TRY THIS Subtract by adding an inverse.

7. $8 - (-9)$ ₁₇   **8.** $23.7 - 5.9$ 17.8   **9.** $-\dfrac{11}{16} - \left(-\dfrac{23}{12}\right)$ 59/48

Expressions and Number Properties

The Subtraction Theorem (Theorem 1–1) tells us that the expressions $m - n$ and $m + (-n)$ will have the same value whenever we make the same substitutions in both expressions. Such expressions, expressions that always have the same value, are said to be equivalent.

In algebra it is important to know when expressions are equivalent. We use the properties of numbers to determine whether expressions are equivalent. The Subtraction Theorem is thus an important number property.

EXAMPLES

Use the Subtraction Theorem to write equivalent expressions.

8. $4y - x = 4y + (-x)$ Adding an inverse

9. $3p + 5q = 3p - (-5q)$ Subtracting an inverse

TRY THIS Use the Subtraction Theorem to write equivalent expressions.

10. $-5x - 3y$ **11.** $3x + (-2y)$ **12.** $-6p + 5t$
$\quad$ $-5x + (-3y)$ $\qquad$ $3x - 2y$ $\qquad\qquad$ $-6p - (-5t)$

The commutative and associative laws of addition are important number properties. These laws allow us to determine whether certain expressions are equivalent.

The Commutative Law of Addition

For any real numbers a and b, $a + b = b + a$. (Numbers can be added in any order without affecting the answer.)

The Associative Law of Addition

For any real numbers a, b, and c, $a + (b + c) = (a + b) + c$. (Numbers can be grouped in any manner for addition.)

EXAMPLES

Use the commutative and associative laws of addition to write equivalent expressions.

10. $y + 3x = 3x + y$ Using the commutative law to change order

11. $3p + (r + 5t) = (3p + r) + 5t$ Using the associative law to move parentheses

12. $3p + (r + 5t) = (5t + 3p) + r$ Using both laws to change grouping and order

TRY THIS Use the commutative and associative laws of addition to write equivalent expressions. Indicate which number properties you use.

13. $5y + 4x$ **14.** $3m + (2n + 4)$ **15.** $(6x + 5y) + 2z$
$4x + 5y$; commutative $(3m + 2n) + 4$; associative $(2z + 6x) + 5y$; commutative and associative

Two more familiar but important properties are the following.

The Additive Property of Zero

For any real number a, $a + 0 = a$. (Adding 0 to any real number gives that same real number.)

Property of Additive Inverses

For each number a, there is one and only one additive inverse, $-a$, for which $a + (-a) = 0$.

1–3	

Exercises
Add.

1. $-12 + (-16)$ -28 **2.** $-11 + (-18)$ -29 **3.** $-8 + (-8)$ -16 **4.** $-6 + (-6)$ -12

5. $8 + (-3)$ 5 **6.** $9 + (-4)$ 5 **7.** $11 + (-7)$ 4 **8.** $12 + (-8)$ 4

9. $-16 + 9$ -7 **10.** $-23 + 8$ -15 **11.** $-24 + 0$ -24 **12.** $-34 + 0$ -34

13. $-8.4 + 9.6$ 1.2 **14.** $-6.3 + 8.2$ 1.9

15. $-2.62 + (-6.24)$ -8.86 **16.** $-5.83 + (-7.43)$ -13.26

17. $-\frac{2}{7} + \frac{3}{7}$ **18.** $-\frac{5}{6} + \frac{1}{6}$ **19.** $-\frac{11}{12} + \left(-\frac{5}{12}\right)$

20. $-\frac{3}{8} + \left(-\frac{7}{8}\right)$ **21.** $\frac{2}{5} + \left(-\frac{3}{10}\right)$ **22.** $-\frac{3}{4} + \frac{1}{8}$

17. $\frac{1}{7}$ 20. $-\frac{10}{8} = -\frac{5}{4}$

18. $-\frac{4}{6} = -\frac{2}{3}$ 21. $\frac{1}{10}$

19. $-\frac{16}{12} = -\frac{4}{3}$ 22. $-\frac{5}{8}$

Subtract.

23. $5 - 7$ -2 **24.** $9 - 12$ -3 **25.** $-5 - 7$ -12 **26.** $-9 - 12$ -21

27. $-6 - (-11)$ 5 **28.** $-7 - (-12)$ 5 **29.** $10 - (-5)$ 15 **30.** $28 - (-16)$ 44

31. $15.8 - 27.4$ –11.6   **32.** $17.2 - 34.9$ –17.7

33. $-18.01 - 11.24$ **34.** $-19.04 - 15.76$ –34.80
–29.25

35. $-\frac{21}{4} - \left(-\frac{7}{4}\right)$ –$\frac{14}{4}$ = –$\frac{7}{2}$ **36.** $-\frac{16}{5} - \left(-\frac{3}{5}\right)$ –$\frac{13}{5}$ **37.** $-\frac{1}{2} - \left(-\frac{1}{12}\right)$ –$\frac{5}{12}$ **38.** $-\frac{3}{4} - \left(-\frac{3}{2}\right)\frac{3}{4}$

Use properties of real numbers to write equivalent expressions.
Indicate which number properties you use. Answers may vary.

39. $-3x - 4y$ **40.** $5y + (-2x)$ **41.** $3m + (-n)$ **42.** $4y + (-2)$

43. $5a + 3b$ **44.** $6t + 8s$ **45.** $3x + 0$ **46.** $5y + (-5y)$

47. $3x + (4y + 5)$ **48.** $-9a + (4b + 5c)$

49. $(4x + 5y) + 7z$ **50.** $(9p + 5q) + 2r$

Extension

Find the value of each of the following expressions.

51. $(8 - 10) - (-6 + 2)$ 2   **52.** $|8 - 10| - |-6 + 2|$ –2

53. $-10 + 18 - 6 - 14 + 31$ 19   **54.** $-10 + 18 - (6 - 14) + 31$ 47

55. $-10 + 18 - 6 - (14 + 31)$ –43 **56.** $|(8 - |-9|)| + |-6 + 12|$ 7

57. $|-6 - (-3)| - |3 - 6|$ 0   **58.** Find a number that is 27 less than -6. –33

59. What number can be added to 11.7 to obtain $-7\frac{3}{4}$? –19.45

60. Is subtraction a commutative operation? no

61. Is subtraction an associative operation? no

62. Is there a subtractive property of zero (if we subtract 0 from any number do we get that same number)? yes

39. $-3x + (-4y)$, Thm. 1–1
40. $-2x + 5y$, commutative law
41. $3m - n$, Thm. 1–1
42. $4y - 2$, Thm. 1–1
43. $3b + 5a$, commutative law
44. $8s + 6t$, commutative law
45. $3x$, additive property of 0
46. 0, property of additive inverses
47. $(3x + 4y) + 5$, associative law
48. $(-9a + 4b) + 5c$, associative law
49. $(4x + 7z) + 5y$, associative and commutative laws
50. $(5q + 9p) + 2r$, commutative law

Challenge

63. Consider the expressions $-|x|$ and $|x|$.
   a. Evaluate for several numbers and compare the value of the two expressions.
   b. Are the expressions equivalent? Why or why not? no
   c. If they are not equivalent, are there any real numbers for which they have the same value? no

64. Consider the expressions $|x|$ and $|-x|$.
   a. Evaluate for several numbers and compare the value of the two expressions.
   b. Are the expressions equivalent? Why or why not? yes
   c. If they are not equivalent, are there any real numbers for which they have the same value?

Use a calculator to find decimal notation. Round to four decimal places. Then add.

65. $-459\frac{178}{256} + 356\frac{2345}{2667}$ **66.** $-7899\frac{9876}{9934} + \left(-5672\frac{6732}{7342}\right)$ –13572.911
–102.816

1–4 Multiplication and Division

Multiplication of Real Numbers

For review, we summarize the rules of signs for multiplying.

> **Rules for Multiplication of Real Numbers**
>
> 1. To multiply a positive number and a negative number, we multiply their absolute values and take the additive inverse of the result. (The answer is negative.)
> 2. To multiply two negative numbers or two positive numbers, we multiply their absolute values. (The answer is positive.)

When we multiply any number by 0, the answer is 0. The number 1 is also important.

> **The Multiplicative Property of Zero**
>
> For any real number a, $a \cdot 0 = 0$.
>
> **The Multiplicative Property of One**
>
> For any real number a, $a \cdot 1 = a$. (Multiplying any real number by 1 gives that same real number.)

Because of the multiplicative property of 1, the number 1 is sometimes called the multiplicative identity.
The number 1 can be named in many ways with fractional notation.

Here are some examples.

$$\frac{3}{3}, \frac{-5}{-5}, \frac{x}{x}$$

EXAMPLES
Multiply.

1. $6(-7) = -42$ Multiplying absolute values and changing the sign

2. $-5.2(-10) = 52$ Multiplying absolute values

16 CHAPTER 1 REAL NUMBERS AND THEIR PROPERTIES

3. $14.5(x - x) - 14.5 \times 0 = 0$ Using the multiplicative property of 0

4. $9y \cdot \frac{x}{x} = 9y$ Using the multiplicative property of 1

5. $\frac{2}{3} \cdot \frac{5}{5} = \frac{10}{15}$ Since we multiplied by 1, we know $\frac{2}{3} = \frac{10}{15}$.

6. $\frac{-4}{5} \cdot \frac{-1}{-1} = \frac{4}{-5}$ Since we multiplied by 1, we know $\frac{-4}{5} = \frac{4}{-5}$.

TRY THIS Multiply.

1. $-4 \cdot 6$ $_{-24}$ **2.** 8.1×3.5 $_{28.35}$**3.** $\left(-\frac{4}{5}\right)\left(-\frac{2}{3}\right)$ $_{\frac{8}{15}}$ **4.** $-4.7(-9.1)$ $_{42.77}$

5. 6.921436×0 $_0$ **6.** $\frac{3}{4} \cdot \frac{7}{7}$ $_{\frac{3}{4}}$ **7.** $\frac{-17}{-25} \cdot \frac{-1}{-1}$ $_{\frac{17}{25}}$

The commutative and associative laws hold for multiplication as well as addition.

The Commutative Law of Multiplication

For any real numbers a and b, $a \cdot b = b \cdot a$. (Numbers can be multiplied in any order without affecting the answer.)

The Associative Law of Multiplication

For any real numbers a, b, and c, $a \cdot (b \cdot c) = (a \cdot b) \cdot c$. (Numbers can be grouped in any manner for multiplication.)

Division of Real Numbers

Division is defined in terms of multiplication. Division and multiplication are opposite operations.

DEFINITION

Definition of Division

The quotient $\frac{p}{q}$, or $p \div q$, is that number which when multiplied by q gives p.

EXAMPLES

Divide.

7. $\frac{10}{-2}$ Since $-5 \cdot (-2) = 10$, $\frac{10}{-2} = -5$

8. $-32 \div 4$ Since $-8 \cdot 4 = -32$, $-32 \div 4 = -8$

9. $\frac{-5.6}{-7}$ Since $0.8(-7) = -5.6$, $\frac{-5.6}{-7} = 0.8$

TRY THIS Divide.

8. $\frac{24}{-8}$ -3 9. $\frac{-10}{5}$ -2 10. $\frac{-10}{-40}$ $\frac{1}{4} = 0.25$

For review, we summarize the rules for dividing.

Rules for Division of Real Numbers

1. To divide one number by another, divide the absolute values.
2. If both numbers are positive or both are negative, the quotient is positive.
3. If one number is positive and the other negative, the quotient is negative.

When we divide 0 by any nonzero number, the answer is 0. To see that this is so, consider $\frac{0}{a}$, where a is any nonzero real number. By the definition of division, the quotient is some number b for which $b \cdot a = 0$. By the multiplicative property of zero, the number b is 0.

To subtract, we can add an inverse. To divide, we can multiply by a multiplicative inverse, which we call a reciprocal.

Property of Reciprocals

For each nonzero number a, there is one and only one reciprocal $\frac{1}{a}$, for which $a \cdot \frac{1}{a} = 1$.

To find the reciprocal of a number, we can divide 1 by that number. If we have fractional notation for the number, we can find the reciprocal by inverting.

EXAMPLES

Find the reciprocal of each number.

10. 8   The reciprocal of 8 is $\frac{1}{8}$ or 0.125, because $8 \cdot \frac{1}{8} = 1$.

11. $-\frac{2}{3}$ The reciprocal of $-\frac{2}{3}$ is $-\frac{3}{2}$, because $\left(-\frac{2}{3}\right)\left(-\frac{3}{2}\right) = 1$.

12. 0.25   The reciprocal of 0.25 is $\frac{1}{0.25}$ or 4.   Dividing 1 by 0.25

The reciprocal of a positive number is positive. The reciprocal of a negative number is negative.

TRY THIS Find the reciprocal of each number.

11. $\frac{3}{8}$ $\frac{8}{3}$ **12.** -27 $-\frac{1}{27}$ **13.** $-\frac{112}{234}$ **14.** 5.6 13. $-\frac{234}{112}$ 14. $\frac{10}{56}$

THEOREM 1–2

The Division Theorem

For any real numbers p and q, $q \neq 0$,

$$\frac{p}{q} = p \cdot \frac{1}{q}.$$

(To divide, we can multiply by a reciprocal.)

EXAMPLES

Divide by multiplying by a reciprocal.

13. $\frac{1}{4} \div \frac{3}{5} = \frac{1}{4} \times \frac{5}{3} = \frac{5}{12}$

14. $\frac{2}{3} \div \left(-\frac{4}{9}\right) = \frac{2}{3} \times \left(-\frac{9}{4}\right) = -\frac{18}{12}$

$$= -\frac{3 \cdot 6}{2 \cdot 6}$$

$$= -\frac{3}{2} \cdot \frac{6}{6}$$

$$= -\frac{3}{2}$$

TRY THIS Divide by multiplying by a reciprocal.

15. $-\frac{3}{4} \div \frac{7}{8}$ $-\frac{6}{7}$ **16.** $-\frac{12}{5} \div \left(-\frac{7}{15}\right)$ $\frac{36}{7}$

Division by Zero

We do not divide by zero. Let's see why. By the definition of division, $\frac{n}{0}$ would have to be some number c for which $c \cdot 0 = n$. But $c \cdot 0 = 0$ for any number c, so the only possible number n which could be divided by 0 would be 0. Let's consider what $\frac{0}{0}$ might be.

$\frac{0}{0}$ might be 5 because $0 = 0 \cdot 5$

$\frac{0}{0}$ might be 567 because $0 = 0 \cdot 567$

It looks as if $\frac{0}{0}$ could be *any* number. Thus we agree to exclude division by 0. Zero is the only real number that does not have a reciprocal.

Division by 0 is not defined, so any division with a divisor of 0 is not possible.

EXAMPLES
Which of the following divisions are possible?

15. $\frac{7}{0}$ Not possible   16. $\frac{0}{7}$ Possible   17. $\frac{4}{x - x}$ Not possible

TRY THIS Which of the following divisions are possible?

17. $\frac{0}{8}$ 18. $\frac{0}{0}$ 19. $\frac{8}{0}$ 20. $\frac{17}{2x - 2x}$

Possible   Not possible   Not possible   Not possible

Expressions and Number Properties

Number properties can be used to obtain expressions equivalent to a given expression. They can also be used to determine whether two expressions are equivalent. For example, we know that the expressions

$xy + 3$ and $3 + yx$

are equivalent by the commutative laws of addition and multiplication. (The order of both operations has been changed, but nothing else has been changed.)

EXAMPLES
Determine whether the two expressions are equivalent.

18. $y(x + 3), (3 + x)y$ Equivalent; commutative law of addition and commutative law of multiplication

19. $5(x - 3), 5(3 - x)$ Not equivalent; subtraction is not commutative.

20. $\frac{7a}{b}, \frac{7ac}{bc}$ Equivalent; the multiplicative property of 1

TRY THIS Determine whether the two expressions are equivalent, and give reasons.

21. $2x + (y + 5), 2x + (5 + y)$ Equivalent; commutative law

22. $9y + (5a + b), (b + 5a) + 9y$ Equivalent; commutative law

23. $3x - (2x - x), (3x - 2x) - x$ Not equivalent; subtraction is not commutative

24. $\frac{x + 2y}{2a}, (2y + x) \cdot \frac{1}{2a}$ Equivalent; Theorem 1–2 and commutative law

25. $\frac{3xy}{2xy}, \frac{3x}{2x}$ Equivalent; The multiplicative property of 1

<table>
<tr><td>**1–4**</td><td></td></tr>
</table>

Exercises

Multiply.

1. $3(-7)$ -21 **2.** $5(-8)$ -40 **3.** $-2 \cdot 4$ -8

4. $-5 \cdot 9$ -45 **5.** $(-8)(-2)$ 16 **6.** $(-7)(-3)$ 21

7. $(-9)(-14)$ 126 **8.** $(-8)(-17)$ 136 **9.** $(-6)(-5.7)$ 34.2

10. $(-7)(-6.1)$ 42.7 **11.** $-4.2(-6.3)$ 26.46 **12.** $-7.4(-9.6)$ 71.04

13. $-3\left(-\frac{2}{3}\right)$ 2 **14.** $-5\left(-\frac{3}{5}\right)$ 3 **15.** $-3(-4)(5)$ 60

16. $-6(-8)(9)$ 432 **17.** $4(-3) \cdot (-2)(1)$ 24 **18.** $-3 \cdot (-6)(8)(0)$ 0

19. $-\frac{3}{5} \cdot \frac{4}{7}$ $\frac{-12}{35}$ **20.** $-\frac{5}{4} \cdot \frac{11}{3}$ $\frac{-55}{12}$ **21.** $-\frac{9}{11} \cdot \left(-\frac{11}{9}\right)$ 1

22. $-\frac{13}{7} \cdot \left(-\frac{5}{2}\right)$ $\frac{65}{14}$ **23.** $-\frac{2}{3} \cdot \left(-\frac{2}{3}\right) \cdot \left(-\frac{2}{3}\right)$ $-\frac{8}{27}$ **24.** $-\frac{4}{5} \cdot \left(-\frac{4}{5}\right) \cdot \left(-\frac{4}{5}\right)$ $-\frac{64}{125}$

Divide.

25. $\frac{-8}{4}$ -2 **26.** $\frac{-16}{2}$ -8 **27.** $\frac{56}{-8}$ -7

28. $\frac{63}{-7}$ -9 **29.** $\frac{-77}{-11}$ 7 **30.** $\frac{-48}{-6}$ 8

31. $\dfrac{-5.4}{-18}$ 0.3

32. $\dfrac{-8.4}{-12}$ 0.7

33. $18.6 \div (-3.1)$ −6

34. $39.9 \div (-13.3)$ −3

35. $(-75.5) \div (-15.1)$ 5

36. $(-12.1) \div (-0.11)$ 110

Name the reciprocal of each.

37. $\dfrac{3}{4}$ $\frac{4}{3}$

38. $-\dfrac{7}{8}$ $-\frac{8}{7}$

39. 26 $\frac{1}{26}$

40. -97 $-\frac{1}{97}$

Divide by multiplying by a reciprocal.

41. $\dfrac{2}{7} \div \left(-\dfrac{11}{3}\right)$ $-\frac{6}{77}$

42. $\dfrac{3}{5} \div \left(-\dfrac{6}{7}\right)$ $-\frac{7}{10}$

43. $-\dfrac{10}{3} \div \left(-\dfrac{2}{15}\right)$ 25

44. $-\dfrac{12}{5} \div \left(-\dfrac{3}{10}\right)$ 8

Which of these divisions are possible?

45. $\dfrac{9}{0}$ Not possible

46. $\dfrac{0}{16}$ 0

47. $\dfrac{a-a}{28}$ 0

48. $\dfrac{2x-2x}{2x-2x}$ Not possible

Determine whether the two expressions are equivalent, and give reasons.

49. $y \cdot (s \cdot t), \quad y \cdot (t \cdot s)$

50. $(4y + 2) + x, \quad (2 + 4y) + x$

51. $(a + b) \cdot c, \quad a + (b \cdot c)$

52. $5 \cdot (x - y), \quad (5 \cdot x) - y$

53. $2y + (3 + y), \quad (2y + 3) + y$

54. $2y - (3 + y), \quad (2y - 3) + y$

55. $\dfrac{a + 3b}{4x}, \quad (a + 3b)\dfrac{1}{4x}$

56. $\dfrac{1}{ab}(5 - x), \quad \dfrac{5 - x}{ab}$

49. Equivalent. Commutative law
50. Equivalent. Commutative law
51. Not equivalent.
52. Not equivalent.
53. Equivalent. Associative law
54. Not equivalent. Subtraction is not associative.

Extension

Place parentheses in each expression so that it has the given value.

57. $3 \cdot (3 + 10 - 8); \quad 15$

58. $7 \cdot (6 - 1) + 4 \cdot (3 - 12); \quad -1$

59. $20 \div 2 \cdot (5 - 2) + 14; \quad 44$

55. Equivalent. Theorem 1–2
56. Equivalent. Theorem 1–2 property of one

Evaluate each expression using $a = -1, b = 7, c = -6,$ and $d = \frac{1}{2}$.

60. $\dfrac{d(ab - c)}{2a}$ $\frac{1}{4}$

61. $\dfrac{ad + bd}{b - a} - \dfrac{ac}{d}$ $-11\frac{5}{8}$

66. 46,871,451
67. −0.00168012

Determine which values of the variable make the following true.

62. $2x < 3x$ $\quad$ x > 0

63. $\dfrac{x}{2x} < \dfrac{x}{3x}$ $\quad$ Never true

64. $|y| < |2y|$ $\quad$ x ≠ 0

65. $|x| \leq |3x|$ $\quad$ All real values

Challenge

Use a calculator to find the value of each of the following expressions.

66. $-80{,}397 \times (-583)$

67. -0.56004×0.003

68. For which values of x and y is the following true?

$$|x + y| \leq |x| + |y|$$ For all real values

1–5 The Distributive Laws

Multiplication

When multiplying a number by a sum, we can either add first and then multiply or multiply first and then add. The results are the same. We now state the first distributive law.

The Distributive Law of Multiplication Over Addition

For any real numbers a, b and c, $a(b + c) = ab + ac$.

In stating this law we have used an agreement about parentheses. Parentheses, of course, show us which calculations are to be done first. We agree to omit them, however, around products. Thus the expression $ab + ac$ means the same as $(ab) + (ac)$. The products are to be calculated first.

There is another, equally important, distributive law.

The Distributive Law of Multiplication Over Subtraction

For any real numbers a, b and c, $a(b - c) = ab - ac$.

EXAMPLES
Multiply.

1. $4(x + 2) = 4x + 4 \cdot 2 = 4x + 8$
2. $b(s - t + f) = bs - bt + bf$
3. $-3(y + 4) = -3 \cdot y + (-3) \cdot 4 = -3y - 12$
4. $-2x(y - 1) = -2x \cdot y - (-2x) \cdot 1 = -2xy + 2x$

The distributive laws guarantee that the expression with which we begin (showing the multiplication to be done) and the final expression are equivalent. The expressions will always have the same value.

TRY THIS Multiply.

1. $5(x + 9)$ 2. $8(y - 10)$ 3. $a(x + y - z)$
   $5x + 45$ $8y - 80$ $ax + ay - az$

Factoring

The reverse of multiplying is called factoring. To factor an expression means to write an equivalent expression which is a product.

The parts of an expression such as $3x + 4y - 2z$ are called the terms of the expression. In this case the terms are $3x$, $4y$, and $-2z$. Whenever the terms of an expression have a factor in common, we can factor it out using the distributive laws. We usually try to factor out the largest factor common to all the terms.

EXAMPLES

Factor.

5. $cx - cy = c(x - y)$ Using a distributive law

6. $9x + 27y = 9x + 9 \cdot (3y) = 9(x + 3y)$

7. $P + Prt = P \cdot 1 + Prt$ Writing P as a product of P and 1
$ = P(1 + rt)$ Using a distributive law

The expression to be factored and the factored expression are always equivalent (have the same value).

TRY THIS Factor.

4. $2l + 2w$ **5.** $ac - ay$ **6.** $6x - 12$ **7.** $-25y + 15w + 5$
   $2(l + w)$ $a(c - y)$ $6(x - 2)$ $5(-5y + 3w + 1)$

Collecting Like Terms

In expressions like those in the following examples, if two terms have the same variables and no exponents, we say that they are like terms, or similar terms. If two terms have no variable at all, but are just numbers, they are similar terms. We can simplify by collecting like terms, using the distributive laws.

EXAMPLES

Collect like terms.

8. $x - 3x = 1 \cdot x - 3 \cdot x = (1 - 3)x = -2x$

9. $2x + 3y - 5x - 2y$
$ = 2x + 3y + (-5x) + (-2y)$ Subtraction is the same as adding an inverse.
$ = 2x + (-5x) + 3y + (-2y)$ Using the commutative and associative laws
$ = (2 - 5)x + (3 - 2)y$ Using the distributive law
$ = -3x + y$

An expression with like terms collected is equivalent to the original expression.

TRY THIS Collect like terms.

8. $9x + 11x$ 20x **9.** $5x - 12x$ -7x **10.** $22x - 2.5 + 1.4x + 6.4$ 23.4x + 3.9

Factoring can be useful in some practical problems, as shown below.

EXAMPLE 10

A certain amount of money is invested. This is called principal and we shall represent this amount by P. The investment pays 12% simple interest per year. Interest is the money you are paid for your investment. Find an expression for the value of the investment one year later.

$$\text{Principal} + \text{Interest} = P + 12\% \cdot P$$
$$= 1 \cdot P + 0.12P = (1 + 0.12)P = 1.12P$$

Example 10 is concerned with a percent of increase. The Try This exercise that follows is concerned with a percent of decrease, but is similar to Example 10.

TRY THIS

11. The population of a city is P. After an 8% decrease, what is the population? 0.92P

Inverse of a Sum

When we multiply a number by -1, we get the additive inverse of that number.

> **The Multiplicative Property of -1**
>
> For any real number a, $-1 \cdot a = -a$. (Negative 1 times a is the additive inverse of a, or, multiplying a number by -1 changes its sign.)

From the property of -1 we know that we can replace a negative sign by -1.

EXAMPLE 11

Rename this inverse without parentheses.

$$-(-9y) = -1(-9y) \quad \text{Using the property of } -1$$
$$= [-1(-9)]y = 9y$$

TRY THIS Rename without parentheses.

12. $-(9x)$ $-9x$ **13.** $-(-24t)$ 24t

We now consider additive inverses of sums.

EXAMPLES
Find the additive inverse and name it without parentheses.

12. $4 + x$ The inverse is $-(4 + x)$.

$$\begin{aligned}
-(4 + x) &= -1(4 + x) & \text{Using the property of } -1 \\
&= -1 \cdot 4 + (-1) \cdot x \\
&= -4 + (-x) & \text{Using the property of } -1 \\
&= -4 - x & \text{The Subtraction Theorem}
\end{aligned}$$

13. $3x - 2y + 4$ The inverse is $-(3x - 2y + 4)$.

$$\begin{aligned}
-(3x - 2y + 4) &= -1(3x - 2y + 4) \\
&= -1 \cdot 3x - (-1)2y + (-1)4 \\
&= -3x + [-(-2y)] + (-4) \\
&= -3x + 2y - 4
\end{aligned}$$

TRY THIS Find the additive inverse and name it without parentheses.

14. $7 - y$
$-7 + y$

15. $x - y$
$-x + y$

16. $9x + 6y + 11$
$-9x - 6y - 11$

17. $-3x - 2y + 1$
$3x + 2y - 1$

Examples 12–13 illustrate another important property of real numbers.

> **The Inverse of a Sum Property**
>
> For any real numbers a and b, $-(a + b) = -a + (-b)$.
> (The inverse of a sum is the sum of the inverses.)

This property holds when there is a sum of more than two terms. It also holds for differences, because any difference can be expressed as a sum. The property gives us a rule for finding the additive inverse of an expression with more than one term. To find the additive inverse of an expression with more than one term, change the sign of *every* term.

EXAMPLES
Rename the following additive inverses without parentheses.

14. $-(3x - 4y + 5) = -3x + 4y - 5$

15. $-(-9t + 7z - \frac{1}{4}w) = 9t - 7z + \frac{1}{4}w$

TRY THIS Rename the following additive inverses without parentheses.

18. $-(-2x - 5z + 24)$ 19. $-(\frac{1}{4}t + 41w - 5d + 23)$

  $2x + 5z - 24$ $-\frac{1}{4}t - 41w + 5d - 23$

We have already said what we mean by the terms of an expression. When there are only addition signs, the terms are easy to identify. They are the parts separated by addition signs. If there are subtraction signs, we can rename using addition signs.

EXAMPLE 16

What are the terms of $3x - 4y + 2z$?

$$3x - 4y + 2z = 3x + (-4y) + 2z$$

Thus the terms are: $3x$, $-4y$, and $2z$.

TRY THIS What are the terms of the following expressions?

20. $-5x - 7y + 67t - \frac{4}{5}$ 21. $-9a - 4b + 1.7c - 24$

20. $-5x, -7y, 67t, \frac{-4}{5}$
21. $-9a, -4b, 1.7c, -24$

When a sum or difference is being subtracted, as in $5y - (4x - 3)$, we can subtract by adding an inverse, as usual. We can then remove parentheses and collect like terms. Doing all of this gives us an expression equivalent to the original.

EXAMPLES
Remove parentheses and simplify.

17. $6x - (4x + 2) = 6x + [-(4x + 2)]$ Subtracting is adding the additive inverse.
$ = 6x + (-4x) + (-2)$ Renaming an inverse having two terms
$ = 6x - 4x - 2$
$ = 2x - 2$

18. $3y - 4 - (9y - 7) = 3y - 4 - 9y + 7$
$ = -6y + 3$

When removing parentheses preceded by a subtraction sign, or additive inverse sign, the sign of each term inside the parentheses is changed. If parentheses are preceded by an addition sign, no signs are changed.

TRY THIS Remove parentheses and simplify.

22. $6x - (3x - 8)$ **23.** $6x - (9y - 4) - (8x + 10)$

22. $3x + 8$
23. $-2x - 9y - 6$

We now consider subtracting an expression consisting of several terms preceded by a number.

EXAMPLE 19
Remove parentheses and simplify.

$$
\begin{aligned}
x - 3(x + y) &= x + [-3(x + y)] \quad \text{Subtracting is adding an inverse.} \\
&= x + [-3x - 3y] \\
&= x - 3x - 3y \\
&= -2x - 3y
\end{aligned}
$$

TRY THIS Remove parentheses and simplify.

24. $x - 2(y + x)$ **25.** $3x - 5(2y - 4x)$

24. $-x - 2y$
25. $23x - 10y$

Parentheses Within Parentheses

When parentheses occur within parentheses, we may make them of different shapes, such as [ ] (called "brackets") and { } (called "braces"). All of these have the same meaning. When parentheses occur within parentheses, computations in the *innermost* ones are to be done first.

EXAMPLE 20
Simplify.

$$
\begin{aligned}
7 - [3(2 - 5) - 4(2 + 3)] &= 7 - [3(-3) - 4(5)] \quad \begin{array}{l}\text{Doing the calculations} \\ \text{in the innermost parentheses}\end{array} \\
&= 7 - [-9 - 20] \\
&= 7 - [-29] \\
&= 36
\end{aligned}
$$

EXAMPLE 21
Simplify.

$$
\begin{aligned}
6y - \{4[3(y - 2) - 4(y + 2)] - 3\} & \\
= 6y - \{4[3y - 6 - 4y - 8] - 3\} &\quad \begin{array}{l}\text{Multiplying to remove the} \\ \text{innermost parentheses}\end{array} \\
= 6y - \{4[-y - 14] - 3\} &\quad \text{Collecting like terms in the braces} \\
= 6y - \{-4y - 56 - 3\} &\quad \text{Multiplying to remove the braces} \\
= 6y - \{-4y - 59\} & \\
= 6y + 4y + 59 & \\
= 10y + 59 &
\end{aligned}
$$

TRY THIS Simplify. $\qquad$ $23x + 52$ $\qquad$ $12a + 12$

26. $15x - \{2[2(x - 5) - 6(x + 3)] + 4\}$ **27.** $9a + \{3a - 2[(a - 4) - (a + 2)]\}$

1–5

Exercises

Multiply.

1. $3(a + 1)$ **2.** $8(x + 1)$ **3.** $4(x - y)$ **4.** $9(a - b)$

5. $-5(2a + 3b)$ **6.** $-2(3c + 5d)$ **7.** $2a(b - c + d)$ **8.** $5x(y - z + w)$

9. $2\pi r(h + 1)$ **10.** $P(1 + rt)$ **11.** $\frac{1}{2}h(a + b)$ **12.** $\pi r(1 + s)$

Factor.

13. $8x + 8y$ **14.** $7a + 7b$ **15.** $9p - 9$ **16.** $12x - 12$

17. $7x - 21$ **18.** $6y - 36$ **19.** $xy + x$ **20.** $ab + a$

21. $2x - 2y + 2z$ **22.** $3x + 3y - 3z$ **23.** $3x + 6y - 3$ **24.** $4a + 8b - 4$

25. $ab + ac - ad$ **26.** $xy - xz - xw$ **27.** $\pi rr + \pi rs$ **28.** $\frac{1}{2}ah + \frac{1}{2}bh$

Collect like terms.

29. $4a + 5a$ $9a$ **30.** $9x + 3x$ $12x$

31. $8b - 11b$ $-3b$ **32.** $9c - 12c$ $-3c$

33. $14y + y$ $15y$ **34.** $13x + x$ $14x$

35. $12a - a$ $11a$ **36.** $15x - x$ $14x$

37. $t - 9t$ $-8t$ **38.** $x - 6x$ $-5x$

39. $5x - 3x + 8x$ $10x$ **40.** $3x - 11x + 2x$ $-6x$

41. $5x - 8y + 3x$ $8x - 8y$ **42.** $9a - 10b + 4a$ $13a - 10b$

43. $7c + 8d - 5c + 2d$ $2c + 10d$ **44.** $12a + 3b - 5a + 6b$ $7a + 9b$

45. $4x - 7 + 18x + 25$ $22x + 18$ **46.** $13p + 5 - 4p + 7$ $9p + 12$

47. $13x + 14y - 11x - 47y$ $2x - 33y$ **48.** $17a + 17b - 12a - 38b$ $5a - 21b$

Rename each additive inverse without parentheses.

49. $-(-4b)$ **50.** $-(-5x)$ **51.** $-(a + 2)$ **52.** $-(b + 9)$

53. $-(b - 3)$ **54.** $-(x - 8)$ **55.** $-(t - y)$ **56.** $-(r - s)$

Find the additive inverse and name it without parentheses.

57. $a + b + c$ **58.** $x + y + z$ **59.** $8x - 6y + 13$

60. $9a - 7b + 24$ **61.** $-2c + 5d - 3e + 4f$ **62.** $-4x + 8y - 5w + 9z$

1. $3a + 3$
2. $8x + 8$
3. $4x - 4y$
4. $9a - 9b$
5. $-10a - 15b$
6. $-6c - 10d$
7. $2ab - 2ac + 2ad$
8. $5xy - 5xz + 5xw$
9. $2\pi rh + 2\pi r$
10. $P + Prt$
11. $\frac{1}{2}ha + \frac{1}{2}hb$
12. $\pi r + \pi rs$

13. $8(x + y)$
14. $7(a + b)$
15. $9(p - 1)$
16. $12(x - 1)$
17. $7(x - 3)$
18. $6(y - 6)$
19. $x(y + 1)$
20. $a(b + 1)$
21. $2(x - y + z)$
22. $3(x + y - z)$
23. $3(x + 2y - 1)$
24. $4(a + 2b - 1)$
25. $a(b + c - d)$
26. $x(y - z + w)$
27. $\pi r(r + s)$
28. $\frac{1}{2}h(a + b)$
49. $4b$
50. $5x$
51. $-a - 2$
52. $-b - 9$
53. $-b + 3$
54. $-x + 8$
55. $-t + y$
56. $-r + s$
57. $-a - b - c$
58. $-x - y - z$
59. $-8x + 6y - 13$
60. $-9a + 7b - 24$
61. $2c - 5d + 3e - 4f$
62. $4x - 8y + 5w - 9z$

What are the terms of the following?

63. $4a - 5b + 6$ $4a, -5b, 6$

64. $5x - 9y + 12$ $5x, -9y, 12$

65. $2x - 3y - 2z$ $2x, -3y, -2z$

66. $5a - 7b - 9c$ $5a, -7b, -9c$

Subtract and simplify.

67. $a - (2a + 5)$ $-a - 5$

68. $x - (5x + 9)$ $-4x - 9$

69. $4m - (3m - 1)$ $m + 1$

70. $5a - (4a - 3)$ $a + 3$

71. $3d - 7 - (5 - 2d)$ $5d - 12$

72. $8x - 9 - (7 - 5x)$ $13x - 16$

73. $-2(x + 3) - 5(x - 4)$ $-7x + 14$

74. $-9(y + 7) - 6(y - 3)$ $-15y - 45$

75. $5x - 7(2x - 3)$ $-9x + 21$

76. $8y - 4(5y - 6)$ $-12y + 24$

Simplify.

77. $9a - [7 - 5(7a - 3)]$ $44a - 22$

78. $12b - [9 - 7(5b - 6)]$ $47b - 51$

79. $5\{-2 + 3[4 - 2(3 + 5)]\}$ -190

80. $7\{-7 + 8[5 - 3(4 + 6)]\}$ -1449

81. $2y + \{7[3(2y - 5) - (8y + 7)] + 9\}$

82. $7b - \{6[4(3b - 7) - (9b + 10)] + 11\}$

83. $[8(x - 2) + 9x] - \{7[3(2y - 5) - (8y + 7)] + 9\}$ $17x + 14y + 129$

81. $-12y - 145$
82. $-11b + 217$

84. $[11(a - 3) + 12a] - \{6[4(3b - 7) - (9b + 10)] + 11\}$ $23a - 18b + 184$

85. $-3[9(x - 4) + 5x] - 8\{3[5(3y + 4)] - 12\}$ $-42x - 360y - 276$

86. $-6[8(y - 7) + 9y] - 7\{5[7(4z + 3)] - 14\}$ $-102y - 980z - 301$

Simplify. Use a calculator.

87. $(87,573a - 47,924b) + (-578,563a + 903,408b)$ $-490,990a + 855,484b$

88. $-348(107,324x + 57,820) - 927(33,429x - 88,007)$ $-68,337,435x + 61,461,129$

89. $(0.00079x - 0.000843y) - (-0.007943x - 0.000059y)$ $0.008733x - 0.000784y$

Extension

Simplify.

90. $-[-(-(-9))]$ 9

91. $-\{-[-(-(-10))]\}$ -10

92. $-\{-[-(-(-(-8)))]\}$ 8

93. $\frac{2}{3}[2(x + y) + 4(x + 4y)]$

94. $-4[3(x - y - z) - 3(2x + y - 5z)]$

93. $4x + 12y$
94. $12x + 24y - 48z$

95. $[-(7a - b) - (a + 5b)] - \left[2\left(a + \frac{1}{2}b\right) + 3\left(7a - \frac{5}{3}b\right)\right]$ $-31a$

96. $0.01\{0.1(x - 2y) - [0.001(3x + y) - (0.2x - 0.1y)]\} - (x - y)$ $-0.99703x + 0.99699y$

The expression $P + Prt$ gives the value of an account of P dollars principal, invested at a rate r (in percent) for a time t (in years). Find the value of an account under the following conditions.

97. $P = \$120$ $r = 12\%$ $t = 1$ yr
$\$134.40$

98. $P = \$500$ $r = 14\%$ $t = \frac{1}{2}$ yr $\$535.00$

1–6 Exponential Notation

Exponential notation is a shorthand device. When we write 3^4 for $3 \cdot 3 \cdot 3 \cdot 3$, we are using exponential notation. In the expression 3^4, the number 3 is the base and the number 4 is the exponent.

Whole Number Exponents

DEFINITION

Exponential notation a^n, where n is an integer greater than 1, means $\underbrace{a \cdot a \cdot \ldots \cdot a \cdot a.}_{n \text{ factors}}$

EXAMPLES
Write exponential notation.

1. $7 \cdot 7 \cdot 7 = 7^3$ **2.** $2x \cdot 2x \cdot 2x \cdot 2x = (2x)^4$

TRY THIS Write exponential notation.
1. $8 \cdot 8 \cdot 8 \cdot 8$ $\ ^{8^4}$ **2.** mmm $\ _{m^3}$ **3.** $4y \cdot 4y \cdot 4y \cdot 4y \cdot 4y$ $\ _{(4y)^5}$

EXAMPLES
Simplify.

3. $(4x)^2 = 4x \cdot 4x = 16x^2$ **4.** $(-3y)^3 = (-3y)(-3y)(-3y) = -27y^3$

TRY THIS Simplify.
4. $(5y)^2$ $\ _{25y^2}$ **5.** $(-2x)^3$ $\ _{-8x^3}$

When a negative or inverse sign occurs with exponential notation, a certain caution is in order. For example, $(-4)^2$ means $(-4)(-4)$, which is 16, but -4^2 means $-(4^2)$, which is -16.

In general, an exponent tells how many times the base occurs as a factor. What happens when the exponent is 1 or 0? Look for a pattern in the following equations.

$$10^3 = 10 \cdot 10 \cdot 10 = 1000$$
$$10^2 = 10 \cdot 10 = 100$$
$$10^1 = ?$$
$$10^0 = ?$$

For the pattern to continue, 10^1 would have to be 10 and 10^0 would have to be 1. We shall *agree* that exponents of 1 and 0 have that meaning.

> For any number a, we agree that a^1 means a.
> For any nonzero number a, we agree that a^0 means 1.

EXAMPLES

Write an equivalent expression without exponents for each of the following.

5. $4^1 = 4$ 6. $(-9y)^1 = -9y$

7. $6^0 = 1$ 8. $(-37.4)^0 = 1$

TRY THIS Write equivalent expressions without exponents.

6. 8^1 8   7. $(-31)^1$ −31 8. 3^0 1

9. $(-7)^0$ 1   10. y^0, where $y \neq 0$ 1

Negative Integers as Exponents

How shall we define negative integers as exponents? First let us consider the following equations and look for a pattern.

$$10^3 = 1000$$
$$10^2 = 100$$
$$10^1 = 10$$
$$10^0 = 1$$
$$10^{-1} = ?$$
$$10^{-2} = ?$$

For a pattern to continue, 10^{-1} would have to be $\frac{1}{10}$ and 10^{-2} would have to be $\frac{1}{100}$. This leads to the following definition.

DEFINITION

If n is any integer, a^{-n} is given the meaning $1/a^n$. In other words, a^n and a^{-n} are *reciprocals*.

EXAMPLES
Write equivalent expressions without using negative exponents.

9. $(-2)^{-3} = \dfrac{1}{(-2)^3}$, or $\dfrac{1}{-8}$ **10.** $(3x)^{-2} = \dfrac{1}{9x^2}$

TRY THIS Write equivalent expressions without negative exponents.

11. 10^{-4} $\frac{1}{10^4}$ **12.** $(-4)^{-3}$ **13.** $(5y)^{-3}$ 12. $\frac{1}{(-4)^3}$, or $\frac{1}{-64}$ 13. $\frac{1}{5y^3}$

EXAMPLES
Write equivalent expressions with negative exponents.

11. $\dfrac{1}{5^2} = 5^{-2}$ **12.** $\dfrac{1}{(3x)^5} = (3x)^{-5}$

TRY THIS Write equivalent expressions with negative exponents.

14. $\dfrac{1}{4^3}$ 4^{-3} **15.** $\dfrac{1}{(-5)^4}$ **16.** $\dfrac{1}{(2x)^6}$ 15. $(-5)^{-4}$ 16. $(2x)^{-6}$

1–6

Exercises
Write exponential notation.

1. $4 \cdot 4 \cdot 4 \cdot 4 \cdot 4 \cdot 4$ 4^6

2. $6 \cdot 6 \cdot 6$ 6^3

3. $y \cdot y \cdot y \cdot y \cdot y \cdot y$ y^6

4. $x \cdot x \cdot x \cdot x$ x^4

5. $3a \cdot 3a \cdot 3a \cdot 3a$ $(3a)^4$

6. $5x \cdot 5x \cdot 5x \cdot 5x \cdot 5x$ $(5x)^5$

7. $(-4x)(-4x)(-4x)$ $(-4x)^3$

8. $(-3y)(-3y)(-3y)(-3y)(-3y)$ $(-3y)^5$

9. $5 \cdot 5 \cdot x \cdot x \cdot x \cdot y \cdot y \cdot y \cdot y$ $5^2x^3y^4$

Write equivalent expressions without exponents.

10. $(-5)^3$ **11.** $(-3y)^4$ **12.** $-(5b)^3$
    -125 $81yyyy$ $-125bbb$

13. $-5b^3$ **14.** $(5x)^1$ **15.** $(-3p)^0$
    $-5bbb$ $5x$ $1, p \neq 0$

Write equivalent expressions without negative exponents.

16. 6^{-3} **17.** 8^{-4} **18.** 9^{-5} **19.** 16^{-2}

20. 11^{-1} **21.** $(-4)^{-3}$ **22.** $(6x)^{-3}$ **23.** $(-5y)^{-2}$

24. $(3m)^{-4}$ **25.** $(-3m)^{-3}$ **26.** x^2y^{-3} **27.** $2a^2b^{-5}$

28. x^2y^{-2} **29.** $a^2b^{-3}c^4d^{-5}$ **30.** $\dfrac{x^2}{y^{-2}}$ **31.** $\dfrac{a^2b^{-3}}{x^3y^{-2}}$

16. $\frac{1}{6^3}$
17. $\frac{1}{8^4}$
18. $\frac{1}{9^5}$
19. $\frac{1}{16^2}$
20. $\frac{1}{11^1}$
21. $\frac{1}{(-4)^3}$
22. $\frac{1}{(6x)^3}$
23. $\frac{1}{(5y)^2}$
24. $\frac{1}{(3m)^4}$
25. $\frac{1}{(-3m)^3}$
26. $\frac{x^2}{y^3}$
27. $\frac{2a^2}{b^5}$
28. $\frac{x^2}{y^2}$
29. $\frac{a^2c^4}{b^3d^5}$
30. x^2y^2
31. $\frac{a^2y^2}{x^3b^3}$

Write equivalent expressions using negative exponents.

32. $\dfrac{1}{3^4}$ **33.** $\dfrac{1}{9^2}$ **34.** $\dfrac{1}{(-16)^2}$ **35.** $\dfrac{1}{(-8)^6}$

36. $\dfrac{1}{(5y)^3}$ **37.** $\dfrac{1}{(5x)^5}$ **38.** $\dfrac{1}{3y^4}$ **39.** $\dfrac{1}{4b^3}$

32. 3^{-4}
33. 9^{-2}
34. $(-16)^{-2}$
35. $(-8)^{-6}$
36. $(5y)^{-3}$
37. $(5x)^{-5}$
38. $\frac{y^{-4}}{3}$
39. $\frac{b^{-3}}{4}$

Extension

Write equivalent expressions having all exponents negative.

40. x^3y^{-2} **41.** $x^3a^{-2}b^3d^{-4}$ **42.** $\dfrac{x^{-3}}{y^5}$ **43.** $\dfrac{a^2b^{-3}}{x^3y^{-2}}$

40. $\frac{y^{-2}}{x^{-3}}$
41. $\frac{a^{-2}d^{-4}}{x^{-3}b^{-3}}$
42. $x^{-3}y^{-5}$
43. $\frac{x^{-3}b^{-3}}{a^{-2}y^{-2}}$

Evaluate each of the following.

44. x^4; Use $x = 2$ 16

45. $m^3 + 7$; Use $m = 4$ 71

46. $x^3 + y^2$; Use $x = -3$ and $y = 4$ -11

47. $p^4 - q^4$; Use $p = 5$ and $q = -3$ 544

Challenge

Simplify.

48. $(-2)^0 - (-2)^3 - (-2)^{-1} + (-2)^4 - (-2)^{-2}$ $26\frac{3}{4}$

49. $2(6^1 \cdot 6^{-1} - 6^{-1} \cdot 6^0)$ $\frac{5}{3}$

50. $\dfrac{(-8)^{-2} \cdot (8 - 8^0)}{2^{-6}}$ 7

51. $\left[\dfrac{1}{(-3)^{-2}} - (-3)^1\right] \cdot \left[(-3)^2 + (-3)^{-2}\right]$ $\frac{984}{9}$, or $\frac{328}{3}$

52. Evaluate the following when $x = 1$ and $y = -2$.

$(x - y)(x^{y-x} - y^{x-y})$ 27

1–7 Properties of Exponents

Multiplication and Division

To multiply using exponential notation, we add the exponents. For example, $x^3 \cdot x^2 = x^5$.

Let us consider a case in which one exponent is positive and one is negative.

$$b^5 \cdot b^{-2} = b \cdot b \cdot b \cdot b \cdot b \, \frac{1}{b \cdot b} \quad \text{By definition of exponents}$$

$$= \frac{b \cdot b}{b \cdot b} \, b \cdot b \cdot b$$

$$= b^3$$

Adding exponents again gives the correct result. That is always the case, whether exponents are positive, negative or zero.

THEOREM 1–3

In multiplication with exponential notation, we can add exponents if the bases are the same.

$$a^m a^n = a^{m+n}$$

EXAMPLES
Multiply and simplify.

1. $x^4 \cdot x^3 = x^{4+3} = x^7$ 2. $4^5 \cdot 4^{-3} = 4^{5+(-3)} = 4^2$

3. $(-2)^{-3}(-2)^7 = (-2)^{-3+7} = (-2)^4 = 16$

4. $(8x^4y^{-2})(-3x^{-3}y) = 8 \cdot (-3) \cdot x^4 \cdot x^{-3} \cdot y^{-2} \cdot y^1$
$$= -24x^{4-3}y^{2+1} = -24xy^{-1} \text{ or } -\frac{24x}{y}$$

TRY THIS Multiply and simplify.

1. $8^{-3} \cdot 8^7$ 8^4 2. y^7y^{-2} y^5 3. $(9x^4)(-2x^7)$ $-18x^{11}$ 4. $-75x^{-14} = \frac{-75}{x^{14}}$

4. $(-3x^{-4})(25x^{-10})$ 5. $(5x^{-3}y^4)(-2x^{-9}y^{-2})$ 5. $-10x^{-12}y^2 = \frac{-10y^2}{x^{12}}$

We now consider division using exponential notation.

$\frac{8^5}{8^3}$ means $\frac{8 \cdot 8 \cdot 8 \cdot 8 \cdot 8}{8 \cdot 8 \cdot 8}$. This simplifies to $8 \cdot 8$, or 8^2.

We can obtain the result by subtracting exponents. This is always the case, even if exponents are negative or zero.

THEOREM 1–4

In division with exponential notation, we can subtract exponents if the bases are the same.

$$\frac{a^m}{a^n} = a^{m-n}$$

EXAMPLES
Divide and simplify.

5. $\frac{5^7}{5^3} = 5^{7-3} = 5^4$ Subtracting exponents

6. $\frac{5^7}{5^{-3}} = 5^{7-(-3)}$ Subtracting exponents

     $= 5^{7+3}$

     $= 5^{10}$

7. $\frac{9^{-2}}{9^5} = 9^{-2-5} = 9^{-7}$, or $\frac{1}{9^7}$

8. $\frac{7^{-4}}{7^{-5}} = 7^{-4-(-5)} = 7^{-4+5} = 7^1 = 7$

9. $\frac{16x^4y^7}{-8x^3y^9} = \frac{16}{-8} \cdot \frac{x^4}{x^3} \cdot \frac{y^7}{y^9} = -2xy^{-2}$, or $-\frac{2x}{y^2}$

10. $\frac{14x^7y^{-3}}{4x^5y^{-5}} = \frac{14}{4} \cdot \frac{x^7}{x^5} \cdot \frac{y^{-3}}{y^{-5}} = \frac{7}{2}x^2y^2$

TRY THIS Divide and simplify.

6. $\frac{5^4}{5^{-2}}$ 5^6 7. $\frac{10^{-2}}{10^{-8}}$ 10^6 8. $\frac{42y^7x^6}{-21y^{-3}x^{10}}$ 9. $\frac{33a^5b^{-2}}{22a^7b^{-4}}$

8. $-2y^{10}x^{-4} = \frac{-2y^{10}}{x^4}$

9. $\frac{3a^{-2}b^2}{2} = \frac{3b^2}{2a^2}$

We do not define 0^0. Now we can see why. 0^0 would be equal to 0^{1-1}. But 0^{1-1} would also be equal to $\frac{0}{0}$. We have already seen that we must leave $\frac{0}{0}$ undefined, so we also leave 0^0 undefined.

Raising a Power to a Power

Consider the expression $(5^2)^4$. It means $5^2 \cdot 5^2 \cdot 5^2 \cdot 5^2$, or 5^8. We can obtain the result by multiplying the exponents.
Consider $(8^{-2})^3$. It means

$$\frac{1}{8^2} \cdot \frac{1}{8^2} \cdot \frac{1}{8^2}, \text{ or } \frac{1}{8^6}, \text{ which is } 8^{-6}.$$

Again, we could obtain the result by multiplying the exponents. This works in general, whether the exponents are positive, negative, or zero.

THEOREM 1—5

To raise a power to a power we can multiply exponents.

$$(a^m)^n = a^{m \cdot n}$$

EXAMPLES
Simplify.

11. $(3^5)^7 = 3^{5 \cdot 7} = 3^{35}$
12. $(x^{-5})^4 = x^{-5 \cdot 4} = x^{-20}$

TRY THIS Simplify.
10. $(3^7)^6$ 3^{42} 11. $(x^2)^{-7}$ x^{-14} 12. $(t^{-3})^{-2}$ t^6

We consider cases in which there are several factors inside the parentheses. Consider $(5^2 \cdot 7^3)^4$. It means

$$(5^2 \cdot 7^3) \cdot (5^2 \cdot 7^3) \cdot (5^2 \cdot 7^3) \cdot (5^2 \cdot 7^3), \text{ or } 5^8 \cdot 7^{12}.$$

Again, we can obtain the result by multiplying the exponents. That is true in general, for positive, negative, or zero exponents.

THEOREM 1—6

To raise an expression with several factors to a power, raise each factor to the power, multiplying exponents.

$$(a^m b^n)^p = a^{m \cdot p} \cdot b^{n \cdot p}$$

EXAMPLES

Simplify.

13. $(3x^2y^{-2})^3 = 3^3(x^2)^3(y^{-2})^3 = 3^3x^6y^{-6}$, or $27x^6y^{-6}$, or $\dfrac{27x^6}{y^6}$

14. $(5x^3y^{-5}z^2)^4 = 5^4(x^3)^4(y^{-5})^4(z^2)^4$, or $625x^{12}y^{-20}z^8$, or $\dfrac{625x^{12}z^8}{y^{20}}$

TRY THIS Simplify.

13. $(2xy)^3$ $8x^3y^3$ **14.** $(4x^{-2}y^7)^{-2}$ $\frac{x^4}{16y^{14}}$

15. $(-2x^4y^2)^5$ **16.** $(10x^{-4}y^7z^{-2})^3$ 15. $-32x^{20}y^{10}$ 16. $\frac{1000y^{21}}{x^{12}z^6}$

We now consider raising a quotient to a power. Consider $\left(\dfrac{3^2}{5^3}\right)^4$.

This means $\left(\dfrac{3^2}{5^3}\right) \cdot \left(\dfrac{3^2}{5^3}\right) \cdot \left(\dfrac{3^2}{5^3}\right) \cdot \left(\dfrac{3^2}{5^3}\right)$, or $\dfrac{3^8}{5^{12}}$.

Once more, we can obtain the result by multiplying the exponents. This is true in general, for positive, negative, or zero exponents.

THEOREM 1—7

To raise a quotient to a power, raise both numerator and denominator to the power, multiplying exponents.

$$\left(\frac{a^m}{b^n}\right)^p = \frac{a^{m\cdot p}}{b^{n\cdot p}}$$

EXAMPLES

Simplify.

15. $\left(\dfrac{x^2}{y^{-3}}\right)^{-5} = \dfrac{x^{2\cdot(-5)}}{y^{-3\cdot(-5)}} = \dfrac{x^{-10}}{y^{15}}$, or $\dfrac{1}{x^{10}y^{15}}$

16. $\left(\dfrac{2x^3y^{-2}}{3y^4}\right)^5 = \dfrac{(2x^3y^{-2})^5}{(3y^4)^5} = \dfrac{2^5x^{35}y^{-25}}{3^5y^{45}}$

$= \dfrac{32x^{15}y^{-10}}{243y^{20}} = \dfrac{32x^{15}}{243y^{30}}$, or $\dfrac{32}{243}x^{15}y^{-30}$

TRY THIS Simplify.

17. $\left(\dfrac{x^{-3}}{y^4}\right)^{-3}$ **18.** $\left(\dfrac{3x^2y^{-3}}{2y^5}\right)^2$ 17. x^9y^{12} 18. $\frac{9x^4}{4y^{16}}$

Order of Operations

The order of operations is given by the following rules. These rules are particularly helpful when you are using a calculator or learning to write computer programs.

Order of Operations

1. Calculate within innermost parentheses first.
2. Evaluate exponential expressions.
3. Multiply and divide, in order, from left to right.
4. Add and subtract, in order, from left to right.

EXAMPLES

17. $3^2 - 9 \cdot 6 = 9 - 9 \cdot 6$ Evaluating exponential expression first
$= 9 - 54$ Multiplying
$= -45$ Subtracting

18. $(3^2 - 9) \cdot 6 = (9 - 9) \cdot 6$ Evaluating exponential expression first
$= 0 \cdot 6$
$= 0$

19. $3^2 + 2 \cdot 8 - (4 - 1) = 3^2 + 2 \cdot 8 - 3$ Calculating within parentheses first
$= 9 + 2 \cdot 8 - 3$ Then evaluating exponential expression
$= 9 + 16 - 3$
$= 22$

TRY THIS Simplify.

19. $3 \cdot 2^2 + 4$ 16   **20.** $3 \cdot (2^2 + 4)$ 24   **21.** $3 \cdot 4 \div 6 + 9 \cdot 2$ 20

1–7	

Exercises

Multiply and simplify.

1. $5^6 \cdot 5^3$ 5^9 **2.** $6^2 \cdot 6^6$ 6^8 **3.** $8^{-6} \cdot 8^2$ 8^{-4}

4. $9^{-5} \cdot 9^3$ 9^{-2} **5.** $8^{-2} \cdot 8^{-4}$ 8^{-6} **6.** $9^{-1} \cdot 9^{-6}$ 9^{-7}

7. $b^2 \cdot b^{-5}$ b^{-3} **8.** $a^4 \cdot a^{-3}$ a **9.** $a^{-3} \cdot a^4 \cdot a^2$ a^3

10. $x^{-8} \cdot x^5 \cdot x^3$ 1   **11.** $(2x^3)(3x^2)$ $6x^5$ **12.** $(9y^2)(2y^3)$ $18y^5$

13. $(14m^2n^3)(-2m^3n^2)$ $-28m^5n^5$

14. $(6x^5y^{-2})(-3x^2y^3)$ $-18x^7y$

15. $(-2x^{-3})(7x^{-8})$ $-14x^{-11}$

16. $(6x^{-4}y^3)(-4x^{-8}y^{-2})$ $-24x^{-12}y$

Divide and simplify.

17. $\dfrac{6^8}{6^3}$ 6^5

18. $\dfrac{7^9}{7^4}$ 7^5

19. $\dfrac{4^3}{4^{-2}}$ 4^5

20. $\dfrac{5^8}{5^{-3}}$ 5^{11}

21. $\dfrac{10^{-3}}{10^6}$ 10^{-9}

22. $\dfrac{12^{-4}}{12^8}$ 12^{-12}

23. $\dfrac{9^{-4}}{9^{-6}}$ 9^2

24. $\dfrac{2^{-7}}{2^{-5}}$ 2^{-2}

25. $\dfrac{a^3}{a^{-2}}$ a^5

26. $\dfrac{y^4}{y^{-5}}$ y^9

27. $\dfrac{9a^2}{(-3a)^2}$ 1

28. $\dfrac{24a^5b^3}{-8a^4b}$ $-3ab^2$

29. $\dfrac{-24x^6y^7}{18x^{-3}y^9}$ $\frac{-4x^9}{3y^2}$

30. $\dfrac{14a^4b^{-3}}{-8a^8b^{-5}}$ $-\frac{7b^2}{4a^4}$

31. $\dfrac{-18x^{-2}y^3}{-12x^{-5}y^5}$ $\frac{3x^3}{2y^2}$

32. $\dfrac{-14a^{14}b^{-5}}{-18a^{-2}b^{-10}}$ $\frac{7a^{12}b^5}{9}$

Simplify.

33. $(4^3)^2$ 4^6

34. $(5^4)^5$ 5^{20}

35. $(8^4)^{-3}$ 8^{-12}

36. $(9^3)^{-4}$ 9^{-12}

37. $(6^{-4})^{-3}$ 6^{12}

38. $(7^{-8})^{-5}$ 7^{40}

39. $(3x^2y^2)^3$

40. $(2a^3b^4)^5$ $2^5a^{15}b^{20}$ or $32a^{15}b^{20}$

41. $(-2x^3y^{-4})^{-2}$

42. $(-3a^2b^{-5})^{-3}$

43. $(-6a^{-2}b^3c)^{-2}$

44. $(-8x^{-4}y^5z^2)^{-4}$

45. $\left(\dfrac{4^{-3}}{3^4}\right)^3$ $\frac{1}{4^9 \cdot 3^{12}}$

46. $\left(\dfrac{5^2}{4^{-3}}\right)^{-3}$ $\frac{1}{5^6 \cdot 4^9}$

47. $\left(\dfrac{2x^3y^{-2}}{3y^{-3}}\right)^3$ $\frac{8x^9y^3}{27}$

48. $\left(\dfrac{-4x^4y^{-2}}{5x^{-1}y^4}\right)^{-4}$ $\frac{5^4y^{24}}{(-4)^4x^{20}}$

49. $3 \cdot 2 + 4 \cdot 2^2 - 6(3-1)$ 10

50. $3[(2 + 4 \cdot 2^2) - 6(3-1)]$ 18

51. $4(8-6)^2 + 4 \cdot 3 - 2 \cdot 8 \div 4$ 24

52. $[4(8-6)^2 + 4] \cdot (3 - 2 \cdot 8) \div 4$ -65

39. $3^3x^6y^6$ or $27x^6y^6$

41. $(-2)^{-2}x^{-6}y^8$ or $\frac{1}{4}x^{-6}y^8$

42. $(-3)^{-3}a^{-6}b^{15}$ or $-\frac{1}{27}a^{-6}b^{15}$

43. $(-6)^{-2}a^4b^{-6}c^{-2}$ or $\frac{1}{36}a^4b^{-6}c^{-2}$

44. $(-8)^{-4}x^{16}y^{-20}z^{-8}$ or $\frac{1}{4096}x^{16}y^{-20}z^{-8}$

Extension
Simplify.

53. $\dfrac{(2^{-2})^{-4}(2^3)^{-2}}{(2^{-2})^2(2^5)^{-3}}$ 2^{21}

54. $\left\{[(8^{-2})^3]^{-4}\right\}^5 \cdot [(8^0)^{-2}]^6$ 8^{120}

55. $\left[\dfrac{(-3x^2y^5)^{-3}}{(2x^4y^{-8})^{-2}}\right]^2$ $\frac{2^4x^4}{(-3)^6y^{62}}$

56. $\left[\left(\dfrac{a^{-2}}{b^7}\right)^{-3} \cdot \left(\dfrac{a^4}{b^{-3}}\right)^2\right]^{-1}$ $\frac{1}{a^{-14}b^{27}}$

57. $\left[\dfrac{(-4x^2y^3)(-2xy)^{-2}}{(4x^4y^2)(-2x^5y)}\right]^{-2}$ $64x^{22}y^2$

58. $\dfrac{(3xy)^2(6x^2y^2) + 4x^4y^4}{(4xy)^2 + 13x^2y^2}$ $2x^2y^2$

Challenge
Simplify. Assume variables in exponents represent integers.

59. $(x^y \cdot x^{2y})^3$ x^{9y}

60. $(y^x \cdot y^{-x})^4$ 1

61. $(a^{b+x} \cdot a^{b-x})^3$ a^{6b}

62. $(m^{a-b} \cdot m^{2b-a})^p$ m^{bp}

63. $(x^by^a \cdot x^ay^b)^c$ $x^{ca+cb}y^{ca+cb}$

64. $(m^{x-b}n^{x+b})^x(m^bn^{-b})^x$ $mx^{x^2}n^{x^2}$

65. $\left[\dfrac{(2x^ay^b)^3}{(-2x^ay^b)^2}\right]^2$ $4x^{2a}y^{2b}$

66. $\left[\left(\dfrac{x^r}{y^s}\right)^2\left(\dfrac{x^{2r}}{y^{3s}}\right)^{-2}\right]^{-2}$ $\frac{x^{4r}}{y^{8s}}$

1–8 Scientific Notation

Scientific Notation

Scientific notation is based on the properties of exponents which were presented in Chapter 1. It is very useful for calculating with very large or very small numbers. It is also helpful for estimating.

6.4×10^{13} means 64000000000000 4.6×10^{-6} means 0.0000046

DEFINITION

Scientific notation for a number is the product of exponential notation for a power of 10 and decimal notation for a number between 1 and 10.

EXAMPLE 1
Light travels about 9,460,000,000,000 kilometers in one year. Write scientific notation for the number.

We need to move the decimal point 12 places, between the 9 and the 4, so we multiply by 1 in the form $10^{-12} \times 10^{12}$.

$9,460,000,000,000 \times 10^{-12} \times 10^{12}$ Multiplying by 1
$= 9.46 \times 10^{12}$ The 10^{-12} moved the decimal point 12 places to the left and we have scientific notation.

TRY THIS
1. Convert 460,000,000,000 to scientific notation. 4.6×10^{11}
2. The distance from the earth to the sun is about 150,000,000 km. Write scientific notation for this number. 1.5×10^{8}

EXAMPLE 2
Write scientific notation for 0.0000000000156.

We want to move the decimal point 11 places. We choose $10^{11} \times 10^{-11}$ as a name for 1, and then multiply.

$0.0000000000156 \times 10^{11} \times 10^{-11}$ Multiplying by 1
$= 1.56 \times 10^{-11}$ The 10^{11} moved the decimal point 11 places to the right and we have scientific notation.

You should try to make conversions to scientific notation mentally as much as possible.

TRY THIS

3. Convert 0.00000001235 to scientific notation. 1.235×10^{-8}

4. The mass of a hydrogen atom is 0.00000000000000000000000017 grams. Write scientific notation for this number. 1.7×10^{-24}

Multiplying and Dividing

Multiplying and dividing in scientific notation is easy. We use the commutative and associative laws and then use the properties of exponents to simplify the powers of ten.

EXAMPLES

3. Multiply and write scientific notation for the answer.

$$(3.1 \times 10^5)(4.5 \times 10^{-3})$$

We apply the commutative and associative laws.

$$(3.1 \times 10^5)(4.5 \times 10^{-3}) = (3.1 \times 4.5)(10^5 \times 10^{-3})$$
$$= 13.95 \times 10^2$$

To find scientific notation for the result, we convert 13.95 to scientific notation and then simplify.

$$13.95 \times 10^2 = (1.395 \times 10^1) \times 10^2$$
$$= 1.395 \times 10^3$$

4. Divide and write scientific notation for the answer.

$$\frac{6.4 \times 10^{-7}}{8.0 \times 10^6} = \frac{6.4}{8.0} \times \frac{10^{-7}}{10^6} \quad \text{Factoring}$$
$$= 0.8 \times 10^{-13} \quad \text{Doing the divisions separately}$$
$$= (8.0 \times 10^{-1}) \times 10^{-13} \quad \text{Converting 0.8 to scientific notation}$$
$$= 8.0 \times 10^{-14}$$

TRY THIS Multiply or divide and write scientific notation for the answer.

5. $(9.1 \times 10^{-17})(8.2 \times 10^3)$ 6. $(1.12 \times 10^{-8})(5 \times 10^{-7})$ 5. 7.462×10^{-13} 6. 5.6×10^{-15}

7. $\dfrac{4.2 \times 10^5}{2.1 \times 10^2}$ 2×10^3 8. $\dfrac{1.1 \times 10^{-4}}{2.0 \times 10^{-7}}$ 5.5×10^2

1-8	

Exercises

Convert to scientific notation.

1. 47,000,000,000 4.7×10^{10}

2. 2,600,000,000,000 2.6×10^{12}

3. 863,000,000,000,000,000 8.63×10^{17}

4. 957,000,000,000,000,000 9.57×10^{17}

5. 0.000000016 1.6×10^{-8}

6. 0.000000263 2.63×10^{-7}

7. 0.00000000007 7×10^{-11}

8. 0.00000000009 9×10^{-11}

Convert to decimal notation.

9. 4×10^{-4} 0.0004

10. 5×10^{-5} 0.00005

11. 6.73×10^{8} 673,000,000

12. 9.24×10^{7} 92,400,000

13. 8.923×10^{-10} 0.0000000008923

14. 7.034×10^{-2} 0.07034

Write scientific notation for the number in each of the following.

15. The mass of an electron is 0.00000000000000000000000000911 g.

16. The population of the United States is about 224,000,000. 2.24×10^{8}

17. An electron carries a charge of 0.00000000048 electrostatic units. 4.8×10^{-10}

18. A helium atom has a diameter of 0.000000022 cm. 2.2×10^{-8}

Multiply and write scientific notation for the answer.

19. $(2.3 \times 10^{6})(4.2 \times 10^{-11})$ 9.66×10^{-5}

20. $(6.5 \times 10^{3})(5.2 \times 10^{-8})$ 3.38×10^{-4}

21. $(2.34 \times 10^{-8})(5.7 \times 10^{-4})$ 1.3338×10^{-11}

22. $(3.26 \times 10^{-6})(8.2 \times 10^{-6})$ 2.6732×10^{-11}

23. $(3.2 \times 10^{6})(2.6 \times 10^{4})$ 8.34×10^{10}

24. $(3.11 \times 10^{3})(1.01 \times 10^{13})$ 3.1411×10^{16}

Divide and write scientific notation for the answer. 15. 9.11×10^{-28}

25. $\dfrac{8.5 \times 10^{8}}{3.4 \times 10^{5}}$

26. $\dfrac{5.1 \times 10^{6}}{3.4 \times 10^{3}}$

27. $\dfrac{4.0 \times 10^{-6}}{8.0 \times 10^{-3}}$

25. 2.5×10^{3}
26. 1.5×10^{3}
27. 5×10^{-4}
28. 3×10^{-5}

28. $\dfrac{7.5 \times 10^{-9}}{2.5 \times 10^{-4}}$

29. $\dfrac{12.6 \times 10^{8}}{4.2 \times 10^{-3}}$

30. $\dfrac{3.2 \times 10^{-7}}{8.0 \times 10^{8}}$

29. 3×10^{11}
30. 4×10^{-16}

Extension

Estimate.

31. $\dfrac{(6.1 \times 10^{4})(7.2 \times 10^{-6})}{9.8 \times 10^{-4}}$ 4.5×10^{2}

32. $\dfrac{(8.05 \times 10^{-11})(5.9 \times 10^{7})}{3.1 \times 10^{14}}$ 1.6×10^{19}

33. $\dfrac{780,000,000 \times 0.00071}{0.000005}$ 1.1×10^{11}

34. $\dfrac{830,000,000 \times 0.12}{3,100,000}$ 3×10^{1}

35. $\dfrac{43,000,000 \times 0.095}{63,000}$ 6.5×10

36. $\dfrac{0.0073 \times 0.84}{0.000006}$ 1×10^{3}

1–9 Proofs in Algebra (Optional)

Axioms, Theorems, and Definitions

In this chapter we have demonstrated various number properties and laws as they apply to algebra. For example, we learned to factor $4x + 12$ as $4(x + 3)$ using a distributive law. We also learned to simplify $x^5 \cdot x^3$ as x^8, using Theorem 1–3. In each case we were finding equivalent expressions.

The number properties and laws that we accept without proof are called axioms. Others are called theorems, and are proven from the axioms and previously proven theorems. The definitions we make are agreements—usually in the form of an abbreviated way of stating something. For example, we agree to write 3^5 as an abbreviation for $3 \cdot 3 \cdot 3 \cdot 3 \cdot 3$. In some definitions, the agreements are more complicated as in the definition of subtraction in terms of addition.

The axioms that we have been using are those for the real numbers and were listed in Section 1–1. You will need to make reference to that list.

In addition to the important definitions of subtraction, division, absolute value, and exponential notation, we also need a definition of equality and the properties of equality.

DEFINITION

A sentence $a = b$ states that a and b are expressions for the same number.

Properties of Equality

1. Reflexive Property. For any number a, $a = a$.
2. Symmetric Property. For any numbers a and b, if $a = b$ is true, then $b = a$ is true.
3. Transitive Property. For any numbers a, b, and c, if $a = b$ is true and $b = c$ is true, then $a = c$ is true.

EXAMPLES

Which axiom(s) or properties of equality, if any, justify the following statements?

1. $6(x + 3) = 6x + 18$ Axiom 3 (Distributive Law)

2. $5y - x = 5y + (-x)$ We cannot justify this one. We need a theorem for it.

3. $3x^2 \cdot 1 = 3x^2$ Axiom 6 (Multiplicative Property of One)

4. If $2 + 3 = 5$ and $5 = 4 + 1$,   Transitive Property of Equality
   then $2 + 3 = 4 + 1$.

TRY THIS Which axiom(s) or properties of equality, if any, justify the following statements?

1. $5 + (a + b) = (5 + a) + b$ 2. $5(x - 2) = 5x - 10$

3. $5y^3 + 0 = 5y^3$ 4. $(x + 2) \cdot \dfrac{1}{x + 2} = 1$

Proofs

Number properties that can be proved by using axioms and definitions are called theorems.

THEOREM 1–8

For any numbers $a, b, c,$ and d, $a(b + c + d) = ab + ac + ad$.

To prove the theorem, we write a sequence of statements. Each one must be supported by an axiom. Proofs are written in columns to make sure that we support every statement.

EXAMPLE 5
Prove Theorem 1–8.

1. $a(b + c + d) = a[(b + c) + d]$	1. Axiom 2 (Associativity)
2. $a[(b + c) + d] = a(b + c) + ad$	2. Axiom 3 (Distributive Law)
3. $a(b + c) + ad = ab + ac + ad$	3. Axiom 3
4. $a(b + c + d) = ab + ac + ad$	4. By statements 1–3 (The Transitive Property of Equality is used here.)

THEOREM 1–1

The Subtraction Theorem

For any numbers a and b, $a - b = a + (-b)$.

To prove the theorem, we will use the definition of subtraction. It says that $a - b$ is the number which when added to b gives a. We will show that $a + (-b)$ works the same way.

EXAMPLE 6
Prove Theorem 1–1.

1. $[a + (-b)] + b = a + [(-b) + b]$	1. ?
2. $a + [(-b) + b] = a + 0$	2. Axiom 5
3. $a + 0 = a$	3. ?
4. $[a + (-b)] + b = a$	4. Statements 1–3
5. $a + (-b) = a - b$	5. Definition of Subtraction

TRY THIS

5. Supply reasons for steps 1 and 3 of the proof of Theorem 1–1.

We list some further theorems. You will be asked to prove some of them in the exercises. To prove a specific theorem, you may use any preceding theorem for its proof.

Theorem 1–2 The Division Theorem
For any numbers a and b, except that b cannot be 0,

$$a \div b \left(\text{or } \frac{a}{b} \right) = a \cdot \frac{1}{b}.$$

Theorem 1–9 The Multiplicative Property of 0

For any real number a, $a \cdot 0 = 0$.

Theorem 1–10 Inverses of Sums

For any real numbers a and b, $-(a + b) = -a + (-b)$.

Theorem 1–11 The Multiplicative Property of -1

For any real number a, $-1 \cdot a = -a$.

Theorem 1–12 Distributive Law of Multiplication over Subtraction

For any real numbers a, b, and c, $a(b - c) = ab - ac$.

Theorem 1–13 Inverses of Products

For any real numbers a and b, $-(ab) = -a \cdot b = a \cdot (-b)$.

Theorem 1–14 Products of Inverses

For any real numbers a and b, $(-a)(-b) = ab$

1–9	

Exercises

Which axiom(s) or properties of equality, if any, justify the following statements?

1. $6(x + 3) = 6x + 18$
2. $4x + (2y + 5) = (4x + 2y) + 5$
3. $a(-b + b) = a \cdot 0$
4. $x(a + b) = xa + xb$
5. $3x - 2y = 3x + (-2y)$
6. $-1 \cdot 3x = -3x = (-3) \cdot x$

7. $5x - (y - 2) = (5x - y) + 2$
8. $\dfrac{2}{x + 1} = 2 \cdot \dfrac{1}{x + 1}$

9. If $2 = x$, then $x = 2$.
10. $a + b = a + b$
11. $x^2 + y^2 = y^2 + x^2$
12. $(a + b) + c = a + (b + c)$

13. $x^3 - y^3 = x^3 + (-y^3)$
14. $\frac{1}{2}(x + y) = \frac{1}{2}x + \frac{1}{2}y$

15. $x + y = y + x$
16. If $-1 \cdot x = -x$ and $-x = y$, then $-1 \cdot x = y$.

Write proofs for the following.

17. Complete this proof of Theorem 1–10.
    For any real numbers a and b, $-(a - b) = -a + (-b)$.

1. $(a + b) + [-a + (-b)] = [a + (-a)] + [b + (-b)]$	1.
2. $[a + (-a)] + [b + (-b)] = \quad 0 \quad + \quad 0$	2.
3. $0 \quad\quad + \quad 0 \quad = \quad 0$	3.
4. Thus, $-a + (-b)$ is the inverse of $(a + b)$; in other words $-a + (-b) = -(a + b)$.	4.

18. For any numbers a, b, and c $(a + b)c = ac + bc$.

19. Complete this proof of Theorem 1–11.
For any real number a, $-1 \cdot a = -a$.

1. $-1 \cdot a + a$	1. ?
2. $-1 \cdot a + 1 \cdot a = (-1 + 1) \cdot a$	2. Exercise 18
3. $(-1 + 1) \cdot a = 0 \cdot a$	3. ?
4. $0 \cdot a = 0$	4. Theorem 1–9
5. $-1 \cdot a + a = 0$	5. Transitive Property of Equality. Statements 1–4.
6. Thus, $-1 \cdot a$ is the inverse of a; that is, $-1 \cdot a = -a$.	6. ?

20. Complete this proof of Theorem 1–13.

First part of proof:	
1. $-a \cdot b = (-1 \cdot a) \cdot b$	1. Theorem 1–11
2. $(-1 \cdot a) \cdot b = -1 \cdot (a \cdot b)$	2. Axiom 2 (Associativity)
3. $-1 \cdot (a \cdot b) = -(a \cdot b)$	3. Theorem 1–11
4. $-a \cdot b = -(a \cdot b)$	4. Transitive Property of Equality. Statements 1–3.
Second part of proof:	
5. $a \cdot (-b) = a \cdot [(-1) \cdot b]$	5. ?
6. $a \cdot [(-1) \cdot b] = [a \cdot (-1)] \cdot b$	6. ?
7. $[a \cdot (-1)] \cdot b = [(-1) \cdot a] \cdot b$	7. ?
8. $[(-1) \cdot a] \cdot b = -(a \cdot b)$	8. Already proven in statements 1–4 above.

21. Theorem 1–8   **22.** Theorem 1–12   **23.** Theorem 1–14

24. For any number a, $a - a = 0$.

25. For any nonzero number n, $\frac{n}{n} = 1$.

Extension

26. Closure. A set is closed under an operation if whenever the operation is done on elements within the set, the result is also in the set. Determine which of the following sets are closed under the operation.
   a. The set of whole numbers; addition
   b. The set of whole numbers; subtraction
   c. The set of odd integers; addition
   d. The set of even integers; multiplication
   e. The set of rational numbers; multiplication

CAREERS/Forestry

A timber cruiser travels over forest land to estimate the amount of timber available for logging. To make this estimate, the timber cruiser applies established sampling techniques and uses accurate hand instruments.

Among these instruments is the Abney level. It is used to determine the height of a tree.

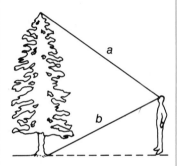

As shown above, the timber cruiser stands 66 feet (1 chain) from the base of the tree. He then uses the Abney level and sights on the top of the tree to get reading a. He sights on the bottom of the tree to get reading b.
Once he has found readings a and b, he uses the methods in Section 1–2 to substitute in the expression $a + b$ and find the height of the tree.

For example: If $a = 104$ and $b = 6$,

$$a + b$$
$$104 + 6$$
$$110$$

The tree is 110 feet tall.

If the timber cruiser looks *down* for both Abney readings, the expression for finding the height of the tree is $b - a$. If he looks *up* for both readings, the expression is $a - b$.

The timber cruiser logs this data with other information about the type of timber and its condition. These facts are used to determine how to best manage the forest's resources.

Exercises
Evaluate each expression.

1. $a - b$; Use $a = 62$ and $b = 15$. 47
2. $b - a$; Use $a = 21$ and $b = 109$. 88
3. $2a - b$; Use $a = 44$ and $b = 80$. 8
4. $2a + 3b$; Use $a = 15$ and $b = 9$. 57
5. $4a - 7b$; Use $a = 51$ and $b = 11$. 127

6. $5a + b$; Use $a = 13$ and $b = 24$. 89
7. $6a + 4b$; Use $a = 16$ and $b = 12$. 144
8. $2a + 3b + c$; Use $a = 9, b = 4$ and $c = 6$. 36
9. $4a + 2b + 5c$; Use $a = 8, b = 7$ and $c = 5$. 71
10. $-a$; Use $a = 53$. −53
11. $-b$; Use $b = -91$. 91
12. $-(-a)$; Use $a = -44$.
13. $-(a + b)$; Use $a = 23$ and $b = 5$. −28
14. $-(b + 6)$; Use $b = -18$. 12
15. $-(a + 4)$; Use $a = 16$. −20
16. $2|a + 5|$; Use $a = 3$. 16
17. $7|b|$; Use $b = 8$. 56
18. $5|a|$; Use $a = -6$. 30
19. $|a| + |b|$; Use $a = 7$ and $b = 15$. 22
20. $|a| + |b|$; Use $a = 14$ and $b = -22$. 36
21. $|b| - |a|$; Use $a = 23$ and $b = 38$. 15
22. $|a| - |b|$; Use $a = -41$ and $b = -19$. 22
23. $|a + b|$; Use $a = 17$ and $b = 20$. 37
24. $|b - a|$; Use $a = -4$ and $b = 15$. 19
25. $6|a + b|$; Use $a = 8$ and $b = -10$. 12
26. $3|a - b|$; Use $a = 16$ and $b = 9$. 21

12. −44

CHAPTER 1 Review

Review the material in the chapter. Then see how you have done by trying these review exercises. If you miss an exercise, restudy the indicated lesson.

1–1

1. Is -3 a natural number? a whole number? an integer? a rational number? No, no, yes, yes

2. Find decimal notation for $\frac{7}{11}$. $0.\overline{63}$ **3.** Find fractional notation for -7.33. $\frac{-733}{100}$

1–1 Which of the following numbers are rational and which are irrational?

4. $\sqrt{7}$ Irrational **5.** $0.\overline{142857}$ Rational **6.** $2.113111311113\ldots$ Irrational

1–1 Insert $<$ or $>$ to make true sentences.

7. $-2.7 \quad -6.1$ $>$ **8.** $\frac{13}{15} \quad \frac{7}{8}$ $<$

1–2 Evaluate each expression for $x = 3$ and $y = -2$.

9. $2x + 1 - 3y$ 13 **10.** $-(x - 1 - y)$ -4 **11.** $2|x - 4| - |y|$ 0

1–3 Add.

12. $-\frac{7}{5} + \left(-\frac{13}{10}\right)$ $-\frac{27}{10}$ **13.** $8.7 + (-7.9)$ 0.8 **14.** $-\frac{7}{8} + \frac{5}{6}$ $-\frac{1}{24}$

1–3 Subtract.

15. $-\frac{6}{7} - \left(-\frac{2}{5}\right)$ $-\frac{16}{35}$ **16.** $-13.8 - 5.9$ 19.7 **17.** $16.56 - (-15.72)$ 32.28

1–3 Use properties of real numbers to write equivalent expressions. Indicate which number properties you use.

18. $-9x + (-5y)$ Ex. $-5y + 9x$, commutative **19.** $3x + (-3x) + y$ Ex. y, add. inverse, add. prop. of zero

1–4 Multiply.

20. $-4(2.1)$ -8.4 **21.** $-\frac{5}{6}\left(-\frac{18}{7}\right)$ $\frac{15}{7}$ **22.** $-6.01(-1000)$ 6010

1–4 Divide.

23. $\frac{-18.72}{3.6}$ -5.2 **24.** $-\frac{7}{8} \div \left(-\frac{3}{4}\right)$ $\frac{7}{6}$ **25.** $\frac{2}{3} \div \left(-\frac{8}{5}\right)$ $-\frac{5}{12}$

1–4 Which of these divisions are possible?

26. $\dfrac{10}{0}$ **27.** $\dfrac{0}{56}$ 0 **28.** $\dfrac{10}{x-x}$ Not possible

Not possible

1–4 Determine whether the two expressions are equivalent and give reasons.

29. $(3x+y)\dfrac{1}{2b}, \dfrac{y+3x}{2b}$ **30.** $2x-(4+y),(y+4)-2x$ Not equiv., substraction is not com.

Equiv. Thm 1–2 and com. law

1–5 Multiply.

31. $6(x-y+z)$ **32.** $-3(s-2t+w)$ **33.** $12\left(\dfrac{a}{2}-\dfrac{b}{3}+\dfrac{c}{4}\right)$ 6a − 4b + 3c

1–5 Factor.

34. $ax-ay$ **35.** $-20x+5y-10z$ **36.** $2ab-6ac-8ad$ 2a(b + 3c − 4d)

1–5 Collect like terms.

37. $-6y-8z-4y+3z$ **38.** $2.3y-8-4y+7.6x-5.8x$ −1.7y + 0.1x − 8

1–5 Rename each additive inverse without parentheses.

39. $-(r-s)$ **40.** $-(-4x+3y)$ 4x − 3y

1–5 Simplify.

41. $2a-(3a-4)$ **42.** $y-3(2y-4x)$ **43.** $5x-[2x-(3x+2)]$ 6x + 2

44. $8x-\{2x-3[(x-4)-(x+2)]\}$ 6x − 18

1–6 Write equivalent expressions using negative exponents.

45. $\dfrac{1}{8^3}$ 8^{-3} **46.** $\dfrac{1}{(-3)^2}$ **47.** $\dfrac{1}{3y^5}$ $\dfrac{y^{-5}}{3}$ **48.** $\dfrac{1}{(3y)^5}$ $(3y)^{-5}$

1–6 Write equivalent expressions without negative exponents.

49. $(-4)^{-3}$ **50.** $\dfrac{x^3}{y^{-4}}$ **51.** $3a^3b^{-5}$ **52.** $a^3b^{-2}c^5d^{-6}$ $\dfrac{a^3c^5}{b^2d^6}$

1–7 Simplify.

53. $(7x^3y^{-1})(-2x^{-4}y)$ **54.** $\dfrac{a^{-2}}{a^{-4}}$ a^2 **55.** $\dfrac{54x^{-5}y^4}{-18x^3y^{-1}}$ $-3x^{-8}y^5$

56. $(-3x^2y^3)^4$ **57.** $(-2x^3)^{-3}$ $\dfrac{1}{8x^9}$ **58.** $\left(\dfrac{2x^3y^{-6}}{-3y^4}\right)^2$ $\dfrac{4x^6}{9y^{20}}$

1–8 Write in scientific notation.

59. 80,200,000 **60.** 0.00000074 **61.** $(1.8\times10^{12})(2.1\times10^{-3})$ **62.** $\dfrac{6.25\times10^{-6}}{2.5\times10^3}$

31. 6x − 6y + 6z
32. −3s + 6t − 3w
34. a(x − y)
35. −5(4x − y + 2z)
37. −10y − 5z
39. s − r
41. a + 4
42. −5y + 12x
46. $(-3)^{-2}$
49. $\dfrac{1}{(-4)^3}$
50. x^3y^4
51. $\dfrac{3a^3}{b^5}$
53. −14x⁻¹
56. 81x⁸y¹²
59. 8.02 × 10⁷
60. 7.4 × 10⁻⁷
61. 3.78 × 10⁹
62. 2.5 × 10⁻⁹

CHAPTER 1 Test

1. Find decimal notation for $\frac{5}{9}$. $0.\bar{5}$ 2. Find fractional notation for 8.03. $\frac{803}{100}$

Which of the following numbers are rational and which are irrational?

3. $\sqrt{5}$ 4. $0.\overline{153846}$ 5. $0.1121231234\ldots$ Irrational

   Irrational   Rational

Insert < or > to make true sentences.

6. -3.7 -5.4 > 7. $\frac{7}{11}$ $\frac{4}{5}$ <

Evaluate each expression for $x = -2$ and $y = 5$.

8. $3x - y + 7$ -4 9. $-(y - x + 1)$ -8 10. $3|x + 1| - |y|$ -2

Add.

11. $-4.9 + (-3.08)$ 12. $\frac{9}{16} + \left(-\frac{7}{10}\right)$ 13. $-\frac{4}{9} + \frac{7}{12}$ $\frac{5}{36}$

Subtract.

14. $-0.74 - (-11.8)$ 15. $\frac{8}{9} - \left(-\frac{5}{6}\right)$ 16. $-30.7 - 6.1$ -36.8

Multiply.

17. $-0.9(3.1)$ 18. $-\frac{2}{7}\left(-\frac{10}{3}\right)$ $\frac{20}{21}$ 19. $0.43(-100)$ -43

Divide.

20. $\frac{4}{3} \div \left(-\frac{8}{15}\right)$ $-\frac{5}{2}$ 21. $\frac{-6.09}{0.29}$ -21

Multiply.

22. $-4(x - y + 8)$ 23. $a(3b - c - d)$ $3ab - ac - ad$

Factor.

24. $2xy - xz$ 25. $6ab - 8bc - 4bd$ $2b(3a - 4c - 2d)$

Collect like terms.

26. $9x - 5x - 6x + 7x$ $5x$ 27. $3.2y - 9 - 5y + 4.8x - 5.7x$ $-1.8y - 0.9x - 9$

Simplify.

28. $3t - (5t - 6)$ 29. $9y - [4y - (2y - 5)]$ $7y - 5$

11. -7.89
12. $-\frac{9}{80}$
14. 11.06
15. $\frac{31}{18}$
17. -2.79
22. $-4x + 4y - 32$
24. $x(2y - z)$
28. $-2t + 6$
30. $-30x^8$
31. $7y^2z^{12}$
33. 9.04×10^7

Simplify.

30. $(5x^3)(-6x^5)$ **31.** $\dfrac{63y^4z^9}{9y^2z^{-3}}$ **32.** $(10 - 3 \cdot 4)^2 \cdot [5(3)^2 + 9]$ 216

Write in scientific notation.

33. 90,400,000   **34.** 0.00000752 7.52×10^{-6}

Challenge

35. Evaluate $(2x + y)(x^{x+y} - y^{y-x})$ when $x = -1$ and $y = 1$.   1

Ready for Solving Equations and Inequalities?

1–2   Simplify.

   1. $|-8|$ 8   **2.** $|0|$ 0   **3.** $|\sqrt{4}|$ $\sqrt{4}$

1–2   Find $-a$ when a stands for

   4. -7 7   **5.** 0   0   **6.** 8 -8

1–3   Add.

   7. $3.8 + (-3.8)$ 0   **8.** $-4.8 + 1.2$ -3.6 **9.** $-\dfrac{3}{8} + \left(-\dfrac{1}{6}\right)$ $-\dfrac{13}{24}$

1–3   Subtract.

10. $8 - (-5)$ 13   **11.** $-18.2 - 4.7$ -22.9 **12.** $-\dfrac{2}{3} - \left(-\dfrac{4}{7}\right)$ $-\dfrac{2}{21}$

1–4   Multiply.

13. $3 \cdot (-8)$ -24 **14.** $-4.7 \cdot 10$ -47 **15.** $-8 \cdot \left(-\dfrac{3}{4}\right)$ 6

1–5   Factor.

16. $3x - 18$ $3(x - 6)$ **17.** $5x - 10y + 15$ $5(x - 2y + 3)$

18. $4x - 8 + 6y$ **19.** $12ab + 4ac - 16ad$ $4a(3b + c - 4d)$
   $2(2x - 4 + 3y)$

1–5   Multiply.

20. $5(y - 4)$ $5y - 20$ **21.** $a(2 - b)$ $2a - ab$

22. $c(x + y - z)$ **23.** $-3(x - y + 1)$ $-3x + 3y - 3$
   $cx + cy - cz$

1–5   Collect like terms.

24. $x + 3x - 5x$ $-x$ **25.** $2y + 3 + 5y - 1$ $7y + 2$

2

CHAPTER TWO

Solving Equations and Inequalities

2–1 Solving Equations

The most common type of sentence used in algebra is an   .
Equations may be true or false. An equation containing a variable
may be neither true nor false. Some replacements may make it true
and some may make it false.

DEFINITION

The replacements that make an equation true are called its
solutions. The set of all possible replacements is called
the *replacement set*. The set of all solutions is called the
solution set.

In this book, unless otherwise stated, the replacement set for
equations and inequalities is the set of all real numbers.

When we find all of the solutions of an equation, we say that we
have solved it, no matter how we find the solutions. There are
various procedures for solving equations.

The Addition Principle

One approach to solving an equation is to transform it to a simpler
equation, one whose solution set is obvious. Then we check by
substituting in the original equation.

One principle used for transforming equations to simpler ones
consists of adding the same number on both sides of the equation.

THEOREM 2–1

The Addition Principle for Equations

If an equation $a = b$ is true, then $a + c = b + c$ is true for
any number c.

EXAMPLE 1

Solve $x + 6 = -15$.

$$x + 6 + (-6) = -15 + (-6) \quad \text{Using the addition principle;}$$
$$x + 0 = -15 + (-6) \quad \text{adding } -6 \text{ on both sides}$$
$$x = -21 \quad \text{Simplifying}$$

Check:
$$\frac{x + 6 = -15}{\begin{array}{c|c} -21 + 6 & -15 \\ -15 & \end{array}}$$

The solution is -21.

In Example 1, to get x alone, we added the inverse of 6. This "got rid of" the 6 on the left.

TRY THIS Solve, using the addition principle.

1. $x + 9 = 2$ ₋₇   **2.** $13 = -25 + y$ ₃₈   **3.** $x + \frac{1}{4} = -\frac{3}{4}$ ₋₁   **4.** $y - 61.4 = 78.9$ ₁₄₀.₃

The Multiplication Principle

Suppose the equation $a = b$ is true and we multiply the number a by some number c. We will get the same answer as if we multiply b by c.

THEOREM 2–2

The Multiplication Principle for Equations

If an equation $a = b$ is true, then $a \cdot c = b \cdot c$ is true for any number c.

EXAMPLE 2

Solve $4x = 9$.

$$\frac{1}{4} \cdot 4x = \frac{1}{4} \cdot 9 \quad \text{Using the multiplication principle;}$$
$$\text{multiplying by } \tfrac{1}{4}$$
$$1 \cdot x = \frac{9}{4}$$
$$x = \frac{9}{4} \quad \text{Simplifying}$$

Check:
$$\frac{4x = 9}{\begin{array}{c|c} 4 \cdot \frac{9}{4} & 9 \\ 9 & \end{array}}$$

The solution is $\frac{9}{4}$.

Checking by substituting in the original equation is an important part of solving.

In Example 2 we multiplied by the reciprocal of 4. When we multiplied we got $1 \cdot x$, which simplified to x.

TRY THIS Solve, using the multiplication principle.

5. $8x = 10$ $\frac{5}{4}$ 6. $-4x = 64$ -16

7. $-3x = -\frac{6}{7}$ $\frac{2}{7}$ 8. $-12.6 = 4.2y$ -3

Using the Principles Together

Let's see how to use the addition and multiplication principles together.

EXAMPLE 3

Solve $3x - 4 = 13$.

$$3x - 4 + 4 = 13 + 4 \qquad \text{Using the addition principle, adding 4}$$
$$3x + (-4) + 4 = 13 + 4$$
$$3x = 17 \qquad \text{Simplifying}$$
$$\frac{1}{3} \cdot 3x = \frac{1}{3} \cdot 17 \qquad \text{Using the multiplication principle, multiplying by } \tfrac{1}{3}$$
$$x = \frac{17}{3} \qquad \text{Simplifying}$$

Check: $\dfrac{3x - 4 = 13}{}$

$$3\left(\frac{17}{3}\right) - 4 \;\Big|\; 13$$
$$17 - 4$$
$$13$$

TRY THIS Solve.

9. $9x - 4 = 8$ $\frac{4}{3}$ 10. $-\frac{1}{4}y + \frac{3}{2} = \frac{1}{2}$ 4

If there are like terms in an equation, they should be collected first. If there are like terms on opposite sides of an equation, we can get them on the same side using the addition principle, and then "combine" them.

EXAMPLE 4

Solve $8x + 6 - 2x = -12 - 4x + 5$.

$$8x - 2x = -12 - 4x + 5 - 6 \quad \text{Adding} -6 \text{ and simplifying}$$
$$8x - 2x + 4x = -12 + 5 - 6 \quad \text{Adding } 4x \text{ and simplifying}$$
$$10x = -13 \quad \text{Collecting like terms and simplifying}$$
$$\frac{1}{10} \cdot 10x = \frac{1}{10} \cdot (-13) \quad \text{Multiplying by } \frac{1}{10}$$
$$x = \frac{-13}{10}, \text{ or } -1.3 \quad \text{Simplifying}$$

Check:

$$8x + 6 - 2x = -12 - 4x + 5$$

$8\left(\dfrac{-13}{10}\right) + 6 - 2\left(\dfrac{-13}{10}\right)$	$-12 - 4\left(\dfrac{-13}{10}\right) + 5$
$\dfrac{-52}{5} + 6 - \dfrac{-13}{5}$	$-12 - \dfrac{-26}{5} + 5$
$\dfrac{-39}{5} + 6$	$-7 + \dfrac{26}{5}$
$\dfrac{-9}{5}$	$\dfrac{-9}{5}$

In Example 4 we used the addition principle to get all terms with the variable on one side of the equation and all other terms on the other side. Then we combined like terms and proceeded as before.

TRY THIS Solve.

11. $30 + 7(x - 1) = 3(2x + 7)$ ₋₂

| **2–1** | |

Exercises

Solve using the addition principle. Check.

1. $y + 11 = 8$ ₋₃   **2.** $t + 13 = 4$ ₉   **3.** $x - 18 = 22$ ₄₀

4. $p - 15 = 11$ ₂₆   **5.** $x + 9 = -6$ ₋₁₅   **6.** $p + 14 = -42$ ₋₅₆

7. $t - 9 = -23$ ₋₁₄ **8.** $y - 7 = -3$ ₄   **9.** $x - 26 = 13$ ₃₉

Solve using the multiplication principle. Check.

10. $5x = 20$ ₄   **11.** $3x = 21$ ₇   **12.** $8y = -72$ ₋₉

13. $9t = -81$ ₋₉   **14.** $-24x = -192$ ₈ **15.** $-13y = 117$ ₋₉

16. $\frac{1}{5}y = 8$ ₄₀   **17.** $\frac{1}{4}x = 9$ ₃₆   **18.** $\frac{2}{3}x = 27$ $\frac{81}{2}$

Solve using both principles. Check.

19. $4x - 12 = 60$ ₁₈
20. $4x - 6 = 70$ ₁₉
21. $5y + 3 = 28$ ₅
22. $7t + 11 = 74$ ₉
23. $2y - 11 = 37$ ₂₄
24. $3x - 13 = 29$ ₁₄
25. $-4x - 7 = -35$ ₇
26. $-9y + 8 = -91$ ₁₁
27. $5x + 2x = 56$ ₈
28. $3x + 7x = 120$ ₁₂
29. $9y - 7y = 42$ ₂₁
30. $8t - 3t = 65$ ₁₃
31. $-6y - 10y = -32$ ₂
32. $-9y - 5y = 28$ ₋₂
33. $7y - 1 = 23 - 5y$ ₂
34. $15x + 20 = 8x - 22$ ₋₆
35. $5 - 4a = a - 13$ $\frac{18}{5}$
36. $8 - 5x = x - 16$ ₄
37. $3m - 7 = -7 - 4m - m$ ₀
38. $5x - 8 = -8 + 3x - x$ ₀
39. $5r - 2 + 3r = 2r + 6 - 4r$ $\frac{4}{5}$
40. $5m - 17 - 2m = 6m - 1 - m$ ₋₈

Extension
Solve.

41. $-\frac{3}{4}x + \frac{1}{8} = -2$ $\frac{17}{6}$
42. $y - \frac{1}{3}y - 15 = 0$ $\frac{45}{2}$
43. $\frac{a}{5} - \frac{a}{25} = 3.1$ $\frac{155}{8}$
44. $\frac{3x}{2} + \frac{5x}{3} - \frac{13x}{6} - \frac{2}{3} = \frac{5}{6}$ $\frac{3}{2}$
45. $\frac{11}{2}x + \frac{1}{2} - \frac{3}{4}x - x - \frac{5}{8} = 2x + \frac{7}{8} - 4x - x - \frac{1}{4} + 6x$ ₁
46. $3x + 2^2 = x + 3^2$ $\frac{5}{2}$
47. $2^3 \cdot x + 9 = 2^2 \cdot x - 23$ ₋₈

Solve. Use a calculator.

48. $4.23x - 17.898 = -1.65x - 42.454$ ₋₄.₁₇₆
49. $-0.00458y + 1.7787 = 13.002y - 1.005$ ₀.₂₁₄₀₂₂

Challenge
Solve.

50. $4x - 2x - 2 = 2x$ No solution
51. $2x + 4 + x = 4 + 3x$ All real numbers

An identity is an equation that is true for all sensible replacements.
Determine which of the following are identities.

52. $2(x - 3) + 5 = 3(x - 2) + 5$ No
53. $3(x - 4) = 3x - 4$ No
54. $5(x + 3) = 5x + 15$ Yes
55. $\frac{6y + 4}{2} = 6y + 2$ No
56. $\frac{3y - 1}{y^2 - y} - \frac{2}{y - 1} = \frac{1}{y}$ Yes
57. $7(x - 3) \cdot \frac{1}{7} = x - 3$ Yes

2-2 More on Solving Equations

We now consider another way to solve equations.

Clearing Fractions or Decimals

When an equation contains fractions or decimals, it helps to eliminate them. To do that, we use the multiplication principle. The process is called clearing the equation of fractions or decimals.

EXAMPLE 1

Clear the equation $\frac{3}{4}x + \frac{1}{2} = \frac{3}{2}$ of fractions.

We multiply on both sides by the least common multiple of the denominators, in this case 4.

$$4\left(\frac{3}{4}x + \frac{1}{2}\right) = 4 \cdot \frac{3}{2} \quad \text{Multiplying by 4}$$

$$4 \cdot \frac{3}{4}x + 4 \cdot \frac{1}{2} = 4 \cdot \frac{3}{2} \quad \text{Using the distributive law}$$

$$3x + 2 = 6 \quad \text{Simplifying}$$

EXAMPLE 2

Clear of decimals and then solve: $12.4 - 3.64x = 1.48$.
We multiply on both sides by a power of ten to get rid of the decimal points.

$$100(12.4 - 3.64x) = 100 \times 1.48 \quad \text{Multiplying by 100}$$
$$1240 - 364x = 148$$
$$1240 - 148 = 364x \quad \text{Using the addition principle}$$
$$1092 = 364x$$
$$3 = x \quad \text{Using the multiplication principle}$$

Check:

$$\begin{array}{c|c} 12.4 - 3.64x = 1.48 \\ \hline 12.4 - 3.64(3) & 1.48 \\ 12.4 - 10.92 & \\ 1.48 & \end{array}$$

TRY THIS Clear of fractions or decimals. Then solve.

1. $\frac{2}{3} - \frac{5}{6}y = \frac{1}{3}$ $\frac{2}{5}$ 2. $6.3x - 9.6 = 3$ 2

Equations with Parentheses

Certain equations with parentheses can be solved by first removing the parentheses and then proceeding as before.

EXAMPLE 3

Solve $3(7 - 2x) = 14 - 8(x - 1)$.

$$21 - 6x = 14 - 8x + 8 \quad \text{Multiplying to remove parentheses}$$
$$21 - 6x = 22 - 8x$$
$$8x - 6x = 22 + (-21) \quad \text{Using the addition principle}$$
$$2x = 1 \quad \text{Collecting like terms and simplifying}$$
$$x = \frac{1}{2}$$

The number checks, so the solution is $\frac{1}{2}$.

TRY THIS Solve.

3. $3(y - 1) - 1 = 2 - 5(y + 5)$ $\quad -\frac{19}{8}$

Methods of Solving Equations

1. Clear of fractions or decimals if necessary.
2. Collect like terms on both sides of the equation.
3. Collect like terms again if necessary.
4. Use the multiplication principle to get the variable alone on one side.

The Principle of Zero Products

When we multiply two numbers, the product will be zero if one of the factors is zero. Furthermore, if a product is zero, then at least one of the factors must be zero.

THEOREM 2–3

The Principle of Zero Products

For any real numbers a and b, if $ab = 0$, then $a = 0$ or $b = 0$, and if $a = 0$ or $b = 0$, then $ab = 0$.

A statement in two parts like the one in Theorem 2–3 is often abbreviated using the words if and only if. For example,

if A, then B and if B, then A

can be abbreviated

A if and only if B
or
B if and only if A.

Theorem 2–3 could be restated as follows.

For any real numbers a and b, $ab = 0$ if and only if $a = 0$ or $b = 0$.

EXAMPLE 4
Solve $(x + 4)(x - 2) = 0$.

Here we have a product which is zero. This equation will become true when either factor is zero. Hence it is true when $x + 4 = 0$ or $x - 2 = 0$. We have applied the principle of zero products. Solving each equation separately we get the following.

$x = -4$ or $x = 2$

There are two solutions, -4 and 2. We can name some sets by listing their members inside braces. The solution set is $\{-4, 2\}$.

EXAMPLE 5
Solve $7x(4x + 2) = 0$.

$7x = 0$ or $4x + 2 = 0$ Using the principle of zero products
$x = 0$ or $4x = -2$

$x = 0$ or $x = -\frac{1}{2}$ Solving each equation separately

The solutions are 0 and $-\frac{1}{2}$.

The solution set is $\{0, -\frac{1}{2}\}$.

TRY THIS   Solve.

4. $(x - 19)(x + 5) = 0$ $19, -5$
5. $x(3x - 17) = 0$ $0, \frac{17}{3}$
6. $(9x + 2)(-6x + 3) = 0$ $-\frac{2}{9}, \frac{1}{2}$

Exercises

Solve.

1. $\frac{1}{4} + \frac{3}{8}y = \frac{3}{4}$ $\frac{4}{3}$

2. $\frac{1}{5} + \frac{3}{10}x = \frac{4}{5}$ 2

3. $-\frac{5}{2}x + \frac{1}{2} = -18$ $\frac{37}{5}$

4. $0.9y - 0.7 = 4.2$ $\frac{49}{9}$

5. $0.8t - 0.3t = 6.5$ 13

6. $1.4x + 5.02 = 0.4x$ $\frac{-502}{100}$

7. $2(x + 6) = 8x$ 2

8. $3(y + 5) = 8y$ 3

9. $80 = 10(3t + 2)$ 2

10. $27 = 9(5y - 2)$ 1

11. $180(n - 2) = 900$ 7

12. $210(x - 3) = 840$ 7

13. $5y - (2y - 10) = 25$ 5

14. $8x - (3x - 5) = 40$ 7

15. $0.7(3x + 6) = 1.1 - (x + 2)$ $-\frac{51}{31}$

16. $0.9(2x + 8) = 20 - (x + 5)$ $\frac{39}{14}$

17. $\frac{1}{8}(16y + 8) - 17 = -\frac{1}{4}(8y - 16)$ 5

18. $\frac{1}{6}(12t + 48) - 20 = -\frac{1}{8}(24t - 144)$ 6

19. $a + (a - 3) = (a + 2) - (a + 1)$ 2

20. $0.8 - 4(b - 1) = 0.2 + 3(4 - b)$ $-\frac{37}{5}$

21. $(x + 2)(x - 5) = 0$ $-2, 5$

22. $(x + 4)(x - 8) = 0$ $-4, 8$

23. $(y - 8)(y - 9) = 0$ 8, 9

24. $(t - 3)(t - 7) = 0$ 3, 7

25. $(2x - 3)(3x - 2) = 0$ $\frac{3}{2}, \frac{2}{3}$

26. $(3y - 4)(4y - 1) = 0$ $\frac{4}{3}, \frac{1}{4}$

27. $m(m - 8) = 0$ 0, 8

28. $p(p - 5) = 0$ 0, 5

29. $x(x - 1)(x + 2) = 0$ 0, 1, -2

30. $y(y - 4)(y + 2) = 0$ 0, 4, -2

Extension

Solve.

31. $2x - 4 - (x + 1) - 3(x - 2) = 6(2x - 3) - 3(6x - 1) - 8$ -6

32. $\frac{1}{7}(a - 3)(7a + 4) = 0$

33. $24\left(\frac{x}{6} - \frac{1}{3}\right) = x - 24$ 32. $3, \frac{-4}{7}$ 33. $\frac{-16}{3}$

34. $0.5(x - 2) - 2(x - 5) = 0.4(x - 5) - 5(x - 2)$ $-\frac{10}{31}$

Solve for x or y.

35. $8x + 3 = c$

36. $16y - 4 = f$

37. $cy + 3h = 5a$

38. $7x - 3 = ax + 5b$

39. $ay - by = 12$

40. $5x + ax = 19$

35. $\frac{c - 3}{8}$

36. $\frac{f + 4}{16}$

37. $\frac{5a - 3h}{c}$

38. $\frac{3 + 5b}{7 - a}$

39. $\frac{12}{a - b}$

40. $\frac{19}{5 + a}$

41. 1, -1
42. 1, 0
43. 0, 2
44. 0

Challenge

Solve.

41. $x \cdot x - 1$

42. $x \cdot x = x$

43. $x(x - 1) = x$

44. $x(x - 1) = x(x + 1)$

2–3 Solving Problems

The first step in solving many problems is to translate to mathematical language. Very often this means translating to an equation. Drawing a picture usually helps a great deal. We solve the equation and then check to see if we have a solution to the problem.

EXAMPLE 1

A 28-foot rope is cut into two pieces. One piece is 3 feet longer than the other. How long are the pieces?

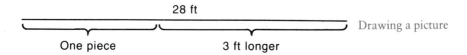

Drawing a picture

The picture can help in translating. Here is one way to do it.

Length of one piece plus length of other is 28.

$$x + (x + 3) = 28 \qquad \text{Translation}$$

We used x for the length of one piece and $x + 3$ for the length of the other.

Now we solve. $x + (x + 3) = 28$

$$2x + 3 = 28$$
$$2x = 25$$
$$x = \frac{25}{2}, \text{ or } 12\frac{1}{2}$$

Do we have an answer to the *problem*? If one piece is $12\frac{1}{2}$ ft long, the one that is 3 ft longer must be $15\frac{1}{2}$ ft long. The lengths of the pieces add up to 28 ft, so this checks.

Steps to Use in Solving a Problem

1. Translate to an equation. (Always draw a picture if it makes sense to do so.) Carefully keep track of what each variable represents.
2. Solve the equation.
3. Check the answer in the original problem.

TRY THIS

1. A 32-ft rope is cut into two pieces, one three times as long as the other. How long are the pieces? 8 ft, 24 ft

EXAMPLE 2

Five plus twice a number is seven times the number. What is the number?

This time it does not make sense to draw a picture.

5 plus twice a number is seven times the number.   Step 1 Translate

$$5 + 2x = 7 \cdot x$$

We have used x to represent the unknown number. Notice that "is" translates to $=$.

$$5 + 2x = 7x \quad \text{Step 2 Solve}$$
$$5 = 7x - 2x$$
$$5 = 5x$$
$$1 = x$$

Twice 1 is 2. If we add 5, we get 7. This is $7 \cdot 1$.   Step 3 Check
This checks so the answer to the *problem* is 1.

TRY THIS

2. If 7 times a certain number is subtracted from 6, the result is 5 times the number. What is the number? $\frac{1}{2}$

EXAMPLE 3

It has been found that the world record for the 10,000-meter run has been decreasing steadily since 1940. The record is 30.18 minutes minus 0.12 times the number of years since 1940. If the record continues to decrease in this way, what will it be in 1990?

Record is 30.18 minutes minus 0.12 times number of years since 1940.

$$R = 30.18 - 0.12 \cdot t$$

$$R = 30.18 - 0.12t$$

In 1990, t will be 50, so we have the following equation.

$$R = 30.18 - 0.12 \cdot 50 \quad \text{This is the translation.}$$

Solving, we get 24.18. The number checks in the problem, so 24.18 minutes is the answer. (In this case it is only a *prediction*.)

TRY THIS

3. It has been found that the world record for the 800-meter run has been decreasing steadily since 1930. The record is 1.82 minutes minus 0.0035 times the number of years since 1930. Predict what the record will be in 1995. 1.5925 min.

4. The County Cab Company charges sixty cents plus eleven cents per km as the fare. What will be the total cost of a 12 km ride? $1.92

EXAMPLE 4

A group of airline pilots once took a pay cut of 11% to a new salary of $48,950 per year. What was their former salary?

Former salary minus 11% of former salary is new salary.

$$x \quad - \quad 11\% \cdot \quad x \quad = \quad 48{,}950 \quad \text{Translation}$$

We have used x to represent the former salary.

$$
\begin{aligned}
x - 11\% \cdot x &= 48{,}950 \quad \text{Solving} \\
1x - 0.11x &= 48{,}950 \quad \text{Replacing 11\% by 0.11} \\
(1 - 0.11)x &= 48{,}950 \\
0.89x &= 48{,}950 \\
x &= 55{,}000
\end{aligned}
$$

The solution of the equation is 55,000.

Check: 11% of 55,000 is 6050. Subtracting from 55,000 we get 48,950. The number checks, so the former salary was $55,000.

TRY THIS

5. A clothing store drops the price of suits 25% to a sale price of $93. What was the former price? $124

6. An investment is made at 12% simple interest. It grows to $812 at the end of 1 year. How much was invested originally? (Hint: Recall the expression $P + Prt$ regarding the return on a principal of P dollars.) $725

EXAMPLE 5

The sum of two consecutive integers is 35. What are the integers? (Consecutive integers are next to each other, such as 4 and 5.)

First integer + second integer = 35

$$x \quad + \quad (x + 1) \quad = 35 \quad \text{Translation}$$

Since the integers are consecutive, we know one of them is 1 greater than the other. We call one of them x and the other $x + 1$.

$$x + (x + 1) = 35$$
$$2x + 1 = 35$$
$$2x = 34$$
$$x = 17$$

Check: The answers are 17 and 18. These are both integers and consecutive. Their sum is 35, so the answers check in the problem.

TRY THIS

7. The sum of two consecutive odd integers is 36. What are the integers? (*Note:* If x is an odd integer, the next consecutive *odd* integer is $x + 2$.) 17, 19

Here is a list of hints for solving problems.

1. If two numbers are consecutive, call one x. Call the other $x + 1$.
2. If two numbers are consecutive odd (or even) numbers, call one x. Call the other $x + 2$.
3. If a number x is increased by $n\%$, the new number is $x + \frac{1}{100}n \cdot x$.
4. Remember that the sum of the measures of the three angles of a triangle is 180°.
5. If a rectangle has length l and width w, then its perimeter is $2l + 2w$ and its area is lw.

2–3

Exercises

Solve.

1. A 12-cm piece of tubing is cut into two pieces. One piece is 4 cm longer than the other. How long are the pieces? 8 cm; 4 cm

2. A 10 meter piece of wire is cut into two pieces. One piece is 2 meters longer than the other. How long are the pieces? 6 m; 4 m

3. A piece of wire four meters long is cut into two pieces so that one piece is two-thirds as long as the other. Find the length of each piece. $1\frac{3}{5}$ m; $2\frac{2}{5}$ m

4. A piece of rope five meters long is cut into two pieces so that one piece is three-fifths as long as the other. Find the length of each piece. $1\frac{7}{8}$ m; $3\frac{1}{8}$ m

5. Tony's baby-sitting service charges $2.50 per day plus $1.75 per hour. What is the cost of a seven hour baby-sitting job? $14.75

6. The cost of renting a rug shampooer is $3.25 per hour plus $2.75 for the shampoo. Find the cost of shampooing if the time involved is 3.5 hours. $14.13

7. Five more than three times a number is the same as ten less than six times the number. What is the number? 5

8. Six more than nine times a number is the same as two less than ten times the number. What is the number? 8

9. A pro shop in a bowling alley drops the price of bowling balls 24% to a sale price of $34.20. What was the former price? $45

10. An appliance store drops the price of a certain type of TV 18% to a sale price of $410. What was the former price? $500

11. Money is borrowed at 11% simple interest. After 1 year $721.50 pays off the loan. How much was originally borrowed? $650

12. Money is borrowed at 12% simple interest. After 1 year $896 pays off the loan. How much was originally borrowed? $800

13. The second angle of a triangle is three times the first and the third is 12° less than twice the first. Find the measures of the angles. 32°, 96°, 52°

14. The second angle of a triangle is four times the first and the third is 5° more than twice the first. Find the measures of the angles. 25°, 100°, 55°

15. The perimeter of a college basketball court is 96 m and the length is 14 m more than the width. What are the dimensions? Length is 31 m; width is 17 m

16. The perimeter of a certain soccer field is 310 m. The length is 65 m more than the width. What are the dimensions? Length is 110 m; width is 45 m

17. Find three consecutive odd integers such that the sum of the first, two times the second, and three times the third is 80. 11, 13, 15

18. Find two consecutive even integers such that two times the first plus three times the second is 76. 14, 16

19. After a person gets a 20% raise in salary the new salary is $9600. What was the old salary? (Hint: What number plus 20% of that number is 9600?) $8000

20. A person gets a 17% raise, bringing the salary to $21, 645. What was the salary before the raise? $18,500

21. The total cost for tuition plus room and board at Southern State University is $2584. Tuition costs $704 more than room and board. What is the tuition fee at the university? $1644

22. The cost of a private pilot course is $1875. The flight portion costs $775 more than the ground school portion. What is the cost of each? Ground school portion costs $550; flight portion costs $1325

Extension

23. A student's scores on five tests are 93%, 89%, 72%, 80%, and 96%. What must the student score on the sixth test so that the average will be 88%? 98%

24. The yearly changes in the population census of a city for three consecutive years are, respectively, 20% increase, 30% increase, and 20% decrease. What is the total percent change from the beginning to the end of the third year, to the nearest percent? 25% increase

25. Three numbers are such that the second is 6 less than 3 times the first and the third is 2 more than $\frac{2}{3}$ the second. The sum of the three numbers is 172. Find the largest number. 84

26. An appliance store is having a sale on 13 TV models. They are displayed left to right in order of increasing prices. The price of each TV differs by $20 from that of each adjacent TV. For the price of the TV at the extreme right a customer can buy both the second and the seventh models. What is the price of the least expensive TV? $100

27. A tank at a marine exhibit contains 2000 gallons of sea water. The sea water is 7.5% salt. How many gallons, to the nearest gallon, of fresh water must be added to the tank so that the mixture contains only 7% salt? 143 gallons

28. The sum of two consecutive odd integers is 137. Find the integers. No solution

29. The perimeter of a square is 12 cm greater than another square. Its area exceeds the area of the other by 39 cm². Find the perimeter of each square. 20 cm and 32 cm

Challenge

30. Diophantos spent $\frac{1}{6}$ of his life as a child, $\frac{1}{12}$ as a young man and $\frac{1}{7}$ as a bachelor. Five years after he was married he had a son who died 4 years before his father at half his father's final age. How long did Diophantos live? 84 years

---

USING A CALCULATOR / Solving Equations

A calculator cannot solve an equation, but it can help you do any computation that is involved. First, solve the equation using algebra. Then do all the calculations.	Problem: Solve $8x - 35 = 9$. Solve for x: $x = \dfrac{9 + 35}{8}$ Enter: 9 ⊞ 35 ⊟ ⊟ 8 ⊟ Display: 9 35 44 8 5.5

2-4 Solving Formulas

A formula is a kind of recipe, or rule, for doing a certain kind of calculation. Formulas are often given by equations. Here is a formula for finding the circumference of a circle.

$$c = \pi d$$

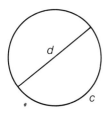

The formula says that to find the circumference, we should multiply the diameter by π.

Suppose we know the circumference of a circle and want to find the diameter. To do so, we can get d alone on one side of the equation. We solve for d.

EXAMPLE 1

Solve the formula $c = \pi d$ for d.

$$c = \pi d \quad \text{We want this letter alone.}$$

$$\frac{1}{\pi} \cdot c = \frac{1}{\pi} \cdot \pi d \quad \text{Multiplying by } \frac{1}{\pi}$$

$$\frac{c}{\pi} = d$$

The new formula says that to find the diameter, we should divide the circumference by π.

When we solve a formula, we do the same things we would do to solve any equation. The idea is to get a certain letter alone on one side of the equals sign.

In most formulas there are several letters. Some of those letters are variables because they can represent various numbers. Other letters represent only one number. Such letters are called constants. In using a formula, we often find that the letters are variables in some applications and constants in others. In $c = \pi d$, the Greek letter π is always a constant.

EXAMPLE 2

Solve for b.

$$A = \frac{5}{2}(b - 20)$$

$$\frac{2}{5}A = b - 20 \quad \text{Multiplying by } \frac{2}{5}$$

$$\frac{2}{5}A + 20 = b \quad \text{Adding 20}$$

TRY THIS

1. A formula for the area of a triangle is $A = \frac{1}{2}bh$. Solve for b. $b = \frac{2A}{h}$

2. Solve for c: $P = \frac{3}{5}(c + 10)$. $c = \frac{5}{3}P - 10$

EXAMPLE 3

Solve for r.

$$H = 2r + 3m \quad \text{We want this letter alone.}$$

$$H - 3m = 2r \quad \text{Adding } -3m$$

$$\frac{H - 3m}{2} = r \quad \text{Multiplying by } \frac{1}{2}$$

TRY THIS Solve for m.

3. $H = 2r + 3m$ $m = \frac{H - 2r}{3}$

EXAMPLE 4

The formula $A = P + Prt$ tells how much a principal P, in dollars, will earn at simple interest at a rate r in t years. Solve the formula for P.

$$A = P + Prt \quad \text{We want this letter alone.}$$

$$A = P(1 + rt) \quad \text{Factoring (or collecting like terms)}$$

$$A \cdot \frac{1}{1 + rt} = P(1 + rt) \cdot \frac{1}{1 + rt} \quad \text{Multiplying by } \frac{1}{1 + rt}$$

$$\frac{A}{1 + rt} = P \quad \text{Simplifying}$$

TRY THIS Solve for Q.

4. $T = Q + Qiy$ $Q = \frac{T}{1 + iy}$

Exercises

Solve.

1. $A = lw$, for l (an area formula) $l = \frac{A}{w}$
2. $A = lw$, for w $w = \frac{A}{l}$
3. $W = EI$, for I (an electricity formula) $I = \frac{W}{E}$
4. $W = EI$, for E $E = \frac{W}{I}$
5. $F = ma$, for m (a physics formula) $m = \frac{F}{a}$
6. $F = ma$, for a $a = \frac{F}{m}$
7. $I = Prt$, for t (an interest formula) $t = \frac{I}{Pr}$
8. $I = Prt$, for P $P = \frac{I}{rt}$
9. $E = mc^2$, for m (a relativity formula) $m = \frac{E}{c^2}$
10. $E = mc^2$, for c^2 $c^2 = \frac{E}{m}$
11. $P = 2l + 2w$, for l (a perimeter formula)
12. $P = 2l + 2w$, for w $w = \frac{P - 2l}{2}$
13. $c^2 = a^2 + b^2$, for a^2 (a geometry formula)
14. $c^2 = a^2 + b^2$, for b^2 $b^2 = c^2 - a^2$
15. $A = \pi r^2$, for r^2 (a circle formula) $r^2 = \frac{A}{\pi}$
16. $A = \pi r^2$, for π $\pi = \frac{A}{r^2}$

17. $C = \frac{5}{9}(F - 32)$, for F (a temperature formula) $F = \frac{9}{5}C + 32$
18. $W = \frac{11}{2}(h - 40)$, for h $h = \frac{2}{11}W + 40$

19. $V = \frac{4}{3}\pi r^3$, for r^3 (a volume formula) $r^3 = \frac{3V}{4\pi}$
20. $V = \frac{4}{3}\pi r^3$, for π $\frac{3V}{4r^3} = \pi$

21. $A = \frac{1}{2}h(a + b)$, for h (an area formula) $h = \frac{2A}{(a + b)}$
22. $A = \frac{1}{2}h(a + b)$, for b $b = \frac{2A - ha}{h}$

23. $F = \frac{mv^2}{r}$, for m (a physics formula) $m = \frac{rF}{v^2}$
24. $F = \frac{mv^2}{r}$, for v^2 $v^2 = \frac{rF}{m}$

11. $l = \frac{P - 2w}{2}$

Extension
13. $a^2 = c^2 - b^2$

Solve.

25. $s = v_i t + \frac{1}{2}at^2$, for a $a = \frac{2s - 2v_i t}{t^2}$

26. $A = \pi rs + r^2$, for s $s = \frac{A - r^2}{\pi r}$

27. In Exercise 7, you solved the formula $I = Prt$ for t. Now use it to find how long it will take a deposit of $75 to earn $3 interest when invested at 10% simple interest. 0.4 yr

28. In Exercise 8, you solved the formula $I = Prt$ for P. Now use it to find how much principal would be needed to earn $6 in two-thirds of a year at 12% simple interest. $75

Challenge

29. In Exercise 13, you solved for a^2. How might you solve for a? Take the square root of both sides.

30. In Exercise 19, you solved for r^3. How might you solve for r? Take the cube root of both sides.

31. A gas formula from physics is $\frac{P_1 V_1}{T_1} = \frac{P_2 V_2}{T_2}$. Solve it for V_1. $V_1 = \frac{T_1 P_2 V_2}{P_1 T_2}$

32. Solve the gas formula of Exercise 31 for T_2. $T_2 = \frac{P_2 V_2 T_1}{P_1 V_1}$

2-5 Solving Inequalities

Solutions and Graphs

Sentences containing $<$, $>$, $\leq$, or $\geq$ are called inequalities. A solution of an inequality is any number that makes it true. The set of all solutions is called the solution set.

EXAMPLES
Determine whether the given number is a solution of the inequality.

1. $x + 3 < 6$; 5
   We substitute and get $5 + 3 < 6$, or $8 < 6$, a false sentence. Therefore 5 is not a solution.

2. $2x - 3 > -3$; 1
   We substitute and get $2(1) - 3 > -3$, or $-1 > -3$, a true sentence. Therefore 1 is a solution.

3. $4x - 1 \leq 3x + 2$; 3
   We substitute and get $4(3) - 1 \leq 3(3) + 2$, or $11 \leq 11$, a true sentence. Therefore 3 is a solution.

TRY THIS Determine whether the specified number is a solution of the inequality.

1. $3 - x < 2$; 4 Yes 2. $3y + 2 > -1$; -2 No 3. $3x + 2 \leq 4x - 3$; 5 Yes

A graph of an inequality shows all of its solutions on a number line. The graph is a picture of the solution set.

EXAMPLE 4
Graph $x < 2$ on a number line. The solutions consist of all numbers less than 2, so we shade all numbers less than 2. Note that 2 is not a solution. We indicate this by using an open circle at 2.

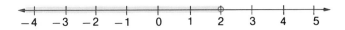

The solution set graphed in Example 4 can be named as follows.

$$\{x \mid x < 2\}$$

The notation is read the set of all x such that x is less than 2. Set notation of this type is written using braces { }. The symbol $\mid$ is read such that.

EXAMPLE 5

Graph $x \le 2$ on a number line. We draw a picture of the set $\{x \mid x \le 2\}$. This time the solution set consists of 2 and also all the numbers less than 2. We shade all numbers less than 2 and use a solid circle at 2 to indicate that it is also a solution.

TRY THIS Graph on a number line.

4. $x < -2$ 5. $x \ge 1$ 6. $\{x \mid x \le 5\}$

The Addition Principle

There is an addition principle for inequalities, similar to the one for solving equations.

THEOREM 2–4

The Addition Principle for Inequalities

If any number is added on both sides of a true inequality, another true inequality is obtained.

To solve inequalities using the addition principle, we do almost exactly what we would do in solving equations. We transform the inequality into a simpler one by adding the same number to both sides of the inequality.

EXAMPLE 6

Solve $x + 3 > 6$. Then graph.

$$x + 3 > 6$$
$$x + 3 + (-3) > 6 + (-3) \quad \text{Using the addition principle, adding } -3$$
$$x > 3$$

The solution set is $\{x \mid x > 3\}$.
The graph is as follows.

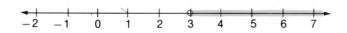

TRY THIS Solve each inequality algebraically. Then graph.

7. $x + 6 > 9$ 8. $x + 4 \le 7$ 9. $3x - 1 \ge 2x - 3$

    $\{x \mid x > 3\}$ $\{x \mid x \le 3\}$ $\{x \mid x \ge 2\}$

The Multiplication Principle

Consider this true inequality.

$$4 < 9$$

If we multiply both numbers by 2, we get another true inequality.

$$8 < 18$$

If we multiply both numbers by -3, we get a false inequality.

$$-12 < -27$$

However, if we now reverse the inequality symbol, we get a true inequality.

$$-12 > -27$$

THEOREM 2–5

The Multiplication Principle for Inequalities

If we multiply on both sides of a true inequality by a positive number, we get another true inequality. If we multiply by a negative number and reverse the inequality symbol, we get another true inequality.

When we solve an inequality using the multiplication principle, we can multiply by any number except zero, provided that we do not multiply by an expression containing a variable.

EXAMPLES
Solve.

7. $3y < \frac{3}{4}$

$$\frac{1}{3} \cdot 3y < \frac{1}{3} \cdot \frac{3}{4} \quad \text{Multiplying by } \frac{1}{3}$$

$$y < \frac{1}{4}$$

Any number less than $\frac{1}{4}$ is a solution. The solution set is $\{y \mid y < \frac{1}{4}\}$.

8. $-4x < \frac{4}{5}$

$\qquad -\frac{1}{4} \cdot (-4x) > -\frac{1}{4} \cdot \frac{4}{5}$ Multiplying by $-\frac{1}{4}$ and reversing the inequality sign

$\qquad x > -\frac{1}{5}$

Any number greater than $-\frac{1}{5}$ is a solution. The solution set is $\{x \mid x > -\frac{1}{5}\}$.

9. $-5x \geq -80$

$\qquad -\frac{1}{5} \cdot (-5x) \leq -\frac{1}{5} \cdot (-80)$ Multiplying by $-\frac{1}{5}$ and reversing $\geq$

$\qquad x \leq 16$

The solution set is $\{x \mid x \leq 16\}$.

TRY THIS Solve.

10. $5y \leq \frac{3}{2}$ **11.** $-2y > \frac{5}{6}$ 10. $\left\{ y \mid y \leq \frac{3}{10} \right\}$ 11. $\left\{ y \mid y < \frac{-5}{12} \right\}$

12. $-\frac{1}{3}x \leq -4$ **13.** $-0.5y \geq -18$ 12. $\{x \mid x \geq 12\}$ 13. $\{y \mid y \geq 36\}$

Using the Principles Together

We use the addition and multiplication principles together in solving inequalities in much the same way as for equations.

EXAMPLE 10

Solve $16 - 7y \geq 10y - 4$.

$\qquad -16 + 16 - 7y \geq -16 + 10y - 4$ Adding -16

$\qquad\qquad -7y \geq 10y - 20$

$\qquad -10y - 7y \geq -10y + 10y - 20$ Adding $-10y$

$\qquad\qquad -17y \geq -20$

$\qquad -\frac{1}{17} \cdot (-17y) \leq -\frac{1}{17} \cdot (-20)$ Multiplying by $-\frac{1}{17}$ and reversing the inequality sign

$\qquad\qquad y \leq \frac{20}{17}$

The solution set is $\{y \mid y \leq \frac{20}{17}\}$.

TRY THIS Solve.

14. $6 - 5y \geq 7$ **15.** $3x + 5x < 4$ **16.** $17 - 5y \leq 8y - 5$

14. $\left\{ y \mid -\frac{1}{5} \geq y \right\}$

15. $\left\{ x \mid x < \frac{1}{2} \right\}$

16. $\left\{ y \mid \frac{22}{13} \leq y \right\}$

Exercises

You may wish to have students write answers in set notation. For example, the answer to Exercise 5 would be $\{x \mid x > -5\}$.

Find the solution set. Then graph.

1. $x \le 4$
2. $y \le -1$
3. $x > 5$
4. $x > 3$

5. $x + 8 > 3$
6. $x + 5 > 2$
7. $y + 3 < 9$
8. $y + 4 < 10$

   5. $x > -5$
   6. $x > -3$
   7. $y < 6$
   8. $y < 6$

9. $a + 9 \le -12$ $a \le -21$
10. $a + 7 \le -13$ $a \le -20$

11. $t + 14 \ge 9$ $t \ge -5$
12. $x - 9 \le 10$ $x \le 19$

13. $y - 8 > -14$ $y > -6$
14. $y - 9 > -18$ $y > -9$

15. $x - 11 \le -2$ $x \le 9$
16. $y - 18 \le -4$ $y \le 14$

17. $8x \ge 24$ $x \ge 3$
18. $9t < -81$ $t < -9$

19. $0.3x < -18$ $x < -60$
20. $0.5x < 25$ $x < 50$

21. $-9x \ge -8.1$ $x \le 0.9$
22. $-8y \le 3.2$ $y \ge -0.4$

23. $-\frac{3}{4}x \ge -\frac{5}{8}$ $x \le \frac{5}{6}$
24. $-\frac{5}{6}y \le -\frac{3}{4}$ $y \ge \frac{5}{8}$

25. $2x + 7 < 19$ $x < 6$
26. $5y + 13 > 28$ $y > 3$

27. $5y + 2y \le -21$ $y \le -3$
28. $-9x + 3x \ge -24$ $x \le 4$

29. $2y - 7 < 5y - 9$ $y > \frac{2}{3}$
30. $8x - 9 < 3x - 11$ $x < -\frac{2}{5}$

31. $0.4x + 5 \le 1.2x - 4$ $x \ge 11.25$
32. $0.2y + 1 > 2.4y - 10$ $y < 5$

33. $3x - \frac{1}{8} \le \frac{3}{8} + 2x$ $x \le \frac{1}{2}$
34. $2x - 3 < \frac{13}{4}x + 10 - 1.25x$ $0 \cdot x < 13$ Real number line

Extension

Solve.

35. $4(3y - 2) \ge 9(2y + 5)$ $y \le -8\frac{5}{6}$
36. $4m + 5 \ge 14(m - 2)$ $m \le 3.3$

37. $3(2 - 5x) + 2x < 2(4 + 2x)$ $x > \frac{-2}{17}$
38. $2(0.5 - 3y) + y > (4y - 0.2)8$ $y < 0.07$

39. $5[3m - (m + 4)] > -2(m - 4)$
40. $[8x - 3(3x + 2)] - 5 \ge 3(x + 4) - 2x$ $x \le -11.5$

              $m > \frac{7}{3}$

Challenge

Solve.

41. $(y + 3)(y - 3) < 0$ $-3 < y < 3$
42. $y(y + 5) > 0$ $y > 0$ or $y < -5$
43. $\frac{x + 3}{x - 3} > 0$
44. $\frac{x - 2}{x + 1} < 0$

   43. $\{x \mid x \le -3 \text{ or } x > 3\}$
   44. $\{x \mid -1 < x \le 2\}$

45. Determine whether the following statements are true or false. If false, give a counterexample.

    a. For any real numbers, a, b, c and d, if $a < b$ and $c < d$, then $a - c < b - d$. True

    b. For any real numbers x and y, if $x < y$ then $x^2 < y^2$.
       False, because $-3 < -2$, but $9 > 4$.

2–6 Solving Problems with Inequalities

Certain problems translate quite naturally to inequalities, rather than equations.

EXAMPLE 1

In a history course, there will be three tests. You must get a total score of 270 for an A. You get 91 and 86 on the first two tests. What scores on the last test will give you an A?

We translate. For an A,

$$\text{Total score} \geq 270$$
$$91 + 86 + x \geq 270$$

We have used x for your score on the last test. Solving the inequality, we get the following.

$$x \geq 93$$

Thus a score of 93 or higher will give you an A.

TRY THIS

1. In a chemistry course, there will be five tests. To get a B, a total of 400 points are needed. You get scores of 91, 86, 73, and 79 on the first four tests. What scores on the last test will give you at least a B? 71 or higher

EXAMPLE 2

On your new job, you can be paid one of two ways.

Plan A: A salary of $600 per month, plus a commission of 4% of gross sales

Plan B: A salary of $800 per month, plus a commission of 6% of gross sales over $10,000

For what gross sales is Plan A better than Plan B, assuming that gross sales are always more than $10,000?

To translate, we will write an inequality that states that the income from Plan A is greater than that from Plan B.

$$\text{Income from A} > \text{Income from B}$$
$$600 + 4\% \cdot x > 800 + (x - 10{,}000) \cdot 6\%$$

We have used x to represent the gross sales for the month. Solving this inequality, we get the following.

$$x < 20,000$$

Thus for gross sales under $20,000, Plan A is better.

TRY THIS

2. A painter can be paid in two ways.

   Plan A: $500 plus $4 per hour   Plan B: Straight $9 per hour

   Suppose the job takes n hours. For what values of n is Plan A better for the painter? $n < 100$

2–6

Exercises

1. A car rents for $13.95 per day, plus 10¢ per mile. You are on a daily budget of $76. What mileages will allow you to stay within the budget? Less than 620 miles

2. You are taking a history course. There will be 4 tests. You have scores of 89, 92, and 95 on the first three. You must make a total of 360 to get an A. What scores on the last test will give you an A? 84 or more

3. You are going to invest $25,000, part at 14% and part at 16%. What is the most that can be invested at 14% in order to make at least $3600 interest per year? $20,000

4. You are going to invest $20,000, part at 12% and part at 16%. What is the most that can be invested at 12% in order to make at least $3000 interest per year? $5000

5. In planning for a school dance, you find that one band will play for $250 plus 50% of the total ticket sales. Another band will play for a flat fee of $550. In order for the first band to produce more profit for the school than the other band, what is the highest price you can charge per ticket, assuming that 300 people attend? $2

6. On your new job, you can be paid in one of two ways.

   Plan A: A salary of $500 per month, plus a commission of 4% gross sales

   Plan B: A salary of $750 per month plus a commission of 5% of gross sales over $8000

   For what gross sales is Plan B better than Plan A, assuming that gross sales are always more than $8000? $15,000 or more

7. A mason can be paid in two ways.

   Plan A: $500 plus $3.00 per hour

   Plan B: Straight $8.00 per hour

   Suppose the job takes n hours. For what values of n is Plan A better for the mason than Plan B? 100 hours or less

8. A mason can be paid in two ways.

   Plan A: $300 plus $3.00 per hour

   Plan B: Straight $8.50 per hour

   Suppose that the job takes n hours. For what values of n is Plan B better for the mason? 55 hours or more

2-7 Compound Inequalities

We now consider compound sentences with conjunctions.

Conjunctions and Intersections

When two sentences are joined by the word and to make a compound sentence, the new sentence is called a conjunction of the two sentences. We consider conjunctions of inequalities. Here is an example.

$$-2 < x \text{ and } x < 1$$

For the conjunction to be true, both parts must be true. Let's look at the solution sets and graphs of the simple inequalities.

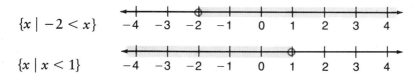

$\{x \mid -2 < x\}$

$\{x \mid x < 1\}$

For a number to be a solution of the conjunction, it must be in *both* solutions sets. The solution set of the conjunction is the part common to the individual solution sets.

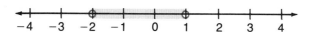

The common part of two or more sets is called their intersection. For two sets A and B, we can name the intersection $A \cap B$. If sets have no common members, we say that their intersection is empty, or the empty set, which can be named $\emptyset$.

The solution set of $-2 < x$ and $x < 1$ is the intersection

$$\{x \mid -2 < x\} \cap \{x \mid x < 1\}.$$

The conjunction "$-2 < x$ and $x < 1$" can be abbreviated as follows.

$$-2 < x < 1$$

EXAMPLE 1
Graph $-3 \le x < 4$.

The inequality is an abbreviation for the following conjunction.

$$-3 \le x \text{ and } x < 4$$

The word and corresponds to set intersection. The solution set is thus the intersection of the solution sets.

$$\{x \mid -3 \le x\} \cap \{x \mid x < 4\}$$

The graph is the intersection of the individual graphs.

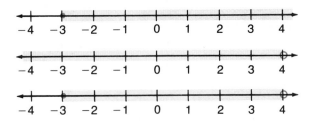

TRY THIS Graph.

1. $-1 < x < 4$ 2. $-2 < y < 5$

EXAMPLE 2

Solve $-3 < 2x + 5 < 7$.

Method 1: We write the conjunction with the word and.

$$-3 < 2x + 5 \text{ and } 2x + 5 < 7$$

Now we solve the individual inequalities separately.

$$
\begin{array}{ccc}
-3 < 2x + 5 & \text{and} & 2x + 5 < 7 \\
-3 + (-5) < 2x + 5 + (-5) & \text{and} & 2x + 5 + (-5) < 7 + (-5) \\
-8 < 2x & \text{and} & 2x < 2 \\
-4 < x & \text{and} & x < 1
\end{array}
$$

We now abbreviate the answer.

$$-4 < x < 1$$

Method 2: In Method 1, we did the same thing to each inequality. We can shorten the writing as follows.

$$
\begin{array}{ll}
-3 < 2x + 5 < 7 & \\
-3 + (-5) < 2x + 5 + (-5) < 7 + (-5) & \text{Adding } -5 \\
-8 < 2x < 2 & \\
-4 < x < 1 & \text{Multiplying by } \frac{1}{2}
\end{array}
$$

The solution set is $\{x \mid -4 < x < 1\}$.

TRY THIS Solve, using both methods as in Example 2.

3. $-2 < 3x + 4 < 7$ $\{x \mid -2 < x < 1\}$

Disjunctions and Unions

When two sentences are joined by the word or, the resulting compound sentence is called a disjunction of the two sentences. Here is an example.

$$x < -3 \text{ or } x > 3$$

A disjunction is true when either or both parts are true. Thus the solution set of a disjunction is the set formed by joining the individual solution sets. The set formed by joining sets A and B is called their union and can be denoted $A \cup B$. The solution set of the disjunction $x < -3$ or $x > 3$ is the following union.

$$\{x \mid x < -3\} \cup \{x \mid x > 3\}$$

The graph is shown below.

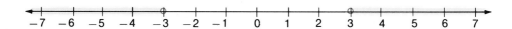

EXAMPLE 3

Graph $x \le 2$ or $x \ge 5$.

The graph consists of the union of their individual graphs.

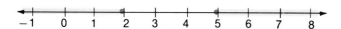

TRY THIS Graph.

4. $x \le -2$ or $x > 4$ 5. $x < -4$ or $x \ge 6$

EXAMPLE 4

Solve $-2x - 5 < -2$ or $x - 3 < 2$.

We solve the individual inequalities separately, but we keep writing the word or.

$$-2x - 5 + 5 < -2 + 5 \text{ or } x - 3 + 3 < 2 + 3$$
$$-2x < 3 \text{ or } x < 5$$
$$x > -\frac{3}{2} \text{ or } x < 5$$

TRY THIS Solve.

6. $x - 4 < -3$ or $x - 4 \ge 3$ 7. $-2x + 4 \le -3$ or $x + 5 < 3$

6. $\{x \mid x < 1 \text{ or } x \ge 7\}$

7. $\left\{ x \ge \dfrac{-7}{2} \text{ or } x < -2 \right\}$

Exercises

Graph. You may wish to have students write answers in set notation. For example, the answer to Exercise 5 would be $\{x \mid -4 < x < 6\}$.

1. $1 < x < 6$ **2.** $0 \le y \le 3$ **3.** $-7 \le y \le -3$ **4.** $-9 \le x < -5$

Solve.

5. $-2 < x + 2 < 8$ $-4 < x < 6$ **6.** $-1 < x + 1 \le 6$ $-2 < x \le 5$

7. $1 < 2y + 5 \le 9$ $-2 < y \le 2$ **8.** $3 \le 5x + 3 \le 8$ $0 \le x \le 1$

9. $-10 \le 3x - 5 \le -1$ $-\frac{5}{3} \le x \le \frac{4}{3}$ **10.** $-18 \le -2x - 7 < 0$ $\frac{11}{2} \ge x > -\frac{7}{2}$

Graph.

11. $x < -1$ or $x > 2$ **12.** $x < -2$ or $x > 0$ 17. $x < -9$ or $x > -5$

13. $x \le -3$ or $x > 1$ **14.** $x \le -1$ or $x > 3$ 18. $x < -13$ or $x > -5$
   19. $x \le \frac{5}{2}$ or $x \ge 11$

15. $x < -8$ or $x > -2$ **16.** $t \le -10$ or $t \ge -5$ 20. $x \le 5$ or $x \ge 3$
   21. $x < \frac{4}{3}$ or $x > 15$

Solve.   22. $x < -1$ or $x > 16$

17. $x + 7 < -2$ or $x + 7 > 2$ **18.** $x + 9 < -4$ or $x + 9 > 4$

19. $2x - 8 \le -3$ or $x - 8 \ge 3$ **20.** $x - 7 \le -2$ or $3x - 7 \ge 2$

21. $3x - 9 < -5$ or $x - 9 > 6$ **22.** $4x - 4 < -8$ or $x - 4 > 12$

Extension

Solve and graph.

23. $4a - 2 \le a + 1 \le 3a + 4$ $-\frac{3}{2} \le a \le 1$ **24.** $4m - 8 > 6m + 5$ or $5m - 8 < -2$ $m < \frac{6}{5}$

25. $x - 10 < 5x + 6 \le x + 10$ $-4 < x \le 1$ **26.** $2[5(3 - y) - 2(y - 2)] > y + 4$ $y < \frac{34}{15}$

27. $-\frac{2}{15} \le \frac{2}{3}x - \frac{2}{5} \le \frac{2}{15}$ $\frac{2}{5} \le x \le \frac{4}{5}$ **28.** $2x - \frac{3}{4} < -\frac{1}{10}$ or $2x - \frac{3}{4} > \frac{1}{10}$ $x < \frac{13}{40}$ or $x > \frac{17}{40}$

29. $3x < 4 - 5x < 5 + 3x$ $-\frac{1}{8} < x < 2$ **30.** $(x + 6)(x - 4) > (x + 1)(x - 3)$ $x > \frac{21}{4}$

True or False. Let a, b, and c represent real numbers.

31. If $b > c$, then $b \not< c$.   T   **32.** If $-b < -a$, then $a < b$.   T

33. If $c \ne a$, then $a < c$.   F   **34.** If $a < c$, and $c < b$, then $b \not< a$.   F

35. If $a < c$ and $b < c$, then $a < b$.   F   **36.** If $-a < c$ and $-c > b$, then $a < b$.   F

Challenge

Solve.

37. $[4x - 2 < 8$ or $3(x - 1) < -2]$ and $-2 \le 5x \le 10$ $-\frac{2}{5} \le x \le 2$

38. $-2 \le 4m + 3 < 7$ and $[m - 5 - 4$ or $3 - m > 12]$ $-\frac{5}{4} \le m \le 1$

2–8 Absolute Value

There are certain properties of absolute value that can be proved using the definition of absolute value. They are stated in the next theorem.

THEOREM 2–6

A. For any real numbers a and b, $|ab| = |a| \cdot |b|$.
   (The absolute value of a product is the product of the absolute values.)

B. $\left|\dfrac{a}{b}\right| = \dfrac{|a|}{|b|}$, assuming that $b \neq 0$.
   (The absolute value of a quotient is the quotient of the absolute values.)

C. $|a^n| = a^n$ if n is an even integer.
   (The absolute value of an even power is that power.)

Theorem 2–6 can be used to simplify or otherwise manipulate expressions containing absolute value.

EXAMPLES
Simplify, leaving as little as possible inside absolute value signs.

1. $|5x| = |5| \cdot |x| = 5|x|$

2. $|x^2| = x^2$

3. $|x^2 y^3| = |x^2 y^2 y| = |x^2| \cdot |y^2| \cdot |y| = x^2 y^2 |y|$

4. $\left|\dfrac{x^2}{y}\right| = \dfrac{|x^2|}{|y|} = \dfrac{x^2}{|y|}$

5. $|-5x| = |-5| \cdot |x| = 5|x|$

TRY THIS Simplify, leaving as little as possible inside absolute value signs.

1. $|7x|$ $7|x|$ 2. $|x^8|$ x^8 3. $|5a^2 b|$ $5a^2|b|$ 4. $\left|\dfrac{7a}{b^2}\right|$ $\dfrac{7|a|}{b^2}$ 5. $|-9x|$ $9|x|$

Distance on a Number Line

On a number line, the number that goes with a point is called its coordinate. To find the distance between two points we can subtract their coordinates and take the absolute value of the result. For example, the distance from 2 to -3 on a number line is $|-3 - 2|$ or $|-5|$, which is 5.

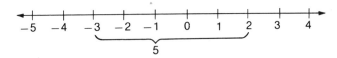

DEFINITION

The distance between any two points of a number line having coordinates a and b is $|a - b|$ or $|b - a|$.

EXAMPLE 6
Find the distance between points having coordinates 10 and 3.

The distance is $|10 - 3|$, or $|7|$, which is 7.

EXAMPLE 7
Find the distance between points having coordinates -8 and -92.

The distance is $|-8 - (-92)|$, which is $|84|$, or 84.

TRY THIS Find the distance between the points having the given coordinates.

6. $-6, -35$ 29 7. $19, 14$ 5 8. $-3, 17$ 20

Equations and Inequalities with Absolute Value

To solve equations or inequalities with absolute value, it may help to think about distance on a number line.

EXAMPLE 8
Solve $|x| = 4$. Then graph, using a number line.
Since $|x| = |x - 0|$, we know that $|x|$ is the distance from x to 0. The solutions of the equation are those numbers x whose distance from 0 is 4. The solution set is $\{4, -4\}$.

The graph consists of just two points, as shown.

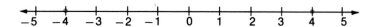

TRY THIS Solve. Then graph using a number line.

9. $|x| = 6$ **10.** $|x| = \frac{1}{2}$ 9. {6, −6}   10. $\left\{-\frac{1}{2}, \frac{1}{2}\right\}$

EXAMPLE 9
Solve $|x| < 4$. Then graph.

Since $|x| = |x - 0|$, we know that $|x|$ is the distance from x to 0. The solutions of $|x| < 4$ are those numbers whose distance from 0 is less than 4. The solution set is

$$\{x \mid -4 < x < 4\}.$$

The graph is as follows.

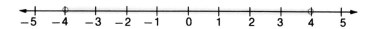

TRY THIS Solve. Then graph.

11. $|x| < 5$ **12.** $|x| < 6.5$ 11. {x | −5 < x < 5}   12. {x | −6.5 < x < 6.5}

EXAMPLE 10
Solve $|x| \geq 4$. Then graph.

Since $|x| = |x - 0|$, the solutions of $|x| \geq 4$ are those numbers whose distance from 0 is greater than or equal to 4; in other words, those numbers x such that $x \leq -4$ or $x \geq 4$. The solution set is

$$\{x \mid x \leq -4 \text{ or } x \geq 4\}.$$

The graph is as follows.

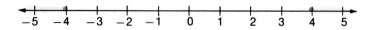

TRY THIS Solve. Then graph.

13. $|y| \geq 8$ **14.** $|x| > \frac{1}{2}$ 13. {y | y ≤ −8 or y ≥ 8}   14. $\left\{x \mid x > \frac{1}{2} \text{ or } x < -\frac{1}{2}\right\}$

86 CHAPTER 2 SOLVING EQUATIONS AND INEQUALITIES

Examples 8–10 illustrate three cases of solving inequalities with absolute value. The expression inside of absolute value signs can be something besides a single variable. The following theorem gives the general principles for solving.

THEOREM 2–7

For any positive number b, and any expression X,

A. The solutions of $|X| = b$ are those numbers that satisfy $X = -b$ or $X = b$.

B. The solutions of $|X| < b$ are those numbers that satisfy $-b < X < b$.

C. The solutions of $|X| > b$ are those numbers that satisfy $X < -b$ or $X > b$.

Parts A and B of Theorem 2–7 show that the solutions of $|X| \leq b$ are those numbers that satisfy $-b \leq X \leq b$. Parts A and C tell us that the solutions of $|X| \geq b$ are those numbers that satisfy $X \leq -b$ or $X \geq b$.

EXAMPLE 11

Solve $|5x - 4| = 11$. Then graph.

We use Theorem 2–7. In this case, b is 11 and X is $5x - 4$.

$$|X| = b$$
$$|5x - 4| = 11 \quad \text{Replacing } X \text{ by } 5x - 4 \text{ and } b \text{ by } 11$$
$$5x - 4 = 11 \text{ or } 5x - 4 = -11 \quad \text{Using Theorem 2–7, part A.}$$
$$5x = 15 \text{ or } \quad 5x = -7 \quad \text{Adding 4}$$
$$x = 3 \text{ or } \quad x = -\frac{7}{5} \quad \text{Multiplying by } \frac{1}{5}$$

The solution set is $\{3, -\frac{7}{5}\}$.

Here is the graph of the solution set.

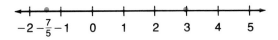

TRY THIS

15. Solve $|3x + 4| = 9$. $\left\{\frac{5}{3}, -\frac{13}{3}\right\}$

EXAMPLE 12

Solve $|3x - 2| < 4$. Then graph.

We use Theorem 2–7, part B. In this case b is 4 and X is $3x - 2$.

$$|X| < b$$
$$|3x - 2| < 4 \quad \text{Replacing } X \text{ by } 3x - 2 \text{ and } b \text{ by } 4$$
$$-4 < 3x - 2 < 4 \quad \text{Using Theorem 2–7, part B.}$$
$$-2 < 3x < 6 \quad \text{Adding 2}$$
$$-\frac{2}{3} < x < 2 \quad \text{Multiplying by } \frac{1}{3}$$

The graph is as follows.

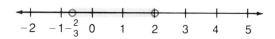

EXAMPLE 13

Solve $|4x + 2| \geq 6$. Then graph.

We use Theorem 2–7. In this case, b is 6 and X is $4x + 2$.

$$|X| \geq b$$
$$|4x + 2| \geq 6 \quad \text{Replacing } X \text{ by } 4x + 2 \text{ and } b \text{ by } 6$$
$$4x + 2 \leq -6 \text{ or } 4x + 2 \geq 6 \quad \text{Theorem 2–7, part C.}$$
$$4x \leq -8 \text{ or } 4x \geq 4 \quad \text{Adding } -2$$
$$x \leq -2 \text{ or } x \geq 1 \quad \text{Multiplying by } \frac{1}{4}$$

The graph is as follows.

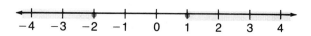

TRY THIS Solve.

16. $|2x - 3| < 7$ $\quad \{x \mid -2 < x < 5\}$

17. $|2x - 4| > 7$ $\quad \left\{ x \mid x > \frac{11}{2} \text{ or } x < -\frac{3}{2} \right\}$

2–8	

Exercises

Simplify, leaving as little as possible inside absolute value signs.

1. $|3x|$ $\quad 3|x|$
2. $|4x|$ $\quad 4|x|$
3. $|y^8|$ $\quad y^8$
4. $|x^6|$ $\quad x^6$

5. $|9x^2y^3|$ $\quad 9x^2y^2|y|$
6. $|10a^4b^7|$ $\quad 10a^4b^6|b|$
7. $\left|\dfrac{a^2}{b}\right|$ $\quad \dfrac{a^2}{|b|}$
8. $\left|\dfrac{y^4}{m}\right|$ $\quad \dfrac{y^4}{|m|}$

9. $|-16m|$ $16|m|$ **10.** $|-9t|$ $9|t|$ **11.** $|t^3|$ $t^2|t|$ **12.** $|p^5|$ $p^4|p|$

13. $|b^9|$ $b^8|b|$ **14.** $|x^6|$ x^6 **15.** $|x^3y^2|$ $x^2y^2|x|$ **16.** $|25n^3|$ $25n^2|n|$

Find the distance between the points having the given coordinates.

17. $-8, -42$ 34 **18.** $-9, -36$ 27 **19.** 26, 15 11 **20.** 54, 18 36

21. $-9, 24$ 33 **22.** $-18, -37$ 19 **23.** $-5, 0$ 5 **24.** 0, 23 23

Solve. Then graph.

25. $|x| = 3$ **26.** $|x| = 5$ **27.** $|x| < 3$ **28.** $|x| \le 5$

29. $|x| \ge 2$ **30.** $|y| > 8$ **31.** $|t| \ge 5.5$ **32.** $|m| > 0$

33. $|x - 3| = 12$ **34.** $|3x - 2| = 6$ **35.** $|2x - 3| \le 4$

36. $|5x + 2| \le 3$ **37.** $|2y - 7| > 10$ **38.** $|3y - 4| > 8$

39. $|4x - 9| \ge 14$ **40.** $|9y - 2| \ge 17$ **41.** $|10x + 8| > 2$

Extension

Solve. Use a calculator.

42. $\left|\dfrac{2x - 1}{0.0059}\right| \le 1$ $0.49705 \le x \le 0.50295$ **43.** $\left|\dfrac{3x - 2}{5}\right| \ge 1$ $x \le -1$ or $x \ge \frac{7}{3}$

44. $\left|\dfrac{0.005x - 0.004}{0.0059}\right| \le 0.0043$ **45.** $3\left|\dfrac{0.0064x - 0.0009}{0.0023}\right| \ge 0.0089$

$0.794926 \le x \le 0.805074$ $\qquad$ $x \le 0.1396$ or $x \ge 0.1417$

Solve.

46. $|m + 5| + 9 \le 16$ **47.** $|t - 7| + 3 \ge 4$

48. $|g + 7| + 13 = 4$ **49.** $2|2x - 7| + 11 = 25$

Challenge

Solve.

50. $|3x - 4| > -2$ **51.** $|x - 6| \le -8$ **52.** $\left|\dfrac{5}{9} + 3x\right| < \dfrac{1}{6}$

53. $1 - \left|\dfrac{1}{4}x + .8\right| > \dfrac{3}{4}$ **54.** $|x + 5| > x$ **55.** $2 \le |x - 1| \le 5$

56. $|7x - 2| = x + 4$ **57.** $|x - 1| - 2 = |2x - 5|$ **58.** $|x + 1| \le |x - 3|$

MATHEMATICAL LANGUAGE/The Inclusive *Or*	
In everyday language, the word *or* is usually used *exclusively*. For example, "We shall have roast or chicken for dinner" means that we are having either roast or chicken, but not both. The word	*or* is used *inclusively* in the sentence "Gravy is good with roast or chicken." The sentence means that gravy is good with both. In mathematics, the inclusive *or* is most frequently used.

2-9 Proofs (Optional)

If, Then Statements

An *If, then* statement,

> *If P, then Q*

is also called a conditional. Such statements occur extensively in mathematics. The sentence P is called the antecedent and the sentence Q is called the consequent.

To prove a statement S, in particular *If P, then Q*, we use any axiom and previously proven theorem and try to deduce S.

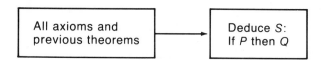

To prove an *If P, then Q* statement we temporarily accept P as an axiom, and use it and all the axioms and previously proven theorems and try to prove Q. This results in a proof of *If P, then Q*.

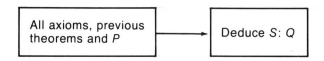

Thus, to prove a conditional, we begin by assuming the antecedent to be true. We call that assumption the hypothesis. Then we try to show that the assumption leads to Q. Then we conclude that *If P, then Q* is true.

EXAMPLE 1
Prove that if $3x + 5 < 38$, then $x < 11$.

1. $3x + 5 < 38$	1. Hypothesis
2. $3x < 33$	2. Using the addition principle by adding -5 on both sides
3. $x < 11$	3. Using the multiplication principle by multiplying by $\frac{1}{3}$
4. If $3x + 5 < 38$, then $x < 11$.	4. Statements $1 - 3$

TRY THIS

1. Prove that if $-3x + 8 > 23$, then $x < -5$.

What does a conditional sentence tell us? Consider the following true statement.

If $x < 3$, then $x < 10$.

If a number makes the antecedent true, it must also make the consequent true. In other words, the solution set of $x < 3$ is a subset of the solution set of $x < 10$. The symbol $\subset$ means is a subset of. We have thus shown that $\{x \mid x < 3\} \subset \{x \mid x < 10\}$.

The conditional does not tell us what happens if the antecedent is false. The chart shows what happens for various replacements.

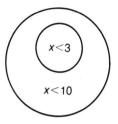

x	Antecedent	Consequent
	$x < 3$	$x < 10$
2	$2 < 5$ True	$2 < 10$ True
7	$7 < 5$ False	$7 < 10$ True
12	$12 < 5$ False	$12 < 10$ False

The chart above shows that there are various possibilities for antecedents and consequences in a true *if, then* statement. The one possibility that cannot occur is a true antecedent and a false consequent.

Converses

From a conditional if P, then Q, we can form a new conditional. We do this by interchanging the antecedent and consequent.

If Q, then P.

The two statements are called converses of each other.

EXAMPLES

Write the converse of each statement.

2. If $x > 5$, then $x > -1$.
   The converse is: If $x > -1$, then $x > 5$.

3. If $3x + 5 = 20$, then $x = 5$.
   The converse is: If $x = 5$, then $3x + 5 = 20$.

TRY THIS Write the converse of each statement.

2. If $x < 12$, then $x < 17$.   3. If $3x + 7 = 37$, then $x = 9$.

2. If $x < 17$, then $x < 12$.
3. If $x = 9$, then $3x + 7 = 37$.

We have already considered this true statement: If $x < 3$, then $x < 10$. Let us now consider the converse.

If $x < 10$, then $x < 3$.

x	Antecedent	Consequent
	$x < 10$	$x < 3$
18	$18 < 10$ False	$18 < 3$ False
6	$6 < 10$ True	$6 < 3$ False
1	$1 < 10$ True	$1 < 3$ True

The replacement 6 gives us a true antecedent and a false consequent. This can happen only because the conditional is false. The solution set of $x < 10$ is not a subset of the solution set of $x < 3$.

Converses of true conditionals may not be true. We have just seen an example in which the converse of a true statement was false. In Example 1, we proved that if $3x + 5 < 38$, then $x < 11$. The converse, if $x < 11$, then $3x + 5 < 38$, is true in this case.

EXAMPLE 4
Prove: If $x < 11$, then $3x + 5 < 38$.
We reverse the steps used in Example 1.

1. $x < 11$	1. Hypothesis
2. $3x < 33$	2. Using the multiplication principle
3. $3x + 5 < 38$	3. Using the addition principle
4. If $x < 11$, then $3x + 5 < 38$	4. Transitive property of inequality

We now know that the solution set of $x < 11$ is a subset of the solution set of $3x + 5 < 38$. Since we already established that the solution set of $x < 11$ is a subset of the solution set of $3x + 5 < 38$, we know that the antecedent and the consequent have the *same* solution set.

TRY THIS

4. In Try This 1 you proved that if $-3x + 8 > 23$, then $x < -5$.
   a. Prove the converse.
   b. Describe the solution sets of the antecedent and consequent.

Solving Equations and Inequalities

When we solve an equation or inequality, in effect we write a proof. We start with the sentence to be solved, using it as hypothesis. From that hypothesis, we try to obtain a very simple statement, one whose solution set is obvious, as in the following example.

EXAMPLE 5

Solve $6x - 2 = 28$.

$$6x - 2 = 28$$
$$6x = 30 \quad \text{Using the addition principle}$$
$$x = 5 \quad \text{Using the multiplication principle}$$

The statement $x = 5$ has a very simple solution set, $\{5\}$. What about the solution set of $6x - 2 = 28$? From the proof we know that it is a subset of $\{5\}$. Thus the only possible solution is 5. To determine whether 5 is actually a solution of $6x - 2 = 28$, we can reverse the steps of the proof (prove the converse), or we can check by substituting. For inequalities we usually cannot check by substituting, because the solution sets are infinite.

EXAMPLE 6

Solve $3x + 5 < 29$ by proving a statement and its converse.

a. We prove this statement: If $3x + 5 < 29$, then $x < 8$. We abbreviate the writing as we ordinarily do in solving.

$$3x + 5 < 29$$
$$3x < 24$$
$$x < 8$$

b. We prove this statement: If $x < 8$, then $3x - 5 < 29$, also abbreviating the writing.

$$x < 8$$
$$3x < 24$$
$$3x + 5 < 29$$

Since we have proved a statement and its converse, we know that $3x + 5 < 29$ and $x < 8$ have the same solution set. Therefore, the solution set of $3x + 5 < 29$ is $\{x \mid x < 8\}$.

TRY THIS

5. Solve $7x - 1 > 34$, by proving a statement and its converse. $\{x \mid x > 5\}$
6. Solve $9x - 5 = 103$ 12
   a. by proving a statement and its converse.
   b. by proving a statement and then substituting.

Equivalent Statements

If two equations or inequalities have the same solution set, they are said to be equivalent. If in solving we know which manipulations give us equivalent statements, we can cut down on the work of proving converses. The following theorem answers that question.

THEOREM 2–8

The use of the addition and multiplication principles for equations and inequalities produces equivalent statements under the following conditions.
A. The expression added or multiplied must have no nonsensible replacements.
B. The expression by which we multiply must never have the value 0.

According to Theorem 2–8, whenever we add any constant or multiply by any nonzero constant, we obtain equivalent statements. Thus in the solving of simple equations or inequalities, we can depend on Theorem 2–8, and need not actually prove a converse.

EXAMPLE 7

To show that multiplying by 0 can be troublesome, prove that if $x = 1$, then $x^2 = x$.

$$x = 1$$
$$x^2 = x \quad \text{Multiplying by } x$$

If $x = 1$, then $x^2 = x$.

The solution set of $x = 1$ is $\{1\}$. The solution set of $x^2 = x$ is $\{0, 1\}$. The statements are not equivalent.

According to Theorem 2–8, if the expressions that we add or that we multiply by in solving do not contain variables (and we do not multiply by 0), then we always obtain equivalent statements.

EXAMPLES

Which of the following will be certain to produce an equivalent equation or inequality?

8. Adding 3 on both sides — Yes

9. Adding $\frac{1}{x}$ on both sides — No, the expression added has a nonsensible replacement.

10. Adding $3x - 3x$ on both sides — Yes

11. Multiplying by $x + 2$ on both sides — No, the expression can have the value 0.

12. Multiplying by $x^2 + 1$ on both sides — Yes, the expression cannot have the value 0.

13. Multiplying by $\frac{3}{x + 2}$ on both sides — No, there is a nonsensible replacement.

TRY THIS Which of the following will be certain to produce an equivalent equation or inequality?

7. Multiplying by -5 on both sides   Yes

8. Multiplying by $3x - 3x$ on both sides   No

9. Adding $\frac{x}{1 - x}$ on both sides   No

10. Adding 7 on both sides   Yes

11. Multiplying by $x + 5$ on both sides   No

12. Multiplying by $\frac{1}{x + 27}$ on both sides   No

2–9

Exercises

Prove the following.

1. If $7x - 12 = 37$, then $x = 7$.

2. If $5y + 16 = 88 - 3y$, then $y = 9$.

3. If $15x - 5 \geq 11 - 2x$, then $x \geq \frac{16}{17}$.

4. If $13x + 12 < 15x - 7$, then $x > \frac{19}{2}$.

Write the converse of each statement.

5. If $3y = 5$, then $6y = 10$.   **7.** If $5x + 3 = 17$, then $2x + 5 = 14$.

6. If $x < 12$, then $x < 20$.   **8.** If $3y + 5 > 17 - y$, then $4y + 2 < 8y + 1$.

Write the converse of each statement and then prove it. Compare with Exercises 1 – 4.

5. If $6y = 10$, then $3y = 5$.
6. If $x < 20$, then $x < 12$.
7. If $2x + 5 = 14$, then $5x + 3 = 17$.
8. If $4y + 2 < 8y + 1$, then $3y + 5 > 17 - y$.

9. If $7x - 12 = 37$, then $x = 7$.   If $x = 7$, then $7x - 12 = 37$.

10. If $5y + 16 = 88 - 3y$, then $y = 9$.   If $y = 9$, then $5y + 16 = 88 - 3y$.

11. If $15x - 5 \geq 11 - 2x$, then $x \geq \frac{16}{17}$.   If $x \geq \frac{16}{17}$, then $15x - 5 \geq 11 - 2x$.

12. If $13x + 12 < 15x - 7$, then $x > \frac{19}{2}$.   If $x > \frac{19}{2}$, then $13x + 12 < 15x - 7$.

Solve, by proving a statement and its converse.

13. $3x - 2 < 5x + 7$ $\left\{ x \mid -\frac{9}{2} < x \right\}$ **14.** $4y + 5 \geq 7y - 2$ $\left\{ y \mid \frac{7}{3} \geq y \right\}$

15. $16x + 3 = 2x - 5$ $-\frac{4}{7}$ **16.** $6y - 12 = 8y + 2$ -7

Solve by proving a statement and then substituting.

17. $14x - 12 = 16x + 5$ $-\frac{17}{2}$ **18.** $7y + 5 = 5y + 7$ 1

19. $-6x - 10 = 6x + 10$ $-\frac{5}{3}$ **20.** $-5y + 7 = 10y - 14$ $\frac{7}{5}$

Which of the following will be certain to produce an equivalent equation or inequality?

21. Multiplying on both sides by -5 Yes

22. Multiplying on both sides by x^2 No

23. Adding $x^2 + 3$ on both sides   Yes

24. Adding $3 - x^2$ on both sides   Yes

25. Adding $\frac{x - 2}{x + 3}$ on both sides   No

26. Multiplying on both sides by $x^2 + 2$ Yes

27. Adding 5 on both sides   Yes

28. Multiplying on both sides by $\frac{1}{x^2 + 1}$ Yes

Extension

29. Solve by proving a statement and its converse.
$16x + 3(x - 2) = 12x - 5$ $\frac{1}{7}$

30. Solve the inequality in the set of integers, by proving a statement and then substituting.

$3x + 7 < 13 + x$ $\{x \mid x < 3\}$

Recall the definition of equality in Section 1–9. Prove the following.

31. The addition principle for equations

32. The multiplication principle for equations

33. The principle of zero products

To prove the addition principle and the multiplication principle for inequalities we need another definition and two more axioms regarding the real numbers.

DEFINITION

For any real numbers a and b, $a < b$ is true if and only if the difference $b - a$ is positive. Also, $a > b$ means that $b < a$.

Axioms for Real Numbers

8. Closure of the Positive Set. For any positive numbers a and b, both the product ab and the sum $a + b$ are in the set of positive numbers.

9. Trichotomy. For any real number a, one and only one of the following is true.
   a. $a > 0$ **b.** $a = 0$ **c.** $a < 0$

Prove the following.

34. Transitive Law for Inequality. For any real numbers a, b, and c, if $a < b$ and $b < c$, then $a < c$.

35. The addition principle for inequalities

36. The multiplication principle for inequalities

37. For any real numbers a and b, $|ab| = |a| \cdot |b|$.

38. For any real numbers a and b, $\left|\dfrac{a}{b}\right| = \dfrac{|a|}{|b|}$.

39. For any real number a, $|a|^2 = a^2$.

Challenge

For each statement, rewrite in *if, then* form and then write the converse.

40. Integers are rational numbers.   Answers may vary.

41. Quitters never win.

42. Birds of a feather flock together.

CAREERS/Clothing Manufacturing

A production superintendent in a clothing factory makes the plans for the manu-facturing of the clothing.

Efficient use of machines, materials, and people is im-portant for the profitable operation of the shop. Know-ing this, the production su-perintendent investigates data about the cost, availability, and quality of materials such as fabric and thread. This in-formation as well as data about labor time and costs and machine time and costs is then analyzed.

This analysis requires that the production superintendent translate production problems into equations using the methods taught in Section 2–3. The solutions to these problems provide the prod-uction superintendent with the information necessary to determine the hours, equip-ment and materials needed to construct each garment.

To complete the planning, the production superintendent co-ordinates production activities with procurement, mainte-nance, and quality control ac-tivities to assure maximum production and the best utili-zation of people, materials, and machines.

Exercises

Translate each problem into an equation or equations. Solve.

1. The cost of equipment maintenance has increased by $6,000 a year for the past 3 years. Three years ago the cost of equipment main-tenance was $78,000. What is the cost this year? $96,000

2. In one day the factory can make 70 of a particular skirt. If this is 40% of an order, how many skirts are in the order?

3. A fabric supplier is dis-counting selected fabrics 30%. What is the sale price on a roll of fabric that was originally $360? $252

4. A 100 meter roll of cloth is to be cut into two pieces. One piece is 3 times as long as the other. How long is each piece? 25 m, 75 m

5. The number of workers the factory employs has de-creased by 12%. There are now 264 employees. What was the former number of employees? 300

6. Two workers can sew 224 sleeves a day. One of the workers sews 16 more than the other. How many sleeves does each sew a day? 104, 120

2. 175

7. Some of the employees got a 10% salary raise. Their new salary is $19,800. What was their salary before the raise? $18,000

8. The factory borrowed money at 14% simple interest to buy a new machine. At the end of one year $52,440 paid off the loan. How much was originally borrowed? $46,000

9. Quality control workers check each garment. On the last four orders quality control passed 97%, 94%, 93%, and 94% of the gar-ments. What percent must they pass on the next order to have passed an average of 95% of the garments? 97%

10. Three of the buttonhole machines at the factory have been named Molly, Burt, and Daisy. Molly can make 140 fewer than twice as many buttonholes as Burt does in a day. Daisy can make 80 more than $\frac{3}{4}$ the number Molly makes. Together they make 1290 buttonholes a day. How many buttonholes does each make? Molly: 580; Burt: 360; Daisy: 350

11. Last week the factory made 3 times as many suits as have been made so far this week. If 180 more suits are made this week, the factory will have made the same number of suits as last week. How many suits have been made so far this week? How many suits were made this week? 90, 270

CHAPTER 2   Review

Review the material in the chapter. Then see how you have done by trying these review exercises. If you miss an exercise, restudy the indicated lesson.

2–1   Solve.

1. $x - \frac{2}{3} = \frac{1}{2}$ $\frac{7}{6}$
2. $-\frac{7}{6} = x - \frac{3}{8}$ $-\frac{19}{24}$
3. $x + 1.8 = 3.2$ 1.4
4. $y - 2.9 = -7.2$ -4.3
5. $7y = -5.6$ -0.8
6. $-1.4y = -12.6$ 9
7. $-\frac{4}{5}y = 72$ -90
8. $-4x = -\frac{6}{5}$ $\frac{3}{10}$
9. $-8x - 19 = 53$ -9
10. $-9t - 74 = -2$ -8
11. $7 - 12x = -x + 5$ $\frac{2}{11}$
12. $-3x - 75 = 7x - 20$ -5.5

2–2

13. $\frac{1}{4} + \frac{1}{2}x = \frac{5}{4}$ 2
14. $\frac{2}{3}x + \frac{1}{6} = 9$ $\frac{53}{4}$
15. $0.6x + 1.5 = 2.1$ 1
16. $2.9y - 4.6 = 0.6y$ 2
17. $300(x + 7) = 350$ $-\frac{35}{6}$
18. $\frac{1}{4}(3x - 5) = 10 - \frac{3}{4}(x - 1)$ 8
19. $(x + 4)(x - 3) = 0$ $-4, 3$
20. $(2x - 5)(3x - 4) = 0$ $\frac{5}{2}, \frac{4}{3}$

2–3

21. One angle of a triangle is five times as large as the first angle. The measure of the third angle is 2° less than that of the first angle. How large are the angles? $26°, 130°, 24°$

22. A retail store decreases the price of suits 20% to a sale price of $120. What was the former price? $\$150$

2–4   Solve for the indicated letter.

23. $A = \frac{1}{2}bh$, for b
24. $V = ah + at$, for a $a = \frac{V}{h+t}$ 23. $b = \frac{2A}{h}$

2–5   Graph on a number line.

25. $x > -1$ 26. $x \le 4$ All points left of, and including 4
   All points right of -1

2–5   Solve.

27. $y + 3 \ge 4$ $y \ge 1$
28. $2x + 7 > x - 9$ $x > -16$
29. $\frac{1}{3}x \ge -9$ $x \ge -27$
30. $-9y \ge -45$ $y \le 5$
31. $-\frac{2}{3}x \ge -20$ $x \le 30$
32. $3x - 8 \le 7x + 5$ $x \ge \frac{13}{4}$

2–6

33. Find all sets of three consecutive positive odd integers whose sum is less than 20. $\{1, 3, 5\}, \{3, 5, 7\}$

2–7   Graph.

34. $-3 < x < 2$ **35.** $x < -2$ or $x > 5$ All points left of -2 and right of 5

All points between -3 and 2

2–7   Solve.

36. $-7 < 2x - 1 < 9$ **37.** $x + 1 < -4$ or $x + 1 > 4$ $x < -5$ or $x > 3$

$-3 < x < 5$

2–8

38. $|y| < 4$ **39.** $|x| \geq 10$ $x \leq -10$ or $x \geq 10$ 38. $-4 < y < 4$

40. $|x - 3| \geq 5$ **41.** $|3x + 5| < 7$ $-4 < x < \frac{2}{3}$ 40. $x \geq 8$ or $x \leq -2$

CHAPTER 2   Test

Solve.

1. $r - 17 = 20$ 37   **2.** $-9x = 450$ -50

3. $3y + 10 = 16$ 2   **4.** $-2z + 5 = 7$ -1

5. $0.8x - 3.7 = 0.3$ 5   **6.** $\frac{1}{5}y - \frac{2}{3} = 6$ $\frac{100}{3}$

7. $8(x + 9) = 112$ 5   **8.** $8y - (5y - 9) = -160$ $-\frac{169}{3}$

9. $(x + 7)(x - 8) = 0$ $-7, 8$ **10.** $(3x + 5)(2x - 6) = 0$ $-\frac{5}{3}, 3$

Solve.

11. A 14-m piece of cable is cut into two pieces. One piece is 4 m longer than the other. How long are the pieces? 5 m, 9 m

12. Solve $Q = P - Prt$ for P. $P = \frac{Q}{1 - rt}$

Solve.

13. $y + 5 \geq 8$ $y \geq 3$ **14.** $4x \geq 28$ $x \geq 7$ **15.** $-8y \leq -40$ $y \geq 5$

16. $4 + 7y \leq 39$ $y \leq 5$ **17.** $2x - 9 \leq 9x + 4$ $x \geq \frac{-13}{7}$

Solve.

18. You have made scores of 81, 76, and 82 on three quizzes. What is the least you can make on the fourth quiz to have an average of at least 80? 81

Solve.

19. $-3 < x + 1 < 8$ **20.** $|y| \geq 8$ $y \leq -8$ or $y \geq 8$ 19. $-4 < x < 7$

21. $x - 2 \leq 6$ $-4 \leq x \leq 8$ **22.** $|2x + 7| < 9$ $-8 < x < 1$

Challenge

23. Solve $(x + 1)(x - 1) < 0.$ $-1 < x < 1$

Ready for Graphs, Relations, and Functions?

1–2 Evaluate each expression when $x = -2$, $y = 3$, and $z = -4$.

1. $y - xz$ -5 **2.** $3x + 2y - z$ 4

1–2 Find $-a$ when a stands for

3. -10 10 **4.** 0 0 **5.** $\frac{1}{2}$ $-\frac{1}{2}$

1–3 Add.

6. $-4 + 0$ -4 **7.** $-2 + (-7)$ -9

8. $-2.7 + (-3.5)$ -6.2 **9.** $15 + (-8)$ 7

10. $-8.1 + 2.4$ -5.7 **11.** $\frac{2}{3} + \left(-\frac{3}{5}\right)$ $\frac{1}{15}$

2–1 Solve.

12. $x + 8 = -12$ -20

13. $3x = 21$ 7

14. $4x - 5 = 11$ 4

15. $9x - 2x = 21$ 3

16. $7x - 4 + 2x = -8 - 3x + 6$ $\frac{1}{6}$

17. $r + \frac{5}{6} = -\frac{3}{12}$ $-\frac{13}{12}$

18. $5t = -12$ $-\frac{12}{5}$

19. $\frac{2}{3}x = 16$ 24

20. $-4y - 3y = 28$ -4

21. $8 - 5x = x - 14$ $\frac{11}{3}$

22. $8a = 3(a + 5)$ 3

2–5 Solve.

23. $x + 2 < 6$ $x < 4$ **24.** $y - 8 \geq 0$ $y \geq 8$

25. $4y \leq -8$ $y \leq -2$ **26.** $-5x > 10$ $x < -2$

27. $3x - 1 > 8$ $x > 3$ **28.** $2 + 7y \leq 3$ $y \leq \frac{1}{7}$

29. $4y - 1 < y + 2$ $y < 1$ **30.** $x - 6 \geq 3x - 10$ $x \leq 2$

3

CHAPTER THREE

Graphs, Relations, and Functions

3–1 Relations and Ordered Pairs

Cartesian Products

Consider the following sets.

$$A = \{1, 2, 3\} \text{ and } B = \{a, b\}$$

From these sets we can form ordered pairs, choosing the first elements from A and the second elements from B.

$(1, a)$ $(2, a)$ $(3, a)$
$(1, b)$ $(2, b)$ $(3, b)$

The set of all ordered pairs formed this way is called the Cartesian product and is denoted as $A \times B$.

DEFINITION

The *Cartesian product* of two sets A and B, symbolized $A \times B$, is defined as the set of all ordered pairs having the first member from set A and the second member from set B.

The two sets used to form a Cartesian product may be the same. If $Q = \{2, 3, 4, 5\}$, then the Cartesian product is called $Q \times Q$.

EXAMPLE 1
Find the Cartesian product $Q \times Q$, where $Q = \{2, 3, 4, 5\}$.
The Cartesian product $Q \times Q$ is as follows.

$(2, 2)$ $(3, 2)$ $(4, 2)$ $(5, 2)$
$(2, 3)$ $(3, 3)$ $(4, 3)$ $(5, 3)$
$(2, 4)$ $(3, 4)$ $(4, 4)$ $(5, 4)$
$(2, 5)$ $(3, 5)$ $(4, 5)$ $(5, 5)$

TRY THIS Find the Cartesian products of the following sets.
1. $A = \{d, e\}$ and $B = \{1, 2\}$. Find $A \times B$. $(d, 1)\,(e, 1)\,(d, 2)\,(e, 2)$
2. $C = \{x, y, z\}$. Find $C \times C$. $(x, x)\,(y, x)\,(z, x)\,(x, y)\,(y, y)\,(z, y)\,(x, z)\,(y, z)\,(z, z)$

Relations

In a Cartesian product we can pick out ordered pairs that make up common relations, such as $=$ or $<$ as in the following examples.

EXAMPLE 2

In the Cartesian product of Example 1 indicate all ordered pairs for which the first member is less than the second. This set of ordered pairs is the relation $<$.

(2, 2)	(3, 2)	(4, 2)	(5, 2)
(2, 3)	(3, 3)	(4, 3)	(5, 3)
(2, 4)	(3, 4)	(4, 4)	(5, 4)
(2, 5)	(3, 5)	(4, 5)	(5, 5)

TRY THIS

3. In the Cartesian product of Example 1 indicate all ordered pairs for which the first member is the same as the second. This is the relation $=$. {(2, 2) (3, 3) (4, 4) (5, 5)}

There are also many relations that do not have common names and relations with which we are not already familiar. Any set of ordered pairs selected from a Cartesian product is called a relation.

DEFINITION

A *relation* from a set A to a set B is defined to be any set of ordered pairs in $A \times B$.

In a relation two other sets are known as the domain and the range.

DEFINITION

The set of all first members in a relation is called its *domain*.
The set of all second members in a relation is called its *range*.

EXAMPLE 3

Find the domain and range of the relation $<$ in Example 2.

Domain: {2, 3, 4}; Range: {3, 4, 5}

TRY THIS

4. Find the domain and range of the relation in Try This 3. Domain: {2, 3, 4, 5}, range: {2, 3, 4, 5}

5. Consider the relation whose ordered pairs are (2, 2), (1, 1), (1, 2), and (1, 3). Find the domain and range. Domain: {1, 2}; range: {1, 2, 3}

Set-Builder Notation

In a set or relation we often need to refer to those elements that satisfy a certain condition. In the set $\{1, 2, 3, 4, 5, 6\}$ we may refer to the set of all x such that x is greater than 3. In symbols we write $\{x \mid x > 3\}$. The numbers 4, 5, and 6 satisfy this condition. We can write

$$\{x \mid x > 3\} = \{4, 5, 6\}.$$

EXAMPLE 4

Use the set $\{1, 2, 3, 4, \ldots, 10\}$. Find $\{x \mid 2 < x < 8\}$. The numbers satisfying both conditions that $x < 8$ and $x < 2$ are 3, 4, 5, 6, and 7.

$$\{x \mid 2 < x < 8\} = \{3, 4, 5, 6, 7\}$$

EXAMPLE 5

Use the relation $Q \times Q$ of Example 1. Find $\{(x, y) \mid y > x + 1\}$. We check each ordered pair in turn to find those that satisfy the condition $y > x + 1$. There are three of them.

$$\{(x, y) \mid y > x + 1\} = \{(2, 5), (2, 4), (3, 5)\}$$

TRY THIS Write the elements indicated by each of the following.

6. In the set $\{1, 2, 3, \ldots, 10\}$, find $\{x \mid 5 < x < 7\}$. {6}

7. In the set $Q \times Q$ of Example 1, find $\{(x, y) \mid x > 2 \text{ and } y > 3\}$. {(3, 4), (3, 5), (4, 4), (4, 5), (5, 4), (5, 5)}

3–1	

Exercises

List all ordered pairs in the following Cartesian products.

1. $A \times B$, where $A = \{0, 2, 4, 5\}$ and $B = \{a, b, c\}$.

2. $A \times B$, where $A = \{1, 3, 5, 9\}$ and $B = \{d, e, f\}$.

3. $B \times C$, where $B = \{x, y, z\}$ and $C = \{1, 2\}$.

4. $B \times C$, where $B = \{5, 7, 10\}$ and $C = \{a, z\}$.

5. $D \times D$, where $D = \{5, 6, 7, 8\}$.

6. $E \times E$, where $E = \{-2, 0, 2, 4\}$.

For Exercises 7–12, consider the set $\{-1, 0, 1, 2\}$.

7. Find the set of ordered pairs determined by the relation $<$ (is less than).

8. Find the set of ordered pairs determined by the relation $>$ (is greater than).

9. Find the set of ordered pairs determined by the relation $\leq$ (is less than or equal to).

10. Find the set of ordered pairs determined by the relation $\geq$ (is greater than or equal to).

11. Find the set of ordered pairs determined by the relation $=$.

12. Find the set of ordered pairs determined by the relation $\neq$.

7. $\{(-1, 0), (-1, 1), (-1, 2), (0, 1), (0, 2), (1, 2)\}$ 8. $\{(2, 1), (2, 0), (2, -1), (1, 0), (1, -1), (0, -1)\}$ 9. $\{(-1, -1), (-1, 0), (-1, 1), (-1, 2), (0, 0), (0, 1), (0, 2), (1, 1), (1, 2), (2, 2)\}$ 10. $\{(2, 2), (2, 1), (2, 0), (2, -1), (1, 1), (1, 0), (1, -1), (0, 0), (0, -1), (-1, -1)\}$ 11. $\{(-1, -1), (0, 0), (1, 1), (2, 2)\}$ 12. $\{(-1, 0), (-1, 1), (-1, 2), (0, -1), (0, 1), (0, 2), (1, -1), (1, 0), (1, 2), (2, -1), (2, 0), (2, 1)\}$

13. Domain: $\{5, 6, 8\}$; range: $\{2, 4, 6\}$ 14. Domain: $\{7, 8, 9\}$; range: $\{1, 2, 5\}$ 15. Domain: $\{6, 7, 8\}$; range: $\{0, 5\}$ 16. Domain: $\{8, 10, 6\}$; range: $\{2, 1, 3\}$ 17. Domain: $\{8, 5\}$; range: $\{1\}$ 18. Domain: $\{6, 2, -3\}$; range: $\{2, 0\}$ 19. Domain: $\{5\}$; range $\{6\}$ 20. Domain: $\{7\}$; range $\{-4\}$

List the domain and range for each of the following relations.

13. $\{(5, 2), (6, 4), (8, 6)\}$

14. $\{(7, 1), (8, 2), (9, 5)\}$

15. $\{(6, 0), (7, 5), (8, 5)\}$

16. $\{(8, 2), (10, 1), (6, 3)\}$

17. $\{(8, 1), (8, 1), (5, 1)\}$

18. $\{(6, 2), (2, 0), (-3, 0)\}$

19. $\{(5, 6)\}$

20. $\{(7, -4)\}$

21. a. List all the ordered pairs in the Cartesian product $D \times D$, where $D = \{-1, 0, 1, 2\}$.
    b. Find the ordered pairs determined by relation $=$. $\{(-1, -1), (0, 0), (1, 1), (2, 2)\}$
    c. List the domain and the range of this relation. Domain: $\{-1, 0, 1, 2\}$; range: $\{-1, 0, 1, 2\}$

22. a. List all the ordered pairs in the Cartesian product $E \times E$, where $E = \{-1, 1, 3, 5\}$.
    b. Find the ordered pairs determined by relation $<$. $\{(-1, 1), (-1, 3), (1, 3), (-1, 5), (1, 5), (3, 5)\}$
    c. List the domain and the range of this relation. Domain: $\{-1, 1, 3\}$; range: $\{1, 3, 5\}$

Consider the set $\{2, 4, 6, 8, 10, 12\}$. Find the sets indicated by each of the following.

23. $\{x \mid x > 7\}$ $\{8, 10, 12\}$

24. $\{x \mid x < 4\}$ $\{2\}$

25. $\{x \mid 3 < x < 10\}$ $\{4, 6, 8\}$

26. $\{x \mid x > 6 \text{ or } x < 3\}$ $\{2, 8, 10, 12\}$

Consider the relation $Q \times Q$ in Example 1. Find the sets indicated by each of the following.

27. $\{2, 2), (2, 3)\}$ 28. $\{(5, 2), (5, 3)\}$ 29. $\{(2, 3), (3, 3)\}$ 30. $\{(2, 4), (2, 5), (3, 4), (3, 5)\}$ 31. $\{(3, 2)\}$ 32. $\{(3, 3), (3, 4)\}$

27. $\{(x, y) \mid x \leq 2 \text{ and } y \leq 3\}$

28. $\{(x, y) \mid x > 4 \text{ and } y < 4\}$

29. $\{(x, y) \mid 2 \leq x \leq 3 \text{ and } y = 3\}$

30. $\{(x, y) \mid x < 4 \text{ and } 4 \leq y \leq 5\}$

31. $\{(x, y) \mid x = 3 \text{ and } y = 2\}$

32. $\{(x, y) \mid 2 < x < 4 \text{ and } 2 < y < 5\}$

3–2 Graphs of Equations

Graphs of Ordered Pairs

We are most interested in relations involving $R \times R$, where R is the set of real numbers. The set R is infinite. Thus relations involving R may be infinite, and therefore cannot be indicated by listing the ordered pairs one at a time. We usually indicate such relations with a graph.

On a number line each point corresponds to a number. On a plane each point corresponds to a number pair from $R \times R$. To represent $R \times R$ we draw an x-axis and a y-axis perpendicular to each other. Their intersection is called the origin and is labeled 0. The arrows show the positive directions.

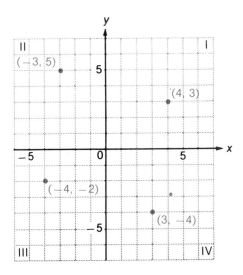

This is called a Cartesian coordinate system. The first member of an ordered pair is called the first coordinate. The second member is called the second coordinate. (The first coordinate is sometimes called the abscissa and the second coordinate the ordinate.) Together these are called the coordinates of a point. The axes divide the plane into four quadrants, indicated by the Roman numerals. The figure shows the graph of the relation {(4, 3), (−3, 5), (−4, −2), (3, −4)}.

TRY THIS

1. Use graph paper.
   a. Draw and label an x-axis and a y-axis.
   b. Label the quadrants.
   c. Plot the points in the relation $\{(3, 2), (-5, -2), (-4, 3)\}$.
   d. Find the domain of the relation. {3, −5, −4}
   e. Find the range of the relation. {2, −2, 3}

Graphing Equations

If an equation has two variables, its solutions are ordered pairs of numbers. A solution is an ordered pair which when substituted alphabetically for the variables produces a true equation.

EXAMPLE 1

Determine whether the following ordered pairs are solutions of the equation $y = 3x - 1$: $(-1, -4)$ and $(7, 5)$.

$$y = 3x - 1$$

-4	$3(-1) - 1$	We substitute -1 for x and -4 for y
-4	$-3 - 1$	(alphabetical order of variables).
	-4	

The equation becomes true: $(-1, -4)$ is a solution.

$$y = 3x - 1$$

5	$3 \cdot 7 - 1$	We substitute.
5	$21 - 1$	
	20	

The equation becomes false: $(7, 5)$ is not a solution.

TRY THIS

2. Determine whether $(1, 7)$ is a solution of $y = 2x + 5$. Yes
3. Determine whether $(-1, 4)$ is a solution of $y = 2x + 5$. No
4. Determine whether $(-2, 5)$ is a solution of $y = x^2$. No

The solutions of an equation are ordered pairs and thus constitute a relation. To graph an equation, or a relation, means to make a drawing of its solutions. Some general suggestions for graphing are as follows.

Graphing suggestions

1. Use graph paper.
2. Label axes with symbols for the variables.
3. Use arrows to indicate positive directions.
4. Mark numbers on the axes.
5. Plot solutions and complete the graph.
6. Label the equation or relation being graphed.

EXAMPLE 2

Graph $y = 3x - 1$.

To begin, we find some ordered pairs that are solutions. To do this we choose *any* number that is a sensible replacement for x and then determine y. For example, if we choose 2 for x, then $y = 3(2) - 1$, or 5. We have found the solution $(2, 5)$. We continue making choices for x, and finding the corresponding values for y. We make some negative choices for x, as well as positive ones. We keep track of the solutions in a table.

x	0	1	2	-1	-2
y	-1	2	5	-4	-7

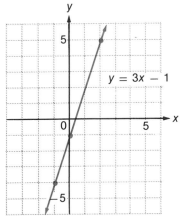

The table gives us the ordered pairs $(0, -1)$, $(1, 2)$, $(2, 5)$, and so on. Next, we plot these points. If we had enough of them, they would make a line. We can draw the line with a ruler, and label it $y = 3x - 1$.

Note that the equation $y = 3x - 1$ has an infinite (unending) set of solutions. The graph of the equation is a drawing of the relation that is the solution set.

Thus the relation consists of all pairs (x, y) such that $y = 3x - 1$ is true. That is, $\{(x, y) \mid y = 3x - 1\}$.

TRY THIS

5. Graph $y = -3x + 1$.

EXAMPLE 3

Graph $y = x^2 - 5$.

We select numbers for x and find the corresponding values for y. The table gives us the ordered pairs $(0, -5)$, $(-1, -4)$, and so on.

x	0	-1	1	-2	2	-3	3
y	-5	-4	-4	-1	-1	4	4

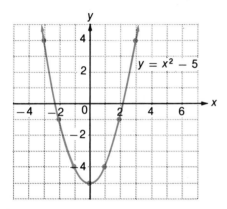

Next we plot these points. We note that as the absolute value of x increases, $x^2 - 5$ also increases. Thus the graph is a curve that rises gradually on either side of the y-axis, as shown above.

This graph shows the relation $\{(x, y) \mid y = x^2 - 5\}$.

TRY THIS

6. Graph $y = 3 - x^2$.

7. Graph $x = y^2 - 5$. [Hint: Select values for y and then find the corresponding values of x. When you plot the points, be sure to find x (horizontally) first.] Compare it with the graph of Example 3.

7. The shapes are the same, but this curve opens to the right instead of up.

You can always use a calculator to find as many values as desired. This can be especially helpful when you are uncertain about the shape of a graph.

Domains and Ranges

In each graph we can see a relation in real numbers, together with its domain and range.

EXAMPLE 4   **EXAMPLE 5**

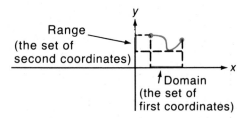   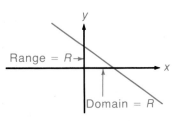

In Example 5 the domain and the range are the set of real numbers.

TRY THIS. Make copies of each relation. Shade the domain on the x-axis and shade the range on the y-axis.

8.

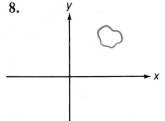

9.

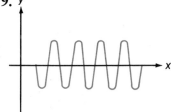

10.

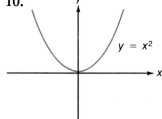

$y = x^2$

3–2	

Exercises

Plot the points in each of the following relations.

1. $\{(3, 0), (4, 2), (5, 4), (6, 6)\}$

2. $\{(1, 1), (2, 3), (3, 5), (4, 7)\}$

3. $\{(3, -4), (3, -3), (3, -2), (3, -1), (3, 0)\}$

4. $\{(-2, 1), (-2, 2), (-2, 3), (-2, 4), (-2, 5)\}$

5. $\{(4, 3), (4, 2), (3, 2), (3, 3), (5, 2), (5, 3)\}$

6. $\{(2, -2), (3, -2), (2, -3), (3, -3), (2, -4), (3, -4)\}$

7. $\{(-1, 1), (-2, 1), (-2, 2), (-3, 1), (-3, 2), (-3, 3)\}$

8. $\{(-1, -1), (-1, -2), (-1, -3), (-2, -2), (-2, -3), (-3, -3)\}$

Determine whether the given ordered pair is a solution of the indicated equation.

9. $(1, -1); y = 2x - 3$ Yes

10. $(2, 5); y = 3x - 1$ Yes

11. $(3, 4); 3s + t = 4$ No

12. $(2, 3); 2p + q = 5$ No

13. $(3, 5); 4x - y = 7$ Yes

14. $(2, 7); 5x - y = 3$ Yes

15. $\left(0, \frac{3}{5}\right); 2a + 5b = 3$ Yes

16. $\left(0, \frac{3}{2}\right); 3f + 4g = 6$ Yes

17. $(2, -1); 4r + 3s = 5$ Yes

18. $(2, -4); 5w + 2z = 2$ Yes

19. $(3, 2); 3x - 2y = -4$ No

20. $(1, 2); 2x - 5y = -6$ No

Graph each of the following. You should obtain a straight line.

21. $y = x$

22. $y = 2x$

23. $y = -2x$

24. $y = -\frac{1}{2}x$

25. $y = x + 3$

26. $y = x - 2$

27. $y = 3x - 2$

28. $y = -4x + 1$

29. $y = -2x + 3$

Graph each of the following. You should obtain a curve like the one in Example 3. Indicate the domain and the range for each.

30. $y = x^2$

31. $y = -x^2$

32. $y = x^2 + 2$

33. $y = x^2 - 2$

34. $x = y^2 + 2$

35. $x = y^2 - 2$

36. Graph a relation as follows.
   a. Draw a triangle with vertices at $(1, 1)$, $(4, 2)$, and $(3, 6)$. Shade the triangle and its interior.
   b. Shade (on the x-axis) the domain. Describe the domain. $\{x \mid 1 \leq x \leq 4\}$
   c. Shade (on the y-axis) the range. Describe the range. $\{y \mid 1 \leq y \leq 6\}$

37. Graph a relation as follows.
   a. Draw a circle with radius of length 2, centered at $(4, 3)$. Shade the circle and its interior.
   b. Shade (on the x-axis) the domain. Describe the domain. $\{x \mid 2 \leq x \leq 6\}$
   c. Shade (on the y-axis) the range. Describe the range. $\{y \mid 1 \leq y \leq 5\}$

Extension

In each of the following, all relations are in $R \times R$, where R is the set of real numbers.

38. Graph the relation in which the second coordinate is always 2 and the first coordinate may be any real number.

39. Graph the relation in which the first coordinate is always -3, and the second coordinate may be any real number.

40. Graph the relation in which the second coordinate is always 1 more than the first coordinate, and the first coordinate may be any real number.

41. Graph the relation in which the second coordinate is always 1 less than the first coordinate, and the first coordinate may be any real number.

42. Graph the relation in which the second coordinate is always twice the first coordinate, and the first coordinate may be any real number.

43. Graph the relation in which the second coordinate is always half the first coordinate, and the first coordinate may be any real number.

44. Graph the relation in which the second coordinate is always the square of the first coordinate, and the first coordinate may be any real number.

45. Graph the relation in which the first coordinate is always the square of the second coordinate, and the second coordinate may be any real number.

Consider $M \times M$ where $M = \{-5, -4, -3, \ldots, 4, 5\}$. Graph each of the following.

46. $\{(x, y) \mid y > 2x\}$

47. $\{(x, y) \mid -3 < x < 3 \text{ and } y = 0\}$

48. $\{(x, y) \mid x^2 + y^2 > 25\}$

49. $\{(x, y) \mid x \cdot y = 0\}$

Challenge
Graph the following relations in $R \times R$.

50. $\{(x, y) \mid 1 \leq x \leq 4 \text{ and } -3 \leq y \leq -1\}$

51. $\{(x, y) \mid -1 \leq x \leq 1 \text{ and } -4 \leq y \leq 4\}$

Use a calculator to find ordered pairs. Find at least 20 values between -5 and 5. Graph.

52. $y = \frac{1}{3}x^3 - x + \frac{2}{3}$

53. $y = \frac{1}{3}x^3 - \frac{1}{2}x^2 - 2x + 1$

DISCOVERY/René Descartes

Cartesian products and the Cartesian coordinate system are named after René Descartes, a French mathematician who lived from 1596 to 1650. Before the time of Descartes, algebra and geometry were separate areas of mathematics.

Algebra dealt with numbers; geometry was the study of points, lines, and curves. By using a coordinate system to combine algebra and geometry, Descartes introduced a new approach to the study of curves.

3-3 Functions

Recognizing Graphs of Functions

A function is a special kind of relation. It is defined as follows.

DEFINITION

A *function* is a relation in which no two ordered pairs have the same first coordinate and different second coordinates.

In a function, given a member of the domain (a first coordinate) there is one and only one member of the range that goes with it (the second coordinate). Thus each member of the domain *determines* exactly one member of the range. Suppose a relation has two ordered pairs with the same first element. Their graphs would be two points on the same vertical line. If there are two or more points of the graph on the same vertical line, then the relation is not a function.

Here are some graphs of functions. In graph **c.** the solid dot indicates that $(-1, 1)$ belongs to the graph. The open dot indicates that $(-1, -2)$ does not belong to the graph. Thus no vertical line crosses the graph more than once.

a.

b.

c.

The following are not graphs of functions, because they fail the vertical line test. That is, we can find a vertical line that meets the graph in more than one point.

a.

b.
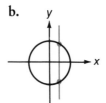

c.
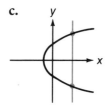

> **The Vertical Line Test**
>
> If it is possible for a vertical line to meet a graph more than once, the graph is not the graph of a function.

TRY THIS

1. Which of the following are graphs of functions?

a. Yes 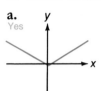 **b.** Yes 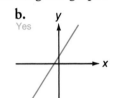 **c.** Yes 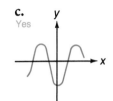 **d.** No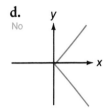

Notation for Functions

Functions are often named by letters, such as f or g. A function f is thus a set of ordered pairs. If we represent the first coordinate of a pair by x, then we may represent the second coordinate by $f(x)$. The symbol $f(x)$ is read "f of x." The number represented by $f(x)$ is called the "value" of the function at x. *Note:* "$f(x)$" does *not* mean "f times x."

EXAMPLE 1
Consider the function g defined as

$$g = \{(1, 4), (2, 3), (3, 2), (4, 4)\}.$$

Here $g(1) = 4$, $g(2) = 3$, $g(3) = 2$, and $g(4) = 4$.

EXAMPLE 2
Let us call the function graphed at the right f. To find function values, we locate x on the x-axis, and then find $f(x)$ on the y-axis.

We see that $f(1) = -1$ and $f(3) = 2$.

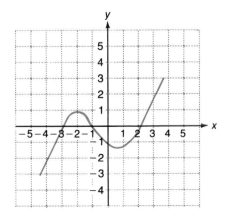

2. Use the graph in Example 2. Find each of the following.

a. $f(-4)$ $_{-2}$ **b.** $f(0)$ $_{-1}$ **c.** $f(2)$ $_{0}$

Mappings and Function Machines

Functions can be thought of as mappings. A function f maps the set of first coordinates (the domain) to the set of second coordinates (the range).

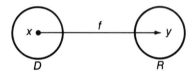

As in this diagram, each x in the domain corresponds to (or is mapped to) just one y in the range. That y is the second coordinate of the ordered pair (x, y).

EXAMPLE 3

Consider the function f for which $f(x) = 2x + 3$.

Since $f(0)$ is 3, this function maps 0 to 3 and gives the ordered pair $(0, 3)$.

Since $f(3)$ is 9, this function maps 3 to 9 and gives the ordered pair $(3, 9)$.

Sometimes it is helpful to think of functions or mappings in terms of function machines. Inputs are entered into the machine. The machine then gives the proper output. The inputs acceptable to the machine are the members of the domain of f. The outputs are members of the range of f.

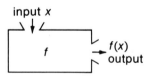

EXAMPLE 4

This function machine is for the function f which maps each input x to the output $\frac{1}{x}$. Find: **a.** $f(2)$; **b.** $f(3)$; and **c.** $f(-2)$.

a. $f(2) = \frac{1}{2}$ **b.** $f(3) = \frac{1}{3}$ **c.** $f(-2) = \frac{1}{-2}$

$$= -\frac{1}{2}$$

Note that f is not defined for $x = 0$.

TRY THIS Find the indicated outputs for the function machines described below.

input x

$g(x) = x - 4 \rightarrow$ $x - 4$ output

3. a. $g(0)$ $_{-4}$ b. $g(-3)$ $_{-7}$ c. $g(7)$ $_3$ d. $g\left(\frac{1}{2}\right)$ $_{-\frac{7}{2}}$

input x

$h(x) = x^2 - x \rightarrow$ $x^2 - x$ output

4. a. $h(1)$ $_0$ b. $h(3)$ $_6$ c. $h(-4)$ $_{20}$ d. $h(5)$ $_{20}$

input x

$f(x) = \dfrac{1}{-x} \rightarrow$ $\dfrac{1}{-x}$ output

5. a. $f(2)$ $_{-\frac{1}{2}}$ b. $f(-4)\frac{1}{4}$ c. $f(-3)\frac{1}{3}$ d. $f\left(\frac{1}{3}\right)$ $_{-3}$

Some functions in real numbers can be defined by formulas or equations. Here are some examples.

$$g(s) = 3 \qquad p(t) = \frac{1}{t} \qquad f(x) = 3x^2 + 4x - 5 \qquad u(y) = |y| + 3$$

Function values can be obtained by making substitutions for the variables.

A function such as g above is called a constant function because all its function values are the same. The range contains only one number, 3.

EXAMPLE 5

Let $f(x) = 2x^2 - 3$. We can find function values as follows.

a. $f(0) = 2 \cdot 0^2 - 3 = -3$
b. $f(-1) = 2(-1)^2 - 3 = 2 \cdot 1 - 3 = -1$
c. $f(5a) = 2(5a)^2 - 3 = 2 \cdot 25a^2 - 3 = 50a^2 - 3$

If you have trouble finding function values when a formula is given, think of the formula, in the case of Example 5, as follows.

$$f(\ \ ) = 2(\ \ )^2 - 3$$

Then whatever goes between parentheses on the left goes between parentheses on the right.

TRY THIS

6. $f(x) = 3x^2 + 1$; find each of the following.
   a. $f(0)$ $_1$ b. $f(1)$ $_4$ c. $f(-1)$ $_4$ d. $f(2a)$ $_{12a^2 + 1}$

Finding the Domain of a Function

When a function in $R \times R$ is given by a formula, the domain is understood to be the set of all real numbers, or inputs, that are sensible replacements. Sometimes certain inputs are not possible when a function is given by a formula.

EXAMPLE 6

Let $f(x) = \frac{x-4}{x+3}$. Notice what happens for $x = -3$.

$$f(-3) = \frac{-3-4}{-3+3} = \frac{-7}{0}$$

Since we cannot divide by 0, the input -3 is *not possible*.

When an input is not possible that number is not in the domain of the function. Thus the domain of f is the set of real numbers except -3. We can name this set $\{x \mid x \neq -3\}$.

TRY THIS

7. Let $g(x) = \frac{x}{(x-1)(x+3)}$. Find $g(1)$ and $g(-3)$. What is the domain of g? They are not possible. $\{x \mid x \neq 1 \text{ and } x \neq -3\}$

Special Functions

Certain functions are known as special functions. The absolute value function is one of these.

EXAMPLE 7

Graph the function $y = |x|$.
We find numbers that satisfy the equation.

x	0	1	-1	2	-2	3	-3	4	-4
y	0	1	1	2	2	3	3	4	4

We plot these points and connect them. To see how to do this, note that as we get farther from the origin, to the left or right, the absolute value of x increases. Thus the graph is a curve that rises to the left and right of the y-axis. It actually consists of parts of two straight lines, as follows.

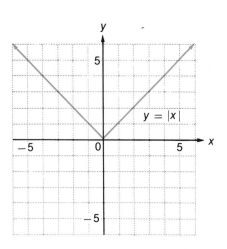

21. $f(x) = \dfrac{1}{5x + 8}$ $\{x \mid x \neq \frac{-8}{5}\}$ **22.** $f(x) = \dfrac{1}{(3 - x)(x + x)}$ $\{x \mid x \neq 3 \text{ and } x \neq 0\}$

23. $f(x) = \dfrac{4x^3 + 4}{x(x + 2)(x - 1)}$ **24.** $f(x) = x^3 - x^2 + x - 2$ R
$\{x \mid x \neq 0, x \neq -2, \text{ and } x \neq 1\}$

Graph. For each graph, tell whether it is a graph of a function.

25. $y = |x - 1|$ Yes   **26.** $x = |y + 1|$ No   **27.** $y = |x| + x$ Yes

28. $x = |y| - 1$ No   **29.** $y = \frac{1}{2}|x|$ Yes   **30.** $y = 2|x| - 2$ Yes

31. $y = [x - 2]$ Yes   **32.** $x = [y] - 1$ No   **33.** $x = [y - 1]$ No

Extension

Composition of Functions. The composition of the functions f and g is the function h where $h(x) = f(g(x))$. To find $h(x)$, begin by finding $g(x)$. Then use this value to evaluate f. Let $f(x) = 2x + 1$ and $g(x) = 1 - x^2$.

34. Show that $f(g(0)) = f(1) = 3.$ **35.** Show that $g(f(0)) = g(1) = 0.$

36. Find $g(g(2))$. -8 **37.** Find $f(f(-3))$. -9 34. $g(0) = 1 - 0^2 = 1;$
                                                             $f(1) = 2(1) + 1 = 3$

38. Find $g(f(3))$. -48 **39.** Find $f(g(3))$. -15 35. $f(0) = 2(0) + 1 = 1;$
                                                              $g(1) = 1 - 1^2 = 0$

Challenge

40. Graph $|x| - |y| = 1.$

41. Graph the relation $\{(x, y) \mid |x| \leq 1 \text{ and } |y| \leq 2\}.$

42. Determine whether the relation $\{(x, y) \mid xy = 0\}$ is a function. No

43. Graph the equation $[y] = [x]$. Is this the graph of a function? No

44. A person's bowling average is defined as follows.

     Bowling average $= [\frac{P}{n}]$, where $P =$ total number of pins knocked over and $n =$ total number of games bowled.

     In each case find the bowling average.
     a. 547 pins in 3 games   182 **b.** 4621 pins in 27 games   171

Find $h(x)$, $f(g(x))$, the composition of $f(x)$ and $g(x)$ as described for Exercises 34–39. For example, if $f(x) = 2x + 1$ and $g(x) = 1 - x^2$, then $h(x) = f(g(x)) = f(1 - x^2) = 2(1 - x^2) + 1 = -2x^2 + 3.$

45. $f(x) = 3x - 4, g(x) = |x|$ $h(x) = 3|x| - 4$

46. $f(x) = \sqrt{x}, g(x) = 2x - 3$ $h(x) = \sqrt{2x - 3}$

47. $f(x) = 2x + 3, g(x) = \dfrac{x - 3}{2}$ $h(x) = 2\left(\dfrac{x - 3}{2}\right) + 3 = x$

48. $f(x) = 5x - 4, g(x) = \dfrac{x + 4}{5}$ $h(x) = 5\left(\dfrac{x + 4}{5}\right) - 4 = x$

3-4 Graphs of Linear Equations

Recognizing Linear Equations

Equations that have straight lines for their graphs are called linear equations. An equation is linear if the variables occur to the first power only. No products of variables nor variables in denominators may appear.

EXAMPLE 1
Which of the following equations are linear?

a. $xy = 9$ **b.** $2r + 7 = 4s$ **c.** $4x^3 = 7y$

d. $8x - 17y = y$ **e.** $q = \dfrac{3}{p}$ **f.** $4x = -3$

Equations **b.**, **d.**, and **f.** are linear equations.

Since in linear equations the variables occur to the first power only, they are also called first degree equations.

TRY THIS Which of these equations are linear (first degree)?
1. $5y + 8x = 9$ Yes **2.** $7y = 11$ Yes

3. $5y^2x = 13$ No   **4.** $x = 4 + \dfrac{7}{y}$ No

5. $xy = 0$ No   **6.** $3x - 2y + 5 = 0$ Yes

Finding the Standard Form

Any linear equation can be written so that the right member is 0. This is called standard form.

DEFINITION

The *standard form* for a linear equation is $Ax + By + C = 0$, where A and B are not both zero.

In the standard form, A, B, and C represent constants.

EXAMPLE 2
Find the standard form for the equation $7x = \frac{1}{4} - 5x$.

$$7x = \frac{1}{4} - 5x$$

$$7x + 5x - \frac{1}{4} = 0 \quad \text{Using the addition principle, adding } 5x - \frac{1}{4}$$

$$12x + 0y - \frac{1}{4} = 0$$

This equation is of the form $Ax + By + C = 0$, where $A = 12$, $B = 0$, and $C = -\frac{1}{4}$.

TRY THIS Find the standard form for each equation.

7. $5y = \frac{1}{2} + 5x$ 8. $8y = 10 + 5y$

7. $-5x + 5y - \frac{1}{2} = 0$
8. $0x + 3y - 10 = 0$

Graphing Linear Equations

THEOREM 3–1

The graph of any linear equation is a straight line.

Since two points determine a line, we can graph a linear equation by finding two points that belong to the graph. Then we draw a line through those points.

A third point should always be used as a check. The easiest points to find are often the intercepts.

DEFINITION

The points where a graph crosses the axes are called the *intercepts*.

To find the y-intercept, let $x = 0$. To find the x-intercept, let $y = 0$.

EXAMPLE 3

Graph $4x + 5y = 20$.

We set $x = 0$ and find that $y = 4$. Thus $(0, 4)$ is a point of the graph (the y-intercept).

We set $y = 0$ and find that $x = 5$. Thus $(5, 0)$ is a point of the graph (the x-intercept). The graph is shown below. The point $(-2, 5\frac{3}{5})$ was used as a check.

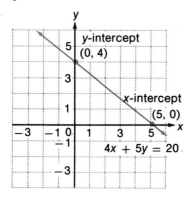

TRY THIS Graph.

9. $2x - 6y = -2$ 10. $3y = 2x - 6$

The graph of any equation $y = mx$ goes through the origin. Thus, the x-intercept and the y-intercept are the same point $(0, 0)$. Other points will be needed for graphing.

EXAMPLE 4

Graph $y = 2x$.

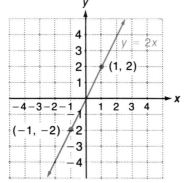

TRY THIS Graph.

11. $y = -x$ 12. $y = \frac{5}{2}x$

We have seen that the graph of any equation $y = mx$ is a straight line through the origin. Notice what happens if we add a number b on the right-hand side to get an equation $y = mx + b$.

EXAMPLE 5

Graph $y = 2x - 3$ and compare it with the graph of $y = 2x$.

We first make a table of values. Then graph and compare.

x	y (or $2x - 3$)
0	-3
1	-1
3	3
-2	-7

The graph of $y = 2x - 3$ is a line moved down 3 units from the graph of $y = 2x$.

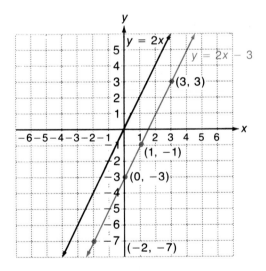

THEOREM 3–2

The graph of an equation $y = mx$ is a line through the origin. Any equation $y = mx + b$ has a graph that is a line parallel to $y = mx$, and it goes through the point $(0, b)$, the y-intercept.

We also refer to the number b as the y-intercept.

TRY THIS

13. Compare the graph of $y = 2x + 1$ with the graph of $y = 2x$.

14. Compare the graph of $y = 2x - 4$ with the graph of $y = 2x$.

Consider the equation $y = 4$. We can think of it as $y = 0 \cdot x + 4$. No matter what number we choose for x, we find y is 4. Thus $(x, 4)$ is a solution no matter what x is.

THEOREM 3–3

If there is no x term in a linear equation, the graph is a line parallel to the x-axis. If there is no y term, the graph is a line parallel to the y-axis.

EXAMPLE 6

Graph $y = 4$.

Any ordered pair $(x, 4)$ is a solution. So the line is parallel to the x-axis with y-intercept $(0, 4)$.

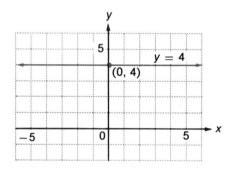

EXAMPLE 7

Graph $x = -2$.

Any ordered pair $(-2, y)$ is a solution. So the line is parallel to the y-axis with x-intercept $(-2, 0)$.

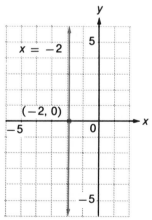

TRY THIS Graph these equations, using the same axes.

15. $x = 4$ **16.** $y = -3$ **17.** $y = 0$

We summarize the quickest procedure for graphing linear equations.

Graphing Linear Equations

1. Is there a variable missing? If so, solve for the other one. The graph will be a line parallel to an axis.
2. If no variable is missing, find the intercepts. Graph using the intercepts if this is feasible.
3. If the intercepts are too close together, choose another point further from the origin.
4. In any case, use a third point as a check.

3–4

Exercises

Which of the following equations are linear? If an equation is not linear, give the reason.

1. $3x - 4 = y$ 　　2. $x = 9$

3. $4r^2 = 2r + 1$ 　　4. $2 + 3pq = -9$

5. $y = 7$ 　　6. $3x^2 + 4y^2 = 16$

7. $4x - 5y = 20$ 　　8. $5 = \dfrac{1}{x}$

9. $3p - 4 = q - 1$ 　　10. $5 = r + 4t$

Find the standard form for each of the following equations.

11. $4x - 8 = y$ 　　12. $x = 2y - 1$

13. $y = 2x + 3$ 　　14. $y = 6x - 2$

15. $y + 4 = 4x + 8$ 　　16. $3x - 8 = x - 2$

17. $x = 6$ 　　18. $y = 9$

19. $\sqrt{2}y = 3x$ 　　20. $\sqrt{3}x = 5y$

Use graph paper. Use a different set of axes to graph each of the following linear equations.

21. $x + 2y = 4$ 　　22. $x + 3y = 9$ 　　23. $-x + 4y = 8$ 　　24. $-x + 2y = 6$

25. $4x + y = 8$ 　　26. $3x + y = 6$ 　　27. $3y - 3 = 6x$ 　　28. $2y - 6 = 4x$

29. $y = -\dfrac{5}{2}x - 4$ 　　30. $y = -\dfrac{2}{5}x + 3$ 　　31. $3x + 6y = 18$ 　　32. $4x + 5y = 20$

1. Yes
2. Yes
3. No, second degree term
4. No, product of variables
5. Yes
6. No, second degree terms
7. Yes
8. No, variable in denominator
9. Yes
10. Yes
11. $4x - y - 8 = 0$
12. $x - 2y + 1 = 0$
13. $-2x + y - 3 = 0$
14. $-6x + y + 2 = 0$
15. $-4x + y - 4 = 0$
16. $2x + 0y - 6 = 0$
17. $x + 0y - 6 = 0$
18. $0x + y - 9 = 0$
19. $-3x + \sqrt{2}y + 0 = 0$
20. $\sqrt{3}x - 5y + 0 = 0$
21. Line through (4, 0) and (0, 2)
22. Line through (9, 0) and (0, 3)
23. Line through (−8, 0) and (0, 2)
24. Line through (−6, 0) and (0, 3)
25. Line through (2, 0) and (0, 8)
26. Line through (2, 0) and (0, 6)
27. Line through (1, 3) and (−1, −1)
28. Line through $\left(-\dfrac{3}{2}, 0\right)$ and (0, 3)
29. Line through $\left(\dfrac{-8}{5}, 0\right)$ and (0, −4)
30. Line through $\left(\dfrac{15}{2}, 0\right)$ and (0, 3)
31. Line through (6, 0) and (0, 3)   32. Line through (5, 0) and (0, 4)

3–4 Graphs of Linear Equations **127**

Find the intercepts. Then use graph paper to graph each equation on different axes. Label the intercepts and a third point used as a check. Each graph is a line through the intercepts given in the answers.

33. $x - 2 = y$
34. $x - 4 = y$
35. $3a - 1 = b$
36. $3a - 4 = b$
37. $5x - 4y = 20$
38. $3x - 5y = 15$
39. $y = -5 - 5x$
40. $y = -2 - 2x$
41. $2p + 7q = 14$
42. $3p + 6q = 12$

Graph the following equations.

43. $x = 2$
44. $x = 4$
45. $y = -6$
46. $y = -3$
47. $x = -5$
48. $x = -3$
49. $y = 7$
50. $y = 5$
51. $3y - 9 = 0$
52. $3x + 15 = 0$
53. $2x - 10 = 0$
54. $6y + 24 = 0$

Extension

Find the intercepts of the following equations.

55. $2x + 5y + 2 = 5x - 10y - 8$
56. $\frac{1}{8}y = -x - \frac{7}{16}$
57. $0.4y - 0.004x = -0.04$
58. $x = \frac{-7}{3}y - \frac{2}{11}$

Use a calculator to find the intercepts of the following equations.

59. $4.92x - 3.07 = y$ (10, −3.07), (0.6239837, 0)
60. $1.706x - 3.481y = 7.283$ (0, −2.0922148), (4.2690504, 0)
61. Which of the graphs in Exercises 43–54 are graphs of functions   The horizontal lines.

Challenge

62. Write the equation $y = mx + b$ in standard form. $-mx + 1y - b = 0$
63. Write the equation $Ax + By + C = 0$ in the form $y = mx + b$. $y = \frac{-A}{B}x - \frac{C}{B}$

Answers:
33. (0, −2), (2, 0)
34. (0, −4), (4, 0)
35. $(0, -1), \left(\frac{1}{3}, 0\right)$
36. $(0, -4), \left(\frac{4}{3}, 0\right)$
37. (0, −5), (4, 0)
38. (0, −3), (5, 0)
39. (0, −5), (−1, 0)
40. (0, −2), (−1, 0)
41. (0, 2), (7, 0)
42. (0, 2), (4, 0)
43. Vertical line through (2, 0)
44. Vertical line through (4, 0)
45. Horizontal line through (0, −6)
46. Horizontal line through (0, −3)
47. Vertical line through (−5, 0)
48. Vertical line through (−3, 0)
49. Horizontal line through (0, 7)
50. Horizontal line through (0, 5)
51. Horizontal line through (0, 3)
52. Vertical line through (−5, 0)
53. Vertical line through (5, 0)
54. Horizontal line through (0, −4)
55. $\left(0, \frac{-2}{3}\right), \left(\frac{10}{3}, 0\right)$
56. $\left(0, \frac{-7}{2}\right), \left(\frac{-7}{16}, 0\right)$
57. (0, −0.1), (10, 0)
58. $\left(0, \frac{-6}{77}\right), \left(\frac{-2}{11}, 0\right)$

PHYSICS/Newton's Second Law of Motion

The acceleration of a body is directly proportional to the net force acting on the body and inversely proportional to the mass of the body. If F represents force, m represents mass, and a is acceleration, the law can be stated as $a = \frac{F}{m}$. If the mass, m, is constant, a is a linear function of F. Can a linear function be derived from the Second Law if the force, F, is constant?   No

3–5 Slope

Finding the Slope of a Line

Graphs of some linear equations slant upward from left to right.
Others slant downward from left to right. Some graphs slant more
steeply than others.

Here is a line with two points marked. As we go from P_1 to P_2,
the change in x is $x_2 - x_1$. Similarily, the change in y is $y_2 - y_1$.
The ratio of the change in y over the change in x is called the slope
of the line.

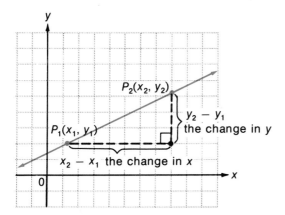

DEFINITION

The slope m of a line is

$$\frac{y_2 - y_1}{x_2 - x_1} \left(\frac{\text{change in } y}{\text{change in } x} \right),$$

where (x_1, y_1) and (x_2, y_2) are any two points on the line.

To find the slope of a line, we find *any* two points on the line. We
use the coordinates of these points to determine the change in y
and the change in x. Then we divide the change in y by the change
in x.

EXAMPLE 1

The points (1, 2) and (3, 6) are on a line. Find its slope.

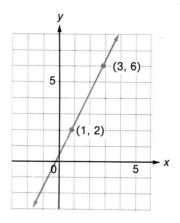

$$\text{The slope, } m = \frac{y_2 - y_1}{x_2 - x_1} \quad \frac{\text{change in } y}{\text{change in } x}$$

$$= \frac{6 - 2}{3 - 1}$$

$$= \frac{4}{2}, \text{ or } 2$$

If we use the points (1, 2) and (3, 6) in opposite order, we find that the change in y is negative and the change in x is negative. We get the same number for the slope.

$$m = \frac{2 - 6}{1 - 3} = \frac{-4}{-2}, \text{ or } 2$$

To compute slope, the order of the points does not matter as long as we take the same order for finding both the differences.

The points (0, 0) and $(-1, -2)$ are also on the line. If we use those points to compute the slope we get the following.

$$m = \frac{-2 - 0}{-1 - 0} = 2$$

The slope will be the same no matter what pair of points we use.

TRY THIS Find the slope of the line containing these points.

1. (1, 1) and (12, 14) $\frac{13}{11}$ 2. (3, 9) and (4, 10) 1

If a line slants up from left to right, it has positive slope, as in Example 1. If a line slants down from left to right, it has a negative slope.

The following diagrams show the relative positions of lines with different positive and negative slopes.

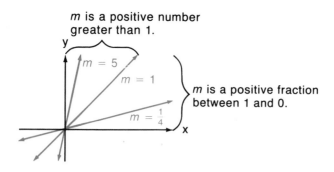

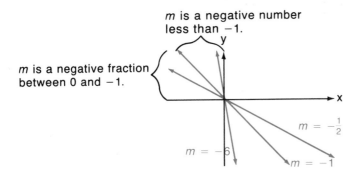

m is a negative number less than -1.

m is a negative fraction between 0 and -1.

$m = -\frac{1}{2}$

$m = -6$

$m = -1$

Horizontal and Vertical Lines

Vertical and horizontal lines do not slant. Let us apply the definition of slope to such lines.

EXAMPLE 2
Find the slope of the line $y = 3$.

$$y_2 - y_1 = 3 - 3$$
$$= 0$$
$$x_2 - x_1 = -2 - 4$$
$$= -6$$
$$\text{slope} = \frac{0}{-6} = 0$$

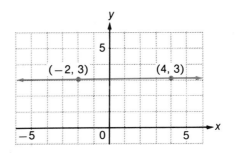

Any two points on a horizontal line have the same second coordinate. Thus the change in y is 0, so the slope is 0.

EXAMPLE 3
Find the slope of the line $x = -4$.

$$y_2 - y_1 = -2 - 3$$
$$= -5$$
$$x_2 - x_1 = -4 - (-4)$$
$$= 0$$
$$\text{slope} = \frac{-5}{0}$$

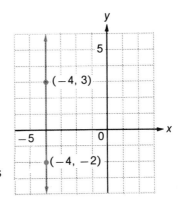

Since division by 0 is not defined, we say that this line has no slope.

Any two points on a vertical line have the same first coordinates. Thus the change in x is 0, so the denominator in the formula for slope would be 0. Since we cannot divide by 0, the line has no slope.

THEOREM 3–4

A horizontal line has slope 0. A vertical line has *no* slope.

TRY THIS Find the slopes, if they exist, of the lines containing these points.

3. (4, 6) and (−2, 6) 0   **4.** (−7, 3) and (−7, 2) No slope

Point-Slope Equations of Lines

If we know the slope of a line and the coordinates of a point on the line, we can find an equation of the line.

THEOREM 3–5

The Point-Slope Equation

A line containing a point (x_1, y_1) with slope m has an equation $(y - y_1) = m(x - x_1)$.

EXAMPLE 4

Find an equation of the line containing the point $(\frac{1}{2}, -1)$ with slope 5.

$$(y - y_1) = m(x - x_1)$$
$$y - (-1) = 5\left(x - \frac{1}{2}\right) \quad \text{Substituting}$$
$$y + 1 = 5\left(x - \frac{1}{2}\right)$$
$$y = 5x - \frac{7}{2} \quad \text{Simplifying}$$

EXAMPLE 5

Find an equation of the line with y-intercept (0, 4) and slope $\frac{3}{5}$.

$$(y - y_1) = m(x - x_1)$$
$$y - 4 = \frac{3}{5}(x - 0) \quad \text{Substituting}$$
$$y = \frac{3}{5}x + 4 \quad \text{Simplifying}$$

TRY THIS

5. Find an equation of the line containing the point $(-2, 4)$ with slope -3. $\quad y = -3x - 2$

6. Find an equation of the line containing the point $(-4, -10)$ with slope $\frac{1}{4}$. $\quad y = \frac{1}{4}x - 9$

7. Find an equation of the line with x-intercept $(5, 0)$ and slope $-\frac{1}{2}$. $\quad y = \frac{-1}{2}x + \frac{5}{2}$

A Proof of Theorem 3–5

We have seen that a line containing a point (x_1, y_1) with slope m has an equation $(y - y_1) = m(x - x_1)$. Let us prove this.

Think of a fixed point P, with coordinates (x_1, y_1), on a nonvertical line. Suppose we have a movable point P on the line with coordinates (x, y). The slope m is

$$\frac{y - y_1}{x - x_1}.$$

This is true only when (x, y) is a point different from (x_1, y_1). Now we can use the multiplication principle.

$$\frac{y - y_1}{x - x_1} = m \quad \text{Definition of slope}$$

$$\frac{(y - y_1)}{(x - x_1)} \cdot (x - x_1) = m(x - x_1) \quad \text{Multiplication principle}$$

$$(y - y_1) \cdot \frac{(x - x_1)}{(x - x_1)} = m(x - x_1) \quad \text{Simplifying}$$

$$(y - y_1) = m(x - x_1)$$

This equation holds even when $(x, y) = (x_1, y_1)$.

3–5

Exercises

Find the slopes, if they exist, of the lines containing these points.

1. $(5, 0)$ and $(6, 8)$ $\quad$ 8

2. $(4, 0)$ and $(7, 3)$ $\quad$ 1

3. $(0, 7)$ and $(-2, 9)$ $\quad$ −1

4. $(0, 8)$ and $(3, 8)$ $\quad$ 0

5. $(4, -3)$ and $(6, -4)$ $-\frac{1}{2}$

6. $(5, -7)$ and $(8, -3)$ $\frac{4}{3}$

7. $(0, 0)$ and $(-4, -8)$ 2

8. $(0, 0)$ and $(-5, -6)$ $\frac{6}{5}$

9. $(-2, -4)$ and $(-9, -7)$ $\frac{3}{7}$

10. $(-3, -7)$ and $(-8, -5)$ $-\frac{2}{5}$

11. $\left(\frac{1}{2}, \frac{1}{4}\right)$ and $\left(\frac{3}{2}, \frac{3}{4}\right)$ $\frac{1}{2}$

12. $\left(\frac{3}{5}, \frac{1}{2}\right)$ and $\left(\frac{1}{5}, -\frac{1}{2}\right)$ $\frac{5}{2}$

13. $\left(\frac{1}{8}, \frac{1}{4}\right)$ and $\left(\frac{3}{4}, \frac{1}{2}\right)$ $\frac{2}{5}$

14. $\left(\frac{1}{3}, -\frac{1}{8}\right)$ and $\left(\frac{5}{6}, -\frac{1}{4}\right)$ $-\frac{1}{4}$

15. $(3.2, -12.8)$ and $(3.2, 2.4)$ No slope

16. $(-16.3, 12.4)$ and $(8.3, 12.4)$ 0

Find the slope, if it exists, of each of these lines.

17. $x = 7$ No slope

18. $x = -4$ No slope

19. $y = -3$ 0

20. $y = 18$ 0

21. $x = 6$ No slope

22. $x = -17$ No slope

23. $y = 20$ 0

24. $y = -31$ 0

25. $5x - 6 = 15$ No slope

26. $-12 = 4x - 7$ No slope

27. $5y = 6$ 0

28. $19 = -6y$ 0

29. $y - 6 = 14$ 0

30. $12 - 4x = 9 + x$ No slope

31. $15 + 7x = 3x - 5$ No slope

32. $3y - 2x = 5 + 9y - 2x$ 0

Find the equations of the lines containing the given points with the indicated slopes.

33. $(3, 2)$; $m = 4$

34. $(4, 7)$; $m = -2$

35. $(-5, -2)$; $m = -1$

36. $(-2, -4)$; $m = 3$

37. $(-6, 4)$; $m = \frac{1}{2}$

38. $(3, -1)$; $m = -\frac{4}{3}$

39. $(0, -7)$; $m = 0$

40. $(3, 0)$; $m = 0$

33. $y = 4x - 10$
34. $y = -2x + 15$
35. $y = -x - 7$
36. $y = 3x + 2$
37. $y = \frac{1}{2}x + 7$
38. $y = -\frac{4}{3}x + 3$
39. $y = -7$
40. $y = 0$

Extension

For each of the following, use a calculator to find the slope of the line containing the given pair of points.

41. $(0.04, 0.08)$ and $(0.47, 0.83)$ 1.7441860

42. $(0.02, 0.8)$ and $(-0.2, -0.04)$ 3.8181818

Use a calculator to find equations of the following lines.

43. Through $(3.014, -2.563)$ with slope 3.516 $y = 3.516x - 13.1602$

44. Through the points $(1.103, 2.443)$ and $(8.114, 11.012)$ $y = 1.2222x + 1.0949$

45. Determine whether these three points are on a line. (Hint: Compare the slopes of $\overline{AB}$ and $\overline{BC}$. $\overline{AB}$ refers to the segment from A to B.)
$A(9, 4)$, $B(-1, 2)$, $C(4, 3)$ Yes

46. Determine whether these three points are on a line. (See hint for Exercise 45.)
$A(-1, -1)$, $B(2, 2)$, $C(-3, -4)$ No

47. Determine a so that the slope of the line through this pair of points has the given value. $\frac{5}{8}$

$$(-2, 3a), (4, -a); m = -\frac{5}{12}$$

48. Find the slope of the line that contains the given pair of points.
   a. $(5b, -6c)$, $(b, -c)$ $\frac{-5c}{4b}$
   b. (b, d), $(b, d + e)$ No slope
   c. $(c + f, a + d)$, $(c - f, -a - d)$ $\frac{2a + 2d}{2f}$

49. A line contains the points $(-100, 4)$ and $(0, 0)$. List four more points of the line. Answers may vary. $(1, -25), (2, -50), (3, -75), (-1, 25)$

Find two solutions of each equation. Use these to find the slope. 50. $m = -\frac{2}{3}$

50. $2x + 3y = 6$ 51. $2x + 5y + 2 = 5x + 10y - 8$ 51. $m = -\frac{3}{5}$

Challenge

52. Use graph paper. Plot the points $A(0, 0)$, $B(8, 2)$, $C(11, 6)$, and $D(3, 4)$. Draw $\overline{AB}$, $\overline{BC}$, $\overline{CD}$, and $\overline{DA}$. Find the slopes of these four segments. Compare the slopes of $\overline{AB}$ and $\overline{CD}$. Compare the slopes of $\overline{BC}$ and $\overline{DA}$.

52. Figure $ABCD$ is a parallelogram and its opposite sides are parallel.
53. Figure $EFGH$ is a rhombus and its diagonals are perpendicular.
54. a. Grade = 4%; $y = 4\%x$
    b. Grade = 6.7%; $y = 6.7\%x$

53. Use graph paper. Plot the points $E(-2, -5)$, $F(2, -2)$, $G(7, -2)$, and $H(3, -5)$. Draw $\overline{EF}$, $\overline{FG}$, $\overline{GH}$, $\overline{HE}$, $\overline{EG}$, and $\overline{FH}$. Compare the slopes of $\overline{EG}$ and $\overline{FH}$.

54. Road grade. Numbers like 2%, 3%, and 6% are often used to represent the *grade* of a road. Such a number is meant to tell how steep a road up a hill or mountain is. For example, a 3% grade means that for every horizontal distance of 100 ft, the road rises 3 ft. In each case find the road grade and an equation giving the height y of a vehicle in terms of a horizontal distance x.

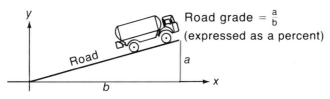

Road grade = $\frac{a}{b}$ (expressed as a percent)

a.
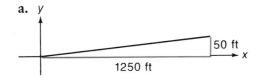
50 ft, 1250 ft

b.
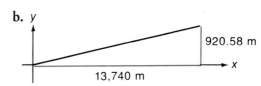
920.58 m, 13,740 m

3–6 More Equations of Lines

Two-Point Equations of Lines

Given two points, we can find an equation of the line containing them. If we find the slope of a line by dividing the change in y by the change in x and substitute this value for m in the point-slope equation, we obtain the two-point equation, which is stated in the following theorem.

THEOREM 3–6

The Two-Point Equation

Any nonvertical line containing the points (x_1, y_1) and (x_2, y_2) has an equation $y - y_1 = \frac{y_2 - y_1}{x_2 - x_1}(x - x_1)$.

EXAMPLE 1

Find an equation of the line containing the points $(2, 3)$ and $(1, -4)$.

a. We take $(2, 3)$ as P_1 and $(1, -4)$ as P_2. Then substitute in the two-point equation.

$$y - 3 = \frac{-4 - 3}{1 - 2}(x - 2)$$

$$y - 3 = \frac{-7}{-1}(x - 2)$$

$$y - 3 = 7(x - 2)$$
$$y - 3 = 7x - 14$$
$$y = 7x - 11$$

b. It doesn't matter which point we take as P_1 and which we take as P_2. If we take $(1, -4)$ as P_1 and $(2, 3)$ as P_2, we get the same equation.

$$y - (-4) = \frac{3 - (-4)}{2 - 1}(x - 1)$$

$$y = 7x - 11 \quad \text{Simplifying}$$

TRY THIS Find an equation of the line containing the points

1. $(1, 4)$ and $(3, -2)$ 2. $(3, -6)$ and $(0, 4)$

1. $y = -3x + 7$

2. $y = -\frac{10}{3}x + 4$

Slope-Intercept Equations of Lines

Given the slope and y-intercept of a line, we can find an equation of the line.

THEOREM 3–7

The Slope-Intercept Equation

A nonvertical line with slope m and y-intercept $(0, b)$ has an equation $y = mx + b$.

For brevity, we often refer to the number b as the intercept. From any equation for a nonvertical line we can find the slope-intercept equation by solving for y.

EXAMPLE 2

Find the slope and y-intercept of the line whose equation is $3x - 6y - 7 = 0$.

First solve for y.

$$-6y = -3x + 7$$

$$-\frac{1}{6} \cdot (-6y) = -\frac{1}{6} \cdot (-3x) + \left(-\frac{1}{6}\right) \cdot 7$$

$$y = \frac{1}{2}x - \frac{7}{6}$$

slope $\frac{1}{2}$ y-intercept $-\frac{7}{6}$

There is no slope-intercept equation for a vertical line because such a line has no slope.

TRY THIS

3. a. Find the slope-intercept equation of the line whose equation is $-2x + 3y - 6 = 0$. $y = \frac{2}{3}x + 2$
   b. Find the slope and y-intercept of this line. $m = \frac{2}{3}, b = 2$

3-6

Exercises

Find an equation of the line containing each of the following pairs of points.

1. $(1, 4)$ and $(5, 6)$
2. $(2, 6)$ and $(4, 1)$
3. $(-1, -1)$ and $(2, 2)$
4. $(-3, -3)$ and $(6, 6)$
5. $(-2, 0)$ and $(0, 5)$
6. $(6, 0)$ and $(0, -3)$
7. $(3, 5)$ and $(-5, 3)$
8. $(4, 6)$ and $(-6, 4)$
9. $(0, 0)$ and $(5, 2)$
10. $(0, 0)$ and $(7, 3)$
11. $(-4, -7)$ and $(-2, -1)$
12. $(-2, -3)$ and $(-4, -6)$

Find the slope and y-intercept of each of the following lines.

13. $y = 2x + 3$
14. $y = 3x + 4$
15. $y = -4x + 9$
16. $y = -5x - 7$
17. $y = 6 - x$
18. $y = 7 - x$
19. $2y = -6x + 10$
20. $-3y = -12x + 6$
21. $3x - 4y = 12$
22. $5x + 2y = -7$
23. $6x + 2y - 8 = 0$
24. $3y - 2x + 5 = 0$
25. $-7x - 3y - 9 = 0$
26. $-8x - 5y - 7 = 0$
27. $y = 7$
28. $y = 9$
29. $3y + 10 = 0$
30. $4y + 11 = 0$

Use a calculator to find the slope and y-intercept of these lines.

31. $2.735x - 1.379y - 6.084 = 0$

$m = 1.9833212, b = -4.4118926$

32. $-4.005x + 2.057y + 8.316 = 0$

$m = 1.9470102, b = -4.0427807$

Find an equation of a line with the given slope and y-intercept.

33. $m = -4$; y-intercept $(0, 3)$ $\quad y = -4x + 3$

34. $m = \frac{2}{5}$; y-intercept $(0, -4)$ $\quad y = \frac{2}{5}x - 4$

35. $m = 75$; y-intercept is -18 $\quad y = 75x - 18$

36. $m = -0.36$; y-intercept is 10 $\quad y = -0.36x + 10$

Extension

Find an equation of the line containing each pair of points.

37. $(-0.2, 0.7)$ and $(-0.7, -0.3)$
38. $\left(\frac{1}{11}, \frac{1}{2}\right)$ and $\left(-\frac{10}{11}, -2\right)$

Answers (margin):

1. $y = \frac{1}{2}x + \frac{1}{2}$
2. $y = \frac{-5}{2}x + 11$
3. $y = x$
4. $y = x$
5. $y = \frac{5}{2}x + 5$
6. $y = \frac{1}{2}x - 3$
7. $y = \frac{1}{4}x + \frac{17}{4}$
8. $y = \frac{1}{5}x + \frac{26}{5}$
9. $y = \frac{2}{5}x$
10. $y = \frac{3}{7}x$
11. $y = 3x + 5$
12. $y = \frac{3}{2}x$
13. $m = 2, b = 3$
14. $m = 3, b = 4$
15. $m = -4, b = 9$
16. $m = -5, b = -7$
17. $m = -1, b = 6$
18. $m = -1, b = 7$
19. $m = -3, b = 5$
20. $m = 4, b = -2$
21. $m = \frac{3}{4}, b = -3$
22. $m = \frac{-5}{2}, b = \frac{-7}{2}$
23. $m = -3, b = 4$
24. $m = \frac{2}{3}, b = \frac{-5}{3}$
25. $m = \frac{-7}{3}, b = -3$
26. $m = \frac{-8}{5}, b = \frac{-7}{5}$
27. $m = 0, b = 7$
28. $m = 0, b = 9$
29. $m = 0, b = \frac{-10}{3}$
30. $m = 0, b = \frac{-11}{4}$
37. $y = 2x + 1.1$
38. $y = \frac{5}{2}x + \frac{3}{11}$

138 CHAPTER 3 GRAPHS, RELATIONS, AND FUNCTIONS

39. Find an equation of the line containing $(2, -3)$ and having the same slope as the line $3x + 4y = 10$. $y = \frac{-3}{4}x - \frac{3}{2}$

40. Find an equation of the line containing $(3, -4)$ and having slope -2. If this line contains the points $(a, 8)$ and $(5, b)$, find a and b. $y = -2x + 2; a = -3, b = -8$

41. Write an equation of the line that has x-intercept $(-3, 0)$ and y-intercept $(0, \frac{2}{5})$. $y = \frac{2}{15}x + \frac{2}{5}$

Challenge

42. Prove that an equation in the form $\frac{x}{a} + \frac{y}{b} = 1$ has x-intercept $(a, 0)$ and y-intercept $(0, b)$.

43. Prove that the slope of the line $Ax + By + C = 0$, $B \neq 0$, is given by $m = \frac{-A}{B}$.

Use the result of Exercise 43 to find the slope of each of the following lines.

44. $5x - 4y - 7 = 0$ $m = \frac{5}{4}$

45. $2y - 3y = 4$ $m = \frac{3}{2}$

46. $0.25y + 7.8x = 4.2x - 18$ $m = -14.4$

42. $\frac{x}{a} + \frac{y}{b} = 1; bx + ay = ab$, multiplying both sides by ab; $y = -\frac{b}{a}x + b$, solving for y; y-intercept is $(0, b)$; setting $y = 0$, $x = a$; x-intercept is $(a, 0)$.

43. $Ax + By + C = 0; By = -Ax - C; y = -\frac{A}{B}x - \frac{C}{B}$, this is slope-intercept equation of the line, so $m = -\frac{A}{B}$, where $B \neq 0$.

USING A CALCULATOR/Power and Memory Keys

Many calculators have a key marked x^2 or x^y. A key marked x^2 replaces the number in the display with its square.

EXAMPLE 1
In this example, an x^y key is used to find values for x^3.
Problem: Graph $y = \frac{1}{3}x^3 - x + \frac{2}{3}$

Let $x = 6$: $y = \frac{1}{3}(6)^3 - 6 + \frac{2}{3}$

Equivalent problem: $(1 \div 3 \times 6^3) - 6 + (2 \div 3)$

Enter: 1 $\div$ 3 $\times$ 6 x^y

Display: 1 $\quad 3$ $\quad 0.333333$ $\quad 6$

Enter: 3 $-$ 6 $+$ 2 $\div$ 3 $=$

Display: 3 $\quad 72$ $\quad 6$ $\quad 66$ $\quad 2$ $\quad 3$ $\quad 66.66667$

Repeat for other values of x until you have enough ordered pairs to draw the graph.

Most calculators have one or more memory keys. A key marked Min or STO stores a number in the memory. A key marked MR or RM or RCL recalls the number in the memory to the display. Many problems with fractions require you to use memory keys to record intermediate results. Denominators are usually computed first.

EXAMPLE 2
Problem: Let $g(x) = \frac{x - 47}{x + 38}$. Find $g(25)$.

Enter: 25 $+$ 38 $=$ Min 25

Display: 25 $\quad 38$ $\quad 63$ $\quad 63$ $\quad 25$

Enter: $-$ 47 $=$ $\div$ MR $=$

Display: $\quad 47$ $\quad -22$ $\quad 63$ $\quad -0.349$

3-7 Parallel and Perpendicular Lines

Parallel Lines

When we graph a pair of linear equations, there are three possibilities.

1. The equations have the same graph.
2. The graphs intersect at exactly one point.
3. The graphs are parallel lines.

THEOREM 3-8

If nonvertical lines have the same slope but different y-intercepts, they are parallel. Also, if nonvertical lines are parallel they have the same slope and different y-intercepts.

EXAMPLE 1

Determine whether the graphs of $y = -3x + 5$ and $4y = -12x + 20$ are parallel.

These equations have the same graph, so the lines are not parallel. We can determine this without looking at the graphs. We find the slope-intercept equations by solving for y.

$$y = -3x + 5$$
$$y = -3x + 5$$

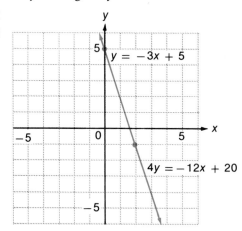

The slope-intercept equations are the same. This tells us that the graphs are the same line.

EXAMPLE 2

Determine whether the graphs of $y - 3x = 1$ and $-2y = 3x + 2$ are parallel.

These graphs intersect. We can determine this without looking at the graphs. We find the slope-intercept equations by solving for y.

$$y = 3x + 1$$
$$y = -\frac{3}{2}x - 1$$

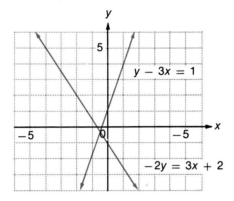

The slopes are different, so the lines are not parallel.

EXAMPLE 3

Determine whether the graphs of $3x - y = -5$ and $y - 3x = -2$ are parallel.

We can determine this without looking at the graphs. We find the slope-intercept equations by solving for y.

$$y = 3x + 5$$
$$y = 3x - 2$$

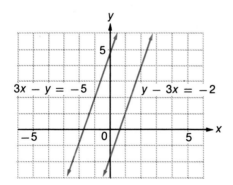

The slopes are the same, but the y-intercepts are different, so the lines are parallel.

TRY THIS Without graphing, tell whether the graphs of each pair of equations are parallel. (Hint: First find the slope-intercept equation.)

1. $x + 4 = y$
   $y - x = -3$ Yes
2. $y + 4 = 3x$
   $4x - y = -7$ No
3. $y = 4x + 5$
   $2y = 8x + 10$ No

Finding Equations of Parallel Lines

EXAMPLE 4

Write an equation of the line parallel to the line $2x + y - 10 = 0$ and containing the point $(-1, 3)$.

a. We first find the slope-intercept equation.

$$y = -2x + 10$$

Now we see that the parallel line must have slope -2.

b. We find the point-slope equation of the line with slope -2 and containing the point $(-1, 3)$.

$$y - y_1 = m(x - x_1) \quad \text{Theorem 3-5}$$
$$y - 3 = -2[x - (-1)] \quad \text{Substituting}$$
$$y = -2x + 1 \quad \text{Simplifying}$$

The equations $y = -2x + 10$ and $y = -2x + 1$ have the same slope and different y-intercepts. Hence their graphs are parallel.

TRY THIS

4. Write an equation of the line parallel to the line $2y + 8x = 6$ and containing the point $(-2, -4)$. $y = -4x - 12$

Perpendicular Lines

If two lines meet at right angles, they are called perpendicular.

THEOREM 3-9

If for two nonvertical lines, the product of the slopes is -1, the lines are perpendicular. Also, if two lines are perpendicular, the product of the slopes is -1.

EXAMPLE 5

Determine whether the lines $5y = 4x + 10$ and $4y = -5x + 4$ are perpendicular.

We find the slope-intercept equations by solving for y.

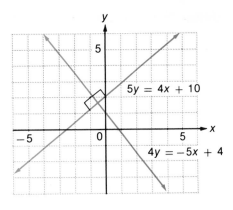

$$y = \frac{4}{5}x + 2, \quad y = -\frac{5}{4}x + 1$$

The product of the slopes is -1; that is,

$$\frac{4}{5} \cdot \left(-\frac{5}{4}\right) = -1.$$

The lines are perpendicular.

Proof of Theorem 3–9

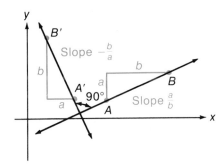

Consider a line $\overleftrightarrow{AB}$ as shown, with slope $\frac{a}{b}$. Then think of rotating the entire figure 90° to get a line perpendicular to $\overleftrightarrow{AB}$. For the new line the roles of a and b are interchanged, but a is now negative. Thus the slope of the new line is $-\frac{b}{a}$. Let us multiply the slopes.

$$\frac{a}{b}\left(-\frac{b}{a}\right) = -1$$

This is the condition under which lines will be perpendicular.

TRY THIS

5. Without graphing, tell whether the graphs of each pair of equations are perpendicular.

   a. $2y - x = 2$ b. $3y = 2x + 15$
   $\quad y + 2x = 4$ Yes $2y = 3x + 10$ No

Finding Equations of Perpendicular Lines

EXAMPLE 6

Write an equation of the line perpendicular to $4y - x = 20$ and containing the point $(2, -3)$.

a. We find the slope-intercept equation for $4y - x = 20$.

$$y = \tfrac{1}{4}x + 5$$

We know that the slope of the perpendicular line is -4, because $\tfrac{1}{4} \cdot (-4) = -1$.

b. We find the point-slope equation of the line having slope -4 and containing the point $(2, -3)$.

$$y - y_1 = m(x - x_1) \quad \text{Theorem 3-5}$$
$$y - (-3) = -4(x - 2) \quad \text{Substituting}$$
$$y = -4x + 5 \quad \text{Simplifying}$$

TRY THIS

6. Write an equation of the line perpendicular to the line $y = \tfrac{7}{8}x - 3$ and containing the point $(-1, 2)$. $y = \tfrac{-8}{7}x + \tfrac{6}{7}$

7. Write an equation of the line perpendicular to the line $4 - y = 2x$ and containing the point $(3, 4)$. $y = \tfrac{1}{2}x + \tfrac{5}{2}$

3-7

Exercises

Without graphing, tell whether the graphs of each pair of equations are parallel.

1. $x + 6 = y$
   $y - x = -2$ Yes

2. $2x - 7 = y$
   $y - 2x = 8$ Yes

3. $y + 3 = 5x$
   $3x - y = -2$ No

4. $y + 8 = -6x$
   $-2x + y = 5$ No

5. $y = 3x + 9$
   $2y = 6x - 2$ Yes

6. $y = -7x - 9$
   $-3y = 21x + 7$ Yes

Write an equation of the line containing the given point and parallel to the given line.

7. $(3, 7)$, $x + 2y = 6$

8. $(0, 3)$, $3x - y = 7$

9. $(2, -1)$, $5x - 7y = 8$

10. $(-4, -5)$, $2x + y = -3$

11. $(-6, 2)$, $3x - 9y = 2$

12. $(-7, 0)$, $5x + 2y = 6$

7. $y = -\tfrac{1}{2}x + \tfrac{17}{2}$
8. $y = 3x + 3$
9. $y = \tfrac{5}{7}x - \tfrac{17}{7}$
10. $y = -2x - 13$
11. $y = \tfrac{1}{3}x + 4$
12. $y = -\tfrac{5}{2}x - \tfrac{35}{2}$

Without graphing, tell whether the graphs of each pair of equations are perpendicular.

13. $y = 4x - 5$ 14. $2x - 5y = -3$ 15. $x + 2y = 5$ 16. $y = -x + 7$

    $4y = 8 - x$ Yes $2x + 5y = 4$ No $2x + 4y = 8$ No $y = x + 3$ Yes

Write an equation of the line containing the given point and perpendicular to the given line.

17. $(2, 5)$, $2x + y = -3$ 18. $(4, 0)$, $x - 3y = 0$

19. $(3, -2)$, $3x + 4y = 5$ 20. $(-3, -5)$, $5x - 2y = 4$

21. $(0, 9)$, $2x + 5y = 7$ 22. $(-3, -4)$, $-3x + 6y = 2$

17. $y = \frac{1}{2}x + 4$
18. $y = -3x + 12$
19. $y = \frac{4}{3}x - 6$
20. $y = -\frac{2}{5}x - \frac{31}{5}$
21. $y = \frac{5}{2}x + 9$
22. $y = -2x - 10$

Extension

23. Find an equation of the line containing $(4, -2)$ and parallel to the line containing $(-1, 4)$ and $(2, -3)$. $y = -\frac{7}{3}x + \frac{22}{3}$

24. Find an equation of the line containing $(-1, 3)$ and perpendicular to the line containing $(3, -5)$ and $(-2, 7)$. $y = \frac{5}{12}x + \frac{41}{12}$

25. Use slopes to show that the triangle with vertices $(-2, 7)$, $(6, 9)$, and $(3, 4)$ is a right triangle.

26. Which pairs out of the following four equations represent perpendicular lines?

    a. $7y - 3x = 21$ b. $-3x - 7y = 12$ c. $7y + 3x = 21$ d. $3y + 7x = 12$

26. a. and d.

27. Write an equation of the line that has y-intercept $\left(0, \frac{5}{7}\right)$ and is parallel to the graph of $6x - 3y = 1$. $y = 2x + \frac{5}{7}$

28. Write an equation of the line that has x-intercept $(-1.2, 0)$ and is perpendicular to the graph of $6x - 3y = 1$. $y = -0.5x - 0.6$

Challenge

29. Find the value of a so that the graphs of $5y = ax + 5$ and $\frac{1}{4}y = \frac{1}{10}x - 1$ are parallel. 2

30. Find the value of k so that the graphs of $x + 7y = 70$ and $y + 3 = kx$ are perpendicular. 7

25. The side which contains $(3, 4)$ and $(6, 9)$ has slope $\frac{5}{3}$. The side which contains $(-2, 7)$ and $(3, 4)$ has slope $-\frac{3}{5}$. Since $\frac{5}{3} \cdot \left(-\frac{3}{5}\right) = -1$, these two sides are perpendicular.

FIELDS OF MATHEMATICS/Projective Geometry

Projective geometry was invented by Girard Desargues about 1640. A surprising fact about this geometry is that it has no parallel lines. Just as the drawing of parallel lines in a picture shows two lines that meet at a point, so Desargues' parallel lines are required to meet in a point that may be infinitely distant but which is nevertheless assumed to exist.

3—8 Applications of Linear Functions

DEFINITION

A *linear function* is a function f given by

$$y = f(x) = mx + b.$$

The graph of a linear function is always a straight line.

Fitting Equations to Data

There are many situations to which linear functions can be applied. How do we know when we have such a situation?

EXAMPLE 1

Plot the following data and determine whether a linear function gives an approximate fit.

Crickets are known to chirp faster when the temperature is higher. Here are some measurements made at different temperatures.

Temperature °C	6	8	10	15	20
Number of chirps per minute	11	29	47	75	107

We make a graph with a T (temperature) axis and an N (number per minute) axis and plot these data. We see that they do lie approximately on a straight line, so we can use a linear function in this situation.

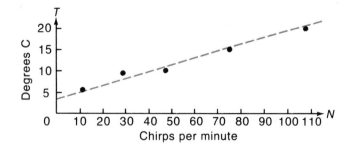

EXAMPLE 2

Wind friction, or resistance, increases with speed. Here are some measurements made in a wind tunnel. Plot the data and determine whether a linear function will give an approximate fit.

Velocity, km/h	10	21	34	40	45	52
Force of resistance, kg	3	4.2	6.2	7.1	15.1	29.0

We make a graph with a V (velocity) axis and an F (force) axis and plot the data. They do not lie on a straight line, even approximately. Therefore we cannot use a linear function in this situation.

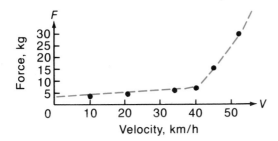

When we have a situation that a linear function fits, we can find a function and use it to solve problems and make predictions.

EXAMPLE 3

When crickets chirp 40 times per minute, the temperature is 10°C. When they chirp 112 times per minute, the temperature is 20°C. We know that a linear function fits this situation. **a.** Find a linear function that fits the data. **b.** From your function, find the temperature when crickets chirp 76 times per minute; 100 times per minute.

a. To find the function, we use the two known ordered pairs (40, 10°) and (112, 20°). We call these data points. We find the two-point equation, using these data points.

$$T - T_1 = \frac{T_2 - T_1}{N_2 - N_1}(N - N_1)$$

$$T - 10 = \frac{20 - 10}{112 - 40}(N - 40) \quad \text{Substituting}$$

$$T - 10 = \frac{5}{36}N - \frac{5}{36} \cdot 40$$

$$T = \frac{5}{36}N + \frac{40}{9}, \text{ or } \frac{5N + 160}{36} \quad \text{Solving for } T$$

b. Using the last equation as a formula, we find T when $N = 76$.

$$T = \frac{5 \cdot 76 + 160}{36} = 15°$$

When $N = 100$, we get the following.

$$T = \frac{5 \cdot 100 + 160}{36} \approx 18.3° \quad \approx \text{means "is approximately equal to"}$$

Physical considerations often limit the domain of a function. For the function of Example 3, any temperature for which the formula gives a negative number of chirps per minute would be meaningless. Also, imagine what would happen to a cricket at $-40°$ or at $100°$!

TRY THIS Records in the 100-meter dash. It has been found that running records change with time according to linear functions. In 1920 the record for the 100-meter dash was 10.43 seconds. In 1970 it was 9.93 seconds.

1. Fit a linear function to the data points. $\quad R = -0.01t + 10.43$

2. Use your function to predict the record in 1990; in 2000. $\quad$ 9.73 seconds; 9.23 seconds

3. In what year will the record be 9.0 seconds? $\quad$ 2063

3–8	

Exercises

Solve.

1. Life expectancy of females in the United States. In 1950, the life expectancy of females was 72 years. In 1970, it was 75 years. Let E represent the life expectancy and t the number of years since 1950 ($t = 0$ gives 1950 and $t = 10$ gives 1960).
   a. Fit a linear function to the data points. [They are $(0, 72)$ and $(20, 75)$.] $\quad E = \frac{3}{20}t + 72$
   b. Use the function of **a.** to predict the life expectancy of females in 1989; in 1992. $\quad$ 77.9 years; 78.3 years

2. Life expectancy of males in the United States. In 1950, the life expectancy of males was 65 years. In 1970, it was 68 years. Let E represent life expectancy and t the number of years since 1950.
   a. Fit a linear function to the data points. $\quad E = \frac{3}{20}t + 65$
   b. Use the function of **a.** to predict the life expectancy of males in 1988; in 1995. $\quad$ 70.7 years; 71.8 years

3. Natural gas demand. In 1950, natural gas demand in the United States was 20 quadrillion joules. In 1960, the demand was 22 quadrillion joules. Let D represent the demand for natural gas t years after 1950.
   a. Fit a linear function to the data points. $D = \frac{1}{5}t + 20$
   b. Use the function of a. to predict the natural gas demand in 1987; in 2000. 27.4 quadrillion joules; 30 quadrillion joules

4. Records in the 1500-meter run. In 1930, the record for the 1500-meter run was 3.85 minutes. In 1950, it was 3.70 minutes. Let R represent the record in the 1500-meter run and t the number of years since 1930.
   a. Fit a linear function to the data points. $R = -0.0075t + 3.85$
   b. Use the function of a. to predict the record in 1984; in 1989. 3.45 minutes, 3.41 minutes
   c. When will the record be 3.3 minutes? 2004

5. Records in the 400-meter run. In 1930, the record for the 400-meter run was 46.8 seconds. In 1970, it was 43.8 seconds. Let R represent the record in the 400-meter run and t the number of years since 1930.
   a. Fit a linear function to the data points. $R = -0.075t + 46.8$
   b. Use the function of a. to predict the record in 1990; in 2000. 42.3 seconds, 41.6 seconds
   c. When will the record be 40 seconds? 2021

6. The cost of a taxi ride. The cost of a taxi ride for 2 miles in Eastridge is $1.75. For 3 miles the cost is $2.00.
   a. Fit a linear function to the data points. $C = 0.25m + 1.25$
   b. Use the function to find the cost of a 7-mile ride. $3.00

7. The cost of renting a car. If you rent a car for one day and drive it 100 miles, the cost is $30. If you drive it 150 miles, the cost is $37.50.
   a. Fit a linear function to the data points. $C = 0.15m + 15$
   b. Use the function to find how much it will cost to rent the car for one day if you drive it 200 miles. $45.00

Extension

Solve each problem assuming a linear function fits the situation.

8. The value of a copying machine is $5200 when it is purchased. After 2 years its value is $4225. Find its value after 8 years. $1300

9. Water freezes at 32° Fahrenheit, and at 0° Celsius. Water boils at 212° F and at 100° C. What Celsius temperature corresponds to a room temperature of 70° Fahrenheit? 21.1°C

10. A business determines that when it sells 7000 units of a product it will take in $22,000. For the sale of 8000 units it will take in $25,000. How much will it take in for the sale of 10,000 units? $31,000

11. A piece of copper pipe has a length of 100 cm at 18°C. At 20°C the length of the pipe changes to 100.00356 cm. Find the length of the pipe at 40°C and at 0°C. 100.03916 cm; 99.96796 cm

12. For a linear function f, $f(-1) = 3$ and $f(2) = 4$.
   a. Find an equation for f. $f(x) = \frac{1}{3}x + 3\frac{1}{3}$
   b. Find $f(3)$. $4\frac{1}{3}$
   c. Find a such that $f(a) = 100$. 290

13. Sales commissions. A person applying for a sales position is offered alternative salary plans.
   Plan A: A base salary of $600 per month plus a commission of 4% of the gross sales for the month
   Plan B: A base salary of $700 per month plus a commission of 6% of the gross sales for the month in excess of $10,000
   a. For each plan formulate a function that expresses monthly earnings as a function of gross sales, x. Plan A: E = 600 + 0.04x; Plan B: E = 100 + 0.06x
   b. For what gross sales values is Plan B preferable? $x \geq 25{,}000$

14. Anthropology—Estimating heights. An anthropologist can use certain linear functions to estimate the height of a male or female, given the length of certain bones. A *humerus* is the bone from the elbow to the shoulder. Let $x =$ length of the humerus in centimeters. Then the height, in centimeters, of a male with a humerus of length x is given by $M(x) = 2.89x + 70.64$. The height, in centimeters, of a female with a humerus of length x is given by $F(x) = 2.75x + 71.48$. A 45-cm humerus was uncovered in some ruins.
   a. Assuming it was from a male, how tall was he? 200.69 cm
   b. Assuming it was from a female, how tall was she? 195.23 cm

CONSUMER APPLICATION/Buying a New Car

Car manufacturers place a sticker on a new car to show the base price, the prices of the optional equipment, and the destination charge. The total of these charges is the sticker price of the car.

Many buyers pay a cash down payment and then finance the rest. The financed amount is paid back in monthly installments which are determined by the amount borrowed, the interest rate, and the term of the loan. This costs more than paying in cash.

After careful shopping, Phil decided to buy a new Stinger X. His purchase price is $6525.00. Added to that are these charges: 5% sales tax, $28.00 license fee, and $139.00 dealer preparation fee.

Total cash price = purchase price + other charges
$$= \$6525.00 + (0.05 \times \$6525.00 + \$28.00 + \$139.00)$$
$$= \$6525.00 + \$493.25 = \$7018.25$$

Phil can put down 20% of the total price and finance the rest.

Amount financed = total price − down payment
$$= \$7018.25 − (0.20 \times \$7018.25)$$
$$= \$7018.25 − \$1403.65 = \$5614.60$$

The bank tells Phil that at the current rate of interest he can repay the loan over three years at $202.98 per month.

Deferred payment price = down payment + total of monthly payments
$$= \$1403.65 + (36 \times \$202.98)$$
$$= \$1403.65 + \$7307.28 = \$8710.93$$

The car actually costs $8710.93.

Exercises

1. Find the total price of this Splasher II: $7200.00 plus 5% sales tax, $25.00 license fee, and $150.00 dealer preparation fee. $7735.00

2. Find the down payment and the amount financed of this Tiger Stripe Coupe: $7995.00, 20% down. $1599.00 down, $6396.00 financed

3. Find the deferred payment price of this Carry-Van. Compare it with the cash price. Cash price $8500.00, $2500.00 down payment, two-year loan at $299.52 per month.

   $ 9688.48 deferred payment price
   −8500.00 cash price
   $ 1188.48 difference

4. Find the total price of this MX-20 sports car: $6550.00 plus 5% sales tax, $35.00 license fee, and $125.00 dealer preparation fee. $7037.50

5. Find the down payment and the amount financed of this Estate Wagon: $12,400.00, 30% down. $3720.00 down, $8680.00 financed

6. Find the deferred payment price of this D-Cruiser. Compare it with the cash price. $2500.00 down payment, two-year loan at $299.52 per month. $ 12,109.80 deferred payment price
$\underline{-10,000.00}$ cash price
$ 2109.80 difference

CHAPTER 3 Review

Review the material in the chapter. Then see how you have done by trying these review exercises. If you miss an exercise, restudy the indicated lesson.

3–1

1. Consider sets A and B, where $A = \{a, b, c\}$ and $B = \{1, 2\}$. List all the ordered pairs in $A \times B$. {(a, 1), (a, 2), (b, 1), (b, 2), (c, 1), (c, 2)}

2. Consider the set $\{-2, -1, 0, 1\}$. Find the set of ordered pairs determined by the relation > (is greater than). {(−1, −2), (0, −2), (0, −1), (1, −2), (1, −1), (1, 0)}

3. List the domain and range of the relation $\{(1, 2), (-1, 4), (0, 5), (2, -4), (-6, \sqrt{3})\}$. Domain: {−6, −1, 0, 1, 2}; range: {−4, √3, 2, 4, 5}

3–2

4. Graph the relation which is the solution set of $y = 2x + 1$. Line through (1, 3) and (0, 1)

5. Graph the relation which is the solution set of $y = x^2 + 1$. A parabola through (−2, 5), (−1, 2), (0, 1), (1, 2), (2, 5)

3–3 Which of the following are graphs of functions?

6. No

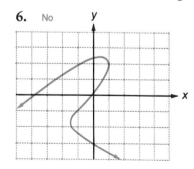

7. Yes

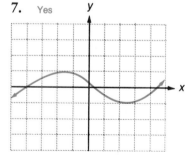

8. No

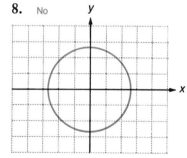

3–3

9. $f(x) = 3\sqrt{x} + 2$. Find the indicated function values.

   a. $f(2)$ 6   b. $f(0)$ 3√2 c. $f(-2)$ 0   d. $f(-5)$ Not a real number

152 CHAPTER 3 GRAPHS, RELATIONS, AND FUNCTIONS

3–4

10. Which of these are linear equations?

　　a. $x - 5y = 8$ Yes **b.** $3xy + y^2 = 0$ No **c.** $2x = 5y - 9$ Yes **d.** $y^2 - 7 = 9y$ No

3–4

11. Find standard form for $y = \frac{2}{9}x + \frac{7}{9}$. $2x - 9y + 7 = 0$

3–4

12. Graph $-5x + 2y = 10$ using intercepts. Line through $(-2, 0)$ and$(0, 5)$

13. Graph $x = 9$. 　**14.** Graph $y = -2$. 13. Vertical line through $(9, 0)$ 14. Horizontal line through $(0, -2)$

3–5

15. Find the slope of the line containing $(8, 2)$ and $(-4, -3)$. $\frac{5}{12}$

16. Find an equation for the line with slope of -3 and containing $(2, 1)$. $y = -3x + 7$

3–6

17. Find an equation of the line containing $(3, 5)$ and $(-2, -4)$. $y = \frac{9}{5}x - \frac{2}{5}$

18. Find the slope and y-intercept of $-5x + 2y = -4$. $\frac{5}{2}, -2$

3–7

19. Determine, without graphing, whether the graphs of the following pairs of equations are parallel or perpendicular.

　　a. $y + 3 = x$ 　　**b.** $7x + 3y = 11$ 　　**c.** $2x - y = 8$
　　　$x - 5 = y$ Parallel 　$3x - 7y = 12$ 　　　　$2y = 6 + 4x$ Parallel
　　　　　　　　　　　Perpendicular

20. Find an equation of the line containing $(-3, 7)$ which is

　　a. parallel to the line $5x + 3y = 8$. $y = \frac{-5}{3}x + 2$

　　b. perpendicular to the line $5x + 3y = 8$. $y = \frac{3}{5}x + \frac{44}{5}$

3–8

21. Records in the 200-meter dash. In 1920 the record for the 200-meter dash was 20.8 seconds. In 1945 is was 20.1 seconds. Let R represent the record in the 200-meter dash and t the number of years since 1920.

　　a. Fit a linear function to the data points. $R = -0.028t + 20.8$

　　b. Use the function of part **a** to predict the record in 1994. 18.7 seconds

　　c. When will the record be 18.5 seconds? 2002

CHAPTER 3 Test

1. Consider the set $\{-4, -2, 0, 2\}$. Find the set of ordered pairs determined by the relation $\leq$ (is less than or equal to). $\{(-4, -4), (-4, -2), (-4, 0), (-4, 2), (-2, -2), (-2, 0), (-2, 2), (0, 0), (0, 2), (2, 2)\}$

2. List the domain and range of the relation $\{(-1, 4), (2, 3), (-2, -3), (1, -2)\}$. Domain: $\{-2, -1, 1, 2\}$; range: $\{-3, -2, 3, 4\}$

3. Graph the relation which is the solution set of $y = 3x - 1$. Line through $(0, -1)$ and $(1, 2)$

4. Graph the relation which is the solution set of $y = x^2 - 1$. A parabola through $(-2, 3)$, $(-1, 0), (0, -1), (1, 0), (2, 3)$

Which of the following are graphs of functions?

5. No

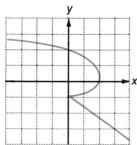

6. Yes

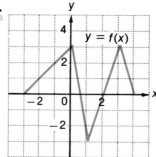

$$f(x) = \frac{1}{(x - 2)(x + 1)}.$$ Find the indicated function values.

7. $f(1)$ $-\frac{1}{2}$ 8. $f(0)$ $-\frac{1}{2}$

9. Which of these are linear equations?
   a. $xy = 5$ No b. $\frac{x}{y} = 4$ Yes
   c. $2x = y$ Yes d. $x = 7$ Yes

10. Find standard form for $y = \frac{3}{5}x - \frac{8}{5}$. $3x - 5y = 8$

11. Graph $6x - 4y = 12$ using intercepts. Line through $(0, -3)$ and $(2, 0)$

12. Graph $y = 3$ and $x = -1$ on the same axes. Vertical line through $(0, 3)$ and $(2, 3)$; horizontal line through $(-1, 0)$ and $(-1, 2)$

13. Find the slope of the line containing $(-8, 3)$ and $(-1, -4)$. -1

14. Find an equation for the line with slope of $\frac{3}{4}$ and containing $(-2, -3)$. Write in standard form. $3x - 4y - 6 = 0$

15. Find an equation of the line containing $(-3, -6)$ and $(2, -5)$. $y = \frac{1}{5}x - \frac{27}{5}$

16. Find the slope and y-intercept of the equation $-3x + 5y - 6 = 0$. $\frac{3}{5}, \frac{6}{5}$

17. Determine, without graphing, whether the graphs of the following pairs of equations are parallel or perpendicular.

   a. $5x - 3y = 12$ b. $7 + 3y = 2x$ c. $-2y - 3 = 4x$
      $3x + 5y = -10$ $-3x - 8 = 2y$ $-6x - 1 = 3y$
      Perpendicular   Perpendicular   Parallel

18. Find an equation of the line containing $(4, -3)$ which is

a. perpendicular to the line $6x - 4y = 1$. $y = -\frac{2}{3}x - \frac{1}{3}$

b. parallel to the line $6x - 4y = 1$. $y = \frac{3}{2}x - 9$

19. The cost of renting a car. If you rent a car for one day and drive it 100 miles, the cost is \$40. If you drive it 150 miles, the cost is \$48.50.

a. Fit a linear function to the data points. $C = 0.17x + 23$

b. Use the function to find how much it will cost to rent the car for one day if you drive it 200 miles. \$57

Challenge

20. Find $h(x)$, the composition of $f(x)$ and $g(x)$, if $f(x) = -3x + 2$ and $g(x) = x^2 - 1$. $-3x^2 + 5$

Ready for Systems of Equations and Inequalities?

1–2 Find the additive inverse of each number.

1. -8 $\quad$ 8 $\quad$ **2.** 7 $\quad$ -7 **3.** $\frac{3}{4}$ $\quad$ $-\frac{3}{4}$ **4.** 0 $\quad$ 0

1–3 Add.

5. $-\frac{3}{4} + \frac{1}{6}$ $\quad$ $-\frac{7}{12}$ **6.** $\frac{4}{5} + \left(-\frac{4}{5}\right)$ $\quad$ 0 $\quad$ **7.** $-8.6 + (-3.4)$ $\quad$ -12

1–3 Subtract.

8. $8 - (-2)$ $\quad$ 10 $\quad$ **9.** $-\frac{2}{3} - \frac{4}{5}$ $\quad$ $-\frac{22}{15}$ **10.** $-3.2 - (-8.1)$ $\quad$ 4.9

3–2 Graph.

11. $y - 3x = 2$ $\quad$ Line through (0, 2) and (−2, −4)

12. $2y = 3x + 2$ $\quad$ Line through (0, 1) and (−2, −2)

13. $\frac{1}{2}x = 4y - 3$ $\quad$ Line through (2, 1) and (−6, 0)

3–4

14. $4y - 4 = 2x$ $\quad$ Line through (−2, 0) and (0, 1)

15. $2y + 4 = 3x$ $\quad$ Line through (1, 2) and (0, −2)

16. $y = -1$ $\quad$ Horizontal line through (0, −1)

2–5 Solve.

17. $3y - 1 > y - 3$ $\quad$ **18.** $2x - 3 > 5$ $\quad$ $x > 4$ **19.** $|x + 2| \leq 6$ $\quad$ $x \leq 4$ or $x \geq 8$ $\quad$ 17. $y > -1$

4

CHAPTER FOUR

Systems of Equations and Inequalities

4–1 Systems of Equations in Two Variables

Identifying Solutions

Recall that a conjunction of sentences is formed by joining sentences with the word and. Here is an example of a conjunction of sentences.

$$x + y = 11 \quad \text{and} \quad 3x - y = 5$$

A solution of a sentence with two variables such as $x + y = 11$ is an ordered pair. Here are some pairs in the solution set of $x + y = 11$.

$$(5, 6) \quad (12, -1) \quad (4, 7) \quad (8, 3)$$

Here are some pairs in the solution set of $3x - y = 5$.

$$(0, -5) \quad (4, 7) \quad (-2, -11) \quad (9, 22)$$

The solution set of the sentence

$$x + y = 11 \quad \text{and} \quad 3x - y = 5$$

consists of all pairs that make both sentences true. That is, it is the intersection of the solution sets. We can write the solution set as follows.

$$\{(x, y) \mid x + y = 11 \quad \text{and} \quad 3x - y = 5\}$$

Note that (4, 7) is a solution of the conjunction; in fact, it is the only solution. If an equation or conjunction has only one solution, it is called the unique solution.

EXAMPLE 1
Determine whether $(-2, 3)$ is a solution of the conjunction.

$$x + y = 1 \quad \text{and} \quad 2x - y = -7$$

We substitute $(-2, 3)$ into the equations.

$$
\begin{array}{c|c}
x + y = 1 & 1 \\
\hline
-2 + 3 & 1 \\
1 &
\end{array}
\qquad
\begin{array}{c|c}
2x \quad - y = -7 & -7 \\
\hline
2(-2) - 3 & -7 \\
-4 \; - 3 & \\
- 7 &
\end{array}
$$

The pair $(-2, 3)$ makes both equations true. Therefore, it is a solution.

TRY THIS

1. Determine whether $(-3, 2)$ is a solution of the conjunction.

$2x - y = -8$ and $3x + 4y = -1$ Yes

2. Determine whether $(0, 1)$ is a solution of the conjunction.

$5x + 12y = 12$ and $3x + 9y = 10$ No

Solving Systems of Equations Graphically

One way to find solutions is to graph the equations and look for points of intersection.

EXAMPLE 2

Solve graphically.

$$y - x = 1 \quad \text{and} \quad y + x = 3$$

The graph shows the solution sets of $y - x = 1$ and $y + x = 3$. Their intersection is the single ordered pair $(1, 2)$.

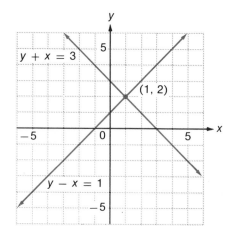

TRY THIS Solve graphically.

3. $x + y = 11 \quad \text{and} \quad 3x - y = 5$ (4, 7)

Recall that the graphs of two linear equations can be two intersecting lines, two parallel lines, or the same line. We will discuss the latter two possibilities in Section 4–5.

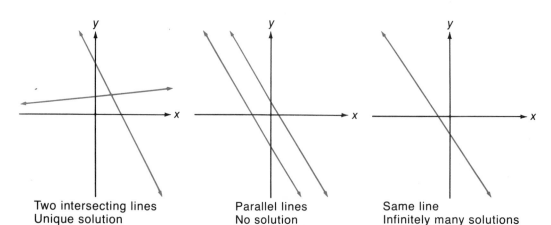

Two intersecting lines
Unique solution

Parallel lines
No solution

Same line
Infinitely many solutions

We often refer to a conjunction of equations as a system of equations. We usually omit the word *and*, and often write one equation under the other.

We now consider two algebraic methods for solving systems of linear equations.

The Substitution Method

To use the substitution method we solve one equation for one of the variables. Then we substitute in the other equation and solve.

EXAMPLE 3
Solve the system.

$$x + y = 11 \quad (1)$$
$$3x - y = 5 \quad (2)$$

First we solve equation (1) for y (we could just as well solve for x).

$$y = 11 - x$$

Then we substitute $11 - x$ for y in equation (2). This gives an equation in one variable, which we know how to solve from earlier work.

$$3x - (11 - x) = 5$$
$$3x - 11 + x = 5$$
$$4x = 16$$
$$x = 4$$

Now substitute 4 for x in either equation (1) or (2) and solve for y. Let us use equation (1).

$$4 + y = 11$$
$$y = 7$$

The solution is the ordered pair (4, 7). Note the alphabetical listing: 4 for x, 7 for y.

Check:

$x + y = 11$		$3x - y = 5$	
$4 + 7$	11	$3 \cdot 4 - 7$	5
11		5	

TRY THIS Solve, using the substitution method.

4. $2x + y = 6$
$3x + 4y = 4$ (4, −2)

5. $8x - 3y = -31$
$2x + 6y = 26$ (−2, 5)

The Addition Method

The substitution method is a useful technique for systems in which it is easy to solve one of the equations for x or y.

If all of the variables have coefficients other than 1, the addition method may be easier to use. The addition method makes use of the addition and multiplication principles for solving equations. Consider the following system.

$$3x - 4y = -1$$
$$-3x + 2y = 0$$

We add the left-hand sides and obtain $-2y$, and add the right-hand sides and obtain -1. When we do this we say that we "add the two equations." Thus we obtain a new equation: $-2y = -1$. We can now solve for y and then substitute into one of the original equations to find x.

$$-2y = -1$$
$$y = \frac{1}{2}$$
$$-3x + 2\left(\frac{1}{2}\right) = 0 \quad \text{Substituting into the second equation}$$
$$-3x + 1 = 0$$
$$-3x = -1$$
$$x = \frac{1}{3}$$

The solution $\left(\frac{1}{3}, \frac{1}{2}\right)$ is also the solution of the original system. We know this because we used only those operations that produce equivalent systems: replacing an equation by an equivalent equation; substituting values or expressions for a variable; and replacing an equation by a *linear combination* of the equations in the system. To obtain a linear combination, we multiply each equation by a constant and add. We choose the constants so that the resulting coefficient of one of the variables will be 0.

EXAMPLE 4
Solve.

$$5x + 3y = 7 \qquad \text{①} \; \text{These numbers indicate the equations in the first and}$$
$$3x - 5y = -23 \quad \text{②} \; \text{second positions, respectively, throughout the solving process.}$$

We first multiply equation ② by 5 to make the x-coefficient a multiple of 5.

$$5x + 3y = 7 \qquad \text{①}$$
$$15x - 25y = -115 \quad \text{②}$$

Now we multiply equation ① by -3 and add it to equation ②. This gets rid of the x-term.

$$5x + 3y = 7 \qquad \begin{array}{l} -15x - 9y = -21 \quad \text{(Multiplying ① by } -3) \\ \underline{15x - 25y = -115} \quad \text{(②)} \end{array}$$
$$-34y = -136 \qquad -34y = -136 \quad \text{(Adding)}$$

Next we solve the second equation for y. Then we substitute the result into the first equation to find x.

$$-34y = -136 \qquad 5x + 3(4) = 7$$
$$y = 4 \qquad 5x + 12 = 7$$
$$5x = -5$$
$$x = -1$$

The solution is $(-1, 4)$.

There are some preliminary things that might be done to make the steps of the addition method simpler. One is to first write the equations in the form $Ax + By = C$. Another is to interchange two equations before beginning. For example, if we have the system

$$5x + y = -2$$
$$x + 7y = 3$$

we may prefer to write the second equation first. This accomplishes two things. One is that the x-coefficient is 1 in the first equation. After y has been found, this will make solving for x easier. The other is that this makes the x-coefficient in the second equation a multiple of the first.

Something else that might be done is to multiply one or more equations by a power of 10 before beginning in order to eliminate decimal points. For example, if we have the system:

$$-0.3x + 0.5y = 0.03$$
$$0.01x - 0.4y = 1.2$$

we can multiply both equations by 100 to clear decimals.

$$-30x + 50y = 3$$
$$x - 40y = 120$$

The method illustrated in Example 4 establishes a step-by-step procedure, or algorithm, which could even be done mechanically by a computer.

TRY THIS Solve.

6. $\quad 4x + 3y = -6 \qquad$ 7. $9x - 2y = -4 \qquad$ 8. $0.2x + 0.3y = 0.1$
$\quad -4x + 2y = 16 \;\; (-3, 2) \quad 3x + 4y = 1 \;\; (-\frac{1}{3}, \frac{1}{2}) \quad 0.3x - 0.1y = 0.7 \;\; (2, -1)$

Exercises

Determine whether the given ordered pair is a solution of the system of equations. Remember to use alphabetical order of variables.

1. $(1, 2)$; $-4x - y = 2$
$10x - 3y = 4$ No

2. $(-1, -2)$; $2x + y = -4$
$x - y = 1$ Yes

3. $(2, 5)$; $y = 3x - 1$
$2x + y = 4$ No

4. $(-1, -2)$; $3x - 2y = 12$
$x + 3y = -7$ No

5. $(1, 5)$; $x + y = 6$
$y = 2x + 3$ Yes

6. $(5, 2)$; $a + b = 7$
$2a - 8 = b$ Yes

7. $(2, -7)$; $3a + b = -1$
$2a - 3b = -8$ No

8. $(2, 1)$; $3p + 2q = 5$
$4p + 5q = 2$ No

Solve graphically.

9. $x + y = 4$
$x - y = 2$ (3, 1)

10. $x - y = 3$
$x + y = 5$ (4, 1)

11. $2x - y = 4$
$5x - y = 13$ (3, 2)

12. $3x + y = 5$
$x - 2y = 4$ (2, −1)

13. $4x - y = 9$
$x - 3y = 16$ (1, −5)

14. $2y = 6 - x$
$3x - 2y = 6$ (3, 3/2)

15. $a = 1 + b$
$b = -2a + 5$ (2, 1)

16. $x = y - 1$
$2x = 3y$ (−3, −2)

17. $2u + v = 3$
$2u = v + 7$ (5/2, −2)

18. $2b + a = 11$
$a - b = 5$ (7, 2)

19. $y = -\frac{1}{3}x - 1$
$4x - 3y = 18$ (3, −2)

20. $y = -\frac{1}{4}x + 1$
$2y = x - 4$ (4, 0)

Solve, using the substitution method.

21. $3x + 5y = 3$
$x = 8 - 4y$

22. $2x - 3y = 13$
$y = 5 - 4x$

21. (−4, 3) 22. (2, −3)

23. $9x - 2y = 3$
$3x - 6 = y$

24. $x = 3y - 3$
$x + 2y = 9$

23. (−3, −15) 24. (21/5, 12/5)

25. $5m + n = 8$
$3m - 4n = 14$

26. $4x + y = 1$
$x - 2y = 16$

25. (2, −2) 26. (2, −7)

27. $4x + 12y = 4$
$5x - y = -11$

28. $3b - a = -7$
$5a + 6b = 14$

27. (−2, 1) 28. (4, −1)

Solve, using the addition method.

29. $x + 3y = 7$
$-x + 4y = 7$ (1, 2)

30. $x + y = 9$
$2x - y = -3$ (2, 7)

31. $2x + y = 6$
$x - y = 3$ (3, 0)

32. $x - 2y = 6$
    $-x + 3y = -4$ (10, 2)

33. $9x + 3y = -3$
    $2x - 3y = -8$ (-1, 2)

34. $6x - 3y = 18$
    $6x + 3y = -12$ ($\frac{1}{2}$, -5)

35. $5x + 3y = -9$
    $2x - 5y = -16$ (-3, 2)

36. $3x + 2y = 22$
    $9x - 8y = -4$ (4, 5)

37. $5r - 3s = 24$
    $3r + 5s = 28$ (6, 2)

38. $5x - 7y = -16$
    $2x + 8y = 26$ (1, 3)

39. $0.3x - 0.2y = 0.3$
    $0.2x + 0.3y = -0.3$ (3, -3)

40. $0.7x - 0.3y = 0.5$
    $-0.4x + 0.7y = 1.3$ (2, 3)

Solve.

41. ($\frac{1}{2}$, $-\frac{1}{2}$)

42. (-2, -9)

43. ($-\frac{4}{3}$, $-\frac{19}{3}$)

41. $5x - 9y = 7$
    $7y - 3x = -5$

42. $a - 2b = 16$
    $b + 3 = 3a$

43. $3(a - b) = 15$
    $4a = b + 1$

44. $1.3x - 0.2y = 12$
    $0.4x + 17y = 89$

44. (10, 5)

45. $x - \frac{1}{10}y = 100$
    $y - \frac{1}{10}x = -100$

45. (90.91, -90.91)

46. $\frac{1}{8}x + \frac{3}{5}y = \frac{19}{2}$
    $-\frac{3}{10}x - \frac{7}{20}y = -1$

46. (-20, 20)

Extension

47. $\frac{x + y}{4} - \frac{x - y}{3} = 1$

    $\frac{x - y}{2} + \frac{x + y}{4} = -9$ (-12, 0)

48. $\frac{x + y}{2} - \frac{y - x}{3} = 0$

    $\frac{x + y}{3} - \frac{x + y}{4} = 0$ (0, 0)

Solve graphically.

49. $3x - y = -5$
    $y - 3x = -2$ No solution

50. $y = -3x + 5$
    $4y + 12x = 20$ Infinitely many solutions; any point on line $y = -3x + 5$

Each of the following is a system of equations that is *not* linear. But each is *linear in form*, because an appropriate substitution (say u for $\frac{1}{x}$ and v for $\frac{1}{y}$) yields a linear system. Solve for the new variable and then solve for the original variable.

51. $\frac{1}{x} - \frac{3}{y} = 2$
    $\frac{6}{x} + \frac{5}{y} = -34$
    $(-\frac{1}{4}, -\frac{1}{2})$

52. $\frac{2}{x} + \frac{1}{y} = 0$
    $\frac{5}{x} + \frac{2}{y} = -5$
    $(-\frac{1}{5}, \frac{1}{10})$

53. $3|x| + 5|y| = 30$
    $5|x| + 3|y| = 34$
    {(5, 3), (-5, 3), (5, -3), (-5, -3)}

Challenge

In each case two solutions of an equation are given. Find the equation using a system of equations.

54. $y = mx + b$; (1, 2) and (-3, 4) $y = -\frac{1}{2}x + \frac{5}{2}$

55. $y = ax^2 + c$; (0, 3) and (-2, 3) $y = 0 \cdot x^2 + 3$ or $y = 3$

4-2 Solving Problems with Two Equations

To solve problems, we often translate to a system of equations in two variables. This can make the translation much easier than if we used just one equation.

EXAMPLE 1

Eight times a certain number added to five times a second number is 184. The first number minus the second number is -3. Find the numbers.

There are two statements in the problem. We translate the first one.

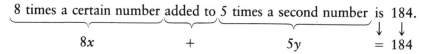

$$8x \qquad + \qquad 5y \qquad = 184$$

Here x represents the first number and y represents the second. Now we translate the second statement, remembering to use x and y.

The first number minus the second number is -3.
$$x \qquad - \qquad y \qquad = -3$$

We now have a system of equations.

$$8x + 5y = 184$$
$$x - y = -3$$

We solve this system, either by substitution or addition. We show the substitution method this time.

$$x = y - 3 \qquad\qquad x - 16 = -3$$
$$8(y - 3) + 5y = 184 \qquad\qquad x = 13$$
$$8y - 24 + 5y = 184$$
$$13y = 208$$
$$y = \frac{208}{13} = 16$$

Now we must check in the *original problem*. Since $8 \cdot 13 = 104$ and $5 \cdot 16 = 80$, the sum is 184. The difference between 13 and 16 is -3, so we have the answer.

TRY THIS

1. One number is 4 times another number. Their sum is 175. Find the numbers. 35, 140

EXAMPLE 2 A mixture problem

Solution A is 2% alcohol. Solution B is 6% alcohol. A service station owner wants to mix the two to get 60 liters of a solution that is 3.2% alcohol. How many liters of each should the owner use?

We can organize information in a table. This will help in translating the problem into equations.

	Amount of solution	Percent of alcohol	Amount of alcohol in solution
A	x liters	2%	$2\%x$ or $0.02x$
B	y liters	6%	$6\%y$ or $0.06y$
Mixture	60 liters	3.2%	0.032×60 or 1.92 liters

Notice we have used x for the number of liters of A and y for the number of liters of B. To get the amount of alcohol, we multiply by the percentages. If we add x and y in the first column we get 60, and this gives us one equation.

$$x + y = 60$$

If we add the amounts of alcohol in the third column we get 1.92, and this gives us another equation.

$$0.02x + 0.06y = 1.92$$

We multiply the second equation by 100.

$$x + y = 60$$
$$2x + 6y = 192$$

When we solve the system we find that $x = 42$ and $y = 18$.
Remember, $x = $ number of liters of 2% solution; $y = $ number of liters of 6% solution.

Check: Total numbers of liters of mixture

$$x + y = 42 + 18$$
$$= 60$$

Amount of alcohol

$$2\% \times 42 + 6\% \times 18 = 0.02 \times 42 + 0.06 \times 18$$
$$= 1.92 \text{ liters}$$

Percentage of alcohol in mixture

$$\frac{1.92}{60} = 0.032, \text{ or } 3.2\%$$

The numbers check in the original problem, so the answer is that the owner should use 42 L of 2% alcohol and 18 L of 6% alcohol.

TRY THIS

2. A gardener has two kinds of solutions containing weedkiller and water. One is 5% weedkiller and the other is 15% weedkiller. The gardener needs 100 liters of a 12% solution and wants to make it by mixing. How much of each solution should be used? 30 liters of 5% and 70 liters of 15%

EXAMPLE 3   A motion problem

A train leaves Sioux City traveling east at 30 km/h. Two hours later another train leaves Sioux City in the same direction on a parallel track at 45 km/h. How far from Sioux City will the faster train catch the slower one?

To translate motion problems we use the definition of distance.

$$\text{Distance} = \text{Rate} \times \text{Time}$$

or

$$d = rt$$

To solve this problem, we first make a drawing.

From the drawing we see that the distances are the same. Let's call the distance d. We don't know the times. Let t represent the time for the faster train. Then the time for the slower one will be $t + 2$. We can organize the information in a table.

	Distance	Rate	Time
Slow train	d	30	$t+2$
Fast train	d	45	t

Using $d = rt$ in each row of the table, we get an equation. Thus we get a system of two equations:

$$d = 30(t + 2) \text{ and } d = 45t \quad \text{This is the translation.}$$

166 CHAPTER 4 SYSTEMS OF EQUATIONS AND INEQUALITIES

We solve.

$$30(t + 2) = 45t \qquad \text{Using substitution}$$
$$30t + 60 = 45t$$
$$60 = 15t$$
$$t = 4$$

Thus the time for the faster train should be 4 hours and the time for the slower train 6 hours. At 45 km/h the faster train would go $45 \cdot 4$, or 180 kilometers in 4 hours. At 30 km/h the slower train would go $30 \cdot 6$, or 180 kilometers in 6 hours. This checks, and the answer is 180 kilometers.

TRY THIS

3. A train leaves Barstow traveling east at 35 km/h. One hour later a faster train leaves Barstow, also traveling east on a parallel track at 40 km/h. How far from Barstow will the faster train catch the slower one? 280 km

---

4–2	

Exercises

Solve.

1. The sum of a certain number and a second number is -42. The first number minus the second is 52. Find the numbers. 5, −47

2. The sum of two numbers is -63. The first number minus the second is -41. Find the numbers. −52, −11

3. The difference between two numbers is 16. Three times the larger number is nine times the smaller. What are the numbers? 24, 8

4. The difference between two numbers is 11. Twice the smaller number plus three times the larger number is 123. What are the numbers? 29, 18

5. Soybean meal is 16% protein; corn meal is 9% protein. How many pounds of each should be mixed together to get a 350-pound mixture that is 12% protein? 150 lb soybean meal; 200 lb corn meal

6. A chemist has one solution that is 25% acid and a second that is 50% acid. How many liters of each should be mixed together to get 10 liters of a solution that is 40% acid?

7. One canned juice drink is 15% orange juice; another is 5% orange juice. How many liters of each should be mixed together to get 10 liters which is 10% orange juice? 5 L of each

8. Antifreeze A is 18% alcohol. Antifreeze B is 10% alcohol. How many liters of each should be mixed to get 20 L of a mixture that is 15% alcohol?

6. 4 L of 25% solution, 6 L of 50% solution

8. $12\frac{1}{2}$ L of A, $7\frac{1}{2}$ L of B

9. Two investments are made totaling $8800. For a certain year these investments yield $1326 in simple interest. Part of the $8800 is invested at 14% and part at 16%. Find the amount invested at each rate. $4100 at 14%, $4700 at 16%

10. Two investments are made totaling $15,000. For a certain year these investments yield $1432 in simple interest. Part of the $15,000 is invested at 9% and part at 10%. Find the amount invested at each rate.

11. $1150 is invested, part of it at 12% and part of it at 11%. The total yield was $133.75. How much was invested at each rate? $725 at 12%, $425 at 11%

12. $27,000 is invested, part of it at 10% and part of it at 12%. The total yield was $2990. How much was invested at each rate? $12,500 at 10%, $14,500 at 12%

13. A train leaves a station and travels north at 75 km/h. Two hours later a second train leaves on a parallel track and travels north at 125 km/h. How far from the station will they meet? 375 km

14. Two cars leave town traveling in opposite directions. One travels 80 km/h and the other 96 km/h. In how many hours will they be 528 kilometers apart? 3

15. Two motorcycles travel toward each other from Chicago and Indianapolis, which are about 350 km apart, at rates of 110 and 90 km/h. They started at the same time. In how many hours will they meet? $1\frac{3}{4}$

16. Two planes travel toward each other from cities which are 780 km apart at rates of 190 and 200 km/h. They started at the same time. In how many hours will they meet? 2

17. One day a store sold 30 sweatshirts. White ones cost $9.95 and yellow ones cost $10.50. In all, $310.60 worth of sweatshirts were sold. How many of each color were sold? 8 white, 22 yellow

18. One week a business sold 40 scarves. White ones cost $4.95 and printed ones cost $7.95. In all, $282 worth of scarves were sold. How many of each kind were sold? 12 white, 28 printed

19. One day a store sold 45 pens, one kind at $8.50 and another kind at $9.75. In all, $398.75 was taken in. How many of each kind were sold? 13 at $9.75; 32 at $8.50

20. At a club play, 117 tickets were sold. Adult tickets cost $1.25 and children's tickets cost $0.75. In all, $129.75 was taken in. How many of each kind of ticket were sold? 84 adult, 33 children

21. Carlos is 8 years older than his sister Maria. Four years ago Maria was $\frac{2}{3}$ as old as Carlos. How old are they now?

22. Paula is 12 years older than her brother Bob. Four years from now Bob will be $\frac{2}{3}$ as old as Paula. How old are they now?

23. The perimeter of a rectangular field is 628 m. The length of the field exceeds its width by 6 m. Find the dimensions.

24. The perimeter of a lot is 190 m. The width is one-fourth the length. Find the dimensions. l = 76 m, w = 19 m

25. The perimeter of a rectangle is 86 cm. The length is 19 cm greater than the width. Find the length and the width.

26. The perimeter of a rectangle is 384 m. The length is 82 m greater than the width. Find the length and the width.

21. Maria 20, Carlos 28   23. l = 160 m; w = 154 m   26. l = 137 m; w = 55 m
22. Paula 32, Bob 20   25. l = 31 cm; w = 12 cm

Extension

27. James Kent and Joan Jensen are mathematics teachers. They have a total of 46 years of teaching. Two years ago James had taught 2.5 times as many years as Joan. How long has each taught? Joan, 14 yrs, James, 32 years

28. Nancy jogs and walks to school each day. She averages 4 km/h walking and 8 km/h jogging. The distance from home to school is 6 km and she makes the trip in 1 hour. How far does she jog in a trip? 4 km

29. The ten's digit of a two-digit positive integer is 2 more than three times the unit's digit. If the digits are interchanged, the new number is 13 less than half the given number. Find the given integer. (*Hint*: Let x = ten's place digit and y = unit's place digit, then $10x + y$ is the number.) 82

30. A limited edition of a book published by a historical society was offered for sale to its membership. The cost was one book for $12 or two books for $20. The society sold 880 books and the total amount of money taken in was $9840. How many members ordered two books? 180

31. The measure of one of two supplementary angles is 8° more than three times the other. Find the measure of the larger of the two angles. 137°

32. The numerator of a fraction is 12 more than the denominator. The sum of the numerator and the denominator is 5 more than three times the denominator. What is the reciprocal of the fraction? $\frac{7}{19}$

Challenge

33. An automobile radiator contains 16 liters of antifreeze and water. This mixture is 30% antifreeze. How much of this mixture should be drained and replaced with pure antifreeze so that there will be 50% antifreeze? $4\frac{4}{7}$ L

34. A train leaves Union Station for Central Station, 216 km away, at 9 A.M. One hour later, a train leaves Central Station for Union Station. They meet at noon. If the second train had started at 9 A.M. and the first train at 10:30 A.M., they would still have met at noon. Find the speed of each train.
First train – 36 km/h; Second train – 54 km/h

4—3 Systems of Equations in Three Variables

Identifying Solutions

A solution of a system of equations in three variables is an ordered triple that makes all three equations true.

EXAMPLE 1

Determine whether $(\frac{3}{2}, -4, 3)$ is a solution of the following system.

$$4x - 2y - 3z = 5$$
$$-8x - y + z = -5$$
$$2x + y + 2z = 5$$

We substitute $(\frac{3}{2}, -4, 3)$ into the three equations, using alphabetical order.

$4x - 2y - 3z = 5$		$-8x - y + z = -5$		$2x + y + 2z = 5$	
$4 \cdot \frac{3}{2} - 2(-4) - 3 \cdot 3$	5	$-8 \cdot \frac{3}{2} - (-4) + 3$	-5	$2 \cdot \frac{3}{2} + (-4) + 2 \cdot 3$	5
$6 + 8 - 9$		$-12 + 4 + 3$		$3 - 4 + 6$	
5		-5		5	

The triple makes all three equations true, so it is a solution.

TRY THIS Consider the following system.

$$4x - y + z = 6$$
$$2x + y + 2z = 3$$
$$3x - 2y + z = 3$$

1. Determine whether $(\frac{5}{2}, 2, -2)$ is a solution. No
2. Determine whether $(2, 1, -1)$ is a solution. Yes

Solving Systems of Equations in Three Variables

Graphical methods for solving linear equations in three variables are unsatisfactory, because a three-dimensional coordinate system is required. The substitution method becomes cumbersome for most systems of more than two equations. Therefore, we will use the addition method. It is essentially the same for systems of three equations as for systems of two equations.

EXAMPLE 2

Solve.

$$x + y + z = 4 \quad ① \quad \text{These numbers indicate}$$
$$x - 2y - z = 1 \quad ② \quad \text{the equations in the first,}$$
$$2x - y - 2z = -1 \quad ③ \quad \text{second, and third positions, respectively.}$$

We begin by multiplying ① by -1, and adding it to ② to eliminate x from the second equation. Equations ① and ③ are unchanged by this step.

$$x + \quad y + \ z = 4 \quad ①$$
$$-3y - 2z = -3 \quad ②$$
$$2x - \quad y - 2z = -1 \quad ③$$

$$-x - \quad y - \ z = -4 \quad \text{(Multiplying ① by } -1\text{)}$$
$$\underline{\quad x - 2y - \ z = 1 \quad ②}$$
$$-3y - 2z = -3 \quad \text{(Adding)}$$

To eliminate x from the third equation we multiply ① by -2 and add it to ③.

$$x + \quad y + \ z = 4 \quad ①$$
$$-3y - 2z = -3 \quad ②$$
$$-3y - 4z = -9 \quad ③$$

$$-2x - 2y - 2z = -8 \quad \text{(Multiplying ① by } -2\text{)}$$
$$\underline{\quad 2x - \quad y - 2z = -1 \quad ③}$$
$$-3y - 4z = -9 \quad \text{(Adding)}$$

Next we eliminate y from the third equation by multiplying ② by -1 and adding the result to ③.

$$x + \quad y + \quad z = 4 \quad ①$$
$$-3y - \quad 2z = -3 \quad ②$$
$$-2z = -6 \quad ③$$

$$3y + \quad 2z = 3 \quad \text{(Multiplying ② by } -1\text{)}$$
$$\underline{-3y - \quad 4z = -9 \quad ③}$$
$$-2z = -6 \quad \text{(Adding)}$$

When the system is in this triangular form, we can easily solve for the three variables.

First we solve ③ for z.

$$x + y + z = 4$$
$$-3y - 2z = -3$$
$$z = 3 \quad \left(\text{Multiplying ③ by } -\frac{1}{2}\right)$$

Next we substitute 3 for z in ② and solve for y.

$$-3y - 2(3) = -3$$
$$-3y - 6 = -3$$
$$-3y = 3$$
$$y = -1$$

Finally, we substitute -1 for y and 3 for z in ①.

$$x + (-1) + 3 = 4$$
$$x + 2 = 4$$
$$x = 2$$

The solution is $(2, -1, 3)$. To be sure computational errors have not been made, you can check by substituting 2 for x, -1 for y, and 3 for z in the three original equations. If all are true, then the triple is a solution.

Below is the algorithm we are using to solve systems of three equations. It can easily be extended to systems of more than three equations.

Triangularization Algorithm For Solving Systems of Linear Equations

Our goal is to obtain an equivalent system of equations in the following form.

$$Ax + By + Cz = D$$
$$Ey + Fz = G$$
$$Hz = J$$

1. First, if possible, interchange equations to make each x-coefficient a multiple of the first.
2. Second, if (1) is not possible, multiply where appropriate to make each x-coefficient a multiple of the first.
3. Multiply and add to eliminate x from the second and third equations.
4. Interchange equations or multiply so the y-coefficient of the third equation is a multiple of the y-coefficient of the second equation.
5. Multiply and add to eliminate y from the third equation.
6. Solve the third equation for z, substitute in the second equation to find y, and then substitute y and z in the first equation to find x.

TRY THIS Solve these systems, using the procedures above.

3. $x + y + z = 2$
   $x - 2y - z = 2$
   $3x + 2y + z = 2$ $(1, -2, 3)$

4. $x + y - z = 2$
   $x - y - 2z = 2$
   $2x + 3y + z = 9$ $(5, -1, 2)$

EXAMPLE 3

Solve.

$$2x - 4y + 6z = 22 \quad ①$$
$$4x + 2y - 3z = 4 \quad ②$$
$$3x + 3y - z = 4 \quad ③$$

We begin by multiplying ③ by 2, to make each x-coefficient a multiple of the first.

$$2x - 4y + 6z = 22$$
$$4x + 2y - 3z = 4$$
$$6x + 6y - 2z = 8$$

Next, we multiply ① by -2 and add it to ②. We also multiply ① by -3 and add it to ③.

$$2x - 4y + 6z = 22$$
$$10y - 15z = -40$$
$$18y - 20z = -58$$

Now we multiply ③ by -5 to make the y-coefficient a multiple of the y-coefficient in ②.

$$2x - 4y + 6z = 22$$
$$10y - 15z = -40$$
$$-90y + 100z = 290$$

Next, we multiply ② by 9 and add it to ③.

$$2x - 4y + 6z = 22$$
$$10y - 15z = -40$$
$$-35z = -70$$

Now we solve ③ for z.

$$-35z = -70$$
$$z = 2$$

Next we substitute 2 for z in ②, and solve for y.

$$10y - 15(2) = -40$$
$$10y - 30 = -40$$
$$y = -1$$

Finally, we substitute -1 for y and 2 for z in ①.

$$2x - 4(-1) + 6(2) = 22$$
$$2x + 4 + 12 = 22$$
$$x = 3$$

The solution is $(3, -1, 2)$.

TRY THIS Solve this system.

5. $\quad x + 2y - z = 5$
$\quad 2x - 4y + z = 0$
$\quad 3x + 2y + 2z = 3$ $\quad (2, \frac{1}{2}, -2)$

4–3	

Exercises

1. Determine whether (30, 50, 100) is a solution of the system.

$x + y + z = 180$
$x - z = -70$
$2y - z = 0$ Yes

2. Determine whether $(2, -1, -2)$ is a solution of the system.

$x + y - 2z = 5$
$2x - y - z = 7$
$-x - 2y + 3z = 6$ No

Solve.

3. $x + y + z = 6$
$2x - y + 3z = 9$ $(1, 2, 3)$
$-x + 2y + 2z = 9$

4. $2x - y + z = 10$
$4x + 2y - 3z = 10$ $(4, 0, 2)$
$x - 3y + 2z = 8$

5. $2x - y - 3z = -1$
$2x - y + z = -9$ $(-1, 5, -2)$
$x + 2y - 4z = 17$

6. $x - y + z = 6$
$2x + 3y + 2z = 2$ $(2, -2, 2)$
$3x + 5y + 4z = 4$

7. $2x - 3y + z = 5$
$x + 3y + 8z = 22$ $(3, 1, 2)$
$3x - y + 2z = 12$

8. $6x - 4y + 5z = 31$
$5x + 2y + 2z = 13$ $(3, -2, 1)$
$x + y + z = 2$

9. $3a - 2b + 7c = 13$
$a + 8b - 6c = -47$ $(-3, -4, 2)$
$7a - 9b - 9c = -3$

10. $x + y + z = 0$
$2x + 3y + 2z = -3$ $(7, -3, -4)$
$-x + 2y - 3z = -1$

11. $2x + 3y + z = 17$
$x - 3y + 2z = -8$ $(2, 4, 1)$
$5x - 2y + 3z = 5$

12. $2x + y - 3z = -4$
$4x - 2y + z = 9$ $(2, 1, 3)$
$3x + 5y - 2z = 5$

13. $2x + y + z = -2$
$2x - y + 3z = 6$ $(-3, 0, 4)$
$3x - 5y + 4z = 7$

14. $2x + y + 2z = 11$
$3x + 2y + 2z = 8$ $(2, -5, 6)$
$x + 4y + 3z = 0$

15. $x - y + z = 4$
$5x + 2y - 3z = 2$ $(2, 2, 4)$
$3x - 7y + 4z = 8$

16. $2x + y + 2z = 3$
$x + 6y + 3z = 4$ $(-2, -1, 4)$
$3x - 2y + z = 0$

17. $4x - y - z = 4$
    $2x + y + z = -1$ $(\frac{1}{2}, 4, -6)$
    $6x - 3y - 2z = 3$

18. $a + 2b + c = 1$
    $7a + 3b - c = -2$ $(3, -5, 8)$
    $a + 5b + 3c = 2$

19. $2r + 3s + 12t = 4$
    $4r - 6s + 6t = 1$ $(\frac{1}{2}, \frac{1}{3}, \frac{1}{6})$
    $r + s + t = 1$

20. $10x + 6y + z = 7$
    $5x - 9y - 2z = 3$ $(\frac{2}{3}, \frac{2}{3}, -3)$
    $15x - 12y + 2z = -5$

Solve.

21. $4a + 9b = 8$
    $8a + 6c = -1$ $(\frac{1}{2}, \frac{2}{3}, -\frac{5}{6})$
    $6b + 6c = -1$

22. $3p + 2r = 11$
    $q - 7r = 4$ $(4, \frac{1}{2}, -\frac{1}{2})$
    $p - 6q = 1$

Extension

23. $\dfrac{x + 2}{3} - \dfrac{y + 4}{2} + \dfrac{z + 1}{6} = 0$

    $\dfrac{x - 4}{3} + \dfrac{y + 1}{4} - \dfrac{z - 2}{2} = -1$

    $\dfrac{x + 1}{2} + \dfrac{y}{2} + \dfrac{z - 1}{4} = \dfrac{3}{4}$ $(1, -1, 2)$

24. $0.2x + 0.3y + 1.1z = 1.6$
    $0.5x - 0.2y + 0.4z = 0.7$
    $-1.2x + y - 0.7z = -0.9$ $(1, 1, 1)$

25. $w + x + y + z = 2$
    $w + 2x + 2y + 4z = 1$
    $w - x + y + z = 6$
    $w - 3x - y + z = 6$ $(1, -2, 4, -1)$

26. $w + x - y + z = 0$
    $w - 2x - 2y - z = -5$
    $w - 3x - y + z = 4$
    $2w - x - y + 3z = 7$ $(-3, -1, 0, 4)$

For Exercises 27 and 28, let u represent $\frac{1}{x}$, v represent $\frac{1}{y}$, and w represent $\frac{1}{z}$. Then solve for u, v, and w.

27. $\dfrac{2}{x} - \dfrac{1}{y} - \dfrac{3}{z} = -1$

    $\dfrac{2}{x} - \dfrac{1}{y} + \dfrac{1}{z} = -9$

    $\dfrac{1}{x} + \dfrac{2}{y} - \dfrac{4}{z} = 17$ $(-1, \frac{1}{5}, -\frac{1}{2})$

28. $\dfrac{2}{x} + \dfrac{2}{y} - \dfrac{3}{z} = 3$

    $\dfrac{1}{x} - \dfrac{2}{y} - \dfrac{3}{z} = 9$

    $\dfrac{7}{x} - \dfrac{2}{y} + \dfrac{9}{z} = -39$ $(-\frac{1}{2}, -1, -\frac{1}{3})$

Challenge

29. Determine a, b, and c if $(2, 3, -4)$ is a solution of the system.

    $ax + by + cz = -11$
    $bx - cy + az = -19$
    $ax + cy - bz = 9$ $a = 2; b = -1; c = 3$

In each case three solutions of an equation are given. Find the equation using a system of equations.

30. $Ax + By + Cz = 12$; $(1, \frac{3}{4}, 3)$, $(\frac{4}{3}, 1, 2)$, and $(2, 1, 1)$ $3x + 4y + 2z = 12$

31. $z = b - mx - ny$; $(1, 1, 2)$, $(4, 1, 0)$, and $(\frac{3}{2}, 1, 1)$ $z = 8 - 2x - 4y$

4–4 Solving Problems with Three Equations

Many problems can be solved by first translating to a system of three equations.

EXAMPLE 1

In a factory there are three machines A, B, and C. When all three are running, they produce 222 suitcases per day. If A and B work but C does not, they produce 159 suitcases per day. If B and C work but A does not, they produce 147 suitcases per day. What is the daily production of each machine?

Let us use x, y, and z for the number of suitcases produced daily by the machines A, B, and C, respectively. There are three statements.

When all three are running, they produce 222 suitcases per day.

$$x + y + z = 222$$

When A and B work, they produce 159 suitcases per day.

$$x + y = 159$$

When B and C work, they produce 147 suitcases per day.

$$y + z = 147$$

We now have a system of three equations.

$$x + y + z = 222$$
$$x + y \phantom{{}+ z} = 159$$
$$\phantom{x + {}} y + z = 147$$

We solve and get $x = 75$, $y = 84$, $z = 63$. These numbers check, so the answer to the problem is that A produces 75 suitcases per day, B produces 84 suitcases per day, and C produces 63 suitcases per day.

TRY THIS

1. There are three machines, A, B, and C, in a factory. When all three work, they produce 287 bolts per hour. When only A and C work, they produce 197 bolts per hour. When A and B work, they produce 202 bolts per hour. How many bolts per hour can each produce alone? A – 112, B – 90, C – 85

Exercises

1. The sum of three numbers is 105. The third is 11 less than 10 times the second. Twice the first is 7 more than 3 times the second. Find the numbers. 17, 9, 79

2. The sum of three numbers is 57. The second is 3 more than the first. The third is 6 more than the first. Find the numbers. 16, 19, 22

3. The sum of three numbers is 5. The first number minus the second plus the third is 1. The first minus the third is 3 more than the second. Find the numbers. 4, 2, −1

4. The sum of three numbers is 26. Twice the first minus the second is 2 less than the third. The third is the second minus three times the first. Find the numbers. 8, 21, −3

5. In triangle ABC, the measure of angle B is 2° more than three times the measure of angle A. The measure of angle C is 8° more than the measure of angle A. Find the angle measures. A = 34°, B = 104°, C = 42°

6. In triangle ABC, the measure of angle B is three times the measure of angle A. The measure of angle C is 30° greater than the measure of angle A. Find the angle measures. A = 30°, B = 90°, C = 60°

7. In triangle ABC, the measure of angle B is twice the measure of angle A. The measure of angle C is 80° more than that of angle A. Find the angle measures. A = 25°, B = 50°, C = 105°

8. In triangle ABC, the measure of angle B is three times that of angle A. The measure of angle C is 20° more than that of angle A. Find the angle measures. A = 32°, B = 96°, C = 52°

9. Gina sells magazines part time. On Thursday, Friday, and Saturday, she sold $66 worth. On Thursday she sold $3 more than on Friday. On Saturday she sold $6 more than on Thursday. How much did she take in each day? $21 on Thur., $18 on Fri., $27 on Sat.

10. Pat picked strawberries on three days. He picked a total of 87 quarts. On Tuesday he picked 15 quarts more than on Monday. On Wednesday he picked 3 quarts fewer than on Tuesday. How many quarts did he pick each day? 20 on Mon., 35 on Tues., 32 on Wed.

11. Linda has a total of 225 on three tests. The sum of the scores on the first and second tests exceeds her third score by 61. Her first score exceeds her second by 6. Find the three scores. 11. first score is 74.5, second score is 68.5, third score is 82

12. Fred, Jane and Mary made a total bowling score of 575. Fred's score was 15 more than Jane's. Mary's was 20 more than Jane's. Find the scores. Fred – 195, Jane – 180, Mary – 200

13. In a factory there are three polishing machines, A, B, and C. When all three of them are working, 5700 lenses can be polished in one week. When only A and B are working, 3400 lenses can be polished in one week. When only B and C are working, 4200 lenses can be polished in one week. How many lenses can be polished in a week by each machine? A – 1500, B – 1900, C – 2300

14. Sawmills A, B and C can produce 7400 board-feet of lumber per day. A and B together can produce 4700 board-feet, while B and C together can produce 5200 board-feet. How many board-feet can each mill produce by itself? A – 2200, B – 2500, C – 2700

15. When three pumps, A, B, and C, are running together, they can pump 3700 gallons per hour. When only A and B are running, 2200 gallons per hour can be pumped. When only A and C are running, 2400 gallons per hour can be pumped. What is the pumping capacity of each pump? A – 900 gal/hr; B – 1300 gal/hr; C – 1500 gal/hr

16. Three welders, A, B, and C, can weld 37 linear feet per hour when working together. A and B together can weld 22 linear feet per hour, while A and C together can weld 25 linear feet per hour. How many linear feet per hour can each weld alone?
16. A – 10; B – 12; C – 15

Extension

17. Tammy's age is the sum of the ages of Carmen and Dennis. Carmen's age is 2 more than the sum of the ages of Dennis and Mark. Dennis' age is four times Mark's age. The sum of all four ages is 42. How old is Tammy? 20

18. Find a three-digit positive integer such that the sum of all three digits is 14, the ten's digit is 2 more than the unit's digit, and if the digits are reversed the number is unchanged. 464

Challenge

19. Hal gives Tom as many raffle tickets as Tom has and Gary as many as Gary has. In like manner, Tom then gives Hal and Gary as many tickets as each then has. Similarly, Gary gives Hal and Tom as many tickets as each then has. If each finally has 40 tickets, with how many tickets does Tom begin? 35

20. At a county fair, adults' tickets sold for $5.50, senior citizens' tickets sold for $4.00, and children's tickets sold for $1.50. On the opening day the number of children's and senior citizens' tickets sold was 30 more than half the number of adults' tickets sold. The number of senior citizens' tickets sold was 5 more than four times the number of children's tickets. How many of each type of ticket was sold if the total receipts from the ticket sales were $14,970. adult's – 2050; senior citizen's – 845; children's – 210

4—5 Inconsistent and Dependent Equations

Inconsistent Equations

DEFINITION

If a system of equations has a solution, we say that it is consistent. If a system does not have a solution, we say that it is inconsistent.

EXAMPLE 1

Determine whether this system is consistent or inconsistent.

$$x - 3y = 1 \quad ①$$
$$-2x + 6y = 5 \quad ②$$

We attempt to find a solution. We multiply ① by 2 and add it to ②.

$$x - 3y = 1$$
$$0 = 7$$

The last equation says that $0 \cdot x + 0 \cdot y = 7$. There are no numbers x and y for which this is true, so there is no solution. The system is inconsistent. Whenever we obtain a statement such as $0 = 7$, which is clearly false, we know that the system we are trying to solve is inconsistent.

We can also consider the problem graphically. The slope-intercept forms of the equations are

$$y = \frac{1}{3}x - \frac{1}{3} \quad ①$$

$$\text{and } y = \frac{1}{3}x + \frac{5}{6} \quad ②$$

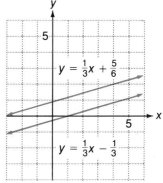

We can see that the lines are parallel. They have no point of intersection, so the system is inconsistent.

TRY THIS Determine whether these systems are consistent or inconsistent.

1. $3x - y = 2$
   $6x - 2y = 3$

2. $x + 4y = 2$
   $2x - y = 1$

1. Inconsistent
2. Consistent

EXAMPLE 2

Determine whether this system is consistent or inconsistent.

$$x + 2y + z = 1 \quad \text{①}$$
$$-x - y + 2z = 0 \quad \text{②}$$
$$y + 3z = 4 \quad \text{③}$$

We attempt to find a solution. We add equation ① to ②.

$$x + 2y + z = 1$$
$$y + 3z = 1$$
$$y + 3z = 4$$

We multiply ② by -1 and add it to ③.

$$x + 2y + z = 1$$
$$y + 3z = 1$$
$$0 = 3$$

The system is inconsistent.

TRY THIS Determine whether these systems are consistent or inconsistent.

3. $x + 2y + z = 1$
   $3x + 3y + z = 2$
   $2x + y = 2$

4. $x + z = 1$
   $y + z = 1$
   $x + y = 1$

3. Inconsistent
4. Consistent

Dependent Equations

DEFINITION

If a system of n linear equations is equivalent to a system of fewer than n of them, we say the system is *dependent*. If such is not the case, we say the system is *independent*.

EXAMPLE 3

Determine whether this system is dependent or independent.

$$2x + 3y = 1 \quad ①$$
$$4x + 6y = 2 \quad ②$$

We attempt to solve. We multiply ① by -2 and add it to ②.

$$2x + 3y = 1$$
$$0 = 0$$

The last equation says that $0 \cdot x + 0 \cdot y = 0$. This is true for all numbers x and y. The system is dependent.

Whenever we get an equation that is true for all numbers x and y, we know that the system we are trying to solve is dependent.

We can also consider the problem graphically. The slope-intercept forms of the equations are

$$y = -\frac{2}{3}x + \frac{1}{3}$$

and

$$y = -\frac{2}{3}x + \frac{1}{3}.$$

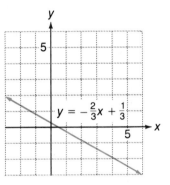

The slope-intercept equations of the lines are the same. This tells us that the graphs are the same. This system of equations has infinitely many solutions. Each point on the line $y = -\frac{2}{3}x + \frac{1}{3}$ is a solution.

TRY THIS Determine whether these systems are dependent or independent.

5. $\quad 3x - 2y = 1$
$\quad -6x + 4y = 2$

6. $x - y = 2$
$\quad x + y = 4$

5. dependent
6. independent

EXAMPLE 4

Determine whether this system is dependent or independent.

$$x + 2y + z = 1 \quad ①$$
$$x - y + z = 1 \quad ②$$
$$2x + y + 2z = 2 \quad ③$$

We attempt to solve. We multiply ① by -1 and add it to ②.

$$x + 2y + z = 1$$
$$-3y = 0$$
$$2x + y + 2z = 2$$

We then multiply ① by -2 and add it to ③.

$$
\begin{aligned}
x + 2y + z &= 1 \\
- 3y \quad\; &= 0 \\
- 3y \quad\; &= 0
\end{aligned}
$$

Since the last two equations are identical, the system of three equations is equivalent to the following system of two equations.

$$
\begin{aligned}
x + \quad 2y + z &= 1 \\
- 3y \quad\;\; &= 0
\end{aligned}
$$

The system is dependent.

In solving a system, how do we know it is dependent? If, at some stage, we find that two of the equations are identical, then we know the system is dependent. If we obtain an obviously true statement, such as $0 = 0$, then we know that the system is dependent. We cannot know whether such a system is consistent or inconsistent without further analysis.

TRY THIS Determine whether these systems are dependent or independent.

7. $\begin{aligned} x + y + 2z &= 1 \\ x - y + z &= 1 \\ 2x \quad + 3z &= 2 \end{aligned}$
8. $\begin{aligned} x + y + 2z &= 1 \\ x - y + z &= 1 \\ x + 2y + z &= 2 \end{aligned}$

7. dependent
8. independent

4–5

Exercises

Determine whether these systems are consistent or inconsistent.

1. $\begin{aligned} x + 2y &= 6 \\ 2x &= 8 - 4y \end{aligned}$
   inconsistent

2. $\begin{aligned} y - 2x &= 1 \\ 2x - 3 &= y \end{aligned}$
   inconsistent

3. $\begin{aligned} y - x &= 4 \\ x + 2y &= 2 \end{aligned}$
   consistent

4. $\begin{aligned} y + x &= 5 \\ y &= x - 3 \end{aligned}$
   consistent

5. $\begin{aligned} x - 3 &= y \\ 2x - 2y &= 6 \end{aligned}$
   consistent

6. $\begin{aligned} 3y &= x - 2 \\ 3x &= 6 + 9y \end{aligned}$
   consistent

7. $\begin{aligned} x + z &= 0 \\ x + y + 2z &= 3 \\ y + z &= 2 \end{aligned}$
   inconsistent

8. $\begin{aligned} x + y &= 0 \\ x + z &= 1 \\ 2x + y + z &= 2 \end{aligned}$
   inconsistent

9. $\begin{aligned} x + z &= 0 \\ x + y &= 1 \\ y + z &= 1 \end{aligned}$
   consistent

Determine whether these systems are dependent or independent.

10. $x - 3 = y$
    $2x - 2y = 6$
    dependent

11. $3y = x - 2$
    $3x = 6 + 9y$
    dependent

12. $y - x = 4$
    $x + 2y = 2$
    independent

13. $y + x = 5$
    $y = x - 3$
    independent

14. $2x + 3y = 1$
    $x + 1.5y = 0.5$
    dependent

15. $15x + 6y = 20$
    $7.5x - 10 = -3y$
    dependent

16. $x + z = 0$
    $x + y = 1$
    $y + z = 1$
    independent

17. $2x + y = 1$
    $x + 2y + z = 0$
    $x + z = 1$
    independent

18. $x + y + z = 1$
    $-x + 2y + z = 2$
    $2x - y = -1$
    dependent

Extension

Solve. If a system has more than one solution, list three of them.

19. $9x - 3y = 15$
    $6x - 2y = 10$ $(0, -5), (1, -2), (-1, -8)$

20. $2s - 3t = 9$
    $4s - 6t = 9$ no solution

21. $x + 2y - z = -8$
    $2x - y + z = 4$
    $8x + y + z = 2$ no solution

22. $2x + y + z = 0$
    $x + y - z = 0$
    $x + 2y + 2z = 0$ $(0, 0, 0)$

23. $2x + 4y + 8z = 5$
    $x + 2y + 4z = 13$
    $4x + 8y + 16z = 10$ no solution

24. $x + y + + = 4$
    $5x + 5y + 5z = 15$
    $2x + 2y + 2z = 6$ no solution

25. Classify each of the systems in Exercises 19, 21, and 23 as consistent or inconsistent, dependent or independent.   dependent: 19, 23 consistent: 19

26. Classify each of the systems in Exercises 20, 22, and 24 as consistent or inconsistent, dependent or independent.   dependent: 24 consistent: 20

Challenge

Determine the constant k such that each system is dependent.

27. $6x - 9y = -3$
      $-4x + 6y = k$ 2

28. $8x - 16y = 20$
      $10x - 20y = k$ 25

Consider the following dependent systems. For each system, find an ordered pair in terms of y that describes the entire solution set of the system.

29. $2x + 3y = 1$
    $4x + 6y = 2$ $\left(\frac{1 - 3y}{2}, y\right)$

30. $-6x + 4y = 10$
    $3x - 2y = -5$ $\left(\frac{2y - 5}{3}, y\right)$

4-6 Matrices and Systems (Optional)

In solving systems of equations, we perform computations with the constants. After the equations are in the form $Ax + By = C$, the variables play no important role in the process. We can simplify writing by omitting the variables. For example, the system

$$\begin{aligned} 3x + 4y &= 5 \\ x - 2y &= 1 \end{aligned} \quad \text{simplifies to} \quad \begin{array}{ccc} 3 & 4 & 5 \\ 1 & -2 & 1 \end{array}$$

In the above example we have written a rectangular array of numbers. Such an array is called a matrix (plural, matrices). We ordinarily write brackets around matrices. The following are matrices.

$$\begin{bmatrix} 4 & 1 & 3 & 5 \\ 1 & 0 & 1 & 2 \\ 6 & 3 & -2 & 0 \end{bmatrix} \quad \begin{bmatrix} 6 & 2 & 1 & 4 & 7 \\ 1 & 2 & 1 & 3 & 1 \\ 4 & 0 & -2 & 0 & -3 \end{bmatrix} \quad \begin{bmatrix} 1 & 2 \\ 145 & 0 \\ -7 & 9 \\ 8 & 1 \\ 0 & 0 \end{bmatrix}$$

The rows of a matrix are horizontal, and the columns are vertical.

$$\begin{array}{ccc} \text{column 1} & \text{column 2} & \text{column 3} \\ \downarrow & \downarrow & \downarrow \end{array}$$
$$\begin{bmatrix} 5 & -2 & 2 \\ 1 & 0 & 1 \\ 0 & 1 & 2 \end{bmatrix} \begin{array}{l} \leftarrow \text{row 1} \\ \leftarrow \text{row 2} \\ \leftarrow \text{row 3} \end{array}$$

We can use matrices to solve systems of linear equations. All the operations used correspond to operations with the equations and they produce equivalent systems of equations. We call the matrices row-equivalent, and the operations that produce them row-equivalent operations.

THEOREM 4-1

Each of the following row-equivalent operations produces equivalent matrices:

a. Interchanging any two rows of a matrix;
b. Multiplying each element of a row by the same nonzero constant;
c. Multiplying each element of a row by a nonzero number and adding the result to another row.

EXAMPLE 1

Solve.

$$2x - y + 4z = -3$$
$$x - 4z = 5$$
$$6x - y + 2z = 10$$

We first write a matrix, using only the constants. Note that where there are missing terms we must write 0's.

$$\begin{bmatrix} 2 & -1 & 4 & -3 \\ 1 & 0 & -4 & 5 \\ 6 & -1 & 2 & 10 \end{bmatrix}$$

We do exactly the same calculations using the matrix that we would do if we wrote the entire equations. The first step, if possible, is to interchange the rows so that each number in the first column below the first number is a multiple of that number. We do this by interchanging rows 1 and 2.

$$\begin{bmatrix} 1 & 0 & -4 & 5 \\ 2 & -1 & 4 & -3 \\ 6 & -1 & 2 & 10 \end{bmatrix}$$ This corresponds to interchanging equation ① with equation ②.

Next we multiply the first row by -2 and add it to the second row.

$$\begin{bmatrix} 1 & 0 & -4 & 5 \\ 0 & -1 & 12 & -13 \\ 6 & -1 & 2 & 10 \end{bmatrix}$$ This corresponds to multiplying equation ① by -2 and adding it to equation ②.

Now we multiply the first row by -6 and add it to the third row.

$$\begin{bmatrix} 1 & 0 & -4 & 5 \\ 0 & -1 & 12 & -13 \\ 0 & -1 & 26 & -20 \end{bmatrix}$$ This corresponds to multiplying equation ① by -6 and adding it to equation ③.

Next we multiply row 2 by -1 and add it to the third row.

$$\begin{bmatrix} 1 & 0 & -4 & 5 \\ 0 & -1 & 12 & -13 \\ 0 & 0 & 14 & -7 \end{bmatrix}$$ This corresponds to multiplying equation ② by -1 and adding it to equation ③.

If we now put the variables back, we have the following.

$$x - 4z = 5$$
$$-y + 12z = -13$$
$$14z = -7$$

We solve ③ for z and get $z = -\frac{1}{2}$. Next we substitute $-\frac{1}{2}$ for z in ② and solve for y: $-y + 12(-\frac{1}{2}) = -13$, so $y = 7$. Since there is no y-term in ① we need only substitute $-\frac{1}{2}$ for z in ① and solve for x: $x - 4(-\frac{1}{2}) = 5$, so $x = 3$. The solution is $(3, 7, -\frac{1}{2})$.

Note in the preceding that our goal was to get the matrix in the form where there are just 0's below the main diagonal, formed by a, e, and h. Then we put the variables back and complete the solution.

$$\begin{bmatrix} a & b & c & d \\ 0 & e & f & g \\ 0 & 0 & h & k \end{bmatrix}$$

TRY THIS Solve, using matrices.

1. $5x - 2y = -44$
   $2x + 5y = -6$

2. $x - 2y + 3z = 4$
   $2x - y + z = -1$
   $4x + y + z = 1$

   1. $(-8, 2)$
   2. $(-1, 2, 3)$

4–6

Exercises

Solve, using matrices.

1. $4x + 2y = 11$
   $3x - y = 2$ $(\frac{3}{2}, \frac{5}{2})$

2. $3x - 3y = -6$
   $9x - 2y = 3$ $(1, 3)$

3. $5x + 2 = 3y$
   $4x + 2y - 5 = 0$ $(\frac{1}{2}, \frac{3}{2})$

4. $3x + 3y - 2 = 0$
   $2y = -1 + 5x$ $(\frac{1}{3}, \frac{1}{3})$

5. $3x + y = 7$
   $x + y = 1$ $(3, -2)$

6. $2x + y = 0$
   $x - 5y = -11$ $(-1, 2)$

7. $x + 2y - 3z = 9$
   $2x - y + 2z = -8$
   $3x - y - 4z = 3$ $(-1, 2, -2)$

8. $x - y + 2z = 0$
   $x - 2y + 3z = -1$
   $2x - 2y + z = -3$ $(0, 2, 1)$

9. $4x - y - 3z = 1$
   $8x + y - z = 5$
   $2x + y + 2z = 5$ $(\frac{3}{2}, -4, 3)$

10. $3x + 2y + 2z = 3$
    $x + 2y - z = 5$
    $2x - 4y + z = 0$ $(2, \frac{1}{2}, -2)$

Extension

Solve, using matrices.

11. $0.3x + 0.2y = -0.9$
    $0.2x - 0.3y = -0.6$ $(-3, 0)$

12. $0.2x - 0.3y = 0.3$
    $0.4x + 0.6y = -0.2$ $(\frac{1}{2}, -\frac{2}{3})$

13. $2w - 2x - 2y + 2z = 10$
    $w + x + y + z = -5$
    $3w + x - y + 4z = -2$
    $w + 3x - 2y + 2z = -6$
    $(1, -3, -2, -1)$

14. $w - 2x + 3y - z = 8$
    $w - x - y + z = 4$
    $w + 2x + y + z = 22$
    $w - x + y + z = 14$ $(7, 4, 5, 6)$

4-7 Determinants and Cramer's Rule (Optional)

Determinants of 2 × 2 Matrices

A matrix of m rows and n columns is called an m × n matrix (read "m by n"). If a matrix has the same number of rows and columns, it is called a square matrix. With every square matrix is associated a number called its determinant. The determinant of a 2 × 2 matrix is defined as follows.

DEFINITION

The *determinant* of the matrix $\begin{bmatrix} a & c \\ b & d \end{bmatrix}$ is denoted $\begin{vmatrix} a & c \\ b & d \end{vmatrix}$ and is defined as follows.

$$\begin{vmatrix} a & c \\ b & d \end{vmatrix} = ad - bc$$

EXAMPLE 1

Evaluate $\begin{vmatrix} 7 & -3 \\ -4 & -8 \end{vmatrix}$.

$\begin{vmatrix} 7 & -3 \\ -4 & -8 \end{vmatrix} = 7(-8) - (-4)(-3) = -68$ The arrows indicate the products involved.

TRY THIS Evaluate.

1. $\begin{vmatrix} -4 & -5 \\ -2 & -6 \end{vmatrix}$ 14 2. $\begin{vmatrix} 1 & 2 \\ 3 & 4 \end{vmatrix}$ -2 3. $\begin{vmatrix} -2 & -3 \\ 4 & x \end{vmatrix}$ -2x + 12

Cramer's Rule for Two Equations

Determinants have many uses. One of these is in solving systems of linear equations in which the number of variables is the same as the number of equations. Let us consider a system of two equations.

$$a_1x + b_1y = c_1$$
$$a_2x + b_2y = c_2$$

Using the methods of the preceding sections we can solve. We obtain the following solution.

$$x = \frac{c_1 b_2 - c_2 b_1}{a_1 b_2 - a_2 b_1}$$

and

$$y = \frac{a_1 c_2 - a_2 c_1}{a_1 b_2 - a_2 b_1}.$$

The numerators and denominators of the expressions for x and y are determinants. Thus we have the following theorem.

THEOREM 4–2

Cramer's Rule (2 Equations)

The system of two equations in two variables

$$a_1 x + b_1 y = c_1$$
$$a_2 x + b_2 y = c_2$$

has a solution given by

$$x = \frac{\begin{vmatrix} c_1 & b_1 \\ c_2 & b_2 \end{vmatrix}}{\begin{vmatrix} a_1 & b_1 \\ a_2 & b_2 \end{vmatrix}} \text{ and } y = \frac{\begin{vmatrix} a_1 & c_1 \\ a_2 & c_2 \end{vmatrix}}{\begin{vmatrix} a_1 & b_1 \\ a_2 & b_2 \end{vmatrix}}.$$

The equations in Theorem 4–2 make sense only if the denominator determinant is not 0. If the denominator is 0, then one of two things happens.

1. If the denominator is 0 and the other two determinants are also 0, then the system of equations is dependent.

2. If the denominator is 0 and at least one of the other determinants is not 0, then the system is inconsistent.

To use Cramer's Rule to solve systems of equations, we compute the three determinants and compute x and y as shown above. Note that the denominator in both cases contains the coefficients of x and y, in the same position as in the original equations. For x the numerator is obtained by replacing the x-coefficients (the a's) by the c's. For y the numerator is obtained by replacing the y-coefficients (the b's) by the c's.

EXAMPLE 2

Solve, using Cramer's Rule.

$$2x + 5y = 7$$
$$5x - 2y = -3$$

$$x = \frac{\begin{vmatrix} 7 & 5 \\ -3 & -2 \end{vmatrix}}{\begin{vmatrix} 2 & 5 \\ 5 & -2 \end{vmatrix}} = \frac{7(-2) - (-3)5}{2(-2) - 5 \cdot 5} = -\frac{1}{29}$$

$$y = \frac{\begin{vmatrix} 2 & 7 \\ 5 & -3 \end{vmatrix}}{\begin{vmatrix} 2 & 5 \\ 5 & -2 \end{vmatrix}} = \frac{2(-3) - 5 \cdot 7}{-29} = \frac{41}{29}$$

The solution is $\left(-\frac{1}{29}, \frac{41}{29}\right)$.

TRY THIS Solve, using Cramer's Rule.

4. $2x - y = 5$ 5. $3x + 4y = -2$
   $x - 2y = 1$ (3, 1) $5x - 7y = 1$ $\left(-\frac{10}{41}, -\frac{13}{41}\right)$

Determinants of 3 × 3 Matrices

DEFINITION

The *determinant* of a 3 × 3 matrix is defined as follows.

$$\begin{vmatrix} a_1 & b_1 & c_1 \\ a_2 & b_2 & c_2 \\ a_3 & b_3 & c_3 \end{vmatrix} = a_1 \cdot \begin{vmatrix} b_2 & c_2 \\ b_3 & c_3 \end{vmatrix} - a_2 \cdot \begin{vmatrix} b_1 & c_1 \\ b_3 & c_3 \end{vmatrix} + a_3 \cdot \begin{vmatrix} b_1 & c_1 \\ b_2 & c_2 \end{vmatrix}$$

The 2 × 2 determinants are obtained by crossing out the row and column in which the a-coefficients occur.

EXAMPLE 3

Evaluate.

$$\begin{vmatrix} -1 & 0 & 1 \\ -5 & 1 & -1 \\ 4 & 8 & 1 \end{vmatrix} = -1 \cdot \begin{vmatrix} 1 & -1 \\ 8 & 1 \end{vmatrix} - (-5) \cdot \begin{vmatrix} 0 & 1 \\ 8 & 1 \end{vmatrix} + 4 \cdot \begin{vmatrix} 0 & 1 \\ 1 & -1 \end{vmatrix}$$

$$= -1(1 + 8) + 5(-8) + 4(-1) = -53$$

TRY THIS Evaluate.

6. $\begin{vmatrix} 3 & 2 & 2 \\ -2 & 1 & 4 \\ 4 & -3 & 3 \end{vmatrix}$ 93   7. $\begin{vmatrix} -5 & 0 & 0 \\ 4 & 2 & 0 \\ -3 & 5 & -6 \end{vmatrix}$ 60   8. $\begin{vmatrix} x & 0 & x \\ 0 & x & 0 \\ 1 & 0 & x \end{vmatrix}$ $x^3 - x^2$

Cramer's Rule for Three Equations

THEOREM 4—3

Cramer's Rule (3 Equations)

The system of three equations in three variables:

$$a_1 x + b_1 y + c_1 z = d_1$$
$$a_2 x + b_2 y + c_2 z = d_2$$
$$a_3 x + b_3 y + c_3 z = d_3$$

has a solution given by

$$x = \frac{D_x}{D}, \quad y = \frac{D_y}{D}, \quad z = \frac{D_z}{D}, \text{ where}$$

$$D = \begin{vmatrix} a_1 & b_1 & c_1 \\ a_2 & b_2 & c_2 \\ a_3 & b_3 & c_3 \end{vmatrix}, D_x = \begin{vmatrix} d_1 & b_1 & c_1 \\ d_2 & b_2 & c_2 \\ d_3 & b_3 & c_3 \end{vmatrix},$$

$$D_y = \begin{vmatrix} a_1 & d_1 & c_1 \\ a_2 & d_2 & c_2 \\ a_3 & d_3 & c_3 \end{vmatrix}, D_z = \begin{vmatrix} a_1 & b_1 & d_1 \\ a_2 & b_2 & d_2 \\ a_3 & b_3 & d_3 \end{vmatrix}.$$

Note that we obtain the determinant D_x in the numerator for x from D by replacing the x-coefficients by d_1, d_2, and d_3. A similar thing happens with D_y and D_z. We have thus extended Cramer's Rule to solve systems of three equations in three variables. As before, when $D = 0$, Cramer's Rule cannot be used. If $D = 0$, and D_x, D_y, and D_z are 0, the system is dependent. If $D = 0$ and one of D_x, D_y, or D_z is not zero, then the system is inconsistent.

EXAMPLE 4
Solve, using Cramer's Rule.

$$x - 3y + 7z = 13$$
$$x + y + z = 1$$
$$x - 2y + 3z = 4$$

$$D = \begin{vmatrix} 1 & -3 & 7 \\ 1 & 1 & 1 \\ 1 & -2 & 3 \end{vmatrix} = -10 \qquad D_x = \begin{vmatrix} 13 & -3 & 7 \\ 1 & 1 & 1 \\ 4 & -2 & 3 \end{vmatrix} = 20$$

$$D_y = \begin{vmatrix} 1 & 13 & 7 \\ 1 & 1 & 1 \\ 1 & 4 & 3 \end{vmatrix} = -6 \qquad D_z = \begin{vmatrix} 1 & -3 & 13 \\ 1 & 1 & 1 \\ 1 & -2 & 4 \end{vmatrix} = -24$$

$$x = \frac{D_x}{D} = \frac{20}{-10} = -2, \, y = \frac{D_y}{D} = \frac{-6}{-10} = \frac{3}{5}, \, z = \frac{D_z}{D} = \frac{-24}{-10} = \frac{12}{5}$$

The solution is $(-2, \frac{3}{5}, \frac{12}{5})$. In practice, it is not necessary to evaluate D_z. When we have found values for x and y we can substitute them into one of the equations and find z.

TRY THIS Solve, using Cramer's Rule.

9. $x - 3y - 7z = 6$
$2x + 3y + z = 9$
$4x + y = 7$ $(1, 3, -2)$

4—7

Exercises
Evaluate.

1. $\begin{vmatrix} 2 & 7 \\ 1 & 5 \end{vmatrix}$ 3

2. $\begin{vmatrix} 3 & 2 \\ 2 & -3 \end{vmatrix}$ −13

3. $\begin{vmatrix} 6 & -9 \\ 2 & 3 \end{vmatrix}$ 36

4. $\begin{vmatrix} 3 & 2 \\ -7 & 5 \end{vmatrix}$ 29

5. $\begin{vmatrix} 1.3 & 2.7 \\ 4.2 & 0.8 \end{vmatrix}$ −10.3

6. $\begin{vmatrix} 2.4 & 1.6 \\ 0.9 & 1.8 \end{vmatrix}$ 2.88

7. $\begin{vmatrix} -7 & -7 \\ 3 & 3 \end{vmatrix}$ 0

8. $\begin{vmatrix} 8 & -1 \\ 8 & -1 \end{vmatrix}$ 0

Solve, using Cramer's Rule.

9. $3x - 4y = 6$
$5x + 9y = 10$ $(2, 0)$

10. $5x + 8y = 1$
$3x + 7y = 5$ $(-3, 2)$

11. $2x - 2y = 2$
$6x - 5y = 1$ $(-4, -5)$

12. $5x - 6y = 8$
$2x - 5y = -2$ $(4, 2)$

13. $4x - 4y = 4$
$7x + 2y = 1$ $(\frac{1}{3}, -\frac{2}{3})$

14. $-2x + 4y = 3$
$3x - 7y = 1$ $(-\frac{25}{2}, -\frac{11}{2})$

Evaluate.

15. $\begin{vmatrix} 0 & 2 & 0 \\ 3 & -1 & 1 \\ 1 & -2 & 2 \end{vmatrix}$ −10

16. $\begin{vmatrix} 3 & 0 & -2 \\ 5 & 1 & 2 \\ 2 & 0 & -1 \end{vmatrix}$ 1

17. $\begin{vmatrix} -1 & -2 & -3 \\ 3 & 4 & 2 \\ 0 & 1 & 2 \end{vmatrix}$ −30

18. $\begin{vmatrix} 1 & 2 & 2 \\ 2 & 1 & 0 \\ 3 & 3 & 1 \end{vmatrix}$ 3

19. $\begin{vmatrix} 3 & 2 & 2 \\ -2 & 1 & 4 \\ 4 & -3 & 3 \end{vmatrix}$ 93

20. $\begin{vmatrix} 2 & -1 & 1 \\ 1 & 2 & -1 \\ 3 & 4 & -3 \end{vmatrix}$ −6

Solve, using Cramer's Rule.

21. $2x - 3y + 5z = 27$
$x + 2y - z = -4$
$5x - y + 4z = 27$ $(2, -1, 4)$

22. $x - y + 2z = -3$
$x + 2y + 3z = 4$
$2x + y + z = -3$ $(-3, 2, 1)$

23. $r - 2s + 3t = 6$
$2r - s - t = -3$
$r + s + t = 6$ $(1, 2, 3)$

24. $a - 3c = 6$
$b + 2c = 2$
$7a - 3b - 5c = 14$ $(3, 4, -1)$

25. $3x + 2y - z = 4$
$3x - 2y + z = 5$
$4x - 5y - z = -1$ $(\frac{3}{2}, \frac{13}{14}, \frac{33}{14})$

26. $3x - y + 2z = 1$
$x - y + 2z = 3$
$-2x + 3y + z = 1$ $(-1, -\frac{9}{7}, \frac{11}{7})$

Extension

Evaluate.

27. $\begin{vmatrix} x & 4 \\ x & x^2 \end{vmatrix}$ $x^3 - 4x$

28. $\begin{vmatrix} y^2 & -2 \\ y & 3 \end{vmatrix}$ $3y^2 + 2y$

29. $\begin{vmatrix} z & -3 \\ z^2 & 1 \end{vmatrix}$ $z + 3z^2$

Solve for x.

30. $\begin{vmatrix} 4 & 2 \\ 3 & x \end{vmatrix} = x$ 2

31. $\begin{vmatrix} x & 5 \\ -4 & x \end{vmatrix} = 24$ 2 or −2

32. $\begin{vmatrix} x + 3 & 4 \\ x - 3 & 5 \end{vmatrix} = -7$ −34

33. Solve, using Cramer's Rule.
$\sqrt{3}x + \pi y = -5$
$\pi x - 3y = 4$ $\left(\frac{15 - 4\pi}{-3\sqrt{3} - \pi^2}, \frac{4\sqrt{3} + 5\pi}{-3\sqrt{3} - \pi^2} \right)$

Rewrite each expression using determinants. Answers may vary.

34. $2L + 2W$ $\begin{vmatrix} L & -W \\ 2 & 2 \end{vmatrix}$

35. $a^2 + b^2$ $\begin{vmatrix} a & b \\ -b & a \end{vmatrix}$

Challenge

36. Evaluate. $\begin{vmatrix} 1 & x & y \\ 1 & x & y \\ 1 & 1 & 1 \end{vmatrix}$ 0

37. Verify. $\begin{vmatrix} 1 & x & x^2 \\ 1 & y & y^2 \\ 1 & z & z^2 \end{vmatrix} = (x - y)(y - z)(z - x)$

38. Use the addition method to prove Cramer's Rule for a system of two equations. That is, verify that the solution of the system:

$ax + by = c$ is given by $x = \dfrac{ce - bf}{ae - db}$ and $y = \dfrac{af - dc}{ae - db}$,

$dx + ey = f$

when $ae - db \neq 0$.

4-8 Systems of Inequalities

Graphs of Inequalities in Two Variables

A solution of an inequality in two variables is an ordered pair of numbers that makes the inequality true.

EXAMPLE 1

Determine whether $(-3, 2)$ is a solution of the inequality $5x - 4y \leq 13$.

We replace x by -3 and y by 2.

$$
\begin{array}{c|c}
5x - 4y & \leq 13 \\
\hline
5(-3) - 4 \cdot 2 & 13 \\
-15 - 8 & \\
-23 &
\end{array}
$$

Since -23 is less than 13, $(-3, 2)$ makes the inequality true.

TRY THIS

1. Determine whether $(1, -4)$ is a solution of the inequality. $4x - 5y < 12$ no

To graph inequalities, we use our knowledge and skill in graphing equations. In fact, the first step in graphing an inequality is usually the graphing of an equation.

EXAMPLE 2

Graph $y < x$.

We first graph the equation $y = x$, drawing the line dashed. For any point above the line, y is greater than x, or $y > x$. For any point below the line, y is less than x, or $y < x$. Thus the graph is the half-plane below the line $y = x$. We show this by shading the lower half-plane. The dashed lines mean that the points on the line are not in the graph.

The graph of any linear inequality in two variables is either a half-plane or a half-plane together with the line along the edge.

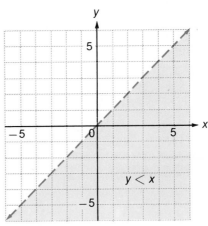

EXAMPLE 3

Graph $6x - 2y \leq 12$.

Method 1. Solve for y.

$$y \geq 3x - 6$$

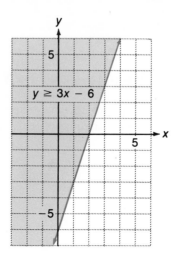

Now graph the line $y = 3x - 6$. For any point on the line the value of y is $3x - 6$. Such values make the inequality true, hence are in the graph. Therefore we draw the line solid this time.

For any point above the line the value of y is greater than $3x - 6$. Hence any such point is in the graph. The graph of the inequality is the half-plane above the line, together with the line.

Method 2. We are to graph $6x - 2y \leq 12$. We graph the line $6x - 2y = 12$, by any method. This time let us find the intercepts. They are $(0, -6)$, $(2, 0)$. We plot them and then use them to draw the line.

Next, we know that the rest of the graph is a half-plane, but we need to determine which one. All we need to do is choose any point on one of the half-planes, substitute it into the inequality, and see if we get a true sentence. The origin is an easy point to use, if the line doesn't contain the origin. We try $(0, 0)$.

$$6 \cdot 0 - 2 \cdot 0 \leq 12 \quad \text{or} \quad 0 \leq 12$$

This gives us a true sentence. Hence $(0, 0)$ is a solution. Thus we shade the half-plane containing $(0, 0)$.

TRY THIS Graph.

2. $y > -2x$ **3.** $2x + y \geq 2$ **4.** $3x - y > -3$

EXAMPLE 4

Graph $-1 < y \leq 2$.

This is a conjunction of two inequalities.

$$-1 < y \quad \text{and} \quad y \leq 2$$

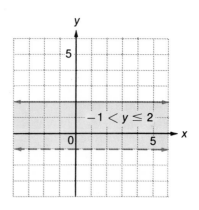

It will be true for any y that is both greater than -1 and less than or equal to 2. Since our inequality is a conjunction, the graph is the intersection of the graphs of the two inequalities.

TRY THIS Graph.

5. $y > -\frac{1}{2}$ 6. $-4 \le x < 1$ 7. $1 \le y \le 2\frac{1}{2}$

Systems of Inequalities

To get a picture of the solution set of a system or conjunction of inequalities, we will graph the inequalities separately and find their intersection. A system of linear inequalities may have a graph that is a polygon and its interior. Sometimes it is important to find the vertices.

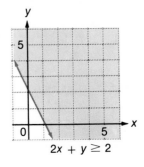
$2x + y \ge 2$

EXAMPLE 5
Graph this system of inequalities. Find the coordinates of any vertices formed.

$$2x + y \ge 2$$
$$4x + 3y \le 12$$
$$\frac{1}{2} \le x \le 2$$
$$y \ge 0$$

The separate graphs are shown at the right and the graph of the intersection, which is the graph of the system, is shown below.

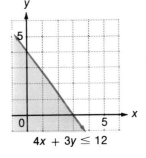
$4x + 3y \le 12$

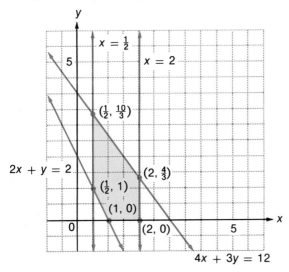

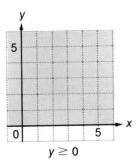
$y \ge 0$

We find the vertex $(\frac{1}{2}, 1)$ by solving the following system.

$$2x + y = 2$$
$$x = \frac{1}{2}$$

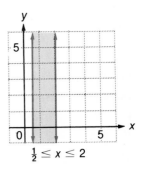
$\frac{1}{2} \le x \le 2$

We find the vertex (1, 0) by solving the following system.

$$2x + y = 2$$
$$y = 0$$

We find the vertex (2, 0) from the following system.

$$x = 2$$
$$y = 0$$

The vertices $(2, \frac{4}{3})$ and $(\frac{1}{2}, \frac{10}{3})$ were found by solving, respectively, the following two systems.

$$x = 2 \qquad\qquad x = \frac{1}{2}$$
$$\text{and}$$
$$4x + 3y = 12 \qquad 4x + 3y = 12$$

TRY THIS Graph. If a polygon is formed, find the vertices.

8. $x + y \geq 1$
   $y - x \geq 2$

9. $5x + 6y \leq 30$
   $0 \leq y \leq 3$
   $0 \leq x \leq 4$ Vertices: (0, 0), (4, 0), (4, $\frac{5}{3}$), (0, 3), ($\frac{12}{5}$, 3)

4–8

Exercises

Determine whether the ordered pair is a solution of the inequality.

1. $(-4, 2); 2x + y < -5$ yes
2. $(3, -6); 4x + 2y \geq 0$ yes
3. $(8, 14); 2y - 3x > 5$ no
4. $(7, 20); 3x - y > -1$ yes

Use graph paper. Graph these inequalities.

5. $y > 2x$
6. $y < 3x$
7. $y < x + 1$
8. $y \leq x - 3$
9. $y > x - 2$
10. $y \geq x + 4$
11. $x + y < 4$
12. $x - y \geq 3$
13. $3x + 4y \leq 12$
14. $2x + 3y < 6$
15. $2y - 3x > 6$
16. $2y - x \leq 4$
17. $3x - 2 \leq 5x + y$
18. $2x - 2y \geq 8 + 2y$
19. $x < -4$
20. $y \geq 5$
21. $x > -2$
22. $-4 < y < -1$
23. $-2 < y < 3$
24. $-3 \leq x \leq 3$
25. $-4 \leq x \leq 4$

Graph.

26. $y < x$
    $y > -x + 3$

27. $y > x$
    $y < -x + 1$

28. $y \geq x$
    $y < -x + 4$

29. $y \geq x$
    $y < -x + 2$

30. $y \geq -2$
    $x > 1$

31. $y \leq -2$
    $x > 2$

32. $x < 3$
    $y \geq -3x + 2$

33. $x > -2$
    $y \leq -2x + 3$

34. $y \geq -2$
    $y \geq x + 3$

35. $y \leq 4$
    $y \geq -x + 2$

36. $x + y \leq 1$
    $x - y \leq 2$

37. $x + y < 3$
    $x - y < 4$

38. $y - 2x > 1$
    $y - 2x < 3$

39. $y + 3x > 0$
    $y + 3x < 2$

40. $2y - x \leq 2$
    $y - 3x \geq -1$

Graph. Find the coordinates of any vertices formed.

41. $y \leq 2x + 1$
    $y \geq -2x + 1$
    $x \leq 2$

42. $x - y \leq 2$
    $x + 2y \geq 8$
    $y \leq 4$

43. $x + 2y \leq 12$
    $2x + y \leq 12$
    $x \geq 0$
    $y \geq 0$

44. $4y - 3x \geq -12$
    $4y + 3x \geq -36$
    $y \leq 0$
    $x \leq 0$

45. $8x + 5y \leq 40$
    $x + 2y \leq 8$
    $x \geq 0$
    $y \geq 0$

46. $3x + 4y \geq 12$
    $5x + 6y \leq 30$
    $1 \leq x \leq 3$

41. $(0, 1), (2, -5), (2, 5)$
42. $(0, 4), (4, 2), (6, 4)$
43. $(0. 0), (0, 6), (4, 4), (6, 0)$
44. $(0, 0), (0, -3), (-4, -6), (12, 0)$
45. $(0, 0), (0, 4), (\frac{40}{11}, \frac{24}{11}), (5, 0)$
46. $(1, \frac{9}{4}), (1, \frac{25}{6}), (3, \frac{3}{4}), (3, \frac{15}{6})$

Challenge
Graph.

47. $y \geq |x|$

48. $y > |x| + 3$

49. $|x + y| \leq 1$

50. $|x| + |y| \leq 1$

51. $|x| > |y|$

DISCOVERY/Early Perspectives

We speak of x^2 as "x-squared" and x^3 as "x-cubed" rather than saying "x second" or "x third" because mathematics had strong roots in Greek geometry. In fact, the geometrical base for serious mathematics prevailed until about 1600. Early Greeks could not see that the product of four or more numbers had any meaning, because there was

no geometrical significance to the fourth power.
   In Egypt things were more practical, and calculation flourished as a science of its own, unbounded by geometric constraints. For example, Heron of Alexandria is credited with the formula for the area of a triangle given the three sides a, b, and c, and the semiperim-

eters, equal to $\frac{1}{2}(a + b + c)$.
$$A = \sqrt{s(s - a)(s - b)(s - c)},$$
a product with four factors. Thus it was from the mathematicians in Alexandria that developments were made in calendar-reckoning, time measurement, navigation, optics, geography, and other practical sciences.

4—9 Linear Programming

You are taking a test in which items of type A are worth 10 points and items of type B are worth 15 points. It takes 3 minutes for each item of type A and 6 minutes for each item of type B. Total time allowed is 60 minutes and you may not answer more than 16 questions. Assuming all of your answers are correct, how many items of each type should you answer to get the best score?

A kind of mathematics called linear programming provides the answer.

Let x = the number of items of type A, and
y = the number of items of type B.

The total score T is given by $T = 10x + 15y$. The set of ordered pairs (x, y) for which this equation makes sense is determined by the following inequalities, called constraints.

Total number of questions allowed, not more than 16: $x + y \leq 16$
Time, not more than 60 minutes: $3x + 6y \leq 60$
Number of items of type A, not negative: $x \geq 0$
Number of items of type B, not negative: $y \geq 0$

We now graph the system of inequalities and determine the vertices, if any are formed.

The graph consists of a polygon and its interior. Under this condition, T has a maximum value and a minimum value. Moreover, the maximum and minimum values occur at the vertices of the polygon. All we need to do is find the vertices and substitute the coordinates in $T = 10x + 15y$.

Vertices: (x, y)	Score: $T = 10x + 15y$	
(0, 0)	0	Minimum
(16, 0)	160	
(12, 4)	180	Maximum
(0, 10)	150	

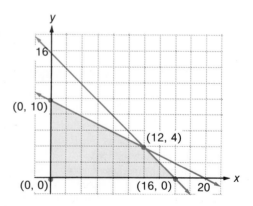

The maximum score is 180. To get this you would answer 12 items of type A and 4 items of type B.

The following is the main theorem used to solve linear programming problems.

THEOREM 4-4

Suppose a quantity F is given by a linear equation $F = ax + by + c$, and that the set of ordered pairs (x, y) for which the equation makes sense can be described by a system of linear inequalities (called *constraints*). If the graph of this system consists of a polygon and its interior, then F has a maximum and a minimum value, and they occur at the vertices.

EXAMPLE 1

A company manufactures motorcycles and bicycles. To stay in business it must produce at least 10 motorcycles each month, but it does not have facilities to produce more than 60 motorcycles. It also does not have facilities to produce more than 120 bicycles. The total production of motorcycles and bicycles cannot exceed 160. The profit on a motorcycle is $134 and on a bicycle is $20. Find the number of each that should be manufactured to maximize profit.

Let x = the number of motorcycles to be produced, and y = the number of bicycles to be produced.

The profit P is $P = 134x + 20y$, subject to these constraints.

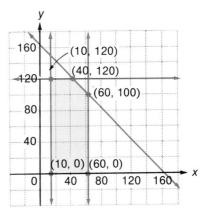

$$10 \leq x \leq 60$$
$$0 \leq y \leq 120$$
$$x + y \leq 160$$

Vertices: (x, y)	Profit $P = 134x + 20y$	
(10, 0)	1340	
(60, 0)	8040	
(60, 100)	10,040	Maximum
(40, 120)	7760	
(10, 120)	3740	

The company will make a maximum profit of $10,040 by producing 60 motorcycles and 100 bicycles.

TRY THIS

1. A snack bar cooks and sells hamburgers and hot dogs during football games. To stay in business it must sell at least 10 hamburgers but cannot cook more than 40. It must also sell at least 30 hot dogs but cannot cook more than 70. It cannot cook more than 90 sandwiches all together. The profit on a hamburger is $0.33 and on a hot dog it is $0.21. How many of each kind of sandwich should it sell to make the maximum profit?

1. The snack bar will make a maximum profit of $23.70 by selling 40 hamburgers and 50 hot dogs.

4-9

Exercises

Solve.

1. You are about to take a test that contains questions of type A worth 4 points and questions of type B worth 7 points. You must do at least 5 questions of type A but time restricts doing more than 10. You must do at least 3 questions of type B but time restricts doing more than 10. In total, you can do no more than 18 questions. How many of each type of question must you do to maximize your score? What is this maximum score?

2. You are about to take a test that contains questions of type A worth 10 points and questions of type B worth 25 points. You must do at least 3 questions of type A but time restricts doing more than 12. You must do at least 4 questions of type B but time restricts doing more than 15. In total you can do no more than 20 questions. How many of each type of question must you do to maximize your score? What is this maximum score?

3. A man is planning to invest up to $22,000 in bank X or bank Y or both. He wants to invest at least $2000 but no more than $14,000 in bank X. Bank Y does not insure more than a $15,000 investment so he will invest no more than that in bank Y. The interest in bank X is 6% and in bank Y it is $6\frac{1}{2}\%$ and this will be simple interest for one year. How much should he invest in each bank to maximize his income? What is the maximum income?

4. A woman is planning to invest up to $40,000 in corporate or municipal bonds or both. The least she is allowed to invest in corporate bonds is $6000 and she does not want to invest more than $22,000 in corporate bonds. She also does not want to invest more than $30,000 in municipal bonds. The interest on corporate bonds is 8% and on municipal bonds it is $7\frac{1}{2}\%$. This is simple interest for one year. How much should she invest in each type of bond to maximize her income? What is the maximum income?

Extension

Solve.

5. It takes a tailoring firm 2 hr of cutting and 4 hr of sewing to make a knit suit. To make a worsted suit it takes 4 hr of cutting and 2 hr of sewing. At most, 20 hr per day are available for cutting and, at most, 16 hr per day are available for sewing. The

profit on a knit suit is $34 and on a worsted suit is $31. How many of each kind of suit should be made to maximize profit? What is the maximum profit? Maximum $192, 2 knits; 4 worsteds

6. A nut company has 3000 lb of peanuts, 2040 lb of pecans, and 480 lb of cashew nuts. To make one batch of mix A it takes 12 lb of peanuts and 4 lb of cashews. To make one batch of mix B it takes 8 lb of peanuts and 8 lb of pecans. The profit is $10.00 per batch for mix A and $6.00 per batch of mix B. How many batches of each mix should be made to maximize profit? What is the maximum profit? 120 of A, 195 of B; $2370

Challenge

Solve.

7. An airline with two types of airplanes, P-1 and P-2, has contracted with a tour group to provide accommodations for a minimum of each of 2000 first-class, 1500 tourist, and 2400 economy-class passengers. Airplane P-1 costs $12,000 per mile to operate and can accommodate 40 first-class, 40 tourist, and 120 economy-class passengers, whereas airplane P-2 costs $10,000 per mile to operate and can accommodate 80 first-class, 30 tourist, and 40 economy-class passengers. How many of each type of airplane should be used to minimize the operating cost? 30 P-1 airplanes and 10 P-2 airplanes to minimize cost at $460,000

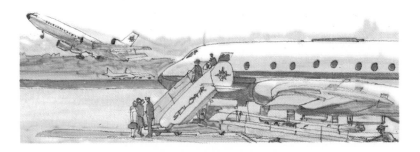

8. The recommended minimum daily allowance of protein for a 16-year old male is 56 g. For calcium it is 0.8 g. Every gram of ground beef contains 0.0001 g of calcium and 0.270 g of protein, and costs 0.28¢. Every gram of cheddar cheese contains 0.007g of calcium and 0.247 g of protein, and costs 0.64¢. To avoid gaining weight, one should eat no more than 2000 g of beef and 1100 g of cheddar cheese. Assuming only beef and cheddar cheese are eaten, how many grams of each should be eaten to minimize the cost of obtaining the recommended minimum daily allowance?

CHAPTER 4 Review

Review the material in the chapter. Then see how you have done by trying these review exercises. If you miss an exercise, restudy the indicated lesson.

4–1 Solve graphically.

1. $-2x + y = 1$
   $3x + y = 1$ (0, 1)

2. $x = y$
   $3x + y = 12$ (3, 3)

4–1 Solve using the substitution method.

3. $2x - y = -9$
   $3x - 8y = -7$
   (−5, −1)

4. $x + y = 6$
   $y = x + 2$ (2, 4)

5. $y = 7 - x$
   $2x - y = 8$ (5, 2)

4–1 Solve using the addition method.

6. $2x + 7y = 2$
   $3x + 5y = -8$ (−6, 2)

7. $5x + 3y = 17$
   $-5x + 3y = 3$ (1, 4)

8. $-3a + 2b = 0$
   $3a - 4b = -1$ $\left(\frac{1}{3}, \frac{1}{2}\right)$

4–2

9. On a recent trip, Ellie drove 273 km in the same length of time that Carol took to drive 270 km. Ellie's speed was 17 km/h greater than Carol's speed. Find the rate of each.   Ellie, 62 km/h; Carol, 45 km/h

4–3 Solve.

10. $2a - b + c = 7$
    $a + 2b + 2c = 3$
    $7a - 3b - 3c = 4$ (1, −2, 3)

11. $2x - y - 4z = 0$
    $x - y + 2z = 5$
    $3x + 2y + 2z = 3$ $(2, -2, \frac{1}{2})$

4–4

12. The sum of three numbers is 135. The third is ten greater than twice the first. The second is ten less than the third. Find the numbers.   25, 50, 60

4–5 Which system is inconsistent? Which is dependent?

13. $2x - y = 4$
    $2x - y = 6$
    Inconsistent

14. $x - 2y = 3$
    $4x - 8y = 12$
    Dependent

4–7 Evaluate.

15. $\begin{bmatrix} 2 & 3 \\ 7 & 8 \end{bmatrix}$ −5

16. $\begin{bmatrix} 2 & -1 & 1 \\ 1 & 2 & -1 \\ 3 & 4 & -3 \end{bmatrix}$ −6

4–7 Solve using Cramer's rule.

17. $5x - 2y = 19$
$7x + 3y = 15$ 3, –2

18. $2x - y + z = -1$
$x - 2y + 3z = 4$
$4x + y + 2z = 4$ (–1, 2, 3)

19. All points above line through (–2, 0) and (0, 2)
20. All points below and on line through (5, 0) and (0, –3)
21. All points above and on line through (0, 0) and (1, 2) and also below line through (0. 3) and (3, 0)
22. All points below and on line $y = 3$ and also to the left of and on line $x = -5$

4–8 Graph.

19. $y > x + 2$

20. $3x - 5y \leq 15$

21. $y \geq 2x$
$y < -x + 3$

22. $y \leq 3$
$x \geq -5$

CHAPTER 4 Test

Solve.

1. $x + y = 2$
$x - y = 4$

2. $x + y = 7$
$2x - y = 8$

3. $-2x + y = 4$ $\left(\frac{1}{2}, 5\right)$
$2x - 3y = -14$

4. The perimeter of a rectangular field is $606 \, m$. The length is 42 m more than twice the width. Find the dimensions.   width 87 m, length 216 m

5. $x + y - 3z = 8$ (2, 3, –1)
$2x - 3y + z = -6$
$3x + 4y - 2z = 20$

Evaluate.

6. $\begin{vmatrix} 3 & 1 \\ 2 & 5 \end{vmatrix}$ 13

7. $\begin{vmatrix} 3 & 4 & 2 \\ 5 & -2 & 0 \\ 4 & 3 & -3 \end{vmatrix}$ 124

Solve using Cramer's Rule.

8. $3x + 2y = 13$
$2x - 5y = 15$

9. $x + y - z = 6$ (3, 1, –2)
$2x - y + z = 3$
$x + 3y - 2z = 10$

1. (3, –1)
2. (5, 2)
8. (5, –1)
10. All points below line through (0, 3) and (3, 0)
11. All points below and on line through (0, 9) and (2, 6)
12. All points above line through (0, 0) and (1, 1) and also below and on line through (0, –2) and (–1, 0)
13. All points below and on line $y = 2$ and also to the right of and on line $x = -4$

Graph on a plane.

10. $y < -x + 3$

11. $3x + 2y \leq 18$

12. $y > x$
$y \leq -2x - 2$

13. $y \leq 2$
$x \geq -4$

Challenge

14. Determine a, b, and c if $(1, -1, 2)$ is a solution of the system.

$ax + bg + cz = -1$
$cx - ay + bz = 3$
$bx + cy - az = -2$ a = 2, b = 1, c = –1

CHAPTERS 1–4 Cumulative Review

1–2 Evaluate each expression for $x = -1$ and $y = 4$.

1. $-(2x - y - 6)$ ₁₂ **2.** $2|y - 8| - |x|$ ₇

1–5 Simplify.

3. $3x - 2(5y - 4x)$ **4.** $8y - [2y - (5y - 7)]$ ₁₁ᵧ ₊ ₇

1–7

5. $(2x^2y)(-5x^{-5}y^6)$ **6.** $\dfrac{-28x^{-3}y^2}{4x^5y^{-3}}$ **7.** $(8x^3)^{-2}$ $\frac{1}{64x^6}$

2–2 Solve.

8. $-7t + 23 = -33$ ₈ **9.** $\frac{1}{8}x + \frac{3}{2} = \frac{1}{3} - \frac{1}{6}x$ ₋₄ **10.** $(x - 7)(2x + 1) = 0$ $7, -\frac{1}{2}$

2–5 Solve.

11. $3x - 8 > 2x - 1$ **12.** $-\frac{2}{3}y \le 12$ **13.** $-3 + 7x < 2x + 9$ $x < \frac{12}{5}$

2–6

14. The sum of three consecutive odd integers is greater than 30. What are the least possible values for the integers? 9, 11, 13

2–7 Solve.

15. $-3 < 4x + 1 < 6$ **16.** $2x + 1 < -1$ or $x - 3 > 4$ $x < -1$ or $x > 7$

2–8

17. $|x| < \frac{1}{2}$ **18.** $|14 - y| < 10$ $-6 < y < 14$

3–2 Graph.

19. $-x + 2y = 1$ **20.** $2x - y = -4$ Line through (0, 4) and (−2, 0)

3–4 Graph using intercepts.

21. $5x - 3y = 15$ **22.** $-2x + 7y = 14$ Line through (0, 2) and (−7, 0)

3–6 Find an equation of each line. Write in standard form.

23. Line with slope $-\frac{1}{2}$ and containing $(-8, 0)$ $y = -\frac{1}{2}x - 4$
24. Line containing $(-2, -1)$ and $(-3, 7)$ $y = -8x - 17$

4–1 Solve.

25. $2x - y = 8$ (5, 2) **26.** $x - 3y = 2$ (−7, −3)
    $-x + 3y = 1$ $2x + 3y = -23$

4–3 Solve.

27. $2x - y - t = -11$ **28.** $3x + y - 2z = 1$
    $x + 2y - 3z = -13$ (−1, 3, 6) $x - y - z = -6$ (−2, 5, −1)
    $-x - y + 4z = 22$ $-x + y - 3z = 10$

4–8 Graph.

29. $-3x + y > 1$ **30.** $y > x - 1$
                $2x + y < 5$

Ready for Polynomials and Factoring?

1–5

1. Evaluate $xy - xz$ when $x = -2$, $y = 4$, $z = 3$. −2

1–5 Factor.

2. $5x + 5y$ **3.** $10x + 15y = 5$ $5(2x + 3y - 1)$

2. $5(x + y)$
4. $3y - 6$
5. $4x + 48$
10. $x - 4$
16. $-8y^3$

1–5 Multiply.

4. $3(y - 2)$ **5.** $4(x + 12)$ **6.** $c(t + s - f)$ $ct + cs - cf$

1–5 Collect like terms.

7. $3y + 2y$ 5y **8.** $a + 4a$ 5a **9.** $b - 4b + 3b$ 0

1–5 Remove parentheses and simplify.

10. $3x - (2x + 4)$ **11.** $7y - 2 - (8y - 4)$ $-y + 2$

1–7 Multiply and simplify.

12. $3^{-2} \cdot 3^5$ 3³ **13.** $(4a^7b^{-2})(2a^2b^3)$ 8a⁹b **14.** $(8x^{-3}y^4)(3x^{-9}y^{-2})$ 24x⁻¹²y²

1–7 Simplify.

15. $(3a)^2$ 9a² **16.** $(-2y)^3$ **17.** $(2^{-3})^4$ 2⁻¹² **18.** $(x^{-2})^{-4}$ x⁸

2–2 Solve.

19. $(x - 3)(x + 5) = 0$ **20.** $3x(2x + 10) = 0$ 0, −5
3, −5

5

CHAPTER FIVE

Polynomials and Factoring

5–1 Addition and Subtraction of Polynomials

Polynomials

Expressions like these are called polynomials in one variable.

$$5x^2, \quad 8a, \quad 2, \quad 2x + 3, \quad -7x + 5, \quad 2y^2 + 5y - 3,$$
$$5a^4 - 3a^2 + \frac{1}{4}a - 8, \quad b^6 + 3b^5 - 8b + 7b^4 + \frac{1}{2}$$

Expressions like these are called polynomials in several variables.

$$5x - xy^2 + 7y + 2, \quad 9xy^2z - 4x^3z + (-14x^4y^2) + 9, \; 15x^3y^2$$

The polynomial $5x^3y - 7xy^2 + 2$ has three terms.

$$5x^3, \; -7xy^2, \text{ and } 2$$

The coefficients of the terms are 5, -7, and 2.

The degree of a term is the sum of the exponents of the variables. The degree of a polynomial is the same as its term of highest degree. The polynomial 0 has no degree.

EXAMPLE 1

Determine the degree of each term and the degree of the polynomial: $6x^2 + 8x^2y^3 - 17xy - 24xy^2z^4 + 2y + 3$.

Term	$6x^2$	$8x^2y^3$	$-17xy$	$-24xy^2z^4$	$2y$	3
Degree	2	5	2	7	1	0

The degree of the polynomial is 7.

TRY THIS

1. Determine the degree of each term and the degree of the polynomial: $2y + 4 - 5x + 7x^2y^3z^2 + 5xy^2$. 1, 0, 1, 7, 3; 7

A polynomial with a single term is called a monomial. A polynomial of two terms is a binomial, and one with three terms is a trinomial. We usually arrange polynomials in one variable so that the exponents decrease (descending order) or so that they increase (ascending order).

For polynomials in several variables we choose one of the variables and arrange the terms in ascending or descending order with respect to it.

EXAMPLE 2

Arrange $y^4 + 2 - 5x^3 + 3x^3y + 7xy$ in descending powers of x.

$$3x^3y - 5x^3 + 7xy + y^4 + 2$$

TRY THIS

2. Arrange $-8xy^2 + 3xy + 7xy^4 - 2xy^3$ in descending powers of y. $\quad$ $7xy^4 - 2xy^3 - 8xy^2 + 3xy$

3. Arrange $4x^2yz + 5xy^2 + 5x^3yz^2 - 4$ in ascending powers of x. $\quad$ $-4 + 5xy^2 + 4x^2yz + 5x^3yz^2$

We now give a precise definition of polynomials in one variable.

DEFINITION

A *polynomial in x* is any expression equivalent to

$$a_nx^n + a_{n-1}x^{n-1} + \cdots + a_1x + a_0,$$

where n is a nonnegative integer and the coefficients $a_0, \ldots, a_n$ are real numbers.

Addition

If two terms of a polynomial have the same letters raised to the same powers, the terms are called similar, or like terms. Similar terms can be "combined" or "collected" using the distributive laws.

EXAMPLES

Combine similar terms.

3. $3x^2 - 4y + 2x^2 = 3x^2 + 2x^2 - 4y \quad$ Rearranging using the commutative and associative laws
$= (3 + 2)x^2 - 4y \quad$ Using a distributive law
$= 5x^2 - 4y$

4. $4x^3 + 5x - 4x^2 - 2x^3 + 5x^2 = 2x^3 + x^2 + 5x$

5. $3x^2y + 5xy^2 - 3x^2y - xy^2 = 4xy^2$

TRY THIS Combine similar terms.

4. $5x^2 + 3x^4 - 2x^2 - x^4$ $3x^2 + 2x^4$

5. $5x^3y^2 - 2x^2y^3 + 4x^3y^2$ $9x^3y^2 - 2x^2y^3$

6. $3xy^2 - 4x^2y + 4xy^2 + 2x^2y$ $7xy^2 - 2x^2y$

The sum of two polynomials can be found by writing a plus sign between them and then combining similar terms. Ordinarily this can be done mentally.

EXAMPLE 6

Add $-3x^3 + 2x - 4$ and $4x^3 + 3x^2 + 2$.

$$(-3x^3 + 2x - 4) + (4x^3 + 3x^2 + 2) = x^3 + 3x^2 + 2x - 2$$

The use of columns is often helpful. To do this we write the polynomials one under the other, writing like terms under one another and leaving spaces for missing terms. Let us do the addition in Example 6 using columns.

$$
\begin{array}{r}
-3x^3 \qquad + 2x - 4 \\
4x^3 + 3x^2 \qquad + 2 \\
\hline
x^3 + 3x^2 + 2x - 2
\end{array}
$$

EXAMPLE 7

Add $4ax^2 + 4bx - 5$ and $3ax^2 + 5bx + 8$.

$$
\begin{array}{r}
4ax^2 + 4bx - 5 \\
3ax^2 + 5bx + 8 \\
\hline
7ax^2 + 9bx + 3
\end{array}
$$

Although the use of columns is helpful for complicated examples, you should attempt to write only the answer when you can.

EXAMPLE 8

Add.

$$(13x^3y + 3x^2y - 5y) + (x^3y + 4x^2y - 3xy + 3y)$$
$$= 14x^3y + 7x^2y - 3xy - 2y$$

TRY THIS Add.

7. $3x^3 + 4x^2 - 7x - 2$ and $-7x^3 - 2x^2 + 3x + \frac{1}{2}$ $-4x^3 + 2x^2 - 4x - \frac{3}{2}$

8. $5p^2q^4 - 2p^2q^2 - 3q$ and $-6pq^2 + 3p^2q^2 + 5$ $5p^2q^4 + p^2q^2 - 6pq^2 - 3q + 5$

Additive Inverses

The additive inverse of a polynomial can be found as described in the following theorem.

THEOREM 5–1

The additive inverse of a polynomial can be found by replacing every term by its additive inverse.

EXAMPLE 9

The additive inverse of $7xy^2 - 6xy - 4y + 3$ can be symbolized as $-(7xy^2 - 6xy - 4y + 3)$.

$$-(7xy^2 - 6xy - 4y + 3) = -7xy^2 + 6xy + 4y - 3$$

The preceding example may bring to mind a rule that says: To remove parentheses preceded by an additive inverse sign, change the sign of every term inside the parentheses.

TRY THIS

9. Find the additive inverse. $5x^2t^2 - 4xy^2t - 3xt + 6x - 5$ $\quad -5x^2t^2 + 4xy^2t + 3xt - 6x + 5$

10. Remove the parentheses. $-(-3x^2y + 5xy - 7x + 4y + 2)$ $\quad 3x^2y - 5xy + 7x - 4y - 2$

Subtraction

By Theorem 1–1 we can subtract by adding an inverse. Thus to subtract one polynomial from another, we add its additive inverse. We change the sign of each term of the polynomial to be subtracted and then add. In simple cases this can be done mentally.

EXAMPLE 10

Subtract.

$$
\begin{aligned}
(-9x^5 - x^3 + 2x^2 + 4) &- (2x^5 - x^4 + 4x^3 - 3x^2) \\
&= (-9x^5 - x^3 + 2x^2 + 4) + [-(2x^5 - x^4 + 4x^3 - 3x^2)] \\
&= (-9x^5 - x^3 + 2x^2 + 4) + (-2x^5 + x^4 - 4x^3 + 3x^2) \\
&= -11x^5 + x^4 - 5x^3 + 5x^2 + 4
\end{aligned}
$$

On occasion, it may be helpful to write polynomials to be subtracted with similar terms in columns.

EXAMPLE 11

Subtract the second polynomial from the first.

$$4x^2y - 6x^3y^2 \qquad\qquad + x^2y^2 - 5y$$
$$4x^2y + \; x^3y^2 + 3x^2y^3 \qquad\qquad + \; 6y \qquad \text{Mentally, change signs and add.}$$
$$\overline{\qquad - 7x^3y^2 - 3x^2y^3 + x^2y^2 - 11y \qquad}$$

TRY THIS

11. Subtract.
$$(5xy^4 - 7xy^2 + 4x^2 - 3) - (-3xy^4 + 2xy^2 - 2y + 4) \quad {\scriptstyle 8xy^4 \,-\, 9xy^2 \,+\, 4x^2 \,+\, 2y \,-\, 7}$$

12. Subtract.
$$5x^2y - 7x^3y^2 \qquad\qquad -x^2y^2 + 4y$$
$$-2x^2y + 2x^3y^2 - 5x^2y^3 \qquad\qquad - \; 5y \quad {\scriptstyle 7x^2y \,-\, 9x^3y^2 \,+\, 5x^2y^3 \,-\, x^2y^2 \,+\, 9y}$$

5–1

Exercises

Determine the degree of each term and the degree of the polynomial.

1. $-11x^4 - x^3 + x^2 + 3x - 9$ {\scriptstyle 4, 3, 2, 1, 0; 4}

2. $t^3 - 3t^2 + t + 1$ {\scriptstyle 3, 2, 1, 0; 3}

3. $y^3 + 2y^6 + x^2y^4 - 8$ {\scriptstyle 3, 6, 6, 0; 6}

4. $u^2 + 3v^5 - u^3v^4 - 7$ {\scriptstyle 2, 5, 7, 0; 7}

5. $a^5 + 4a^2b^4 + 6ab + 4a - 3$ {\scriptstyle 5, 6, 2, 1, 0; 6}

6. $8p^6 + 2p^4t^4 - 7p^3t + 5p^2 - 14$
{\scriptstyle 6, 8, 4, 2, 0; 8}

Add.

7. $5x^2y - 2xy^2 + 3xy - 5$ and
$-2x^2y - 3xy^2 + 4xy + 7$

8. $6x^2y - 3xy^2 + 5xy - 3$ and
$-4x^2y - 4xy^2 + 3xy + 8$

9. $2x + 3y + z - 7$ and
$4x - 2y - z + 8$ and $-3x + y - 2z - 4$

10. $2x^2 + 12xy - 11$ and
$6x^2 - 2x + 4$ and $-x^2 - y - 2$

11. $1.23y^4 - 2.25y^3 - 3.4y - 5.2$ and
$8.23y^4 + 4.75y^3 - 8.4y + 2.1$

12. $\frac{1}{3}x^5 - \frac{1}{5}x^3 - \frac{1}{2}x^2 - 8$ and
$\frac{1}{6}x^5 - \frac{1}{10}x^3 + \frac{1}{4}x^2 + \frac{2}{3}x - 11$

Rename each additive inverse without parentheses.

13. $-(5x^3 - 7x^2 + 3x - 6)$ {\scriptstyle -5x^3 + 7x^2 - 3x + 6}

14. $-(-4y^4 + 7y^2 - 2y - 1)$
{\scriptstyle 4y^4 - 7y^2 + 2y + 1}

Subtract.

15. $(3x^2 - 2x - x^3 + 2)$
$- (5x^2 - 8x - x^3 + 4)$ {\scriptstyle -2x^2 + 6x - 2}

16. $(5x^2 + 4xy - 3y^2 + 2)$ {\scriptstyle -4x^2 + 8xy - 5y^2 + 3}
$- (9x^2 - 4xy + 2y^2 - 1)$

17. $(5a^2 + 4ab - 3b^2) - (9a^2 - 4ab + 2b^2)$
{\scriptstyle -4a^2 + 8ab - 5b^2}

18. $8x^4 - (2x^4 + 8x^2 - 9x + 4)$
{\scriptstyle 6x^4 - 8x^2 + 9x - 4}

19. $(0.09y^4 - 0.052y^3 + 0.93) - (0.03y^4 - 0.084y^3 + 0.94y^2)$ $\quad$ 0.06y⁴ + 0.032y³ − 0.94y² + 0.93

20. $\left(\frac{5}{8}x^4 - \frac{1}{4}x^2 - \frac{1}{2}\right) - \left(-\frac{3}{8}x^4 + \frac{3}{4}x^2 + \frac{1}{2}\right)$ $\quad$ x⁴ − x² − 1

Use a calculator to simplify.

21. $(0.565p^2q - 2.167pq^2 + 16.02pq - 17.1)$
    $+ (-1.612p^2q - 0.312pq^2 - 7.141pq - 87.044)$ $\quad$ −1.047p²q − 2.479pq² + 8.879pq − 104.144

22. $(8{,}479{,}768y^4 - 56{,}009{,}728y^2 - 19{,}429{,}009y)$
    $- (12{,}049{,}778y^4 - 19{,}118{,}979y^2 + 26{,}047{,}972y)$ $\quad$ −3,570,010y⁴ − 36,890,749y² − 45,476,981y

Extension

A polynomial function is a function described by a polynomial in one variable.

23. If there are n teams in a league and each team plays each other once in a season, the total number of games played can be found by a polynomial function $f(n) = \frac{1}{2}(n^2 - n)$. Find the number of games played when there are 8 teams, 20 teams. $\quad$ 28; 190

24. The cost, in cents per kilometer, of operating an automobile at speed s is approximated by the polynomial function $C(s) = 0.002s^2 - 0.21s + 15$. How much does it cost to operate at 50 km/h? 80 km/h? $\quad$ 9.5¢ per km; 11¢ per km

For the polynomial functions $P(x)$ and $Q(x)$, find each of the following.

$$P(x) = 13x^5 - 22x^4 - 36x^3 + 40x^2 - 16x + 75$$
$$Q(x) = 42x^5 - 37x^4 + 50x^3 - 28x^2 + 34x + 100$$

25. $P(x) + Q(x)$ $\qquad$ 26. $P(x) - Q(x)$ $\qquad$ 27. $Q(x) - P(x)$ $\qquad$ 28. $4[P(x)] + 3[Q(x)]$

Challenge

29. Express the area of this box as a polynomial. The box is rectangular with an open top, and dimensions as shown. $\quad$ x² + 4hx

30. A box is to be made from a piece of cardboard 12 inches square. Corners are cut out and the sides are folded up. Express the volume of the box as a polynomial. $\quad$ 6x² − ½x³

Add. Assume variables in the exponents represent positive integers.

31. $(2x^{2a} + 4x^a + 3) + (6x^{2a} + 3x^a + 4)$ $\quad$ 8x²ᵃ + 7xᵃ + 7

32. $(47x^{4a} + 3x^{3a} + 22x^{2a} + x^a + 1) + (37x^{3a} + 8x^{2a} + 3)$
    $\quad$ 47x⁴ᵃ + 40x³ᵃ + 30x²ᵃ + xᵃ + 4

Subtract. Assume variables in the exponents represent positive integers.

33. $(3x^{6a} - 5x^{5a} + 4x^{3a} + 8) - (2x^{6a} + 4x^{4a} + 3x^{3a} + 2x^{2a})$ $\quad$ x⁶ᵃ − 5x⁵ᵃ − 4x⁴ᵃ + x³ᵃ − 2x²ᵃ + 8

34. $(2x^{5b} + 4x^{4b} + 3x^{3b} + 8) - (x^{5b} + 2x^{3b} + 6x^{2b} + 9x^b + 8)$ $\quad$ x⁵ᵇ + 4x⁴ᵇ + x³ᵇ − 6x²ᵇ − 9xᵇ

5–2 Multiplication of Polynomials

Multiplication of Any Two Polynomials

Multiplication of polynomials is based on the distributive laws. To multiply two polynomials, we multiply each term of one by every term of the other and then add the results.

EXAMPLE 1
Multiply $4x^4y - 7x^2y + 3y$ by $2y - 3x^2y$.

$$
\begin{array}{r}
4x^4y - 7x^2y + 3y \\
2y - 3x^2y \\
\hline
8x^4y^2 - 14x^2y^2 + 6y^2 \\
-12x^6y^2 + 21x^4y^2 - 9x^2y^2 \\
\hline
-12x^6y^2 + 29x^4y^2 - 23x^2y^2 + 6y^2 \\
\end{array}
$$

Multiplying by $2y$
Multiplying by $-3x^2y$
Adding

TRY THIS Multiply.

1. $3x^2y - 2xy + 3y$ and $xy + 2y$ $\quad 3x^3y^2 + 4x^2y^2 - xy^2 + 6y^2$
2. $p^2q + 2pq + 2q$ and $2p^2q - pq + q$ $\quad 2p^4q^2 + 3p^3q^2 + 3p^2q^2 + 2q^2$

Products of Two Binomials

We can find a product of two binomials mentally.

> To multiply any two polynomials we multiply each term of one by every term of the other. For two binomials we can think of it this way: Multiply the first terms, then the outside terms, then the inside terms, then the last terms. We abbreviate this FOIL.
>
> $$(A + B)(C + D) = \underset{\text{F}}{AC} + \underset{\text{O}}{AD} + \underset{\text{I}}{BC} + \underset{\text{L}}{BD}$$

EXAMPLES
Multiply.

2. $(3xy + 2x)(x^2 + 2xy^2) = \underset{\text{F}}{3x^3y} + \underset{\text{O}}{6x^2y^3} + \underset{\text{I}}{2x^3} + \underset{\text{L}}{4x^2y^2}$

3. $(2x - 3)(y + 2) = 2xy + 4x - 3y - 6$

4. $(2x + 3y)(x - 4y) = 2x^2 - 5xy - 12y^2$

TRY THIS Multiply.

3. $(2xy + 3x)(x^2 - 2)$ 4. $(3x - 2y)(5x + 3y)$ 5. $(2x + 20)(3y - 20)$

Squares of Binomials

Note the following.

$$(A + B)^2 = (A + B)(A + B)$$
$$= A^2 + AB + AB + B^2$$
$$= A^2 + 2AB + B^2$$

$$(A + B)^2 = A^2 + 2AB + B^2$$
$$(A - B)^2 = A^2 - 2AB + B^2$$

The square of a binomial is the square of the first expression, plus or minus twice the product of the expressions, plus the square of the second expression.

EXAMPLES
Multiply.

$$(A - B)^2 = A^2 - 2\ A\ B + B^2$$
$$\downarrow \quad \downarrow \quad\quad \downarrow \quad \downarrow\ \downarrow\ \downarrow \quad\quad \downarrow$$

5. $(y - 5)^2 = y^2 - 2\ (5)\ (y) + 5^2$

6. $(2x + 3y)^2 = (2x)^2 + 2(2x)(3y) + (3y)^2$
$$= 4x^2 + 12xy + 9y^2$$

7. $(3x^2 - 5xy^2)^2 = (3x^2)^2 - 2(3x^2)(5xy^2) + (5xy^2)^2$
$$= 9x^4 - 30x^3y^2 + 25x^2y^4$$

TRY THIS Multiply.

6. $(4x - 5y)^2$ 7. $(2y^2 + 6x^2y)^2$

Products of Sums and Differences

Note the following.

$$\begin{array}{cccc} & \text{F} & \text{O} & \text{I} & \text{L} \end{array}$$
$$(A + B)(A - B) = A^2 - AB + AB - B^2$$
$$= A^2 - B^2$$

$$(A + B)(A - B) = A^2 - B^2$$

The product of the sum and difference of two expressions is the square of the first expression minus the square of the second.

EXAMPLES

Multiply.

$$(A + B)(A - B) = A^2 - B^2$$

8. $(y + 5)(y - 5) = y^2 - 5^2$
$$= y^2 - 25$$

9. $(2xy^2 + 3x)(2xy^2 - 3x) = (2xy^2)^2 - (3x)^2$
$$= 4x^2y^4 - 9x^2$$

10. $(5y + 4 + 3x)(5y + 4 - 3x) = (5y + 4)^2 - (3x)^2$
$$= 25y^2 + 40y + 16 - 9x^2$$

11. $(3xy^2 + 4y)(-3xy^2 + 4y) = -(3xy^2)^2 + (4y)^2$
$$= 16y^2 - 9x^2y^4$$

TRY THIS Multiply.

8. $(4x + 7)(4x - 7)$ $\quad 16x^2 - 49$

9. $(5x^2y + 2y)(5x^2y - 2y)$ $\quad 25x^4y^2 - 4y^2$

10. $(2x + 3 + 5y)(2x + 3 - 5y)$ $\quad 4x^2 + 12x + 9 - 25y^2$

11. $(-2x^3y^2 + 5t)(2x^3y^2 + 5t)$ $\quad 25t^2 - 4x^6y^4$

Cubing a Binomial

The following multiplication gives another result to be remembered.

$$
\begin{aligned}
(A + B)^3 &= (A + B)(A + B)^2 \\
&= (A + B)(A^2 + 2AB + B^2) \\
&= (A + B)A^2 + (A + B)2AB + (A + B)B^2 \\
&= A^3 + A^2B + 2A^2B + 2AB^2 + AB^2 + B^3 \\
&= A^3 + 3A^2B + 3AB^2 + B^3
\end{aligned}
$$

The result to be remembered is as follows.

$$(A + B)^3 = A^3 + 3A^2B + 3AB^2 + B^3$$

EXAMPLES

Multiply.

12. $(x + 2)^3 = x^3 + 3x^2(2) + 3x(2)^2 + 2^3$
$= x^3 + 6x^2 + 12x + 8$

13. $(x - 2)^3 = [x + (-2)]^3$
$= x^3 + 3x^2(-2) + 3x(-2)^2 + (-2)^3$
$= x^3 - 6x^2 + 12x - 8$

14. $(5m^2 - 4n^3)^3 = (5m^2)^3 + 3(5m^2)^2(-4n^3) + 3(5m^2)(-4n^3)^2 + (-4n^3)^3$
$= 125m^6 - 300m^4n^3 + 240m^2n^6 - 64n^9$

Note in Examples 13 and 14 that a separate formula for $(A - B)^3$ need not be memorized. We can think of $(A - B)^3$ as $[A + (-B)]^3$.

TRY THIS Multiply.

12. $x^3 + 3x^2 + 3x + 1$ 14. $t^6 - 9t^4b + 27t^2b^2 - 27b^3$
13. $x^3 - 3x^2 + 3x - 1$ 15. $8a^9 - 60a^6b^2 + 150a^3b^4 - 125b^6$

12. $(x + 1)^3$ 13. $(x - 1)^3$ 14. $(t^2 - 3b)^3$ 15. $(2a^3 - 5b^2)^3$

In the following exercises you should do mentally as much of the calculating as you can. If possible, write only the answer. Work for speed with accuracy.

5–2

Exercises

Multiply.

1. $6x^3 + 4x^2 + 32x - 64$ 3. $4a^3b^2 - 10a^2b^2 + 3ab^3 + 4ab^2 - 6b^3 + 4a^2b - 2ab + 3b^2$
2. $6y^3 + 3y^2 + 9y + 27$ 4. $2x^4 - x^2y^2 - 4x^3y - 2y^4 + 3xy^3$

1. $2x^2 + 4x + 16$ and $3x - 4$ 2. $3y^2 - 3y + 9$ and $2y + 3$

3. $4a^2b - 2ab + 3b^2$ and $ab - 2b + 1$ 4. $2x^2 + y^2 - 2xy$ and $x^2 - 2y^2 - xy$

5. $(a - b)(a^2 + ab + b^2)$ $a^3 - b^3$ 6. $(t + 1)(t^2 - t + 1)$ $t^3 + 1$

7. $(2x + 3y)(2x + y)$ $4x^2 + 8xy + 3y^2$ 8. $(2a - 3b)(2a - b)$ $4a^2 - 8ab + 3b^2$

9. $\left(4x^2 - \frac{1}{2}y\right)\left(3x + \frac{1}{4}y\right)$ $12x^3 + x^2y - \frac{3}{2}xy^2 - \frac{1}{8}y^2$ 10. $\left(2y^3 + \frac{1}{5}x\right)\left(3y - \frac{1}{4}x\right)$ $6y^4 - \frac{1}{2}xy^3 + \frac{3}{5}xy - \frac{1}{20}x^2$

11. $(2x^2 - y^2)(2x - 2y)$ $4x^3 - 4x^2y - 2xy^2 + 2y^3$ 12. $(3y^2 - 2)(3y - x)$ $9y^3 - 3y^2x - 6y + 2x$

13. $(2x + 3y)^2$ $4x^2 + 12xy + 9y^2$ 14. $(5x + 2y)^2$ $25x^2 + 20xy + 4y^2$

15. $(2x^2 - 3y)^2$ $4x^4 - 12x^2y + 9y^2$ 16. $(4x^2 - 5y)^2$ $16x^4 - 40x^2y + 25y^2$

17. $(2x^3 + 3y^2)^2$ $4x^6 + 12x^3y^2 + 9y^4$ 18. $(5x^3 + 2y^2)^2$ $25x^6 + 20x^3y^2 + 4y^4$

19. $(3x - 2y)(3x + 2y)$ $9x^2 - 4y^2$ 20. $(3x + 5y)(3x - 5y)$ $9x^2 - 25y^2$

21. $(x^2 + yz)(x^2 - yz)$

22. $(2x^2 + 5xy)(2x^2 - 5xy)$

23. $(3x^2 - 2)(3x^2 + 2)$

24. $(5x^2 - 3)(5x^2 + 3)$

25. $(y + 5)^3$

26. $(t - 7)^3$

27. $(m^2 - 2n)^3$

28. $(3t^2 + 4)^3$

Use a calculator to multiply.

29. $(0.051x + 0.04y)^2$

30. $(1.032x - 2.512y)^2$

31. $(37.86x + 1.42)(65.03x - 27.4)$

32. $(3.601x - 17.5)(47.105x + 31.23)$

Extension

Multiply.

33. $\left(\frac{1}{2}x^2 - \frac{3}{5}y\right)^2$

34. $\left(\frac{1}{4}x^2 - \frac{2}{3}y\right)^2$

35. $(0.5x + 0.7y^2)^2$

36. $(0.3x + 0.8y^2)^2$

37. $(2x + 3y + 4)(2x + 3y - 4)$

38. $(x^2 + 3y + y^2)(x^2 + 3y - y^2)$

39. $(x + 1)(x - 1)(x^2 + 1)$

40. $(y - 2)(y + 2)(y^2 + 4)$

41. $(2x + y)(2x - y)(4x^2 + y^2)$

42. $(5x + y)(5x - y)(25x^2 + y^2)$

Challenge

Multiply. Assume that variables in exponents represent positive integers.

43. $[(2x - 1)^2 - 1]^2$

44. $[(a + b)(a - b)][5 - (a + b)][5 + (a + b)]$

45. $(x - 1)(x^2 + x + 1)(x^3 + 1)$

46. $[2(y - 3) - 6(x + 4)][5(y - 3) - 4(x + 4)]$

47. $y^3z^n(y^{3n}z^3 - 4yz^{2n})$

Let $P(x) = x^2$, $Q(x) = x^3$, $H(x) = x + 2$, and $J(x) = x - 1$.

Find each of the following composition functions.

48. $P(H(x))$ 49. $H(P(x))$ 50. $Q(Q(x))$ 51. $Q(J(x))$

52. The amount to which $1000 will grow in b years, when interest is compunded annually, is given by the polynomial function A for which

$$A(r) = \$1000(1 + r)^b,$$

where r is the interest rate.

a. Find the amount to which $1000 will grow in 2 years at 17%.

b. Find the amount to which $1000 will grow in 3 years at 11%.

c. Find the amount to which $1000 will grow in 4 years at 8%.

d. Find expanded forms of $A(r)$ for $b = 2, 3,$ and 4 years.

5-3 Factoring

Terms with Common Factors

Factoring is the reverse of multiplication. To factor an expression means to write it as as a product. When factoring polynomials first look for common factors.

EXAMPLE 1

Factor out a common factor.

$$4y^2 - 8 = 4 \cdot y^2 - 4 \cdot 2 \quad \text{4 is a common factor}$$
$$= 4(y^2 - 2)$$

In some cases there is more than one common factor. In the following expression, 5 is a common factor, and x^3 is also a common factor. You should try to write the answer directly.

EXAMPLES

Factor out a common factor.

2. $5x^4 - 20x^3 = 5x^3(x - 4)$

3. $12x^2y - 20x^3y = 4x^2y(3 - 5x)$

4. $10p^6q^2 - 4p^5q^3 + 2p^4q^4 = 2p^4q^2(5p^2 - 2pq + q^2)$

TRY THIS Factor out a common factor.

1. $3x^2 - 6x$ **2.** $P + Prt$

3. $9y^4 - 15y^3 + 3y^2$ **4.** $6x^2y - 21x^3y^2 + 3x^2y^3$

1. $3x(x - 2)$
2. $P(1 + rt)$
3. $3y^2(3y^2 - 5y + 1)$
4. $3x^2y(2 - 7xy + y^2)$

Differences of Squares

To factor a difference of squares, we use the result established in the last section, in reverse.

$$A^2 - B^2 = (A + B)(A - B)$$

To factor the difference of two squares, write the square root of the first expression *plus* the square root of the second, times the square root of the first *minus* the square root of the second.

EXAMPLE 5

Factor $x^2 - 9$.

$$x^2 - 9 = x^2 - 3^2 = (x + 3)(x - 3)$$

EXAMPLE 6

Factor $25y^6 - 49x^2$.

$$A^2 - B^2 = (A + B)(A - B)$$
$$25y^6 - 49x^2 = (5^3 + 7x)(5y^3 - 7x)$$

TRY THIS Factor.

5. $y^2 - 4$ 6. $49x^4 - 25y^{10}$ 7. $36x^4 - 16y^6$

5. $(y + 2)(y - 2)$
6. $(7x^2 + 5y^5)(7x^2 - 5y^5)$
7. $(6x^2 + 4y^3)(6x^2 - 4y^3)$

Factoring Squares of Binomials

Some trinomials are squares of binomials. Here are two examples.

$$x^2 + 6x + 9 = (x + 3)^2$$
$$x^2 - 22x + 121 = (x - 11)^2$$

Trinomials like this are sometimes called trinomial squares. They have the form $A^2 + 2AB + B^2$ or $A^2 - 2AB + B^2$. We must first be able to recognize when a trinomial is a square of a binomial.

For a trinomial to be square, three conditions must be true.

1. Two of the terms must be squares (A^2 and B^2).
2. There must be no minus sign before A^2 or B^2.
3. If we multiply A and B (the square roots of these expressions) and double the result, we get the remaining term, $2 \cdot A \cdot B$, or its additive inverse, $-2 \cdot A \cdot B$.

EXAMPLE 7

Is $x^2 + 10x + 25$ the square of a binomial?

1. x^2 and 25 are squares.
2. There is no minus sign before x^2 or 25.
3. If we multiply the square roots, x and 5, and then double this quantity, we get the remaining term: $2 \cdot 5 \cdot x$ or $10x$.

Thus $x^2 + 10x + 25$ is the square of a binomial.

EXAMPLE 8

Is $x^2 + 8x + 13$ the square of a binomial?
The answer is no, since 13 is not a square.

TRY THIS Which of the following are trinomial squares?

8. $x^2 + 6x + 9$ Yes

9. $x^2 - 8x + 16$ Yes

10. $x^2 + 6x + 11$ No

11. $4x^2 - 20x + 25$ Yes

12. $16x^2 - 20x + 25$ No

13. $5x^2 + 14x + 16$ No

14. $x^2 + 8x - 16$ No

15. $x^2 - 8x - 16$ No

To factor squares of binomials we use the following equations.

$$A^2 + 2 \cdot A \cdot B + B^2 = (A + B)^2$$
$$A^2 - 2 \cdot A \cdot B + B^2 = (A - B)^2$$

EXAMPLES

Factor.

9. $x^2 - 10x + 25 = (x - 5)^2$

10. $16y^2 + 49 + 56y = 16y^2 + 56y + 49$ Rearranging terms
$$= (4y + 7)^2$$

11. $-20xy + 4y^2 + 25x^2 = 4y^2 - 20xy + 25x^2$ Rearranging terms
$$= (2y - 5x)^2$$

TRY THIS Factor.

16. $x^2 + 14x + 49$ $(x + 7)^2$

17. $9y^2 + 25 - 30y$ $(3y - 5)^2$

18. $72xy + 16x^2 + 81y^2$ $(9y + 4x)^2$

EXAMPLES

Factor.

12. $25x^4 + 70x^2y^3 + 49y^6 = (5x^2 + 7y^3)^2$

13. $-4y^2 - 144y^8 + 48y^5 = -4y^2(1 - 12y^3 + 36y^6)$ Removing a common factor first
$$= -4y^2(1 - 6y^3)^2$$

TRY THIS Factor.

19. $16x^4 - 40x^2y^3 + 25y^6$ $(4x^2 - 5y^3)^2$

20. $24ab - 8a^2 - 18b^2$ $-2(2a - 3b)^2$

21. $-12x^4y^2 + 60x^2y^5 - 75y^8$ $-3y^2(2x^2 - 5y^3)^2$

5–3

Exercises

Factor.

1. $y^2 - 5y$
2. $x^2 + 9x$
3. $4a^2 + 2a$
4. $6y^2 + 3y$
5. $y^3 + 9y^2$
6. $x^3 + 8x^2$
7. $3y^2 - 3y - 9$
8. $5x^2 - 5x + 15$
9. $6x^2 - 3x^4$
10. $8y^2 + 4y^4$
11. $4ab - 6ac + 12ad$
12. $8xy + 10xz - 14xw$
13. $4x^2y - 12xy^2$
14. $5x^2y^3 + 15x^3y^2$
15. $x^6 + x^5 - x^3 + x^2$
16. $y^4 - y^3 + y^2 + y$
17. $24x^3 - 36x^2 + 72x$
18. $10a^4 + 15a^2 - 25a - 30$

Factor. Remember to look first for a common factor.

19. $x^2 - 16$
20. $y^2 - 9$
21. $9x^2 - 25$
22. $4a^2 - 49$
23. $4x^2 - 25$
24. $100y^2 - 81$
25. $6x^2 - 6y^2$
26. $8x^2 - 8y^2$
27. $3x^8 - 3y^8$
28. $5x^4 - 5y^4$
29. $4xy^4 - 4xz^4$
30. $9a^4 - a^2b^2$

Factor. Remember to look first for a common factor.

31. $y^2 - 6y + 9$
32. $x^2 - 8x + 16$
33. $x^2 + 14x + 49$
34. $x^2 + 16x + 64$
35. $x^2 + 1 + 2x$
36. $x^2 + 1 - 2x$
37. $a^2 + 4a + 4$
38. $a^2 - 4a + 4$
39. $y^2 + 36 - 12y$
40. $y^2 + 36 + 12y$
41. $-18y^2 + y^3 + 81y$
42. $24a^2 + a^3 + 144a$
43. $12a^2 + 36a + 27$
44. $20y^2 + 100y + 125$
45. $2x^2 - 40x + 200$
46. $32x^2 + 48x + 18$
47. $1 - 8d + 16d^2$
48. $64 + 25y^2 - 80y$

Extension

Factor.

49. $\frac{4}{7}x^6 - \frac{6}{7}x^4 + \frac{1}{7}x^2 - \frac{3}{7}x$
50. $\frac{1}{25} - x^2$
51. $0.25 - y^2$

52. $0.04x^2 - 0.09y^2$
53. $x^4y^4 - 8x^2y^2 + 16$
54. $-24ab + 16a^2 + 9b^2$

55. $9y^8 + 12y^4 + 4$
56. $\frac{1}{36}x^8 + \frac{4}{18}x^4 + \frac{4}{9}$
57. $0.25x^2 + 0.30x + 0.09$

Challenge

Factor. Assume that variables in the exponents represent positive integers.

58. $(x - 3)^2 - 9$
59. $(3x + 9)^2 - 81$
60. $a^{16} - 1$
61. $y^{32} - 1$
62. $(x^{2a} - y^2)$
63. $(x^{4a} - y^{2b})$
64. $(y^{2a} - 5y^a)$
65. $(y^{2a} - 6y^a + 9)$
66. $(y^2 - 2ay + a^2)$

5-4 More Factoring

Trinomials of the Type $x^2 + ax + b$

Consider this product.

$$\begin{array}{c} \text{F} \quad\ \text{O} \quad\ \text{I} \quad\ \text{L} \\ (x + 3)(x + 5) = x^2 + 5x + 3x + 15 \\ = x^2 + 8x + 15 \end{array}$$

Note that the coefficient 8 is the sum of 3 and 5, and the constant term 15 is the product of 3 and 5. In general, $(x + a)(x + b) = x^2 + (a + b)x + ab$. To factor we can use this equation in reverse.

$$x^2 + (a + b)x + ab = (x + a)(x + b)$$

EXAMPLE 1
Factor $x^2 - 3x - 10$.

We look for pairs of integers whose product is -10 and whose sum is -3.

Pairs of Factors	Sum of Factors
$-2, \ \ 5$	3
$2, -5$	-3
$10, -1$	9
$-10, \ \ 1$	-9

Thus the desired integers are 2 and -5.

$$x^2 - 3x - 10 = (x + 2)(x - 5)$$

We can check by multiplying.

TRY THIS Factor. Check by multiplying.

1. $x^2 + 5x - 14$ 2. $x^2 + 21 - 10x$ 3. $y^2 - y - 2$

1. $(x + 7)(x - 2)$
2. $(x - 7)(x - 3)$
3. $(y - 2)(y + 1)$

Trinomials of the Type $ax^2 + bx + c$

In the trinomial $ax^2 + bx + c$, the x^2 term has a coefficient.

$$\begin{array}{c} \text{F} \quad\ \ \text{O} \quad\ \ \text{I} \quad\ \ \text{L} \\ (2x + 3)(5x + 4) = 10x^2 + 8x + 15x + \ \ 12 \end{array}$$

To factor $ax^2 + bx + c$ we look for binomials

$$(\_x + \_)(\_x + \_)$$

where products of numbers in the blanks are as follows.
1. The numbers in the *first* blanks have product a.
2. The *outside* product and the *inside* product add up to b.
3. The numbers in the *last* blanks have product c.

EXAMPLE 2
Factor $12x^2 + 34x + 14$.

We first note that the number 2 is a common factor, so we factor it out. $2(6x^2 + 17x + 7)$. Now we consider $6x^2 + 17x + 7$. We look for numbers whose product is 6. These are 6, 1 and 2, 3. We then have these possibilities.

$$(6x + \ )(x + \ ) \text{ and } (2x + \ )(3x + \ )$$

Next we look for pairs of numbers whose product is 7.

$7, 1 \qquad -7, -1$ Both positive or both negative

By multiplying, we find that the answer is $2(2x + 1)(3x + 7)$.

EXAMPLE 3
Factor $x^2y^2 + 5xy + 4$.

In this case, we treat xy as if it were a single variable.

$$x^2y^2 + 5xy + 4 = (xy)^2 + (4 + 1)xy + 4 \cdot 1$$
$$= (xy + 4)(xy + 1)$$

TRY THIS Factor.

4. $3x^2 + 5x + 2$

5. $4x^2 - 3 + 4x$

6. $24y^2 - 46y + 10$

7. $2x^4y^6 - 3x^2y^3 - 20$

4. $(3x + 2)(x + 1)$
5. $(2x + 3)(2x - 1)$
6. $2(4y - 1)(3y - 5)$
7. $(2x^2y^2 + 5)(x^2y^3 - 4)$

5–4

Exercises
Factor.

1. $x^2 + 9x + 20$

2. $y^2 + 8y + 15$

3. $y^2 - 8y + 16$

4. $a^2 - 10a + 25$

5. $x^2 - 27 - 6x$

6. $t^2 - 15 - 2t$

7. $m^2 - 3m - 28$

8. $x^2 - 2x - 8$

9. $14x + x^2 + 45$

10. $12y + y^2 + 32$

11. $y^2 + 2y - 63$

12. $x^2 + 3x - 40$

13. $t^2 - 11t + 28$

14. $y^2 - 14y + 45$

15. $3x + x^2 - 10$

16. $x + x^2 - 6$

17. $x^2 + 5x + 6$

18. $y^2 + 8y + 7$

19. $32 + 4y - y^2$

20. $56 + x - x^2$

21. $15 + t^2 + 8t$

Factor. Remember to look first for a common factor.

22. $3b^2 + 8b + 4$

23. $9x^2 + 15x + 4$

24. $6y^2 - y - 2$

25. $3a^2 - a - 4$

26. $-7a + 6a^2 - 10$

27. $-35z + 12z^2 - 3$

28. $9a^2 + 6a - 8$

29. $4t^2 + 4t - 15$

30. $3x^2 - 16x - 12$

31. $6x^2 - 5x - 25$

32. $6x^2 - 15 - x$

33. $10y^2 - 12 - 7y$

34. $3a^2 - 10a + 8$

35. $12a^2 - 7a + 1$

36. $35y^2 + 34y + 8$

37. $9a^2 + 18a + 8$

38. $2t + 5t^2 - 3$

39. $4x + 15x^2 - 3$

40. $8x^2 - 16 - 28x$

41. $18x^2 - 24 - 6x$

42. $3x^3 - 5x^2 - 2x$

43. $18y^3 - 3y^2 - 10y$

44. $24x^2 - 2 - 47x$

45. $15y^2 - 10 - 19y$

46. $21x^2 + 37x + 12$

47. $10y^2 + 23y + 12$

48. $17x + 40x^2 - 12$

49. $2y + 24y^2 - 15$

50. $12a^2 - 17a + 6$

51. $20a^2 - 23a + 6$

Extension

Factor.

52. $x^4 + 11x^2 - 80$

53. $y^4 + 5y^2 - 84$

54. $x^2 - \frac{4}{25} + \frac{3}{5}x$

55. $y^2 - \frac{8}{49} + \frac{2}{7}y$

56. $y^2 + 0.4y - 0.05$

57. $t^2 + 0.6t - 0.27$

58. $2x^2 + xy - 6y^2$

59. $2m^2 + mn + 10n^2$

60. $-6xy + 8x^2 - 9y^2$

61. $-7ts + 2t^2 - 4s^2$

62. $7a^2b^2 + 6 + 13ab$

63. $9x^2y^2 - 4 + 5xy$

Challenge

Factor. Assume variables in exponents represent positive integers.

64. $3x^2 + 12x - 495$

65. $-225x + x^3$

66. $4y^3 - 96y^2 + 576y$

67. $3xy^2 - 150xy + 1875x$

68. $7x^2 - 4375y^2$

69. $12x^2 - 72xy + 108y^2$

70. $15t^3 - 60t^2 - 315t$

71. $216x + 78x^2 + 6x^3$

72. $x^{2a} + 5x^a - 24$

73. $x^2 + ax + bx + ab$

74. $4x^{2a} - 4x^a - 3$

75. $bdx^2 + adx + bcx + ac$

76. $\frac{1}{4}p^2 - \frac{2}{5}p + \frac{4}{25}$

77. $\frac{4}{27}r^2 + \frac{5}{9}rs + \frac{1}{12}s^2 - \frac{1}{3}rs$

5–5 Factoring by Grouping

Finding a Common Factor

Sometimes an expression of four or more terms can be grouped in such a way that common factors can be found. The common factor may itself be a binomial.

In the following expression we note that 4 is a factor of the last two terms and y is a factor of the first two terms.

$$\begin{aligned} y^2 + 3y + 4y + 12 &= (y^2 + 3y) + (4y + 12) \\ &= y(y + 3) + 4(y + 3) \quad \text{Factoring} \\ &= (y + 4)(y + 3) \quad \text{Factoring out } (y + 3) \end{aligned}$$

EXAMPLES

Factor.

1. $\begin{aligned} 4x^2 - 3x + 20x - 15 &= 4x^2 + 20x - 3x - 15 \\ &= 4x(x + 5) - 3(x + 5) \\ &= (4x - 3)(x + 5) \end{aligned}$

2. $\begin{aligned} ax^2 + ay - bx^2 - by &= ax^2 + ay + (-bx^2 - by) \\ &= a(x^2 + y) - b(x^2 + y) \quad \text{Factoring out } a \text{ and } -b \\ &= (a - b)(x^2 + y) \end{aligned}$

Not all expressions with four terms can be factored by grouping.

TRY THIS Factor.

1. $x^2 + 5x + 4x + 20$ 2. $5y^2 + 2y + 10y + 4$ 3. $px + py - qx - qy$

1. $(x + 4)(x + 5)$
2. $(y + 2)(5y + 2)$
3. $(p - q)(x + y)$

Factoring Differences of Squares

A difference of two squares can have more than two terms.

EXAMPLE 3

Factor.

$$\begin{aligned} x^2 + 6x + 9 - 25 &= (x^2 + 6x + 9) - 25 \\ &= (x + 3)^2 - 5^2 \end{aligned}$$

This is now a difference of two squares, one of which is a square of a binomial. When we factor, we get

$(x + 3 + 5)(x + 3 - 5)$, or $(x + 8)(x - 2)$.

TRY THIS Factor.

4. $x^2 + 2x + 1 - p^2$ 5. $64 - (x^2 + 8x + 16)$ 4. $(x + 1 - p)(x + 1 + p)$
5. $(4 - x)(12 + x)$

Completing the Square

The trinomial $x^2 + 10x + 25$ is the square of a binomial, because $x^2 + 10x + 25 = (x + 5)^2$. Given the first two terms of a trinomial, we can find the third term that will make it a square.

EXAMPLE 4
What must be added to $x^2 + 12x$ to make it a trinomial square?
We take half the coefficient of x and square it.

$$x^2 + 12x$$
$$\downarrow$$

Half of 12 is 6, and $6^2 = 36$. We add 36.
$x^2 + 12x + 36$ is a trinomial square. It is equal to $(x + 6)^2$.

The process illustrated in Example 4 is called completing the square. Completing the square can be used in factoring.

EXAMPLE 5
Complete the square for $x^2 - 8ax$.

Half of $-8a$ (the coefficient of x) is $-4a$.

$$(-4a)^2 = 16a^2$$

We add the result, to obtain $x^2 - 8ax + 16a^2$. This is a trinomial square, because it is equal to $(x - 4a)^2$.

EXAMPLE 6
Complete the square for $y^2 + \frac{3}{4}y$.

Half of $\frac{3}{4}$ (the coefficient of y) is $\frac{1}{2} \cdot \frac{3}{4} = \frac{3}{8}$.

$$\left(\frac{3}{8}\right)^2 = \frac{9}{64}$$

Thus $y^2 + \frac{3}{4}y + \frac{9}{64}$ is a trinomial square.

TRY THIS Complete the square.

6. $x^2 + 14x$ 7. $y^2 - 10by$ 8. $x^2 - \frac{2}{5}x$ 9. $x^2 + 4.2x$

6. $x^2 + 14x + 49$
7. $y^2 - 10by + 25b^2$
8. $x^2 - \frac{2}{5}x + \frac{1}{25}$
9. $x^2 + 4.2x + 4.41$

226 CHAPTER 5 POLYNOMIALS AND FACTORING

Factoring by Completing the Square

Completing the square can be used to factor trinomials.

EXAMPLE 7
Factor $x^2 - 22x + 112$ by completing the square.

We first complete the square for $x^2 - 22x$. We take half of -22, which is -11.

$$(-11)^2 = 121$$

Now we add 0 to the original trinomial, naming it $121 - 121$.

$$
\begin{aligned}
x^2 - 22x + 112 &= x^2 - 22x + 112 + (121 - 121) &&\text{Adding } 121 - 121 \\
&= (x^2 - 22x + 121) + 112 - 121 &&\text{Grouping} \\
&= (x^2 - 22x + 121) - 9 \\
&= (x - 11)^2 - 3^2 \\
&= (x - 11 + 3)(x - 11 - 3), \text{ or } (x - 8)(x - 14)
\end{aligned}
$$

EXAMPLE 8
Factor $2x^2 + 80x + 768$ by completing the square.

$$2x^2 + 80x + 768 = 2(x^2 + 40x + 384) \quad \text{Removing the common factor 2}$$

To complete the square we take half of 40 to obtain 20.

$$20^2 = 400$$

We add 0, naming it $400 - 400$.

$$
\begin{aligned}
2(x^2 + 40x + 384) &= 2(x^2 + 40x + 400 - 400 + 384) &&\text{Adding } 400 - 400 \\
&= 2(x^2 + 40x + 400 - 16) &&\text{Grouping} \\
&= 2[(x + 20)^2 - 4^2] \\
&= 2(x + 20 + 4)(x + 20 - 4) \\
&= 2(x + 24)(x + 16)
\end{aligned}
$$

TRY THIS Factor by completing the square.

10. $x^2 + 26x + 120$ 11. $2x^2 - 48x + 126$ 12. $x^2 + 8.4x + 13.64$

10. $(x + 20)(x + 6)$
11. $2(x - 3)(x - 21)$
12. $(x + 2.2)(x + 6.2)$

5–5

Exercises

Factor.

1. $a(b - 2) + c(b - 2)$

2. $a(x^2 - 3) - 2(x^2 - 3)$

3. $(x - 2)(x + 5) + (x - 2)(x + 8)$

4. $(m - 4)(m + 3) + (m - 4)(m - 3)$

1. $(a + c)(b - 2)$
2. $(a - 2)(x^2 - 3)$
3. $(x - 2)(2x + 13)$
4. $2m(m - 4)$

5. $a^2(x - y) + a^2(x - y)$ <small>$2a^2(x - y)$</small>   6. $3x^2(x - 6) + 3x^2(x - 6)$ <small>$6x^2(x - 6)$</small>

7. $ac + ad + bc + bd$ <small>$(a + b)(c + d)$</small>   8. $xy + xz + wy + wz$ <small>$(x + w)(y + z)$</small>

9. $b^3 - b^2 + 2b - 2$ <small>$(b^2 + 2)(b - 1)$</small>   10. $y^3 - y^2 + 3y - 3$ <small>$(y^2 + 3)(y - 1)$</small>

11. $y^2 - 8y - y + 8$ <small>$(y - 1)(y - 8)$</small>   12. $t^2 + 6t - 2t - 12$ <small>$(t - 2)(t + 6)$</small>

13. $2y^4 + 6y^2 + 5y^2 + 15$ <small>$(2y^2 + 5)(y^2 + 3)$</small>   14. $2xy - x^2y - 6 + 3x$ <small>$(xy - 3)(2 - x)$</small>

Factor.
<small>15. $(a + b + 3)(a + b - 3)$ 18. $(c + 2d - 3p)(c + 2d + 3p)$ 21. $(3 - a - b)(3 + a + b)$
16. $(x - y - 5)(x - y + 5)$ 19. $2(m + n - 5b)(m + n + 5b)$ 22. $(4 - x + y)(4 + x - y)$
17. $(r - 1 - 2s)(r - 1 + 2s)$ 20. $3(2x + 1 - y)(2x + 1 + y)$ 23. $(5y - x - 4)(5y + x + 4)$</small>

15. $a^2 + 2ab + b^2 - 9$ 16. $x^2 - 2xy + y^2 - 25$ 17. $r^2 - 2r + 1 - 4s^2$

18. $c^2 + 4cd + 4d^2 - 9p^2$ 19. $2m^2 + 4mn + 2n^2 - 50b^2$ 20. $12x^2 + 12x + 3 - 3y^2$

21. $9 - (a^2 + 2ab + b^2)$ 22. $16 - (x^2 - 2xy + y^2)$ 23. $25y^2 - (x^2 + 8x + 16)$

Complete the square.   <small>24. $x^2 + 16x + 64$ 26. $x - 4.2x + 4.41$ 28. $(x + 7)(x + 17)$
25. $y^2 - 24y + 144$ 27. $y^2 + 3.6y + 324$ 30. $2(x + 9)(x + 19)$</small>

24. $x^2 + 16x$ 25. $y^2 - 24y$ 26. $x^2 - 4.2x$ 27. $y^2 + 3.6y$
<small>31. $2(x - 12a)(x - 4a)$
32. $3(x - 16b)(x - 4b)$
33. $3(x - 1)(x - 13)$
34. $2(x - 6)(x - 12)$
36. $8(x + 1)(x - 9)$</small>

Factor by completing the square.

28. $x^2 + 24x + 119$ 29. $x^2 - 26x + 105$ <small>$(x - 21)(x - 5)$</small>   30. $2x^2 + 56x + 342$

31. $2x^2 - 32ax + 96a^2$ 32. $3x^2 - 60bx + 192b^2$ 33. $3x^2 + 39 - 42x$

34. $2x^2 + 144 - 36x$ 35. $5a^2 - 40a - 420$ <small>$5(a + 6)(a - 14)$</small>   36. $8x^2 - 64x - 72$

Factor by completing the square. Use a calculator.

37. $x^2 + 4.482x - 7.403544$ 38. $x^2 - 0.78x + 0.1232$ <small>37. $(x + 5.766)(x - 1.284)$</small>

39. $5.72x^2 + 35.464x - 1319.2608$ <small>38. $(x - 0.56)(x - 0.22)$
39. $5.72(x + 18.6)(x - 12.4)$</small>

Extension

Complete the square.

<small>40. $x^2 + \frac{2}{3}bx + \frac{1}{9}b^2$ 45. $(x - 2.6)(x - 0.6)$
41. $y^2 + \frac{3}{4}ay + \frac{9}{64}a^2$ 46. $\left(x + \frac{1}{5}\right)\left(x + \frac{2}{5}\right)$</small>

40. $x^2 + \frac{2}{3}bx$ 41. $y^2 + \frac{3}{4}ay$ <small>42. $\left(x - \frac{1}{2}\right)\left(x - \frac{5}{2}\right)$ 47. $\left(x - \frac{9}{4}\right)\left(x - \frac{5}{4}\right)$
43. $\left(x - \frac{9}{2}\right)\left(x - \frac{1}{2}\right)$ 48. $(4y^{2a} + 10)(y^{2a} + 3)$
44. $(x + 2.3)(x + 0.3)$ 49. $(5y^a - x^b + 1)(5y^a + x^b + 1)$</small>

Factor.   <small>50. $(x^a + 5)(x^a + 9)$
51. $(x - 3a)(x + a)$</small>

42. $x^2 - 3x + \frac{5}{4}$ 43. $x^2 - 5x + \frac{9}{4}$ 44. $x^2 + 2.6x + 0.69$

45. $x^2 - 3.2x + 1.56$ 46. $x^2 + \frac{3}{5}x + \frac{8}{100}$ 47. $x^2 - \frac{7}{2}x + \frac{45}{16}$

Challenge

Assume variables in exponents represent positive integers.
Factor.

48. $4y^{4a} + 12y^{2a} + 10y^{2a} + 30$ 49. $25y^{2a} - (x^{2b} - 2x^b + 1)$

Factor by completing the square.

50. $x^{2a} + 14x^a + 45$ 51. $x^2 - 2ax - 3a^2$

228   CHAPTER 5   POLYNOMIALS AND FACTORING

5–6 Sums or Differences of Two Cubes

Note the following products.

$$(A + B)(A^2 - AB + B^2) = A(A^2 - AB + B^2) + B(A^2 - AB + B^2)$$
$$= A^3 - A^2B + AB^2 + A^2B - AB^2 + B^3 .$$
$$= A^3 + B^3$$

and

$$(A - B)(A^2 + AB + B^2) = A(A^2 + AB + B^2) - B(A^2 + AB + B^2)$$
$$= A^3 + A^2B + AB^2 - A^2B - AB^2 - B^3$$
$$= A^3 - B^3$$

The above equations (reversed) show how we can factor a sum or a difference of two cubes.

$$A^3 + B^3 = (A + B)(A^2 - AB + B^2)$$
$$A^3 - B^3 = (A - B)(A^2 + AB + B^2)$$

This table of cubes will help in the following problems.

N	0.2	0.1	0	1	2	3	4	5	6	7	8
N^3	0.008	0.001	0	1	8	27	64	125	216	343	512

EXAMPLE 1

Factor $x^3 - 27$.

$$x^3 - 27 = x^3 - 3^3$$

In one set of parentheses we write the cube root of the first term, x. Then we write the cube root of the second term, -3. This gives us the expression $x - 3$.

$$(x - 3)(\quad)$$

To get the next factor we think of $x - 3$ and do the following.

1. Square the first term: x^2.
2. Multiply the terms and then change the sign: $3x$.
3. Square the second term: 9.

$$(x - 3)(x^2 + 3x + 9)$$

Note that we cannot factor $x^2 + 3x + 9$. It is not the square of a binomial.

TRY THIS Factor.

1. $x^3 - 8$ **2.** $y^3 - 27$ 1. $(x - 2)(x^2 + 2x + 4)$ 2. $(y - 3)(y^2 + 3y + 9)$

EXAMPLE 2

Factor $125x^3 + y^3$.

$$125x^3 + y^3 = (5x + y)(\qquad)\quad \text{Writing the sum of the cube roots}$$

Now we think of $5x + y$ and get the next factor.

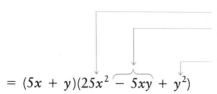

1. Square the first term: $25x^2$.
2. Take the product of the first and second terms, $5xy$, and change the sign: $-5xy$.
3. Square the last term: y^2.

$$= (5x + y)(25x^2 - 5xy + y^2)$$

TRY THIS Factor.

3. $27x^3 + y^3$ **4.** $8y^3 + z^3$ 3. $(3x + y)(9x^2 - 3xy + y^2)$ 4. $(2y + z)(4y^2 - 2yz + z^2)$

EXAMPLE 3

Factor $128y^7 - 250x^6y$.

We first look for a common factor.

$$2y(64y^6 - 125x^6) = 2y[(4y^2)^3 - (5x^2)^3]$$
$$= 2y(4y^2 - 5x^2)(16y^4 + 20x^2y^2 + 25x^4)$$

Some powers such as a^6 or a^9 can be thought of as cubes:
$a^6 = (a^2)^3$ and $a^9 = (a^3)^3$.

EXAMPLE 4

Factor $64a^6 - 729b^6$.

We can write this as a difference of cubes.

$$(4a^2)^3 - (9b^2)^3$$
$$(4a^2 - 9b^2)(16a^4 + 36a^2b^2 + 81b^4)\quad \text{Factoring the difference of cubes}$$
$$(2a + 3b)(2a - 3b)(16a^4 + 36a^2b^2 + 81b^4)\quad \text{Factoring first factor as the differences of squares}$$

EXAMPLE 5

Factor $y^3 + 0.008$.

We note that $0.008 = (0.2)^3$. Thus we have a sum of two cubes, and we factor as follows.

$$(y + 0.2)(y^2 - 0.2y + 0.04)$$

TRY THIS Factor.

5. $16x^7y + 54xy^7$ **6.** $729x^6 - 64y^6$ **7.** $x^3 - 0.027$

5. $2xy(2x^2 + 3y^2)(4x^4 - 6x^2y^2 + 9y^4)$
6. $(9x^2 - 4y^2)(81x^4 + 36x^2y^2 + 16y^4)$
7. $(x - 0.3)(x^2 + 0.3x + 0.09)$

Remember the following about factoring sums or differences of squares and cubes.

> Sum of cubes: $A^3 + B^3 = (A + B)(A^2 - AB + B^2)$
> Difference of cubes: $A^3 - B^3 = (A - B)(A^2 + AB + B^2)$
> Difference of squares: $A^2 - B^2 = (A + B)(A - B)$
> Sum of squares: $A^2 + B^2$ *cannot be factored*

5–6

Exercises

Factor. Remember to look first for a common factor.

1. $x^3 + 8$ **2.** $c^3 + 27$ **3.** $y^3 - 64$

4. $z^3 - 1$ **5.** $w^3 + 1$ **6.** $x^3 + 125$

7. $8a^3 + 1$ **8.** $27x^3 + 1$ **9.** $y^3 - 8$

10. $p^3 - 27$ **11.** $8 - 27b^3$ **12.** $64 - 125x^3$

13. $64y^3 + 1$ **14.** $125x^3 + 1$ **15.** $8x^3 + 27$

16. $27y^3 + 64$ **17.** $a^3 - b^3$ **18.** $x^3 - y^3$

19. $a^3 + \dfrac{1}{8}$ **20.** $b^3 + \dfrac{1}{27}$ **21.** $8x^3 - 27y^3$

1. $(x + 2)(x^2 - 2x + 4)$
2. $(c + 3)(c^2 - 3c + 9)$
3. $(y - 4)(y^2 + 4y + 16)$
4. $(z - 1)(z^2 + z + 1)$
5. $(w + 1)(w^2 - w + 1)$
6. $(x + 5)(x^2 - 5x + 25)$
7. $(2a + 1)(4a^2 - 2a + 1)$
8. $(3x + 1)(9x^2 - 3x + 1)$
9. $(y - 2)(y^2 + 2y + 4)$
10. $(p - 3)(p^2 + 3p + 9)$
11. $(2 - 3b)(4 + 6b + 9b^2)$
12. $(4 - 5x)(16 + 20x + 25x^2)$
13. $(4y + 1)(16y^2 - 4y + 1)$
14. $(5x + 1)(25x^2 - 5x + 1)$
15. $(2x + 3)(4x^2 - 6x + 9)$
16. $(3y + 4)(9y^2 - 12y + 16)$
17. $(a - b)(a^2 + ab + b^2)$
18. $(x - y)(x^2 + xy + y^2)$

Extension

Factor.

22. $rs^3 + 64r$ **23.** $ab^3 + 125a$ **24.** $5x^3 - 40z^3$ **25.** $2y^3 - 54z^3$

26. $x^3 + 0.001$ **27.** $y^3 + 0.125$ **28.** $64x^6 - 8t^6$ **29.** $125c^6 - 8d^6$

19. $\left(a + \dfrac{1}{2}\right)\left(a^2 - \dfrac{1}{2}a + \dfrac{1}{4}\right)$
20. $\left(b + \dfrac{1}{3}\right)\left(b^2 - \dfrac{1}{3}b + \dfrac{1}{9}\right)$
21. $(2x - 3y)(4x^2 + 6xy + 9y^2)$
22. $r(s + 4)(s^2 - 4s + 16)$
23. $a(b + 5)(b^2 - 5b + 25)$
24. $5(x - 2z)(x^2 + 2xz + 4z^2)$
25. $2(y - 3z)(y^2 + 3yz + 9z^2)$
26. $(x + 0.1)(x^2 - 0.1x + 0.01)$
27. $(y + 0.5)(y^2 - 0.5y + 0.25)$
28. $8(2x^2 - t^2)(4x^4 + 2x^2t^2 + t^4)$

Challenge

29. $(5c^2 - 2d^2)(25c^4 + 10c^2d^2 + 4d^4)$
30. $(x^{2a} + y^b)(x^{4a} - x^{2a}y^b + y^{2b})$
31. $(ax - by)(a^2x^2 + axby + b^2y^2)$

Factor. Assume variables in exponents represent positive integers.

30. $x^{6a} + y^{3b}$ **31.** $a^3x^3 - b^3y^3$ **32.** $3x^{3a} + 24y^{3b}$

33. $\dfrac{8}{27}x^3 + \dfrac{1}{64}y^3$ **34.** $\dfrac{1}{24}x^3y^3 + \dfrac{1}{3}z^3$ **35.** $\dfrac{1}{16}x^{3a} + \dfrac{1}{2}y^{6a}z^{9b}$

32. $3(x^a + 2y^b)(x^{2a} - 2x^ay^b + 4y^{2b})$
33. $\left(\dfrac{2}{3}x + \dfrac{1}{4}y\right)\left(\dfrac{4}{9}x^2 - \dfrac{1}{6}xy + \dfrac{1}{16}y^2\right)$
34. $\dfrac{1}{3}\left(\dfrac{1}{2}xy - z\right)\left(\dfrac{1}{4}x^2y^2 + \dfrac{1}{2}xyz + z^2\right)$
35. $\dfrac{1}{2}\left(\dfrac{1}{2}x^a + y^{2a}z^{3b}\right)\left(\dfrac{1}{4}x^{2a} - \dfrac{1}{2}x^ay^{2a}z^{3b} + y^{4a}z^{6b}\right)$

5-7 Factoring: A General Strategy

A. Always look first for a common factor.

B. Then proceed by considering the number of terms.

Two terms
Try factoring as a difference of two squares, or a sum or difference of two cubes.

Three terms
1. Is it a square of a binomial? If so, you know how to factor.
2. Is it a square of a binomial? If not, use trial and error.

More than three terms
1. Try grouping.
2. Try differences of squares again.

C. Always factor completely. By this we mean whenever you obtain a factor that can still be factored, you should factor it.

EXAMPLE 1

Factor $10a^2x - 40b^2x$.

A. We look first for a common factor: $10x(a^2 - 4b^2)$.

B. The factor $a^2 - 4b^2$ has only two terms. It is a difference of squares. We factor it: $10x(a + 2b)(a - 2b)$.

C. Have we factored completely? Yes, because no factor can be factored further.

EXAMPLE 2

Factor $x^6 - y^6$.

A. We look for a common factor. There isn't one.

B. There are only two terms. It is a difference of squares: $(x^3)^2 - (y^3)^2$. We factor it: $(x^3 + y^3)(x^3 - y^3)$.

One factor is a sum of two cubes, and the other factor is a difference of two cubes. We factor them.

$$(x + y)(x^2 - xy + y^2)(x - y)(x^2 + xy + y^2)$$

C. We have factored completely because no factor can be factored further.

TRY THIS Factor completely.

1. $2(1 + 4x^2)(1 + 2x)(1 - 2x)$
2. $7(a + 1)(a^2 - a + 1)(a - 1)(a^2 + a + 1)$
3. $(3 + x)(4 + x)$
4. $(c - d + t + 4)(c - d - t - 4)$

1. $2 - 32x^4$
2. $7a^6 - 7$
3. $3x + 12 + 4x + x^2$
4. $c^2 - 2cd + d^2 - t^2 - 8t - 16$

5–7

Exercises

Factor completely. Remember to look first for a common factor.

1. $x^2 - 144$
2. $2x^2 + 11x + 12$
3. $3x^4 - 12$
4. $2xy^2 - 50x$
5. $a^2 + 25 + 10a$
6. $p^2 + 64 + 16p$
7. $2x^2 - 10x - 132$
8. $3y^2 - 15y - 252$
9. $9x^2 - 25y^2$
10. $16a^2 - 81b^2$
11. $4c^2 - 4cd + d^2$
12. $70b^2 - 3ab - a^2$
13. $-7x^2 + 2x^3 + 4x - 14$
14. $9m^2 + 3m^3 + 8m + 24$
15. $x^2 - 27x + 25$
16. $3y^2 + 15y - 42$
17. $8m^3 + m^6 - 20$
18. $-37x^2 + x^4 + 36$
19. $ac + cd - ab - bd$
20. $xw - yw + xz - yz$
21. $m^6 - 1$
22. $64t^6 - 1$
23. $x^2 + 6x - y^2 + 9$
24. $t^2 + 10t - p^2 + 25$
25. $36y^2 - 35 + 12y$
26. $2b - 28a^2b + 10ab$
27. $a^8 - b^8$
28. $2x^4 - 32$
29. $8p^3 + 27q^3$
30. $125x^3 + 64y^3$
31. $64p^3 - 1$
32. $8y^3 - 125$
33. $a^3b - 16ab^3$
34. $x^3y - 25xy^3$
35. $-23xy + 20x^2y^2 + 6$
36. $42ab + 27a^2b^2 + 8$
37. $2x^3 + 6x^2 - 8x - 24$
38. $3x^3 + 6x^2 - 27x - 54$
39. $250x^3 - 128y^3$
40. $27a^3 - 343b^3$
41. $16x^3 + 54y^3$
42. $250a^3 + 54b^3$

Extension

Factor.

43. $(x - p)^2 - p^2$
44. $30y^4 - 97xy^2 + 60x^2$
45. $5c^{100} - 80d^{100}$
46. $3a^2 + 3b^2 - 3c^2 - 3d^2 + 6ab - 6cd$
47. $8(a - 3)^2 - 64(a - 3) + 128$
48. $-16 + 17(5 - y^2) - (5 - y^2)^2$

Challenge

Factor. Assume variables in exponents represent positive integers.

49. $x^6 - 2x^5 + x^4 - x^2 + 2x - 1$
50. $(a + 2)^3 - (a - 2)^3$
51. $(y - 1)^4 - (y - 1)^2$
52. $27x^{6s} + 64y^{3t}$
53. $c^{2w+1}2c^{w+1}c$
54. $24x^{2a} - 6$

5-8 Solving Equations by Factoring

We restate an important theorem from Chapter 2.

THEOREM 2-3

The Principle of Zero Products

A product is 0 if and only if one of the factors is 0.

Theorem 2-3 says that if a product is 0, then one of the factors must be 0; and also that if a factor is 0, then the product is 0.

To use this principle in solving equations, we make sure that there is 0 on one side of the equation and then factor the other side.

Using the Principle of Zero Products

What does this mean for solving equations? Suppose we have an equation $A \cdot B = 0$. Theorem 2-3 says that if either of the factors is 0 it will be true. It also says that if it is true, then at least one of the factors must be 0. Thus we get solutions by setting the factors equal to 0, and we get *all* of the solutions that way. Thus the statements $A \cdot B = 0$ and $A = 0$ or $B = 0$ are equivalent statements and have the same solutions.

EXAMPLE 1

Solve $x^2 - 3x - 28 = 0$.

First we factor the polynomial.

$$x^2 - 3x - 28 = 0$$
$$(x - 7)(x + 4) = 0 \quad \text{Factoring}$$

The expressions $x^2 - 3x - 28$ and $(x - 7)(x + 4)$ name the same number for any replacement. Hence the equations have the same solutions.

$$x - 7 = 0 \quad \text{or} \quad x + 4 = 0 \quad \text{Using the principle of zero products}$$
$$x = 7 \quad \text{or} \quad x = -4$$

Check:
$$\begin{array}{c|c} x^2 - 3x - 28 = 0 & \\ \hline 7^2 - 3(7) - 28 & 0 \\ 49 - 21 - 28 & \\ 0 & \end{array} \qquad \begin{array}{c|c} x^2 - 3x - 28 = 0 & \\ \hline (-4)^2 - 3(-4) - 28 & 0 \\ 16 + 12 - 28 & \\ 0 & \end{array}$$

The solutions are 7 and -4.

TRY THIS Solve.

1. $x^2 + 8 = 6x$ 4, 2

EXAMPLE 2

Solve $3y^2 + 7y + 2 = 0$.

$$(3y + 1)(y + 2) = 0 \quad \text{Factoring}$$

$$3y + 1 = 0 \quad \text{or } y + 2 = 0 \quad \text{Using the principle of zero products}$$

$$y = -\frac{1}{3} \quad \text{or} \quad y = -2$$

The solutions are $-\frac{1}{3}$ and -2.

TRY THIS Solve.

2. $5y + 2y^2 = 3$ $\frac{1}{2}, -3$

EXAMPLE 3

Solve $5b^2 - 10b = 0$.

$$5b(b - 2) = 0 \quad \text{Factoring}$$

$$5b = 0 \quad \text{or} \quad b - 2 = 0 \quad \text{Using the principle of zero products}$$

$$b = 0 \quad \text{or} \quad b = 2$$

The solutions are 0 and 2.

TRY THIS Solve.

3. $8b^2 - 16b = 0$ 0, 2

EXAMPLE 4

Solve $x^2 - 6x + 9 = 0$.

$$(x - 3)(x - 3) = 0 \quad \text{Factoring}$$

$$x - 3 = 0 \quad \text{or} \quad x - 3 = 0 \quad \text{Using the principle of zero products}$$

$$x = 3 \quad \text{or} \quad x = 3$$

There is only one solution, 3.

TRY THIS Solve.

4. $25 + x^2 = -10x$ **5.** $4x^2 - 9 = 0$ 4. -5 5. $-\frac{3}{2}, \frac{3}{2}$

5–8

Exercises
Solve.

1. $x^2 + 3x - 28 = 0$ $-7, 4$ **2.** $y^2 - 4y - 45 = 0$ $9, -5$ **3.** $y^2 - 8y + 16 = 0$ 4

4. $r^2 - 2r + 1 = 0$ 1 **5.** $x^2 - 12x + 36 = 0$ 6 **6.** $y^2 + 16y + 64 = 0$ -8

7. $9x + x^2 + 20 = 0$ $-5, -4$ **8.** $8y + y^2 + 15 = 0$ $-5, -3$ **9.** $x^2 + 8x = 0$ $0, -8$

10. $t^2 + 9t = 0$ $0, -9$ **11.** $x^2 - 9 = 0$ $-3, 3$ **12.** $p^2 - 16 = 0$ $-4, 4$

13. $z^2 = 36$ $-6, 6$ **14.** $y^2 = 81$ $-9, 9$ **15.** $x^2 + 14x + 45 = 0$ $-5, -9$

16. $y^2 + 12y + 32 = 0$ **17.** $y^2 + 2y = 63$ $-9, 7$ **18.** $a^2 + 3a = 40$ $-8, 5$

19. $p^2 - 11p = -28$ $7, 4$ **20.** $x^2 - 14x = -45$ $9, 5$ **21.** $32 + 4x - x^2 = 0$ $8, -4$

22. $27 + 12t + t^2 = 0$ **23.** $3b^2 + 8b + 4 = 0$ **24.** $9y^2 + 15y + 4 = 0$ $-\frac{4}{3}, -\frac{1}{3}$

25. $8y^2 - 10y + 3 = 0$ **26.** $4x^2 + 11x + 6 = 0$ **27.** $6z - z^2 = 0$ $0, 6$

28. $8y - y^2 = 0$ $0, 8$ **29.** $12z^2 + z = 6$ $-\frac{3}{4}, \frac{2}{3}$ **30.** $6x^2 - 7x = 10$ $-\frac{5}{6}, 2$

31. $5x^2 - 20 = 0$ $-2, 2$ **32.** $6y^2 - 54 = 0$ $-3, 3$ **33.** $2x^2 - 15x = -7$ $\frac{1}{2}, 7$

34. $x^2 - 9x = -8$ $8, 1$ **35.** $21r^2 + r - 10 = 0$ **36.** $12a^2 - 5a - 28 = 0$ $\frac{7}{4}, -\frac{4}{3}$

37. $15y^2 = 3y$ $0, \frac{1}{5}$ **38.** $18x^2 = 9x$ $0, \frac{1}{2}$ **39.** $100x^2 = 81$ $-\frac{9}{10}, \frac{9}{10}$

Extension   16. $-8, -4$ 25. $\frac{3}{4}, \frac{1}{2}$
Solve.   22. $-9, -3$
   23. $-\frac{2}{3}, -2$ 26. $-\frac{3}{4}, -2$ 35. $-\frac{5}{7}, \frac{2}{3}$

40. $x^2 - \frac{1}{25} = 0$ **41.** $y^2 - \frac{1}{64} = 0$

40. $-\frac{1}{5}, \frac{1}{5}$

41. $-\frac{1}{8}, \frac{1}{8}$

42. $x(x + 8) = 16(x - 1)$ **43.** $m(m + 9) = 4(2m + 5)$

42. 4

44. $(a - 5)^2 = 36$ **45.** $(x - 6)^2 = 81$

43. $-5, 4$
44. $-1, 11$
45. $-3, 15$

46. $(3x^2 - 7x - 20)(x - 5) = 0$ **47.** $(8x + 11)(12x^2 - 5x - 2) = 0$

46. $-\frac{5}{3}, 5, 4$

48. $16x^3 = x$ **49.** $9x^3 = x$

47. $-\frac{1}{4}, \frac{2}{3}, -\frac{11}{8}$

48. $0, \frac{1}{4}, -\frac{1}{4}$

Challenge
Solve.

49. $\frac{1}{3}, -\frac{1}{3}, 0$

50. $(x + 1)^3 = (x - 1)^3 + 26$ $2, -2$ **51.** $(x - 2)^3 = x^3 - 2$ 1

5-9 Solving Problems

To solve some problems we can first translate the problem situation to an equation and then solve the equation. Then we check to see if the solution(s) satisfies the conditions of the problem.

EXAMPLE 1

The square of a number minus the number is 20. Find the number.

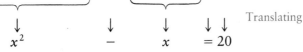

$$\underbrace{\text{The square of a number}} \text{ minus } \underbrace{\text{the number}} \text{ is 20.}$$

$$x^2 \qquad\qquad - \qquad x \qquad = 20 \qquad \text{Translating}$$

We solve the equation.

$$x^2 - x = 20$$
$$x^2 - x - 20 = 0 \quad \text{Adding } -20$$
$$(x - 5)(x + 4) = 0 \quad \text{Factoring}$$
$$x - 5 = 0 \quad \text{or} \quad x + 4 = 0 \quad \text{Using the principle of zero products}$$
$$x = 5 \quad \text{or} \qquad x = -4$$

5 and -4 both check. They are the answers to the problem.

TRY THIS

1. The square of a number minus twice the number is 48. Find the number. 8, −6

EXAMPLE 2

The width of a rectangle is 2 m less than the length. The area is 15 m². Find the dimensions.

$$\underbrace{\text{The length}} \text{ times the } \underbrace{\text{length minus}} \text{ 2 is 15.} \quad \text{Rewording}$$

$$\ell \qquad \cdot \qquad (\ell - 2) \qquad = 15 \quad \text{Translating}$$

We solve the equation.

$$\ell \cdot (\ell - 2) = 15$$
$$\ell^2 - 2\ell - 15 = 0 \quad \text{Multiplying and adding } -15$$
$$(\ell - 5)(\ell + 3) = 0 \quad \text{Factoring}$$
$$\ell - 5 = 0 \quad \text{or} \quad \ell + 3 = 0 \quad \text{Using the principle of zero products}$$
$$\ell = 5 \quad \text{or} \qquad \ell = -3$$

The solutions of the equation are 5 and -3. Now we check in the problem. The length of a rectangle cannot be negative. Thus the length is 5 m. Since the width is 2 m less than the length, the width is 3 m.

TRY THIS

2. The width of a rectangle is 5 cm less than the length. The area is 24 cm². Find the dimensions. Length is 8 cm; width is 3 cm

5–9

Exercises

Solve these problems.

1. Four times the square of a number is 21 more than eight times the number. What is the number? $\frac{7}{2}, -\frac{3}{2}$

2. Four times the square of a number is 45 more than eight times the number. What is the number? $\frac{9}{2}, -\frac{5}{2}$

3. The square of a number plus the number is 132. What is the number? $-12, 11$

4. The square of a number plus the number is 156. What is the number? $-13, 12$

5. The length of the top of a table is 5 cm more than the width. Find the length and width if the area is 84 cm². Length is 12 cm; width is 5 cm

6. The length of the top of a workbench is 4 cm greater than the width. The area is 96 cm². Find the length and the width. Length is 12 cm; width is 8 cm

7. Sam Stratton is planning a garden 25 m longer than it is wide. The garden will have an area of 7500 m². What will its dimensions be? Length is 100 m; width is 75 m

8. A flower bed is to be 3 m longer than it is wide. The flower bed will have an area of 108 m². What will its dimensions be? Length is 12 m; width is 9 m

9. The sum of the squares of two consecutive odd positive integers is 202. Find the integers. 9 and 11

10. The sum of the squares of two consecutive odd positive integers is 394. Find the integers. 13 and 15

11. If the sides of a square are lengthened by 4 cm the area becomes 49 cm². Find the length of a side of the original square. 3 cm

12. If the sides of a square are lengthened by 6 m the area becomes 144 m². Find the length of a side of the original square. 6 m

13. The base of a triangle is 9 cm greater than the height. The area is 56 cm². Find the height and base. Height is 7 cm; base is 16 cm

14. The base of a triangle is 5 cm less than the height. The area is 18 cm². Find the height and base. Height is 9 cm; base is 4 cm

15. The perimeter of a square is 4 more than its area. Find the length of a side. 2

16. The area of a square is 12 more than its perimeter. Find the length of a side. 6

17. Three consecutive even integers are such that the square of the first plus the square of the third is 136. Find the three integers. −10, −8, and −6; 6, 8, 10

18. Three consecutive even integers are such that the square of the third is 76 more than the square of the second. Find the three integers. 16, 18, and 20

19. Find three consecutive integers such that the product of the first and third minus the second is one more than 10 times the third. 11, 12, and 13; −2, −1, and 0

20. Find three consecutive integers such that four times the square of the third less three times the square of the first minus 41 is twice the square of the second. 9, 10, and 11; 3, 4, and 5

Extension

21. The sum of two numbers is 17, and the sum of their squares is 205. Find the numbers. 3; 14

22. A rectangular piece of tin is twice as long as it is wide. Squares 2 cm on a side are cut out of each corner and the ends are turned up to make a box whose volume is 480 cm^2. What are the dimensions of the piece of tin? Length is 28 cm; width is 14 cm

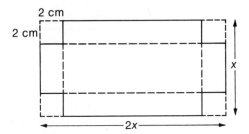

Challenge

Solve for x.

23. $(x + 6)(x − 3) + b = (x − 5)(x − 2) − 3b$ $x = \frac{14 − 2b}{5}$

24. $x^2 − 3(x − b) + c = (x − b)^2$ $x = \frac{b^2 − 3b − c}{2b − 3}$

25. The top and base of a fish tank are rectangles whose length is 10 inches more than the width. If the depth and the width of the tank total 50 inches and the combined area of the top and base is 400 square inches less than the total area of the four sides, what are the dimensions of the tank? Width is 30 in.; length is 40 in.; depth is 20 in.

26. A rectangular swimming pool with dimensions 11 meters and 8 meters is built in a rectangular backyard. The area of the backyard is 1120 square meters. If the strip of yard surrounding the pool is of uniform width, how wide is the strip? 12 m

27. The hypotenuse of a right triangle is 3 cm more than one of its legs and 6 cm more than the other leg. What is the area of the triangle? 54 cm^2

CAREERS/Railroad Traffic Control

Railroad traffic-control operators coordinate railroad traffic on each section of the railroad line. They know the destinations of the trains, and the arrival and departure times. They use schedules to decide which trains have the highest priorities. Traffic control operators then monitor the panelboard on a centralized traffic-control unit. This unit electrically activates railroad tracks and switches. As trains pass specific positions, their locations are shown on the panelboard.

Knowing the location of each train, traffic-control operators are able to determine necessary speed changes, reroutings, or stops for each train, depending on traffic conditions.

For example, a train making a 5 hour, 360 km trip is traveling at 60 km/h. The traffic control operator knows that the train needs to speed up to 80 km/h to arrive on time.

To find how long the train travels at each speed, we can write the following two equations.

$$60a + 80b = 360$$
$$a + b = 5$$

As you learned in Section 4–2, the equations can be solved either by addition or by substitution. For this problem we will use substitution.

$$a + b = 5$$
$$a = 5 - b$$
$$60(5 - b) + 80b = 360$$
$$300 - 60b + 80b = 360$$
$$20b = 60$$
$$b = 3 \text{ hours}$$
$$a = 5 - 3$$
$$= 2 \text{ hours}$$

The train travels at 60 km/h for 2 hours and at 80 km/h for 3 hours.

Traffic-control operators often record the time each train reaches specified points or they may chart train movements on graphs.

Exercises

Solve each problem.

1. A train leaves Westwood traveling east at 40 km/h. Two hours later, another train leaves Westwood in the same direction on a parallel track at 60 km/h. How far from Westwood will the faster train catch the slower one? 240 km

2. Two trains travel toward each other on parallel tracks from cities which are 165 km apart. One train is traveling at 60 km/h; the other at 50 km/h. If they start at the same time, in how many hours will they pass each other? $1\frac{1}{2}$ hr

3. Two trains are traveling in opposite directions. One travels at 75 km/h and the other at 85 km/h. In how many hours will they be 640 km apart? 4hr

4. A train usually makes a 360-km trip in 6 hours. One day, after traveling for 2 hours, the train was delayed for 1 hour. At what speed did the train have to travel for the rest of the trip to arrive on time? 80 km/h

5. A train leaves Centerville for Williamsburg, which is 675 km away, at 7 A.M. Two hours later, another train leaves Williamsburg. They meet at noon. If the second train had started at 6 A.M. and the first at 11 A.M. they would still have met at noon. Find the speed of each train. First: 75 km/h, second: 100 km/h

CHAPTER 5 Review

Review the material in the chapter. Then see how you have done by trying these review exercises. If you miss an exercise, restudy the indicated lesson.

5–1 Add.

1. $5x^2 - 8x^3 + 3x - 2$ and $4x^3 + 5x^2 + 9 - x$ $\quad -4x^3 + 10x^2 + 2x + 7$
2. $5a^4 + 7a^3 + 6a^2 - 7$ and $3a^4 - 5a^2 + 2 - a^3$ $\quad 8a^4 + 6a^3 + a^2 - 5$
3. $8y^2 - 4xy - 5x^2 + 8x^3$ and $7x^3 + 2x^2 - 8xy + 6y^2$ $\quad 14y^2 - 12xy - 3x^2 + 15x^3$
4. $p^3 - 5q^2 + 2pq$ and $3pq^3 - p^3 - 6$ and $4pq^2 + 5p^3 - pq + 6$ $\quad 5p^3 + 5q^2 + pq + 3pq^3 + 4pq^2$

5–1 Subtract.
  5. $13y^2 - y + 9$ $\qquad$ 7. $10a - 4b - 9c$
  6. $6p - 10q + 11r$ $\qquad$ 8. $4x^2 + 3xy + y^2$

5. $(8y^2 + 3y + 6) - (-5y^2 + 4y - 3)$ $\qquad$ 6. $(8p - 5q + 7r) - (2p - 5p - 4r)$
7. $(15a - 5c + 4b) - (8b + 4c + 5a)$ $\qquad$ 8. $(8x^2 - 3xy - 7y^2) - (4x^2 - 6xy - 8y^2)$

13. $8x^2 - 2x - 21$
14. $4t^2 - 9x^4y^6$
11. $-9x^2 + 6xy - 3xz - 8yz + 20z^2$
12. $30y^6 - 2y^4 - y^3 - 12y^2 + 45y - 42$
15. $49x^2 - 70xy + 25y^2$

5–2 Multiply.

9. $(-8x^2y)(4xy^2)$ $\quad 32x^3y^3$ $\qquad$ 10. $(3xy + 4y)(x^2 - 2)$ $\quad 3x^3y + 4x^2y - 6xy - 8y$
11. $(3x - 2y + 5z)(-3x + 4z)$ $\qquad$ 12. $(5y^3 + 3y - 6)(6y^3 - 4y + 7)$
13. $(a - b)(a^2 + ab + b^2)$ $\qquad$ 14. $(-3x^2y^3 + 2t)(3x^2y^3 + 2t)$ $\qquad$ 15. $(7x - 5y)^2$
16. $(7a - 3b)(4a - 6b)$ $\qquad$ 17. $(x + 3)^3$ $\quad x^3 + 9x^2 + 27x + 27$ $\qquad$ 18. $(2x + 1)^3$

5–3 Factor.

19. $49y^4 - 81$ $\qquad$ 20. $9y^2 - 64$ $\qquad$ 21. $x^2 - 14x + 49$ $\qquad$ 22. $8x^2 + 50 + 40x$

5–4

23. $a^2b^2 + 7ab + 12$ $\qquad$ 24. $72 - x - x^2$ $\qquad$ 25. $2y^2 - 3y - 2$ $\qquad$ 26. $8b^2 + 9 - 18b$

5–5

27. Factor $2y^6 + 6y^4 + 5y^2 + 15$ by grouping. $\quad (2y^4 + 5)(y^2 + 3)$

28. Factor $3a^2 + 6ab + 3b^2 - 75c^2)$. $\quad 3(a + b + 5c)(a + b - 5c)$

16. $28a^2 - 54ab + 18b^2$
18. $8x^3 + 12x^2 + 6x + 1$
19. $(7y^2 + 9)(7y^2 - 9)$
20. $(3y + 8)(3y - 8)$
21. $(x + 7)^2$
22. $2(2x + 5)^2$
23. $(ab + 3)(ab + 4)$
24. $(8 - x)(9 + x)$
25. $(2y - 1)(y - 2)$
26. $(4b - 3)(2b - 3)$
29. $(2x^2 + 3y^2)(4x^4 - 6x^2y^2 + 9y^4)$
30. $(a + 2b)(a^2 - 2ab + 4b^2)$
31. $(3b - 4c)(9b^2 + 16bc + 16c^2)$
32. $(c^2 - d^2)(c^4 + c^2d^2 + d^4)$
33. $(a + b + x + 3)(a + b - x - 3)$

5–6 Factor.

29. $8x^6 + 27y^6$ $\qquad$ 30. $a^3 + 8b^3$ $\qquad$ 31. $27b^3 - 64c^3$

5–7

32. $c^6 - d^6$ $\qquad$ 33. $a^2 + 2ab + b^2 - x^2 + 6x - 9$

5–8 Solve.

34. $2x^2 + 9x = -4$ **35.** $x^2 - 8x = 0$ 0, 8   34. $-4, -\frac{1}{2}$

5–9 Solve.

36. The square of a number plus 7 times the number is -12. Find The number. $-4, -3$

37. The length of a rectangle is 3 *cm* more than the width and the area is 54 cm². Find its dimensions.   Length is 9 cm; width is 6 cm

---

CHAPTER 5   Test

Add.

1. $3x^2 - 4x^3 + 2x - 1$ and $5x^3 + 4x^2 + 3 - x$ $x^3 + 7x^2 + x + 2$

2. $4y^2 - 3xy - 4x^2 + 7x^3$ and $5x^3 + 3x^2 - 2xy + 5y^2$ $9y^2 - 5xy - x^2 + 12x^3$

Subtract.

3. $(7x^2 + 2x + 4) - (-2x^2 + 2x - 2)$ $9x^2 + 6$

4. $(5r^2 - 2rs - 6s^2) - (3r^2 - 4rs - 7s^2)$ $2r^2 + 2rs + s^2$

Multiply.

5. $(14x^2y)(3xy^2)$ $-12x^3y^3$

6. $(-4x + 3z)(2x - 3y + 4z)$ $-8x^2 + 12xy - 10xz - 9yz + 12z^2$

7. $(3x^3 + 2x - 4)(5x^2 - 2x + 4)$ $15x^4 + 4x^3 - 12x^2 + 16x - 16$

8. $(3x - 5)(3x + 5)$ $9x^2 - 25$

9. $(5x + 2y)^2$ $25x^2 + 20xy + 4y^2$

10. $(9x - 5y)(2x - 7y)$ $18x^2 - 73xy + 35y^2$

Factor.

11. $(9t - 27)$ $9(t - 3)$ **12.** $16x^2 - 81$ $(4x - 9)(4x + 9)$

13. $9x^2 + 24x + 16$ **14.** $x^2y^2 - 2xy - 15$

15. $6x^2 + 11x - 10$ **16.** $36 - 16x - x^2$

17. $64p^3 - 125q^3$ **18.** $y^6 - z^6$

19. $x^2 - 6x + 9 - a^2 + 2a - 1$ $(x - y + a + 1)(x - y - a - 1)$

13. $(3x + 4)^2$
14. $(xy - 5)(xy + 3)$
15. $(3x - 2)(2x + 5)$
16. $(2 + x)(18 - x)$
17. $(4p - 5q)(16p^2 + 20pq + 25q^2)$
18. $(y^2 - z^2)(y^4 + y^2z^2 + y^4)$
20. $7, -3$

Solve.

20. $x^2 - 21 = 4x$ **21.** $y^2 - 9y = 0$ 0, 9

242 CHAPTER 5   POLYNOMIALS AND FACTORING

Solve.

22. The square of a number plus 9 times the number is -8. Find the number. $-1, -8$

23. The length of a rectangle is 5 cm more than the width and the area is 84 cm². Find its dimensions. 7 cm, 12 cm

Challenge

24. Factor $(x - 1)^3 - (x + 1)^3$. $-2(3x^2 + 1)$

Ready for Fractional Expressions and Equations?

1–3   Add or subtract.

1. $\frac{2}{7} + \left(-\frac{7}{9}\right)$ $-\frac{31}{63}$ **2.** $\frac{5}{3} - \left(-\frac{3}{5}\right)$ $-\frac{16}{15}$

1–4   Multiply.

3. $7 \cdot \left(-\frac{2}{3}\right)$ $-\frac{14}{3}$ **4.** $-\frac{3}{8} \cdot \left(-\frac{4}{7}\right)$ $\frac{3}{14}$

1–4   Divide.

5. $\frac{2}{3} \div \frac{3}{4}$ $\frac{8}{9}$ **6.** $-\frac{7}{8} \div \frac{1}{2}$ $-\frac{7}{4}$ **7.** $\frac{3}{4} \div \left(-\frac{1}{4}\right)$ -3

1–5

8. Evaluate $xy - xz$ when $x = 3$, $y = -2$, $z = 4$. -18

1–5   Factor.

9. $4x + 4y$ **10.** $3y + 6$ **11.** $cx - cr + cw$ $c(x - r + w)$ 9. $4(x + y)$ 10. $3(y + 2)$

1–7   Simplify.

12. $(7x^3y^{-2})(2x^{-2}y^4)$ **13.** $\dfrac{10x^5y^2}{2xy^4}$ **14.** $(2x^2y^{-4}z^3)^4$ $16x^8y^{-16}z^{12}$ 12. $14xy^2$ 13. $5x^4y^{-2}$

2–2

24. Solve: $8 - 3(a - 1) = 2 + 4(3 - a)$ 3

2–4

25. Solve $E = mc^2$, for m. $m = \dfrac{E}{c^2}$

6

CHAPTER SIX

Fractional Expressions and Equations

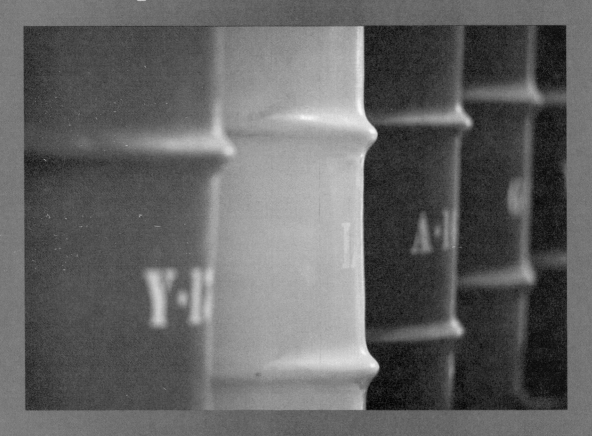

6–1 Multiplying and Simplifying

A fractional expression is a quotient of two polynomials. The following are examples of fractional expressions.

$$\frac{7}{8}, \frac{a}{b}, \frac{8}{y+5}, \frac{x^2 + 7xy - 4}{x^3 - y^3}$$

A fractional expression always indicates division.

$\frac{a}{b}$ means $a \div b$ and $\frac{x^2 + 7xy - 4}{x^3 - y^3}$ means $(x^2 + 7xy - 4) \div (x^3 - y^3)$

Recall that we can divide by multiplying by a reciprocal.

$\frac{a}{b}$ means ab^{-1} and $\frac{x^2 + 7xy - 4}{x^3 - y^3}$ means $(x^2 + 7xy - 4)(x^3 - y^3)^{-1}$

Certain substitutions are not sensible in fractional expressions. Since division by 0 is not defined, any number that makes a denominator 0 is not a sensible replacement.

Multiplying

In arithmetic, to multiply two fractions, we multiply numerators and denominators. We do the same with fractional expressions.

THEOREM 6–1

For any fractional expressions $\frac{a}{b}$ and $\frac{c}{d}$, $\frac{a}{b} \cdot \frac{c}{d} = \frac{a \cdot c}{b \cdot d}$.

EXAMPLE 1
Multiply. Do not carry out the multiplications in the numerator and denominator.

$$\frac{x + 3}{y - 4} \cdot \frac{x^3}{y + 5} = \frac{(x + 3)x^3}{(y - 4)(y + 5)} \quad \text{Multiplying numerators and multiplying denominators}$$

TRY THIS Multiply.

1. $\dfrac{x - 2}{5} \cdot \dfrac{x + 2}{x + 4}$ 2. $\dfrac{x + y}{x + 3} \cdot \dfrac{x + y}{x - 3}$ 1. $\dfrac{(x - 2)(x + 2)}{5(x + 4)}$ 2. $\dfrac{(x + y)(x + y)}{(x + 3)(x - 3)}$

Any number multiplied by 1 is that same number. Any fractional expression with the same numerator and denominator names the number 1.

$$\frac{y + 5}{y + 5}, \frac{4x^2 - 5}{4x^2 - 5}, \frac{-1}{-1}$$ All name the number 1 for all sensible replacements

We can multiply by 1 to get equivalent expressions. For example, let us multiply $\frac{x + y}{5}$ by 1.

$$\frac{x + y}{5} \cdot \frac{x - y}{x - y} = \frac{(x + y)(x - y)}{5(x - y)}$$ Multiplying; $\frac{x - y}{x - y} = 1$

We know now that $\frac{x + y}{5}$ and $\frac{(x + y)(x - y)}{5(x - y)}$ are equivalent. This means that they will name the same number for all replacements, except those that make a denominator zero.

EXAMPLES
Multiply to obtain equivalent expressions.

2. $\frac{x^2 + 3}{x - 1} \cdot \frac{x + 1}{x + 1} = \frac{(x^2 + 3)(x + 1)}{(x - 1)(x + 1)}$ 3. $\frac{-1}{-1} \cdot \frac{x - 4}{x - y} = \frac{-1 \cdot (x - 4)}{-1 \cdot (x - y)}$

TRY THIS Multiply.

3. $\frac{3x + 2y}{5x + 4y} \cdot \frac{x}{x}$ 4. $\frac{2x^2 - y}{3x + 4} \cdot \frac{3x + 2}{3x + 2}$ 5. $\frac{-1}{-1} \cdot \frac{2a - 5}{a - b}$

3. $\frac{(3x + 2y)x}{(5x + 4y)x}$

4. $\frac{(2x^2 - y)(3x + 2)}{(3x + 4)(3x + 2)}$

5. $\frac{-1 \cdot (2a - 5)}{-1 \cdot (a - b)}$

Simplifying Fractional Expressions

We can simplify fractional expressions by reversing the procedure of multiplying by 1. First we factor numerator and denominator, then factor the fractional expression, so that a factor is equal to 1.

EXAMPLES
Simplify. Identify factors equal to 1.

4. $\frac{5x^2}{x} = \frac{5x \cdot x}{1 \cdot x}$ Factoring numerator and denominator

$= \frac{5x}{1} \cdot \frac{x}{x}$ Factoring the fractional expression

$= 5x$ $\frac{x}{x} = 1$ for all sensible replacements

5. $\frac{4a + 8}{2} = \frac{2 \cdot 2a + 2 \cdot 4}{2 \cdot 1} = \frac{2(2a + 4)}{2 \cdot 1} = \frac{2}{2} \cdot \frac{2a + 4}{1} = 2a + 4$

TRY THIS Simplify.

6. $\dfrac{7x^2}{x}$ 7. $\dfrac{6a + 9}{3}$ 6. $7x$ 7. $2a + 3$

EXAMPLE 6

$$\frac{x^2 - 1}{2x^2 - x - 1} = \frac{(x - 1)(x + 1)}{(2x + 1)(x - 1)} \quad \text{Factoring numerator and denominator}$$

$$= \frac{x - 1}{x - 1} \cdot \frac{x + 1}{2x + 1} \quad \text{Factoring the fractional expression}$$

$$= \frac{x + 1}{2x + 1} \quad \text{Removing a factor of 1}$$

Identifying a numerator factor and a denominator factor that form a factor of 1 is sometimes called cancelling

EXAMPLE 7

$$\frac{9x^2 + 6xy - 3y^2}{12x^2 - 12y^2} = \frac{3(x + y)(3x - y)}{12(x + y)(x - y)} \quad \text{Factoring}$$

$$= \frac{3(x + y)}{3(x + y)} \cdot \frac{3x - y}{4(x - y)}$$

$$= \frac{3x - y}{4(x - y)} \quad \text{"Removing" a factor of 1}$$

After finding all possible factors of 1, we usually multiply out the numerator and the denominator. Then the final answer is $\frac{3x - y}{4x - 4y}$.

TRY THIS Simplify.

8. $\dfrac{6x^2 + 4x}{2x^2 + 4x}$ 9. $\dfrac{y^2 + 3y + 2}{y^2 - 1}$ 8. $\dfrac{3x + 2}{x + 2}$ 9. $\dfrac{y + 2}{y - 1}$

Multiplying and Simplifying

EXAMPLES
Multiply and simplify.

8. $\dfrac{x + 2}{x - 2} \cdot \dfrac{x^2 - 4}{x^2 + x - 2} = \dfrac{(x + 2)(x^2 - 4)}{(x - 2)(x^2 + x - 2)}$ Multiplying numerators and also denominators

$$= \frac{(x + 2)(x - 2)(x + 2)}{(x - 2)(x + 2)(x - 1)} \quad \text{Factoring numerators and denominators}$$

$$= \frac{(x + 2)(x - 2)}{(x + 2)(x - 2)} \cdot \frac{x + 2}{x - 1}$$

$$= \frac{x + 2}{x - 1} \quad \text{Simplifying}$$

9. $\dfrac{a^3 - b^3}{a^2 - b^2} \cdot \dfrac{a^2 + 2ab + b^2}{a^2 + ab + b^2} = \dfrac{(a^3 - b^3)(a^2 + 2ab + b^2)}{(a^2 - b^2)(a^2 + ab + b^2)}$

$$= \dfrac{(a - b)(a^2 + ab + b^2)(a + b)(a + b)}{(a - b)(a + b)(a^2 + ab + b^2)}$$

$$= \dfrac{(a - b)(a^2 + ab + b^2)(a + b)}{(a - b)(a^2 + ab + b^2)(a + b)} \cdot \dfrac{a + b}{1}$$

$$= a + b$$

TRY THIS Multiply and simplify.

10. $\dfrac{(x - y)^2}{x + y} \cdot \dfrac{3x + 3y}{x^2 - y^2}$ **11.** $\dfrac{a^3 + b^3}{a^2 - b^2} \cdot \dfrac{a^2 - 2ab + b^2}{a^2 - ab + b^2}$ 10. $\dfrac{3(x - y)}{x + y}$ 11. $a - b$

Dividing and Simplifying

Two expressions are reciprocals of each other if their product is 1. In arithmetic, the reciprocal of a fraction $\frac{a}{b}$ is the fraction $\frac{b}{a}$. For fractional expressions this is also the case.

THEOREM 6–2

For any fractional expression $\frac{a}{b}$, which is nonzero, its reciprocal is $\frac{b}{a}$.

EXAMPLES

10. The reciprocal of $\dfrac{x + 2y}{3x^2y + 7}$ is $\dfrac{3x^2y + 7}{x + 2y}$.

11. The reciprocal of $y - 8$ is $\dfrac{1}{y - 8}$.

12. The reciprocal of $\dfrac{1}{x^2 + 3}$ is $x^2 + 3$.

TRY THIS Find the reciprocal.

12. $\dfrac{x + 3}{x - 5}$ **13.** $x + 7$ **14.** $\dfrac{1}{y^3 - 9}$ 12. $\dfrac{x - 5}{x + 3}$ 13. $\dfrac{1}{x + 7}$ 14. $y^3 - 9$

In arithmetic, we know that we can always divide by multiplying by a reciprocal. It can be proved that the same is true for fractional expressions.

THEOREM 6-3

For any fractional expressions $\frac{a}{b}$ and $\frac{c}{d}$, for which $\frac{c}{d}$ is nonzero,

$$\frac{a}{b} \div \frac{c}{d} = \frac{a}{b} \cdot \frac{d}{c}.$$

(We can divide by multiplying by a reciprocal.)

EXAMPLES

Divide. Simplify by removing a factor of 1 if possible. Then multiply out the numerator and denominator.

13. $\dfrac{x-2}{x+1} \div \dfrac{x+5}{x-3} = \dfrac{x-2}{x+1} \cdot \dfrac{x-3}{x+5}$ Multiplying by the reciprocal

$= \dfrac{x^2 - 5x + 6}{x^2 + 6x + 5}$ Multiplying numerators and denominators

14. $\dfrac{a^2-1}{a+1} \div \dfrac{a^2 - 2a + 1}{a+1} = \dfrac{a^2-1}{a+1} \cdot \dfrac{a+1}{a^2 - 2a + 1}$ Multiplying by the reciprocal

$= \dfrac{(a+1)(a-1)}{a+1} \cdot \dfrac{a+1}{(a-1)(a-1)}$ Factoring numerator and denominator

$= \dfrac{(a+1)(a-1)}{(a+1)(a-1)} \cdot \dfrac{a+1}{a-1}$

$= \dfrac{a+1}{a-1}$ Simplifying

TRY THIS Divide and simplify.

15. $\dfrac{x^2 + 7x + 10}{2x - 4} \div \dfrac{x^2 - 3x - 10}{x - 2}$

16. $\dfrac{a^2 - b^2}{ab} \div \dfrac{a^2 - 2ab + b^2}{2a^2b^2}$

15. $\dfrac{(x+5)}{2(x-5)}$ 16. $\dfrac{2ab(a+b)}{(a-b)}$

6-1

Exercises

Multiply to obtain equivalent expressions. Do not simplify.

1. $\dfrac{3x}{3x} \cdot \dfrac{x+1}{x+3}$ 2. $\dfrac{4-y^2}{6-y} \cdot \dfrac{-1}{-1}$ 3. $\dfrac{t-3}{t+2} \cdot \dfrac{t+3}{t+3}$ 4. $\dfrac{p-4}{p-5} \cdot \dfrac{p+5}{p+5}$

Simplify by removing factors equal to 1.

5. $\dfrac{9y^2}{15y}$ 6. $\dfrac{2a-6}{2}$ 7. $\dfrac{3a-6}{3}$

1. $\dfrac{3x(x+1)}{3x(x+3)}$

2. $\dfrac{(4-y^2)\cdot(-1)}{(6-y)\cdot(-1)}$

3. $\dfrac{(t-3)(t+3)}{(t+2)(t+3)}$

4. $\dfrac{(p-4)(p+5)}{(p-5)(p+5)}$

5. $\dfrac{3y}{5}$

6. $a-3$

7. $a-2$

8. $\dfrac{4y - 12}{4y + 12}$

9. $\dfrac{8x + 16}{8x - 16}$

10. $\dfrac{t^2 - 16}{t^2 - 8t + 16}$

11. $\dfrac{p^2 - 25}{p^2 + 10p + 25}$

12. $\dfrac{x^2 + 7x - 8}{4x^2 - 8x + 4}$

13. $\dfrac{y^2 + 4y - 12}{3y^2 - 12y + 12}$

14. $\dfrac{x^4 - 4x^2}{x^3 + 2x^2}$

15. $\dfrac{a^3 - b^3}{a^2 - b^2}$

16. $\dfrac{x^3 + y^3}{x^2 - y^2}$

Multiply and simplify.

17. $\dfrac{x^2 - 16}{x^2} \cdot \dfrac{x^2 - 4x}{x^2 - x - 12}$

18. $\dfrac{y^2 + 10y + 25}{y^2 - 9} \cdot \dfrac{y + 3}{y + 5}$

19. $\dfrac{y^2 - 16}{2y + 6} \cdot \dfrac{y + 3}{y - 4}$

20. $\dfrac{m^2 - n^2}{4m + 4n} \cdot \dfrac{m + n}{m - n}$

21. $\dfrac{x^2 - 2x - 35}{2x^3 - 3x^2} \cdot \dfrac{4x^3 - 9x}{7x - 49}$

22. $\dfrac{y^2 - 10y + 9}{y^2 - 1} \cdot \dfrac{y + 4}{y^2 - 5y - 36}$

23. $\dfrac{c^3 + 8}{c^2 - 4} \cdot \dfrac{c^2 - 4c + 4}{c^2 - 2c + 4}$

24. $\dfrac{x^3 - 27}{x^2 - 9} \cdot \dfrac{x^2 - 6x + 9}{x^2 + 3x + 9}$

25. $\dfrac{x^2 - y^2}{x^3 - y^3} \cdot \dfrac{x^2 + xy + y^2}{x^2 + 2xy + y^2}$

26. $\dfrac{4x^2 - 9y^2}{8x^3 - 27y^3} \cdot \dfrac{4x^2 + 6xy + 9y^2}{4x^2 + 12xy + 9y^2}$

Divide and simplify.

27. $\dfrac{3y + 15}{y} \div \dfrac{y + 5}{y}$

28. $\dfrac{6x + 12}{x} \div \dfrac{x + 2}{x^3}$

29. $\dfrac{y^2 - 9}{y} \div \dfrac{y + 3}{y + 2}$

30. $\dfrac{x^2 - 4}{x} \div \dfrac{x - 2}{x + 4}$

31. $\dfrac{4a^2 - 1}{a^2 - 4} \div \dfrac{2a - 1}{a - 2}$

32. $\dfrac{25x^2 - 4}{x^2 - 9} \div \dfrac{5x - 2}{x + 3}$

33. $\dfrac{x^2 - 16}{x^2 - 10x + 25} \div \dfrac{3x - 12}{x^2 - 3x - 10}$

34. $\dfrac{y^2 - 36}{y^2 - 8y + 16} \div \dfrac{3y - 18}{y^2 - y + 12}$

35. $\dfrac{y^3 + 3y}{y^2 - 9} \div \dfrac{y^2 + 5y - 14}{y^2 + 4y - 21}$

36. $\dfrac{a^3 + 4a}{a^2 - 16} \div \dfrac{a^2 + 8a + 15}{a^2 + a - 20}$

37. $\dfrac{x^3 - 64}{x^3 + 64} \div \dfrac{x^2 - 16}{x^2 - 4x + 16}$

38. $\dfrac{8y^3 + 27}{64y^3 - 1} \div \dfrac{4y^2 - 9}{16y^2 + 4y + 1}$

Multiply or divide. Use a calculator.

39. $\dfrac{834x}{y - 427.2} \cdot \dfrac{26.3x}{y + 427.2}$

40. $\dfrac{0.0049t}{t + 0.007} \cdot \dfrac{27,000t}{t - 0.007}$

41. $\dfrac{527}{x + 93.87} \div \dfrac{x - 93.87}{468}$

42. $\dfrac{y + 924.6}{0.003} \div \dfrac{0.421}{y - 924.6}$

Extension

Simplify.

43. $\left[\dfrac{r^2 - 4s^2}{r + 2s} \div (r + 2s) \right] \cdot \dfrac{2s}{r - 2s}$

44. $\left[\dfrac{d^2 - d}{d^2 - 6d + 8} \cdot \dfrac{d - 2}{d^2 + 5d} \right] \div \dfrac{5d}{d^2 - 9d + 20}$

45. $\dfrac{x(x + 1) - 2(x + 3)}{(x + 1)(x + 2)(x + 3)}$

46. $\dfrac{2x - 5(x + 2) - (x - 2)}{x^2 - 4}$

8. $\dfrac{y - 3}{y + 3}$

9. $\dfrac{x + 2}{x - 2}$

10. $\dfrac{t + 4}{t - 4}$

11. $\dfrac{p - 5}{p + 5}$

12. $\dfrac{x + 8}{4(x - 1)}$

13. $\dfrac{y + 6}{3(y - 2)}$

14. $x - 2$

15. $\dfrac{a^2 + ab + b^2}{a + b}$

16. $\dfrac{x - xy + y^2}{x - y}$

17. $\dfrac{(x + 4)(x - 4)}{x(x + 3)}$

18. $\dfrac{y + 5}{y - 3}$

19. $\dfrac{y + 4}{2}$

20. $\dfrac{m + n}{4}$

21. $\dfrac{(x + 5)(2x + 3)}{7x}$

22. $\dfrac{1}{y + 1}$

23. $c - 2$

24. $\dfrac{(x - 3)^2}{x + 3}$

25. $\dfrac{1}{x + y}$

26. $\dfrac{1}{2x + 3y}$

27. 3

28. $6x^2$

29. $\dfrac{(y - 3)(y + 2)}{y}$

30. $\dfrac{(x + 2)(x + 4)}{x}$

31. $\dfrac{2a + 1}{a + 2}$

32. $\dfrac{5x + 2}{x - 3}$

33. $\dfrac{(x + 4)(x + 2)}{3(x - 5)}$

34. $\dfrac{(y + 6)(y + 3)}{3(y - 4)}$

35. $\dfrac{y(y^2 + 3)}{(y + 3)(y - 2)}$

36. $\dfrac{a(a^2 + 4)}{(a + 4)(a + 3)}$

37. $\dfrac{x^2 + 4x + 16}{(x + 4)^2}$

38. $\dfrac{4y^2 - 6y + 9}{(4y - 1)(2y - 3)}$

39. $\dfrac{21,934.2x^2}{y^2 - 182,499.84}$

40. $\dfrac{132.3t^2}{t^2 - 0.000049}$

41. $\dfrac{246,636}{x^2 - 8811.5769}$

42. $\dfrac{y^2 - 854,885.16}{0.001263}$

43. $\dfrac{2s}{r + 2s}$

44. $\dfrac{(d - 1)(d - 5)}{5d(d + 5)}$

45. $\dfrac{x - 3}{(x + 1)(x + 3)}$

46. $\dfrac{-4}{x - 2}$

47. $\dfrac{m^2 - t^2}{m^2 + t^2 + m + t + 2mt}$

48. $\dfrac{a^3 - 2a^2 + 2a - 4}{a^3 - 2a^2 - 3a + 6}$

49. $\dfrac{x^3 + x^2 - y^3 - y^2}{x^2 - 2xy + y^2}$

50. $\dfrac{u^6 + v^6 + 2u^3v^3}{u^3 - v^3 + u^2v - uv^2}$

47. $\dfrac{m - t}{m + t + 1}$

48. $\dfrac{a^2 + 2}{a^2 - 3}$

49. $\dfrac{x^2 + xy + y^2 + x + y}{x - y}$

50. $\dfrac{u^2 + uv + v^2}{u^2 - v^2}$

51. $\dfrac{-2x}{x - 1}$

52. $2x + h$

53. $3x^2 + 3xh + h^2$

54. $2x + h + 3$

55. $3x^2 + 3xh + h^2 - 2x - h$

Challenge

Simplify.

51. $\dfrac{x^5 - x^3 + x^2 - 1 - (x^3 - 1)(x + 1)^2}{(x^2 - 1)^2}$

For each of the following functions, find and simplify.

$$\dfrac{f(x + h) - f(x)}{h}$$

52. $f(x) = x^2$ **53.** $f(x) = x^3$ **54.** $f(x) = x^2 + 3x$ **55.** $f(x) = x^3 - x^2$

Prove the following theorems.

56. Theorem 6–1   **57.** Theorem 6–2   **58.** Theorem 6–3

59. For any fractional expressions a and b, $(ab)^{-1} = a^{-1}b^{-1}$.
Prove this theorem by showing that the product of $a^{-1}b^{-1}ab$ is 1.

USING A CALCULATOR/Algebraic Logic

If you enter $10 - 3 \times 2$ on your calculator and the result is 4, your calculator follows the algebraic order of operations you have learned in this book. If the result is 14 (or some other result), then your calculator does not use algebraic logic.

EXAMPLE 1
This calculator does not have algebraic logic.
Problem: $10 - 3 \times 2$

Enter: 3 $\boxed{\times}$ 2 $\boxed{=}$ $\boxed{\text{Min}}$ 10 $\boxed{-}$

Display: 3   2   6   6   10

Enter: $\boxed{\text{MR}}$ $\boxed{=}$

Display: 6   4

The example above uses memory. Some problems can be solved by using the equals key instead. (For a calculator without algebraic logic, the first equals sign of Example 2 may

be omitted.)

EXAMPLE 2
This calculator has algebraic logic.
Problem: Evaluate $\dfrac{2(3x + 5)}{9}$ for $x = 4.569$.

Enter: 3 $\boxed{\times}$ 4.569 $\boxed{+}$ 5 $\boxed{=}$

Display: 3   4.569 13.707 5 18.707

Enter: $\boxed{\times}$ 2 $\boxed{\div}$ 9 $\boxed{=}$

Display: 2 37.414 9 4.1571111

EXAMPLE 3
This calculator has algebraic logic.
Problem: Check that 8.7 is a solution of

$$x + \dfrac{46.11}{x} = 14.$$

Enter: 8.7 $\boxed{+}$ 46.11 $\boxed{\div}$ 8.7 $\boxed{=}$

Display: 8.7   46.11   8.7   14

6-2 Least Common Multiples

To add fractional expressions we first find a common denominator. Consider $\frac{5}{42} + \frac{7}{12}$. We look for a common multiple of 42 and 12. Usually we try to get the smallest such number, or the least common multiple (LCM). To find the LCM we first factor each of the numbers.

$$42 = 2 \cdot 3 \cdot 7$$
$$12 = 2 \cdot 2 \cdot 3$$

The LCM is the number that has 2 as a factor twice, 3 as a factor once, and 7 as a factor once.

The LCM is $2 \cdot 2 \cdot 3 \cdot 7$, or 84.

> To obtain the LCM of two or more numbers we use each factor the greatest number of times it occurs in any one of the factorizations.

EXAMPLE 1
Find the LCM of 18 and 24.

$$18 = 3 \cdot 3 \cdot 2$$
$$24 = 2 \cdot 2 \cdot 2 \cdot 3$$

The LCM is $3 \cdot 3 \cdot 2 \cdot 2 \cdot 2$, or 72.

TRY THIS Find the LCM by factoring.
1. 18, 30 90 **2.** 12, 18, 24 72

To find the LCM of two or more algebraic expressions we factor them. Then we use each factor the greatest number of times it occurs in any one expression.

EXAMPLES
2. Find the LCM of $12xy^2$ and $15x^2y$.

$$12xy^2 = 2 \cdot 2 \cdot 3 \cdot x \cdot y \cdot y$$
$$15x^3y = 3 \cdot 5 \cdot x \cdot x \cdot x \cdot y$$

The LCM is $2 \cdot 2 \cdot 3 \cdot 5 \cdot x \cdot x \cdot x \cdot y \cdot y$, or $60x^3y^2$.

3. Find the LCM of $x^2 + 2x + 1$, $5x^2 - 5x$, and $x^2 - 1$.

$$x^2 + 2x + 1 = (x + 1)(x + 1)$$
$$5x^2 - 5x = 5x(x - 1) \qquad \text{Factoring}$$
$$x^2 - 1 = (x + 1)(x - 1)$$

The LCM is $5x(x + 1)(x + 1)(x - 1)$.

4. Find the LCM of $x^2 - y^2$, $x^3 + y^3$, and $x^2 + 2xy + y^2$.

$$x^2 - y^2 = (x - y)(x + y)$$
$$x^3 + y^3 = (x + y)(x^2 - xy + y^2)$$
$$x^2 + 2xy + y^2 = (x + y)(x + y)$$

The LCM is $(x - y)(x + y)(x + y)(x^2 - xy + y^2)$.

In finding LCMs, if factors that are additive inverses occur, we do not use them both. For example, if $(a - b)$ occurs in one factorization and $(b - a)$ occurs in another, we do not use them both, since $b - a = -(a - b)$.

EXAMPLE 5
Find the LCM of $x^2 - y^2$ and $3y - 3x$.

$$x^2 - y^2 = (x + y)(x - y) \quad \text{We can use } (x - y) \text{ or } (y - x),$$
$$3y - 3x = 3(y - x) \qquad\qquad \text{but we do not use them both.}$$

The LCM is $3(x + y)(x - y)$, or $3(x + y)(y - x)$.

TRY THIS Find the LCM.

3. a^2b^2, $5a^3b$ $\quad$ 5a³b²

4. $y^2 + 7y + 12$, $y^2 + 8y + 16$, $y + 4$ $\quad$ (y + 4)²(y + 3)

5. $x^2 - 9$, $x^3 - x^2 - 6x$, $2x^2$ $\quad$ 2x²(x − 3)(x + 3)(x + 2)

6. $a^2 - b^2$, $2b - 2a$ $\quad$ 2(a − b)(a + b)

6–2

Exercises
Find the LCM.

1. 12, 18 $\quad$ 2² · 3²

2. 15, 20 $\quad$ 2² · 3 · 5

3. 18, 48 $\quad$ 2⁴ · 3²

4. 45, 54 $\quad$ 2 · 3³ · 5

5. 24, 36 $\quad$ 2³ · 3²

6. 30, 75 $\quad$ 2 · 3 · 5²

7. 9, 15, 5 $\quad$ 3² · 5

8. 27, 35, 63 $\quad$ 3³ · 5 · 7

9. 24, 36, 42 $\quad$ 504

10. 24, 42, 60 $\quad$ 840

11. $8x^2$, $12x^3$ $\quad$ 24x³

12. $4y^2$, $24y^3$ $\quad$ 24y³

13. $12x^2y$, $4xy$ $12x^2y$

14. $18r^2s$, $12rs^3$ $36r^2s^3$

15. $15ab^2$, $3ab$, $10a^3b$ $30a^3b^2$

16. $6x^2y^2$, $9x^3y$, $15y^3$ $90x^3y^3$

17. $a + b$, $a - b$ $(a + b)(a - b)$

18. $x - 4$, $x + 4$ $(x - 4)(x + 4)$

19. $3(y - 2)$, $6(2 - y)$ $6(y - 2)$ or $6(2 - y)$

20. $5(y - 1)$, $10(1 - y)$ $10(y - 1)$ or $10(1 - y)$

21. $y^2 - 9$, $3y + 9$ $3(y + 3)(y - 3)$

22. $a^2 - b^2$, $ab + b^2$ $b(a + b)(a - b)$

23. $5y - 15$, $y^2 - 6y + 9$ $5(y - 3)(y - 3)$

24. $4x - 16$, $x^2 - 8x + 16$ $4(x - 4)(x - 4)$

25. $(a + 1)$, $(a - 1)^2$, $a^2 - 1$

26. $(x - 2)$, $(x + 2)^2$, $x^2 - 4$

27. $x^2 - 4$, $2 - x$

28. $y^2 - 9$, $3 - y$

29. $x^2 + 10x + 25$, $x^2 + 2x - 15$

30. $y^2 + 8x + 16$, $y^2 - 3y - 28$

31. $2r^2 - 5r - 12$, $3r^2 - 13r + 4$

32. $3x^2 - 4x - 4$, $4x^2 - 5x - 6$

25. $(a + 1)(a - 1)(a - 1)$
26. $(x - 2)(x + 2)(x + 2)$
27. $(x + 2)(x - 2)$ or $(x + 2)(2 - x)$
28. $(y + 3)(y - 3)$ or $(y + 3)(3 - y)$

Extension

Find the LCM.

33. $2x^2 - 5x - 3$, $2x^2 - x - 1$,
$x^2 - 6x + 9$
$(2x + 1)(x - 3)(x - 3)(x - 1)$

34. $3x^2 + 4x - 4$, $2x^2 + 7x + 6$,
$x^2 - 4x + 4$
$(3x - 2)(x + 2)(2x + 3)(x - 2)(x - 2)$

29. $(x + 5)(x + 5)(x - 3)$
30. $(y + 4)(y + 4)(y - 7)$
31. $(2r + 3)(r - 4)(3r - 1)$
32. $(3x + 2)(x - 2)(4x + 3)$

Challenge

Find the LCM.

35. $x^8 - x^4$, $x^5 - x^2$, $x^5 - x^3$, $x^5 + x^2$ $x^4(x^2 + 1)(x^2 - 1)(x^2 + x + 1)(x^2 - x + 1)$

36. The LCM of two expressions is $8a^4b^7$. One of the expressions is $2a^3b^7$. List all the possibilities for the other expression. $8a^4$, $8a^4b$, $8a^4b^2$, $8a^4b^3$, $8a^4b^4$, $8a^4b^5$, $8a^4b^6$, $8a^4b^7$

DISCOVERY/Diophantine Equations

Diophantus of Alexandria was one of the greatest mathematicians of Greek civilization. He lived about the year 250 and collected and solved a wide variety of problems. He was one of the first writers to use algebraic symbols and he had special symbols for an unknown quantity, for a minus sign, and for the reciprocal of a number.

Diophantus was particularly interested in solving equations with integral coefficients, and for identifying those solutions which are integers. Thus, equations of the form $ax + by = c$ are called *diophantine*. The coefficients a, b, and c are integers and only those pairs (x, y) in which both x and y are integers are considered solutions. For example, all integral solutions of $31x - 164y = 7$ are given by the two equa-

tions below, where p is any integer:

$x = -259 + 164p$
$y = -49 + 31p$ $(-95, -18)$, $(69, 13)$, $(233, 44)$

Find x and y for $p = 1, 2$, and 3. Then show that x and y solve the equation $31x - 164y = 7$.

Very little is known about the life of Diophantus. In fact the only information about him comes from a book of problems written in the 5th century. The book says that his boyhood lasted $\frac{1}{6}$ of his life, his beard grew after $\frac{1}{12}$ more, after $\frac{1}{7}$ more he was married, 5 years later his son was born, the son lived to half his father's age, and the father died 4 years after his son. It is usually agreed that Diophantus married at 33 and died at 84.

6-3 Addition and Subtraction

When Denominators Are the Same

When we add or subtract fractional expressions with the same denominator, we add or subtract the numerators and keep the same denominator.

THEOREM 6-4

For any fractional expressions $\frac{a}{c}$ and $\frac{b}{c}$, for which c is nonzero,

$$\frac{a}{c} + \frac{b}{c} = \frac{a + b}{c}$$

and

$$\frac{a}{c} - \frac{b}{c} = \frac{a - b}{c}.$$

EXAMPLES
Add.

1. $\dfrac{3 + x}{x} + \dfrac{4}{x} = \dfrac{7 + x}{x}$

Example 1 shows that $\frac{3 + x}{x} + \frac{4}{x}$ and $\frac{7 + x}{x}$ are equivalent expressions. This means that both expressions name the same number for all replacements except 0.

2. $\dfrac{4x^2 - 5xy}{x^2 - y^2} + \dfrac{2xy - y^2}{x^2 - y^2} = \dfrac{4x^2 - 3xy - y^2}{x^2 - y^2}$

$$= \dfrac{(4x + y)(x - y)}{(x + y)(x - y)}$$

$$= \dfrac{x - y}{x - y} \cdot \dfrac{4x + y}{x + y}$$

$$= \dfrac{4x + y}{x + y}$$

TRY THIS Add.

1. $\dfrac{5 + y}{y} + \dfrac{7}{y}$ 2. $\dfrac{2x^2 + 5x - 9}{x - 5} + \dfrac{x^2 - 19x + 4}{x - 5}$ 1. $\dfrac{12 + y}{y}$ 2. $3x + 1$

EXAMPLE 3

Subtract.

$$\frac{4x+5}{x+3} - \frac{x-2}{x+3} = \frac{4x+5-(x-2)}{x+3} \quad \text{Subtracting numerators}$$

$$= \frac{4x+5-x+2}{x+3} = \frac{3x+7}{x+3}$$

TRY THIS Subtract.

3. $\dfrac{a}{b+2} - \dfrac{b}{b+2}$ **4.** $\dfrac{4y+7}{x^2+y^2} - \dfrac{3y-5}{x^2+y^2}$ 3. $\frac{a-b}{b+2}$ 4. $\frac{y+12}{x^2+y^2}$

When one denominator is the additive inverse of the other, we first multiply one expression by $\frac{-1}{-1}$. This will give us a common denominator.

EXAMPLE 4

Add.

$$\frac{a}{2a} + \frac{a^3}{-2a} = \frac{a}{2a} + \frac{-1}{-1} \cdot \frac{a^3}{-2a} \quad \text{Multiplying by } \frac{-1}{-1}$$

$$= \frac{a}{2a} + \frac{-a^3}{2a}$$

$$= \frac{a-a^3}{2a} \quad \text{Adding numerators}$$

$$= \frac{a(1-a^2)}{2a} \quad \text{Factoring}$$

$$= \frac{a}{a} \cdot \frac{1-a^2}{2} = \frac{1-a^2}{2}$$

EXAMPLE 5

Subtract.

$$\frac{5x}{x-2y} - \frac{3y-7}{2y-x} = \frac{5x}{x-2y} - \frac{-1}{-1} \cdot \frac{3y-7}{2y-x}$$

$$= \frac{5x}{x-2y} - \frac{7-3y}{x-2y}$$

$$= \frac{5x-(7-3y)}{x-2y} \quad \begin{array}{l}\text{Subtracting numerators}\\ \text{(remember the parentheses)}\end{array}$$

$$= \frac{5x-7+3y}{x-2y}$$

TRY THIS

5. $\dfrac{3x^2+4}{x-5} + \dfrac{x^2-7}{5-x}$ **6.** $\dfrac{4x^2}{2x-y} - \dfrac{7x^2}{y-2x}$ 5. $\frac{2x^2+11}{x-5}$ 6. $\frac{11x^2}{2x-y}$

When Denominators Are Different

When we add or subtract fractional expressions with different denominators which are not additive inverses of each other, we first find a common denominator, using the LCM, and then add or subtract the numerators.

EXAMPLE 6
Add.

$$\frac{2a}{5} + \frac{3b}{2a}$$

First find the LCM of the denominators.

$\begin{aligned}5\\2a\end{aligned}$ The LCM is $5 \cdot 2a$ or $10a$.

Now we multiply each expression by 1. For each expression we choose whatever symbol for 1 will give us the LCM in each denominator.

$$\frac{2a}{5} \cdot \frac{2a}{2a} + \frac{3b}{2a} \cdot \frac{5}{5} = \frac{4a^2}{10a} + \frac{15b}{10a}$$

$$= \frac{4a^2 + 15b}{10a}$$

EXAMPLE 7
Add.

$$\frac{1}{2x} + \frac{5x}{x^2 - 1} + \frac{3}{x + 1}$$

We first find the LCM of the denominators.

$$\left.\begin{aligned}2x &= 2x\\x^2 - 1 &= (x - 1)(x + 1)\\x + 1 &= x + 1\end{aligned}\right\}\quad \text{The LCM is } 2x(x - 1)(x + 1).$$

Now we multiply by 1 to get the LCM in each expression. Then we add and simplify. We leave the denominator factored to ease possible simplifying at the end.

$$\frac{1}{2x} \cdot \frac{(x - 1)(x + 1)}{(x - 1)(x + 1)} + \frac{5x}{(x - 1)(x + 1)} \cdot \frac{2x}{2x} + \frac{3}{x + 1} \cdot \frac{2x(x - 1)}{2x(x - 1)}$$

$$= \frac{(x - 1)(x + 1)}{2x(x - 1)(x + 1)} + \frac{10x^2}{2x(x - 1)(x + 1)} + \frac{6x(x - 1)}{2x(x - 1)(x + 1)}$$

$$= \frac{x^2 - 1}{2x(x - 1)(x + 1)} + \frac{10x^2}{2x(x - 1)(x + 1)} + \frac{6x^2 - 6x}{2x(x - 1)(x + 1)}$$

$$= \frac{17x^2 - 6x - 1}{2x(x - 1)(x + 1)}$$

TRY THIS Add. Leave denominators factored.

7. $\dfrac{3x}{7} + \dfrac{4y}{3x}$ 8. $\dfrac{2xy - 2x^2}{x^2 - y^2} + \dfrac{2x + 3}{x + y}$ 7. $\frac{9x^2 + 28y}{21x}$ 8. $\frac{3}{x + y}$

EXAMPLE 8
Subtract.

$$\frac{2y + 1}{y^2 - 7y + 6} - \frac{y + 3}{y^2 - 5y - 6} = \frac{2y + 1}{(y - 6)(y - 1)} - \frac{y + 3}{(y - 6)(y + 1)} \quad \begin{array}{l}\text{The LCM is}\\ (y - 6)(y - 1)(y + 1).\end{array}$$

$$= \frac{2y + 1}{(y - 6)(y - 1)} \cdot \frac{y + 1}{y + 1} - \frac{y + 3}{(y - 6)(y + 1)} \cdot \frac{y - 1}{y - 1}$$

$$= \frac{(2y + 1)(y + 1) - (y + 3)(y - 1)}{(y - 6)(y - 1)(y + 1)}$$

$$= \frac{2y^2 + 3y + 1 - (y^2 + 2y - 3)}{(y - 6)(y - 1)(y + 1)}$$

$$= \frac{2y^2 + 3y + 1 - y^2 - 2y + 3}{(y - 6)(y - 1)(y + 1)}$$

$$= \frac{y^2 + y + 4}{(y - 6)(y - 1)(y + 1)}$$

TRY THIS Subtract.

9. $\dfrac{4y - 5}{y^2 - 7y + 12} - \dfrac{y + 7}{y^2 + 2y - 15}$ 10. $\dfrac{a}{a + 3} - \dfrac{a - 4}{a}$ 9. $\frac{3y^2 + 12y + 3}{(y - 4)(y - 3)(y + 5)}$ 10. $\frac{a + 12}{a(a + 3)}$

6–3

Exercises
Perform the indicated operations. Simplify when possible. If a denominator has three or more factors (other than monomials) leave it factored.

1. $\dfrac{a - 3b}{a + b} + \dfrac{a + 5b}{a + b}$ 2

2. $\dfrac{x - 5y}{x + y} + \dfrac{x + 7y}{x + y}$ 2

3. $\dfrac{4y + 3}{y - 2} - \dfrac{y - 2}{y - 2}$ $\frac{3y + 5}{y - 2}$

4. $\dfrac{3t + 2}{t - 4} - \dfrac{t - 4}{t - 4}$ $\frac{2t + 6}{t - 4}$

5. $\dfrac{a^2}{a - b} + \dfrac{b^2}{b - a}$ $a + b$

6. $\dfrac{r^2}{r - s} + \dfrac{s^2}{s - r}$ $r + s$

7. $\dfrac{3}{x} - \dfrac{8}{-x}$ $\frac{11}{x}$

8. $\dfrac{2}{a} - \dfrac{5}{-a}$ $\frac{7}{a}$

9. $\dfrac{2x - 10}{x^2 - 25} - \dfrac{5 - x}{25 - x^2}$ $\frac{1}{x + 5}$

10. $\dfrac{y - 9}{y^2 - 16} - \dfrac{7 - y}{16 - y^2}$ $\frac{-2}{y^2 - 16}$

11. $\dfrac{y - 2}{y + 4} + \dfrac{y + 3}{y - 5}$ $\frac{2y^2 + 22}{y^2 - y - 20}$

12. $\dfrac{x - 2}{x + 3} + \dfrac{x + 2}{x - 4}$ $\frac{2x^2 - x + 14}{x^2 - x - 12}$

13. $\dfrac{4xy}{x^2 - y^2} + \dfrac{x - y}{x + y}$ $\dfrac{x + y}{x - y}$

14. $\dfrac{5ab}{a^2 - b^2} + \dfrac{a + b}{a - b}$ $\dfrac{a^2 + 7ab + b^2}{a^2 - b^2}$

15. $\dfrac{3x - 4}{x^2 - 3x + 2}$

15. $\dfrac{9x + 2}{3x^2 - 2x - 8} + \dfrac{7}{3x^2 + x - 4}$

16. $\dfrac{3y + 2}{2y^2 - y - 10} + \dfrac{8}{2y^2 - 7y + 5}$ $\dfrac{3y^2 + 7y + 14}{(2y - 5)(y + 2)(y - 1)}$

17. $\dfrac{4}{x + 1} + \dfrac{x + 2}{x^2 - 1} + \dfrac{3}{x - 1}$ $\dfrac{8x + 1}{x^2 - 1}$

18. $\dfrac{-2}{y + 2} + \dfrac{5}{y - 2} + \dfrac{y + 3}{y^2 - 4}$ $\dfrac{4y + 17}{y^2 - 4}$

19. $\dfrac{x - 1}{3x + 15} - \dfrac{x + 3}{5x + 25}$ $\dfrac{2x - 14}{15x + 75}$

20. $\dfrac{y - 2}{4y + 8} - \dfrac{y + 6}{5y + 10}$ $\dfrac{y - 34}{20y + 40}$

21. $\dfrac{5ab}{a^2 - b^2} - \dfrac{a - b}{a + b}$ $\dfrac{-a^2 + 7ab - b^2}{a^2 - b^2}$

22. $\dfrac{6xy}{x^2 - y^2} - \dfrac{x + y}{x - y}$ $\dfrac{-x^2 + 4xy - y^2}{x^2 - y^2}$

23. $\dfrac{3y}{y^2 - 7y + 10} - \dfrac{2y}{y^2 - 8y + 15}$

24. $\dfrac{5x}{x^2 - 6x + 8} - \dfrac{3x}{x^2 - x - 12}$ $\dfrac{2x^2 + 21x}{(x - 2)(x - 4)(x + 3)}$

25. $\dfrac{y}{y^2 - y - 20} + \dfrac{2}{y + 4}$ $\dfrac{3y - 10}{y^2 - y - 20}$

26. $\dfrac{6}{y^2 + 6y + 9} + \dfrac{5}{y^2 - 9}$ $\dfrac{11y - 3}{(y + 3)^2(y - 3)}$

27. $\dfrac{3y + 2}{y^2 + 5y - 24} + \dfrac{7}{y^2 + 4y - 32}$

28. $\dfrac{3y + 2}{y^2 - 7y + 10} + \dfrac{2y}{y^2 - 8y + 15}$ $\dfrac{5y^2 - 11y - 6}{(y - 2)(y - 5)(y - 3)}$

29. $\dfrac{3x - 1}{x^2 + 2x - 3} - \dfrac{x + 4}{x^2 - 9}$

30. $\dfrac{3p - 2}{p^2 + 2p - 24} - \dfrac{p - 3}{p^2 - 16}$ $\dfrac{2p^2 + 7p + 10}{(p - 4)(p + 6)(p + 4)}$

31. $\dfrac{1}{x + 1} - \dfrac{x}{x - 2} + \dfrac{x^2 + 2}{x^2 - x - 2}$ 0

32. $\dfrac{2}{y + 3} - \dfrac{y}{y - 1} + \dfrac{y^2 + 2}{y^2 + 2y - 3}$ $\dfrac{-y}{y^2 + 2y - 3}$

33. $\dfrac{4x}{x^2 - 1} + \dfrac{3x}{1 - x} - \dfrac{4}{x - 1}$

34. $\dfrac{5y}{1 - 2y} - \dfrac{2y}{2y + 1} + \dfrac{3}{4y^2 - 1}$ $\dfrac{-14y^2 - 3y + 3}{4y^2 - 1}$

23. $\dfrac{y}{(y - 2)(y - 3)}$

29. $\dfrac{2x^2 - 13x + 7}{(x + 3)(x - 1)(x - 3)}$

Extension
Perform the indicated operations and simplify.

27. $\dfrac{3y^2 - 3y - 29}{(y - 3)(y + 8)(y - 4)}$

33. $\dfrac{-3x^2 - 3x - 4}{x^2 - 1}$

35. $2x^{-2} + 3x^{-2}y^{-2} - 7xy^{-1}$ $\dfrac{2y^2 + 3 - 7x^3y}{x^2y^2}$

36. $5(x - 3)^{-1} + 4(x + 3)^{-1} - 2(x + 3)^{-2}$ $\dfrac{9x^2 - 28x + 15}{(x - 3)(x + 3)^2}$

37. $4(y - 1)(2y - 5)^{-1} + 5(2y + 3)(5 - 2y)^{-1} + (y - 4)(2y - 5)^{-1}$ $\dfrac{5y + 23}{5 - 2y}$

Simplify each of the following, using $A = x + y$ and $B = x - y$.

38. $\dfrac{A + B}{A - B} - \dfrac{A - B}{A + B}$ $\dfrac{x^2 - y^2}{xy}$

39. $\left(\dfrac{1}{A} + \dfrac{x}{B}\right) \div \left(\dfrac{1}{B} - \dfrac{x}{A}\right)$ $\dfrac{x - y + x^2 + xy}{x + y - x^2 + xy}$

Challenge
Consider the following polynomial functions.

$$p(x) = x, \; g(x) = x^2 - 16, \; h(x) = x^2 + x - 20, \; d(x) = x^2 - 25$$

A *rational function* is given by a ratio of two polynomials. Find a simplified expression for each rational function given below.

40. $\dfrac{x - 4}{x - 5}$

41. $\dfrac{x + 4}{x + 5}$

42. $\dfrac{x^2 - 30}{x^2 - 11}$

40. $R(x) = \dfrac{h(x)}{d(x)}$

41. $R(x) = \dfrac{g(x)}{h(x)}$

42. $R(x) = \dfrac{d(d(x))}{h(g(x))}$

43. Prove the first part of Theorem 6–4.

44. Prove the second part of Theorem 6–4.

6–4 Complex Fractional Expressions

DEFINITION

A *complex fractional expression* is one that has a fractional expression in its numerator or its denominator, or both.

The following are examples of complex fractional expressions.

$$\frac{x}{x - \frac{1}{3}}, \quad \frac{2x - \frac{4x}{3y}}{\frac{5x^2 + 2x}{6y^2}}, \quad \frac{a^{-1} + b^{-1}}{a^{-3}b^{-3}}, \quad \frac{\frac{5}{x}}{\frac{x}{y}}$$

We will show two different methods for simplifying complex fractional expressions.

Simplifying Complex Fractional Expressions

METHOD 1
1. Simplify numerator and denominator separately to obtain a single fractional expression in each.
2. Treat the result as a division.
3. Factor and simplify as usual.

METHOD 2
1. Find the LCM of all denominators appearing in the complex fractional expression.
2. Multiply the complex fractional expression by 1, using $\frac{n}{n}$ when n is the LCM found in step 1. The distributive property is important here.
3. Factor and simplify as usual.

EXAMPLE 1

Simplify $\dfrac{1 + \frac{1}{x}}{1 - \frac{1}{x^2}}$.

METHOD 1

$$\frac{1 + \frac{1}{x}}{1 - \frac{1}{x^2}} = \frac{\frac{x}{x} + \frac{1}{x}}{\frac{x^2}{x^2} - \frac{1}{x^2}} = \frac{\frac{x + 1}{x}}{\frac{x^2 - 1}{x^2}} \quad \text{Step 1}$$

$$= \frac{x + 1}{x} \div \frac{x^2 - 1}{x^2} = \frac{x + 1}{x} \cdot \frac{x^2}{x^2 - 1} \quad \text{Step 2}$$

$$= \frac{(x + 1)x^2}{x(x + 1)(x - 1)} = \frac{(x + 1)x}{(x + 1)x} \cdot \frac{x}{x - 1} = \frac{x}{x - 1} \quad \text{Step 3}$$

METHOD 2

$$\frac{1 + \frac{1}{x}}{1 - \frac{1}{x^2}} \text{ has denominators } x \text{ and } x^2; \text{ LCM is } x^2. \quad \text{Step 1}$$

$$\frac{\left(1 + \frac{1}{x}\right)}{\left(1 - \frac{1}{x^2}\right)} \cdot \frac{x^2}{x^2} = \frac{\left(1 + \frac{1}{x}\right)x^2}{\left(1 - \frac{1}{x^2}\right)x^2} = \frac{x^2 + x}{x^2 - 1} \quad \text{Step 2}$$

$$= \frac{x(x + 1)}{(x + 1)(x - 1)} = \frac{(x + 1)}{(x + 1)} \cdot \frac{x}{x - 1} = \frac{x}{x - 1} \quad \text{Step 3}$$

TRY THIS Simplify. Use either method.

1. $\dfrac{y + \frac{1}{2}}{y - \frac{1}{7}}$ 2. $\dfrac{1 - \frac{1}{x}}{1 - \frac{1}{x^2}}$ 1. $\frac{14y + 7}{14y - 2}$ 2. $\frac{x}{x + 1}$

When simplifying fractional expressions that have negative integers
as exponents, first rename the expression to remove the negative
integer exponents. Then simplify the new complex fractional
expression by using either method described above.

6–4

Exercises

Simplify.

1. $\dfrac{\frac{1}{x} + 4}{\frac{1}{x} - 3}$ 2. $\dfrac{\frac{1}{y} + 7}{\frac{1}{y} - 5}$ 3. $\dfrac{x - \frac{1}{x}}{x + \frac{1}{x}}$ 4. $\dfrac{y + \frac{1}{y}}{y - \frac{1}{y}}$

1. $\frac{1 + 4x}{1 - 3x}$
2. $\frac{1 + 7y}{1 - 5y}$
3. $\frac{x^2 - 1}{x^2 + 1}$
4. $\frac{y^2 + 1}{y^2 - 1}$

5. $\dfrac{\dfrac{3}{x}+\dfrac{4}{y}}{\dfrac{4}{x}-\dfrac{3}{y}}$

6. $\dfrac{\dfrac{2}{y}+\dfrac{5}{z}}{\dfrac{1}{y}-\dfrac{4}{z}}$

7. $\dfrac{\dfrac{x^2-y^2}{xy}}{\dfrac{x-y}{y}}$

8. $\dfrac{\dfrac{a^2-b^2}{ab}}{\dfrac{a+b}{b}}$

5. $\dfrac{3y+4x}{4y-3x}$

6. $\dfrac{2z+5y}{z-4y}$

7. $\dfrac{x+y}{x}$

8. $\dfrac{a-b}{a}$

9. $\dfrac{a^2(b-3)}{b^2(a-1)}$

10. $\dfrac{3}{3x+2}$

11. $\dfrac{1}{a-b}$

12. $\dfrac{-1}{x+y}$

13. $\dfrac{1+x^2}{x}$

14. $\dfrac{1+y^4}{y(1+y^2)}$

15. $\dfrac{y-3}{y+5}$

9. $\dfrac{a-\dfrac{3a}{b}}{b-\dfrac{b}{a}}$

10. $\dfrac{1-\dfrac{2}{3x}}{x-\dfrac{4}{9x}}$

11. $\dfrac{\dfrac{1}{a}+\dfrac{1}{b}}{\dfrac{a^2-b^2}{ab}}$

12. $\dfrac{\dfrac{1}{x}-\dfrac{1}{y}}{\dfrac{x^2-y^2}{xy}}$

13. $\dfrac{x^{-3}-x}{x^{-2}-1}$

14. $\dfrac{y^{-3}+y}{y^{-2}+1}$

15. $\dfrac{\dfrac{y^2-y-6}{y^2-5y-14}}{\dfrac{y^2+6y+5}{y^2-6y-7}}$

16. $\dfrac{\dfrac{x^2-x-12}{x^2-2x-15}}{\dfrac{x^2+8x+12}{x^2-5x-14}}$

16. $\dfrac{(x-4)(x-7)}{(x-5)(x+6)}$

17. $\dfrac{1+x}{1-x}$

18. $\dfrac{x^3(x+y)}{yx^3-2xy^3+y^4}$

19. $\dfrac{3}{4}$

20. $\dfrac{5(y-x-2)}{6(x+2)}$

21. $\dfrac{6x-2}{5x+6}$

22. $\dfrac{-4a-4}{8a-5}$

17. $\dfrac{\dfrac{x}{1-x}+\dfrac{1+x}{x}}{\dfrac{1-x}{x}+\dfrac{x}{1+x}}$

18. $\dfrac{\dfrac{y}{x-y}+\dfrac{x+y}{y}}{\dfrac{x-y}{x}+\dfrac{y}{x+y}}$

19. $\dfrac{3a^{-1}+3b^{-1}-6a^{-1}b^{-1}}{4a^{-1}+4b^{-1}-8a^{-1}b^{-1}}$

20. $\dfrac{5x^{-1}-5y^{-1}+10x^{-1}y^{-1}}{6y^{-1}+12x^{-1}y^{-1}}$

21. $\dfrac{\dfrac{4}{x-5}+\dfrac{2}{x+2}}{\dfrac{2x}{x^2-3x-10}+\dfrac{3}{x-5}}$

22. $\dfrac{\dfrac{4a}{2a^2-a-1}-\dfrac{4}{a-1}}{\dfrac{1}{a-1}+\dfrac{6}{2a+1}}$

Extension

Find the reciprocal of each of the following.

23. $\dfrac{1}{x}+1$

24. $x^2-\dfrac{1}{x}$

25. $\dfrac{1-\dfrac{1}{a}}{a-1}$

26. $\dfrac{a^3+b^3}{a+b}$

23. $\dfrac{x}{x+1}$

24. $\dfrac{x}{x^3+1}$

25. a

26. $\dfrac{1}{a^2-ab+b^2}$

30. $\dfrac{-6x-3h}{x^2(x+h)^2}$

31. $\dfrac{-5}{x(x+h)}$

32. $\dfrac{1}{(1-x-h)(1-x)}$

33. $\dfrac{1}{(1+x)(1+x+h)}$

Challenge
Simplify.

27. $1+\dfrac{1}{1+\dfrac{1}{1+\dfrac{1}{1+\dfrac{1}{x}}}}$ $\dfrac{5x+3}{3x+2}$

28. $(a^2-ab+b^2)^{-1}(a^2b^{-1}+b^2a^{-1})(a^{-2}-b^{-2})(a^{-2}+2a^{-1}b^{-1}+b^{-2})^{-1}$ $\dfrac{b-a}{ab}$

29. For $f(x)=\dfrac{1}{1-x}$, find $f(f(x))$ and $f(f(f(x)))$. $\dfrac{x-1}{x};x$

Find and simplify $\dfrac{f(x+h)-f(x)}{h}$ for each rational function f.

30. $f(x)=\dfrac{3}{x^2}$

31. $f(x)=\dfrac{5}{x}$

32. $f(x)=\dfrac{1}{1-x}$

33. $f(x)=\dfrac{x}{1+x}$

6–5 Division of Polynomials

Divisor a Monomial

Remember that fractional expressions indicate division. Division by a monomial can be done by first writing a fractional expression.

EXAMPLE 1
Divide $12x^3 + 8x^2 + x + 4$ by $4x$.

$$\frac{12x^3 + 8x^2 + x + 4}{4x} \quad \text{Writing a fractional expression}$$

$$= \frac{12x^3}{4x} + \frac{8x^2}{4x} + \frac{x}{4x} + \frac{4}{4x} \quad \text{Theorem 6–4}$$

$$= 3x^2 + 2x + \frac{1}{4} + \frac{1}{x} \quad \text{Doing the four indicated divisions}$$

TRY THIS Divide. 1. $\frac{x^2}{2} + 8x + 3$ 2. $4x^2 + x + 2$ 3. $2x^6 + \frac{3}{2}x^5 + 3x^4 + 6x^3 + x^2 + \frac{1}{2}x + 1$

1. $\frac{x^3 + 16x^2 + 6x}{2x}$ **2.** $12x^3 + 3x^2 + 6x \div 3x$

3. $4x^7 + 3x^6 + 6x^5 + 12x^4 + 2x^3 + x^2 + 2x \div 2x$

EXAMPLE 2
Divide $(8x^4 - 3x^3 + 5x^2)$ by x^2.

$$\frac{8x^4 - 3x^3 + 5x^2}{x^2} = \frac{8x^4}{x^2} - \frac{3x^3}{x^2} + \frac{5x^2}{x^2}$$

$$= 8x^2 - 3x + 5$$

You should try to write only the answer.

> To divide a polynomial by a monomial we can divide each term by the monomial.

TRY THIS Divide.

4. $(15y^5 - 6y^4 + 18y^3) \div 3y^2$ **5.** $(x^4 + 10x^3 + 16x^2) \div 2x^2$

6. $\frac{16y^4 + 4y^3 + 2y^2}{4y}$ 4. $5y^3 - 2y^2 + 6y$ 5. $\frac{x^2}{2} + 5x + 8$ 6. $4y^3 + y^2 + \frac{1}{2}y$

Divisor Not a Monomial

When the divisor is not a monomial, we use a procedure very much like long division in arithmetic.

EXAMPLE 3

Divide $x^2 + 5x + 6$ by $x + 3$.

$$
\begin{array}{r}
x \quad\quad\quad\quad \longleftarrow \text{Divide first term by first term: } \frac{x^2}{x} = x \\
x + 3\overline{)x^2 + 5x + 6} \\
\underline{x^2 + 3x} \longleftarrow \text{Multiply } x \text{ by divisor} \\
2x \longleftarrow \text{Subtract}
\end{array}
$$

We now "bring down" the next term of the dividend, 6.

$$
\begin{array}{r}
x \; + 2 \longleftarrow \text{Divide first term by first term: } \frac{2x}{x} = 2 \\
x + 3\overline{)x^2 + 5x + 6} \\
\underline{x^2 + 3x} \\
2x + 6 \\
\underline{2x + 6} \longleftarrow \text{Multiply 2 by divisor} \\
0 \longleftarrow \text{Subtract}
\end{array}
$$

Answer: Quotient $x + 2$, remainder 0.

To check, we multiply quotient by divisor and add the remainder, if any, to see if we get the dividend. This answer checks.

TRY THIS Divide and check.

7. $x - 2\overline{)x^2 + 3x - 10}$ $x + 5$

Always remember to arrange polynomials in descending order and to leave space for missing terms in the dividend (or write them with 0 coefficients).

EXAMPLE 4

Divide $(125y^3 - 8)$ by $(5y - 2)$.

$$
\begin{array}{r}
25y^2 + 10y + 4 \\
5y - 2\overline{)125y^3 \quad\quad\quad\quad - 8} \\
\underline{125y^3 - 50y^2} \longleftarrow \text{Leave space for missing terms} \\
50y^2 \\
\underline{50y^2 - 20y} \\
20y - 8 \\
\underline{20y - 8} \\
0
\end{array}
$$

EXAMPLE 5

Divide $(x^4 - 9x^2 - 5)$ by $(x - 2)$.

$$
\begin{array}{r}
x^3 + 2x^2 - 5x - 10 \\
x - 2\overline{)x^4 \qquad - 9x^2 \qquad - 5}
\end{array}
$$

$\underline{x^4 - 2x^3}$ The first subtraction is $x^4 - (x^4 - 2x^3)$.

$2x^3 - 9x^2$

$\underline{2x^3 - 4x^2}$ The second subtraction is $(2x^3 - 9x^2) - (2x^3 - 4x^2)$.

$-5x^2$

$\underline{-5x^2 + 10x}$

$-10x - 5$

$\underline{-10x + 20}$

-25

The answer is $x^3 + 2x^2 - 5x - 10$, R -25, or

$$x^3 + 2x^2 - 5x - 10 + \frac{-25}{x - 2}.$$

TRY THIS Divide and check.

8. $(9y^4 + 14y^2 - 8) \div (3y + 2)$ 9. $(y^3 - 11y^2 + 6) \div (y - 3)$ 8. $3y^3 - 2y^2 + 6y - 4$
9. $y^2 - 8y - 24$, R -66

When dividing, we continue until the degree of the remainder is less than the degree of the divisor. The answer can be written as the quotient and remainder, or as a fractional expression.

EXAMPLE 6

Divide $(x^3 + 9x^2 - 5)$ by $(x^2 - 1)$.

$$
\begin{array}{r}
x + 9 \\
x^2 - 1\overline{)x^3 + 9x^2 + 0x - 5}
\end{array}
$$

$\underline{x^3 \qquad - x}$ Again we have a missing term, so we can write it in.

$9x^2 + x - 5$

$\underline{9x^2 \qquad - 9}$

$x + 4$ The degree of the remainder is less than the degree of the divisor, so we are finished.

The answer is $x + 9$, with R $x + 4$, or

$$x + 9 + \frac{x + 4}{x^2 - 1}$$ This expression is the remainder over the divisor.

TRY THIS Divide and check.

10. $(y^3 - 11y^2 + 6) \div (y^2 - 3)$ $y - 11 + \frac{3y - 27}{y^2 - 3}$

6–5

Exercises

Divide.

1. $\dfrac{30x^8 - 15x^6 + 40x^4}{5x^4}$

2. $\dfrac{24y^6 + 18y^5 - 36y^2}{6y^2}$

3. $\dfrac{-14a^3 + 28a^2 - 21a}{7a}$

4. $\dfrac{-32x^4 - 24x^3 - 12x^2}{4x}$

5. $(9y^4 - 18y^3 + 27y^2) \div 9y$

6. $(24a^3 + 28a^2 - 20a) \div 2a$

7. $(36x^6 - 18x^4 - 12x^2) \div -6x$

8. $(18y^7 - 27y^4 - 3y^2) \div -3y^2$

9. $(a^2b - a^3b^3 - a^5b^2) \div a^2b$

10. $(x^3y^2 - x^3y^3 - x^4y^2) \div x^2y^2$

11. $(6p^2q^2 - 9p^2q + 12pq^2) \div -3pq$

12. $(16y^4z^2 - 8y^6z^4 + 12y^8z^3) \div 4y^4z$

Divide and check.

13. $(x^2 + 10x + 21) \div (x + 3)$

14. $(y^2 - 8y + 16) \div (y - 4)$

15. $(a^2 - 8a - 16) \div (a + 4)$

16. $(y^2 - 10y - 25) \div (y - 5)$

17. $(y^2 - 25) \div (y + 5)$

18. $(a^2 - 81) \div (a - 9)$

19. $(y^3 - 4y^2 + 3y - 6) \div (y - 2)$

20. $(x^3 - 5x^2 + 4x - 7) \div (x - 3)$

21. $(a^3 - a + 12) \div (a - 4)$

22. $(x^3 - x + 6) \div (x + 2)$

23. $(8x^3 + 27) \div (2x + 3)$

24. $(64y^3 - 8) \div (4y - 2)$

25. $(x^4 - x^2 - 42) \div (x^2 - 7)$

26. $(y^4 - y^2 - 54) \div (y^2 - 3)$

27. $(x^4 - x^2 - x + 2) \div (x - 1)$

28. $(y^4 - y^2 - y + 3) \div (y + 1)$

29. $(10y^3 + 6y^2 - 9y + 10) \div (5y - 2)$ $\quad 2y^2 + 2y - 1 + \dfrac{8}{5y-2}$

30. $(6x^3 - 11x^2 + 11x - 2) \div (2x - 3)$ $\quad 3x^2 - x + 4 + \dfrac{10}{2x-3}$

31. $(2x^4 - x^3 - 5x^2 + x - 6) \div (x^2 + 2)$ $\quad 2x^2 - x - 9 + \dfrac{3x+12}{x^2+2}$

32. $(3x^4 + 2x^3 - 11x^2 - 2x + 5) \div (x^2 - 2)$ $\quad 3x^2 + 2x - 5 + \dfrac{2x-5}{x^2-2}$

Extension

Divide.

33. $(x^4 - x^3y + x^2y^2 + 2x^2y - 2xy^2 + 2y^3) \div (x^2 - xy + y^2)$ $\quad x^2 + 2y$

34. $(4a^3b + 5a^2b^2 + a^4 + 2ab^3) \div (a^2 + 2b^2 + 3ab)$ $\quad a^2 + ab$

35. $(x^4 - y^4) \div (x - y)$ $\quad x^3 + x^2y + xy^2 + y^3$

36. $(a^7 + b^7) \div (a + b)$ $\quad a^6 - a^5b + a^4b^2 - a^3b^3 + a^2b^4 - ab^5 + b^6$

Challenge

37. Find k so that when $x^3 - kx^2 + 3x + 7k$ is divided by $x + 2$ the remainder will be 0. $\quad \frac{14}{3}$

38. When $x^2 - 3x + 2k$ is divided by $x + 2$ the remainder is 7. Find the value of k. $\quad -\frac{3}{2}$

6-6 Solving Fractional Equations

A fractional equation is an equation which contains one or more fractional expressions. These are fractional equations.

$$\frac{2}{3} + \frac{5}{6} = \frac{1}{x}, \frac{x-1}{x-5} = \frac{4}{x-5}$$

To solve a fractional equation we multiply on both sides by the LCM of all the denominators. This is called clearing fractions

EXAMPLE 1

Solve $\frac{2}{3} - \frac{5}{6} = \frac{1}{x}$.

The LCM of all denominators is $6x$, or $2 \cdot 3 \cdot x$.

$$(2 \cdot 3 \cdot x) \cdot \left(\frac{2}{3} - \frac{5}{6}\right) = (2 \cdot 3 \cdot x) \cdot \frac{1}{x} \quad \text{Multiplying by LCM}$$

$$2 \cdot 3 \cdot x \cdot \frac{2}{3} - 2 \cdot 3 \cdot x \cdot \frac{5}{6} = 2 \cdot 3 \cdot x \cdot \frac{1}{x} \quad \text{Multiplying to remove parentheses}$$

$$\frac{2 \cdot 3 \cdot x \cdot 2}{3} - \frac{2 \cdot 3 \cdot x \cdot 5}{6} = \frac{2 \cdot 3 \cdot x}{x}$$

$$4x - 5x = 6 \quad \text{Simplifying}$$
$$-x = 6$$
$$x = -6$$

Check:

$$\frac{2}{3} - \frac{5}{6} = \frac{1}{x}$$

$$\begin{array}{c|c} \frac{2}{3} - \frac{5}{6} & \frac{1}{-6} \\ \frac{4}{6} - \frac{5}{6} & -\frac{1}{6} \\ -\frac{1}{6} & \end{array}$$

When clearing fractions, be sure to multiply every term in the equation by the LCM. Note that when we clear fractions all the denominators disappear. Thus we have an equation without fractional expressions, which we know how to solve.

TRY THIS Solve.

1. $\frac{2}{3} + \frac{5}{6} = \frac{1}{x}$ $\frac{2}{3}$

EXAMPLE 2

Solve $\dfrac{x-1}{x-5} = \dfrac{4}{x-5}$.

The LCM of the denominators is $x-5$. We multiply by $x-5$.

$$(x-5) \cdot \dfrac{x-1}{x-5} = (x-5) \cdot \dfrac{4}{x-5}$$

$$x - 1 = 4$$

$$x = 5$$

Check: $\dfrac{x-1}{x-5} = \dfrac{4}{x-5}$

$$\begin{array}{c|c} \dfrac{5-1}{5-5} & \dfrac{4}{5-5} \\[2ex] \dfrac{4}{0} & \dfrac{4}{0} \end{array}$$

5 is not a solution of the original equation because it results in division by 0. In fact, the equation has no solution.

TRY THIS Solve.

2. $\dfrac{y-2}{5} - \dfrac{y-5}{4} = -2$ 3. $\dfrac{x-7}{x-9} = \dfrac{2}{x-9}$ 2. $y = 57$ 3. No solution

In general, when in solving an equation we multiply by an expression containing a variable, we may not get equivalent equations. We may get an equation having solutions that the original one does not. Thus we must always check possible solutions in the original equation.

EXAMPLES

3. Solve $\dfrac{x^2}{x-2} = \dfrac{4}{x-2}$.

The LCM of all the denominators is $x-2$. We multiply by $x-2$ to clear of fractions.

$$(x-2) \cdot \dfrac{x^2}{x-2} = (x-2) \cdot \dfrac{4}{x-2}$$

$$x^2 = 4$$

$$x^2 - 4 = 0$$

$$(x+2)(x-2) = 0$$

$$x = -2 \text{ or } x = 2 \quad \text{Using the principle of zero products}$$

The number -2 checks, but 2 does not (it results in division by 0). The solution is -2.

4. Solve $x + \frac{6}{x} = 5$.

The LCM of the denominators is x. We multiply on both sides by x.

$$x\left(x + \frac{6}{x}\right) = 5 \cdot x \quad \text{Multiplying on both sides by } x$$

$$x^2 + x \cdot \frac{6}{x} = 5x$$

$$x^2 + 6 = 5x \quad \text{Simplifying}$$
$$x^2 - 5x + 6 = 0 \quad \text{Getting 0 on one side}$$
$$(x - 3)(x - 2) = 0 \quad \text{Factoring}$$
$$x = 3 \text{ or } x = 2 \quad \text{Using the principle of zero products}$$

Check:
$$\begin{array}{c|c} x + \dfrac{6}{x} = 5 & \\ \hline 3 + \dfrac{6}{3} & 5 \\ 5 & \end{array} \qquad \begin{array}{c|c} x + \dfrac{6}{x} = 5 & \\ \hline 2 + \dfrac{6}{2} & 5 \\ 5 & \end{array}$$

The solutions are 2 and 3.

TRY THIS Solve.

4. $\dfrac{x^2}{x + 3} = \dfrac{9}{x + 3}$ 3   **5.** $x - \dfrac{12}{x} = 1$ $x = 4, x = -3$

EXAMPLE 5

Solve $\dfrac{2}{x + 5} + \dfrac{1}{x - 5} = \dfrac{16}{x^2 - 25}$.

The LCM is $(x + 5)(x - 5)$. We multiply by $(x + 5)(x - 5)$.

$$(x + 5)(x - 5) \cdot \left[\frac{2}{x + 5} + \frac{1}{x - 5}\right] = (x + 5)(x - 5) \cdot \frac{16}{x^2 - 25}$$

$$(x + 5)(x - 5) \cdot \frac{2}{x + 5} + (x + 5)(x - 5) \cdot \frac{1}{x - 5} = (x + 5)(x - 5) \cdot \frac{16}{x^2 - 25}$$

$$2(x - 5) + (x + 5) = 16$$
$$2x - 10 + x + 5 = 16$$
$$x = 7$$

This checks in the original equation, so the solution is 7.

TRY THIS Solve.

6. $\dfrac{2}{x - 1} = \dfrac{3}{x + 2}$ **7.** $\dfrac{2}{x^2 - 9} + \dfrac{5}{x - 3} = \dfrac{3}{x + 3}$ 6. $x = 7$ 7. $x = -13$

Exercises

Solve.

1. $\frac{2}{5} + \frac{7}{8} = \frac{y}{20}$ $\frac{51}{2}$ 2. $\frac{1}{3} - \frac{5}{6} = \frac{1}{x}$ -2 3. $\frac{5}{8} - \frac{2}{5} = \frac{1}{y}$ $\frac{40}{9}$

4. $\frac{x}{3} - \frac{x}{4} = 12$ 144 5. $y + \frac{5}{y} = -6$ $-5, -1$ 6. $\frac{y+2}{4} - \frac{y-1}{5} = 15$ 286

7. $\frac{x+1}{3} - \frac{x-1}{2} = 1$ -1 8. $\frac{4}{3y} - \frac{3}{y} = \frac{10}{3}$ $-\frac{1}{2}$ 9. $\frac{x-3}{x+2} = \frac{1}{5}$ $\frac{17}{4}$

10. $\frac{y-5}{y+1} = \frac{3}{5}$ 14 11. $\frac{y-1}{y-3} = \frac{2}{y-3}$ 12. $\frac{3}{y+1} = \frac{2}{y-3}$ 11

$\qquad\qquad\qquad\qquad\qquad\qquad\qquad$ No solution

13. $\frac{x+1}{x} = \frac{3}{2}$ 2 14. $\frac{y+2}{y} = \frac{5}{3}$ 3 15. $\frac{2}{x} - \frac{3}{x} + \frac{4}{x} = 5$ $\frac{3}{5}$ 16. $\frac{4}{y} - \frac{6}{y} + \frac{8}{y} = 8$ $\frac{3}{4}$

17. $\frac{1}{2} + \frac{2}{x} = \frac{1}{3} + \frac{3}{x}$ 6 18. $-\frac{1}{3} - \frac{5}{4y} = \frac{3}{4} - \frac{1}{6y}$ -1 19. $\frac{60}{x} - \frac{60}{x-5} = \frac{2}{x}$ -145

20. $\frac{50}{y} - \frac{50}{y-2} = \frac{4}{y}$ -23 21. $\frac{7}{5x-2} = \frac{5}{4x}$ $-\frac{10}{3}$ 22. $\frac{1}{2t} - \frac{2}{5t} = \frac{1}{10t} - 3$ No solution

23. $\frac{x}{x-2} + \frac{x}{x^2-4} = \frac{x+3}{x+2}$ -3 24. $\frac{3}{y-2} + \frac{2y}{4-y^2} = \frac{5}{y+2}$ 4

25. $\frac{a}{2a-6} - \frac{3}{a^2-6a+9} = \frac{a-2}{3a-9}$ 26. $\frac{2}{x+4} + \frac{2x-1}{x^2+2x-8} = \frac{1}{x-2}$ 3

$\qquad\qquad\qquad\qquad\qquad\qquad -6, 5$

27. $\frac{2x+3}{x-1} = \frac{10}{x^2-1} + \frac{2x-3}{x+1}$ No solution   28. $\frac{y}{y+1} + \frac{3y+5}{y^2+4y+3} = \frac{2}{y+3}$ $-3, -1$

Extension

Solve. Use a calculator for Exercises 29 and 30.

29. $\frac{2.315}{y} - \frac{12.6}{17.4} = \frac{6.71}{7} + 0.763$ 30. $\frac{6.034}{x} - 43.17 = \frac{0.793}{x} + 18.15$ 0.0855

$\qquad\qquad\qquad\qquad\qquad 0.947$

31. $\frac{x^3+8}{x+2} = x^2 - 2x + 4$ 32. $\frac{(x-3)^2}{x-3} = x - 3$

$\quad$ All real numbers except -2 All real numbers except 3

Equations that are true for all sensible replacements of the variables are called *identities*. Determine which equations are identities.

33. $\frac{x^2+6x-16}{x-2} = x + 8$ Yes   34. $\frac{x^3+8}{x^2-4} = \frac{x^2-2x+4}{x-2}$ Yes

Challenge

Solve.

35. $\frac{x+3}{x+2} - \frac{x+4}{x+3} = \frac{x+5}{x+4} - \frac{x+6}{x+5}$ $-\frac{7}{2}$

6–7 Solving Problems

Work Problems

Suppose a machine can do a certain job in 5 hours. Then in 1 hour it can do $\frac{1}{5}$ of the job. In 3 hours it can do $\frac{3}{5}$ of the job, and so on. This reasoning gives us a principle for solving certain problems.

If a job can be done in t hours (or days), then $\frac{1}{t}$ of it can be done in 1 hour (or day).

EXAMPLE 1

Tom can mow a lawn in 4 hours. Penny can mow the same lawn in 5 hours. How long would it take both of them, working together with 2 lawnmowers, to mow the lawn?

Tom can mow the lawn in 4 hours, so he can mow $\frac{1}{4}$ of it in 1 hour. Penny can mow the lawn in 5 hours, so she can mow $\frac{1}{5}$ of it in 1 hour. Thus they can mow $\frac{1}{4} + \frac{1}{5}$ of it in 1 hour working together.

Let t represent the number of hours it takes them, working together. Then they mow $\frac{1}{t}$ of it in 1 hour. We now have an equation.

$$\frac{1}{4} + \frac{1}{5} = \frac{1}{t} \quad \text{This is the translation to mathematical language.}$$

We solve the equation.

$$20t\left(\frac{1}{4} + \frac{1}{5}\right) = 20t \cdot \frac{1}{t}$$

$$\frac{20t}{4} + \frac{20t}{5} = \frac{20t}{t} \qquad \text{Multiplying on both sides by the LCM of denominators and clearing of fractions}$$

$$5t + 4t = 20$$

$$9t = 20$$

$$t = \frac{20}{9}, \text{ or } 2\frac{2}{9} \text{ hours}$$

Now we check in the original problem.

Tom does $\frac{1}{4}$ of the lawn in 1 hour. In $\frac{20}{9}$ hr he does $\frac{1}{4} \cdot \frac{20}{9}$, or $\frac{5}{9}$ of it.

Penny does $\frac{1}{5}$ of the job in 1 hour. In $\frac{20}{9}$ hr she does $\frac{1}{5} \cdot \frac{20}{9}$, or $\frac{4}{9}$ of it.

Altogether they do $\frac{5}{9} + \frac{4}{9}$ of the job, or all of it. The number checks.

TRY THIS

1. Fred does a certain typing job in 6 hours. Bruce can do the same job in 4 hours. How long would it take them to do the same amount of typing working together with 2 typewriters? $2\frac{2}{5}$ hours

EXAMPLE 2

At a factory, smokestack A pollutes the air twice as fast as smokestack B. When the stacks operate together they yield a certain amount of pollution in 15 hours. Find the time it would take each to yield that same amount of pollution operating alone.

Let x represent the number of hours it takes A to yield the pollution. Then $2x$ is the number of hours it takes B to yield the same amount of pollution.

$\frac{1}{x}$ is the fraction of the pollution by A in 1 hour.

$\frac{1}{2x}$ is the fraction of the pollution by B in 1 hour.

Together, the stacks yield $\frac{1}{x} + \frac{1}{2x}$ of the pollution in 1 hour. They also yield $\frac{1}{15}$ of it in 1 hour. We now have an equation.

$\frac{1}{x} + \frac{1}{2x} = \frac{1}{15}$ This is the translation.

$30x\left(\frac{1}{x} + \frac{1}{2x}\right) = 30x \cdot \frac{1}{15}$ Multiplying on both sides by the LCM of denominators and clearing fractions

Solving for x we get $x = 22\frac{1}{2}$ hours for smokestack A, and $2x = 45$ hours for smokestack B. This checks.

TRY THIS

2. Two pipes carry water to the same tank. Pipe A can fill the tank three times as fast as pipe B. Together they can fill the tank in 24 hours. Find the time it takes each to fill the tank alone. A, 32 hours, B, 96 hours

Motion Problems

Recall from Chapter 4 the equation for distance, $d = rt$. From this we can easily obtain fractional equations for time and for rate.

$t = \frac{d}{r}$ and $r = \frac{d}{t}$

We can use these equations to solve motion problems.

EXAMPLE 3

An airplane flies 1062 km with the wind. In the same amount of time it can fly 738 km against the wind. The speed of the plane in still air is 200 km/h. Find the speed of the wind.

We first make a drawing. We let r represent the speed of the wind, and organize the facts in a chart.

1062 km $\qquad$ t_1 hours

$200 + r$ (The wind increases the speed.)

t_2 hours $\qquad$ 738 km

$200 - r$ (The wind decreases the speed.)

	Distance	Rate	Time
With wind	1062	$200 + r$	t
Against wind	738	$200 - r$	t

The times are the same, so using the equation for time with each row of the table, we get a system of equations.

$$t = \frac{1062}{200 + r} \text{ and } t = \frac{738}{200 - r} \qquad \text{This is the translation.}$$

We solve. $\dfrac{1062}{200 + r} = \dfrac{738}{200 - r}$ Using substitution

Solving for r we get 36. This checks. Thus the speed of the wind is 36 km/h.

TRY THIS

3. A boat travels 246 miles downstream in the same time that it takes to travel 180 miles upstream. The speed of the current in the stream is 5.5 mi/h. Find the speed of the boat in still water. 35.5 mi/h

---

6–7	

Exercises

Solve.

1. The reciprocal of 5 plus the reciprocal of 7 is the reciprocal of what number? $\frac{35}{12}$

2. The reciprocal of 3 plus the reciprocal of 6 is the reciprocal of what number? 2

3. The sum of a number and 6 times its reciprocal is -5. Find the number. $-3, -2$

4. The sum of a number and 21 times its reciprocal is -10. Find the number. $-3, -7$

5. In a fractional numeral the numerator is 3 more than the denominator. If 2 is added to both numerator and denominator, the result is $\frac{3}{2}$. Find the original fractional numeral. $\frac{7}{4}$

6. In a fractional numeral the denominator is 8 more than the numerator. If 5 is subtracted from both numerator and denominator, the result is $\frac{1}{2}$. Find the original fractional numeral. $\frac{13}{21}$

7. The speed of a stream is 3 km/h. A boat travels 4 km upstream in the same time it takes to travel 10 km downstream. What is the speed of the boat in still water? 7 km/h

8. The speed of a stream is 4 km/h. A boat travels 6 km upstream in the same time it takes to travel 12 km downstream. What is the speed of the boat in still water? 12 km/h

9. The speed of Train A is 12 km/h slower than the speed of Train B. Train A travels 230 km in the same time it takes Train B to travel 290 km. Find the speed of each train. Train A 46 km/h, Train B 58 km/h

10. The speed of Train X is 14 km/h faster than the speed of Train Y. Train X travels 400 km in the same time it takes Train Y to travel 330 km. Find the speed of each train. Train X 80 km/h, Train Y 66 km/h

11. George has a boat that can move at a speed of 15 km/h in still water. He rides 140 km downstream in a river in the same time it takes to ride 35 km upstream. What is the speed of the river? 9 km/h

12. A paddleboat can move at a speed of 2 km/h in still water. The boat is paddled 4 km downstream in a river in the same time it takes to go 1 km upstream. What is the speed of the river? $1\frac{1}{5}$ km/h

13. Derek has just enough money to rent a canoe for $1\frac{1}{2}$ hours. How far out on a lake can he paddle and return on time if he paddles out at 2 km/h and back at 4 km/h? 2 km

14. Kelly has just enough money to rent a canoe for $2\frac{1}{2}$ hours. How far out on the lake can she paddle and return on time if she paddles out at 3 km/h and back at 2 km/h? 3 km

15. Jim, an experienced shipping clerk, can fill a certain order in 5 hours. Pat, a new clerk, needs 9 hours to do the same job. Working together, how long would it take them to fill the order? $3\frac{3}{14}$ hours

16. Maria can paint a room in 4 hours. Paula can paint the same room in 3 hours. Working together, how long would it take them to paint the room? $1\frac{5}{7}$ hours

17. Sheila can frame in a room in 5 hours. David can do the same job in 4 hours. Working together, how long will it take them to frame in a room? $2\frac{2}{9}$ hours

18. Andrew can complete a plumbing job in 6 hours. Vivian can do the same job in 4 hours. Working together, how long will it take them to complete the job? $2\frac{2}{5}$ hours

19. A swimming pool can be filled using either a pipe or a hose, or both. Using the pipe alone it takes 12 hours. Using both it takes $8\frac{4}{7}$ hours. How long does it take using the hose alone? 30 hours

20. A tank can be filled using pipes A or B or both. It takes pipe A, working alone, 18 hours to fill the tank. It takes both pipes, working together, 9.9 hours to fill the tank. How long does it take pipe B, working alone, to fill the tank? 22 hours

21. One car travels 25 km/h faster than another. While one travels 300 km the other travels 450 km. Find their speeds. 50 km/h and 75 km/h

22. One car travels 30 km/h faster than another. While one travels 450 km the other travels 600 km. Find their speeds. 90 km/h and 120 km/h

6–9 Variation

Direct Variation

A plumber earns $18 per hour. In 1 hour $18 is earned. In 2 hours $36 is earned. In 3 hours $54 is earned, and so on. This gives rise to a set of ordered pairs of numbers, all having the same ratio.

$(1, 18), (2, 36), (3, 54), (4, 72),$ and so on

The ratio of earnings to time is $\frac{18}{1}$ in every case.

Whenever a situation gives rise to pairs of numbers in which the ratio is constant, we say that there is direct variation. Here the earnings vary directly as the time.

$$\frac{E}{t} = 18 \text{ (a constant), or } E = 18t$$

Note that the constant, 18, is positive. Note also that when one variable increases, so does the other. When one decreases, so does the other.

Whenever a situation gives rise to a linear function $f(x) = kx$, or $y = kx$, where k is a positive constant, we say that there is *direct variation*, or that *y varies directly as x*. The number k is called the *variation constant*.

EXAMPLE 1

Find the variation constant and an equation of variation where y varies directly as x, and where $y = 32$ and $x = 2$.

We know that $(2, 32)$ is a solution of $y = kx$.

$32 = k \cdot 2$ Substituting

$\frac{32}{2} = k$, or $k = 16$ Solving for k

The variation constant is 16. The equation of variation is $y = 16x$.

TRY THIS

1. Find the variation constant and an equation of variation where y varies directly as x, and $y = 8$ when $x = 20$. $y = 0.4x$

Direct-Variation Problems

EXAMPLE 2

The number of centimeters W of water produced from melting snow varies directly as S, the number of centimeters of snow. Meteorologists have found that 150 cm of snow will melt to 16.8 cm of water. How many cm of water will 200 cm of snow melt to?

First find the variation constant using the data, and then an equation of variation.

$$W = kS$$
$$16.8 = k \cdot 150 \quad \text{Substituting}$$
$$\frac{16.8}{150} = k \quad \text{Solving for } k$$
$$0.112 = k \quad \text{This is the variation constant}$$

The equation of variation is $W = 0.112S$.

Next, use the equation to find how many cm of water will result from melting 200 cm of snow.

$$W = 0.112S$$
$$W = 0.112(200) \quad \text{Substituting}$$
$$W = 22.4$$

Thus 200 cm of snow will melt to 22.4 cm of water.

TRY THIS Solve.

2. Ohm's law states that the voltage V in an electric circuit varies directly as the number of amperes I of electric current in the circuit. If the voltage is 10 volts when the current is 3 amperes, what is the voltage when the current is 15 amperes? 50 volts

Inverse Variation

A bus is traveling a distance of 20 mi. At a speed of 20 mi/h it will take 1 hour. At 40 mi/h it will take $\frac{1}{2}$ hour. At 60 mi/h it will take $\frac{1}{3}$ hour, and so on. This gives rise to a set of pairs of numbers all having the same product.

$$(20, 1), \left(40, \frac{1}{2}\right), \left(60, \frac{1}{3}\right), \left(80, \frac{1}{4}\right), \text{ and so on}$$

Whenever a situation gives rise to pairs of numbers whose product is constant, we say that there is inverse variation. Here the time varies inversely as the speed.

$$rt = 20 \text{ (a constant) or } t = \frac{20}{r}$$

Note that the constant, 20, is positive. Note also that when one variable increases, the other decreases.

> Whenever a situation gives rise to a rational function $f(x) = \frac{k}{x}$, or $y = \frac{k}{x}$, where k is a positive constant, we say that there is *inverse variation*, or that y *varies inversely as* x. The number k is called the *variation constant*.

EXAMPLE 3

Find the variation constant and then an equation of variation where y varies inversely as x, and $y = 32$ when $x = 0.2$. We know that $(0.2, 32)$ is a solution of $y = \frac{k}{x}$.

$$32 = \frac{k}{0.2} \quad \text{Substituting}$$
$$(0.2)32 = k$$
$$6.4 = k \quad \text{Solving}$$

The variation constant is 6.4.
The equation of variation is $y = \frac{6.4}{x}$.

TRY THIS

3. Find the variation constant and an equation of variation where y varies inversely as x and $y = 0.012$ when $x = 50$. $\quad y = \frac{0.6}{x}$

Inverse-Variation Problems

EXAMPLE 4

The time t required to do a certain job varies inversely as the number of people P who work on the job (assuming that all do the same amount of work). It takes 4 hours for 12 people to erect some football bleachers. How long would it take 3 people to do the same job?

First find the variation constant, using the data, and then an equation of variation.

$$t = \frac{k}{P}$$

$$4 = \frac{k}{12} \quad \text{Substituting}$$

$$48 = k \quad \text{Solving for } k, \text{ the variation constant}$$

The equation of variation is $t = \frac{48}{P}$.

Next, use the equation to find the time it would take 3 people to do the job.

$$t = \frac{48}{P}$$

$$t = \frac{48}{3} \quad \text{Substituting}$$

$$t = 16$$

It would take 16 hours.

TRY THIS Solve.

4. The time t required to drive a fixed distance varies inversely as the speed r. It takes 5 hours at 60 km/h to drive a fixed distance. How long would it take to drive that same distance at 40 km/h? $7\frac{1}{2}$ hr

---

6–9

Exercises

Find the variation constant and an equation of variation where y varies directly as x and the following are true.

1. $y = 24$ when $x = 3$ $y = 8x$ 2. $y = 5$ when $x = 12$ $y = \frac{5}{12}x$

3. $y = -16$ when $x = 1$ $y = -6x$ 4. $y = 2$ when $x = 5$ $y = \frac{2}{5}x$

5. $y = 15$ when $x = 3$ $y = 5x$ 6. $y = 1$ when $x = -2$ $y = -\frac{1}{2}x$

7. $y = 30$ when $x = 8$ $y = \frac{15}{4}x$ 8. $y = -1$ when $x = 1$ $y = -x$

9. $y = 0.8$ when $x = 0.5$ $y = \frac{8}{5}x$ 10. $y = 0.6$ when $x = 0.4$ $y = \frac{3}{2}x$

Solve.

11. The electric current I, in amperes, in a circuit varies directly as the voltage V. When 12 volts are applied, the current is 4 amperes. What is the current when 18 volts are applied? 6 amperes

12. Hooke's law states that the distance d a spring is stretched by a hanging object varies directly as the weight w of the object. If the distance is 40 cm when the weight is 3 kg, what is the distance when the weight is 5 kg? $66\frac{2}{3}$ cm

13. The number N of plastic straws produced by a machine varies directly as the amount of time t the machine is operating. If the machine produces 20,000 straws in 8 hours, how many straws can it produce in 50 hours? 125,000

14. The number N of aluminum cans used each year varies directly as the number of people using the cans. If 250 people use 60,000 cans in one year, how many cans are used each year in a city with population 850,000? 204,000,000

15. The amount of pollution A entering the atmosphere varies directly as the number of people N living in an area. If 60,000 people result in 42,600 tons of pollutants entering the atmosphere, how many tons enter the atmosphere in a city with a population of 750,000? 532,500 tons

16. The weight M of an object on the moon varies directly as its weight E on earth. A person who weighs 95 kg on earth weighs 15.2 kg on the moon. How much would a 105 kg person weigh on the moon? 16.8 kg

17. The weight M of an object on Mars varies directly as its weight E on earth. A person who weighs 95 kilograms on earth weighs 38 kg on Mars. How much would a 100 kg person weigh on Mars? 40 kg

18. The number of kilograms of water W in a human body varies directly as the total weight. A person weighing 96 kg contains 64 kg of water. How many kilograms of water are in a person weighing 75 kg? 50 kg

Find the variation constant and an equation of variation where y varies inversely as x, and the following are true.

19. $y = 6$ when $x = 10$ $y = \frac{60}{x}$

20. $y = 16$ when $x = 4$ $y = \frac{64}{x}$

21. $y = 4$ when $x = 3$ $y = \frac{12}{x}$

22. $y = 4$ when $x = 9$ $y = \frac{36}{x}$

23. $y = 12$ when $x = 3$ $y = \frac{36}{x}$

24. $y = 9$ when $x = 5$ $y = \frac{45}{x}$

25. $y = 27$ when $x = \frac{1}{3}$ $y = \frac{9}{x}$

26. $y = 81$ when $x = \frac{1}{9}$ $y = \frac{9}{x}$

Solve.

27. The current I in an electrical conductor varies inversely as the resistance R of the conductor. If the current is $\frac{1}{2}$ ampere when the resistance is 240 ohms, what is the current when the resistance is 540 ohms? $\frac{2}{9}$ ampere

28. The time t required to empty a tank varies inversely as the rate r of pumping. If a pump can empty a tank in 45 minutes at the rate of 600 kl per minute, how long will it take the pump to empty the same tank at the rate of 1000 kl per minute? 27 minutes

29. The volume V of a gas varies inversely as the pressure P upon it. The volume of a gas is 200 cm^3 under a pressure of 32 kg/cm^2. What will be its volume under a pressure of 40 kg/cm^2? 160 cm³

30. The time T required to do a job varies inversely as the number of people P working. It takes 5 hours for 7 bricklayers to complete a certain job. How long would it take 10 bricklayers to complete the job? 3.5 hours

31. The time t required to drive a fixed distance varies inversely as the speed r. It takes 5 hours at 80 km/h to drive a fixed distance; how long would it take to drive the fixed distance at 60 km/h? $6\frac{2}{3}$ hours

32. The wavelength W of a radio wave varies inversely as its frequency F. A wave with a frequency of 1200 kilohertz per second has a length of 300 meters. What is the length of a wave with a frequency of 800 kilohertz per second? 450 m

Extension

A *unit price* is the price of one of something. It is also the ratio of price to the number of units.

$$\text{Unit Price} = \frac{\text{Price}}{\text{Number of Units}}$$

33. A customer bought a 15 oz box of raisin bran for $1.47. What is the unit price in cents per ounce? Round to the nearest hundredth. 10 cents per ounce

34. A 14 oz can of baked beans costs 39¢. A 31 oz can of the same kind of beans costs 63¢. Which has the lower unit price? Find a way to use proportions to solve this problem. 31 oz can is 2.03¢/oz; 14 oz can is 2.79¢/oz

35. To determine the number of deer in a forest, a conservationist catches 612 deer, tags them, and releases them. Later, 244 deer are caught, and it is found that 72 of them are tagged. Estimate how many deer are in the forest. 2074

36. It is known that it takes 60 ounces of grass seed to seed 3000 square feet of lawn. At this rate, how much would be needed for 5000 feet of lawn? 100 lb

37. Explain how you might use a proportion to estimate the number of words in a novel.

38. A loan of $9000 earns simple interest of $1665. Find an equation of variation that describes the simple interest I in terms of the loan principal P. $I = 0.185P$

Challenge

39. Show that if P varies directly as Q, then Q varies directly as P.

40. Show that if A varies inversely as B, then B varies inversely as A, and $1/A$ varies directly as B.

CONSUMER APPLICATION/Understanding Life Insurance

Term Life Insurance
Term insurance provides coverage for a certain period of time. The premium is paid during the term of the insurance. Unless the policy is renewed, the insurance coverage ends when the term ends. At each renewal, the premium is higher in price.

Whole (Straight) Life Insurance
This provides coverage until the insured dies (or cancels the policy). The premium is set at the time of purchase and is paid as long as the policy is in effect. The policy builds up a cash value so that the insured can receive some money if the policy is cancelled.

Limited Payment Life Insurance
This insurance provides coverage until the insured dies. The premium is set at the time of purchase, but is paid for a limited time only, usually 20 or 30 years. Then the insurance is paid up and the coverage continues until death.

Endowment Life Insurance
Endowment insurance provides coverage for a certain amount of time, usually 20 or 30 years. The premium is set and paid throughout that time. At the end of the specified time, the insured collects the value of the policy and the coverage ends.

Annual premiums are calculated from tables. The amount is determined by sex, age, and the type and amount of insurance.

Annual Premium for Each $1000 of Insurance							
Age purchased	Term		Whole life	Limited pay		Endowment	
	5 Year	10 Year		20 Year	30 Year	20 Year	30 Year
M F 15 18	—	—	$11.20	$28.10	$22.10	$49.50	$31.90
20 22	$4.75	$5.10	$12.10	$30.60	$24.00	$49.80	$32.40
25 28	$5.50	$6.10	$13.80	$33.30	$26.25	$50.30	$33.20
30 33	$6.70	$7.60	$15.80	$36.50	$28.90	$51.10	$34.40
35 38	$8.50	$9.80	$19.40	$40.15	$32.15	$52.30	$36.20

The annual premium for each $1000 of whole life insurance at age 22 is $12.10. The annual premium for a $30,000.00 policy is:

$$30 \times \$12.10 \text{ or } \$363.$$

Exercises

Use the table to find the annual premium.

1. David Yawger, age 20, purchased a $5000 5-year term insurance policy. $23.75
2. Rose Mastro, age 25, purchased a $10,000 whole life policy. $121.00
3. Sally Snyder, age 30, purchased a $15,000 20-year limited payment policy. $499.50
4. Matt Owen, age 35, purchased a $20,000 30-year endowment policy. $724

Solve.

5. Carl Fischer, age 35, purchased a 20-year $20,000 limited payment policy. What is the annual premium? At what age will he stop paying the premium? $803.00; 55
6. Joanna Kingsman, age 40, purchased a $50,000 20-year endowment policy. What is the annual premium? What is the total of her premiums for the 20 years? How much will she receive in 20 years? $2615; $52,300; $50,000

CHAPTER 6   Review

Review the material in the chapter. Then see how you have done by trying these review exercises. If you miss an exercise, restudy the indicated lesson.

6–1 Multiply.

1. $\dfrac{y}{y} \cdot \dfrac{4y - 3}{2y + 5}$
2. $\dfrac{4x - 3}{x + 5} \cdot \dfrac{x^2 - 1}{x^2 - 1}$ $\dfrac{4x^3 - 3x^2 - 4x + 3}{x^3 + 5x^2 - x - 5}$

6–1 Simplify.

1. $\dfrac{4y^2 - 3y}{2y^2 + 5y}$

3. $\dfrac{3a^2 - 3b^2}{4a^2 + 8ab + b^2}$
4. $\dfrac{3x^2 - 4x - 4}{4x^2 - 3x - 10}$ $\dfrac{3x + 2}{4x + 5}$
3. $\dfrac{3(a - b)}{4(a + b)}$

286 CHAPTER 6 FRACTIONAL EXPRESSIONS AND EQUATIONS .

6–1 Multiply and simplify.

5. $\dfrac{x^3 - 64}{8x^3 + 1} \cdot \dfrac{x^2 - 1}{x^2 - 4}$ $\dfrac{(2x - 1)(x^2 + 4x + 16)}{(x + 4)(4x^2 + 2x + 1)}$

6–1 Divide and simplify.

6. $\dfrac{6y^4}{y^2 - 9} \div \dfrac{3y^2}{2y^2 + 7y + 3}$ $\dfrac{2y^2(2y + 1)}{y - 3}$

6–2 Find the LCM.

7. $18a^2b^2, 15a^3b$ 8. $x^2 + 2x + 1, x^2 + 5x + 4$ 9. $x^2 + 10, x - 3, 5$

6–3 Add.

10. $\dfrac{a + 9}{a + 3} + \dfrac{12 - 5a}{a + 3}$ 11. $\dfrac{y + 2}{y - 3} + \dfrac{y}{3 - y}$ 12. $\dfrac{5}{4x - 2} + \dfrac{x + 3}{4x^2 - 4x + 1}$

6–3 Subtract.

13. $\dfrac{a + 5}{a - 7} - \dfrac{a}{7 - a}$ 14. $\dfrac{7}{x^2 - 81} - \dfrac{x - 4}{3x^2 - 25 - 18}$ $\dfrac{-x^2 + 16x + 50}{(x + 9)(x - 9)(3x + 2)}$

6–3 Simplify.

15. $\dfrac{1}{3y} + \dfrac{4y}{y^2 - 1} + \dfrac{7}{y - 1}$ $\dfrac{34y^2 + 21y - 1}{3y(y - 1)(y + 1)}$

6–4 Simplify.

16. $\dfrac{\dfrac{1}{a} + \dfrac{1}{b}}{\dfrac{1}{a} - \dfrac{1}{b}}$ 17. $\dfrac{\dfrac{1}{a} - \dfrac{1}{a + h}}{h}$ 18. $\dfrac{\dfrac{1}{a} - \dfrac{1}{b}}{\dfrac{1}{a^3} - \dfrac{1}{b^3}}$ $\dfrac{a^2b^2}{b^2 + ab + a^2}$

6–5 Divide and check.

19. $(10y^4 - 8y^3 + 12y^2) \div 2y^2$ $5y^2 - 4y + 6$

20. $2x - 3\overline{)4x^4 - 5x^2 + 2x - 10}$ $2x^3 + 3x^2 + 2x + 4 + \dfrac{2}{2x - 3}$

6–6 Solve.

21. $\dfrac{x^2}{x + 3} = \dfrac{9}{x + 3}$ 3   22. $\dfrac{15}{y} - \dfrac{15}{y - 2} = -2$ 23. $\dfrac{2}{y + 4} + \dfrac{2y - 1}{y^2 + 2y - 8} = \dfrac{1}{y - 2}$ 3

6–7 Solve.

24. One car travels 90 km in the same time a car going 10 km/h slower travels 60 km. Find the speed of each. 30 km/h and 20 km/h

6–8 Solve each formula for the given letter.

25. $T = Rn + \dfrac{mn}{P}; P$ 26. $\dfrac{1}{p} + \dfrac{1}{q} = \dfrac{1}{f}; q$ $\dfrac{fp}{p - f}$ 25. $P = \dfrac{mn}{T - Rn}$

7. $90a^3b^2$
8. $(x + 1)(x + 1)(x + 4)$
9. $5(x - 3)(x^2 + 10)$
10. $\dfrac{21 - 4a}{a + 3}$
11. $\dfrac{2}{y - 3}$
12. $\dfrac{12x + 1}{2(2x - 1)^2}$
13. $\dfrac{2a + 5}{a - 7}$
16. $\dfrac{b + a}{b - a}$
17. $\dfrac{1}{a(a + h)}$
22. $5, -3$

6–9 Solve.

27. The number N of parts a punch press can produce varies directly as it operates. It can produce 1150 parts in 2 hours. How many can it produce in 5.5 hours? 3162

28. The time T required to do a certain job varies inversely as the number of people P working. It takes 16 hours for 2 people to repaint a gymnasium. How long would it take 6 people to do the job? $5\frac{1}{3}$ hours

CHAPTER 6 Test

Simplify.

1. $\dfrac{5x^2 + 38x + 21}{3x^2 + 22x + 7}$ $\frac{5x+3}{3x+1}$

Multiply and simplify.

2. $\dfrac{y^3 + 27}{9y} \cdot \dfrac{3y}{y + 3}$ $\frac{y^2-3y+9}{3}$

Divide and simplify.

3. $\dfrac{8t^5}{t^2 - 25} \div \dfrac{4t^2}{7t^2 - 34t - 5}$ $\frac{4t^3(7t+1)}{t+5}$

Add or subtract.

4. $\dfrac{t + 9}{t - 5} + \dfrac{2t}{5 - t}$

5. $\dfrac{4}{5x - 15} + \dfrac{x + 8}{4x^2 - 11x - 3}$ $\frac{21x+44}{5(x-3)(4x+1)(x-3)}$ 4. $\frac{-t+9}{t-5}$

6. $\dfrac{8}{y^2 - 64} - \dfrac{y - 5}{2y^2 - 15y - 8}$

7. $\dfrac{1}{2x} + \dfrac{4x}{x^2 - 1} + \dfrac{2}{x + 1}$ $\frac{5x-1}{2x(x-1)}$ 6. $\frac{-y^2+13y+48}{(y+8)(y-8)(2y+1)}$

Simplify.

8. $\dfrac{\dfrac{1}{3a} - 4}{\dfrac{1}{2a} - 1}$ $\frac{2(1-12a)}{3(1-2a)}$

Divide.

9. $(2a^3 - 13a + 15) \div (a + 3)$ $2a^2 - 6a + 5$

Solve.

10. $\dfrac{x}{x - 1} = \dfrac{7}{1 - x}$ −7

11. $\dfrac{12}{x - 1} - \dfrac{8}{x} = 2$ 4, −1

288 CHAPTER 6 FRACTIONAL EXPRESSIONS AND EQUATIONS

12. Solve $\dfrac{E}{e} = \dfrac{t + r}{r}$ for T. $\quad T = \frac{Er}{e} - r$

6–9 Solve.

13. One car travels 90 km in the same time a car going 10 km/h slower travels 60 km. Find the speed of each. $\quad$ 30 km/h, 20 km/h

Challenge

14. Find and simplify $\dfrac{f(x + h) - f(x)}{h}$ for $f(x) = \dfrac{x - 1}{x}$. $\quad -1$

Ready for Powers, Roots, and Complex Numbers?

1–2 Simplify.

1. $|-8|$ $\;$ 8 $\quad$ 2. $|0|$ $\;$ 0 $\qquad$ 3. $|\sqrt{3}|$ $\;$ $\sqrt{3}$

1–7 Simplify.

4. $y^7 \cdot y^3$ $\;$ y^{10}
5. $8^3 \cdot 8^{-2}$ $\;$ 8
6. $(3x^2 y^{-4})(4x^3 y^2)$ $\;$ $12x^5 y^{-2}$
7. $\dfrac{4^8}{4^2}$ $\;$ 4^6 $\quad$ 8. $\dfrac{3^{-4}}{3^{-6}}$ $\;$ 3^2 $\quad$ 9. $\dfrac{32x^3 y^{10}}{4x^4 y^4}$ $\;$ $8x^{-1} y^6$

1–7 Simplify.

10. $(4^2)^4$ $\;$ 4^8 $\quad$ 11. $(a^{-3})^{-4}$ $\;$ a^{12} $\quad$ 12. $(4xy^{-3})^3$ $\quad$ 13. $(10x^3 y^{-2} z^{-4})^2$ $\;$ $100x^6 y^{-4} z^{-8}$ $\quad$ 12. $64x^3 y^{-9}$

2–2 Solve.

14. $2(8 - 3x) = 3 - 5(x - 1)$ $\;$ 8 $\quad$ 15. $9x + 7 - 2x = -12 - 4x + 5$ $\;$ $-\frac{14}{11}$
16. $(x - 5)(x + 3) = 0$ $\;$ $-3, 5$ $\qquad$ 17. $(x + 5)(x - 7) = 0$ $\;$ $-5, 7$

5–2 Multiply.

18. $2 + 5y - 12y^2$
19. $9x^2 + 48x + 64$
20. $4x^2 - 9$

18. $(2 - 3y)(1 + 4y)$ $\quad$ 19. $(3x + 8)^2$ $\quad$ 20. $(2x - 3)(2x + 3)$

5–4 Factor.

21. $x^2 - 1$ $\;$ $(x + 1)(x - 1)$ $\qquad$ 22. $16x^4 - 40x^2 y^4 + 25y^8$ $\;$ $(4x^2 - 5y^4)^2$
23. $-27x^2 + 36x - 12$ $\;$ $-3(3x - 2)^2$ $\qquad$ 24. $x^2 - 13x + 36$ $\;$ $(x - 4)(x - 9)$

7

CHAPTER SEVEN

Powers, Roots, and Complex Numbers

7-1 Radical Expressions

Square Roots

A square root of a number a is a number c whose second power is a, that is, $c^2 = a$.

> 5 is a square root of 25 because $5 \cdot 5 = 25$.
> -5 is a square root of 25 because $(-5)(-5) = 25$.
> -4 does not have a real number square root because there is no real number such that $c^2 = -4$.

Later in this chapter we shall see that there is a number system, other than the real number system, in which negative numbers do have square roots.

THEOREM 7-1

Every positive real number has two real number square roots. The number 0 has just one square root, 0 itself. Negative numbers do not have real number square roots.

EXAMPLE 1

Find the two square roots of 64.

The square roots are 8 and -8, because $8^2 = 64$ and $(-8)^2 = 64$.

TRY THIS Find the square roots of each number.

1. 9   2. 36   3. 121   1. 3, −3   2. 6, −6   3. 11, −11

DEFINITION

The *principal square root* of a nonnegative number is its nonnegative square root. The symbol $\sqrt{a}$ represents the principal square root of a. To name the negative square root of a we write $-\sqrt{a}$.

EXAMPLES

Simplify. Remember, $\sqrt{}$ indicates the principal square root.

2. $\sqrt{25} = 5$ **3.** $-\sqrt{64} = -8$ **4.** $\sqrt{\dfrac{25}{64}} = \dfrac{5}{8}$ **5.** $\sqrt{0.0049} = 0.07$

TRY THIS Simplify.

4. $\sqrt{1}$ ₁ **5.** $-\sqrt{36}$ ₋₆ **6.** $\sqrt{\dfrac{81}{100}}$ _{9/10} **7.** $-\sqrt{0.0064}$ _{-0.08}

DEFINITION

The symbol $\sqrt{}$ is called a *radical sign*. An expression written with a radical sign is called a *radical expression*. The expression written under the radical sign is called the *radicand*.

These are radical expressions.

$$\sqrt{5}, \qquad \sqrt{a}, \qquad -\sqrt{5x}, \qquad \sqrt{\dfrac{y^2 + 7}{\sqrt{x}}}$$

Finding $\sqrt{a^2}$

In the expression $\sqrt{a^2}$, the radicand is a perfect square.

Suppose $a = 5$. Then we have $\sqrt{5^2}$, which is $\sqrt{25}$, or 5.
Suppose $a = -5$. Then we have $\sqrt{(-5)^2}$, which is $\sqrt{25}$, or 5.
Suppose $a = 0$. Then we have $\sqrt{0^2}$, which is $\sqrt{0}$, or 0.

The symbol $\sqrt{a^2}$ does not represent a negative number. It represents the principal square root of a^2. Note that if $a \geq 0$, then $\sqrt{a^2} = a$. If $a < 0$, then $\sqrt{a^2} = -a$. In all cases the radical expression $\sqrt{a^2}$ represents the absolute value of a.

THEOREM 7–2

For any real number a, $\sqrt{a^2} = |a|$. The principal (nonnegative) square root of a^2 is the absolute value of a.

EXAMPLES

Find the following. Assume that variables represent any real numbers.

6. $\sqrt{(-16)^2} = |-16|$, or 16   7. $\sqrt{(3b)^2} = |3b|$, or $3|b|$

8. $\sqrt{(x-1)^2} = |x-1|$ 9. $\sqrt{x^2 + 8x + 16} = \sqrt{(x+4)^2} = |x+4|$

TRY THIS Find the following. Assume that variables represent any real numbers.

8. $\sqrt{(-24)^2}$ 24 9. $\sqrt{(5y)^2}$ 5|y| 10. $\sqrt{16y^2}$ 4|y| 11. $\sqrt{(x+7)^2}$ |x + 7|

Cube Roots

The number c is the cube root of a if its third power is a, that is, $c^3 = a$.

$\quad$ 2 is the cube root of 8 because $2^3 = 2 \cdot 2 \cdot 2 = 8$.

$\quad$ -4 is the cube root of -64 because $(-4)^3 = (-4)(-4)(-4) = -64$.

We use the word "the" with cube roots because of Theorem 7–3. The symbol $\sqrt[3]{a}$ represents the cube root of a.

THEOREM 7–3

Every real number has exactly one cube root in the system of real numbers.

EXAMPLES

Find the following.

10. $\sqrt[3]{8} = 2$ 11. $\sqrt[3]{-27} = -3$ 12. $\sqrt[3]{-\dfrac{216}{125}} = -\dfrac{6}{5}$ 13. $\sqrt[3]{-8y^3} = -2y$

No absolute value signs are needed when finding cube roots, because a real number has just one cube root. The cube root of a positive number is positive. The cube root of a negative number is negative.

TRY THIS Find the following.

12. $\sqrt[3]{-64}$ -4 13. $\sqrt[3]{27y^3}$ 3y 14. $\sqrt[3]{-\dfrac{343}{64}}$ $-\dfrac{7}{4}$

Odd and Even k-th Roots

The fifth root of a number a is the number c for which $c^5 = a$. There are also 7th roots, 9th roots and so on. Whenever the number k in $\sqrt[k]{\ }$ is an odd number, we say that we are taking an odd root. The number k is called the index. When the index is 2 we do not write it.

When we take any odd root of a number, we find that there is just one answer. If the number is positive, the root is positive. If the number is negative, the root is negative.

EXAMPLES
Find the following.

14. $\sqrt[5]{32} = 2$

15. $\sqrt[5]{-32} = -2$

16. $-\sqrt[5]{32} = -2$

17. $-\sqrt[5]{-32} = -(-2) = 2$

18. $\sqrt[7]{x^7} = x$

19. $\sqrt[9]{(x-1)^9} = x - 1$

Absolute value signs are never needed when finding odd roots.

TRY THIS Find the following. Assume that variables represent any real numbers.

15. $\sqrt[5]{243}$ ₃

16. $\sqrt[5]{-243}$ ₋₃

17. $-\sqrt[5]{243}$ ₋₃

18. $-\sqrt[5]{-32}$ ₂

19. $\sqrt[5]{-32x^5}$ ₋₂ₓ

20. $\sqrt[7]{(3x+2)^7}$ · ₃ₓ ₊ ₂

When the index k in $\sqrt[k]{\ }$ is an even number, we say that we are taking an even root. Every positive real number has two k-th roots when k is even. One of those roots is positive and one is negative. Negative real numbers do not have k-th roots when k is even. When finding even k-th roots, absolute value signs are sometimes necessary, as with square roots.

EXAMPLES
Find the following. Assume that variables represent any real numbers.

20. $\sqrt[4]{16} = 2$

21. $-\sqrt[4]{16} = -2$

22. $\sqrt[4]{-16}$

23. $\sqrt[4]{81x^4} = 3|x|$

24. $\sqrt[6]{(y+7)^6} = |y+7|$

TRY THIS Find the following.

21. $\sqrt[4]{81}$ ₃

22. $-\sqrt[4]{81}$ ₋₃

23. $\sqrt[4]{-81}$ Does not exist

24. $\sqrt[4]{16(x-2)^4}$ 2|x − 2|

25. $\sqrt[6]{x^6}$ |x|

26. $\sqrt[8]{(x+3)^8}$ |x + 3|

THEOREM 7-4

For any real number a, the following statements are true.
1. $\sqrt[k]{a^k} = |a|$ when k is even. We use absolute value when k is even unless a is nonnegative.
2. $\sqrt[k]{a^k} = a$ when k is odd. We do not use absolute value when k is odd.

7-1

Exercises

Find the square roots of each number.

1. 16 $\quad$ 2. 225 $\quad$ 3. 144 $\quad$ 4. 9 $\quad$ 5. 400 $\quad$ 6. 81
   4, −4 $\qquad$ 15, −15 $\qquad$ 12, −12 $\qquad$ 3, −3 $\qquad$ 20, −20 $\qquad$ 9, −9

Find the following.

7. $-\sqrt{\dfrac{49}{36}}$ $\;-\frac{7}{6}$ $\quad$ 8. $-\sqrt{\dfrac{361}{9}}$ $\;-\frac{19}{3}$ $\quad$ 9. $\sqrt{196}$ 14 $\quad$ 10. $\sqrt{441}$ 21 $\quad$ 11. $-\sqrt{\dfrac{16}{81}}$ $\;-\frac{4}{9}$

12. $-\sqrt{\dfrac{81}{144}}$ $\;-\frac{9}{12}$ 13. $\sqrt{0.09}$ 0.3 $\quad$ 14. $\sqrt{0.36}$ 0.6 $\quad$ 15. $-\sqrt{0.0049}$ $\;-0.07$ $\quad$ 16. $\sqrt{0.0144}$ 0.12

Find the following. Assume that variables represent any real number.

17. $\sqrt{16x^2}$ $\;4|x|$ $\qquad$ 18. $\sqrt{25t^2}$ $\;5|t|$ $\qquad$ 19. $\sqrt{(-7c)^2}$ $\;7|c|$

20. $\sqrt{(-6b)^2}$ $\;6|b|$ $\qquad$ 21. $\sqrt{(a+1)^2}$ $\;|a+1|$ $\qquad$ 22. $\sqrt{(5-b)^2}$ $\;|5-b|$

23. $\sqrt{x^2 - 4x + 4}$ $\;|x-2|$ $\qquad$ 24. $\sqrt{y^2 + 16y + 64}$ $\;|y+8|$ $\qquad$ 25. $\sqrt{4x^2 + 28x + 49}$ $\;|2x+7|$

Simplify.

26. $\sqrt[3]{27}$ 3 $\qquad$ 27. $-\sqrt[3]{64}$ $\;-4$ $\qquad$ 28. $\sqrt[3]{-64x^3}$ $\;-4x$

29. $\sqrt[3]{-125y^3}$ $\;-5y$ 30. $\sqrt[3]{-216}$ $\;-6$ $\qquad$ 31. $-\sqrt[3]{-1000}$ 10

32. $\sqrt[3]{-64x^3y^6}$ $\;-4xy^2$ $\qquad$ 33. $\sqrt[3]{0.343(x+1)^3}$ $\;0.7(x+1)$ $\qquad$ 34. $\sqrt[3]{0.000008(y-2)^3}$ $\;0.02(y-2)$

Find the following. Assume that variables represent any real number.

35. $\sqrt[4]{625}$ 5 $\qquad$ 36. $-\sqrt[4]{256}$ $\;-4$ $\qquad$ 37. $\sqrt[5]{-1}$ $\;-1$

38. $-\sqrt[5]{-32}$ 2 $\qquad$ 39. $\sqrt[5]{-\dfrac{32}{243}}$ $\;-\frac{2}{3}$ $\qquad$ 40. $\sqrt[5]{-\dfrac{1}{32}}$ $\;-\frac{1}{2}$

41. $\sqrt[6]{x^6}$ $\;|x|$ $\qquad$ 42. $\sqrt[8]{y^8}$ $\;|y|$ $\qquad$ 43. $\sqrt[4]{(5a)^4}$ $\;5|a|$

44. $\sqrt[4]{(7b)^4}$ $\;7|b|$ $\qquad$ 45. $\sqrt[10]{(-6)^{10}}$ 6 $\qquad$ 46. $\sqrt[12]{(-10)^{12}}$ 10

47. $\sqrt[414]{(a + b)^{414}}$ $\ |a + b|$ **48.** $\sqrt[1976]{(2a + b)^{1976}}$ $\ |2a + b|$ **49.** $\sqrt[7]{y^7}$ y

50. $\sqrt[3]{(-6)^3}$ $\ -6$ **51.** $\sqrt[5]{(x - 2)^5}$ $\ x - 2$ **52.** $\sqrt[9]{(2xy)^9}$ $\ 2xy$

Extension

53. Parking. A parking lot has attendants to park the cars. The number N of temporary stalls needed for waiting cars before attendants can get to them is given by the formula $N = 2.5\sqrt{A}$, where A is the number of arrivals in peak hours. Find the number of spaces needed for the given average number of arrivals in peak hours.

   a. 25 $\ 12.5$ **b.** 36 $\ 15$ **c.** 49 $\ 17.5$ **d.** 64 $\ 20$

Find the domain of each function.

54. $f(x) = \sqrt{x}$ **55.** $f(x) = \sqrt[3]{x}$

56. $f(x) = \sqrt{2x + 8}$ **57.** $f(x) = \sqrt{4 - 3x}$

58. $f(x) = \sqrt{-3x^2}$ **59.** $f(x) = \sqrt{x^2 + 1}$

54. $\{x \mid x \geq 0\}$
55. All real numbers
56. $\{x \mid x \geq -4\}$
57. $\left\{x \mid x \leq \dfrac{4}{3}\right\}$
58. The set containing 0
59. All real numbers

Challenge

Find the domain of each function.

60. $\left\{x \mid x \geq 0 \text{ and } x \neq \dfrac{5}{2}\right\}$
61. $\{x \mid x \geq -3 \text{ and } x \neq 2 \text{ and } x \neq -1\}$
62. $\{x \mid x > 0\}$

60. $f(x) = \dfrac{\sqrt{x}}{2x^2 - 3x - 5}$ **61.** $f(x) = \dfrac{\sqrt{x + 3}}{x^2 - x - 2}$ **62.** $f(x) = \dfrac{\sqrt{x + 1}}{x + |x|}$

USING A CALCULATOR / The Square Root Key

A square root key can be used to compute with radicals and evaluate radical expressions. Pressing the key replaces the displayed number with its positive square root. In the examples below, displays are shown to three decimal places.

Example 1

Problem: Find $x + \sqrt{3}$ for $x = 0.843$.

Enter: 0.843   (+)   3   (√)   (=)

Display: 0.843   3   1.732   2.575

Example 2

Problem: Find $\sqrt{x + 3}$ for $x = 0.843$.

Enter: 0.843   (+)   3   (=)   (√)

Display: 0.843   3   3.843   1.960

Example 3

In this problem, the memory keys are used to

store and recall the value of x. Notice that the denominator is evaluated first.

Problem: Let $f(x) = \dfrac{\sqrt{x + 3}}{x^2 - x - 2}$. Find $f(0.843)$.

Enter: 0.843   (Min)   (x²)   (−)   (MR)

Display: 0.843   0.710   0.843

Enter: (−)   2   (=)   (Min)

Display: −0.132   2   −2.132

The number −2.132351 is now stored in the memory.

Enter: 0.843   (+)   3   (=)   (√)

Display: 0.843   3   3.843   1.960

Enter: (÷)   (MR)   (=)

Display: 1.960   −2.132   −0.919

7–2 Multiplying and Simplifying

Multiplying

Notice that $\sqrt{4}\sqrt{25} = 2 \cdot 5 = 10$.
Also $\sqrt{4 \cdot 25} = \sqrt{100} = 10$.
Likewise, $\sqrt[3]{27}\sqrt[3]{8} = 3 \cdot 2 = 6$ and $\sqrt[3]{27 \cdot 8} = \sqrt[3]{216} = 6$.

These examples suggest the following theorem.

THEOREM 7–5

For any nonnegative real numbers a and b, and any index k,
$\sqrt[k]{a} \cdot \sqrt[k]{b} = \sqrt[k]{ab}$.

EXAMPLES
Multiply.

1. $\sqrt{x + 2}\sqrt{x - 2} = \sqrt{(x + 2)(x - 2)} = \sqrt{x^2 - 4}$

2. $\sqrt[3]{4}\sqrt[3]{5} = \sqrt[3]{4 \cdot 5} = \sqrt[3]{20}$

3. $\sqrt[4]{\dfrac{y}{5}}\sqrt[4]{\dfrac{7}{x}} = \sqrt[4]{\dfrac{y}{5} \cdot \dfrac{7}{x}} = \sqrt[4]{\dfrac{7y}{5x}}$

TRY THIS Multiply.

1. $\sqrt{19}\sqrt{7}$ 2. $\sqrt{x + 2y}\sqrt{x - 2y}$ 3. $\sqrt[4]{403}\sqrt[4]{7}$ 4. $\sqrt[3]{8x}\sqrt[3]{x^4 + 5}$

1. $\sqrt{133}$
2. $\sqrt{x^2 - 4y^2}$
3. $\sqrt[4]{2821}$
4. $\sqrt[3]{8x^5 + 40x}$

Simplifying by Factoring

Turning around the equation of Theorem 7–5 we have
$\sqrt[k]{ab} = \sqrt[k]{a} \cdot \sqrt[k]{b}$. This shows a way to factor and thus simplify
radical expressions. Consider $\sqrt{20}$. The number 20 has the factor
4, which is a perfect square.

$\sqrt{20} = \sqrt{4 \cdot 5}$ Factoring the radicand (4 is a perfect square.)

$= \sqrt{4} \cdot \sqrt{5}$ Factoring into two radicals

$= 2\sqrt{5}$ Taking the square root of 4

> To simplify a radical expression by factoring, look for factors of the radicand that are perfect k-th powers (where k is the index). Then remove those factors by taking the k-th root.

EXAMPLES

Simplify by factoring.

4. $\sqrt{50} = \sqrt{25 \cdot 2} = \sqrt{25} \cdot \sqrt{2} = 5\sqrt{2}$ Finding a perfect square factor

5. $\sqrt[3]{32} = \sqrt[3]{8 \cdot 4} = \sqrt[3]{8} \cdot \sqrt[3]{4} = 2\sqrt[3]{4}$ Finding a perfect cube factor

TRY THIS Simplify by factoring.

5. $\sqrt{32}$ **6.** $\sqrt[3]{80}$ 5. $4\sqrt{2}$ 6. $2\sqrt[3]{10}$

EXAMPLE 6

Simplify by factoring. Assume that all expressions under radical signs represent nonnegative numbers. Hence no absolute value signs will be needed.

$$\sqrt{2x^2 - 4x + 2} = \sqrt{2(x - 1)^2}$$
$$= \sqrt{(x - 1)^2} \cdot \sqrt{2} = (x - 1) \cdot \sqrt{2}$$

TRY THIS Simplify by factoring. Assume that all expressions represent nonnegative numbers. Hence no absolute value signs will be needed.

7. $\sqrt{300}$ **8.** $\sqrt{3x^2 + 12x + 12}$ **9.** $\sqrt{12ab^3c^2}$ 7. $10\sqrt{3}$ 8. $(x + 2)\sqrt{3}$ 9. $2bc\sqrt{3ab}$

10. $\sqrt[3]{16}$ **11.** $\sqrt[4]{81x^4y^8}$ **12.** $\sqrt[3]{(a + b)^4}$ 10. $2\sqrt[3]{2}$ 11. $3xy^2$ 12. $(a + b)\sqrt[3]{a + b}$

Multiplying and Simplifying

Sometimes after we multiply we can then simplify by factoring.

EXAMPLES

Multiply and then simplify by factoring. Assume that all expressions under radical signs represent nonnegative numbers.

7. $\sqrt{15}\sqrt{6} = \sqrt{15 \cdot 6} = \sqrt{90} = \sqrt{9 \cdot 10} = 3\sqrt{10}$

8. $3\sqrt[3]{25} \cdot 2\sqrt[3]{5} = 6 \cdot \sqrt[3]{25 \cdot 5}$ Multiplying radicands
$$= 6 \cdot \sqrt[3]{125}$$
$$= 6 \cdot 5, \text{ or } 30 \quad \text{Taking cube root of 125}$$

9. $\sqrt[3]{18y^3}\,\sqrt[3]{4x^2} = \sqrt[3]{18y^3 \cdot 4x^2} = \sqrt[3]{72y^3x^2}$ Multiplying radicands
$= \sqrt[3]{8y^3 \cdot 9x^2}$ Factoring the radicand
$= \sqrt[3]{8y^3}\,\sqrt[3]{9x^2}$ Factoring into 2 radicals
$= 2y\sqrt[3]{9x^2}$ Taking cube root

TRY THIS Multiply and then simplify by factoring. Assume that all expressions under radical signs represent nonnegative numbers.

13. $\sqrt{3}\,\sqrt{6}$ 14. $\sqrt{18y}\,\sqrt{14y}$ 15. $\sqrt[3]{3x^2y}\,\sqrt[3]{36x}$ 16. $\sqrt{7a}\,\sqrt{21b}$

13. $3\sqrt{2}$
14. $6y\sqrt{7}$
15. $3x\sqrt[3]{4y}$
16. $7\sqrt{3ab}$

Approximating Square Roots

Table 1 in the back of the book contains approximate square roots for 1 through 100. If a radicand is not listed in the table we can factor the radical expression, find exact or approximate square roots of the factors, and then find the product of these square roots.

EXAMPLE 10
Approximate to the nearest tenth.

$\sqrt{275} = \sqrt{25 \cdot 11}$ Factoring the radicand
$= \sqrt{25} \cdot \sqrt{11}$ Factoring into two radicals
$\approx 5 \times 3.317 \approx 16.6$ $\approx$ means approximately equal

TRY THIS Approximate to the nearest tenth.

17. $\sqrt{160}$ 12.6   18. $\sqrt{341}$ (Hint: $341 = 11 \cdot 31$)   18.5   19. $\dfrac{16 - \sqrt{640}}{4}$ −2.3

7–2	

Exercises
Multiply.

1. $\sqrt{3}\,\sqrt{2}$ $\sqrt{6}$
2. $\sqrt{5}\,\sqrt{7}$ $\sqrt{35}$
3. $\sqrt[3]{2}\,\sqrt[3]{5}$ $\sqrt[3]{10}$
4. $\sqrt[3]{7}\,\sqrt[3]{2}$ $\sqrt[3]{14}$
5. $\sqrt[4]{8}\,\sqrt[4]{9}$ $\sqrt[4]{72}$
6. $\sqrt[4]{6}\,\sqrt[4]{3}$ $\sqrt[4]{18}$
7. $\sqrt{3a}\,\sqrt{10b}$ $\sqrt{30ab}$
8. $\sqrt{2x}\,\sqrt{13y}$ $\sqrt{26xy}$
9. $\sqrt[5]{9t^2}\,\sqrt[5]{2t}$ $\sqrt[5]{18t^3}$
10. $\sqrt[3]{8y^3}\,\sqrt[3]{10y}$ $\sqrt[3]{80y^4}$
11. $\sqrt{x-a}\,\sqrt{x+a}$ $\sqrt{x^2-a^2}$
12. $\sqrt{y-b}\,\sqrt{y+b}$ $\sqrt{y^2-b^2}$
13. $\sqrt[3]{0.3x}\,\sqrt[3]{0.2x}$ $\sqrt[3]{0.06x^2}$
14. $\sqrt[3]{0.7y}\,\sqrt[3]{0.3y}$ $\sqrt[3]{0.21y^2}$
15. $\sqrt[4]{x-1}\,\sqrt[4]{x^2+x+1}$ $\sqrt[4]{x^3-1}$
16. $\sqrt[5]{x-2}\,\sqrt[5]{(x-2)^2}$ $\sqrt[5]{(x-2)^3}$
17. $\sqrt{\dfrac{6}{x}}\,\sqrt{\dfrac{y}{5}}$ $\sqrt{\dfrac{6y}{5x}}$
18. $\sqrt{\dfrac{7}{t}}\,\sqrt{\dfrac{s}{11}}$ $\sqrt{\dfrac{7s}{11t}}$

Simplify by factoring. Assume that all expressions represent nonnegative numbers.

19. $\sqrt{8}$ $\ _{2\sqrt{2}}$

20. $\sqrt{18}$ $\ _{3\sqrt{2}}$

21. $\sqrt{24}$ $\ _{2\sqrt{6}}$

22. $\sqrt{20}$ $\ _{2\sqrt{5}}$

23. $\sqrt{180x^4}$ $\ _{6x^2\sqrt{5}}$

24. $\sqrt{175y^6}$ $\ _{5y^3\sqrt{7}}$

25. $\sqrt[3]{54x^8}$ $\ _{3x^2\sqrt[3]{2x^2}}$

26. $\sqrt[3]{40y^3}$ $\ _{2y\sqrt[3]{5}}$

27. $\sqrt[3]{80x^8}$ $\ _{2x^2\sqrt[3]{10x^2}}$

28. $\sqrt[3]{108m^5}$ $\ _{3m\sqrt[3]{4m^2}}$

29. $\sqrt[4]{32}$ $\ _{2\sqrt[4]{2}}$

30. $\sqrt[4]{80}$ $\ _{2\sqrt[4]{5}}$

31. $\sqrt[4]{162c^4d^6}$ $\ _{3cd\sqrt[4]{2d^2}}$

32. $\sqrt[4]{243x^8y^{10}}$ $\ _{3x^2y^2\sqrt[4]{3y^2}}$

33. $\sqrt[3]{(x+y)^4}$ $\ _{(x+y)\sqrt[3]{x+y}}$

Multiply and simplify by factoring. Assume that all expressions represent nonnegative numbers.

34. $\sqrt{3}\sqrt{6}$ $\ _{3\sqrt{2}}$

35. $\sqrt{5}\sqrt{10}$ $\ _{5\sqrt{2}}$

36. $\sqrt{15}\sqrt{6}$ $\ _{3\sqrt{10}}$

37. $\sqrt{2}\sqrt{32}$ $\ _{8}$

38. $\sqrt{6}\sqrt{8}$ $\ _{4\sqrt{3}}$

39. $\sqrt{18}\sqrt{14}$ $\ _{6\sqrt{7}}$

40. $\sqrt[3]{3}\sqrt[3]{18}$ $\ _{3\sqrt[3]{2}}$

41. $\sqrt{45}\sqrt{60}$ $\ _{30\sqrt{3}}$

42. $\sqrt{5b^3}\sqrt{10c^4}$ $\ _{5bc^2\sqrt{2b}}$

43. $\sqrt{2x^3y}\sqrt{12xy}$ $\ _{2x^2y\sqrt{6}}$

44. $\sqrt[3]{y^4}\sqrt[3]{16y^5}$ $\ _{2y^3\sqrt[3]{2}}$

45. $\sqrt[3]{5^2t^4}\sqrt[3]{5^4t^6}$ $\ _{25t^3\sqrt[3]{t}}$

46. $\sqrt[3]{(b+3)^4}\sqrt[3]{(b+3)^2}$ $\ _{(b+3)^2}$

47. $\sqrt[3]{(x+y)^3}\sqrt[3]{(x+y)^5}$ $\ _{(x+y)^2\sqrt[3]{(x+y)^2}}$

48. $\sqrt{12a^3b}\sqrt{8a^4b^2}$ $\ _{4a^3b\sqrt{6ab}}$

Approximate to the nearest tenth.

49. $\sqrt{180}$ $\ _{13.4}$ 50. $\sqrt{124}$ $\ _{11.1}$ 51. $\sqrt{195}$ $\ _{14.0}$ 52. $\sqrt{115}$ $\ _{10.7}$ 53. $\dfrac{10+\sqrt{20}}{4}$ $\ _{3.6}$

Extension

54. Speed of a skidding car. After an accident, police can estimate the speed that a car was traveling by measuring its skid marks. The formula $r = 2\sqrt{5L}$ can be used, where r is the speed in mi/hr, and L is the length of the skid marks in feet. Estimate the speed of a car that left skid marks of the following lengths.

    a. 20 ft   b. 70 ft   c. 90 ft

    20 mi/hr   37.4 mi/hr   42.4 mi/hr

Challenge

55. Wind Chill Temperature. In cold weather we feel colder if there is wind than if there is not. *Wind chill temperature* is the temperature at which, without wind, we would feel as cold in an actual situation with wind. Here is a formula for finding wind chill temperature.

$$T_w = 33 - \frac{(10.45 + 10\sqrt{v} - v)(33 - T)}{22}$$

    T is the actual temperature given in degrees Celsius and v is the wind speed in m/s. Find the wild chill temperature for the given actual temperatures and wind speeds. Use a calculator.

    a. $T = 7°C$, $v = 8$ m/s $\ _{-3.3°C}$ b. $T = 0°C$, $v = 12$ m/s $\ _{-16.6°C}$

    c. $T = -5°C$, $v = 14$ m/s   d. $T = -23°C$, $v = 15$ m/s $\ _{-54.0°C}$
    $_{-25.5°C}$

7–3 Dividing and Simplifying

Roots of Quotients

Notice that

$$\sqrt{\frac{16}{9}} = \frac{4}{3} \text{ and } \frac{\sqrt{16}}{\sqrt{9}} = \frac{4}{3}$$

$$\sqrt[3]{\frac{27}{8}} = \frac{3}{2} \text{ and } \frac{\sqrt[3]{27}}{\sqrt[3]{8}} = \frac{3}{2}$$

These examples suggests the following theorem.

THEOREM 7–6

For any nonnegative number a, and any positive number b, and any index k,

$$\sqrt[k]{\frac{a}{b}} = \frac{\sqrt[k]{a}}{\sqrt[k]{b}}.$$

From Theorem 7–6 we have the following rule.

To take the k-th root of a quotient, take the k-th root of the numerator and denominator separately.

EXAMPLES

Simplify by taking roots of numerator and denominator. Assume that all expressions under radical signs represent positive numbers.

1. $\sqrt[3]{\frac{27}{125}} = \frac{\sqrt[3]{27}}{\sqrt[3]{125}} = \frac{3}{5}$ We take the cube root of the numerator and denominator.

2. $\sqrt{\frac{25}{y^2}} = \frac{\sqrt{25}}{\sqrt{y^2}} = \frac{5}{y}$ We take the square root of the numerator and denominator.

3. $\sqrt{\frac{16x^3}{y^4}} = \frac{\sqrt{16x^3}}{\sqrt{y^4}} = \frac{\sqrt{16x^2 \cdot x}}{\sqrt{y^4}} = \frac{4x\sqrt{x}}{y^2}$

4. $\sqrt[3]{\frac{27y^5}{343x^3}} = \frac{\sqrt[3]{27y^5}}{\sqrt[3]{343x^3}} = \frac{\sqrt[3]{27y^3 \cdot y^2}}{\sqrt[3]{343x^3}} = \frac{\sqrt[3]{27y^3} \cdot \sqrt[3]{y^2}}{\sqrt[3]{343x^3}} = \frac{3y\sqrt[3]{y^2}}{7x}$

TRY THIS Simplify by taking roots of numerator and denominator. Assume that all expressions under radical signs represent positive numbers.

1. $\sqrt{\dfrac{25}{36}}$ 2. $\sqrt[3]{\dfrac{1000}{27}}$ 3. $\sqrt{\dfrac{x^2}{100}}$ 4. $\sqrt{\dfrac{4a^3}{b^4}}$ 1. $\frac{5}{6}$ 2. $\frac{10}{3}$ 3. $\frac{x}{10}$ 4. $\frac{2a\sqrt{a}}{b^2}$

Dividing Radical Expressions

Turning around the equation of Theorem 7–6, we have

$$\frac{\sqrt[k]{a}}{\sqrt[k]{b}} = \sqrt[k]{\frac{a}{b}}.$$

This gives us a rule for dividing radical expressions.

> To divide radical expressions with the same index, we can divide the radicands.

After dividing radicands, we can sometimes simplify.

EXAMPLES
Divide. Then simplify by taking roots if possible. Assume that all expressions under radical signs represent positive numbers.

5. $\dfrac{\sqrt{80}}{\sqrt{5}} = \sqrt{\dfrac{80}{5}} = \sqrt{16} = 4$

6. $\dfrac{5\sqrt[3]{32}}{\sqrt[3]{2}} = 5\sqrt[3]{\dfrac{32}{2}} = 5\sqrt[3]{16} = 5\sqrt[3]{8 \cdot 2} = 5\sqrt[3]{8}\,\sqrt[3]{2} = 5 \cdot 2\sqrt[3]{2} = 10\sqrt[3]{2}$

7. $\dfrac{\sqrt[4]{32a^5b^3}}{\sqrt[4]{2b^{-1}}} = \sqrt[4]{\dfrac{32a^5b^3}{2b^{-1}}} = \sqrt[4]{16a^5b^4} = \sqrt[4]{16a^4b^4 \cdot a} = \sqrt[4]{16a^4b^4}\,\sqrt[4]{a} = 2ab\sqrt[4]{a}$

TRY THIS Divide. Then simplify by taking roots, if possible. Assume that all expressions under radical signs represent positive numbers.

5. $\dfrac{\sqrt{75}}{\sqrt{3}}$ 5   6. $\dfrac{14\sqrt{128xy}}{2\sqrt{2}}$ $56\sqrt{xy}$ 7. $\dfrac{\sqrt{50a^3}}{\sqrt{2a}}$ $5a$

8. $\dfrac{4\sqrt[3]{250}}{7\sqrt[3]{2}}$ $\frac{20}{7}$ 9. $\dfrac{\sqrt[3]{8a^3b}}{\sqrt[3]{27b^{-2}}}$ $\frac{2ab}{3}$ 10. $\dfrac{\sqrt[3]{750}}{\sqrt[3]{3}}$ $5\sqrt[3]{2}$

7-3

Exercises

Simplify by taking roots of numerator and denominator. Assume that all expressions under radical signs represent positive numbers.

1. $\sqrt{\dfrac{16}{25}}$
2. $\sqrt{\dfrac{100}{81}}$
3. $\sqrt[3]{\dfrac{64}{27}}$
4. $\sqrt[3]{\dfrac{343}{512}}$
5. $\sqrt{\dfrac{49}{y^2}}$

6. $\sqrt{\dfrac{121}{x^2}}$
7. $\sqrt{\dfrac{25y^3}{x^4}}$
8. $\sqrt{\dfrac{36a^5}{b^6}}$
9. $\sqrt[3]{\dfrac{8x^5}{27y^3}}$
10. $\sqrt[3]{\dfrac{64x^7}{216y^6}}$

Divide. Then simplify by taking roots if possible. Assume that all expressions under radical signs represent positive numbers.

11. $\dfrac{\sqrt{21a}}{\sqrt{3a}}$
12. $\dfrac{\sqrt{28y}}{\sqrt{4y}}$
13. $\dfrac{\sqrt[3]{54}}{\sqrt[3]{2}}$
14. $\dfrac{\sqrt[3]{40}}{\sqrt[3]{5}}$

15. $\dfrac{\sqrt{40xy^3}}{\sqrt{8x}}$
16. $\dfrac{\sqrt{56ab^3}}{\sqrt{7a}}$
17. $\dfrac{\sqrt[3]{96a^4b^2}}{\sqrt[3]{12a^2b}}$
18. $\dfrac{\sqrt[3]{189x^5y^7}}{\sqrt[3]{7x^2y^2}}$

19. $\dfrac{\sqrt{72xy}}{2\sqrt{2}}$
20. $\dfrac{\sqrt{75ab}}{3\sqrt{3}}$
21. $\dfrac{\sqrt{x^3-y^3}}{\sqrt{x-y}}$
22. $\dfrac{\sqrt{r^3+s^3}}{\sqrt{r+s}}$

Answers (margin):

1. $\frac{4}{5}$
2. $\frac{10}{9}$
3. $\frac{4}{3}$
4. $\frac{7}{8}$
5. $\frac{7}{y}$
6. $\frac{11}{x}$
7. $\frac{5y\sqrt{y}}{x^2}$
8. $\frac{6a^2\sqrt{a}}{b^3}$
9. $\frac{2x\sqrt[3]{x^2}}{3y}$
10. $\frac{4x^2\sqrt[3]{x}}{6y^2}$
11. $\sqrt{7}$
12. $\sqrt{7}$
13. 3
14. 2
15. $y\sqrt{5y}$
16. $2b\sqrt{2b}$
17. $2\sqrt[3]{a^2b}$
18. $3xy\sqrt[3]{y^2}$
19. $3\sqrt{xy}$
20. $\frac{5\sqrt{ab}}{3}$
21. $\sqrt{x^2+xy+y^2}$
22. $\sqrt{r^2-rs+s^2}$

Extension

23. Pendulums. The *period* of a pendulum is the time it takes to complete one cycle, swinging to and fro. If a pendulum consists of a ball on a string, the period T is given by the following formula.

$$T = 2\pi\sqrt{\dfrac{L}{980}}$$

T is in seconds and L is the length of the pendulum in centimeters. Find the period of a pendulum of the given lengths. Use 3.14 for π.

a. 65 cm   **b.** 98 cm   **c.** 120 cm
   1.62 sec   1.99 sec   2.20 sec

DISCOVERY/Oscillatory Motion

The motion of a pendulum is an example of *oscillatory motion*. In the history of mathematics, people studied oscillatory motions because they wanted to improve their methods of telling time.

In the early 1600s, the scientist Galileo had noticed the swinging of the lamps in church. The motion of the lamps caused him to investigate properties of pendulums. Many years after he had discovered the formula in Exercise 23, Galileo designed the first practical pendulum clock and had his students build it.

7–4 Operations with Radical Expressions

Addition and Subtraction

Any two real numbers can be added. For example, the sum of 7 and $\sqrt{3}$ can be expressed as $7 + \sqrt{3}$. We cannot simplify this name for the sum. However, when we have like radical terms (radical terms having the same index and radicand) we can use the distributive laws to simplify, collecting like radical terms.

EXAMPLES

Add or subtract. Simplify by collecting like radical terms if possible.

1. $6\sqrt{7} + 4\sqrt{7} = (6 + 4)\sqrt{7}$ Using the distributive law
$$= 10\sqrt{7}$$

2. $8\sqrt[3]{2} - 7x\sqrt[3]{2} + 5\sqrt[3]{2} = (8 - 7x + 5)\sqrt[3]{2}$ Factoring out $\sqrt[3]{2}$
$$= (13 - 7x)\sqrt[3]{2}$$

3. $6\sqrt[5]{4x} + 4\sqrt[5]{4x} - \sqrt[3]{4x} = (6 + 4)\sqrt[5]{4x} - \sqrt[3]{4x}$
$$= 10\sqrt[5]{4x} - \sqrt[3]{4x}$$

TRY THIS   Add or subtract. Simplify if possible by collecting like radical terms.

1. $5\sqrt{2} + 8\sqrt{2}$ 2. $7\sqrt[4]{5x} + 3\sqrt[4]{5x} - \sqrt{7}$ 1. $13\sqrt{2}$ 2. $10\sqrt[4]{5x} - \sqrt{7}$

Sometimes we need to factor in order to have terms with like radical terms.

EXAMPLES

Add or subtract. Simplify by collecting like radical terms if possible.

4. $3\sqrt{8} - 5\sqrt{2} = 3\sqrt{4 \cdot 2} - 5\sqrt{2}$ Factoring 8
$$= 3\sqrt{4} \cdot \sqrt{2} - 5\sqrt{2}$$ Factoring $\sqrt{4 \cdot 2}$ into 2 radicals
$$= 3 \cdot 2\sqrt{2} - 5\sqrt{2}$$ Taking the square root of 4
$$= 6\sqrt{2} - 5\sqrt{2}$$
$$= (6 - 5)\sqrt{2}$$
$$= \sqrt{2}$$ Collecting like radical terms

5. $5\sqrt{2} - 4\sqrt{3}$ No simplification possible

6. $5\sqrt[3]{16y^4} + 7\sqrt[3]{2y} = 5\sqrt[3]{8y^3 \cdot 2y} + 7\sqrt[3]{2y}$ Factoring the first radical

$\qquad\qquad\qquad\quad = 5\sqrt[3]{8y^3} \cdot \sqrt[3]{2y} + 7\sqrt[3]{2y}$

$\qquad\qquad\qquad\quad = 5 \cdot 2y \cdot \sqrt[3]{2y} + 7\sqrt[3]{2y}$ Taking the cube root of $8y^3$

$\qquad\qquad\qquad\quad = 10y\sqrt[3]{2y} + 7\sqrt[3]{2y}$

$\qquad\qquad\qquad\quad = (10y + 7)\sqrt[3]{2y}$ Collecting like radical terms

TRY THIS Add or subtract. Simplify if possible by collecting like radical terms.

3. $19\sqrt{5}$
4. $(3y + 4)\sqrt[3]{y^2} + 2y^2$
5. $2\sqrt{x} - 1$

3. $7\sqrt{45} - 2\sqrt{5}$ **4.** $3\sqrt[3]{y^5} + 4\sqrt[3]{y^2} + \sqrt[3]{8y^6}$ **5.** $\sqrt{25x - 25} - \sqrt{9x - 9}$

Multiplication

To multiply radical expressions in which some factors contain more than one term, we use the procedures for multiplying polynomials.

EXAMPLES
Multiply.

7. $\sqrt[3]{y}(\sqrt[3]{y^2} + \sqrt[3]{2}) = \sqrt[3]{y} \cdot \sqrt[3]{y^2} + \sqrt[3]{y} \cdot \sqrt[3]{2}$ Using the distributive law

$\qquad\qquad\qquad\quad = \sqrt[3]{y^3} + \sqrt[3]{2y}$ Multiplying radicals

$\qquad\qquad\qquad\quad = y + \sqrt[3]{2y}$ Simplifying $\sqrt[3]{y^3}$

8. $(4\sqrt{3} + \sqrt{2})(\sqrt{3} - 5\sqrt{2}) = \overset{F}{4(\sqrt{3})^2} - \overset{O}{20\sqrt{3} \cdot \sqrt{2}} + \overset{I}{\sqrt{2} \cdot \sqrt{3}} - \overset{L}{5(\sqrt{2})^2}$

$\qquad\qquad\qquad\qquad\qquad = 4 \cdot 3 - 20\sqrt{6} + \sqrt{6} - 5 \cdot 2$

$\qquad\qquad\qquad\qquad\qquad = 12 - 20\sqrt{6} + \sqrt{6} - 10$

$\qquad\qquad\qquad\qquad\qquad = 2 - 19\sqrt{6}$

9. $(\sqrt{5} + \sqrt{7})(\sqrt{5} - \sqrt{7}) = (\sqrt{5})^2 - (\sqrt{7})^2$ This is now a difference

$\qquad\qquad\qquad\qquad\qquad = 5 - 7$ of two squares.

$\qquad\qquad\qquad\qquad\qquad = -2$

TRY THIS Multiply.

6. $5\sqrt{6} + 3\sqrt{14}$
7. $3\sqrt{ab} + 6\sqrt{3b} - 4\sqrt{3a} - 24$
8. $20 - 4y\sqrt{5} + y^2$

6. $\sqrt{2}(5\sqrt{3} + 3\sqrt{7})$ **7.** $(\sqrt{a} + 2\sqrt{3})(3\sqrt{b} - 4\sqrt{3})$ **8.** $(2\sqrt{5} - y)^2$

Rationalizing Denominators

When performing operations with radical expressions it is standard to write the result without radicals in the denominator. The idea in rationalizing a denominator is to multiply by 1, to make the denominator a perfect power.

EXAMPLE 10

Rationalize the denominator.

$$\sqrt[3]{\frac{7}{9}} = \sqrt[3]{\frac{7}{3\cdot 3}\cdot\frac{3}{3}} \quad \text{Multiplying by } \frac{3}{3} \text{ to make the denominator a perfect cube}$$

$$= \sqrt[3]{\frac{21}{3\cdot 3\cdot 3}}$$

$$= \frac{\sqrt[3]{21}}{\sqrt[3]{3^3}}$$

$$= \frac{\sqrt[3]{21}}{3} \quad \text{Taking the cube root of } 3^3$$

TRY THIS Rationalize the denominator.

9. $\sqrt{\frac{2}{3}}$ **10.** $\sqrt{\frac{10}{7}}$ **11.** $\sqrt[3]{\frac{3}{6}}$ 9. $\frac{\sqrt{6}}{3}$ 10. $\frac{\sqrt{70}}{7}$ 11. $\frac{\sqrt[3]{4}}{2}$

In Example 10 we multiplied by 1 under the radical sign. We can also multiply by 1 outside the radical sign, as in Example 11.

EXAMPLE 11

Rationalize the denominator. Assume that all expressions under radicals represent positive numbers.

$$\sqrt{\frac{2a}{5b}} = \frac{\sqrt{2a}}{\sqrt{5b}} \quad \text{Converting to a quotient of radicals}$$

$$= \frac{\sqrt{2a}}{\sqrt{5b}}\cdot\frac{\sqrt{5b}}{\sqrt{5b}} \quad \text{Multiplying by 1}$$

$$= \frac{\sqrt{10ab}}{\sqrt{25b^2}} \quad \text{The radicand in the denominator is a perfect square.}$$

$$= \frac{\sqrt{10ab}}{5|b|} \quad \text{Taking the square root of } 25b^2$$

TRY THIS Rationalize the denominator. Assume that all expressions under radicals represent positive numbers.

12. $\sqrt{\frac{4a}{3b}}$ **13.** $\frac{\sqrt{4x^5}}{\sqrt{3y^3}}$ 12. $\frac{2\sqrt{3ab}}{3|b|}$ 13. $\frac{2x^2\sqrt{3xy}}{3y^2}$

EXAMPLE 12

Rationalize the denominator.

To choose the symbol for 1, we look at the radicand $9x$. This is $3\cdot 3\cdot x$. To make it a cube we need another 3 and two more x's. Thus we multiply by $\sqrt[3]{3x^2}/\sqrt[3]{3x^2}$.

$$\frac{\sqrt[3]{a}}{\sqrt[3]{9x}} = \frac{\sqrt[3]{a}}{\sqrt[3]{9x}} \cdot \frac{\sqrt[3]{3x^2}}{\sqrt[3]{3x^2}} \quad \text{Multiplying by 1}$$

$$= \frac{\sqrt[3]{3ax^2}}{3x} \quad \text{Simplifying}$$

TRY THIS Rationalize the denominator.

14. $\dfrac{\sqrt[3]{7}}{\sqrt[3]{2}}$ 15. $\sqrt[7]{\dfrac{3x^5}{2y}}$ 14. $\dfrac{\sqrt[3]{28}}{2}$ 15. $\dfrac{\sqrt[7]{192y^6x^5}}{2y}$

When the denominator to be rationalized has two terms, choose a symbol for 1 as illustrated below.

EXAMPLE 13
Rationalize the denominator.

$$\frac{4 + \sqrt{2}}{\sqrt{5} - \sqrt{2}} = \frac{4 + \sqrt{2}}{\sqrt{5} - \sqrt{2}} \cdot \frac{\sqrt{5} + \sqrt{2}}{\sqrt{5} + \sqrt{2}} \qquad \text{Multiplying by 1}$$

$$= \frac{(4 + \sqrt{2})(\sqrt{5} + \sqrt{2})}{(\sqrt{5} - \sqrt{2})(\sqrt{5} + \sqrt{2})} \qquad \text{Multiplying numerators and denominators}$$

$$= \frac{4\sqrt{5} + 4\sqrt{2} + \sqrt{2}\sqrt{5} + (\sqrt{2})^2}{(\sqrt{5})^2 - (\sqrt{2})^2} \qquad \text{Using FOIL}$$

$$= \frac{4\sqrt{5} + 4\sqrt{2} + \sqrt{10} + 2}{5 - 2} \qquad \text{Squaring in the denominator}$$

$$= \frac{4\sqrt{5} + 4\sqrt{2} + \sqrt{10} + 2}{3}$$

Note that the denominator in this example was $\sqrt{5} - \sqrt{2}$. We chose a symbol for 1 which had $\sqrt{5} + \sqrt{2}$ in the numerator and denominator. If the denominator had been $\sqrt{5} + \sqrt{2}$ we would have chosen $\dfrac{5 - \sqrt{2}}{5 - \sqrt{2}}$ for 1.

EXAMPLES
What symbol for 1 would you use to rationalize the denominator?

Expression	Symbol for 1	Expression	Symbol for 1
14. $\dfrac{3}{2 + \sqrt{7}}$	$\dfrac{2 - \sqrt{7}}{2 - \sqrt{7}}$	15. $\dfrac{4 + \sqrt{3}}{\sqrt{3} - \sqrt{11}}$	$\dfrac{\sqrt{3} + \sqrt{11}}{\sqrt{3} + \sqrt{11}}$

TRY THIS Choose an appropriate symbol for 1 and rationalize the denominator.

16. $\dfrac{5}{1 - \sqrt{2}}$ 17. $\dfrac{1}{\sqrt{2} + \sqrt{3}}$ 18. $\dfrac{\sqrt{5} + 1}{\sqrt{3} - 1}$

16. $\dfrac{1 + \sqrt{2}}{1 \pm \sqrt{2}}, -5(1 + \sqrt{2})$
17. $\dfrac{\sqrt{2} - \sqrt{3}}{\sqrt{2} - \sqrt{3}}, -\sqrt{2} + \sqrt{3}$
18. $\dfrac{\sqrt{3} + 1}{\sqrt{3} + 1}, \dfrac{\sqrt{15} + \sqrt{3} + \sqrt{5} + 1}{2}$

7-4

Exercises

Add or subtract. Simplify by collecting like radical terms, if possible, assuming that all expressions under radical signs represent nonnegative numbers.

1. $6\sqrt{3} + 2\sqrt{3}$ $\quad 8\sqrt{3}$
2. $8\sqrt{5} + 9\sqrt{5}$ $\quad 17\sqrt{5}$
3. $9\sqrt[3]{5} - 6\sqrt[3]{5}$ $\quad 3\sqrt[3]{5}$
4. $14\sqrt[5]{2} - 6\sqrt[5]{2}$ $\quad 8\sqrt[5]{2}$
5. $4\sqrt[3]{y} + 9\sqrt[3]{y}$ $\quad 13\sqrt[3]{y}$
6. $6\sqrt[4]{t} - 3\sqrt[4]{t}$ $\quad 3\sqrt[4]{t}$
7. $8\sqrt{2} - 6\sqrt{2} + 5\sqrt{2}$ $\quad 7\sqrt{2}$
8. $2\sqrt{6} + 8\sqrt{6} - 3\sqrt{6}$ $\quad 7\sqrt{6}$
9. $4\sqrt[3]{5} - \sqrt{3} + 2\sqrt[3]{5} + \sqrt{3}$ $\quad 6\sqrt[3]{5}$
10. $5\sqrt{7} - 8\sqrt[4]{11} + \sqrt{7} + 9\sqrt[4]{11}$ $\quad 6\sqrt{7} + \sqrt[4]{11}$
11. $6\sqrt{8} + 11\sqrt{2}$ $\quad 23\sqrt{2}$
12. $2\sqrt{12} + 5\sqrt{3}$ $\quad 9\sqrt{3}$
13. $8\sqrt{27} - 3\sqrt{3}$ $\quad 21\sqrt{3}$
14. $9\sqrt{50} - 4\sqrt{2}$ $\quad 41\sqrt{2}$
15. $8\sqrt{45} + 7\sqrt{20}$ $\quad 38\sqrt{5}$
16. $9\sqrt{12} + 16\sqrt{27}$ $\quad 66\sqrt{3}$
17. $18\sqrt{72} + 2\sqrt{98}$ $\quad 122\sqrt{2}$
18. $12\sqrt{45} - 8\sqrt{80}$ $\quad 4\sqrt{5}$
19. $3\sqrt[3]{16} + \sqrt[3]{54}$ $\quad 9\sqrt[3]{2}$
20. $\sqrt[3]{27} - 5\sqrt[3]{8}$ $\quad -7$
21. $5\sqrt[3]{32} - 2\sqrt[3]{108}$ $\quad 4\sqrt[3]{4}$
22. $9\sqrt[3]{40} - 7\sqrt[3]{135}$ $\quad -3\sqrt[3]{5}$
23. $2\sqrt{128} - \sqrt{18} + 4\sqrt{32}$ $\quad 29\sqrt{2}$
24. $5\sqrt{50} - 2\sqrt{18} + 9\sqrt{32}$ $\quad 55\sqrt{2}$
25. $\sqrt{5a} + 2\sqrt{45a^3}$ $\quad (1 + 6a)\sqrt{5a}$
26. $4\sqrt{3x^3} - \sqrt{12x}$ $\quad (4x - 2)\sqrt{3x}$
27. $\sqrt[3]{24x} - \sqrt[3]{3x^4}$ $\quad (2 - x)\sqrt[3]{3x}$
28. $\sqrt[3]{54x} - \sqrt[3]{2x^4}$ $\quad (3 - x)\sqrt[3]{2x}$
29. $2\sqrt[3]{125a^4} - 5\sqrt[3]{8a}$ $\quad 10(a - 1)\sqrt[3]{a}$
30. $9\sqrt[3]{16x^5y} - 2\sqrt[3]{128x^2y}$ $\quad 2(9x - 4)\sqrt[3]{2x^2y}$
31. $\sqrt{8y - 8} + \sqrt{2y - 2}$ $\quad 3\sqrt{2y - 2}$
32. $\sqrt{12t + 12} + \sqrt{3t + 3}$ $\quad 3\sqrt{3t + 3}$
33. $\sqrt{x^3 - x^2} + \sqrt{9x - 9}$ $\quad (x + 3)\sqrt{x - 1}$
34. $\sqrt{4x - 4} - \sqrt{x^3 - x^2}$ $\quad (2 - x)\sqrt{x - 1}$

Multiply.

35. $\sqrt{6}(2 - 3\sqrt{6})$ $\quad 2\sqrt{6} - 18$
36. $\sqrt{3}(4 + \sqrt{3})$ $\quad 4\sqrt{3} + 3$
37. $\sqrt{2}(\sqrt{3} - \sqrt{5})$ $\quad \sqrt{6} - \sqrt{10}$
38. $\sqrt{5}(\sqrt{5} - \sqrt{2})$ $\quad 5 - \sqrt{10}$
39. $\sqrt{3}(2\sqrt{5} - 3\sqrt{4})$ $\quad 2\sqrt{15} - 6\sqrt{3}$
40. $\sqrt{2}(3\sqrt{10} - 2\sqrt{2})$ $\quad 6\sqrt{5} - 4$
41. $\sqrt[3]{2}(\sqrt[3]{4} - 2\sqrt[3]{32})$ $\quad -6$
42. $\sqrt[3]{3}(\sqrt[3]{9} - 4\sqrt[3]{21})$ $\quad 3 - 4\sqrt[3]{63}$
43. $\sqrt[3]{a}(\sqrt[3]{2a^2} + \sqrt[3]{16a^2})$ $\quad 3a\sqrt[3]{2}$
44. $\sqrt[3]{x}(\sqrt[3]{3x^2} - \sqrt[3]{81x^2})$ $\quad -2x\sqrt[3]{3}$
45. $(\sqrt{3} - \sqrt{2})(\sqrt{3} + \sqrt{2})$ $\quad 1$
46. $(\sqrt{5} + \sqrt{6})(\sqrt{5} - \sqrt{6})$ $\quad -1$
47. $(\sqrt{8} + 2\sqrt{5})(\sqrt{8} - 2\sqrt{5})$ $\quad -12$
48. $(\sqrt{18} + 3\sqrt{7})(\sqrt{18} - 3\sqrt{7})$ $\quad -45$
49. $(\sqrt{a} + \sqrt{b})(\sqrt{a} - \sqrt{b})$ $\quad a - b$
50. $(\sqrt{x} - \sqrt{y})(\sqrt{x} + \sqrt{y})$ $\quad x - y$
51. $(3 - \sqrt{5})(2 + \sqrt{5})$ $\quad 1 + \sqrt{5}$
52. $(2 + \sqrt{6})(4 - \sqrt{6})$ $\quad 2 + 2\sqrt{6}$
53. $(\sqrt{3} + 1)(2\sqrt{3} + 1)$ $\quad 7 + 3\sqrt{3}$
54. $(4\sqrt{3} + 5)(\sqrt{3} - 2)$ $\quad 2 - 3\sqrt{3}$
55. $(2\sqrt{7} - 4\sqrt{2})(3\sqrt{7} + 6\sqrt{2})$ $\quad -6$
56. $(4\sqrt{5} + 3\sqrt{3})(3\sqrt{5} - 4\sqrt{3})$ $\quad 24 - 7\sqrt{15}$

57. $(\sqrt{a} + \sqrt{2})(\sqrt{a} + \sqrt{3})$

58. $(2 - \sqrt{x})(1 - \sqrt{x})$ $\quad 2 - 3\sqrt{x} + x$

59. $(2\sqrt[3]{3} + \sqrt[3]{2})(\sqrt[3]{3} - 2\sqrt[3]{2})$

60. $(3\sqrt[4]{7} + \sqrt[4]{6})(2\sqrt[4]{9} - 3\sqrt[4]{6})$ $\quad 6\sqrt[4]{63} - 9\sqrt[4]{42} + 2\sqrt[4]{54} - 3\sqrt[4]{36}$

61. $(2 + \sqrt{3})^2$ $\quad 7 + 4\sqrt{3}$

62. $(\sqrt{5} + 1)^2$ $\quad 6 + 2\sqrt{5}$

63. $(3\sqrt{2} - \sqrt{3})^2$ $\quad 21 - 6\sqrt{6}$

64. $(5\sqrt{3} + 3\sqrt{5})^2$ $\quad 120 + 30\sqrt{15}$

57. $a + \sqrt{3a} + \sqrt{2a} + \sqrt{6}$
59. $2\sqrt[3]{9} - 3\sqrt[3]{6} - 2\sqrt[3]{4}$

Rationalize the denominator.

65. $\sqrt{\dfrac{6}{5}}$

66. $\sqrt{\dfrac{11}{6}}$

67. $\sqrt{\dfrac{10}{7}}$

68. $\sqrt{\dfrac{22}{3}}$

69. $\dfrac{6\sqrt{5}}{5\sqrt{3}}$

70. $\dfrac{2\sqrt{3}}{5\sqrt{2}}$

71. $\sqrt[3]{\dfrac{16}{9}}$

72. $\sqrt[3]{\dfrac{3}{9}}$

73. $\dfrac{\sqrt[3]{3a}}{\sqrt[3]{5c}}$

74. $\dfrac{\sqrt[3]{7x}}{\sqrt[3]{3y}}$

75. $\dfrac{\sqrt[3]{2y^4}}{\sqrt[3]{6x^4}}$

76. $\dfrac{\sqrt[3]{3a^4}}{\sqrt[3]{7b^2}}$

77. $\dfrac{1}{\sqrt[3]{xy}}$

78. $\dfrac{1}{\sqrt[3]{ab}}$

79. $\dfrac{5}{8 - \sqrt{6}}$

80. $\dfrac{7}{9 + \sqrt{10}}$

81. $\dfrac{-4\sqrt{7}}{\sqrt{5} - \sqrt{3}}$

82. $\dfrac{-3\sqrt{2}}{\sqrt{3} - \sqrt{5}}$

83. $\dfrac{\sqrt{5} - 2\sqrt{6}}{\sqrt{3} - 4\sqrt{5}}$

84. $\dfrac{\sqrt{6} - 3\sqrt{5}}{\sqrt{3} - 2\sqrt{7}}$

85. $\dfrac{\sqrt{x} - \sqrt{y}}{\sqrt{x} + \sqrt{y}}$

86. $\dfrac{\sqrt{a} + \sqrt{b}}{\sqrt{a} - \sqrt{b}}$

87. $\dfrac{5\sqrt{3} - 3\sqrt{2}}{3\sqrt{2} - 2\sqrt{3}}$

88. $\dfrac{7\sqrt{2} + 4\sqrt{3}}{4\sqrt{3} - 3\sqrt{2}}$

65. $\dfrac{\sqrt{30}}{5}$
66. $\dfrac{\sqrt{66}}{6}$
67. $\dfrac{\sqrt{70}}{7}$
68. $\dfrac{\sqrt{66}}{3}$
69. $\dfrac{2\sqrt{15}}{5}$
70. $\dfrac{\sqrt{6}}{5}$
71. $\dfrac{2\sqrt[3]{6}}{3}$
72. $\dfrac{\sqrt[3]{9}}{3}$
73. $\dfrac{\sqrt[3]{75ac^2}}{5c}$
74. $\dfrac{\sqrt[3]{63xy^2}}{3y}$
75. $\dfrac{y\sqrt[3]{9yx^2}}{3x^2}$
76. $\dfrac{a\sqrt[3]{147ab}}{7b}$
77. $\dfrac{\sqrt[3]{x^2y^2}}{xy}$
78. $\dfrac{\sqrt[3]{a^2b^2}}{ab}$
79. $\dfrac{5(8 + \sqrt{6})}{58}$
80. $\dfrac{7(9 - \sqrt{10})}{71}$
81. $-2\sqrt{7}(\sqrt{5} + \sqrt{3})$
82. $\dfrac{3\sqrt{2}(\sqrt{3} + \sqrt{5})}{2}$

Extension

Rationalize the numerator.

89. $\dfrac{\sqrt{7}}{\sqrt{3}}$

90. $\sqrt{\dfrac{14}{21}}$

91. $\dfrac{4\sqrt{13}}{3\sqrt{7}}$

92. $\dfrac{\sqrt[3]{7}}{\sqrt[3]{2}}$

93. $\sqrt{\dfrac{7x}{3y}}$

94. $\dfrac{\sqrt[3]{5y^4}}{\sqrt[3]{6x^5}}$

95. $\dfrac{\sqrt{3} + 5}{8}$

96. $\dfrac{\sqrt{3} - 5}{\sqrt{2} + 5}$

97. $\dfrac{\sqrt{5} - \sqrt{2}}{\sqrt{2} + \sqrt{3}}$

98. **a.** Find as many pairs of numbers, a and b, as you can for which $\sqrt{a} + \sqrt{b} = \sqrt{a + b}$. $\quad a = 0$ and $b \geq 0$, or $a \geq 0$ and $b = 0$

b. Find several pairs of numbers for which the above equation is false. Any pair of numbers that does not satisfy the conditions stated in answer to 98a.

Challenge

Multiply.

99. $(\sqrt{x + 3} - 3)(\sqrt{x + 3} + 3)$

100. $(\sqrt{x + h} - \sqrt{x})(\sqrt{x + h} + \sqrt{x})$

99. $x - 6$
100. h

Rationalize the numerator. Assume all expressions represent nonnegative numbers.

101. $\dfrac{\sqrt{x + 1} + 1}{\sqrt{x}}$ $\quad \dfrac{x}{\sqrt{x}(\sqrt{x + 1} - 1)}$

102. $\dfrac{\sqrt{a + h} - \sqrt{a}}{h}$ $\quad \dfrac{1}{\sqrt{a + h} + \sqrt{a}}$

7–5 Rational Numbers as Exponents

Combinations of Powers and Roots

Consider the following.

$$\sqrt[3]{8^2} = \sqrt[3]{64} = 4$$
$$(\sqrt[3]{8})^2 = 2^2 = 4$$

This example suggests another important theorem about radical notation.

THEOREM 7–7

For any nonnegative number a, any index k, and any natural number m,

$$\sqrt[k]{a^m} = (\sqrt[k]{a})^m.$$

(We can raise to a power and then take a root, or we can take a root and then raise to a power.)

In some cases one way of calculating is easier than the other.

EXAMPLES

Calculate as shown. Then use Theorem 7–7 to calculate another way. Assume that all expressions under radical signs are positive.

1. $\sqrt[3]{27^2} = \sqrt[3]{729} = 9$
   $(\sqrt[3]{27})^2 = (3)^2 = 9$

2. $\sqrt[3]{2^6} = \sqrt[3]{64} = 4$
   $(\sqrt[3]{2})^6 = \sqrt[3]{2} \cdot \sqrt[3]{2} \cdot \sqrt[3]{2} \cdot \sqrt[3]{2} \cdot \sqrt[3]{2} \cdot \sqrt[3]{2} = 2 \cdot 2 = 4$

3. $(\sqrt{5x})^3 = \sqrt{5x} \cdot \sqrt{5x} \cdot \sqrt{5x} = \sqrt{5^3x^3} = \sqrt{5^2x^2}\sqrt{5x} = 5x\sqrt{5x}$
   $\sqrt{(5x)^3} = \sqrt{5^3x^3} = \sqrt{5^2x^2} \cdot \sqrt{5x} = 5x\sqrt{5x}$

TRY THIS Calculate as shown. Then use Theorem 7–7 to calculate another way.

1. $(\sqrt[3]{125})^2$ 2. $(\sqrt{6y})^3$

1. $(\sqrt[3]{125})^2 = 25,$
   $\sqrt[3]{125^2} = 25$
2. $(\sqrt{6y})^3 = 6y\sqrt{6y},$
   $\sqrt{(6y)^3} = 6y\sqrt{6y}$

Fractional Exponents

Consider $a^{\frac{1}{2}} \cdot a^{\frac{1}{2}}$. If we still want to multiply by adding exponents it must follow that $a^{\frac{1}{2}} \cdot a^{\frac{1}{2}} = a^{\frac{1}{2}+\frac{1}{2}}$, or a^1. Thus we should define $a^{\frac{1}{2}}$ to be a square root of a, $\sqrt{a}$ or $-\sqrt{a}$. Similarly, $a^{\frac{1}{3}} \cdot a^{\frac{1}{3}} \cdot a^{\frac{1}{3}} = a^{\frac{1}{3}+\frac{1}{3}+\frac{1}{3}}$, or a^1, so $a^{\frac{1}{3}}$ should be defined to mean $\sqrt[3]{a}$.

DEFINITION

For any nonnegative number a, and any index k, $a^{\frac{1}{k}}$ means $\sqrt[k]{a}$ (the nonnegative kth root of a).

EXAMPLES

Rewrite without fractional exponents.

4. $x^{\frac{1}{2}} = \sqrt{x}$ **5.** $27^{\frac{1}{3}} = \sqrt[3]{27}$, or 3   **6.** $(abc)^{\frac{1}{5}} = \sqrt[5]{abc}$

Rewrite with fractional exponents.

7. $\sqrt[5]{7xy} = (7xy)^{\frac{1}{5}}$ **8.** $\sqrt[7]{\dfrac{x^3y}{9}} = \left(\dfrac{x^3y}{9}\right)^{\frac{1}{7}}$

TRY THIS Write an equivalent form of each of the following expressions using the definition of fractional exponents.

3. $y^{\frac{1}{4}}$ **4.** $(3a)^{\frac{1}{2}}$ **5.** $16^{\frac{1}{4}}$ **6.** $(125)^{\frac{1}{3}}$

7. $(a^3b^2c)^{\frac{1}{5}}$ **8.** $\sqrt[3]{19}$ **9.** $\sqrt{abc}$ **10.** $\sqrt[5]{\dfrac{x^2y}{16}}$

3. $\sqrt[4]{y}$
4. $\sqrt{3a}$
5. $\sqrt[4]{16}$ or 2
6. $\sqrt[3]{125}$ or 5
7. $\sqrt[5]{a^3b^2c}$
8. $19^{1/3}$
9. $(abc)^{1/2}$
10. $\left(\dfrac{x^2y}{16}\right)^{1/5}$

How should we define $a^{\frac{2}{3}}$? If the usual properties of exponents are to hold, we have $a^{\frac{2}{3}} = (a^{\frac{1}{3}})^2$, or $(\sqrt[3]{a})^2$, or $\sqrt[3]{a^2}$.

DEFINITION

For any natural numbers m and k, and any nonnegative number a, $a^{\frac{m}{k}}$ means $\sqrt[k]{a^m}$.

Thus $a^{\frac{m}{k}}$ represents the principal kth root of a^m. Since, by Theorem 7-7, we know that $\sqrt[k]{a^m} = (\sqrt[k]{a})^m$ it follows that $a^{\frac{m}{k}}$ also represents $(\sqrt[k]{a})^m$.

EXAMPLES

Rewrite without fractional exponents.

9. $(27)^{\frac{2}{3}} = (\sqrt[3]{27})^2$ or $(27)^{\frac{2}{3}} = \sqrt[3]{27^2}$
$\qquad = (3)^2 \qquad\qquad = \sqrt[3]{729}$
$\qquad = 9 \qquad\qquad\quad = 9$

10. $4^{\frac{3}{2}} = (\sqrt[2]{4})^3$ or $4^{\frac{3}{2}} = \sqrt[2]{4^3}$
$\qquad = 2^3 \qquad\qquad = \sqrt{64}$
$\qquad = 8 \qquad\qquad\; = 8$

Rewrite with fractional exponents.

11. $\sqrt[3]{8^4} = 8^{\frac{4}{3}}$ 12. $(\sqrt[4]{7xy})^5 = (7xy)^{\frac{5}{4}}$

TRY THIS Write an equivalent form of each of the following expressions using the definition of fractional exponents.

11. $x\sqrt{x}$ 14. $(7abc)^{4/3}$
12. 4   15. $6^{7/5}$
13. 32   16. $x^{1/2}y^{3/4}$

11. $x^{\frac{3}{2}}$ 12. $8^{\frac{2}{3}}$ 13. $4^{\frac{5}{2}}$ 14. $(\sqrt[3]{7abc})^4$ 15. $\sqrt[5]{6^7}$ 16. $\sqrt[4]{x^2y^3}$

Negative Rational Exponents

Negative fractional exponents have a meaning similar to that of negative integer exponents. Changing the sign of an exponent amounts to finding a reciprocal.

DEFINITION

For any rational number $\frac{m}{n}$ and any positive real number a,
$a^{-\frac{m}{n}}$ means $\frac{1}{a^{\frac{m}{n}}}$ ($a^{\frac{m}{n}}$ and $a^{-\frac{m}{n}}$ are reciprocals).

EXAMPLES

Rewrite with positive exponents.

13. $4^{-\frac{1}{2}} = \frac{1}{4^{\frac{1}{2}}}$ $4^{-\frac{1}{2}}$ is the reciprocal of $4^{\frac{1}{2}}$.

Since $4^{\frac{1}{2}} = \sqrt{4} = 2$, the answer simplifies to $\frac{1}{2}$.

14. $(5xy)^{-\frac{4}{3}} = \frac{1}{(5xy)^{\frac{4}{3}}}$ $(5xy)^{-\frac{4}{3}}$ is the reciprocal of $(5xy)^{\frac{4}{3}}$.

TRY THIS Rewrite with positive exponents.

17. $5^{-\frac{1}{4}}$ $\frac{1}{5^{1/4}}$ 18. $(3xy)^{-\frac{7}{8}}$ $\frac{1}{(3xy)^{7/8}}$

The properties of exponents that hold for integer exponents also hold for rational exponents.

EXAMPLES

Use the properties of exponents to simplify.

15. $3^{\frac{1}{5}} \cdot 3^{\frac{3}{5}} = 3^{\frac{1}{5}+\frac{3}{5}} = 3^{\frac{4}{5}}$ Adding exponents

16. $\frac{7^{\frac{1}{4}}}{7^{\frac{1}{2}}} = 7^{\frac{1}{4}-\frac{1}{2}} = 7^{\frac{1}{4}-\frac{2}{4}} = 7^{-\frac{1}{4}}$ Subtracting exponents

17. $(7.2^{\frac{2}{3}})^{\frac{3}{4}} = 7.2^{\frac{2}{3}\cdot\frac{3}{4}} = 7.2^{\frac{6}{12}} = 7.2^{\frac{1}{2}}$ Multiplying exponents

TRY THIS Use the properties of exponents to simplify.

19. $7^{\frac{1}{3}} \cdot 7^{\frac{3}{5}}$ **20.** $\frac{5^{\frac{7}{6}}}{5^{\frac{5}{6}}}$ **21.** $(9^{\frac{3}{5}})^{\frac{2}{3}}$ 19. $7^{14/15}$ 20. $5^{1/3}$ 21. $9^{2/5}$

Simplifying Radical Expressions

Fractional exponents can be used to simplify some radical expressions. The procedure is as follows.

> 1. Convert radical expressions to exponential expressions.
> 2. Use arithmetic and the properties of exponents to simplify.
> 3. Convert back to radical notation when appropriate.

We confine our examples to nonnegative radicands so absolute value signs will not be needed.

EXAMPLES

Use fractional exponents to simplify.

18. $\sqrt[6]{x^3} = x^{\frac{3}{6}}$ Converting to an exponential expression

$= x^{\frac{1}{2}}$ Using arithmetic to simplify the exponent

$= \sqrt{x}$ Converting back to radical notation

19. $\sqrt[6]{4} = 4^{\frac{1}{6}}$

$= (2^2)^{\frac{1}{6}}$

$= 2^{\frac{2}{6}}$

$= 2^{\frac{1}{3}}$

$= \sqrt[3]{2}$

TRY THIS Use fractional exponents to simplify.

22. $\sqrt[4]{a^2}$ $\sqrt{a}$ **23.** $\sqrt[4]{x^4}$ x **24.** $\sqrt[6]{8}$ $\sqrt{2}$

EXAMPLE 20

Use fractional exponents to simplify.

$$\sqrt[8]{a^2b^4} = (a^2b^4)^{\frac{1}{8}}$$
$$= a^{\frac{2}{8}} \cdot b^{\frac{4}{8}}$$
$$= a^{\frac{1}{4}} \cdot b^{\frac{2}{4}}$$
$$= (ab^2)^{\frac{1}{4}}$$
$$= \sqrt[4]{ab^2}$$

TRY THIS Use fractional exponents to simplify.

25. $\sqrt[5]{a^5b^{10}}$ ab^2 **26.** $\sqrt[4]{x^4y^{12}}$ xy^3 **27.** $\sqrt[12]{x^3y^6}$ $x^{1/4}y^{1/2}$

We can use properties of fractional exponents to write a single radical expression for a product or quotient.

EXAMPLES

Use fractional exponents to write a single radical expression.

21. $\sqrt[3]{5} \cdot \sqrt{2} = 5^{\frac{1}{3}} \cdot 2^{\frac{1}{2}}$
$$= 5^{\frac{2}{6}} 2^{\frac{3}{6}}$$
$$= (5^2 \cdot 2^3)^{\frac{1}{6}}$$
$$= \sqrt[6]{5^2 \cdot 2^3}$$
$$= \sqrt[6]{200}$$

22. $\sqrt{x - 2} \cdot \sqrt[4]{3y} = (x - 2)^{\frac{1}{2}}(3y)^{\frac{1}{4}}$
$$= (x - 2)^{\frac{2}{4}}(3y)^{\frac{1}{4}}$$
$$= [(x - 2)^2 (3y)]^{\frac{1}{4}}$$
$$= \sqrt[4]{(x^2 - 4x + 4) \cdot 3y}$$
$$= \sqrt[4]{3x^2y - 12xy + 12y}$$

23. $\dfrac{\sqrt[4]{(x + y)^3}}{\sqrt{x + y}} = \dfrac{(x + y)^{\frac{3}{4}}}{(x + y)^{\frac{1}{2}}}$
$$= (x + y)^{\frac{3}{4} - \frac{1}{2}}$$
$$= (x + y)^{\frac{1}{4}}$$
$$= \sqrt[4]{x + y}$$

TRY THIS Use fractional exponents to write a single radical expression.

28. $\sqrt[4]{7} \cdot \sqrt{3}$ $\sqrt[4]{63}$ **29.** $\dfrac{\sqrt[4]{(a - b)^5}}{a - b}$ $\sqrt[4]{a - b}$

EXAMPLE 24

Write a single radical expression.

$$a^{\frac{1}{2}}b^{-\frac{1}{2}}c^{\frac{5}{6}} = a^{\frac{3}{6}}b^{-\frac{3}{6}}c^{\frac{5}{6}} \qquad \text{Rewriting exponents with a common denominator}$$
$$= (a^3b^{-3}c^5)^{\frac{1}{6}} \qquad \text{Using the properties of exponents}$$
$$= \sqrt[6]{a^3b^{-3}c^5} \qquad \text{Converting to radical notation}$$

TRY THIS Write a single radical expression.

30. $x^{\frac{2}{3}}y^{\frac{1}{2}}z^{\frac{5}{6}}$ **31.** $\dfrac{a^{\frac{1}{2}}b^{\frac{3}{8}}}{a^{\frac{1}{4}}b^{\frac{1}{8}}}$ 30. $\sqrt[6]{x^4y^3z^5}$ 31. $\sqrt[4]{ab}$

We have now seen four different methods of simplifying radical expressions.

Methods of Simplifying Radical Expressions

1. Simplifying by Factoring. We factor the radicand, looking for factors that are perfect powers.
2. Rationalizing Denominators. We multiply the radical expression by 1 to make the denominator a perfect power. Then we simplify the expression.
3. Collecting Like Radical Terms. We use the distributive laws to collect terms with the same radicand and index.
4. Using Fractional Exponents. We convert to exponential notation and use arithmetic and the properties of exponents to simplify. Then we convert back to radical notation.

7–5

Exercises

Calculate as shown. Then use Theorem 7–7 to calculate another way. Assume that all expressions under radical signs represent positive numbers.

1. $\sqrt{(6a)^3}$ **2.** $\sqrt{(7y)^3}$ **3.** $(\sqrt[3]{16b^2})^2$ **4.** $(\sqrt[3]{25r^2})^2$

5. $\sqrt{(18a^2b)^3}$ **6.** $\sqrt{(12x^2y)^3}$ **7.** $(\sqrt[3]{12c^2d})^2$ **8.** $(\sqrt[3]{9x^2y})^2$

Rewrite without fractional exponents.

9. $x^{\frac{1}{4}}$ **10.** $y^{\frac{1}{5}}$ **11.** $(8)^{\frac{1}{3}}$ **12.** $(16)^{\frac{1}{2}}$ **13.** $(a^2b^2)^{\frac{1}{5}}$

14. $(x^3y^3)^{\frac{1}{4}}$ **15.** $a^{\frac{2}{3}}$ **16.** $b^{\frac{3}{2}}$ **17.** $16^{\frac{3}{4}}$ **18.** $4^{\frac{7}{2}}$

Rewrite with fractional exponents.

19. $\sqrt[3]{20}$ **20.** $\sqrt[3]{19}$ **21.** $\sqrt{17}$ **22.** $\sqrt{6}$

23. $\sqrt[4]{cd}$ **24.** $\sqrt[5]{xy}$ **25.** $\sqrt[5]{xy^2z}$ **26.** $\sqrt[7]{x^3y^2z^2}$

27. $(\sqrt{3mn})^3$ **28.** $(\sqrt[3]{7xy})^4$ **29.** $(\sqrt[7]{8x^2y})^5$ **30.** $(\sqrt[6]{2a^5b})^7$

Rewrite with positive exponents.

31. $x^{-\frac{1}{3}}$ **32.** $y^{-\frac{1}{4}}$ **33.** $(2rs)^{-\frac{3}{4}}$ **34.** $(5xy)^{-\frac{5}{6}}$

35. $\left(\frac{1}{10}\right)^{-\frac{2}{3}}$ **36.** $\left(\frac{1}{8}\right)^{-\frac{3}{4}}$ **37.** $\frac{1}{x^{-\frac{2}{3}}}$ **38.** $\frac{1}{x^{-\frac{5}{6}}}$

Use the properties of exponents to simplify.

39. $5^{\frac{3}{4}} \cdot 5^{\frac{1}{8}}$ **40.** $11^{\frac{2}{3}} \cdot 11^{\frac{1}{2}}$ **41.** $\frac{7^{\frac{5}{8}}}{7^{\frac{3}{8}}}$ **42.** $\frac{9^{\frac{9}{11}}}{9^{\frac{7}{11}}}$

43. $\frac{8.3^{\frac{3}{4}}}{8.3^{\frac{2}{3}}}$ **44.** $\frac{3.9^{\frac{3}{8}}}{3.9^{\frac{1}{4}}}$ **45.** $(10^{\frac{3}{5}})^{\frac{2}{3}}$ **46.** $(5^{\frac{5}{4}})^{\frac{3}{7}}$

Write an exponential expression. Then simplify if possible. Assume variables stand for nonnegative numbers. Write radical notation for the answer, if appropriate.

47. $\sqrt[6]{a^4}$ **48.** $\sqrt[6]{y^2}$ **49.** $\sqrt[3]{8y^6}$ **50.** $\sqrt{x^4y^6}$

51. $\sqrt[5]{32c^{10}d^{15}}$ **52.** $\sqrt[4]{16x^{12}y^{16}}$ **53.** $\sqrt[6]{\frac{m^{12}n^{24}}{64}}$ **54.** $\sqrt[5]{\frac{x^{15}y^{20}}{32}}$

55. $\sqrt[8]{r^4s^2}$ **56.** $\sqrt[3]{27a^3b^9}$ **57.** $\sqrt[12]{64t^6s^6}$ **58.** $\sqrt[4]{81x^8y^8}$

Write a single radical expression.

59. $\sqrt{x}\ \sqrt[3]{x-2}$ **60.** $\sqrt[4]{3x}\ \sqrt{y+4}$ **61.** $\frac{\sqrt[3]{(a+b)^2}}{\sqrt[4]{(a+b)}}$ **62.** $\frac{\sqrt[3]{(x+y)^2}}{\sqrt[4]{(x+y)^3}}$

63. $a^{\frac{2}{3}} \cdot b^{\frac{3}{4}}$ **64.** $x^{\frac{1}{3}} \cdot y^{\frac{1}{4}} \cdot z^{\frac{1}{6}}$ **65.** $\frac{s^{\frac{7}{12}} \cdot t^{\frac{5}{6}}}{s^{\frac{3}{4}} \cdot t^{-\frac{1}{6}}}$ **66.** $\frac{x^{\frac{8}{15}} \cdot y^{\frac{4}{5}}}{x^{\frac{1}{3}} \cdot y^{-\frac{1}{5}}}$

Challenge

67. Road Pavement Messages. In a psychological study it was determined that the proper length L of the letters of a word printed on pavement is given by

$$L = \frac{(0.00252)d^{2.27}}{h},$$

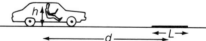

where d is the distance of a car from the lettering and h is the height of the eye above the surface of the road. All units are in meters. This formula says that if a person is h meters above the surface of the road and is to be able to recognize a message d meters away, that message will be the most recognizable if the length of the letters is L. Find L, given the values of d and h. Use a calculator.

  a. $h = 1$ m, $d = 60$ m   27.4 m   **b.** $h = 0.9906$ m, $d = 75$ m   45.9 m
  c. $h = 2.4$ m, $d = 80$ m   21.9 m   **d.** $h = 1.1$ m, $d = 100$ m   79.4 m
  e. Find a road pavement message near the school. See if it conforms to this formula.
  (Caution: Don't do your measurements in the middle of a road.)

Answers (right margin):

31. $\frac{1}{x^{1/3}}$
32. $\frac{1}{y^{1/4}}$
33. $\frac{1}{(2rs)^{3/4}}$
34. $\frac{1}{(5xy)^{5/6}}$
35. $10^{2/3}$
36. $8^{3/4}$
37. $x^{2/3}$
38. $x^{5/6}$
39. $5^{7/8}$
40. $11^{7/6}$
41. $7^{1/4}$
42. $9^{2/11}$
43. $8.3^{7\cdot 20}$
44. $3.9^{7\cdot 20}$
45. $10^{6\cdot 25}$
46. $5^{15\cdot 28}$
47. $\sqrt[3]{a^2}$
48. $\sqrt[3]{y}$
49. $2y^2$
50. x^2y^3
51. $2c^2d^3$
52. $2x^3y^4$
53. $\frac{m^2n^4}{2}$
54. $\frac{x^3y^4}{2}$
55. $\sqrt[4]{r^2s}$
56. $3ab^3$
57. $\sqrt{2ts}$
58. $3x^2y^2$
59. $\sqrt[6]{x^5 - 4x^4 + 4x^3}$
60. $\sqrt[4]{3xy^2 + 24xy + 48x}$
61. $\sqrt[12]{a+b}$
62. $\sqrt[12]{(x+y)^{-1}}$
63. $\sqrt[12]{a^8b^9}$
64. $\sqrt[12]{x^4y^3z^2}$
65. $\sqrt[12]{st^4}$
66. $\sqrt[5]{xy^5}$

7–6 Solving Radical Equations

The Principle of Powers

These are radical equations.

$$\sqrt{2x} + 1 = 5, \quad \sqrt[3]{x} + \sqrt[3]{4x - 2} = 7$$

A radical equation is an equation in which variables occur in one or more radicands. To solve such equations we need a new principle for equations. Suppose the equation $a = b$ is true. When we square both sides we still get a true equation, $a^2 = b^2$.

THEOREM 7–8

The Principle of Powers

For any natural number n, if an equation $a = b$ is true, then the equation $a^n = b^n$ is true.

EXAMPLES
Solve.

1. $\sqrt{x} - 3 = 4$

   $\sqrt{x} = 7$ Adding 3

   $x = 7^2$, or 49 Principle of powers

   Check: $\dfrac{\sqrt{x} - 3 = 4}{\begin{array}{c|c} \sqrt{49} - 3 & 4 \\ 7 - 3 & \\ 4 & \end{array}}$

The solution is 49.

2. $\sqrt{x} = -3$

We might observe at the outset that this equation has no solution because the principal square root of a number is never negative. Let us continue as above, for comparison.

$$x = (-3)^2, \text{ or } 9 \quad \text{Principle of powers}$$

Check: $\dfrac{\sqrt{x} = -3}{\begin{array}{c|c} \sqrt{9} & -3 \\ 3 & \end{array}}$

The number 9 does not check. Hence the equation has no solution.

Example 2 shows that since the converse of Theorem 7–8 is not true, the principle of powers does *not* always give equivalent equations. In solving radical equations, possible solutions found using the principle of powers *must* be checked!

TRY THIS Solve.

1. $\sqrt{x} - 7 = 3$ ~100~

EXAMPLE 3

Solve $x - 5 = \sqrt{x + 7}$.

$$x - 5 = \sqrt{x + 7} \qquad \text{The radical is already isolated.}$$
$$(x - 5)^2 = (\sqrt{x + 7})^2 \qquad \text{Principle of powers: squaring both sides}$$
$$x^2 - 10x + 25 = x + 7$$
$$x^2 - 11x + 18 = 0$$
$$(x - 9)(x - 2) = 0 \qquad \text{Factoring}$$

$$x = 9 \text{ or } x = 2 \qquad \text{Using the principle of zero products}$$

The possible solutions are 9 and 2. Let us check.

$$
\begin{array}{c|c}
x - 5 = \sqrt{x + 7} & \\
\hline
9 - 5 & \sqrt{9 + 7} \\
4 & \sqrt{16} \\
& 4
\end{array}
\qquad
\begin{array}{c|c}
x - 5 = \sqrt{x + 7} & \\
\hline
2 - 5 & \sqrt{2 + 7} \\
-3 & \sqrt{9} \\
& 3
\end{array}
$$

Since 9 checks but 2 does not, the solution is 9.

TRY THIS Solve.

2. $\sqrt{x} = -2$ 3. $x - 1 = \sqrt{x + 5}$ 2. No solution   3. 4

Equations with Two Radical Terms

A general strategy for solving equations with two radical terms is as follows.

1. Isolate one of the radical terms.
2. Use Theorem 7–8, the principle of powers.
3. If a radical remains, perform steps 1 and 2 again.
4. Check possible solutions.

EXAMPLES

Solve.

4. $\sqrt{x-3} + \sqrt{x+5} = 4$

$\sqrt{x-3} = 4 - \sqrt{x+5}$ Adding $-\sqrt{x+5}$; this isolates one of the radical terms

$(\sqrt{x-3})^2 = (4 - \sqrt{x+5})^2$ Principle of powers; squaring both sides

$x - 3 = 16 - 8\sqrt{x+5} + (x+5)$

$-24 = -8\sqrt{x+5}$ Isolating the remaining radical term

$3 = \sqrt{x+5}$

$3^2 = x + 5$ Squaring

$4 = x$

The number 4 checks and is the solution.

5. $\sqrt{2x-5} = 1 + \sqrt{x-3}$

One radical is already isolated; we square both sides.

$(\sqrt{2x-5})^2 = (1 + \sqrt{x-3})^2$

$2x - 5 = 1 + 2\sqrt{x-3} + (x-3)$

$x - 3 = 2\sqrt{x-3}$ Isolating the remaining radical

$(x-3)^2 = (2\sqrt{x-3})^2$ Squaring both sides.

$x^2 - 6x + 9 = 4(x-3)$

$x^2 - 6x + 9 = 4x - 12$

$x^2 - 10x + 21 = 0$

$(x-7)(x-3) = 0$ Factoring

$x = 7 \text{ or } x = 3$ Using the principle of zero products

The numbers 7 and 3 check and are the solutions.

TRY THIS Solve.

4. $\sqrt{x} - \sqrt{x-5} = 1$ 9   **5.** $\sqrt{3x+1} = 1 + \sqrt{x+4}$ 5

7–6	

Exercises

Solve.

1. $\sqrt{2x-3} = 1$ 2

2. $\sqrt{x+3} = 6$ 33

3. $\sqrt{y+1} - 5 = 8$ 168

4. $\sqrt{x-2} - 7 = -4$ 11

5. $\sqrt[3]{x+5} = 2$ 3

6. $\sqrt[3]{x-2} = 3$ 29

7. $\sqrt[4]{y-3} = 2$ 19

8. $\sqrt[4]{x+3} = 3$ 78

9. $\sqrt{3y + 1} = 9$ $\frac{80}{3}$

10. $\sqrt{2y + 1} = 13$ 84

11. $3\sqrt{x} = 6$ 4

12. $8\sqrt{y} = 2$ $\frac{1}{16}$

13. $\sqrt[3]{x} = -3$ -27

14. $\sqrt[3]{y} = -4$ -64

15. $\sqrt{y + 3} - 20 = 0$ 397

16. $\sqrt{x + 4} - 11 = 0$ 117

17. $\sqrt{x + 2} = -4$ No solution

18. $\sqrt{y - 3} = -2$ No solution

19. $8 = \dfrac{1}{\sqrt{x}}$ $\frac{1}{64}$

20. $3 = \dfrac{1}{\sqrt{y}}$ $\frac{1}{9}$

21. $\sqrt[3]{6x + 9} + 8 = 5$ -6

22. $\sqrt[3]{3y + 6} + 2 = 3$ $-\frac{5}{3}$

23. $\sqrt{3y + 1} = \sqrt{2y + 6}$ 5

24. $\sqrt{5x - 3} = \sqrt{2x + 3}$ 2

25. $2\sqrt{1 - x} = \sqrt{5}$ $-\frac{1}{4}$

26. $2\sqrt{2y - 3} = \sqrt{4y}$ 3

27. $2\sqrt{t - 1} = \sqrt{3t - 1}$ 3

28. $\sqrt{y + 10} = 3\sqrt{2y + 3}$ -1

29. $\sqrt{y - 5} + \sqrt{y} = 5$ 9

30. $\sqrt{x - 9} + \sqrt{x} = 1$ No solution

31. $3 + \sqrt{z - 6} = \sqrt{z + 9}$ 7

32. $\sqrt{4x - 3} = 2 + \sqrt{2x - 5}$ 7, 3

33. $\sqrt{20 - x} + 8 = \sqrt{9 - x} + 11$ $\frac{80}{9}$

34. $4 + \sqrt{10 - x} = 6 + \sqrt{4 - x}$ $\frac{15}{4}$

35. $\sqrt{x + 2} + \sqrt{3x + 4} = 2$ -1

36. $\sqrt{6x + 7} - \sqrt{3x + 3} = 1$ $\frac{1}{3}$

37. $\sqrt{4y + 1} - \sqrt{y - 2} = 3$ 6, 2

38. $\sqrt{y + 15} - \sqrt{2y + 7} = 1$ 1

39. $\sqrt{3x - 5} + \sqrt{2x + 3} + 1 = 0$ No solution

40. $\sqrt{2m - 3} = \sqrt{m + 7} - 2$ 2

Extension

The formula $V = 1.2\sqrt{h}$ can be used to approximate the distance V, in miles, that a person can see to the horizon from a height h, in feet. Use a calculator for Exercises 41–42.

41. How far can you see to the horizon through an airplane window at a height of 30,000 feet?   208 mi

42. How far can a sailor see to the horizon from the top of a 72-ft mast?   10 mi

Solve.

43. $x^{\frac{1}{3}} + 5 = 7$ 8

44. $(x - 5)^{\frac{1}{5}} - 3 = 7$ $5 + 10^5$

45. $(x - 5)^{\frac{2}{3}} = 2$ $5 \pm 2\sqrt{2}$

46. $(x - 3)^{\frac{2}{3}} = 2$ $3 \pm 2\sqrt{2}$

47. $\dfrac{x + \sqrt{x + 1}}{x - \sqrt{x + 1}} = \dfrac{5}{11}$ $-\frac{8}{9}$

48. $\sqrt{\sqrt{x + 25}} - \sqrt{x} = 5$ No solution

49. $\sqrt{x + 2} - \sqrt{x - 2} = \sqrt{2x}$ 2

50. $2\sqrt{x + 3} = \sqrt{x} + \sqrt{x + 8}$ 1

51. $\sqrt[4]{x + 2} = \sqrt{3x + 1}$ $\frac{-5 + \sqrt{61}}{18}$

52. $\sqrt[3]{2x - 1} = \sqrt[6]{x + 1}$ $\frac{5}{4}$

Challenge

53. Prove Theorem 7–8.

7–7 Imaginary and Complex Numbers

Imaginary Numbers

In the set of real numbers, negative numbers do not have square roots. An equation like

$$x^2 = -1$$

has no solution. A new kind of number, called imaginary, was invented so that negative numbers would have square roots and certain equations would have solutions. These numbers were devised, starting with an imaginary unit, named i, with the agreement that

$$i^2 = -1, \text{ or } i = \sqrt{-1}.$$

We assume that i acts like a real number in other respects. Square roots of all negative numbers can then be expressed as a product of i and a real number.

EXAMPLES

Express these numbers in terms of i.

1. $\sqrt{-5} = \sqrt{-1 \cdot 5}$
   $= \sqrt{-1}\sqrt{5}$
   $= i\sqrt{5} \text{ or } \sqrt{5}i$

2. $-\sqrt{-7} = -\sqrt{-1 \cdot 7}$
   $= -\sqrt{-1}\sqrt{7}$
   $= -i\sqrt{7} \text{ or } -\sqrt{7}i$

3. $\sqrt{-99} = \sqrt{-1 \cdot 9 \cdot 11}$
   $= i\sqrt{9}\sqrt{11}$
   $= 3i\sqrt{11} \text{ or } 3\sqrt{11}i$

TRY THIS Express these numbers in terms of i.

1. $\sqrt{-7}$ $i\sqrt{7}$ 2. $-\sqrt{-36}$ $-6i$ 3. $\sqrt{-160}$ $4i\sqrt{10}$

DEFINITION

The *imaginary* numbers consist of all numbers bi, where b is a real number and i is the imaginary unit, with the property that $i^2 = -1$.

Products

To multiply imaginary numbers or an imaginary number by a real number, it is important first to express the imaginary numbers in terms of i.

EXAMPLES
Multiply.

4. $47i \cdot 2 = 94i$

5. $\sqrt{-5} \cdot 2i = \sqrt{5}i \cdot 2i$
$= 2\sqrt{5}i^2$
$= -2\sqrt{5}$

6. $-\sqrt{-3} \cdot \sqrt{-7} = -i\sqrt{3} \cdot i\sqrt{7}$
$= -i^2\sqrt{21}$
$= -(-1)\sqrt{21}$
$= \sqrt{21}$

TRY THIS Multiply.

4. $6i \cdot 3i$ **5.** $\sqrt{-3} \cdot 3i$ **6.** $\sqrt{-3} \cdot \sqrt{-6}$ 4. -18 5. $-3\sqrt{3}$ 6. $-3\sqrt{2}$

Complex Numbers

To construct a complete number system, we shall define sums of real and imaginary numbers. We call these complex numbers.

> **DEFINITION**
>
> The *complex* numbers consist of all sums $a + bi$, where a and b are real numbers and i is the imaginary unit. a is called the real part and bi is called the imaginary part.

Every real number a is a complex number because $a = a + 0 \cdot i$. Thus the complex numbers are an extension of the real number system. All imaginary numbers bi are also complex because $bi = 0 + bi$.

We assume that i acts like a real number, obeying the commutative, associative, and distributive laws. Thus to add or subtract complex numbers we can treat i as we would treat a variable. We combine like terms.

EXAMPLES
Add.

7. $7i + 9i = (7 + 9)i$
$= 16i$

8. $(-5 + 6i) + (2 - 11i) = -5 + 6i + 2 - 11i$
$= -3 - 5i$

322 CHAPTER 7 POWERS, ROOTS, AND COMPLEX NUMBERS

TRY THIS Add.

7. $3i + 4i$ ₇ᵢ $\rightarrow$ **8.** $(2 + 3i) + (2 + 4i)$ ₄₊₇ᵢ

9. $(-7 + 4i) + (5 - 9i)$ **10.** $(-2 + 3i) + (2 - 3i)$ ₀
    -2 - 5i

EXAMPLES
Subtract.

9. $7i - 9i = (7 - 9)i$
$$= -2i$$

10. $(2 + 3i) - (4 + 2i) = 2 + 3i - 4 - 2i$
$$= -2 + i$$

11. $(-6 + 5i) - (-6 + 5i) = -6 + 5i + 6 - 5i$
$$= 0$$

TRY THIS Subtract.

11. $3i - 4i$ ₋ᵢ   **12.** $(2 - 3i) - (5 - 8i)$ ₋₃₊₅ᵢ

13. $(-4 + 10i) - (-2 + 3i)$ **14.** $(9 - 7i) - (15 + 2i)$ ₋₆₋₉ᵢ
    -2 + 7i

7–7

Exercises

Express these numbers in terms of i.

1. $\sqrt{-2}$ $i\sqrt{2}$ **2.** $\sqrt{-3}$ $i\sqrt{3}$ **3.** $\sqrt{-36}$ $6i$ **4.** $\sqrt{-25}$ $5i$

5. $-\sqrt{-9}$ ₋₃ᵢ   **6.** $-\sqrt{-16}$ ₋₄ᵢ   **7.** $\sqrt{-128}$ $8i\sqrt{2}$ **8.** $\sqrt{-12}$ $2i\sqrt{3}$

9. $\sqrt{-\dfrac{9}{16}}$ $\frac{3}{4}i$ **10.** $\sqrt{-\dfrac{25}{4}}$ $\frac{5}{2}i$ **11.** $-\sqrt{-80}$ **12.** $-\sqrt{-75}$ ₋₅ᵢ√₃
                                        -4i√5

Multiply.

13. $23i \cdot 4$ $92i$ **14.** $-12i \cdot (-3)$ $36i$ **15.** $\sqrt{-3} \cdot 4i$ ₋₄√₃

16. $\sqrt{-5} \cdot 6i$ ₋₆√₅   **17.** $\sqrt{-2}\sqrt{-3}$ ₋√₆   **18.** $\sqrt{-5}\sqrt{-3}$ ₋√₁₅

19. $-\sqrt{-2}\sqrt{-18}$ ₆   **20.** $-\sqrt{-3}\sqrt{-15}$ $3\sqrt{5}$ **21.** $\sqrt{-3}\sqrt{-15}$ ₋₃√₅

22. $\sqrt{-10}\sqrt{-2}$ ₋₂√₅   **23.** $-\sqrt{-10}(-\sqrt{-10})$ ₋₁₀   **24.** $-\sqrt{-7}(-\sqrt{-7})$ ₋₇

Add.

25. $5i + 4i$ $9i$ **26.** $-7i + 10i$ $3i$ **27.** $4i + (-10i)$ ₋₆ᵢ

28. $-2i + (-3i)$ ₋₅ᵢ   **29.** $3i + (8 - 5i)$ ₈₋₂ᵢ   **30.** $-2i + (-3 + 8i)$ ₉₋₅ᵢ

31. $(3 + 2i) + (5 - i)$ ₈₊ᵢ   **32.** $(-2 + 3i) + (7 + 8i)$ **33.** $(4 - 3i) + (5 - 2i)$
                                       5 + 11i   -3 + 6i

Subtract.

34. $5i - 4i$ i

35. $-7i - 10i$ $-17i$

36. $6i - (-8i)$ $14i$

37. $-3i - (-4i)$ i

38. $2i - (4 - 3i)$ $-4 + 5i$

39. $3i - (5 - 2i)$ $-5 + 5i$

40. $(3 - i) - (5 + 2i)$ $-2 - 3i$

41. $(-2 + 8i) - (7 + 3i)$ $-9 + 5i$

42. $(4 - 2i) - (5 - 3i)$ $-1 + i$

43. $(-2 - 3i) - (1 - 5i)$ $-3 + 2i$

44. $(9 + 5i) - (-2 - i)$ $11 + 6i$

45. $(6 - 3i) - (2 + 4i)$ $4 - 7i$

Use a calculator to simplify.

46. $(56.4325 + 789.5097i) + (-456.892 + 809.0568i)$ $-400.4595 + 1598.5665i$

47. $(76.5773 - 567.9076i) - (907.238 - 7890.67i)$ $-830.6607 + 7322.7624i$

Extension

Powers of i. These four powers of i are the keys to finding higher powers of i.

$$i^1 = i, \quad i^2 = -1, \quad i^3 = -i, \quad i^4 = 1$$

For example, $i^{31} = i^{28} \cdot i^3 = (i^4)^7 \cdot i^3 = 1^7 \cdot (-i) = 1 \cdot (-i) = -i.$

Simplify.

48. i^{13} i

49. i^{20} 1

50. i^{18} -1

51. i^{27} $-i$

52. i^{99} $-i$

53. $i^{71} - i^{49}$ $-2i$

54. $i^{68} - i^{72} + i^{76} - i^{80}$ 0

HISTORY/The Idea of Number

When early mathematicians began to study equations, they found that an equation of the form $ax + b = 0$ could not be solved with positive rational numbers. Greek mathematicians, who were more interested in geometry than in algebra, believed that an equation such as $2x + 3 = 0$ had no solution. They rejected the idea of *negative numbers* because negative numbers cannot be represented by drawings. Later mathematicians saw that negative numbers could stand for practical ideas such as temperatures below zero and so the negative whole numbers and fractions were allowed into mathematics as acceptable members of the number family. Eventually even *irrational numbers* were accepted, for you can draw a picture of a number such as the square root of 2. (Construct a square with sides of length 1. The diagonal has length $\sqrt{2}$.)

If early mathematicians were uncomfortable

with the idea of a number such as -1, they were even more upset with the concept of a number like $\sqrt{-1}$. Although people knew that equations of the form $x^2 + a = 0$, where a is greater than 0, could not be solved without inventing a new type of number, many mathematicians preferred to say that $x^2 + a = 0$ has no solution, or that it was an "absurd" equation. Solutions of an equation of this type were called meaningless, or impossible, or imaginary.

And yet an *imaginary number* is a precise mathematical idea. Like all other numbers, i is a symbol which represents an abstract concept. It obeys all the rules of arithmetic and its many uses in solving equations have justified it being admitted into mathematics along with the more "real" whole numbers, rationals, and irrationals.

7-8 More About Complex Numbers

Equality for Complex Numbers

Equality for complex numbers is based on equality for real numbers. A sentence $a + bi = c + di$ says that $a + bi$ and $c + di$ are two names of the same number. For this to be true, a and c must be the same and b and d must be the same. Thus $a + bi = c + di$ when $a = b$ and $c = d$.

EXAMPLE 1
Suppose that $3x + yi = 5x + 1 + 2i$. Find x and y.
We equate the real parts.   We equate the imaginary parts.

$$3x = 5x + 1 \qquad\qquad yi = 2i$$
$$x = -\frac{1}{2} \text{ Solving} \qquad y = 2 \text{ Solving}$$

TRY THIS Solve.

1. Suppose $3x + 1 + (y + 2)i = 2x + 2yi$. Find x and y. $\quad x = -1, y = 2$

Multiplication

We multiply complex numbers as we would multiply monomials or binomials, treating the imaginary parts as like terms. Of course, we remember that $i^2 = -1$.

EXAMPLES
Multiply.

2. $3i \cdot 4i = (3 \cdot 4)i^2 \qquad$ 3. $(7i)^2 = 7^2 i^2$
$\qquad\qquad = 12(-1) \qquad\qquad\qquad = 49(-1)$
$\qquad\qquad = -12 \qquad\qquad\qquad\quad = -49$

4. $(4 + 3i) \cdot (7 + 2i) = 28 + 8i + 21i + 6i^2$
$\qquad\qquad\qquad\quad = 28 + (8i + 21i) + 6(-1) \quad \text{Since } i^2 = -1$
$\qquad\qquad\qquad\quad = 28 + 29i - 6$
$\qquad\qquad\qquad\quad = 22 + 29i$

TRY THIS Multiply.

2. $5i \cdot 6i \qquad$ 3. $(10i)^2 \qquad$ 4. $(-2 - 3i)(6 + 5i)$ $\quad$ 2. $-30 \quad$ 3. $-100 \quad$ 4. $3 - 28i$

Conjugates

DEFINITION

The *conjugate* of a complex number $a + bi$ is $a - bi$ and the conjugate of $a - bi$ is $a + bi$.

EXAMPLES

5. The conjugate of $3 + 4i$ is $3 - 4i$.

6. The conjugate of $-4 - 7i$ is $-4 + 7i$.

7. The conjugate of $5i$ is $-5i$.

8. The conjugate of 6 is 6.

TRY THIS Find the conjugate of each number.

5. $6 + 3i$ 6. $-9 - 5i$ 7. $-7i$ 8. -8

5. $6 - 3i$ 6. $-9 + 5i$ 7. $7i$ 8. -8

The special product $(A + B)(A - B) = A^2 - B^2$ applies to multiplying a number by its conjugate.

EXAMPLES
Multiply.

9. $(5 + 7i)(5 - 7i) = 5^2 - (7i)^2$
$= 25 - (49i^2)$
$= 25 + 49$
$= 74$

10. $(a + bi)(a - bi) = a^2 - (bi)^2$
$= a^2 - b^2i^2$
$= a^2 + b^2$

THEOREM 7-9

The product of a nonzero complex number $a + bi$ and its conjugate $a - bi$ is the positive real number $a^2 + b^2$.

TRY THIS Multiply.

9. $(7 - 2i)(7 + 2i)$ 53   10. $(-3 + i)(-3 - i)$ 10   11. $(p - qi)(p + qi)$ $p^2 + q^2$

Division

To divide complex numbers we can multiply by 1. In choosing a symbol for 1, we use the conjugate of the divisor.

EXAMPLES
Divide.

11. $\dfrac{-5 + 9i}{1 - i} = \dfrac{-5 + 9i}{1 - i} \cdot \dfrac{1 + i}{1 + i}$

$= \dfrac{-14 + 4i}{1 - i^2}$

$= \dfrac{-14 + 4i}{2}$

$= -7 + 2i$

12. $\dfrac{2 - 3i}{3 + 5i} = \dfrac{2 - 3i}{3 + 5i} \cdot \dfrac{3 - 5i}{3 - 5i}$

$= \dfrac{-9 - 19i}{9 - 25i^2}$

$= \dfrac{-9 - 19i}{34}$

$= \dfrac{-9}{34} - \dfrac{19}{34}i$

TRY THIS Divide.

12. $\dfrac{6 + 2i}{1 - 3i}$ $\quad 2i$ 13. $\dfrac{2 + 3i}{-1 + 4i}$ $\quad \frac{10}{17} - \frac{11}{17}i$

Reciprocals

The reciprocal of a number $a + bi$ is of course that number by which we multiply $a + bi$ to get 1. By definition of division this is $\frac{1}{a + bi}$. To express it in the form $a + bi$ we can do this division.

EXAMPLE 13
Find the reciprocal of $2 - 3i$ and express it in the form $a + bi$.

The reciprocal of $2 - 3i$ is $\dfrac{1}{2 - 3i}$.

$\dfrac{1}{2 - 3i} = \dfrac{1}{2 - 3i} \cdot \dfrac{2 + 3i}{2 + 3i}$

$= \dfrac{2 + 3i}{2^2 - 3^2 i^2}$

$= \dfrac{2 + 3i}{4 + 9}$

$= \dfrac{2}{13} + \dfrac{3}{13}i$

TRY THIS

14. Find the reciprocal of $3 + 4i$ and express it in the form $a + bi$. $\quad \frac{3}{25} - \frac{4}{25}i$

Exercises

Solve for x and y.

1. $4x + 7i = -6 + yi$ $x = -\frac{3}{2}, y = 7$
2. $8 + 8yi = 4x - 2i$ $x = 2, y = -\frac{1}{4}$
3. $-5x - yi = 10 + 8i$ $x = -2, y = -8$
4. $-3y - 4xi = 2 + 2i$ $x = -\frac{1}{2}, y = -\frac{2}{3}$
5. $3x + 4y - 7i = 18 + (x - 3y)i$
   5. $x = 2, y = 3$
6. $-4 + (x + y)i = 2x - 5y + 5i$ $x = 3, y = 2$

Multiply.

7. $7i \cdot 9i$ -63
8. $3i \cdot i$ -3
9. $(9i)^2$ -81
10. $(13i)^2$ -169
11. $(-3i)^2$ -9
12. $(-5i)^2$ -25
13. $(3 + 2i)(1 + i)$ $1 + 5i$
14. $(4 + 3i)(2 + i)$ $5 + 10i$
15. $(6 - 5i)(3 + 4i)$ $38 + 9i$
16. $(5 - 6i)(4 + 8i)$
    16. $68 + 16i$
17. $(5 - 2i)^2$ $21 - 20i$
18. $(-2 + 2i)^2$ $-8i$

Find the conjugate of each number.

19. $-4 + 8i$
20. $-8 + 5i$
21. $6 - 5i$
22. $7 - i$
23. $\sqrt{2} - \frac{1}{2}i$
24. $\sqrt{3} + 0.4i$
25. $r - ti$
26. $-m + ni$

19. $-4 - 8i$
20. $-8 - 5i$
21. $6 + 5i$
22. $7 + i$
23. $\sqrt{2} + \frac{1}{2}i$
24. $\sqrt{3} - 0.4i$
25. $r + ti$
26. $-m - ni$

Multiply.

27. $(1 - i)(1 + i)$
28. $(6 + 3i)(6 - 3i)$
29. $\left(\frac{1}{2} + i\right)\left(\frac{1}{2} - i\right)$
30. $\left(1 + \frac{1}{3}i\right)\left(1 - \frac{1}{3}i\right)$
31. $(\sqrt{3} - i)(\sqrt{3} + i)$
32. $(3 - \sqrt{2}i)(3 + \sqrt{2}i)$

27. 2
28. 45
29. $\frac{5}{4}$
30. $\frac{10}{9}$
31. 4
32. 11

Divide.

33. $\dfrac{1 + i}{1 - i}$
34. $\dfrac{3 + 2i}{2 + i}$
35. $\dfrac{8 - 3i}{-2 + 7i}$
36. $\dfrac{5 - 10i}{-3 + 4i}$
37. $\dfrac{\sqrt{2} + i}{\sqrt{2} - i}$
38. $\dfrac{\sqrt{3} - i}{\sqrt{3} + i}$
39. $\dfrac{3 + 2i}{i}$
40. $\dfrac{i}{2 + i}$

33. i
34. $\frac{8}{5} + \frac{1}{5}i$
35. $-\frac{37}{53} - \frac{50}{53}i$
36. $-\frac{11}{5} + \frac{2}{5}i$
37. $\frac{1}{3} + \frac{2}{3}\sqrt{2}i$
38. $\frac{1}{2} - \frac{1}{2}\sqrt{3}i$
39. $2 - 3i$
40. $\frac{1}{5} + \frac{2}{5}i$
41. $-i$
42. i
43. $\frac{1}{10} + \frac{2}{5}i$

Find the reciprocal of each number and express it in the form $a + bi$.

41. i
42. $-i$
43. $2 - 4i$
44. $-3 - 5i$
45. $-4 + 7i$
46. $-2 + 6i$

Extension

Simplify to the form $a + bi$.

47. i^{-3}
48. i^2
49. $\dfrac{1 - i}{(1 + i)^2}$
50. $\dfrac{1 + i}{(1 - i)^2}$

51. Let $z = a + bi$. Find a general expression for $\frac{1}{z}$. $\frac{a}{a^2 + b^2} - \frac{b}{a^2 + b^2}i$

52. Show that the general rule for radicals, in real numbers, $\sqrt{a \cdot b} = \sqrt{a} \cdot \sqrt{b}$, does not hold for complex numbers.
    52. For example, $\sqrt{-1}\sqrt{-1} = i^2 = -1$, but $\sqrt{(-1)(-1)} = \sqrt{1} = 1$.

44. $-\frac{3}{34} + \frac{5}{34}i$
45. $-\frac{4}{65} - \frac{7}{65}i$
46. $-\frac{1}{20} - \frac{3}{20}i$
47. i
48. -1
49. $-\frac{1}{2} - \frac{1}{2}i$
50. $-\frac{1}{2} + \frac{1}{2}i$

7-9 Solutions of Equations

Complex Numbers as Solutions of Equations

EXAMPLE 1

Determine whether $1 + \sqrt{7}i$ is a solution of $x^2 - 2x + 8 = 0$.

$$
\begin{array}{c|c}
x^2 - 2x + 8 = 0 & \\
\hline
(1 + \sqrt{7}i)^2 - 2(1 + \sqrt{7}i) + 8 & 0 \\
1 + 2(\sqrt{7}i) + (\sqrt{7}i)^2 - 2 - 2\sqrt{7}i + 8 & \\
1 + 2\sqrt{7}i - 7 - 2 - 2\sqrt{7}i + 8 & \\
0 & \\
\end{array}
$$

$1 + \sqrt{7}i$ is a solution.

TRY THIS

1. Determine whether $1 + i$ is a solution of $x^2 - 2x + 2 = 0$.
2. Determine whether $1 - i$ is a solution of $x^2 + 2x + 1 = 0$.

1. $(1 + i)^2 - 2(1 + i) + 2 = 1 + 2i + i^2 - 2 - 2i + 2 = 0$ 2. $(1 - i)^2 + 2(1 - i) + 1 = 1 - 2i + i^2 + 2 - 2i + 1 = 3 - 4i$; Therefore $(1 - i)$ is not a solution of $x^2 + 2x + 1 = 0$.

Writing Equations with Given Solutions

The principle of zero products for real numbers states that a product is 0 if and only if at least one of the factors is 0. This principle also holds for complex numbers. Since the principle holds for complex numbers we can write equations having given solutions.

EXAMPLE 2

Find an equation having -1, i, and $1 + i$ as solutions.

The factors we use will be $x - (-1)$, $x - i$, and $x - (1 + i)$.
Next we set the product of these factors equal to 0.

$$[x - (-1)](x - i)[x - (1 + i)] = 0$$

Now we multiply and simplify.

$$(x^2 + x - ix - i)(x - 1 - i) = 0$$
$$x^3 - 2ix^2 - ix - 2x - 1 + i = 0$$

TRY THIS Find an equation having the given numbers as solutions.

3. $i, 1 + i$ 4. $2, i, -i$

3. $x^2 - 2ix - x + i - 1 = 0$
4. $x^3 - 2x^2 + x - 2 = 0$

Solving Equations

First-degree equations in complex numbers are solved very much like first-degree equations in real numbers.

EXAMPLE 3

Solve $3ix + 4 - 5i = (1 + i)x + 2i$.

$$3ix - (1 + i)x = -4 + 7i \quad \text{Adding } -(1 + i)x \text{ and } -(-4 - 5i)$$
$$(-1 + 2i)x = -4 + 7i \quad \text{Simplifying}$$
$$x = \frac{-4 + 7i}{-1 + 2i} \quad \text{Dividing}$$
$$x = \frac{-4 + 7i}{-1 + 2i} \cdot \frac{-1 - 2i}{-1 - 2i}$$
$$x = \frac{18 + i}{5}$$
$$x = \frac{18}{5} + \frac{1}{5}i$$

TRY THIS Solve.

5. $3 - 4i + 2ix = 3i - (1 - i)x$ 2 + 5i

Linear equations always have solutions. Complex numbers were invented so that certain other equations would have solutions. Suppose we ask what kinds of equations do have solutions. The answer depends upon a very important theorem.

THEOREM 7–10

The Fundamental Theorem of Algebra

Every polynomial with complex coefficients and of degree n (where $n > 1$) can be factored into n linear factors.

The factors of a polynomial are not always easy to find, but they exist.

EXAMPLE 4

Show that $(x + i)(x - i)$ is a factorization of $x^2 + 1$.

We multiply.

$$(x + i)(x - i) = x^2 + ix - ix - i^2 = x^2 + 1$$

TRY THIS

6. Show that $(x + 2i)(x - 2i)$ is a factorization of $x^2 + 4$. $\quad$ $(x + 2i)(x - 2i) = x^2 + 2ix - 2ix - 4i^2$
$$= x^2 + 4$$

We can now answer the question about solutions of equations.

THEOREM 7–11

Every polynomial equation of degree n ($n \geq 1$) with complex coefficients has at least one solution and at most n solutions in the system of complex numbers.

A Proof of Theorem 7–11

Let us consider a polynomial equation of degree n, $P(x) = 0$. The polynomial $P(x)$ is either of degree 1, in which case there is a solution, or by the fundamental theorem of algebra, it can be factored into n linear factors. We then have

$$(x - a_1)(x - a_2) \ldots (x - a_n) = 0.$$

By the principle of zero products, we get

$$x = a_1 \text{ or } x = a_2 \text{ or } x = a_3 \text{ or } \ldots \text{ or } x = a_n.$$

Thus the equation has solutions $a_1, a_2, \ldots, a_n$. Some of these may be the same. So there is at least one solution, and there are not more than n solutions.

Square Roots of Complex Numbers

The fundamental theorem of algebra can be used to show that all complex numbers have square roots.

THEOREM 7–12

Every nonzero complex number has two square roots. They are additive inverses of each other. Zero has just one square root.

EXAMPLE 5

Show that $1 + i$ is a square root of $2i$. Find the other square root.

We square $(1 + i)$ to show that we get $2i$.

$$(1 + i)^2 = 1 + 2i + i^2 = 1 + 2i - 1 = 2i$$

By Theorem 7–12, the other square root of $2i$ is the additive inverse of $1 + i$, so it is $-1 - i$.

TRY THIS

7. Show that $(-1 + i)$ is a square root of $-2i$. Then find the other square root. $\quad (-1 + i)^2 = 1 - 2i + i^2 = 1 - 2i - 1 = -2i, 1 - i$

7–9

Exercises

Determine whether the given numbers are solutions of the equation.

1. $2i, -2i; x^2 + 4 = 0$ Yes, yes
2. $4i, -4i; x^2 + 16 = 0$ Yes, yes
3. $\sqrt{2}i, -\sqrt{3}i; x^2 + 3 = 0$ No, yes
4. $\sqrt{3}i, -\sqrt{2}i; x^2 + 2 = 0$ No, yes
5. $-1 + i, -1 - i; z^2 + 2z + 2 = 0$ Yes, yes
6. $2 - i, 2 + i; z^2 - 4z + 5 = 0$ Yes, yes

Find an equation having the specified numbers as solutions.

7. $5i, -5i$
8. $7i, -7i$
9. $1 + i, 1 - i$
10. $2 + i, 2 - i$
11. $2 + 3i, 2 - 3i$
12. $4 + 3i, 4 - 3i$
13. $3, i$
14. $5, i$
15. $1, 3i, -3i$
16. $1, 2i, -2i$
17. $2, 1 + i, i$
18. $i, 2i, -i$

Solve.

19. $(3 + i)x + i = 5i$
20. $(2 + i)x - i = 5 + i$
21. $2ix + 5 - 4i = (2 + 3i)x - 2i$
22. $5ix + 3 + 2i = (3 - 2i)x + 3i$
23. $(1 + 2i)x + 3 - 2i = 4 - 5i + 3ix$
24. $(1 - 2i)x + 2 - 3i = 5 - 4i + 2x$
25. $(5 + i)x + 1 - 3i = (2 - 3i)x + 2 - i$
26. $(5 - i)x + 2 - 3i = (3 - 2i)x + 3 - i$

27. Show that $(2x + i)(2x - i)$ is a factorization of $4x^2 + 1$. $\quad (2x + i)(2x - i) = 4x^2 - 2ix + 2ix - i^2 = 4x^2 + 1$

28. Show that $(2x + 2i)(2x - 2i)$ is a factorization of $4x^2 + 4$. $\quad (2x + 2i)(2x - 2i) = 4x^2 - 4ix + 4ix - 4i^2 = 4x^2 + 4$

29. Show that $(2 + i)$ is a square root of $3 + 4i$. Then find the other square root. $\quad (2 + i)^2 = 4 + 4i + i^2 = 3 + 4i, -2 - i$

30. Show that $(2 - i)$ is a square root of $3 - 4i$. Then find the other square root. $\quad (2 - i)^2 = 4 - 4i + i^2 = 3 - 4i, -2 + i$

7–10 Graphical Representation

Graphical Representation

The real numbers are graphed on a line. We graph $a + bi$ in the same way we graph ordered pairs of real numbers (a, b). In place of an x-axis we have a real axis, and in place of a y-axis we have an imaginary axis.

EXAMPLE 1

Graph.

A: $3 + 2i$
B: $-4 + 5i$
C: $-5 - 4i$
D: i

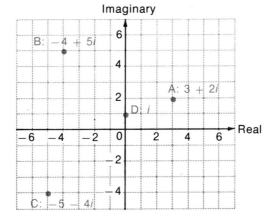

Horizontal distance corresponds to the real part of a number. Vertical distance corresponds to the imaginary part.

TRY THIS

1. Graph.
   A: $5 - 3i$ B: $-3 + 4i$ C: $-5 - 2i$ D: $-5i$

Absolute Value

From the graph at the right we see that the length of the line drawn from the origin to $a + bi$ is $\sqrt{a^2 + b^2}$. Note that this quantity is a real number. It is called the absolute value of $a + bi$ and is denoted $|a + bi|$.

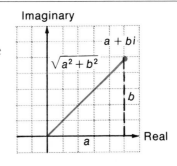

DEFINITION

The *absolute value* of a complex number $a + bi$ is denoted $|a + bi|$ and is defined to be $\sqrt{a^2 + b^2}$.

EXAMPLE 2

Find $|-3 + 4i|$.

$$|-3 + 4i| = \sqrt{(-3)^2 + 4^2} = \sqrt{9 + 16} = \sqrt{25} = 5$$

TRY THIS Find the following absolute values.

2. $|4 - 3i|$ 5   3. $|-12 - 5i|$ 13   4. $|1 + i|$ $\sqrt{2}$

7–10

Exercises

Graph.

1. $3 + 2i, 2 - 5i, -4 - 2i$ 2. $3 - 4i, -5 + 3i, -2 - 3i$
3. $-4 + 2i, -3 - 4i, 2 - 3i$ 4. $-5 + 4i, 3 - 2i, -5 + 5i$
5. $-2 - 5i, 5 + 3i, -3 - 4i$ 6. $2 + 2i, -3 - 3i, 2 - 3i$

Find the following absolute values.

7. $|-4 - 3i|$ 5   8. $|-3 - 4i|$ 5   9. $|8 + 15i|$ 17   10. $|7 - 24i|$ 25

11. $|1 - 3i|$ $\sqrt{10}$ 12. $|-2 + i|$ $\sqrt{5}$ 13. $|3i|$ 3   14. $|-2i|$ 2

15. $|c - di|$ $\sqrt{c^2 + d^2}$ 16. $|-c + di|$ $\sqrt{c^2 + d^2}$ 17. $|4c + 2i|$ $2\sqrt{4c^2 + 1}$ 18. $|-4p - 3qi|$ $\sqrt{16p^2 + 9q^2}$

Extension

19. Show that for any complex number z, $|z| = |-z|$. (Hint: Let $z = a + bi$.)

20. Show that for any complex number z, $|z| = |$the conjugate of $z|$. (Hint: Let $z = a + bi$.)

21. Let $z = a + bi$ and $w = c + di$. Find a general formula for $z \cdot w$.

22. Let $z = a + bi$ and $w = c + di$. Find a general formula for $\frac{z}{w}$.

23. Show that $|z \cdot w| = |z| \cdot |w|$.   24. Show that $\left|\frac{z}{w}\right| = \frac{|z|}{|w|}$.

7–11 Conjugates of Polynomials

We can name a complex number $a + bi$ as z. For the conjugate of z, we write $\bar{z}$, or $\overline{a + bi}$. By definition of conjugates,

$$\overline{a + bi} = a - bi \text{ and } \overline{a - bi} = a + bi.$$

We have already noted (Theorem 7–9) that the product of a number and its conjugate is a real number. We restate that theorem and consider some others.

THEOREM 7–13

For any complex number z, $z \cdot \bar{z}$ is a real number.

The sum of a number and its conjugate is also always real.

THEOREM 7–14

For any complex number, z, $z + \bar{z}$ is a real number.

A Proof of Theorem 7–13

We have said that for any complex number z, $z \cdot \bar{z}$ is a real number. Let us prove this.

Let $z = a + bi$. Then $(a - bi)$ is $\bar{z}$.

$$\begin{aligned} z \cdot \bar{z} &= (a + bi)(a - bi) \\ &= a^2 - b^2 i^2 \\ &= a^2 + b^2 \end{aligned}$$

Since a and b are real numbers, so is $a^2 + b^2$. Thus $z \cdot \bar{z}$ is a real number.

Taking the conjugate of a sum gives the same result as adding the conjugates.

THEOREM 7–15

For any complex numbers z and w, $\overline{z + w} = \bar{z} + \bar{w}$.

EXAMPLE 1

Compare $\overline{(2 + 4i) + (5 + i)}$ and $\overline{(2 + 4i)} + \overline{(5 + i)}$

$$\overline{(2 + 4i) + (5 + i)} = \overline{7 + 5i} \quad \text{Adding the complex numbers}$$
$$= 7 - 5i \quad \text{Taking the conjugate}$$

$$\overline{(2 + 4i)} + \overline{(5 + i)} = (2 - 4i) + (5 - i) \quad \text{Taking conjugates}$$
$$= 7 - 5i \quad \text{Adding}$$

TRY THIS

$\overline{(3 + 2i) + (4 - 5i)} = \overline{(7 - 3i)} = 7 + 3i,$
$\overline{(3 + 2i)} + \overline{(4 - 5i)} = (3 - 2i) + (4 + 5i) = 7 + 3i$

1. Compare $\overline{(3 + 2i) + (4 - 5i)}$ with $\overline{(3 + 2i)} + \overline{(4 - 5i)}$.

A Proof of Theorem 7–15

We have said that for any complex numbers z and w,
$\overline{z + w} = \bar{z} + \bar{w}$. Let us prove this.

Let $z = a + bi$ and $w = c + di$.

$$\overline{z + w} = \overline{(a + bi) + (c + di)}$$
$$= \overline{(a + c) + (b + d)i} \quad \text{Adding}$$
$$= (a + c) - (b + d)i \quad \text{Taking the conjugate}$$

$$\bar{z} + \bar{w} = \overline{(a + bi)} + \overline{(c + di)}$$
$$= (a - bi) + (c - di) \quad \text{Taking the conjugates}$$
$$= (a + c) - (b + d)i \quad \text{Adding}$$

This is the same result as before. Thus $\overline{z + w} = \bar{z} + \bar{w}$.

Let us next consider the conjugate of a product. The conjugate of a product is the product of the conjugates.

THEOREM 7–16

For any complex numbers z and w, $\overline{z \cdot w} = \bar{z} \cdot \bar{w}$.

EXAMPLE 2

Compare $\overline{(3 + 2i)(4 - 5i)}$ and $\overline{(3 + 2i)} \cdot \overline{(4 - 5i)}$.

$$\overline{(3 + 2i)(4 - 5i)} = \overline{22 - 7i} \quad \text{Multiplying}$$
$$= 22 + 7i \quad \text{Taking the conjugate}$$

$$\overline{(3 + 2i)} \cdot \overline{(4 - 5i)} = (3 - 2i)(4 + 5i) \quad \text{Taking conjugates}$$
$$= 12 + 15i - 8i - 10i^2 \quad \text{Multiplying}$$
$$= 22 + 7i \quad \text{Simplifying}$$

TRY THIS

2. Compare $\overline{(2 + 5i)(1 + 3i)}$ and $\overline{(2 + 5i)} \cdot \overline{(1 + 3i)}$. $\quad \overline{(2 + 5i)(1 + 3i)} = \overline{(-13 + 11i)} = -13 - 11i$, $\overline{(2 + 5i)} \cdot \overline{(1 + 3i)} = (2 - 5i)(1 - 3i) = -13 - 11i$

Let us now consider conjugates of powers, using the preceding result. The conjugate of a power is the power of the conjugate.

THEOREM 7–17

For any complex number z, $\overline{z^n} = \overline{z}^n$, where n is a natural number.

EXAMPLE 3

Show that for any complex number z, $\overline{z^2} = \overline{z}^2$

$$\overline{z^2} = \overline{z \cdot z} \quad \text{By definition of exponents}$$
$$= \overline{z} \cdot \overline{z} \quad \text{Using Theorem 7–16}$$
$$= \overline{z}^2 \quad \text{By definition of exponents}$$

TRY THIS

3. Show that for any complex number z, $\overline{z^3} = \overline{z}^3$. $\quad \overline{z^3} = \overline{z \cdot z \cdot z} = \overline{z} \cdot \overline{z} \cdot \overline{z} = \overline{z}^3$

The conjugate of a real number $a + 0i$ is $a - 0i$, and both are equal to a. Thus a real number is its own conjugate.

THEOREM 7–18

If z is a real number, then $\overline{z} = z$.

Conjugates of Polynomials

Given a polynomial in z, where z is a variable for a complex number, we can find its conjugate in terms of $\bar{z}$.

EXAMPLE 4

Find a polynomial in $\bar{z}$ that is the conjugate of $3z^2 + 2z - 1$. We write the expression for the conjugate and then use the properties of conjugates.

$$\overline{3z^2 + 2z - 1} = \overline{3z^2} + \overline{2z} - \overline{1} \qquad \text{Using Theorem 7–15}$$
$$= \overline{3} \cdot \overline{z^2} + \overline{2} \cdot \overline{z} - \overline{1} \qquad \text{Using Theorem 7–16}$$
$$= 3\overline{z^2} + 2\overline{z} - 1 \qquad \text{Using Theorem 7–18}$$
$$= 3\bar{z}^2 + 2\bar{z} - 1 \qquad \text{Using Theorem 7–17}$$

TRY THIS Find a polynomial in $\bar{z}$ that is the conjugate of the following.

4. $5z^3 + 4z^2 - 2z + 1$ **5.** $7z^5 - 3z^3 + 8z^2 + z$

4. $5\bar{z}^3 + 4\bar{z}^2 - 2\bar{z} + 1$
5. $7\bar{z}^5 - 3\bar{z}^3 + 8\bar{z}^2 + \bar{z}$

7–11

Exercises

Find a polynomial in $\bar{z}$ that is the conjugate.

1. $z^2 - 3z + 5$

2. $z^2 + 4z - 1$

3. $3z^5 - 4z^2 + 3z - 5$

4. $5z^4 - 2z^3 + 5z - 3$

5. $7z^4 + 5z^3 - 12z$

6. $4z^7 - 3z^5 + 4z$

7. $5z^{10} - 7z^8 + 13z^2 - 4$

8. $8z^{12} - 8z^7 + 12z^5 - 8$

9. $7z^{100} - 15z^{89} + z^2$

10. $17z^{45} + 70z^3 - 14z + 2$

1. $\bar{z}^2 - 3\bar{z} + 5$
2. $\bar{z}^2 + 4\bar{z} - 1$
3. $3\bar{z}^5 - 4\bar{z}^2 + 3\bar{z} - 5$
4. $5\bar{z}^4 - 2\bar{z}^3 + 5\bar{z} - 3$
5. $7\bar{z}^4 + 5\bar{z}^3 - 12\bar{z}$
6. $4\bar{z}^7 - 3\bar{z}^5 + 4\bar{z}$
7. $5\bar{z}^{10} - 7\bar{z}^8 + 13\bar{z}^2 - 4$
8. $8\bar{z}^{12} - 8\bar{z}^7 + 12\bar{z}^5 - 8$
9. $7\bar{z}^{100} - 15\bar{z}^{89} + \bar{z}^2$
10. $17\bar{z}^{45} + 70\bar{z}^3 - 14\bar{z} + 2$

15. Let $z = a + bi$. Then $(a - bi)$ is $\bar{z}$, and $z + \bar{z} = (a + bi) + (a - bi)$ $= 2a$. Since a is a real number, so is $2a$. Thus $z + \bar{z}$ is a real number.

Extension

11. Solve $z + 6\bar{z} = 7$. $z = 1$

12. Solve $5z - 4\bar{z} = 7 + 8i$. $7 + \frac{8}{9}i$

13. Let $z = a + bi$. Find $\frac{1}{2}(z + \bar{z})$. a

14. Find $f(3 + i)$, where $f(z) = \dfrac{\bar{z}}{z - 1}$. $\frac{3-i}{2+i}$, or $1 - i$

15. Prove Theorem 7–14.

16. Prove Theorem 7–16.

Challenge

17. State and prove a theorem about the conjugate of a polynomial.   Answers may vary.

CAREERS/Oceanography

Oceanographers study the sea plants and animals and their habitats. They investigate the mountains and valleys of the ocean floor and explore mineral and oil deposits. They conduct surveys and experiments and collect data about the waves, currents, and tides of the ocean.

The movement of tides has a great effect on the plants and animals living at the edge of the sea. For example, when the tide is in, the algae on the rocks swell with water and become active, some filtering food from the water, others moving about searching for prey.

Once the tide recedes, the algae gradually dry out and must find moist areas to wait for the return of the water.

Oceanographers understand that tides are caused by the fact that gravitational attractions of the sun and moon vary from place to place on the earth. The closer a point on the earth is to the sun, the more strongly it is pulled toward the sun.

Oceanographers know that the relationship among the variables for this part of the tide producing force is $r^2 = \frac{GM}{A}$ where

$A =$ average gravitational attraction
$r =$ the distance between the centers of the earth and sun
$G =$ the universal constant of gravitation
$M =$ the mass of the sun

To find the formula for the average gravitational attraction, the oceanographer can solve this formula for A using the methods you learned in Section 6–8.

$$r^2 = \frac{GM}{A}$$
$$A \cdot r^2 = A \cdot \frac{GM}{A}$$
$$A \cdot r^2 = GM$$
$$\frac{1}{r^2} \cdot A \cdot r^2 = GM \cdot \frac{1}{r^2}$$
$$A = \frac{GM}{r^2}$$

The earth is similarly acted upon by the moon. The combination of the forces produces the earth's tides.

Oceanographers study the flow of currents and tides to better learn how to make effective use of the sea.

Exercises

Solve each formula for the given letter.

1. $M = \frac{(a_1 + a_2)f}{3}$; f $f = \frac{3M}{a_1 + a_2}$

2. $\frac{1}{S} = \frac{1}{S_1} + \frac{1}{S_2}$; S_1 $S_1 = \frac{SS_2}{S_2 - S}$

3. $\frac{A_1}{A_2} = \frac{B_1}{B_2}$; B_1 $B_1 = \frac{B_2 A_1}{A_2}$

4. $K = \frac{k_b}{k_b + k_c}$; k_c

5. $V_m = A + \frac{B}{R}$; B

6. $N = \frac{xy}{x + y}$; y $y = \frac{Nx}{x - N}$

7. $S = \frac{3d}{W + 3s}$; s $s = \frac{3d - SW}{3S}$

8. $\frac{1}{B} = \frac{1}{B_1} + \frac{1}{B_2}$; B $B = \frac{B_1 B_2}{B_2 + B_1}$

9. $\frac{1}{V} + \frac{1}{W} = \frac{1}{X}$; X $X = \frac{VW}{V + W}$

10. $C = \frac{p^F}{Z + pt}$; t $t = \frac{p^F - CZ}{Cp}$

11. $R = \frac{c - cx^2}{1 - x}$; c $c = \frac{R - Rx}{1 - x^2}$

12. $L = \frac{a}{n(b_1 - b_2)}$; a

13. $F = \frac{d(mv)}{dt}$; t $t = \frac{d(mv)}{Fd}$

14. $V = \frac{m_1 v_1 + m_2 v_2}{m_1 + m_2}$; v_1

15. $m = P\left(\frac{b + a}{b - a}\right)$; a

16. $f = A + \frac{B}{r^2}$; B $B = r^2(f - a)$

17. $C = \frac{wv^2}{q}$; w $w = \frac{cg}{v^2}$

18. $P = \frac{b}{2}(h^3 - m^3)$; b

19. $M = \frac{Wa_1 a_2}{(a_1 + a_2)}$; a_1

20. $C = \frac{ad^2}{b}$; d $d = \sqrt{\frac{Cb}{a}}$

CHAPTER 7 Review

Review the material in the chapter. Then see how you have done by trying these review exercises. If you miss an exercise, restudy the indicated lesson.

7-1 Simplify.

1. $\sqrt{(-36)^2}$ 36 **2.** $\sqrt{16x^2}$ 4|x| **3.** $\sqrt[3]{\dfrac{-8x^3}{27}}$ $-\frac{2x}{3}$ **4.** $\sqrt[5]{-243}$ −3 **5.** $\sqrt[4]{(-2x)^4}$ 2|x|

7-2 Multiply and simplify.

6. $\sqrt{18x}\,\sqrt{12x}$ $6x\sqrt{6}$ **7.** $\sqrt[3]{a^2b}\,\sqrt[3]{a^4b^6}$ $a^2b^2\sqrt[3]{b}$ **8.** $\sqrt[3]{3c^2d^5}\,\sqrt[3]{16c^2d^2}$ $2cd^2\sqrt[3]{bcd}$

7-2 Approximate to the nearest tenth.

9. $\dfrac{20 + \sqrt{44}}{4}$ 6.7 **10.** $\dfrac{12 - \sqrt{45}}{6}$ 0.9

7-3 Divide and simplify.

11. $\dfrac{\sqrt[3]{32}}{\sqrt[3]{2}}$ **12.** $\sqrt{\dfrac{12a^3}{b^7}}$ **13.** $\dfrac{\sqrt{40x^5}}{\sqrt{32x^3}}$ $\frac{2x\sqrt{5}}{4}$

11. $2\sqrt[3]{2}$
12. $\frac{2a}{b^3}\frac{\sqrt{3a}}{b}$

7-4 Add or subtract.

14. $2\sqrt{32} - \sqrt{50} + \sqrt{162}$ $12\sqrt{2}$ **15.** $\sqrt[3]{24} - \sqrt[3]{81}$ $-\sqrt[3]{3}$ **16.** $5\sqrt{3y^3} - \sqrt{12y}$ $(5y - 2)\sqrt{3y}$

7-4 Multiply.

17. $(7 - 4\sqrt{3})(7 + 4\sqrt{3})$ 1   **18.** $(3\sqrt{6} + 2)^2$ $58 + 12\sqrt{6}$ **19.** $(2\sqrt[3]{2} + \sqrt[3]{3})(\sqrt[3]{2} + 3\sqrt[3]{3})$ $2\sqrt[3]{4} + 7\sqrt[3]{6} + 3\sqrt[3]{9}$

7-4 Rationalize the denominator.

20. $\dfrac{\sqrt{8}}{\sqrt{3}}$ **21.** $\dfrac{6}{3 - \sqrt{17}}$ **22.** $\dfrac{\sqrt{3} + 5}{7 + \sqrt{3}}$ $\frac{\sqrt{3} + 16}{23}$

20. $\frac{2\sqrt{6}}{3}$
21. $9 + 3\sqrt{7}$

7-5 Simplify.

23. $(\sqrt[3]{16})^2$ $\sqrt[3]{4}$ **24.** $(\sqrt{3x})^3$ $3x\sqrt{3x}$

25. $\sqrt{a^6b^4}$ a^3b^2 **26.** $\sqrt[3]{\dfrac{27}{a^6}}$ $\frac{3}{a^2}$

7-5 Write a single radical expression.

27. $\sqrt[3]{x}\,\sqrt{x - 1}$ $\sqrt[6]{x^2(x - 1)^3}$ **28.** $a^{\frac{1}{2}}b^{\frac{2}{3}}$ $\sqrt[6]{a^3b^4}$ **29.** $\dfrac{\sqrt[4]{(x + y)^3}}{\sqrt{x + y}}$ $\sqrt[4]{x + y}$

340 CHAPTER 7 POWERS, ROOTS, AND COMPLEX NUMBERS

7–6 Solve.

30. $\sqrt{5 - 3x} = 6$ $-\frac{31}{3}$ **31.** $\sqrt{7 - 4x} - \sqrt{3 - 2x} = 1$ $-\frac{1}{2}, \frac{3}{2}$

7–7 Simplify.

32. $\sqrt{-6} \cdot 6i$ $-6\sqrt{6}$ **33.** $(6 + 2i) + (-4 - 3i)$ $2 - i$ **34.** $(3 - 5i) - (2 - i)$ $1 - 4i$

7–8 Simplify.

35. $(2 - 2i)(3 + 4i)$ $14 + 2i$ **36.** $(2 - 3i)(2 + 3i)$ 13 **37.** $\frac{2 - 3i}{1 - 3i}$ $\frac{11}{10} + \frac{3}{10}i$

7–9 Solve.

38. $2ix - 5 + 3i = (2 - i)x + i$ $\frac{-16}{13} - \frac{11}{13}i$

7–10

39. Find $|4 - 8i|$. $4\sqrt{5}$

7–11

40. Find a polynomial in $\bar{z}$ that is the conjugate of $3z^2 + z - 7$. $3\bar{z}^2 + \bar{z} - 7$

CHAPTER 7   Test

Simplify.

1. $-\sqrt{121}$ -11 **2.** $\sqrt[3]{-0.027}$ -0.3 **3.** $\sqrt{20}\sqrt{18}$ $6\sqrt{10}$

4. $\sqrt[3]{x^2y^4}\sqrt[3]{x^5y^2}$ $x^2y^2\sqrt[3]{x}$ **5.** $\frac{\sqrt{8x^2}}{\sqrt{2x}}$ $2\sqrt{x}$ **6.** $\frac{\sqrt[3]{750}}{\sqrt[3]{3}}$ $5\sqrt[3]{2}$

Add or subtract.

7. $\sqrt{27} + \sqrt{108}$ $9\sqrt{3}$ **8.** $\sqrt[3]{40} - \sqrt[3]{135}$ $-\sqrt[3]{5}$

Multiply.

9. $(8 + 5\sqrt{6})(8 - 5\sqrt{6})$ -86 **10.** $(2\sqrt{7} - 3\sqrt{5})(\sqrt{7} - \sqrt{5})$ $29 - 5\sqrt{35}$

Rationalize the denominator.

11. $\frac{\sqrt{5}}{\sqrt{7}}$ **12.** $\frac{\sqrt{3} + 7}{8 - \sqrt{5}}$ $\frac{8\sqrt{3} + \sqrt{15} + 56 + 7\sqrt{5}}{59}$

11. $\frac{1}{7}\sqrt{35}$

14. $\frac{n^8\sqrt[3]{a}}{a^3}$

Simplify.

13. $\sqrt[3]{9a^2b^4}$ $b\sqrt[3]{9a^2b}$ **14.** $\sqrt[3]{\frac{n^{24}}{a^8}}$ **15.** $\sqrt[4]{81x^8y^8}$ $3x^2y^2$

Solve.

16. $x - 5 = \sqrt{x + 7}$ ₉ **17.** $\sqrt{2x - 5} = 1 + \sqrt{x - 3}$ ₇

Add or subtract.

18. $(3 + 2i) + (2 - 3i)$ ₅ᵢ **19.** $(9 - 4i) - (3 + 2i)$ ₆ ₋ ₆ᵢ

Multiply.

20. $(1 - 2i)(2 - i)$ ₋₅ᵢ **21.** $(2 + 5i)(2 - 5i)$ ₂₉

22. Solve $-5ix + 8i - 4 = (7 + i)x + 10i$. $-\frac{8}{17} + \frac{2}{17}i$

23. Find $|4 + 2i|$. $2\sqrt{5}$

24. Find a polynomial in $\bar{z}$ that is the conjugate of $2z^6 - 4z^3 + z + 1$. $2\bar{z}^6 - 4\bar{z}^3 + \bar{z} + 1$

Challenge
25. Multiply $(\sqrt{x - 1} - 2)(\sqrt{x - 1} + 2)$. $x - 5$

CHAPTERS 1–7 Cumulative Review

1–1 Which of the following numbers are rational and which are irrational?

1. -0.625 **2.** π **3.** $0.\overline{2}$ **4.** $\sqrt{1.44}$ Rational
Rational   Irrational Rational

1–2 Evaluate each expression for $x = -2$ and $y = -3$.

5. $3|y - 5| + |x|$ ₂₆ **6.** $-(y - 2 - x)$ ₃

1–5 Simplify.

7. $-18x - (-3 - 5x)$ **8.** $4x - 5(3y - 2x)$ **9.** $-6z - [7z - (8z - 3)]$
$-13x + 3$ $14x - 15y$ $-5z - 3$

1–7

10. $(6x^4y^{-2})(-3x^{-4}y^3)$ **11.** $\dfrac{-48x^{-4}y^{-3}}{14x^3y^{-2}}$ **12.** $(-3x^4)^{-2}$ $\frac{1}{9x^8}$
$-18y$ $-\frac{24}{7x^7y}$

2–2 Solve.

13. $8x - (3x + 2) = -7.5$ **14.** $\frac{3}{4}x + \frac{5}{12} = \frac{2}{3}x - \frac{1}{6}$ ₋₇ **15.** $(4x - 1)(6x + 5) = 0$ $\frac{1}{4}, \frac{-5}{6}$
-1.1

2–4 Solve for the indicated letter.

16. $a = \dfrac{-ks}{m}$ for k **17.** $b = \frac{1}{2}gt^2$ for t^2 $\frac{2h}{g}$ 16. $\frac{-am}{s}$

2–5   Solve.

18. $5y + 3 \leq 4y - 7$ **19.** $\frac{-3}{4}x \leq 60$ **20.** $-4.8x - 3 < 0.2x - 1$ $\quad x > -0.4$

$\quad y \leq -10$ $\quad x \geq -80$

2–7   Solve.

21. $-1 < 2x + 5 < 7$ **22.** $4x - 9 < -3$ or $x - 5 > -2$ **23.** $|3x - 2| < 6$

$\quad x < \frac{3}{2}$ or $x > 3$

21. $-3 < x < 1$

23. $-\frac{4}{3} < x < \frac{8}{3}$

3–4

24. Graph $-6x + 5y = 60$ using intercepts. $\quad$ Line through (0, 12), and (−10, 0)

3–5

25. Find the slope of the line containing $(-6, -5)$ and $(3, -4)$. $\frac{1}{9}$

3–6

26. Find an equation of the line containing $(2, -3)$ and $(-4, 1)$. Write in standard form. $\quad 2x + 3y + 5 = 0$

3–7

27. Find an equation of the line containing $(2, -5)$ which is

  a. parallel to the line $4x + 5y = 8$; $\quad y = \frac{-4}{5}x - \frac{17}{5}$

  b. perpendicular to the line $4x + 5y = 8$. $\quad y = \frac{5}{4}x - \frac{15}{12}$

4–1   Solve.

28. $5x - 2y = 10$ **29.** $-2x + 3y = -18$

$\quad 3x - 5y = -13$ $\;$ (4, 5) $\quad -4x - 5y = -3$ $\;\left(\frac{9}{2}, -3\right)$

4–3   Solve.

30. $2x + y - z = 5$ **31.** $5x + 3y + 2z = 1$

$\quad y - 2z = 7$ $\quad 2x - y + z = -1$

$\quad 2y + 3z = 0$ $\;$ (0, 3, −2) $\quad -2x + 2y - z = 2$ $\;$ (−2, 1, 4)

4–7   Solve using Cramer's rule.

32. $2x - 5y = 9$ **33.** $5x + 3y + 2z = 1$

$\quad 3x + 4y = 25$ $\;$ (7, 1) $\quad 2x - y + z = -1$

$\qquad\qquad\qquad\qquad -2x + 2y - z = 2$ $\;$ −2, 1, 4

34. All points above, and including,

a line through (0, −5) and $\left(\frac{5}{4}, 0\right)$

4–8   Graph.

35. All points above line $y = x - 2$

34. $4x - y \geq 5$ **35.** $x - y < 2$

$\qquad\qquad\qquad\quad x + 2y > 8$

and above line $y = -\frac{1}{2}x + 4$;

intersection of lines at (4, 2)

5–1 Simplify.

36. $-3pq^2 - 5p^2q + 4pq + 3 - 7pq^2 + 3pq - 4p + 2q$ $-10pq^2 - 5p^2q + 7pq + 2q - 4p$

37. $(7x^2 - 3x^2y + 2xy^2 - y^2) - (-3xy^2 + 5x^2 - 4y^2 - x^2y - 6)$ $-2x^2y + 2x^2 + 5xy^2 + 3y^2 + 6$

5–2 Multiply.

38. $(2x^2y - 3xy + 4y)(xy + 3y)$ $2x^3y^2 + 3x^2y^2 - 5xy^2 + 12y^2$

39. $(4x^2 - 5xy^2)^2$ $16x^2 - 40x^3y^2 + 25x^2y^4$

40. $(x^2 + 3y)^3$ $x^6 + 9x^4y + 27x^2y^2 + 27x^3$

5–3 to 5–7 Factor.

41. $5x^4 - 5y^4$

42. $-3y + 12y^3 - 12y^5$ $-3y(1 - 2y^2)^2$ 41. $5(x^2 + y^2)(x + y)(x - y)$

43. $5x^2 - 9x - 2$ $(x - 2)(5x + 1)$

44. $8x^2 + 14xy - 15y^2$ $(4x - 3y)(2x + 5)$

45. $ax^2 - ay + bx^2 - by$

46. $2x^2y - 2x^2 - y + 1$ $(2x^2 - 1)(y - 1)$ 45. $(a + b)(x^2 - 1)$

47. $x^2 - 6.2x + 8.61$ $(x - 2.1)(x - 4.1)$

48. $2x^2 - 4xy + 2y^2 - 18b^2$ $2(x - y + 3b)(x - y - 3b)$

49. $64x^3 + y^3$

50. $x^2 - 2xy + y^2 - b^2 + 8b - 16$

49. $(4x + y)(16x^2 - 4xy + y^2)$ 50. $(x - y + b - 4)(x - y - b + 4)$

5–8 Solve.

51. $4x^2 + 11x + 6 = 0$ $-2, -\frac{3}{4}$

52. $3x^2 + 36x = 0$ $0, 12$

6–1 to 6–4 Simplify.

53. $\dfrac{3a^2 + ab - 2b^2}{a^2 - b^2}$ $\dfrac{3a - 2b}{a - b}$

54. $\dfrac{8x^3 - 27}{64x^3 + 1} \div \dfrac{4x^2 - 12x + 9}{16x^2 + 8x + 1}$

55. $\dfrac{x - 1}{x - 2} - \dfrac{x + 1}{x + 2} + \dfrac{x - 6}{x^2 - 4}$

56. $\dfrac{\dfrac{1}{x} + \dfrac{1}{y}}{\dfrac{x^2 - y^2}{xy}}$

54. $\dfrac{(4x + 1)(4x^2 + 6x + 9)}{(2x - 3)(16x^2 - 4x + 1)}$

55. $\dfrac{5}{x + 2}$

56. $\dfrac{1}{x - y}$

57. $6y - 2x + 3x^2y^2$

58. $16x^2 + 12x + 9$

59. $y^2 - 2y + 3$

6–5 Divide.

57. $\dfrac{18xy^2 - 6x^2y + 9x^3y^3}{3xy}$

58. $4x - 3\overline{)64x^3 - 27}$

59. $(y^3 - y + 6) \div (y + 2)$

6–6 Solve.

60. $-\dfrac{1}{3} - \dfrac{5}{4x} = \dfrac{3}{4} - \dfrac{1}{6x}$ -1

61. $\dfrac{x}{2x - 6} - \dfrac{3}{x^2 - 6x + 9} = \dfrac{x - 2}{3x - 9}$ $-6, 5$

6–9

62. Find the variation constant and an equation of variation where y varies directly as x, and $y = 5.6$ when $x = 8$. $0.7, y = 0.7x$

7–1 to 7–4 Simplify.

63. $\sqrt{(-25t)^2}$ $25|t|$

64. $-\sqrt[5]{-32}$ 2

65. $\sqrt[4]{16x^8y^4}$ $2x^2y$

344 CHAPTER 7 POWERS, ROOTS, AND COMPLEX NUMBERS

66. $\sqrt[3]{12x^3}\,\sqrt[3]{2x^4}$ **67.** $\dfrac{\sqrt{60a^5}}{\sqrt{72a^2}}$ **68.** $\dfrac{\sqrt{y^3+x^3}}{\sqrt{y+x}}\,\sqrt{y^2-xy+y^2}$ 66. $2x^2\sqrt[3]{3x}$

69. $\sqrt[3]{108}-2\sqrt{75}+\sqrt{147}$ **70.** $\sqrt[3]{x}(\sqrt[3]{3x^2}+\sqrt[3]{12x})$ $3x+2\sqrt[3]{3x^2}$ 67. $\dfrac{a^3}{6}\sqrt{30a}$

69. $15\sqrt{3}$

7–5   Write a single radical expression.

71. $x^{\frac{2}{3}}y^{\frac{3}{4}}z^2$ **72.** $\dfrac{\sqrt[3]{(x-y)^2}}{\sqrt{x-y}}$ **73.** $\sqrt{y}\,\sqrt[3]{y+3}$ $\sqrt[6]{y^3(y+3)^2}$ 71. $z^2\sqrt[12]{x^8y^9}$

72. $\sqrt[6]{x-y}$

7–6   Solve.

74. $\sqrt{5x+4}=12$ 28   **75.** $\sqrt{4x+1}-\sqrt{x-2}=3$ 6, 2

7–7, 7–8   Simplify.

76. $\sqrt{-3}\cdot 5i$ $-5\sqrt{3}$ **77.** $(8-5i)-(-1+3i)$ $9-8i$

78. $(-1-2i)(4-3i)$ **79.** $(x+yi)(x-yi)$ **80.** $\dfrac{2-4i}{1+i}$ $-1-3i$

$-10-5i$ x^2+y^2

7–9

81. Find an equation with the solutions $2+i,\,2-i$. $x^2-4x+5=0$

82. Show that $(3+i)$ is a square root of $8+6i$. Then find the other square root. $(3+i)^2=8+6i,\,-3-i$

7–10

83. Find $|2-3i|$. $\sqrt{13}$

Ready for Quadratic Equations?

5–8   Solve.

1. $x^2-5x-14=0$ $7,-2$ **2.** $4x^2-8x=0$ $0, 2$

3. $x^2+10x+25=0$ -5 **4.** $x^2-9=0$ $3,-3$

7–1, 7–2   Simplify. Approximate to the nearest tenth.

5. $\sqrt{49}$ 7   **6.** $\sqrt{88}$ **7.** $\dfrac{14-\sqrt{88}}{10}$ $\dfrac{7-\sqrt{22}}{5},0.5$

$2\sqrt{22}, 9.4$

7–7   Express in terms of i.

8. $\sqrt{-7}$ $\sqrt{7}i$ **9.** $\sqrt{-20}$ $2\sqrt{5}i$

8

CHAPTER EIGHT

Quadratic Equations

8–1 Introduction to Quadratic Equations

Equations of second degree are called quadratic.

DEFINITION

An equation of the type $ax^2 + bx + c = 0$, where a, b and c are constants and $a \neq 0$, is called the *standard form of a quadratic equation*.

Equations of the Type $ax^2 + bx + c = 0$

By the fundamental theorem of algebra, every quadratic polynomial $ax^2 + bx + c$ with complex coefficients can be factored into two linear factors. Some equations are solved easily by factoring.

EXAMPLE 1

Solve $3x^2 + x - 2 = 0$.

$(3x - 2)(x + 1) = 0$ Factoring

$3x - 2 = 0$ or $x + 1 = 0$ Principle of zero products

$x = \frac{2}{3}$ or $x = -1$

These numbers check, so the solutions are $\frac{2}{3}$ and -1.

TRY THIS Solve.

1. $5x^2 - 8x + 3 = 0$ $\frac{3}{5}, 1$

Sometimes it helps to find the standard form before factoring.

EXAMPLE 2

Solve $(x - 1)(x + 1) = 5(x - 1)$.

$x^2 - 5x + 4 = 0$ Finding a standard form

$(x - 4)(x - 1) = 0$ Factoring

$x = 4$ or $x = 1$ Principle of zero products

These numbers check, so the solutions are 4 and 1.

TRY THIS Solve.

2. $6(y - 3) = (y - 3)(y - 2)$ 3, 8

Equations of the Type $ax^2 + c = 0$

We next consider equations in which $b = 0$, that is equations $ax^2 + c = 0$. In other words, equations in which ax^2 equals some constant. In order to solve equations of this type we often need to take the square root of both sides of an equation. Consider the equation $x^2 = k$, where k can be any complex number.

$$x^2 = k$$
$$x^2 - k = 0$$
$$(x - \sqrt{k})(x + \sqrt{k}) = 0$$
$$x - \sqrt{k} = 0 \text{ or } x + \sqrt{k} = 0$$
$$x = \sqrt{k} \quad \text{or} \quad x = -\sqrt{k}$$

Both these solutions check.

EXAMPLE 3
Solve $3x^2 = 6$.

$$x^2 = 2 \quad \text{Multiplying by } \tfrac{1}{3}$$
$$x = \sqrt{2} \text{ or } x = -\sqrt{2}$$

These numbers check, so the solutions are $\sqrt{2}$ and $-\sqrt{2}$. We often write the solutions as $\pm\sqrt{2}$.

TRY THIS Solve.

3. $5x^2 = 15$ **4.** $7x^2 = 0$ 3. $\pm\sqrt{3}$ 4. 0

Sometimes we get solutions that are complex numbers.

EXAMPLE 4
Solve $4x^2 + 9 = 0$.

$$x^2 = -\frac{9}{4} \quad \text{Adding } -9 \text{ and multiplying by } \tfrac{1}{4}$$
$$x = \sqrt{-\frac{9}{4}} \text{ or } x = -\sqrt{-\frac{9}{4}} \quad \text{Taking square roots}$$
$$x = \frac{3}{2}i \quad \text{or } x = -\frac{3}{2}i$$

TRY THIS Solve.

5. $2x^2 + 1 = 0$ $\pm\frac{i\sqrt{2}}{2}$

Equations of the Type $ax^2 + bx = 0$

When c is 0 ($a \neq 0$, $b \neq 0$), we can factor $ax^2 + bx$ as $x(ax + b)$ and use the principle of zero products.

$$x(ax + b) = 0$$
$$x = 0 \text{ or } ax + b = 0$$
$$x = 0 \text{ or } \quad ax = -b$$
$$x = 0 \text{ or } \quad x = -\frac{b}{a}$$

EXAMPLE 5

Solve $3x^2 + 5x = 0$.

$$x(3x + 5) = 0 \quad \text{Factoring}$$
$$x = 0 \text{ or } 3x + 5 = 0 \quad \text{Principle of zero products}$$
$$x = 0 \text{ or } \quad x = -\frac{5}{3}$$

These numbers check, so the solutions are 0 and $-\frac{5}{3}$.

A quadratic equation of this type will always have 0 as one solution and a nonzero number as the other solution.

TRY THIS Solve.

6. $4x^2 - 3x = 0$ $\quad 0, \frac{3}{4}$

Applying Quadratic Equations

EXAMPLE 6

A rectangular garden is 60 m by 80 m. Part of the garden is torn up to install a strip of lawn of uniform width around the garden. The new area of the garden is $\frac{1}{6}$ of the old area. How wide is the strip of lawn?

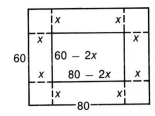

First make a drawing. Let x represent the width of the strip of lawn.

$$\text{Area of old garden} = 60 \cdot 80 \quad \text{Multiplying length and width}$$
$$\text{Area of new garden} = (60 - 2x)(80 - 2x)$$

Since the new garden is $\frac{1}{6}$ of the old we have the following equation.

$$(60 - 2x)(80 - 2x) = \frac{1}{6} \cdot 60 \cdot 80$$
$$4800 - 160x - 120x + 4x^2 = 800$$
$$4x^2 - 280x + 4000 = 0 \quad \text{Writing the standard form}$$
$$x^2 - 70x + 1000 = 0$$
$$(x - 20)(x - 50) = 0$$

$$x = 20 \text{ or } x = 50$$

Checking in the original problem we see that 50 is not a solution because when $x = 50$, $60 - 2x = -40$, and the width of the garden cannot be negative. The number 20 checks. Thus the width of the strip of lawn is 20 m.

TRY THIS

7. An open box is to be made from a 10 cm by 20 cm rectangular piece of cardboard by cutting a square from each corner. The area of the bottom of the box is 96 cm². What is the length of the sides of the squares which are cut from the corners? 2 cm

EXAMPLE 7

Bicyclists A and B leave the same point P at the same time at right angles. B travels 7 km/h faster than A. After 3 hours they are 39 km apart. Find the speed of each.

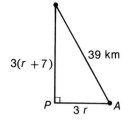

We first make a drawing, letting r be the speed of A and $r + 7$ be the speed of B. Since they both travel 3 hr, their distances from P are $3r$ and $3(r + 7)$, respectively. To translate we use the Pythagorean Theorem.

$$[3(r + 7)]^2 + [3r]^2 = 39^2$$
$$9(r + 7)^2 + 9r^2 = 1521$$
$$(r + 7)^2 + r^2 = 169 \quad \text{Multiplying by } \frac{1}{9}$$
$$r^2 + 14r + 49 + r^2 = 169$$
$$2r^2 + 14r + 49 = 169$$

We write the equation in standard form.

$$2r^2 + 14r - 120 = 0$$
$$r^2 + 7r - 60 = 0 \quad \text{Multiplying by } \frac{1}{2}$$
$$(r + 12)(r - 5) = 0$$

$$r = -12 \text{ or } r = 5$$

The solutions of the equation are -12 and 5. Since speed cannot be negative in this problem, -12 is not a solution. The number 5 checks, so the speed of A is 5 km/h and the speed of B is 12 km/h.

TRY THIS

8. Joggers A and B leave the same point P at right angles. A jogs 1 km/h faster than B. After 2 hours they are 10 km apart. Find the speed of each. $A: 4$ km/h; $B: 3$ km/h

8–1

Exercises

Solve.

1. $x^2 - 6x + 5 = 0$

2. $x^2 - 7x + 6 = 0$

3. $x^2 - 4x - 5 = 0$

4. $x^2 - 6x - 7 = 0$

5. $x^2 + 8x + 15 = 0$

6. $x^2 + 9x + 14 = 0$

7. $6x^2 - x - 2 = 0$

8. $2x^2 + 13x + 15 = 0$

9. $9t^2 + 15t + 4 = 0$

10. $3y^2 + 10y - 8 = 0$

11. $6x^2 + 4x = 10$

12. $3x^2 + 7x = 20$

13. $2x(4x - 5) = 3$

14. $t(2t + 9) = -7$

15. $(p - 3)(p - 4) = 42$

16. $16(t - 1) = t(t + 8)$

17. $4x(x - 2) - 5x(x - 1) = 2$

18. $14(x - 4) - (x + 2) = (x + 2)(x - 4)$

1. 5, 1
2. 6, 1
3. 5, −1
4. 7, −1
5. −5, −3
6. −7, −2
7. $\frac{2}{3}, -\frac{1}{2}$
8. $-\frac{3}{2}, -5$
9. $-\frac{4}{3}, -\frac{1}{3}$
10. $\frac{2}{3}, -4$
11. $-\frac{5}{3}, 1$
12. $\frac{5}{3}, -4$
13. $-\frac{1}{4}, \frac{3}{2}$
14. $-\frac{7}{2}, -1$
15. 10, −3
16. 4
17. −2, −1
18. 10, 5

Solve.

19. $4x^2 = 20$

20. $3x^2 = 21$

21. $10x^2 = 0$

22. $9x^2 = 0$

23. $2x^2 - 3 = 0$

24. $3x^2 - 7 = 0$

25. $-3x^2 + 5 = 0$

26. $-2x^2 + 1 = 0$

27. $25x^2 + 4 = 0$

28. $9x^2 + 16 = 0$

29. $3x^2 + 1 = 0$

30. $5x^2 + 1 = 0$

31. $x^2 + 5 = 0$

32. $x^2 + 6 = 0$

33. $2x^2 + 14 = 0$

34. $3x^2 + 15 = 0$

35. $\frac{4}{9}x^2 - 1 = 0$

36. $\frac{16}{25}x^2 - 1 = 0$

19. $\pm\sqrt{5}$
20. $\pm\sqrt{7}$
21. 0
22. 0
23. $\pm\frac{\sqrt{6}}{2}$
24. $\pm\frac{\sqrt{21}}{3}$
25. $\pm\frac{\sqrt{15}}{3}$
26. $\pm\frac{\sqrt{2}}{2}$
27. $\pm\frac{2}{5}i$
28. $\pm\frac{4}{3}i$
29. $\pm\frac{i\sqrt{3}}{3}$
30. $\pm\frac{i\sqrt{5}}{5}$
31. $\pm i\sqrt{5}$
32. $\pm i\sqrt{6}$
33. $\pm i\sqrt{7}$
34. $\pm i\sqrt{5}$
35. $\pm\frac{3}{2}$
36. $\pm\frac{5}{4}$

Solve.

37. $x^2 - 5x = 0$

38. $x^2 - 6x = 0$

39. $5x^2 + 10x = 0$

40. $3x^2 + 12x = 0$

41. $3x^2 - 2x = 0$

42. $7x^2 - 3x = 0$

43. $14x^2 + 9x = 0$

44. $19x^2 + 8x = 0$

45. $11x^2 - 55x = 0$

37. 0, 5
38. 0, 6
39. 0, −2
40. 0, −4
41. $0, \frac{2}{3}$
42. $0, \frac{3}{7}$
43. $0, -\frac{9}{14}$
44. $0, -\frac{8}{19}$
45. 0, 5

Solve.

46. A picture frame measures 14 cm by 20 cm. 160 cm² of picture shows. Find the width of the frame. 2 cm

47. A picture frame measures 12 cm by 20 cm. 84 cm² of picture shows. Find the width of the frame. 3 cm

48. The width of a rectangle is 4 cm less than the length. The area is 12 m^2. Find the length and width. Length is 6 m; width is 2 m

49. The width of a rectangle is 5 m less than the length. The area is 24 m^2. Find the length and width. Length is 8 m; width is 3 m

50. The length of a rectangle is twice the width. The area is 288 m^2. Find the length and width. Length is 24 m; width is 12 m

51. The length of a rectangle is twice the width. The area is 338 km^2. Find the length and width. Length is 26 m; width is 13 m

52. The hypotenuse of a right triangle is 5 m long. One leg is 1 m less than the other. Find the lengths of the legs. 4 m and 3 m

53. The hypotenuse of a right triangle is 13 m long. One leg is 7 m longer than the other. Find the lengths of the legs. 12 m and 5 m

54. The hypotenuse of a right triangle is 26 m long. The length of one leg is 14 m longer than the other. Find the lengths of the legs. 24 m and 10 m

55. The hypotenuse of a right triangle is 25 km long. The length of one leg is 17 km less than the other. Find the lengths of the legs. 24 km and 7 km

56. Boats A and B leave the same point at the same time at right angles. B travels 7 km/h slower than A. After 4 hr they are 68 km apart. Find the speed of each boat. A : 15 km/h; B 8 km/h

Extension

Solve.

57. Find three consecutive integers such that the square of the first plus the product of the other two is 46. 4, 5, and 6

58. A bicyclist travels 280 km at a certain speed. If the speed had been increased 5 km/h, the trip could have been made in 1 hour less time. Find the actual speed. 35 km/h

59. Airplane A travels 2800 km at a certain speed. Airplane B travels 2000 km at a speed which is 50 km/h faster than Plane A in 3 hours less time. Find the speed of each plane. A : 350 km/h; B : 400 km/h

Challenge

Solve.

60. $(3x^2 - 7x - 20)(2x - 5) = 0$ $-\frac{5}{3}, 4, \frac{5}{2}$

61. $x(2x^2 + 9x - 56)(3x + 10) = 0$ $-8, -\frac{10}{3}, 0, \frac{7}{2}$

62. $\left(x - \frac{1}{3}\right)\left(x - \frac{1}{3}\right) + \left(x - \frac{1}{3}\right)\left(x + \frac{2}{9}\right) = 0$ $\frac{1}{18}, \frac{1}{3}$

Solve for x.

63. $ax^2 - b = 0$ **64.** $ax^2 - bx = 0$ 63. $\pm\sqrt{\frac{b}{a}}$ 64. $0, -\frac{b}{a}$

8-2 The Quadratic Formula

Solving Equations Using the Quadratic Formula

Here is a formula for finding the solutions of any quadratic equation.

THEOREM 8-1

The Quadratic Formula

The solutions of any quadratic equation (with complex coefficients), $ax^2 + bx + c = 0$ are given by the *quadratic formula*:

$$x = \frac{-b \pm \sqrt{b^2 - 4ac}}{2a}.$$

EXAMPLE 1

Solve $3x^2 + 5x = -1$.

First find the standard form and determine a, b, and c.

$$3x^2 + 5x + 1 = 0 \qquad a = 3, b = 5, c = 1$$

Then use the quadratic formula.

$$x = \frac{-b \pm \sqrt{b^2 - 4ac}}{2a}$$

$$x = \frac{-(5) \pm \sqrt{(5)^2 - 4 \cdot 3 \cdot 1}}{2 \cdot 3}$$

$$x = \frac{-5 \pm \sqrt{25 - 12}}{6} = \frac{-5 \pm \sqrt{13}}{6}$$

The solutions are $\dfrac{-5 + \sqrt{13}}{6}$ and $\dfrac{-5 - \sqrt{13}}{6}$.

When using the quadratic formula, the solutions obtained are always solutions of the original equation unless a computational error has been made. Therefore, it is better to check your work than to substitute into the original equation.

TRY THIS Solve using the quadratic formula.

1. $3x^2 + 2x = 7$ $\quad \frac{-1 \pm \sqrt{22}}{3}$

When the expression under the radical sign is negative, we get complex solutions.

EXAMPLE 2

Solve $x^2 + x + 1 = 0$.

$$a = 1, b = 1, c = 1$$

$$x = \frac{-b \pm \sqrt{b^2 - 4ac}}{2a}$$

$$x = \frac{-1 \pm \sqrt{1^2 - 4 \cdot 1 \cdot 1}}{2 \cdot 1}$$

$$x = \frac{-1 \pm \sqrt{1 - 4}}{2}$$

$$x = \frac{-1 \pm \sqrt{-3}}{2}$$

$$x = \frac{-1 \pm i\sqrt{3}}{2}$$

The solutions are $\frac{-1 + i\sqrt{3}}{2}$ and $\frac{-1 - i\sqrt{3}}{2}$.

TRY THIS Solve.

2. $x^2 - x + 2 = 0$ $\frac{1 \pm i\sqrt{7}}{2}$

Approximating Solutions

A square root table can be used to find rational number approximations to the exact solutions given by the formula.

EXAMPLE 3

Approximate the solutions of the equation in Example 1. From Table 1 in the back of the book, $\sqrt{13} \approx 3.606$.

$$\frac{-5 + \sqrt{13}}{6} \approx \frac{-5 + 3.606}{6} \qquad\qquad \frac{-5 - \sqrt{13}}{6} \approx \frac{-5 - 3.606}{6}$$

$$= \frac{-1.394}{6} \qquad\qquad\qquad = \frac{-8.606}{6}$$

$$\approx -0.2 \quad \text{Rounded to} \qquad\qquad \approx -1.4 \quad \text{Rounded to}$$
$$\text{the nearest tenth} \qquad\qquad\qquad\qquad \text{the nearest tenth}$$

TRY THIS

3. Approximate the solutions to Try This exercise 1. Round to the nearest tenth.   1.2, −1.9

A Proof of Theorem 8–1

Consider any quadratic equation in standard form:
$ax^2 + bx + c = 0, a > 0$. (If $a < 0$, we first multiply on both sides of the equation by -1.)

Let's solve by completing the square.

$$x^2 + \frac{b}{a}x + \frac{c}{a} = 0 \quad \text{Multiplying by } \frac{1}{a}$$

$$x^2 + \frac{b}{a}x = -\frac{c}{a} \quad \text{Adding } -\frac{c}{a}$$

Half of $\frac{b}{a}$ is $\frac{b}{2a}$. The square is $\frac{b^2}{4a^2}$. We add $\frac{b^2}{4a^2}$ on both sides to complete the square.

$$x^2 + \frac{b}{a}x + \frac{b^2}{4a^2} = -\frac{c}{a} + \frac{b^2}{4a^2}$$

$$\left(x + \frac{b}{2a}\right)^2 = -\frac{4ac}{4a^2} + \frac{b^2}{4a^2}$$

$$\left(x + \frac{b}{2a}\right)^2 = \frac{b^2 - 4ac}{4a^2}$$

$$x + \frac{b}{2a} = \sqrt{\frac{b^2 - 4ac}{4a^2}} \text{ or } x + \frac{b}{2a} = -\sqrt{\frac{b^2 - 4ac}{4a^2}}$$

$$x + \frac{b}{2a} = \frac{\sqrt{b^2 - 4ac}}{2a} \text{ or } x + \frac{b}{2a} = -\frac{\sqrt{b^2 - 4ac}}{2a} \quad \begin{array}{l}\text{Since}\\ a > 0,\\ |a| = a.\end{array}$$

$$x = -\frac{b}{2a} + \frac{\sqrt{b^2 - 4ac}}{2a} \text{ or } x = -\frac{b}{2a} - \frac{\sqrt{b^2 - 4ac}}{2a}$$

The solutions are given by

$$x = \frac{-b \pm \sqrt{b^2 - 4ac}}{2a}.$$

8–2

Exercises
Solve.

1. $x^2 + 6x + 4 = 0$ $-3 \pm \sqrt{5}$

2. $x^2 - 6x - 4 = 0$ $3 \pm \sqrt{13}$

3. $x^2 + 4x - 5 = 0$ $1, -5$

4. $x^2 - 2x - 15 = 0$ $5, -3$

5. $y^2 + 7y = 30$ $3, -10$

6. $y^2 - 7y = 30$ $10, -3$

7. $2t^2 - 3t - 2 = 0$ $2, -\frac{1}{2}$

8. $5m^2 + 3m - 2 = 0$ $\frac{2}{5}, -1$

9. $3p^2 = -8p - 5$ $-1, -\frac{5}{3}$

10. $3u^2 = 18u - 6$ $3 \pm \sqrt{7}$

11. $x^2 - x + 1 = 0$ $\frac{1 \pm i\sqrt{3}}{2}$ 12. $x^2 + x + 2 = 0$ $\frac{-1 \pm i\sqrt{7}}{2}$

13. $1 + \frac{2}{x} + \frac{5}{x^2} = 0$ $-1 \pm 2i$ 14. $1 + \frac{5}{x^2} = \frac{2}{x}$ $1 \pm 2i$

15. $x^2 - 2x + 5 = 0$ $1 \pm 2i$ 16. $x^2 - 4x + 5 = 0$ $2 \pm i$

17. $x^2 + 13 = 4x$ $2 \pm 3i$ 18. $x^2 + 13 = 6x$ $3 \pm 2i$

19. $z^2 + 5 = 0$ $\pm i\sqrt{5}$ 20. $t^2 + 3 = 0$ $\pm i\sqrt{3}$

21. $r^2 + 3r = 8$ $\frac{-3 \pm \sqrt{41}}{2}$ 22. $h^2 + 4 = 6h$ $3 \pm \sqrt{5}$

23. $2x^2 = 5$ $\pm \frac{\sqrt{10}}{2}$ 24. $3x^2 = 2$ $\pm \frac{\sqrt{6}}{3}$

25. $3x + x(x - 2) = 0$ $0, -1$ 26. $4x + x(x - 3) = 0$ $0, -1$

27. $5x^2 + 2x + 1 = 0$ $\frac{-1 \pm 2i}{5}$ 28. $3x^2 + x + 2 = 0$ $\frac{-1 \pm \sqrt{23}i}{6}$

29. $(2t - 3)^2 + 17t = 15$ $\frac{3}{4}, -2$ 30. $2y^2 - (y + 2)(y - 3) = 12$ $2, -3$

31. $(x - 2)^2 + (x + 1)^2 = 0$ $\frac{1 \pm 3i}{2}$ 32. $(x + 3)^2 + (x - 1)^2 = 0$ $-1 \pm 2i$

33. $x + \frac{1}{x} = \frac{13}{6}$ $\frac{3}{2}, \frac{2}{3}$ 34. $\frac{3}{x} + \frac{x}{3} = \frac{5}{2}$ $6, \frac{3}{2}$

Use the square root table, Table 1, in the back of the book to approximate solutions to the nearest tenth.

35. $x^2 + 4x - 7 = 0$ 36. $x^2 + 6x + 4 = 0$ 37. $x^2 - 6x + 4 = 0$

38. $x^2 - 4x + 1 = 0$ 39. $2x^2 - 3x - 7 = 0$ 40. $3x^2 - 3x - 2 = 0$

Extension

Use a calculator to solve.

41. $t^2 + 0.2t - 0.3 = 0$ 42. $p^2 + 0.3p - 0.2 = 0$

43. $x^2 - 0.75x - 0.5 = 0$ 44. $z^2 + 0.84z - 0.4 = 0$

Solve.

45. $x^2 + x - \sqrt{2} = 0$ 46. $x^2 - x - \sqrt{3} = 0$

47. $x^2 + \sqrt{5}x - \sqrt{3} = 0$ 48. $\sqrt{2}x^2 + 5x + \sqrt{2} = 0$

49. $x^2 + 3x + i = 0$ 50. $ix^2 - 2x + 1 = 0$

51. A boat travels 2 km upstream and 2 km downstream. The total time for both parts of the trip is 1 hour. The speed of the stream is 2 km/h. What is the speed of the boat in still water? Round to the nearest tenth. 4.8 km/h

Challenge

52. Solve $3x^2 + xy + 4y^2 - 9 = 0$ for x in terms of y. $x = \frac{-y \pm \sqrt{-47y^2 + 108}}{6}$

53. One solution of $kx^2 + 3x - k = 0$ is -2. Find the other. $\frac{1}{2}$

54. Prove that the solutions of $ax^2 + bx + c = 0$ are the reciprocals of the solutions of $cx^2 - bx + a = 0$.

35. 1.3, −5.3
36. −0.8, −5.2
37. 5.2, 0.8
38. 3.7, 0.3
39. 2.8, −1.3
40. 1.5, −0.5
41. 0.4567764, −0.6567764
42. 0.321699, −0.621699
43. 1.1753905, −0.4253905
44. −1.179201, 0.33921
45. $\frac{-1 \pm \sqrt{1 + 4\sqrt{2}}}{2}$
46. $\frac{1 \pm \sqrt{1 + 4\sqrt{3}}}{2}$
47. $\frac{-\sqrt{5} \pm \sqrt{5 + 4\sqrt{3}}}{2}$
48. $\frac{-5\sqrt{2} \pm \sqrt{34}}{4}$
49. $\frac{-3 \pm \sqrt{9 - 4i}}{2}$
50. $\frac{1 \pm \sqrt{1 - i}}{i}$

8–3 Solutions of Quadratic Equations

The Discriminant

The quadratic formula can be used when the coefficients are any complex numbers. Now we restrict our attention to equations with real number coefficients. The expression $b^2 - 4ac$ in the quadratic formula is called the discriminant. From this number we can determine the nature of the solutions of a quadratic equation.

THEOREM 8–2

An equation $ax^2 + bx + c = 0$, with $a \neq 0$ and all coefficients real numbers, has

1. Exactly one real number solution if $b^2 - 4ac = 0$.
2. Two real number solutions if $b^2 - 4ac > 0$.
3. Two complex, but not real, number solutions that are conjugates of each other if $b^2 - 4ac < 0$.

EXAMPLE 1

Determine the nature of the solutions of $9x^2 - 12x + 4 = 0$.

$$a = 9, b = -12, \text{ and } c = 4$$

We compute the discriminant.

$$b^2 - 4ac = (-12)^2 - 4 \cdot 9 \cdot 4 = 144 - 144 = 0$$

By Theorem 8–2, there is just one solution and it is a real number.

EXAMPLE 2

Determine the nature of the solutions of $x^2 + 5x + 8 = 0$.

$$a = 1, b = 5, \text{ and } c = 8$$

We compute the discriminant.

$$b^2 - 4ac = 5^2 - 4 \cdot 1 \cdot 8 = 25 - 32 = -7$$

Since the discriminant is negative, there are two nonreal solutions that are complex conjugates of each other.

EXAMPLE 3

Determine the nature of the solutions of $x^2 + 5x + 6 = 0$.

$$a = 1, b = 5, \text{ and } c = 6$$
$$b^2 - 4ac = 5^2 - 4 \cdot 1 \cdot 6 = 1$$

Since the discriminant is positive, there are two solutions and they are real numbers.

TRY THIS Determine the nature of the solutions of each equation.

1. $x^2 + 5x - 3 = 0$ **2.** $9x^2 - 6x + 1 = 0$ **3.** $3x^2 - 2x + 1 = 0$

1. Two real
2. One real
3. Two nonreal

Sum and Product of Solutions

THEOREM 8–3

For the equation $ax^2 + bx + c = 0$, the sum of the solutions is $-\frac{b}{a}$, and the product of the solutions is $\frac{c}{a}$.

Note that if we express $ax^2 + bx + c = 0$ in the equivalent form,

$$x^2 + \frac{b}{a}x + \frac{c}{a} = 0,$$

then the sum of the solutions is the additive inverse of the x coefficient and the product of the solutions is the constant term.

EXAMPLE 4

Without solving, find the sum and product of the solutions of $2x^2 = 6x + 5$.

Let x_1 and x_2 represent the solutions.

Since $2x^2 - 6x - 5 = 0$, we have $a = 2$, $b = -6$, and $c = -5$.

$$x_1 + x_2 = -\frac{b}{a} = -\left(\frac{-6}{2}\right) = 3 \qquad x_1 \cdot x_2 = \frac{c}{a} = \frac{-5}{2}$$

TRY THIS Find, without solving, the sum and product of the solutions.

4. $3x^2 + 4 = 12x$ **5.** $x^2 + \sqrt{2}x - 4 = 0$

4. Sum = 4; product = $\frac{4}{3}$
5. Sum = $-\sqrt{2}$; product = -4

Sum and Product Given

EXAMPLE 5

Find a quadratic equation for which the sum of the solutions is $-\frac{4}{5}$ and the product of the solutions is $\frac{2}{3}$.

$$x^2 - \left(-\frac{b}{a}\right)x + \frac{c}{a} = x^2 - \left(-\frac{4}{5}\right)x + \frac{2}{3} = x^2 + \frac{4}{5}x + \frac{2}{3} = 0$$

Thus we have $x^2 + \frac{4}{5}x + \frac{2}{3} = 0$, or $15x^2 + 12x + 10 = 0$.

TRY THIS

6. Find a quadratic equation for which the sum of the solutions is 3 and the product is $-\frac{1}{4}$. $4x^2 - 12x - 1 = 0$

Writing Equations from Solutions

We can use the principle of zero products to write a quadratic equation whose solutions are known.

EXAMPLE 6

Find a quadratic equation whose solutions are 3 and $-\frac{2}{5}$.

$$x = 3 \text{ or } \qquad x = -\frac{2}{5}$$

$$x - 3 = 0 \text{ or } x + \frac{2}{5} = 0$$

$$(x - 3)\left(x + \frac{2}{5}\right) = 0 \quad \text{Multiplying}$$

$$x^2 - \frac{13}{5}x - \frac{6}{5} = 0, \text{ or } 5x^2 - 13x - 6 = 0$$

When radicals are involved, it is sometimes easier to use the properties of the sum and product.

EXAMPLE 7

Find a quadratic equation whose solutions are $2 + \sqrt{5}$ and $2 - \sqrt{5}$.

$$x_1 + x_2 = (2 + \sqrt{5}) + (2 - \sqrt{5})$$
$$= 4$$

$$x_1 \cdot x_2 = (2 + \sqrt{5}) \cdot (2 - \sqrt{5})$$
$$= 4 - 5 = -1$$

$$x^2 - \left(-\frac{b}{a}\right)x + \frac{c}{a} = x^2 - (4)x + (-1) = 0; \text{ or } x^2 - 4x - 1 = 0$$

TRY THIS Find a quadratic equation whose solutions are the following.

7. $-4, \frac{5}{3}$ **8.** $-7, 8$ **9.** m, n **10.** $8, -9$

11. $3 + \sqrt{2}, 3 - \sqrt{2}$ **12.** $\frac{2 + \sqrt{5}}{2}, \frac{2 - \sqrt{5}}{2}$

7. $3x^2 + 7x - 20 = 0$
8. $x^2 - x - 56 = 0$
9. $x^2 - (m + n)x + mn = 0$
10. $x^2 + x - 72 = 0$
11. $x^2 - 6x + 7 = 0$
12. $4x^2 - 8x - 1 = 0$

8–3

Exercises

Determine the nature of the solutions of each equation.

1. One real
2. One real
3. Two nonreal
4. Two nonreal
5. Two real
6. Two real
7. One real
8. Two real
9. Two nonreal
10. Two nonreal
11. Two real
12. Two real
13. Two real
14. Two real
15. One real

1. $x^2 - 6x + 9 = 0$ **2.** $x^2 + 10x + 25 = 0$ **3.** $x^2 + 7 = 0$

4. $x^2 + 2 = 0$ **5.** $x^2 - 2 = 0$ **6.** $x^2 - 5 = 0$

7. $4x^2 - 12x + 9 = 0$ **8.** $4x^2 + 8x - 5 = 0$ **9.** $x^2 - 2x + 4 = 0$

10. $x^2 + 3x + 4 = 0$ **11.** $9t^2 - 3t = 0$ **12.** $4m^2 + 7m = 0$

13. $y^2 = \frac{1}{2}y + \frac{3}{5}$ **14.** $y^2 + \frac{9}{4} = 4y$ **15.** $4x^2 - 4\sqrt{3}x + 3 = 0$

Without solving, find the sum and product of the solutions.

16. $x^2 + 7x + 8 = 0$ **17.** $x^2 - 2x + 10 = 0$ **18.** $x^2 - x + 1 = 0$

19. $x^2 + x - 1 = 0$ **20.** $8 - 2x^2 + 4x = 0$ **21.** $4 + x + 2x^2 = 0$

22. $m^2 = 25$ **23.** $t^2 = 49$ **24.** $(2 + 3x)^2 = 7x$

25. $2x - 1 = (1 - 5x)^2$ **26.** $5(t - 3)^2 = 4(t + 3)^2$ **27.** $3(y + 4)^2 = 2(y + 5)^2$

Find a quadratic equation for which the sum and product of the solutions are as given.

28. Sum of solutions $= -5$; product $= \frac{1}{2}$ **29.** Sum of solutions $= -\pi$; product $= \frac{1}{4}$

30. Sum of solutions $= \sqrt{3}$; product $= 8$ **31.** Sum of solutions $= 5$; product $= -\sqrt{2}$

Find a quadratic equation whose solution or solutions are the following.

32. $-11, 9$ **33.** $-4, 4$ **34.** 7 (only solution)   **35.** -5 (only solution)

36. $-\frac{2}{5}, \frac{6}{5}$ **37.** $-\frac{1}{4}, -\frac{1}{2}$ **38.** $\frac{c}{2}, \frac{d}{2}$ **39.** $\frac{k}{3}, \frac{m}{4}$

40. $\sqrt{2}, 3\sqrt{2}$ **41.** $-\sqrt{3}, 2\sqrt{3}$ **42.** $\pi, -2\pi$ **43.** $-3\pi, 4\pi$

Use the sum and product properties to write a quadratic equation whose solutions are the following.

44. 4, 3

44. $x^2 - 7x + 12 = 0$
45. $x^2 - 11x + 30 = 0$
46. $4x^2 + 3x - 10 = 0$
47. $4x^2 + 23x - 6 = 0$

45. 5, 6

46. $-2, \dfrac{5}{4}$

47. $-6, \dfrac{1}{4}$

48. $x^2 - 2x - 1 = 0$
49. $x^2 - 4x + 1 = 0$

48. $1 + \sqrt{2}, 1 - \sqrt{2}$

49. $2 + \sqrt{3}, 2 - \sqrt{3}$

50. $\dfrac{2 + \sqrt{3}}{2}, \dfrac{2 - \sqrt{3}}{2}$

51. $\dfrac{1 + \sqrt{13}}{2}, \dfrac{1 - \sqrt{13}}{2}$

52. $\dfrac{m}{n}, -\dfrac{n}{m}$

53. $\dfrac{g}{h}, -\dfrac{h}{g}$

54. $2 - 5i, 2 + 5i$

55. $4 + 3i, 4 - 3i$

50. $4x^2 - 8x + 1 = 0$
51. $x^2 - x - 3 = 0$
52. $mnx^2 - (m^2 - n^2)x - mn = 0$

53. $ghx^2 - (g^2 - h^2)x - gh = 0$
54. $x^2 - 4x + 29 = 0$
55. $x^2 - 8x + 25 = 0$

Extension

In each of the following find k so that: **a.** there are two real number solutions, **b.** there is one real number solution, and **c.** there are two solutions which are complex conjugates.

56. $x^2 + 3x + k = 0$

57. $x^2 + x + k = 0$

58. $kx^2 - 4x + 1 = 0$

59. $x^2 - x + 3x + k = 0$

60. $x^2 + x = 1 - k$

61. $3x^2 + 4x = k - 5$

For each equation under the given condition, find the other solution, and find k.

62. $kx^2 - 17x + 33 = 0$; one solution is $3 \frac{11}{2}, k = 2$

63. $kx^2 - 2x + k = 0$; one solution is $-3 -\frac{1}{3}, k = -\frac{3}{5}$

64. $x^2 - kx - 25 = 0$; one solution is -5 $5, k = 0$

65. Find k if $kx^2 - 4x + (2k - 1) = 0$ and the product of the solutions is 3. -1

Challenge

Suppose in a quadratic equation $ax^2 + bx + c = 0$, a, b, and c are integers.

66. Prove that the quadratic equation has two rational number solutions if the discriminant is positive and a perfect square.

67. Use the result of Exercise 66 to determine if each equation has rational solutions.
   a. $6x^2 + 5x + 1 = 0$ **b.** $x^2 + 4x - 2 = 0$

68. Prove that every polynomial equation with rational coefficients is equivalent to one with integer coefficients.

69. Prove Theorem 8–2. (Hint: Use the quadratic formula.)

70. Find h and k if $3x^2 - hx + 4k = 0$ and the sum of the solutions is -12 and the product of the solutions is 20.

71. One solution of the equation $p(q - r)y^2 + q(r - p)y + r(p - q) = 0$ is 2. Find the other.

8-4 Equations in Quadratic Form

Look for a pattern.

$$x^4 - 9x^2 + 8 = 0, \text{ let } u = x^2. \text{ Then } u^2 - 9u + 8 = 0$$
$$x - 5\sqrt{x} + 4 = 0, \text{ let } u = \sqrt{x}. \text{ Then } u^2 - 5u + 4 = 0$$
$$(x^2 - 1)^2 - (x^2 - 1) - 2 = 0, \text{ let } u = x^2 - 1. \text{ Then } u^2 - u - 2 = 0$$

The equations on the left are not quadratic, but after a substitution we get quadratic equations. Such equations are said to be quadratic in form.

> To solve such equations, we first make a substitution, solve for the new variable, then solve for the original variable.

EXAMPLE 1

Solve $x^4 - 9x^2 + 8 = 0$.

Let $u = x^2$. Then we solve the equation found by substituting u for x^2.

$$u^2 - 9u + 8 = 0$$
$$(u - 8)(u - 1) = 0$$

$$u - 8 = 0 \text{ or } u - 1 = 0$$
$$u = 8 \text{ or } \quad u = 1$$

Now we substitute x^2 for u and solve these equations.

$$x^2 = 8 \quad \text{ or } x^2 = 1$$
$$x = \pm\sqrt{8} \quad \text{ or } x = \pm 1$$
$$x = \pm 2\sqrt{2} \text{ or } x = \pm 1$$

These four numbers check. The solutions are 1, -1, $2\sqrt{2}$, and $-2\sqrt{2}$.

TRY THIS Solve.

1. $x^4 - 10x^2 + 9 = 0$ ±3, ±1

EXAMPLE 2

Solve $x - 3\sqrt{x} - 4 = 0$.

Let $u = \sqrt{x}$. Then we solve the equation found by substituting u for $\sqrt{x}$.

$$u^2 - 3u - 4 = 0$$
$$(u - 4)(u + 1) = 0$$

$$u = 4 \text{ or } u = -1$$

$\sqrt{x} = 4 \text{ or } \sqrt{x} = -1$ Substituting $\sqrt{x}$ for u

Squaring the first equation we get $x = 16$. The second equation has no real solution since principal square roots are never negative. The number 16 checks and is the solution.

TRY THIS

2. Solve $x + 3\sqrt{x} - 10 = 0$. Be sure to check.   4

EXAMPLE 3

Solve $(x^2 - 1)^2 - (x^2 - 1) - 2 = 0$.

Let $u = x^2 - 1$.

$$u^2 - u - 2 = 0$$
$$(u - 2)(u + 1) = 0$$

$$u = 2 \text{ or } u = -1$$

Now we substitute $x^2 - 1$ for u and solve these equations.

$$x^2 - 1 = 2 \quad \text{or } x^2 - 1 = -1$$
$$x^2 = 3 \quad \text{or} \quad x^2 = 0$$
$$x = \pm\sqrt{3} \text{ or} \quad x = 0$$

The numbers $\sqrt{3}$, $-\sqrt{3}$, and 0 check. They are the solutions.

TRY THIS Solve.

3. $(x^2 - x)^2 - 14(x^2 - x) + 24 = 0$ 4, 2, −1, −3

EXAMPLE 4

Solve $t^{\frac{2}{5}} - t^{\frac{1}{5}} - 2 = 0$.

Let $u = t^{\frac{1}{5}}$. Then solve the equation found by substituting u for $t^{\frac{1}{5}}$.

$$u^2 - u - 2 = 0$$
$$(u - 2)(u + 1) = 0$$

$$u = 2 \text{ or } u = -1$$

$t^{\frac{1}{5}} = 2$ or $t^{\frac{1}{5}} = -1$ Substituting $t^{\frac{1}{5}}$ for u

$t = 32$ or $t = -1$ Principle of powers; raising to the 5th power

The numbers 32 and -1 check and are the solutions.

TRY THIS Solve.

4. $t^{\frac{2}{3}} - 3t^{\frac{1}{3}} - 10 = 0$ 125, −8

$\boxed{8\text{--}4}$

Exercises

Solve.

1. 81, 1
2. $\frac{1}{4}$, 16
3. $\pm\sqrt{5}$
4. $\pm\sqrt{2}$, ±1
5. −27, 8
6. 64, −8
7. 16
8. 729
9. 7, −1, 5, 1
10. 1
11. 4, 1, 6, −1

12. $-\frac{3}{2}$, 1, $\frac{1}{2}$, −1
13. $\pm\sqrt{2+\sqrt{6}}$, $\pm\sqrt{2-\sqrt{6}}$
14. $\pm\sqrt{\frac{5+\sqrt{5}}{2}}$, $\pm\sqrt{\frac{5-\sqrt{5}}{2}}$
15. $\frac{1}{3}$, $-\frac{1}{2}$
16. $\frac{4}{5}$, −1
17. 2, −1
18. $-\frac{1}{10}$, 1

1. $x - 10\sqrt{x} + 9 = 0$

2. $2x - 9\sqrt{x} + 4 = 0$

3. $x^4 - 10x^2 + 25 = 0$

4. $x^4 - 3x^2 + 2 = 0$

5. $t^{\frac{2}{3}} + t^{\frac{1}{3}} - 6 = 0$

6. $w^{\frac{2}{3}} - 2w^{\frac{1}{3}} - 8 = 0$

7. $z^{\frac{1}{2}} - z^{\frac{1}{4}} - 2 = 0$

8. $m^{\frac{1}{3}} - m^{\frac{1}{6}} - 6 = 0$

9. $(x^2 - 6x)^2 - 2(x^2 - 6x) - 35 = 0$

10. $(1 + \sqrt{x})^2 + (1 + \sqrt{x}) - 6 = 0$

11. $(y^2 - 5y)^2 - 2(y^2 - 5y) - 24 = 0$

12. $(2t^2 + t)^2 - 4(2t^2 + t) + 3 = 0$

13. $w^4 - 4w^2 - 2 = 0$

14. $t^4 - 5t^2 + 5 = 0$

15. $x^{-2} - x^{-1} - 6 = 0$

16. $4x^{-2} - x^{-1} - 5 = 0$

17. $2x^{-2} + x^{-1} - 1 = 0$

18. $m^{-2} + 9m^{-1} - 10 = 0$

Extension

Use a calculator to solve. Check possible solutions by substituting into the original equation.

19. $6.75x - 35\sqrt{x} - 5.36 = 0$ 28.5

20. $\pi x^4 - \pi^2 x^2 - \sqrt{99.3} = 0$ ±2.0

Solve.   22. $\frac{9 \pm \sqrt{89}}{2}$, $-1 \pm \sqrt{3}$ 23. $\frac{5 \pm \sqrt{21}}{2}$, $\frac{3 \pm \sqrt{5}}{2}$

21. $\left(\frac{x^2 - 1}{x}\right)^2 - \left(\frac{x^2 - 1}{x}\right) - 2 = 0$ $1 \pm \sqrt{2}$

22. $\left(\frac{x^2 - 2}{x}\right)^2 - 7\left(\frac{x^2 - 2}{x}\right) - 18 = 0$

23. $\left(\frac{x^2 + 1}{x}\right)^2 - 8\left(\frac{x^2 + 1}{x}\right) + 15 = 0$

24. $\frac{x}{x - 1} - 6\sqrt{\frac{x}{x - 1}} - 40 = 0$ $\frac{100}{99}$

25. $\left(\frac{x + 1}{x - 1}\right)^2 + \left(\frac{x + 1}{x - 1}\right) - 2 = 0$ $\frac{1}{3}$

26. $5\left(\frac{x + 2}{x - 2}\right)^2 - 3\left(\frac{x + 2}{x - 2}\right) - 2 = 0$ $-\frac{6}{7}$

Challenge

Solve.

27. $9x^{\frac{3}{2}} - 8 = x^3$ 1, 4

28. $\sqrt[3]{2x + 3} = \sqrt[6]{2x + 3}$ $-\frac{3}{2}$, −1

29. $\sqrt{x - 3} - \sqrt[4]{x - 3} = 2$ 19

30. $a^3 - 26a^{\frac{3}{2}} - 27 = 0$ 9

31. $\frac{2x + 1}{x} = 3 + 7\sqrt{\frac{2x + 1}{x}}$ $\frac{2}{51 + 7\sqrt{61}}$ or $\frac{7\sqrt{61} - 51}{194}$

364 CHAPTER 8 QUADRATIC EQUATIONS

8-5 Formulas and Problems

Formulas

To solve a formula for a given variable, we try to get the variable alone on one side of the equation. When square roots appear, we can usually get rid of the radical signs by squaring both sides.

EXAMPLE 1

Solve $T = 2\pi\sqrt{\dfrac{m}{g}}$, for m.

$$T^2 = \left(2\pi\sqrt{\dfrac{m}{g}}\right)^2 \quad \text{Squaring both sides}$$

$$T^2 = 4\pi^2 \cdot \dfrac{m}{g}$$

$$gT^2 = 4\pi^2 m \quad \text{Clearing of fractions}$$

$$\dfrac{gT^2}{4\pi^2} = m \quad \text{Multiplying by } \dfrac{1}{4\pi^2}$$

In most formulas the variables represent nonnegative numbers, so absolute values are not needed when taking principal square roots.

EXAMPLE 2

Solve $c^2 = a^2 + b^2$, for c.

$$c = \sqrt{a^2 + b^2} \quad \text{Taking square root}$$

EXAMPLE 3

Solve $h = v_0 t + 16t^2$, for t.

$$16t^2 + v_0 t - h = 0 \quad \text{Finding standard form}$$

$$a = 16,\, b = v_0,\, c = -h$$

$$t = \dfrac{-b \pm \sqrt{b^2 - 4ac}}{2a}$$

$$t = \dfrac{-v_0 \pm \sqrt{v_0^2 - 4 \cdot 16 \cdot (-h)}}{2 \cdot 16} \quad \text{Substituting into the quadratic formula}$$

$$t = \dfrac{-v_0 \pm \sqrt{v_0^2 + 64h}}{32}$$

We choose the plus sign,

$$\dfrac{-v_0 + \sqrt{v_0^2 + 64h}}{32},$$

because the negative square root would give a negative answer.

TRY THIS Solve for the indicated letter.

1. $A = \sqrt{\dfrac{w_1}{w_2}}; w_2$ **2.** $V = \pi r^2 h; r$ **3.** $Ls^2 - Rs = C; s$

1. $w_2 = \dfrac{w_1}{A^2}$

2. $r = \sqrt{\dfrac{V}{\pi h}}$

3. $s = \dfrac{R \pm \sqrt{R^2 + 4LC}}{2L}$

Problems

When an object is dropped or thrown downward, the distance, in meters, that it falls in t seconds is given by

$$s = 4.9t^2 + v_0 t.$$

In this formula v_0 is the initial velocity.

EXAMPLE 4

a. An object is dropped from the top of the Gateway Arch in St. Louis, which is 195 meters high. How long does it take to reach the ground?

Since the object was dropped, its initial velocity was 0. So we substitute 0 for v_0 and 195 for s and then solve for t.

$$195 = 4.9t^2 + 0 \cdot t$$
$$195 = 4.9t^2$$
$$t^2 \approx 39.8$$
$$t \approx \sqrt{39.8} \quad \text{We take the positive square root because } t$$
$$t \approx 6.31 \quad \text{cannot be negative.}$$

Thus it takes about 6.31 seconds to reach the ground.

b. An object is thrown downward from the top of the arch at an initial velocity of 16 meters per second (m/s). How long does it take to reach the ground?

We substitute 195 for s and 16 for v_0 and solve for t.

$$195 = 4.9t^2 + 16t$$
$$0 = 4.9t^2 + 16t - 195$$

By the quadratic formula we obtain $t = -8.15$ or $t = 4.88$. The negative answer is meaningless in this problem, so the answer is 4.88 seconds.

c. How far will an object fall in 3 seconds if it is thrown downward from the top of the arch at an initial velocity of 16 m/s?

We substitute 16 for v_0 and 3 for t and solve for s.

$$s = 4.9t^2 + v_0 t$$
$$= 4.9(3)^2 + 16 \cdot 3 = 92.1$$

Thus the object falls 92.1 meters in 3 seconds.

TRY THIS Solve.

4. **a.** An object is dropped from the top of the Statue of Liberty, which is 92 meters high. How long does it take to reach the ground? 4.33 s

   b. An object is thrown downward from the top of the statue at an initial velocity of 40 m/s. How long does it take to reach the ground? 1.87 s

   c. How far will an object fall in 1 second, thrown downward from the top of the statue at an initial velocity of 40 m/s? 44.9 m

---

8–5	

Exercises

Solve for the indicated letter.

1. $P = 4s^2$; s

2. $A = \pi r^2$; r

3. $F = \dfrac{Gm_1m_2}{r^2}$; r

4. $K = \dfrac{Qab}{t^2}$; t

5. $T = 4\pi\sqrt{\dfrac{L}{g}}$; L

6. $\sqrt{\dfrac{E}{m}} = c$; E

7. $x^2 + y^2 = r^2$; r

8. $a^2 + b^2 = h^2$; h

9. $x^2 + y^2 + z^2 = d^2$; z

10. $a^2 + b^2 + c^2 = t^2$; b

11. $h = v_0 t - 16t^2$; t

12. $A = \pi rs + \pi r^2$; r

13. $S = \frac{1}{2}gt^2$; t

14. $h = \dfrac{V^2}{2g}$; V

15. $A = 2\pi r^2 + 2\pi rh$; r

16. $h = 2v_0 + 10t^2$; t

17. $\sqrt{2}t^2 + 3k = \pi t$; t

18. $\sqrt{3}t^2 - 4\pi = 0.2t$; t

Solve. Use the formula $s = 4.9t^2 + v_0 t$.

19. **a.** An object is dropped 75 m from an airplane. How long does it take to reach the ground? 3.91 s

   b. An object is thrown downward 75 m from the plane at an initial velocity of 30 m/s. How long does it take to reach the ground? 1.91 s

   c. How far will an object fall in 2 seconds, thrown downward at an initial velocity of 30 m/s? 79.6 m

20. **a.** An object is dropped 500 m from an airplane. How long does it take to reach the ground? 10.10 s

   b. An object is thrown downward 500 m from the plane at an initial velocity of 30 m/s. How long does it take to reach the ground? 7.49 s

   c. How far will an object fall in 5 seconds, thrown downward at an initial velocity of 30 m/s? 272.5 m

Answers (right margin):

1. $s = \dfrac{\sqrt{P}}{2}$

2. $r = \sqrt{\dfrac{A}{\pi}}$

3. $r = \sqrt{\dfrac{Gm_1m_2}{F}}$

4. $t = \sqrt{\dfrac{Qab}{K}}$

5. $L = \dfrac{gT^2}{16\pi^2}$

6. $E = mc^2$

7. $r = \sqrt{x^2 + y^2}$

8. $h = \sqrt{a^2 + b^2}$

9. $z = \sqrt{d^2 - x^2 - y^2}$

10. $b = \sqrt{t^2 - a^2 - c^2}$

11. $t = \dfrac{v_0 \pm \sqrt{v_0^2 - 64h}}{32}$

12. $r = \dfrac{-\pi s + \sqrt{\pi^2 s^2 + 4\pi A}}{2\pi}$

13. $t = \sqrt{\dfrac{2S}{g}}$

14. $V = \sqrt{2gh}$

15. $r = \dfrac{-\pi h + \sqrt{\pi^2 h^2 + 2\pi A}}{2\pi}$

16. $t = \sqrt{\dfrac{h - 2V_0}{10}}$

17. $t = \dfrac{\pi \pm \sqrt{\pi^2 - 12k\sqrt{2}}}{2\sqrt{2}}$

18. $t = \dfrac{0.2 \pm \sqrt{0.04 + 16\pi\sqrt{3}}}{2\sqrt{3}}$

21. An amount of money P is invested at interest rate r. In t years it will grow to the amount A given by $A = P(1 + r)^t$, where interest is compounded annually. For the following situations, find the interest rate if interest is compounded annually.
    a. $2560 grows to $3610 in 2 years 18.75%
    b. $1000 grows to $1210 in 2 years 10%
    c. $8000 grows to $9856.80 in 2 years (Use a calculator.) 11%
    d. $1000 grows to $1271.26 in 2 years (Use a calculator.) 12.75%

22. A ladder 10 ft long leans against a wall. The bottom of the ladder is 6 ft from the wall. How much would the lower end of the ladder have to be pulled away so that the top end would be pulled down the same amount? 2 ft

23. A ladder 13 ft long leans against a wall. The bottom of the ladder is 5 ft from the wall. How much would the lower end of the ladder have to be pulled away so that the top end would be pulled down the same amount? 7 ft

24. The area of a triangle is 18 cm^2. The base is 3 cm longer than the height. Find the height. 4.685 cm

25. A baseball diamond is a square 90 ft on a side. How far is it directly from second base to home? $90\sqrt{2} \approx 127.28$ ft

26. Trains A and B leave the same city at right angles at the same time. Train B travels 5 mi/h faster than train A. After 2 hr they are 50 mi apart. Find the speed of each train. A: 15 mi/h; B: 20 mi/h

27. Trains A and B leave the same city at right angles at the same time. Train A travels 14 km/h faster than train B. After 5 hr they are 130 km apart. Find the speed of each train. A: 24 km/h; B: 10 km/h

28. The diagonal of a square is 1.341 cm longer than a side. Use a calculator to find the length of the side. 3.237 cm

29. The hypotenuse of a right triangle is 8.312 cm long. The sum of the lengths of the legs is 10.23 cm. Use a calculator to find the lengths of the legs. 2.2199 cm; 8.0101 cm

Extension

Solve for the indicated letter.

30. $m = \dfrac{m_0}{\sqrt{1 - \dfrac{v^2}{c^2}}}$; v 31. $T = \sqrt{\dfrac{a^2 + b^2}{a^2}}$; a

Solve for x.

32. $kx^2 + (3 - 2k)x - 6 = 0$ 33. $x^2 - 2x + kx + 1 = kx^2$

34. $(m + n)^2 x^2 + (m + n)x = 2$ 35. Solve $x^2 - 3xy - 4y^2 = 0$
　　　　　　　　　　　　　　　　　　　　a. for x.　　b. for y.

36. For interest compounded annually, use a calculator to find the interest rate when $9826 grows to $13,704 in 3 years. 11.7%

For Exercises 37 and 38 use the formula $T = c \cdot N$, where T is the total cost, c is the cost per item or cost per person, and N is the number of items or number of persons.

37. A group of students share equally in the $140 cost of a boat. At the last minute 3 students drop out and this raises the share of each remaining student $15. How many students were in the group at the outset? 7

38. An investor bought a group of lots for $8400. All but 4 of them were sold for $8400. The selling price for each lot was $350 greater than the cost. How many lots were bought? 12

Challenge

39. A rectangle of 12-cm^2 area is inscribed in the right triangle ABC as shown in the drawing. What are its dimensions? 3 cm × 4 cm

40. The world record for free-fall to earth without a parachute by a woman is 175 ft and is held by Kitty O'Neill. Approximately how long did the fall take? 3.3 sec

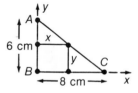

THE GOLDEN SECTION

The Parthenon, which sits on top of a hill overlooking Athens, Greece, is one of the most beautiful buildings ever constructed. The ratio of the width to the height of the Parthenon is especially pleasing to the eye. The Greeks called this ratio the Golden Section and they obtained it by dividing a line segment into two parts. The ratio of the lesser part to the greater part equals the ratio of the greater part to the whole length.

$$\frac{1 - x}{x} = \frac{x}{1} \text{ or } x^2 + x - 1 = 0$$

Solving for x gives a value of 0.618 for the Golden Section.

8–6 Quadratic Variation

Direct Variation

Recall from Chapter 6 that the equation

$$y = kx$$

where k is a constant, expresses a relation between x and y called direct variation. We say that y varies directly as x.

We now consider variation when the equations involved are of second degree, or higher.

DEFINITION

y varies directly as the square of x if there is some positive number k such that $y = kx^2$.

Consider the equation for the area of a circle.

$$a = \pi r^2$$

It shows that the area varies directly as the square of the radius and π is the variation constant.

EXAMPLE 1
Find an equation of variation where y varies directly as the square of x, and $y = 12$ when $x = 2$.

We write an equation of variation and find k.

$$y = kx^2$$
$$12 = k \cdot 2^2 \quad \text{Substituting}$$
$$3 = k \quad \text{Solving for } k$$

Now we write an equation.
$$y = 3x^2 \quad \text{Substituting for } k \text{ in the original equation}$$

TRY THIS

1. Find an equation of variation where y varies directly as the square of x and $y = 175$ when $x = 5$. $y = 7x^2$

Inverse and Joint Variation

DEFINITION

y *varies inversely* as the square of x if there is some positive number k such that $y = \frac{k}{x^2}$.

From the law of gravity, we know that the weight W of an object varies inversely as the square of the distance d from the center of the earth.

$$W = \frac{k}{d^2}$$

EXAMPLE 2

Find an equation of variation where W varies inversely as the square of d, and $W = 3$ when $d = 5$.

$W = \frac{k}{d^2}$, so $3 = \frac{k}{5^2}$ and $75 = k$. Solving for k

Thus $W = \frac{75}{d^2}$.   Substituting for k in the original equation

TRY THIS

2. Find an equation of variation where y varies inversely as the square of x, and $y = \frac{1}{4}$ when $x = 6$. $y = \frac{9}{x^2}$

Consider the equation for the area A of a triangle with height h and base b.

$$A = \frac{1}{2}bh$$

We say that the area varies jointly as the height and the base.

DEFINITION

y *varies jointly* as x and z if there is some positive number k such that $y = kxz$.

EXAMPLE 3

Find an equation of variation where y varies jointly as x and z, and $y = 42$ when $x = 2$ and $z = 3$.

$y = kxz$, so $42 = k \cdot 2 \cdot 3$ and $7 = k$.   Solving for k

Thus $y = 7xz$.   Substituting for k in the original equation

TRY THIS

3. Find an equation of variation where y varies jointly as x and z, and $y = 65$ when $x = 10$ and $z = 13$. $y = \frac{1}{2}xz$

The following equation asserts that y varies jointly as x and the cube of z, and inversely as w. Note that all these values are factors. There is no addition in the equation.

$$y = k \cdot \frac{xz^3}{w}$$

EXAMPLE 4

Find an equation of variation where y varies jointly as x and z and inversely as the square of w, and $y = 105$ when $x = 3$, $z = 20$ and $w = 2$.

$y = k \cdot \frac{xz}{w^2}$, so $105 = k \cdot \frac{3 \cdot 20}{2^2}$ and $k = 7$.

Thus $y = 7 \cdot \frac{xz}{w^2}$.

TRY THIS

4. Find an equation of variation where y varies jointly as x and the square of z and inversely as w, and $y = 80$ when $x = 4$, $z = 10$, and $w = 25$. $y = \frac{5xz^2}{w}$

Solving Problems

Many problem situations can be described with equations of variation.

EXAMPLE 5

The volume of wood V in a tree varies jointly as the height h and the square of the girth g (girth is distance around). If the volume of a tree is 216 m^3 when the height is 30 m and the girth is 1.5 m, what is the height of a tree whose volume is 960 m^3 and girth is 2 m?

First find k using the first set of data. Then solve for h using the second set of data.

$$V = khg^2$$
$$216 = k \cdot 30 \cdot 1.5^2$$
$$3.2 = k \qquad \text{Solving for } k$$

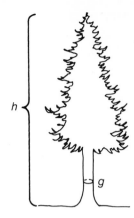

Then

$$960 = 3.2 \cdot h \cdot 2^2 \quad \text{Using 3.2 for } k \text{ to solve for } h$$
$$75 = h$$

Proportions can be used to solve variation problems. In Example 5 the volume of the two trees are proportional.

EXAMPLE 6

Use proportions to solve the problem in Example 5.

Let h_1 represent the height of the first tree and h_2 the height of the second tree.

$$\frac{V_1}{V_2} = \frac{k \cdot h_1 \cdot g_1^2}{k \cdot h_2 \cdot g_2^2}$$
$$= \frac{h_1 g_1^2}{h_2 g_2^2} \frac{k}{k} = 1$$

Now we can solve directly for the unknown height h_2 without first finding the constant of variation.

$$\frac{216}{960} = \frac{30 \cdot 1.5^2}{h_2 \cdot 2^2}$$
$$h_2 = \frac{960 \cdot 67.5}{4 \cdot 216}$$
$$h_2 = 75 \text{ m}$$

EXAMPLE 7

The intensity I of a TV signal varies inversely as the square of the distance d from the transmitter. If the intensity is 23 watts per square meter (W/m^2) at a distance of 2 km, what is the intensity at a distance of 6 km?

We use the proportion.

$$\frac{I_1}{I_2} = \frac{d_2^2}{d_1^2} \qquad I_1 = \frac{k}{d_1^2} \quad I_2 = \frac{k}{d_2^2}$$
$$\frac{I_2}{23} = \frac{2^2}{6^2}$$
$$I_2 = \frac{4 \cdot 23}{36}$$
$$I_2 = 2.56 \text{ W/m}^2 \quad \text{Rounded to the nearest hundredth}$$

TRY THIS

5. The distance s that an object falls when dropped from some point above the ground varies directly as the square of the time t it falls. If the object falls 19.6 m in 2 seconds, how far will the object fall in 10 seconds? 490 m

6. In Example 7 why is the equation not appropriate when the distance is 0 km from a transmitter whose initial signal is 316,000 W/m^2? Division by zero is undefined.

8–6

Exercises

Find an equation of variation where:

1. y varies directly as x, and $y = 0.6$ when $x = 0.4$. $y = \frac{3}{2}x$

2. y varies inversely as x, and $y = 0.4$ when $x = 0.8$. $y = \frac{0.32}{x}$

3. y varies directly as the square of x, and $y = 0.15$ when $x = 0.1$. $y = 15x^2$

4. y varies directly as the square of x, and $y = 6$ when $x = 3$. $y = \frac{2}{3}x^2$

5. y varies inversely as the square of x, and $y = 0.15$ when $x = 0.1$. $y = \frac{0.0015}{x^2}$

6. y varies inversely as the square of x, and $y = 6$ when $x = 3$. $y = \frac{54}{x^2}$

7. y varies jointly as x and z, and $y = 56$ when $x = 7$ and $z = 8$. $y = xz$

8. y varies directly as x and inversely as z, and $y = 4$ when $x = 12$ and $z = 15$. $y = \frac{5x}{z}$

9. y varies jointly as x and the square of z, and $y = 105$ when $x = 14$ and $z = 5$. $y = \frac{3}{10}xz^2$

10. y varies jointly as x and z and inversely as w, and $y = \frac{3}{2}$ when $x = 2$, $z = 3$, and $w = 4$. $y = \frac{xz}{w}$

11. y varies jointly as x and z and inversely as the product of w and p, and $y = \frac{3}{28}$ when $x = 3$, $z = 10$, $w = 7$, and $p = 8$. $y = \frac{1xz}{5wp}$

12. y varies jointly as x and z and inversely as the square of w, and $y = \frac{12}{5}$ when $x = 16$, $z = 3$, and $w = 5$. $y = \frac{5xz}{4w^2}$

Solve.

13. Stopping Distance of a Car. The stopping distance d of a car after the brakes are applied varies directly as the square of the speed r. If a car traveling 60 km/h can stop in 80 m, how many feet will it take the same car to stop when it is traveling 90 km/h? 180 m

14. Area of a Cube. The area of a cube varies directly as the square of the length of a side. If a cube has an area 168.54 m^2 when the length of a side is 5.3 m, what will the area be when the length of a side is 10.2 m? 624.24 m^2

15. Weight of an Astronaut. The weight W of an object varies inversely as the square of the distance d from the center of the earth. At sea level (6400 km from the center of the earth) an astronaut weighs 100 kg. Find the astronaut's weight in a spacecraft 200 km above the surface of the earth when the spacecraft is not in motion. 94.03 kg

16. Intensity of Light. The intensity of light l from a light bulb varies inversely as the square of the distance d from the bulb. Suppose l is 90 W/m^2 when the distance is 5 m. Find the intensity at a distance of 10 m. 22.5 W/m^2

17. Earned Run Average. A pitcher's earned run average A varies directly as the number of earned runs R allowed and inversely as the number I of innings pitched. In a recent year a pitcher had an earned run average of 2.92. He gave up 85 earned runs in 262 innings. How many earned runs would he have given up had he pitched 300 innings? Round to the nearest whole number. 97

18. Volume of a Gas. The volume V of a given mass of a gas varies directly as the temperature T and inversely as the pressure P. If $V = 231$ cm^3 when $T = 42°$ and $P = 20$ kg/cm^2, what is the volume when $T = 30°$ and $P = 15$ kg/cm^2? 220 cm^3

19. Use a calculator. The distance d that one can see to the horizon varies directly as the square root of the height above sea level. If a person 19.5 m above sea level can see 28.97 km, how high above sea level must one be to see 54.32 km? 68.56 m

Extension

20. Suppose y varies directly as x and x is doubled. What is the effect on y? y is doubled.

21. Suppose y varies inversely as x and x is tripled. What is the effect on y? y is multiplied by $\frac{1}{3}$.

22. Suppose y varies inversely as the square of x and x is multiplied by n. What is the effect on y? y is multiplied by $\frac{1}{n^2}$.

23. Suppose y varies directly as the square of x and x is multiplied by n. What is the effect on y? y is multiplied by n^2.

24. Show that if p varies directly as q, then q varies directly as p.

24. If p varies directly as q, then $p = kq$. Thus, $q = \frac{1}{k}p$, so q varies directly as p.

25. Show that if u varies inversely as v, then v varies inversely as u; and $1/u$ varies directly as v. $u = \frac{k}{v}$, so $v = \frac{k}{u}$ and $\frac{1}{u} = \frac{1}{k} \cdot v$

26. The area of a circle varies directly as the square of the length of a diameter. What is the variation constant? $\frac{\pi}{4}$

27. P varies directly as the square of t. How does t vary in relationship to P? t varies directly as $\sqrt{P}$.

Challenge

28. The Gravity Model in Sociology. It has been determined that the average number of telephone calls in a day N, between two cities, is directly proportional to the populations P_1 and P_2 of the cities and inversely proportional to the square of the distance d between the cities. That is,

$$N = \frac{kP_1P_2}{d^2}.$$

Use a calculator to find solutions to these problems.

a. The population of Indianapolis is about 744,624 and the population of Cincinnati is about 452,524 and the distance between the cities is 174 km. The average number of daily phone calls between the two cities is 11,153. Find the value k and write the equation of variation. $N = \frac{0.001P_1P_2}{d^2}$

b. The population of Detroit is about 1,511,482 and it is 446 km from Indianapolis. Find the average number of daily phone calls between Detroit and Indianapolis. 5658

c. The average number of daily phone calls between Indianapolis and New York City is 4270 and the population of New York City is about 7,895,563. Find the distance between Indianapolis and New York City. 1173 km

d. Why is this model not appropriate for adjoining cities such as Minneapolis and St. Paul? (Sociologists say that as the communication between two cities increases, the cities tend to merge.) Division by zero is undefined.

DISCOVERY/Perfect Numbers

The Pythagoreans of ancient Greece said that an integer that was the sum of all its factors except itself is a *perfect number*. The number 28 is perfect because

$14 + 7 + 4 + 2 + 1 = 28.$

Can you find a perfect number between 1 and 10? 6

CHAPTER 8   Review

Review the material in the chapter. Then see how you have done by trying these review exercises. If you miss an exercise, restudy the indicated lesson.

8–1   Solve.

1. $3x^2 + 10x - 8 = 0$ 2. $4x^2 + 2 = 0$ 3. $7x^2 + 6x = 0$ $0, -\frac{6}{7}$

4. The sum of the squares of two consecutive positive integers   1. $\frac{2}{3}, -4$
   is 61. What are the integers? 5 and 6

8–2   Solve.
2. $\pm i\frac{\sqrt{2}}{2}$
5. $-2 \pm \sqrt{11}$
7. $-1 \pm i\sqrt{3}$
16. $h = \frac{v^2}{29}$

5. $x^2 + 4x - 7 = 0$ 6. $x^2 + 3x - 5 = 0$ $\frac{-3 \pm \sqrt{29}}{2}$

7. $x^2 + 2x + 4 = 0$ 8. $x^2 + x + 4 = 0$ $\frac{-1 \pm i\sqrt{15}}{2}$

9. Use the square root table, Table 1, in the back of the book to approximate solutions of $x^2 - 8x + 5 = 0$ to the nearest tenth. 7.3, 0.7

8–3

10. Determine the nature of the solutions of $4y^2 + 5y + 1 = 0$. Two real solutions

11. Without solving, find the sum and product of the solutions of
    $5s^2 - 4s + 2 = 0$. Sum = $\frac{4}{5}$; product = $\frac{2}{5}$

12. Find a quadratic equation for which the sum of the solution is $-\frac{1}{2}$ and the product of the solutions is $\frac{3}{5}$. $10x^2 + 5x + 6 = 0$

13. Find a quadratic equation whose solutions are -3 and $-\frac{1}{2}$. $2x^2 + 7x + 3 = 0$

8–4   Solve.

14. $y^4 - 2y^2 + 1 = 0$ ± 1 15. $(x^2 + 1)^2 - 15(x^2 + 1) + 50 = 0$ $\pm 3, \pm 2$

8–5

16. Solve $v = \sqrt{2gh}$ for h.   17. Solve $A^2 + a^2 = 1$ for A. $A = \sqrt{1 - a^2}$

18. From a height of 200 m, an object is thrown downward at an initial velocity of 20 m/s. How long does it take to reach the ground? Round to the nearest hundredth. Use $s = 4.9t^2 + v_0 t$. 4.67 sec

8–6   Find an equation where:

19. y varies directly as the square of x, and $y = 2$ when $x = 3$. $y = \frac{2}{9}x^2$

Chapter 8 Review   **377**

20. y varies directly as the square of x, and $y = 0.1$ when $x = 0.2$. $y = 2.5x^2$

21. y varies inversely as the square of x, and $y = 0.5$ when $x = 2$. $y = \frac{2}{x^2}$

22. y varies inversely as the square of x, and $y = -0.1$ when $x = 10$. $y = \frac{-10}{x^2}$

8–6 Solve.

23. The area of a sphere varies directly as the square of its radius. If the area is 1257 m^2 when the radius is 10 m, what is the area when the radius is 3 m? 113.13 m²

CHAPTER 8 Test

Solve.

1. $x^2 - 6x + 5 = 0$ 1, 5
2. $16x^2 + 9 = 0$ $\pm\frac{3}{4}i$
3. $5x^2 + 8x = 0$ $0, -\frac{8}{5}$
4. $\frac{2}{5}, -3$
9. $\pm 1, \pm 2$
4. $5x^2 + 13x - 6 = 0$
5. $2x^2 - x - 1 = 0$ $1, -\frac{1}{2}$

6. Determine the nature of the solutions of $t^2 - 12t + 12 = 0$. Two real solutions

7. Without solving, find the sum and product of the solutions of $6y^2 + 8y - 7$. $-\frac{4}{3}, -\frac{7}{6}$

8. Find a quadratic equation whose solutions are $3 + \sqrt{2}$ and $3 - \sqrt{2}$. $x^2 - 6x + 7 = 0$

Solve.

9. $x^4 - 5x^2 + 4 = 0$
10. $u + \sqrt{u} - 6 = 0$ 4
11. Solve $A^2 + a^2 = 1$ for A. $A = \sqrt{1 - a^2}$

Find an equation where:

12. y varies directly as the square of x, and $y = 4$ when $x = 2$. $y = 2x$

13. y varies inversely as the square of x, and $y = \frac{1}{3}$ when $x = 3$. $y = \frac{1}{x}$

Solve.

14. The distance s that an object falls when dropped from some point above the ground varies directly as the square of the time t it falls. If the object falls 14.7 m in 3 seconds, how far will it fall in 5 seconds? Use $s = 4.9t^2 + v_0 t$. 245 m

Challenge

15. Solve $(3x^2 - x)(x^2 + 7x - 15) = 0$. $0, \frac{1}{3}, \frac{7 \pm \sqrt{109}}{2}$

Ready for Quadratic Functions?

3–2 Graph.

1. $2y = \frac{1}{3}x - 1$ **2.** $y = -2x + 3$

3–3 Tell whether or not each graph is the graph of a function.

3. No

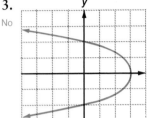

4. Yes

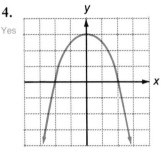

5. Yes

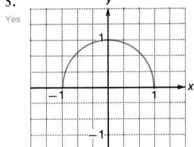

3–4 Find the x- and y-intercepts of each.

6. $2x - 5y = 10$ **7.** $3x + y = 6$ (2, 0), (0, 6)

8. $-4x + 3y = 12$ **9.** $-x + 2y = 4$ (−4, 0), (0, 2)

10. $3x + 5y = 10$ **11.** $x - 7y = 4$ (4, 0), $\left(0, -\frac{4}{7}\right)$

5–5 Factor by completing the square.

12. $x^2 - 8x + 12$ (x − 2)(x − 6)

13. $x^2 - 3x - 4$ (x − 4)(x + 1)

14. $x^2 - 6x + 8$ (x − 4)(x − 2)

15. $x^2 - 4x - 5$ (x − 5)(x + 1)

16. $x^2 - 2x - 24$ (x − 6)(x + 4)

17. $x^2 - x - 6$ (x − 3)(x + 2)

9

CHAPTER NINE

Quadratic Functions

9-1 Symmetry

In this chapter we consider how changes in the equation $y = f(x)$ affect the graph of the function. Then we use this information to graph quadratic functions, $y = f(x) = ax^2 + bx + c$, $a \neq 0$.

Symmetry with Respect to the Axes

Points P and P_1 are symmetric with respect to line ℓ.

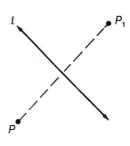

DEFINITION

Two points P and P_1 are *symmetric with respect to a line ℓ* when they are the same distance from ℓ, measured along a perpendicular to ℓ. Line ℓ is known as a *line* or *axis of symmetry*. P_1 is said to be the *image* of P. A figure, or set of points, is symmetric with respect to a line when the image of each point in the set is also in the set.

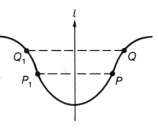

We say that two points symmetric with respect to a line are reflections of each other across the line. The line is known as a line of reflection.

The figure at the right is symmetric with respect to line ℓ. Imagine picking this figure up and flipping it over. Points P and P_1 would be interchanged. Points Q and Q_1 would be interchanged. These are pairs of symmetric points. The entire figure would look exactly like it did before flipping.

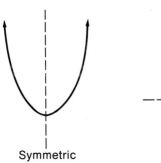

Symmetric

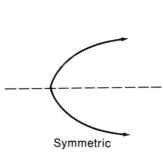

Symmetric

Not symmetric

There are special and interesting kinds of symmetry in which the x-axis or the y-axis is a line of symmetry.

> ## THEOREM 9–1
>
> Two points are symmetric with respect to the x-axis if and only if their y-coordinates are additive inverses and they have the same x-coordinate. Two points are symmetric with respect to the y-axis if and only if their x-coordinates are additive inverses and they have the same y-coordinate.

EXAMPLE 1

Plot the point $(2, -5)$ and the point symmetric to it with respect to the x-axis.

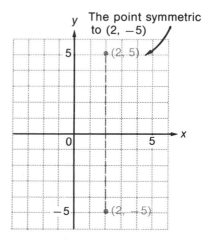

TRY THIS

1. Plot the point $(4, -2)$ and the point symmetric to it with respect to the y-axis.

EXAMPLE 2

In the relation $y = x^2$ there are points $(2, 4)$ and $(-2, 4)$. The first coordinates, 2 and -2, are additive inverses of each other, while the second coordinates are the same. For every point of the relation (x, y), there is another point $(-x, y)$. So the relation $y = x^2$ is symmetric with respect to the y-axis.

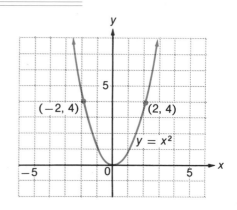

382 CHAPTER 9 QUADRATIC FUNCTIONS

THEOREM 9–2

When a relation is defined by an equation,
1. its graph is symmetric with respect to the y-axis if and only if replacing x by $-x$ produces an equivalent equation.
2. its graph is symmetric with respect to the x-axis if and only if replacing y by $-y$ produces an equivalent equation.

We thus have a means of testing a relation for symmetry with respect to the x- and y-axes when the relation is defined by an equation.

EXAMPLE 3

Test $y = x^2 + 2$ for symmetry with respect to the axes.

We replace x by $-x$, and obtain $y = (-x)^2 + 2$, which is equivalent to $y = x^2 + 2$. Therefore the graph is symmetric with respect to the y-axis.

We replace y by $-y$ and obtain $-y = x^2 + 2$, which is not equivalent to $y = x^2 + 2$. Therefore the graph is not symmetric with respect to the x-axis.

TRY THIS Test for symmetry with respect to the x-axis and y-axis.

2. $y = x^2 + 3$ **3.** $x^2 + y^2 = 2$ 2. Symmetric with respect to y-axis
3. Symmetric with respect to both axes

Symmetry with Respect to the Origin

We now define symmetry with respect to a point.

DEFINITION

Two points P and P_1 are *symmetric with respect to a point Q* when they are the same distance from Q, and all three points are on a line. P_1 is said to be the *image* of P. A figure or set of points is symmetric with respect to a point when the image of each point in the set is also in the set.

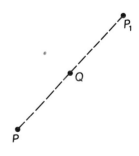

The figure at the right is symmetric with respect to point O. Imagine sticking a pin in this figure at O and then rotating the figure 180°. Points P and P_1 would be interchanged. Points Q and Q_1 would be interchanged. These are pairs of symmetric points. The entire figure would look exactly as it did before rotating. This means that the image of each point of the figure is also on the figure.

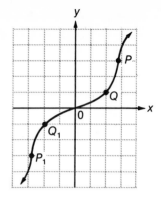

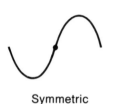
Symmetric

Symmetric

Not symmetric

A special kind of symmetry with respect to a point is symmetry with respect to the origin.

THEOREM 9–3

Two points are symmetric with respect to the origin if and only if both their x and y coordinates are additive inverses of each other.

EXAMPLE 4

Plot the point $(3, 5)$ and the point symmetric to it with respect to the origin.

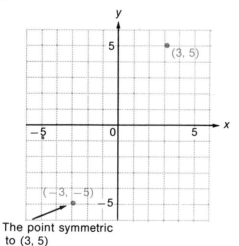

The point symmetric to $(3, 5)$

TRY THIS

4. Plot the point $(4, -2)$ and the point symmetric to it with respect to the origin.

THEOREM 9–4

A graph of a relation defined by an equation is symmetric with respect to the origin if and only if replacing x by $-x$ and replacing y by $-y$ produces an equivalent equation.

This gives us a means for testing a relation for symmetry with respect to the origin, when it is defined by an equation.

EXAMPLE 5

Test $x^2 = y^2 + 2$ for symmetry with respect to the origin.

We replace x by $-x$ and y by $-y$, and obtain $(-x)^2 = (-y)^2 + 2$, which is equivalent to $x^2 = y^2 + 2$, the original equation. Therefore the graph is symmetric with respect to the origin.

TRY THIS Test each equation for symmetry with respect to the origin.

5. $y^2 + x^2 = 16$ Yes 6. $y = x^3$ Yes

7. $y = x^2$ No   8. $\frac{1}{2}y^2 + x = \frac{3}{4}$ No

Even and Odd Functions

If the graph of a function is symmetric with respect to the y-axis, it is an even function. If we have an even function given by $y = f(x)$, then $y = f(-x)$ will give the same function.

DEFINITION

A function is an *even function* when $f(x) = f(-x)$ for all x in the domain of f.

If the graph of a function is symmetric with respect to the origin, it is an odd function. If we have an odd function given by $y = f(x)$, then $-y = f(-x)$.

DEFINITION

A function is an *odd function* when $f(-x) = -f(x)$ for all x in the domain of f.

EXAMPLE 6
Determine whether $f(x) = x^2 + 1$ is even, odd, or neither.

Find $f(-x)$ and $-f(x)$ and simplify.
$$f(-x) = (-x)^2 + 1 = x^2 + 1$$
$$-f(x) = -(x^2 + 1) = -x^2 - 1$$

Compare $f(-x)$ and $-f(x)$. They are not the same for all x in the domain, so f is not odd.

Compare $f(x)$ and $f(-x)$. They are the same for all x in the domain, so f is an even function.

TRY THIS Determine whether each function is even, odd, or neither.

9. $f(x) = x^4 - x^6$ 10. $f(x) = 3x^2 + 3x^5$ 11. $f(x) = x^3 + x$

9. Even
10. Neither
11. Odd

9–1

Exercises
For each of the following figures, determine whether it is symmetric with respect to the given line and then determine whether it is symmetric with respect to the given point.

1. Yes; no

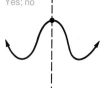

2. Yes; no

3. No; no

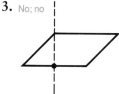

4.  No; yes   **5.** 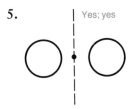 Yes; yes   **6.** 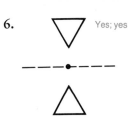 Yes; yes

Use graph paper for Exercises 7–10.

7. Plot $(3, -7)$ and the point symmetric to it with respect to the x-axis. List the coordinates of that point.

8. Plot $(-5, 2)$ and the point symmetric to it with respect to the x-axis. List the coordinates of that point.

9. Plot $(-4, 3)$ and the point symmetric to it with respect to the y-axis. List the coordinates of that point.

10. Plot $(1, -6)$ and the point symmetric to it with respect to the y-axis. List the coordinates of that point.

Test for symmetry with respect to the x-axis and the y-axis.

11. $3y = x^2 + 4$
12. $5y = 2x^2 - 3$
13. $2x^4 + 3 = y^2$
14. $3y^2 = 2x^4 - 5$
15. $2x - 5 = 3y$
16. $5y = 4x + 5$
17. $y^3 = 2x^2$
18. $3y^3 = 4x^2$
19. $2y^2 = 5x^2 + 12$
20. $3x^2 - 2y^2 = 7$
21. $3y^3 = 4y^3 + 2$
22. $x^3 - 4y^3 = 12$

11. y-axis
12. y-axis
13. Both axes
14. Both axes
15. Neither axis
16. Neither axis
17. y-axis
18. y-axis
19. Both axes
20. Both axes
21. Neither axis
22. Neither axis

Use graph paper for Exercises 23–26.

23. Plot the point $(2, -4)$ and the point symmetric to it with respect to the origin.

24. Plot the point $(4, 3)$ and the point symmetric to it with respect to the origin.

25. Plot the point $(-3, 6)$ and the point symmetric to it with respect to the origin.

26. Plot the point $(-4, -3)$ and the point symmetric to it with respect to the origin.

Test for symmetry with respect to the origin.

27. $3x^2 - 2y^2 = 3$ Yes
28. $5y^2 = -7x^2 + 4$ Yes
29. $3x + 3y = 0$ Yes
30. $7x = -7y$ Yes
31. $5x - 5y = 0$ Yes
32. $3x = 3y$ Yes
33. $3x = \dfrac{5}{y}$ Yes
34. $3y = \dfrac{7}{x}$ Yes
35. $3x^2 + 4x = 2y$ No
36. $5y = 7x^2 - 2x$ No
37. $y = |2x|$ No
38. $3x = |y|$ No

Determine whether each function is even, odd, or neither.

39. $f(x) = 2x^2 + 4x$
40. $f(x) = -3x^3 + 2x$ Odd
41. $f(x) = 3x^4 - 4x^2$ Even   39. Neither
42. $f(x) = 4x$ Odd
43. $f(x) = |3x|$ Even
44. $f(x) = x^{24}$ Even

45. $f(x) = x + \dfrac{1}{x}$ Odd   **46.** $f(x) = x - |x|$ Neither   **47.** $f(x) = \sqrt{x}$ Neither

48. $f(x) = \sqrt[3]{x}$ Odd   **49.** $f(x) = 7$ Even   **50.** $f(x) = 0$ Even and odd

For each function, tell whether it is even, odd, or neither.

51. Even
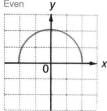

52. Even
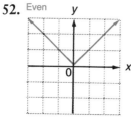

53. Even
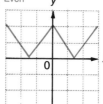

54. Even
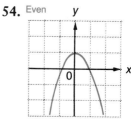

55. Odd
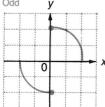

56. Neither
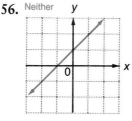

57. Odd
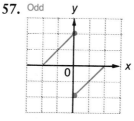

58. Neither
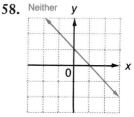

Extension

On a coordinate grid draw the quadrilateral with vertices $(0, 4)$, $(4, 4)$, $(-2, -2)$, and $(1, -2)$.

59. Graph the reflection across the x-axis.

60. Graph the reflection across the y-axis.

61. Graph the figure formed by reflecting each point through the origin.

Challenge

Test for symmetry with respect to the x-axis and the y-axis.

62. $y = |x|$ **63.** $|x| = |y|$ **64.** $y = |x| + 1$

65. $y = |x| - 3$ **66.** $|x| + |y| = 3$ **67.** $|x| - |y| = 5$

62. y-axis
63. Both axes
64. y-axis
65. y-axis
66. Both axes
67. Both axes

FAMILIES OF EQUATIONS

A *family* of equations have one or more property or characteristic in common. For example, $y = ax + 5$ represents a family of lines that all have the y-intercept 5. The equation

$y = a(x - 1)^2$ is a family of parabolas with the same vertex, $(1, 0)$, and the same axis of symmetry, $x = 1$. You will learn about parabolas in Section 9–4.

9-2 Transformations

An alteration of a relation is called a transformation. If such an alteration consists merely of moving the graph without changing its shape and without rotating it, the transformation is called a translation

Vertical Translations

Consider the following relations.

$$y = x^2$$
$$y = 1 + x^2$$

The graphs of these relations are shown at the right.

The graphs have the same shape except that $y = 1 + x^2$ is moved up a distance of 1 unit. Consider any equation $y = f(x)$ and adding a constant a to produce $y = a + f(x)$. This changes each function value by the same amount a, but produces no change in the shape of the graph. If a is positive the graph is translated upward. If a is negative the graph is translated downward.

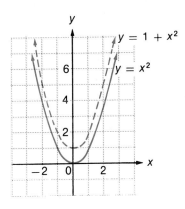

Note that the following equations are equivalent.

$$y = 1 + x^2$$
$$y - 1 = x^2$$

Thus the transformation above amounts to replacing y by $y - 1$ in the original equation.

THEOREM 9-5

In an equation of a relation, replacing y by $y - a$, where a is a constant, translates the graph vertically a distance of $|a|$. If a is positive the translation is in the positive direction (upward). If a is negative the translation is downward.

If in an equation we replace y by $y + 3$, this is the same as replacing it by $y - (-3)$. In this case the constant a is -3 and the translation is downward. If we replace y by $y - 5$, the constant a is 5 and the translation is upward.

EXAMPLE 1

Sketch the graph of $y = |x|$. Then sketch the graph of $y = -2 + |x|$ by translating it.

The graph of $y = |x|$ is shown below on the left. Note that $y = -2 + |x|$ is equivalent to $y + 2 = |x|$ or $y - (-2) = |x|$. This shows the new equation can be obtained by replacing y by $y - (-2)$, so by Theorem 9–5 the translation is downward, two units.

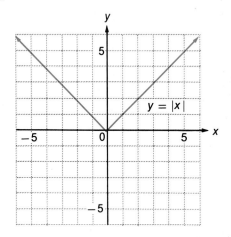
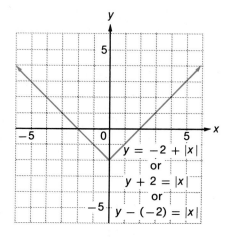

TRY THIS Consider the graph of $y = |x|$ as shown in Example 1. Sketch the graph of each of the following by translating.

1. $y = -1 + |x|$ **2.** $y = 4 + |x|$ 1. Ray from $(0, -1)$ through $(2, 1)$; ray from $(0, -1)$ through $(-2, 1)$ 2. Ray from $(0, 4)$ through $(2, 6)$; ray from $(0, 4)$ through $(-2, 6)$

Horizontal Translations

Translations can also be horizontal. If we replace x by $x - b$ everywhere it occurs in an equation, we translate a distance of $|b|$ horizontally.

THEOREM 9–6

In an equation of a relation, replacing x by $x - b$, where b is a constant, translates the graph horizontally a distance of $|b|$. If b is positive, the translation is in the positive direction (to the right). If b is negative, the translation is to the left.

EXAMPLE 2

Sketch the graph of $y = |x|$. Then sketch the graph of $y = |x + 2|$ by translating it.

Here we note that x is replaced by $x + 2$, or $x - (-2)$. Thus $b = -2$, and by Theorem 9–6 the translated graph will be moved two units in the negative direction (to the left).

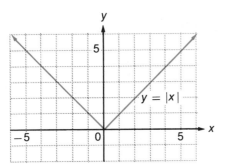
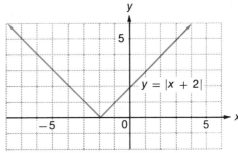

TRY THIS Consider the graph of $y = |x|$ as shown in Example 2. Sketch the graph of each of the following by translating it.

3. $y = |x + 3|$ 4. $y = |x - 1|$

3. Ray from $(-3, 0)$ through $(0, 3)$; ray from $(-3, 0)$ through $(-6, 3)$.   4. Ray from $(1, 0)$ through $(4, 3)$; ray from $(1, 0)$ through $(-2, 3)$

Relations other than functions can be translated. Theorems 9–5 and 9–6 hold for any relations. A relation may be translated both horiziontally and vertically.

9–2

Exercises

Here is a graph of $y = |x|$. Sketch graphs of the following by translating this one.

1. $y = 2 + |x|$ 2. $y = 3 + |x|$
3. $y = -2 + |x|$ 4. $y = -3 + |x|$
5. $y = 5 + |x|$ 6. $y = 6 + |x|$
7. $y = -4 + |x|$ 8. $y = -5 + |x|$
9. $y = \frac{1}{2} + |x|$ 10. $y = \frac{3}{4} + |x|$

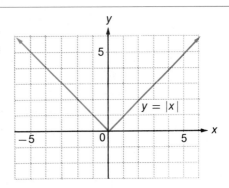

Consider the graph of $y = |x|$ as shown on page 391. Sketch graphs of the following by translating this one.

11. $y = |x - 3|$ 12. $y = |x - 2|$ 13. $y = |x + 2|$

14. $y = |x + 4|$ 15. $y = |x - 4|$ 16. $y = |x - 5|$

17. $y = |x + 5|$ 18. $y = |x + 6|$ 19. $y = \left|x - \frac{1}{2}\right|$

Extension

A circle centered at the origin with radius of length 1 has an equation $x^2 + y^2 = 1$.

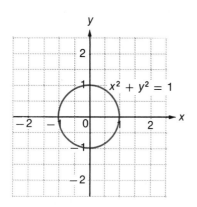

20. Sketch the graph of $(x - 1)^2 + (y + 2)^2 = 1$.

21. Consider the circle $x^2 + y^2 = 1$ centered at the origin. If we replace x by $x - 2$ and y by $y + 3$, what are the coordinates of the center of the translated circle? (2, −3)

22. Consider a circle with center at (2, 4). What are the coordinates of the center of the translated circle if we replace x with $x - 3$ and y with $y + 5$ in the equation of the circle? (5, −1)

ASTRONOMY/Halley's Comet

In 1985 you will have a chance to see a once-in-a-lifetime event, Halley's comet. Halley's comet follows a path through the solar system. Its path is near the sun at one end and near the planet Pluto at the other.

Edmund Halley was born in London, England, in 1658 and his career included work in many areas of science and mathematics. He studied the orbits of 24 different comets. Three of these were so much alike that he decided the comets of 1531, 1607, and 1682 were the same body. Halley predicted the comet would return in 1758 and on Christmas Day of that year he was proved right. The comet has since appeared in 1835 and 1910.

Stretching and Shrinking

Vertical Stretchings and Shrinkings

Compare the graphs of $y = f(x)$, $y = 2f(x)$, and $y = \frac{1}{2}f(x)$. The graph of $y = 2f(x)$ looks like that of $y = f(x)$ but is stretched in a vertical direction. The graph of $y = \frac{1}{2}f(x)$ is flattened or shrunk in a vertical direction.

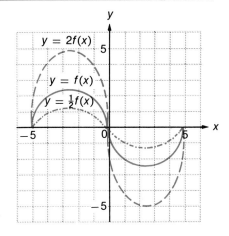

Consider any equation such as $y = f(x)$. Multiplying on the right by the constant 2 will double every function value, thus stretching the graph both ways away from the horizontal axis. A similar thing is true for any constant greater than 1.

Multiplying on the right by $\frac{1}{2}$ will halve every function value, thus shrinking the graph both ways toward the horizontal axis. A similar thing is true for any constant between 0 and 1.

Now compare the graphs of $y = f(x)$, $y = -2f(x)$, and $y = -\frac{1}{2}f(x)$.

When we multiply by a negative constant, the graph is reflected across the x-axis as well as being stretched or shrunk. Note that if we multiply by -1, this has the effect of replacing y by $-y$ and we obtain a reflection without stretching or shrinking.

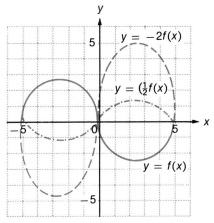

Multiplying $f(x)$ by a constant a is the same as dividing y by a. In an equation of any relation, dividing y by 2 will stretch the graph in the y-direction. Dividing y by $\frac{1}{2}$ will shrink the graph in the y-direction.

THEOREM 9-7

In an equation of a relation, dividing y by a constant does the following to the graph.
1. If $|c| > 1$, the graph is stretched vertically.
2. If $|c| < 1$, the graph is shrunk vertically.
3. If c is negative, the graph is also reflected across the x-axis.

EXAMPLE 1

Here is a graph of $y = f(x)$. Sketch a graph of $y = 2f(x)$.

$y = 2f(x)$ is equivalent to $\frac{y}{2} = f(x)$. By Theorem 9–7 the graph is stretched vertically. Every function value is doubled.

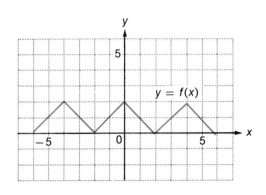
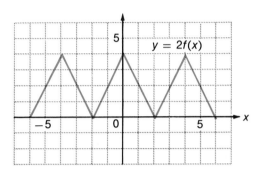

EXAMPLE 2

Here is a graph of $y = g(x)$. Sketch a graph of $y = -\frac{1}{2}g(x)$.

$y = -\frac{1}{2}g(x)$ is equivalent to $\frac{y}{-\frac{1}{2}} = g(x)$. By Theorem 9–7 the graph is shrunk in the y-direction and also reflected across the x-axis. We halve each function value and change its sign.

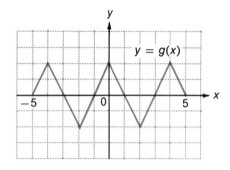
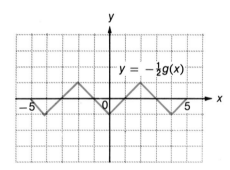

TRY THIS Consider the graph of $y = f(x)$ as shown in Example 1.

1. Sketch a graph of $y = 3f(x)$.

2. Sketch a graph of $y = \frac{1}{2}f(x)$.

3. Sketch a graph of $y = -\frac{1}{2}f(x)$.

1. Graph consists of segments from $(-6, 0)$ to $(-4, 6)$ to $(-2, 0)$ to $(0, 6)$ to $(2, 0)$ to $(4, 6)$ to $(6, 0)$ 2. Graph consists of segments from $(-6, 0)$ to $(-4, 1)$ to $(-2, 0)$ to $(0, 1)$ to $(2, 0)$ to $(4, 1)$ to $(6, 0)$ 3. Graph consists of segments from $(-6, 0)$ to $(-4, -1)$ to $(-2, 0)$ to $(-1, -1)$ to $(2, 0)$ to $(4, -1)$ to $(6, 0)$

394 CHAPTER 9   QUADRATIC FUNCTIONS

Horizontal Stretchings and Shrinkings

If we divide y by a constant, a graph is stretched or shrunk vertically. If we divide x by a constant, a graph will be stretched or shrunk horizontally.

THEOREM 9–8

In an equation of a relation, dividing x wherever it occurs by a constant d does the following to the graph.
1. If $|d| > 1$, the graph is stretched horizontally.
2. If $|d| < 1$, the graph is shrunk horizontally.
3. If d is negative, the graph is also reflected across the y-axis.

Note that if $d = -1$, this has the effect of replacing x by $-x$ and we obtain a reflection without stretching or shrinking.

EXAMPLE 3

Here is a graph of $y = f(x)$. Sketch a graph of each of the following.

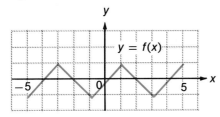

a. $f(2x) = f\left(\dfrac{x}{\frac{1}{2}}\right)$. By Theorem 9–8 the graph will be shrunk. Each x-coordinate will be halved.

b. $f(\frac{1}{2}x) = f\left(\dfrac{x}{2}\right)$. The graph will be stretched. Each x-coordinate will be doubled.

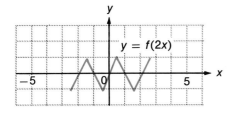

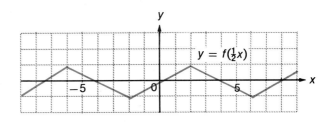

c. $f\left(-\frac{1}{2}x\right) = f\left(\frac{x}{-2}\right)$. The graph will be stretched and reflected.

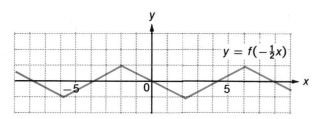

$y = f\left(-\frac{1}{2}x\right)$

4. Graph consists of segments from $(-2, 0)$ to $\left(-\frac{3}{2}, 2\right)$ to $\left(-\frac{1}{2}, -2\right)$ to $\left(\frac{1}{2}, 2\right)$ to $\left(\frac{3}{2}, -2\right)$ to $(2, 0)$ 5. Graph consists of segments from $(-8, 0)$ to $(-6, 2)$ to $(-2, -2)$ to $(2, 2)$ to $(6, -2)$ to $(8, 0)$.   6. Graphs consists of segments from $(-8, 0)$ to $(-6, -2)$ to $(-2, 2)$ to $(2, -2)$ to $(6, 2)$ to $(8, 0)$

TRY THIS Here is a graph of $y = f(x)$.

4. Sketch a graph of $y = f(2x)$.

5. Sketch a graph of $y = f\left(\frac{1}{2}x\right)$.

6. Sketch a graph of $y = f\left(-\frac{1}{2}x\right)$.

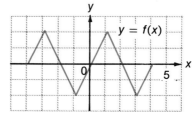

$y = f(x)$

9–3

Exercises

Here is a graph of $y = |x|$. Sketch graphs by transforming this one.

1. $y = 4|x|$
2. $y = 3|x|$
3. $y = 5|x|$

4. $y = 6|x|$
5. $y = \frac{1}{4}|x|$
6. $y = \frac{1}{3}|x|$

7. $y = -3|x|$
8. $y = -4|x|$
9. $y = -\frac{1}{4}|x|$

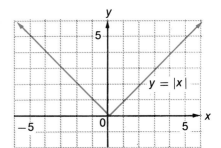

$y = |x|$

Here is a graph of $y = f(x)$. Sketch graphs by transforming this one.

10. $y = 3f(x)$
11. $y = 2f(x)$
12. $y = -2f(x)$
13. $y = -3f(x)$
14. $y = 4f(x)$
15. $y = 5f(x)$

16. $y = \frac{1}{2}f(x)$
17. $y = \frac{1}{3}f(x)$
18. $y = -\frac{1}{2}f(x)$

Consider the graph of $y = |x|$ above. Sketch graphs by transforming this one.

19. $y = |2x|$
20. $y = |3x|$
21. $y = \left|\frac{1}{2}x\right|$

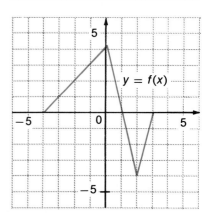

$y = f(x)$

Consider the graph of $y = f(x)$ above. Sketch graphs by transforming this one.

22. $y = f(3x)$ **23.** $y = f(2x)$ **24.** $y = f\left(\frac{1}{2}x\right)$

25. $y = f\left(\frac{1}{3}x\right)$ **26.** $y = f(-2x)$ **27.** $y = f(-3x)$

23. Graph consists of segments from $(-2, 0)$ to $(0, 4)$ to $(1, -4)$ to $\left(\frac{3}{2}, 0\right)$

24. Graph consists of segments from $(-8, 0)$ to $(0, 4)$ to $(4, -4)$ to $(6, 0)$

25. Graph consists of segments from $(-12, 0)$ to $(0, 4)$ to $(6, -4)$ to $(9, 0)$

26. Graph consists of segments from $\left(-\frac{3}{2}, 0\right)$ to $(-1, -4)$ to $(0, 4)$ to $(2, 0)$

27. Graph consists of segments from $(-1, 0)$ to $\left(-\frac{2}{3}, -4\right)$ to $(0, 4)$ to $\left(\frac{4}{3}, 0\right)$

Extension

For Exercises 28–39, sketch graphs by transforming this one.

28. $y = 2 + f(x)$ **29.** $y + 1 = f(x)$

30. $y = f(x - 1)$ **31.** $y = f(x + 2)$

32. $\frac{y}{-2} = f(x)$ **33.** $y = \frac{1}{3}f(x)$

34. $y = 3f(x)$ **35.** $y = -\frac{1}{2}f(x)$

36. $y = f(x - 2) + 3$ **37.** $y = -3f(x - 2)$

38. $y = 2 \cdot f(x + 1) - 2$ **39.** $y = \frac{1}{2}f(x + 2) - 1$

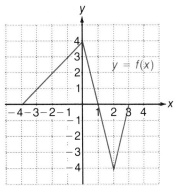

Challenge

For Exercises 40–42, sketch graphs by transforming this one.

40. $y = -2f(x + 1) - 1$ **41.** $y = 3f(x + 2) + 1$

42. $y = \frac{5}{2}f(x - 3) - 2$ **43.** $y = \frac{-1}{2}f(x + 2) - 3$

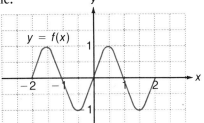

DISCOVERY/Sophie Germain

Sophie Germain was born in France in the 1700's. Although her parents felt mathematics was dangerous to women, and restricted her to home as a child, she educated herself in her father's library. When France established a training academy for mathematics and science, women were not admitted. She obtained lecture notes from friends and submitted reports under an assumed name. One paper so impressed the French mathemetician Joseph Lagrange that he asked to meet the author. His shock at finding the identity of the writer and the risk to his own career did not prevent Lagrange from assisting her. Sophie went on to win prizes for her work in physics under her own name.

9-4 Graphs of $f(x) = ax^2$

Graphs of $f(x) = ax^2$

A *quadratic function* is a function that can be described as follows: $f(x) = ax^2 + bx + c, a \neq 0$.

Graphs of quadratic functions are called parabolas.

Consider the graph of $f(x) = x^2$ shown among those at the right. This function is even because $f(-x) = -f(x)$ for all x. Thus the y-axis is a line of symmetry. The point $(0, 0)$, where the graph crosses the line of symmetry, is called the vertex of the parabola.

Next consider $f(x) = ax^2$, where a is a positive number. By Theorem 9-7 we know the following about its graph.

Compared with the graph of $f(x) = x^2$,
1. if $|a| > 1$, the graph is stretched vertically.
2. if $|a| < 1$, the graph is shrunk vertically.

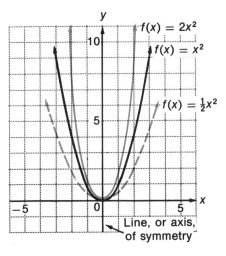

TRY THIS

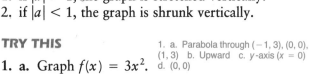

1. a. Parabola through $(-1, 3), (0, 0)$, $(1, 3)$ b. Upward c. y-axis $(x = 0)$ d. $(0, 0)$

1. **a.** Graph $f(x) = 3x^2$.
   b. Does the graph open upward or downward?
   c. What is the line of symmetry?
   d. What is the vertex?

Now consider $f(x) = ax^2$, where a is negative. By Theorem 9-7 we know the following.

Compared with the graph of $f(x) = x^2$,
1. if $|a| > 1$, the graph is stretched vertically.
2. if $|a| < 1$, the graph is shrunk vertically.
3. since $a < 0$, the graph is reflected across the x-axis.

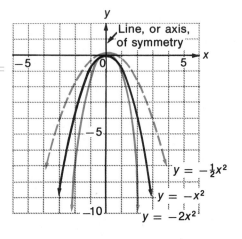

TRY THIS

2. a. Graph $f(x) = -\frac{1}{4}x^2$.

b. Does the graph open upward or downward?

c. What is the line of symmetry?

d. What is the vertex?

2. a. Parabola through $(-4, -4)$, $(0, 0)$, $(4, -4)$ b. Downward
c. y-axis $(x = 0)$ d. $(0, 0)$

Graphs of $f(x) = a(x - h)^2$

In $f(x) = ax^2$, let us replace x by $x - h$. By Theorem 9–6, if h is positive, the graph will be translated to the right. If h is negative, the translation will be to the left. The line, or axis, of symmetry and the vertex will also be translated the same way. Thus for $f(x) = a(x - h)^2$ the line, or axis, of symmetry is $x = h$, and the vertex is $(h, 0)$.

EXAMPLE 1

a. Graph $f(x) = 2x^2$.

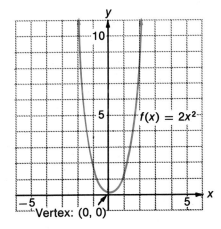

b. Use the graph in a. to graph $f(x) = 2(x + 3)^2$.

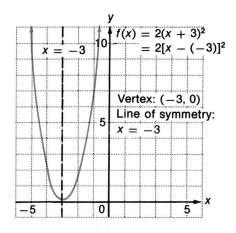

c. Use the graph in a. to graph $f(x) = -2(x - 1)^2$.

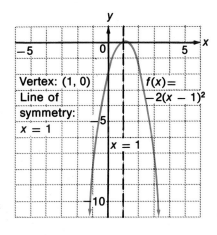

TRY THIS

3. a. Graph $f(x) = 3x^2$.
   b. Use the graph in a. to graph $f(x) = 3(x - 2)^2$.
   c. What is the vertex?
   d. What is the line of symmetry?
   e. Does the graph open upward or downward?
   f. Is the graph of $f(x) = 3(x - 2)^2$ a horizontal translation to the left or to the right?

3. a. Parabola through $(-1, 3)$, $(0, 0)$, $(1, 3)$ b. Parabola through $(1, 3)$, $(2, 0)$, $(3, 3)$ c. $(2, 0)$ d. $x = 2$ e. Upward   f. To the right
4. Parabola through $(-1, -3)$, $(0, 0)$, $(1, -3)$ b. Parabola through $(-3, -3)$, $(-2, 0)$, $(-1, -3)$ c. $(-2, 0)$ d. $x = -2$ e. Downward   f. To the left

4. a. Graph $f(x) = -3x^2$.
   b. Use the graph in a. to graph $f(x) = -3(x + 2)^2 = -3[x - (-2)]^2$.
   c. What is the vertex?
   d. What is the line of symmetry?
   e. Does the graph open upward or downward?
   f. Is the graph of $f(x) = -3(x + 2)^2$ a horizontal translation to the left or to the right?

9–4	

Exercises

For each of the following functions, graph the function, find the vertex, and find the line of symmetry.

1. $f(x) = x^2$
2. $f(x) = -x^2$
3. $f(x) = -4x^2$
4. $f(x) = 2x^2$
5. $f(x) = (x - 3)^2$
6. $f(x) = (x - 7)^2$
7. $f(x) = -(x + 4)^2$
8. $f(x) = -(x - 2)^2$
9. $f(x) = 2(x - 3)^2$
10. $f(x) = -4(x - 7)^2$
11. $f(x) = -2(x + 9)^2$
12. $f(x) = 2(x + 7)^2$
13. $f(x) = 3(x - 1)^2$
14. $f(x) = -4(x - 2)^2$
15. $f(x) = -3\left(x - \frac{1}{2}\right)^2$
16. $f(x) = -2\left(x + \frac{1}{2}\right)^2$
17. $f(x) = \frac{1}{2}(x + 1)^2$
18. $f(x) = \frac{1}{3}(x - 2)^2$

Extension

Graph these quadratic inequalities.

19. $y \le x^2$
20. $y > x^2$
21. $y > 2x^2$
22. $y \le 2x^2$
23. $y < -x^2$
24. $y \ge -x^2$
25. $y < -\frac{1}{3}x^2$
26. $y > -\frac{1}{2}x^2$
27. $y \le 3(x + 4)^2$

Graphs of $f(x) = a(x - h)^2 + k$

Graphs of $f(x) = a(x - h)^2 + k$

In $f(x) = a(x - h)^2$, let us replace $f(x)$ by $f(x) - k$. This amounts to the same thing as replacing the right side by $a(x - h)^2 + k$. By Theorem 9–5 we know that the graph will be translated upward if k is positive and downward if k is negative.

The vertex will be translated the same way. The line, or axis, of symmetry will not be affected. Thus, for $f(x) = a(x - h)^2 + k$, the line of symmetry is $x = h$ and the vertex is (h, k).

The maximum or the minimum function value occurs at the vertex. If a graph opens upward ($a > 0$), there is a minimum function value, k. If a graph opens downward ($a < 0$), there is a maximum function value k.

EXAMPLE 1

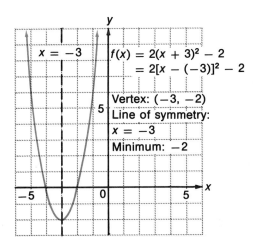

EXAMPLE 2

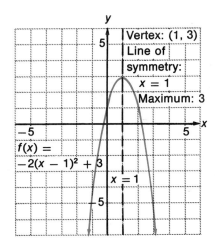

TRY THIS

1. **a.** Graph $f(x) = 3(x - 2)^2 + 4$.
   b. What is the vertex?
   c. What is the line of symmetry?

   d. Is there a minimum? If so, what is it?
   e. Is there a maximum? If so, what is it?

2. **a.** Graph $f(x) = -3(x + 2)^2 - 1$
   $= -3[x - (-2)]^2 - 1$.
   b. What is the vertex?
   c. What is the line of symmetry?

   d. Is there a minimum? If so, what is it?
   e. Is there a maximum? If so, what is it?

Analyzing $f(x) = a(x - h)^2 + k$ Without Graphing

Without actually graphing, we can determine a lot of information about a function such as $f(x) = a(x - h)^2 + k$.

EXAMPLES

Function	3. $f(x) = 3\left(x - \frac{1}{4}\right)^2 - 2$	4. $g(x) = -3(x + 5)^2 + 7$ $= -3[x - (-5)]^2 + 7$
a. What is the vertex?	$\left(\frac{1}{4}, -2\right)$	$(-5, 7)$
b. What is the line of symmetry?	$x = \frac{1}{4}$	$x = -5$
c. Is there a maximum? What is it?	No, graph extends upward, $3 > 0$	Yes, 7, graph extends downward, $-3 < 0$
d. Is there a minimum? What is it?	Yes, -2, graph extends upward, $3 > 0$	No, graph extends downward, $-3 < 0$

TRY THIS Without graphing, answer the following questions for each function.

a. What is the vertex?
b. What is the line of symmetry?
c. Is there a minimum? If so, what is it?
d. Is there a maximum? If so, what is it?

3. $f(x) = (x - 5)^2 + 40$ 4. $f(x) = -3(x - 5)^2$

5. $f(x) = 2\left(x + \frac{3}{4}\right)^2 - 6$ 6. $f(x) = -\frac{1}{4}(x + 9)^2 + 3$

3. a. $(5, 40)$
   b. $x = 5$
   c. Yes, 40
   d. No

4. a. $(5, 0)$
   b. $x = 5$
   c. No
   d. Yes, 0

5. a. $\left(-\frac{3}{4}, -6\right)$
   b. $x = -\frac{3}{4}$
   c. Yes, -6
   d. No

6. a. $(-9, 3)$
   b. $x = -9$
   c. No
   d. Yes, 3

9–5	

Exercises

For each of the following, graph the function, find the vertex, find the line of symmetry, and find the maximum value, or the minimum value.

1. $f(x) = (x - 3)^2 + 1$ 2. $f(x) = (x + 2)^2 - 3$
3. $f(x) = (x + 1)^2 - 2$ 4. $f(x) = (x - 1)^2 + 2$

5. $f(x) = 2(x - 1)^2 - 3$ 6. $f(x) = 2(x + 1)^2 + 4$

7. $f(x) = -3(x + 4)^2 + 1$ 8. $f(x) = -2(x - 5)^2 - 3$

Without graphing, find the vertex, find the line of symmetry, and find the maximum value, or the minimum value.

9. $f(x) = 8(x - 9)^2 + 5$ 10. $f(x) = 10(x + 5)^2 - 8$

11. $f(x) = 5\left(x + \frac{1}{4}\right)^2 - 13$ 12. $f(x) = 6\left(x - \frac{1}{4}\right)^2 + 19$

13. $f(x) = -7(x - 10)^2 - 20$ 14. $f(x) = -9(x + 12)^2 + 23$

15. $f(x) = \sqrt{2}(x + 4.58)^2 + 65\pi$ 16. $f(x) = 4\pi(x - 38.2)^2 - \sqrt{34}$

Extension

For each of the following, write the equation of the parabola that is a translation of $f(x) = 2x^2$ and has a maximum or minimum value at the given point.

17. Maximum: $(0, 4)$ 18. Minimum: $(2, 0)$ 19. Minimum: $(6, 0)$

20. Maximum: $(0, 3)$ 21. Maximum: $(3, 8)$ 22. Minimum: $(-2, 3)$

23. Minimum: $(-3, 6)$ 24. Maximum: $(-4, -3)$ 25. Minimum: $(2, -3)$

Challenge

For each of the following, write the equation of the parabola.

26. The parabola has a minimum value at the same point as $f(x) = 3(x - 4)^2$, but for all x in the domain except 4 the function values are doubled. $y = 6(x - 4)^2$

27. The parabola is a translation of $f(x) = -\frac{1}{2}(x - 2)^2 + 4$ and has a maximum value at the same point as $f(x) = -2(x - 1)^2 - 6$. $y = -\frac{1}{2}(x - 1)^2 - 6$

COMPUTERS AND CHESS

Have you ever played checkers with a much better player? If so, you probably looked at the risk of each move. You asked yourself, "What's the worst that can happen if I move there?" And you looked at the maximum risks of other moves. Computers play checkers and chess in the same way. They look at the maximum risks of various moves.

Around 1910, Leonardo Torres, a Spanish mathematician and engineer, built what was probably the first decision-making machine. His machine was an early computer and could play—and win—simple games of chess with human opponents. In 1915, Torres was interviewed for a magazine and predicted: "At least in theory most or all of the operations of a large establishment could be done by machine, even those which are supposed to need the intervention of a considerable intellectual capacity."

9–6 Standard Form for Quadratic Equations

Completing the Square

Consider a quadratic function described by $f(x) = ax^2 + bx + c$.
By completing the square we can describe it $f(x) = a(x - h)^2 + k$.

EXAMPLE 1
For $f(x) = x^2 - 6x + 4$,
a. find an equation of the type $f(x) = a(x - h)^2 + k$.
b. find the vertex, line of symmetry, and the maximum or minimum value.

a. $f(x) = x^2 - 6x + 4 = (x^2 - 6x) + 4$

We complete the square inside the parentheses. We take half the x coefficient and square it to get 9. Then we add $9 - 9$ inside the parentheses.

$$f(x) = (x^2 - 6x + 9 - 9) + 4$$
$$= (x^2 - 6x + 9) + (-9 + 4) \quad \text{Rearranging terms}$$
$$= 1 \cdot (x - 3)^2 - 5$$

b. The vertex is $(3, -5)$.
The line of symmetry is $x = 3$.
Since the coefficient, 1, is positive, there is a minimum function value. It is -5.

TRY THIS

1. For $f(x) = x^2 - 4x + 7$,
   a. find an equation of the type $f(x) = a(x - h)^2 + k$. $\quad f(x) = (x - 2)^2 + 3$
   b. find the vertex, line of symmetry, and the maximum or minimum value. $\quad (2, 3), x = 2, \text{Min.} = 3$

EXAMPLE 2
For $f(x) = -2x^2 + 10x - 7$,
a. find an equation of the type $f(x) = a(x - h)^2 + k$.
b. find the vertex, line of symmetry, and the maximum or minimum value.

a. We first factor the expression $-2x^2 + 10x$. We "remove" -2 from the first two terms. This makes the coefficient of x^2 inside the parentheses 1.

$$f(x) = -2(x^2 - 5x) - 7$$

We take half of the x-coefficient and square it, to get $\frac{25}{4}$. Then we add $\frac{25}{4} - \frac{25}{4}$ inside the parentheses.

$$f(x) = -2\left(x^2 - 5x + \frac{25}{4} - \frac{25}{4}\right) - 7$$

$$= -2\left(x^2 - 5x + \frac{25}{4}\right) + 2\left(\frac{25}{4}\right) - 7 \quad \text{Multiplying by } -2, \text{ using the distributive law, and rearranging terms}$$

$$= -2\left(x - \frac{5}{2}\right)^2 + \frac{11}{2}$$

b. The vertex is $\left(\frac{5}{2}, \frac{11}{2}\right)$. The line of symmetry is $x = \frac{5}{2}$. The coefficient -2 is negative, so there is a maximum. It is $\frac{11}{2}$.

TRY THIS

2. For $f(x) = -4x^2 + 12x - 5$,
   a. find an equation of the type $f(x) = a(x - h)^2 + k$. $f(x) = -4\left(x - \frac{3}{2}\right)^2 + 4$
   b. find the vertex, line of symmetry, and the maximum or minimum value. $\left(\frac{3}{2}, 4\right), x = \frac{3}{2}, \text{Max.} = 4$

Maximum and Minimum Problems

Some maximum or minimum problems involve quadratic functions. To solve such a problem, we translate by finding the appropriate function. Then we find the maximum or minimum value of that function.

EXAMPLE 3

What are the dimensions of the largest rectangular pen that can be enclosed with 64 meters of fence?

We make a drawing and label it. The perimeter must be 64 m, so we have $2w + 2l = 64$.

We wish to find the maximum area, so we try to find a quadratic function for the area.

$$A = lw$$

Solving $2w + 2l = 64$ for l, we get $l = 32 - w$. We substitute for l in the area formula.

$$a = (32 - w)w = -w^2 + 32w$$

Then we complete the square.

$$A = -(w - 16)^2 + 256$$

The maximum function value is 256. It occurs when $w = 16$. Thus the dimensions are 16 m by 16 m.

TRY THIS

3. What is the maximum product of two numbers whose sum is 30? 225

4. What are the dimensions of the largest rectangular pen that can be enclosed with 100 meters of fence? 25 m by 25 m

9–6	

Exercises

For each function, find an equation of the type $f(x) = a(x - h)^2 + k$, and then find the vertex, line of symmetry, and the maximum or minimum value.

1. $f(x) = x^2 - 2x - 3$
2. $f(x) = x^2 + 2x - 5$
3. $f(x) = -x^2 + 4x + 6$
4. $f(x) = -x^2 - 4x + 3$
5. $f(x) = x^2 + 3x - 10$
6. $f(x) = x^2 + 5x + 4$
7. $f(x) = x^2 - 9x$
8. $f(x) = x^2 + x$
9. $f(x) = 3x^2 - 24x + 50$

10. $f(x) = 4x^2 + 8x - 3$
11. $f(x) = \frac{3}{4}x^2 + 9x$
12. $f(x) = -2x^2 + 2x + 1$

13. A rancher is fencing off a rectangular area with a fixed perimeter of 76 m. What dimensions would yield the maximum area? What is the maximum area? 19 m by 19 m; 361 m²

14. A carpenter is building a rectangular room with a fixed perimeter of 68 m. What dimensions would yield the maximum area? What is the maximum area? 17 m by 17 m; 289 m²

15. What is the maximum product of two numbers whose sum is 22? What numbers yield this product? 121; 11 and 11

16. What is the maximum product of two numbers whose sum is 45? What numbers yield this product? 506.25; 22.5 and 22.5

17. What is the minimum product of two numbers whose difference is 4? What are the numbers? −4; 2 and −2

18. What is the minimum product of two numbers whose difference is 6? What are the numbers? −9; 3 and −3

19. What is the minimum product of two numbers whose difference is 5? What are the numbers? $-\frac{25}{4}; \frac{5}{2}$ and $-\frac{5}{2}$

20. What is the minimum product of two numbers whose difference is 7? What are the numbers? $-\frac{49}{4}; \frac{7}{2}$ and $-\frac{7}{2}$

Extension

Find an equation of the type $f(x) = a(x - h)^2 + k$.

21. $f(x) = ax^2 + bx + c$
22. $f(x) = 3x^2 + mx + m^2$

21. $f(x) = a\left[x - \left(-\frac{b}{2a}\right)\right]^2 + \frac{4ac - b^2}{4a}$

22. $f(x) = 3\left(x + \frac{m}{6}\right)^2 + \frac{11m^2}{12}$

Graph.

23. $f(x) = |x^2 - 1|$
24. $f(x) = |3 - 2x - x^2|$

1. $f(x) = (x - 1)^2 - 4; (1, -4), x = 1,$ min. $= -4$ 2. $f(x) = (x + 1)^2 - 6;$ $(-1, -6); x = -1,$ min. $= -6$
3. $f(x) = -(x - 2)^2 + 10; (2, 10),$ $x = 2,$ max. $= 10$ 4. $f(x) =$ $-(x + 2)^2 + 7; (-2, 7), x = -2,$ max. $= 7$ 5. $f(x) = \left(x + \frac{3}{2}\right)^2 - \frac{49}{4};$ $\left(-\frac{3}{2}, -\frac{49}{4}\right), x = -\frac{3}{2},$ min. $= -\frac{49}{4}$

Use a calculator to find the maximum or minimum value for each of the following functions.

25. $f(x) = 2.31x^2 - 3.135x - 5.89$ 26. $f(x) = -18.8x^2 + 7.92x + 6.18$

27. What is the minimum product of two numbers whose difference is 4.932? What are the numbers?   Minimum, -6.081; ± 2.466

25. Min, -6.95
26. Max, 7.014

28. What is the maximum product of two numbers whose sum is 21.355? What are the numbers?   Maximum, 114.009; both 10.678

Challenge

29. Maximizing yield. An orange grower finds that she gets an average yield of 40 bu per tree when she plants 20 trees on an acre of ground. Each time she adds a tree to an acre the yield per tree decreases by 1 bu, due to congestion. How many trees per acre should she plant for maximum yield?   30

30. Maximizing revenue. When a theater owner charges $2 for admission he averages 100 people attending. For each 10¢ increase in admission price the average number attending decreases by 1. What should he charge to make the most money? $6

31. Find the dimensions and area of the largest rectangle that can be inscribed as shown in a right triangle ABC whose sides have lengths 9 cm, 12 cm, and 15 cm.   6 cm by 4.5 cm; 27 cm²

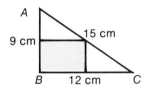

32. A farmer wants to build a rectangular fence near a river, and will use 120 ft of fencing. What is the area of the largest region that can be enclosed? (The side next to the river is not fenced.)   1800 ft²

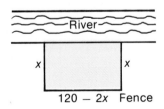

33. The sum of the base and the height of a triangle is 38 cm. Find the dimensions for which the area is a maximum and find the maximum area.   19 cm by 19 cm; 180.5 cm²

34. The perimeter of rectangle $RSTV$ is 44 ft. Find the least value of the diagonal RT. $11\sqrt{2}$ ft

x-intercepts and Graphs

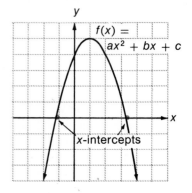

The points at which a graph crosses the x-axis are called its x-intercepts. These are the points at which $y = 0$.

To find the x-intercepts of a quadratic function $f(x) = ax^2 + bx + c$ we solve the equation $0 = ax^2 + bx + c$.

EXAMPLE 1

Find the x-intercepts of the graph of $f(x) = x^2 - 2x - 2$.

We solve the equation $0 = x^2 - 2x - 2$.

The equation is difficult to factor, so we use the quadratic formula and get $x = 1 \pm \sqrt{3}$. Thus the x-intercepts are $(1 - \sqrt{3}, 0)$ and $(1 + \sqrt{3}, 0)$. We sometimes refer to the x-coordinates of these points as intercepts.

TRY THIS Find the x-intercepts.

1. $f(x) = x^2 - 2x - 5$ $\quad (1 + \sqrt{6}, 0), (1 - \sqrt{6}, 0)$

The discriminant, $b^2 - 4ac$, tells us how many real number solutions the equation $0 = ax^2 + bx + c$ has, so it also indicates how many intercepts there are. Compare.

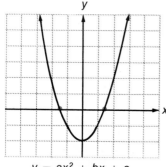

$y = ax^2 + bx + c$
$b^2 - 4ac > 0$
Two real solutions
Two x-intercepts

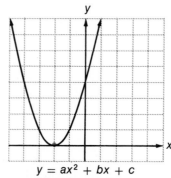

$y = ax^2 + bx + c$
$b^2 - 4ac = 0$
One real solution
One x-intercept

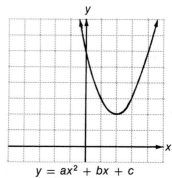

$y = ax^2 + bx + c$
$b^2 - 4ac < 0$
No real solutions
No x-intercepts

TRY THIS Find the x-intercepts, if they exist.

2. $f(x) = x^2 - 2x - 3$ (3, 0), (−1, 0)

3. $f(x) = x^2 + 8x + 16$ (−4, 0)

4. $f(x) = -2x^2 - 4x - 3$ None

9–7

Exercises

Find the x-intercepts.

1. $(2 + \sqrt{3}, 0), (2 - \sqrt{3}, 0)$ 5. $(4, 0), (−1, 0)$
2. None   6. $(4 + \sqrt{11}, 0), (4, -\sqrt{11}, 0)$
3. $(3, 0), (−1, 0)$ 7. $(4, 0), (−1, 0)$
4. $(1 - \sqrt{6}, 0), (1 + \sqrt{6}, 0)$ 8. None
9. $\left(\dfrac{-2 + \sqrt{6}}{2}, 0\right), \left(\dfrac{-2 - \sqrt{6}}{2}, 0\right)$
10. None
11. None

1. $f(x) = x^2 - 4x + 1$ **2.** $f(x) = x^2 + 6x + 10$ **3.** $f(x) = -x^2 + 2x + 3$

4. $f(x) = x^2 - 2x - 5$ **5.** $f(x) = x^2 - 3x - 4$ **6.** $f(x) = x^2 - 8x + 5$

7. $f(x) = -x^2 + 3x + 4$ **8.** $f(x) = 2x^2 - 4x + 6$ **9.** $f(x) = 2x^2 + 4x - 1$

10. $f(x) = x^2 - x + 2$ **11.** $f(x) = x^2 - x + 1$ **12.** $f(x) = 4x^2 + 12x + 9$

13. $f(x) = -x^2 - 3x - 3$ **14.** $f(x) = -5x^2 + 6x - 5$ **15.** $f(x) = 3x^2 - 6x + 1$

Extension

12. $\left(-\dfrac{3}{2}, 0\right)$ 14. None
13. None   15. $\left(\dfrac{3 + \sqrt{6}}{3}, 0\right), \left(\dfrac{3 - \sqrt{6}}{3}, 0\right)$
16. (62.75820, 0), (31.941480, 0)
17. (1.5571557, 0), (−4.042996, 0)

Use a calculator to find the x-intercepts.

16. $f(x) = 0.05x^2 - 4.735x + 100.23$ **17.** $f(x) = 1.13x^2 + 2.809x - 7.114$

18. $f(x) = 2.12x^2 + 3.21x + 9.73$ None   **19.** $f(x) = 0.13x^2 - 0.071x - 0.12$ (1.27200, 0), (−0.72575, 0)

20. Graph the function $f(x) = x^2 - x - 6$. Use your graph to
approximate solutions to the following equations.   Answers may vary.

   a. $x^2 - x - 6 = 2$ 3.4, −2.4   **b.** $x^2 - x - 6 = -3$ 2.3, −1.3

21. Graph the function $f(x) = \dfrac{x^2}{8} + \dfrac{x}{4} - \dfrac{3}{8}$. Use your graph to
approximate solutions to the following equations.   Answers may vary.

   a. $\dfrac{x^2}{8} + \dfrac{x}{4} - \dfrac{3}{8} = 0$ **b.** $\dfrac{x^2}{8} + \dfrac{x}{4} - \dfrac{3}{8} = 1$ **c.** $\dfrac{x^2}{8} + \dfrac{x}{4} - \dfrac{3}{8} = 2$

a. 1, −3
b. 2.5, −4.5
c. 3.5, −5.5

Challenge

Graph these quadratic inequalities.

22. $y < x^2 - 4x - 1$ **23.** $y \geq x^2 + 3x - 4$

24. $y \leq x^2 + 5x + 6$ **25.** $y < -x^2 - 2x + 3$

26. $y > 3x^2 + 6x + 2$ **27.** $y > 2x^2 + 4x - 2$

28. $y \geq 4x^2 + 8x + 3$ **29.** $y < 2x^2 - 4x + 2$

25. All points below parabola through (−3, 0), (−1, 4), (1, 0)
26. All points above parabola through (−2, 2), (−1, −1), (0, 2)
27. All points above parabola through (−2, −2), (−1, −4), (0, −2)
28. All points above, and including parabola through (−2, 3), (−1, −1), (0, 3)
29. All points below, and including parabola through (0, 2), (1, 0), (2, 2)

9–8 Applications of Quadratic Functions

Fitting Quadratic Functions to Data

In many problems, a quadratic function can be used to describe the situation. We can find a quadratic function if we know three inputs and their outputs. Each such ordered pair is called a data point.

EXAMPLE 1
A pizza restaurant has the following prices for pizzas.

Diameter in cm	Price
20	$3.00
30	$4.25
40	$5.75

Is price a quadratic function of diameter? Probably so, because the price should be proportional to the area, and the area is a quadratic function of the diameter. $\left(\text{The area of a circular region is given by }\right.$

$A = \pi r^2 \text{ or } A = \frac{\pi}{4}d^2. \Big)$

a. Fit a quadratic equation to the data points $(20, 3)$, $(30, 4.25)$, and $(40, 5.75)$.

b. Use the function to find the price of a 35 cm pizza.

a. We use the three data points in $f(x) = ax^2 + bx + c$.

$$3.00 = a \cdot 20^2 + b \cdot 20 + c$$
$$4.25 = a \cdot 30^2 + b \cdot 30 + c$$
$$5.75 = a \cdot 40^2 + b \cdot 40 + c$$

Simplifying, we get the following system.

$$3.00 = 400a + 20b + c$$
$$4.25 = 900a + 30b + c$$
$$5.75 = 1600a + 40b + c$$

We solve this system obtaining

$a = 0.00125,$
$b = 0.0625,$ and
$c = 1.25.$

Thus the function $f(x) = 0.00125x^2 + 0.0625x + 1.25.$

b. To find the price of 35-cm pizza, we find $f(35)$.

$$f(35) = 0.00125(35)^2 + 0.0625(35) + 1.25$$
$$= \$4.97 \quad \text{Rounded to the nearest cent}$$

It should be noted that this price function always gives results greater than \$1.25 since $f(0) = 1.25$. The \$1.25 is the fixed cost involved in making a pizza.

TRY THIS

1. Find the quadratic function that fits the data points $(1, 0)$, $(-1, 4)$, and $(2, 1)$. $f(x) = x^2 - 2x + 1$
2. The following table shows the accident records in a city. It has values that a quadratic function will fit.

Age of driver	Number of accidents (in a year)
20	250
40	150
60	200

   a. Assuming that a quadratic function will describe the situation, find the number of accidents as a function of age. $f(x) = 0.1875x^2 - 16.25x + 500$
   b. Use the function to calculate the number of accidents a typical 16-year-old is involved in.   288

Solving Problems

A theory from physics shows that when an object such as a ball is thrown upward with an initial velocity v_0, its height is given, approximately, by a quadratic function.

$$s = -4.9t^2 + v_0 t + h$$

In the formula h is the starting height (in meters), s is the actual height (in meters), and t is the time from projection in seconds.

EXAMPLE 2
A model rocket is fired upward. At the end of the burn it has an upward velocity of 49 m/s and is 155 m high. Find
a. its maximum height and when it is attained.
b. when it reaches the ground.

a. We will start counting time at the end of the burn. Thus $v_0 = 49$ and $h = 155$. We will graph the appropriate function, and we begin by completing the square.

$$s = -4.9t^2 + 49t + 155$$
$$= -4.9\left(t^2 - \frac{49}{4.9}t\right) + 155$$
$$= -4.9(t^2 - 10t) + 155$$
$$= -4.9(t^2 - 10t + 25 - 25) + 155$$
$$= -4.9(t^2 - 10t + 25) + (-4.9)(-25) + 155$$
$$= -4.9(t - 5)^2 + 122.5 + 155$$
$$= -4.9(t - 5)^2 + 277.5$$

The vertex of the graph is the point $(5, 277.5)$. The graph is shown at the right. The maximum height reached is 277.5 m and it is attained 5 seconds after the end of the burn.

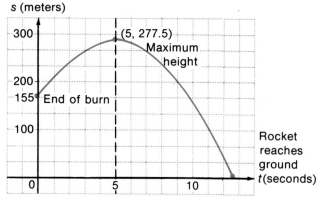

b. To find when the rocket reaches the ground, we set $s = 0$ in our equation and solve for t.

$$-4.9(t - 5)^2 + 277.5 = 0$$
$$(t - 5)^2 = \frac{277.5}{4.9}$$
$$t - 5 = \sqrt{\frac{277.5}{4.9}}$$
$$t - 5 \approx 7.525$$
$$t \approx 12.525$$

The rocket will reach the ground about 12.525 seconds after the end of the burn.

TRY THIS

3. A ball is thrown upward from the top of a cliff 12 meters high, at a velocity of 2.8 m/s. Find
   a. its maximum height and when it is attained. Max. height = 12.4 m in 0.286 s
   b. when it reaches the ground. 1.876 s

Exercises

Find the quadratic function which fits each set of data points.

1. $(1, 4), (-1, -2), (2, 13)$ 2. $(1, 4), (-1, 6), (-2, 16)$

1. $f(x) = 2x^2 + 3x - 1$
2. $f(x) = 3x^2 - x + 2$
3. $f(x) = -3x^2 + 13x - 5$
4. $f(x) = x^2 - 5x$

3. $(1, 5), (2, 9), (3, 7)$ 4. $(1, -4), (2, -6), (3, -6)$

5. Predicting earnings. A business earns $38 in the first week, $66 in the second week, and $86 in the third week. The manager graphs the points $(1, 38)$, $(2, 66)$, and $(3, 86)$.
   a. Find a quadratic function that fits the data. $f(x) = -4x^2 + 40x + 2$
   b. Using the function, predict the earnings for the fourth week. $98

6. Predicting earnings. A business earns $1000 in its first month, $2000 in the second month, and $8000 in the third month. The manager plots the points $(1, 1000)$, $(2, 2000)$, and $(3, 8000)$.
   a. Find a quadratic function that fits the data. $f(x) = 2500x^2 - 6500x + 5000$
   b. Using the function, predict the earnings for the fourth month. $19,000

7. a. Find a quadratic function that fits the following data. $f(x) = 0.05x^2 - 10.5x + 650$

8. a. Find a quadratic function that fits the following data. $f(x) = \frac{3}{16}x^2 - \frac{135}{4}x + 1750$

Travel Speed in km/h	Number of Daytime Accidents (For every 200 million km)
60	200
80	130
100	100

Travel Speed in km/h	Number of Nighttime Accidents (For every 200 million km)
60	400
80	250
100	250

7. b. Use your function to calculate the number of daytime accidents which occur at 50 km/h. 250

8. b. Use the function to calculate the number of nighttime accidents which occur at 50 km/h. 531.25

9. A rocket is fired upward from ground level at a velocity of 147 m/s. Find
   a. its maximum height and when it is attained; Max. height = 1102.5 m in 15 s
   b. when it reaches the ground. 30 s

10. A rocket is fired upward from ground level at a velocity of 245 m/s. Find
   a. its maximum height and when it is attained; Max. height = 3062.5 m in 25 s
   b. when it reaches the ground. 50 s

Extension

Use a calculator to find the quadratic function which fits each set of data points.

11. $(20.34, -5.86), (34.67, -6.02), (28.55, -8.46)$ $f(x) = 0.0499218x^2 - 2.7573651x + 29.571379$

12. $(0.789, 245), (0.988, 350), (1.233, 404)$ $f(x) = -691.96016x^2 + 1757.2031x - 710.6735$

Challenge

13. Maximizing area. A farmer wants to enclose two adjacent rectangular regions, as shown below, near a river, one for sheep and one for cattle. No fencing will be used next to the river, but 60 m of fencing will be used. What is the area of the largest region that can be enclosed? 300 m²

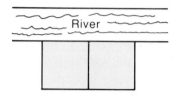

14. A city council is planning to use 200 yd of fencing to enclose an outdoor exercise area for physically handicapped citizens. The exercise area will be adjacent to the community center and will have two rectangular areas connected by a bridge crossing a creek that is 10 yd from the building. The area next to the community center can have a length no greater than the length of the building, which is 75 yd, but the area across the creek may have any dimensions. What is the total area of the largest exercise area they may enclose? Be sure to use a drawing. 5550 yd²

15. Let $y = (x - p)^2 + (x - q)^2$ where p and q are constants. For what value of x is y a minimum? $\frac{p+q}{2}$

PHYSICS/Gravity, Weight, and Mass

If a ball is dropped from a distance d above the ground, then the height h, in feet, of the ball above the ground t seconds after it is dropped is given by the following equation.

$$h = -16t^2 + d$$

The equation is only an approximate one, for it does not include the effects of friction. According to the equation, a ball dropped from a height of 400 feet is 384 feet above the ground after 1 second has passed. How many seconds does it take for the ball to hit the ground? 5 sec

The physical force that acts on a falling object is called *gravity*. On Earth, the pull of gravity is inversely proportional to the square of the distance from the center of the Earth. In the equation

above, the coefficient -16 represents the force of gravity.

Weight in pounds or tons is a measure of the pull of gravity on an object. The farther you are from the center of the Earth, the less you weigh. So, you might weigh several pounds less if you were standing on a mountain top than you would at sea level. On the moon, the pull of gravity is about only $\frac{1}{6}$ of that of Earth, so you would weigh $\frac{1}{6}$ of your weight on the moon.

The amount of matter in an object is its *mass*. It is not changed by gravity. Your mass on the moon is the same as it is anywhere else. Grams and kilograms are actually measures of mass, but they are often incorrectly used to measure weight.

CAREERS/Communications

Telephone cable testers test insulated wires in aerial, underground, or under-water conductor cables. Their objective is to determine whether or not the cable or its insulation is damaged and to check that the cable load is correct.

Cable testers are sometimes able to locate defects in the cable by listening for the sound of insulating gas escaping from a hole. More often, they use testing procedures that require the use of resistance meters, frequency oscillating meters, and impedance meters.

A cable tester knows that an alternating current flowing through a circuit is opposed by a resistance component and an inductive reactance component. The combined opposition is called impedance.

The relationship among resistance, inductive reaction and impedance is

$$Z^2 = R^2 + X_L^2$$

Z = impedance (in ohms)
R = resistance (in ohms)
X_L = inductive reactance (in ohms)

To find the resistance R in a circuit with an impedance of 780 ohms and an inductive reactance of $2R + 120$, solve the equation as you learned to do in Section 8–1.

$Z^2 = R^2 + X_L^2$
$Z = 780$
$R = R$
$X_L = 2R + 120$

$780^2 = R^2 + (2R + 120)^2$
$608,400 = R^2 + 4R^2 + 480R + 14,400$
$0 = 5R^2 + 480R - 594,000$
$0 = R^2 + 96R - 118,800$
$0 = (R + 396)(R - 300)$
$R = -396$ or $R = 300$

The resistance, R, in the circuit is 300 ohms. The inductive reactance, $2R + 120$, is 720 ohms.

The cable tester tests each strand of cable and prepares reports to identify the location and cause of any malfunctions.

Exercises

Solve.

1. $x^2 + x - 20 = 0$ $-5, 4$
2. $x^2 - 7x + 12 = 0$ $3, 4$
3. $3x^2 - 13x - 30 = 0$ $6, -\frac{5}{3}$
4. $16x^2 - 1 = 0$ $\pm\frac{1}{4}$
5. $8x^2 - 10x - 3 = 0$ $-\frac{1}{4}, \frac{3}{2}$
6. $3x^2 + 2x - 5 = 0$ $-\frac{5}{3}, 1$
7. $3x(3x + 5) + 4 = 0$ $-\frac{4}{3}, -\frac{1}{3}$
8. $(x - 5)(x - 8) = 10$ $10, 3$
9. $x(3x + 7) = 20$ $\frac{5}{3}, -4$
10. $x(3x - 1) = 2$ $1, -\frac{2}{3}$
11. $x(x + 4) + 5(x + 2)$
    $= -4$ $-7, -2$
12. $5x^2 = 30$ $\pm\sqrt{6}$
13. $17x^2 = 0$ 0
14. $2x^2 - 1 = 0$ $\pm\frac{1}{2}\sqrt{2}$
15. $4x^2 + 9 = 0$ $\pm\frac{3}{2}$
16. $2x^2 - (x + 2)(x - 3)$
    $= 12$ $2, -3$
17. $3x^2 - 2 = 0$ $\pm\frac{\sqrt{6}}{3}$
18. $4x^2 = 10$ $\pm\frac{\sqrt{10}}{2}$
19. $x^2 - 7x = 0$ $0, 7$
20. $2x^2 + 6x = 0$ $0, -3$
21. $10x^2 + 40x = 0$ $0, -4$
22. $4x^2 - 20x = 0$ $0, 5$
23. $7x^2 - 5x = 0$ $0, \frac{5}{7}$
24. $17x^2 + 51x = 0$ $0, -3$
25. $\frac{9}{16}x^2 - 1 = 0$ $\pm\frac{4}{3}$

CHAPTER 9   Review

Review the material in the chapter. Then see how you have done by trying these review exercises. If you miss an exercise, restudy the indicated lesson.

9–1   Plot the given point and the point symmetric to it with respect to the x-axis; to the y-axis. List the coordinates of the point.

1. $(4, -2)$ 2. $(-3, -7)$ 3. $(5, 1)$ (5, -1); (-5, 1)

4. $(-2, 8)$ 5. $(-4, -3)$ 6. $(-2, -5)$ (-2, 5); (2, -5)

7. $(2, 2)$ 8. $(1, -1)$ 9. $(-6, -7)$ (-6, 7); (6, -7)

1. (4, 2); (-4, -2)
2. (-3, 7); (3, -7)
4. (-2, -8); (2, 8)
5. (-4, 3); (4, -3)
7. (2, -2); (-2, 2)
8. (1, 1); (-1, -1)
14. Neither
18. (-1, -5)
19. (4, 3)
21. (-6, 5)
22. (1, 1)

9–1   Test for symmetry with respect to the x-axis and the y-axis.

10. $y = 7$ y-axis
11. $y^2 = x^2 + 3$ Both
12. $x^2 + y^2 = 4$ Both
13. $x = 3$ x-axis
14. $x^3 = y^3 - y$
15. $x^2 = y + 3$ y-axis
16. $x - y = 1$ Neither
17. $3 - x^2 = y$ Both

9–1   Plot each point and the point symmetric to it with respect to the origin. List the coordinates of the point.

18. $(1, 5)$ 19. $(-4, -3)$ 20. $(-3, 2)$ (3, -2)

21. $(6, -5)$ 22. $(-1, -1)$ 23. $(5, 4)$ (-5, -4)

9–1   Test for symmetry with respect to the origin.

24. $x + y = 3$ No
25. $y = x^3$ Yes
26. $x = 2$ No
27. $y = -4$ No
28. $x^2 - y^2 = 1$ Yes
29. $1 - y^3 = x$ No

9–2, 9–3 Here is a graph of $g(x)$. Sketch graphs of the following equations.

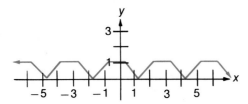

30. $y = g(x) + 2$

31. $y = g(x - 1)$

9–4 For each function, graph the function, find the vertex, and find the line of symmetry.

32. $f(x) = -2x^2$

33. $f(x) = \frac{1}{4}x^2$

34. $f(x) = -2(x + 1)^2$

35. $f(x) = 3(x - 2)^2$

9–5 For each of the following, graph the function, find the vertex, find the line of symmetry, and find the maximum or minimum value.

36. $f(x) = -2(x + 1)^2 + 3$

37. $f(x) = \frac{1}{2}(x - 1)^2 + 5$

38. $f(x) = -3(x + 2)^2 + 1$

9–6 For each equation, find an equation of the type $f(x) = a(x - h)^2 + k$, and then find the vertex, line of symmetry, and the maximum or minimum value.

39. $f(x) = x^2 - 8x + 5$

40. $f(x) = -\frac{1}{2}x^2 + 6x - 16$

41. $f(x) = -2x^2 - 4x + 3$

9–6 Solve.

42. What is the maximum product of two numbers whose sum is 32? What numbers yield this product? 256; 16 and 16

43. What is the minimum product of two numbers whose difference is 8? What are the numbers? −16; 4 and −4

9–7 Find the x-intercepts, if they exist.

44. $f(x) = -2x^2 - 4x + 3$
45. $f(x) = -x^2 - 2x + 4$
46. $f(x) = x^2 - 4x + 3$

9–8 Find the quadratic function that fits each set of data points.

47. $(1, -3), (-1, 5), (2, 13)$
48. $(1, 2), (0, 5), (-1, 14)$
49. $(3, 7), (4, 8), (5, 7)$

9–8 Solve.

50. A rocket is fired upward from ground level at the velocity of 98 m/s. Find

a. its maximum height and when it is attained; 490 m in 10 s
b. when it reaches the ground. 20 s

CHAPTER 9 Test

Plot the given point and the point symmetric to it with respect to the x-axis; to the y-axis. List the coordinates of each point.

1. $(3, 1)$ **2.** $(-4, -2)$ (−4, 2); (4, −2)
(3, −1); (−3, 1)

Test for symmetry with respect to the x-axis and the y-axis.

3. $y = 4$ **4.** $y^2 = x^2 + 8$ Both **5.** $x^2 + y^2 = 9$ Both **6.** $x = 5$ **7.** $x^5 = y^5 - y$

Plot each point and the point symmetric to it with respect to the origin. List the coordinates of the point.

8. $(-3, 2)$ **9.** $(5, -3)$ (−5, 3)
(3, −2)

Test for symmetry with respect to the origin.

10. $x + y = 7$ No **11.** $y = 2x^3$ Yes **12.** $x = 4$ No

For each function, graph the function, find the vertex, and find the line of symmetry.

13. $f(x) = 2x^2$ **14.** $f(x) = 2(x - 5)^2$

For each of the following, graph the function, find the vertex, find the line of symmetry, and find the maximum or minimum value.

15. $f(x) = 2(x - 5)^2 - 4$ **16.** $f(x) = -3(x + 1)^2 - 2$

For each equation, find an equation of the type $f(x) = a(x - h)^2 + k$, and then find the vertex, line of symmetry, and the maximum or minimum value.

17. $f(x) = -x^2 - 6x + 7$ **18.** $f(x) = 2x^2 - 10x - 7$

Solve.

19. What is the maximum product of two numbers whose sum is 40? What numbers yield this product? 400; 20 and 20

15. Parabola through $(4, -2)$, $(5, -4)$, $(6, -2)$; $(5, -4)$; $x = 5$; min $= -4$
16. Parabola through $(-2, -5)$, $(-1, -2)$, $(0, -5)$; $(-1, -2)$; $x = -1$; max. $= -2$
17. $f(x) = -(x + 3)^2 + 16$; $(-3, 16)$; $x = -3$; max. $= 16$
18. $f(x) = 2\left(x - \frac{5}{2}\right)^2 - \frac{39}{2}$; $\left(\frac{5}{2}, -\frac{39}{2}\right)$; $x = \frac{5}{2}$; min. $= -\frac{39}{2}$

Find the x-intercepts, if they exist.

20. $f(x) = 2x^2 - 5x + 8$ None   **21.** $f(x) = -x^2 - 2x + 2$ $(-1 + \sqrt{3}, 0)$, $(-1 - \sqrt{3}, 0)$

Challenge

22. The sum of the lengths of base and the height of a triangle is 24 cm. Find the dimensions for which the area is a maximum and find the maximum area. $b = h = 12$ cm, 72 cm²

Ready for Equations of Second Degree?

7–1, 7–2   Simplify.

1. $\sqrt{169}$ 13   **2.** $\sqrt{48}$ $4\sqrt{3}$

5–5   Factor by completing the square.

3. $x^2 - 2x - 15$ $(x - 5)(x + 3)$ **4.** $y^2 - 9y + 14$ $(y - 7)(y - 2)$

3–2, 9–4   Graph.

5. $y = 3x - 1$ **6.** $y = 3x^2$

5. Line through $(2, 5)$ and $(0, -1)$
6. Parabola through $(-1, 3)$, $(0, 0)$, $(1, 3)$

4–1, 5–8, 8–1, 8–4   Solve.

7. $\left(\frac{1}{2}, -5\right)$

7. $6x + 3y = -12$
   $6x - 3y = 18$

8. $x^2 - 9x + 14 = 0$ 2, 7   **9.** $x^2 = 5$ $\sqrt{5}, -\sqrt{5}$

10

CHAPTER TEN

Equations of Second Degree

10–1 Coordinate Geometry

The Distance Formula

THEOREM 10–1

The Distance Formula

The distance between any two points (x_1, y_1) and (x_2, y_2) is given by $d = \sqrt{(x_1 - x_2)^2 + (y_1 - y_2)^2}$.

Proof of Theorem 10–1

The proof of this theorem involves two cases, one where the points are on either a horizontal or vertical line, and the other where the points are not on a horizontal or vertical line. We prove the latter case as follows.

Consider any two points not on a horizontal or vertical line, (x_1, y_1) and (x_2, y_2). These points are vertices of a right triangle as shown. The other vertex is (x_2, y_1). The legs of the triangle have lengths $|x_1 - x_2|$ and $|y_1 - y_2|$. By the Pythagorean Theorem, $d^2 = |x_1 - x_2|^2 + |y_1 - y_2|^2$. Since squares of numbers are never negative, $d^2 = (x_1 - x_2)^2 + (y_1 - y_2)^2$. Taking the principal square root, we get $d = \sqrt{(x_1 - x_2)^2 + (y_1 - y_2)^2}$.

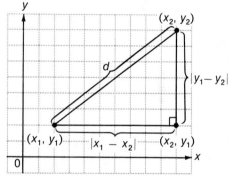

EXAMPLE 1

Find the distance between the points $(8, 7)$ and $(3, -5)$.

We substitute the coordinates into the distance formula.

$$d = \sqrt{(8 - 3)^2 + [7 - (-5)]^2}$$
$$= \sqrt{25 + 144}$$
$$= \sqrt{169}$$
$$= 13$$

TRY THIS Find the distance between the points.

1. $(-5, 3)$ and $(2, -7)$ **2.** $(3, 3)$ and $(-3, -3)$ 1. $\sqrt{149}$ 2. $6\sqrt{2}$

Midpoints of Segments

The distance formula can be used to verify a formula for finding the coordinates of the midpoint of a segment when the coordinates of the endpoints are known.

THEOREM 10–2

The Midpoint Formula

If the endpoints of a segment are (x_1, y_1) and (x_2, y_2), then the coordinates of the midpoint are

$$\left(\frac{x_1 + x_2}{2}, \frac{y_1 + y_2}{2}\right).$$

The coordinates of the midpoint can be found by averaging those of the endpoints.

EXAMPLE 2

Find the midpoint of the segment with endpoints $(-3, 5)$ and $(4, -7)$.

Using the midpoint formula, we get

$$\left(\frac{-3 + 4}{2}, \frac{5 + (-7)}{2}\right), \text{ or } (\tfrac{1}{2}, -1).$$

TRY THIS Find the midpoints of the segments having endpoints as given.

3. $(-2, 1)$ and $(5, -6)$ **4.** $(9, -6)$ and $(9, -4)$ 3. $\left(\frac{3}{2}, -\frac{5}{2}\right)$ 4. $(9, -5)$

10–1

Exercises

Find the distance between the points.

1. $(-3, -2)$ and $(1, 1)$ 5   **2.** $(5, 9)$ and $(-1, 6)$ $3\sqrt{5}$

3. $(0, -7)$ and $(3, -4)$ $3\sqrt{2}$ **4.** $(2, 2)$ and $(-2, -2)$ $4\sqrt{2}$

5. $(9, 5)$ and $(6, 1)$ 5

6. $(1, 10)$ and $(7, 2)$ 10

7. $(5, 6)$ and $(5, -2)$ 8

8. $(5, 6)$ and $(0, 6)$ 5

9. $(a, -3)$ and $(2a, 5)$ $\sqrt{a^2 + 64}$

10. $(5, 2k)$ and $(-3, k)$ $\sqrt{64 + k^2}$

11. $(0, 0)$ and (a, b) $\sqrt{a^2 + b^2}$

12. $(\sqrt{2}, \sqrt{3})$ and $(0, 0)$ $\sqrt{5}$

13. $(\sqrt{a}, \sqrt{b})$ and $(-\sqrt{a}, \sqrt{b})$ $2\sqrt{a}$

14. $(c - d, c + d)$ and $(c + d, d - c)$ $2\sqrt{d^2 + c^2}$

Use a calculator to find the distance between the points.

15. $(7.3482, -3.0991)$ and $(18.9431, -17.9054)$ 18.8061

16. $(-25.414, 175.31)$ and $(275.34, -95,144)$ 404.4729

Find the midpoint of the segments having the following endpoints.

17. $(-4, 7)$ and $(3, -9)$ $\left(-\frac{1}{2}, -1\right)$

18. $(4, 5)$ and $(6, -7)$ $(5, -1)$

19. $(2, -5)$ and $(-9, -10)$ $\left(-\frac{7}{2}, -\frac{15}{2}\right)$

20. $(8, -4)$ and $(-3, 9)$ $\left(\frac{5}{2}, \frac{5}{2}\right)$

21. $(2, 2)$ and $(6, 6)$ $(4, 4)$

22. $(-2, 0)$ and $(3, 0)$ $\left(\frac{1}{2}, 0\right)$

23. (a, b) and $(a, -b)$ $(a, 0)$

24. $(-c, d)$ and (c, d) $(0, d)$

Extension

The converse of the Pythagorean Theorem is true. That is, if the sides of a triangle have lengths a, b, and c and $a^2 + b^2 = c^2$, then the triangle is a right triangle. Determine whether the points are vertices of a right triangle.

25. $(9, 6)$, $(-1, 2)$, $(1, -3)$ Yes

26. $(-8, -5)$, $(6, 1)$, $(-4, 5)$ Yes

27. Prove that the Distance Formula holds when two points are on either a vertical or a horizontal line.

28. Prove the Midpoint Formula, Theorem 10–2.

29. Prove that the diagonals of a rectangle bisect each other. [Hint: Locate the rectangle on the x- and y-axes of a graph as shown.]

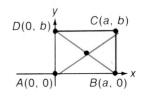

30. Find the point on the x-axis that is equidistant from the points $(1, 3)$ and $(8, 4)$. $(5, 0)$

31. Find the point on the y-axis that is equidistant from the points $(-2, 0)$ and $(4, 6)$. $(0, 4)$

Challenge

32. Consider any right triangle with base b and height h, situated as shown. Show that the midpoint of the hypotenuse P is equidistant from the three vertices of the triangle.

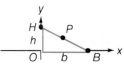

33. Consider any quadrilateral situated as shown. Show that the segments joining the midpoints of the sides, in order as shown, form a parallelogram.

10—2 Conic Sections: Circles

The nonempty intersection of any plane with a cone is a conic section. Some conic sections are shown as follows.

In this chapter we study certain equations of second degree and their graphs. Graphs of most such equations are conic sections.

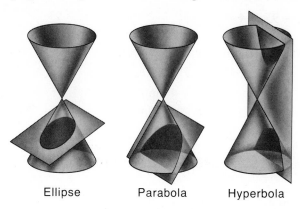

Ellipse   Parabola   Hyperbola

Equations of Circles

Some equations of second degree have graphs that are circles. Circles are defined as follows.

DEFINITION

A *circle* is the set of all points in a plane that are at a fixed distance from a fixed point in that plane.

When a plane intersects a cone as shown, perpendicular to the axis of the cone, a circle is formed.

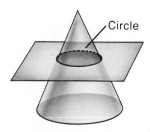

Circle

We first obtain an equation for a circle centered at the origin.

THEOREM 10–3

The equation (in standard form) of the circle centered at the origin with radius r is $x^2 + y^2 = r^2$.

Proof of Theorem 10–3

We must prove that a point (x, y) is on the circle centered at the origin with radius r if and only if $x^2 + y^2 = r^2$. To prove a sentence 'P if and only if Q' we must prove 'If P, then Q' and 'If Q, then P'. Thus there are two parts to the proof.

1. Assume (x, y) is on the circle. Then it is a distance r from $(0, 0)$. By the distance formula, we get the following.

$$r = \sqrt{(x - 0)^2 + (y - 0)^2}$$
$$r^2 = x^2 + y^2$$

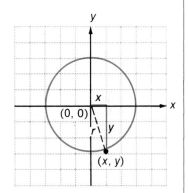

We have now shown that if (x, y) is on the circle then $x^2 + y^2 = r^2$.

2. Now assume $x^2 + y^2 = r^2$ is true for a point (x, y). This can be expressed as

$$(x - 0)^2 + (y - 0)^2 = r^2.$$

Taking the principal square root we get

$$\sqrt{(x - 0)^2 + (y - 0)^2} = r.$$

Thus the distance from (x, y) to $(0, 0)$ is r, so (x, y) is on the circle. We have now shown that if $x^2 + y^2 = r^2$, then (x, y) is on the circle.

The two parts of the proof together show that the equation

$$x^2 + y^2 = r^2$$

gives *all* the points of the circle, *and no others*.

When a circle is translated so its center is (h, k), we can find an equation for it by replacing x by $x - h$ and y by $y - k$.

THEOREM 10–4

The equation (in standard form) of a circle with center (h, k) and radius r is $(x - h)^2 + (y - k)^2 = r^2$.

EXAMPLE 1

Find an equation of a circle with center at $(-1, 3)$ and radius $\sqrt{2}$.

$$[x - (-1)]^2 + (y - 3)^2 = (\sqrt{2})^2$$
$$(x + 1)^2 + (y - 3)^2 = 2$$

TRY THIS Find an equation of a circle with center and radius as given.

1. Center: $(-3, 7)$, Radius: 5 $(x + 3)^2 + (y - 7)^2 = 25$
2. Center: $(5, -2)$, Radius: $\sqrt{3}$ $(x - 5)^2 + (y + 2)^2 = 3$
3. Center: $(-2, -6)$, Radius: $\sqrt{7}$ $(x + 2)^2 + (y + 6)^2 = 7$

Finding Center and Radius

EXAMPLE 2

Find the center and radius of $(x - 2)^2 + (y + 3)^2 = 16$. Then graph the circle.

We may first write standard form: $(x - 2)^2 + [y - (-3)]^2 = 4^2$. Then the center is $(2, -3)$ and the radius is 4. The graph is then easy to draw, as shown, using a compass.

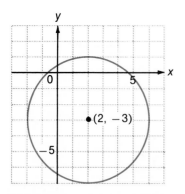

TRY THIS

4. Find the center and radius of $(x + 1)^2 + (y - 3)^2 = 4$. Then graph the circle. $(-1, 3), 2$

Standard Form by Completing the Square

Completing the square allows us to find the standard form for the equation of a circle.

EXAMPLE 3

Find the center and radius of the circle.

$$x^2 + y^2 + 8x - 2y + 15 = 0$$

We complete the square twice to get standard form.

$$(x^2 + 8x + \quad) + (y^2 - 2y \quad) = -15$$

We take half the coefficient of the x-term and square it, obtaining 16. We add $16 - 16$ in the first parentheses. Similarly, we add $1 - 1$ in the second parentheses.

$$(x^2 + 8x + 16 - 16) + (y^2 - 2y + 1 - 1) = -15$$

Now we do some rearranging and factoring.

$$(x^2 + 8x + 16) + (y^2 - 2y + 1) - 16 - 1 = -15$$
$$(x + 4)^2 + (y - 1)^2 = 2 \quad \text{This is standard form.}$$

The center is $(-4, 1)$ and the radius is $\sqrt{2}$.

TRY THIS

5. Find the center and radius of the circle
   $x^2 + y^2 - 14x + 4y - 11 = 0$. $(7, -2), 8$
6. Find the center and radius of the circle
   $x^2 + y^2 - 12x - 8x + 27 = 0$. $(6, 4), 5$

10–2	

Exercises

Find an equation of a circle with center and radius as given.

1. Center: $(0, 0)$ 2. Center: $(0, 0)$ 3. Center: $(-2, 7)$ 4. Center: $(5, 6)$
   Radius: 7   Radius: π Radius: $\sqrt{5}$ Radius: $2\sqrt{3}$

1. $x^2 + y^2 = 49$ 2. $x^2 + y^2 = \pi^2$ 3. $(x + 2)^2 + (y - 7)^2 = 5$ 4. $(x - 5)^2 + (y - 6)^2 = 12$

Find the center and radius of each circle. Then graph the circle.

5. $(x + 1)^2 + (y + 3)^2 = 4$ $(-1, -3), 2$ 6. $(x - 2)^2 + (y + 3)^2 = 1$ $(2, -3), 1$

7. $(x - 8)^2 + (y + 3)^2 = 40$ 8. $(x + 5)^2 + (y - 1)^2 = 75$ $(-5, 1), 5\sqrt{3}$

9. $x^2 + y^2 = 2$ $(0, 0), \sqrt{2}$ 10. $x^2 + y^2 = 3$ $(0, 0), \sqrt{3}$

11. $(x - 5)^2 + y^2 = \frac{1}{4}$ $(5, 0), \frac{1}{2}$ 12. $x^2 + (y - 1)^2 = \frac{1}{25}$ $(0, 1), \frac{1}{5}$

13. $x^2 + y^2 + 8x - 6y - 15 = 0$ 14. $x^2 + y^2 + 6x - 4y - 15 = 0$ $(-3, 2), 2\sqrt{7}$

15. $x^2 + y^2 - 8x + 2y + 13 = 0$ 16. $x^2 + y^2 + 6x + 4y + 12 = 0$ $(-3, -2), 1$

17. $x^2 + y^2 - 4x = 0$ $(2, 0), 2$ 18. $x^2 + y^2 + 10y - 75 = 0$ $(0, -5), 10$

7. $(8, -3), 2\sqrt{10}$ 13. $(-4, 3), 2\sqrt{10}$ 15. $(4, -1), 2$

Extension

Find an equation of a circle satisfying the given conditions.

19. Center $(0, 0)$, passing through $(-3, 4)$ $x^2 + y^2 = 25$

20. Center $(3, -2)$, passing through $(11, -2)$ $(x - 3)^2 + (y + 2)^2 = 64$

21. Center $(2, 4)$ and tangent (touching at one point) to the x-axis $(x - 2)^2 + (y - 4)^2 = 16$

22. Center $(-3, -2)$ and tangent to the y-axis $(x + 3)^2 + (y + 2)^2 = 9$

23. Find an equation of a circle such that the endpoints of a diameter are $(5, -3)$ and $(-3, 7)$. $(x - 1)^2 + (y - 2)^2 = 41$

24. **a.** Graph $x^2 + y^2 = 4$. Is this relation a function? No

   b. Solve $x^2 + y^2 = 4$ for y. $y = \pm\sqrt{4 - x^2}$

   c. Graph $y = \sqrt{4 - x^2}$ and determine whether it is a graph of a function. Find the domain and range. This is a graph of a function; Domain $\{x \mid -2 < x \le 2\}$; Range $\{y \mid 0 \le y \le 2\}$

   d. Graph $y = -\sqrt{4 - x^2}$ and determine whether it is a graph of a function. Find the domain and range. This is a graph of a function; Domain $\{x \mid -2 \le x \le 2\}$; Range $\{y \mid -2 \le y \le 0\}$

Determine whether each of the following points lies on the *unit circle* $x^2 + y^2 = 1$.

25. $(0, -1)$ 26. $\left(\frac{\sqrt{3}}{2}, -\frac{1}{2}\right)$ 27. $(\sqrt{2} + \sqrt{3}, 0)$ 28. $\left(\frac{\pi}{4}, \frac{4}{\pi}\right)$

Challenge

29. A circular swimming pool is being constructed in the corner of a lot as shown. In laying out the pool the contractor wishes to know the distances a_1 and a_2. Find them.

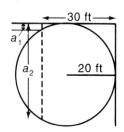

30. Prove that $\angle ABC$ is a right angle. Asssume point B is on the circle whose radius is a and whose center is at the origin. (Hint: Use slopes and an equation of the circle.)

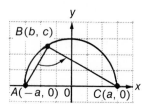

10-3 Ellipses

Some equations of second degree have graphs that are ellipses. Ellipses are defined as follows.

DEFINITION

An ellipse is the set of all points P in a plane such that the sum of the distances from P to two fixed points F_1 and F_2 is constant. Each fixed point is called a *focus* (plural: *foci*) of the ellipse.

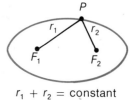

$r_1 + r_2 = $ constant

We first obtain an equation of an ellipse whose center is at the origin and whose foci lie on one of the coordinate axes.

THEOREM 10-5

The equation (in standard form) of the ellipse centered at the origin with foci on the x-axis is

$$\frac{x^2}{a^2} + \frac{y^2}{b^2} = 1.$$

From this equation, we see that the graph is symmetric with respect to both axes and the origin. The longer axis of symmetry $\overline{A'A}$ is called the major axis. The shorter axis of symmetry $\overline{B'B}$ is called the minor axis. The intersection of these axes is called the center. The points A, A', B, and B' are called vertices. The constant distance, $F_1P + F_2P$, is $2a$ and $c^2 = a^2 - b^2$.

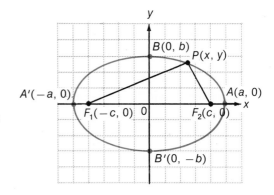

EXAMPLE 1
For the ellipse $x^2 + 16y^2 = 16$, find the vertices and the foci. Then graph the ellipse.

a. We first multiply by $\frac{1}{16}$ to find standard form.

$$\frac{x^2}{16} + \frac{y^2}{1} = 1 \text{ or } \frac{x^2}{4^2} + \frac{y^2}{1^2} = 1$$

Thus $a = 4$ and $b = 1$. Then two of the vertices are $(-4, 0)$ and $(4, 0)$. These are also x-intercepts. The other vertices are $(0, 1)$ and $(0, -1)$. These are also y-intercepts. Since we know that $c^2 = a^2 - b^2$, we have $c^2 = 16 - 1$, so $c = \sqrt{15}$ and the foci are $(-\sqrt{15}, 0)$ and $(\sqrt{15}, 0)$.

b. The graph is as follows.

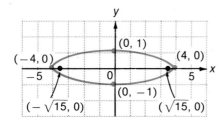

TRY THIS For each ellipse find the vertices and the foci, and draw a graph.

1. $x^2 + 9y^2 = 9$ **2.** $9x^2 + 25y^2 = 225$ **3.** $2x^2 + 4y^2 = 8$

1. Vertices: $(-3, 0), (3, 0),$ $(0, 1), (0, -1);$ Foci: $(-2\sqrt{2}, 0), (2\sqrt{2}, 0)$
2. Vertices: $(-5, 0), (5, 0),$ $(0, -3), (0, 3);$ Foci: $(-4, 0), (4, 0)$
3. Vertices: $(-2, 0), (2, 0),$ $(0, -\sqrt{2}), (0, \sqrt{2});$ Foci: $(-2, 0), (\sqrt{2}, 0)$

EXAMPLE 2

Graph this ellipse and its foci: $9x^2 + 2y^2 = 18$.

a. We first multiply by $\frac{1}{18}$.

$$\frac{x^2}{2} + \frac{y^2}{9} = 1 \quad \text{or} \quad \frac{x^2}{(\sqrt{2})^2} + \frac{y^2}{3^2} = 1$$

Thus $a = \sqrt{2}$ and $b = 3$.

b. Since $b > a$ the foci are on the y-axis and the major axis lies along the y-axis. To find c in this case we proceed as follows.

$$c^2 = b^2 - a^2 = 9 - 2 = 7$$
$$c = \sqrt{7}$$

c. The graph is at the right.

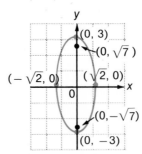

TRY THIS For each ellipse find the center, the vertices, and the foci, and draw a graph.

4. $9x^2 + y^2 = 9$ **5.** $25x^2 + 9y^2 = 225$

6. $4x^2 + 2y^2 = 8$ **7.** $x^2 + 3y^2 = 48$

4. Center: (0, 0); Vertices:
   $(-1, 0)$, $(1, 0)$, $(0, -3)$, $(0, 3)$;
   Foci: $(0, -2\sqrt{2})$, $(0, 2\sqrt{2})$
5. Center: (0, 0); Vertices:
   $(-3, 0)$, $(3, 0)$, $(0, -5)$, $(0, 5)$;
   Foci: $(0, -4)$, $(0, 4)$
6. Center: (0, 0); Vertices:
   $(-\sqrt{2}, 0)$, $(\sqrt{2}, 0)$, $(0, -2)$,
   $(0, 2)$; Foci: $(0, -\sqrt{2})$, $(0, \sqrt{2})$
7. Center: (0, 0); Vertices:
   $(-4\sqrt{3}, 0)$, $(4\sqrt{3}, 0)$, $(0, 4)$,
   $(0, -4)$; Foci: $(0, 4\sqrt{2})$,
   $(0, -4\sqrt{2})$

Standard Form by Completing the Square

If the center of an ellipse is not at the origin but at some point (h, k), then the standard form of the equation is as follows.

THEOREM 10–6

The equation (in standard form) of an ellipse with center (h, k) is

$$\frac{(x - h)^2}{a^2} + \frac{(y - k)^2}{b^2} = 1.$$

EXAMPLE 3

For the ellipse

$$16x^2 + 4y^2 + 96x - 8y + 84 = 0,$$

find the center, vertices, and foci. Then graph the ellipse.

a. We first complete the square to get standard form.

$$16(x^2 + 6x +) + 4(y^2 - 2y +) = -84$$
$$16\,(x^2 + 6x + 9 - 9) + 4(y^2 - 2y + 1 - 1) = -84$$
$$16(x^2 + 6x + 9) + 4(y^2 - 2y + 1) = -84 + 16 \cdot 9 + 4 \cdot 1$$
$$16(x^2 + 6x + 9) + 4(y^2 - 2y + 1) = -84 + 144 + 4$$
$$16(x + 3)^2 + 4(y - 1)^2 = 64$$
$$\frac{16(x + 3)^2}{64} + \frac{4(y - 1)^2}{64} = 1$$
$$\frac{(x + 3)^2}{2^2} + \frac{(y - 1)^2}{4^2} = 1$$

The center is $(-3, 1)$, $a = 2$, and $b = 4$.

b. The vertices of $\frac{x^2}{2^2} + \frac{y^2}{4^2} = 1$ are $(2, 0)$, $(-2, 0)$, $(0, 4,)$ and

$(0, -4)$; and since $c^2 = 16 - 4 = 12$, $c = 2\sqrt{3}$, and its foci

are $(0, 2\sqrt{3})$ and $(0, -2\sqrt{3})$.

c. Then the vertices and foci of the translated ellipse are found by translation in the same way in which the center has been translated.

Thus the vertices are

$$(-3 + 2, 1), \quad (-3 - 2, 1), \quad (-3, 1 + 4), \text{ and } (-3, 1 - 4),$$

or

$$(-1, 1), \quad (-5, 1), \quad (-3, 5), \text{ and } (-3, -3).$$

The foci are $(-3, 1 + 2\sqrt{3})$ and $(-3, 1 - 2\sqrt{3})$.

d. The graph is as follows.

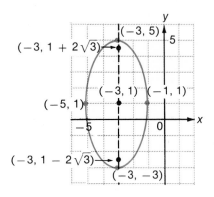

TRY THIS For each ellipse find the center, the vertices, and the foci, and graph the ellipse.

8. $25x^2 + 9y^2 + 150x - 36y + 260 = 0$ **9.** $9x^2 + 25y^2 - 36x + 150y + 260 = 0$

Applications

Ellipses have many applications. Earth satellites travel around the Earth in elliptical orbits. The planets of the solar system travel around the sun in elliptical orbits with the sun located at one focus.

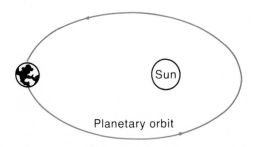

Planetary orbit

An interesting attraction found in museums is the whispering gallery. It is elliptical. Persons with their heads at the foci can whisper and hear each other clearly, while persons at other positions cannot hear them. This happens because sound waves emanating from one focus are reflected to the other focus, being concentrated there.

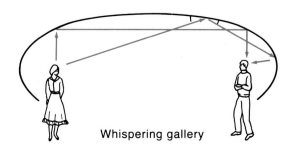

Whispering gallery

10–3

Exercises

For each ellipse find the vertices and the foci, and draw a graph.

1. $\frac{x^2}{4} + \frac{y^2}{1} = 1$ **2.** $\frac{x^2}{1} + \frac{y^2}{4} = 1$ **3.** $16x^2 + 9y^2 = 144$ **4.** $9x^2 + 16y^2 = 144$

5. $2x^2 + 3y^2 = 6$ **6.** $5x^2 + 7y^2 = 35$ **7.** $4x^2 + 9y^2 = 1$ **8.** $25x^2 + 16y^2 = 1$

Find the center, vertices, and foci, and draw a graph.

9. $\frac{(x-1)^2}{4} + \frac{(y-2)^2}{1} = 1$ **10.** $\frac{(x-1)^2}{1} + \frac{(y-2)^2}{4} = 1$

11. $\frac{(x+3)^2}{25} + \frac{(y-2)^2}{16} = 1$ **12.** $\frac{(x-2)^2}{25} + \frac{(y+3)^2}{16} = 1$

13. $3(x+2)^2 + 4(y-1)^2 = 192$ **14.** $4(x-5)^2 + 3(y-5)^2 = 192$

15. $4x^2 + 9y^2 - 16x + 18y - 11 = 0$ **16.** $x^2 + 2y^2 - 10x + 8y + 29 = 0$

17. $4x^2 + y^2 - 8x - 2y + 1 = 0$ **18.** $9x^2 + 4y^2 + 54x - 8y + 49 = 0$

For each ellipse find the center and vertices. Use a calculator.

19. $4x^2 + 9y^2 - 16.025x + 18.0927y - 11.346 = 0$

20. $9x^2 + 4y^2 + 54.063x - 8.016y + 49.872 = 0$

Extension

Find equations of the ellipses with the following vertices. (Hint: Graph the vertices.)

21. $(2, 0), (-2, 0), (0, 3), (0, -3)$
22. $(1, 0), (-1, 0), (0, 4), (0, -4)$
23. $(1, 1), (5, 1), (3, 6), (3, -4)$
24. $(-1, -1), (-1, 5), (-3, 2), (1, 2)$

Find equations of the ellipses satisfying the given conditions.

25. Center at $(-2, 3)$ with major axis of length 4 and parallel to the y-axis, minor axis of length 1 $\quad (x + 2)^2 + \frac{(y - 3)^2}{16} = 1$

26. Vertices $(3, 0)$ and $(-3, 0)$ and containing the point $\left(2, \frac{22}{3}\right)$ $\quad \frac{x^2}{9} + \frac{y^2}{\frac{484}{5}} = 1$

27. **a.** Graph $9x^2 + y^2 = 9$. Is this relation a function? No

    b. Solve $9x^2 + y^2 = 9$ for y. $\quad y = \pm 3\sqrt{1 - x^2}$

    c. Graph $y = 3\sqrt{1 - x^2}$ and determine whether it is a graph of a function. Find the domain and range. This is a graph of a function; Domain $\{x \mid -1 \le x \le 1\}$; Range $\{y \mid 0 \le y \le 3\}$

    d. Graph $y = -3\sqrt{1 - x^2}$ and determine whether it is a graph of a function. Find the domain and range. This is a graph of a function; Domain $\{x \mid -1 \le x \le 1\}$; Range $\{y \mid -3 \le y \le 0\}$

28. Describe the graph of $\frac{x^2}{a^2} + \frac{y^2}{b^2} = 1$ when $a^2 = b^2$. The graph is a circle.

29. Draw a large-scale precise graph of $\frac{x^2}{25} + \frac{y^2}{16} = 1$ by calculating and plotting a large number of points. Use a calculator to find the points.

30. The maximum distance of the earth from the sun is 9.3×10^7 miles. The minimum distance is 9.1×10^7 miles. The sun is at one focus of the elliptical orbit. Find the distance from the sun to the other focus. 2.0×10^6 miles

Challenge

31. An ellipse has foci $F_1 (-c, 0)$ and $F_2 (c, 0)$. $P(x, y)$ is a point on the ellipse and $F_1P + F_2P$ is the given constant distance. Let $F_1P + F_2P = 2a$. Use the distance formula to derive the standard form equation of the ellipse as given in Theorem 10–5. (Hint: $F_1P = \sqrt{(x + c)^2 + y^2}$)

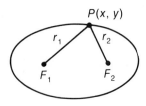

32. The unit square on the left is transformed to the rectangle on the right by a stretch or shrink in the x-direction and a stretch or shrink in the y-direction.

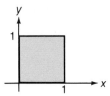 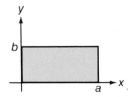

a. Use the above result to develop a formula for the area of the ellipse $\dfrac{x^2}{a^2} + \dfrac{y^2}{b^2} = 1$. (Hint: The area of the circle $x^2 + y^2 = r^2$ is $\pi \cdot r \cdot r$.) $A = \pi ab$

b. Use the result of **a.** to find the area of the ellipse $\dfrac{x^2}{16} + \dfrac{y^2}{25} = 1$. 20π

c. Use the result of **a.** to find the area of the ellipse $\dfrac{x^2}{4} + \dfrac{y^2}{3} = 1$. $2\pi\sqrt{3}$

33. The toy pictured here is called a "vacuum grinder." It consists of a rod hinged on two blocks A and B that slide in perpendicular grooves. The person playing with the toy grasps the knob at C and grinds. Determine (and prove) whether the path of the handle C is an ellipse.

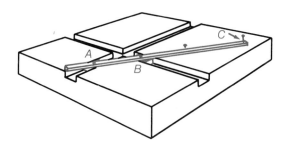

CONIC SECTIONS/Paths of Motion

From about 350 B.C., mathematicians had known about the conic sections. But it took two thousand years for the conics to be recognized for what they were—a way to describe the path of any moving body, whether on earth or in the solar system. In the 17th century the astronomer Kepler discovered that the path of each planet around the sun is an ellipse. In the same century, Galileo proved that an object shot into the air will follow a parabola.

10-4 Hyperbolas

Some equations of second degree have graphs that are hyperbolas. When a plane intersects a cone as shown at the beginning of Section 10-2, parallel to the axis of the cone, a hyperbola is formed.

Equations of Hyperbolas

DEFINITION

A *hyperbola* is a set of all points P in a plane such that the absolute value of the difference of the distances from P to two fixed points F_1 and F_2 is constant. The fixed points F_1 and F_2 are called *foci*. The midpoint of the segment F_1F_2 is called the *center*.

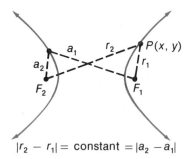

$|r_2 - r_1| = \text{constant} = |a_2 - a_1|$

We first obtain an equation of a hyperbola whose center is at the origin and whose foci lie on one of the coordinate axes.

THEOREM 10-7

The equation (in standard form) of a hyperbola centered at the origin with foci on the x-axis is

$$\frac{x^2}{a^2} - \frac{y^2}{b^2} = 1.$$

The two parts of the hyperbola are called branches. Points $(a, 0)$ and $(-a, 0)$ are called the vertices, and the line segment joining them is called the transverse axis. The line segment from $(0, b)$ to $(0, -b)$ is called the conjugate axis.

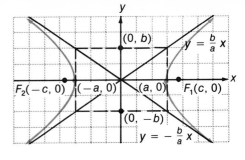

By looking at the equation, we can see that the hyperbola is symmetric with respect to the origin, and that the x-axis and y-axis are lines of symmetry.

The lines $y = \left(\frac{b}{a}\right)x$ and $y = -\left(\frac{b}{a}\right)x$ are called asymptotes. They have slopes $\frac{b}{a}$ and $-\frac{b}{a}$.

The constant distance, $|PF_2 - PF_1|$, is $2a$ and $c^2 = a^2 + b^2$.

EXAMPLE 1

For the hyperbola $9x^2 - 16y^2 = 144$, find the vertices, the foci, and the asymptotes. Then graph the hyperbola.

a. We first multiply the equation by $\frac{1}{144}$ to find the standard form.

$$\frac{x^2}{16} - \frac{y^2}{9} = 1$$

Thus, $a = 4$ and $b = 3$. The vertices are $(4, 0)$ and $(-4, 0)$. Since $b^2 = c^2 - a^2$, $c = \sqrt{a^2 + b^2} = \sqrt{4^2 + 3^2} = 5$. Thus the foci are $(5, 0)$ and $(-5, 0)$. The asymptotes are $y = \frac{3}{4}x$ and $y = -\frac{3}{4}x$.

b. To graph the hyperbola it is helpful to first graph the asymptotes. An easy way to do this is to draw the rectangle shown below. Then draw the branches of the hyperbola outward from the vertices toward the asymptotes.

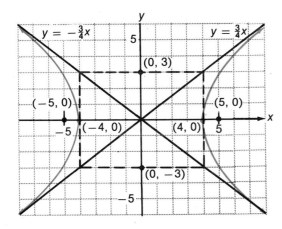

Why are $y = (b/a)x$ and $y = -(b/a)x$ asymptotes? To answer this we solve $x^2/16 - y^2/9 = 1$ for y^2.

$$-16y^2 = 144 - 9x^2$$
$$16y^2 = 9x^2 - 144$$
$$y^2 = \frac{1}{16}(9x^2 - 144) = \frac{9x^2 - 144}{16}$$

From this last equation, we see that as $|x|$ gets larger the term -144 is very small compared to $9x^2$, so y^2 gets close to $\frac{9x^2}{16}$. That is, when $|x|$ is large,

$$y^2 \approx \frac{9x^2}{16}, \qquad \text{so} \qquad y \approx \left|\frac{3}{4}x\right| \text{ or } y \approx \pm\frac{3}{4}x.$$

Thus the lines $y = \frac{3}{4}x$ and $y = -\frac{3}{4}x$ are asymptotes.

TRY THIS For each hyperbola find the vertices, the foci, and the asymptotes. Then draw a graph.

1. $4x^2 - 9y^2 = 36$ **2.** $x^2 - y^2 = 16$

The foci of a hyperbola can be on the y-axis.

THEOREM 10–8

The equation (in standard form) of a hyperbola centered at the origin with foci on the y-axis is $\frac{y^2}{b^2} - \frac{x^2}{a^2} = 1$.

The slopes of the asymptotes are still $\pm b/a$ and it is still true that $c^2 = a^2 + b^2$. There are now y-intercepts and they are $\pm b$.

EXAMPLE 2
For the hyperbola $25y^2 - 16x^2 = 400$, find the vertices, the foci, and the asymptotes. Then draw a graph.

a. We first multiply by $\frac{1}{400}$ to find the standard form.

$$\frac{y^2}{16} - \frac{x^2}{25} = 1$$

Thus $a = 5$ and $b = 4$. The vertices are $(0, 4)$ and $(0, -4)$. Since $c = \sqrt{4^2 + 5^2} = \sqrt{41}$, the foci are $(0, \sqrt{41})$ and $(0, -\sqrt{41})$. The asymptotes are $y = \frac{4}{5}x$ and $y = -\frac{4}{5}x$.

b. The graph is as shown.

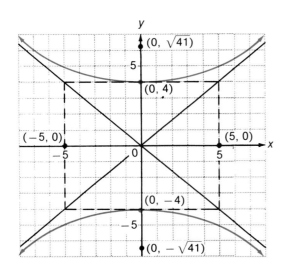

TRY THIS

3. Find the vertices, the foci, and the asymptotes. Then draw a graph.
$$9y^2 - 25x^2 = 225$$

4. Find the vertices, the foci, and the asymptotes. Then draw a graph.
$$y^2 - x^2 = 25$$

EXAMPLE 3

For the hyperbola
$$4x^2 - y^2 + 24x + 4y + 28 = 0,$$
find the center, the vertices, the foci, and the asymptotes. Then graph the hyperbola.

a. First, we complete the square to find standard form.

$$4(x^2 + 6x + \quad) - (y^2 - 4y + \quad) = -28$$
$$4(x^2 + 6x + 9 - 9) - (y^2 - 4y + 4 - 4) = -28$$
$$4(x^2 + 6x + 9) - (y^2 - 4y + 4) = -28 + 36 - 4$$
$$4(x + 3)^2 - (y - 2)^2 = 4$$
$$\frac{(x + 3)^2}{1} - \frac{(y - 2)^2}{4} = 1$$

The center is $(-3, 2)$.

b. Consider $\frac{x^2}{1} - \frac{y^2}{4} = 1$. We have $a = 1$ and $b = 2$. The vertices of this hyperbola are $(1, 0)$ and $(-1, 0)$. Also, $c = \sqrt{1^2 + 2^2} = \sqrt{5}$, so the foci are $(\sqrt{5}, 0)$ and $(-\sqrt{5}, 0)$. The asymptotes are $y = 2x$ and $y = -2x$.

c. The vertices, foci, and asymptotes of the translated hyperbola are found in the same way in which the center has been translated. The vertices are $(-3 + 1, 2)$, $(-3 - 1, 2)$, or $(-2, 2)$, $(-4, 2)$. The foci are $(-3 + \sqrt{5}, 2)$ and $(-3 - \sqrt{5}, 2)$. The asymptotes are

$$y - 2 = 2(x + 3) \text{ and } y - 2 = -2(x + 3).$$

d. The graph is as follows.

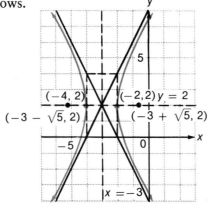

TRY THIS For each hyperbola, find the center, the vertices, the foci, and the asymptotes. Then draw a graph.

5. $4x^2 - 25y^2 - 8x - 100y - 196 = 0$ 6. $\dfrac{(y - 2)^2}{9} - \dfrac{(x + 1)^2}{16} = 1$

Asymptotes on the Coordinate Axes

If a hyperbola has its center at the origin and its axes at $45°$ to the coordinate axes, it has a simple equation. The coordinate axes are its asymptotes.

THEOREM 10–9

The equation of a hyperbola with asymptotes on the coordinate axes is $xy = c$, where $c \neq 0$.

If c is positive, the branches of the hyperbola lie in the first and third quadrants. If c is negative, the branches lie in the second and fourth quadrants. In either case the asymptotes are the x-axis and the y-axis.

10-5 Parabolas

Equations of Parabolas

Some equations of second degree have graphs that are parabolas. Parabolas are defined as follows.

DEFINITION

A *parabola* is a locus or set of all points P in a plane equidistant from a fixed line and a fixed point in the plane. The fixed line is called the *directrix* and the fixed point is called the *focus*.

When a plane intersects a cone parallel to an element of the cone, a parabola is formed. We first obtain an equation of a parabola with focus on the y-axis, directrix parallel to the x-axis, and vertex at the origin.

THEOREM 10-10

The equation (in standard form) of a parabola with focus at $(0, p)$, directrix $y = -p$, vertex $(0, 0)$, and y-axis as the only line of symmetry is $x^2 = 4py$.

If $p > 0$, the graph opens upward. If $p < 0$, the graph opens downward and the focus and directrix exchange sides of the x-axis. The inverse of the above parabola is described as follows.

THEOREM 10-11

The equation (in standard form) of a parabola with focus $(p, 0)$, directrix $x = -p$, vertex $(0, 0)$, and x-axis as the line of symmetry is $y^2 = 4px$.

EXAMPLE 1

For the parabola $y = x^2$, find the vertex, the focus, and the directrix, and draw a graph.

$$x^2 = 4py \qquad \text{Vertex: } (0, 0)$$
$$x^2 = 4\left(\tfrac{1}{4}\right)y \qquad \text{Focus: } \left(0, \tfrac{1}{4}\right)$$
$$\text{Directrix: } y = -\tfrac{1}{4}$$

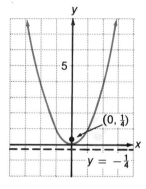

EXAMPLE 2

For the parabola $y^2 = -12x$, find the vertex, the focus, and the directrix, and draw a graph.

$$y^2 = 4px \qquad \text{Vertex: } (0, 0)$$
$$y^2 = 4(-3)x \qquad \text{Focus: } (-3, 0)$$
$$\text{Directrix: } x = -(-3)$$
$$= 3$$

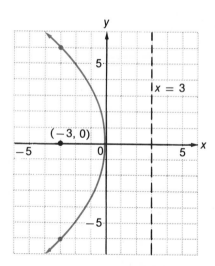

TRY THIS For each parabola find the vertex, the focus, and the directrix, and draw a graph.

1. $8y = x^2$ 2. $y = 2x^2$ 3. $y^2 = -6x$

1. Vertex: (0, 0); Focus: (0, 2); Directrix: $y = -2$

2. Vertex: (0, 0); Focus: $\left(0, \tfrac{1}{8}\right)$; Directrix: $y = -\tfrac{1}{8}$

3. Vertex: (0, 0); Focus: $\left(-\tfrac{3}{2}, 0\right)$; Directrix: $x = \tfrac{3}{2}$

Focus and Directrix Known

EXAMPLE 3
Find an equation of a parabola with focus $(5, 0)$ and directrix $x = -5$.

The focus is on the x-axis and $x = -5$ is the directrix, so the line of symmetry is the x-axis. Thus the equation is of the type

$$y^2 = 4px.$$

Since $p = 5$, the equation is $y^2 = 20x$.

EXAMPLE 4
Find an equation of a parabola with focus $(0, -7)$ and directrix $y = 7$.

The focus is on the y-axis and $y = 7$ is the directrix, so the line of symmetry is the y-axis. Thus the equation is of the type

$$x^2 = 4py.$$

Since $p = -7$, we obtain $x^2 = -28y$.

TRY THIS Find an equation of a parabola satisfying the given conditions.

4. Focus $(3, 0)$, directrix $x = -3$ 5. Focus $\left(0, \frac{1}{2}\right)$, directrix $y = -\frac{1}{2}$

6. Focus $(-6, 0)$, directrix $x = 6$ 7. Focus $(0, -1)$, directrix $y = 1$

4. $y^2 = 12x$ 5. $x^2 = 2y$
6. $y^2 = -24x$ 7. $x^2 = -4y$

Standard Form by Completing the Square

THEOREM 10–12

If a parabola is translated so that its vertex is (h, k) and its axis of symmetry is parallel to the y-axis, it has an equation as follows:

$$(x - h)^2 = 4p(y - k),$$

where the vertex is (h, k), the focus is $(h, k + p)$, and the directrix is $y = k - p$.

THEOREM 10-13

If a parabola is translated so that its vertex is (h, k) and its axis of symmetry is parallel to the x-axis, it has an equation as follows:

$$(y - k)^2 = 4p(x - h),$$

where the vertex is (h, k), the focus is $(h + p, k)$, and the directrix is $x = h - p$.

EXAMPLE 5

For the parabola $x^2 + 6x + 4y + 5 = 0$, find the vertex, the focus, and the directrix, and graph the parabola.

First, we complete the square.

$$
\begin{aligned}
x^2 + 6x &= -4y - 5 \\
x^2 + 6x + 9 - 9 &= -4y - 5 \\
x^2 + 6x + 9 &= -4y + 4 \\
(x + 3)^2 &= -4y + 4 = 4(-1)(y - 1)
\end{aligned}
$$

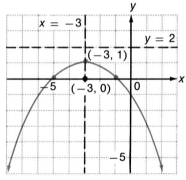

Vertex: $(-3, 1)$
Focus: $(-3, 1 + (-1))$ or $(-3, 0)$
Directrix: $y = 2$

EXAMPLE 6

For the parabola $y^2 + 6y - 8x - 31 = 0$, find the vertex, the focus, and the directrix, and draw a graph.

We complete the square.

$$
\begin{aligned}
y^2 + 6y &= 8x + 31 \\
y^2 + 6y + 9 - 9 &= 8x + 31 \\
y^2 + 6y + 9 &= 8x + 40 \\
(y + 3)^2 &= 8x + 40 \\
&= 8(x + 5) \\
&= 4(2)(x + 5)
\end{aligned}
$$

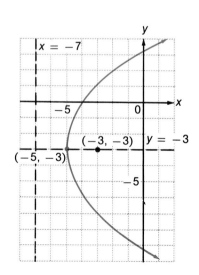

Vertex: $(-5, -3)$
Focus: $(-5 + 2, -3)$ or
$\qquad (-3, -3)$
Directrix: $x = -5 - 2 = -7$

TRY THIS For each parabola find the vertex, the focus, and the directrix, and graph the parabola.

8. $x^2 + 2x - 8y - 3 = 0$ **9.** $y^2 + 2y + 4x - 7 = 0$

8. Vertex $= (-1, -\frac{1}{2})$; Focus: $(-1, \frac{3}{2})$; Directrix: $y = -\frac{5}{2}$
9. Vertex: $(2, -1)$; Focus: $(1, -1)$; Directrix: $x = 3$

Applications

Parabolas have many applications. Cross sections of headlights are parabolas. The bulb is located at the focus. All light from that point is reflected outward, parallel to the axis of symmetry.

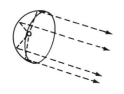 

Radar and radio antennas may have cross sections that are parabolas. Incoming radio waves are reflected and concentrated at the focus. Cables hung between structures to form suspension bridges form parabolas. When a cable supports only its own weight, it does not form a parabola, but rather a curve called a catenary.

10–5	

Exercises

For each parabola find the vertex, the focus, and the directrix, and graph the parabola.

1. $x^2 = 8y$ $V(0, 0); F(0, 2); y = -2$

2. $x^2 = 16y$ $V(0, 0); F(0, 4); y = -4$

3. $y^2 = -6x$ $V(0, 0); F(-\frac{3}{2}, 0); x = \frac{3}{2}$

4. $y^2 = -2x$ $V(0, 0); F(-\frac{1}{2}, 0); x = \frac{1}{2}$

5. $x^2 - 4y = 0$ $V(0, 0); F(0, 1); y = -1$

6. $y^2 + 4x = 0$ $V(0, 0); F(-1, 0); x = 1$

7. $y = 2x^2$ $V(0, 0); F(0, \frac{1}{8}); y = -\frac{1}{8}$

8. $y = \frac{1}{2}x^2$ $V(0, 0); F(0, \frac{1}{2}); y = -\frac{1}{2}$

Find an equation of a parabola satisfying the given conditions.

9. Focus $(4, 0)$, directrix $x = -4$ $y^2 = 16x$

10. Focus $\left(0, \frac{1}{4}\right)$, directrix $y = -\frac{1}{4}$ $x^2 = -y$

11. Focus $(-\sqrt{2}, 0)$, directrix $x = \sqrt{2}$ $y^2 = -4\sqrt{2}x$

12. Focus $(0, -\pi)$, directrix $y = \pi$ $x^2 = -4\pi y$

13. Focus $(3, 2)$, directrix $x = -4$ $(y - 2)^2 = 14(x + \frac{1}{2})$

14. Focus $(-2, 3)$, directrix $y = -3$ $(x + 2)^2 = 12y$

10–5 Parabolas **447**

Find the vertex, focus, and directrix, and graph.

15. $(x + 2)^2 = -6(y - 1)$

16. $(y - 3)^2 = -20(x + 2)$

17. $x^2 + 2x + 2y + 7 = 0$

18. $y^2 + 6y - x + 16 = 0$

19. $x^2 - y - 2 = 0$

20. $x^2 - 4x - 2y = 0$

21. $y = x^2 + 4x + 3$

22. $y = x^2 + 6x + 10$

23. $4y^2 - 4y - 4x + 24 = 0$

24. $4y^2 + 4y - 4x - 16 = 0$

Extension

For each parabola find the vertex, the focus, and the directrix. Use a calculator.

25. $x^2 = 8056.25y$

26. $y^2 = -7645.88x$

27. Graph each of the following, using the same set of axes.
$$x^2 - y^2 = 0, \quad x^2 - y^2 = 1$$
$$x^2 + y^2 = 1, \quad y = x^2$$

28. Graph each of the following, using the same set of axes.
$$x^2 - 4y^2 = 0, \quad x^2 - 4y^2 = 1$$
$$x^2 + 4y^2 = 1, \quad x = 4y^2$$

29. Find equations of the following parabola: Line of symmetry parallel to the y-axis, vertex $(-1, 2)$, and passing through $(-3, 1)$. $(x + 1)^2 = -4(y - 2)$

30. a. Graph $(y - 3)^2 = -20(x + 1)$. Is this relation a function? No
    b. In general, is $(y - k)^2 = 4p(x - h)$ a function? No, unless $p = 0$

31. The cables of a suspension bridge are 50 ft above the roadbed at the ends of the bridge and 10 ft above it in the center of the bridge. The roadbed is 200 ft long. Vertical cables are to be spaced every 20 ft along the bridge. Calculate the lengths of these vertical cables.
    10 ft, 11.6 ft, 16.4 ft, 24.4 ft, 35.6 ft, 50 ft

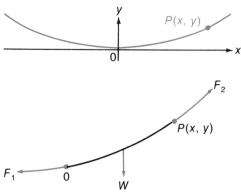

Challenge

32. Prove that when a cable supports a load distributed uniformly horizontally, it hangs in the shape of a parabola. Proceed as follows.

    a. Place a coordinate system with the origin at the lowest point of the cable.
    b. For a point $P(x, y)$ on the cable write an equation of rotational equilibrium. The forces involved are the tensions in the cable, F_1 and F_2, and the weight supported, W (which is a function of x). The weight of the cable is essentially neglected. Use point P as the center of rotation.
    c. Solve for y.

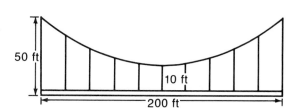

The Addition Method

To solve systems of two second-degree equations we can use either the substitution or the addition method.

EXAMPLE 2

Solve this system of equations.

$$2x^2 + 5y^2 = 22 \quad (1)$$
$$3x^2 - y^2 = -1 \quad (2)$$

Here we use the addition method.

$$
\begin{array}{ll}
2x^2 + 5y^2 = 22 & \\
15x^2 - 5y^2 = -5 & \text{Multiplying (2) by 5} \\
\hline
17x^2 = 17 & \text{Adding} \\
x^2 = 1 & \\
x = \pm 1 &
\end{array}
$$

If $x = 1$, $x^2 = 1$, and if $x = -1$, $x^2 = 1$, so we substitute 1 or -1 for x in equation (2).

$$3 \cdot 1^2 - y^2 = -1$$
$$y^2 = 4$$
$$y = \pm 2$$

Thus, if $x = 1$, $y = 2$ or $y = -2$, and if $x = -1$, $y = 2$ or $y = -2$. The possible solutions are $(1, 2)$, $(1, -2)$, $(-1, 2)$, and $(-1, -2)$.

Check: Since $(2)^2 = 4$, $(-2)^2 = 4$, $(1)^2 = 1$, and $(-1)^2 = 1$, we can check all four pairs at one time.

$$
\begin{array}{c|c}
\multicolumn{2}{c}{2x^2 + 5y^2 = 22} \\
\hline
2(\pm 1)^2 + 5(\pm 2)^2 & 22 \\
2 + 20 & \\
22 &
\end{array}
$$

$$
\begin{array}{c|c}
\multicolumn{2}{c}{3x^2 - y^2 = -1} \\
\hline
3(\pm 1)^2 - (\pm 2)^2 & -1 \\
3 - 4 & \\
-1 &
\end{array}
$$

TRY THIS Solve each system.

3. $x^2 + y^2 = 4$
   $\dfrac{x^2}{25} + \dfrac{y^2}{-4} = 1$

4. $2y^2 - 3x^2 = 6$
   $5y^2 + 2x^2 = 53$

3. $(0, -4), (0, 4)$
4. $(-2, -3), (-2, 3), (2, -3), (2, 3)$

The Substitution Method

EXAMPLE 3

Solve this system of equations.

$$x^2 + 4y^2 = 20 \quad (1)$$
$$xy = 4 \quad (2)$$

Here we use the substitution method. Firse we solve equation (2) for y.

$$y = \frac{4}{x}$$

Then substitute $\frac{4}{x}$ for y in equation (1) and solve for x.

$$x^2 + 4\left(\ \right)^2 = 20$$

$$x^2 + \frac{64}{x^2} = 20$$

$$x^4 + 64 = 20x^2$$
$$x^4 - 20x^2 + 64 = 0$$
$$u^2 - 20u + 64 = 0$$
$$(u - 16)(u - 4) = 0$$

Then $x = 4$ or $x = -4$ or $x = 2$ or $x = -2$. Since $y = 4/x$, if $x = 4$, $y = 1$; if $x = -4$, $y = -1$; if $x = 2$, $y = 2$; if $x = -2$, $y = -2$. The solutions are $(4, 1)$, $(-4, -1)$, $(2, 2)$, and $(-2, -2)$.

TRY THIS

5. Solve this system.

$$x^2 + xy + y^2 = 19$$
$$xy = 6 \quad (-3, -2), (-2, -3), (3, 2), (2, 3)$$

An Applied Problem

EXAMPLE 4

The area of a rectangle is 300 yd^2 and the length of a diagonal is 25 yd. Find the dimensions.

First make a drawing.

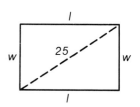

We use l for the length and w for the width and translate to equations.

From the Pythagorean Theorem: $l^2 + w^2 = 25^2$

Area: $lw = 300$

Now we solve the system:

$$l^2 + w^2 = 625$$
$$lw = 300$$

and get the solutions $(15, 20)$ and $(-15, -20)$. Now we check in the original problem: $15^2 + 20^2 = 25^2$ and $15 \cdot 20 = 300$ so $(15, 20)$ is a solution of the problem. Lengths of sides cannot be negative, so $(-15, -20)$ is not a solution. The answer is $l = 20$ yd and $w = 15$ yd.

TRY THIS

6. The area of a rectangle is 2 ft^2 and the length of a diagonal is $\sqrt{5}$ ft. Find the dimensions of the rectangle. $l = 1$ ft, $w = 2$ ft

10-7

Exercises

Solve each system graphically. Then solve algebraically.

1. $x^2 + y^2 = 25$
   $y^2 = x + 5$ $(4, -3), (4, 3), (-5, 0)$

2. $y = x^2$
   $x = y^2$ $(1, 0), (0, 0)$

3. $x^2 + y^2 = 9$
   $x^2 - y^2 = 9$ $(-3, 0), (3, 0)$

4. $y^2 - 4x^2 = 4$
   $4x^2 + y^2 = 4$ $(0, -2), (0, 2)$

5. $x^2 + y^2 = 25$
   $xy = 12$ $(-4, -3), (-3, -4), (3, 4), (4, 3)$

6. $x^2 - y^2 = 16$
   $x + y^2 = 4$ $(-5, -3), (-5, 3), (4, 0)$

7. $x^2 + y^2 = 4$
   $16x^2 + 9y^2 = 144$ No solution

8. $x^2 + y^2 = 25$
   $25x^2 + 16y^2 = 400$ $(0, -5), (0, 5)$

Solve.

9. $x^2 + y^2 = 16$
   $y^2 - 2x^2 = 10$

10. $x^2 + y^2 = 14$
    $x^2 - y^2 = 4$

9. $(-\sqrt{2}, -\sqrt{14}), (-\sqrt{2}, \sqrt{14}), (\sqrt{2}, -\sqrt{14}), (\sqrt{2}, \sqrt{14})$
10. $(-3, -\sqrt{5}), (-3, \sqrt{5}), (3, -\sqrt{5}), (3, \sqrt{5})$
11. $(-2, -1), (-1, -2), (1, 2), (2, 1)$
12. $(-4, -2), (-2, -4), (2, 4), (4, 2)$
13. $(-3, -2), (-2, -3), (2, 3), (3, 2)$
14. $(-2, -2), (2, 2), (4, 1), (-4, -1)$

11. $x^2 + y^2 = 5$
    $xy = 2$

12. $x^2 + y^2 = 20$
    $xy = 8$

13. $x^2 + y^2 = 13$
    $xy = 6$

14. $x^2 + 4y^2 = 20$
    $xy = 4$

15. $\left(\dfrac{5 - 9\sqrt{15}}{20}, \dfrac{-45 + 3\sqrt{15}}{20} \right),$
    $\left(\dfrac{5 + 9\sqrt{15}}{20}, \dfrac{-45 - 3\sqrt{15}}{20} \right)$

15. $x^2 + y^2 + 6y + 5 = 0$
    $x^2 + y^2 - 2x - 8 = 0$

16. $2xy + 3y^2 = 7$
    $3xy - 2y^2 = 4$ $(-2, -1), (2, 1)$

Use a calculator in Exercises 17 and 18.

17. Solve this system of equations.

$$18.465x^2 + 788.723y^2 = 6408$$
$$106.535x^2 - 788.723y^2 = 2692$$

(8.53, 2.53), (8.53, −2.53), (−8.53, 2.53), (−8.53, −2.53)

Solve.

19. Find two numbers whose product is 156 if the sum of their squares is 313.

21. The area of a rectangle is $\sqrt{3}$ m^2 and the length of a diagonal is 2 m. Find the dimensions. $l = \sqrt{3}$ m, $w = 1$ m

23. A garden contains two square peanut beds. Find the length of each bed if the sum of their areas is 832 ft^2, and the difference of their areas is 320 ft^2. 16 ft, 24 ft

19. 12, 13 and −12, −13   20. 6, 10 and −6, −10

18. Solve this system of equations.

$$0.319x^2 + 2688.7y^2 = 56{,}548$$
$$0.306x^2 - 2688.7y^2 = 43{,}452$$

(400, 1.43), (400, −1.43)
(−400, 1.43), (−400, −1.43)

20. Find two numbers whose product is 60 if the sum of their squares is 136.

22. The area of a rectangle is $\sqrt{2}$ m^2 and the length of a diagonal is $\sqrt{3}$ m. Find the dimensions. $l = \sqrt{2}$ m, $w = 1$ m

24. A certain amount of money saved for 1 yr at a certain interest rate yielded $7.50. If the principal had been $25 more and the interest rate 1% less, the interest would have been the same. Find the principal and the rate. $125, 6%

Extension

25. Find an equation of the circle that passes through the points (4, 6), (−6, 2), and (1, −3).

$$\left(x + \frac{5}{13}\right)^2 + \left(y - \frac{32}{13}\right)^2 = \frac{5365}{169}$$

26. Find an equation of the circle that passes through the points (2, 3), (4, 5), and (0, −3).

$$(x - 10)^2 + (y + 3)^2 = 100$$

DISCOVERY/Doubling the Cube

Given a cube in which each side has length b, how would you construct the side of another cube that is double the volume of the first? If y is the side of the new cube, then this problem can be expressed in the equation $y^3 = 2b^3$. Given b, find y so that $y^3 = 2b^3$.

From the 5th to the 3rd centuries B.C., many Greek mathematicians tried to solve this problem. But none were successful. They found the problem difficult because algebra had not yet been invented. Also, the Greeks believed that the only correct solution was one that could be accomplished with a compass and unmarked straightedge.

About 350 B.C., the mathematician Menaechmus was struggling with the cube problem and dreamed up the idea of cutting a cone with a plane. The resulting sections are the conics—the parabola, hyperbola, and ellipse. For some time it had been known that doubling the cube was related to the problem of finding two mean proportionals between two given lines. Algebraically, this means finding x and y in the equations $\frac{a}{x} = \frac{x}{y} = \frac{y}{b}$. The equations give the following system of equations.

$$y^2 = bx \quad \text{(a parabola)}$$
$$xy = ab \quad \text{(an hyperbola)}$$
$$y^3 = ab^2 \quad \text{(a cubic equation)}$$

Menaechmus is said to have solved the third equation by finding the intersection of the parabola and the hyperbola. If $a = 2b$, then $y^3 = 2b^3$ and the problem becomes that of doubling the cube.

CONSUMER APPLICATION/Financing a Home

When most people buy a home, they make a down payment and finance the rest of the cost with a mortgage loan. The mortgage loan is repaid with interest in monthly payments, usually over 25 or 30 years.

The Busfields have decided to purchase a $75,000.00 home. A 20% down payment is required.

Down Payment $= 0.20 \times \$75,000.00$
$= \$15,000.00$

Amount of Mortgage $= \$75,000.00 - \$15,000.00$
$= \$60,000.00$

Monthly payment on mortgage loans can be found by using this table.

Monthly Payment Per $1000			
Interest Rate	20 years	25 years	30 years
15%	$13.17	$12.81	$12.64
16%	13.91	13.59	13.45
17%	14.67	14.38	14.26
18%	15.40	15.17	15.07
19%	16.21	15.98	15.89
20%	16.99	16.78	16.71
21%	17.78	17.60	17.53
22%	18.57	18.41	18.36

At 18%, the Busfield's monthly payment on a $60,000.00 loan for 30 years is

$60 \times \$15.07 = \$904.20$

Lending institutions lend money only to those who prove they are able to make regular payments. Many factors are considered, but an approximate guideline is to calculate one-fourth of the applicant's monthly income. If that amount is greater than or equal to the monthly payment, then the loan is granted.

The Busfield's monthly income is $3895.00

Maximum monthly payment $=$ Monthly income $\div$ 4
$= \$3895.00 \div 4 = \$973.75$

The monthly payment, $904.20, is less than one-fourth of their monthly income, so the Busfields qualify for the loan.

In addition to the down payment, the Busfields must pay closing costs such as these: the title search, $125.00; deed recording fee, $50.00; credit report, $45.00; legal fees, $250.00; taxes, $465.00; and home insurance, $375.00. These costs vary considerably from region to region.

$$\begin{aligned}
\text{Total Cash Needed} &= \text{Down Payment} + \text{Closing Costs}\\
&= \$15,000,00 + (\$125.00 + 50.00 + 45.00\\
&\quad + 250.00 + 465.00 + 375.00)\\
&= \$16,260.00
\end{aligned}$$

The Busfields must be prepared to pay $16,260.00 at the closing.

Exercises

Use the table to find the monthly payment on these mortgage loans.

Monthly Payment Per $1000			
Interest Rate	20 years	25 years	30 years
15%	$13.17	$12.81	$12.64
16%	13.91	13.59	13.45
17%	14.67	14.38	14.26
18%	15.40	15.17	15.07
19%	16.21	15.98	15.89
20%	16.99	16.78	16.71
21%	17.78	17.60	17.53
22%	18.57	18.41	18.36

1. $35,000 at 20% for 20 years $594.65
2. $50,000 at 19% for 25 years $799.00
3. $47,000 at 21% for 30 years $823.91
4. $63,000 at 18% for 30 years $949.41
5. $56,000 at 16% for 20 years $778.96
6. $84,000 at 15% for 30 years $1061.76
7. $60,000 at 19% for 25 years $958.80
8. $45,000 at 17% for 30 years $641.70
9. $78,000 at 22% for 25 years $1435.98
10. $36,000 at 20% for 30 years $601.56
11. $91,000 at 18% for 25 years $1380.47
12. $42,000 at 21% for 25 years $739.20

Determine whether these applicants qualify for these mortgage loans.

13. Lee and Al Deltz want to purchase a condominium for $65,000.00. They can make a 20% down payment and finance the rest with a 20-year loan at 19%. Their monthly income is $3500.00. Yes. Monthly payment, $842.92, is less than $3500 ÷ 4.

CHAPTER 10   Review

Review the material in the chapter. Then see how you have done by trying these review exercises. If you miss an exercise, restudy the indicated lesson.

$10-1$ Find the distance between the points.

1. $(-3, 4)$ and $(7, 0)$ $2\sqrt{29}$
2. $(0, 3)$ and $(4, 0)$ 5
3. $(2, -4)$ and $(-9, 6)$ $\sqrt{221}$

Find the midpoint of the segments having the following endpoints.

4. $(-3, 4)$ and $(7, 0)$ $(2, 2)$
5. $(-2, 4)$ and $(6, 8)$ $(2, 6)$
6. $(-8, -1)$ and $(4, 5)$ $(5, -2)$
7. $(0, 3)$ and $(10, -7)$ $(-2, 2)$

$10-2$ Find an equation of the circle with center and radius as given.

8. $(-2, 6)$; $\sqrt{13}$ **9.** $(3, -1)$; 2 $(x - 3)^2 + (y + 1)^2 = 4$ 8. $(x + 2)^2 + (y - 6)^2 = 13$

$10-2$ Find the center and radius of each circle.

10. $(x - 4)^2 + (y + 3)^2 = 12$
11. $x^2 + y^2 = 36$ $(0, 0); 6$
12. $2x^2 + 2y^2 - 3x - 5y + 3 = 0$ 10. $(4 - 3); 2\sqrt{3}$
13. $x^2 + y^2 - 6x + 10y + 24 = 0$ $(3, -5); 2\sqrt{2}$ 12. $\left(\frac{3}{4}, \frac{5}{4}\right); \frac{\sqrt{10}}{4}$

$10-3$ For each ellipse find the center, vertices, and foci and draw a graph.

14. $16x^2 + 25y^2 - 64x + 50y - 311 = 0.$
15. $9x^2 + 16y^2 + 36x - 32y - 92 = 0.$

10–4 For each hyperbola, find the center, vertices, foci, and asymptotes and graph the hyperbola.

16. $x^2 - 2y^2 + 4x + y - \frac{1}{8} = 0$

17. $8x^2 - 3y^2 = 48$

10–5 For each parabola find the vertex, focus, and directrix, and graph the parabola.

18. $y^2 = -12x$

19. $(x - 1)^2 - 2(y + 1)$

20. $y^2 + 2y + 4x - 8 = 0$

10–6 Solve.

21. $\frac{x^2}{16} + \frac{y^2}{9} = 1$ (4, 0), (0, 3)
$3x + 4y = 12$

22. $x^2 + y^2 = 16$ (4, 0), (−4, 0)
$\frac{x^2}{16} + \frac{y^2}{9} = 1$

10–7 Solve.

23. The sides of a triangle are 8, 10, and 14. Find the altitude to the longest side. $\frac{16\sqrt{6}}{7}$

24. The area of a rectangle is 240 cm^2 and the length of a diagonal is 26 cm. Find the dimensions of the rectangle. Length is 24 cm, width is 10 cm

CHAPTER 10   Test

Find the distance between the points.

1. $(-3, 4)$ and $(7, 6)$ $2\sqrt{26}$
2. $(4, -1)$ and $(-2, 0)$ $\sqrt{37}$

Find the midpoint of the segment having the following endpoints.

3. $(-3, 4)$ and $(7, 6)$ (2, 5)
4. $(-2, -3)$ and $(0, 1)$ (−1, −1)

5. Find an equation of the circle with center $(4, -1)$ and radius 5. $(x - 4)^2 + (y + 1)^2 = 25$

6. Find the center and radius of the circle Center $(4, -6), r = \sqrt{3}$
$x^2 + y^2 - 8x + 12y + 49 = 0$.

7. Find the center, vertices, and foci of the ellipse
$x^2 + 4y^2 - 6x + 24y + 41 = 0$. Then graph the ellipse.

8. Find the center, vertices, foci, and asymptotes of the hyperbola
$25x^2 - 9y^2 = 225$.

9. Find the vertex, focus, and directrix of the parabola
$x^2 + 2x + 6y - 11 = 0$. Then graph the parabola.

10. Solve: $x^2 + y^2 = 74$ $(-5, -7), (7, 5)$
$x - y = 2$

7. Center $(3, -3)$; vertices $(5, -3), (1, -3)$
$(3, 1), (3, -7)$; foci $(3, -3 + \sqrt{3}), (3, -3, -\sqrt{3})$
8. Center $(0, 0)$; vertices $(3, 0), (-3, 0)$;
foci $(\sqrt{34}, 0), (-\sqrt{34}, 0)$; asymptotes $y = \pm\frac{5}{3}x$
9. Vertex $(-1, 2)$; focus $\left(-1, \frac{1}{2}\right)$; directrix $y = \frac{7}{2}$

11. Two squares whose sides differ in length by 9 m have areas 13 m and 4 m
that differ by 153 m². Find the length of a side of each.

Challenge

12. Find the equation of a circle that passes through the points $(x - 3)^2 + (y - 2)^2 = 25$
$(0, -2)$ and $(6, 6)$ and whose center is on the line $x - y = 1$.

Ready for Polynomial Functions?

5–4   Factor.

1. $x^2 + x - 6$ 2. $x^2 - 5x + 4$ 3. $3x^2 + 2x - 1$
4. $2x^2 + 7x + 6$ 5. $4x^2 + x - 5$ 6. $x^2 - 11x + 24$

1. $(x + 3)(x - 2)$
2. $(x - 4)(x - 1)$
3. $(3x - 1)(x + 1)$
4. $(x + 2)(2x + 3)$
5. $(x - 1)(4x + 5)$
6. $(x - 3)(x - 8)$

7–8   Find the conjugate of each.

7. $-3 + 8i$ 8. $2 - 4i$ $2 + 4i$
   $-3 - 8i$

7–8   Multiply.

9. $(1 - 5i)(1 + 5i)$ 26   10. $(3 - 2i)(3 + 2i)$ 13   11. $(-6 - i)(-6 + i)$ 37

7–9   Determine whether each of the following is a solution of
$x^2 - 2x + 1 = 0$.

12. 1   Yes   13. $1 + i$ No   14. $1 - i$ No

15. Find an equation having -2, i, and $3i$ as solutions. $x^3 - 4ix^2 + 2x^2 - 8ix - 3x - 6$

16. Show that $-1 - i$ is a square root of $2i$. Then find the other
square root. $(-1, -i)^2 = 2i ; 1 + i$

8–3   Find a quadratic equation having the given solutions.

17. $-5, \frac{2}{3}$ 18. $\frac{1}{2}, -\frac{3}{2}$ 19. $\sqrt{2}, -\sqrt{2}$ $x^2 - 2 = 0$

17. $3x^2 + 13x - 10 = 0$
18. $4x^2 + 4x - 3 = 0$

11

CHAPTER ELEVEN

Polynomial Functions

11–1 Polynomials and Polynomial Functions

Recall the definition of a polynomial: A polynomial in x is any expression equivalent to one of this form.

$$a_n x^n + a_{n-1} x^{n-1} + a_{n-2} x^{n-2} + \cdots + a_1 x + a_0$$

We will usually assume the coefficients are complex numbers, but in some cases will consider them to be real numbers, or rational numbers, or integers. Some or all of the coefficients may be 0. If all of the coefficients are 0, the polynomial is called the zero polynomial. The coefficient of the term of highest degree, a_n, is called the leading coefficient

Roots of Polynomials

When a number is substituted for the variable in a polynomial, the result is some unique number. Thus every polynomial defines a function. We often refer to polynomials, therefore, using function notation $P(x)$.

DEFINITION

If a number a makes a polynomial 0, then a is called a *root*, or a *zero*, of the polynomial; that is, a root is a solution of the equation $P(x) = 0$.

EXAMPLES

$P(x) = x^3 + 2x^2 - 5x - 6$

1. Is 3 a root of $P(x)$? We substitute 3 into the polynomial.

$$P(3) = 3^3 + 2(3)^2 - 5 \cdot 3 - 6 = 24$$

Since $P(3) \neq 0$, 3 is not a root.

2. Is -1 a root of $P(x)$?

$$P(-1) = (-1)^3 + 2(-1)^2 - 5(-1) - 6 = 0$$

Since $P(-1) = 0$, -1 is a root of the polynomial.

TRY THIS

1. Determine whether the following numbers are roots of the polynomial $P(x) = x^2 - 4x - 21$.
   a. 7   **b.** 3   **c.** -3 a. Yes b. No c. Yes

2. Determine whether the following numbers are roots of the polynomial $P(x) = x^4 - 16$.
   a. 2   **b.** -2 **c.** -1 **d.** 0   a. Yes b. Yes c. No d. No

Factors and Division

When we divide one polynomial by another we obtain a quotient and a remainder. If the remainder is 0, then the divisor is a factor of the dividend.

EXAMPLE 3

Divide, to find whether $x^2 + 9$ is a factor of $x^4 - 81$.

$$
\begin{array}{r}
x^2 - 9 \\
x^2 + 9 \overline{)x^4 \qquad\qquad - 81} \\
\underline{x^4 \qquad + 9x^2} \\
-9x^2 - 81 \\
\underline{-9x^2 - 81} \\
0
\end{array}
$$

Spaces have been left for missing terms in the dividend.

Since the remainder is 0, we know that $x^2 + 9$ is a factor of $x^4 - 81$. That is, $x^4 - 81 = (x^2 + 9)(x^2 - 9)$.

EXAMPLE 4

Divide, to find whether $x^2 + 3x - 1$ is a factor of $x^4 - 81$.

$$
\begin{array}{r}
x^2 - 3x + 10 \\
x^2 + 3x - 1 \overline{)x^4 \qquad\qquad\qquad - 81} \\
\underline{x^4 + 3x^3 - \quad x^2} \\
-3x^3 + \quad x^2 \\
\underline{-3x^3 - \quad 9x^2 + \quad 3x} \\
10x^2 - \quad 3x - 81 \\
\underline{10x^2 + 30x - 10} \\
-33x - 71
\end{array}
$$

Since the remainder is not 0, we know that $x^2 + 3x - 1$ is not a factor of $x^4 - 81$.

TRY THIS

3. By division, determine whether the following polynomials are factors of the polynomial $x^3 + 2x^2 - 5x - 6$.
   a. $x - 3$ b. $x + 1$ c. $x^2 + 3x - 1$ a. No b. Yes c. No

When we divide a polynomial $P(x)$ by a divisor $d(x)$ we obtain a polynomial $Q(x)$ for a quotient and a polynomial $R(x)$ for a remainder . The remainder must either be 0 or have degree less than that of $d(x)$. To check, we multiply the quotient by the divisor and add the remainder, to see if we get the dividend.

$$P(x) = d(x) \cdot Q(x) + R(x)$$

EXAMPLE 5

If $P(x) = x^4 - 81$ and $d(x) = x^2 + 9$, find $Q(x)$ and $R(x)$.

$$x^4 - 81 = (x^2 + 9) \cdot (x^2 - 9) + 0$$
$$P(x) = \quad d(x) \quad \cdot \quad Q(x) \quad + R(x)$$

TRY THIS

4. Divide $x^3 + 2x^2 - 5x - 6$ by $x - 3$. Then express the dividend as $P(x) = d(x) \cdot Q(x) + R(x)$. $x^3 + 2x^2 - 5x - 6 = (x - 3)(x^2 + 5x + 10) + 24$

11–1

Exercises

Determine whether the given numbers are roots of the polynomial $P(x)$.

1. $2, 3, -1$;   Yes, no, no
   $P(x) = x^3 + 6x^2 - x - 30$

2. $2, 3, -1$;   No, no, no
   $P(x) = 2x^3 - 3x^2 + x - 1$

3. $0, -1, 1 + i\sqrt{7}, 1 - i\sqrt{7}$;
   $P(x) = x^3 - 2x^2 + 8x$ Yes, no, yes, yes

4. $0, -2, 1 + i, 1 - i$;   Yes, no, yes, yes
   $P(x) = x^3 - 2x^2 + 2x$

By division, determine whether the polynomials are factors of the polynomial $P(x)$.

5. $P(x) = x^3 + 6x^2 - x - 30$
   a. $x - 2$ Yes b. $x - 3$ No c. $x + 1$ No

6. $P(x) = 2x^3 - 3x^2 + x - 1$
   a. $x - 2$ No b. $x - 3$ No c. $x + 1$ No

7. $P(x) = x^4 - 81$
   a. $x - 3$ Yes b. $x + 3$ Yes c. $x + 9$ No

8. $P(x) = x^5 + 32$
   a. $x - 2$ No b. $x + 2$ Yes c. $x - 4$ No

In each of the following, a polynomial $P(x)$ and a divisor $d(x)$ are given. Find the quotient $Q(x)$ and the remainder $R(x)$ when $P(x)$ is divided by $d(x)$ and express $P(x)$ in the form $d(x) \cdot Q(x) + R(x)$.

9. $P(x) = x^3 + 6x^2 - x - 30$
  a. $d(x) = x - 2$
  b. $d(x) = x - 3$

10. $P(x) = 2x^3 - 3x^2 + x - 1$
  a. $d(x) = x - 2$
  b. $d(x) = x - 3$

11. $P(x) = x^3 - 8$
  $d(x) = x + 2$

12. $P(x) = x^3 + 27$
  $d(x) = x + 1$

13. $P(x) = x^4 + 9x^2 + 20$
  $d(x) = x^2 + 4$

14. $P(x) = x^4 + x^2 + 2$
  $d(x) = x^2 + x + 1$

15. $P(x) = 5x^7 - 3x^4 + 2x^2 - 3$
  $d(x) = 2x^2 - x + 1$

16. $P(x) = 6x^5 + 4x^4 - 3x^2 + x - 2$
  $d(x) = 3x^2 + 2x - 1$

Extension

17. $P(x) = x^5 - 64$
  a. Find $P(2)$. -32
  b. Find the remainder when $P(x)$ is divided by $x - 2$, and compare your answer to a. -32
  c. Find $P(-1)$. -65
  d. Find the remainder when $P(x)$ is divided by $x + 1$, and compare your answer to c. -65

18. $P(x) = x^3 + x^2$
  a. Find $P(-1)$. 0
  b. Find the remainder when $P(x)$ is divided by $x + 1$ and compare your answer to a. 0
  c. Find $P(2)$. 12
  d. Find the remainder when $P(x)$ is divided by $x - 2$, and compare your answer to c. 12

Challenge

19. $P(x) = 2x^2 - ix + 1$
  a. Find $P(-i)$. -2
  b. Find the remainder when $P(x)$ is divided by $x + i$. -2

20. $P(x) = 2x^2 + ix - 1$
  a. Find $P(i)$. -4
  b. Find the remainder when $P(x)$ is divided by $x - i$. -4

21. Under what conditions is a polynomial function of real variables an even function, that is, $P(x) = P(-x)$ for all x? Does your answer still hold for complex variables? All exponents even; yes

22. Under what conditions is a polynomial function of real variables an odd function, that is $-P(x) = P(-x)$ for all x? Does your answer still hold for complex variables? All exponents odd; yes

9. a. $x^3 + 6x^2 - x - 30 =$
  $(x - 2)(x^2 + 8x + 15) + 0$
  b. $x^3 + 6x^2 - x - 30 =$
  $(x - 3)(x^2 + 9x + 26) + 48$

10. a. $2x^3 - 3x^2 + x - 1 =$
  $(x - 2)(2x^2 + x + 3) + 5$
  b. $2x^3 - 3x^2 + x - 1 =$
  $(x - 3)(2x^2 + 3x + 10) + 29$

11. $x^3 - 8 = (x + 2)(x^2 - 2x + 4)$
  $+ (-16)$

12. $x^3 + 27 = (x + 1)(x^2 - x + 1)$
  $+ 26$

13. $x^4 + 9x^2 + 20 = (x^2 + 4)(x^2 + 5)$
  $+ 0$

14. $x^4 + x^2 + 2 = (x^2 + x + 1)$
  $(x^2 - x + 1) + 1$

15. $5x^7 - 3x^4 + 2x^2 - 3 = (2x^2 - x$
  $+ 1)\left(\frac{5}{2}x^5 + \frac{5}{4}x^4 - \frac{5}{8}x^3 - \frac{39}{16}x^2 - \right.$
  $\left. \frac{29}{32}x + \frac{113}{64} + \frac{171x - 305}{64}\right)$

16. $6x^5 + 4x^4 - 3x^2 + x - 2 = (3x^2$
  $+ 2x - 1)\left(2x^3 + \frac{2}{3}x - \frac{13}{9}\right) +$
  $\frac{41x - 31}{9}$

11-2 The Remainder and Factor Theorems

Skill in dividing one polynomial by another is important in applying several important theorems. Before developing these theorems we show a rapid method of dividing a polynomial by $x - r$.

Synthetic Division

To streamline division, we can arrange the work so that duplicate writing is avoided. Compare the following.

A
$$
\begin{array}{r}
4x^2 + 5x + 11 \\
x - 2\overline{)4x^3 - 3x^2 + x + 7} \\
\underline{4x^3 - 8x^2} \\
5x^2 + x \\
\underline{5x^2 - 10x} \\
11x + 7 \\
\underline{11x - 22} \\
29 \quad \text{remainder}
\end{array}
$$

B
$$
\begin{array}{r}
4 \quad 5 \quad 11 \\
1 - 2\overline{)4 - 3 + 1 + 7} \\
\underline{4 - 8} \\
5 + 1 \\
\underline{5 - 10} \\
11 + 7 \\
\underline{11 - 22} \\
29 \quad \text{remainder}
\end{array}
$$

In **A** we performed a division. In **B** we performed the same division, but we wrote only the coefficients. If there had been any missing terms, we would have written 0's. Note that the numerals in color are duplicated. There would be no loss of understanding if we did not write them twice. Note also that when we subtract we add an additive inverse. We can accomplish this by using the additive inverse of -2, and then adding instead of subtracting.

C Synthetic Division. Write down the 2 of the divisor and the coefficients. Bring down the first coefficient (4), then multiply it by the 2 and write the result under the next coefficient (-3). Add -3 and 8, multiply the sum (5) by the 2, and write the result under the next coefficient (1). Add 1 and 10, multiply the sum (11) by 2, and write the result under the next coefficient (7). Then add.

$$
\begin{array}{r|rrrr}
2 & 4 & -3 & 1 & 7 \\
 & & 8 & 10 & 22 \\
\hline
 & 4 & 5 & 11 & 29
\end{array}
$$

The last number (29) is the remainder. The others are the coefficients of the quotient.

EXAMPLE 1

Use synthetic division to find the quotient and remainder:
$(2x^3 + 7x^2 - 5) \div (x + 3)$.

First note that $x + 3 = x - (-3)$.

$$
\begin{array}{r|rrrr}
-3 & 2 & +7 & +0 & -5 \\
   &   & -6 & -3 & +9 \\
\hline
   & 2 & +1 & -3 & +4 \\
\end{array}
$$

Note: We must write 0's for missing terms.

The quotient is $2x^2 + 1x - 3$. The remainder is 4.

TRY THIS Use synthetic division to find the quotient and remainder.

1. $(x^3 + 6x^2 - x - 30) \div (x - 2)$ Q: $x^2 + 8x + 15$, R: 0
2. $(y^3 + 1) \div (y + 1)$ Q: $y^2 - y + 1$, R: 0

Function Values for Polynomials

We can now use synthetic division to find function values for polynomials.

THEOREM 11–1

The Remainder Theorem

For a polynomial $P(x)$, the function value $P(r)$ is the remainder when $P(x)$ is divided by $x - r$.

EXAMPLE 2

$P(x) = 2x^5 - 3x^4 + x^3 - 2x^2 + x - 8$. Find $P(10)$.

By Theorem 11–1, $P(10)$ is the remainder when $P(x)$ is divided by $x - 10$. We use synthetic division to find that remainder.

$$
\begin{array}{r|rrrrrr}
10 & 2 & -3 & 1 & -2 & 1 & -8 \\
   &   & 20 & 170 & 1710 & 17{,}080 & 170{,}810 \\
\hline
   & 2 & 17 & 171 & 1708 & 17{,}081 & 170{,}802 \\
\end{array}
$$

Thus $P(10) = 170{,}802$.

TRY THIS Let $P(x) = x^5 - 2x^4 - 7x^3 + x^2 + 20$.

3. Use synthetic division to find $P(10)$ and $P(-8)$. 73,120; -37,292

Roots

EXAMPLE 3
Determine whether -4 is a zero or root of $P(x)$, where
$P(x) = x^3 + 8x^2 + 8x - 32$.

We use synthetic division and Theorem 11–1 to find $P(-4)$.

$$
\begin{array}{r|rrrr}
-4 & 1 & 8 & 8 & -32 \\
   &   & -4 & -16 & 32 \\
\hline
   & 1 & 4 & -8 & 0
\end{array}
$$

Since $P(-4) = 0$, the number -4 is a root of $P(x)$.

TRY THIS Let $P(x) = x^3 + 6x^2 - x - 30$. Using synthetic division, determine whether the given numbers are roots of $P(x)$.

4. 2 Yes **5.** 5 No **6.** -3 Yes

Proof of Theorem 11–1

The equation $P(x) = d(x) \cdot Q(x) + R(x)$ is the basis of this proof. If we divide $P(x)$ by $x - r$, we obtain a quotient $Q(x)$ and a remainder $R(x)$ related as follows.

$$P(x) = (x - r) \cdot Q(x) + R(x)$$

The remainder $R(x)$ must either be 0 or have degree less than $x - r$. Thus $R(x)$ must be a constant. Let us call this constant R. In the above expression we get a true sentence whenever we replace x by any number. Let us replace x by r.

$$
\begin{aligned}
P(r) &= (r - r) \cdot Q(r) + R \\
P(r) &= 0 \cdot Q(r) + R \\
P(r) &= R
\end{aligned}
$$

This tells us that the function value $P(r)$ is the remainder obtained when we divide $P(x)$ by $x - r$.

Finding Factors of Polynomials

The next theorem follows from the Remainder Theorem.

THEOREM 11–2

The Factor Theorem

For a polynomial $P(x)$, if $P(r) = 0$, then the polynomial $x - r$ is a factor of $P(x)$.

This theorem is very useful in factoring polynomials, and hence in the solving of equations.

EXAMPLE 4

Let $P(x) = x^3 + 2x^2 - 5x - 6$. Factor $P(x)$ and thus solve the equation $P(x) = 0$.

We look for linear factors of the form $x - r$. Let us try $x - 1$. We use synthetic division to see whether $P(1) = 0$.

$$
\begin{array}{r|rrrr}
1 & 1 & 2 & -5 & -6 \\
  &   & 1 & 3 & -2 \\
\hline
  & 1 & 3 & -2 & -8
\end{array}
$$

We know that $x - 1$ is not a factor of $P(x)$. We try $x + 1$.

$$
\begin{array}{r|rrrr}
-1 & 1+2 & -5 & -6 \\
   & -1 & -1 & 6 \\
\hline
   & 1 & 1 & -6 & 0
\end{array}
$$

We know that $x + 1$ is one factor and the quotient, $x^2 + x - 6$, is another.

$$P(x) = (x + 1)(x^2 + x - 6)$$

The trinomial is easily factored.

$$P(x) = (x + 1)(x + 3)(x - 2)$$

To solve the equation $P(x) = 0$, we use the principle of zero products.

$$x + 1 = 0 \quad \text{or } x + 3 = 0 \quad \text{or } x - 2 = 0$$
$$x = -1 \text{ or} \quad x = -3 \text{ or} \quad x = 2$$

The solutions are -1, -3, and 2.

TRY THIS

7. Determine whether $x - \frac{1}{2}$ is a factor of $4x^4 + 2x^3 + 8x - 1$. No

8. Determine whether $x + 5$ is a factor of $x^4 + 625$. Yes

9. Let $P(x) = x^3 + 6x^2 - x - 30$.
   a. Determine whether $x - 2$ is a factor of $P(x)$.   b. Find another factor of $P(x)$.
   c. Find a complete factorization of $P(x)$.   d. Solve the equation $P(x) = 0$.

9. a. Yes
   b. $x^2 + 8x + 15$
   c. $(x - 2)(x + 5)(x + 3)$
   d. $2, -5, -3$

Proof of Theorem 11–2

If we divide $P(x)$ by $x - r$, we obtain a quotient and remainder, related as follows.

$$P(x) = (x - r) \cdot Q(x) + P(r)$$

Then if $P(r) = 0$, we have

$$P(x) = (x - r) \cdot Q(x),$$

so $x - r$ is a factor of $P(x)$.

11–2

Exercises

Use synthetic division to find the quotient and remainder.

1. $(2x^4 + 7x^3 + x - 12) \div (x + 3)$
2. $(x^3 - 7x^2 + 13x + 3) \div (x - 2)$
3. $(x^3 - 2x^2 - 8) \div (x + 2)$
4. $(x^3 - 3x + 10) \div (x - 2)$
5. $(x^4 - 1) \div (x - 1)$
6. $(x^5 + 32) \div (x + 2)$
7. $(2x^4 + 3x^2 - 1) \div \left(x - \frac{1}{2}\right)$
8. $(3x^4 - 2x^2 + 2) \div \left(x - \frac{1}{4}\right)$
9. $(x^4 - y^4) \div (x - y)$
10. $(x^3 + 3ix^2 - 4ix - 2) \div (x + i)$

Use synthetic division to find the function values.

11. $P(x) = x^3 - 6x^2 + 11x - 6$
    Find $P(1)$, $P(-2)$, $P(3)$.
12. $P(x) = x^3 + 7x^2 - 12x - 3$
    Find $P(-3)$, $P(-2)$, $P(1)$.
13. $P(x) = 2x^5 - 3x^4 + 2x^3 - x + 8$
    Find $P(20)$ and $P(-3)$.
14. $P(x) = x^5 - 10x^4 + 20x^3 - 5x - 100$
    Find $P(-10)$ and $P(5)$.

Using synthetic division, determine whether the numbers are roots of the polynomials.

15. $-3, 2; P(x) = 3x^3 + 5x^2 - 6x + 18$
Yes; no

16. $-4, 2; P(x) = 3x^3 + 11x^2 - 2x + 8$
Yes; no

17. $-3, \frac{1}{2}; P(x) = x^3 - \frac{7}{2}x^2 + x - \frac{3}{2}$
No; no

18. $i, -i, -2; P(x) = x^3 + 2x^2 + x + 2$
Yes; yes; yes

Determine whether the expressions of the type $x - r$ are factors of the polynomial $P(x)$.

19. $P(x) = x^3 - 3x^2 - 4x - 12; x + 2$ No

20. $P(x) = x^3 - 4x^2 + 3x + 8; x + 1$ Yes

21. $P(x) = 2x^2 + 2x + 1; x - \left(-\frac{1}{2} - \frac{1}{2}i\right)$ Yes

22. $P(x) = 9x^2 + 6x + 2; x - \left(\frac{1}{3} - \frac{1}{3}i\right)$ No

23. $P(x) = x^5 - 1; x - 1$ Yes

24. $P(x) = x^5 + 1; x + 1$ Yes

25. Let $P(x) = x^3 + 2x^2 - x - 2$.
  a. Determine whether $x - 1$ is a factor of $P(x)$.
  b. Find another factor of $P(x)$.
  c. Find a complete factorization of $P(x)$.
  d. Solve the equation $P(x) = 0$.
  a. Yes b. $x^2 + 3x + 2$ c. $(x - 1)(x + 2)(x + 1)$ d. $1, -2, -1$

26. Let $P(x) = x^3 + 4x^2 - x - 4$.
  a. Determine whether $x + 1$ is a factor of $P(x)$.
  b. Find another factor of $P(x)$.
  c. Find a complete factorization of $P(x)$.
  d. Solve the equation $P(x) = 0$.
  a. Yes b. $x^2 + 3x - 4$ c. $(x + 1)(x + 4)(x - 1)$ d. $-1, -4, 1$

Factor the polynomial $P(x)$. Then solve the equation $P(x) = 0$.

27. $P(x) = x^3 + 4x^2 + x - 6$

28. $P(x) = x^3 + 5x^2 - 2x - 24$

29. $P(x) = x^3 - 6x^2 + 3x + 10$

30. $P(x) = x^3 + 2x^2 - 13x + 10$

31. $P(x) = x^3 - x^2 - 14x + 24$

32. $P(x) = x^3 - 3x^2 - 10x + 24$

33. $P(x) = x^4 - x^3 - 19x^2 + 49x - 30$

34. $P(x) = x^4 + 11x^3 + 41x^2 + 61x + 30$

27. $P(x) = (x - 1)(x + 2)(x + 3)$; 1, $-2, -3$
28. $P(x) = (x - 2)(x + 3)(x + 4)$; 2, $-3, -4$
29. $P(x) = (x - 2)(x - 5)(x + 1)$; 2, 5, -1
30. $P(x) = (x - 1)(x - 2)(x + 5)$; 1, 2, -5
31. $P(x) = (x - 2)(x - 3)(x + 4)$; 2, 3, -4

Extension

Solve.

35. $x^3 + 2x^2 - 13x + 10 > 0$

36. $x^4 - x^3 - 19x^2 + 49x - 30 < 0$

37. Find k so that $x + 2$ is a factor of $x^3 - kx^2 + 2x + 7k$. 4

38. Find k so that $x - 1$ is a factor of $x^3 - 3x^2 + kx - 1$. 3

39. For what values of k will the remainder be the same when $x^2 + kx + 4$ is divided by $x - 1$ or $x + 1$? None

40. When $x^2 - 3x + 2k$ is divided by $x + 2$ the remainder is 7. Find the value of k. $-\frac{3}{2}$

41. Given that $f(x) = 2.13x^5 - 42.1x^3 + 17.5x^2 + 0.953x - 1.98$, use a calculator to find $f(3.21)$
  a. by synthetic division. -485.1587
  b. by substitution. -485.1588

32. $P(x) = (x - 2)(x - 4)(x + 3)$; 2, $-3, 4$
33. $P(x) = (x - 1)(x - 2)(x - 3)$ $(x + 5)$; 1, 2, 3, -5
34. $P(x) = (x + 1)(x + 2)(x + 3)$ $(x + 5)$; $-1, -2, -3, -5$

Challenge

42. Use the Factor Theorem to prove that $x - a$ is a factor of $x^n - a^n$, for any natural number n.
$P(a) = a^n - a^n = 0$. Since $P(a) = 0$, $x - a$ is a factor of $x^n - a^n$.

11–3 Theorems About Roots

Finding Roots by Factoring

Let us recall Theorem 7–10.

THEOREM 7–10

The Fundamental Theorem of Algebra

Every polynomial with complex coefficients and of degree n (where $n \geq 1$) can be factored into n linear factors.

Once a polynomial is factored into linear factors, its roots are easy to find, using the principle of zero products.

EXAMPLES

Polynomial   Roots

1. $P_1(x) = x^4 + x^3 - 13x^2 - x + 12$
$ = (x - 3)(x + 4)(x + 1)(x - 1)$ $3, -4, -1, 1$

2. $P_2(x) = 3x^4 - 15x^3 + 18x^2 + 12x - 24$
$ = 3(x - 2)(x - 2)(x - 2)(x + 1)$
$ = 3(x - 2)^3(x + 1)$ $2, -1$

Note that while the polynomial $P_2(x)$ has 4 linear factors, it has only 2 roots. The factor $x - 2$ occurs three times. We say that 2 is a root of multiplicity 3 and -1 is a root of multiplicity 1.

THEOREM 11–3

Every polynomial of degree n (where $n \geq 0$) has at least one root and at most n roots.

TRY THIS Find the roots, stating the multiplicity of each.

1. $P(x) = 4(x + 7)^2(x - 3)$ 2. $P(x) = (x^2 - 7x + 12)^2$ 3. $P(x) = 5x^2 - 5$

1. -7(multiplicity 2), 3(multiplicity 1)
2. 4(multiplicity 2), 3(multiplicity 2)
3. 1(multiplicity 1), -1(multiplicity 1)

Finding Polynomials with Specified Roots

Given several numbers, we can find a polynomial having them as its roots.

EXAMPLE 3

Find a polynomial of degree three, having the roots -2, 1, and $3i$.

By Theorem 11–2, such a polynomial has factors $x + 2$, $x - 1$, and $x - 3i$, so we have the polynomial $P(x)$.

$$P(x) = a_n(x + 2)(x - 1)(x - 3i)$$

The number a_n can be any nonzero number. The simplest polynomial will be obtained if we let it be 1. If we then multiply the factors we obtain the following.

$$P(x) = x^3 + (1 - 3i)x^2 + (-2 - 3i)x + 6i$$

EXAMPLE 4

Find a polynomial of degree 5 with -1 as the root of multiplicity 3, 4 as a root of multiplicity 1, and 0 as a root of multiplicity 1.

We proceed as in Example 3, letting $a_n = 1$.

$$(x + 1)^3(x - 4)(x - 0) = x^5 - x^4 - 9x^3 - 11x^2 - 4x$$

TRY THIS

4. Find a polynomial of degree 3 that has -1, 2, and 5 as roots. $\quad (x + 1)(x - 2)(x - 5) = x^3 - 6x^2 + 3x + 10$

5. Find a polynomial of degree 5 with -2 as a root of multiplicity 3 and 0 as a root of multiplicity 2. $\quad x^2(x + 2)^3 = x^5 + 6x^4 + 12x^3 + 8x^2$

Real and Rational Coefficients

Consider the quadratic equation $x^2 - 2x + 2 = 0$, with real coefficients. Its roots are $1 + i$, and $1 - i$. Note that they are complex conjugates. This generalizes to any polynomial with real coefficients.

THEOREM 11–4

If a complex number z is a root of a polynomial $P(x)$ of degree greater than or equal to 1 with real coefficients, then its conjugate $\bar{z}$ is also a root. (Complex roots occur in conjugate pairs.)

To apply Theorem 11–4, it is essential that the coefficients be real numbers. This can be seen by considering Example 3. In that polynomial the root $3i$ occurs but its conjugate does not. This can happen because some of the coefficients of the polynomial are not real.

When a polynomial has rational numbers for coefficients, certain irrational roots also occur in pairs, as described in the following theorem.

THEOREM 11–5

Suppose $P(x)$ is a polynomial with rational coefficients and of degree greater than or equal to 1. Then if either of the following is a root, so is the other: $a + c\sqrt{b}, a - c\sqrt{b}$.

EXAMPLE 5

Suppose a polynomial of degree 6 with rational coefficients has $-2 + 5i$, $-i$, and $1 - \sqrt{3}$ as some of its roots. Find the other roots.

By Theorem 11–4, the conjugates of $-2 + 5i$ and $-i$ are roots. They are $-2 - 5i$ and i. By Theorem 11–5, since $1 - \sqrt{3}$ is a root, $1 + \sqrt{3}$ is also a root. There are no other roots since the degree is 6.

TRY THIS

6. Suppose a polynomial of degree 5 with rational coefficients has -4, $7 - 2i$, and $3 + \sqrt{5}$ as roots. Find the other roots. $7 + 2i, 3 - \sqrt{5}$

Finding Polynomials

EXAMPLE 6

Find a polynomial of lowest degree with rational coefficients which has $1 - \sqrt{2}$ and $1 + 2i$ as some of its roots.

By Theorem 11–4, $1 - 2i$ is a root. By Theorem 11–5, $1 + \sqrt{2}$ is a root. Thus the polynomial is as follows.

$$
\begin{aligned}
P(x) &= [x - (1 - \sqrt{2})][x - (1 + \sqrt{2})][x - (1 + 2i)][x - (1 - 2i)] \\
&= (x^2 - 2x - 1)(x^2 - 2x + 5) \\
&= x^4 - 4x^3 + 8x^2 - 8x - 5
\end{aligned}
$$

TRY THIS

7. Find a polynomial of lowest degree with rational coefficients which has $2 + \sqrt{3}$ and $1 - i$ as some of its roots. $x^4 - 6x^3 + 11x^2 - 10x + 2$

8. Find a polynomial of lowest degree with real coefficients which has $2i$ and 2 as some of its roots. $x^3 - 2x^2 + 4x - 8$

Finding Roots

EXAMPLE 7

Let $P(x) = x^4 - 5x^3 + 10x^2 - 20x + 24$. Find the other roots of $P(x)$, given that $2i$ is a root.

Since $2i$ is a root, we know that $-2i$ is also a root.

$$P(x) = (x - 2i)(x + 2i) \cdot Q(x), \text{ for some } Q(x)$$

Since $(x - 2i)(x + 2i) = x^2 + 4$, we write $P(x)$ as follows.

$$P(x) = (x^2 + 4) \cdot Q(x)$$

We find, using division, that $Q(x) = x^2 - 5x + 6$. We factor $x^2 - 5x + 6$.

$$P(x) = (x^2 + 4)(x - 2)(x - 3)$$

Thus the other roots are $-2i$, 2, and 3.

TRY THIS

9. Find the other roots of $x^4 + x^3 - x^2 + x - 2$ given that i is a root. $-i, -2, 1$

11–3

Exercises

Find the roots of each polynomial and state the multiplicity of each.

1. $(x + 3)^2(x - 1)$
2. $-4(x + 2)(x - \pi)^5$
3. $-8(x - 3)^2(x + 4)^3 x^4$
4. $x^3(x - 1)^2(x + 4)$
5. $(x^2 - 5x + 6)^2$
6. $(x^2 - x - 2)^2$

Find a polynomial of degree 3 with the given numbers as roots.

7. $-2, 3, 5$ $x^3 - 6x^2 - x + 30$

8. $3, 2, -1$ $x^3 - 4x^2 + x + 6$

9. $2, i, -i$ $x^3 - 2x^2 + x - 2$

10. $-3, 2i, -2i$ $x^3 + 3x^2 + 4x + 12$

11. $2 + i, 2 - i, 3$ $x^3 - 7x^2 + 17x - 15$

12. $1 + 4i, 1 - 4i, -1$ $x^3 - x^2 + 15x + 17$

13. $\sqrt{2}, -\sqrt{2}, \sqrt{3}$. $x^3 - \sqrt{3}x^2 - 2x + 2\sqrt{3}$, No
Are the coefficients rational?

14. $\sqrt{3}, -\sqrt{3}, \sqrt{2}$. $x^3 - \sqrt{2}x^2 - 3x + 3\sqrt{2}$, No
Are the coefficients rational?

15. Find a polynomial of degree 4 with 0 as a root of multiplicity 2 and 5 as a root of multiplicity 2. $x^4 - 10x^3 + 25x^2$

16. Find a polynomial of degree 4 with 0 as a root of multiplicity 4. x^4

17. Find a polynomial of degree 4 with -2 as a root of multiplicity 1, 3 as a root of multiplicity 2, and -1 as a root of multiplicity 1. $x^4 - 3x^3 - 7x^2 + 15x + 18$

18. Find a polynomial of degree 5 with 4 as a root of multiplicity 3 and -2 as a root of multiplicity 2. $x^5 - 8x^4 + 4x^3 + 80x^2 - 64x - 256$

Suppose a polynomial of degree 6 with real coefficients has the given roots. Find the other roots.

19. $-5, 6, 5 + i, -2i$ $5 - i, 2i$

20. $8, 6, -3 - 2i, 4i$ $-3 + 2i, -4i$

Suppose a polynomial of degree 5 with rational coefficients has the given roots. Find the other roots.

21. $6, -3 + 4i, 4 - \sqrt{5}$ $-3 - 4i, 4 + \sqrt{5}$

22. $8, 6 - 7i, \frac{1}{2} + \sqrt{11}$ $6 + 7i, \frac{1}{2} - \sqrt{11}$

23. $-2, 3, 4, 1 - i$ $1 + i$

24. $3, 4, -5, 7 + i$ $7 - i$

Find a polynomial of lowest degree with rational coefficients that has the given numbers as some of its roots.

25. $1 + i, 2$ $x^3 - 4x^2 + 6x - 4$

26. $2 - i, -1$ $x^3 - 3x^2 + x + 5$

27. $3i, -2$ $x^3 + 2x^2 + 9x + 18$

28. $-4i, 5$ $x^3 - 5x^2 + 16x - 80$

29. $2 - \sqrt{3}, 1 + i$ $x^4 - 6x^3 + 11x^2 - 10x + 2$

30. $3 + \sqrt{2}, 2 - i$ $x^4 - 10x^3 + 36x^2 - 58x + 35$

31. $\sqrt{5}, -3i$ $x^4 + 4x^2 - 45$

32. $-\sqrt{2}, 4i$ $x^4 + 14x^2 - 32$

33. $-\sqrt{2}, 2 + \sqrt{7}i$ $x^4 - 4x^3 + 9x^2 + 8x - 22$

34. $3i, -3 - \sqrt{5}i$ $x^4 + 6x^3 + 23x^2 + 54x + 126$

Given that the polynomial has the given root, find the other roots.

35. $x^4 - 5x^3 + 7x^2 - 5x + 6; -i$ $i, 3, 2$

36. $x^3 - 4x^2 + x - 4; -i$ $i, 4$

37. $x^4 - 16; 2i$ $-2i, 2, -2$

38. $x^4 - 1; i$ $-i, 1, -1$

39. $x^3 - x^2 - 7x + 15; -3$ $2 + i, 2 - i$

40. $x^3 - 6x^2 + 13x - 20; 4$ $1 + 2i, 1 - 2i$

41. $x^3 - 8; 2$ $-1 + i\sqrt{3}, -1 - i\sqrt{3}$

42. $x^3 + 8; -2$ $1 + i\sqrt{3}, 1 - i\sqrt{3}$

43. $x^4 - 2x^3 + 17x^2 + 6x - 30; -\sqrt{3}$ $\sqrt{3}, 1 + 3i, 1 - 3i$

44. $x^4 + 4x^3 + 2x^2 - 28x - 63; \sqrt{7}$ $-\sqrt{7}, -2 + \sqrt{5}i, -2 - \sqrt{5}i$

Extension

Solve.

45. $x^3 - 4x^2 + x - 4 = 0$ $\quad$ 4, i, -i

46. $x^3 - x^2 - 7x + 15 = 0$ $\quad$ -3, 2 + i, 2 - i

47. $x^4 - 2x^3 - 2x - 1 = 0$ $\quad$ i, -i, 1 + $\sqrt{2}$, 1 - $\sqrt{2}$

48. The equation $x^2 + 2ax + b = 0$ has a root of multiplicity 2. Find it. $\quad$ -a

Challenge

49. Prove that a polynomial with positive coefficients cannot have a positive root.

50. Prove that every polynomial of odd degree, with real coefficients, has at least one real root.

51. Prove Theorem 11–4.

52. Prove Theorem 11–5.

49. For $P(x) = a_n x^n + a_{n-1}x^{n-1} + \cdots + a_o$ with a_i positive, consider any positive x. Every term will be positive, hence $P(x) > 0$.

50. By Theorem 11–3, $P(x)$ can be factored into n linear factors, where n is the degree of $P(x)$. Since by Theorem 11–5 the nonreal roots occur in conjugate pairs, there is at least one factor $(x - a)$ with a real.

TWO-VARIABLE POLYNOMIALS/Identifying Conic Sections

The roots of a polynomial in one variable, $P(x)$, can be found by solving the equation $P(x) = 0$. For example, if $Q(x) = 8x^2 - 2x - 15$, the roots of $Q(x)$ are the solutions of $8x^2 - 2x - 15 = 0$. Find the roots of $Q(x)$. $\quad \frac{3}{2}, \frac{-5}{4}$

In this chapter, you have studied polynomials in one variable. However, some of the properties of one-variable polynomials can be applied to polynomials in more than one variable. The following is an example of a polynomial in two variables.

$$Q(x, y) = 2x^2 - 9y^2 + 4x + 18y + 1$$

The "roots" of this polynomial are all the solutions of the equations $Q(x, y) = 0$. To find these solutions, you can graph the corresponding polynomial equation.

$$2x^2 - 9y^2 + 4x + 18y + 1 = 0$$

By completing the squares in x and y, you can write the equation in the following form.

$$\frac{(y - 1)^2}{\frac{8}{9}} - \frac{(x + 1)^2}{4} = 1$$

Thus, the graph of the equation is a hyperbola.

For an equation $ax^2 + by^2 + cx + dy + e = 0$ (a and c not both 0), the product ac can help you identify the shape of the graph. If $ac < 0$, the graph is a hyperbola. If $ac = 0$, it is a parabola. And if $ac > 0$, it is an ellipse. In the polynomial $Q(x, y)$ above, notice that $a = 2$ and $c = -9$. So, the product $ac < 0$, and the graph is a hyperbola.

Use the product ac to identify the graph of each of the following conic sections.

1. $16x^2 + 4y^2 + 96x - 8y + 84 = 0$ $\quad$ ellipse
2. $y^2 + 6y - x + 16 = 0$ $\quad$ parabola
3. $9x^2 - 4y^2 + 54x + 8y + 45 = 0$ $\quad$ hyperbola
4. $x^2 + 6x - y + 10 = 0$ $\quad$ parabola

Draw a graph of the polynomial equation that corresponds to each of the following polynomials.

5. $P(x, y) = 16x^2 + 4y^2 + 96x - 8y + 84$
6. $P(x, y) = y^2 + 6y - x + 16$
7. $P(x, y) = 9x^2 - 4y^2 + 54x + 8y + 45$
8. $P(x, y) = x^2 + 6x - y + 10$

11–4 Rational Roots

Finding the roots of a polynomial is not always easy. However, if a polynomial has integer coefficients, there is a procedure for finding all of the rational roots.

THEOREM 11–6

Rational Roots Theorem

Let $P(x) = a_n x^n + a_{n-1} x^{n-1} + \cdots + a_1 x + a_0$, where all the coefficients are integers. Consider a rational number denoted by $\frac{c}{d}$, where c and d have no common factor besides 1 and -1. If $\frac{c}{d}$ is a root of $P(x)$, then c is a factor of a_0 and d is a factor of a_n.

EXAMPLE 1

Let $P(x) = 3x^4 - 11x^3 + 10x - 4$. Find the rational roots of $P(x)$. If possible, find the other roots.

By the Rational Roots Theorem, if $\frac{c}{d}$ is a root of $P(x)$, then c must be a factor of -4 and d must be a factor of 3. Thus the possibilities for c and d are as follows.

$$c: \quad 1, -1, 4, -4, 2, -2 \qquad d: \quad 1, -1, 3, -3$$

Then the resulting possibilities for $\frac{c}{d}$ are

$$1, -1, 4, -4, \tfrac{1}{3}, -\tfrac{1}{3}, \tfrac{4}{3}, -\tfrac{4}{3}, \tfrac{2}{3}, -\tfrac{2}{3}, 2, \text{ and } -2.$$

Of these 12 possibilities, we know that at most 4 of them could be roots because $P(x)$ is of degree 4. To find which are roots we can use synthetic division.

We try 1.

$$
\begin{array}{r|rrrrr}
1 & 3 & -11 & 0 & 10 & -4 \\
  &   & 3 & -8 & -8 & 2 \\
\hline
  & 3 & -8 & -8 & 2 & -2
\end{array}
$$

$P(1) = -2$, so 1 is not a root.

We try -1.

$$
\begin{array}{r|rrrrr}
-1 & 3 & -11 & 0 & 10 & -4 \\
  &   & -3 & 14 & -14 & 4 \\
\hline
  & 3 & -14 & 14 & -4 & \big|\ 0
\end{array}
$$

$P(-1) = 0$, so -1 is a root, and

$$P(x) = (x + 1)(3x^3 - 14x^2 + 14x - 4).$$

We now use $3x^3 - 14x^2 + 14x - 4$ and check the other possible roots.

We try $\frac{2}{3}$.

$$
\begin{array}{r|rrrr}
\frac{2}{3} & 3 & -14 & 14 & -4 \\
  &   & 2 & -8 & 4 \\
\hline
  & 3 & -12 & 6 & 0
\end{array}
$$

$P\left(\frac{2}{3}\right) = 0$, so $\frac{2}{3}$ is a root. We now know that

$$P(x) = (x + 1)\left(x - \frac{2}{3}\right)(3x^2 - 12x + 6).$$

Since the factor $3x^2 - 12x + 6$ is quadratic, we can use the quadratic formula to find the other roots. They are $2 + \sqrt{2}$ and $2 - \sqrt{2}$. Thus the rational roots are -1 and $\frac{2}{3}$.

TRY THIS Let $P(x) = 2x^4 - 7x^3 - 35x^2 + 13x + 3$ and $\frac{c}{d}$ be a rational root of $P(x)$.

1. What are the possibilities for c?   2. What are the possibilities for d?
3. What are the possibilities for $\frac{c}{d}$?   4. Find the rational roots.
5. If possible, find the other roots. $\ 3 + \sqrt{10}, 3 - \sqrt{10}$

1. $-1, 3, -3$
2. $1, -1, 2, -2$
3. $1, -1, \frac{1}{2}, -\frac{1}{2}, 3, -3, \frac{3}{2}, -\frac{3}{2}$
4. $-3, \frac{1}{2}$

EXAMPLE 2
Let $P(x) = x^3 + 6x^2 + x + 6$. Find the rational roots of $P(x)$. If possible, find the other roots.

By the Rational Roots Theorem, if $\frac{c}{d}$ is a root of $P(x)$, then c must be a factor of 6 and d must be a factor of 1. Thus the possibilities for c and d are as follows.

$$c: 1, -1, 2, -2, 3, -3, 6, -6 \qquad d: 1, -1$$

Find the rational roots, if they exist, of each polynomial. If possible, find the other roots.

5. $x^3 + 3x^2 - 2x - 6$ $\ -3, \sqrt{2}, -\sqrt{2}$
6. $x^3 - x^2 - 3x + 3$ $\ 1, \sqrt{3}, -\sqrt{3}$
7. $5x^4 - 4x^3 + 19x^2 - 16x - 4$ $\ 7. \ 1, -\frac{1}{5}, 2i, -2i$
8. $3x^4 - 4x^3 + x^2 + 6x - 2$
9. $x^4 - 3x^3 - 20x^2 - 24x - 8$
10. $x^4 + 5x^3 - 27x^2 + 31x - 10$
11. $x^3 + 3x^2 - x - 3$ $\ 1, -1, -3$
12. $x^3 + 5x^2 - x - 5$ $\ 1, -1, -5$
13. $x^3 + 8$ $\ -2, 1 + i\sqrt{3}, 1 - i\sqrt{3}$
14. $x^3 - 8$ $\ 2, -1 + i\sqrt{3}, -1 - i\sqrt{3}$
15. $4x^3 - 3x^2 + 4x - 3$ $\ \frac{3}{4}, i, -i$
16. $2x^3 - 3x^2 - x + 1$ $\ \frac{1}{2}, \frac{1 + \sqrt{5}}{2}, \frac{1 - \sqrt{5}}{2}$

Find only the rational roots.

8. $-1, \frac{1}{3}, 1 + i, 1 - i$ 9. $-1, -2, 3 + \sqrt{13}, 3 - \sqrt{13}$
10. $1, 2, -4 + \sqrt{21}, -4 - \sqrt{21}$

17. $x^5 - 5x^4 + 5x^3 + 15x^2 - 36x + 20$ $\ 1, 2, -2$
18. $x^5 - 3x^4 - 3x^3 + 9x^2 - 4x + 12$ $\ 2, -2, 3$
19. $x^4 + 32$ $\ $ No rational
20. $x^6 + 8$ $\ $ No rational
21. $x^3 - x^2 - 4x + 3$ $\ $ No rational
22. $2x^3 + 3x^2 + 2x + 3$ $\ -\frac{3}{2}$
23. $x^4 + 2x^3 + 2x^2 - 4x - 8$ $\ $ No rational
24. $x^4 + 6x^3 + 17x^2 + 36x + 66$ $\ $ No rational

Extension

25. Rational Coefficients. $P(x) = \frac{1}{12}x^3 - \frac{1}{12}x^2 - \frac{2}{3}x + 1$ does not have all integer coefficients, but they are all rational. If we multiply by the LCM of the denominators, 12, we get a polynomial which does have all integer coefficients. Any rational root of $12P(x)$ is a rational root of $P(x)$, and conversely. Find the rational roots of each polynomial. $\ $ a. 2(multiplicity 2), -3(multiplicity 1) b. $1, -1, \frac{2}{3}, -\frac{1}{2}$ c. $\frac{1}{2}$, d. $\frac{3}{4}$

    a. $\frac{1}{12}x^3 - \frac{1}{12}x^2 - \frac{2}{3}x + 1$
    b. $x^4 - \frac{1}{6}x^3 - \frac{4}{3}x^2 + \frac{1}{6}x + \frac{1}{3}$
    c. $\frac{1}{3}x^3 - \frac{1}{2}x^2 - \frac{1}{6}x + \frac{1}{6}$
    d. $\frac{2}{3}x^3 - \frac{1}{2}x^2 + \frac{2}{3}x - \frac{1}{2}$

26. The volume of a cube is 64 cm³. Find the length of a side. (Hint: Solve $x^3 - 64 = 0$.) $\ $ 4 cm

27. The volume of a cube is 125 cm³. Find the length of a side. $\ $ 5 cm

28. An open box of volume 48 cm³ can be made from a piece of tin 10 cm on a side by cutting a square from each corner and folding up the edges. What is the length of a side of the squares? $\ $ 3 cm, $\frac{7 - \sqrt{33}}{2}$ cm

29. An open box of volume 500 cm³ can be made from a piece of tin 20 cm on a side by cutting a square from each corner and folding up the edges. What is the length of a side of the squares? $\ $ 5 cm

Challenge

30. Show that $\sqrt{5}$ is irrational, by considering the equation $x^2 - 5 = 0$. $\ $ The possible rational roots of $x^2 - 5 = 0$ are $\pm 1, \pm 5$. None of these are roots.

11–5 Descartes' Rule and Bounds on Roots

Descartes' Rule of Signs

A rule that helps determine the number of positive real roots of a polynomial is known as Descartes' Rule of Signs. To use the rule we must have the polynomial arranged in descending or ascending order, with no zero terms included. Then we determine the number of variations of sign, that is, the number of times that successive coefficients are of different sign.

For example, in the polynomial $2x^6 - 3x^2 + x + 4$ the number of variations is 2. In the polynomial $3x^5 - 2x^3 - x^2 + x - 2$ there are three variations.

We now state Descartes' Rule.

THEOREM 11–7

Descartes' Rule of Signs

The number of positive real roots of a polynomial with real coefficients is either

1. The same as the number of its variations of sign, or
2. Less than the number of its variations of sign by a positive even integer.

A root of multiplicity m must be counted m times.

EXAMPLES
1. $2x^5 - 5x^2 + 3x + 6$

   The number of variations of sign is two. Therefore the number of positive real roots either is 2 or is less than 2 by 2, 4, 6, etc. Thus the number of positive roots is either 2 or 0, a negative number of roots having no meaning. (Thus, if one positive root is known, you can be sure there is one more.)

2. $5x^4 - 3x^3 + 7x^2 - 12x + 4$

   There are four variations of sign. Thus the number of positive real roots is 4, $4 - 2$, or $4 - 4$; there are 4, 2, or 0 roots.

3. $6x^5 - 2x - 5 = 0$

The number of variations of sign is 1. Therefore there is exactly one positive real root.

TRY THIS In each case, what does Descartes' Rule of Signs tell you about the number of positive real roots?

1. $5x^3 - 4x - 5$ **2.** $6p^6 - 5p^4 + 3p^3 - 7p^2 + p - 2$ **3.** $3x^2 - 2x + 4$

  1   5, 3, or 1   2 or 0

Negative Roots

Descartes' Rule can also be used to help determine the number of negative roots of a polynomial. Recall that the graph of $P(-x)$ is the reflection of the graph of $P(x)$ across the y-axis. The points at which the graph crosses the x-axis are the roots of the polynomial. Thus positive roots of $P(-x)$ are the negative roots of the original polynomial $P(x)$.

THEOREM 11–8

Corollary to Descartes' Rule of Signs

The number of negative real roots of a polynomial $P(x)$ with real coefficients is either

1. The number of variations of sign of $P(-x)$, or
2. Less than the number of variations of sign of $P(-x)$ by a positive even integer.

To apply Theorem 11–8, we construct $P(-x)$ by replacing x by $-x$ wherever it occurs and then count the variations of sign.

EXAMPLES
In each case, what does Descartes' Rule of Signs tell you about the number of negative real roots?

4. $5x^4 + 3x^3 + 7x^2 + 12x + 4$

$\quad P(-x) = 5(-x)^4 + 3(-x)^3 + 7(-x)^2 + 12(-x) + 4$ Replacing x by $-x$

$\qquad\qquad = 5x^4 - 3x^3 + 7x^2 - 12x + 4$ Simplifying

There are four variations of sign, so the number of negative roots is either 4 or 2 or 0.

5. $2x^5 - 5x^2 + 3x + 6$

$$P(-x) = 2(-x)^5 - 5(-x)^2 + 3(-x) + 6 \quad \text{Replacing } x \text{ by } -x$$
$$= -2x^5 - 5x^2 - 3x + 6 \quad \text{Simplifying}$$

There is one variation of sign, so there is exactly one negative root.

TRY THIS In each case, what does Descartes' Rule of Signs tell you about the number of negative real roots?

4. $5x^3 - 4x - 5$ **5.** $6p^6 - 5p^4 + 3p^3 - 7p^2 + p - 2$ **6.** $3x^2 - 2x + 4$
   2 or 0   1   0

Upper Bounds on Roots

Suppose you perform the synthetic division using $x - a$ as a divisor for some positive number a, and the result is a quotient with non-negative coefficients and remainder.

$$P(x) = (x - a) \cdot Q(x) + R$$

positive   0 or positive

all positive coefficients

This shows that there can be no root of $P(x)$ greater than the positive number a. If there were such a root r, we would have $P(r) = 0$. But $(r - a) > 0$, $Q(r) > 0$, and $R \geq 0$, so the expression $(r - a) \cdot Q(r) + R$ could not be zero. (We know $Q(r)$ is positive because all the coefficients are nonnegative and the number r is assumed to be positive.)

The number a is an upper bound to all the roots of $P(x)$.

THEOREM 11–9

Upper Bound Theorem

If when a polynomial is divided by $x - a$, where a is positive, the remainder and all coefficients of the quotient are non-negative, the number a is an upper bound to the roots of the polynomial (all of the roots are less than or equal to a).

EXAMPLE 6

Determine an upper bound to the roots of $3x^4 - 11x^3 + 10x - 4$.

We use synthetic division to divide by some *positive a*, say 4.

$$\begin{array}{r|rrrrr} 4 & 3 & -11 & 0 & 10 & -4 \\ & & 12 & 4 & 16 & 104 \\ \hline & 3 & 1 & 4 & 26 & 100 \end{array}$$

Since there are no negative numbers in the bottom row, 4 is an upper bound.

> Remember, in applying Theorem 11–9 the number a must be a *positive* number.

TRY THIS In each case, determine an upper bound to the roots. Answers may vary.

7. $5x^4 - 18x^2 + 3x - 2$ 8. $x^3 - 75x^2 + 3$
   2 or 3   75

Lower Bounds

We now apply Theorem 11–9 to $P(-x)$. If the number a is an upper bound for $P(-x)$, then $-a$ is a lower bound for $P(x)$.

EXAMPLE 7
Determine a lower bound to the roots of $P(x)$, where
$P(x) = 3x^4 + 11x^3 + 10x - 4$.

We first construct $P(-x)$ by replacing x by $-x$.

$$\begin{aligned} P(-x) &= 3(-x)^4 + 11(-x)^3 + 10(-x) - 4 \\ &= 3x^4 - 11x^3 - 10x - 4 \quad \text{Simplifying} \end{aligned}$$

Next, we use synthetic division, dividing by $x - 4$.

$$\begin{array}{r|rrrrr} 4 & 3 & -11 & 0 & -10 & -4 \\ & & 12 & 4 & 16 & 24 \\ \hline & 3 & 1 & 4 & 6 & 20 \end{array}$$

Since none of the numbers in the bottom row is negative, 4 is an upper bound to the roots of $P(-x)$. Thus -4 is a lower bound to the roots of $3x^4 + 11x^3 + 10x - 4$, which is $P(x)$.

When the leading coefficient is itself negative, it would be impossible to get $Q(x)$ with all positive coefficients. We can consider $-P(x)$, which is a reflection of $P(x)$ across the x-axis, and so has the same roots.

TRY THIS Determine a lower bound to the roots.

9. $5x^4 + 18x^3 + 3x - 2$ −4 10. $4x^3 + 7x^2 + 3x + 5$ −2

Exercises

What does Descartes' Rule of Signs tell you about the number of positive real roots?

1. $3x^5 - 2x^2 + x - 1$ ₃ or 1 — 3 or 1
2. $5x^6 - 3x^3 + x^2 - x$ 3 or 1
3. $6x^7 + 2x^2 + 5x + 4 = 0$ 0
4. $-3x^5 - 7x^3 - 4x - 5 = 0$ 0
5. $3p^{18} + 2p^4 - 5p^2 + p + 3$ 2 or 0
6. $5t^{12} - 7t^4 + 3t^2 + t + 1$ 2 or 0

What does Descartes' Rule of Signs tell you about the number of negative real roots?

7. $3x^5 - 2x^2 + x - 1$ 0
8. $5x^6 - 3x^3 + x^2 - x$ 0
9. $6x^7 + 2x^2 + 5x + 4 = 0$ 3 or 1
10. $-3x^5 - 7x^3 - 4x - 5 = 0$ 1
11. $3p^{18} + 2p^3 - 5p^2 + p + 3$ 2 or 0
12. $5t^{11} - 7t^4 + 3t^2 + t + 1$ 3 or 1

Determine an upper bound to the roots. Answers may vary.

13. $3x^4 - 15x^2 + 2x - 3$ 3
14. $4x^4 - 14x^2 + 4x - 2$ 3
15. $6x^3 - 17x^2 - 3x - 1$ 4
16. $5x^3 - 15x^2 + 5x - 4$ 3

Determine a lower bound to the roots. Answers may vary.

17. $3x^4 - 15x^3 + 2x - 3$ −1
18. $4x^4 - 17x^3 + 3x - 2$ −1
19. $6x^3 + 15x^2 + 3x - 1$ −3
20. $6x^3 + 12x^2 + 5x - 3$ −3

What does Descartes' Rule of Signs tell you about the roots of the polynomial or equation? Find upper and lower bounds to the real roots.

21. $x^4 - 2x^2 + 12x - 8$
22. $x^4 - 6x^2 + 20x - 24$
23. $x^4 - 2x^2 - 8 = 0$
24. $3x^4 - 5x^2 - 4 = 0$
25. $x^4 - 9x^2 - 6x + 4$
26. $x^4 - 21x^2 + 4x + 6$
27. $x^4 + 3x^2 + 2 = 0$
28. $x^4 + 5x^2 + 6 = 0$

21. 3 or 1 positive; 1 negative; upper bound 2; lower bound −3
22. 3 or 1 positive; 1 negative; upper bound 3; lower bound −4
23. 1 positive; 1 negative; 2 nonreal; upper bound 2; lower bound −2
24. 1 positive; 1 negative; upper bound 2; lower bound −2
25. 2 or 0 positive; 2 or 0 negative; upper bound 4; lower bound −3
26. 2 or 0 positive; 2 or 0 negative; upper bound 5; lower bound −5
27. 0 positive; 0 negative; 4 nonreal
28. 0 positive; 0 negative; 4 nonreal
29. Let $P(x) = x^n - 1$. There is one variation of sign, so there is just one positive root. Since n is even, $P(-x) = P(x)$. Hence $P(-x)$ has just one variation of sign, and there is just one negative root. Zero is not a root, so the total number of real roots is two.
30. Let $P(x) = x^n - 1$. There is one variation of sign, hence one positive root. $P(-x) = (-x)^n - 1$ has no variation, so there is no negative root.

Extension

29. Prove that for n a positive even integer, $x^n - 1$ has only two real roots.

30. Prove that for n an odd positive integer, $x^n - 1$ has only one real root.

Challenge

31. Show that $x^4 + ax^2 + bx - c$, where a, b, and c are positive, has just two nonreal roots.

11–6 Graphs of Polynomial Functions

Graphs of first-degree polynomial functions are lines; graphs of second-degree, or quadratic, functions are parabolas. We now consider polynomials of higher degree. We begin with some general principles to be kept in mind while graphing. We consider only polynomials with real coefficients.

1. Every polynomial has as its domain the set of real numbers. The graph of any function is a continuous unbroken curve that must pass the vertical line test.

2. Unless a polynomial function is linear, no part of its graph is straight.

3. A polynomial of degree n cannot have more than n real roots. This means that the graph cannot cross the x-axis more than n times, so we know something about the shape of the curve. Third-degree, or cubic, functions have graphs like the following.

 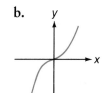 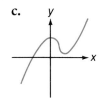

a.   b.   c.

In **a.** the graph crosses the axis three times, so there are three real roots. In **b.** and **c.** there is only one x-intercept, so there is only one real root in each case.

Graphs of fourth-degree, or quartic, polynomials look like these.

 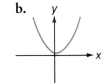 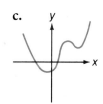

a.   b.   c.

In **a.** there are four real roots, in **b.** there is one, and in **c.** there are two.

Multiple roots occur at points like the following.

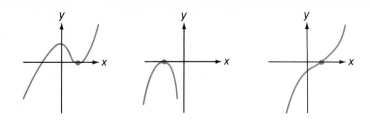

Graphing Polynomials

To graph polynomials, keep in mind previously established results and proceed as follows.

Graphing Polynomials

1. Look at the degree of the polynomial and its leading coefficient. This gives a lot of information about the general shape of the graph.
2. Look for symmetries, as covered in Chapter 9.
3. Make a table of values using synthetic division.
4. Find the y-intercept and as many x-intercepts as possible (the latter are roots of the polynomial). In doing this, recall the theorems about roots, including Descartes' Rule of Signs.
5. Plot the points and connect them appropriately.

EXAMPLE 1

Graph $P(x) = 2x^3 - x + 2$.

1. This polynomial is of degree 3 with leading coefficient positive. Thus as we move far to the right, function values increase in the positive direction. As we move far left, they will be negative and decrease. The curve will have the general shape of a cubic.

2. The function is not odd or even. However, $2x^3 - x$ is an odd function, with the origin as a point of symmetry. $P(x)$ is a translation of this upward 2 units; hence the point $(0, 2)$ is a point of symmetry.

3. From a table of values we find $(0, 2)$, the y-intercept. An upper bound is 1 and a lower bound is -2. The points $(1, 3)$, $(2, 16)$, $(-1, 1)$ and $(-2, -12)$ are on the graph.

4. Descartes' Rule tells us that there are 2 or 0 positive roots and that there is just one negative root.

5. We plot this information and consider the three possibilities.

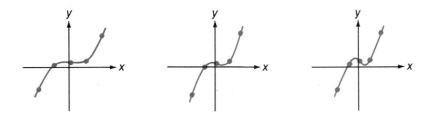

In this example it is not easy to see how to draw the graph, because we do not know the shape of the curve between $(-1, 1)$ and $(0, 2)$ and between $(0, 2)$ and $(1, 3)$. We therefore need to plot some more points between -1 and 1. After we determine the points using a calculator, the complete graph is sketched as follows.

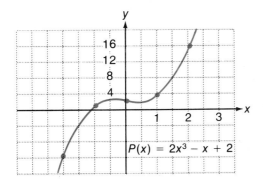

$$P(x) = 2x^3 - x + 2$$

TRY THIS Graph.

1. $P(x) = x^3 - 4x^2 - 3x + 12$

Solving Equations

Whenever we find the roots, or zeros, of a function $P(x)$ we have solved the equation $P(x) = 0$. One means of finding approximate solutions of polynomial equations is by graphing. We graph the function $y = P(x)$ and note where the graph crosses the x-axis. In Example 1, there is a real solution of the equation $2x^3 - x + 2 = 0$ at about -1.1.

We can approximate roots more precisely by further calculation.

EXAMPLE 2

Use a calculator to find a better approximation of the solution of $2x^3 - x + 2 = 0$, which is near -1.1.

We know that $P(-1) = 1$ and $P(-2) = -12$, so there must be a root between -1 and -2. To find a better approximation we use synthetic division.

$P(-1.1) = 0.44$ and $P(-1.2) = -0.26$. Therefore, the graph crosses the x-axis between -1.1 and -1.2. Further calculation shows $P(-1.16) = 0.04$ and $P(-1.17) = -0.03$, so we have a root between -1.16 and -1.17.

We now have an approximation to hundredths, -1.16. In this manner the approximation can be made as close as we please.

TRY THIS

2. **a.** Graph $P(x) = x^3 - 3x^2 + 1$.
   b. Use the graph to approximate the roots to tenths. $\quad$ 0.7, $-$0.5, 2.9

11–6	

Exercises

Graph.

1. $P(x) = x^3 - 3x^2 - 2x - 6$ $\qquad$ 2. $P(x) = x^3 + 4x^2 - 3x - 12$

3. $P(x) = 2x^4 + x^3 - 7x^2 - x + 6$ $\qquad$ 4. $P(x) = 3x^4 + 5x^3 + 5x^2 - 5x - 6$

5. $P(x) = x^5 - 2x^4 - x^3 + 2x^2$ $\qquad$ 6. $P(x) = x^5 - 2x^4 + x^3 - 2x^2$

Graph the corresponding polynomial functions, in order to find approximate solutions of the equations.

7. $x^3 - 3x - 2 = 0$ $\quad$ $-1, 2$ $\qquad$ 8. $x^3 - 3x^2 + 3 = 0$ $\quad$ $-0.9, 1.4, 2.7$

9. $x^3 - 3x - 4 = 0$ $\quad$ 2.2 $\qquad$ 10. $x^3 - 3x^2 + 5 = 0$ $\quad$ -1.1

11. $x^4 + x^2 + 1 = 0$ $\quad$ No real solution $\qquad$ 12. $x^4 + 2x^2 + 2 = 0$ $\quad$ No real solution

13. $x^4 - 6x^2 + 8 = 0$ $\quad$ $\pm 1.4, \pm 2$ $\qquad$ 14. $x^4 - 4x^2 + 2 = 0$ $\quad$ $\pm 0.7, \pm 1.7$

15. $x^5 + x^4 - x^3 - x^2 - 2x - 2 = 0$ $\quad$ $1, \pm 1.4$ $\qquad$ 16. $x^5 - 2x^4 - 2x^3 + 4x^2 - 3x + 6 = 0$ $\quad$ $\pm 1.7, 2$

Extension

17. The equation $2x^5 + 2x^3 - x^2 - 1 = 0$ has a solution between 0 and 1. Use a calculator to approximate it, to hundredths. $\quad$ 0.75

18. The equation $x^4 - 2x^3 - 3x^2 + 4x + 2 = 0$ has a solution between 1 and 2. Use a calculator to approximate it, to hundredths. 1.41

In each of the following, graph and then approximate the irrational roots, to hundredths. Use a calculator.

19. $P(x) = x^3 - 2x^2 - x + 4$ −1.27
20. $P(x) = x^3 - 4x^2 + x + 3$ −0.7, 1.24, 3.46

Challenge

21. Use a calculator to graph $P(x) = 5.8x^4 - 2.3x^2 - 6.1$.
22. Nested evaluation. A procedure for evaluating a polynomial is as follows. Given a polynomial, such as $3x^4 - 5x^3 + 4x^2 - 5$, successively factor out x, as shown.

$$x(x(x(3x - 5) + 4)) - 5$$

Given a value of x, substitute it in the innermost parentheses and work your way out, at each step multiplying, then adding or subtracting. Show that this process is identical to synthetic division.

USING A CALCULATOR/Evaluating Polynomials

A calculator with power and memory keys can be used to evaluate polynomials.

EXAMPLE 1
Problem: Let $P(x) = 2x^3 - x + 2$.
        Find $P(-1.16)$.

Enter: 1.16 [+/−]   [Min]   [x^y] 3
Display: 1.16 −1.16 −1.16   3

Enter: [×]   2   [−]   [MR]
Display: −1.560896 2 −3.121792 −1.16

Enter: [+]   2   [=]
Display: −1.961792 2 0.038208

If your calculator does not have an x^y key, you can use it to evaluate polynomials by first rewriting them in *nested form*.

EXAMPLE 2
Problem: Let $Q(x) = 2x^5 + 2x^3 - x^2 - 1$.
        Find $Q(0.75)$.

Nested polynomial: $((2x^2 + 2)x - 1)x^2 - 1$

Enter: 2 [×] 0.75 [×] 0.75 [+]
Display: 2   0.75 1.5 0.75 1.125

Enter: 2 [=]   [×] 0.75 [−]
Display: 2 3.125   0.75 2.34375

Enter: 1 [=]   [×] 0.75 [×]
Display: 1 1.34375   0.75 1.0078125

Enter: 0.75 [−] 1 [=]
Display: 0.75 0.7558593 1 −0.2441406

CAREERS/Astronomy

Astronomers study celestial bodies using telescopes equipped with devices such as cameras, spectrometers (for measuring wave lengths of radiant energy), and photometers (for measuring light intensity). Instruments carried into space in balloons, satellites, or space probes provide additional information for astronomers to use to determine sizes, brightnesses, shapes, motions, and positions of celestial bodies.

All astronomers are interested in the orbits of the planets, the sun, asteroids, and comets; but astronomers who specialize in celestial mechanics have a particular interest in the calculation of orbits of

earth-launched satellites. To perform their calculations, astronomers first observe the motions and positions of the space vehicle. For instance, an orbiting solar observatory launched by the United States was found to have an apogee (point farthest from the earth) of 358 miles and a perigee (point closest to the earth) of 205 miles. Astronomers use the equation $\frac{x^2}{a^2} + \frac{y^2}{b^2} = 1$, which you learned in Section 10–3, to find vertices and foci of an elliptical orbit.

$$\frac{x^2}{a^2} + \frac{y^2}{b^2} = 1$$

Let $a = 358$ and $b = 205$.

$$\frac{x^2}{358^2} + \frac{y^2}{205^2} = 1$$

The vertices are $(-358, 0)$, $(358, 0)$, $(0, 205)$, and $(0, -205)$.

The foci are found using the equation $c^2 = a^2 - b^2$.

$c^2 = 358^2 - 205^2$
$c^2 = 128,164 - 42,025$
$c^2 = 86,139$
$c = \sqrt{86,139}$
$c \approx 293.49$

The foci are $(-293.49, 0)$ and $(293.49, 0)$.

Knowledge about the orbital motion, the size, the shape, and the structure of satellites and celestial bodies is gathered and computerized. It is

then used by astronomers researching subjects such as the statistical theory of motion of celestial bodies.

Exercises

For each ellipse find the center, vertices, and foci. Then graph the ellipse.

1. $\frac{x^2}{49} + \frac{y^2}{16} = 1$

2. $\frac{(x-3)^2}{4} + \frac{(y-1)^2}{25} = 1$

3. $4x^2 + 16y^2 = 64$

4. $2(x+2)^2 + 3(y-1)^2 = 6$

5. $9x^2 + 16y^2 + 36x - 32y - 92 = 0$

6. A large piece of space debris is found to be orbiting the earth. It has an apogee of 700 kilometers and a perigee of 400 kilometers. What are the vertices and foci of its elliptical orbit? Graph the ellipse.

CHAPTER 11 Review

Review the material in the chapter. Then see how you have done by trying these review exercises. If you miss an exercise, restudy the indicated lesson.

11–1 By division, determine whether the following polynomials are factors of the polynomial $P(x) = x^4 - 16$.

1. $x - 2$ Yes **2.** $x^2 + 3x - 1$ No

11–2

3. Use synthetic division to find the quotient and remainder: $(5x^6 - 6x^4 + 1) \div (x + 1)$. Q: $5x^5 - 5x^4 - x^3 + x^2 - x + 1$, R = 0

4. Use synthetic division to find $P(-4)$ if $P(x) = -2x^4 - 8x^3 + 4x^2 - 2x + 1$. 73

5. Determine whether $x + i$ is a factor of $P(x) = x^4 - 1$. Yes

11–3

6. Find a polynomial of degree 4 with roots $1, -1, i,$ and $-i$. $x^4 - 1$

7. Find a polynomial of degree 3 with -1 as a root of multiplicity 1 and 1 as a root of multiplicity 2. $x^3 - x^2 - x + 1$

8. Suppose a polynomial of degree 5 with rational coefficients has roots $7, -3 + 4i, 2 - \sqrt{5}$. Find the other roots. $-3 - 4i, 2 + \sqrt{5}$

9. Find the other roots of $x^4 - x^3 + 2x^2 - 4x - 8$ given that one root is $2i$. $-2i, -1, 2$

11–4

10. Find the rational roots of $20x^3 - 30x^2 + 12x - 1$, if they exist. If possible, find the other roots. $\frac{1}{2}, \frac{5 + \sqrt{15}}{10}, \frac{5 - \sqrt{15}}{10}$

11–5

11. What does Descartes' Rule of Signs tell you about the number of positive real roots of $4x^5 - 3x^2 + x - 3$? 3 or 1

12. Determine an upper bound and a lower bound to the roots of $5x^4 + 4x^3 + 5x + 1$. Answers may vary; 1, -2

11–6

13. Sketch the graph of $f(x) = x(x + 1)(x - 1)$.

CHAPTER 11 Test

1. Is $2i$ a root of $P(x) = x^2 + 2$? No

2. Is $x + 1$ a factor of $P(x) = x^3 + 6x^2 + x + 30$? No

3. Use synthetic division to find the quotient and remainder:
   $(2x^4 - 6x^3 + 7x^2 - 5x + 1) \div (x + 2)$. Q: $2x^3 - 10x^2 + 27x - 59$, R: 119

4. Use synthetic division to find $P(3)$: $P(x) = 2x^4 - 3x^3 + x^2 - 3x + 7$. 88

5. Find a polynomial of degree 3 with roots 0, 1, and i. $x^3 - x^2i - x^2 + xi$

6. Find a polynomial of degree 7 with 1 as a root of multiplicity 1, -1 as a root of multiplicity 1, 2 as a root of multiplicity 2, and -3 as a root of multiplicity 3. $x^7 + 5x^6 - 6x^5 - 50x^4 + 5x^3 + 153x^2 - 108$

7. Suppose a polynomial of degree 4 with rational coefficients has roots $-8 - 7i$ and $10 + \sqrt{3}$. Find the other roots. $-8 + 7i$, $10 - \sqrt{3}$

8. Find the other roots of $x^3 - 1$ given that one of the roots is 1. $\frac{-1 + i\sqrt{3}}{2}, \frac{-1 - i\sqrt{3}}{2}$

9. Find the rational roots of $x^3 - 7x^2 + 16x - 12$, if they exist. If possible, find the other roots. 2(multiplicity 2), 3(multiplicity 1)

10. What does Descartes' Rule of Signs tell you about the number of positive real roots of $3x^5 - x^4 + 2x^3 - 5x^2 - 3x - 1$? What about the number of negative real roots? 2 or 0; 2 or 0

11. Graph $x^3 - 2x^2 + x + 1 = 0$. Find approximate solutions. -0.5

Challenge

12. Use a calculator to graph $P(x) = 2.4x^4 - 1.6x^2 - 0.8$.

CHAPTERS 1–11 Cumulative Review

1–2 Evaluate each expression for $a = 5$ and $c = -2$.

1. $-|a + c| + (3a + c)$ 6

2. $ac + c^2 + |6c|$ 6

3. $|a + c| - |a| - |c|$ -4

4. $|a - c| + |c - a|$ 14

1–5 Simplify.

5. $3a + 6(a - 2)$ 9a − 12

6. $10x - (9x - 3x)$ 4x

7. $-3y - [6y - (2y + 7)]$ $-7y + 7$

2–5, 2–7 Solve.

8. $4x - 3 \leq 5x + 2$ 8. $-5 \leq x$

9. $-2x \leq 2(x + 3) - 1$ 9. $x \geq -\frac{5}{4}$

10. $-\frac{2}{5}x < -24$ x > 60

3–6 Find an equation in standard form for each line.

11. Line containing $(-1, 1)$ and $(-2, 1)$ 12. Line containing $(6, 3)$ and $(6, -3)$
$g - 1 = 0$ $x - 6 = 0$

4–1 Solve.

13. $4x - 2y = 10$ 14. $16x + 6y = -11$ 15. $19x + 18y = -12$
    $-x + 2y = -7$ $(3, -2)$ $-7x + 9y = -1$ $\left(-\frac{1}{2}, -\frac{1}{2}\right)$ $14x + 9y = -6$ $\left(0, -\frac{2}{3}\right)$

4–2

16. Solution A is 12% acid and Solution B is 60% acid. How many liters of each should be mixed together to get 24 liters of a solution that is 50% acid? 5 liters of A and 19 liters of B

4–3 Solve.

17. $2x + y - z = 2$ 18. $2x + y - z = -10$
    $x - y = -1$ $4x - 2y - 3z = -5$
    $y + 3z = -2$ $(0, 1, -1)$ $6x - y + z = 4$ $\left(\frac{1}{2}, -4, 5\right)$

4–8 Graph.

19. $x < y$ 20. $x - y > 0$ 21. $y + x < 1$

5–2 Multiply.

22. $(2z + 4y)^2$ 23. $(x - 5)^3$ 24. $(a^2 + 2b)^3$

5–3 Factor.

25. $400x^2 - 441y^2$ 26. $a^{16} - 1$ 27. $x^4y^2 - x^2$
28. $y^3 + 125$ 29. $y^3 + 2y^2 - 4y - 8$ 30. $4x^3 - 16x^2 - 9x + 36$

5–8 Solve.

31. $2x^2 = 15 + x$ 32. $3x^2 + 6 = 19x$ 33. $20x^2 - 3 = -28x$ $-\frac{3}{2}, \frac{1}{10}$

6–1 to 6–4 Simplify.

34. $\dfrac{4x^2 - xy - 3y^2}{x^2 - y^2}$ 35. $\dfrac{2a}{a^2 - 8a + 15} - \dfrac{3a}{a^2 - 7y + 10}$ 36. $\dfrac{x + y}{x - y} + \dfrac{5xy}{x^2 - y^2}$

37. $\dfrac{a^2 - b^2}{ab} \div \left(\dfrac{1}{a} + \dfrac{1}{b}\right)$ 38. $\left(\dfrac{3x}{y} - x\right) \div \left(\dfrac{y}{x} - y\right)$

39. $\left(\dfrac{x - 1}{x} + \dfrac{x}{1 + x}\right) \div \left(\dfrac{x}{1 - x} + \dfrac{1 + x}{x}\right)$ 39. $\frac{(2x^2 - 1)(1 - x)}{1 + x}$

6–5 Divide.

40. $(2x^4 + 7x^3 + 5x^2 - 17x - 9)$ by $(2x + 1)$ $x^3 + 3x^2 + x - 9$

22. $4z^2 + 16yz + 16y^2$
23. $x^3 - 15x^2 + 75x - 125$
24. $a^6 + 6a^4b + 12a^2b^2 + 8b^3$
25. $(20x + 21y)(20x - 21y)$
26. $(a^8 + 1)(a^4 + 1)(a^2 + 1)(a + 1)(a - 1)$
27. $x^2(y + 1)(y - 1)$
28. $(y + 5)(y^2 - 5y + 25)$
29. $(y + 2)^2(y - 2)$
30. $(x - 4)(2x + 3)(2x - 3)$
31. $3, -\dfrac{5}{2}$
32. $\dfrac{1}{3}, 6$
34. $\dfrac{4x + 3y}{x + y}$
35. $\dfrac{-a}{(a - 2)(a - 3)}$
36. $\dfrac{x^2 + 7xy + y^2}{x^2 - y^2}$
37. $a - b$
38. $\dfrac{x^2(y - 3)}{y^2(x - 1)}$

6–6 Solve.

41. $x = -\frac{10}{3}$
48. $4|y|\sqrt{3y}$
50. $6 + \sqrt{35}$
56. $21 + 20i$
57. $\frac{-1 + 5i}{13}$

41. $\dfrac{7}{5x - 2} = \dfrac{5}{4x}$ 42. $\dfrac{1}{x} + \dfrac{2x + 3}{2} = 8x$ $x = \frac{1}{2}, x = -\frac{2}{7}$

7–1, 7–4 Simplify.

43. $\sqrt{36x^2}$ $6|x|$ 44. $\sqrt[3]{-125}$ -5 45. $\sqrt[4]{16x^4y^8}$ $2|x|y^2$ 46. $\sqrt{(-3)^2}$ 3

47. $\sqrt{45x}$ $3\sqrt{5x}$ 48. $\sqrt{48y^3}$ 49. $\sqrt{18} - \sqrt{50} + 2\sqrt{8} + \sqrt{8}$ $4\sqrt{2}$

50. $\dfrac{\sqrt{7} + \sqrt{5}}{\sqrt{7} - \sqrt{5}}$ 51. $\dfrac{\sqrt{10}}{\sqrt{15}}$ $\frac{\sqrt{6}}{3}$ 52. $\dfrac{\sqrt{48a^5}}{\sqrt{36a^3}}$ 53. $\dfrac{\sqrt[3]{96x^6}}{\sqrt{72x^2}}$ $\frac{x}{3}\sqrt[3]{36x}$

7–6 Solve.

54. $\sqrt{5x + 39} = x - 9$ 55. $\sqrt[3]{4x + 7} + 2 = 5$ $x = 5$
$x = 21$

7–8 Simplify.

56. $(5 + 2i)^2$ 57. $(1 + i) \div (2 - 3i)$ 58. $-(-i^9)(i^4)$ i

8–1, 8–2 Solve.

59. $4x^2 - 5x - 6 = 0$ 60. $5x^2 - 4x = 0$ 61. $2x^2 + 2x + 3 = 0$ $\frac{-1 \pm i\sqrt{5}}{2}$

8–3 Find a quadratic equation whose solutions are the following. 59. $-\frac{3}{4}, 2$

60. $0, \frac{4}{5}$

62. $\dfrac{3}{4}, \dfrac{-5}{3}$ 63. $1 + \sqrt{3}, 1 - \sqrt{3}$ $x^2 - 2x - 2 = 0$

62. $12x^2 + 11x - 15 = 0$

72.a. $\left(-\frac{3}{2}, 0\right)$

8–4 Solve.

64. $x + 6\sqrt{x} - 16 = 0$ 4

9–1 Test the following equations for symmetry with respect to the x-axis and the y-axis.

65. $4y = 3x^2 - 1$ 66. $2x^2 - 3y^2 = 5$ 67. $x^3 + 3y^3 = 10$ Neither axis
y-axis   Both axes

9–1 Determine whether each function is even, odd, or neither.

68. $f(x) = 5$ Even 69. $f(x) = x^{23}$ Odd 70. $f(x) = \sqrt{x} + 1$ Neither

9–6

71. For $f(x) = -3x^2 + 12x - 5$
   a. find an equation of the type $a(x - h)^2 + k$. $-3(x - 2)^2 + 7$
   b. find the vertex, the line of symmetry, and the maximum or minimum value. $(2, 7), x = 2, \text{max } 7$

500 CHAPTER 11 POLYNOMIAL FUNCTIONS

9–7

72. Find the x-intercepts, if they exist.

    a. $f(x) = 4x^2 + 12x + 9$ **b.** $f(x) = 9x^2 - 12x - 1$ $\left(\frac{2+\sqrt{5}}{3}, 0\right)\left(\frac{2-\sqrt{5}}{3}, 0\right)$

10–1 to 10–5   Solve.

73. Find the distance between the points $(-2, 5)$ and $(3, -4)$. $\sqrt{106}$

74. Find the vertices, the foci, and the asymptotes of the hyperbola
$8x^2 - 3y^2 = 48$. Then graph the hyperbola.
Center: $(0, 0)$; vertices: $(\sqrt{6}, 0)$, $(-\sqrt{6}, 0)$; foci: $(\sqrt{22}, 0)$, $(-\sqrt{22}, 0)$; asymptotes $y = \frac{2\sqrt{6}}{3}x$, $y = \frac{-2\sqrt{6}}{3}x$

75. Find the vertex, focus, and directrix of the parabola
$x^2 + 2x + 6y - 11 = 0$. Then graph the parabola.
Vertex: $(-1, 2)$; focus: $(-1, 0.5)$; directrix: $y = 3.5$

10–6, 10–7   Solve the system.

76. $y^2 + x^2 = 13$ **77.** $x^2 + y^2 = 20$
$x - 2y = 1$ $(-3, -2), \left(\frac{17}{5}, \frac{6}{5}\right)$ $xy = 8$ $(2, 4), (-2, -4), (4, 2), (-4, -2)$

11–2 to 11–5   Solve.

78. Use synthetic division to find $P(-3)$ if $P(x) = -2x^3 + x^2 - 1$.   62

79. Find a polynomial of degree 3 with roots $3, i, -i$. $x^3 - 3x^2 + x - 3 = 0$

80. Find all roots of $2x^4 - 7x^3 + 5x^2 + 9x - 5$. $\frac{1}{2}, -1, 2 + i, 2 - i$

81. What does Descartes' Rule of Signs tell you about the number
of positive real roots and negative real roots of $4x^5 + 3x^4 - 2x^3 + 2x^2 + 3x - 1$?   3 or 1 positive roots, 2 or 0 negative roots

---

Ready for Exponential and Logarithm Functions?

1–6   Rename without using an exponent.

1. 5^1 5   **2.** 8^0 1   **3.** 2^{-3} $\frac{1}{8}$

1–7   Simplify.

4. $x^{-5} \cdot x^3$ x^{-2} **5.** $\dfrac{x^{-3}}{x^4}$ x^{-7} **6.** $(x^{-3})^4$ x^{-12}

1–8

7. 8.45×10^{-2}
8. 433,500

7. Convert 0.0845 to scientific notation.   **8.** Convert 4.335×10^5 to decimal notation.

12

CHAPTER TWELVE

Exponential and Logarithmic Functions

12–1 Inverse Relations and Functions

Inverses of Relations

DEFINITION

If, in a relation, we interchange first and second members in each ordered pair, then we obtain a relation called the *inverse* of the original relation.

EXAMPLE 1

Find the inverse of the relation {(2, 1), (3, 1), (4, 2)}. The inverse is {(1, 2), (1, 3), (2, 4)}.

TRY THIS

1. Find the inverse of the relation {(0, 1), (−2, 5), (5, −2)}. {(1, 0), (5, −2), (−2, 5)}

THEOREM 12–1

Interchanging x and y in the equation of a relation produces an equation of the inverse relation.

EXAMPLE 2

Find an equation of the inverse of $y = x^2 - 5$.

We interchange x and y, and obtain $x = y^2 - 5$. This is an equation of the inverse relation.

TRY THIS

2. Find an equation of the inverse of $y = x^2 + 4$. $x = y^2 + 4$

Inverses and Symmetry

Interchanging first and second coordinates in each ordered pair of a relation has the effect of interchanging the x-axis and the y-axis.

Interchanging the x-axis and the y-axis has the effect of reflecting across the diagonal line whose equation is $y = x$, as shown below. Thus the graphs of a relation and its inverse are always reflections of each other across the line $y = x$.

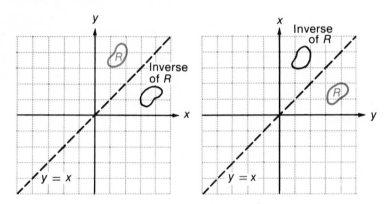

Here are some other graphs of relations and their inverses.

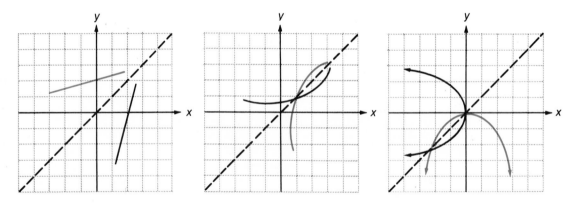

It can happen that a relation is its own inverse: that is, when the relation is reflected across the line $y = x$, there is no change. Such a relation is symmetric with respect to the line $y = x$.

EXAMPLE 3

Test the relation $3x + 3y = 5$ for symmetry with respect to the line $y = x$.

We interchange x and y in the equation, obtaining $3y + 3x = 5$. This is equivalent to the original equation, so the graph is symmetric with respect to the line $y = x$.

TRY THIS Test the relations defined by these equations for symmetry with respect to the line $y = x$.

3. $4x + 4y = 6$ Yes **4.** $y = 2x^2$ No

Inverses of Functions

All functions have inverses, but the inverse is not necessarily a function. If the inverse of a function f is also a function we denote it by f^{-1} (read "f inverse"). Recall that we obtain the inverse of a relation by interchanging the coordinates of each ordered pair. Thus the domain of a function f is the range of f^{-1} and the range of f is the domain of f^{-1}.

Let us consider inverses of functions in terms of function machines. Suppose that the function f programmed into the machine has an inverse that is also a function. Suppose then that the function machine has a reverse switch. When the switch is thrown the machine is programmed to do the inverse mapping f^{-1}. Inputs then enter at the opposite end and the entire process is reversed.

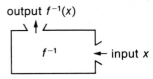

When a function is defined by an equation, we can sometimes find an equation for its inverse by thinking of interchanging x and y.

EXAMPLE 4
Given $f(x) = 3x + 1$, find an equation for $f^{-1}(x)$.

a. Let us think of this as $y = 3x + 1$.
b. To find the inverse we interchange x and y: $x = 3y + 1$.

c. Now we solve for y: $y = \dfrac{x - 1}{3}$.

d. Thus $f^{-1}(x) = \dfrac{x - 1}{3}$.

In Example 4 f maps any x onto $3x + 1$ (this function multiplies each number of the domain by 3 and adds 1). Its inverse, f^{-1}, maps any number x onto $\frac{x-1}{3}$ (this inverse function subtracts 1 from each member of its domain and divides by 3.). Thus the function and its inverse do opposite things.

TRY THIS

5. Given $g(x) = x + 2$, find an equation for $g^{-1}(x)$. $g^{-1}(x) = x - 2$
6. Let $g(x) = 5x + 2$. Find a formula for $g^{-1}(x)$. $g^{-1}(x) = \frac{1}{5}(x - 2)$

EXAMPLE 5

Let $S(x) = \sqrt{x}$. Find an equation for $S^{-1}(x)$.

a. Let us think of this as $y = \sqrt{x}$. Note that the domain and range both consist of nonnegative numbers only.
b. To find the inverse we interchange x and y: $x = \sqrt{y}$.
c. Now we solve for y, squaring both sides: $y = x^2$.
d. Thus $S^{-1}(x) = x^2$, with the understanding that x cannot be negative.

In Example 5, S maps any x onto $\sqrt{x}$ (this function takes the square root of any input). Its inverse, S^{-1}, maps any number x onto x^2 (this function squares each input); thus the function and its inverse do opposite things.

TRY THIS

7. Let $f(x) = \sqrt{x + 1}$. Find an equation for $f^{-1}(x)$. $f^{-1}(x) = x^2 - 1$

Suppose the inverse of a function f is also a function. Let us suppose that we do the mapping f and then do the inverse mapping f^{-1}. We will be back where we started. In other words, if we find $f(x)$ for some x and then find f^{-1} for this number, we will be back at x. In function notation the statement looks like the following equation.

$$f^{-1}(f(x)) = x$$

This is read "f inverse of f of x equals x." It means, working from the inside out, to take x, then find $f(x)$, and then find f^{-1} for that number. When we do, we will be back where we started, at x. For similar reasons, the following is also true.

$$f(f^{-1}(x)) = x$$

For the statements above to be true, x must of course be in the domain of the function being considered. We summarize these ideas by stating the following theorem.

THEOREM 12–2

For any function f whose inverse is a function: $f^{-1}(f(a)) = a$ for any a in the domain of f. Also $f(f^{-1}(a)) = a$ for any a in the domain of f^{-1}.

EXAMPLE 6

For the function f of Example 4, find $f^{-1}(f(283))$. Find also $f(f^{-1}(-12,045))$.

We note that every real number is in the domain of both f and f^{-1}. Thus, using Theorem 12–2, we may immediately write the answers, without calculating.

$$f^{-1}(f(283)) = 283$$
$$f(f^{-1}(-12,045)) = -12,045$$

TRY THIS

8. For the function f of Example 4, find $f^{-1}(f(579))$ and $f(f^{-1}(-83,479))$. $\quad f^{-1}(f(579)) = 579, f(f^{-1}(-83,479)) = -83,479$

12–1

Exercises

Find the inverse of each of the following relations.

1. $\{(0, 1), (5, 6), (-2, -4)\}$ 2. $\{(-1, -2), (0, 0), (3, 1)\}$ 3. $\{(-1, -1), (\div 3, -4)\}$

Write an equation of the inverse relation of the following.

4. $y = 4x - 5$ 5. $y = 3x + 5$ 6. $y = 3x^2 + 2$
7. $y = 5x^2 - 4$ 8. $x^2 - 3y^2 = 3$ 9. $2x^2 + 5y^2 = 4$
10. $xy = 7$ 11. $xy = -5$ 12. $xy^2 = 1$

Test for symmetry with respect to the line $y = x$.

13. $3x + 2y = 4$ 14. $5x - 2y = 7$ 15. $xy = 10$
16. $xy = 12$ 17. $4x + 4y = 3$ 18. $5x + 5y = -1$

19. $3x = \dfrac{4}{y}$ 20. $4y = \dfrac{5}{x}$ 21. $4x^2 + 4y^2 = 3$

22. $3x^2 + 3y^2 = 5$ 23. $y = |2x|$ 24. $3x = |2y|$

In each of the following, find equations for $f^{-1}(x)$

25. $f(x) = x - 1$ 26. $f(x) = x - 2$ 27. $f(x) = x + 4$
28. $f(x) = x + 3$ 29. $f(x) = x + 8$ 30. $f(x) = x + 7$
31. $f(x) = 2x + 5$ 32. $f(x) = 3x + 2$ 33. $f(x) = 3x - 1$

34. $f(x) = 4x - 3$

35. $f(x) = 0.5x + 2$

36. $f(x) = 0.7x + 4$

37. $f(x) = \sqrt{x} - 1$

38. $f(x) = \sqrt{x - 2}$

39. $f(x) = \sqrt{x + 2}$

40. $f(x) = 35x - 173$. Find $f^{-1}(f(3))$.
Find $f(f^{-1}(-125))$. 3, −125

41. $g(x) = \dfrac{-173x + 15}{3}$. Find $g^{-1}(g(5))$.
Find $g(g^{-1}(-12))$. 5, −12

42. $f(x) = x^3 + 2$. Find $f^{-1}(f(12,053))$.
Find $f(f^{-1}(-17,243))$. 12,053, −17,243

43. $g(x) = x^3 - 486$. Find $g^{-1}(g(489))$.
Find $g(g^{-1}(-17,422))$. 489, −17,422

Extension

44. Graph $y = x^2 + 1$. Then by reflection across the line $y = x$, graph its inverse.

45. Graph $y = x^2 - 3$. Then by reflection across the line $y = x$, graph its inverse.

46. Graph $y = |x|$. Then by reflection across the line $y = x$, graph its inverse.

47. Graph $x = |y|$. Then by reflection across the line $y = x$, graph its inverse.

For each of the following, find the composition functions $f(g(x))$ and $g(f(x))$.

48. $f(x) = 3x + 1, g(x) = \dfrac{x - 1}{3}$

49. $f(x) = x^3 - 5, g(x) = \sqrt[3]{x + 5}$

50. $f(x) = 2x, g(x) = x^2 + 1$

51. $f(x) = x^2, g(x) = x + 3$

52. $f(x) = 2x + 3, g(x) = x - 4$

53. $f(x) = 3x^2 + 2, g(x) = 2x - 1$

54. $f(x) = 4x^2 - 1, g(x) = \dfrac{2}{x}$

55. $f(x) = x^2 - 1, g(x) = x^2 - 1$

Challenge

Graph each equation and its inverse. Then test for symmetry with respect to the x-xis, y-axis, the origin, and the line $y = x$.

56. $y = \dfrac{1}{x^2}$

57. $|x| - |y| = 1$

58. $y = x^3$

59. $y = \dfrac{|x|}{x}$

USING A CALCULATOR/Power and Log Keys

Most scientific calculators have keys marked x^y, $\sqrt{\ }$, 10^x, e^x, log, and ln.

Problem: Find $8^{\sqrt{3}}$.

Enter: 8 [x^y] 3 [$\sqrt{\ }$] [=]

Display: 8   3 1.7320508 36.660446

If you wanted to find the square root of 8^3, you would need to hit the equals key before pressing the square root key.

Problem: Find $\sqrt{8^3}$.

Enter: 8 [x^y] 3 [=] [$\sqrt{\ }$]

Display: 8   3 512 22.627417

When uncertain about the order of operations to use with a problem, experiment with a problem for which you know the answer. For the problems above, you could use $8^{\sqrt{2}}$ and $\sqrt{8^2}$.

12–2 Exponential and Logarithmic Functions

We have defined exponential notation for rational exponents. We now consider irrational exponents. Let us consider 2^π. The number π has an unending decimal representation.

$$3.1415926535\ldots$$

Now consider this sequence of numbers.

$$3, \quad 3.1, \quad 3.14, \quad 3.141, \quad 3.1415, \quad 3.14159,\ldots$$

Each of these numbers is an approximation to π, the more decimal places the better the approximation. Let us use these (rational) numbers to form a sequence as follows.

$$2^3, \quad 2^{3.1}, \quad 2^{3.14}, \quad 2^{3.1415}, \quad 2^{3.14159}, \ldots$$

Each of the numbers in this sequence is already defined, the exponent being rational. The numbers in this sequence get closer and closer to some real number. We define that number to be 2^π.

We can define exponential notation for any irrational exponent in a similar way. Thus any exponential expression a^x, $a > 0$, now has meaning, whether the exponent is rational or irrational.

Exponential Functions

Exponential functions are defined using exponential notation.

DEFINITION

The function $f(x) = a^x$, where a is some positive constant different from 1, is called the *exponential function, base a*.

Here are some exponential functions.

$$f(x) = 2^x \qquad g(x) = 3^x \qquad h(x) = (0.178)^x$$

Note that the variable is the exponent. The following are *not* exponential functions.

$$f(x) = x^2 \qquad g(x) = x^3 \qquad h(x) = x^{0.178}$$

Note that the variable is not the exponent.

EXAMPLE 1

Graph $y = 2^x$. Use the graph to approximate 2^π.

We find some solutions, plot them, and then draw the graph.

x	0	1	2	3	-1	-2	-3
y	1	2	4	8	$\frac{1}{2}$	$\frac{1}{4}$	$\frac{1}{8}$

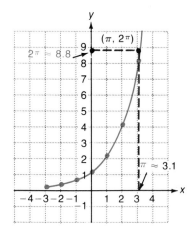

Note that as x increases, the function values increase. Check this on a calculator. As x decreases, the function values decrease toward 0.

To approximate 2^π, we locate π on the x-axis, at about 3.1. Then we find the corresponding function value. It is about 8.8.

TRY THIS

1. Use the graph of $y = 2^x$.
   a. What is the domain?   b. What is the range?   c. What is the y-intercept?
   d. Use the graph to approximate $2^{\sqrt{3}}$ ($\sqrt{3} \approx 1.732$).

1. a. set of all real numbers
   b. set of all positive numbers
   c. 1
   d. 3.3

Let us now look at some other exponential functions. We will make comparisons, using transformations.

EXAMPLE 2

Graph $y = 4^x$.

We could plot points and connect them, but let us be more clever. We note that $4^x = (2^2)^x = 2^{2x}$. Compare this with $y = 2^x$, graphed in Example 1. Notice that the graph of $y = 2^{2x}$ approaches the y-axis more rapidly than the graph of $y = 2^x$. The graph of $y = 2^{2x}$ is called a shrinking of the graph of $y = 2^x$.

Knowing this allows us to graph $y = 2^{2x}$ at once. Each point on the graph of 2^x is moved half the distance to the y-axis.

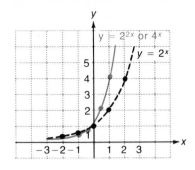

TRY THIS

2. Graph $y = 8^x$. Use graph paper.

EXAMPLE 3

Graph $y = \left(\frac{1}{2}\right)^x$.

We could plot points and connect them, but again let us be more clever. We note that $\left(\frac{1}{2}\right)^x = \frac{1}{2^x} = 2^{-x}$. Compare this with the graph of $y = 2^x$ in Example 1. The graph of $y = 2^{-x}$ is a reflection, across the y-axis, of the graph of $y = 2^x$. Knowing this allows us to graph $y = 2^{-x}$ at once.

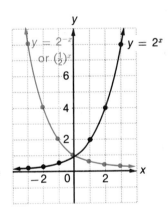

TRY THIS

3. Graph $y = \left(\frac{1}{3}\right)^x$. $\left[\text{Hint: } \left(\frac{1}{3}\right)^x = 3^{-x}\right]$

The preceding examples and exercises illustrate exponential functions of various bases. If $a = 1$, then $f(x) = a^x = 1^x = 1$ and the graph is a horizontal line. This is why we exclude 1 as a base for an exponential function.

As an application of exponential functions we consider the compound interest formula, $A = P(1 + i)^t$. Suppose principal P of $1000 is invested at an interest rate of 13%, compounded annually. Then the amount A in the account after time t, in years, is given by the exponential function $A = \$1000\ (1.13)^t$.

Logarithmic Functions

DEFINITION

A *logarithmic function* is the inverse of an exponential function.

One way to describe a logarithmic function is to interchange variables in the equation $y = a^x$. Thus, the following equation is logarithmic.

$$x = a^y$$

The most useful and interesting logarithmic functions are those for which $a > 1$. The graph of such a function is a reflection of $y = a^x$ across the line $y = x$. The domain of a logarithmic function is the set of all positive real numbers.

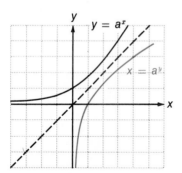

For logarithmic functions we use the notation $\log_a(x)$ or $\log_a x$. That is, we use the symbol $\log_a x$ to denote the second coordinates of a function $x = a^y$. In other words, a logarithmic function can be described as $y = \log_a x$. The parentheses in $\log_a(x)$ are like those in $f(x)$. In the case of logarithmic functions we usually omit the parentheses.

THEOREM 12–3

The following are equivalent.
1. $x = a^y$; and
2. $y = \log_a x$ (read "y equals the log, base a, of x")

Thus $\log_a x$ represents the exponent in the equation $x = a^y$, so the logarithm, base a, of a number x is the power to which a is raised to get x.

EXAMPLE 4

Graph $y = \log_3 x$.

The equation $y = \log_3 x$ is equivalent to $x = 3^y$. The graph is a reflection of $y = 3^x$ across the line $y = x$. We make a table of values for $y = 3^x$ and then interchange x and y.

For $y = 3^x$:

x	0	1	2	-1	-2
y	1	3	9	$\frac{1}{3}$	$\frac{1}{9}$

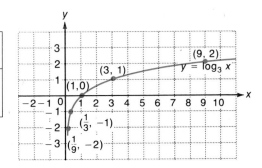

For $y = \log^3 x$ (or $x = 3^y$):

x	1	3	9	$\frac{1}{3}$	$\frac{1}{9}$
y	0	1	2	-1	-2

The graph of $y = \log_a x$, for any a, has the x-intercept $(1, 0)$.

TRY THIS

4. Graph $y = \log_2 x$. What is the domain of this function? What is the range?

5. Graph $y = \log_4 x$. What is the domain of this function? What is the range?

4. domain: positive real numbers; range: all real numbers
5. domain: positive real numbers; range: all real numbers

12-2

Exercises

Graph. Where possible, use transformations.

1. $y = 2^x$ **2.** $y = 3^x$ **3.** $y = 5^x$ **4.** $y = 6^x$

5. $y = \left(\frac{1}{4}\right)^x$ **6.** $y = \left(\frac{1}{5}\right)^x$ **7.** $y = (0.4)^x$ **8.** $y = (0.3)^x$

Consider the graph of $y = 4^x$ in Example 2.

9. What is the domain of $y = 4^x$?   set of all real numbers

10. What is the range?   set of all positive numbers

11. What is the y-intercept?   1

12. Use the graph to approximate $4^{0.7}$.   2.6

Graph. Where possible, use transformations.

13. $y = \log_2 x$ **14.** $y = \log_5 x$ **15.** $y = \log_3 x$

16. $y = \log_4 x$ **17.** $y = \log_7 x$ **18.** $y = \log_{10} x$

Extension

Graph.

19. $y = 2^{x-1}$ **20.** $y = 2^{x+1}$ **21.** $y = 3^{x+1}$

22. $y = \log_2(x + 1)$ **23.** $y = \log_3(x - 2)$ **24.** $f(x) = 3^{|x|}$

25. $f(x) = 2^{|x-1|}$ **26.** $y = 2^x + 2^{-x}$ **27.** $y = \log_2|x|$

What is the domain of each function?

28. $f(x) = 3^x$ **29.** $f(x) = \log_{10} x$ **30.** $f(x) = \log_a x^2$

31. $f(x) = \log_4 x^3$ **32.** $f(x) = \log_{10}(3x - 4)$ **33.** $f(x) = \log_5|x|$

28. All real numbers
29. $\{x \mid x > 0\}$
30. $\{x \mid x \neq 0\}$
31. $\{x \mid x > 0\}$
32. $\left\{x \mid x > \frac{4}{3}\right\}$
33. $\{x \mid x \neq 0\}$
34. a. 8
    b. 8.574188
    c. 8.815241
    d. 8.821353
    e. 8.824411
    f. 8.824962

34. Use a calculator to estimate each of the following to six decimal places.

   a. 2^3 **b.** $2^{3.1}$ **c.** $2^{3.14}$ **d.** $2^{3.141}$ **e.** $2^{3.1415}$ **f.** $2^{3.14159}$

Use a calculator to determine which of the two numbers is larger.

35. 5^π or π^5 π^5 **36.** $\sqrt{8^3}$ or $8^{\sqrt{3}}$ $8^{\sqrt{3}}$

Challenge

Graph.

37. $y = 2^{-x^2}$ **38.** $y = 3^{-(x+1)^2}$ **39.** $y = |2^{x^2} - 8|$

12-3 Exponential and Logarithmic Relationships

Converting Exponential and Logarithmic Equations

It is important to be able to convert from an exponential equation to a logarithmic equation.

EXAMPLES
Convert to logarithmic equations.

1. $8 = 2^x \rightarrow x = \log_2 8$ It helps in such conversions, to remember that the *logarithm is the exponent*.

2. $y^{-1} = 4 \rightarrow -1 = \log_y 4$

3. $a^b = c \rightarrow b = \log_a c$

TRY THIS Write equivalent logarithmic equations.

1. $6^0 = 1$ 2. $10^{-3} = 0.001$ 3. $16^{\frac{1}{4}} = 2$ 4. $\left(\dfrac{6}{5}\right)^{-2} = \dfrac{25}{36}$

1. $\log_6 1 = 0$
2. $\log_{10} 0.001 = -3$
3. $\log_{16} 2 = \frac{1}{4}$
4. $\log_{6/5} \frac{25}{36} = -2$

It is also important to be able to convert from a logarithmic equation to an exponential equation.

EXAMPLES
Convert to exponential equations.

4. $y = \log_3 5 \rightarrow 3^y = 5$ Again, it helps to remember that the *logarithm is the exponent.*

5. $-2 = \log_a 7 \rightarrow a^{-2} = 7$

6. $a = \log_b d \rightarrow b^a = d$

5. $2^5 = 32$
6. $10^3 = 1000$
7. $10^{-2} = 0.01$
8. $(\sqrt{5})^2 = 5$

TRY THIS Write equivalent exponential equations.

5. $\log_2 32 = 5$ 6. $\log_{10} 1000 = 3$ 7. $\log_{10} 0.01 = -2$ 8. $\log_{\sqrt{5}} 5 = 2$

Solving Logarithmic Equations

Certain equations containing logarithmic notation can be solved by first converting to exponential notation.

EXAMPLES

7. Solve $\log_2 x = -3$.

   $\log_2 x = -3$ is equivalent to $2^{-3} = x$. So $x = \frac{1}{8}$.

8. Solve $\log_{27} 3 = x$.

   $\log_{27} 3 = x$ is equivalent to $27^x = 3$. Since $27^{\frac{1}{3}} = 3$, we have $x = \frac{1}{3}$.

9. Solve $\log_x 4 = \frac{1}{2}$.

   $\log_x 4 = \frac{1}{2}$ is equivalent to $x^{\frac{1}{2}} = 4$. Since $(x^{\frac{1}{2}})^2 = 4^2$, we have $x = 16$.

TRY THIS Solve.

9. $\log_{10} x = 4$ 10. $\log x\ 81 = 4$ ₃ 11. $\log_2 16 = x$ ₄ 12. $\log_5 \frac{1}{25} = x$ ₋₂
        10,000

Simplifying the Expressions $a^{\log_a x}$ and $\log_a a^x$

The exponential and logarithm functions are inverses of each other. Let us recall an important fact about functions and their inverses. If the domains are suitable, then for any x, $f(f^{-1}(x)) = x$ and $f^{-1}(f(x)) = x$. We apply this fact to exponential and logarithm functions. Suppose f is the exponential function, base a: $f(x) = a^x$. Then f^{-1} is the logarithm function, base a: $f^{-1}(x) = \log_a x$.

Now let us find $f(f^{-1}(x))$ and $f^{-1}(f(x))$.

$$f(f^{-1}(x)) = a^{f^{-1}(x)} = a^{\log_a x} = x$$

Thus for any suitable base a, $a^{\log_a x} = x$ for any positive number x (negative numbers and 0 do not have logarithms).

$$f^{-1}(f(x)) = \log_a f(x) = \log_a a^x = x$$

Thus for any suitable base a, $\log_a a^x = x$ for any number x whatever.

THEOREM 12–4

For any number a, suitable as a logarithm base,
1. $a^{\log_a x} = x$, for any positive number x; and
2. $\log_a a^x = x$, for any number x.

EXAMPLES
Simplify.

10. $2^{\log_2 5} = 5$ 11. $10^{\log_{10} t} = t$ 12. $\log_{10} 10^{5.6} = 5.6$

TRY THIS Simplify.

13. $4^{\log_4 3}$ ₃ **14.** $b^{\log_b 42}$ ₄₂ **15.** $\log_5 5^{37}$ ₃₇ **16.** $\log_{10} 10^{3.2}$ 3.2

12–3

Exercises

Convert to logarithmic equations.

1. $10^3 = 1000$

2. $10^2 = 100$

3. $8^{\frac{1}{3}} = 2$

4. $16^{\frac{1}{4}} = 2$

5. $5^{-3} = \dfrac{1}{125}$

6. $4^{-5} = \dfrac{1}{1024}$

7. $10^{0.3010} = 2$

8. $10^{0.4771} = 3$

9. $a^{-b} = c$

Convert to exponential equations.

10. $t = \log_3 8$

11. $h = \log_7 10$

12. $\log_5 25 = 2$

13. $\log_6 6 = 1$

14. $\log_{10} 0.1 = -1$

15. $\log_{10} 0.01 = -2$

16. $\log_{10} 7 = 0.845$

17. $\log_{10} 3 = 0.4771$

18. $\log_k A = c$

Solve.

19. $\log_3 x = 2$ ₉

20. $\log_4 x = 3$ ₆₄

21. $\log_x 16 = 2$ ₄

22. $\log_x 64 = 3$ ₄

23. $\log_2 x = -1$ $\frac{1}{2}$

24. $\log_3 x = -2$ $\frac{1}{9}$

25. $\log_8 x = \dfrac{1}{3}$ ₂

26. $\log_{32} x = \dfrac{1}{5}$ ₂

27. $\log_9 x = \dfrac{1}{2}$ ₃

Find.

28. $\log_2 64$ ₆

29. $\log_4 64$ ₃

30. $\log_{10} 10^2$ ₂

31. $\log_3 3^4$ ₄

32. $\log_{10} 0.1$ ₋₁

33. $\log_{10} 10{,}000$ ₄

34. $\log_{10} 1$ ₀

35. $\log_{10} 10$ ₁

36. $\log_{10} 1000$ ₃

Simplify.

37. $3^{\log_3 4}$ ₄

38. $7^{\log_7 10}$ ₁₀

39. $\log_t t^9$ ₉

40. $\log_p p^a$ ₐ

Extension

Solve using graphing.

41. $2^x > 1$
$\{x \mid x \geq 0\}$

42. $3^x \leq 1$
$\{x \mid x \leq 0\}$

43. $\log_2 x < 0$
$\{x \mid x < 1\}$

44. $\log_2 x \geq 4$
$\{x \mid x \geq 16\}$

Challenge

Solve.

45. $3^{3^x} = 1$ ∅

Answers (right margin):

1. $3 = \log_{10} 1000$
2. $2 = \log_{10} 100$
3. $\dfrac{1}{3} = \log_8 2$
4. $\dfrac{1}{4} = \log_{16} 2$
5. $-3 = \log_5 \dfrac{1}{125}$
6. $-5 = \log_4 \dfrac{1}{1024}$
7. $0.3010 = \log_{10} 2$
8. $0.4771 = \log_{10} 3$
9. $-b = \log_a c$
10. $3^t = 8$
11. $7^h = 10$
12. $5^2 = 25$
13. $6^1 = 6$
14. $10^{-1} = 0.1$
15. $10^{-2} = 0.01$
16. $10^{0.845} = 7$
17. $10^{0.4771} = 3$
18. $k^c = A$

12–3 Exponential and Logarithmic Relationships **517**

12–4 Properties of Logarithmic Functions

Let us now establish some basic properties of logarithmic functions.

THEOREM 12–5

For any positive numbers x and y,

$$\log_a (x \cdot y) = \log_a x + \log_a y,$$

where a is any positive number different from 1.

Theorem 12–5 says that the logarithm of a product is the sum of the logarithms of the factors. Note that the base a must remain constant. The logarithm of a sum is *not* the sum of the logarithms of the addends.

Proof of Theorem 12–5

Since a is positive and different from 1, it can serve as a logarithm base. Since x and y are assumed positive, they are in the domain of $f(x) = \log_a x$. Now let $b = \log_a x$ and $c = \log_a y$. We write equivalent exponential equations.

$$x = a^b \text{ and } y = a^c$$

Next we multiply.

$$xy = a^b a^c = a^{b+c}$$

Now writing an equivalent logarithmic equation, we obtain

$$\log_a (xy) = b + c, \text{ or}$$

$$\log_a (xy) = \log_a x + \log_a y,$$

which was to be shown.

EXAMPLE 1

Express as a sum of logarithms and simplify.

$$\log_2 (4 \cdot 16) = \log_2 4 + \log_2 16$$
$$= 2 + 4 = 6$$

TRY THIS

1. Express as a sum of logarithms.
   a. $\log_a MN$ b. $\log_5 (25 \cdot 5)$
2. Express as a single logarithm.
   a. $\log_3 7 + \log_3 5$ b. $\log_a C + \log_a A + \log_a B + \log_a I + \log_a N$

1. a. $\log_a M + \log_a N$
   b. $\log_5 25 + \log_5 5$
2. a. $\log_3 35$
   b. $\log_a CABIN$

THEOREM 12–6

For any positive number x and any number p,

$$\log_a x^p = p \cdot \log_a x,$$

where a is any logarithm base.

Theorem 12–6 says that the logarithm of a power of a number is the exponent times the logarithm of the number.

Proof of Theorem 12–6

Let $b = \log_a x$. Then, writing an equivalent exponential equation, we have $x = a^b$. Next we raise both sides of the latter equation to the pth power.

$$x^p = (a^b)^p, \text{ or } a^{bp}$$

Now we can write an equivalent logarithmic equation.

$$\log_a x^p = \log_a a^{bp} = bp$$

But $b = \log_a x$, so we have $\log_a x^p = p \cdot \log_a x$, which was to be shown.

EXAMPLES

Express as products.

2. $\log_b 9^{-5} = -5 \cdot \log_b 9$
3. $\log_a \sqrt[4]{5} = \log_a 5^{\frac{1}{4}} = \frac{1}{4} \log_a 5$

TRY THIS Express each as a product.

3. $\log_7 4^5$ 4. $\log_a \sqrt{5}$ 3. $5\log_7 4$ 4. $\frac{1}{2}\log_a 5$

THEOREM 12–7

For any positive numbers x and y,

$$\log_a \frac{x}{y} = \log_a x - \log_a y,$$

where a is any logarithm base.

Theorem 12–7 says that the logarithm of a quotient is the logarithm of the dividend minus the logarithm of the divisor.

Proof of Theorem 12–7

$\frac{x}{y} = x \cdot y^{-1}$, so

$$\log_a \frac{x}{y} = \log_a (xy^{-1}).$$

By Theorem 12–5,

$$\log_a (xy^{-1}) = \log_a x + \log_a y^{-1},$$

and by Theorem 12–6,

$$\log_a y^{-1} = -1 \cdot \log_a y,$$

so we have

$$\log_a \frac{x}{y} = \log_a x - \log_a y,$$

which was to be shown.

EXAMPLE 4

Express in terms of logarithms of x, y, and z.

$$\log_a \sqrt[4]{\frac{xy}{z^3}} = \log_a \left(\frac{xy}{z^3}\right)^{\frac{1}{4}}$$

$$= \frac{1}{4} \cdot \log_a \frac{xy}{z^3}$$

$$= \frac{1}{4} [\log_a xy - \log_a z^3]$$

$$= \frac{1}{4} [\log_a x + \log_a y - 3 \log_a z]$$

$$= \frac{1}{4} \log_a x + \frac{1}{4} \log_a y - \frac{3}{4} \log_a z$$

EXAMPLE 5

Express as a single logarithm.

$$\frac{1}{2}\log_a x - 7\log_a y + \log_a z = \log_a \sqrt{x} - \log_a y^7 + \log_a z$$
$$= \log_a \frac{\sqrt{x}}{y^7} + \log_a z$$
$$= \log_a \frac{z\sqrt{x}}{y^7}$$

TRY THIS

5. Express as a difference.

   a. $\log_a \frac{M}{N}$ **b.** $\log_c \frac{1}{4}$ a. $\log_a M - \log_a N$ b. $\log_c 1 - \log_c 4$

6. Express as sums and differences of logarithms and without exponential notation or radicals.

   $\log_{10} \frac{4\pi}{\sqrt{23}}$ $\log_{10} 4 + \log_{10} \pi - \frac{1}{2}\log_{10} 23$

7. Express in terms of logarithms of x, y, and z.

   $\log_a \sqrt{\frac{z^3}{xy}}$ $\frac{1}{2}[3\log_a z - \log_a x - \log_a y]$

8. Express as a single logarithm.

   $5\log_a x - \log_a y + \frac{1}{4}\log_a z$ $\log_a \frac{x^5\sqrt[4]{z}}{y}$

EXAMPLE 6

Given that $\log_a 2 = 0.301$ and $\log_a 3 = 0.477$, find the following.

a. $\log_a 6 = \log_a 2 \cdot 3$
$= \log_a 2 + \log_a 3$
$= 0.301 + 0.477 = 0.778$

b. $\log_a \sqrt{3} = \log_a 3^{\frac{1}{2}} = \frac{1}{2} \cdot \log_a 3 = \frac{1}{2} \cdot 0.477 = 0.2385$

c. $\log_a \frac{2}{3} = \log_a 2 - \log_a 3 = 0.301 - 0.477 = -0.176$

d. $\log_a 5$ No way to find, using Theorems 12–5, 12–6, or 12–7
$(\log_a 5 \neq \log_a 2 + \log_a 3)$

e. $\frac{\log_a 2}{\log_a 3} = \frac{0.301}{0.477} = 0.63$ Note that we could not use Theorems 12–5, 12–6, 12–7; we simply divided.

TRY THIS

9. Given that $\log_a 2 = 0.301$ and $\log_a 3 = 0.477$, find the following.

   a. $\log_a 9$ b. $\log_a \sqrt{2}$ c. $\log_a \sqrt[3]{2}$ d. $\log_a \frac{3}{2}$ e. $\frac{\log_a 3}{\log_a 2}$

For any base a, $\log_a a = 1$. This is easily seen by writing an equivalent exponential equation, $a^1 = a$. Similarly, for any base a, $\log_a 1 = 0$. These facts are important and should be remembered.

THEOREM 12–8

For any base a,

$\log_a a = 1$ and $\log_a 1 = 0$.

TRY THIS Simplify.

10. $\log_\pi \pi$ 1   11. $\log_9 1$ 0   12. $\log_{\frac{1}{4}} \frac{1}{4}$ 1

12–4

Exercises

Express as a sum of logarithms.

1. $\log_2 (32 \cdot 8)$ 2. $\log_3 (27 \cdot 81)$ 3. $\log_4 (64 \cdot 16)$
4. $\log_5 (25 \cdot 125)$ 5. $\log_c Bx$ 6. $\log_t 5Y$

Express as a single logarithm.

7. $\log_a 6 + \log_a 70$ 8. $\log_b 65 + \log_b 2$ 9. $\log_c K + \log_c y$

Express as a product.

10. $\log_a x^3$ 11. $\log_b t^5$ 12. $\log_c y^6$

Express as a difference of logarithms.

13. $\log_a \frac{67}{5}$ 14. $\log_t \frac{T}{7}$ 15. $\log_b \frac{3}{4}$

Express in terms of logarithms of x, y, and z.

16. $\log_a x^2 y^3 z$

17. $\log_a 5xy^4 z^3$

18. $\log_b \dfrac{xy^2}{z^3}$

Express as a single logarithm and simplify if possible.

19. $\dfrac{2}{3} \log_a x - \dfrac{1}{2} \log_a y$

20. $\dfrac{1}{2} \log_a x + 3 \log_a y - 2 \log_a x$

21. $\log_a 2x + 3(\log_a x - \log_a y)$

22. $\log_a x^2 - 2 \log_a \sqrt{x}$

23. $\log_a \dfrac{a}{\sqrt{x}} = \log_a \sqrt{ax}$

24. $\log_a (x^2 - 4) - \log_a (x - 2)$

Given $\log_{10} 2 = 0.301$, $\log_{10} 3 = 0.477$, and $\log_{10} 10 = 1$, find the following.

25. $\log_{10} 4$

26. $\log_{10} 5$

27. $\log_{10} 50$

28. $\log_{10} 12$

29. $\log_{10} 60$

30. $\log_{10} \dfrac{1}{3}$

31. $\log_{10} \sqrt{\dfrac{2}{3}}$

32. $\log_{10} \sqrt[5]{12}$

33. $\log_{10} 90$

34. $\log_{10} \dfrac{9}{8}$

35. $\log_{10} \dfrac{1}{4}$

36. $\log_{10} \dfrac{9}{10}$

Extension

Which of the following are false?

37. $\dfrac{\log_a M}{\log_a N} = \log_a M - \log_a N$ False

38. $\dfrac{\log_a M}{\log_a N} = \log_a \dfrac{M}{N}$ False

39. $\log_a 2x = 2 \log_a x$ False

40. $\log_a 2x = \log_a 2 + \log_a x$ True

41. $\log_a (M + N) = \log_a M + \log_a N$ False

42. $\log_a x^3 = 3 \log_a x$ True

Solve.

43. $\log_\pi \pi^{2x+3} = 4$ $\dfrac{1}{2}$

44. $3^{\log_3 (8x-4)} = 5$ $\dfrac{9}{8}$

45. $4^{2 \log_4 \pi} = 7$ $\sqrt{7}$

46. $8^{2 \log_8 x + \log_8 x} = 27$ 3

47. $(x + 3) \cdot \log_a a^x = x$ −2, 0

48. $\log_a 5x = \log_a 5 + \log_a x$ $\{x \mid x > 0\}$

Challenge

49. If $\log_a x = 2$, what is $\log_a \left(\dfrac{1}{x}\right)$? −2

50. If $\log_a x = 2$, what is $\log_{\frac{1}{a}} x$? −2

Prove the following for any base a and any positive number x.

51. $\log_a \left(\dfrac{1}{x}\right) = -\log_a x$

52. $\log_a \left(\dfrac{1}{x}\right) = \log_{\frac{1}{a}} x$

53. Show that $\log_a \left(\dfrac{x + \sqrt{x^2 - 5}}{5}\right) = -\log_a (x - \sqrt{x^2 - 5})$.

12–5 Common Logarithms

Base ten logarithms are known as common logarithms. Tables for these logarithms are readily available (Table 2 at the back of this book).

John Napier invented logarithms about 1614. The word logarithm was derived from two Greek words, logos, which means "ratio," and arithmos, which means "number."

Before calculators and computers became readily available, common logarithms were used extensively to do certain kinds of calculations. Although today computations with logarithms are mainly of historical interest, logarithmic functions are of modern importance. The study of computations with logarithms is helpful in learning the properties of logarithmic functions.

The following is a table of powers of 10, or logarithms base 10.

$$
\begin{aligned}
1 &= 10^{0.0000}, \text{ or } \log_{10} 1 = 0.0000 \\
2 &= 10^{0.3010}, \text{ or } \log_{10} 2 = 0.3010 \\
3 &= 10^{0.4771}, \text{ or } \log_{10} 3 = 0.4771 \\
4 &= 10^{0.6021}, \text{ or } \log_{10} 4 = 0.6021 \\
5 &= 10^{0.6990}, \text{ or } \log_{10} 5 = 0.6990 \\
6 &= 10^{0.7782}, \text{ or } \log_{10} 6 = 0.7782 \\
7 &= 10^{0.8451}, \text{ or } \log_{10} 7 = 0.8451 \\
8 &= 10^{0.9031}, \text{ or } \log_{10} 8 = 0.9031 \\
9 &= 10^{0.9542}, \text{ or } \log_{10} 9 = 0.9542 \\
10 &= 10^{1.0000}, \text{ or } \log_{10} 10 = 1.0000 \\
11 &= 10^{1.0414}, \text{ or } \log_{10} 11 = 1.0414 \\
12 &= 10^{1.0792}, \text{ or } \log_{10} 12 = 1.0792 \\
13 &= 10^{1.1139}, \text{ or } \log_{10} 13 = 1.1139 \\
14 &= 10^{1.1461}, \text{ or } \log_{10} 14 = 1.1461 \\
15 &= 10^{1.1761}, \text{ or } \log_{10} 15 = 1.1761 \\
16 &= 10^{1.2041}, \text{ or } \log_{10} 16 = 1.2041
\end{aligned}
$$

The exponents are approximate, but accurate to four decimal places. To illustrate how logarithms can be used for computation we will use the above table and do some easy calculations.

EXAMPLE 1

Find 3×4 using the table of exponents.

$$
\begin{aligned}
3 \times 4 &= 10^{0.4771} \times 10^{0.6021} \\
&= 10^{1.0792} \quad \text{Adding exponents}
\end{aligned}
$$

From the table we see that $10^{1.0792} = 12$, so $3 \times 4 = 12$.

TRY THIS

1. Find 2×8 using the table. 16

Note from Example 1 that we can find a product by adding the logarithms of the factors and then finding the number having the result as its logarithm; that is, we found the number $10^{1.0792}$. This number is often referred to as the antilogarithm of 1.0792. In other words, if

$$f(x) = \log_{10} x, \text{ then } f^{-1}(x) = \text{antilog}_{10} x = 10^x.$$

Therefore, an antilogarithm function is simply an exponential function.

EXAMPLE 2

Find $\frac{14}{2}$, using base 10 logarithms.

$$\log_{10} \frac{14}{2} = \log_{10} - \log_{10} 2$$
$$= 1.1461 - 0.3010$$
$$\log_{10} \frac{14}{2} = 0.8451$$
$$\frac{14}{2} = \text{antilog}_{10}\ 0.8451 = 7$$

EXAMPLE 3

Find $\sqrt[4]{16}$, using base 10 logarithms.

$$\log_{10} \sqrt[4]{16} = \log_{10} 16^{\frac{1}{4}} = \frac{1}{4} \cdot \log_{10} 16 = \frac{1}{4} \cdot 1.2041$$
$$\log_{10} \sqrt[4]{16} = 0.3010 \quad \text{Rounded to four decimal places}$$
$$\sqrt[4]{16} = \text{antilog}_{10}\ 0.3010 = 2$$

EXAMPLE 4

Find 2^3, using base 10 logarithms.

$$\log_{10} 2^3 = 3 \cdot \log_{10} 2 = 3 \cdot 0.3010 = 0.9030$$
$$\log_{10} 2^3 = 0.9030$$
$$2^3 = \text{antilog}_{10}\ 0.9030 \approx 8$$

Note the rounding error.

TRY THIS Using base 10 logarithms, find the following.

2. 4×2 8   3. $\frac{15}{3}$ 5   4. $\sqrt[3]{8}$ 2   5. 3^2 9

Finding Common Logarithms Using Tables

We often omit the base, 10, when working with common logarithms.

Table 2 contains logarithms of numbers from 1 to 10. Part of that table is shown below. To illustrate the use of the table, let us find log 5.24. We locate the row headed 5.2, then move across to the column headed 4. We find log 5.24 as the colored entry in the table.

x	0	1	2	3	4	5	6	7	8	9
5.0	0.6990	0.6998	0.7007	0.7016	0.7024	0.7033	0.7042	0.7050	0.7059	0.7067
5.1	0.7076	0.7084	0.7093	0.7101	0.7110	0.7118	0.7126	0.7135	0.7143	0.7152
5.2	0.7160	0.7168	0.7177	0.7185	0.7193	0.7202	0.7210	0.7218	0.7226	0.7235
5.3	0.7243	0.7251	0.7259	0.7267	0.7275	0.7284	0.7292	0.7300	0.7308	0.7316
5.4	0.7324	0.7332	0.7340	0.7348	0.7356	0.7364	0.7372	0.7380	0.7388	0.7396

We can find antilogarithms by reversing this process. For example, antilog $0.7193 = 10^{0.7193} = 5.24$. Similarly, antilog $0.7292 = 5.36$.

TRY THIS

6. Use Table 2 to find each logarithm.
   a. log 3.14   **b.** log 9.99   **c.** log 4.00

7. Use Table 2 to find each antilogarithm.
   a. antilog 0.7589   **b.** antilog 0.0000   **c.** antilog 0.5587

6. a. 0.4969
   b. 0.9996
   c. 0.6021

7. a. 5.74
   b. 1.00
   c. 3.62

Using Table 2 and scientific notation we can approximate logarithms of numbers that are not between 1 and 10. First recall the following.

$$\log_a a^k = k \text{ for any number } k \quad \text{Theorem 12–4}$$

Thus

$$\log_{10} 10^k = k \text{ for any number } k.$$

EXAMPLES

5. $\log 52.4 = \log (5.24 \times 10^1)$ Converting to scientific notation
   $= \log 5.24 + \log 10^1$ Theorem 12–5
   $= 0.7193 + 1$

6. $\log 0.524 = \log (5.24 \times 10^{-1})$
   $= \log 5.24 + \log 10^{-1}$
   $= 0.7193 + (-1)$

7. $\log 52{,}400 = \log (5.24 \times 10^4)$
$= \log 5.24 + \log 10^4$
$= 0.7193 + 4$

8. $\log 0.00524 = \log (5.24 \times 10^{-3})$
$= \log 5.24 + \log 10^{-3}$
$= 0.7193 + (-3)$

TRY THIS Use scientific notation and Table 2 to find each logarithm.

8. $\log 289$ **9.** $\log 0.000289$ 8. $0.4609 + 2$ 9. $0.4609 + (-4)$

The preceding examples illustrate the importance of using the base 10 for computation. It allows great economy in the printing of tables. If we know the logarithm of a number from 1 to 10 we can multiply that number by any power of ten and easily determine the logarithm of the resulting number. For any base other than 10 this would not be the case. In each of Examples 5–8, the integer part of the logarithm is the exponent in the scientific notation. This integer is called the characteristic of the logarithm. The other part of the logarithm, a number between 0 and 1, is called the mantissa of the logarithm. Table 2 contains only mantissas.

EXAMPLE 9

Find $\log 0.0538$, indicating the characteristic and mantissa.

We first write scientific notation for the number.

5.38×10^{-2}

Then we find $\log 5.38$. This is the mantissa.

$\log 5.38 = 0.7308$

The characteristic of the logarithm is the exponent -2. Now $\log 0.0538 = 0.7308 + (-2)$, or -1.2692. When negative characteristics occur, it is often best to name the logarithm so that the characteristic and mantissa are preserved.

$\log 0.0538 = 0.7308 + (-2) = -1.2692$

The latter notation displays neither the characteristic nor the mantissa. We can rename the characteristic, -2, as $8 - 10$, and then add the mantissa to preserve both the mantissa and characteristic.

$8.7308 - 10$

The characteristic and mantissa are useful when working with logarithm tables, but are not needed on a calculator. For example, on a calculator with a ten-digit readout, we find the following.

$$\log 0.0538 = -1.269217724$$

This shows neither the characteristic nor the mantissa. Check this on your calculator. How can you find the characteristic and mantissa?

EXAMPLE 10
Find $\log 0.00687$.

We write scientific notation (or at least visualize it).

$$0.00687 = 6.87 + 10^{-3}$$

The characteristic is

$$-3, \text{ or } 7 - 10.$$

The mantissa, from the table, is

$$0.8370.$$

Thus $\log 0.00687 = 7.8370 - 10$.

TRY THIS Find the following. Use Table 2 and try to write only the answer. Where appropriate, name so that positive mantissas are preserved.

10. $\log 67,800$ 11. $\log 892,000$ 12. $\log 45.9$

10. 4.8312
11. 5.9504
12. 1.6618

Antilogarithms

To find antilogarithms, we reverse the procedure for finding logarithms.

EXAMPLE 11
Find antilog 2.6085 (or find x such that $\log x = 2.6085$).

$$\begin{aligned}
\text{antilog } 2.6085 &= 10^{2.6085} \\
&= 10^{(2 + 0.6085)} \\
&= 10^2 \cdot 10^{0.6085}
\end{aligned}$$

From the table we can find $10^{0.6085}$, or antilog 0.6085. It is 4.06.

$$\text{antilog } 2.6085 = 10^2 \times 4.06, \text{ or } 406$$

Note that in this example, we in effect separate the number 2.6085 into an integer and a number between 0 and 1. We use the latter with the table, after which we have scientific notation for our answer.

EXAMPLE 12

Find antilog 3.7118.

From the table we find that antilog 0.7118 = 5.15.

$$\text{antilog } 3.7188 = 5.15 \times 10^3 \quad \text{Note that 3 is the characteristic.}$$
$$= 5150$$

EXAMPLE 13

Find antilog (7.7143 − 10).

The characteristic is −3 and the mantissa is 0.7143.
From the table we find that antilog 0.7143 = 5.18.

$$\text{antilog } (7.7143 - 10) = 5.18 \times 10^{-3}$$
$$= 0.00518$$

EXAMPLE 14

Find antilog −2.2857.

We are to find the antilog of a number, but the number is named so that the mantissa is not apparent. To find the mantissa we add 0, naming it 10 − 10.

$$-2.2857 = -2.2857 + (10 - 10)$$
$$= (-2.2857 + 10) - 10 = 7.7143 - 10$$

Then we proceed as in Example 13. The answer is 0.00518.

TRY THIS Find the following. Use Table 2. Try to write only the answer.

13. If $\log x = 4.8069$, find x.
14. $10^{4.8069}$
15. $10^{3.9325}$
16. antilog 6.6284 − 10
17. antilog −1.9788

13. 64,100
14. 64,100
15. 8560
16. 0.000425
17. 0.0105

12–5

Exercises

Use Table 2 to find each of the following.

1. log 2.46 0.3909
2. log 7.65 0.8837
3. log 5.31 0.7251
4. log 8.57 0.9330
5. log 3.72 0.5705
6. log 9.04 0.9562
7. log 1.07 0.0294
8. log 4.60 0.6628
9. log 6.32 0.8007
10. antilog 0.8657 7.34
11. antilog 0.3502 2.24
12. antilog 0.6803 4.79
13. antilog 0.1399 1.38
14. antilog 0.7574 5.72
15. antilog 0.9191 8.30

16. $10^{0.5551}$ 3.59   **17.** $10^{0.8021}$ 6.34   **18.** $10^{0.5911}$ 3.90

19. $10^{0.9609}$ 9.14   **20.** $10^{0.3502}$ 2.24   **21.** $10^{0.8657}$ 7.34

Find these logarithms using Table 2. Try to write only the answers. Where appropriate, name the answers so that positive mantissas are preserved.

22. log 347   **23.** log 8720   **24.** log 52.5

25. log 20.6   **26.** log 834   **27.** log 92.4

28. log 3870   **29.** log 624,000   **30.** log 0.00134

31. log 0.0702   **32.** log 0.64   **33.** log 0.000216

34. log 0.173   **35.** log 0.00347   **36.** log 0.0000404

Find these antilogarithms using Table 2. Try to write only the answers.

37. antilog 3.3674   **38.** antilog 4.9222   **39.** antilog 1.2553

40. antilog 2.6294   **41.** antilog 9.7875 − 10   **42.** antilog 8.9881 − 10

43. $10^{1.4014}$ **44.** $10^{2.5391}$ **45.** $10^{7.9881-10}$

46. $10^{8.5391-10}$ **47.** $10^{6.7875-10}$ **48.** $10^{4.6294-10}$

Extension

Find x.

49. $\log x = 0.8021$ **50.** $\log x = 4.1903$ **51.** $\log x = 9.7875 - 10$

52. $\log x = -1.0218$ **53.** $10^x = 345$ **54.** $10^x = 5670$

Use a calculator to find each of the following. Round to six decimal places.

55. log 56,789   **56.** log 0.0111347   **57.** log (log 3)

Use a calculator to find each antilogarithm. Since $\text{antilog}_{10} x = 10^x$, you can find the antilogarithm, base 10, of any number x by raising 10 to the power x.

58. $10^{0.4356}$ **59.** antilog_{10} 7.8943

60. $\text{antilog}_{10} (-7.5689)$ **61.** $10^{-3.23445678}$

THE NUMBER e

In Section 12−8, you will read about the function e^x. Like the number π, e is a *transcendental number*. That is, it can never be completely expressed in a finite number of digits or as the solution of an algebraic equation with integers as coefficients. One way of expressing the value of e uses factorials. In the expression below, 3! (3 factorial) equals $3 \times 2 \times 1$;

$4! = 4 \times 3 \times 2 \times 1$; and so on.

$$e = 1 + \frac{1}{1!} + \frac{1}{2!} + \frac{1}{3!} + \frac{1}{4!} + \frac{1}{5!} + \frac{1}{6!} + \frac{1}{7!} + \cdots$$

Thus, the value of e can be approximated as closely as needed by continuing the series above. To the tenth decimal place, $e = 2.7182818285$.

12–6 Interpolation

Tables are often prepared giving function values for a continuous function. Suppose the table gives four-digit precision. By using a procedure called interpolation, we can estimate values between those listed in the table, obtaining four-digit precision.

Interpolation can be done in various ways, the simplest and most common being linear interpolation. We describe it now in relation to Table 2 for common logarithms. Remember that what we say applies to a table for *any* continuous function.

Linear Interpolation

Let us consider how a table of values for any function is made. We select members of the domain x_1, x_2, x_3, and so on. Then we compute or somehow determine the corresponding function values $f(x_1)$, $f(x_2)$, $f(x_3)$, and so on. Then we tabulate the results. We might also graph the results.

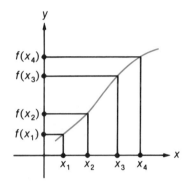

x	x_1	x_2	x_3	x_4	...
$f(x)$	$f(x_1)$	$f(x_2)$	$f(x_3)$	$f(x_4)$	...

Suppose we want to find the function value $f(x)$ for an x not in the table. If x is halfway between x_1 and x_2, then we can take the number halfway between $f(x_1)$ and $f(x_2)$ as an approximation to $f(x)$. If x is one-fifth of the way between x_2 and x_3, we take the number that is one-fifth of the way between $f(x_2)$ and $f(x_3)$ as an approximation to $f(x)$. What we do is divide the length from x_2 to x_3 in a certain ratio, and then divide the length from $f(x_2)$ to $f(x_3)$ in the same ratio. This is linear interpolation.

We can show this geometrically. The length from x_1 to x_2 is divided in a certain ratio by x. The length from $f(x_1)$ to $f(x_2)$ is divided in the same ratio by y. The number y approximates $f(x)$ with the noted error.

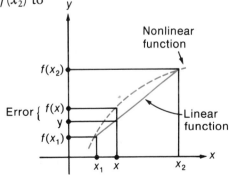

Note the slanted line in the figure. The approximation y comes from this line. This explains the use of the term linear interpolation. Let us apply linear interpolation to Table 2 of common logarithms.

EXAMPLE 1

Find log 34,870.

a. Since $34,870 = 3.487 \times 10^4$, the characteristic is 4.

b. Find the mantissa. From Table 2 we have:

$$
0.01 \begin{cases} 0.007 \begin{cases} \log 3.480 = 0.5416 \\ \log 3.487 = 0.54?? \\ \log 3.490 = 0.5428 \end{cases} \end{cases} \quad \text{The tabular difference is } 0.0012.
$$

The tabular difference (difference between consecutive values in the table) is 0.0012. Now 3.487 is $\frac{7}{10}$ of the way from 3.480 to 3.490. So we take 0.7 of 0.0012, which is 0.00084, and round it to 0.0008. We add this to 0.5416 and get 0.5424.

c. Add the characteristic and mantissa.

$$\log 34,870 = 4.5424$$

With practice you will take 0.7 of 12, forgetting the zeros but adding in the same way.

EXAMPLE 2

Find log 0.009543.

a. Since $0.009543 = 9.543 \times 10^{-3}$, the characteristic is -3, or $7 - 10$.

b. Find the mantissa. From Table 2 we have:

$$
0.01 \begin{cases} 0.003 \begin{cases} \log 9.540 = 0.9795 \\ \log 9.543 = 0.97?? \\ \log 9.550 = 0.9800 \end{cases} \end{cases} \quad \text{The tabular difference is } 0.0005.
$$

Now 9.543 is $\frac{3}{10}$ of the way from 9.540 to 9.550, so we take 0.3 of 0.0005, which is 0.00015, and round it to 0.0002. We add this to 0.9795. The mantissa that results is 0.9797.

c. Add the characteristic and the mantissa.

$$\log 0.009543 = 7.9797 - 10$$

TRY THIS

1. Find log 4562. 3.6592

2. Find log 0.02387. 8.3779 − 10

Antilogarithms

We interpolate when finding antilogarithms, using the table in reverse.

EXAMPLE 3
Find antilog 4.9164.

a. The characteristic is 4. The mantissa is 0.9164.
b. Find the antilog of the mantissa, 0.9164. From Table 2, we have:

$$\left. \begin{array}{l} 0.0006 \quad\quad 0.0005 \left[\begin{array}{l} \text{antilog } 0.9159 = 8.240 \\ \text{antilog } 0.9164 = 8.24? \\ \text{antilog } 0.9165 = 8.250 \end{array} \right. \end{array} \right\} \begin{array}{l} \text{The tabular difference} \\ \text{is } 0.010. \end{array}$$

0.9164 is $\frac{0.0005}{0.0006}$, or $\frac{5}{6}$, of the way between 0.9159 and 0.9165. Then antilog 0.9164 is $\frac{5}{6}$ of the way between 8.240 and 8.250, or $\frac{5}{6}(0.010)$, which is 0.00833 ..., and rounds to 0.008. Thus the antilog of the mantissa is 8.248.

Thus antilog $4.9164 = 8.248 \times 10^4 = 82{,}480$.

TRY THIS

3. Find $10^{3.4557}$. 2856

EXAMPLE 4
Find antilog (7.4122 − 10).

a. The characteristic is −3. The mantissa is 0.4122.
b. Find the antilog of the mantissa, 0.4122. From Table 2 we have:

$$\left. \begin{array}{l} 0.0017 \quad\quad 0.0006 \left[\begin{array}{l} \text{antilog } 0.4116 = 2.580 \\ \text{antilog } 0.4122 = 2.58? \\ \text{antilog } 0.4133 = 2.590 \end{array} \right. \end{array} \right\} \begin{array}{l} \text{The tabular difference} \\ \text{is } 0.010. \end{array}$$

The difference between 0.4116 and 0.4133 is 0.0017. Thus 0.4122 is $\frac{0.0006}{0.0017}$, or $\frac{6}{17}$, of the way between 0.4116 and 0.4133. Then antilog 0.4122 is $\frac{6}{17}$ of the way between 2.580 and 2.590, or $\frac{6}{17}(0.010)$, which is 0.0035, to four places. We round it to 0.004. Thus the antilog of the mantissa is 2.584.

So antilog $(7.4122 - 10) = 2.584 \times 10^{-3} = 0.002584$.

TRY THIS

4. Find antilog $(6.7749 - 10)$. 0.0005956

12–6

Exercises

Find each of the following logarithms using interpolation and Table 2.

1. log 41.63 1.6194
2. log 472.1 2.6740
3. log 2.944 0.4689
4. log 21.76 1.3377
5. log 650.2 2.8130
6. log 37.37 1.5725
7. log 0.1425 9.1538 − 10
8. log 0.09045 8.9564 − 10
9. log 0.004257 7.6291 − 10
10. log 4518 3.6549
11. log 0.1776 9.2494 − 10
12. log 0.08356 8.9220 − 10
13. log 600.6 2.7786
14. log 500.2 2.6991
15. log 800.1 2.9032

Find each of the following antilogarithms using interpolation and Table 2.

16. antilog 1.6350 43.15
17. antilog 2.3512 224.5
18. antilog 0.6478 4.444
19. antilog 1.1624 14.53
20. antilog 0.0342 1.082
21. antilog 4.8453 70,030
22. antilog 9.8564 − 10
23. antilog 8.9659 − 10
24. antilog 7.4128 − 10
25. antilog 9.7278 − 10
26. antilog 8.2010 − 10
27. antilog 7.8630 − 10

Extension

Find.

28. log (log 3) 9.6786 − 10
29. log (log 5) 9.8445 − 10
30. log (log 7) 9.9269 − 10

Challenge

Use logarithms and interpolation to do the following calculations. Use four-digit precision. Answers may be checked using a calculator.

31. $\dfrac{35.24 \times (16.77)^3}{12.93 \times \sqrt{276.2}}$
32. $\sqrt[5]{\dfrac{16.79 \times (4.234)^3}{18.81 \times 175.3}}$

22. 0.7185
23. 0.09245
24. 0.002587
25. 0.5343
26. 0.01589
27. 0.007295

31. 773.2
32. 0.8268

12–7 Exponential and Logarithmic Equations

Exponential Equations

An equation with variables in exponents, such as $3^{2x-1} = 4$, is called an exponential equation. We can solve such equations by taking logarithms on both sides and then using Theorem 12–6.

EXAMPLE 1

Solve $3^x = 8$.

$$\log 3^x = \log 8 \quad \text{Taking log on both sides. Remember } \log m = \log_{10} m.$$

$$x \log 3 = \log 8 \quad \text{Using Theorem 12–6}$$

$$x = \frac{\log 8}{\log 3} \quad \text{Solving for } x$$

$$x \approx \frac{0.9031}{0.4771} \approx 1.8929 \quad \text{We look up the logs, or find them on a calculator, and divide.}$$

TRY THIS

1. Solve $2^x = 7$. 2.8076

EXAMPLE 2

Solve $2^{3x-5} = 16$.

$$\log 2^{3x-5} = \log 16 \quad \text{Taking log on both sides}$$

$$(3x - 5) \log 2 = \log 16 \quad \text{Using Theorem 12–6}$$

$$3x - 5 = \frac{\log 16}{\log 2}$$

$$3x = \frac{\log 16}{\log 2} + 5$$

$$x = \frac{\frac{\log 16}{\log 2} + 5}{3}$$

$$\approx \frac{\frac{1.2041}{0.3010} + 5}{3} \quad \text{Solving for } x \text{ and evaluating logarithms}$$

$$x \approx 3.0001 \quad \text{Calculating}$$

The answer is approximate because the logarithms are approximate.

The following is another method of solving exponential equations.

EXAMPLE 3
Solve $2^{3x-5} = 16$.

Note that $16 = 2^4$. Then we have $2^{3x-5} = 2^4$.

Since the base is the same, 2, on both sides, the exponents must be the same. Thus, we can solve for x as follows.

$$3x - 5 = 4$$
$$x = 3$$

TRY THIS

2. Solve $4^{2x-3} = 64$. Use Table 2 and the method in Example 2. 2.9999
3. Solve $4^{2x-3} = 64$. Use the method in Example 3. 3

Logarithmic Equations

Equations that contain logarithmic expressions are called logarithmic equations. We solve them by converting to an equivalent exponential equation. For example, to solve $\log_2 x = -3$, we convert to $x = 2^{-3}$ and find that $x = \frac{1}{8}$.

> To solve logarithmic equations we first try to obtain a single logarithmic expression on one side of the equation and then write an equivalent exponential equation.

EXAMPLE 4
Solve $\log_3 (5x + 7) = 2$.

We already have a single logarithmic expression, so we write an equivalent exponential equation.

$$5x + 7 = 3^2$$
$$5x + 7 = 9$$
$$x = \frac{2}{5}$$

Check:
$$\log_3 (5x + 7) = 2$$
$$\log_3 \left(5 \cdot \frac{2}{5} + 7\right) \Big| 2$$
$$\log_3 (2 + 7)$$
$$\log_3 9$$
$$2 \Big|$$

TRY THIS Solve.

4. $\log_5 x = 3$ 125 5. $\log_4 (8x - 6) = 3$ 8.75

EXAMPLE 5

Solve $\log x + \log (x - 3) = 1$.

Here we must first obtain a single logarithmic equation.

$$\log x + \log (x - 3) = 1$$
$$\log x \, (x - 3) = 1 \quad \text{Using Theorem 12-5 to obtain a single logarithm}$$
$$\log_{10} x\,(x - 3) = 1$$
$$x\,(x - 3) = 10^1 \quad \text{Converting to an equivalent exponential equation}$$
$$x^2 - 3x = 10$$
$$x^2 - 3x - 10 = 0$$
$$(x + 2)(x - 5) = 0 \quad \text{Factoring and principle of zero products}$$
$$x = -2 \text{ or } x = 5$$

Possible solutions to logarithmic equations must be checked because domains of logarithmic functions consist only of positive numbers.

Check:
$$\begin{array}{c|c} \log x + \log (x - 3) = 1 \\ \hline \log (-2) + \log (-2 - 3) & 1 \end{array} \qquad \begin{array}{c|c} \log x + \log (x - 3) = 1 \\ \hline \log 5 + \log (5 - 3) & 1 \\ \log 5 + \log 2 \\ \log 10 \\ 1 \end{array}$$

The number -2 is not a solution because negative numbers do not have logarithms. The solution is 5.

TRY THIS

6. Solve $\log x + \log (x + 3) = 1$. ₂

Applications

Exponential and logarithmic functions and equations have many applications.

EXAMPLE 6   Compound Interest

The amount A that principal P will be worth after t years at interest rate r, compounded annually, is given by the formula $A = P(1 + r)^t$.

Suppose \$4000 principal is invested at 6% interest and yields \$5353. For how many years was it invested?

We use the formula $A = P(1 + r)^t$.

$$5353 = 4000(1 + 0.06)^t, \text{ or } 5353 = 4000(1.06)^t$$

Then we solve for t.

$$\log 5353 = \log 4000(1.06)^t \quad \text{Taking log on both sides}$$

$$\log 5353 = \log 4000 + t \log 1.06 \quad \text{Theorems 12–5 and 12–6}$$

$$\frac{\log 5353 - \log 4000}{\log 1.06} = t \quad \text{Solving for } t$$

$$\frac{3.7286 - 3.6021}{0.0253} \approx t \quad \text{Evaluating logarithms}$$

$$5 \approx t$$

The money was invested for 5 years. We can use a calculator for an approximate check.

TRY THIS

7. $5000 was invested at 14%, compounded annually, and it yielded $18,540. For how long was it invested? 10 years

EXAMPLE 7 Loudness of Sound

The sensation of loudness of sound is not proportional to the energy intensity, but rather is a logarithmic function. Loudness in bels (after Alexander Graham Bell) of a sound of intensity I is defined to be

$$L = \log \frac{I}{I_0},$$

where I_0 is the minimum intensity detectable by the human ear (such as the tick of a watch at 6 meters under quiet conditions). When a sound is 10 times as intense as another, its loudness is 1 bel greater. If a sound is 100 times as intense as another, it is louder by 2 bels, and so on. The bel is a large unit, so a subunit one tenth as large (a decibel) is usually used. For L in decibels, the formula is as follows.

$$L = 10 \log \frac{I}{I_0}$$

a. Find the loudness in decibels of the background noise in a radio studio, for which the intensity I is 199 times I_0.

We substitute into the formula and calculate, using Table 2.

$$L = 10 \log \frac{199 \cdot I_0}{I_0}$$
$$= 10 \log 199$$
$$\approx 10(2.2989)$$
$$\approx 23 \text{ decibels}$$

b. Find the loudness of the sound of a heavy truck, for which the intensity is 10^9 times I_0.

$$L = 10 \log \frac{10^9 \cdot I_0}{I_0}$$
$$= 10 \log 10^9$$
$$= 10 \cdot 9$$
$$= 90 \text{ decibels}$$

TRY THIS

8. Find the loudness in decibels of the sound in a library, for which the intensity I is 2510 times I_0. 34 decibels

9. Find the loudness in decibels of conversational speech, for which the intensity is 10^6 times I_0. 60 decibels

EXAMPLE 8   Earthquake Magnitude

The magnitude R (on the Richter scale) of an earthquake of intensity I is defined as follows:

$$R = \log \frac{I}{I_0},$$

where I_0 is a minimum intensity used for comparison.

An earthquake has an intensity $10^{8.6}$ times I_0. What is its magnitude on the Richter scale?

We substitute into the formula.

$$R = \log \frac{10^{8.6} \cdot I_0}{I_0} = \log 10^{8.6} = 8.6$$

TRY THIS

10. The earthquake in Anchorage, Alaska on March 27, 1964 had an intensity $10^{8.4}$ times I_0. What was its magnitude on the Richter scale? 8.4

12–7

Exercises

Solve.

1. $2^x = 8$

2. $2^x = 32$

3. $2^x = 10$

4. $2^x = 33$

5. $5^{4x-7} = 125$

6. $4^{3x+5} = 16$

1. 3
2. 5
3. 3.3223
4. 5.0449
5. $\frac{5}{2}$
6. -1

7. $3^{x^2+4x} = \dfrac{1}{27}$ **8.** $3^{5x} \cdot 9^{x^2} = 27$ **9.** $4^x = 7$ 7. $-3, -1$

8. $-3, \frac{1}{2}$

10. $8^x = 10$ **11.** $2^x = 3^{x-1}$ **12.** $3^{x+2} = 5^{x-1}$ 9. 1.4036

10. 1.1073

13. $(2.8)^x = 41$ **14.** $(3.4)^x = 80$ **15.** $(1.7)^x = 20$ 11. 2.7093

12. 7.4502

13. 3.6064

14. 3.5806

15. 5.6467

Solve.

16. $\log x + \log (x - 9) = 1$ 10   **17.** $\log x + \log (x + 9) = 1$ 1

18. $\log x - \log (x + 3) = -1$ $\frac{1}{3}$ **19.** $\log (x + 9) - \log x = 1$ 1

20. $\log_4 (x + 3) + \log_4 (x - 3) = 2$ 5   **21.** $\log_5 (x + 4) + \log_5 (x - 4) = 2$ $\sqrt{41}$

22. $\log \sqrt[3]{x} = \sqrt{\log x}$ 1, 10^9 **23.** $\log \sqrt[4]{x} = \sqrt{\log x}$ 1, 10^{16}

24. $\log_5 \sqrt{x^2 + 1} = 1$ $\pm 2\sqrt{6}$ **25.** $\log \sqrt[3]{x^2} + \log \sqrt[3]{x^4} = \log 2^{-3}$ $\pm\frac{\sqrt{2}}{4}$

Solve.

26. Doubling time. How many years will it take an investment of $1000 to double itself when interest is compounded annually at 6%?   11.9

27. Tripling time. How many years will it take an investment of $1000 to triple itself when interest is compounded annually at 5%?   22.5

28. Find the loudness in decibels of the sound of an automobile having an intensity 3,100,000 times I_0.   65 decibels

29. Find the loudness in decibels of the sound of a dishwasher having an intensity 2,500,000 times I_0.   64 decibels

30. Find the loudness in decibels of the threshold of sound pain, for which the intensity is 10^{14} times I_0.   140 decibels

31. Find the loudness in decibels of a jet aircraft having an intensity 10^{12} times I_0.   120 decibels

32. The Los Angeles earthquake of 1971 had an intensity $10^{6.7}$ times I_0. What was its magnitude on the Richter scale?   6.7

33. The San Francisco earthquake of 1906 had an intensity $10^{8.25}$ times I_0. What was its magnitude on the Richter scale?   8.25

34. An earthquake has a magnitude of 5 on the Richter scale. What is its intensity? 10^5 times i_0

35. An earthquake has a magnitude of 7 on the Richter scale. What is its intensity? 10^7 times I_0

In chemistry, pH is defined as follows:

$$\text{pH} = -\log [\text{H}^+],$$

where $[\text{H}^+]$ is the hydrogen ion concentration in moles per liter. For example, the hydrogen ion concentration in milk is 4×10^{-7} moles per liter, so $\text{pH} = -\log (4 \times 10^{-7}) = -[\log 4 + (-7)] \approx 6.4$.

36. For tomatoes, $[\text{H}^+]$ is about 6.3×10^{-5}. Find the pH.   4.2

37. For eggs, $[\text{H}^+]$ is about 1.6×10^{-8}. Find the pH.   7.8

Extension

Solve.

38. $\log \sqrt{x} = \sqrt{\log x}$

39. $\log_5 \sqrt{x^2 + 1} = 1$

40. $(\log_a x)^{-1} = \log_a x^{-1}$

41. $|\log_5 x| = 2$

42. $\log_3 |x| = 2$

43. $\log x^{\log x} = 4$

44. $\dfrac{\sqrt{(a^{2x} \cdot a^{-5x})^{-4}}}{a^x \div a^{-x}} = a^7$

45. $\dfrac{(a^{3x+1})^2}{a^4} = a^{10x}$

46. Solve $y = ax^n$, for n. Use $\log_x$.

47. Solve $y = kb^{at}$, for t. Use $\log_b$.

48. Solve for t. $T = T_0 + (T_1 - T_0)10^{-kt}$

49. Solve for n. Use $\log_V$. $PV^n = c$

50. Solve for Q. $\log_a Q = \frac{1}{3}\log_a y + b$

51. Solve for y. $\log_a y = 2x + \log_a x$

Solve for x.

52. $x^{\log x} = \dfrac{x^3}{100}$

53. $x^{\log x} = 100x$

Challenge

54. $|\log_5 x| + 3\log_5 |x| = 4$

55. $|\log_a x| = \log_a |x|$

56. $(0.5)^x < \dfrac{4}{5}$

57. $8x^{0.3} - 8x^{-0.3} = 63$

58. Solve the system of equations.
$$5^{x+y} = 100$$
$$3^{2x-y} = 1000$$

59. Given that
$$\log_2 [\log_3 (\log_4 x)] =$$
$$\log_3 [\log_2 (\log_4 y)] =$$
$$\log_4 [\log_3 (\log_2 z)] = 0,$$
find $x + y + z$.

60. If $2\log_3 (x - 2y) = \log_3 x + \log_3 y$, find $\dfrac{x}{y}$.

61. Find the ordered pair (x, y) for which $4^{\log_{16} 27} = 2^x 3^y$.

LOGARITHMS/Taking the Base of a Power

Suppose we have an equation such as the following.

$$x^5 = 1000$$

We can use logarithms to find the base x. To do so, take the log of both sides and then use Theorem 12–6.

$$\log x^5 = \log 1000$$
$$5 \log x = \log 1000$$

$$\log x = \frac{\log 1000}{5}$$

$$\log x = \frac{3}{5} = 0.6$$

$$x = 10^{0.6}$$
$$x \approx 3.981$$

In general, for $x^a = b$, $x = 10^{\frac{\log b}{a}}$.

12–8 The Number *e* and Applications

Exponential Functions, Base *e*

One of the most important numbers is a certain irrational number, with a nonrepeating decimal representation. This number is usually called *e* and is approximated as follows.

$$e = 2.718281828459\ldots$$

The exponential function, base e, is important in many applications, and its inverse, the logarithm function base e, is also important in mathematical theory and in applications as well. Logarithms to the base e are called natural logarithms. Most scientific calculators have an $\boxed{e^x}$ key. Table 4 at the back of the book gives function values for e^x and e^{-x}. Using a calculator or these tables we can construct graphs of $y = e^x$ and $y = \log_e x$.

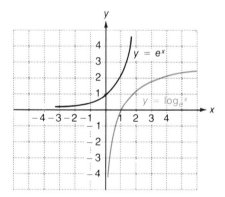

TRY THIS

1. Using the same axes, graph each of the following.
   a. $y = 2^x$ **b.** $y = 4^x$ **c.** $y = e^x$
   Use Table 4 to obtain values of e^x.
2. Graph $y = e^{-x}$.

Natural Logarithms

The number $\log_e x$ is abbreviated $\ln x$; that is, $\ln x = \log_e x$. If you have an $\boxed{\ln}$ key on your calculator, you can find such logarithms directly. You can also use Table 5 at the back of the book.

EXAMPLES

Use a calculator or Table 5 to find each of the following.

1. $\ln 5.24 = 1.656321$ **2.** $\ln 52.4 = 3.958907$ **3.** $\ln 0.001277 = -6.663242$

From $\ln 5.24$ and $\ln 52.4$ we note that natural logarithms do not have characteristics and mantissas. Common logarithms have characteristics and mantissas because our numeration system is based on 10. For any base other than 10, logarithms have neither characteristics nor mantissas.

TRY THIS Use a calculator to find each logarithm. Round to six decimal places.

3. $\ln 2$ **4.** $\ln 100$ **5.** $\ln 0.07432$ **6.** $\ln 0.9999$

3. 0.693147 4. 4.605170
5. −2.599375 6. −0.000100

Applications

There are many applications of exponential functions, base e. We consider a few.

EXAMPLE 4 Population growth

One mathematical model for describing population growth is the formula

$$P = P_0 e^{kt},$$

where P_0 is the number of people at time 0, P is the number of people at time t, and k is a positive constant depending on the situation. The population of the United States in 1970 was 208 million. In 1980 it was 225 million. Use these data to find the value of k and then use the model to predict the population in 2000.

  Time t begins with 1970. That is, $t = 0$ in 1970, $t = 10$ in 1980, and so on. Substituting the data into the formula, we get the equation $225 = 208e^{k \cdot 10}$

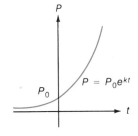

We solve for k.

$\ln 225 = \ln 208 e^{10k}$ Taking the natural logarithm on both sides
$\ln 225 = \ln 208 + \ln e^{10k}$ Theorem 12–5
$\ln 225 = \ln 208 + 10k$ Theorem 12–4

$$k = \frac{\ln 225 - \ln 208}{10}$$ Solving for k

$$k = \frac{5.4161 - 5.3375}{10}$$ Using a calculator or Table 5

$$k = 0.008$$ Calculating

12–8 The Number e and Applications **543**

To find the population in 2000, we will use $P_0 = 208$ (population in the year 1970).

$$P = 208e^{0.008t}$$

In 2000, t will be 30.

$$P = 208e^{0.008(30)} = 208e^{0.24}$$

Using a calculator or Table 4, we find that $e^{0.24} = 1.2712$. Multiplying by 208 gives us about 264 million. This is our prediction for the population of the United States in the year 2000.

TRY THIS

7. The population of Tempe, Arizona, was 25,000 in 1960. In 1969 it was 52,000.
   a. Use these data to determine k in the growth model. 0.08
   b. Use these data to predict the population of Tempe in 1990. 275,580

EXAMPLE 5   Radioactive decay

In a radioactive element some of the atoms are always transforming themselves into other elements. Thus the amount of a radioactive substance decreases. This is called radioactive decay. A model for radioactive decay is as follows:

$$N = N_0 e^{-kt},$$

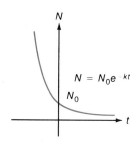

where N_0 is the amount of a radioactive substance at time 0, N is the amount at time t, and k is a positive constant depending on the rate that a particular element decays. Strontium-90, a radioactive substance, has a half-life of 25 years. This means that half of a sample of the substance will remain as the original element in 25 years. Find k in the formula and then use the formula to find how much of a 36-gram sample will remain after 100 years.

When $t = 25$ (half-life), N will be half of N_0.

$$\frac{1}{2} N_0 = N_0 e^{-25k} \text{ or } \frac{1}{2} = e^{-25k}$$

We take the natural log on both sides.

$$\ln \frac{1}{2} = \ln e^{-25k} = -25k$$

Thus

$$k = -\frac{\ln 0.5}{25} \approx 0.0277$$

Now to find the amount remaining after 100 years, we use the following formula.

$$N = 36e^{-0.0277 \cdot 100}$$
$$= 36e^{-2.77}$$

From a calculator or Table 4 we find that $e^{-2.8} = 0.0608$, and thus

$$N \approx 2.2 \text{ grams.}$$

TRY THIS

8. Radioactive bismuth has a half-life of 5 days. A scientist buys 224 grams of it. How much of it will remain as the original bismuth in 30 days? 3.5 grams

Logarithm Tables and Change of Base

The following theorem shows how we can change logarithm bases. The theorem can be applied to find the logarithm of a number to any base, using a table of common or natural logarithms.

THEOREM 12–9

For any bases a and b, and any positive number M,

$$\log_b M = \frac{\log_a M}{\log_a b}.$$

Proof of Theorem 12–9

Let $x = \log_b M$.
Then $b^x = M$, so that

$$\log_a M = \log_a b^x, \text{ or } x \log_a b.$$

We now solve for x.

$$x = \log_b M = \frac{\log_a M}{\log_a b}$$

This is the desired formula.

EXAMPLE 6

Find $\log_5 346$.

$$\log_5 346 = \frac{\log_{10} 346}{\log_{10} 5} = \frac{2.5391}{0.6990} \approx 3.6325$$

TRY THIS

9. Find $\log_5 125$.   10. Find $\log_6 4870$.   11. Use 2.718 for e. Find $\log_{10} e$.

If in Theorem 12–9 we let $a = 10$ and $b = e$, we obtain a formula for changing from common to natural logarithms.

$$\log_e M = \frac{\log_{10} M}{\log_{10} e}$$

Now $\log_{10} e \approx 0.4343$, so we have the following.

THEOREM 12–10

$$\log_e M = \frac{\log_{10} M}{0.4343}$$

EXAMPLE 7

Find $\log_e 257$.

$$\log_e 257 = \frac{\log_{10} 257}{0.4343} = \frac{2.4099}{0.4343} = 5.5489$$

We can make use of this change-of-base procedure to solve certain exponential equations.

EXAMPLE 8

Solve $3^x = 8$.

$$
\begin{aligned}
\log_3 3^x &= \log_3 8 \quad \text{Taking logarithms, base 3, on both sides} \\
x &= \log_3 8 \quad \text{Theorem 12–4} \\
&= \frac{\log_{10} 8}{\log_{10} 3} = \frac{0.9031}{0.4771} = 1.8929
\end{aligned}
$$

Compare this with Example 1 in Section 12–7.

TRY THIS

12. Find $\log_e 1030$.   13. Find $\log_e 0.457$.   14. Solve $2^x = 7$.

Exercises

Graph.

1. $y = e^{2x}$ **2.** $y = e^{0.5x}$ **3.** $y = e^{-2x}$

4. $y = e^{-0.5x}$ **5.** $y = 1 - e^{-x}$, for $x \geq 0$ **6.** $y = 2(1 - e^{-x})$, for $x \geq 0$

Find each natural logarithm to four decimal places. Use a calculator or Table 5.

7. ln 1.88   **8.** ln 18.8   **9.** ln 0.0188   **10.** ln 0.188   **11.** ln 2.13

12. ln 213   **13.** ln 0.213   **14.** ln 0.00213   **15.** ln 4500   **16.** ln 81,000

17. ln 0.00056   **18.** ln 0.999   **19.** ln 0.08   **20.** ln 0.0471   **21.** ln 980,000

Solve.

22. Population growth. The approximate population of Dallas was 680,000 in 1960. In 1969 it was 815,000. Find k in the growth formula and estimate the population in 1990.

23. Population growth. The approximate population of Kansas City was 475,000 in 1960. In 1970 it was 507,000. Find k in the growth formula and estimate the population in 2000.

24. Radioactive decay. The half-life of polonium-218 is 3 minutes. After 30 minutes, how much of a 410-gram sample will remain as the original polonium?

25. Radioactive decay. The half-life of a lead isotope is 22 yr. After 66 yr, how much of a 1000-gram sample will remain as the original isotope?

26. Radioactive decay. A certain radioactive substance decays from 66,560 grams to 6.5 grams in 16 days. What is its half-life?

27. Radioactive decay. Ten grams of uranium will decay to 2.5 grams in 496,000 years. What is its half-life?

28. Radiocarbon dating. Carbon-14 has a half-life of 5750 years. Organic objects contain carbon-14 as well as nonradioactive carbon, in known proportions. When an organism dies, it takes in no more carbon. The carbon-14 decays, changing the proportions of the kinds of carbon in the organism. By determining the amount of carbon-14 it is possible to determine how long the organism has been dead, hence how old it is.

    a. How old is an animal bone that has lost 30% of its carbon-14?

    b. A mummy discovered in the pyramid Khufu in Egypt had lost 46% of its carbon-14. Determine its age.

Answers here have been found using Table 5. If students use a calculator, there may be some variance in the last decimal place.

7. 0.6313
8. 2.9339
9. −3.9739
10. −1.6713
11. 0.7561
12. 5.3613
13. −1.5465
14. −6.1517
15. 8.4119
16. 11.3022
17. −7.4875
18. −0.001
19. −2.5258
20. −3.0555
21. 13.7953
22. $k = 0.0201$; $P = 1,243,000$
23. $k = 0.0065$; $P = 616,040$
24. 0.4 gram
25. 125 grams
26. 1.2 days
27. 248,000 years

28. a. 3000 years (rounding to the nearest hundred)
    b. 5100 years (rounding to the nearest hundred)

29. Radiocarbon dating.
   a. How old is an animal bone that has lost 20% of its carbon-14?
   b. The Statue of Zeus at Olympia in Greece is one of the seven wonders of the world. It is made of gold and ivory. The ivory was found to have lost 35% of its carbon-14. Determine the age of the statue.

30. Consumer price index. The *consumer price index* compares the costs of goods and services over various years. The base year is 1967. The same goods and services that cost \$100 (P_0) in 1967 cost \$184.50 in 1977. Assuming the exponential model:
   a. Find the value k and write the equation.
   b. Estimate what the same goods and services will cost in 1987.
   c. When did the same goods and services cost double that of 1967?

Find the following.

31. $\log_4 20$ **32.** $\log_8 0.99$ **33.** $\log_5 0.78$

34. $\log_{12} 15{,}000$ **35.** $\log_e 12$ (Do not use Table 5.)   **36.** $\log_e 0.77$ (Do not use Table 5.)

Extension

Solve for t.

37. $P = P_0 e^{kt}$ $t = \dfrac{\ln P - \ln P_0}{k}$

38. $P = P_0 e^{-kt}$ $t = \dfrac{\ln P_0 - \ln P}{k}$

Verify each of the following.

39. $\ln x = \dfrac{\log x}{\log e} \approx 2.3026 \log x$

40. $\log x = \dfrac{\ln x}{\ln 10} \approx 0.4343 \ln x$

Use a calculator for the following exercises.

41. Which is larger, e^π or π^e?

42. Which is larger, $e^{\sqrt{\pi}}$ or $\sqrt{e^\pi}$?

43. Given $f(x) = (1 + x)^{1/x}$, find $f(1)$, $f(0.5)$, $f(0.2)$, $f(0.1)$, $f(0.01)$, and $f(0.001)$ to six decimal places. This sequence of numbers approaches the number e.

44. Given $f(t) = t^{1/(t-1)}$, find $f(0.5)$, $f(0.9)$, $f(0.99)$, $f(0.999)$, and $f(0.9999)$ to six decimal places. This sequence of numbers approaches the number e.

Challenge

45. Find a (simple) formula for radioactive decay involving H, the half-life.

Prove the following for any logarithm bases a and b.

46. $\log_a b = \dfrac{1}{\log_b a}$

47. $a^{(\log_b M) \div (\log_b a)} = M$

48. $a^{(\log_b M)(\log_b a)} = M^{(\log_b a)^2}$

49. $\log_a (\log_a x) = \log_a (\log_b x) - \log_a (\log_b a)$

CONSUMER APPLICATION/Finding a Job

Most people have jobs to earn the money they need for living expenses. One of the ways to find a job is to use the "Help-Wanted" advertisements found in newspapers. Here are some typical ads.

EXECUTIVE SECRETARY	JEWELRY SALES	CASHIER
Typing (50 wpm) and shorthand required. Excellent benefits, potential for advancement. Salary $13,500.	$15,000 or more! Leading firm seeks salesperson to sell to distributors. Sales experience required. 25% commission.	Quality department store. $6.25/hr. for 40-hour week, time and a half overtime. No experience necessary.

Note how earnings are calculated in different ways. To see how similar jobs differ in pay, we can compare them for the same time period.

Receptionist, X Co.: salary $11,200.00 per year

Receptionist, Y Co.: $4.85 per hour, 40-hour week
Yearly earnings $= (40 \times \$4.85) \times 52$
$= \$10,088.00$

The receptionist at X Co. makes $1112.00 more per year.

Salesperson A: 20% commission, $95,000.00 per year projected sales
Yearly earnings $= 0.20 \times \$95,000.00$
$= \$19,000.00$

Salesperson B: salary $1665.00 per month
Yearly salary $= 12 \times 1665.00$
$= \$19,980.00$

Salesperson B makes $980.00 more per year.

Many factors besides earnings must be considered in choosing a job. Some are as follows.

Hours—regular? nights? holidays?
Working conditions—pleasant? indoor/outdoor?
Location—travel time? transportation expense?
Benefits—vacation? insurance?
Career potential—fits personal career goals? advancement?

When all factors are considered, then a true comparison can be made.

Exercises

Compare these jobs by finding the difference in earnings.

1. File clerk. Job A: $3.85 per hour, 40-hour week
   Job B: $4.00 per hour, 35-hour week   Job A pays $14 more per week.

2. Computer service representative. Job A: salary $17,500.00 per year
   Job B: salary $1350.00
   per month   Job A pays $1300 more per year.

3. Service station attendant. Job A: $225.00 per week
   Job B: $5.25 per hour, 40-hour week   Job A pays $15 more per week.

4. Salesperson. Job A: 15% commission, $115,000 projected sales
   Job B: salary $1550.00 per month   Job B pays $1350 more per month.

5. Secretary. Job A: $6.50 per hour, 40-hour week
   Job B: $280 per week   Job B pays $20 more per week

6. Typist. Job A: $5.60 per hour, 40-hour week
   Job B: $5.00 per page, for 50 pages   Job B pays $26 more.

7. House painter. Job A: $8.25 per hour, 40-hour week
   Job B: $300 per week   Job A pays $30 more per week.

8. Inventory clerk. Job A: $9800 per year
   Job B: $800 per month   Job A pays $200 more per year.

9. Bank loan officer. Job A: $18,400 per year
   Job B: $1560 per month   Job B pays $320 more per year.

10. Find employment ads in local newspapers for jobs you might be interested in. Compare earnings.

11. Obtain job application forms from local employers. Compare the types of information required.

12. Select a career that appeals to you. Check library sources such as the *Occupational Outlook Handbook* (U.S. Bureau of Labor Statistics) for information on required training, annual employment outlook, current salaries, and so on.

CHAPTER 12 Review

Review the material in the chapter. Then see how you have done by trying these review exercises. If you miss an exercise, restudy the indicated lesson.

12–1 Write an equation of the inverse relation of each of the following.

1. $y = 3x - 1$ 2. $y = 3x^2 + 2x - 1$ $x = 3y^2 + 2y - 1$ 1. $y = \frac{1}{3}x + \frac{1}{3}$

Find the inverse of the relation of each of the following.

3. $(4, 1), (-3, 8), (-1, -5)$ **4.** $(2, 3), (5, 7), (6, -4)$ (3, 2), (7, 5), (-4, 6)
(1, 4), (8, -3), (-5, -1)

12–1   Test each of the following for symmetry with respect to the line $y = x$.

5. $6x + 6y = 7$ Yes **6.** $2x - y = 1$ No

7. Given $g(x) = \dfrac{\sqrt{x}}{2} + 2$. Find an equation for $g^{-1}(x)$. $g^{-1}(x) = 4x^2 - 16x + 16$

8. Given $h(x) = 0.5x - 1$. Find an equation for $h^{-1}(x)$. $y = 2x + 2$

12–2

9. Graph $y = 5^x$. Give the domain, range, and y-intercept.   9. Curve through $\left(-1, \frac{1}{5}\right)$, (0, 1), (1, 5); set of all real numbers; set of all positive numbers; 1

10. Graph $y = \log_5 x$.   Curve through $\left(\frac{1}{5}, -1\right)$, (1, 0), (5, 1)

12–3   Write equivalent logarithmic equations.

11. $7^{2.3} = x$ **12.** $8^{\frac{1}{3}} = 2$ $\frac{1}{3} = \log_8 2$ 11. $2.3 = \log_7 x$

12–3   Write equivalent exponential equations.

13. $\log_3 81 = 4$ **14.** $\log_8 M = t$ $8^t = M$ 13. $3^4 = 81$

12–3

15. Solve $\log_x 64 = 3$.   4   **16.** Solve $\log_{16} 4 = x$. $\frac{1}{2}$ **17.** Simplify $\log_h h^3$.   3

12–4

18. Express as a single logarithm: $\dfrac{1}{2} \log_b a + \dfrac{3}{2} \log_b c - 4 \log_b d$. $\log_b \frac{\sqrt{a} \cdot c^{3/2}}{d^4}$

19. Express in terms of logarithms of M and N: $\log \sqrt[3]{\dfrac{M^2}{N}}$. $\frac{1}{3}[2 \log M - \log N]$

12–4   Given that $\log_a 2 = 0.301$, $\log_a 3 = 0.447$, and $\log_a 7 = 0.845$, find the following:

20. 1.255
21. 0.544
22. −0.602

20. $\log_a 18$ **21.** $\log_a \dfrac{7}{2}$ **22.** $\log_a \dfrac{1}{4}$ **23.** $\log_a \sqrt{3}$ 0.2385

12–5   Use Table 2 to find each of the following.

24. $\log 26.2$ **25.** $\log 0.00806$ **26.** $10^{1.8686}$ 73.9
    1.4183   7.9063 − 10

27. $\log 2904$ **28.** antilog $8.4414 - 10$ 0.02763
    3.4630

12–6   Find each of the following using interpolation and Table 2.

29. $\log 18.75$ **30.** antilog 1.1629 14.56
    1.2730

12–7 Solve.

31. $3^{-1-x} = 9^{2x}$ $-\frac{1}{5}$ 32. $\log (x^2 - 1) - \log (x - 1) = 1$ 9

33. How many years will it take an investment of $1000 to double itself if interest is compounded annually at 5%? 14.2

12–8 Find each natural logarithm to four decimal places.

34. ln 1.6   35. ln 1600 7.3778   30. 0.4700

36. Find $\log_4 80$. 3.1109

CHAPTER 12 Test

1. Write an equation of the inverse relation of $y = 2x^2 - 3x + 1$. $x = 2y^2 - 3y + 1$

2. Test $x + y = 7$ for symmetry with respect to the line $y = x$. Yes

3. Given $f(x) = \dfrac{\sqrt{x}}{3} + 1$. Find an equation for $f^{-1}(x)$. $f^{-1}(x) = 9x^2 - 18x + 9$

Write equivalent logarithmic equations.

4. $3^x = 25$ $x = \log_3 25$ 5. $25^{\frac{1}{2}} = 5$ $\frac{1}{2} = \log_{25} 5$

Write equivalent exponential equations.

6. $\log_3 9 = 2$ $3^2 = 9$ 7. $\log_6 x = y$ $6^y = x$

Solve.

8. $\log_x 125 = 3$ 5   9. $\log_{25} 5 = x$ $\frac{1}{2}$ 10. Simplify $14^{\log_{14} 7t}$ 7t

Given that $\log_a 3 = 0.451$ and $\log_a 4 = 0.510$, find the following.

11. $\log_a 9$ 0.902   12. $\log_a \dfrac{4}{3}$ 0.059

Use Table 2 to find each of the following.

13. log 14.3 1.553   14. antilog 7.5340 − 10 0.00342

Solve.

15. $2^{x-1} = 32$ 6   16. $\log 4x + \log x = 2$ 5

Find each natural logarithm to four decimal places.

17. ln 1.7 0.5306   18. ln 1700 7.4384

552 CHAPTER 12 EXPONENTIAL AND LOGARITHMIC FUNCTIONS

Challenge

19. If $\log_a x = 1$, what is $\log_a \left(\frac{1}{x}\right)$?

Ready for Sequences, Series, and Probability?

1–1 Find decimal notation for each.

1. $\frac{1}{4}$ 0.25 **2.** $\frac{2}{3}$ 0.6̄ **3.** $\frac{3}{11}$ 0.27̄ **4.** $\frac{7}{20}$ 0.35

1–2 Evaluate each expression for $n = 5$.

5. $n(n-1)$ 20 **6.** $n(n-1)(n-2)$ 60

1–6 Evaluate each expression for $n = 5$ and $r = 3$.

7. n^r 125 **8.** $(r-1)^n$ 32

1–7 Simplify.

9. $(5x)^3$ 125x³ **10.** $(-2y)^4$ 16y⁴

4–1 Solve.

11. $x + 15y = 47$ **12.** $2x + y = -7$
     $x + 2y = 8$ (2, 3) $x + 4y = 7$ (−5, 3)

3–3 Given each function f, find $f(1)$, $f(2)$, and $f(3)$.

13. $f(x) = 3x + 2$ 5, 8, 11   **14.** $f(x) = 3x^2 - 1$ 2, 11, 26

12–2

15. $f(x) = 3^x$ 3, 9, 27   **16.** $f(x) = (-2)^x$ −2, 4, −8

5–2 Multiply.

17. $(a + b)^2$ a² + 2ab + b²   **18.** $(a + b)(a^2 + 2ab + b^2)$ a³ + 2a²b + 2ab² + b³

7–1, 7–2 Simplify.

19. $\sqrt{1}$ 1   **20.** $\sqrt{4}$ 2   **21.** $\sqrt{196}$ 14

7–2

22. $\sqrt{56}$ 2√14   **23.** $\sqrt{80}$ 4√5   **24.** $\sqrt{108}$ 6√3

13

CHAPTER THIRTEEN

Sequences, Series, and Probability

13–1 Sequences and Series

Sequences

DEFINITION

A *sequence* is an ordered set of numbers.

Here is an example of a sequence.

$$3, 5, 7, 9, \ldots$$

The dots mean that there are more numbers in the sequence. A sequence that does not end is called infinite.

Each number is called a term of the sequence. The first term is 3, the second term is 5, the third term is 7, and so on. We can think of a sequence as a function a whose domain is a set of consecutive natural numbers.

Some sequences have a rule which describes the nth term. The above sequence could be described $3, 5, 7, 9, \ldots, 2n + 1, \ldots$ where the nth term is $2n + 1$. We also say

$$a_n = 2n + 1.$$

We can find the terms of the sequence by consecutively substituting the numbers $1, 2, 3, \ldots, n$, and so on.

$$a_1 = 2 \cdot 1 + 1, \text{ or } 3$$
$$a_2 = 2 \cdot 2 + 1, \text{ or } 5$$
$$a_3 = 2 \cdot 3 + 1, \text{ or } 7$$
$$\vdots \qquad \vdots$$

The nth term is also called the general term. The letter k is often used instead of n.

EXAMPLE 1

Find the first two terms of the sequence whose general term is given by $a_n = \dfrac{(-1)^n}{n + 1}$.

$$a_1 = \frac{(-1)^1}{1 + 1} = \frac{-1}{2} = -\frac{1}{2} \qquad a_2 = \frac{(-1)^2}{2 + 1} = \frac{(-1)^2}{3} = \frac{1}{3}$$

TRY THIS

1. A sequence is given by $a_n = 2n - 1$.
   a. Find the first three terms. 1, 3, 5
   b. Find the 34th term. 67

2. A sequence is given by $a_n = (-1)^n n^2$. Find the first four terms. −1, 4, −9, 16

Finding General Terms

We may know the first few terms of a sequence, but not the general term. In such a case we cannot know for sure what the general term is, but we can make a guess by looking for a pattern.

EXAMPLES

For each sequence, make a guess at the general term.

2. 1, 4, 9, 16, 25, . . .
   These are squares of numbers, so the general term may be n^2.

3. −1, 2, −4, 8, −16, . . .
   These are powers of 2 with alternating signs, so the general term may be $(-1)^n 2^{n-1}$.

TRY THIS For each sequence try to find a rule for finding the general term or the nth term. Answers may vary.

3. 2, 4, 6, 8, 10, . . . $2n$ 4. 1, 2, 3, 4, 5, 6, . . . n

5. 1, 8, 27, 64, 125, . . . n^3 6. 1, 2, 4, 8, 16, 32, . . . 2^{n-1}

Series

With any sequence there is associated another sequence, obtained by taking sums of terms of the given sequence. The general term of this sequence of "partial sums" is denoted S_n. Consider the following sequence.

$$3, 5, 7, 9, \ldots, 2n + 1$$

We construct some terms of the sequence of partial sums.

$S_1 = 3$ This is the first term of the given sequence.
$S_2 = 3 + 5 = 8$ This is the sum of the first two terms.
$S_3 = 3 + 5 + 7 = 15$ The sum of the first three terms
$S_4 = 3 + 5 + 7 + 9 = 24$ The sum of the first four terms

A sum of terms of a sequence is also known as a series.

EXAMPLE 4

Find S_5 for the sequence $-2, 4, -6, 8, -10, 12, -14, \ldots$.

$$S_5 = -2 + 4 + (-6) + 8 + (-10) = -6$$

TRY THIS

7. Find S_1, S_2, S_3, and S_4 for the sequence $\frac{1}{2}, \frac{1}{4}, \frac{1}{8}, \frac{1}{16}, \frac{1}{32}, \ldots$. $\quad S_1 = \frac{1}{2}, S_2 = \frac{3}{4}, S_3 = \frac{7}{8}, S_4 = \frac{15}{16}$

Sigma Notation

The Greek letter Σ (sigma) can be used to simplify notation when a series has a formula for the general term.

The sum of the first four terms of the sequence $3, 5, 7, 9, \ldots$, $2k + 1$ can be named as follows.

$$\sum_{k=1}^{4} (2k + 1)$$

This is read "the sum as k goes from 1 to 4 of $(2k + 1)$."

EXAMPLES

Rename the following sums without using sigma notation.

5. $\displaystyle\sum_{k=1}^{5} k^2 = 1^2 + 2^2 + 3^2 + 4^2 + 5^2$

6. $\displaystyle\sum_{k=1}^{4} (-1)^k(2k) = (-1)^1(2 \cdot 1) + (-1)^2(2 \cdot 2) + (-1)^3(2 \cdot 3) + (-1)^4(2 \cdot 4)$
$$= -2 + 4 - 6 + 8$$

Write sigma notation for each sum.

7. $1 + 4 + 9 + 16 + 25$; This is a sum of squares, $1^2 + 2^2 + 3^2 + 4^2 + 5^2$, so the general term is k^2. Sigma notation is $\displaystyle\sum_{k=1}^{5} k^2$.

8. $-1 + 3 - 5 + 7$; These are odd integers with alternating signs. The general term is $(-1)^k(2k - 1)$ beginning with $k = 1$.
Sigma notation is $\displaystyle\sum_{k=1}^{4} (-1)^k(2k - 1)$.

TRY THIS Rename each of the following sums.

8. $\displaystyle\sum_{k=1}^{3} 2 + \frac{1}{k}$

9. $\displaystyle\sum_{k=0}^{4} 5^k$

10. $2 + 4 + 6 + 8 + 10$

11. $2 - 3 + 4 - 5 + \cdots + n$

8. $3 + 2\frac{1}{2} + 2\frac{1}{3}$

9. $5^0 + 5^1 + 5^2 + 5^3 + 5^4$

Answers may vary.

10. $\displaystyle\sum_{k=1}^{5} 2k$

11. $\displaystyle\sum_{k=1}^{n} (-1)^{k+1}(k + 1)$

13-1

Exercises

8. $1, -\dfrac{1}{2}, \dfrac{1}{4}, -\dfrac{1}{8}, -\dfrac{1}{512}, \dfrac{1}{16{,}384}$

In each of the following the nth term of a sequence is given. In each case find the first four terms, the 10th term, and the 15th term.

1. 4, 7, 10, 13; 31; 46
2. 2, 5, 8, 11; 29; 44
3. $\dfrac{1}{2}, \dfrac{2}{3}, \dfrac{3}{4}, \dfrac{4}{5}; \dfrac{10}{11}; \dfrac{15}{16}$
4. 2, 5, 10, 17; 101; 226
5. -1, 0, 3, 8; 80; 195

1. $a_n = 3n + 1$ 2. $a_n = 3n - 1$ 3. $a_n = \dfrac{n}{n + 1}$ 4. $a_n = n^2 + 1$

5. $a_n = n^2 - 2n$ 6. $a_n = \dfrac{n^2 - 1}{n^2 + 1}$ 7. $a_n = n + \dfrac{1}{n}$ 8. $a_n = \left(-\dfrac{1}{2}\right)^{n-1}$

For each sequence, find a rule for finding the general term. Answers may vary.

6. $0, \dfrac{3}{5}, \dfrac{4}{5}, \dfrac{15}{17}, \dfrac{99}{101}; \dfrac{112}{113}$

9. 1, 3, 5, 7, 9, . . . $2n - 1$ 10. 3, 9, 27, 81, 243, . . . 3^n

7. $2, 2\dfrac{1}{2}, 3\dfrac{1}{3}, 4\dfrac{1}{4}; 10\dfrac{1}{10}; 15\dfrac{1}{15}$

11. $\dfrac{2}{3}, \dfrac{3}{4}, \dfrac{4}{5}, \dfrac{5}{6}, \dfrac{6}{7}, \ldots$ $\dfrac{n+1}{n+2}$ 12. $\sqrt{2}, \sqrt{4}, \sqrt{6}, \sqrt{8}, \sqrt{10}, \ldots$ $\sqrt{2n}$

13. $\sqrt{3}, 3, 3\sqrt{3}, 9, 9\sqrt{3}, \ldots$ $3^{n/2}$ 14. $1 \cdot 2, 2 \cdot 3, 3 \cdot 4, 4 \cdot 5, \ldots$ $n(n + 1)$

15. $-1, -4, -7, -10, -13, \ldots$ 16. log 1, log 10, log 100, log 1000, . . .

15. $-(3n - 2)$
16. $n - 1$

Rename each series without using Σ.

17. $\dfrac{1}{2} + \dfrac{1}{4} + \dfrac{1}{6} + \dfrac{1}{8} + \dfrac{1}{10}$
18. $\dfrac{1}{3} + \dfrac{1}{5} + \dfrac{1}{7} + \dfrac{1}{9} + \dfrac{1}{11} + \dfrac{1}{13}$
19. $2^0 + 2^1 + 2^2 + 2^3 + 2^4 + 2^5$
20. $\sqrt{7} + \sqrt{9} + \sqrt{11} + \sqrt{13}$
21. $\log 7 + \log 8 + \log 9 + \log 10$
22. $0 + \pi + 2\pi + 3\pi + 4\pi$

17. $\displaystyle\sum_{k=1}^{5} \dfrac{1}{2k}$ 18. $\displaystyle\sum_{k=1}^{6} \dfrac{1}{2k + 1}$ 19. $\displaystyle\sum_{k=0}^{5} 2^k$ 20. $\displaystyle\sum_{k=4}^{7} \sqrt{2k - 1}$ 21. $\displaystyle\sum_{k=7}^{10} \log k$ 22. $\displaystyle\sum_{k=0}^{4} \pi k$

Write sigma notation. Answers may vary.

25. $\displaystyle\sum_{k=1}^{6} (-1)^k 2^k$

26. $\displaystyle\sum_{k=1}^{5} \dfrac{1}{k^2}$

23. $\dfrac{1}{2} + \dfrac{2}{3} + \dfrac{3}{4} + \dfrac{4}{5} + \dfrac{5}{6} + \dfrac{6}{7}$ $\displaystyle\sum_{k=1}^{6} \dfrac{k}{k+1}$ 24. $3 + 6 + 9 + 12 + 15$ $\displaystyle\sum_{k=1}^{5} 3k$

27. $\displaystyle\sum_{k=2}^{n} (-1)^k k^2$

25. $-2 + 4 - 8 + 16 - 32 + 64$ 26. $\dfrac{1}{1^2} + \dfrac{1}{2^2} + \dfrac{1}{3^2} + \dfrac{1}{4^2} + \dfrac{1}{5^2}$

28. $\displaystyle\sum_{k=3}^{n} (-1)^{k+1} k^2$

27. $4 - 9 + 16 - 25 + \cdots (-1)^n n^2$ 28. $9 - 16 + 25 + \cdots + (-1)^{n+1} n^2$

Extension

Find the first five terms of each sequence.

29. $\dfrac{3}{2}, \dfrac{3}{2}, \dfrac{3}{2}, \dfrac{3}{2}, \dfrac{3}{2}$
30. $i, -1, -i, 1, i$
31. 0, 0.693, 1.792, 3.178, 4.787
32. 2, 2.25, 2.37037, 2.441406, 2.488320, 2.521626, 14.071722

29. $a_n = \dfrac{1}{2n} \log 1000^n$ 30. $a_n = i^n, i = \sqrt{-1}$ 31. $a_n = \ln(1 \cdot 2 \cdot 3 \cdots n)$

33. 0.414214, 0.317837, 0.267949, 0.236068, 0.213422, 0.196262, 1.645751

Use a calculator to find S_6 rounded to six decimal places.

32. $a_n = \left(1 + \dfrac{1}{n}\right)^n$ 33. $a_n = \sqrt{n + 1} - \sqrt{n}$

Challenge

34. Find a formula for S_n, given that $a_n = \dfrac{1}{n} \cdot \dfrac{1}{n + 1}$. $1 - \dfrac{1}{n+1}$

13–2 Arithmetic Sequences and Series

Arithmetic Sequences

Look at the following sequence.

2, 5, 8, 11, 14, . . .

Note that 3 can be added to each term to get the next term. In other words, the difference between any two consecutive terms is 3.

DEFINITION

A sequence in which a constant d can be added to each term to get the next is called an *arithmetic sequence*. The constant d is called the *common difference*.

The following notation is used with arithmetic sequences.

a_1 is the first term.
a_2 is the second term.
a_3 is the third term.
a_n is the nth term.
n is the number of terms from a_1 up to and including a_n.

To find the common difference, subtract any term from the one that follows it.

EXAMPLES
The following are arithmetic sequences. Identify the first term and the common difference.

	Sequence	First term	Common difference
1.	4, 9, 14, 19, 24, . . .	4	5
2.	34, 27, 20, 13, 6, -1, -8, . . .	34	-7
3.	2, $2\frac{1}{2}$, 3, $3\frac{1}{2}$, 4, $4\frac{1}{2}$, . . .	2	$\frac{1}{2}$

TRY THIS Identify the first term and the common difference of each arithmetic sequence.

1. 2, 3, 4, 5, 6, . . .

2. 1, 4, 7, 10, 13, . . .

3. 19, 14, 9, 4, -1, -6, . . .

4. 10, $9\frac{1}{2}$, 9, $8\frac{1}{2}$, 8, $7\frac{1}{2}$, . . .

1. $a_1 = 2, d = 1$
2. $a_1 = 1, d = 3$
3. $a_1 = 19, d = -5$
4. $a_1 = 10, d = -\frac{1}{2}$

The *n*th Term

The first term of an arithmetic sequence is a_1. We add d to get the next term, $a_1 + d$. We add d again to get the next term, $(a_1 + d) + d$, and so on. There is a pattern.

$$a_1$$
$$a_2 = a_1 + d$$
$$a_3 = (a_1 + d) + d = a_1 + 2d$$
$$a_4 = (a_1 + d) + d + d = a_1 + 3d$$
$$\vdots$$
$$a_n = a_1 + (n - 1)d$$

THEOREM 13–1

The nth term of an arithmetic sequence is given by
$a_n = a_1 + (n - 1)d.$

EXAMPLE 4
Find the 14th term of the arithmetic sequence 4, 7, 10, 13, ...

First note that $a_1 = 4$, $d = 3$, and $n = 14$. Then using the formula of Theorem 13–1 we have the following.

$$a_{14} = 4 + (14 - 1)3 = 4 + 39 = 43$$

EXAMPLE 5
In the sequence of Example 4, which term is 301? That is, what is n if $a_n = 301$?

$$a_n = a_1 + (n - 1)d \quad \text{Theorem 13–1}$$
$$301 = 4 + (n - 1)3 \quad \text{Substituting}$$
$$300 = 3n$$
$$100 = n$$

Thus the 100th term is 301.

In a similar manner we can find a_1 if we know n, a_n, and d. Also, we can find d if we know a_1, n, and a_n.

TRY THIS

5. Find the 13th term of the sequence 2, 6, 10, 14, ... 50
6. In the sequence of Try This 5, what term is 298? That is, what is n if $a_n = 298$? 75th
7. Find a_7 when $a_1 = 5$ and $d = 2$. 17
8. Find a_1 when $d = \frac{1}{2}$, $n = 7$, and $a_n = 16$. 13

Constructing Sequences

Given two terms and their places in a sequence, we can find a_1 and d and then construct the sequence.

EXAMPLE 6

The 3rd term of an arithmetic sequence is 8 and the 16th term is 47. Find a_1 and d. Construct the sequence.

We use the formula $a_n = a_1 + (n - 1)d$, where $a_3 = 8$.

$$8 = a_1 + (3 - 1)d \text{ or } 8 = a_1 + 2d$$

We use the same formula where $a_{16} = 47$.

$$47 = a_1 + (16 - 1)d \text{ or } 47 = a_1 + 15d$$

Now we solve the system of equations.

$$a_1 + 15d = 47$$
$$a_1 + 2d = 8$$

$$
\begin{aligned}
a_1 + 15d &= 47 \\
-a_1 - 2d &= -8 \quad \text{Multiplying by } -1 \\
\hline
13d &= 39 \quad \text{Adding} \\
d &= 3
\end{aligned}
$$

$$a_1 + 2 \cdot 3 = 8$$
$$a_1 = 2$$

Thus a_1 is 2, d is 3, and the sequence is 2, 5, 8, 11, 14, ...

TRY THIS

9. The 7th term of an arithmetic sequence is 79 and the 13th term is 151. Find a_1 and d. Construct the sequence. $a_1 = 7, d = 12; 7, 19, 31, 43, ...$

An arithmetic mean of two numbers a and b is simply their average, $\frac{a+b}{2}$. Notice that the numbers a, $\frac{a+b}{2}$, b form an arithmetic sequence. Numbers m_1, m_2, m_3, ... are called arithmetic means between a and b if a, m_1, m_2, m_3, ..., b forms an arithmetic sequence.

EXAMPLE 7

Insert three arithmetic means between 8 and 16.

Let 8 be the 1st term. Then 16 will be the 5th term. We use the formula $a_n = a_1 + (n-1)d$.

$$16 = 8 + (5-1)d \text{ or } d = 2$$

So we have 8, 10, 12, 14, 16.

TRY THIS

10. Insert two arithmetic means between 3 and 24. 3, 10, 17, 24

Arithmetic Series

An arithmetic series is a series associated with an arithmetic sequence. Two theorems give useful formulas for finding the sum of the first n terms.

THEOREM 13–2

The sum of the first n terms of an arithmetic series is given by
$$S_n = \frac{n}{2}(a_1 + a_n).$$

This formula is useful when we know a_1 and a_n.

THEOREM 13–3

The sum of the first n terms of an arithmetic series is given by
$$S_n = \frac{n}{2}[2a_1 + (n-1)d].$$

This formula is useful when we do not know a_n.

EXAMPLE 8

Find the sum of the first 100 natural numbers.

The sum of the first 100 natural numbers is $1 + 2 + 3 + \cdots + 100$. This is an arithmetic series.
$a_1 = 1$, $a_n = 100$, and $n = 100$. We use Theorem 13–2.

$$S_n = \frac{n}{2}(a_1 + a_n)$$

Substituting, we get the following.

$$S_{100} = \frac{100}{2}(1 + 100) = 50(101), \text{ or } 5050$$

TRY THIS

11. Find the sum of the first 200 natural numbers. 20,100

EXAMPLE 9

Find the sum of the first 14 terms of the arithmetic series $2 + 5 + 8 + 11 + 14 + 17 + \cdots$.

Note that $a_1 = 2$, $d = 3$, and $n = 14$. We use Theorem 13–3.

$$S_n = \frac{n}{2}[2a_1 + (n - 1)d]$$

$$S_{14} = \frac{14}{2} \cdot [2 \cdot 2 + (14 - 1)3]$$

$$= 7 \cdot [4 + 13 \cdot 3]$$

$$= 7 \cdot 43$$

$$S_{14} = 301$$

TRY THIS

12. Find the sum of the first 15 terms of the arithmetic series
$1 + 3 + 5 + 7 + 9 + \cdots$. 225

EXAMPLE 10

Find the sum of the series $\sum\limits_{k=1}^{13} (4k + 5)$.

First find a few terms.

$$9 + 13 + 17 + \cdots$$

We see that this is an arithmetic series with $a_1 = 9$, $d = 4$, and $n = 13$. We use Theorem 13–3.

$$S_n = \frac{n}{2}[2a_1 + (n-1)d]$$

$$S_{13} = \frac{13}{2}[2 \cdot 9 + (13-1)4]$$

$$= \frac{13}{2}[18 + 12 \cdot 4]$$

$$= \frac{13}{2} \cdot 66$$

$$S_{13} = 429$$

TRY THIS

13. Find the sum of the series $\sum\limits_{k=1}^{10} (9k - 4)$. 455

13–2

Exercises

For the arithmetic sequences in Exercises 1–6, find the first term and the common difference.

1. 2, 7, 12, 17, ... $a_1 = 2, d = 5$

2. 1.06, 1.12, 1.18, 1.24, ... $a_1 = 1.06, d = 0.06$

3. 7, 3, −1, −5, ... $a_1 = 7, d = -4$

4. −9, −6, −3, 0, ... $a_1 = -9, d = 3$

5. $\frac{3}{2}, \frac{9}{4}, 3, \frac{15}{4}, \ldots$ $a_1 = \frac{3}{2}, d = \frac{3}{4}$

6. $\frac{3}{5}, \frac{1}{10}, -\frac{2}{5}, \ldots$ $a_1 = \frac{3}{5}, d = -\frac{1}{2}$

7. Find the 12th term of the arithmetic sequence 2, 6, 10, ... 46

8. Find the 11th term of the arithmetic sequence 0.07, 0.12, 0.17, ... 0.57

9. Find the 17th term of the arithmetic sequence 7, 4, 1, ... −41

10. Find the 14th term of the arithmetic sequence $3, \frac{7}{3}, \frac{5}{3}, \ldots$ $-\frac{17}{3}$

11. In the sequence of Exercise 7, what term is 106? 27th

12. In the sequence of Exercise 8, what term is 1.67? 33rd

13. In the sequence of Exercise 9, what term is −296? 102nd

14. In the sequence of Exercise 10, what term is −27? 46th

15. Find a_{17} when $a_1 = 5$ and $d = 6$. 101

16. Find a_{20} when $a_1 = 14$ and $d = -3$. −43

17. Find a_1 when $d = 4$ and $a_8 = 33$. 5

18. Find d when $a_1 = 8$ and $a_{11} = 26$. 1.8

19. Find n when $a_1 = 5$, $d = -3$, and $a_n = -76$. 28

20. Find n when $a_1 = 25$, $d = -14$, and $a_n = -507$. 39

21. In an arithmetic sequence $a_{17} = -40$ and $a_{28} = -73$. Find a_1 and d. Write the first 5 terms of the sequence. 8, 5, 2, −1, −4

22. In an arithmetic sequence $a_{17} = \frac{25}{3}$ and $a_{32} = \frac{95}{6}$. Find a_1 and d. Write the first 5 terms of the sequence. $\frac{1}{3}, \frac{5}{6}, \frac{4}{3}, \frac{11}{6}, \frac{7}{3}$

23. Insert three arithmetic means between 2 and 22. 2, 7, 12, 17, 22

24. Insert four arithmetic means between 8 and 23. 8, 11, 14, 17, 20, 23

25. Find the sum of the first 20 terms of the series $5 + 8 + 11 + 14 + \cdots$. 670

26. Find the sum of the first 14 terms of the series $11 + 7 + 3 + \cdots$. −210

27. Find the sum of the even numbers from 2 to 100, inclusive. 2550

28. Find the sum of the odd numbers from 1 to 99, inclusive. 2500

29. If an arithmetic series has $a_1 = 2$, $d = 5$, and $n = 20$, find S_n. 990

30. If an arithmetic series has $a_1 = 7$, $d = -3$, and $n = 32$, find S_n. −1264

Find the sum of each series.

31. $\sum\limits_{k=1}^{12} (6k - 3)$ 432

32. $\sum\limits_{k=1}^{16} (7k - 76)$ −264

33. $\sum\limits_{k=1}^{18} 5k$ 855

34. $\sum\limits_{k=1}^{20} 3k$ 630

35. How many poles will be in a pile of telephone poles if there are 30 in the first layer, 29 in the second, and so on until there is one in the last layer? 465

36. If 10¢ is saved on October 1, 20¢ on October 2, 30¢ on October 3, and so on, how much is saved during October? (October has 31 days.) $49.60

Extension

37. Find a formula for the sum of the first n odd natural numbers. n^2

38. Find three numbers in an arithmetic sequence such that the sum of the first and third is 10 and the product of the first and second is 15. 3, 5, 7

39. Insert enough arithmetic means between 1 and 50 so the sum of the resulting arithmetic series will be 459. 16 means, $d = \frac{49}{17}$

40. Find the first term and the common difference for the arithmetic sequence $3x + 2y, 4x + y, 5x, 6x - y. \ldots$ $a_1 = 3x + 2y, d = x - y$

41. Find the first term and the common difference for the arithmetic sequence where $a_2 = 4p - 3q$ and $a_4 = 10p + q$. $a_1 = p - 5q, d = 3p + 2q$

42. Use a calculator to find the first 10 terms of the arithmetic sequence for which $a_1 = \$8760$ and $d = -\$798.23$.

42. 8760, 7961.77, 7163.54, 6365.31, 5567.08, 4768.85, 3970.62, 3172.39, 2374.16, 1575.93

43. Use a calculator to find the sum of the first ten terms of the sequence given in Exercise 42. 51,679.65

44. p, m, q are in arithmetic sequence, so $m = p + d, q = p + 2d$. Now $\frac{p + q}{2} = \frac{p + (p + 2d)}{2} = p + d = m$.

Challenge

44. Prove that if p, m, and q form an arithmetic sequence, then

$$m = \frac{p + q}{2}.$$

13–3 Geometric Sequences and Series

Geometric Sequences

The following sequence is not arithmetic.

$$3, 6, 12, 24, 48, 96, \ldots$$

If we multiply each term by 2 we get the next term. In other words, the ratio of any term and the preceding one is 2.

DEFINITION

A sequence in which a constant r can be multiplied by each term to get the next is called a *geometric sequence*. The constant r is called the *common ratio*.

The notation for geometric sequences is the same as the notation for arithmetic sequences; a_1 is the first term, a_2 is the second term, a_3 is the third term, and so on.

To find the common ratio, divide any term by the one before it.

EXAMPLES

Each of the following are geometric sequences. Identify the common ratio.

	Sequence	Common ratio
1.	$3, 6, 12, 24, \ldots$	2
2.	$3, -6, 12, -24, \ldots$	-2
3.	$1, \frac{1}{2}, \frac{1}{4}, \frac{1}{8}, \ldots$	$\frac{1}{2}$

TRY THIS Identify the common ratio of each geometric sequence.

1. $1, 5, 25, 125, \ldots$ 5   2. $3, -9, 27, -81, \ldots$ -3

3. $48, -12, 3, \ldots$ $-\frac{1}{4}$ 4. $54, 18, 6, \ldots$ $\frac{1}{3}$

The nth Term

If we let a_1 be the first term and r be the common ratio, then a_1r is the second term, a_1r^2 is the third term, and so on. Generalizing, we have the following.

> ## THEOREM 13-4
>
> In a geometric sequence, the nth term is given by $a_n = a_1 r^{n-1}$.

Note that the exponent is one less than the number of the term.

EXAMPLE 4

Find the 11th term of the geometric sequence 64, -32, 16, $-8, \ldots$. Note that the $a_1 = 64$, $n = 11$, and $r = \frac{-32}{64}$, or $-\frac{1}{2}$.

$$a_n = a_1 r^{n-1} \qquad \text{Theorem 13-4}$$

$$a_{11} = 64 \cdot \left(-\frac{1}{2}\right)^{11-1}$$

$$= 64 \cdot \left(-\frac{1}{2}\right)^{10}$$

$$= 2^6 \cdot \frac{1}{2^{10}} = 2^{-4}, \text{ or } \frac{1}{16}$$

TRY THIS

5. Find the 6th term of the geometric sequence 3, -15, 75, ... $\quad -9375$

Numbers m_1, m_2, m_3, ... are called geometric means of the numbers a and b if a, m_1, m_2, m_3, ... , b forms a geometric sequence. We can use the nth term to insert geometric means between two numbers. The two numbers and their geometric means are terms of a geometric sequence.

EXAMPLE 5

Insert two geometric means between 3 and 24.

3 is the 1st term and 24 is the 4th term.

$$24 = 3(r)^{4-1}$$
$$8 = r^3$$
$$2 = r$$

So we have 3, 6, 12, 24.

TRY THIS

6. Insert one geometric mean between 5 and 20. 10 or −10

EXAMPLE 6

A college student borrows $600 at 14% interest compounded annually. The student pays off the loan at the end of 3 years. How much does the student pay?

For any principal P, at 14% interest, the student will owe $P + 0.14P$ at the end of 1 year, or $1.14P$. Then $1.14P$ is the principal for the second year. So at the end of the second year the student owes $1.14(1.14P)$. Then the principal at the beginning of consecutive years is

$$P, 1.14P, 1.14(1.14P), \ldots .$$

This is a geometric sequence with $a_1 = 600$, $n = 4$, $r = 1.14$. We use Theorem 13−4.

$$a_n = a_1 r^{n-1}$$
$$a_4 = 600 \cdot (1.14)^{4-1}$$
$$= 600 \cdot 1.481544 \approx 888.93$$

Thus the student pays $888.93.

TRY THIS

7. A college student borrows $400 at 11% interest compounded annually. The loan is paid in full at the end of 3 years. How much has the student paid? $547.05

Geometric Series

A geometric series is a series associated with a geometric sequence. The next theorem gives a formula for the first n terms of a geometric series.

THEOREM 13−5

The sum of the first n terms of a geometric series is given by

$$S_n = \frac{a_1 - a_1 r^n}{1 - r}.$$

EXAMPLE 7

Find the sum of the first 6 terms of the geometric series $3 + 6 + 12 + 24 + \dots$.

$a_1 = 3, n = 6,$ and $r = \frac{6}{3},$ or 2

$$S_n = \frac{a_1 - a_1 r^n}{1 - r} \quad \text{Using Theorem 13-5}$$

$$S_6 = \frac{3 - 3 \cdot 2^6}{1 - 2}$$

$$= \frac{3 - 192}{-1}$$

$$= 189$$

TRY THIS

8. Find the sum of the first 6 terms of the geometric series $3 + 15 + 75 + 375 + \dots$. 11,718

9. Find the sum of the first 10 terms of the geometric series $2 - 1 + \frac{1}{2} - \frac{1}{4} + \dots$. $\frac{341}{256}$

A Proof of Theorem 13-5

Let us describe the sum of a geometric series as follows.

$$S_n = a_1 + a_1 r + a_1 r^2 + \dots + a_1 r^{n-2} + a_1 r^{n-1}$$

We multiply on both sides by $-r$.

$$-rS_n = -a_1 r - a_1 r^2 - \dots - a_1 r^{n-1} - a_1 r^n$$

Next, we add the two equations and solve for S_n.

$$S_n - rS_n = a_1 - a_1 r + a_1 r + a_1 r^2 - a_1 r^2 + \dots - a_1 r^n$$

$$= a_1 - a_1 r^n$$

$$S_n = \frac{a_1 - a_1 r^n}{1 - r}$$

EXAMPLE 8

Find the sum of the series $\sum_{k=1}^{5} \left(\frac{1}{2}\right)^{k+1}$.

First find a few terms.

$$\left(\frac{1}{2}\right)^2 + \left(\frac{1}{2}\right)^3 + \left(\frac{1}{2}\right)^4 + \dots$$

We see that this is a geometric series with $a_1 = \frac{1}{4}$, $n = 5$, and $r = \frac{1}{2}$.

$$S_n = \frac{a_1 - a_1 r^n}{1 - r} \quad \text{Using Theorem 13-5}$$

$$S_5 = \frac{\frac{1}{4} - \frac{1}{4} \cdot \left(\frac{1}{2}\right)^5}{1 - \frac{1}{2}}$$

$$= \frac{31}{64}$$

TRY THIS

10. Find the sum of the geometric series $\sum_{k=1}^{5} 3^k$. 363

13-3

Exercises

For the geometric sequences in Exercises 1–6, find the common ratio.

1. 4, 8, 16, 32, . . . 2

2. 12, -4, $\frac{4}{3}$, $-\frac{4}{9}$, . . . $-\frac{1}{3}$

3. 1, -1, 1, -1, 1, . . . -1

4. -5, -0.5, -0.05, -0.005, . . . 0.1

5. $\frac{1}{x}$, $\frac{1}{x^2}$, $\frac{1}{x^3}$, . . . $\frac{1}{x}$

6. 5, $\frac{5m}{2}$, $\frac{5m^2}{4}$, $\frac{5m^3}{8}$, . . . $\frac{m}{2}$

7. Find the 6th term of the geometric sequence 1, 3, 9, . . . 243

8. Find the 10th term of the geometric sequence $\frac{8}{243}$, $\frac{4}{81}$, $\frac{2}{27}$, . . . $\frac{81}{64}$

9. Find the 5th term of the geometric sequence 2, -10, 50, . . . 1250

10. Find the 9th term of the geometric sequence 2, $2\sqrt{3}$, 6, . . . 162

11. Insert one geometric mean between 3 and 48. 3, 12, 48

12. Insert two geometric means between 4 and 32. 4, 8, 16, 32

13. A college student borrows $800 at 18% interest compounded annually. The loan is paid in full at the end of 2 years. How much has the student paid? $1113.92

14. A college student borrows $1000 at 13% interest compounded annually. The loan is paid in full at the end of 4 years. How much has the student paid? $1630.47

15. Find the sum of the first 7 terms of the geometric series $6 + 12 + 24 + \cdots$. 762

16. Find the sum of the first 6 terms of the geometric series $16 - 8 + 4 - \cdots$. $10\frac{1}{2}$

17. Find the sum of the first 7 terms of the geometric series $\frac{1}{18} - \frac{1}{6} + \frac{1}{2} - \cdots$. $\frac{547}{18}$

18. Find the sum of the first 5 terms of the geometric series $6 + 0.6 + 0.06 + \cdots$. $\frac{33,333}{5000}$

19. Find the sum of the first 8 terms of the series $1 + x + x^2 + x^3 + \cdots$. $\frac{1 - x^8}{1 - x}$

20. Find the sum of the first 10 terms of the series $1 + x^2 + x^4 + x^6 + \cdots$. $\frac{1 - x^{20}}{1 - x^2}$

Find the sum of each geometric series.

21. $\sum_{k=1}^{6} \left(\frac{1}{2}\right)^{k-1}$ 22. $\sum_{k=1}^{8} 2^k$ 23. $\sum_{k=1}^{7} 4^k$ 24. $\sum_{k=1}^{5} \left(\frac{1}{3}\right)^{k-1}$

21. $\frac{63}{32}$
22. 510
23. 21,844
24. $\frac{121}{81}$

Extension

25. A Ping-Pong ball is dropped from a height of 16 ft and always rebounds $\frac{1}{4}$ of the distance of the previous fall. What distance does it rebound the 6th time? $\frac{1}{256}$ ft

26. A town has a population of 100,000 now and the population is increasing 10% every year. What will be the population in 5 years? 161,051

27. Use a calculator to find the sum of the first 5 terms of each geometric sequence. Round to the nearest cent.
    a. $1000, $1000(1.08), $1000(1.08)^2, ...   b. $200, $200(1.13), $200(1.13)^2, ...
    a. $5866.60
    b. $1296.05

28. Find the sum of $-8 + 4 - 2 + \cdots - \frac{1}{32}$. $-\frac{171}{32}$

29. Find the sum of the first n terms of $1 + x + x^2 + x^3 + \cdots$. $\frac{1 - x^n}{1 - x}$

30. Find the geometric mean between each pair or numbers.

    a. 4 and 9   6   b. 2 and 6 $2\sqrt{3}$ c. $\frac{1}{2}$ and $\frac{1}{3}$ $\sqrt{\frac{1}{6}}$ d. $\sqrt{5} + \sqrt{2}$ and $\sqrt{5} - \sqrt{2}$ $\sqrt{3}$

Challenge

31. Show that each sequence is a geometric sequence, given that a_1, $a_2, a_3, \ldots$ is a geometric sequence.
    a. $a_1^2, a_2^2, a_3^2, \ldots$ b. $a_1^{-3}, a_2^{-3}, a_3^{-3}, \ldots$

31. a. $\frac{a_n}{a_{n+1}} = r$, so $\frac{a_n^2}{a_{n+1}^2} = r^2$; hence $a_1^2 a_2^2, \ldots$, is geometric, with ratio r^2.
    b. $\frac{a_n}{a_{n+1}} = r$, so $\frac{a_n^{-3}}{a_{n+1}^{-3}} = r^{-3}$; thus $a_1^{-3}, a_2^{-3}, \ldots$ is geometric.

32. A piece of paper is 0.01 in. thick. It is folded in such a way that its thickness is doubled each time for 20 times. How thick is the result? (Use a calculator.) 10,485.76 in.

33. An annuity. A person decides to save money in a savings account for retirement. At the beginning of each year $1000 is invested at 14% compounded annually. How much is in the retirement fund at the end of 40 years? $1,529,908.60

13-4 Infinite Geometric Series

Convergent Geometric Series

Let us consider an infinite (unending) geometric series.

$$2 + 4 + 8 + 16 + 32 + 64 + \cdots + 2^n + \cdots$$

As we take n larger and larger, the sum of the first n terms gets large without bound. The next example, however, is different.

$$\frac{1}{2} + \frac{1}{4} + \frac{1}{8} + \frac{1}{16} + \cdots + \frac{1}{2n} + \cdots$$

Let us look at the sum of the first n terms for some values of n.

$$S_1 = \frac{1}{2}$$

$$S_2 = \frac{1}{2} + \frac{1}{4} = \frac{3}{4}$$

$$S_3 = \frac{1}{2} + \frac{1}{4} + \frac{1}{8} = \frac{7}{8}$$

$$S_4 = \frac{1}{2} + \frac{1}{4} + \frac{1}{8} + \frac{1}{16} = \frac{15}{16}$$

We see a pattern, which we can describe as $S_n = \frac{2^n - 1}{2^n}$. As n gets very large, S_n gets very close to 1. We say S_n approaches a limit of 1. We *define* the sum of the infinite series to be 1.

DEFINITION

If, in an infinite series, S_n approaches some limit as n becomes very large, that limit is defined to be the *sum* of the series. If an infinite series has a sum, it is said to *converge* or to be *convergent*.

TRY THIS Consider the infinite geometric series $1 - \frac{1}{2} + \frac{1}{4} - \frac{1}{8} + \cdots + (-1)^{n-1}(\frac{1}{2})^{n-1} + \cdots$.

1. Find S_1, S_2, S_3, S_4, and S_5. $1, \frac{1}{2}, \frac{3}{4}, \frac{5}{8}, \frac{11}{16}$
2. What appears to be the sum of the series? $\frac{2}{3}$

Some infinite series have sums (converge) and some do not.

THEOREM 13–6

An infinite geometric series has a sum (is convergent) if and only if $|r| < 1$. (The absolute value of the common ratio is less than 1.)

EXAMPLES
Determine which series have sums.

1. $1 - \frac{1}{2} + \frac{1}{4} - \frac{1}{8} + \frac{1}{16} + \cdots$

   $r = -\frac{1}{2}, |r| < 1$

   Series has a sum, by Theorem 13–6.

2. $1 + 5 + 25 + 125 + \cdots$
   $r = 5, |r| > 1$
   Series does not have a sum.

3. $1 + (-1) + 1 + (-1) + \cdots$
   $r = -1, |r| = 1$
   Series does not have a sum.

TRY THIS Decide which geometric series have sums.

3. $4 + 16 + 64 + \cdots$ No 4. $5 - 30 + 180 - \cdots$ No 5. $1 + \frac{1}{3} + \frac{1}{9} + \frac{1}{27} + \cdots$ Yes

Finding Sums

THEOREM 13–7

The sum of an infinite geometric series, with $|r| < 1$, is given by

$$S = \frac{a_1}{1 - r}.$$

EXAMPLE 4

Find the sum of the infinite geometric series $5 + \frac{5}{2} + \frac{5}{4} + \frac{5}{8} + \cdots$.

Note that $a_1 = 5$ and $r = \frac{1}{2}$. We use Theorem 13-7.

$$S = \frac{5}{1 - \frac{1}{2}} \quad \text{Substituting}$$

$$S = 10$$

TRY THIS Find the sum of each geometric series.

6. $1 + \frac{1}{3} + \frac{1}{9} + \frac{1}{27} + \cdots$ $\frac{3}{2}$ 7. $4 - 1 + \frac{1}{4} - \frac{1}{16} + \cdots$ $\frac{16}{5}$

A Proof of Theorem 13–7

We look at the sum of the first n terms of an infinite geometric series.

$$S_n = \frac{a_1 - a_1 r^n}{1 - r}$$

As n gets very large, we look at r^n, and see that, since $|r| < 1$, r^n gets very small, approaching 0. Thus the numerator approaches a_1. The limit of S_n as n gets very large is therefore $\frac{a_1}{1 - r}$, and we have $S = \frac{a_1}{1 - r}$.

13–4

Exercises

In each geometric series find r and determine which series have sums (converge).

1. $5 + 10 + 20 + 40 + \cdots$ 2, No   2. $16 + 8 + 4 + 2 + \cdots$ $\frac{1}{2}$, Yes

3. $6 + 2 + \frac{2}{3} + \frac{3}{9} + \cdots$ $\frac{1}{3}$, Yes   4. $2 - 4 + 8 - 16 + 32 - \cdots$ -2, No

5. $1 + 0.1 + 0.01 + 0.001 + \cdots$ 0.1, Yes   6. $-\frac{5}{3} - \frac{10}{9} - \frac{20}{27} - \frac{40}{81} - \cdots$ $\frac{2}{3}$, Yes

7. $1 - \frac{1}{5} + \frac{1}{25} - \frac{1}{125} + \cdots$ $-\frac{1}{5}$, Yes   8. $6 + \frac{42}{5} + \frac{294}{25} + \cdots$ $\frac{7}{5}$, No

Find the sum of each geometric series.

9. $4 + 2 + 1 + \cdots$ ₈ 10. $7 + 3 + \frac{9}{7} + \cdots$ $\frac{49}{4}$ 11. $1 + \frac{1}{2} + \frac{1}{4} + \cdots$ ₂

12. $\frac{8}{3} + \frac{4}{3} + \frac{2}{3} + \cdots$ $\frac{16}{3}$ 13. $16 + 1.6 + 0.16 + \cdots$ $\frac{160}{9}$ 14. $4 + 2.4 + 1.44 + \cdots$ ₁₀

Extension

Repeating decimals represent infinite geometric series. For example, 0.666666 ... represents $0.6 + 0.06 + 0.006 + 0.0006 + \cdots$. We can use Theorem 13–7 to find fractional notation, using 0.6 for a_1 and 0.1 for r. Find fractional notation for each number.

15. $0.7\overline{777}$ $\frac{7}{9}$ 16. $0.3\overline{333}$ $\frac{1}{3}$ 17. $0.21\overline{2121}$ $\frac{7}{33}$

18. $0.63\overline{6363}$ $\frac{7}{11}$ 19. $5.15\overline{1515}$ $\frac{170}{33}$ 20. $4.125\overline{125}$ $\frac{4121}{999}$

21. How far up and down will a ball travel before stopping if it is dropped from a height of 12 m, and each rebound is $\frac{1}{3}$ of the previous distance? (Hint: Use an infinite geometric series.) 24 m

22. The sides of a square are each 16 cm long. A second square is inscribed by joining the midpoints of the sides, successively. In the second square we repeat the process, inscribing a third square. If this process is continued indefinitely, what is the sum of all of the area of all the squares? (Hint: Use an infinite geometric series.) 512 cm²

Challenge

23. The infinite series

$$2 + \frac{1}{2} + \frac{1}{2 \cdot 3} + \frac{1}{2 \cdot 3 \cdot 4} + \frac{1}{2 \cdot 3 \cdot 4 \cdot 5} + \frac{1}{2 \cdot 3 \cdot 4 \cdot 5 \cdot 6} + \cdots$$

is not geometric, but does have a sum. Find values of S_1, S_2, S_3, S_4, S_5, and S_6. Make a conjecture about the value of S. $2\frac{3}{4}$

MATHEMATICAL NOTATION/Leonhard Euler

The acceptance of the symbol π for the ratio of the circumference of a circle to its diameter; the first use of i for an imaginary number; the use of small letters a, b, c for the sides of a triangle and the capitals A, B, and C for the opposite angles; the notation $f(x)$ for function; and the symbol e for the base of a natural logarithm are all contributions of the mathematician Leonhard Euler.

During his life (1707–1783), Euler published more than 530 books and papers on mathematics. Although he lost his eyesight completely in 1766, he continued to dictate his important discoveries.

13—5 Permutations

The Fundamental Counting Principle

We shall develop means of determining the number of ways a set of objects can be arranged or combined, the number of ways certain objects can be chosen, or the number of ways a succession of events can occur. The study of such things is called combinatorics

EXAMPLE 1
How many 3-letter code symbols can be formed with the letters A, B, and C without repetition?

We can select any of the 3 letters for the first letter in the symbol. Once this letter has been selected, the second is selected from the remaining 2 letters. Then the third is already determined since there is only 1 letter left. The possibilities are illustrated in the tree diagram at the right.

$$A \begin{cases} B \text{---} C \\ C \text{---} B \end{cases}$$
$$B \begin{cases} A \text{---} C \\ C \text{---} A \end{cases}$$
$$C \begin{cases} A \text{---} B \\ B \text{---} A \end{cases}$$

There are $3 \cdot 2 \cdot 1$, or 6, possibilities. The set of all of them is

$$\{ABC, ACB, BAC, BCA, CAB, CBA\}.$$

Suppose we perform an experiment such as selecting letters (as in the preceding example), flipping a coin, or drawing a card. Each result is called an outcome. An event is a set of outcomes. When several events occur together, we say the event is compound. The following principle concerns compound events.

THEOREM 13—8

Fundamental Counting Principle

In a compound event in which the first event may occur independently in n_1 ways, the second may occur independently in n_2 ways, and so on, and the kth event may occur independently in n_k ways, the total number of ways the compound event may occur is $n_1 \cdot n_2 \cdot n_3 \cdots n_k$.

EXAMPLE 2
How many 3-letter code symbols can be formed with the letters A, B, and C with repetition?

There are 3 choices for the first letter, and since we allow repetition, 3 choices for the second, and 3 for the third. Thus by the Fundamental Counting Principle there are $3 \cdot 3 \cdot 3$, or 27, choices.

TRY THIS

1. How many 3-digit numbers can be named using all the digits 5, 6, 7 without repetition? with repetition? 6, 27

2. In how many ways can 5 different cars be parked in a row in a parking lot? 120

Permutations

DEFINITION

A *permutation* of a set of n objects is an ordered arrangement of the objects.

Consider, for example, a set of 4 objects $\{A, B, C, D\}$. Here are some ordered arrangements of these objects.

$$ABDC \quad DBAC \quad ADBC$$
$$BACD \quad CBDA \quad DCAB$$

To find the number of ordered arrangements of the set we select a first one; there are 4 choices. Then we select a second one; there are 3 choices. Then we select a third one; there are 2 choices. Finally there is 1 choice for the last selection. Thus by the Fundamental Counting Principle, there are $4 \cdot 3 \cdot 2 \cdot 1$, or 24 permutations of a set of 4 objects.

We can generalize this to a set of n objects. We have n choices for the first selection, $n - 1$ for the second, $n - 2$ for the third, and so on. For the nth selection there is only one choice.

THEOREM 13—9

The total number of permutations of a set of n objects, denoted $_nP_n$, is given by $_nP_n = n(n - 1)(n - 2) \cdots 3 \cdot 2 \cdot 1$.

EXAMPLES

Find the following.

3. $_4P_4 = 4 \cdot 3 \cdot 2 \cdot 1 = 24$ **4.** $_7P_7 = 7 \cdot 6 \cdot 5 \cdot 4 \cdot 3 \cdot 2 \cdot 1 = 5040$

TRY THIS Evaluate.

3. $_3P_3$ 6   **4.** $_5P_5$ 120 **5.** $_6P_6$ 720

EXAMPLE 5

How many ways can 5 paintings be lined up on a wall?

By Theorem 13–9, there are $_5P_5$ ways.

$$_5P_5 = 5 \cdot 4 \cdot 3 \cdot 2 \cdot 1 = 120$$

TRY THIS

6. In how many ways can 6 people line up at a ticket window?   720

Factorial Notation

For the product $5 \cdot 4 \cdot 3 \cdot 2 \cdot 1$ we write 5!, read "5-factorial."

DEFINITION

$$n! = n(n - 1)(n - 2) \cdots 3 \cdot 2 \cdot 1$$

EXAMPLES

6. $7! = 7 \cdot 6 \cdot 5 \cdot 4 \cdot 3 \cdot 2 \cdot 1 = 5040$ **7.** $3! = 3 \cdot 2 \cdot 1 = 6$ **8.** $1! = 1 = 1$

We also define 0! to be 1, so that certain formulas and theorems can be stated concisely. We now simplify Theorem 13–9.

THEOREM 13—9

The total number of permutations of a set of n objects, denoted $_nP_n$, is given by $n!$

7. Evaluate 9! 362,880

8. Using factorial notation only, represents the number of permutations of 18 objects. 18!

Note that $8! = 8 \cdot 7!$ We can see this as follows.

$$8! = 8 \cdot 7 \cdot 6 \cdot 5 \cdot 4 \cdot 3 \cdot 2 \cdot 1 = 8 \cdot (7 \cdot 6 \cdot 5 \cdot 4 \cdot 3 \cdot 2 \cdot 1) = 8 \cdot 7!$$

Generalizing gives us the following theorem.

THEOREM 13–10

For any natural number n,
$$n! = n(n - 1)!$$

By using Theorem 13–10 repeatedly, we can further manipulate factorial notation.

EXAMPLE 9

Rewrite 7! with a factor of 5!

$$7! = 7 \cdot 6 \cdot 5!$$

9. Represent 10! in the form $n(n - 1)!$ 10·9!

10. Rewrite 11! with a factor of 8! $11 \cdot 10 \cdot 9 \cdot 8!$

13–5

Exercises

1. How many 4-letter code symbols can be formed with the letters P, D, Q, X without repetition? with repetition? 24, 256

2. How many 5-digit numbers can be formed using all the digits 0, 1, 2, 3, 4 without repetition? with repetition? 120, 3125

3. How many ways can 6 bicycles be parked in a row? 720

4. How many ways can 7 different cards be laid out on a table in a row? 5040

5. A woman is going out for the evening. She will put on one of 6 pantsuits, one pair out of 8 pairs of shoes, and go to one of 7 restaurants. In how many ways can this be done? 336

6. A man is going out for the evening. He will put on one of 7 suits, one pair out of 4 pairs of shoes, and go to one of 10 restaurants. In how many ways can this be done? 280

Evaluate.

7. $_6P_6$ 720   8. $_5P_5$ 120   9. $_4P_4$ 24   10. $_2P_2$ 2

11. How many ways can 7 people line up in a row? 5040

12. How many ways can 8 motorcycles be parked in a row? 40,320

13. How many permutations are there of the set $\{R, S, T, U, V, W\}$? 720

14. How many permutations are there of the set $\{M, N, O, P, Q, R, S\}$? 5040

15. The owner of a business hires 8 secretaries, one for each of 8 department managers. How many different assignments of the secretaries are possible? 40,320

16. A fruit stand sells 9 different varieties of apples. How many different ways can the names of the apples be arranged on the sign? 362,880

Evaluate.

17. 5! 120   18. 6! 720   19. 1! 1   20. 0! 1

Represent each in the form $n(n - 1)!$

21. 9!   22. 13!   23. $a!$ 24. $m!$

21. $9 \cdot 8!$
22. $13 \cdot 12!$
23. $a \cdot (a - 1)!$
24. $m \cdot (m - 1)!$

25. Rewrite 27! with a factor of 22!
$27 \cdot 26 \cdot 25 \cdot 24 \cdot 23 \cdot 22!$

26. Rewrite 13! with a factor of 5!
$13 \cdot 12 \cdot 11 \cdot 10 \cdot 9 \cdot 8 \cdot 7 \cdot 6 \cdot 5!$

Extension

27. How many 7-digit telephone numbers can be formed, assuming that no digit is used more than once and the first digit is not 0? $9 \cdot 9 \cdot 8 \cdot 7 \cdot 6 \cdot 5 \cdot 4$, or 544,320

28. a. How many ways can a penny, nickel, dime, quarter, and half dollar be arranged in a straight line? 120
    b. Considering the coins and heads and tails, in how many ways can they be lined up? 3840

RANDOM WALKS

Imagine a blindfolded person who walks away from a lamppost, now and then changing direction in a random or wholly irregular manner. The *law of disorder* predicts that as long as he keeps walking he will keep returning to the lamppost. Random walks are useful for obtaining probabilistic solutions to many mathematical or physical problems.

13-6 Permutations of n Objects r at a Time

Permutations of n Objects r at a Time

Consider a set of 6 objects. In how many ways can we construct an ordered subset having three members? We can select the first object in 6 ways. There are then 5 choices for the second and then 4 choices for the third. By the Fundamental Counting Principle, there are then $6 \cdot 5 \cdot 4$ ways to construct the subset. In other words, there are $6 \cdot 5 \cdot 4$ permutations of a set of 6 objects taken three at a time. Note that $6 \cdot 5 \cdot 4$ is equal to $\frac{6 \cdot 5 \cdot 4 \cdot 3!}{3!}$, or $\frac{6!}{3!}$.

DEFINITION

$_nP_r$ denotes the number of permutations of a set of n objects taken r at a time. Each permutation is an ordered arrangement of r objects taken from the set.

Generalizing the above result gives us a theorem.

THEOREM 13-11

The number of permutations of a set of n objects taken r at a time is given by

$$_nP_r = \frac{n!}{(n-r)!}.$$

EXAMPLES
Compute.

1. $_6P_4 = \dfrac{6!}{(6-4)!}$ By Theorem 13-11

    $= \dfrac{6!}{2!}$

    $= \dfrac{6 \cdot 5 \cdot 4 \cdot 3 \cdot 2!}{2!}$ By Theorem 13-10

    $= 6 \cdot 5 \cdot 4 \cdot 3 = 360$

2. $_5P_2 = \dfrac{5!}{(5-2)!}$ By Theorem 13-11

    $= \dfrac{5!}{3!}$

    $= \dfrac{5 \cdot 4 \cdot 3!}{3!}$ By Theorem 13-10

    $= 5 \cdot 4 = 20$

TRY THIS Compute.

1. $_7P_3$ **2.** $_{10}P_4$ **3.** $_8P_2$ **4.** $_{11}P_5$ 1. 210   2. 5040   3. 56   4. 55,440

EXAMPLE 3

How many ways can letters of the set $\{A, B, C, D, E, F, G\}$ be arranged to form code symbols of **a.** 7 letters? **b.** 5 letters? **c.** 2 letters?

a. $_7P_7 = 7 \cdot 6 \cdot 5 \cdot 4 \cdot 3 \cdot 2 \cdot 1 = 5040$

b. $_7P_5 = 7 \cdot 6 \cdot 5 \cdot 4 \cdot 3 = 2520$

c. $_7P_2 = 7 \cdot 6 = 42$

TRY THIS

5. A teacher wants to write a 6-question test from a pool of 10 questions. How many different forms of the test can the teacher write? 151,200

6. How many 7-digit numbers can be named, without repetition, using the digits 2, 3, 4, 5, 6, 7, and 8 if the even digits come first? 144

Repeated Use of the Same Object

For an arrangement of objects to be a permutation, we can not repeat any of the objects. Sometimes we want to be able to repeat, so we have another theorem.

EXAMPLE 4

How many 5-letter code symbols can be formed with the letters A, B, C, and D if we allow repeated use of the same letter?

We can select the first letter in 4 ways, the second in 4 ways, and so on. Thus there are 4^5, or 1024, arrangements. Generalizing gives us a theorem.

THEOREM 13–12

The number of arrangements of n objects taken r at a time, with repetition, is n^r.

TRY THIS

7. How many 5-letter code symbols can be formed by repeated use of the letters of the alphabet? Just find an expression. Do not evaluate. 26^5

EXAMPLE 5

A standard deck of cards has 52 different cards. How many 3-card ordered arrangements can be made by selecting the 3 cards
a. without replacement? b. with replacement?

a. The case 'without replacement' is the number of permutations of 52 things taken 3 at a time.

$$_{52}P_3 = 52 \cdot 51 \cdot 50 = 132,600 \quad \text{By Theorem 13–11}$$

b. The case 'with replacement' is the number of arrangements of 52 objects taken 3 at a time, with repetition.

$$52 \cdot 52 \cdot 52 = 52^3 = 140,608 \quad \text{By Theorem 13–12}$$

Thus there are 140,608 possible ordered arrangements.

TRY THIS

8. How many 2-card ordered arrangements can be made by selecting 2 cards from a deck of 52
   a. without replacement? 2652
   b. with replacement? 2704

13–6

Exercises

Evaluate.

1. 24
2. 2520
3. 604,800
4. 720
5. 380
6. 870
7. 336
8. 840

1. $_4P_3$ 2. $_7P_5$ 3. $_{10}P_7$ 4. $_{10}P_3$ 5. $_{20}P_2$ 6. $_{30}P_2$ 7. $_8P_3$ 8. $_7P_4$

9. How many ways can the letters of the set {M, N, O, P, Q} be arranged to form code symbols of 4 letters? 3 letters? 120, 60

10. How many ways can the letters of the set {P, D, Q, W, T, Z} be arranged to form code symbols of 3 letters? 5 letters? 120,720

11. How many ways can 4 people be assigned to 6 one-person offices? 360

12. How many ways can 3 people be assigned to 5 one-person offices? 60

13. A special classroom has 8 sets of head-phones for students who have difficulty hearing. How many possible combinations of students and headphones are there if 6 students in a class need to use headphones? 20,160

14. A special classroom has 10 sets of headphones for students who have difficulty hearing. How many possible combinations of students and headphones are there if 7 students in a class need to use headphones? 604,800

15. How many 4-number license plates can be made using the digits 0, 1, 2, 3, 4, 5 if repetitions are allowed? not allowed? 1296, 360

16. How many 5-number license plates can be made using the digits, 1, 2, 3, 4, 5, 6, 7 if repetitions are allowed? not allowed? 16,807, 2520

17. A teacher wants to write a 4-question test from a pool of 12 questions. How many different forms of the test can the teacher write? 11,880

18. A teacher wants to write a 5-question test from a pool of 8 questions. How many different forms of the test can the teacher write? 6720

19. As in Exercise 15, but an even digit must come first. 648, 180

20. As in Exercise 16, but an odd digit must come first. 9604, 1440

21. As in Exercise 15, but the license number must be even. 648, 180

22. As in Exercise 16, but the license number must be odd. 9604, 1440

23. A state forms its license plates by first listing a number that corresponds to the county in which the owner lives, then listing a letter of the alphabet, and finally a number from 1 to 9999. How many such plates are possible if there are 80 counties? (Use a calculator.) $80 \cdot 26 \cdot 9999 = 20{,}797{,}920$

24. How many code symbols can be formed using 4 out of 5 letters of A, B, C, D, E if the letters
   a. are not repeated? 120
   b. can be repeated? 625
   c. are not repeated but must begin with D? 24
   d. are not repeated but must end with DE? 6

Extension

Solve for n.

25. $_nP_5 = 7 \cdot {_nP_4}$ 11

26. $_nP_4 = 8 \cdot {_{n-1}P_3}$ 8

27. $_nP_5 = 9 \cdot {_{n-1}P_4}$ 9

28. $_nP_4 = 8 \cdot {_nP_3}$ 11

Challenge

For each problem, express your answer in terms of n.

29. In a single-elimination sports tournament consisting of n teams, a team is eliminated when it loses one game. How many games are required to complete the tournament? $n - 1$

30. In a double-elimination softball tournament consisting of n teams, a team is eliminated when it loses two games. At most, how many games are required to complete the tournament? $2n - 1$

13-7 Combinatorial Algebra: Combinations

Permutations of a set are ordered subsets. Unordered subsets are called combinations

EXAMPLE 1

How many combinations are there of the set $\{A, B, C, D\}$ taken 3 at a time?

The combinations are the following subsets.

$$\{A, B, C\} \quad \{B, C, D\} \quad \{A, C, D\} \quad \{A, B, D\}$$

Note that the set $\{A, B, C\}$ is the same at the set $\{B, A, C\}$ since they contain the same objects.

TRY THIS

1. Consider the set $\{A, B, C, D\}$. How many combinations are there taken
   a. 4 at a time? ₁ b. 3 at a time? ₄ c. 2 at a time? ₆
   d. 1 at a time? ₄ e. 0 at a time? ₁

DEFINITION

The number of combinations of a set of n objects taken r at a time, denoted $_nC_r$, is the number of subsets that contain r objects.

A general formula for $_nC_r$ is given in Theorem 13-13. First we define some convenient symbolism.

DEFINITION

$\binom{n}{r}$ is defined to mean $\dfrac{n!}{r!(n-r)!}$.

The notation $\binom{n}{r}$ is read "n over r," or (for reasons we see later) "binomial coefficient n over r."

EXAMPLES

Evaluate.

2. $\binom{5}{2} = \dfrac{5!}{2!(5-2)!}$ By definition of $\binom{5}{2}$

$\quad = \dfrac{5!}{2!3!}$

$\quad = \dfrac{5 \cdot 4 \cdot 3!}{2!3!}$ By Theorem 13–10

$\quad = 10$

3. $\binom{7}{4} = \dfrac{7!}{4!(7-4)!} = \dfrac{7!}{4!3!} = \dfrac{7 \cdot 6 \cdot 5 \cdot 4!}{3!4!} = \dfrac{7 \cdot 6 \cdot 5}{3 \cdot 2 \cdot 1} = 35$

TRY THIS Evaluate.

2. $\binom{10}{8}$ **3.** $\binom{10}{2}$ 2. 45   3. 45

THEOREM 13–13

The number of combinations of a set of n objects taken r at a time is given by $_nC_r = \binom{n}{r}$.

TRY THIS Evaluate.

4. $_7C_5$ **5.** $_7C_2$ 4. 21   5. 21

EXAMPLE 4

For a sociological study 4 people are chosen at random from a group of 10 people. How many ways can this be done?

No order is implied here so the number of ways 4 people can be selected is $_{10}C_4$.

$$_{10}C_4 = \binom{10}{4} \quad \text{By Theorem 13–13}$$

$$= \frac{10!}{4!6!}$$

$$= \frac{10 \cdot 9 \cdot 8 \cdot 7 \cdot 6!}{4!6!}$$

$$= \frac{10 \cdot 9 \cdot 8 \cdot 7}{4 \cdot 3 \cdot 2 \cdot 1} = 210$$

TRY THIS

6. How many ways can a 5-player starting unit be selected from a 12-member basketball squad? 792

EXAMPLE 5

How many committees can be formed from a set of 5 governors and 7 senators if each committee contains 3 governors and 4 senators?

The 3 governors can be selected in $_5C_3$ ways and the 4 senators can be selected in $_7C_4$ ways. We use the Fundamental Counting Principle.

$$_5C_3 \cdot {_7C_4} = 10 \cdot 35$$
$$= 350$$

TRY THIS

7. A committee is to be chosen from 12 men and 8 women and is to consist of 3 men and 2 women. How many ways can this committee be formed? 6160

EXAMPLE 6

A hamburger restaurant advertises "We Fix Hamburgers 256 Ways!" This is accomplished using various combinations of catsup, onion, mustard, pickle, mayonnaise, relish, tomato, or lettuce. Of course, one can also have a plain hamburger. Use combination notation to show the number of possible hamburgers. Do not evaluate. (We will show an easy way in Lesson 13–8.)

There are 8 basic seasonings. Each way of fixing a hamburger is a combination, or subset, of these seasonings. There are $\binom{8}{0}$ subsets with 0 seasonings, $\binom{8}{1}$ subsets with 1 seasoning, $\binom{8}{2}$ subsets with 2 seasonings, and so on, up to $\binom{8}{8}$ subsets with 8 seasonings. Thus the total number of combinations, or subsets, is given by the following expression.

$$\binom{8}{0} + \binom{8}{1} + \binom{8}{2} + \cdots + \binom{8}{8}$$

TRY THIS

8. Including cheese as a possibility, use combination notation to show the number of ways the restaurant could fix hamburgers. You do not need to evaluate your expression. $\binom{9}{0} + \binom{9}{1} + \binom{9}{2} + \cdots + \binom{9}{9}$ or 512

13-7

Exercises

Evaluate.

1. $_9C_5$ **2.** $_{14}C_2$ **3.** $\binom{50}{2}$ **4.** $\binom{40}{3}$ **5.** $\binom{12}{8}$ **6.** $\binom{14}{9}$ **7.** $_nC_3$ **8.** $_nC_2$

9. There are 23 students in a club. How many ways can 4 officers be selected? 8855

10. On a test a student is to select 6 out of 10 questions, without regard to order. How many ways can this be done? 210

11. How many basketball games can be played in a 9-team league if each team plays all other teams twice? 72

12. How many basketball games can be played in a 10-team league if each team plays all other teams twice? 90

13. How many lines are determined by 8 points, no three of which are collinear? How many triangles are determined by the same points if no four are coplanar? 28, 56

14. How many lines are determined by 7 points, no three of which are collinear? How many triangles are determined by the same points if no four are coplanar? 21, 35

15. Of the first 10 questions on a test, a student must answer 7. On the second 5 questions, 3 must be answered. In how many ways can this be done? 1200

16. Of the first 8 questions on a test, a student must answer 6. On the second 4 questions, 3 must be answered. In how many ways can this be done? 112

17. Suppose the Senate of the United States consisted of 58 Democrats and 42 Republicans. How many committees consisting of 6 Democrats and 4 Republicans could be formed? You do not need to simplify the expression. $\binom{58}{6} \cdot \binom{42}{4}$

18. Suppose the Senate of the United States consisted of 63 Republicans and 37 Democrats. How many committees consisting of 12 Republicans and 8 Democrats could be formed? You need not simplify the expression. $\binom{63}{12} \cdot \binom{37}{8}$

Extension

19. There are 8 points on a circle. How many triangles can be inscribed with these points as vertices? 56

Solve for n.

20. $\binom{n+1}{3} = 2 \cdot \binom{n}{2}$ 5   **21.** $\binom{n}{n-2} = 6$ 4   **22.** $\binom{n+2}{4} = 6 \cdot \binom{n}{2}$ 7

1. 126
2. 91
3. 1225
4. 9880
5. 495
6. 2002
7. $\dfrac{n(n-1)(n-2)}{6}$
8. $\dfrac{n(n-1)}{2}$

Challenge

23. How many line segments are determined by the n vertices of an n-gon? Of these, how many are diagonals? $\dfrac{n(n-1)}{2}; \dfrac{n(n-3)}{2}$

24. Prove: For any natural numbers n and $r \le n$,

$$\binom{n}{r} = \binom{n}{n-r}.$$

$$\binom{n}{r} = \frac{n!}{r!(n-r)!} = \frac{n!}{(n-r)!r!}$$
$$= \frac{n!}{(n-r)![n-(n-r)]!} = \binom{n}{n-r}$$

13–8 The Binomial Theorem

Consider the following expanded powers of $(a + b)^n$, where $a + b$ is any binomial. Look for patterns.

$$(a + b)^0 = 1$$
$$(a + b)^1 = a + b$$
$$(a + b)^2 = a^2 + 2ab + b^2$$
$$(a + b)^3 = a^3 + 3a^2b + 3ab^2 + b^3$$
$$(a + b)^4 = a^4 + 4a^3b + 6a^2b^2 + 4ab^3 + b^4$$
$$(a + b)^5 = a^5 + 5a^4b + 10a^3b^2 + 10a^2b^3 + 5ab^4 + b^5$$

Note that each expansion is a polynomial. It is also a series, though not arithmetic or geometric. There are some patterns to be noted.

1. In each term, the sum of the exponents is n.

2. The exponents of a start with n and decrease to 0. The last term has no factor of a. The first term has no factor of b. The exponents of b start in the second term with 1 and increase to n.

3. There is one more term than the degree of the polynomial. The expansion of $(a + b)^n$ has $n + 1$ terms.

4. If a and b are positive, all the terms are positive. If b is negative, its odd powers are negative, so the terms would alternate from positive to negative.

The next theorem shows how to determine the coefficients.

THEOREM 13–14

The Binomial Theorem

For any binomial $(a + b)$ and any natural number n,

$$(a + b)^n = \binom{n}{0}a^n + \binom{n}{1}a^{n-1}b + \binom{n}{2}a^{n-2}b^2 + \cdots + \binom{n}{n}b^n.$$

The statement of Theorem 13–14 in sigma notation is as follows.

$$(a + b)^n = \sum_{r=0}^{n} \binom{n}{r}a^{n-r}b^r$$

Because of this theorem $\binom{n}{r}$ is called a binomial coefficient

Finding the rth Term

Look at the theorem. We see that the $(r + 1)$st term is $\binom{n}{r}a^{n-r}b^r$. That is, the 1st term is $\binom{n}{0}a^{n-0}b^0$, the 2nd term is $\binom{n}{1}a^{n-1}b^1$, the 3rd term is $\binom{n}{2}a^{n-2}b^2$, the 8th term is $\binom{n}{7}a^{n-7}b^7$, and so on.

EXAMPLE 1
Find the 7th term of $(4x - y^2)^9$.

We let $r = 6$, $n = 9$, $a = 4x$, and $b = -y^2$ in the formula $\binom{n}{r}a^{n-r}b^r$.

$$\binom{9}{6}(4x)^3(-y^2)^6 = \frac{9!}{6!3!}(4x)^3(-y^2)^6$$

$$= \frac{9 \cdot 8 \cdot 7 \cdot 6!}{3! \cdot 6!}(64x^3y^{12})$$

$$= 5376x^3y^{12}$$

TRY THIS

1. Find the 4th term of $(x - 3)^8$. $\quad -1512x^5$ 2. Find the 6th term of $(y^2 + 2)^{10}$. $\quad 8064y^{10}$

Binomial Expansion

Let us now find an expansion.

EXAMPLE 2
Expand $(x^2 - 2y)^5$.

Note that $a = x^2$, $b = -2y$, and $n = 5$.

$$(x^2 - 2y)^5 = \binom{5}{0}(x^2)^5 + \binom{5}{1}(x^2)^4(-2y) + \binom{5}{2}(x^2)^3(-2y)^2 +$$

$$\binom{5}{3}(x^2)^2(-2y)^3 + \binom{5}{4}x^2(-2y)^4 + \binom{5}{5}(-2y)^5 \quad \text{Theorem 13–14}$$

$$= \frac{5!}{0!5!}x^{10} + \frac{5!}{1!4!}x^8(-2y) + \frac{5!}{2!3!}x^6(-2y)^2 +$$

$$\frac{5!}{3!2!}x^4(-2y)^3 + \frac{5!}{4!1!}x^2(-2y)^4 + \frac{5!}{5!0!}(-2y)^5$$

$$= x^{10} - 10x^8y + 40x^6y^2 - 80x^4y^3 + 80x^2y^4 - 32y^5$$

TRY THIS Expand.

3. $(x^2 - 1)^5$ 4. $\left(2x + \dfrac{1}{y}\right)^4$
3. $x^{10} - 5x^8 + 10x^6 - 10x^4 + 5x^2 - 1$
4. $16x^4 + 32\dfrac{x^3}{y} + 24\dfrac{x^2}{y^2} + 8\dfrac{x}{y^3} + \dfrac{1}{y^4}$

A Proof of Theorem 13–14

Consider the nth power of a binomial $(a + b)$.

$$(a + b)^n = \underbrace{(a + b)(a + b)(a + b)(a + b) \cdots (a + b)}_{n \; factors}$$

When we multiply, we will find all possible products of a's and b's. For example, when we multiply all the first terms we will get n factors of a, or a^n. Thus the first term in the expansion is a^n. The binomial coefficient $\binom{n}{0}$ is 1; this establishes that the first term mentioned in the theorem is correct.

To get a term such as the $a^{n-r}b^r$ term, we will take a's from $n - r$ factors and b's from r factors. Thus we take n objects, $n - r$ of them a's and r of them b's. The number of ways we can do this is

$$\frac{n!}{(n - r)!r!}.$$

This is $\binom{n}{r}$. Thus the $a^{n-r}b^r$ term in the expansion has the coefficient $\binom{n}{r}$.

Subsets

Suppose a set has n objects. The number of subsets containing r members is $\binom{n}{r}$, by Theorem 13–13. The total number of subsets of a set is the number with 0 elements, plus the number with 1 element, plus the number with two elements, and so on. The total number of subsets of a set with n members is

$$\binom{n}{0} + \binom{n}{1} + \binom{n}{2} + \cdots + \binom{n}{n}.$$

Now let us expand $(1 + 1)^n$.

$$(1 + 1)^n = \binom{n}{0} + \binom{n}{1} + \binom{n}{2} + \cdots + \binom{n}{n}$$

Thus the total number of subsets is $(1 + 1)^n$ or 2^n. We have proved the following theorem.

THEOREM 13–15

The total number of subsets of a set with n members is 2^n.

EXAMPLE 3

How many subsets are in the set $\{A, B, C, D, E\}$? The set has 5 members, so the number of subsets is 2^5, or 32.

EXAMPLE 4

Show how a restaurant makes hamburgers 256 ways using 8 seasonings.

$$\binom{8}{0} + \binom{8}{1} + \cdots + \binom{8}{8} = 2^8 = 256$$

TRY THIS

5. How many subsets are in the set of states of the United States? 2^{50}

13-8

Exercises

1. $15a^4b^2$
2. $21x^2y^5$
3. $-745,472a^3$
4. $3,897,234x^2$
5. $-1,959,552u^5v^{10}$
6. $30x\sqrt{x},\ 30x\sqrt{3}$

Find the indicated term of the binomial expression.

1. 3rd, $(a + b)^6$
2. 6th, $(x + y)^7$
3. 12th, $(a - 2)^{14}$
4. 11th, $(x - 3)^{12}$
5. Middle, $(2u - 3v^2)^{10}$
6. Middle two, $(\sqrt{x} + \sqrt{3})^5$

Expand.

7. $m^5 + 5m^4n + 10m^3n^2 + 10m^2n^3 + 5mn^4 + n^5$
8. $a^4 - 4a^3b + 6a^2b^2 - 4ab^3 + b^4$
9. $x^{10} - 15x^8y + 90x^6y^2 - 270x^4y^3 + 405x^2y^4 - 243y^5$

7. $(m + n)^5$
8. $(a - b)^4$
9. $(x^2 - 3y)^5$
10. $(3c - d)^6$
11. $(1 - 1)^n$
12. $(1 + 3)^n$
13. $(\sqrt{2} + 1)^6$
14. $(1 - \sqrt{2})^4$

13. $99 + 70\sqrt{2}$ 14. $17 - 12\sqrt{2}$

10. $729c^6 - 1458c^5d + 1215c^4d^2 - 540c^3d^3 + 135c^2d^4 - 18cd^5 + d^6$

11. $\binom{n}{0} - \binom{n}{1} + \binom{n}{2} - \binom{n}{3} + \cdots + \binom{n}{n}(-1)^n$

Determine the number of subsets of each of the following sets.

15. A set of 7 members 128
16. A set of 6 members 64
17. A set of 26 letters 2^{26}
18. A set of 24 letters 2^{24}

12. $\binom{n}{0} + \binom{n}{1}3 + \binom{n}{2}9 + \binom{n}{3}27 + \cdots + \binom{n}{n}3^n$

Extension

19. $-7 - 4\sqrt{2}i$
20. $-8i$

19. Expand $(\sqrt{2} - i)^4$, where $i^2 = -1$.
20. Expand $(1 + i)^6$, where $i^2 = -1$.
21. Find a formula for $(a - b)^n$. Use sigma notation. $\sum_{r=0}^{n}\binom{n}{r}(-1)^r a^{n-r}b^r$
22. Expand and simplify $\dfrac{(x + h)^n - x^n}{h}$. Use sigma notation. $\sum_{r=1}^{n}\binom{n}{r}x^{n-r}h^{r-1}$

Challenge

Solve for x.

23. $\sum_{r=0}^{8}\binom{8}{r}x^{8-r}3^r = 0$ -3
24. $\sum_{r=0}^{4}\binom{4}{r}5^{4-r}x^r = 64$ $-5 + \sqrt{8}$
25. $\sum_{r=0}^{5}\binom{5}{r}(-1)^r x^{5-r}3^r = 32$ 5

592 CHAPTER 13 SEQUENCES, SERIES, AND PROBABILITY

13-9 Probability

Defining Probability

Suppose we perform an experiment such as flipping a coin, throwing a dart, drawing a card from a deck, or checking an item from an assembly line for quality. The result of an experiment is called an outcome. The set of all possible outcomes is called a sample space. An event is a set of outcomes, that is, a subset of the sample space. For example, for the experiment "throwing a dart" at a 3-colored dart board, the sample space is made up of the three outcomes: {red, yellow, blue}.

We denote the probability that an event E occurs $P(E)$. When the outcomes of an experiment all have the same probability of occurring, we say that they are *equally likely*.

DEFINITION

If an event E can occur m ways out of n possible equally likely outcomes of sample space S, the *probability* of that event is given by

$$P(E) = \frac{m}{n}.$$

A die (plural, dice) is a cube, with six faces, each containing a number of dots from 1 to 6.

EXAMPLE 1
What is the probability of rolling a 3 on a die? On a fair die there are 6 equally likely outcomes and there is 1 way to get a 3. By the definition of probability, $P(3) = \frac{1}{6}$.

EXAMPLE 2
What is the probability of rolling an even number on a die?

The event $P(\text{even})$ can occur in 3 ways (getting a 2, 4, or 6). The number of possible outcomes is 6.

$$P(\text{even}) = \frac{3}{6} = \frac{1}{2}$$

TRY THIS

1. What is the probability of rolling a prime number on a die? $\frac{1}{2}$

EXAMPLE 3

What is the probability of drawing an ace from a well-shuffled deck of 52 cards?

An ace can be drawn in 4 ways. There are 52 equally likely outcomes (cards in the deck).

$$P(\text{drawing an ace}) = \frac{4}{52}, \text{ or } \frac{1}{13}$$

THEOREM 13–16

The probability of any event is a number from 0 to 1. If an event cannot occur its probability is 0. If an event is certain to occur its probability is 1.

EXAMPLE 4

Suppose 2 cards are drawn from a well-shuffled deck of 52 cards. What is the probability that both of them are spades?

13 of the 52 cards are spades, so the number m of ways of drawing 2 spades is $_{13}C_2$.

$$P(\text{getting 2 spades}) = \frac{m}{n} = \frac{_{13}C_2}{_{52}C_2} = \frac{78}{1326} = \frac{1}{17}$$

EXAMPLE 5

What is the probability of getting 8 on a roll of a pair of dice?

On each die there are 6 possible outcomes. There are $6 \cdot 6$, or 36, possible outcomes for the pair. There are 5 ways of getting a total of 8: (2, 6), (3, 5), (4, 4), (5, 3), and (6, 2). So the probability of getting an 8 is $\frac{5}{36}$.

TRY THIS

2. Suppose 3 cards are drawn from a deck of 52 cards. What is the probability that all three of them are spades? $\frac{11}{850}$

3. What is the probability of getting a total of 7 on a roll of a pair of dice? $\frac{1}{6}$

13–9

Exercises

Suppose we draw a card from a deck of 52 cards. What is the probability of drawing

1. a heart? $\frac{1}{4}$ 2. a queen? $\frac{1}{13}$ 3. a 4? $\frac{1}{13}$ 4. a club? $\frac{1}{4}$

5. a black card? $\frac{1}{2}$ 6. a red card? $\frac{1}{2}$ 7. a 9 or a king? $\frac{2}{13}$ 8. an ace or a deuce? $\frac{2}{13}$

Suppose we select, without looking, one marble from a bag containing 4 red marbles and 10 green marbles. What is the probability of selecting

9. a red marble? $\frac{2}{7}$ 10. a green marble? $\frac{5}{7}$ 11. a purple marble? 0

Suppose 4 cards are drawn from a deck of 52 cards. What is the probability that

12. all 4 are spades? $\frac{11}{4165}$

13. all 4 are hearts? $\frac{11}{4165}$

14. If marbles are drawn at random all at once from a bag containing 8 white marbles and 6 black marbles, what is the probability that 2 will be white and 2 will be black? $\frac{60}{143}$

15. From a group of 8 men and 7 women, a committee of 4 is chosen. What is the probability that 2 men and 2 women will be chosen? $\frac{28}{65}$

16. What is the probability of getting a total of 6 on a roll of a pair of dice? $\frac{5}{36}$

17. What is the probability of getting a total of 3 on a roll of a pair of dice? $\frac{1}{18}$

18. From a bag containing 5 nickels, 8 dimes, and 7 quarters, 5 coins are drawn at random all at once. What is the probability of getting 2 nickels, 2 dimes, and 1 quarter? $\frac{245}{1938}$

19. From a bag containing 6 nickels, 10 dimes, and 4 quarters, 6 coins are drawn at random all at once. What is the probability of getting 3 nickels, 2 dimes, and 1 quarter? $\frac{30}{323}$

Extension

There are 52 colored balls in a large tumbler: 13 red, 13 blue, 13 yellow, and 13 green. The balls of each color are lettered A through M. Five balls are chosen at random.

20. How many 5-ball choices are there? (Use a calculator.) $2{,}598{,}960$

21. a. How many 5-ball choices consist of exactly four balls with the same letter? $13 \cdot 48 = 624$

    b. What is the probability of choosing exactly four balls with the same letter? $\frac{624}{2{,}598{,}950}$

Challenge

22. a. How many 5-ball choices have two of the same letter and three other, different letters? $\binom{13}{1}\binom{4}{2}\binom{12}{3}\binom{4}{1}\binom{4}{1}\binom{4}{1} = 1{,}098{,}240$

    b. What is the probability of choosing two of the same letter and three other, different letters? 0.423

CAREERS/Engineering

Acoustical engineers plan structures with the idea of controlling the sounds in the environment and providing proper hearing conditions.

Every home, office, airport terminal, hospital, and so on, has noise control problems from both internal and external sources. In some structures such as high school auditoriums the acoustical engineer's objective is to distribute sound for clear hearing. This might be partially accomplished with sound reflective ceilings and walls. In other structures, such as library reading rooms, the objective is to absorb sound. In this instance, sound absorbing materials may be part of the solution.

No matter what acoustical environment is desired, acoustical engineers need to know the loudness in decibels of the sounds in and around the structure.

For example, in an accounting office the intensity I is 1,990,000 times I_0. In Section 12–7 you learned to find the

loudness in decibels by substituting into this formula.

$$L = 10 \log \frac{I}{I_0}$$

Substituting $I = 1,990,000 \cdot I_0$, we have the following.

$$L = 10 \log \frac{1,990,000 \cdot I_0}{I_0}$$

$$L = 10 \log 1,990,000$$
$$L \approx 10 \, (6.2989)$$
$$L \approx 63 \text{ decibels}$$

The loudness in decibels of the accounting office is 63 decibels.

By finding the loudness of the sound, the source of the sound, the path of the sound and the barriers to sound such as walls, windows, doors, and so on, acoustical engineers can determine the criteria for suitable sound control.

Exercises

Solve. Round answers to the nearest decibel.

1. Find the loudness in decibels of a weaving room for which the intensity is 10^{10} times I_0. 100

2. Find the loudness in decibels of a broadcasting studio for which the intensity is 310 times I_0. 25

3. Find the loudness in decibels of a grocery store for which the intensity is 63,000,000 times I_0. 78

4. Find the loudness in decibels for a machine shop for which the intensity is 10^{12} times I_0. 120

5. Find the loudness in decibels for a home for which the intensity is 25,000 times I_0. 44

6. Find the loudness in decibels for a boiler room for which the intensity is 10^{11} times I_0. 110

7. Find the loudness in decibels for a private office for which the intensity is 10^5 times I_0. 50

8. Find the loudness in decibels for a card shop for which the intensity is 630,000 times I_0. 58

9. You are having a conversation with your friend who is standing three feet from you. The intensity of the sound in an average conversation is 1,000,000 I_0. Heavy traffic is going by 50 feet away with a sound intensity of 316,228,000 I_0. Find the loudness in decibels for each. 60, 85

10. A drill on the street is operating with a loudness of 70 decibels. What is the intensity I in terms of I_0?

11. The drill in exercise 10 is replaced by a drill which has a loudness of 75 decibels. What is the intensity I in terms of I_0 for the new drill?

10. $10^7 = 10,000,000$
11. $10^{7.5} = 31,622,777$

CHAPTER 13   Review

Review the material in the chapter. Then see how you have done by trying these review exercises. If you miss an exercise, restudy the indicated lesson.

13–1   The nth term of a sequence is given. Find the first four terms, the 10th term, and the 15th term.

1. $a_n = \dfrac{n-1}{n+1}$ **2.** $a_n = n - \dfrac{1}{n}$ $0, 1\frac{1}{2}, 2\frac{2}{3}, 3\frac{3}{4}; 9\frac{9}{10}; 14\frac{14}{15}$ 1. $0, \frac{1}{3}, \frac{2}{4}, \frac{3}{5}; \frac{9}{11}; \frac{14}{16}$

For each sequence find a rule for finding the nth term.   Answers may vary.

3. 0, 3, 8, 15, 24, . . .   **4.** 2, $\dfrac{3}{2}, \dfrac{4}{3}, \dfrac{5}{4}, \dfrac{6}{5},$ . . . $\dfrac{n+1}{n}$ 3. $n^2 - 1$

5. Rename $\sum\limits_{k=1}^{3} 3^k$ without using Σ.   3, 9, 27

6. Write sigma notation for $4^2 + 4^3 + 4^4 + 4^5 + 4^6$.   Answers may vary. Ex: $\sum\limits_{k=1}^{5} 4^{k+1}$

13–2   Use the arithmetic sequence 3, $4\frac{1}{2}$, 6, $7\frac{1}{2}$, ...

7. Find the first term and the common difference.   3, $1\frac{1}{2}$

8. Find the 10th term. $16\frac{1}{2}$ **9.** What term is 24?   15th

13–2

10. Insert three arithmetic means between 3 and 23.   3, 8, 13, 18, 23

11. Find the sum of the first 30 positive integers.   465

13–3   Use the geometric sequence 4, -8, 16, -32, ...

12. Find the common ratio. -2 **13.** Find the 7th term.   256

14. Find the sum of the first six terms. -84

13–3

15. Insert two geometric means between 72 and 9.   72, 36, 18, 9

13–4

16. Find the sum of the infinite geometric series $18 + 6 + 2 + $ 27

13–5

17. How many different displays are possible using 9 signal flags in a row?   362,880

13–5, 13–6 Evaluate.

18. 3^P3 6 **19.** $8!$ **20.** 6^P3 120 **21.** 8^P6 56   19. 40,320

13–6

22. How many ways can the letters $\{M, N, O, P, Q, R\}$ be arranged to form code symbols of 4 letters, without repetition? 360

13–7 Evaluate.

23. $\binom{10}{3}$ 120 **24.** $\binom{12}{5}$ 792

13–7

25. Six people are chosen at random from a group of 15 people. How many ways can this be done? 5005

13–8

26. Find the fifth term of $(a + x)^7$. $210a^3x^4$

27. Expand $(x^2 - 3)^4$. $x^8 - 12x^6 + 54x^4 - 108x^2 + 81$

13–9

28. A bag contains 4 white balls, 3 blue balls, and 7 red balls. A ball is drawn at random. What is the probability that it is red? $\frac{1}{2}$

CHAPTER 13 Test

The nth term of a sequence is given. Find the first four terms, the 10th term, and the 15th term.

1. $a_n = \dfrac{1}{2n + 1}$ $\frac{1}{3}, \frac{1}{5}, \frac{1}{7}, \frac{1}{9}; \frac{1}{21}; \frac{1}{31}$

2. $a_n (-1)^n 3^n$ $-3, 9, -27, 81; 59{,}049; -14{,}348{,}907$

3. Find a rule for finding the nth term of $-1, \dfrac{1}{2}, -\dfrac{1}{3}, \dfrac{1}{4}, -\dfrac{1}{5}, \ldots$ Answers may vary. $\frac{(-1)^n}{n}$

4. Rename $\displaystyle\sum_{k=1}^{4} 2^{k-1}$ without using Σ. 1, 2, 4, 8

Use the arithmetic sequence $x - y, x, x + y, \ldots$.

5. Find the first term and the common difference $x - y, y$

6. Find the 7th term. $x + 5y$

7. What term is $x + 10y$? 12th

8. Insert three arithmetic means between -3 and 11. $-3, 0.5, 4, 7.5, 11$

9. Find the sum of the first 10 even integers. 110

10. Find the common ratio for this geometric sequence: 24, 16, $10\frac{2}{3}$, ... $\frac{2}{3}$

11. Find the 6th term of the geometric sequence $-2, -4, -8, ...$ -64

12. Find the sum of the first 9 terms of the geometric series
$1 + x^3 + x^6 + x^9 + x^{12} + ...$ $\frac{1-x^{27}}{1-x^3}$

13. Insert a geometric mean between 12 and 27. 18

14. Find the sum of the infinite geometric series $64 - 8 + 1 - 0.125 + ...$ $\frac{512}{9}$

Evaluate.

15. $5^P P$ 120 16. $6!$ 720 17. $4^P 2$ 12 18. $\binom{8}{3}$ 56 19. $\binom{9}{6}$ 84

20. How many ways can the letters of the set $\{D, E, F, G, H\}$ be arranged to form code symbols of 3 letters, without repetition? 60

Evaluate.

21. If you win a contest, you can choose any 8 of 15 prizes. How many different selections can you make? 6435

22. Find the fourth term of $(a + x)^{12}$. $220a^9x^3$

23. Expand $(x^2 + 3y)^4$. $x^8 + 12x^6y + 54x^4y^2 + 108x^2y^3 + 81y^4$

Challenge

24. Find the geometric mean between $\sqrt{3} + 1$ and $\sqrt{3} - 1$. $\sqrt{2}$

Ready for Matrices?

1–5 Evaluate.

1. $x(y + z)$ when $x = -2$, $y = 3$, and $z = 8$. -22

2. $xy + xz$ when $x = -2$, $y = 3$, and $z = 8$. -22

4–1, 4–3 Solve.

3. $5x + 3y = 7$
   $3x - 5y = -23$ $(-1, 4)$

4. $2x - y + 4z = -3$
   $x - 4z = 5$
   $6x - y + 2z = 10$ $\left(3, 7, -\frac{1}{2}\right)$

5. $x + y - 2z = 9$
   $2x + y - z = 4$
   $x + 2y + z = 5$ $(-2, 5, -3)$

14

Matrices

14-1 Addition and Subtraction of Matrices

Dimensions of a Matrix

We began a study of matrices in Chapter 4 where we used them to solve systems of equations.

DEFINITION

A matrix of m rows and n columns is called a matrix with *dimensions $m \times n$* (read "m by n").

EXAMPLES
Find the dimensions of each matrix.

1. $\begin{bmatrix} 2 & -3 & 4 \\ -1 & \frac{1}{2} & \pi \end{bmatrix}$
2. $\begin{bmatrix} -3 & 8 & 9 \\ \pi & -2 & 5 \\ -6 & 7 & 8 \end{bmatrix}$
3. $\begin{bmatrix} 10 \\ -7 \end{bmatrix}$
4. $[-3 \quad 4]$

2×3 matrix $\qquad$ 3×3 matrix $\qquad$ 2×1 matrix $\quad$ 1×2 matrix

Note that the row dimension is always listed first.

TRY THIS Find the dimensions of each matrix.

1. $\begin{bmatrix} -3 & 5 \\ 4 & \frac{1}{4} \\ -\pi & 0 \end{bmatrix}$ 3×2
2. $\begin{bmatrix} -3 & 0 \\ 0 & 3 \end{bmatrix}$ 2×2
3. $\begin{bmatrix} 1 & 2 & 3 \\ 0 & 1 & 8 \\ 0 & 0 & 1 \end{bmatrix}$ 3×3

4. $[\pi \quad \sqrt{2}]$ 1×2
5. $\begin{bmatrix} -5 \\ \pi \end{bmatrix}$ 2×1
6. $[-3]$ 1×1

Matrix Addition

DEFINITION

To *add* matrices, we add the corresponding members. The matrices must have the same dimensions.

EXAMPLES

Add.

5. $\begin{bmatrix} -5 & 0 \\ 4 & 1 \end{bmatrix} + \begin{bmatrix} 6 & -3 \\ 2 & 3 \end{bmatrix} = \begin{bmatrix} -5+6 & 0-3 \\ 4+2 & 1+3 \end{bmatrix} = \begin{bmatrix} 1 & -3 \\ 6 & 4 \end{bmatrix}$

6. $\begin{bmatrix} 1 & 3 & 2 \\ -1 & 5 & 4 \\ 6 & 0 & 1 \end{bmatrix} + \begin{bmatrix} -1 & -2 & 1 \\ 1 & -2 & 2 \\ -3 & 1 & 0 \end{bmatrix} = \begin{bmatrix} 0 & 1 & 3 \\ 0 & 3 & 6 \\ 3 & 1 & 1 \end{bmatrix}$

Addition of matrices is both commutative and associative.

TRY THIS

7. Let $\mathbf{A} = \begin{bmatrix} 4 & -1 \\ 6 & -3 \end{bmatrix}$ and $\mathbf{B} = \begin{bmatrix} -6 & -5 \\ 7 & 3 \end{bmatrix}$.   7. a. $\begin{bmatrix} -2 & -6 \\ 13 & 0 \end{bmatrix}$ b. $\begin{bmatrix} -2 & -6 \\ 13 & 0 \end{bmatrix}$

    a. Find $\mathbf{A} + \mathbf{B}$.   b. Find $\mathbf{B} + \mathbf{A}$.

A matrix having zeros for all of its members is called a zero matrix and is often denoted by $\mathbf{O}$. When a zero matrix is added to another matrix of the same dimensions, that same matrix is obtained. Thus, a zero matrix is an additive identity

EXAMPLE 7

$\begin{bmatrix} 2 & -1 & 3 \\ 1 & 0 & -1 \end{bmatrix} + \begin{bmatrix} 0 & 0 & 0 \\ 0 & 0 & 0 \end{bmatrix} = \begin{bmatrix} 2 & -1 & 3 \\ 1 & 0 & -1 \end{bmatrix}$

TRY THIS

8. Let $\mathbf{A} = \begin{bmatrix} 4 & -3 \\ 5 & 8 \end{bmatrix}$ and $\mathbf{O} = \begin{bmatrix} 0 & 0 \\ 0 & 0 \end{bmatrix}$. $\mathbf{A} + \mathbf{O} = \begin{bmatrix} 4 & -3 \\ 5 & 8 \end{bmatrix} = \mathbf{O} + \mathbf{A} = \mathbf{A}$

    a. Find $\mathbf{A} + \mathbf{O}$.   b. Find $\mathbf{O} + \mathbf{A}$.

Inverses and Subtraction

To subtract matrices, we subtract the corresponding members. Of course, the matrices must have the same dimensions for this to be possible.

EXAMPLE 8

$\begin{bmatrix} 1 & 2 \\ -2 & 0 \\ -3 & -1 \end{bmatrix} - \begin{bmatrix} 1 & -1 \\ 1 & 3 \\ 2 & 3 \end{bmatrix} = \begin{bmatrix} 0 & 3 \\ -3 & -3 \\ -5 & -4 \end{bmatrix}$

TRY THIS Subtract.

9. $\begin{bmatrix} 1 & 3 & -2 \\ 4 & 0 & 5 \end{bmatrix} - \begin{bmatrix} 2 & -1 & 5 \\ 6 & 4 & -3 \end{bmatrix}$

10. $\begin{bmatrix} 1 & 2 \\ 4 & 1 \\ -5 & 4 \end{bmatrix} - \begin{bmatrix} 7 & -4 \\ 3 & 5 \\ 2 & -1 \end{bmatrix}$

9. $\begin{bmatrix} -1 & 4 & -7 \\ -2 & -4 & 8 \end{bmatrix}$

10. $\begin{bmatrix} -6 & 6 \\ 1 & -4 \\ -7 & 5 \end{bmatrix}$

The additive inverse of a matrix can be obtained by replacing each member by its additive inverse. Of course, when two matrices that are additive inverses of each other are added, a zero matrix is obtained.

EXAMPLE 9

$$\begin{bmatrix} 1 & 0 & 2 \\ 3 & -1 & 5 \end{bmatrix} + \begin{bmatrix} -1 & 0 & -2 \\ -3 & 1 & -5 \end{bmatrix} = \begin{bmatrix} 0 & 0 & 0 \\ 0 & 0 & 0 \end{bmatrix}$$

$$\quad\quad \mathbf{A} \quad\quad + \quad\quad (-\mathbf{A}) \quad\quad = \quad\quad \mathbf{O}$$

TRY THIS

11. Find the additive inverse.

$\begin{bmatrix} 2 & -1 & 5 \\ 6 & 4 & -3 \end{bmatrix}$ $\begin{bmatrix} -2 & 1 & -5 \\ -6 & -4 & 3 \end{bmatrix}$

12. Add.

$\begin{bmatrix} 2 & -1 & 5 \\ 6 & 4 & -3 \end{bmatrix} + \begin{bmatrix} -2 & 1 & -5 \\ -6 & -4 & 3 \end{bmatrix}$ $\begin{bmatrix} 0 & 0 & 0 \\ 0 & 0 & 0 \end{bmatrix}$

With numbers, we can subtract by adding an inverse. This is also true of matrices. If we denote matrices by $\mathbf{A}$ and $\mathbf{B}$ and an additive inverse by $-\mathbf{B}$, this fact can be stated as a theorem.

THEOREM 14–1

For any matrices $\mathbf{A}$ and $\mathbf{B}$, $\mathbf{A} - \mathbf{B} = \mathbf{A} + (-\mathbf{B})$.

EXAMPLE 10

$$\begin{bmatrix} 3 & -1 \\ -2 & 4 \end{bmatrix} - \begin{bmatrix} 2 & 1 \\ 3 & -2 \end{bmatrix} = \begin{bmatrix} 1 & -2 \\ -5 & 6 \end{bmatrix} \quad\quad \begin{bmatrix} 3 & -1 \\ -2 & 4 \end{bmatrix} + \begin{bmatrix} -2 & -1 \\ -3 & 2 \end{bmatrix} = \begin{bmatrix} 1 & -2 \\ -5 & 6 \end{bmatrix}$$

$$\quad\quad \mathbf{A} \quad\quad - \quad\quad \mathbf{B} \quad\quad\quad\quad\quad\quad\quad \mathbf{A} \quad\quad + \quad\quad (-\mathbf{B})$$

TRY THIS Add. Compare with Try This 9.

13. $\begin{bmatrix} 1 & 3 & -2 \\ 4 & 0 & 5 \end{bmatrix} + \begin{bmatrix} -2 & 1 & -5 \\ -6 & -4 & 3 \end{bmatrix}$ $\begin{bmatrix} -1 & 4 & -7 \\ -2 & -4 & 8 \end{bmatrix}$

14-1

Exercises

For Exercises 1–36, let

$$A = \begin{bmatrix} 1 & 2 \\ 4 & -3 \end{bmatrix} \quad B = \begin{bmatrix} -3 & -5 \\ 2 & -1 \end{bmatrix} \quad C = \begin{bmatrix} 1 & -1 \\ -1 & 1 \end{bmatrix} \quad D = \begin{bmatrix} 1 & 1 \\ 1 & 1 \end{bmatrix} \quad E = \begin{bmatrix} 1 & 3 \\ 2 & 6 \end{bmatrix}$$

$$F = \begin{bmatrix} 3 & 3 \\ -1 & -1 \end{bmatrix} \quad G = \begin{bmatrix} 1 & 0 & -2 \\ 0 & -1 & 3 \\ 3 & -2 & 4 \end{bmatrix} \quad H = \begin{bmatrix} -1 & -2 & 5 \\ 1 & 0 & -1 \\ -2 & -3 & 1 \end{bmatrix} \quad M = \begin{bmatrix} -4 & 5 & -2 \\ 1 & 0 & -4 \\ -2 & -3 & -5 \end{bmatrix}$$

$$O = \begin{bmatrix} 0 & 0 \\ 0 & 0 \end{bmatrix} \quad P = \begin{bmatrix} -2 & 3 & 4 \\ 8 & 0 & -1 \end{bmatrix} \quad Q = \begin{bmatrix} -3 & -3 & 7 \\ -5 & 2 & 1 \end{bmatrix} \quad R = \begin{bmatrix} -1 & 0 & 0 \\ 0 & 2 & 0 \end{bmatrix}$$

Find the dimensions of each matrix.

1. A 2×2
2. G 3×3
3. Q 2×3
4. O 2×2

Add.

5. A + B 6. B + C 7. D + F 8. E + F
9. P + Q 10. R + P 11. H + G 12. M + H

Add.

13. A + O 14. O + B 15. O + C 16. D + O

Subtract.

17. A − B 18. C − B 19. F − D 20. E − F
21. H − M 22. G − H 23. Q − P 24. R − Q

Find the additive inverse of each matrix.

25. D 26. Q 27. E 28. M

Subtract by adding an additive inverse.

29. D − C 30. C − E 31. M − H 32. H − G
33. P − Q 34. R − P 35. O − F 36. O − A

Extension

Find the value of each sum.

37. (A + F) + C and A + (F + C)
38. (G + H) + M and (M + H) + G
39. Why does A + H not exist?

14–2 Multiplying Matrices and Numbers

Multiplying Matrices

There are two kinds of products involving matrices. First we define a product of a matrix and a number.

DEFINITION

The *product of a number k and a matrix* $\mathbf{A}$ is the matrix, denoted $k\mathbf{A}$, obtained by multiplying each number in $\mathbf{A}$ by the number k.

EXAMPLES

Let $\mathbf{A} = \begin{bmatrix} -3 & 0 \\ 4 & 5 \end{bmatrix}$. Then

1. $3\mathbf{A} = 3\begin{bmatrix} -3 & 0 \\ 4 & 5 \end{bmatrix} = \begin{bmatrix} -9 & 0 \\ 12 & 15 \end{bmatrix}$

2. $(-1)\mathbf{A} = -1\begin{bmatrix} -3 & 0 \\ 4 & 5 \end{bmatrix} = \begin{bmatrix} 3 & 0 \\ -4 & -5 \end{bmatrix}$

TRY THIS Compute these products.

1. $5\begin{bmatrix} 1 & -2 & x \\ 4 & y & 1 \\ 0 & -5 & x^2 \end{bmatrix}$

2. $t\begin{bmatrix} 1 & -1 & 4 & x \\ y & 3 & -2 & y \\ 1 & 4 & -5 & y \end{bmatrix}$

1. $\begin{bmatrix} 5 & -10 & 5x \\ 20 & 5y & 5 \\ 0 & -25 & 5x^2 \end{bmatrix}$

2. $\begin{bmatrix} t & -t & 4t & xt \\ yt & 3t & -2t & yt \\ t & 4t & -5t & yt \end{bmatrix}$

Now we consider the product of two matrices. We do not multiply two matrices by multiplying their corresponding members. The motivation for defining matrix products comes from systems of equations.

Let us begin by considering the following equation.

$$3x + 2y - 2z = 4$$

We will write the coefficients on the left side in a 1×3 matrix (a row matrix) and the variables in a 3×1 matrix (a column matrix). The 4 on the right is written in a 1×1 matrix.

$$\begin{bmatrix} 3 & 2 & -2 \end{bmatrix}\begin{bmatrix} x \\ y \\ z \end{bmatrix} = \begin{bmatrix} 4 \end{bmatrix}$$

We can return to our original equation by multiplying the members of the row matrix by those of the column matrix, and adding.

$$[3 \quad 2 \quad -2] \begin{bmatrix} x \\ y \\ z \end{bmatrix} = [3x + 2y - 2z] = [4]$$

We define multiplication accordingly. In this special case, we have a row matrix A and a column matrix B. Their product AB is a 1×1 matrix, having the single member 4 (also called $3x + 2y - 2z$).

EXAMPLE 3
Find the product of these matrices.

$$[3 \quad 2 \quad -1] \begin{bmatrix} 1 \\ -2 \\ 8 \end{bmatrix} = [3 \cdot 1 + 2(-2) + (-1) \cdot 8] = [-9]$$

TRY THIS Multiply.

3. $[4 \quad -2 \quad 3] \begin{bmatrix} 2 \\ 3 \\ -5 \end{bmatrix}$ 4. $[-2 \quad 1] \begin{bmatrix} x \\ y \end{bmatrix}$ 3. $[-13]$ 4. $[-2x + y]$

Let us continue by considering a system of equations.

$$\begin{align} 3x + 2y - 2z &= 4 \\ 2x - y + 5z &= 3 \\ -x + y + 4z &= 7 \end{align}$$

Consider the following matrices.

$$\underset{A}{\begin{bmatrix} 3 & 2 & -2 \\ 2 & -1 & 5 \\ -1 & 1 & 4 \end{bmatrix}} \quad \underset{X}{\begin{bmatrix} x \\ y \\ z \end{bmatrix}} \quad \underset{B}{\begin{bmatrix} 4 \\ 3 \\ 7 \end{bmatrix}}$$

If we multiply the first row of A by X, as we did above, we get $3x + 2y - 2z$. If we multiply the second row of A by X, we get $2x - y + 5z$. If we then multiply the third row of A by X, we get $-x + y + 4z$.

Note that the first members are multiplied, the second members are multiplied, the third members are multiplied, and the results are added to get a single number with three terms.

We define the product AX to be the following column matrix.

$$\begin{bmatrix} 3x + 2y - 2z \\ 2x - y + 5z \\ -x + y + 4z \end{bmatrix}$$

Now consider this matrix equation.

$$\begin{bmatrix} 3x + 2y - 2z \\ 2x - y + 5z \\ -x + y + 4z \end{bmatrix} = \begin{bmatrix} 4 \\ 3 \\ 7 \end{bmatrix}$$

Equality for matrices is the same as for numbers. In the above equation, the "two" matrices are really the same one. This means that $3x + 2y - 2z$ is 4, $2x - y + 5z$ is 3, and $-x + y + 4z$ is 7.

$$3x + 2y - 2z = 4$$
$$2x - y + 5z = 3$$
$$-x + y + 4z = 7$$

Thus the matrix equation $AX = B$ is equivalent to the original system of equations.

EXAMPLE 4

Multiply.

$$\begin{bmatrix} 3 & 1 & -1 \\ 1 & 2 & 2 \\ -1 & 0 & 5 \\ 4 & 1 & 2 \end{bmatrix} \begin{bmatrix} 1 \\ 2 \\ 1 \end{bmatrix} = \begin{bmatrix} 3 \cdot 1 + 1 \cdot 2 - 1 \cdot 1 \\ 1 \cdot 1 + 2 \cdot 2 + 2 \cdot 1 \\ -1 \cdot 1 + 0 \cdot 2 + 5 \cdot 1 \\ 4 \cdot 1 + 1 \cdot 2 + 2 \cdot 1 \end{bmatrix} = \begin{bmatrix} 4 \\ 7 \\ 4 \\ 8 \end{bmatrix}$$

TRY THIS Multiply.

5. $\begin{bmatrix} 1 & 4 & 2 \\ -1 & 6 & 3 \\ 3 & 2 & -1 \\ 5 & 0 & 2 \end{bmatrix} \begin{bmatrix} 2 \\ 1 \\ 3 \end{bmatrix}$ 5. 12
                                                          13
                                                           5
                                                          16

In all the examples discussed so far, the second matrix had only one column. If it has more than one column, we treat it in the same way when multiplying that we treated the single column. The product matrix will have as many columns as the second matrix.

EXAMPLE 5

Multiply. (Compare with Example 4.)

$$\underset{\mathbf{A}}{\begin{bmatrix} 3 & 1 & -1 \\ 1 & 2 & 2 \\ -1 & 0 & 5 \\ 4 & 1 & 2 \end{bmatrix}} \underset{\mathbf{B}}{\begin{bmatrix} 1 & 0 \\ 2 & 1 \\ 1 & 3 \end{bmatrix}} = \begin{bmatrix} 4 \\ 7 \\ 4 \\ 8 \end{bmatrix} \begin{matrix} 3 \cdot 0 + 1 \cdot 1 + (-1)3 \\ 1 \cdot 0 + 2 \cdot 1 + 2 \cdot 3 \\ -1 \cdot 0 + 0 \cdot 1 + 5 \cdot 3 \\ 4 \cdot 0 + 1 \cdot 1 + 2 \cdot 3 \end{matrix} = \begin{bmatrix} 4 & -2 \\ 7 & 8 \\ 4 & 15 \\ 8 & 7 \end{bmatrix}$$

Same as in
Example 4

The rows of **A** multiplied by
the second column of **B**

TRY THIS Multiply.

6. $\begin{bmatrix} 4 & 1 & 2 \\ -3 & 2 & 3 \\ 2 & 0 & 5 \\ 3 & 1 & 4 \end{bmatrix} \begin{bmatrix} 1 & 4 \\ 2 & 0 \\ -3 & 5 \end{bmatrix}$

7. $[4 \quad 1 \quad 0 \quad 2] \begin{bmatrix} 1 & 0 & 1 \\ 2 & -1 & 0 \\ 3 & 5 & 1 \\ 1 & 3 & 0 \end{bmatrix}$

6. $\begin{array}{rr} 0 & 26 \\ -8 & 3 \\ -13 & 33 \\ -7 & 32 \end{array}$ 7. $[8 \quad 5 \quad 4]$

EXAMPLE 6

Multiply.

$$\begin{bmatrix} 3 & 1 & -1 \\ 2 & 0 & 3 \end{bmatrix} \begin{bmatrix} 1 & 4 & 6 \\ 3 & -1 & 9 \\ 2 & 5 & 1 \end{bmatrix}$$

$$= \begin{bmatrix} 3 \cdot 1 + 1 \cdot 3 - 1 \cdot 2 & 3 \cdot 4 + 1(-1) - 1 \cdot 5 & 3 \cdot 6 + 1 \cdot 9 - 1 \cdot 1 \\ 2 \cdot 1 + 0 \cdot 3 + 3 \cdot 2 & 2 \cdot 4 + 0 \cdot (-1) + 3 \cdot 5 & 2 \cdot 6 + 0 \cdot 9 + 3 \cdot 1 \end{bmatrix}$$

$$= \begin{bmatrix} 4 & 6 & 26 \\ 8 & 23 & 15 \end{bmatrix}$$

If matrix $\mathbf{A}$ has n columns and matrix $\mathbf{B}$ has n rows, then we can compute the product $\mathbf{AB}$, regardless of the other dimensions. The product will have as many rows as $\mathbf{A}$ and as many columns as $\mathbf{B}$.

$\mathbf{A} + \mathbf{B}$ and $\mathbf{A} - \mathbf{B}$ exist only when the dimensions are the same. $\mathbf{AB}$ exists only when the number of columns in $\mathbf{A}$ is the same as the number of rows in $\mathbf{B}$. Consider matrices $\mathbf{A}$ and $\mathbf{B}$ below.

$$\mathbf{A} = \begin{bmatrix} 3 & 1 & -1 \\ 2 & 0 & 3 \end{bmatrix} \quad \text{and} \quad \mathbf{B} = \begin{bmatrix} 1 & 4 & 6 \\ 3 & -1 & 9 \\ 2 & 5 & 1 \end{bmatrix}$$

$\mathbf{A} + \mathbf{B}$ and $\mathbf{A} - \mathbf{B}$ do not exist because the dimensions of $\mathbf{A}$ and $\mathbf{B}$ are not the same. $\mathbf{AB}$ does exist because the number of columns in $\mathbf{A}$, 3, is the same as the number of rows in $\mathbf{B}$, 3. But $\mathbf{BA}$ does not exist because the number of columns in $\mathbf{B}$, 3, is not the same as the number of rows in $\mathbf{A}$, 2. Since $\mathbf{AB}$ exists, and $\mathbf{BA}$ does not, $\mathbf{AB} \neq \mathbf{BA}$. Matrix multiplication is not commutative.

8. $\mathbf{AB} = \begin{bmatrix} 2 & 8 & 6 \\ -29 & -34 & -7 \end{bmatrix}$; $\mathbf{BA}$ not possible

9. $\mathbf{AB} = \begin{bmatrix} -2 & 32 \\ 4 & 16 \end{bmatrix}$

$\mathbf{BA} = \begin{bmatrix} 8 & -13 \\ -16 & 6 \end{bmatrix}$

TRY THIS

8. Find $\mathbf{AB}$ and $\mathbf{BA}$ if possible.

$$\mathbf{A} = \begin{bmatrix} -2 & 4 & 0 \\ -3 & 0 & -8 \end{bmatrix} \quad \mathbf{B} = \begin{bmatrix} -1 & -2 & -3 \\ 0 & 1 & 0 \\ 4 & 5 & 2 \end{bmatrix}$$

9. Find $\mathbf{AB}$ and $\mathbf{BA}$ and compare.

$$\mathbf{A} = \begin{bmatrix} -8 & 3 \\ -4 & 4 \end{bmatrix} \quad \mathbf{B} = \begin{bmatrix} 1 & -4 \\ 2 & 0 \end{bmatrix}$$

Equivalent Matrix Equations

The following theorem summarizes some of the properties of square matrices of the same dimensions whose elements are real numbers. We restrict the theorem to square matrices so that all additions and multiplications are possible. Some of the proofs will be considered in the Challenge Exercises. Note that not all the field properties hold.

THEOREM 14–2

For any square matrices A, B, and C of the same dimensions, the following laws hold.

Commutative Law

$A + B = B + A$

Associative Law

$A + (B + C) = (A + B) + C$, $A(BC) = (AB)C$

Identity

There exists a unique matrix O, such that

$A + O = O + A = A.$

Inverses

There exists a unique matrix $-A$, such that

$A + (-A) = -A + A = O.$

Distributive Law

$A(B + C) = AB + AC$

For any square matrices A and B, of the same dimensions, and any real numbers k and m, $k(A + B) = kA + kB$, $(k + m)A = kA + mA$, and $(km)A = k(mA)$.

For later purposes it is important to be able to write a matrix equation equivalent to a system of equations.

EXAMPLE 7

Write a matrix equation equivalent to this system of equations.

$$\begin{array}{rrrrl} 4x & + 2y & - & z & = 3 \\ 9x & & + & z & = 5 \\ 4x & + 5y & - & 2z & = 1 \\ x & + y & + & z & = 0 \end{array}$$

We write the coefficients on the left in a matrix. We write the product of that matrix by the column matrix containing the variables, and set the result equal to the column matrix containing the constants on the right.

$$\begin{bmatrix} 4 & 2 & -1 \\ 9 & 0 & 1 \\ 4 & 5 & -2 \\ 1 & 1 & 1 \end{bmatrix} \begin{bmatrix} x \\ y \\ z \end{bmatrix} = \begin{bmatrix} 3 \\ 5 \\ 1 \\ 0 \end{bmatrix}$$

TRY THIS Write a matrix equation equivalent to this system of equations.

10. $3x + 4y - 2z = 5$
$\quad 2x - 2y + 5z = 3$
$\quad 6z + 7y - z = 0$

$$\begin{bmatrix} 3 & 4 & -2 \\ 2 & -2 & 5 \\ 6 & 7 & -1 \end{bmatrix} \begin{bmatrix} x \\ y \\ z \end{bmatrix} = \begin{bmatrix} 5 \\ 3 \\ 0 \end{bmatrix}$$

14–2

Exercises

For Exercises 1–28, let $A = \begin{bmatrix} 1 & 2 \\ 4 & 3 \end{bmatrix}$ $B = \begin{bmatrix} -3 & 5 \\ 2 & -1 \end{bmatrix}$ $C = \begin{bmatrix} 1 & -1 \\ -1 & 1 \end{bmatrix}$ $D = \begin{bmatrix} 1 & 1 \\ 1 & 1 \end{bmatrix}$

$E = \begin{bmatrix} 1 & 3 \\ 2 & 6 \end{bmatrix}$ $F = \begin{bmatrix} 3 & 3 \\ -1 & -1 \end{bmatrix}$ $I = \begin{bmatrix} 1 & 0 \\ 0 & 1 \end{bmatrix}$ $G = \begin{bmatrix} 1 & 0 & -2 \\ 0 & -1 & 3 \\ 3 & 2 & 4 \end{bmatrix}$ $H = \begin{bmatrix} -1 & -2 & 5 \\ 1 & 0 & -1 \\ 2 & -3 & 1 \end{bmatrix}$

$J = [-2 \quad 3 \quad -4]$ $K = [8 \quad -1]$ $L = [-1 \quad -2 \quad -3 \quad 4]$

$M = \begin{bmatrix} -2 \\ -4 \\ 7 \end{bmatrix}$ $N = \begin{bmatrix} 8 \\ -6 \\ \frac{1}{2} \end{bmatrix}$ $P = \begin{bmatrix} -3 \\ -2 \end{bmatrix}$ $Q = \begin{bmatrix} 10 \\ -4 \\ 5 \\ 2 \end{bmatrix}$ $Z = \begin{bmatrix} -2 & 9 & 6 \\ -3 & 3 & 4 \\ 2 & -2 & 1 \end{bmatrix}$

Multiply.

1. $(-2)A$
2. $(-5)B$
3. $14C$
4. $12D$
5. tE
6. pF
7. $(-1)Z$
8. $(-1)H$

Multiply.

9. KP
10. JM
11. JN
12. LQ

Multiply, if possible.

13. AB
14. BC
15. CD
16. EF
17. JG
18. KF
19. JZ
20. FP
21. FI
22. IB
23. GH
24. HG
25. AP
26. KC
27. HA
28. CG

Write a matrix equation equivalent to each of the following systems of equations.

29. $3x - 2y + 4z = 17$
$2x + y - 5z = 13$

30. $3x + 2y + 5z = 9$
$4x - 3y + 2z = 10$

31. $x - y + 2z - 4w = 12$
$2x - y - z + w = 0$
$x + 4y - 3z - w = 1$
$3x + 5y - 7z + 2w = 9$

32. $2x + 4y - 5z + 12w = 2$
$4x - y + 12z - w = 5$
$-x + 4y + 2w = 13$
$2x + 10y + z = 5$

Extension

For Exercise 33, let

$$A = \begin{bmatrix} 3 & 1 & 0 \\ 6 & 4 & 0 \\ 2 & 3 & 1 \end{bmatrix} \text{ and } B = \begin{bmatrix} 2 & 1 & 0 \\ 3 & 3 & 9 \\ 6 & 4 & 6 \end{bmatrix}.$$

33. Compute: $3A + 2B$; $B - 2A$.

33. $\begin{bmatrix} 13 & 5 & 0 \\ 24 & 18 & 18 \\ 18 & 17 & 15 \end{bmatrix}$; $\begin{bmatrix} -4 & -1 & 0 \\ -9 & -5 & 9 \\ 2 & -2 & 4 \end{bmatrix}$

34. Use A and I, below. Find AI and IA.

$$A = \begin{bmatrix} 3 & 2 \\ -1 & 5 \end{bmatrix} \qquad I = \begin{bmatrix} 1 & 0 \\ 0 & 1 \end{bmatrix} \qquad AI = \begin{bmatrix} 3 & 2 \\ -1 & 5 \end{bmatrix} = IA = A$$

35. What can you conclude about matrix I in Exercise 34?

Do the following products exist? If they do, determine how many rows and columns are in the product matrix. Do not carry out the multiplication.

36. $\begin{bmatrix} 3 & 6 & 1 \\ 4 & 9 & 0 \\ 2 & 8 & 3 \end{bmatrix} \begin{bmatrix} 2 & 3 & 6 \\ 4 & 9 & 1 \end{bmatrix}$ No

37. $\begin{bmatrix} 4 & 3 & 2 & 1 & 5 \\ 6 & 9 & 3 & 25 & 6 \\ 4 & 18 & 2 & 18 & 2 \\ 3 & 6 & 1 & 1 & 2 \\ 2 & 4 & 8 & 25 & 23 \end{bmatrix} \begin{bmatrix} 6 & 3 & 7 & 9 & 11 & 24 \\ 4 & 7 & 59 & 8 & 2 & 12 \\ 3 & 2 & 6 & 0 & 1 & 7 \\ 2 & 19 & 4 & 2 & 4 & 1 \\ 1 & 23 & 3 & 9 & 0 & 1 \end{bmatrix}$ Yes; 5 rows and 6 columns

Challenge

38. Let $A = \begin{bmatrix} -1 & 0 \\ 2 & 1 \end{bmatrix}$ and $B = \begin{bmatrix} 1 & -1 \\ 0 & 2 \end{bmatrix}$.

a. Show that $(A + B)(A - B) \neq A^2 - B^2$, where $A^2 = AA$ and $B^2 = BB$.

b. Show that $(A + B)(A + B) \neq A^2 + 2AB + B^2$.

a. $(A + B)(A - B) = \begin{bmatrix} 0 & -1 \\ 2 & 3 \end{bmatrix} \begin{bmatrix} -2 & 1 \\ 2 & -1 \end{bmatrix} = \begin{bmatrix} -2 & 1 \\ 2 & -1 \end{bmatrix}$, $A^2 - B^2 = \begin{bmatrix} 1 & 0 \\ 0 & 1 \end{bmatrix} - \begin{bmatrix} 1 & -3 \\ 0 & 4 \end{bmatrix} = \begin{bmatrix} 0 & 3 \\ 0 & -3 \end{bmatrix}$

For Exercises 39–44, let

$$A = \begin{bmatrix} a & c \\ b & d \end{bmatrix}, B = \begin{bmatrix} e & g \\ f & h \end{bmatrix}, \text{ and } C = \begin{bmatrix} p & r \\ q & s \end{bmatrix}.$$

b. $(A + B)(A + B) = \begin{bmatrix} 0 & -1 \\ 2 & 3 \end{bmatrix} \begin{bmatrix} 0 & -1 \\ 2 & 3 \end{bmatrix} = \begin{bmatrix} -2 & -3 \\ 6 & 7 \end{bmatrix}$,

Prove.

$A^2 + 2AB + B^2 = \begin{bmatrix} 1 & 0 \\ 0 & 1 \end{bmatrix} + 2\begin{bmatrix} -1 & 1 \\ 2 & 0 \end{bmatrix} + \begin{bmatrix} 1 & -3 \\ 0 & 4 \end{bmatrix} = \begin{bmatrix} 0 & -1 \\ 4 & 5 \end{bmatrix}$

39. $A + B = B + A$
40. $(A + B) + C = A + (B + C)$
41. $A - B = A + (-B)$
42. $(-1)A = -A$
43. $k(A + B) = kA + kB$
44. $(k + m)A = kA + mA$

14–2 Multiplying Matrices and Numbers **611**

14–3 Inverses of Matrices

Inverses

We use the symbol I to represent matrices of the type shown below.

$$\begin{bmatrix} 1 & 0 \\ 0 & 1 \end{bmatrix} \qquad \begin{bmatrix} 1 & 0 & 0 \\ 0 & 1 & 0 \\ 0 & 0 & 1 \end{bmatrix}$$

Note that these are square matrices with 1's from the upper left to the lower right along the main diagonal, and 0's elsewhere.

THEOREM 14–3

For any $n \times n$ matrices A and I, $AI = IA = A$ (I is a multiplicative identity).

Usually we say that I is an identity matrix

Suppose a matrix A has a multiplicative inverse, or simply inverse, A^{-1}. Then A^{-1} is a matrix for which $A \cdot A^{-1} = A^{-1} \cdot A = I$.

EXAMPLE 1
For the matrix

$$A = \begin{bmatrix} 5 & 3 \\ 3 & 2 \end{bmatrix}, \qquad \text{we have } A^{-1} = \begin{bmatrix} 2 & -3 \\ -3 & 5 \end{bmatrix}.$$

We can check that $A \cdot A^{-1} = 1$ by multiplying.

$$A \cdot A^{-1} = \begin{bmatrix} 5 & 3 \\ 3 & 2 \end{bmatrix}\begin{bmatrix} 2 & -3 \\ -3 & 5 \end{bmatrix} = \begin{bmatrix} 1 & 0 \\ 0 & 1 \end{bmatrix} = I$$

We leave it to the student to verify that $A^{-1} \cdot A = I$.

TRY THIS

1. Let $A = \begin{bmatrix} 3 & 1 & 0 \\ 1 & -1 & 2 \\ 1 & 1 & 1 \end{bmatrix}$ and $A^{-1} = \dfrac{1}{8}\begin{bmatrix} 3 & 1 & -2 \\ -1 & -3 & 6 \\ -2 & 2 & 4 \end{bmatrix}$. a. $\begin{bmatrix} 1 & 0 & 0 \\ 0 & 1 & 0 \\ 0 & 0 & 1 \end{bmatrix} = I$; b. I; c. both equal I

   a. Find AA^{-1}.   b. Find $A^{-1}A$.   c. Compare AA^{-1} and $A^{-1}A$.

Calculating Matrix Inverses

In this section we consider a way of calculating the inverse of a square matrix, if it exists. In Chapter 4 we discussed determinants of matrices. The inverse of a square matrix exists only when the determinant of the matrix is nonzero.

Suppose we want to find the inverse of the following matrix.

$$A = \begin{bmatrix} 2 & -1 & 1 \\ 1 & -2 & 3 \\ 4 & 1 & 2 \end{bmatrix}$$

First we form a new augmented matrix consisting, on the left, of the matrix A and, on the right, of the corresponding identity matrix I.

$$\begin{bmatrix} 2 & -1 & 1 \\ 1 & -2 & 3 \\ 4 & 1 & 2 \end{bmatrix} \begin{bmatrix} 1 & 0 & 0 \\ 0 & 1 & 0 \\ 0 & 0 & 1 \end{bmatrix}$$

The matrix A The identity matrix I

We now proceed in a manner very much like that described in Section 4–6. We attempt to transform A into an identity matrix by using row-equivalent operations to obtain a matrix which consists of only 0's, except for the main diagonal which consists of only 1's. Whatever operations we perform, we do on the entire augmented matrix. We will get a matrix like the following.

$$\begin{bmatrix} 1 & 0 & 0 & a & b & c \\ 0 & 1 & 0 & d & e & f \\ 0 & 0 & 1 & g & h & i \end{bmatrix}$$

Elements of the identity matrix I.   Elements of the matrix A^{-1}.

EXAMPLE 2

Find A^{-1}.

$$A = \begin{bmatrix} 2 & -1 & 1 \\ 1 & -2 & 3 \\ 4 & 1 & 2 \end{bmatrix}$$

a. We find the augmented matrix consisting of A and I.

$$\begin{bmatrix} 2 & -1 & 1 & 1 & 0 & 0 \\ 1 & -2 & 3 & 0 & 1 & 0 \\ 4 & 1 & 2 & 0 & 0 & 1 \end{bmatrix}$$

b. We interchange the first and second rows so the elements of the first column are multiples of the top number on the main diagonal.

$$\begin{bmatrix} 1 & -2 & 3 & 0 & 1 & 0 \\ 2 & -1 & 1 & 1 & 0 & 0 \\ 4 & 1 & 2 & 0 & 0 & 1 \end{bmatrix}$$

c. Next we obtain 0's in the rest of the first column. We multiply the first row by -2 and add it to the second row. Then we multiply the first row by -4 and add it to the third row.

$$\begin{bmatrix} 1 & -2 & 3 & 0 & 1 & 0 \\ 0 & 3 & -5 & 1 & -2 & 0 \\ 0 & 9 & -10 & 0 & -4 & 1 \end{bmatrix}$$

d. Next we move down the main diagonal to the number 3. We note that the number below it, 9, is a multiple of 3. We multiply the second row by -3 and add it to the third to obtain 0 below the diagonal.

$$\begin{bmatrix} 1 & -2 & 3 & 0 & 1 & 0 \\ 0 & 3 & -5 & 1 & -2 & 0 \\ 0 & 0 & 5 & -3 & 2 & 1 \end{bmatrix}$$

e. Now we move down the main diagonal to the number 5. We check to see if each number above 5 in the third column is a multiple of 5. Since it is not, we multiply the first row by -5.

$$\begin{bmatrix} -5 & 10 & -15 & 0 & -5 & 0 \\ 0 & 3 & -5 & 1 & -2 & 0 \\ 0 & 0 & 5 & -3 & 2 & 1 \end{bmatrix}$$

f. Now we work back up. We add the third row to the second. We also multiply the third row by 3 and add it to the first.

$$\begin{bmatrix} -5 & 10 & 0 & -9 & 1 & 3 \\ 0 & 3 & 0 & -2 & 0 & 1 \\ 0 & 0 & 5 & -3 & 2 & 1 \end{bmatrix}$$

g. We move back to the number 3 on the main diagonal. We multiply the first row by -3, so the element on the top of the second column is a multiple of 3.

$$\begin{bmatrix} 15 & -30 & 0 & 27 & -3 & -9 \\ 0 & 3 & 0 & -2 & 0 & 1 \\ 0 & 0 & 5 & -3 & 2 & 1 \end{bmatrix}$$

h. We multiply the second row by 10 and add it to the first.

$$\begin{bmatrix} 15 & 0 & 0 & 7 & -3 & 1 \\ 0 & 3 & 0 & -2 & 0 & 1 \\ 0 & 0 & 5 & -3 & 2 & 1 \end{bmatrix}$$

i. Finally, we get all 1's on the main diagonal. We multiply the first row by $\frac{1}{15}$, the second by $\frac{1}{3}$, and the third by $\frac{1}{5}$.

$$\begin{bmatrix} 1 & 0 & 0 & \frac{7}{15} & -\frac{1}{5} & -\frac{1}{15} \\ 0 & 1 & 0 & -\frac{2}{3} & 0 & \frac{1}{3} \\ 0 & 0 & 1 & -\frac{3}{5} & \frac{2}{5} & \frac{1}{5} \end{bmatrix}$$

We now have the matrix $\mathbf{I}$ on the left and $\mathbf{A}^{-1}$ on the right.

$$\mathbf{A}^{-1} = \begin{bmatrix} \frac{7}{15} & -\frac{1}{5} & \frac{1}{15} \\ -\frac{2}{3} & 0 & \frac{1}{3} \\ -\frac{3}{5} & \frac{2}{5} & \frac{1}{5} \end{bmatrix}$$

The student can check by doing the multiplication $\mathbf{A}^{-1}\mathbf{A}$ or $\mathbf{A}\mathbf{A}^{-1}$. If we cannot obtain the identity matrix on the left, as would be the case when a system has no solution or infinitely many solutions, then $\mathbf{A}^{-1}$ does not exist.

TRY THIS Find $\mathbf{A}^{-1}$.

2. $\mathbf{A} = \begin{bmatrix} 1 & 0 & 1 \\ 2 & 1 & 0 \\ 1 & -1 & 1 \end{bmatrix}$ **3.** $\mathbf{A} = \begin{bmatrix} 3 & 5 \\ 2 & 4 \end{bmatrix}$ 2. $\mathbf{A}^{-1} = \begin{bmatrix} -\frac{1}{2} & \frac{1}{2} & \frac{1}{2} \\ 1 & 0 & -1 \\ \frac{3}{2} & -\frac{1}{2} & -\frac{1}{2} \end{bmatrix}$ 3. $\mathbf{A}^{-1} = \begin{bmatrix} 2 & -\frac{5}{2} \\ -1 & \frac{3}{2} \end{bmatrix}$

Solving Systems Using Inverses

One application of inverses of square matrices is the solving of certain kinds of systems of equations.

EXAMPLE 3
Consider this system.

$$3x + 5y = -1$$
$$x - 2y = 4$$

We write a matrix equation equivalent to this system.

$$\begin{bmatrix} 3 & 5 \\ 1 & -2 \end{bmatrix} \cdot \begin{bmatrix} x \\ y \end{bmatrix} = \begin{bmatrix} -1 \\ 4 \end{bmatrix}$$

Now we let

$$\begin{bmatrix} 3 & 5 \\ 1 & -2 \end{bmatrix} = \mathbf{A}, \begin{bmatrix} x \\ y \end{bmatrix} = \mathbf{X}, \text{ and } \begin{bmatrix} -1 \\ 4 \end{bmatrix} = \mathbf{B}.$$

Then we have the following equation.

$$\mathbf{A} \cdot \mathbf{X} = \mathbf{B}$$

To solve this equation, we first find A^{-1}.

$$A^{-1} = \frac{1}{11}\begin{bmatrix} 2 & 5 \\ 1 & -3 \end{bmatrix}$$

We solve the matrix equation $A \cdot X = B$.

$$\begin{aligned} A^{-1} \cdot A \cdot X &= A^{-1} \cdot B & \text{Multiplying by } A^{-1} \\ I \cdot X &= A^{-1} \cdot B & \text{Since } A^{-1} \cdot A = I \\ X &= A^{-1} \cdot B & \text{Since I is an identity} \end{aligned}$$

Now we substitute.

$$X = A^{-1} \cdot B$$

$$\begin{bmatrix} x \\ y \end{bmatrix} = \frac{1}{11}\begin{bmatrix} 2 & 5 \\ 1 & -3 \end{bmatrix} \cdot \begin{bmatrix} -1 \\ 4 \end{bmatrix}$$

$$y = \frac{1}{11}\begin{bmatrix} 18 \\ -13 \end{bmatrix}$$

$$= \begin{bmatrix} \dfrac{18}{11} \\ -\dfrac{13}{11} \end{bmatrix}$$

The solution of the system of equations is $x = \frac{18}{11}$ and $y = -\frac{13}{11}$.

TRY THIS

4. Consider this system: $\begin{aligned} 4x - 2y &= -1 \\ x + 5y &= 1 \end{aligned}$

   a. Write a matrix equation equivalent to the system.
   b. Find the coefficient matrix A.   c. Find A^{-1}.
   d. Use the inverse of the coefficient matrix to solve the system.

a. $\begin{bmatrix} 4 & -2 \\ 1 & 5 \end{bmatrix}\begin{bmatrix} x \\ y \end{bmatrix} = \begin{bmatrix} -1 \\ 1 \end{bmatrix}$;

b. $A = \begin{bmatrix} 4 & -2 \\ 1 & 5 \end{bmatrix}$;

c. $A^{-1} = \frac{1}{22}\begin{bmatrix} 5 & 2 \\ -1 & 4 \end{bmatrix}$;

d. $x = -\frac{3}{22}, y = \frac{5}{22}$

14–3

Exercises

Verify that $AA^{-1} = I$.

1. $A = \begin{bmatrix} 1 & 2 \\ 3 & 4 \end{bmatrix}$

   $A^{-1} = \begin{bmatrix} -2 & 1 \\ \dfrac{3}{2} & -\dfrac{1}{2} \end{bmatrix}$

2. $A = \begin{bmatrix} 3 & 4 \\ 2 & 6 \end{bmatrix}$

   $A^{-1} = \begin{bmatrix} \dfrac{6}{10} & -\dfrac{4}{10} \\ -\dfrac{2}{10} & \dfrac{3}{10} \end{bmatrix}$

3. $\mathbf{A} = \begin{bmatrix} 7 & 4 \\ 3 & 2 \end{bmatrix}$
$\mathbf{A}^{-1} = \begin{bmatrix} 1 & -2 \\ -\frac{3}{2} & \frac{7}{2} \end{bmatrix}$

4. $\mathbf{A} = \begin{bmatrix} 2 & 3 \\ 3 & 6 \end{bmatrix}$
$\mathbf{A}^{-1} = \begin{bmatrix} 2 & -1 \\ -1 & \frac{2}{3} \end{bmatrix}$

Find $\mathbf{A}^{-1}$, if it exists. Check your answers by calculating $\mathbf{AA}^{-1}$ and $\mathbf{A}^{-1}\mathbf{A}$.

5. $\mathbf{A} = \begin{bmatrix} 3 & 2 \\ 5 & 3 \end{bmatrix}$

6. $\mathbf{A} = \begin{bmatrix} 3 & 5 \\ 1 & 2 \end{bmatrix}$

7. $\mathbf{A} = \begin{bmatrix} 11 & 3 \\ 7 & 2 \end{bmatrix}$

8. $\mathbf{A} = \begin{bmatrix} 8 & 5 \\ 5 & 3 \end{bmatrix}$

9. $\mathbf{A} = \begin{bmatrix} 4 & -3 \\ 1 & 2 \end{bmatrix}$

10. $\mathbf{A} = \begin{bmatrix} 0 & -1 \\ 1 & 0 \end{bmatrix}$

11. $\mathbf{A} = \begin{bmatrix} 3 & 1 & 0 \\ 1 & 1 & 1 \\ 1 & -1 & 2 \end{bmatrix}$

12. $\mathbf{A} = \begin{bmatrix} 1 & 0 & 1 \\ 2 & 1 & 0 \\ 1 & -1 & 1 \end{bmatrix}$

13. $\mathbf{A} = \begin{bmatrix} 1 & -1 & 2 \\ 0 & 1 & 3 \\ 2 & 1 & -2 \end{bmatrix}$

For Exercises 14 and 15, write a matrix equation equivalent to the system. Find the inverse of the coefficient matrix. Use the inverse of the coefficient matrix to solve each system.

14. $7x - 2y = 10$
$9x + 3y = 24$ (2, 2)

15. $5x + 3y = 29$
$4x - y = 13$ (4, 3)

Extension

For Exercises 16 and 17, follow the instructions for 14 and 15 above.

16. $x \qquad + z = 1$
$2x + y \qquad = 3$
$x - y + z = 4$ (3, −3, −2)

17. $x + 2y + 3z = -1$
$2x - 3y + 4z = 2$
$-3x + 5y - 6z = 4$ (124, 14, −51)

18. Let $\mathbf{A} = \begin{bmatrix} a & b \\ c & d \end{bmatrix}$ and $\mathbf{I} = \begin{bmatrix} 1 & 0 \\ 0 & 1 \end{bmatrix}$.
a. Find $\mathbf{AI}$. b. Find $\mathbf{IA}$.
c. Compare $\mathbf{AI}$ and $\mathbf{IA}$. a. $\mathbf{A}$; b. $\mathbf{A}$; c. both equal $\mathbf{A}$

19. Let $\mathbf{A} = \begin{bmatrix} a & b & c \\ d & e & f \\ g & h & i \end{bmatrix}$ and $\mathbf{I} = \begin{bmatrix} 1 & 0 & 0 \\ 0 & 1 & 0 \\ 0 & 0 & 1 \end{bmatrix}$.
Show that $\mathbf{AI} = \mathbf{IA} = \mathbf{A}$. Find $\mathbf{AI}$ and $\mathbf{IA}$ and compare with $\mathbf{A}$.

Challenge

In Exercises 20–23, find a formula for $\mathbf{A}^{-1}$.

20. $\mathbf{A} = [x]$

21. $\mathbf{A} = \begin{bmatrix} x & 0 \\ 0 & y \end{bmatrix}$

22. $\mathbf{A} = \begin{bmatrix} 0 & x \\ y & 0 \end{bmatrix}$

23. $\mathbf{A} = \begin{bmatrix} x & 0 & 0 \\ 0 & y & 0 \\ 0 & 0 & z \end{bmatrix}$

24. Let $\mathbf{A} = \begin{bmatrix} a & b \\ c & d \end{bmatrix}$.

a. Show that $\mathbf{A}^{-1} = \dfrac{1}{\begin{vmatrix} a & b \\ c & d \end{vmatrix}} \begin{bmatrix} d & -b \\ -c & a \end{bmatrix}$.

b. Use this formula to find $\mathbf{A}^{-1}$ if $\mathbf{A} = \begin{bmatrix} 5 & 3 \\ 6 & 4 \end{bmatrix}$.

20. $\begin{bmatrix} \frac{1}{x} \end{bmatrix}$
21. $\begin{bmatrix} \frac{1}{x} & 0 \\ 0 & \frac{1}{y} \end{bmatrix}$
22. $\begin{bmatrix} 0 & \frac{1}{y} \\ \frac{1}{x} & 0 \end{bmatrix}$
23. $\begin{bmatrix} \frac{1}{x} & 0 & 0 \\ 0 & \frac{1}{y} & 0 \\ 0 & 0 & \frac{1}{z} \end{bmatrix}$

$\begin{vmatrix} 5 & 3 \\ 6 & 4 \end{vmatrix} \begin{bmatrix} 4 & -3 \\ -6 & 5 \end{bmatrix} = \frac{1}{2}\begin{bmatrix} 4 & -3 \\ -6 & 5 \end{bmatrix} = \begin{bmatrix} 2 & -\frac{3}{2} \\ -3 & \frac{5}{2} \end{bmatrix}$

CAREERS/Stress Analysis

Stress analysts often use a computer to evaluate the ability of a structure to withstand stress.

Consider this problem: 5 beams of length L are pin-jointed to the surrounding structure. They are acted upon by a force P at the center.

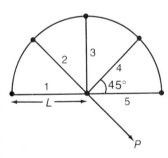

Stress analysts need to know the maximum allowable pull, P, the beams can take before they collapse or fail. The computer program first evaluates an element stiffness ma-

trix for each beam. For example: for beam 1 in the figure above, k_1, the beam's stiffness matrix, is given by the following, where

A = cross sectional area of beam

E = Young's modulus of elasticity

L = beam length

$$k_1 = \frac{AE}{L} \begin{bmatrix} 1 & 0 & -1 & 0 \\ 0 & 0 & 0 & 0 \\ -1 & 0 & 1 & 0 \\ 0 & 0 & 0 & 0 \end{bmatrix}$$

Similarly, for beam 4, k_4 is as follows.

$$k_4 = \frac{AE}{L} \begin{bmatrix} \frac{1}{2} & \frac{1}{2} & -\frac{1}{2} & -\frac{1}{2} \\ \frac{1}{2} & \frac{1}{2} & -\frac{1}{2} & -\frac{1}{2} \\ -\frac{1}{2} & -\frac{1}{2} & \frac{1}{2} & \frac{1}{2} \\ -\frac{1}{2} & -\frac{1}{2} & \frac{1}{2} & \frac{1}{2} \end{bmatrix}$$

The next step in the programming is the formation of a 4×1 deflection matrix U.

$$U = \begin{bmatrix} U_1 \\ U_2 \\ U_3 \\ U_4 \end{bmatrix}$$

F_H and F_V are the horizontal and vertical forces on beam 1.

To find the force terms, k is multiplied by U.

$$F_1 = \frac{AE}{L} \begin{bmatrix} 1 & 0 & -1 & 0 \\ 0 & 0 & 0 & 0 \\ -1 & 0 & 1 & 0 \\ 0 & 0 & 0 & 0 \end{bmatrix} \begin{bmatrix} U_1 \\ U_2 \\ U_3 \\ U_4 \end{bmatrix}$$

$$= \begin{bmatrix} F_H \\ F_V \\ F_H \\ F_V \end{bmatrix} = \begin{bmatrix} \frac{AE}{L}(U_1 - U_3) \\ 0 \\ \frac{AE}{L}(-U_1 + U_3) \\ 0 \end{bmatrix}$$

Exercises

1. Determine the beam stiffness matrix for beam 1 given $A = 100 \text{ cm}^2$, $E = 2.1 \times 10^6 \text{ kg/cm}^2$ and $L = 210 \text{ cm}$.

2. Determine the beam stiffness matrix for beam 4 given $A = 100 \text{ cm}^2$, $E = 2.1 \times 10^6 \text{ kg/cm}^2$ and $L = 210 \text{ cm}$.

3. For beam 1, the structural member is a 2 cm diameter aluminim rod 210 cm long. Determine the beam stiffness matrix given $E = 0.7 \times 10^6 \text{ kg/cm}^2$.

4. The deflection matrix in Exercise 1 is

$$U_1 = \begin{bmatrix} 0.01 \\ 0.01 \\ -0.01 \\ -0.01 \end{bmatrix}.$$

Determine the horizontal and vertical forces F_H and F_V for beam 1.

CHAPTER 14 Review

Review the material in the chapter. Then see how you have done by
trying these review exercises. If you miss an exercise, restudy the
indicated lesson.

1. $\begin{bmatrix} 1 & 6 & 1 \\ 1 & 2 & 1 \\ -2 & 3 & 1 \end{bmatrix}$ 2. $\begin{bmatrix} 2 & 1 & 1 \\ -1 & 4 & -1 \\ 2 & -2 & 3 \end{bmatrix}$ 3. $\begin{bmatrix} 1 & 2 & -1 \\ 2 & 0 & 1 \\ -2 & 1 & 0 \end{bmatrix}$

14–1 Let $A = \begin{bmatrix} 1 & 2 & -1 \\ 2 & 0 & 1 \\ -2 & 1 & 0 \end{bmatrix}$, $B = \begin{bmatrix} 0 & 4 & 2 \\ -1 & 2 & 0 \\ 0 & 2 & 1 \end{bmatrix}$, and $0 = \begin{bmatrix} 0 & 0 & 0 \\ 0 & 0 & 0 \\ 0 & 0 & 0 \end{bmatrix}$.

1. Find $A + B$. **2.** Find $A - B$, **3.** Find $A + 0$.

14–2 Find each product.

4. $3B$ **5.** $-2A$ **6.** AB

4. $\begin{bmatrix} 0 & 12 & 6 \\ -3 & 6 & 0 \\ 0 & 6 & 3 \end{bmatrix}$ 5. $\begin{bmatrix} -2 & -4 & 2 \\ -4 & 0 & -2 \\ 4 & -2 & 0 \end{bmatrix}$ 6. $\begin{bmatrix} -2 & 6 & 1 \\ 0 & 10 & 5 \\ -1 & -6 & -4 \end{bmatrix}$

14–2 Write a matrix equation equivalent to this system of equations.

7. $\begin{aligned} 5x + 2y - 4z &= 0 \\ -3x - 4y - 2z &= 6 \\ 6x + 7y + 5z &= 15 \end{aligned}$ **8.** $\begin{aligned} -x + 4y + 9z &= 10 \\ -9x + 5y - 6z &= 5 \\ 5x + 8y - 2z &= 7 \end{aligned}$

7. $\begin{bmatrix} 5 & 2 & -4 \\ -3 & -4 & -2 \\ 6 & 7 & 5 \end{bmatrix} \begin{bmatrix} x \\ y \\ x \end{bmatrix} = \begin{bmatrix} 0 \\ 6 \\ 15 \end{bmatrix}$

8. $\begin{bmatrix} -1 & 4 & 9 \\ -9 & 5 & -6 \\ 5 & 8 & -2 \end{bmatrix} \begin{bmatrix} x \\ y \\ z \end{bmatrix} = \begin{bmatrix} 10 \\ 5 \\ 7 \end{bmatrix}$

14–3 Find A^{-1}.

9. $\begin{bmatrix} 2 & 3 \\ 1 & 2 \end{bmatrix}$ **10.** $\begin{bmatrix} 1 & 0 & 1 \\ 0 & 1 & -1 \\ 2 & -1 & 1 \end{bmatrix}$

9. $\begin{bmatrix} 2 & -3 \\ -1 & 2 \end{bmatrix}$ 10. $\begin{bmatrix} 0 & \frac{1}{2} & \frac{1}{2} \\ 1 & \frac{1}{2} & -\frac{1}{2} \\ 1 & -\frac{1}{2} & -\frac{1}{2} \end{bmatrix}$

14–3

11. Solve the system using an inverse matrix.

$\begin{aligned} 2x + 3y &= 6 \\ x + 2y &= 2 \end{aligned}$ $(6, -2)$

CHAPTER 14 Test

Let $A = \begin{bmatrix} 2 & 3 & -4 \\ 6 & -5 & 2 \\ 1 & -2 & -3 \end{bmatrix}$, $B = \begin{bmatrix} -4 & 2 & 5 \\ -5 & 6 & -3 \\ 2 & 5 & 4 \end{bmatrix}$, and $0 = \begin{bmatrix} 0 & 0 & 0 \\ 0 & 0 & 0 \\ 0 & 0 & 0 \end{bmatrix}$.

1. $\begin{bmatrix} 2 & 3 & -4 \\ 6 & -5 & 2 \\ 1 & -2 & -3 \end{bmatrix}$

1. Find $A + 0$. **2.** Find $A + B$. **3.** Find $A - B$.

2. $\begin{bmatrix} -2 & 5 & 1 \\ 1 & 1 & -1 \\ 3 & 3 & 1 \end{bmatrix}$

4. Find $2A$. **5.** Find $-3B$. **6.** Find AB.

3. $\begin{bmatrix} 6 & 1 & -9 \\ 11 & -11 & 5 \\ -1 & -7 & -7 \end{bmatrix}$

7. Write a matrix equation equivalent to this system of equations.

$$\begin{aligned} x + y - 2z &= 3 \\ 2x - y + z &= 5 \\ 5x + 4y - 3z &= -8 \end{aligned}$$

7. $\begin{bmatrix} 1 & 1 & -2 \\ 2 & -1 & 1 \\ 5 & 4 & -3 \end{bmatrix} \begin{bmatrix} x \\ y \\ z \end{bmatrix} = \begin{bmatrix} 3 \\ 5 \\ -8 \end{bmatrix}$ 9. $\begin{bmatrix} \frac{1}{x} & 0 \\ 0 & \frac{1}{2y} \end{bmatrix}$

8. Solve the system using an inverse matrix.

$$\begin{aligned} 2x + 3y &= -5 \quad (-4, 1) \\ 3x + 5y &= -7 \end{aligned}$$

Challenge

9. If $A = \begin{bmatrix} x & 0 \\ 0 & 2y \end{bmatrix}$, find a formula for A^{-1}.

CHAPTERS 1–14 Cumulative Review

1–3, 1–7 Simplify.

1. $-(x - y) + (x - y)$ 0
2. $2x + [4 - 3(4x - 5)]$ $-10x + 19$
3. $12x - [9 - 7(5x - 6)]$ $47x - 51$

4. $\dfrac{9y^2}{(-3y)^2}$ 1
5. $\dfrac{24x^5y^3}{-8x^4y}$ $-3xy^2$
6. $\dfrac{1.08 \times 10^{12}}{9.0 \times 10^{-8}}$ 1.2×10^{20}

2–3 Solve.

7. Framing material 2 inches wide is being used to frame a painting 42 inches by 25 inches. What is the outside perimeter of the finished work? 150 inches

2–5 Solve. 8. $a < \frac{20}{17}$ 9. $2 < y \le 4$

8. $10a - 4 \le 16 - 7a$
9. $2 < 5y - 8 \le 12$
10. $\left| \dfrac{3m - 2}{5} \right| \ge 1$ $x \le -1 \text{ or } x \ge \frac{7}{3}$

3–4, 3–5 Solve.

11. Write the equation in standard form for a line perpendicular to the line $y = -\frac{1}{3}x + 2$, and which passes through $(2, 5)$. $x - 3y + 13 = 0$
12. What is the slope of the line perpendicular to the line through $(6, 0)$ and $(-1, -1)$? 7

4–1 Solve. 13. $(4, -1)$ 14. $(-3, -15)$ 15. $(-21, -21)$

13. $\begin{aligned} 3x - y &= -7 \\ 5y + 6x &= 14 \end{aligned}$
14. $\begin{aligned} 3a - 6 &= b \\ 9a - 2b &= 3 \end{aligned}$
15. $\begin{aligned} \tfrac{1}{7}x - \tfrac{1}{3}y &= -10 \\ \tfrac{2}{3}x + \tfrac{1}{7}y &= -11 \end{aligned}$

4–5   Graph the following inequalities.

16. $x \geq 5$ **17.** $x \geq 0$ **18.** $x \geq 0$
   $y \leq -1$ $y \geq 0$ $y \leq x$
   $y > \frac{1}{2}x$ $x + y = 5$ $x + y = 6$

5–2   Simplify.

19. $(a + 8b)(2a - 7b)$ **20.** $-9x(-x^3 - x - 4)$ **21.** $(y + 2)(y^2 + 5y + 10)$
   $2a^2 + 9ab - 56b^2$ $9x^4 + 9x^2 + 36x$ $y^3 + 7y^2 + 20y + 20$

5–3 to 5–5   Factor.

22. $y^3 - y^2 + 3y - 3$ **23.** $\frac{1}{25} - m^2$ **24.** $(a + 3)^2 - 16$
   $(y^2 + 3)(y - 1)$ $\left(\frac{1}{5} + m\right)\left(\frac{1}{5} - m\right)$ $(a + 7)(a - 1)$

6–3 to 6–5   Simplify.

25. $\dfrac{a^2 - b^2}{a^3 - b^3} \cdot \dfrac{a^2 + ab + b^2}{a^2 + 2ab + b^2}$ $\frac{1}{a+b}$ **26.** $\dfrac{x - 1}{x - 2} - \dfrac{x + 1}{x + 2} + \dfrac{x - 6}{x^2 - 4}$ $\frac{3}{x+2}$ **27.** $(a^8 - 1) \div (a^2 + 1)$
   $a^6 - a^4 + a^2 - 1$

7–4   Simplify.

28. $8\sqrt{45} - 7\sqrt{20}$ **29.** $(2 + \sqrt{10})(3 - \sqrt{10})$ **30.** $\dfrac{a}{\sqrt{3} + 1}$ **31.** $(5^2 \cdot 2^3)^{\frac{1}{6}}$
   $10\sqrt{5}$ $-4 + \sqrt{10}$ $\frac{a}{2}(\sqrt{3} - 1)$ $5^3 2^{\frac{1}{2}}$

7–6   Solve.

32. $2\sqrt{x - 1} = \sqrt{3x - 1}$ $_3$ **33.** $\sqrt{a + 9} = 3 + \sqrt{a - 6}$ $_7$

7–7   Simplify.

34. $\sqrt{-4}\sqrt{-5}$ **35.** $(4 + 2i) - (5 - 3i)$ **36.** $\sqrt{-2} \cdot 3i$
   $2i\sqrt{5}$ $9 - i$ $-3\sqrt{2}$

8–1, 8–3, 8–6   Solve.

37. $x^2 + 37 = 2x$ **38.** $4x^3 - 7x^2 = 0$ 39. $(1 - 6i)(1 + 6i)$ 40. $0, \frac{7}{4}$

39. Write a quadratic equation in standard form whose solutions
   are $\frac{2}{3} + i$ and $\frac{2}{3} - i$. $9x^2 - 12x + 13 = 0$

40. Write an equation of variation where M varies as the square of
   $(k + h)$ and $m = 12$ when $k = -1$ and $h = 5$. $m = 3(k + h)$

9–3   Suppose the points $(1, 3)$ and $(6, 0)$ are on the graph of
   $y = f(x)$. Name two points on each of the following graphs.

   41. $\left(1, \frac{3}{2}\right)$, $(6, 0)$

41. $y = \frac{1}{2}f(x)$ **42.** $y = f(x - 2)$ **43.** $y = -f(2x)$ 42. $(3, 3)$, $(8, 0)$

   43. $\left(\frac{1}{2}, -3\right)$, $(3, 0)$

10–2 to 10–5   Solve.

44. Find an equation of a circle with center at $(-2, 7)$ and radius $\sqrt{5}$.
   $(x + 2)^2 + (y - 7)^2 = 5$

45. Find the vertices and foci for the ellipse $16x^2 + 9y^2 = 122$.

vertices: $(-3, 0), (3, 0), (0, 4), (0, -4)$ foci: $(0, \sqrt{7}), (0, -\sqrt{7})$

46. Find the focus of the parabola $y^2 + 4x = 0$. $(-1, 0)$

11–1 to 11–4   Solve.

47. Use synthetic division to find $P(-3)$ where $P(x) = x^3 + 7x^2 - 12x - 3$. 69

48. Find a polynomial of degree 4 with 0 as a root of multiplicity 2, and 5 as a root of multiplicity 2. $x^4 - 10x^3 + 25x^2$

49. Find a polynomial of lowest degree with rational coefficients that has $3 + \sqrt{2}$ and $2 - i$ as roots. $x^4 - 10x^3 + 36x^2 - 58x + 35$

12–1   In each of the following, find equations for $f^{-1}(x)$.

50. $f(x) = 3x - 4$ **51.** $f(x) = \sqrt{x + 1}$

12–3   Solve.

52. $\log_x 64 = 6$ 2   **53.** $\log_3 x = 4$ 81   **54.** $\log_{16} x = \dfrac{1}{4}$ 2

12–3   Find.

55. $\log_{10} 0.01$ -2 **56.** $\log_3 27$ 3   **57.** $6^{\log_6 10}$ 10

12–4   Express as a single logarithm and simplify if possible.

58. $\log_a x^3 + 4\log_a \sqrt{x}$ **59.** $\log_a(x^2 - 1) - \log_a(x + 1)$

$\log_a x^5$ $\log_a x - 1$

12–7   Solve.

60. $3^{2x-5} = 27$ 4   **61.** $\log_3(x + 2) + \log_3(x - 2) = 2$ $\pm 2\sqrt{3}$

13–1   The nth term of a sequence is given. Find the first four terms, the 10th term, and the 15th term.

62. $a_n = \dfrac{1}{3n - 1}$ **63.** $a_n = (-1)^n 2^n$

64. Write sigma notation for $-1, 8, -27, 64, -125, \ldots$ $\displaystyle\sum_{k=1}^{5}(-1)^n n^3$

13–2 to 13–4   Solve.

65. Find the 12th term of the arithmetic sequence $\dfrac{3}{4}, \dfrac{1}{4}, -\dfrac{1}{4}, -\dfrac{3}{4}, -\dfrac{5}{4}, -\dfrac{7}{4}, \ldots$ $-\dfrac{19}{4}$

66. Find the sum of the series $\displaystyle\sum_{k=1}^{9} 2(k - 3)$. 36

67. Find the 7th term of the geometric sequence $3, 3\sqrt{2}, 6, \ldots$ 24

68. Find the sum of the geometric series $\sum_{k=1}^{5} \left[\frac{1}{4}\right]^{k-1}$. $\frac{341}{256}$

69. Find the sum of the infinite geometric series $8 - 2 + 0.5 - \dots$. 6.4

$13-5$ to $13-8$ Evaluate.

70. $_7P_7$ 5040 **71.** $4!$ 24 **72.** $_8P_3$ 336 **73.** $_8C_3$ 56 **74.** $\binom{9}{5}$ 126

75. Find the fourth term of $(b - y)^5$. $-10b^2y^3$

$14-1$ Let $A = \begin{bmatrix} 2 & 0 & -1 \\ 1 & 3 & 0 \\ -1 & 1 & 2 \end{bmatrix}$ and $B = \begin{bmatrix} 4 & 1 & -1 \\ 0 & 2 & 1 \\ 3 & -1 & -2 \end{bmatrix}$

76. $\begin{bmatrix} 2 & 1 & 0 \\ -1 & -1 & 1 \\ 4 & -2 & -4 \end{bmatrix}$

77. $\begin{bmatrix} -12 & -3 & 3 \\ 0 & -6 & -3 \\ -9 & 3 & 6 \end{bmatrix}$

76. Find $B - A$.   **77.** Find $-3B$.   **78.** Find AB.

78. $\begin{bmatrix} 5 & 3 & 0 \\ 4 & 7 & 2 \\ 2 & -1 & -2 \end{bmatrix}$

Ready for Trigonometric Functions?

$3-3$

1. Given $f(x) = 2x^2 + 1$, find $f(3)$ and $f(-2)$. 19, 9

2. Show that $f(x) = x^3 - x$ is odd. $f(-x) = (-x)^3 - (-x) = -x^3 + x = -(x^3 - x) = -f(x)$

3. Show that $g(x) = 2x^2 - x^4$ is even. $g(-x) = 2(-x)^2 - (-x)^4 = 2x^2 - x^4 = g(x)$

$5-7$ Factor completely.

4. $24a^2 - 96b^2$ **5.** $3x^3y - 15x^2y^2 + 18xy^3$
$24(a - 2b)(a + 2b)$ $3xy(x - 3y)(x - 2y)$

$5-2, 6-1, 6-3$ Simplify.

6. $(3t + 2)(t - 4)$ $3t^2 - 10t - 8$

7. $\frac{(a^2 - 4)}{-2a - 6} \cdot \frac{a + 3}{a - 2}$ $\frac{a + 2}{2}$

8. $\frac{4}{-x} + \frac{6}{x}$ $\frac{2}{x}$ **9.** $\frac{5cd}{4c^2 - 1} - \frac{c - d}{2c + 1}$ $\frac{-2c^2 + 7dc + c - d}{(2c - 1)(2c + 1)}$

$8-1, 8-2$ Solve.

10. $a^2 + a - 12 = 0$ **11.** $6y^2 + 20y = 16$ 10. $3, -4$ 11. $\frac{2}{3}, -4$

12. $1 + \frac{3}{x^2} = \frac{1}{x}$ **13.** $2x + x(x - 1) = 1$ 12. $\frac{1 \pm i\sqrt{11}}{2}$ 13. $\frac{-1 \pm \sqrt{5}}{2}$

15

CHAPTER FIFTEEN

Trigonometric Functions

15–1 Trigonometric Functions in Triangles

We now consider an important class of functions known as the trigonometric functions. They are based on certain properties of right triangles.

Trigonometric Ratios

In a right triangle the side opposite the right angle is called the hypotenuse. In the right triangle shown, a is the side *opposite* θ, and b is the side *adjacent* to θ. The ratio $\frac{a}{c}$ of the side opposite θ to the hypotenuse depends on the size of θ. In other words, this ratio is a function of θ. This function is called the sine function. There are six such ratios, or functions. Three of them, the sine, cosine, and tangent functions, are defined as follows.

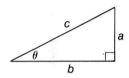

DEFINITION

sine function: $\quad \sin \theta = \dfrac{\text{side opposite } \theta}{\text{hypotenuse}}$

cosine function: $\quad \cos \theta = \dfrac{\text{side adjacent to } \theta}{\text{hypotenuse}}$

tangent function: $\tan \theta = \dfrac{\text{side opposite } \theta}{\text{side adjacent to } \theta}$

Because all right triangles with an angle of measure θ are similar, function values depend only on the size of the angle, not the size of the triangle.

EXAMPLE 1

In this triangle find $\sin \theta$, $\cos \theta$, and $\tan \theta$.

$$\sin \theta = \frac{\text{side opposite } \theta}{\text{hypotenuse}} = \frac{3}{5}$$

$$\cos \theta = \frac{\text{side adjacent to } \theta}{\text{hypotenuse}} = \frac{4}{5}$$

$$\tan \theta = \frac{\text{side opposite } \theta}{\text{side adjacent to } \theta} = \frac{3}{4}$$

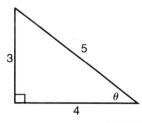

TRY THIS

1. In this triangle find sin θ, cos θ, and tan θ.

Special Angles

Our knowledge of triangles enables us to determine trigonometric function values for certain angles. First recall the Pythagorean Theorem. It says that in any right triangle $a^2 + b^2 = c^2$, where c is the length of the hypotenuse.

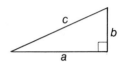

In a 45° right triangle the legs are the same length. Let us consider such a triangle whose legs have length 1. Then its hypotenuse has length c.

$$1^2 + 1^2 = c^2, \text{ or } c^2 = 2, \text{ or } c = \sqrt{2}$$

Such a triangle is shown below. From this diagram we can easily determine the trigonometric function values for 45°. These function values should be memorized.

$$\sin 45° = \frac{1}{\sqrt{2}} = \frac{\sqrt{2}}{2}$$

$$\cos 45° = \frac{1}{\sqrt{2}} = \frac{\sqrt{2}}{2}$$

$$\tan 45° = \frac{1}{1} = 1$$

Next we consider an equilateral triangle with sides of length 2. If we bisect one angle, we obtain a right triangle that has a hypotenuse of length 2 and a leg of length 1. The other leg has length a, given by the Pythagorean Theorem as follows.

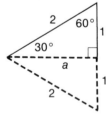

$$a^2 + 1^2 = 2^2, \text{ or } a^2 = 3, \text{ or } a = \sqrt{3}$$

The acute angles of this triangle have measures of 30° and 60°. We can now determine function values for 30° and 60°. These function values should be memorized.

$$\sin 30° = \frac{1}{2} \qquad \sin 60° = \frac{\sqrt{3}}{2}$$

$$\cos 30° = \frac{\sqrt{3}}{2} \qquad \cos 60° = \frac{1}{2}$$

$$\tan 30° = \frac{1}{\sqrt{3}} = \frac{\sqrt{3}}{3} \qquad \tan 60° = \sqrt{3}$$

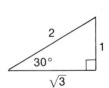

We can use what we have learned about trigonometry to solve problems.

EXAMPLE 2

In $\triangle ABC$, $b = 40$ cm and $m\angle A = 60°$. What is the length of side c?

$$\cos A = \frac{b}{c}$$

$$\cos 60° = \frac{40}{c} \quad \text{Substituting}$$

$$\frac{1}{2} = \frac{40}{c} \quad \text{Using } \cos 60° = \frac{1}{2}$$

$$c = 80 \text{ cm}$$

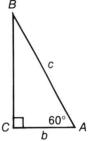

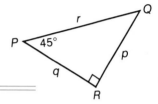

TRY THIS

2. In $\triangle PQR$, $q = 12$ ft. Use the cosine function to find the length of side r. $r = 12\sqrt{2}$

Reciprocal Functions

We define the three other trigonometric functions by taking the reciprocals of the sine, cosine, and tangent functions.

DEFINITION

The *cotangent, secant,* and *cosecant* functions are the respective reciprocals of the tangent, cosine, and sine functions.

$$\cot \theta = \frac{1}{\tan \theta} = \frac{\text{side adjacent to } \theta}{\text{side opposite } \theta}$$

$$\sec \theta = \frac{1}{\cos \theta} = \frac{\text{hypotenuse}}{\text{side adjacent to } \theta}$$

$$\csc \theta = \frac{1}{\sin \theta} = \frac{\text{hypotenuse}}{\text{side opposite } \theta}$$

EXAMPLE 3

Find the cotangent, secant, and cosecant of the angle shown; approximate to two decimal places.

$$\cot \theta = \frac{\text{side adjacent to } \theta}{\text{side opposite } \theta} = \frac{3}{4} = 0.75$$

$$\sec \theta = \frac{\text{hypotenuse}}{\text{side adjacent to } \theta} = \frac{5}{3} \approx 1.67$$

$$\csc \theta = \frac{\text{hypotenuse}}{\text{side opposite } \theta} = \frac{5}{4} = 1.25$$

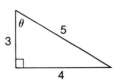

TRY THIS

3. Find cot θ, sec θ, and csc θ for the angle shown in this triangle. Find decimal values approximate to two decimal places.

cot $\theta \approx 1.33$, sec $\theta = 1.25$, csc $\theta \approx 1.67$

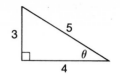

By using the Pythagorean Theorem, we can find all six trigonometric function values of θ when one of the ratios is known.

EXAMPLE 4

If $\sin \theta = \frac{12}{13}$, find the other five trigonometric function values of θ.

We know from the definition of the sine function that the ratio

$$\frac{\text{side opposite } \theta}{\text{hypotenuse}} \text{ is } \frac{12}{13}.$$

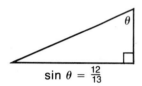

$$\sin \theta = \frac{12}{13}$$

Let us consider a similar right triangle in which the hypotenuse has length 13 and the side opposite θ has length 12. To find the length of the side adjacent to θ, we use the Pythagorean Theorem.

$$a^2 + 12^2 = 13^2$$
$$a^2 = 169 - 144 = 25$$
$$a = 5 \quad \text{Choosing the positive square root since we are finding length}$$

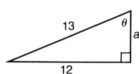

We can use $a = 5$, $b = 12$, and $c = 13$ to find five of the ratios in our original triangle.

$$\sin \theta = \frac{12}{13} \qquad \csc \theta = \frac{13}{12}$$

$$\cos \theta = \frac{5}{13} \qquad \sec \theta = \frac{13}{5}$$

$$\tan \theta = \frac{12}{5} \qquad \cot \theta = \frac{5}{12}$$

TRY THIS

4. If $\cos \theta = \frac{8}{17}$, find the other five trigonometric function values for θ.

$\sin \theta = \frac{15}{17}$, tan $\theta = \frac{15}{8}$, csc $\theta = \frac{17}{15}$, sec $\theta = \frac{17}{8}$, cot $\theta = \frac{8}{15}$

Exercises

Find the indicated trigonometric function values for θ in each of the following triangles. Use fractional notation.

1. Find $\sin \theta$, $\cos \theta$, and $\tan \theta$.

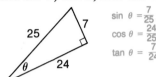

$\sin \theta = \frac{7}{25}$

$\cos \theta = \frac{24}{25}$

$\tan \theta = \frac{7}{24}$

2. Find $\sin \theta$, $\cos \theta$, and $\tan \theta$.

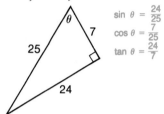

$\sin \theta = \frac{24}{25}$

$\cos \theta = \frac{7}{25}$

$\tan \theta = \frac{24}{7}$

3. Find $\sin \theta$, $\cos \theta$, and $\tan \theta$.

$\sin \theta = \frac{8}{17}$

$\cos \theta = \frac{15}{17}$

$\tan \theta = \frac{8}{15}$

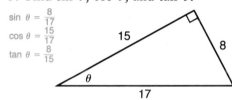

4. Find $\sin \theta$, $\cos \theta$, and $\tan \theta$.

$\sin \theta = \frac{15}{17}$

$\cos \theta = \frac{8}{17}$

$\tan \theta = \frac{15}{8}$

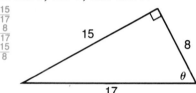

Find the length of each labeled side.

5. $a = 3$

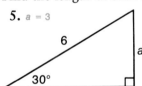

6.

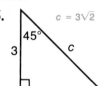

$c = 3\sqrt{2}$

7.

$b = 9\sqrt{3}$

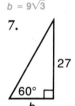

8.

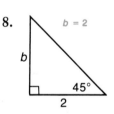

$b = 2$

For Exercises 9–12, use decimal notation.

9. Find $\cot \theta$, $\sec \theta$, $\csc \theta$ for the triangle in Exercise 1. 3.43 1.04 3.57

10. Find $\cot \theta$, $\sec \theta$, $\csc \theta$ for the triangle in Exercise 2. 0.29 3.57 1.04

11. Find $\cot \theta$, $\sec \theta$, $\csc \theta$ for the triangle in Exercise 3. 1.88 1.13 2.13

12. Find $\cot \theta$, $\sec \theta$, $\csc \theta$ for the triangle in Exercise 4. 0.53 2.13 1.13

For Exercises 13–16, do not convert values to decimal notation.

13. If $\tan \theta = \frac{\sqrt{3}}{1}$, find the other five trigonometric function values for θ.

14. If $\cos \theta = \frac{\sqrt{2}}{2}$, find the other five trigonometric function values for θ.

15. If $\sin \theta = \frac{1}{2}$, find the other five trigonometric function values for θ.

16. If $\sec \theta = 2$, find the other five trigonometric function values for θ.

Extension

Find the six trigonometric function values for each of the following angles. Do not convert the values to decimal notation.

17. 30°   **18.** 60°   **19.** 45°

19. $\sin \theta = \dfrac{\sqrt{2}}{2}$

$\cos \theta = \dfrac{\sqrt{2}}{2}$

$\tan \theta = 1$

$\cot \theta = 1$

$\sec \theta = \sqrt{2}$

$\csc \theta = \sqrt{2}$

Challenge

20. A guy wire is attached to a pole, and makes an angle of 60° with the ground. Find:

a. the distance b from A to the pole; $\frac{28\sqrt{3}}{3}$ ft

b. the length of the wire. $\frac{56\sqrt{3}}{3}$ ft

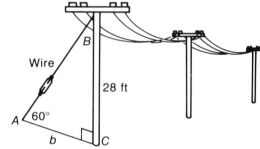

21. A 16 ft ladder is placed against a house so that its base is 8 ft from the house. What angle does the ladder make with the ground? 60°

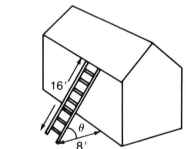

22. An observer stands 120 meters from a tree, and finds that the line of sight to the top of the tree is 30° above the horizontal. Find the height of the tree above eye level. $40\sqrt{3}$ m

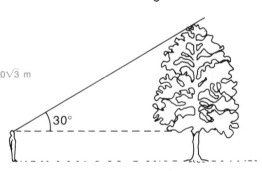

23. Find a. (Hint: Recall from geometry that the altitude of an isosceles triangle from the vertex angle bisects the base and the vertex angle.) $5\sqrt{3}$

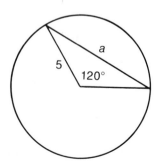

More On Trigonometric Functions

Consider a rotating ray, with its endpoint at the origin of an xy-plane. The ray starts in position along the positive half of the x-axis. Counterclockwise rotations will be called positive. Clockwise rotations will be called negative.

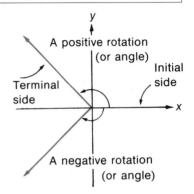

Note that the rotating ray and the positive half of the x-axis form an angle. Thus we often speak of "rotations" and "angles" interchangeably. The rotating ray is often called the terminal side of the angle, and the positive half of the x-axis is called the initial side.

Measures of Rotations or Angles

The measure of an angle, or rotation, may be given in degrees. For example, a complete revolution has a measure of 360°, half a revolution has a measure of 180°, a triple revolution has a measure of $360° \cdot 3$ or 1080°, and so on. We also speak of angles of 90°, or 720°, or $-240°$.

An angle between 0° and 90° has its terminal side in the first quadrant. An angle between 90° and 180° has its terminal side in the second quadrant. An angle between 0° and $-90°$ has its terminal side in the fourth quadrant, and so on.

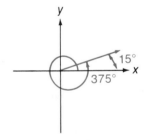

When the measure of an angle is greater than 360°, the rotating ray has gone through at least one complete revolution. For example, an angle of 375° will have the same terminal side as an angle of 15°. Thus, the terminal side will be in the first quadrant.

EXAMPLES
In which quadrant does the terminal side of each angle lie?

1. 53°	First quadrant		**2.** 253°	Third quadrant
3. $-126°$	Third quadrant		**4.** $-373°$	Fourth quadrant
5. 460°	Second quadrant			

TRY THIS
In which quadrant does the terminal side of each angle lie?

1. 47°   **2.** 212°   **3.** $-43°$

4. $-135°$ **5.** 365°   **6.** 740°

1. First
2. Third
3. Fourth
4. Third
5. First
6. First

Trigonometric Functions of Rotations

In the preceding discussion of trigonometric functions we worked with right triangles, so the angle θ was always less than 90°. We can use rotations to apply trigonometric functions to angles of any measure.

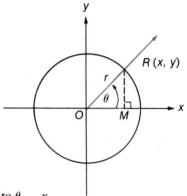

Consider a right triangle with one vertex at the origin of a coordinate system and one vertex on the positive x-axis. The other vertex is at R, a point of the circle whose center is at the origin and whose radius, r, is equal to the hypotenuse of the triangle.

Note that three of the trigonometric functions of θ are defined as follows.

$$\sin \theta = \frac{\text{side opposite } \theta}{\text{hypotenuse}} = \frac{y}{r} \qquad \cos \theta = \frac{\text{side adjacent to } \theta}{\text{hypotenuse}} = \frac{x}{r}$$

$$\tan \theta = \frac{\text{side opposite } \theta}{\text{side adjacent to } \theta} = \frac{y}{x}$$

Since x and y are coordinates of the point R, we could also define these functions as follows.

$$\sin \theta = \frac{y\text{-coordinate}}{\text{radius}} \qquad \cos \theta = \frac{x\text{-coordinate}}{\text{radius}}$$

$$\tan \theta = \frac{y\text{-coordinate}}{x\text{-coordinate}}$$

We will use these definitions for functions of angles of any measure. Note that while x and y may be either positive, negative, or 0, r is always positive.

EXAMPLE 6
Find $\sin \theta$, $\cos \theta$, and $\tan \theta$ for these angles.

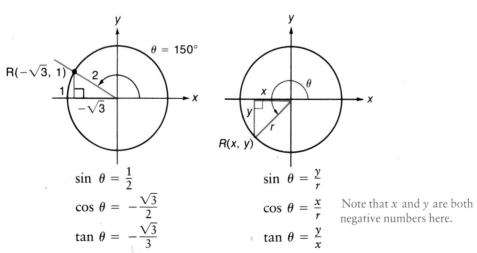

$$\sin \theta = \frac{1}{2} \qquad\qquad \sin \theta = \frac{y}{r}$$

$$\cos \theta = -\frac{\sqrt{3}}{2} \qquad\qquad \cos \theta = \frac{x}{r} \quad \text{Note that } x \text{ and } y \text{ are both negative numbers here.}$$

$$\tan \theta = -\frac{\sqrt{3}}{3} \qquad\qquad \tan \theta = \frac{y}{x}$$

TRY THIS

7. Find $\sin \theta$, $\cos \theta$, and $\tan \theta$ for the angle θ shown.

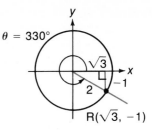

7. $\sin \theta = -\frac{1}{2}$
$\cos \theta = \frac{\sqrt{3}}{2}$
$\tan \theta = -\frac{\sqrt{3}}{3}$

The cosecant, secant, and cotangent functions can also be defined in terms of x, y, and r.

$$\csc \theta = \frac{r}{y} \qquad \sec \theta = \frac{r}{x} \qquad \cot \theta = \frac{x}{y}$$

The values of the trigonometric functions can be positive, negative, or zero, depending on where the terminal side of the angle lies. The figure at the right shows which of the trigonometric function values are positive in each of the quadrants. These relationships should be memorized.

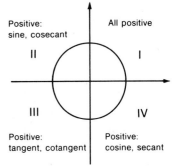

EXAMPLE 7

Give the sign of the six trigonometric function values for a rotation of 225°.

$180 < 225 < 270$, so R(x,y) is in the third quadrant.

The tangent and cotangent are positive and the other four function values are negative.

TRY THIS

8. Give the signs of the six trigonometric function values for a rotation of $-30°$.

8. Cosine and secant values are positive, the other four function values are negative.

Terminal Side on an Axis

If the terminal side of an angle falls on one of the axes, the definitions of the functions still apply, but in some cases functions will not be defined because a denominator will be 0. Notice the coordinates of the points for angles of 0°, 90°, 180°, and 270°. For example, the coordinates for an angle of 90° are $x = 0$ and $y = r$.

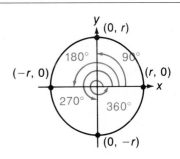

EXAMPLE 8

Find the sine, cosine, and tangent function values for $0°$ and $90°$.

$$\sin 0° = \frac{y}{r} = \frac{0}{r} = 0 \qquad \sin 90° = \frac{y}{r} = \frac{r}{r} = 1$$

$$\cos 0° = \frac{x}{r} = \frac{r}{r} = 1 \qquad \cos 90° = \frac{x}{r} = \frac{0}{r} = 0$$

$$\tan 0° = \frac{y}{x} = \frac{0}{r} = 0 \qquad \tan 90° = \frac{y}{x} = \frac{r}{0} \quad \text{undefined}$$

TRY THIS

9. Find the sine, cosine, and tangent function values for $180°$ and $270°$.

Reference Angles

We can now determine the trigonometric function values for angles in other quadrants by using the values of the functions for angles between $0°$ and $90°$. We do so by using a reference angle.

DEFINITION

The reference angle for a rotation is the acute angle formed by the terminal side and the x-axis.

EXAMPLES

Find the reference angle for θ.

9.

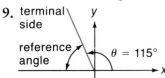

To find the measure of the acute angle formed by the terminal side and the x-axis we subtract the measure of θ from $180°$.

$$180 - 115 = 65$$

The reference angle is $65°$.

10.

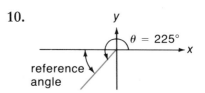

We are looking for the acute angle formed by the terminal side and the x-axis. We subtract $180°$ from $225°$ to get the reference angle.

$$225 - 180 = 45$$

The reference angle is $45°$.

634 CHAPTER 15 TRIGONOMETRIC FUNCTIONS

TRY THIS Find the reference angle for θ.

10. 30°

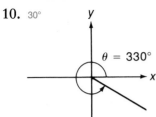

$\theta = 330°$

11. 30°

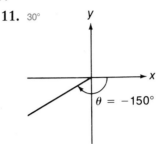

$\theta = -150°$

We now use the reference angle to determine trigonometric function values. Consider, for example, an angle of 150°. The terminal side makes a 30° angle with the x-axis, since $180 - 150 = 30$. As the diagram shows, triangle ONR is congruent to triangle $ON'R'$; hence the ratios of the sides of the two triangles are the same, although the ratios may have different signs.

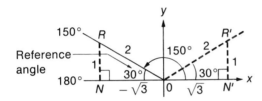

We could determine the function values directly from triangle ONR, but this is not necessary. If we remember that the sine is positive in quadrant II and that the cosine and tangent are negative, we can simply use the values for 30°, prefixing the appropriate sign. The triangle ONR is called a reference triangle. Its acute angle at the origin is called a reference angle

EXAMPLE 11
Find the sine, cosine, and tangent of 600°.
We find the multiple of 180 nearest 600.

$$180 \times 2 = 360$$
$$180 \times 3 = 540$$
$$180 \times 4 = 720$$

The nearest multiple is 540. The difference between 600 and 540 is 60. This gives us the reference angle of 60°. Because 600° is in the third quadrant, $\sin 600° = -\frac{\sqrt{3}}{2}$, $\cos 600° = -\frac{1}{2}$, $\tan 600° = \sqrt{3}$.

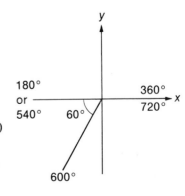

> In general, to find the function values of an angle, we find them for the reference angle and prefix the appropriate sign.

TRY THIS

12. Find the sine, cosine, and tangent of $-765°$.

12. Reference angle is 45°; $-765°$ is in fourth quadrant

$\sin -765° = -\dfrac{\sqrt{2}}{2}$, $\cos -765° = \dfrac{\sqrt{2}}{2}$, $\tan -765° = -1$

15–2

Exercises

For angles of the following measures, state the quadrant in which the terminal side lies.

1. $34°$ **2.** $320°$ **3.** $-120°$ **4.** $-175°$ **5.** $60°$ **6.** $-135°$

7. $495°$ **8.** $855°$ **9.** $160°$ **10.** $230°$ **11.** $-400°$ **12.** $-555°$

1. first
2. fourth
3. third
4. third
5. first
6. third
7. second
8. second
9. second
10. third
11. fourth
12. second

Find the sin, cos, and tan function values for the angle θ shown.

13.

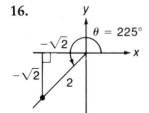

14.

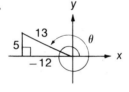

15.

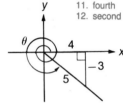

16.

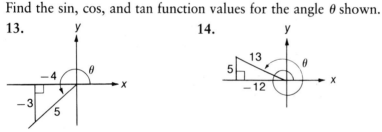

17.

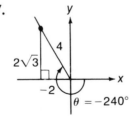

18.

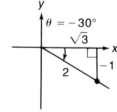

Give the sign of the six trigonometric function values for the following angles of rotation.

19. $57°$ **20.** $-57°$ **21.** $315°$ **22.** $-100°$ **23.** $760°$ **24.** $460°$

25. Construct a table as follows. For horizontal heads use θ, $\cot \theta$, $\sec \theta$, $\csc \theta$. Under θ, write 0, $90°$, $180°$, and $270°$. Fill in the table.

Find the reference angle for the following angles of rotation.

26. $405°$ 45° **27.** $210°$ 30° **28.** $-300°$ 60° **29.** $315°$ 45° **30.** $240°$ 60° **31.** $-225°$ 45°

Find each of the following or indicate if it is undefined.

32. $\cos 180°$ −1 **33.** $\sin 360°$ 0 **34.** $\tan 90°$ undefined **35.** $\cot 180°$ undefined

36. $\sec 720°$ 1 **37.** $\csc 720°$ undefined **38.** $\sin(-135°)$ $-\frac{\sqrt{2}}{2}$ **39.** $\cos 135°$ $-\frac{\sqrt{2}}{2}$

40. $\sin 150°$ $\frac{1}{2}$ **41.** $\cos 150°$ $-\frac{\sqrt{3}}{2}$ **42.** $\tan 240°$ $\sqrt{3}$ **43.** $\cot 240°$ $\frac{\sqrt{3}}{3}$

44. $\sec 315°$ $\sqrt{2}$ **45.** $\csc 315°$ $-\sqrt{2}$ **46.** $\tan(-315°)$ 1 **47.** $\cot(-315°)$ 1

48. $\sin(-210°)$ $\frac{1}{2}$ **49.** $\cos(-210°)$ $-\frac{\sqrt{3}}{2}$ **50.** $\tan 210°$ $\frac{\sqrt{3}}{3}$ **51.** $\cot 210°$ $\sqrt{3}$

52. $\sin 495°$ $\frac{\sqrt{2}}{2}$ **53.** $\cos 495°$ $\frac{\sqrt{2}}{2}$ **54.** $\tan 330°$ $-\frac{\sqrt{3}}{3}$ **55.** $\cot(-30°)$ $-\sqrt{3}$

Extension

Find decimal notation to three places for the six trigonometric functions of each of the following angles. Use the fact that $\sqrt{2} \approx 1.414$ and $\sqrt{3} \approx 1.732$.

56. $30°$ **57.** $60°$ **58.** $120°$ **59.** $225°$

Find the six trigonometric function values for the angle θ shown.

60.

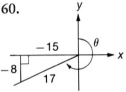

61.

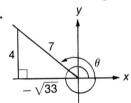

62.

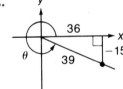

Given that $\tan \theta = \frac{2}{\sqrt{5}}$ and that the terminal side is in quadrant III, find the following.

63. $\sin \theta$ $-\frac{2}{3}$ **64.** $\cos \theta$ $-\frac{\sqrt{5}}{3}$ **65.** $\cot \theta$ $\frac{\sqrt{5}}{2}$ **66.** $\sec \theta$ $-\frac{3}{\sqrt{5}}$ **67.** $\csc \theta$ $-\frac{3}{2}$

Challenge

68. The valve cap on a bicycle wheel is 24.5 in. from the center of the wheel. From the position shown, the wheel starts rolling. After the wheel has turned $390°$, how far above the ground is the valve cap? Assume that the outer radius of the tire is 26 in. 38.25 in.

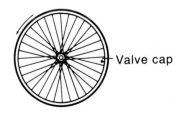

Valve cap

15–3 Radians, Cofunctions, and Tables

Radian Measure

So far we have measured angles using degrees. Another useful angle measure is a *radian*. Consider a circle of radius 1, a unit circle. Since the circumference of a circle is $2\pi r$, the unit circle has a circumference of 2π. A rotation of 360° (1 revolution) has a measure of 2π radians. Half of a revolution is a rotation of 180° or π radians. A quarter revolution is a rotation of 90°, or $\frac{\pi}{2}$ radians, and so on.

When the distance around the circle from the initial side to the terminal side equals 1, the measure of θ is called 1 radian. One radian is about 57°. To convert between degrees and radians we can use the notion of "multiplying by one."

$$\frac{1 \text{ revolution}}{1 \text{ revolution}} = 1 = \frac{2\pi \text{ radians}}{360 \text{ degrees}} = \frac{\pi \text{ radians}}{180 \text{ degrees}}$$

The following equation is also true.

$$\frac{180 \text{ degrees}}{\pi \text{ radians}} = 1$$

When a rotation is given in radians, the word "radians" is optional and often omitted. Thus if no unit is given for a rotation, it is understood to be in radians.

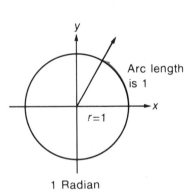

EXAMPLE 1
Convert 60° to radians.

$$60° = 60° \cdot \frac{\pi \text{ radians}}{180°} \quad \text{Multiplying by 1}$$

$$= \frac{60°}{180°} \pi \text{ radians}$$

$$= \frac{\pi}{3} \text{ radians, or } \frac{\pi}{3}$$

TRY THIS Convert to radian measure. Give answers in terms of π.
1. 225° $\frac{5}{4}\pi$ **2.** 300° $\frac{5}{3}\pi$ **3.** −315° $-\frac{7}{4}\pi$

---

638 CHAPTER 15 TRIGONOMETRIC FUNCTIONS

EXAMPLE 2

Convert $\frac{3\pi}{4}$ to degrees.

$$\frac{3\pi}{4} \text{ radians} = \frac{3\pi}{4} \text{ radians} \cdot \frac{180°}{\pi \text{ radians}} \quad \text{Multiplying by 1}$$

$$= \frac{3\pi}{4\pi} \cdot 180°$$

$$= 135°$$

TRY THIS Convert to degree measure.

4. $\frac{4\pi}{3}$ radians 240° **5.** $\frac{5\pi}{2}$ radians 450° **6.** $-\frac{4\pi}{5}$ radians −144°

The diagrams below show unit circles marked in both radians and degrees. These relationships should be memorized.

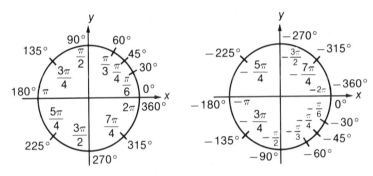

Cofunctions and Complements

In a right triangle the acute angles are complementary, since the sum of all three angle measures is $180°$ and the right angle accounts for $90°$ of this total. Thus if one acute angle of a right triangle is θ, the other is $90° - \theta$, or $\frac{\pi}{2} - \theta$. Note that the sine of $\angle A$ is also the cosine of $\angle B$, its complement.

$$\sin \theta = \frac{a}{c} \qquad \cos(90° - \theta) = \frac{a}{c}$$

Similarly, the tangent of $\angle A$ is the cotangent of its complement and the secant of $\angle A$ is the cosecant of its complement.

These pairs of functions are called *co*functions. The name *cosine* originally meant the sine of the complement. The name *cotangent* meant the tangent of the complement, and *cosecant* meant the secant of the complement. A complete list of the cofunction relations follows. Equations that hold for all sensible replacements for the variables are known as identities.

$$\sin \theta = \cos (90° - \theta) \qquad \cos \theta = \sin (90° - \theta)$$
$$\tan \theta = \cot (90° - \theta) \qquad \cot \theta = \tan (90° - \theta)$$
$$\sec \theta = \csc (90° - \theta) \qquad \csc \theta = \sec (90° - \theta)$$

EXAMPLES

Find the function values.

3. $\cot 60° = \tan (90° - 60°) = \tan 30° = \dfrac{\sqrt{3}}{3}$

4. $\csc 30° = \sec (90° - 30°) = \sec 60° = \dfrac{1}{\cos 60°} = \dfrac{1}{\frac{1}{2}} = 2$

TRY THIS Find the function values.

7. $\sec 60°$ 2 **8.** $\cot 30°$ $\sqrt{3}$ **9.** $\csc 45°$ $\sqrt{2}$

Using a Table

In Sections 15–1 and 15–2 you learned to find trigonometric function values for angles of 30°, 45°, and 60° as well as for any angle that has one of these for its reference angle. To find trigonometric function values for other angles we refer to tables, such as Table 3 at the back of the book. Study the table below.

Degrees	Radians	Sin	Cos	Tan	Cot	Sec	Csc		
43° 00'	0.7505	0.6820	0.7314	0.9325	1.072	1.367	1.466	0.8203	47° 00'
10	534	841	294	380	066	371	462	174	50
20	563	862	274	435	060	375	457	145	40
30	0.7592	0.6884	0.7254	0.9490	1.054	1.379	1.453	0.8116	30
40	621	905	234	545	048	382	448	087	20
50	650	926	214	601	042	386	444	058	10
44° 00'	0.7679	0.6947	0.7193	0.9657	1.036	1.390	1.440	0.8029	46° 00'
10	709	967	173	713	030	394	435	999	50
20	738	988	153	770	024	398	431	970	40
30	0.7767	0.7009	0.7133	0.9827	1.018	1.402	1.427	0.7941	30
40	796	030	112	884	012	406	423	912	20
50	825	050	092	942	006	410	418	883	10
45° 00'	0.7854	0.7071	0.7071	1.0000	1.000	1.414	1.414	0.7854	45° 00'
		Cos	Sin	Cot	Tan	Csc	Sec	Radians	Degrees

The headings on the left of Table 3 range from 0° to 45° only. For angles from 45° to 90° the headings on the right are used, together with the headings at the bottom, because these values are the same as the cofunction values of their complements. For example, sin 43° is found to be 0.6820 using the top and left headings. The cosine of 47° (the complement of 43°) is found also to be 0.6820 using the bottom and right headings.

EXAMPLE 5

Find cos 37°20′.

We find 37°20′ in the left column of Table 3 and then Cos at the top. At the intersection of this row and column we find the entry we seek.

$$\cos 37°20' = 0.7951$$

TRY THIS Use Table 3 to find the following.

10. sin 15°20′ 0.2644 **11.** cot 64°50′ 0.4699

Table 3 gives function values for angles from 0° to 90°. To find the function value for any other angle, we first find the reference angle, which is the angle the terminal side makes with the x-axis. We then look up the function values for the reference angle in the table and use the appropriate sign, depending on the quadrant in which the terminal side lies.

EXAMPLE 6

Find sin 285°40′.

To find sin 285°40′, we determine that the terminal side of the angle is in the fourth quadrant.

$$360° = 359°60'$$
$$\underline{- 285°40'}$$
$$74°20'$$

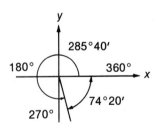

The reference angle is 74°20′.

We find sin 74°20′ = 0.9628. In quadrant IV the sine is negative, so sin 285°40′ = −0.9628.

TRY THIS

12. Find cos 410°20′. 0.6383

Interpolation

The process of linear interpolation can be applied to tables of any function. In particular, we can use it with tables of the trigonometric functions.

EXAMPLE 7

Find tan 27°43′.

$$
10' \left\{
\begin{array}{l}
3' \left[
\begin{array}{l}
\tan 27°40' = 0.5243 \\
\tan 27°43' = 0.52?? \\
\end{array}
\right. \\
\tan 27°50' = 0.5280
\end{array}
\right\} \quad \text{Tabular difference is } 0.0037.
$$

Because 43′ is $\frac{3}{10}$ of the way from 40′ to 50′, we take $\frac{3}{10}$ of 0.0037, the tabular difference. This is 0.0011.

$$\tan 27°43' = 0.5243 + 0.0011, \text{ or } 0.5254$$

To interpolate where a function is decreasing there is a slight difference as the next example shows.

EXAMPLE 8

Find cot 29°44′.

$$
10' \left\{
\begin{array}{l}
4' \left[
\begin{array}{l}
\cot 29°40' = 1.756 \\
\cot 29°44' = 1.7?? \\
\end{array}
\right. \\
\cot 29°50' = 1.744
\end{array}
\right\} \quad \text{Tabular difference is } 0.012.
$$

We take 0.4 of the tabular difference, 0.012, and obtain 0.0048, or 0.005. Because the cotangent function is decreasing for inputs between 0° and 90°, we subtract 0.005 from 1.756. Thus cot 29°44′ = 1.751.

TRY THIS Use Table 3 and interpolation to find the following.

13. sin 38°47′ 0.6264 **14.** cot 27°45′ 1.900

Once the process of interpolation is understood, it will not be necessary to write as much as we did in the examples above. After a bit of practice, you will find that interpolation is rather easy, and you can accomplish some of the steps without writing. Let us look at an example of using the tables in reverse, that is, given a function value, to find the measure of an angle.

EXAMPLE 9
Given $\tan B = 0.3727$, find $m \angle B$ (between $0°$ and $90°$).

$$
\left.
\begin{array}{c}
\tan 20°20' = 0.3706 \\
\tan B \;\;\;\;\; = 0.3727 \\
\tan 20°30' = 0.3739
\end{array}
\right\} \quad \text{Tabular difference is 0.0033.}
$$

with $10'$ bracket, and 0.0021 difference.

We find that B is $\frac{21}{33}$ or $\frac{7}{11}$ of the way from $20°20'$ to $20°30'$. The tabular difference is $10'$, so we take $\frac{7}{11}$ of $10'$ and obtain $6'$. Thus $m \angle B = 20°26'$.

TRY THIS
15. Given $\sin \theta = 0.3624$, find θ. 21°15'
16. Given $\cot \theta = 1.614$, find θ. 31°47'

15–3

Exercises

Convert to radian measure. Give answers in terms of π. Then give each answer using 3.14 for π.

1. $30°$
2. $15°$
3. $100°$
4. $200°$
5. $75°$
6. $105°$
7. $120°$
8. $240°$
9. $-320°$
10. $-250°$
11. $-85°$
12. $-175°$

1. $\frac{\pi}{6} \approx 0.52$
2. $\frac{\pi}{12} \approx 0.26$
3. $\frac{5\pi}{9} \approx 1.74$
4. $\frac{10\pi}{9} \approx 3.49$
5. $\frac{5\pi}{12} \approx 1.31$
6. $\frac{7\pi}{12} \approx 1.83$
7. $\frac{2\pi}{3} \approx 2.10$
8. $\frac{4\pi}{3} \approx 4.19$
9. $-\frac{16\pi}{9} \approx -5.58$
10. $-\frac{25\pi}{18} \approx -4.36$
11. $-\frac{17\pi}{36} \approx -1.48$
12. $-\frac{35\pi}{36} \approx -3.05$

Convert to degree measure.

13. 1 radian
14. 2 radians
15. 8
16. -12
17. $\frac{3}{4}$
18. $\frac{5}{4}$

13. 57.3°
14. 114.6°
15. 1440°
16. $-2160°$
17. 135°
18. 225°

For each of the following, find the function value using cofunctions.

19. tan 60°   **20.** csc 60°   **21.** sec 30°   19. $\sqrt{3}$ 20. $\frac{2\sqrt{3}}{3}$ 21. $\frac{2\sqrt{3}}{3}$

22. csc 30°   **23.** cot 45°   **24.** sec 45°   22. 2   23. 1   24. $\sqrt{2}$

25. cot 60°   **26.** sec 60°   **27.** cos 90°   25. $\frac{\sqrt{3}}{3}$ 26. 2   27. 0

28. 0.2306
29. 0.6648
30. 0.5519

Use Table 3 to find each of the following.

31. 0.3118
32. 0.5467

28. sin 13°20′   **29.** sin 41°40′   **30.** cos 56°30′   **31.** cos 71°50′   33. 1.550

32. tan 28°40′   **33.** tan 57°10′   **34.** csc 62°30′   **35.** csc 70°10′   34. 1.127   35. 1.063

36. −0.7969

Use Table 3 to find each of the following.

37. −0.3987
38. 0.6383

36. sin 307°10′   **37.** sin 336°30′   **38.** cos 410°20′   **39.** cos 456°40′   39. −0.1161

Use Table 3 and interpolation to find each of the following.

40. sin 28°31′   **41.** sin 36°42′   **42.** cos 53°55′   40. 0.4775   41. 0.5977   42. 0.5889

43. cos 80°33′   **44.** tan 24°12′   **45.** cot 54°18′   43. 0.1642   42. 0.4494   45. 0.7186

For each of the following, find θ in degrees and minutes between 0° and 90°.

46. sin θ = 0.2368   **47.** sin θ = 0.3864   **48.** cos θ = 0.3749   46. 13°42′   47. 22°44′

49. cos θ = 0.3538   **50.** cos θ = 0.6348   **51.** cos θ = 0.9678   48. 67°59′   49. 69°17′   50. 50°36′   51. 14°34′

Extension

52. 0.2095π
53. 0.0707222π

Use a calculator to convert to radian measure. Leave answers in terms of π.   54. 1.1922222π 55. 0.4103888π

52. 37.71°   **53.** 12.73°   **54.** 214.6°   **55.** 73.87°   56. 74.694267°   57. 134.54140°   58. 2172.0382°

Use a calculator to convert these radian measures to degree measure.   59. 401.56050°   60. 1477.08°

56. 1.303   **57.** 2.347   **58.** 37.89   **59.** 7.005   61. −2543.4°   62. 135.576°

60. 8.206π **61.** −14.13π **62.** 0.7532π **63.** −1.205π 63. −216.9°

The expressions below are in radians. Use Table 3 to find each value.

64. 0.4176
65. 0.8441

64. tan 0.3956   **65.** tan 0.7010   **66.** cos 0.9134   **67.** cot 1.0443   66. 0.6111   67. 0.5812

Use Table 3 to find each of the following. First convert to degrees and minutes. For example, 63.25° = 63° + (60 × 0.25)′ = 63°15′.   68. 0.2563   69. 0.1407   70. 0.2995

68. cos 75.15°   **69.** cos 81.91°   **70.** sin 17.43°   **71.** sin 38.72°   71. 0.6255

72. What is the angle between the hands of a clock at 7:45? $\frac{5\pi}{24}$ or 37.5°

73. Through how many radians does the minute hand of a clock rotate in 50 min? $\frac{15\pi}{9}$ ≈ 5.233

74. Copy and complete the table.

θ	$\dfrac{\pi}{6}$	$\dfrac{\pi}{4}$	$\dfrac{\pi}{3}$	$\dfrac{\pi}{2}$	$\dfrac{3\pi}{4}$	π	$\dfrac{5\pi}{4}$	$\dfrac{3\pi}{2}$	2π
$\sin\theta$	$\dfrac{1}{2}$	$\dfrac{\sqrt{2}}{2}$	$\dfrac{\sqrt{3}}{2}$	1	$\dfrac{\sqrt{2}}{2}$	0	$-\dfrac{\sqrt{2}}{2}$	-1	0
$\cos\theta$	$\dfrac{\sqrt{3}}{2}$	$\dfrac{\sqrt{2}}{2}$	$\dfrac{1}{2}$	0	$-\dfrac{\sqrt{2}}{2}$	-1	$-\dfrac{\sqrt{2}}{2}$	0	1
$\tan\theta$	$\dfrac{\sqrt{3}}{3}$	1	$\sqrt{3}$	—	-1	0	1	—	0
$\cot\theta$	$\sqrt{3}$	1	$\dfrac{\sqrt{3}}{3}$	0	-1	—	1	0	—
$\sec\theta$	$\dfrac{2\sqrt{3}}{3}$	$\sqrt{2}$	2	—	$-\sqrt{2}$	-1	$-\sqrt{2}$	—	1
$\csc\theta$	2	$\sqrt{2}$	$\dfrac{2\sqrt{3}}{3}$	1	$\sqrt{2}$	—	$-\sqrt{2}$	-1	—

In which quadrant does the terminal side of each angle lie?

75. $\dfrac{5\pi}{4}$ **76.** $\dfrac{17\pi}{8}$ **77.** $-\dfrac{\pi}{15}$ **78.** 37.3π 75. third   76. first   77. fourth   78. third

Find the reference angles for each of the following angles.

79. $\dfrac{5\pi}{6}$ **80.** $\dfrac{9\pi}{4}$ **81.** $-\dfrac{4\pi}{3}$ **82.** $-\dfrac{13\pi}{2}$ 79. $\dfrac{\pi}{6}$ 80. $\dfrac{\pi}{4}$ 81. $\dfrac{\pi}{3}$ 82. $\dfrac{\pi}{2}$

Find the trigonometric function values for each of the following angles.

83. $\sin\dfrac{\pi}{9}$ **84.** $\cot\dfrac{5\pi}{12}$ **85.** $\cot\left(-\dfrac{10\pi}{9}\right)$ **86.** $\sec\dfrac{9\pi}{4}$ 83. 0.3420   84. 0.2679   85. 2.747   86. 1.414

Find the function values for each of the following using cofunctions.

87. $\cot\dfrac{\pi}{3}$ **88.** $\cot\dfrac{\pi}{6}$ **89.** $\tan\dfrac{\pi}{3}$ **90.** $\csc\dfrac{\pi}{4}$ 87. $\dfrac{\sqrt{3}}{3}$ 88. $\sqrt{3}$ 89. $\sqrt{3}$ 90. $\sqrt{2}$

Challenge

91. The formula $\sin x = x - \dfrac{x^3}{6} + \dfrac{x^5}{120}$

gives an approximation for sine values when x is in radians. Use a calculator to calculate $\sin 0.5$ and compare your answer with Table 3.   0.4794

92. For any acute angle θ, we know that $\cos(90° - \theta) = \sin\theta$. Consider angles other than acute angles. Does this relation still hold, and if so to what extent?   Yes, for all angles.

15–4 Graphs of Trigonometric Functions

The Sine and Cosine Functions

Graphs of the trigonometric functions can be constructed by plotting and connecting points.

EXAMPLE 1

Graph the sine function. First we look at special angles in the first two quadrants. We will use radian measure for the angles.

θ	0	$\frac{\pi}{6}$	$\frac{\pi}{4}$	$\frac{\pi}{3}$	$\frac{\pi}{2}$	$\frac{2\pi}{3}$	$\frac{3\pi}{4}$	$\frac{5\pi}{6}$	π
$\sin\theta$ exact	0	$\frac{1}{2}$	$\frac{\sqrt{2}}{2}$	$\frac{\sqrt{3}}{2}$	1	$\frac{\sqrt{3}}{2}$	$\frac{\sqrt{2}}{2}$	$\frac{1}{2}$	0
$\sin\theta$ approximate	0	0.5	0.7	0.8	1	0.8	0.7	0.5	0

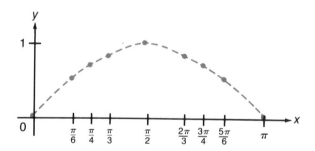

In Section 15–3 we used tables that gave us the values for all angles between 0 and $\frac{\pi}{2}$. So it seems reasonable that we join the above points with a smooth curve. If we choose negative values for θ, we will be choosing rotations from the third and fourth quadrants.

θ	$-\pi$	$-\frac{5\pi}{6}$	$-\frac{3\pi}{4}$	$-\frac{2\pi}{3}$	$-\frac{\pi}{2}$	$-\frac{\pi}{3}$	$-\frac{\pi}{4}$	$-\frac{\pi}{6}$	0
$\sin\theta$ exact	0	$-\frac{1}{2}$	$-\frac{\sqrt{2}}{2}$	$-\frac{\sqrt{3}}{2}$	-1	$-\frac{\sqrt{3}}{2}$	$-\frac{\sqrt{2}}{2}$	$-\frac{1}{2}$	0
$\sin\theta$ approximate	0	-0.5	-0.7	-0.8	-1	-0.8	-0.7	-0.5	0

Choosing values of θ between π and 2π would also give us values for third and fourth quadrants. We can see that the values repeat. Here is an extended graph of the sine function.

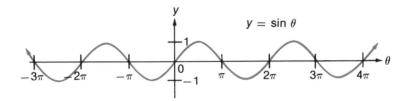

Function values increase to a maximum of 1 at $\frac{\pi}{2}$, then decrease to 0 at π, decrease further to -1 at $\frac{3}{2}\pi$, then increase 0 at 2π, and so on.

TRY THIS

1. What is the domain of the sine function? The set of all real numbers

2. What is the range of the sine function? The set of all real numbers from -1 to 1, inclusive, $\{y \mid -1 \le y \le 1\}$

The cosine function can be graphed in the same way. Here is the graph of the cosine function. Notice that is has the same shape as the sine function, but the graph is shifted $\frac{\pi}{2}$ units to the left.

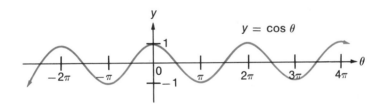

Period and Amplitude

The function values for the sine and cosine functions repeat themselves at regular intervals. Such functions are called periodic. If we translate any part of the sine graph 2π units to the right or to the left, we obtain the original graph. In the graph of the cosine function, the function values also repeat themselves every 2π units.

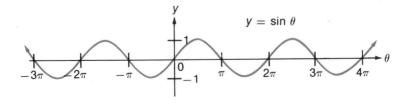

If we shift the graph of either the sine or cosine functions 4π units to the left or right, we obtain the original graphs. The smallest positive shift that gives the original function is called the period of the function.

DEFINITION

If a function f has the property that $f(x + p) = f(x)$ for all x in the domain, where p is a constant, then f is said to be *periodic*. The smallest positive number p (if there is one) for which $f(x + p) = f(x)$ for all x is called the *period* of the function.

From the graphs we have the following.

THEOREM 15–1

The sine function is periodic with period 2π.
The cosine function is periodic with period 2π.
$\sin \theta = \sin (\theta + 2\pi) = \sin (\theta - 2\pi) = \sin (\theta + 4\pi)$, and so on, or $\sin \theta = \sin (\theta \pm 2\pi k)$, where k is an integer.
$\cos \theta = \cos (\theta + 2\pi) = \cos (\theta - 2\pi) = \cos (\theta + 4\pi)$, and so on, or $\cos \theta = \cos (\theta \pm 2\pi k)$, where k is an integer.

Looking at the graph of the cosine function, we see that the function value at 0, 2π, and -2π is 1 and that the function value at π, 3π, and $-\pi$ is -1. The value of the function increases and decreases between these points, but never becomes greater than 1 or less than -1. Thus, the maximum value of the cosine function is 1, while the minimum value is -1.

DEFINITION

The *amplitude* of a trigonometric function is defined by the following equation.

$$\text{amplitude} = \frac{\text{maximum} - \text{minimum}}{2}$$

EXAMPLE 2

What is the amplitude of the cosine function?

$$\text{amplitude} = \frac{\text{maximum} - \text{minimum}}{2} = \frac{1 - (-1)}{2} = 1$$

TRY THIS

3. What is the amplitude of the sine function? 1

Graphs of Other Trigonometric Functions

Not every angle has a tangent. For example, using the relationship $\tan \theta = \frac{\sin \theta}{\cos \theta}$, the tangent ratio for $\frac{\pi}{2}$ would be

$$\frac{\sin \frac{\pi}{2}}{\cos \frac{\pi}{2}}, \text{ or } \frac{1}{0}.$$

But division by 0 is undefined, so $\tan \frac{\pi}{2}$ is meaningless. In this graph of the tangent function we use x instead of θ. The variable x represents any real number. Note that the function value is 0 when $x = 0$, and the values increase as x increases toward $\frac{\pi}{2}$. As we approach $\frac{\pi}{2}$ the tangent values become very large. In fact, they increase without bound. The dashed vertical lines are not part of the graph. They are asymptotes. The graph approaches each asymptote, but never reaches it because there are no values of the function for $\frac{\pi}{2}, \frac{3\pi}{2}$, etc.

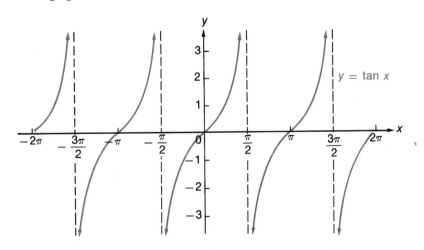

EXAMPLE 3

Is the tangent function periodic? If so, what is its period? What is its domain? What is its range?

We see that the graph from $\frac{-\pi}{2}$ to $\frac{\pi}{2}$ repeats in the interval from $\frac{\pi}{2}$ to $\frac{3\pi}{2}$. Consequently, the tangent function is periodic, with a period of π. Its domain is $\{x \mid x \neq \frac{\pi}{2} + k\pi, k \text{ an integer}\}$. Its range is the set of all real numbers.

TRY THIS

4. Is the tangent function even or odd? odd

The secant and cosine functions are reciprocals.

$$\sec 0 = \frac{1}{\cos 0} = \frac{1}{1} = 1$$

This function is undefined for those numbers for which $\cos x = 0$.

Here is a graph of the secant function. The cosine graph is drawn in for reference, since these functions are reciprocals.

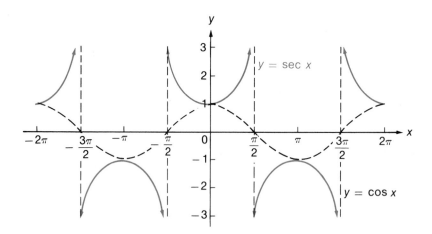

EXAMPLE 4

What is the domain of the secant function?

The domain of the secant function is the set of all real numbers except $\frac{\pi}{2} + k\pi$, k an integer; that is $\{x \mid x \neq \frac{\pi}{2} + k\pi, k \text{ an integer}\}$.

TRY THIS

5. What is the period of the secant function? 2π

6. What is the range of the secant function? $\{x \mid x \geq 1 \text{ or } x \leq -1\}$

Exercises

1. Copy and complete this table of values for the cosine function in the first and second quadrants.

θ	0	$\dfrac{\pi}{6}$	$\dfrac{\pi}{4}$	$\dfrac{\pi}{3}$	$\dfrac{\pi}{2}$	$\dfrac{2\pi}{3}$	$\dfrac{3\pi}{4}$	$\dfrac{5\pi}{6}$	π
$\cos\theta$ exact	1	$\dfrac{\sqrt{3}}{2}$	$\dfrac{\sqrt{2}}{2}$	$\dfrac{1}{2}$	0	$-\dfrac{1}{2}$	$-\dfrac{\sqrt{2}}{2}$	$-\dfrac{\sqrt{3}}{2}$	-1
$\cos\theta$ approximate	1	0.866	0.707	0.5	0	-0.5	-0.707	-0.866	-1

2. Copy and complete this table of values for the cosine function in the third and fourth quadrants.

θ	$-\pi$	$-\dfrac{5\pi}{6}$	$-\dfrac{3\pi}{4}$	$-\dfrac{2\pi}{3}$	$-\dfrac{\pi}{2}$	$-\dfrac{\pi}{3}$	$-\dfrac{\pi}{4}$	$-\dfrac{\pi}{6}$	0
$\cos\theta$ exact	-1	$-\dfrac{\sqrt{3}}{2}$	$-\dfrac{\sqrt{2}}{2}$	$-\dfrac{1}{2}$	0	$\dfrac{1}{2}$	$\dfrac{\sqrt{2}}{2}$	$\dfrac{\sqrt{3}}{2}$	1
$\cos\theta$ approximate	-1	-0.866	-0.707	-0.5	0	0.5	0.707	0.866	1

3. Plot the points in Exercise 1 and sketch the cosine curve.
4. Plot the points in Exercise 2 and sketch the cosine curve.
5. What is the domain of the cosine function? The set of all real numbers
6. What is the range of the cosine function? $\{y \mid -1 \le y \le 1\}$
7. What is the period of the cosine function? 2π
8. What is the amplitude of the cosine function? 1

Which of the following functions are periodic?

9. yes

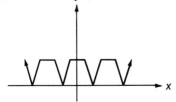

10. no

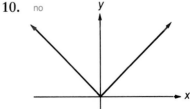

11. What is the period of this function? 4

12. What is the period of this function? 2

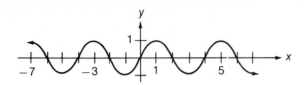

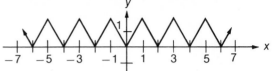

13. What is the amplitude of the function in Exercise 11? 1

14. What is the amplitude of the function in Exercise 12? 1

Here is a table of approximate values of functions. Use the table, plus your knowledge of the properties of the functions, to make graphs.

	$\frac{\pi}{16}$	$\frac{\pi}{8}$	$\frac{\pi}{6}$	$\frac{\pi}{4}$	$\frac{\pi}{3}$	$\frac{3}{8}\pi$	$\frac{7}{16}\pi$	$-\frac{\pi}{16}$	$-\frac{\pi}{8}$	$-\frac{\pi}{6}$	$-\frac{\pi}{4}$
tan	0.2	0.4	0.6	1	1.7	2.4	4.9	-0.2	-0.4	-0.6	-1
cot	4.9	2.4	1.7	1	0.6	0.4	0.2	-4.9	-2.4	-1.7	-1
sec	1.02	1.1	1.2	1.4	2	2.6	5.0	1.02	1.1	1.2	1.4
csc	5.0	2.6	2	1.4	1.2	1.08	1.02	-5.0	-2.6	-2	-1.4

15. Graph the tangent function between -2π and 2π.

16. Graph the cotangent function between -2π and 2π.

17. Graph the secant function between -2π and 2π.

18. Graph the cosecant function between -2π and 2π.

19. What is the domain of the cotangent function?

20. What is the range of the cotangent function?

21. Is the cotangent function periodic? If so, what is its period?

22. Is the cotangent function even? odd?

23. What is the domain of the cosecant function?

24. What is the range of the cosecant function?

25. Is the cosecant function periodic? If so, what is its period?

26. Is the cosecant function even? odd?

Extension

27. a. Sketch a graph of $y = \sin x$.
   b. By reflecting the graph in **a.**, sketch a graph of $y = \sin(-x)$.
   c. By reflecting the graph in **a.**, sketch a graph of $y = -\sin x$.
   d. How do the graphs in **b.** and **c.** compare?

28. a. Sketch a graph of $y = \cos x$.
   b. By reflecting the graph in **a.**, sketch a graph of $y = \cos(-x)$.
   c. By reflecting the graph in **a.**, sketch a graph of $y = -\cos x$.
   d. How do the graphs in **a.** and **b.** compare?

29. a. Sketch a graph of $y = \sin x$.
    b. By translating, sketch a graph of $y = \sin (x + \pi)$.
    c. By reflecting the graph of a., sketch a graph of $y = -\sin x$.
    d. How do the graphs in b. and c. compare?

30. a. Sketch a graph of $y = \sin x$.
    b. By translating, sketch a graph of $y = \sin (x - \pi)$.
    c. By reflecting the graph of a., sketch a graph of $y = -\sin x$.
    d. How do the graphs in b. and c. compare?

31. a. Sketch a graph of $y = \cos x$.
    b. By translating, sketch a graph of $y = \cos (x + \pi)$.
    c. By reflecting the graph of a., sketch a graph of $y = -\cos x$.
    d. How do the graphs in b. and c. compare?

32. a. Sketch a graph of $y = \cos x$.
    b. By translating, sketch a graph of $y = \cos (x - \pi)$.
    c. By reflecting the graph of a., sketch a graph of $y = -\cos x$.
    d. How do the graphs in b. and c. compare?

33. For which numbers is
    a. $\sin x = 1$?   b. $\sin x = -1$?

34. For which numbers is
    a. $\cos x = 1$?   b. $\cos x = -1$?

35. Solve for x. $\sin x = 0$

36. Solve for x. $\cos x = 0$

37. Describe how the graphs of the tangent and cotangent functions are related.

38. Describe how the graphs of the secant and cosecant functions are related.

39. Which pairs of circular functions have the same zeros? (A "zero" of a function is an input that produces an output of 0.)

40. Graph $f(x) = |\tan x|$.

Challenge

41. Solve $\cos x \leq \sec x$.

42. Solve $\sin x > \csc x$.

43. Construct a graph of the sine function by copying the coordinate axes on other paper. Then, from the unit circle shown here, transfer vertical distances with a compass.

44. Construct a graph of the cosine function. Follow the instructions for Exercise 43, but transfer *horizontal* distances from the unit circle with a compass.

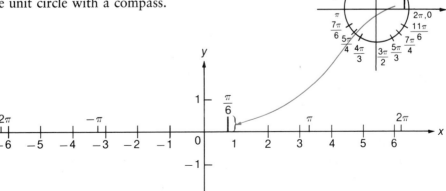

15–5 Trigonometric Function Relationships

We have already seen some of the important relationships that exist among the six trigonometric functions. There are certain other relationships, called *identities*. Recall that an identity is an equation that holds for all sensible replacements for the variables. We use the sign $\equiv$ to indicate that an equation is an identity.

Quotient and Pythagorean Identities

The tangent and cotangent functions can be expressed in terms of the sine and cosine functions.

THEOREM 15–2

The Quotient Identities

$$\tan \theta \equiv \frac{\sin \theta}{\cos \theta}, \cos \theta \neq 0 \qquad \cot \theta \equiv \frac{\cos \theta}{\sin \theta}, \sin \theta \neq 0$$

EXAMPLE 1

Derive an identity that gives $\sin \theta$ in terms of $\tan \theta$ and $\cos \theta$. By Theorem 15–2 we have $\tan \theta \equiv \frac{\sin \theta}{\cos \theta}$. Solving for $\sin \theta$ we have $\sin \theta \equiv \tan \theta \cdot \cos \theta$.

TRY THIS

1. Derive an identity that gives $\cos \theta$ in terms of $\sin \theta$ and $\cot \theta$. $\cos \theta = \cot \theta \cdot \sin \theta$

Suppose θ determines a point T on the unit circle, with coordinates (x, y). By the Pythagorean Theorem, $x^2 + y^2 = 1$. Since $x = \cos \theta$ and $y = \sin \theta$, we obtain the following identity.

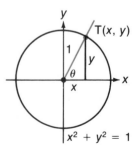

$$\sin^2 \theta + \cos^2 \theta \equiv 1$$

(When exponents are used with the trigonometric functions, we write $\sin^2 \theta$ instead of $(\sin \theta)^2$.) This identity relates the sine and cosine of any angle. It is known as one of the Pythagorean Identities. Now we will divide the above identity by $\sin^2 \theta$.

$$\frac{\sin^2 \theta}{\sin^2 \theta} + \frac{\cos^2 \theta}{\sin^2 \theta} \equiv \frac{1}{\sin^2 \theta}$$

Since the cosecant is the reciprocal of the sine, this can be further simplified.

$$1 + \cot^2 \theta \equiv \csc^2 \theta$$

This relationship is valid for any rotation θ for which $\sin^2 \theta \neq 0$, since we divided by $\sin^2 \theta$.

The third Pythagorean identity is obtained by dividing the first by $\cos^2 \theta$.

$$1 + \tan^2 \theta \equiv \sec^2 \theta$$

THEOREM 15–3

The Pythagorean Identities

$$\sin^2 \theta + \cos^2 \theta \equiv 1$$
$$1 + \cot^2 \theta \equiv \csc^2 \theta$$
$$1 + \tan^2 \theta \equiv \sec^2 \theta$$

EXAMPLE 2

Derive identities that give $\cos^2 \theta$ and $\cos \theta$ in terms of $\sin \theta$.

$$\sin^2 \theta + \cos^2 \theta \equiv 1 \quad \text{Pythagorean Identity}$$
$$\cos^2 \theta \equiv 1 - \sin^2 \theta \quad \text{Solving for } \cos^2 \theta$$
$$|\cos \theta| \equiv \sqrt{1 - \sin^2 \theta} \quad \text{Taking the principal square root}$$
$$\cos \theta \equiv \pm\sqrt{1 - \sin^2 \theta}$$

The sign of $\cos \theta$ is positive if the terminal side of θ is in the first or fourth quadrant. Otherwise, it is negative.

TRY THIS

2. Derive an identity for $\sin^2 \theta$ in terms of $\cos \theta$. $\sin^2 \theta \equiv 1 - \cos^2 \theta$

3. Derive an identity for $\sin \theta$ in terms of $\cos \theta$. $\sin \theta \equiv \pm\sqrt{1 - \cos^2 \theta}$

EXAMPLE 3

Obtain identities from $1 + \cot^2 \theta \equiv \csc^2 \theta$.

We obtain

$$\csc^2 \theta - \cot^2 \theta \equiv 1 \text{ and } \cot^2 \theta \equiv \csc^2 \theta - 1.$$

TRY THIS

4. From the identity $1 + \tan^2 \theta \equiv \sec^2 \theta$, derive two other identities. $\sec^2 \theta - \tan^2 \theta \equiv 1$ $\tan^2 \theta \equiv \sec^2 \theta - 1$

The Cofunction Identities

The sine and cosine are called cofunctions of each other. Another class of identities gives functions in terms of their cofunctions. Consider this graph. The graph of $y = \sin \theta$ has been translated to the left a distance of $\frac{\pi}{2}$. Thus, we obtain the graph of $y = \sin (\theta + \frac{\pi}{2})$. The latter is also a graph of the cosine function. Thus we obtain the identity $\sin (\theta + \frac{\pi}{2}) \equiv \cos \theta$.

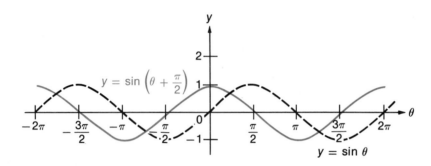

EXAMPLE 4
Check the identity $\sin (\theta + \frac{\pi}{2}) \equiv \cos \theta$ by using $\theta = \frac{\pi}{6}$.

$$\sin\left(\theta + \frac{\pi}{2}\right) = \sin\left(\frac{\pi}{6} + \frac{\pi}{2}\right) = \sin\left(\frac{2\pi}{3}\right) = \frac{\sqrt{3}}{2} = \cos\frac{\pi}{6}$$

By translating the graph of $y = \cos \theta$ to the right a distance of $\frac{\pi}{2}$, we obtain the following identity.

$$\cos\left(\theta - \frac{\pi}{2}\right) \equiv \sin \theta$$

TRY THIS
5. Check the identity $\cos (\theta - \frac{\pi}{2}) = \sin \theta$ by using $\theta = 0°$. $\cos\left(0 - \frac{\pi}{2}\right) = \cos -\frac{\pi}{2} = 0 = \sin 0$

If the graph of $y = \sin \theta$ is translated to the right a distance of $\frac{\pi}{2}$, we obtain the graph of $y = \sin (\theta - \frac{\pi}{2})$. The latter is a reflection of the cosine function across the x-axis. In other words, it is a graph of $y = -\cos \theta$. We thus obtain the following identity.

$$\sin\left(\theta - \frac{\pi}{2}\right) \equiv -\cos \theta$$

By means similar to those above, we obtain this identity.

$$\cos\left(\theta + \frac{\pi}{2}\right) \equiv -\sin \theta$$

We now consider function values at $\frac{\pi}{2} - \theta$. Since the sine function is odd, we know the following.

$$\sin\left(\frac{\pi}{2} - \theta\right) \equiv \sin\left[-\left(\theta - \frac{\pi}{2}\right)\right] \equiv -\sin\left(\theta - \frac{\pi}{2}\right)$$

Now consider the identity already established.

$$\sin\left(\theta - \frac{\pi}{2}\right) \equiv -\cos\theta$$

This is equivalent to the following.

$$-\sin\left(\theta - \frac{\pi}{2}\right) \equiv \cos\theta \quad \text{Multiplying by } -1$$

We now have the following identity.

$$\sin\left(\frac{\pi}{2} - \theta\right) \equiv \cos\theta \quad \text{Algebraic manipulation}$$

Similarly, we can establish the identity $\cos\left(\frac{\pi}{2} - \theta\right) \equiv \sin\theta$.

The following theorem summarizes the cofunction identities. These identities should be memorized.

THEOREM 15–4

The Cofunction Identities

$$\sin\left(\theta + \frac{\pi}{2}\right) \equiv \cos\theta \qquad \cos\left(\theta + \frac{\pi}{2}\right) \equiv -\sin\theta$$

$$\sin\left(\theta - \frac{\pi}{2}\right) \equiv -\cos\theta \qquad \cos\left(\theta - \frac{\pi}{2}\right) \equiv \sin\theta$$

$$\sin\left(\frac{\pi}{2} - \theta\right) \equiv \cos\theta \qquad \cos\left(\frac{\pi}{2} - \theta\right) \equiv \sin\theta$$

EXAMPLE 5

Find an identity for $\tan\left(\theta + \frac{\pi}{2}\right)$.

$$\tan\left(\theta + \frac{\pi}{2}\right) \equiv \frac{\sin\left(\theta + \frac{\pi}{2}\right)}{\cos\left(\theta + \frac{\pi}{2}\right)} \quad \text{Theorem 15–2 (quotient identity)}$$

$$\equiv \frac{\cos\theta}{-\sin\theta} \quad \text{Theorem 15–4 (cofunction identity)}$$

$$\equiv -\cot\theta \quad \text{Theorem 15–2 (quotient identity)}$$

TRY THIS

6. Find an identity for $\cot\left(\theta + \frac{\pi}{2}\right)$. $\cot\left(\theta + \frac{\pi}{2}\right) \equiv -\tan\theta$

15–5

Exercises

1. Write a simpler expression for $1 - \cos^2\theta$. $\sin^2\theta$
2. Write a simpler expression for $1 - \sin^2\theta$. $\cos^2\theta$
3. Derive an identity for $\cos\theta$ in terms of $\sin\theta$ and $\tan\theta$. $\cos\theta \equiv \frac{\sin\theta}{\tan\theta}$
4. Derive an identity for $\sin\theta$ in terms of $\cot\theta$ and $\cos\theta$. $\sin\theta \equiv \frac{\cos\theta}{\cot\theta}$

Derive the following.

5. An identity for $\csc\theta$ in terms of $\cot\theta$ $\csc\theta \equiv \pm\sqrt{1 + \cot^2\theta}$
6. An identity for $\tan\theta$ in terms of $\sec\theta$ $\tan\theta \equiv \pm\sqrt{\sec^2\theta - 1}$
7. An identity for $\cot\theta$ in terms of $\csc\theta$ $\cot\theta \equiv \pm\sqrt{\csc^2\theta - 1}$
8. An identity for $\sec\theta$ in terms of $\tan\theta$ $\sec\theta \equiv \pm\sqrt{1 + \tan^2\theta}$

9. Check the identity
$$\sin\left(\theta - \frac{\pi}{2}\right) \equiv -\cos\theta$$
by using $\theta = \frac{\pi}{4}$.

10. Check the identity
$$\cos\left(\theta - \frac{\pi}{2}\right) \equiv \sin\theta$$
by using $\theta = 0$.

11. Check the identity
$$\sin\left(\frac{\pi}{2} - \theta\right) \equiv \cos\theta$$
by using $\theta = \frac{5\pi}{4}$.

12. Check the identity
$$\cos\left(\frac{\pi}{2} - \theta\right) \equiv \sin\theta$$
by using $\theta = \frac{\pi}{3}$.

Use the given function values to find the six function values of the complement angle.

13. $\sin 65° = 0.9063$ $\cos 65° = 0.4226$
$\tan 65° = 2.145$ $\cot 65° = 0.4663$
$\sec 65° = 2.366$ $\csc 65° = 1.103$

14. $\sin 32° = 0.5299$ $\cos 32° = 0.8480$
$\tan 32° = 0.6249$ $\cot 32° = 1.600$
$\sec 32° = 1.179$ $\csc 32° = 1.887$

13. $\sin 25° = 0.4226$, $\cos 25° = 0.9063$, $\tan 25° = 0.4663$, $\cot 25° = 2.145$, $\sec 25° = 1.103$, $\csc 25° = 2.366$
14. $\sin 58° = 0.8480$, $\cos 58° = 0.5299$, $\tan 58° = 1.600$, $\cot 58° = 0.6249$, $\sec 58° = 1.887$, $\csc 58° = 1.179$

15. $\sin 52° = 0.7880$ $\cos 52° = 0.6157$
     $\tan 52° = 1.280$ $\cot 52° = 0.7813$
     $\sec 52° = 1.624$ $\csc 52° = 1.269$

15. $\sin 38° = 0.6157$, $\cos 38° = 0.7880$, $\tan 38° = 0.7813$, $\cot 38° = 1.280$, $\sec 38° = 1.269$, $\csc 38° = 1.624$
16. $\sin 63° = 0.8910$, $\cos 63° = 0.4540$, $\tan 63° = 1.963$, $\cot 63° = 0.5095$, $\sec 63° = 2.203$, $\csc 63° = 1.122$

16. $\sin 27° = 0.4540$ $\cos 27° = 0.8910$
     $\tan 27° = 0.5095$ $\cot 27° = 1.963$
     $\sec 27° = 1.122$ $\csc 27° = 2.203$

Find identities for the following.

17. $\tan\left(\theta - \dfrac{\pi}{2}\right)$ $\tan\left(\theta - \frac{\pi}{2}\right) \equiv -\cot\theta$

18. $\cot\left(\theta - \dfrac{\pi}{2}\right)$ $\cot\left(\theta - \frac{\pi}{2}\right) \equiv -\tan\theta$

19. $\sec\left(\dfrac{\pi}{2} - \theta\right)$ $\sec\left(\frac{\pi}{2} - \theta\right) \equiv \csc\theta$

20. $\csc\left(\dfrac{\pi}{2} - \theta\right)$ $\csc\left(\frac{\pi}{2} - \theta\right) \equiv \sec\theta$

Extension

21. For the six trigonometric functions, list the cofunction identities involving $\frac{\pi}{2} - \theta$.

22. Describe the pattern you see in Exercise 21.

Write an equivalent expression for each of the following.

23. $\sin(\theta + \pi)$ $-\sin\theta$

24. $\sin(\theta - \pi)$ $-\sin\theta$

25. $\cos(\pi - \theta)$ $-\cos\theta$

26. $\sin(\pi - \theta)$ $\sin\theta$

Write an equivalent expression for each of the following. Check the identities obtained.

27. $\cos(\theta + 2k\pi)$ $\cos\theta$

28. $\sin(\theta + 2k\pi)$ $\sin\theta$

29. $\cos(\theta - \pi)$ $-\cos\theta$

30. $\cos(\theta + \pi)$ $-\cos\theta$

Given that $\sin\frac{\pi}{8} = 0.38268$, use identities to find each of the following.

31. $\cos\dfrac{\pi}{8}$ 0.92388

32. $\cos\dfrac{5\pi}{8}$ -0.38268

33. $\sin\dfrac{5\pi}{8}$ 0.92388

34. $\sin\left(-\dfrac{3\pi}{8}\right)$ -0.92388

35. $\cos\left(-\dfrac{3\pi}{8}\right)$ 0.38268

36. $\cos\left(-\dfrac{\pi}{8}\right)$ 0.92388

Challenge

Choose values for θ or x. Then check these identities.

37. $\dfrac{1 - \sin\theta}{\cos\theta} \equiv \dfrac{\cos\theta}{1 + \sin\theta}$

38. $\dfrac{1 - \cos\theta}{\sin\theta} \equiv \dfrac{\sin\theta}{1 + \cos\theta}$

39. $\csc x - \cos x \cot x \equiv \sin x$

40. $\sec x - \sin x \tan x \equiv \cos x$

15–6 More Graphs

We will consider graphs of some variations of the sine and cosine function. In particular, we are interested in $y = A \sin (B\theta)$ and $y = A \cos (B\theta)$, where A and B are constants.

Change of Amplitude or Period

Changing the constant A in $y = A \sin \theta$ causes a vertical stretching or shrinking of the graph and thus a change in the amplitude.

EXAMPLE 1

Sketch a graph of $y = 2 \sin \theta$. What is the amplitude?

The function $y = 2 \sin \theta$ is equivalent to $\frac{y}{2} = \sin \theta$. The graph is a vertical stretching of the graph of $y = \sin \theta$. The amplitude of this function is 2. That is, $A = 2$.

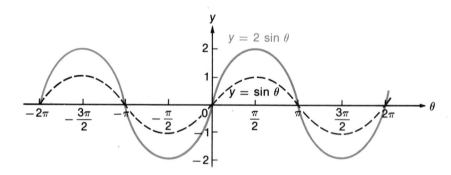

If the constant A in $y = A \sin x$ is negative, there will also be a reflection across the x-axis. If the absolute value of A is less than 1, then there will be a vertical shrinking. The amplitude will be $|A|$. Thus the graph of $y = -\frac{1}{2} \sin \theta$ is a reflection of $y = \sin \theta$ and has an amplitude of $\left| -\frac{1}{2} \right|$ or $\frac{1}{2}$.

TRY THIS

1. Sketch a graph of $y = 2 \cos \theta$. What is the amplitude? 2

Changing the constant B in $y = \sin B\theta$ causes a horizontal stretching or shrinking of the graph and thus a change in the period.

EXAMPLE 2

Sketch a graph of $y = \sin 2\theta$. What is the period? The function $y = \sin 2\theta$ is equivalent to $y = \sin \frac{\theta}{\frac{1}{2}}$. The graph is a horizontal

shrinking of the graph of $y = \sin \theta$. The period of this function is π.

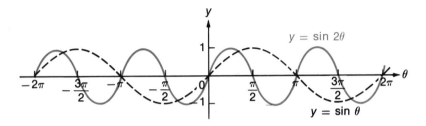

If $|B| > 1$, there will be a horizontal shrink. If $|B| < 1$, there will be a horizontal stretch. If B is negative, there will also be a reflection across the y-axis. The period will be $\frac{2\pi}{|B|}$. Thus the graph of $y = \sin\left(-\frac{1}{2}\theta\right)$ is a reflection of $y = \sin \theta$ and has a period of $\frac{2\pi}{|-\frac{1}{2}|}$ or 4π.

TRY THIS

2. Sketch a graph of $y = \cos 2\theta$. What is the period? π

Change of Amplitude and Period

Changing the constants A and B in $y = A \sin B\theta$ causes both a vertical and a horizontal stretching or shrinking of the graph.

EXAMPLE 3

Sketch a graph of $y = 3 \sin (2\theta)$. What is the amplitude and period? The graph is a vertical stretching and a horizontal shrinking of the graph of $y = \sin \theta$. The function $y = 3 \sin (2\theta)$ is equivalent to

$$\frac{y}{3} = \sin \frac{\theta}{\frac{1}{2}}.$$

Amplitude $= 3$.
Period is π.

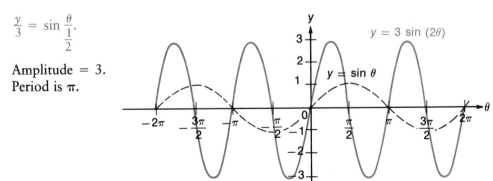

TRY THIS

3. Sketch a graph of $y = 3 \cos 2\theta$.

What is the amplitude and the period? $A = 3$, period $= \pi$

15–6

Exercises

Sketch graphs of these functions. Determine the amplitude.

1. $y = \frac{1}{2} \sin \theta$ $A = \frac{1}{2}$
2. $y = \frac{1}{2} \cos \theta$ $A = \frac{1}{2}$
3. $y = 3 \sin \theta$ $A = 3$

4. $y = 3 \cos \theta$ $A = 3$
5. $y = -\frac{1}{3} \sin \theta$ $A = \frac{1}{3}$
6. $y = -\frac{1}{3} \cos \theta$ $A = \frac{1}{3}$

7. $y = 4 \sin \theta$ $A = 4$
8. $y = 4 \cos \theta$ $A = 4$
9. $y = -2 \sin \theta$ $A = 2$

Sketch graphs of these functions. Determine the period.

10. $y = \sin 3\theta$ $\frac{2\pi}{3}$
11. $y = \cos 3\theta$ $\frac{2\pi}{3}$
12. $y = \sin \frac{1}{2}\theta$ 4π

13. $y = \cos \frac{1}{2}\theta$ 4π
14. $y = \sin \left(-\frac{1}{3}\theta\right)$ 6π
15. $y = \cos \left(-\frac{1}{3}\theta\right)$ 6π

16. $y = \sin (-2\theta)$ π
17. $y = \cos (-2\theta)$ π
18. $y = \sin (-3\theta)$ $\frac{2\pi}{3}$

Sketch graphs of these functions. Determine the amplitude and the period.

19. $y = 2 \sin (2\theta)$
20. $y = 2 \cos (2\theta)$
21. $y = \frac{1}{2} \sin (2\theta)$

22. $y = \frac{1}{2} \cos (2\theta)$
23. $y = -2 \sin \left(\frac{1}{2}\theta\right)$
24. $y = -2 \cos \left(\frac{1}{2}\theta\right)$

25. $y = \frac{1}{2} \sin (-2\theta)$
26. $y = \frac{1}{2} \cos (-2\theta)$
27. $y = -\frac{1}{2} \sin (-2\theta)$

19. $A = 2$, period $= \pi$
20. $A = 2$, period $= \pi$
21. $A = \frac{1}{2}$, period $= \pi$
22. $A = \frac{1}{2}$, period $= \pi$
23. $A = 2$, period $= 4\pi$
24. $A = 2$, period $= 4\pi$
25. $A = \frac{1}{2}$, period $= \pi$
26. $A = \frac{1}{2}$, period $= \pi$
27. $A = \frac{1}{2}$, period $= \pi$

Extension

Sketch graphs of these functions.

28. $y = \cos (2\theta - \pi)$
29. $y = \sin (2\theta + \pi)$
30. $y = 2 + \sin \theta$

Challenge

Sketch graphs of these functions. Determine the amplitude and period.

31. $y = 2 + 2 \sin (2\theta + \pi)$
$A = 2$, period $= \pi$

32. $y = -3 + \frac{1}{2} \sin \left(\frac{1}{2}\theta - \pi\right)$
$A = \frac{1}{2}$, period $= 4\pi$

15–7 Algebraic Manipulations

Trigonometric expressions such as $\sin 2\theta$ or $\tan (x - \pi)$ represent numbers, just as algebraic expressions represent numbers. Thus we can work with trigonometric expressions in much the same way as we work with purely algebraic expressions.

Computing and Simplifying

EXAMPLE 1

Multiply and simplify $\cos y (\tan y - \sec y)$.

$$\cos y (\tan y - \sec y) = \cos y \tan y - \cos y \sec y \quad \text{Multiplying}$$
$$= \cos y \frac{\sin y}{\cos y} - \cos y \frac{1}{\cos y} \quad \text{Simplifying}$$
$$= \sin y - 1$$

In Example 1 we used certain identities to accomplish simplification. There is no general rule for doing this, but it is often helpful to put everything in terms of sines and cosines, as we did here.

TRY THIS Multiply and simplify.

1. $\sin x (\cot x + \csc x)$ $\cos x + 1$

EXAMPLE 2

Factor and simplify $\sin^2 x \cos^2 x + \cos^4 x$.

$$\sin^2 x \cos^2 x + \cos^4 x = \cos^2 x (\sin^2 x + \cos^2 x) \quad \text{Factoring}$$
$$= \cos^2 x (1) \quad \text{Substituting 1 for } \sin^2 x + \cos^2 x; \text{ Pythagorean Identity}$$
$$= \cos^2 x$$

EXAMPLE 3

Factor and simplify $\tan x + \cos \left(\frac{\pi}{2} - x \right)$.

$$\tan x + \cos \left(\frac{\pi}{2} - x \right) = \tan x + \sin x \quad \text{Using an identity for } \cos \left(\frac{\pi}{2} - x \right)$$
$$= \frac{\sin x}{\cos x} + \sin x \quad \text{Using an identity for } \tan x$$
$$= \sin x \left(\frac{1}{\cos x} + 1 \right) \quad \text{Factoring}$$
$$= \sin x (\sec x + 1)$$

TRY THIS Factor and simplify.

2. $\sin^3 \theta + \sin \theta \cos^2 \theta$ $\quad$ $\sin \theta$

3. $\cot x - \sin \left(\frac{\pi}{2} - x\right)$ $\quad$ $\cos x \, (\csc x - 1)$

Solving Equations

EXAMPLE 4
Solve for $\tan x$: $\tan^2 x + \tan x = 56$.

$$\tan^2 x + \tan x - 56 = 0 \quad \text{Rewriting as a quadratic equation}$$
$$(\tan x + 8)(\tan x - 7) = 0 \quad \text{Factoring}$$
$$\tan x + 8 = 0 \quad \text{or} \quad \tan x - 7 = 0$$
$$\tan x = -8 \quad \text{or} \quad \tan x = 7$$

EXAMPLE 5
Solve for $\sec x$: $\sec^2 x - \frac{3}{4} \sec x = \frac{1}{2}$.

$$\sec^2 x - \frac{3}{4} \sec x - \frac{1}{2} = 0$$

We now use the quadratic formula, and obtain

$$\sec x = \frac{\frac{3}{4} \pm \sqrt{\frac{9}{16} - 4 \cdot 1 \cdot \left(-\frac{1}{2}\right)}}{2} = \frac{\frac{3}{4} \pm \sqrt{\frac{41}{16}}}{2}$$

$$= \frac{\frac{3}{4} \pm \frac{\sqrt{41}}{4}}{2} = \frac{3 \pm \sqrt{41}}{8}$$

TRY THIS

4. Solve for $\cot x$ in $\cot^2 x + \cot x = 12$. $\quad$ $\cot x = -4$ or $\cot x = 3$

15–7

Exercises
Multiply and simplify.

1. $(\sin x - \cos x)(\sin x + \cos x)$ $\quad$ $\sin^2 x - \cos^2 x$ $\quad$ **2.** $(\tan \theta - \cot \theta)(\tan \theta + \cot \theta)$ $\quad$ $\tan^2 \theta - \cot^2 \theta$

3. $\tan x \, (\cos x - \csc x)$ $\quad$ $\sin x - \sec x$ $\quad$ **4.** $\cot x \, (\sin x + \sec x)$ $\quad$ $\cos x + \csc x$

5. $\cos \theta \sin \theta \, (\sec \theta + \csc \theta)$ $\quad$ $\sin \theta + \cos \theta$ $\quad$ **6.** $\tan y \sin y \, (\cot y - \csc y)$ $\quad$ $\sin y - \tan y$

7. $(\sin x + \cos x)(\csc x - \sec x)$ $\cot x - \tan x$

8. $(\sin x + \cos x)(\sec x + \csc x)$

9. $(\sin y - \cos y)^2$ $1 - 2 \sin y \cos y$

10. $(\sin \theta + \cos \theta)^2$ $1 + 2 \sin \theta \cos \theta$

11. $(1 + \tan \theta)^2$ $\sec^2 \theta + 2 \tan \theta$

12. $(1 + \cot x)^2$ $\csc^2 x + 2 \cot x$
$8. \tan x + \cot x + 2$

Factor and simplify.

13. $\sin x \cos x + \cos^2 x$ $\cos x (\sin x + \cos x)$

14. $\sec x \csc x - \csc^2 x$ $\csc x (\sec x - \csc x)$

15. $\sin^2 y - \cos^2 y$ $(\sin y - \cos y)(\sin y + \cos y)$

16. $\tan^2 y - \cot^2 y$ $(\tan y - \cot y)(\tan y + \cot y)$

17. $\tan x + \sin (\pi - x)$ $\tan x + \sin x$

18. $\cot \theta - \cos (\pi - \theta)$ $\cot \theta + \cos \theta$

19. $\sin^4 \theta - \cos^4 \theta$ $\sin^2 \theta - \cos^2 \theta)$

20. $\tan^4 x - \sec^4 x$ $-(\tan^2 x + \sec^2 x)$

21. $3 \cot^2 y + 6 \cot y + 3$ $3 (\cot y + 1)^2$

22. $4 \sin^2 y + 8 \sin y + 4$ $4 (\sin y + 1)^2$

23. $\csc^4 \theta + 4 \csc^2 \theta - 5$ $(\csc^2 \theta + 5)(\cot^2 \theta)$

24. $\tan^4 x - 2 \tan^2 x - 3$ $(\tan^2 x - 3)(\sec^2 x)$

Simplify.

25. $\dfrac{\sin^2 x \cos x}{\cos^2 x \sin x}$ $\tan x$

26. $\dfrac{\cos^2 x \sin x}{\sin^2 x \cos x}$ $\cot x$

27. $\dfrac{4 \sin \theta \cos^3 \theta}{18 \sin^2 \theta \cos \theta}$ $\frac{2}{9} \cos \theta \cot \theta$

28. $\dfrac{30 \sin^3 x \cos x}{6 \cos^2 x \sin x}$ $5 \tan x \sin x$

29. $\dfrac{\cos^2 x - 2 \cos x + 1}{\cos x - 1}$ $\cos x - 1$

30. $\dfrac{\sin^2 x + 2 \sin x + 1}{\sin x + 1}$ $\sin x + 1$

31. $\dfrac{\cos^2 x - 1}{\cos x - 1}$ $\cos x + 1$

32. $\dfrac{\sin^2 \theta - 1}{\sin \theta + 1}$ $\sin \theta - 1$

Solve for the indicated trigonometric expression.

33. $\tan^2 x + 4 \tan x = 21$, for $\tan x$

34. $\sec^2 \theta - 7 \sec \theta = -10$, for $\sec \theta$

35. $8 \sin^2 \theta - 2 \sin \theta = 3$, for $\sin \theta$

36. $6 \cos^2 x + 17 \cos x = -5$, for $\cos x$

37. $\cot^2 x + 9 \cot x - 10 = 0$, for $\cot x$

38. $\csc^2 \theta + 3 \csc \theta - 10 = 0$, for $\csc \theta$

39. $\sin^2 \theta + \cos \left(\theta + \dfrac{\pi}{2}\right) = 6$, for $\sin \theta$

40. $2 \cos^2 \left(x - \dfrac{\pi}{2}\right) - 3 \cos \left(x - \dfrac{\pi}{2}\right) - 2 = 0$, for $\sin x$

41. $\tan^2 \theta - 6 \tan \theta = 4$, for $\tan \theta$

42. $2 \csc^2 x - 3 \csc x - 4 = 0$, for $\csc x$

Extension

43. Show that $\csc \theta - \cos \theta \cot \theta$ is equal to $\sin \theta$.

44. Show that $\sec \theta - \sin \theta \tan \theta$ is equal to $\cos \theta$.

Check the following identities by testing the equality of cross products.

45. $\dfrac{1 - \sin \theta}{\cos \theta} = \dfrac{\cos \theta}{1 + \sin \theta}$

46. $\dfrac{1 - \cos \theta}{\sin \theta} = \dfrac{\sin \theta}{1 + \cos \theta}$

CAREERS/Aerial Surveying

From an airplane aerial surveyors determine the relationships among features on the earth's surface. They then make maps showing the contours of the region. These maps show depressions and elevations in the land as well as features such as forests, rivers, roads, buildings, and other significant landmarks. Aerial surveying is especially useful in charting inaccessible regions.

Here is an example of information an aerial surveyor may gather while flying over an area: To the west are two ponds. The angles of depression to the ponds are 46°10′ and 63°50′. The airplane is flying at a height of 600 meters.

To find the distance between the two ponds to the nearest meter, the aerial surveyor would use the methods taught in Section 16–6.

$$\cot \theta_1 = \frac{d_1}{600}$$

$$\cot \theta_2 = \frac{d_2}{600}$$
$$d_1 = 600 \cot \theta_1$$
$$d_2 = 600 \cot \theta_2$$
$$d = d_2 - d_1$$
$$d = 600 \cot 46°10' - 600 \cot 63°50'$$
$$= 600(\cot 46°10' - \cot 63°50')$$
$$= 600(0.9601 - 0.4913)$$
$$= 600(0.4688)$$
$$= 281.28$$
$$\approx 281 \text{ m}$$

The distance between the two ponds is about 281 meters.

The aerial surveyor also takes photographs from the air. Special photographic equipment installed in the airplane makes possible photographs of large areas. From these photographs accurate measurements of the landscape and any identifying features can be made.

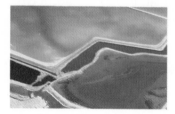

Exercises

Solve. Find answers to the nearest meter.

1. From an airplane 800 meters high, a house is seen at a 43°20′ angle of depression. How far is it from a point on the ground directly below the airplane to the house? 848 m

2. An airplane flying at a height of 1000 meters is just above a crossroads. The angle of depression to the next crossroads is 25°30′. What is the distance between the two crossroads? 2097 m

3. From an airplane flying 700 meters above the ground, one can see to the south a barn at a 72°50′ angle of depression and a cabin at 35°40′ angle of depression. What is the distance between the cabin and the barn? 759 m

4. From an airplane flying 1000 meters above the ground one can see to the east a fork in the river at an angle of depression of 55°20′. To the west at an angle of depression of 68°50′ is the mouth of the river. What is the distance between the fork and the mouth of the river? 1004 m

5. An airplane is flying at an altitude of 850 meters. To the north at an angle of depression of 17°10′ is a hunting lodge. To the south at an angle of depression of·81°40′ is the intersection of the driveway to the lodge and the road. How long is the driveway? 2876 m

CHAPTER 15 Review

Review the material in the chapter. Then see how you have done by trying these review exercises. If you miss an exercise, restudy the indicated lesson.

15-1 Solve.

1. In triangle ABC, $\angle C$ is a right angle, $b = 10$ cm and $m\angle A = 60°$. (Sides a, b, and c are opposite angles A, B, and C respectively. What is the length of side c? 20 cm

2. If $\tan \theta = \dfrac{\sqrt{3}}{3}$, find the other five trigonometric function values.

$\sin \theta = \frac{1}{2}$, $\cos \theta = \frac{\sqrt{3}}{2}$, $\cot \theta = \sqrt{3}$, $\sec \theta = \frac{2\sqrt{3}}{3}$, $\csc \theta = 2$

15-2 In which quadrant does the terminal side of each angle lie?

3. $14°$ 4. $201°$ 5. $116°$ 6. $-131°$
First   Third   Second   Third

7. Find the six trigonometric function values for the angle θ shown.

$\sin \theta = \frac{-4}{7}$, $\cos \theta = \frac{\sqrt{33}}{7}$, $\tan \theta = \frac{-4}{\sqrt{33}}$, $\cot \theta = \frac{\sqrt{33}}{-4}$, $\sec \theta = \frac{7}{\sqrt{33}}$, $\csc \theta = \frac{7}{-4}$

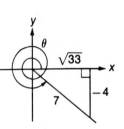

Find the reference angle for the following angles of rotation.

8. $330°$ 30° 9. $-510°$ 30° 10. $220°$ 40°

15-2 Find each of the following function values or indicate if it is undefined.

11. $\tan 270°$ 12. $\tan -315$ 1   13. $\sin 495°$ $\frac{\sqrt{2}}{2}$
Undefined

15-3 Convert to radian measure. Give answers in terms of π.

14. $45°$ $\frac{\pi}{4}$ 15. $150°$ $\frac{5\pi}{6}$ 16. $270°$ $\frac{3\pi}{2}$ 17. $-60°$ $-\frac{\pi}{3}$

15-3 Convert to degree measure.

18. $\dfrac{7\pi}{6}$ radians 210°   19. $-\dfrac{\pi}{3}$ radians -60°   20. 4π radians 720°

15-3 Find the function value using cofunctions.

21. $\csc 45°$ $\sqrt{2}$ 22. $\cot 30°$ $\sqrt{3}$ 23. $\sin 90°$ 1

15-3 Use Table 3 to find each of the following.

24. $\sin 8°20'$ 0.0449   25. $\cos 391°30'$ 0.8526

15-3 Use Table 3 and interpolation to find each of the following.

26. $\tan 27°14'$ 0.515   27. $\sin 42°18'$ 0.6730

15–3   Find θ degrees and minutes between $0°$ and $90°$.

28. $\cos \theta = 0.9094$ **29.** $\tan \theta = 1.103$ 47°48'
24°35'

15–4

30. Sketch a graph of the secant function. See Example 4 in Section 15–4.

15–5   Check each identity by using $\theta = \frac{\pi}{4}$.

31. $\tan \theta \equiv \dfrac{\sin \theta}{\cos \theta}$ **32.** $\sin \left(\dfrac{\pi}{2} - 0 \right) \equiv \cos \theta$ $\sin \left(\frac{\pi}{2} - \frac{\pi}{4} \right) = \sin \frac{\pi}{4} = \frac{\sqrt{2}}{2}$ 31. $\dfrac{\frac{\sqrt{2}}{2}}{\frac{\sqrt{2}}{2}} = 1$

15–5

33. Use the given function values to find the six function values of the complement of $75°$. $\sin 75° = 0.9659$, $\cos 75° = 0.2588$, $\tan 75° = 3.732$, $\cot 75° = 0.2679$, $\sec 75° = 3.864$, $\csc 75° = 1.035$. $\sin 15° = 0.2588$, $\cos 15° = 0.9659$, $\tan 15° = 0.2679$, $\cot 15° = 3.732$, $\sec 15° = 1.035$, $\csc 15° = 3.864$

15–6

34. Sketch a graph of $y = 3 \cos \theta$. What is the amplitude of the function?

35. Sketch a graph of $y = \sin \theta$. What is the period of the function?

36. Simplify $\cos \theta (\tan \theta + \cot \theta)$ **37.** Solve $3 \tan^2 \theta - 2 = 0$ for $\tan \theta$. $\frac{1 \pm \sqrt{7}}{3}$ 36. $\csc \theta$

CHAPTER 15   Test

1. In triangle ABC, $\angle C$ is a right angle, $b = 10$ cm and $m \angle A = 45°$. What is the length of side c? $10\sqrt{2}$ cm

2. If $\sin \theta = \dfrac{1}{\sqrt{5}}$, find the other five trigonometric function values.

3. Find the six trigonometric function values for the angle θ shown.

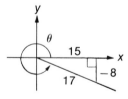

Find each of the following function values or indicate if it is undefined.

4. $\sin -135°$ **5.** $\tan 540°$ 0   6. $\frac{-\sqrt{2}}{2}$

6. Convert $-225°$ to radian measure, in terms of π. $\frac{-5\pi}{4}$

7. Convert $-\dfrac{3\pi}{2}$ to degree measure. $-270°$

Use Table 3 and interpolation to find each of the following.

8. cos 32°40' 0.8444   **9.** tan 54°18' 1.391

Find θ in degrees and minutes between 0° and 90°.

10. sin θ = 0.6259   **11.** tan θ = 1.331 53°05'

12. Use the given function values to find the six function values of the complement of 54°. sin 54° = 0.8090, cos 54° = 0.5878, tan 54° = 1.376, cot 54° = 0.7265, sec 54° = 1.701, csc 54° = 1.236 sin 36° = 0.5878, cos 36° = 0.8090, tan 36° = 0.7265, cot 36° = 1.376, sec 36° = 1.236, csc 36° = 1.701

13. Sketch a graph of $y = 4 \sin \theta$. What is the amplitude of the function? Sine curve with amplitude 4 through $(-\pi, 0), \left(-\frac{\pi}{2}, -4\right), (0, 0), \left(\frac{\pi}{2}, 4\right), (\pi, 0)$

14. Sketch a graph of $y = \sin \frac{1}{2}\theta$. What is the period of the function? Sin curve with period 4π through $(-2\pi, 0), (-\pi, -1), (0, 0), (\pi, 1),$ and $(2\pi, 0)$

15. Simplify $\dfrac{\csc \theta(\sin^2 \theta + \cos^2 \theta \tan \theta)}{\sin \theta + \cos \theta}$. 1

16. Solve $6 \sec^2 \theta - 5 \sec \theta - 2 = 0$ for sec θ. $\frac{5 \pm \sqrt{73}}{12}$

Challenge

17. Solve $2 \sin^2 \theta - 3 \sin \theta + 1 = \theta$ for θ. $\theta = 30°$ or $90°$

Ready for Trigonometric Identities and Equations?

7–1 Simplify.

1. $\sqrt{(-81)^2}$ 81   **2.** $\sqrt{(9c)^2}$ 9|c|

7–4 Simplify by rationalizing the denominators.

3. $\dfrac{\sqrt[3]{4m}}{\sqrt[3]{5n}}$ **4.** $\dfrac{5\sqrt{5} - 2\sqrt{3}}{2\sqrt{3} - 3\sqrt{5}}$ $\frac{63 + 4\sqrt{15}}{-33}$

12–1 Find $f^{-1}(x)$.

5. $f(x) = 3x - 2$ **6.** $f(x) = 2 + \sqrt{x + 3}$ $f^{-1}(x) = x^2 - 4x + 1$

7–10 Find the absolute value of each complex number.

7. $|-a + bi|$ **8.** $|5 - 12i|$ 13

16

CHAPTER SIXTEEN

Trigonometric Identities and Equations

16-1 Sum and Difference Identities

We will now consider some important identities involving sums or differences of angles or rotations.

Cosines of Sums or Differences

A basic identity shows that the cosine of the difference of two angles is related to the cosines and sines of the angles themselves. This identity can be used to simplify expressions.

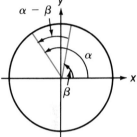

$$\cos (\alpha - \beta) \equiv \cos \alpha \cos \beta + \sin \alpha \sin \beta$$

EXAMPLE 1

Simplify $\cos \left(\dfrac{3\pi}{4} - \dfrac{\pi}{3}\right)$.

$$\cos \left(\frac{3\pi}{4} - \frac{\pi}{3}\right) = \cos \frac{3\pi}{4} \cdot \cos \frac{\pi}{3} + \sin \frac{3\pi}{4} \cdot \sin \frac{\pi}{3} \quad \text{Applying the identity above}$$

$$= -\frac{\sqrt{2}}{2} \cdot \frac{1}{2} + \frac{\sqrt{2}}{2} \cdot \frac{\sqrt{3}}{2} \quad \text{Evaluating each factor}$$

$$= \frac{\sqrt{2}}{4}(-1 + \sqrt{3}) \text{ or } \frac{\sqrt{2}}{4}(\sqrt{3} - 1) \text{ or } \frac{\sqrt{6} - \sqrt{2}}{4}$$

TRY THIS

1. Simplify $\cos \left(\dfrac{\pi}{2} - \dfrac{\pi}{6}\right)$. $\frac{1}{2}$

EXAMPLE 2

Find $\cos 15°$.

$$\cos 15° = \cos (45° - 30°) \quad \begin{array}{l}\text{Writing } 15° \text{ in terms of angles} \\ \text{with known function values.}\end{array}$$

$$= \cos 45° \cos 30° + \sin 45° \sin 30°$$

$$= \frac{\sqrt{2}}{2} \cdot \frac{\sqrt{3}}{2} + \frac{\sqrt{2}}{2} \cdot \frac{1}{2}$$

$$= \frac{\sqrt{2}}{4}(\sqrt{3} + 1), \text{ or } \frac{\sqrt{6} + \sqrt{2}}{4}$$

TRY THIS

2. Find $\cos 105°$ by evaluating $\cos (150° - 45°)$. $\frac{\sqrt{2} - \sqrt{6}}{4}$

A Proof of the Cosine Identity

We have seen that $\cos(\alpha - \beta) \equiv \cos\alpha\cos\beta + \sin\alpha\sin\beta$. Let us see how this identity is developed.

Suppose angles α and β have coordinates as shown.

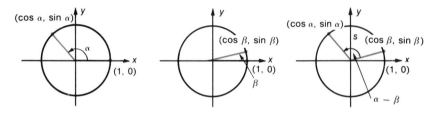

The figure on the right shows these angles on the same coordinate axes. Notice that the size of the angle between them is $\alpha - \beta$. We use the distance formula to write an expression for the length s.

$$
\begin{aligned}
s^2 &= (\cos\alpha - \cos\beta)^2 + (\sin\alpha - \sin\beta)^2 \\
&= (\cos^2\alpha - 2\cos\alpha\cos\beta + \cos^2\beta) + (\sin^2\alpha - 2\sin\alpha\sin\beta + \sin^2\beta) \\
&= (\cos^2\alpha + \sin^2\alpha) + (\cos^2\beta + \sin^2\beta) - 2\cos\alpha\cos\beta - 2\sin\alpha\cos\beta \\
&= 1 + 1 - 2\cos\alpha\cos\beta - 2\sin\alpha\sin\beta \\
&= 2 - 2(\cos\alpha\cos\beta + \sin\alpha\sin\beta)
\end{aligned}
$$

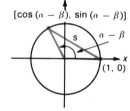

Now imagine that the unit circle above is rotated so that $(\cos\beta, \sin\beta)$ is at $(1, 0)$. The length s has not changed.

$$
\begin{aligned}
s^2 &= [\cos(\alpha - \beta) - 1]^2 + [\sin(\alpha - \beta) - 0]^2 \\
&= [\cos^2(\alpha - \beta) - 2\cos(\alpha - \beta) + 1] + \sin^2(\alpha - \beta) \\
&= [\cos^2(\alpha - \beta) + \sin^2(\alpha - \beta)] + 1 - 2\cos(\alpha - \beta) \\
&= 2 - 2\cos(\alpha - \beta)
\end{aligned}
$$

Equating our two expressions for s^2, we obtain

$$
\begin{aligned}
2 - 2\cos(\alpha - \beta) &= 2 - 2(\cos\alpha\cos\beta + \sin\alpha\sin\beta), \\
\cos(\alpha - \beta) &= \cos\alpha\cos\beta + \sin\alpha\sin\beta.
\end{aligned}
$$

Next let us consider $\cos(\alpha + \beta)$. This is equal to $\cos[\alpha - (-\beta)]$, and by the cosine of a difference identity, we have the following.

$$\cos(\alpha + \beta) \equiv \cos\alpha\cos(-\beta) + \sin\alpha\sin(-\beta)$$

But

$$\cos(-\beta) \equiv \cos\beta \quad \text{and} \quad \sin(-\beta) \equiv -\sin\beta$$

so the identity we seek is the following.

$$\cos(\alpha + \beta) \equiv \cos\alpha\cos\beta - \sin\alpha\sin\beta$$

EXAMPLE 3

Find cos 105°.

$$\begin{aligned}
\cos 105° &= \cos (60° + 45°) \\
&= \cos 60° \cos 45° - \sin 60° \sin 45° \quad \text{Writing 105° in terms of} \\
&= \frac{1}{2} \cdot \frac{\sqrt{2}}{2} - \frac{\sqrt{3}}{2} \cdot \frac{\sqrt{2}}{2} \quad\quad\quad \text{angles with known function values} \\
&= \frac{\sqrt{2} - \sqrt{6}}{4}
\end{aligned}$$

TRY THIS

3. Find cos 75° by evaluating cos (30° + 45°). $\frac{\sqrt{6} - \sqrt{2}}{4}$

Other Identities

To develop an identity for the sine of a sum, we recall the following.

$$\sin \theta \equiv \cos \left(\frac{\pi}{2} - \theta \right)$$

In this identity we shall substitute $\alpha + \beta$ for θ.

$$\sin (\alpha + \beta) \equiv \cos \left[\frac{\pi}{2} - (\alpha + \beta) \right]$$

We can now use the identity for the cosine of a difference.

$$\begin{aligned}
\sin (\alpha + \beta) &\equiv \cos \left[\frac{\pi}{2} - (\alpha + \beta) \right] \\
&\equiv \cos \left[\left(\frac{\pi}{2} - \alpha \right) - \beta \right] \\
&\equiv \cos \left(\frac{\pi}{2} - \alpha \right) \cos \beta + \sin \left(\frac{\pi}{2} - \alpha \right) \sin \beta \\
&\equiv \sin \alpha \cos \beta + \cos \alpha \sin \beta
\end{aligned}$$

Thus, $\sin (\alpha + \beta) \equiv \sin \alpha \cos \beta + \cos \alpha \sin \beta$

EXAMPLE 4

Simplify $\sin \left(\frac{5\pi}{4} + \frac{\pi}{3} \right)$.

$$\begin{aligned}
\sin \left(\frac{5\pi}{4} + \frac{\pi}{3} \right) &= \sin \frac{5\pi}{4} \cos \frac{\pi}{3} + \cos \frac{5\pi}{4} \sin \frac{\pi}{3} \\
&= -\frac{\sqrt{2}}{2} \cdot \frac{1}{2} + \left(-\frac{\sqrt{2}}{2} \right) \frac{\sqrt{3}}{2} \\
&= \frac{-\sqrt{2}}{4} - \frac{\sqrt{6}}{4} = \frac{-\sqrt{2} - \sqrt{6}}{4}
\end{aligned}$$

TRY THIS

4. Simplify $\sin\left(\frac{\pi}{4} + \frac{\pi}{3}\right)$. $\frac{\sqrt{2} + \sqrt{6}}{4}$

To find an identity for the sine of a difference, we can use the identity just derived, substituting $-\beta$ for β.

$$\sin(\alpha - \beta) \equiv \sin \alpha \cos \beta - \cos \alpha \sin \beta$$

An identity for the tangent of a sum can be derived as follows, using identities already established.

$$\tan(\alpha + \beta) \equiv \frac{\sin(\alpha + \beta)}{\cos(\alpha + \beta)}$$

$$\equiv \frac{\sin \alpha \cos \beta + \cos \alpha \sin \beta}{\cos \alpha \cos \beta - \sin \alpha \sin \beta} \cdot \frac{\dfrac{1}{\cos \alpha \cos \beta}}{\dfrac{1}{\cos \alpha \cos \beta}}$$

$$\equiv \frac{\dfrac{\sin \alpha \cos \beta}{\cos \alpha \cos \beta} + \dfrac{\cos \alpha \sin \beta}{\cos \alpha \cos \beta}}{\dfrac{\cos \alpha \cos \beta}{\cos \alpha \cos \beta} - \dfrac{\sin \alpha \sin \beta}{\cos \alpha \cos \beta}}$$

$$\equiv \frac{\dfrac{\sin \alpha}{\cos \alpha} + \dfrac{\sin \beta}{\cos \beta}}{1 - \dfrac{\sin \alpha \sin \beta}{\cos \alpha \cos \beta}}$$

$$\equiv \frac{\tan \alpha + \tan \beta}{1 - \tan \alpha \tan \beta}$$

Similarly, an identity for the tangent of a difference can be established. The following theorem summarizes the sum and difference formulas. These should be memorized.

THEOREM 16–1

$$\cos(\alpha - \beta) \equiv \cos \alpha \cos \beta + \sin \alpha \sin \beta$$
$$\cos(\alpha + \beta) \equiv \cos \alpha \cos \beta - \sin \alpha \sin \beta$$
$$\sin(\alpha - \beta) \equiv \sin \alpha \cos \beta - \cos \alpha \sin \beta$$
$$\sin(\alpha + \beta) \equiv \sin \alpha \cos \beta + \cos \alpha \sin \beta$$
$$\tan(\alpha - \beta) \equiv \frac{\tan \alpha - \tan \beta}{1 + \tan \alpha \tan \beta}$$
$$\tan(\alpha + \beta) \equiv \frac{\tan \alpha + \tan \beta}{1 - \tan \alpha \tan \beta}$$

The identities involving sines and tangents can be used in the same way as those involving cosines in the earlier examples. Simply write the angle as a sum or difference of angles with known function values.

EXAMPLE 5
Find tan 15°.

$$\tan 15° = \tan (45° - 30°)$$

$$= \frac{\tan 45° - \tan 30°}{1 + \tan 45° \tan 30°}$$

$$= \frac{1 - \frac{\sqrt{3}}{3}}{1 + \frac{\sqrt{3}}{3}} = \frac{3 - \sqrt{3}}{3 + \sqrt{3}} = 2 - \sqrt{3}$$

TRY THIS

5. Find tan 105° by evaluating tan (45° + 60°). $-2 - \sqrt{3}$

16–1

Exercises

Use the cosine sum and difference identities to simplify the following.

1. $\cos (A - B)$
2. $\cos (A + B)$
3. $\cos (45° + 30°)$
4. $\cos (45° - 30°)$
5. $\cos (45° + 60°)$
6. $\cos (60° - 45°)$
7. $\cos \left(\frac{\pi}{4} + \frac{\pi}{3}\right)$
8. $\cos \left(\frac{\pi}{4} - \frac{\pi}{3}\right)$

Use the cosine sum and difference identities to find the following.

9. $\cos 165°$
10. $\cos 195°$
11. $\cos 135°$
12. $\cos 225°$

Use sine and tangent sum and difference identities to simplify the following.

13. $\sin (P + Q)$
14. $\sin (P - Q)$
15. $\tan (P - Q)$
16. $\tan (P + Q)$
17. $\sin (45° + 60°)$
18. $\sin (45° - 30°)$
19. $\tan (45° + 30°)$
20. $\tan (45° - 30°)$
21. $\sin P \cos Q + \sin Q \cos P$
22. $\cos Q \sin P - \cos P \sin Q$

1. $\cos A \cos B + \sin A \sin B$
2. $\cos A \cos B - \sin A \sin B$
3. $\frac{\sqrt{6} - \sqrt{2}}{4}$
4. $\frac{\sqrt{6} + \sqrt{2}}{4}$
5. $\frac{\sqrt{2} - \sqrt{6}}{4}$
6. $\frac{\sqrt{2} + \sqrt{6}}{4}$
7. $\frac{\sqrt{2} - \sqrt{6}}{4}$
8. $\frac{\sqrt{2} + \sqrt{6}}{4}$
9. $\frac{-\sqrt{2} - \sqrt{6}}{4}$
10. $\frac{-\sqrt{6} - \sqrt{2}}{4}$
11. $-\frac{\sqrt{2}}{2}$
12. $-\frac{\sqrt{2}}{2}$
13. $\sin P \cos Q + \cos P \sin Q$
14. $\sin P \cos Q - \cos P \sin Q$
15. $\frac{\tan P - \tan Q}{1 + \tan P \tan Q}$
16. $\frac{\tan P + \tan Q}{1 - \tan P \tan Q}$
17. $\frac{\sqrt{2} + \sqrt{6}}{4}$
18. $\frac{\sqrt{6} - \sqrt{2}}{4}$
19. $2 + \sqrt{3}$
20. $2 - \sqrt{3}$
21. $\sin (P + Q)$
22. $\sin (P - Q)$

Use sum and difference formulas to find the following.

23. sin 15°   **24.** sin 105°   **25.** sin 135°   **26.** sin 150°   **27.** tan 75°   **28.** tan 105°

23. $\dfrac{\sqrt{6}-\sqrt{2}}{4}$ 26. $\dfrac{1}{2}$

Extension

Use the cosine, sine, and tangent sum and difference identities to simplify each of the following.

24. $\dfrac{\sqrt{6}+\sqrt{2}}{4}$ 27. $2+\sqrt{3}$

25. $\dfrac{\sqrt{2}}{2}$ 28. $-2-\sqrt{3}$

29. $\sin\left(-\dfrac{5\pi}{2}\right)\cdot\sin\dfrac{\pi}{2}+\cos\dfrac{\pi}{2}\cdot\cos\left(-\dfrac{5\pi}{2}\right)$ **30.** $\sin\dfrac{\pi}{3}\cdot\sin\left(-\dfrac{\pi}{4}\right)+\cos\left(-\dfrac{\pi}{4}\right)\cdot\cos\dfrac{\pi}{3}$

31. $\cos A\cos B+\sin A\sin B$ **32.** $\cos A\cos B-\sin A\sin B$

29. $\cos\pi=-1$

30. $\cos\dfrac{7\pi}{12}=\dfrac{-\sqrt{6}+\sqrt{2}}{4}$

33. $\cos(\alpha+\beta)+\cos(\alpha-\beta)$ **34.** $\cos(\alpha+\beta)-\cos(\alpha-\beta)$

35. $\dfrac{\tan A-\tan B}{1+\tan A\tan B}$ **36.** $\dfrac{\tan A+\tan B}{1-\tan A\tan B}$

31. $\cos(A-B)$
32. $\cos(A+B)$
33. $2\cos\alpha\cos\beta$
34. $-2\sin\alpha\sin\beta$
35. $\tan(A-B)$
36. $\tan(A+B)$
37. $\tan 52°=1.280$

37. $\dfrac{\tan 20°+\tan 32°}{1-\tan 20°\tan 32°}$ **38.** $\dfrac{\tan 35°-\tan 12°}{1+\tan 35°\tan 12°}$

39. $\sin(\alpha+\beta)+\sin(\alpha-\beta)$ **40.** $\sin(\alpha+\beta)-\sin(\alpha-\beta)$

41. $\sin\dfrac{\pi}{3}\cdot\cos\pi+\sin\pi\cdot\cos\dfrac{\pi}{3}$ **42.** $\sin\dfrac{\pi}{2}\cdot\cos\dfrac{\pi}{3}-\sin\dfrac{\pi}{3}\cdot\cos\dfrac{\pi}{2}$

43. Find an identity for sin 2θ. [Hint: $2\theta=\theta+\theta$.] $2\sin\theta\cos\theta$

44. Find an identity for cos 2θ. [Hint: $2\theta=\theta+\theta$.] $\cos^2\theta-\sin^2\theta$

45. Derive an identity for cot (α + β) in terms of cot α and cot β. $\dfrac{\cot\alpha\cot\beta-1}{\cot\beta+\cot\alpha}$

46. Derive an identity for cot (α − β) in terms of cot α and cot β. $\dfrac{\cot\alpha\cot\beta+1}{\cot\beta-\cot\alpha}$

38. $\tan 23°=0.425$
39. $2\sin\alpha\cos\beta$
40. $2\sin\beta\cos\alpha$

The cofunction identities can be derived from the sum and difference formulas. Derive the following cofunction identities.

41. $-\dfrac{\sqrt{3}}{2}$

42. $\dfrac{1}{2}$

47. $\sin\left(\dfrac{\pi}{2}-x\right)$ **48.** $\sin\left(x-\dfrac{\pi}{2}\right)$ **49.** $\cos\left(\dfrac{\pi}{2}-x\right)$ **50.** $\cos\left(x+\dfrac{\pi}{2}\right)$

51. Find sin 45° + sin 30° and compare with sin 75°. (Use Table 3.) $1.2071;\,0.9659$

52. Find cos 45° − cos 30° and compare with cos 15°. (Use Table 3.) $-0.1589;\,0.9659$

Challenge

Given that sin θ = 0.6249 and cos φ = 0.1102, and that θ and φ are both first-quadrant angles, use a calculator to find the following.

53. $\sin(\theta+\phi)$ **54.** $\cos(\theta+\phi)$ 53. 0.8448 54. -0.5351

Use the idea of *composition of functions* to find a formula for each of the following. You may use the following substitution.

      Let $u=\sin x$ and $v=\sin y$.

55. $\sin(\sin x+\sin y)$ **56.** $\cos(\cos x+\cos y)$ **57.** $\sin(x+y+z)$

16-2 Double-Angle and Half-Angle Identities

Two important classes of trigonometric identities are known as the double-angle identities and the half-angle identities.

Double-Angle Identities

Identities involving $\sin 2\theta$ or $\cos 2\theta$ are called double-angle identities. To develop these identities we shall use the sum formulas from the preceding lesson.

We first develop a formula for $\sin 2\theta$. We shall consider an angle θ and substitute it for both α and β in the identity for $\sin (\alpha + \beta)$.

$$\begin{aligned}
\sin 2\theta &\equiv \sin (\theta + \theta) \\
&\equiv \sin \theta \cos \theta + \cos \theta \sin \theta \\
&\equiv 2 \sin \theta \cos \theta
\end{aligned}$$

Thus, we have the following identity.

$$\sin 2\theta \equiv 2 \sin \theta \cos \theta$$

EXAMPLE 1

If $\sin \theta = \frac{3}{8}$ and θ is in the first quadrant, what is $\sin 2\theta$?
From the diagram, we see that $\cos \theta = \frac{\sqrt{55}}{8}$.

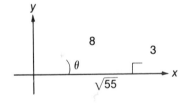

$$\sin 2\theta = 2 \sin \theta \cos \theta = 2 \cdot \frac{3}{8} \cdot \frac{\sqrt{55}}{8} = \frac{3\sqrt{55}}{32}$$

TRY THIS

1. If $\sin \theta = \frac{3}{5}$ and θ is in the first quadrant, what is $\sin 2\theta$? $\frac{24}{25}$

Double-angle identities for the cosine and tangent functions can be derived in much the same way as the identity above.

$$\begin{aligned}
\cos 2\theta &\equiv \cos (\theta + \theta) \\
&\equiv \cos \theta \cos \theta - \sin \theta \sin \theta \\
&\equiv \cos^2 \theta - \sin^2 \theta
\end{aligned}$$

Thus, we have the following identity.

$$\cos 2\theta \equiv \cos^2 \theta - \sin^2 \theta$$

By using the same kind of substitution, we can derive the double-angle identity for the tangent function.

$$\tan 2\theta \equiv \frac{2 \tan \theta}{1 - \tan^2 \theta}$$

EXAMPLE 2

Given that $\tan \theta = -\frac{3}{4}$ and θ is in the second quadrant, find $\sin 2\theta$, $\cos 2\theta$, $\tan 2\theta$, and the quadrant in which 2θ lies.

By drawing a diagram as shown, we find that $\sin \theta = \frac{3}{5}$ and $\cos \theta = -\frac{4}{5}$.

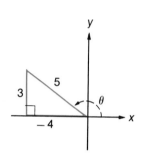

$$\sin 2\theta = 2 \sin \theta \cos \theta = 2 \cdot \frac{3}{5} \cdot \left(-\frac{4}{5}\right) = -\frac{24}{25}$$

$$\cos 2\theta = \cos^2 \theta - \sin^2 \theta = \left(-\frac{4}{5}\right)^2 - \left(\frac{3}{5}\right)^2 = \frac{16}{25} - \frac{9}{25} = \frac{7}{25}$$

$$\tan 2\theta = \frac{2 \tan \theta}{1 - \tan^2 \theta} = \frac{2 \cdot \left(-\frac{3}{4}\right)}{1 - \left(-\frac{3}{4}\right)^2} = \frac{-\frac{3}{2}}{1 - \frac{9}{16}} = -\frac{24}{7}$$

Since $\sin 2\theta$ is negative and $\cos 2\theta$ is positive, we know that 2θ is in quadrant IV. Note that $\tan 2\theta$ could have been found more easily in this case by dividing the values of $\sin 2\theta$ and $\cos 2\theta$; that is, $-\frac{24}{25} \div \frac{7}{25} = -\frac{24}{7}$.

TRY THIS

2. Given that $\cos \theta = -\frac{5}{13}$ with θ in the third quadrant. Find $\sin 2\theta$, $\cos 2\theta$, and $\tan 2\theta$. Also, determine the quadrant in which 2θ lies.

2. $\sin 2\theta = \frac{120}{169}$, $\cos 2\theta = -\frac{119}{169}$,

$\tan 2\theta = -\frac{120}{119}$, second quadrant

Two other useful identities for $\cos 2\theta$ can easily be derived as follows.

$$\cos 2\theta \equiv \cos^2 \theta - \sin^2 \theta$$
$$\equiv (1 - \sin^2 \theta) - \sin^2 \theta \quad \text{Using } \sin^2 \theta + \cos^2 \theta \equiv 1$$
$$\equiv 1 - 2 \sin^2 \theta$$

$$\cos 2\theta \equiv \cos^2 \theta - \sin^2 \theta$$
$$\equiv \cos^2 \theta - (1 - \cos^2 \theta) \quad \text{Using } \sin^2 \theta + \cos^2 \theta \equiv 1$$
$$\equiv 2 \cos^2 \theta - 1$$

Solving these two identities for $\sin^2 \theta$ and $\cos^2 \theta$, respectively, we obtain two more identities that are often useful. The following theorem summarizes the double-angle identities. They should be memorized.

THEOREM 16–2

$$\sin 2\theta \equiv 2 \sin \theta \cos \theta \qquad \tan 2\theta \equiv \frac{2 \tan \theta}{1 - \tan^2 \theta}$$

$$\cos 2\theta \equiv \cos^2 \theta - \sin^2 \theta$$
$$\cos 2\theta \equiv 1 - 2 \sin^2 \theta \qquad \sin^2 \theta \equiv \frac{1 - \cos 2\theta}{2}$$
$$\cos 2\theta \equiv 2 \cos^2 \theta - 1$$

$$\cos^2 \theta \equiv \frac{1 + \cos 2\theta}{2}$$

By dividing the last two identities, it is easy to derive the following useful identity.

$$\tan^2 \theta \equiv \frac{1 - \cos 2\theta}{1 + \cos 2\theta}$$

From the basic identities listed in Theorem 16–1 and Theorem 16–2, others can be obtained.

EXAMPLE 3
Find a formula for $\sin 3\theta$ in terms of function values of θ.

$$\begin{aligned}
\sin 3\theta &\equiv \sin (2\theta + \theta) \\
&\equiv \sin 2\theta \cos \theta + \cos 2\theta \sin \theta \\
&\equiv (2 \sin \theta \cos \theta) \cos \theta + (2 \cos^2 \theta - 1) \sin \theta \\
&\equiv 2 \sin \theta \cos^2 \theta + 2 \sin \theta \cos^2 \theta - \sin \theta \\
&\equiv 4 \sin \theta \cos^2 \theta - \sin \theta
\end{aligned}$$

TRY THIS

3. Find a formula for $\cos 3\theta$ in terms of function values of θ.

3. $\cos^3 \theta - 3 \sin^2 \theta \cos \theta$, $\cos \theta - 4 \sin^2 \theta \cos \theta$ or $2 \cos^3 \theta - \cos \theta - 2 \sin^2 \theta \cos \theta$

Half-Angle Identities

To develop these identities, we use previously developed ones. Consider the following identity.

$$\sin^2 \theta \equiv \frac{1 - \cos 2\theta}{2}$$

Note that the right side of this identity is in terms of 2θ. Letting $2\theta = \phi$ we have $\theta = \frac{\phi}{2}$. Taking the square roots gives the following.

$$\left| \sin \frac{\phi}{2} \right| \equiv \sqrt{\frac{1 - \cos \phi}{2}}$$

Similarly for cosine and tangent, by taking square roots and replacing θ by $\frac{\phi}{2}$ we have the following.

$$\left|\cos \frac{\phi}{2}\right| \equiv \sqrt{\frac{1 + \cos \phi}{2}} \qquad \left|\tan \frac{\phi}{2}\right| \equiv \sqrt{\frac{1 - \cos \phi}{1 + \cos \phi}}$$

We can eliminate the absolute value signs by introducing $\pm$ signs with the understanding that we use $+$ or $-$ depending on the quadrant in which the angle lies. We thus obtain the formulas summarized in the following theorem. They should be memorized.

THEOREM 16–3

$$\sin \frac{\phi}{2} \equiv \pm \sqrt{\frac{1 - \cos \phi}{2}} \qquad \cos \frac{\phi}{2} \equiv \pm \sqrt{\frac{1 + \cos \phi}{2}}$$

$$\tan \frac{\phi}{2} \equiv \pm \sqrt{\frac{1 - \cos \phi}{1 + \cos \phi}}$$

Two other formulas for $\tan \frac{\phi}{2}$ can be obtained.

THEOREM 16–4

$$\tan \frac{\phi}{2} \equiv \frac{\sin \phi}{1 + \cos \phi} \qquad \tan \frac{\phi}{2} \equiv \frac{1 - \cos \phi}{\sin \phi}$$

These formulas give the correct sign of $\tan \left(\frac{\phi}{2}\right)$ directly.

TRY THIS

4. Let $\phi = 30°$. Use Theorem 16–3 to find $\sin 15°$. $\frac{\sqrt{2 - \sqrt{3}}}{2}$

5. Let $\phi = 90°$. Use Theorem 16–4 to find $\tan 45°$. 1

16–2

Exercises

Find $\sin 2\theta$, $\cos 2\theta$, $\tan 2\theta$, and the quadrant in which 2θ lies.

1. $\sin \theta = \frac{4}{5}$ (θ in quadrant I)

2. $\sin \theta = \frac{5}{13}$ (θ in quadrant I)

3. $\cos \theta = -\dfrac{4}{5}$ (θ in quadrant III)

4. $\cos \theta = -\dfrac{3}{5}$ (θ in quadrant III)

5. $\tan \theta = \dfrac{4}{3}$ (θ in quadrant III)

6. $\tan \theta = \dfrac{3}{4}$ (θ in quadrant III)

Find the following without using tables.

7. $\sin 75°$ $\left[Hint: 75 = \dfrac{150}{2}\right]$ $\quad \dfrac{\sqrt{2+\sqrt{3}}}{2}$

8. $\cos 75°$ $\quad \dfrac{\sqrt{2-\sqrt{3}}}{2}$

9. $\tan 75°$ $\quad 2+\sqrt{3}$

10. $\tan 67.5°$ $\left[Hint: 67.5 = \dfrac{135}{2}\right]$ $\quad \sqrt{2}+1$

11. $\sin \dfrac{5\pi}{8}$ $\quad \dfrac{\sqrt{2+\sqrt{2}}}{2}$

12. $\cos \dfrac{5\pi}{8}$ $\quad -\dfrac{\sqrt{2-\sqrt{2}}}{2}$

13. $\sin \dfrac{3\pi}{8}$ $\quad \dfrac{\sqrt{2+\sqrt{2}}}{2}$

14. $\cos \dfrac{3\pi}{8}$ $\quad \dfrac{\sqrt{2-\sqrt{2}}}{2}$

15. $\cos 15°$ $\quad \dfrac{\sqrt{2+\sqrt{3}}}{2}$

16. $\tan \dfrac{\pi}{8}$ $\left[Hint: \dfrac{\pi}{8} = \dfrac{1}{2} \cdot \dfrac{\pi}{4}\right]$ $\quad \sqrt{2}-1$

Answer column (between problems):
1. $\dfrac{24}{25}, -\dfrac{7}{25}, -\dfrac{24}{7}$, II
2. $\dfrac{120}{169}, \dfrac{119}{169}, \dfrac{120}{119}$, I
3. $\dfrac{24}{25}, \dfrac{7}{25}, \dfrac{24}{7}$, I
4. $\dfrac{24}{25}, -\dfrac{7}{25}, -\dfrac{24}{7}$, II
5. $\dfrac{24}{25}, -\dfrac{7}{25}, -\dfrac{24}{7}$, II
6. $\dfrac{24}{25}, \dfrac{7}{25}, \dfrac{24}{7}$, I

Extension

Find these formulas.

17. Find a formula for $\sin 4\theta$ in terms of function values of θ.

18. Find a formula for $\cos 4\theta$ in terms of function values of θ.

19. Find a formula for $\sin^4 \theta$ in terms of function values of θ or 2θ or 4θ, raised only to the first power.

20. Find a formula for $\cos^4 \theta$ in terms of function values of θ or 2θ or 4θ, raised only to the first power.

21. Derive the formula for $\tan 2\theta$ given in Theorem 16–2.

Answers:
17. $8 \sin \theta \cos^3 \theta - 4 \sin \theta \cos \theta$, or $4 \sin \theta \cos^3 \theta - 4 \sin^3 \theta \cos \theta$, or $4 \sin \theta \cos \theta - 8 \sin^3 \theta \cos \theta$

18. (Answers may vary.) $\cos^4 \theta - 6 \cos^2 \theta \sin^2 \theta + \sin^4 \theta$, or $8 \cos^4 \theta - 8 \cos^2 \theta + 1$

19. $\dfrac{1}{8}(3 - 4 \cos 2\theta + \cos 4\theta)$

20. $\dfrac{1}{8}(3 + 4 \cos 2\theta + \cos 4\theta)$

Simplify.

22. $1 - 2 \sin^2 \dfrac{x}{2}$ $\quad \cos x$

23. $2 \cos^2 \dfrac{x}{2} - 1$ $\quad \cos x$

24. $2 \sin \dfrac{x}{2} \cos \dfrac{x}{2}$ $\quad \sin x$

25. $2 \sin 2x \cos 2x$ $\quad \sin 4x$

26. $\cos^2 \dfrac{x}{2} - \sin^2 \dfrac{x}{2}$ $\quad \cos x$

27. $2 \sin^2 \dfrac{x}{2} + \cos x$ $\quad 1$

28. $\cos^4 x - \sin^4 x$ $\quad 1$

29. $(\sin x + \cos x)^2 - \sin 2x$ $\quad 1$

30. $(\sin x - \cos x)^2 + \sin 2x$ $\quad 1$

21. Use Theorem 16–1 using θ for both α and β.

31. $(-4 \cos x \sin x + 2 \cos 2x)^2 + (2 \cos 2x + 4 \sin x \cos x)^2$ $\quad 8$

32. $(-4 \cos 2x + 8 \cos x \sin x)^2 + (8 \sin x \cos x + 4 \cos 2x)^2$ $\quad 32$

33. $2 \sin x \cos^3 x + 2 \sin^3 x \cos x$ $\quad \sin 2x$

34. $2 \sin x \cos^3 x - 2 \sin^3 x \cos x$ $\quad \sin 2x \cos 2x$

16-3 Proving Identities

Basic Identities

One should remember certain trigonometric identities. Then as the occasion arises, other identities can be proved using those memorized. Following is a minimal list of identities that should be learned. Note that most formulas involving cotangents, secants, and cosecants are not in the list. That is because these functions are reciprocals of the sine, cosine, and tangent, and thus formulas for the former can easily be derived from those for the latter.

Pythagorean identities

$$\sin(-x) \equiv -\sin x$$
$$\cos(-x) \equiv \cos x$$
$$\tan(-x) \equiv -\tan x$$

$$\sin^2 x + \cos^2 x \equiv 1$$
$$1 + \tan^2 x \equiv \sec^2 x$$
$$1 + \cot^2 x \equiv \csc^2 x$$

Cofunction identities

$$\sin\left(x \pm \frac{\pi}{2}\right) \equiv \pm\cos x$$
$$\cos\left(x \pm \frac{\pi}{2}\right) \equiv \mp\sin x$$

Sum and difference identities

$$\sin(\alpha \pm \beta) \equiv \sin\alpha\cos\beta \pm \cos\alpha\sin\beta$$
$$\cos(\alpha \pm \beta) \equiv \cos\alpha\cos\beta \mp \sin\alpha\sin\beta$$
$$\tan(\alpha \pm \beta) \equiv \frac{\tan\alpha \pm \tan\beta}{1 \mp \tan\alpha\tan\beta}$$

Double-angle identities

$$\sin 2x \equiv 2\sin x\cos x$$
$$\cos 2x \equiv \cos^2 x - \sin^2 x \equiv 1 - 2\sin^2 x$$
$$\equiv 2\cos^2 x - 1$$
$$\tan 2x \equiv \frac{2\tan x}{1 - \tan^2 x}$$
$$\sin^2 x \equiv \frac{1 - \cos 2x}{2}$$
$$\cos^2 x \equiv \frac{1 + \cos 2x}{2}$$

Half-angle identities

$$\sin\frac{x}{2} \equiv \pm\sqrt{\frac{1 - \cos x}{2}}$$
$$\cos\frac{x}{2} \equiv \pm\sqrt{\frac{1 + \cos x}{2}}$$
$$\tan\frac{x}{2} \equiv \pm\sqrt{\frac{1 - \cos x}{1 + \cos x}} \equiv \frac{\sin x}{1 + \cos x} \equiv \frac{1 - \cos x}{\sin x}$$

EXAMPLE 1
Prove the following identity.

$$\tan^2 x - \sin^2 x \equiv \sin^2 x \tan^2 x$$

$\dfrac{\sin^2 x}{\cos^2 x} - \sin^2 x$	$\sin^2 x \dfrac{\sin^2 x}{\cos^2 x}$	Writing each side in terms of $\sin x$ and $\cos x$
$\dfrac{\sin^2 x - \sin^2 x \cos^2 x}{\cos^2 x}$		Finding common denominators and subtracting
$\dfrac{\sin^2 x (1 - \cos^2 x)}{\cos^2 x}$		
$\dfrac{\sin^2 x (\sin^2 x)}{\cos^2 x}$		
$\sin^2 x \dfrac{\sin^2 x}{\cos^2 x}$		

Therefore, $\tan^2 x - \sin^2 x \equiv \sin^2 x \tan^2 x$.

TRY THIS Prove the following identity.

1. $\cot^2 x - \cos^2 x \equiv \cos^2 x \cot^2 x$

1. $\cot^2 x - \cos^2 x$ | $\cos^2 x \cot^2 x$

$\dfrac{\cos^2 x}{\sin^2 x} - \cos^2 x$ | $\cos^2 x \dfrac{\cos^2 x}{\sin^2 x}$

$\dfrac{\cos^2 x - \cos^2 x \sin^2 x}{\sin^2 x}$

$\dfrac{\cos^2 x (1 - \sin^2 x)}{\sin^2 x}$

$\dfrac{\cos^2 x \cos^2 x}{\sin^2 x}$

The next identity shows the use of double-angle formulas.

EXAMPLE 2
Prove the following identity.

$$\frac{\sin 2\theta}{\sin \theta} - \frac{\cos 2\theta}{\cos \theta} \equiv \sec \theta$$

$\dfrac{2 \sin \theta \cos \theta}{\sin \theta} - \dfrac{\cos^2 \theta - \sin^2 \theta}{\cos \theta}$	$\dfrac{1}{\cos \theta}$
$\dfrac{2 \cos^2 \theta - \cos^2 \theta + \sin^2 \theta}{\cos \theta}$	
$\dfrac{\cos^2 \theta + \sin^2 \theta}{\cos \theta}$	
$\dfrac{1}{\cos \theta}$	

Therefore, $\dfrac{\sin 2\theta}{\sin \theta} - \dfrac{\cos 2\theta}{\cos \theta} \equiv \sec \theta$.

TRY THIS Prove the following identity.

2. $\dfrac{\sin 2\theta + \sin \theta}{\cos 2\theta + \cos \theta + 1} \equiv \tan \theta$

2. $\dfrac{\sin 2\theta + \sin \theta}{\cos 2\theta + \cos \theta + 1}$ | $\tan \theta$

$\dfrac{2 \sin \theta \cos \theta + \sin \theta}{2 \cos^2 \theta + \cos \theta}$ | $\dfrac{\sin \theta}{\cos \theta}$

$\dfrac{\sin \theta (2 \cos \theta + 1)}{\cos \theta (2 \cos \theta + 1)}$

$\dfrac{\sin \theta}{\cos \theta}$

16-3

Exercises

Prove the identities.

1. $\csc x - \cos x \cot x \equiv \sin x$

2. $\sec x - \sin x \tan x \equiv \cos x$

3. $\dfrac{1 + \cos \theta}{\sin \theta} + \dfrac{\sin \theta}{\cos \theta} \equiv \dfrac{\cos \theta + 1}{\sin \theta \cos \theta}$

4. $\dfrac{1}{\sin \theta \cos \theta} - \dfrac{\cos}{\sin \theta} \equiv \dfrac{\sin \theta \cos \theta}{1 - \sin^2 \theta}$

5. $\dfrac{1 - \sin x}{\cos x} \equiv \dfrac{\cos x}{1 + \sin x}$

6. $\dfrac{1 - \cos x}{\sin x} \equiv \dfrac{\sin x}{1 + \cos x}$

7. $\dfrac{1 + \tan \theta}{1 + \cot \theta} \equiv \dfrac{\sec \theta}{\csc \theta}$

8. $\dfrac{\cot \theta - 1}{1 - \tan \theta} \equiv \dfrac{\csc \theta}{\sec \theta}$

9. $\dfrac{\sin x + \cos x}{\sec x + \csc x} \equiv \dfrac{\sin x}{\sec x}$

10. $\dfrac{\sin x - \cos x}{\sec x - \csc x} \equiv \dfrac{\cos x}{\csc x}$

11. $\dfrac{1 + \tan \theta}{1 - \tan \theta} + \dfrac{1 + \cot \theta}{1 - \cot \theta} \equiv 0$

12. $\dfrac{\cos^2 \theta + \cot \theta}{\cos^2 \theta - \cot \theta} \equiv \dfrac{\cos^2 \theta \tan \theta + 1}{\cos^2 \theta \tan \theta - 1}$

13. $\dfrac{1 + \cos 2\theta}{\sin 2\theta} \equiv \cot \theta$

14. $\dfrac{2 \tan \theta}{1 + \tan^2 \theta} \equiv \sin 2\theta$

15. $\sec 2\theta \equiv \dfrac{\sec^2 \theta}{2 - \sec^2 \theta}$

16. $\cot 2\theta \equiv \dfrac{\cot^2 \theta - 1}{2 \cot \theta}$

Extension

17. $\dfrac{\sin (\alpha + \beta)}{\cos \alpha \cos \beta} \equiv \tan \alpha + \tan \beta$

18. $\dfrac{\cos (\alpha - \beta)}{\cos \alpha \sin \beta} \equiv \tan \alpha + \cot \beta$

19. $1 - \cos 5\theta \cos 3\theta - \sin 5\theta \sin 3\theta \equiv 2 \sin^2 \theta$

20. $2 \sin \theta \cos^3 \theta + 2 \sin^3 \theta \cos \theta \equiv \sin 2\theta$

21. $\dfrac{\tan \theta + \sin \theta}{2 \tan \theta} \equiv \cos^2 \dfrac{\theta}{2}$

22. $\dfrac{\tan \theta - \sin \theta}{2 \tan \theta} \equiv \sin^2 \dfrac{\theta}{2}$

23. $\cos^4 x - \sin^4 x \equiv \cos 2x$

24. $\dfrac{\cos^4 x - \sin^4 x}{1 - \tan^4 x} \equiv \cos^4 x$

25. $\dfrac{\tan 3\theta - \tan \theta}{1 + \tan 3\theta \tan \theta} \equiv \dfrac{2 \tan \theta}{1 - \tan^2 \theta}$

26. $\left(\dfrac{1 + \tan \theta}{1 - \tan \theta}\right)^2 \equiv \dfrac{1 + \sin 2\theta}{1 - \sin 2\theta}$

27. $\sin (\alpha + \beta) \sin (\alpha - \beta) \equiv \sin^2 \alpha - \sin^2 \beta$

28. $\cos (\alpha + \beta) \cos (\alpha - \beta) \equiv \cos^2 \alpha - \sin^2 \beta$

29. $\cos (\alpha + \beta) + \cos (\alpha - \beta) \equiv 2 \cos \alpha \cos \beta$

30. $\sin (\alpha + \beta) + \sin (\alpha - \beta) \equiv 2 \sin \alpha \cos \beta$

Challenge

31. Show that
$$\begin{vmatrix} \cos x & \sin x \\ -\sin x & \cos x \end{vmatrix} = \begin{vmatrix} \cos x & -\sin x \\ \sin x & \cos x \end{vmatrix}.$$

16-4 Inverses of the Trigonometric Functions

Finding Inverse Values

To obtain the inverse of any relation we interchange the first and second members of each ordered pair in the relation. If a relation is defined by an equation, say in x and y, interchanging x and y produces an equation of the inverse relation. The graphs of a relation and its inverse are reflections of each other across the line $y = x$.

Let us consider the inverse of the sine function, $y = \sin x$. The inverse may be denoted several ways, as follows.

$$x = \sin y \qquad y = \sin^{-1} x \qquad y = \arcsin x$$

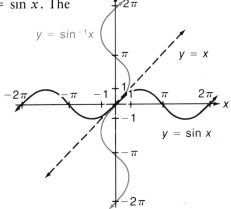

Thus $\sin^{-1} x$ is a number whose sine is x. The notation $\sin^{-1} x$ is not exponential notation. It does *not* mean $\frac{1}{\sin x}$. Either of the latter two kinds of notation above can be read "the inverse sine of x" or "the arc sine of x" or "the number (or angle) whose sine is x." Notation is chosen similarly for the inverses of the other trigonometric functions: $\cos^{-1} x$ or $\arccos x$, $\tan^{-1} x$ or $\arctan x$, and so on.

EXAMPLE 1

Sketch a graph of $y = \cos^{-1} x$. Is this relation a function? First sketch a graph of $y = \cos x$.

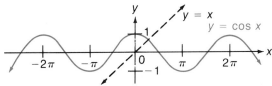

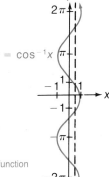

Then reflect this graph over the line $y = x$. The graph is not a function because there is more than one value of y for each x.

TRY THIS

1. Sketch a graph of $y = \cot^{-1} x$. Is this relation a function? Not a function

We can find inverse values using either a graph or a unit circle. In practice the unit circle is easier to use.

EXAMPLE 2

Find all values of arccos $\frac{1}{2}$ using the graph in Example 1. On the graph of $y = \text{arccos } x$, we draw a vertical line at $x = \frac{1}{2}$. It intersects the graph at points whose y-value is arccos $\frac{1}{2}$. Some of the numbers whose cosine is $\frac{1}{2}$ are seen to be $\frac{\pi}{3}, \frac{5\pi}{3}, -\frac{\pi}{3}$, and so on. From the graph in Example 1 we can see that $\frac{\pi}{3}$ plus any multiple of 2π is such a number. Also $\frac{5\pi}{3}$ plus any multiple of 2π is such a number. The complete set of values is given by $\{x \mid (x = \frac{\pi}{3} + 2k\pi)$ or $(x = \frac{5\pi}{3} + 2k\pi), k$ an integer$\}$.

TRY THIS

2. Find all values of arcsin $\frac{1}{2}$. $\quad \{x \mid x = \frac{\pi}{6} + 2k\pi \text{ or } x = \frac{5\pi}{6} + 2k\pi, k \text{ an integer}\}$

We can use the unit circle to find inverse values. On the unit circle there are two points at which the sine is $\frac{1}{2}$. The rotation for the point in the first quadrant is $\frac{\pi}{6}$ plus any multiple of 2π. The rotation for the point in the second quadrant is $\frac{5\pi}{6}$ plus any multiple of 2π. Hence we obtain all values of arcsin $\frac{1}{2}$ as follows:

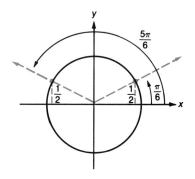

$$\frac{\pi}{6} + 2k\pi \text{ and } \frac{5\pi}{6} + 2k\pi, k \text{ an integer.}$$

In degree notation, we write $30° + k \cdot 360°$ and $150° + k \cdot 360$.

Principal Values

The inverses of the trigonometric functions are not themselves functions. However, if we restrict the ranges of these relations, we can obtain functions. The following graphs show how this restriction is made.

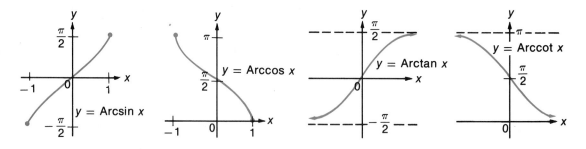

These relations with their ranges so restricted are functions, and the values in these restricted ranges are called principal values. To denote principal values we shall capitalize, as follows: Arcsin x, $\text{Sin}^{-1} x$, Arccos x, $\text{Cos}^{-1} x$, and so on. Thus whereas arcsin $(\frac{1}{2})$ represents an infinite set of numbers, Arcsin $(\frac{1}{2})$ represents the single number $\frac{\pi}{6}$.

Note that for the function $y = $ Arcsin x the range is $\{y \mid -\frac{\pi}{2} \le y \le \frac{\pi}{2}\}$. For the function $y = $ Arctan x the range is $\{y \mid -\frac{\pi}{2} < y < \frac{\pi}{2}\}$. For the function $y = $ Arccos x the range is $\{y \mid 0 \le y \le \pi\}$, and for $y = $ Arccot x the range is $\{y \mid 0 < y < \pi\}$.

EXAMPLE 3

Find Arcsin $\frac{\sqrt{2}}{2}$ and $\text{Cos}^{-1} (-\frac{1}{2})$.

In the restricted range as shown in the figure, the only number whose sine is $\frac{\sqrt{2}}{2}$ is $\frac{\pi}{4}$. Hence Arcsin $\frac{\sqrt{2}}{2} = \frac{\pi}{4}$. The only number whose cosine is $-\frac{1}{2}$ in the restricted range is $\frac{2\pi}{3}$. Hence $\text{Cos}^{-1} (-\frac{1}{2}) = \frac{2\pi}{3}$.

TRY THIS Find each of the following.

3. Arcsin $\frac{\sqrt{3}}{2}$ $\frac{\pi}{3}$ 4. $\text{Cos}^{-1} -\frac{\sqrt{2}}{2}$ $\frac{3\pi}{4}$ 5. Arccot (-1) $\frac{3\pi}{4}$ 6. $\text{Tan}^{-1} (-1)$ $-\frac{\pi}{4}$

16–4

Exercises

Find all values of the following by sketching the graphs.

1. arcsin $\frac{\sqrt{2}}{2}$
2. arcsin $\frac{\sqrt{3}}{2}$
3. $\cos^{-1} \frac{\sqrt{2}}{2}$
4. $\cos^{-1} \frac{\sqrt{3}}{2}$

5. arctan 1
6. arctan (-1)
7. $\sin^{-1} \left(-\frac{\sqrt{2}}{2}\right)$
8. $\sin^{-1} \left(-\frac{\sqrt{3}}{2}\right)$

9. arccos $\left(-\frac{\sqrt{2}}{2}\right)$
10. arccos $\left(-\frac{\sqrt{3}}{2}\right)$
11. arctan $\sqrt{3}$
12. arctan $\frac{\sqrt{3}}{3}$

13. $\cot^{-1} 1$
14. $\cot^{-1} \sqrt{3}$
15. arctan $\left(-\frac{\sqrt{3}}{3}\right)$
16. arctan $(-\sqrt{3})$

Find the following without using tables.

17. Arccos $\left(-\frac{\sqrt{3}}{2}\right)$
18. Arcsin $\frac{1}{2}$
19. $\text{Cos}^{-1} \frac{1}{2}$

20. $\text{Cos}^{-1} \frac{\sqrt{2}}{2}$
21. $\text{Sin}^{-1} \left(-\frac{\sqrt{3}}{2}\right)$
22. $\text{Sin}^{-1} \left(-\frac{1}{2}\right)$

23. $\text{Tan}^{-1} \left(-\frac{\sqrt{3}}{3}\right)$
24. $\text{Tan}^{-1} (-\sqrt{3})$
25. Arccot $\left(-\frac{\sqrt{3}}{3}\right)$

17. $\frac{5\pi}{6}$ 18. $\frac{\pi}{6}$ 19. $\frac{\pi}{3}$ 20. $\frac{\pi}{4}$
21. $-\frac{\pi}{3}$ 22. $-\frac{\pi}{6}$ 23. $-\frac{\pi}{6}$ 24. $-\frac{\pi}{6}$ 25. $\frac{2\pi}{3}$

Extension

Use Table 3 to find, in degrees, all the values of each of the following. For example, arcsin $0.4384 = 26° + k360°, 154° + k360°$.

26. arcsin 0.3907
27. arcsin 0.9613
28. $\sin^{-1} 0.6293$

29. $\sin^{-1} 0.8746$
30. arccos 0.7990
31. arccos 0.9265

32. $\cos^{-1} 0.9310$
33. $\cos^{-1} 0.2735$
34. $\tan^{-1} 0.3673$

35. $\tan^{-1} 1.091$
36. $\cot^{-1} 1.265$
37. $\cot^{-1} 0.4770$

38. $\sec^{-1} 1.167$
39. $\sec^{-1} 1.440$
40. arccsc 6.277

Find all values of the following by sketching the graph.

41. arccot (-1)
42. arccot $(-\sqrt{3})$
43. arcsec 1

44. arcsec 2
45. $\csc^{-1} 1$
46. $\csc^{-1} 2$

41. $\frac{3\pi}{4} + k\pi$
42. $\frac{5\pi}{6} + k\pi$
43. $2k\pi$
44. $\frac{\pi}{3} + 2k\pi, \frac{5\pi}{3} + 2k\pi$
45. $\frac{\pi}{2} + 2k\pi$
46. $\frac{\pi}{6} + 2k\pi, \frac{5\pi}{6} + 2k\pi$

For each of the following, indicate on separate graphs of the unit circle where principal values are found.

47. Arcsin
48. Arccos
49. Arctan
50. Arccot

Find the following, in degrees, using tables.

51. Arcsin 0.2334
52. Arcsin 0.4514
53. $\text{Sin}^{-1} (-0.6361)$

54. $\text{Sin}^{-1} (-0.8192)$
55. Arccos (-0.8897)
56. Arccos (-0.2924)

57. $\text{Tan}^{-1} (-0.4074)$
58. $\text{Tan}^{-1} (-0.2401)$
59. $\text{Cot}^{-1} (-5.396)$

51. 13°30'
52. 26°50'
53. −39°30'
54. −55°
55. 152°50'
56. 107°
57. −22°10'
58. −13°30'
59. 169°30'

THE MATHEMATICS OF INVENTORY CONTROL

A person planning a trip to the food store and the manager of a large department store chain have similar decisions to make:

Shall I buy enough for a day or two or enough to last a long time?

There are advantages and disadvantages to either decision. A manager who buys large quantities saves time, reduces shipping or delivery charges, and may qualify for bulk discounts. However, there is a risk that items will deteriorate or become obsolete. There are also costs for adequate storage space, insurance, taxes, and maintenance.

Furthermore, interest is lost on the capital spent for inventory.

But buying for short periods is also bad from an economic standpoint. There are shortage costs which result from being out of a product when it is needed. Customers may be lost to other suppliers. Ordering costs are incurred each time new items are purchased, and inflation may drive up prices.

Mathemetical models can be used to express all these issues as functions, to forecast future needs, and find optimal inventory levels based upon all these variables.

16-5 Trigonometric Equations

Solving Simple Equations

When an equation contains a trigonometric expression with a variable such as sin x, it is called a trigonometric equation. To solve such an equation, we find all replacements for the variable that make the equation true.

EXAMPLE 1

Solve $2 \sin x = 1$.

We first solve for $\sin x$.

$$\sin x = \tfrac{1}{2}$$

Now we note that the solutions are those angles having a sine of $\tfrac{1}{2}$. We look for them. The unit circle is helpful. There are just two points on it for which the sine is $\tfrac{1}{2}$, as shown. They are points for $\tfrac{\pi}{6}$ and $\tfrac{5\pi}{6}$. These angles, plus any multiple of 2π, are the solutions.

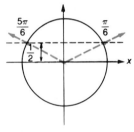

$$\tfrac{\pi}{6} + 2k\pi \text{ and } \tfrac{5\pi}{6} + 2k\pi, \text{ where } k \text{ is any integer}$$

In degrees, the solutions are $30° + k \cdot 360°$ and $150° + k \cdot 360°$, where k is any integer.

EXAMPLE 2

Solve $4 \cos^2 x = 1$.

$$\cos^2 x = \tfrac{1}{4}$$

$$|\cos x| = \tfrac{1}{2} \quad \text{Taking principal square roots}$$

$$\cos x = \pm\tfrac{1}{2}$$

Now we use the unit circle to find those numbers having a cosine of $\pm\tfrac{1}{2}$. The solutions are $\tfrac{\pi}{3}, \tfrac{2\pi}{3}, \tfrac{4\pi}{3}, \tfrac{5\pi}{3}$, plus any multiple of 2π.

> In solving trigonometric equations, it is usually sufficient to find just the solutions from 0 to 2π. We then remember that any multiple of 2π may be added to obtain all the solutions.

TRY THIS Solve.

1. $4 \sin^2 x = 1$ $\quad \frac{\pi}{6}, \frac{5\pi}{6}, \frac{7\pi}{6}, \frac{11\pi}{6}$ plus $2k\pi$

The following example illustrates that when we look for solutions to equations involving a double angle, we must be cautious.

EXAMPLE 3

Find the solutions of $2 \sin 2x = 1$ from 0 to 2π.

We first solve for $\sin 2x$: $\sin 2x = \frac{1}{2}$. Points on the unit circle for which $\sin 2x = \frac{1}{2}$ are points where $2x = \frac{\pi}{6}$ and $2x = \frac{5\pi}{6}$. So $\frac{\pi}{12}$ and $\frac{5\pi}{12}$ are solutions. However, since x values must be in the interval from 0 to 2π, $2x$ must be in the interval from 0 to 4π. Thus, other values of $2x$ are $\frac{13\pi}{6}$ and $\frac{17\pi}{6}$. Thus $\frac{13\pi}{12}$ and $\frac{17\pi}{12}$ are also solutions.

$$x = \frac{\pi}{12}, \frac{5\pi}{12}, \frac{13\pi}{12}, \frac{17\pi}{12}$$

TRY THIS Find all solutions (in terms of π) from 0 to 2π.

2. $2 \cos 2x = 1$ $\quad \frac{\pi}{6}, \frac{5\pi}{6}, \frac{7\pi}{6}, \frac{11\pi}{6}$

In solving trigonometric equations, we often apply some algebra before working with the trigonometric part. In the next example, we recognize that the equation is reducible to a quadratic, with $\cos \theta$ as the variable. We begin by putting the equation in standard form.

EXAMPLE 4

Solve $8 \cos^2 \theta - 2 \cos \theta = 1$.

$$8 \cos^2 \theta - 2 \cos \theta - 1 = 0 \quad \text{Getting 0 on one side}$$
$$(4 \cos \theta + 1)(2 \cos \theta - 1) = 0 \quad \text{Factoring}$$

$4 \cos \theta + 1 = 0 \qquad \text{or} \quad 2 \cos \theta - 1 = 0 \quad \text{Principle of zero products}$

$$\cos \theta = -\frac{1}{4} \qquad \text{or} \qquad \cos \theta = \frac{1}{2}$$

$$= -0.25$$

From Table 3 we find that for $\cos \theta = -0.25$, $\theta = 104°30'$ or $255°30'$. For $\cos \theta = \frac{1}{2}$, $\theta = 60°$ or $300°$. The solutions from 0 to $360°$ are $104°30'$, $255°30'$, $60°$, and $300°$.

TRY THIS Solve.

3. $75°31'$, $284°29'$, $120°$, $240°$

3. $8 \cos^2 \theta + 2 \cos \theta = 1$ $\qquad$ **4.** $2 \cos^2 \phi + \cos \phi = 0$ $\qquad$ 4. $\frac{\pi}{2}, \frac{3\pi}{2}, \frac{2\pi}{3}, \frac{4\pi}{3}$

16–5

Exercises

Solve, finding all solutions from 0 to 2π or $0°$ to $360°$.

1. $2 \sin x + \sqrt{3} = 0$
2. $\sqrt{3} \tan x + 1 = 0$
3. $2 \tan x + 3 = 0$
4. $4 \sin x - 1 = 0$
5. $4 \sin^2 x - 1 = 0$
6. $2 \cos^2 x = 1$
7. $2 \sin^2 x + \sin x = 1$
8. $2 \cos^2 x + 3 \cos x = -1$
9. $\cos^2 x + 2 \cos x = 3$
10. $2 \sin^2 x - \sin x = 3$
11. $2 \sin^2 \theta + 7 \sin \theta = 4$
12. $2 \sin^2 \theta - 5 \sin \theta + 2 = 0$
13. $6 \cos^2 \phi + 5 \cos \phi + 1 = 0$
14. $2 \sin^2 \phi + \sin \phi - 1 = 0$

Find all solutions of the following equations from 0 to 2π.

15. $\cos 2x \sin x + \sin x = 0$
16. $\sin 2x \cos x - \cos x = 0$
17. $\tan x \sin x - \tan x = 0$
18. $2 \sin x \cos x + \sin x = 0$
19. $2 \sec x \tan x + 2 \sec x + \tan x + 1 = 0$
20. $2 \csc x \cos x - 4 \cos x - \csc x + 2 = 0$
21. $\sin 2x \sin x - \cos x = 0$
22. $\sin 2x \cos x - \sin x = 0$
23. $\sin 2x + 2 \sin x \cos x = 0$
24. $\cos 2x \sin x + \sin x = 0$
25. $\cos 2x \cos x + \sin 2x \sin x = 1$
26. $\sin 2x \sin x - \cos 2x \cos x = -\cos x$
27. $\sin 2x + 2 \sin x - \cos x - 1 = 0$
28. $\sin 2x + \sin x + 2 \cos x + 1 = 0$
29. $\sec^2 x = 4 \tan^2 x$
30. $\sec^2 x - 2 \tan^2 x = 0$
31. $\sec^2 x + 3 \tan x - 11 = 0$
32. $\tan^2 x + 4 = 2 \sec^2 x + \tan x$

Extension

Find solutions to the following equations from 0 to 2π.

33. $\cos (\pi - x) + \sin \left(x - \frac{\pi}{2}\right) = 1$
34. $\sin (\pi - x) + \cos \left(\frac{\pi}{2} - x\right) = 1$
35. $2 \cos x + 2 \sin x = \sqrt{6}$
36. $2 \cos x + 2 \sin x = \sqrt{2}$
37. $\sqrt{3} \cos x - \sin x = 1$
38. $\sqrt{2} \cos x - \sqrt{2} \sin x = 2$

Challenge

Solve, restricting solutions to 0 to 2π or $0°$ to $360°$ where sensible to do so.

39. $|\sin x| = \frac{\sqrt{3}}{2}$
40. $|\cos x| = \frac{1}{2}$
41. $\sqrt{\tan x} = \sqrt[4]{3}$
42. $12 \sin x - 7 \sqrt{\sin x} + 1 = 0$
43. $16 \cos^4 x - 16 \cos^2 x + 3 = 0$
44. $\text{Arccos } x = \text{Arccos } \frac{3}{5} - \text{Arcsin } \frac{4}{5}$

16-6 Solving Right Triangles and Applications

Solving Triangles

In Section 15-1 the trigonometric functions were defined and the solving of right triangles was introduced. Tables of the trigonometric functions were considered in Section 15-3. We continue consideration of solving right triangles, a topic important in many applications of trigonometry. The word trigonometry actually means "triangle measurement."

The precision to which we can find an angle, using a ratio of sides, such as the sine ratio, depends on how precisely we know the lengths of the sides. The following table shows the relationship.

Number of Digits in Ratio	Precision of Angle Measure
4	To nearest minute
3	To nearest ten minutes
2	To nearest degree

The table can also be read in reverse. For example, if we know an angle to the nearest ten minutes, then the number of significant digits in a value obtained from the table is 3, and hence the number of significant digits obtained for the length of a side of a triangle is 3.

When we have four-digit precision, but a number itself has fewer than four digits, we often indicate the precision by writing 0's after the decimal point, as in 18.00 or 7.000.

Some of the exercises of this section may use unwarranted precision, from the standpoint of reality, in order to provide valid practice in calculating.

EXAMPLE 1

Find the length b in this triangle. Use four-digit precision.
The known side is the hypotenuse. The side we seek is adjacent to the known angle. Thus we shall use the cosine: $\cos A = b/70$. We solve for b.

$$b = 70 \times \cos 19° = 70 \times 0.9455 = 66.19$$

When we solve a triangle, we find the *measures* of its sides and angles not already known. We sometimes shorten this to saying that we "find the angles" or "find the sides."

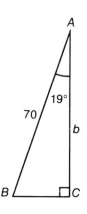

1. Find the lengths a and b in this triangle. Angle A is given to the nearest minute, and length AB to four-digit precision.
$a = 38.43, b = 54.89$

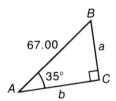

2. Solve this triangle. Use four-digit precision. $m\angle A = 56°19'$, $m\angle B = 33°41'$, $c = 7.211$

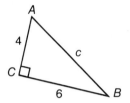

Applications of Solving Triangles

In many applied problems, unknown parts of right triangles are to be found.

EXAMPLE 2

Finding cloud height   A device for measuring cloud height at night consists of a vertical beam of light, which makes a spot on the clouds. The spot is viewed from a point 135 m away. The angle of elevation is $67°40'$. (The angle between the horizontal and a line of sight is called an angle of elevation or an angle of depression, the latter if the line of sight is below the horizontal.) Find the height of the clouds.

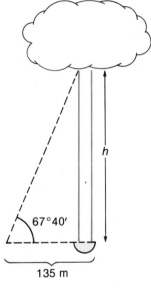

From the drawing we have:

$$\frac{h}{135} = \tan 67°40'$$
$$h = 135 \times \tan 67°40'$$
$$= 135 \times 2.434 = 329 \text{ m}$$

Note that distances are precise to three digits and the angle to the nearest ten minutes.

Following is a general procedure for solving triangle problems.

To solve a triangle problem
1. Draw a sketch of the problem situation.
2. Look for triangles and sketch them in.
3. Mark the known and unknown sides and angles.
4. Express the desired side or angle in terms of known trigonometric ratios. Then solve.

TRY THIS

3. The length of a guy wire to a pole is 12.6 m. It makes an angle of $71°20'$ with the ground, which is horizontal. How high above the ground is it attached to the pole?

11.9 m

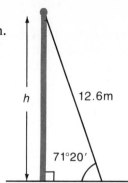

Calculators

A calculator would be most convenient for use with Example 3. The same is true for most of the examples and exercises of this chapter, and the use of a calculator is recommended.

If function values are obtained from a calculator, rather than Table 3, it should be kept in mind that the number of decimal places will be different; hence answers may vary because of rounding-error differences. The answers in the book are computed using Table 3.

It is vital to note whether the calculator requires parts of degrees to be entered in tenths and hundredths or minutes and seconds.

EXAMPLE 3

Two markers at ground level are viewed in one direction from an observation tower. The markers and the base of the tower are on a line and the observer's eye is 21.3 m above the ground. The angles of depression to the markers are $53°10'$ and $27°50'$. How far is one marker from the other?

From the drawing we see that the distance we seek is d, which is $d_1 - d_2$. From the right triangles in the drawing, we have

$$\frac{d_1}{21.3} = \cot \theta_1 \text{ and } \frac{d_2}{21.3} = \cot \theta_2.$$

Then $d_1 = 21.3 \cot 27°50'$
and $d_2 = 21.3 \cot 53°10'$.

$$
\begin{aligned}
d &= d_1 - d_2 \\
&= 21.3 \cot 27°50' - 21.3 \cot 53°10' \\
&= 21.3(\cot 27°50' - \cot 53°10') \\
&= 21.3(1.894 - 0.7490) = 24.4 \text{ m}
\end{aligned}
$$

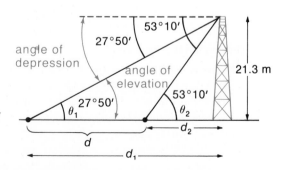

TRY THIS

4. From an airplane flying 2.4 km above level ground, one can see two towns directly to the east. The angles of depression to the towns are 5°10′ and 77°30′. How far apart are the towns, to the nearest kilometer? 26 km

In aerial navigation, directions are given in degrees, clockwise from north. Thus east is 90°, south is 180°, and so on. In some applications directions, or bearings, are given by reference to north or south using an acute angle. For example, N 40°W means 40° west of north and S 30° E means 30° east of south. Both these ideas appear in some of the exercises that follow.

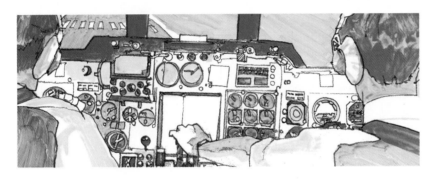

16–6

Exercises

In Exercises 1–18, standard lettering for a right triangle will be used: A, B, and C are the angles, C being the right angle. The sides opposite A, B, and C are a, b, and c, respectively. Solve the triangles, using three-digit precision.

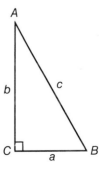

1. $m \angle A = 36°10′$, $a = 27.2$
2. $m \angle A = 87°40′$, $a = 9.73$
3. $m \angle B = 12°40′$, $b = 98.1$
4. $m \angle B = 69°50′$, $b = 127$
5. $m \angle A = 17°20′$, $b = 13.6$
6. $m \angle A = 78°40′$, $b = 1340$
7. $m \angle B = 23°10′$, $a = 0.0345$
8. $m \angle B = 69°20′$, $a = 0.00488$
9. $m \angle A = 47°30′$, $c = 48.3$
10. $m \angle A = 88°50′$, $c = 3950$
11. $m \angle B = 82°20′$, $c = 0.982$
12. $m \angle B = 56°30′$, $c = 0.0447$
13. $a = 12.0$, $b = 18.0$
14. $a = 10.0$, $b = 20.0$
15. $a = 16.0$, $c = 20.0$
16. $a = 15.0$, $c = 45.0$
17. $b = 1.80$, $c = 4.00$
18. $b = 100$, $c = 450$

Solve.

19. A guy wire to a pole makes an angle of 73°10′ with the level ground, and is 4.8 m from the pole at the ground. How far above the ground is the wire attached to the pole? 15.9 m

20. A kite string makes an angle of 31°40′ with the (level) ground, and 148 m of string is out. How high is the kite? 77.7 m

21. A road rises 3 m per 100 horizontal m (it has a 3% grade). What angle does it make with the horizontal? 1°40′

22. A kite is 60 m high when 220 m of string is out. What angle does the kite string make with the ground? 15°50′

23. What is the angle of elevation of the sun when a 2 m person casts a 3.1 m shadow? 32°50′

24. What is the angle of elevation of the sun when a 11.5 m mast casts a 6 m shadow? 62°30′

25. From a balloon 835 m high, a command post is seen with an angle of depression of 7°40′. How far is it from a point on the ground below the balloon to the command post? 6203 m

26. From a lighthouse 18 m above sea level, the angle of depression to a small boat is 11°20′. How far from the foot of the lighthouse is the boat? 89.8 m

27. An airplane travels at 120 km/h for 2 hr in a direction of 243° from Chicago. At the end of this time, how far south of Chicago is the plane? 109 km

28. An airplane travels at 150 km/h for 2 hr in a direction of 138° from Omaha. At the end of this time, how far east of Omaha is the plane? 201 km

29. Ship A is due west of a lighthouse. Ship B is 12 km south of ship A. From ship B the bearing to the lighthouse is N 63°20′E. How far is ship A from the lighthouse? 23.9 km

30. Lookout station A is 15 km west of station B. The bearing from A to a fire directly south of B is S 37°50′E. How far is the fire from B? 19.3 km

31. In one direction from a balloon 2 km high, the angles of depression to two towns in line with the balloon are 81°20′ and 13°40′. How far apart are the towns? 7.92 km

32. In one direction from a balloon 1000 m high, the angles of depression to two observation posts in line with the balloon are 11°50′ and 84°10′. How far apart are the observation posts? 4671 km

33. A weather balloon is directly west of two observing stations 10 km apart. The angles of elevation of the balloon from the two stations are 17°50′ and 78°10′. How high is the balloon? 3.45 km

34. Two points are south of a hill; they are on level ground and 325 m apart. From these two points the angles of elevation of the hill are 12°20′ and 82°40′. How high is the hill? 73.1 km

35. Horizontal distances must often be measured, even though terrain is not level. One way of doing it is as follows. Distance down a slope is measured with a surveyor's tape, and the distance d is measured by making a level sighting from A to a pole held vertically at B, or the angle α is measured by an instrument placed at A. Suppose that a slope distance L is measured to be 121.3 ft and the angle α is measured to be 3°25′. Find the horizontal distance from A to B. 121.1 ft

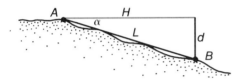

36. A downslope distance is measured to be 241.3 ft and the angle of depression α is measured to be 5°15′. Find the horizontal distance. 240.4 ft

Extension

37. Show that the area of a right triangle is $\frac{1}{4}c^2 \sin 2A$.

38. Show that the area of a right triangle is $bc \sin A/2$.

39. Use the information given to find the distance y without using Table 3 or a calculator. (Hint: Use the double-angle identity for tangent.) $y = 5.2180$

tan 13°30′ = 0.2401

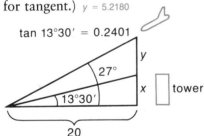

Challenge

Solve.

40. Find a formula for the distance to the horizon, as a function of the height of the observer above the earth. Calculate the distance to the horizon from an airplane at an altitude of 1000 ft.

41. In finding horizontal distance from slope distance (see Exercise 35) $H = L - C$, where C is a correction. Show that a good approximation to C is $d^2/2L$.

16-7 The Law of Sines

The trigonometric functions can be used to solve triangles that are not right triangles (oblique triangles). In order to solve oblique triangles we need to derive some properties, one of which is called the law of sines. We shall consider any oblique triangle. It may or may not have an obtuse angle. We will consider both cases, but the derivations are essentially the same.

The triangles are lettered in the standard way, with angles A, B, and C and the sides opposite them a, b, and c, respectively. The altitude from vertex C has length h. In either triangle we now have, from triangle ADC,

$$\frac{h}{b} = \sin A \text{ or } h = b \sin A.$$

From triangle DBC we have $\frac{h}{a} = \sin B$, or $h = a \sin B$. On the right we have $\frac{h}{a} = \sin \angle CBD = \sin (180° - B) = \sin B$. So in either kind of triangle we now have

$$h = b \sin A \text{ and } h = a \sin B.$$

Thus it follows that

$$b \sin A = a \sin B \qquad \frac{a}{\sin A} = \frac{b}{\sin B} \qquad \text{Dividing by } \sin A \sin B$$

There is no danger of dividing by 0 here because we are dealing with triangles whose angles are never 0° or 180°.

If we were to consider an altitude from vertex A in the triangles shown, the same argument would give us the following.

$$\frac{b}{\sin B} = \frac{c}{\sin C}$$

We combine these results to obtain the law of sines, which holds for right triangles as well as oblique triangles.

THEOREM 16-5

The Law of Sines

In any triangle ABC, $\dfrac{a}{\sin A} = \dfrac{b}{\sin B} = \dfrac{c}{\sin C}$.

(The sides are proportional to the sines of the opposite angles.)

Solving Triangles (AAS)

When two angles and a side of any triangle are known, the law of sines can be used to solve the triangle.

EXAMPLE 1

In triangle ABC, $a = 4.56$, $A = 43°$, and $C = 57°$. Solve the triangle.

We first draw a sketch. We find B, as follows.

$$m\angle B = 180° - (43° + 57°) = 80°$$

We can now find the other two sides, using the law of sines.

$$\frac{c}{\sin C} = \frac{a}{\sin A}$$

$$c = \frac{a \sin C}{\sin A}$$

$$= \frac{4.56 \sin 57°}{\sin 43°}$$

$$= \frac{4.56 \times 0.8387}{0.6820}$$

$$= 5.61$$

$$\frac{b}{\sin B} = \frac{a}{\sin A}$$

$$b = \frac{a \sin B}{\sin A}$$

$$= \frac{4.56 \sin 80°}{0.6820}$$

$$= \frac{4.56 \times 0.9848}{0.6820}$$

$$= 6.58$$

We have now found the unknown parts of the triangle, $B = 80°$, $c = 5.61$, and $b = 6.58$. A calculator is of great help in doing calculations like this.

TRY THIS

1. In a particular triangle ABC, $m\angle A = 41°$ and the side opposite the vertex A has length 6.53. Solve the triangle.

   $m\angle B = 87°, b = 9.94, c = 7.84$

The Ambiguous Case (SSA)

When two sides of a triangle and an angle opposite one of them are known, the law of sines can be used to solve the triangle. However, there may be more than one solution. Thus this is known as the ambiguous case. Suppose a, b, and $m\angle A$ are given. Then the various possibilities are shown in the four cases below.

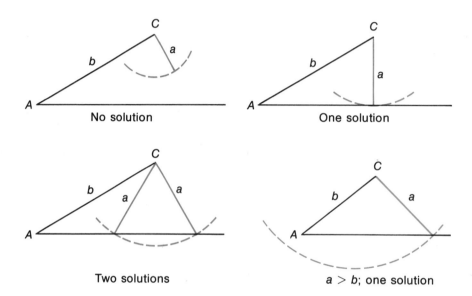

No solution

One solution

Two solutions

$a > b$; one solution

EXAMPLE 2

In triangle ABC, $a = 15$, $b = 25$, and $m\angle A = 47°$. Solve the triangle.

We look for $m\angle B$:

$$\frac{a}{\sin A} = \frac{b}{\sin B} \qquad \text{Then } \sin B = \frac{b \sin A}{a} = \frac{25 \sin 47°}{15} = \frac{25 \times 0.7314}{15} = 1.219.$$

Since there is no angle having a sine greater than 1, there is no solution.

EXAMPLE 3

In triangle ABC, $a = 12$, $b = 5$, and $m\angle B = 24°38'$. Solve the triangle.

We look for $m\angle A$:

$$\frac{a}{\sin A} = \frac{b}{\sin B} \qquad \text{Then } \sin A = \frac{a \sin B}{b} = \frac{12 \sin 24°38'}{5} = \frac{12 \times 0.4168}{5} = 1.000.$$

$$m\angle A = 90°$$

Then $m\angle C = 90° - 24°38' = 65°22'$.

Since $\frac{c}{a} = \cos B$, $c = a \cos B = 12 \times 0.9090 = 10.9$.

EXAMPLE 4

In triangle ABC, $a = 20$, $b = 15$, and $m \angle B = 30°$. Solve the triangle.

We look for $m \angle A$:

$$\frac{a}{\sin A} = \frac{b}{\sin B}$$

$$\sin A = \frac{a \sin B}{b} = \frac{20 \sin 30°}{15} = \frac{20 \times 0.5}{15} = 0.667$$

There are two angles less than $180°$ having a sine of 0.667. They are $42°$ and $138°$. This gives us two possible solutions.

Possible solution 1 We know that $m \angle A = 42°$. Then $m \angle C = 180° - (30° + 42°) = 108°$.

We now find c.

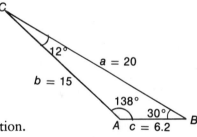

$$\frac{c}{\sin C} = \frac{b}{\sin B}$$

$$c = \frac{b \sin C}{\sin B} = \frac{15 \sin 108°}{\sin 30°} = \frac{15 \times 0.9511}{0.5} = 28.5$$

These parts make a triangle, as shown. Hence we have a solution.

Possible solution 2 $m \angle A = 138°$
$m \angle C = 12°$

We now find c.

$$c = \frac{b \sin C}{\sin B} = \frac{15 \sin 12°}{\sin 30°} = \frac{15 \times 0.2079}{0.5} = 6.2$$

These parts make a triangle. Hence we have a second solution.

TRY THIS

2. In triangle ABC, $a = 25$, $b = 20$ and $m \angle B = 33°$. Solve the triangle. $m \angle A = 42°50', m \angle C = 104°10', = c = 35.6$, or $m \angle A = 137°10', m \angle C = 9°50', c = 6.27$

Area of a Triangle

We can use the law of sines in finding areas of triangles. Look again at the triangles at the beginning of this section. Each triangle has area $\frac{1}{2}hc$. Remember that $h = b \sin A$. So area $= \frac{1}{2}(b \sin A)c$.

$$\text{area} = \frac{1}{2}bc \sin A$$

EXAMPLE 5

In triangle ABC, $b = 9$, $c = 12$, and $m\angle A = 40°$. Find the area.

Using area $= \frac{1}{2}bc \sin A$, we have the following.

$$\text{area} = \frac{1}{2} \times 9 \times 12 \times 0.6428$$

$$= 34.7 \text{ square units}$$

TRY THIS

3. In triangle ABC, $b = 5$, $c = 8$, and $m\angle A = 25°$. Find the area. 8.452

16–7

Exercises

Solve triangle ABC.

1. $m\angle A = 60°$, $m\angle B = 70°$, $b = 20$
2. $m\angle A = 48°$, $m\angle B = 62°$, $b = 35$
3. $m\angle A = 36°$, $m\angle B = 48°$, $a = 12$
4. $m\angle A = 40°$, $m\angle B = 60°$, $b = 100$
5. $m\angle A = 133°$, $m\angle B = 30°$, $b = 18$
6. $m\angle B = 120°$, $m\angle C = 30°$, $a = 16$
7. $m\angle B = 38°$, $m\angle C = 21°$, $b = 24$
8. $m\angle A = 131°$, $m\angle C = 23°$, $b = 10$
9. $m\angle A = 68°30'$, $m\angle C = 42°40'$, $c = 23.5$
10. $m\angle B = 118°20'$, $m\angle C = 45°40'$, $b = 42.1$

Solve triangle ABC.

11. $m\angle B = 150°$, $a = 3$, $b = 7$
12. $m\angle A = 30°$, $a = 6$, $c = 9$
13. $m\angle C = 60°$, $a = 12$, $c = 30$
14. $m\angle B = 45°$, $a = 15$, $b = 17$
15. $m\angle A = 36°$, $a = 24$, $b = 34$
16. $m\angle C = 43°$, $c = 28$, $b = 27$
17. $m\angle A = 116°20'$, $a = 17.2$, $c = 13.5$
18. $m\angle A = 47°50'$, $a = 28.3$, $b = 18.2$
19. $m\angle C = 61°10'$, $c = 30.3$, $b = 24.2$
20. $m\angle B = 58°40'$, $a = 25.1$, $b = 32.6$

Find the area of triangle ABC.

21. $b = 8$, $c = 15$, $m\angle A = 30°$ 30
22. $b = 7$, $c = 18$, $m\angle A = 54°$ 51

Solve.

23. Points A and B are on opposite sides of a lunar crater. Point C is 50 meters from A. The measure of $\angle BAC$ is determined to be 112° and the measure of $\angle ACB$ is determined to be 42°. What is the width of the crater? 76.3 m

702 CHAPTER 16 TRIGONOMETRIC IDENTITIES AND EQUATIONS

24. A guy wire to a pole makes a 71° angle with level ground. At a point 25 ft farther from the pole than the guy wire, the angle of elevation of the top of the pole is 37°. How long is the guy wire? 26.9 ft

25. A pole leans away from the sun at an angle of 7° to the vertical. When the angle of elevation of the sun is 51°, the pole casts a shadow 47 ft long on level ground. How long is the pole? 50.8 ft

26. A vertical pole stands by a road that is inclined 10° to the horizontal. When the angle of elevation of the sun is 23°, the pole casts a shadow 38 ft long directly downhill along the road. How long is the pole? 9.29 ft

27. A reconnaissance airplane leaves its airport on the east coast of the United States and flies in a direction of 085°. Because of bad weather it returns to another airport 230 km to the north of its home base. For the return it flies in a direction of 283°. What was the total distance it flew? 1467 km

28. Lookout station B is 10.2 km east of station A. The bearing of a fire from A is S 10°40′W. The bearing of the fire from B is S 31°20′W. How far is the fire from A? from B? 24.7 km, 28.4 km

29. A boat leaves a lighthouse A and sails 5.1 km. At this time it is sighted from lighthouse B, 7.2 km west of A. The bearing of the boat from B is N 65°10′E. How far is the boat from B? 10.6 km

30. An airplane leaves airport A and flies 200 km. At this time its bearing from airport B, 250 km to the west, is 120°. How far is the airplane from B? 373 km

Extension

Solve.

31. Prove that the area of a parallelogram is the product of two sides and the sine of the included angle.

32. Prove that the area of a quadrilateral is half the product of the lengths of its diagonals and the sine of an angle between the diagonals.

Challenge

Solve.

33. When two objects, such as ships, airplanes, or runners, move in straight-line paths, if the distance between them is decreasing and if the bearing from one of them to the other is constant, they will collide. ("Constant bearing means collision," as mariners put it.) Prove that this statement is true.

16—8 The Law of Cosines

A second property of triangles important in solving oblique triangles is called the law of cosines. To derive this property we shall consider any triangle ABC placed on a coordinate system. We will place the origin at one of the vertices, say C, and the positive half of the x-axis along one of the sides, say CB. Then the coordinates of B are $(a, 0)$, and the coordinates of A are $(b \cos C, b \sin C)$. We will next use the distance formula to determine c^2.

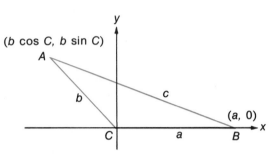

$$c^2 = (b \cos C - a)^2 + (b \sin C - 0)^2$$
$$c^2 = b^2 \cos^2 C - 2ab \cos C + a^2 + b^2 \sin^2 C$$
$$c^2 = a^2 + b^2 (\sin^2 C + \cos^2 C) - 2ab \cos C$$
$$c^2 = a^2 + b^2 - 2ab \cos C$$

Had we placed the origin at one of the other vertices, we would have obtained the following.

$$a^2 = b^2 + c^2 - 2bc \cos A \text{ or } b^2 = a^2 + c^2 - 2ac \cos B$$

This result can be summarized as follows.

THEOREM 16—6

The law of cosines

In any triangle ABC,

$$a^2 = b^2 + c^2 - 2bc \cos A,$$
$$b^2 = a^2 + c^2 - 2ac \cos B, \text{ and}$$
$$c^2 = a^2 + b^2 - 2ab \cos C.$$

(In any triangle, the square of a side is the sum of the squares of the other two sides, minus twice the product of those sides and the cosine of the included angle.)

Only one of the above formulas need be memorized. The other two can be obtained by a change of letters.

Solving Triangles (SAS)

When two sides of a triangle and the included angle are known, we can use the law of cosines to find the third side. The law of sines can then be used to finish solving the triangle.

EXAMPLE 1

In triangle ABC, $a = 24$, $c = 32$, and $m \angle B = 115°$. Solve the triangle.

We first find the third side. From the law of cosines,

$$b^2 = a^2 + c^2 - 2ac \cos B$$
$$= 24^2 + 32^2 - 2 \cdot 24 \cdot 32(-0.4226)$$
$$= 2249$$
$$b = \sqrt{2249} \approx 47.4.$$

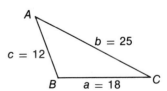

Next, we use the law of sines to find a second angle.

$$\frac{a}{\sin A} = \frac{b}{\sin B}, \quad \sin A = \frac{a \sin B}{b} = \frac{24 \sin 115°}{47.4} = \frac{24 \times 0.9063}{47.4} = 0.4589$$

$$m \angle A = 27°20'$$

$$m \angle C = 180° = (115° + 27°20') = 37°40'$$

TRY THIS Solve the triangle by using the law of cosines.

1. In triangle ABC, $b = 18$, $c = 28$, and $m \angle A = 122°$.
   $a = 40.5, m \angle B = 22°10', m \angle C = 35°50'$

Solving Triangles (SSS)

When all three sides of a triangle are known, the law of cosines can be used to solve the triangle.

EXAMPLE 2

In triangle ABC, $a = 18$, $b = 25$, and $c = 12$. Solve the triangle.

Let us first find $m \angle B$. We select the formula from the law of cosines that contains $\cos B$; in other words, $b^2 = a^2 + c^2 - 2ac \cos B$. We solve this for $\cos B$ and substitute.

$$\cos B = \frac{a^2 + c^2 - b^2}{2ac} = \frac{18^2 + 12^2 - 25^2}{2 \cdot 18 \cdot 12} = -0.3634$$

$$m \angle B = 111°20'$$

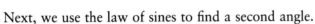

By using the formula that contains $\cos A$ we find that $\cos A = 0.7417$, and so $m \angle A = 42°10'$. Then $m \angle C = 180° - (111°20' + 42°10') = 26°30'$.

TRY THIS Solve the triangle by using the law of cosines.

2. In triangle ABC, $a = 25$, $b = 10$, and $c = 20$. $m\angle A = 108°10'$, $m\angle B = 22°20'$, $m\angle C = 49°30'$

16–8

Exercises

Solve the triangles.

1. $m\angle C = 135°$, $a = 6$, $b = 7$
2. $m\angle A = 116°$, $b = 31$, $c = 25$
3. $m\angle A = 30°$, $b = 12$, $c = 24$
4. $m\angle C = 120°$, $a = 5$, $b = 8$
5. $m\angle A = 133°$, $b = 12$, $c = 15$
6. $m\angle C = 60°$, $a = 15$, $b = 12$
7. $m\angle B = 72°40'$, $c = 16$, $a = 78$
8. $m\angle A = 24°30'$, $b = 68$, $c = 14$

Solve the triangles.

9. $a = 2$, $b = 3$, $c = 4$
10. $a = 7$, $b = 9$, $c = 10$
11. $a = 4$, $b = 6$, $c = 7$
12. $a = 7$, $b = 8$, $c = 10$
13. $a = 12$, $b = 14$, $c = 20$
14. $a = 22$, $b = 22$, $c = 35$
15. $a = 3.3$, $b = 2.7$, $c = 2.8$
16. $a = 16$, $b = 20$, $c = 32$
17. $a = 2.2$, $b = 4.1$, $c = 2.4$
18. $a = 3.6$, $b = 6.2$, $c = 4.1$

Solve.

19. Two ships leave harbor at the same time. The first sails N 15°W at 25 knots (a knot is one nautical mile per hour). The second sails N 32°E at 20 knots. After 2 hr, how far apart are the ships? 3.7 nautical miles

20. Two airplanes leave an airport at the same time. The first flies 150 km/h in a direction of 320°. The second flies 200 km/h in a direction of 200°. After 3 hr, how far apart are the planes? 912 km

21. A hill is inclined 5° to the horizontal. A 45-ft pole stands at the top of the hill. How long a rope will it take to reach from the top of the pole to a point 35 ft downhill from the base of the pole? 59.4 ft

22. A hill is inclined 15° to the horizontal. A 40-ft pole stands at the top of the hill. How long a rope will it take to reach from the top of the pole to a point 68 ft downhill from the base of the pole? 87.4 ft

23. A piece of wire 5.5 m long is bent into a triangular shape. One side is 1.5 m long and another is 2 m long. Find the angles of the triangle. 68°, 68°, 44°

24. A triangular lot has sides 120 ft long, 150 ft long, and 100 ft long. Find the angles of the lot. 52°50', 85°30', 41°40'

25. A slow-pitch softball diamond is a square 60 ft on a side. The pitcher's mound is 46 ft from home. How far is it from the pitcher's mound to first base? 42.6 ft

26. A baseball diamond is a square 90 ft on a side. The pitcher's mound is 60.5 ft from home. How far does the pitcher have to run to cover first? 63.7 ft

27. The longer base of an isosceles trapezoid measures 14 ft. The nonparallel sides measure 10 ft, and the base angles measure 80°.
   a. Find the length of a diagonal. b. Find the area. 118.2 ft²
   15.73 ft

28. An isosceles triangle has a vertex angle of 38° and this angle is included by two sides, each measuring 20 ft. Find the area of the triangle. 123 ft²

29. A field in the shape of a parallelogram has sides that measure 50 yd and 70 yd. One angle of the field measures 78°. Find the area of the field. 3424 yd²

30. After flying 75 miles of a 180-mile trip, an aircraft is 10 miles off course. How much should the heading be corrected to then fly straight to the destination, assuming no wind correction? 13°

Extension

Solve.

31. Find a formula for the area of an isosceles triangle in terms of the congruent sides and their included angle. Under what conditions will the area of a triangle with fixed congruent sides be a maximum? Area = $\frac{1}{2}a^2 \sin \theta$; $\theta = 90°$

32. *Surveying*. In surveying, a series of bearings and distances is called a *traverse*. In the following, measurements are taken as shown.
   a. Compute the bearing BC. b. Compute the distance and bearing AC.
   S87°36'E   526.5 ft, N 77°E

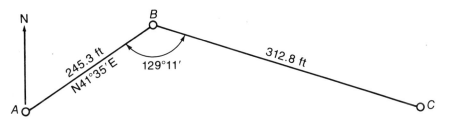

Challenge

Show that in any triangle ABC each of the following is true.

33. $a^2 + b^2 + c^2 = 2(bc \cos A + ac \cos B + ab \cos C)$.

34. $\dfrac{\cos A}{a} + \dfrac{\cos B}{b} + \dfrac{\cos C}{c} = \dfrac{a^2 + b^2 + c^2}{2abc}$

16—9 Vectors

In many applications there arise certain quantities in which a direction is specified. Any such quantity having a *direction* and a *magnitude* is called a *vector quantity,* or *vector*. Here are some examples of vector quantities.

Displacement   An object moves a certain distance in a certain direction.

> A train travels 100 mi to the northeast.
> A person takes 5 steps to the west.
> A batter hits a ball 100 m along the left-field foul line.

Velocity   An object travels at a certain speed in a certain direction.

> The wind is blowing 15 mph from the northwest.
> An airplane is traveling 450 km/h in a direction of 243°.

Force   A push or pull is exerted on an object in a certain direction.

> A 15-kg force is exerted downward on the handle of a jack.
> A 25-lb upward force is required to lift a box.
> A wagon is being pulled up a 30° incline, requiring an effort of 200 kg.

We shall represent vectors abstractly by directed line segments, or arrows. The length is chosen, according to some scale, to represent the magnitude of the vector, and the direction of the arrow represents the direction of the vector. For example, if we let 1 cm represent 5 km/h, then a 15-km/h wind from the northwest would be represented by an arrow 3 cm long, as shown.

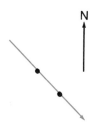

Vector Addition

To "add" vectors, we find a single vector that would have the same effect as the vectors combined. We shall illustrate vector addition for displacements, but it is done the same way for any vector quantities. Suppose a train travels 4 miles east and then 3 miles north. It will then be 5 miles from the starting point in the direction shown. The sum of the two vectors is the vector 5 miles in magnitude and in the direction shown. The sum is also called the resultant of the two vectors.

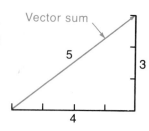

In general, if we have two vectors **a** and **b**, we can add them as in the above example. (It is usual to denote vectors using boldface type, and sometimes in handwriting to write a bar over the letters.) That is, we place the tail of one arrow at the head of the other and then find the vector that forms the third side of a triangle. Or, we can place the tails of the arrows together, complete a parallelogram, and find the diagonal of the parallelogram.

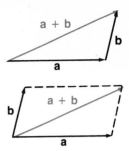

EXAMPLE 1

Forces of 15 kg and 25 kg act on an object at right angles to each other. Find their sum, or resultant, giving the angle that it makes with the larger force.

We make a drawing, this time a rectangle, using s for the length of vector **OB**. Since OAB is a right triangle, we have the following.

$$\tan \theta = \frac{15}{25} = 0.6$$

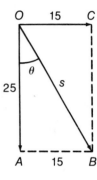

Thus θ, the angle the resultant makes with the larger force, is 31°. Now $s/15 = \csc \theta$, or $s = 15 \csc \theta = 15 \times 1.942 = 29.1$. Thus the resultant **OB** has a magnitude of 29.1 kg and makes an angle of 31° with the larger force.

TRY THIS

1. Two forces of 5.0 kg and 14.0 kg act at right angles to each other. Find the resultant, specifying the angle that it makes with the larger force. 14.9 kg, 19°40′

Applications

EXAMPLE 2

An airplane heads in a direction of 100° at 180-km/h airspeed while a wind is blowing 40 km/h from 220°. Find the speed of the airplane over the ground and the direction of its track over the ground.

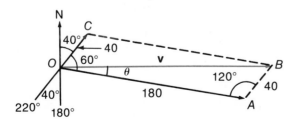

We first make a drawing. The wind is represented by **OC** and the velocity vector of the airplane by **OA**. The resultant velocity is **v**, the sum of the two vectors. We denote the length of **v** by |**v**|. By the law of cosines in $\triangle OAB$, we have the following.

$$|v|^2 = 40^2 + 180^2 - 2 \cdot 40 \cdot 180 \cos 120°$$
$$= 41,200$$

Thus |**v**| is 203 km/h. By the law of sines in the same triangle, we have the following.

$$\frac{40}{\sin \theta} = \frac{203}{\sin 120°} \quad \text{or} \quad \sin \theta = \frac{40 \sin 120°}{203} = 0.1706$$

Thus $\theta = 10°$ to the nearest degree. Therefore the ground speed of the airplane is 203 km/h and its track is in a direction of 90°.

TRY THIS

2. An airplane heads in a direction of 90° at 140-km/h airspeed. The wind is 50 km/h from 210°. Find the direction and speed of the airplane over the ground. 171 km/hr, 75°

16–9

Exercises

In Exercises 1–8, magnitudes of vectors **a** and **b** and the angle between the vectors θ are given. Find the resultant, giving the direction by specifying to the nearest degree the angle it makes with vector **a**.

1. $|a| = 45$, $|b| = 35$, $\theta = 90°$ 57, 38°
2. $|a| = 54$, $|b| = 43$, $\theta = 90°$ 69, 39°
3. $|a| = 10$, $|b| = 12$, $\theta = 67°$ 18.4, 37°
4. $|a| = 25$, $|b| = 30$, $\theta = 75°$ 43.7, 42°
5. $|a| = 20$, $|b| = 20$, $\theta = 117°$ 20.9, 58°
6. $|a| = 30$, $|b| = 30$, $\theta = 123°$ 28.6, 62°
7. $|a| = 23$, $|b| = 47$, $\theta = 27°$ 68.3, 18°
8. $|a| = 32$, $|b| = 74$, $\theta = 72°$ 89.2, 52°

Solve.

9. Two forces of 5 kg and 12 kg act on an object at right angles. Find the magnitude of the resultant and the angle it makes with the smaller force. 13 kg, 67°

10. Two forces of 30 kg and 40 kg act on an object at right angles. Find the magnitude of the resultant and the angle it makes with the smaller force. 50 kg, 53°

11. Forces of 420 kg and 300 kg act on an object. The angle between the forces is 50°. Find the resultant, giving the angle it makes with the larger force. 655 kg, 21°

12. Forces of 410 kg and 600 kg act on an object. The angle between the forces is 47°. Find the resultant, giving the angle it makes with the smaller force. 929 kg, 28°

13. A balloon is rising 12 ft/sec while a wind is blowing 18 ft/sec. Find the speed of the balloon and the angle it makes with the horizontal. 21.6 ft/sec, 34°

14. A balloon is rising 10 ft/sec while a wind is blowing 5 ft/sec. Find the speed of the balloon and the angle it makes with the horizontal. 11.2 ft/sec 63°

15. A boat heads 35°, propelled by a force of 750 lb. A wind from 320° exerts a force of 150 lb on the boat. How large is the resultant force and in what direction is the boat moving? 726 lb, 47°

16. A boat heads 220°, propelled by a 650-lb force. A wind from 080° exerts a force of 100 lb on the boat. How large is the resultant force, and in what direction is the boat moving? 729 lb, 225°

17. A ship sails N 80° E for 120 nautical mi, then S 20° W for 200 nautical mi. How far is it then from the starting point, and in what direction? 174 nautical mi, 516°E

18. An airplane flies 032° for 210 km, then 280° for 170 km. How far is it, then, from the starting point, and in what direction? 215 km, 345°

19. A motorboat has a speed of 15 km/h. It crosses a river whose current has a speed of 3 km/h. In order to cross the river at right angles, the boat should be pointed in what direction? An angle of 11° upstream

20. An airplane has an airspeed of 150 km/h. It is to make a flight in a direction of 080° while there is a 25-km/h wind from 350°. What should be the airplane's heading? 099°

16–10 Vectors and Coordinates

Components of Vectors

Given a vector, it is often convenient to reverse the addition procedure, that is, to find two vectors whose sum is the given vector. Usually the two vectors we seek will be perpendicular. The two vectors we find are called components of the given vector.

EXAMPLE 1

A certain vector **a** has a magnitude of 130 and is inclined 40° with the horizontal. Resolve the vector into horizontal and vertical components.

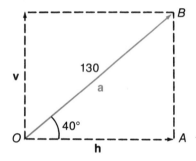

We first make a drawing showing horizontal and vertical vectors whose sum is the given vector **a**. From $\triangle OAB$:

$$|\mathbf{h}| = 130 \cos 40° = 99.6 \quad \text{and} \quad |\mathbf{v}| = 130 \sin 40° = 83.6$$

These are the components we seek.

EXAMPLE 2

An airplane is flying at 200 km/h in a direction of 305°. Find the westerly and northerly components of its velocity.

We first make a drawing showing westerly and northerly vectors whose sum is the given velocity. From $\triangle OAB$:

$$|\mathbf{n}| = 200 \cos 55° = 115 \text{ km/h}$$
$$|\mathbf{w}| = 200 \sin 55° = 164 \text{ km/h}$$

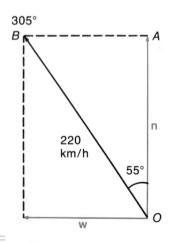

TRY THIS

1. A vector of magnitude 100 points southeast. Resolve the vector into easterly and southerly components. E, $50\sqrt{2}$; S, $50\sqrt{2}$

Analytic Representation of Vectors

If we place a coordinate system so that the origin is at the tail of an arrow representing a vector, we say that the vector is in standard position. Then if we know the coordinates of the other end of the vector, we know the vector. The coordinates will be the x-component and the y-component of the vector. Thus we can consider an ordered pair (a, b) to be a vector. When vectors are given in this form, it is easy to add them. We simply add the respective components.

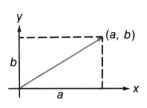

EXAMPLE 3
Find $\mathbf{u} + \mathbf{v}$, where $\mathbf{u} = (3, -7)$ and $\mathbf{v} = (4, 2)$.

The sum is found by adding the x-components and then adding the y-components: $\mathbf{u} + \mathbf{v} = (3, -7) + (4, 2) = (7, -5)$.

TRY THIS Add the vectors, giving answers as ordered pairs.
2. $(7, 2)$ and $(5, -10)$ (12, −8) **3.** $(-2, 7)$ and $(14, -3)$ (12, 4)

Properties of Vectors and Vector Algebra

The system of vectors is not a field, but it does have some of the familiar field properties.

Properties of Vectors

COMMUTATIVE LAW.
Addition of vectors is commutative.

ASSOCIATIVE LAW.
Addition of vectors is associative.

IDENTITY.
There is an additive identity, the vector $(0, 0)$, or $\mathbf{0}$.

INVERSES.
Every vector (a, b) has an additive inverse $(-a, -b)$.

SUBTRACTION.
We define $\mathbf{u} - \mathbf{v}$ to be the vector which when added to $\mathbf{v}$ gives $\mathbf{u}$. Also, $\mathbf{u} - \mathbf{v} = \mathbf{u} + (-\mathbf{v})$.

LENGTH, OR ABSOLUTE VALUE.
If $\mathbf{u} = (a, b)$, then it follows that $|\mathbf{u}| = \sqrt{a^2 + b^2}$.

A vector can be multiplied by a real number. A real number in this context is called a scalar. For example, $2\mathbf{v}$ is a vector in the same direction as $\mathbf{v}$ but twice as long. Analytically, we define scalar multiplication as follows.

DEFINITION

Scalar multiplication.

If r is any real number and $\mathbf{v} = (a, b)$, then $r\mathbf{v} = (ar, br)$.

EXAMPLE 4

Do the following calculations, where $\mathbf{u} = (4, 3)$ and $\mathbf{v} = (-5, 8)$:
a. $\mathbf{u} + \mathbf{v}$; b. $\mathbf{u} - \mathbf{v}$; c. $3\mathbf{u} - 4\mathbf{v}$; d. $|3\mathbf{u} - 4\mathbf{v}|$.

a. $\mathbf{u} + \mathbf{v} = (4, 3) + (-5, 8) = (-1, 11)$

b. $\mathbf{u} - \mathbf{v} = \mathbf{u} + (-\mathbf{v}) = (4, 3) + (5, -8) = (9, -5)$

c. $3\mathbf{u} - 4\mathbf{v} = 3(4, 3) - 4(-5, 8) = (12, 9) - (-20, 32)$
$= (32, -23)$

d. $|3\mathbf{u} - 4\mathbf{v}| = \sqrt{32^2 + (-23)^2} = \sqrt{1553} \approx 39.41$

TRY THIS For $\mathbf{u} = (-3, 5)$ and $\mathbf{v} = (4, 2)$, find the following.

4. $\mathbf{u} + \mathbf{v}$
(1, 7)

5. $\mathbf{v} - \mathbf{u}$
(7, −3)

6. $5\mathbf{u} - 2\mathbf{v}$
(−23, 21)

7. $|3\mathbf{u} + 2\mathbf{v}|$
19.03

16–10	

Exercises

Solve.

1. A vector $\mathbf{u}$ with magnitude 150 is inclined upward $52°$ from the horizontal. Find the horizontal and vertical components of $\mathbf{u}$. h, 92.3; v, 118

2. A vector $\mathbf{u}$ with magnitude 170 is inclined downward $63°$ from the horizontal. Find the horizontal and vertical components of $\mathbf{u}$. h, 77.2; v, 151

3. An airplane is flying $220°$ at 250 km/h. Find the southerly and westerly components of its velocity $\mathbf{v}$. S, 192 km/hr; W, 161 km/hr

4. A wind is blowing from $310°$ at 25 mph. Find the southerly and easterly components of the wind velocity $\mathbf{v}$. S, 16.1 mph; E, 19.2 mph

Add the vectors, giving answers as ordered pairs.

5. $(3, 7) + (2, 9)$ **6.** $(5, -7) + (-3, 2)$

7. $(17, 7.6) + (-12.2, 6.1)$ **8.** $(-15.2, 37.1) + (7.9, -17.8)$

9. $(-650, -750) + (-12, 324)$ **10.** $(-354, -973) + (-75, 256)$

For each of the following do the calculations for the following vectors: $\mathbf{u} = (3, 4)$, $\mathbf{v} = (5, 12)$, and $\mathbf{w} = (-6, 8)$.

11. $3\mathbf{u} + 2\mathbf{v}$ **12.** $3\mathbf{v} - 2\mathbf{w}$ **13.** $(\mathbf{u} + \mathbf{v}) - \mathbf{w}$ **14.** $\mathbf{u} - (\mathbf{v} + \mathbf{w})$

15. $|\mathbf{u}| + |\mathbf{v}|$ **16.** $|\mathbf{u}| - |\mathbf{v}|$ **17.** $|\mathbf{u} + \mathbf{v}|$ **18.** $|\mathbf{u} - \mathbf{v}|$

19. $2|\mathbf{u} + \mathbf{v}|$ **20.** $2|\mathbf{u}| + 2|\mathbf{v}|$ **21.** $|3\mathbf{w} - 2\mathbf{u}|$ **22.** $|2\mathbf{u} - 3\mathbf{w}|$

Extension

23. If $\mathbf{PQ}$ is any vector, what is $\mathbf{PQ} + \mathbf{QP}$? 0

24. The *inner product* of vectors $\mathbf{u} \cdot \mathbf{v}$ is a scalar, defined as follows: $\mathbf{u} \cdot \mathbf{v} = |\mathbf{u}||\mathbf{v}| \cos \theta$, where θ is the angle between the vectors. Show that vectors $\mathbf{u}$ and $\mathbf{v}$ are perpendicular if and only if $\mathbf{u} \cdot \mathbf{v} = 0$.

Challenge

25. Show that scalar multiplication is distributive over vector addition.

26. Let $\mathbf{u} = (3, 4)$. Find a vector that has the same direction as $\mathbf{u}$ but length 1. $\left(\frac{3}{5}, \frac{4}{5}\right)$

27. Prove that for any vectors $\mathbf{u}$ and $\mathbf{v}$, $|\mathbf{u} + \mathbf{v}| \leq |\mathbf{u}| + |\mathbf{v}|$.

Answers (right margin):

5. $(5, 16)$
6. $(2, -5)$
7. $(4.8, 13.7)$
8. $(-7.3, 19.3)$
9. $(-662, -426)$
10. $(-429, -717)$
11. $(19, 36)$
12. $(27, 20)$
13. $(14, 8)$
14. $(4, -16)$
15. 18
16. -8
17. 17.89
18. 8.246
19. 35.78
20. 36
21. 28.84
22. 28.84

24. If $\perp$ then $\theta = 90°$, so $\mathbf{u} \cdot \mathbf{v} = 0$. If $\mathbf{u} \cdot \mathbf{v} = 0$, then, since $|\mathbf{u}| \neq 0$ and $|\mathbf{v}| \neq 0$, $\cos \theta = 0$, and $\theta = 90°$.

25. Consider any vectors (a, b), (c, d), and any scalar s. $s[(a, b) + (c, d)] = s(a + c, b + d) = [s(a + c), s(b + d)]$. Also $s(a, b) + s(c, d) = (sa, sb) + (sc, sd) = [s(a + c), s(b + d)]$.

27. If $\mathbf{u}$ and $\mathbf{v}$ are not collinear, we have a triangle. By the law of cosines $|\mathbf{u} + \mathbf{v}| = |\mathbf{u}|^2 + |\mathbf{v}|^2 - 2|\mathbf{u}||\mathbf{v}| \cos \theta < |\mathbf{u}|^2 + |\mathbf{v}|^2$. If $\mathbf{u}$ and $\mathbf{v}$ are collinear and have opposite directions, equality holds. If collinear and have the same direction, $<$ again holds.

FIELDS OF MATHEMATICS/Game Theory

One of the newest fields in mathematics is game theory, which was developed by John von Neumann forty years ago. In game theory, the word game is given a new meaning. It is not just a pasttime, but a problem of strategy in the context of a competitive situation. The "players" may be individuals, companies, nations, or groups of consumers. Using intricate laws of strategy, each player has a limited number of "moves" or courses of action. After each player has selected a course of action, there is an outcome that results in a gain to each player. Losses are treated as negative gains.

Applications include the areas of sociology, military science, psychology, political science and economics. Through the study of game theory, business executives are being trained to make wide managerial decisions; politicians are improving their campaign strategies, companies are finding better uses for their advertising resources. In a situation that offers no clear-cut way of winning, game theory can show how to find the strategy which will come closest to achieving a stalement. In other words, it can show how to make the best of a bad situation.

Game theory is still in a very active stage of development and is one of the most often applied fields of mathematics.

16–11 Trigonometric Notation

In Chapter 7, we studied complex numbers. We now use our knowledge of trigonometry to develop trigonometric notation for complex numbers.

Consider any complex number $a + bi$. Recall that the length r of the segment from the origin to $a + bi$ is $\sqrt{a^2 + b^2}$. This distance r is called the absolute value of $a + bi$.

Suppose that the segment makes an angle θ with the real axis. As the next diagram shows,

$$a = r \cos \theta \text{ and } b = r \sin \theta.$$

Thus

$$a + bi = r \cos \theta + ir \sin \theta$$
$$= r (\cos \theta + i \sin \theta)$$

This is trigonometric notation for $a + bi$. The angle θ is called the argument.

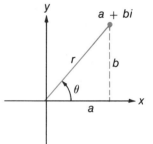

DEFINITION

Trigonometric notation for the complex number $a + bi$ is $r (\cos \theta + i \sin \theta)$, where r is the absolute value and θ is the argument. This is sometimes shortened to $r \operatorname{cis} \theta$.

Change of Notation

To change from trigonometric notation to rectangular notation $a + bi$, we use the formulas $a = r \cos \theta$ and $b = r \sin \theta$.

EXAMPLE 1
Write rectangular notation for $2 (\cos 120° + i \sin 120°)$.

$$a = 2 \cos 120° = -1 \quad \text{Identifying and evaluating } a \text{ and } b$$
$$b = 2 \sin 120° = \sqrt{3}$$

Thus $2 (\cos 120° + i \sin 120°) = -1 + i \sqrt{3}$

To change from rectangular notation to trigonometric notation, we remember that $r = \sqrt{a^2 + b^2}$ and θ is an angle for which $\sin \theta = \frac{b}{r}$ and $\cos \theta = \frac{a}{r}$.

EXAMPLE 2

Find trigonometric notation for $1 + i$.

We note that $a =$ and $b =$.

$$r = \sqrt{^2 + ^2} = \sqrt{2}$$

$$\sin \theta = \frac{1}{\sqrt{2}} \text{ and } \cos \theta = \frac{1}{\sqrt{2}}$$

Thus $\theta = \frac{\pi}{4}$, or $45°$, and we have the following.

$$1 + i = \sqrt{2} \text{ cis } \frac{\pi}{4} \text{ or } 1 + i = \sqrt{2} \text{ cis } 45°$$

TRY THIS

1. Write rectangular notation for $\sqrt{2} (\cos 315° + i \sin 315°)$. $1 - i$
2. Write trigonometric notation for $1 - i$. $\sqrt{2}(\cos 315° + i \sin 315°)$

In changing to trigonometric notation, note that there are many angles satisfying the given conditions. We ordinarily choose the smallest positive angle.

Multiplication and Trigonometric Notation

Multiplication of complex numbers is somewhat easier to do with trigonometric notation than with rectangular notation. We simply multiply the absolute values and add the arguments. To divide, we do the reverse.

THEOREM 16–7

For any complex numbers r_1 cis θ_1 and r_2 cis θ_2,

$$(r_1 \text{ cis } \theta_1)(r_2 \text{ cis } \theta_2) = r_1 \cdot r_2 \text{ cis } (\theta_1 + \theta_2).$$

THEOREM 16–8

For any complex numbers r_1 cis θ_1 and r_2 cis θ_2, $(r_2 \neq 0)$,

$$\frac{r_1 \text{ cis } \theta_1}{r_2 \text{ cis } \theta_2} = \frac{r_1}{r_2} \text{ cis } (\theta_1 - \theta_2).$$

EXAMPLE 3

Find the product of 3 cis 40° and 7 cis 20°.

$$3 \text{ cis } 40° \cdot 7 \text{ cis } 20° = 3 \cdot 7 \text{ cis } (40° + 20°)$$
$$= 21 \text{ cis } 60°$$

EXAMPLE 4

Divide 2 cis π by 4 cis $\frac{\pi}{2}$.

$$\frac{2 \text{ cis } \pi}{4 \text{ cis } \frac{\pi}{2}} = \frac{2}{4} \text{ cis } \left(\pi - \frac{\pi}{2} \right) = \frac{1}{2} \text{ cis } \frac{\pi}{2}$$

TRY THIS

3. Multiply 5 cis 25° by 4 cis 30°. 20 cis 55°

4. Divide 10 cis $\frac{\pi}{2}$ by 5 cis $\frac{\pi}{4}$. 2 cis $\frac{\pi}{4}$

DeMoivre's Theorem

An important theorem about powers and roots of complex numbers is named for French mathematician DeMoivre (1667–1754). Let us consider a number r cis θ and its square.

$$(r \text{ cis } \theta)^2 = (r \text{ cis } \theta)(r \text{ cis } \theta)$$
$$= r \cdot r \text{ cis } (\theta + \theta)$$
$$= r^2 \text{ cis } 2\theta$$

Similarly, we see that $(r \text{ cis } \theta)^3 = r \cdot r \cdot r \text{ cis } (\theta + \theta + \theta) = r^3 \text{ cis } 3\theta$. The generalization of this is DeMoivre's Theorem.

THEOREM 16–9

DeMoivre's Theorem
For any complex number r cis θ and any natural number n,
$(r \text{ cis } \theta)^n = r^n \text{ cis } n\theta$.

EXAMPLE 5

Find $(1 + i)^9$. We first find polar notation.

$$1 + i = \sqrt{2} \text{ cis } 45°$$

Then

$$(1 + i)^9 = (\sqrt{2} \text{ cis } 45°)^9$$
$$= (\sqrt{2})^9 \text{cis } 9 \cdot 45°$$
$$= 2^{\frac{9}{2}} \text{ cis } 405°$$
$$= 16 \sqrt{2} \text{ cis } 45° \quad \text{405° has the same terminal side as 45°}$$

TRY THIS

5. Find $(1 - i)^{10}$.   6. Find $(\sqrt{3} + i)^4$.   5. 32 cis 270°   6. 16 cis 120°

As we shall see, every nonzero complex number has two square roots, three cube roots, four fourth roots, and so on. In general a nonzero complex number has n different nth roots. These can be found by the formula which we now state and prove.

THEOREM 16–10

The nth roots of a complex number r cis θ are given by

$$r^{\frac{1}{n}} \text{ cis } \left(\frac{\theta}{n} + k \cdot \frac{360°}{n} \right), \text{ where } k = 0, 1, 2, \ldots, n - 1.$$

Proof

We show that this formula gives us n different roots, by using DeMoivre's Theorem. We take the expression for the nth roots and raise it to the nth power, to show that we get r cis θ.

$$\left[r^{\frac{1}{n}} \text{ cis } \left(\frac{\theta}{n} + k \cdot \frac{360°}{n} \right) \right]^n = (r^{\frac{1}{n}})^n \text{ cis } \left(\frac{\theta}{n} \cdot n + k \cdot n \cdot \frac{360°}{n} \right)$$
$$= r \text{ cis } (\theta + k \cdot 360°) = r \text{ cis } \theta$$

Thus we know that the formula gives us nth roots for any natural number k. Next we show that there are at least n different roots. To see this, consider substituting 0, 1, 2, and so on, for k. From 0 to $n - 1$ the angles obtained and their sines and cosines are all different. But when $k = n$ the cycle begins to repeat. There cannot be more than n different nth roots. This fact follows from the Fundamental Theorem of Algebra, considered in Chapter 7.

EXAMPLE 6

Find the square roots of $2 + 2\sqrt{3}i$. We first find trigonometric notation.

$$2 + 2\sqrt{3}i = 4 \text{ cis } 60°$$

Then

$$(4 \text{ cis } 60°)^{\frac{1}{2}} = 4^{\frac{1}{2}} \text{ cis} \left(\frac{60°}{2} + k \cdot \frac{360°}{2} \right), k = 0, 1$$

$$= 2 \text{ cis} \left(30° + k \cdot \frac{360°}{2} \right), k = 0, 1$$

Thus the roots are 2 cis 30° and 2 cis 210°, or $\sqrt{3} + i$ and $-\sqrt{3} - i$.

TRY THIS

7. Find the square roots of $2i$.

16–11

Exercises

Find rectangular notation.

1. $3 (\cos 30° + i \sin 30°)$ $\frac{3\sqrt{3}}{2} + \frac{3}{2}i$
2. $5 (\cos 60° + i \sin 60°)$ $\frac{5}{2} + \frac{5\sqrt{3}}{2}i$
3. $4 (\cos 135° + i \sin 135°)$ $-2\sqrt{2} + 2i\sqrt{2}$
4. $6 (\cos 150° + i \sin 150°)$ $-3\sqrt{3} + 3i$
5. $10 \text{ cis } 270°$ $-10i$
6. $12 \text{ cis } 90°$ $12i$
7. $5 \text{ cis } (-45°)$ $\frac{5\sqrt{2}}{2} - \frac{5\sqrt{2}}{2}i$
8. $5 \text{ cis } (-60°)$ $\frac{5}{2} - \frac{5\sqrt{3}}{2}i$
9. $\sqrt{8} \left(\cos \frac{\pi}{4} + i \sin \frac{\pi}{4} \right)$ $2 + 2i$
10. $\sqrt{8} \left(\cos \frac{3\pi}{4} + i \sin \frac{3\pi}{4} \right)$ $-2 + 2i$
11. $4 \left(\cos \frac{\pi}{6} + i \sin \frac{\pi}{6} \right)$ $2\sqrt{3} + 2i$
12. $5 \left(\cos \frac{\pi}{3} + i \sin \frac{\pi}{3} \right)$ $\frac{5}{2} + \frac{5\sqrt{3}}{2}i$
13. $\sqrt{8} \text{ cis } \frac{5\pi}{4}$ $-2 - 2i$
14. $\sqrt{8} \text{ cis } \left(-\frac{\pi}{4} \right)$ $2 - 2i$

Find trigonometric notation.

15. $1 - i$ $\sqrt{2} \text{ cis } \frac{7\pi}{4}$ or $\sqrt{2} \text{ cis } 315°$
16. $-1 - i$ $\sqrt{2} \text{ cis } \frac{5\pi}{4}$ or $\sqrt{2} \text{ cis } 225°$
17. $\sqrt{3} + i$ $2 \text{ cis } \frac{\pi}{6}$ or 2 cis 30°
18. $-\sqrt{3} + i$ $2 \text{ cis } \frac{5\pi}{6}$ or 2 cis 150°
19. $10\sqrt{3} - 10i$ $20 \text{ cis } \frac{11\pi}{6}$ or 20 cis 330°
20. $-10\sqrt{3} + 10i$ $20 \text{ cis } \frac{5\pi}{6}$ or 20 cis 150°
21. $2i$ $2 \text{ cis } \frac{\pi}{2}$ or 2 cis 90°
22. $3i$ $3 \text{ cis } \frac{\pi}{2}$ or 3 cis 90°
23. -5 5 cis π or 5 cis 180°
24. -10 10 cis π or 10 cis 180°
25. $-4i$ $4 \text{ cis } \frac{3\pi}{2}$ or 4 cis 270°
26. $-5i$ $5 \text{ cis } \frac{3\pi}{2}$ or 5 cis 270°

Convert to trigonometric notation and then multiply or divide.

27. $(1 - i)(2 + 2i)$ **28.** $(\sqrt{3} + i)(1 + i)$ **29.** $(10\sqrt{3} + 10i)(\sqrt{3} - i)$

30. $(1 + i\sqrt{3})(1 + i)$ **31.** $(2\sqrt{3} + 2i)(2i)$ **32.** $(3\sqrt{3} - 3i)(2i)$

33. $\dfrac{1 + i}{1 - i}$ **34.** $\dfrac{1 - i}{1 + i}$ **35.** $\dfrac{-1 + i}{\sqrt{3} + i}$

36. $\dfrac{1 - i}{\sqrt{3} - i}$ **37.** $\dfrac{2\sqrt{3} - 2i}{1 + \sqrt{3}i}$ **38.** $\dfrac{3 - 3\sqrt{3}i}{\sqrt{3} - i}$

Raise the number to the power. Give your answer in polar notation.

39. $\left(2 \text{ cis } \dfrac{\pi}{3}\right)^3$ **40.** $\left(3 \text{ cis } \dfrac{\pi}{2}\right)^4$ **41.** $\left(2 \text{ cis } \dfrac{\pi}{6}\right)^6$

42. $\left(2 \text{ cis } \dfrac{\pi}{5}\right)^5$ **43.** $(1 + i)^6$ **44.** $(1 - i)^6$

Raise the number to the power. Give your answer in rectangular notation.

45. $(2 \text{ cis } 240°)^4$ **46.** $(2 \text{ cis } 120°)^4$ **47.** $(1 + \sqrt{3}i)^4$ **48.** $(-\sqrt{3} + i)^6$

49. $\left(\dfrac{1}{\sqrt{2}} + \dfrac{1}{\sqrt{2}}i\right)^{10}$ **50.** $\left(\dfrac{1}{\sqrt{2}} - \dfrac{1}{\sqrt{2}}i\right)^{12}$ **51.** $\left(\dfrac{\sqrt{3}}{2} + \dfrac{1}{2}i\right)^{12}$ **52.** $\left(\dfrac{\sqrt{3}}{2} - \dfrac{1}{2}i\right)^{14}$

Answers in margin:
27. 4 cis 0
28. $2\sqrt{2}$ cis $\dfrac{5\pi}{12}$
29. 40 cis 0
30. $2\sqrt{2}$ cis $\dfrac{7\pi}{12}$
31. 8 cis $\dfrac{2\pi}{3}$
32. 12 cis $\dfrac{\pi}{3}$
33. cis $\dfrac{\pi}{2}$
34. cis $\dfrac{3\pi}{2}$
35. $\dfrac{\sqrt{2}}{2}$ cis $\dfrac{7\pi}{12}$
36. $\dfrac{\sqrt{2}}{2}$ cis $\dfrac{23\pi}{12}$
37. 2 cis $\dfrac{3\pi}{2}$
38. 3 cis $\dfrac{11\pi}{6}$
39. 8 cis π or 8 cis 180°
40. 81 cis 0 or 81 cis 0°
41. 64 cis π or 64 cis 180°
42. 32 cis π or 32 cis 180°
43. 8 cis $\dfrac{3\pi}{2}$ or 8 cis 270°
44. 8 cis $\dfrac{\pi}{2}$ or cis 90°

Find the following.

53. The square roots of $-1 + \sqrt{3}i$ **54.** The square roots of $-\sqrt{3} - i$

55. The cube roots of i **56.** The cube roots of $-i$

57. The fourth roots of 16   **58.** The fourth roots of -16

Extension

59. Every complex number including $1 = 1 + 0i$ has three different cube roots. Show that the three cube roots of 1 are $1, -\dfrac{1}{2} + \dfrac{\sqrt{3}}{2}i$, and $-\dfrac{1}{2} - \dfrac{\sqrt{3}}{2}i$, by raising each to the third power. Locate them on a graph.

60. Write -1 as -1 cis $180°$ to find the three cube roots of -1. Graph the roots.

61. Find the fourth roots of 1.

62. Show that for any complex numbers z, w, $|z \cdot w| = |z| \cdot |w|$. [*Hint*: Let $z = r_1$ cis θ_1 and $w = r_2$ cis θ_2.]

63. Show that for any complex number z and any nonzero complex number w, $\left|\dfrac{z}{w}\right| = \dfrac{|z|}{|w|}$.

64. Find the cube roots of 68.4321.   **65.** Find the cube roots of 456.86.

Challenge

66. Find polar notation for $(\cos \theta + i \sin \theta)^{-1}$.
$\cos \theta - i \sin \theta$

67. Compute $\begin{bmatrix} i & 0 \\ 0 & -i \end{bmatrix}^3 \cdot \begin{bmatrix} -i & 0 \\ 0 & -i \end{bmatrix}$

CONSUMER APPLICATION/Filing Income Tax Returns

Federal law requires that most wage earners file an income tax return each year. This return determines how much tax is to be paid to the government.

In each pay period, your employer withholds a portion of your earnings and sends it to the Internal Revenue Service (IRS). At the end of the year, the employer provides a Wage and Tax Statement called a W-2 form which states how much you earned and how much has been withheld. You need this form when you file your tax return.

Form **W-2 Wage and Tax Statement 1982** Copy D For employer Department of the Treasury Internal Revenue Service

Many wage earners file a 1040A income tax form. Line 11 of form 1040A is the total of your income from all sources. Your tax is figured from the tax tables on this amount and entered in line 14a. Line 12b is the tax already withheld. If your tax, line 15, is greater than what you have paid, line 13, then you have a balance due. If your tax is less than what you have already paid, then you will receive a refund.

Exercises

Determine whether there will be a refund or a balance due.

1. Line 13, tax withheld: $1025.
   Line 15, tax due: $1062. Balance due, $37

2. Line 13, tax withheld: $779.
   Line 15, tax due: $845. Balance due, $66

3. Line 13, tax withheld: $406.
   Line 15, tax due: $391. Refund, $15

4. Line 13, tax withheld: $1873
   Line 15, tax due: $2017 Balance due, $144

5. Obtain copies of the latest 1040A form and the 1040E form with instructions from a local Internal Revenue Service office. Compare the 1040A and the 1040E forms. Who can use a 1040A form? Who can use a 1040E form? When should a 1040 form be used?

CHAPTER 16   Review

Review the material in the chapter. Then see how you have done by trying these review exercises. If you miss an exercise, restudy the indicated lesson.

16–1   Use sum and difference identities to simplify the following.

1. $\cos (x + y)$ **2.** $\tan (45° - 30°)$ $-2 + \sqrt{3}$ 1. $\cos x \cos y - \sin x \sin y$

Use sum and difference identities to find the following.

3. $\sin 75°$ **4.** $\cos 105°$ **5.** $\tan 15°$ $2 - \sqrt{3}$

3. $\dfrac{\sqrt{2} + \sqrt{6}}{4}$

4. $\dfrac{\sqrt{2} - \sqrt{6}}{4}$

16–2   Find $\sin 2\theta$, $\cos 2\theta$, $\tan 2\theta$, and the quadrant in which 2θ lies.

6. $\sin \theta = \dfrac{3}{5}$ (θ in Quadrant I)   **7.** $\tan \theta = \dfrac{4}{3}$ (θ in Quadrant III)

6. $\sin 2\theta = \dfrac{24}{25}$, $\cos 2\theta = \dfrac{7}{25}$, $\tan 2\theta = \dfrac{24}{7}$, θ in Quadrant 1   7. $\sin 2\theta = \dfrac{24}{25}$, $\cos 2\theta = -\dfrac{7}{25}$, $\tan 2\theta = -\dfrac{24}{7}$, θ in Quadrant 1

16–2   Find the following without using tables.

8. $\cos 15°$ **9.** $\sin \dfrac{\pi}{8}$ $\dfrac{\sqrt{2 - \sqrt{2}}}{2}$ 8. $\dfrac{1}{2}\sqrt{2 + \sqrt{3}}$ 10. $\tan 2\theta$ $\left| \begin{array}{l} \dfrac{2 \tan \theta}{1 - \tan 2\theta} \\ \dfrac{2 \tan \theta}{1 - \tan^2 \theta} \end{array} \right.$

16–3

$\tan (\theta + \theta)$ $\left| \begin{array}{l} \dfrac{2 \tan \theta}{1 - \tan^2 \theta} \end{array} \right.$

$\dfrac{\tan \theta + \tan \theta}{1 - \tan \theta \tan \theta}$

10. Prove the identity $\tan 2\theta = \dfrac{2 \tan \theta}{1 - \tan^2 \theta}$. $\dfrac{2 \tan \theta}{1 - \tan^2 \theta}$

16–4   Find all values of the following.

11. $\sin^{-1} \dfrac{1}{2}$ **12.** $\arccos \left(-\dfrac{\sqrt{2}}{2} \right)$ $\dfrac{3\pi}{4} + 2k\pi$ and $\dfrac{5\pi}{4} + 2k\pi$ 11. $\dfrac{\pi}{6} + 2k\pi$ and $\dfrac{5\pi}{6} + 2k\pi$

16–4   Find the following.

13. $\text{Arcsin} -\dfrac{\sqrt{2}}{2}$ $-\dfrac{\pi}{4}$ **14.** $\text{Cos}^{-1} \dfrac{\sqrt{3}}{2}$ $\dfrac{\pi}{6}$

16–5   Solve, finding all solutions from 0 to 2π.

15. $\sin^2 x - 7 \sin x = 0$ **16.** $\sin 2x - \cos x = 0$ $\dfrac{\pi}{6}, \dfrac{5\pi}{6}, \dfrac{\pi}{2}, \dfrac{3\pi}{2}$ 15. $(0, \pi)$

16–6   Solve the triangles. Angle C is a right angle. Use three-digit precision.

17. $m \angle A = 42°30'$, $a = 1200$ $m \angle B = 47°30', b = 1310, c \doteq 1780$

18. $a = 7.3, c = 8.6$ $m \angle A = 58°10', m \angle B = 31°50', b = 4.54$

19. $a = 30.5, m \angle B = 51°10'$ $m \angle A = 38°50', b = 37.8, c = 48.6$

16–7, 16–8   Solve triangle ABC.

20. $M \angle A = 40°, m \angle B = 80°, b = 25$ $m \angle C = 60°, a = 16.3, c = 22.0$

21. $m \angle B = 118°20', m \angle C = 27°40', b = 0.974$ $m \angle A = 34°, a = 0.619, c = 0.514$

22. $m \angle A = 72°, a = 5, b = 4$ $m \angle B = 49°30', m \angle C = 58°30', c = 4.5$

23. Find the area of triangle ABC. $b = 5, c = 9, m \angle A = 65°$ 20

24. $m \angle B = 135°, a = 3.7, c = 4.9$ $b = 7.96, m \angle A = 19°10', m \angle C = 25°50'$

25. $a = 5, b = 8, c = 9$ $m \angle A = 33°30', m \angle B = 28°, m \angle C = 118°30'$

16–9

26. Vectors a and b have magnitudes $|a| = 15$ and $|b| = 20$. The angle between the vectors is $\theta = 90°$. Find the resultant, giving the direction by specifying to the nearest degree the angle it makes with vector **a**. 25, 37°

16–10   Add the vectors, giving answers as ordered pairs.

27. $(4, 9) + (5, -3)$ (9, 6) **28.** $(16.2, -38.1) + (-9.7, 16.2)$ (6.5, −21.9)

16–10   Let **u** $= (2, 1)$, **v** $= (-2, 5)$, and **w** $= (3, -1)$. Find each of the following.

29. $(\mathbf{u} + \mathbf{v}) - \mathbf{w}$ (−3, 7)   **30.** $2 |\mathbf{v}| + 3|\mathbf{w}|$ $2\sqrt{29} + 3\sqrt{10}$

16–11

31. Find rectangular notation for $2(\cos 135° + i \sin 135°)$. $-\sqrt{2} + \sqrt{2}i$

32. Find trigonometric notation for $1 + i$. $\sqrt{2}$ cis $\frac{\pi}{4}$ or $\sqrt{2}$ cis 45°

33. Find $(2 \text{ cis } 120°)^3$. Give your answer in rectangular notation. 8

34. Find the cube roots of $1 + i$. $\sqrt[6]{2}$ cis 15°, $\sqrt[6]{2}$ cis 135°, and $\sqrt[6]{2}$ cis 255°

CHAPTER 16   Test

Use sum and difference identities to simplify the following.

1. $\sin (x - y)$ **2.** $\cos \left(\dfrac{\pi}{2} + \dfrac{\pi}{3} \right)$ $-\dfrac{\sqrt{3}}{2}$ 1. sin x cos y − cos x sin y
3. −2 − $\sqrt{3}$

3. $\tan 105°$ **4.** $\sin 15°$ $\dfrac{\sqrt{6} - \sqrt{2}}{4}$

Find $\sin 2\theta$, $\cos 2\theta$, $\tan 2\theta$, and the quadrant in which 2θ lies.

5. $\cos \theta = \frac{4}{5}$ (θ in Quadrant I) $\frac{24}{25}, \frac{7}{25}, \frac{24}{7}$, Quadrant I

6. $\tan \theta = -\frac{3}{4}$ (θ in Quadrant II) $-\frac{24}{25}, \frac{7}{25}, -\frac{24}{7}$, Quadrant IV

Find the following without using tables.

7. $\sin \frac{\pi}{12}$ **8.** $\sin \frac{7\pi}{8}$ $\frac{\sqrt{2-\sqrt{2}}}{2}$ 7. $\frac{1}{2}\sqrt{2-\sqrt{3}}$

9. Prove the identity $\tan \theta \equiv \dfrac{\sin 2\theta}{1 + \cos 2\theta}$.

9. $\tan \theta \quad \dfrac{\sin 2\theta}{1 + \cos 2\theta}$

$\tan \theta \left| \begin{array}{c} \dfrac{2 \sin \theta \cos \theta}{1 + \cos^2 \theta - \sin^2 \theta} \\ \dfrac{2 \sin \theta \cos \theta}{2 \cos^2 \theta} \\ \dfrac{\sin \theta}{\cos \theta} \\ \tan \theta \end{array} \right.$

Find the following.

10. $\arccos \frac{1}{2}$ **11.** $\arccos \frac{\sqrt{3}}{2}$ $\frac{\pi}{6}$ 10. $\frac{\pi}{3} + 2k\pi$ and $\frac{5\pi}{3} + 2k\pi$

Solve, finding all solutions from 0 to 2π.

12. $2 \cos^2 x + 1 = -3 \cos x$ $\frac{2\pi}{3}, \frac{4\pi}{3}, \pi$
13. $\cos^2 x = 1 + \sin^2 x$ $0, \pi, 2\pi$

Solve the triangles. Angle C is a right triangle. Use three-digit precision.

14. $a = 9.2, c = 10.1$ **15.** $a = 28.5, m\angle B = 49°10'$

14. $m\angle A = 65°40', m\angle B = 24°20', b = 4.16$
15. $m\angle A = 40°50', b = 33.0, c = 43.6$

Solve triangle ABC.

16. $m\angle B = 117°10', m\angle C = 26°50', b = 0.9763$ $m\angle A = 36°, a = 0.636, c = 0.489$
17. $m\angle A = 50°, a = 9, b = 10$ $m\angle B = 58°20', m\angle C = 71°40', c = 11.2$
18. $a = 3.8, c = 4.6, m\angle B = 132°$ $b = 7.68, m\angle A = 21°34', m\angle C = 26°26'$
19. $a = 9, b = 10, c = 13$ $m\angle B = 50°10', m\angle A = 43°40', m\angle C = 86°20'$

Let $\mathbf{u} = (-3, 2)$, $\mathbf{v} = (5, 1)$, and $\mathbf{w} = (6, -4)$.
Find each of the following.

20. $\mathbf{u} + \mathbf{v}$ (2, 3)   **21.** $\mathbf{u} - (\mathbf{v} + \mathbf{w})$ $(-14, 5)$
22. $|\mathbf{v} + \mathbf{w}|$ $\sqrt{130}$ **23.** $3|\mathbf{u}| - 2|\mathbf{w}|$ $-\sqrt{13}$
24. Find rectangular notation for $3(\cos 120° + i \sin 102°)$. $-\frac{3}{2} + \frac{3\sqrt{3}}{2}i$
25. Find trigonometric notation for $1 - i$. $\sqrt{2}\, \text{cis}\, \frac{7\pi}{4}$
26. Find $(2 \text{ cis } 150°)^3$. Give your answer in rectangular notation. $8i$
27. Find the cube roots of $1 - i$. $\sqrt[6]{2}\, \text{cis}\, 105°, \sqrt[6]{2}\, \text{cis}\, 225°,$ and $\sqrt[6]{2}\, \text{cis}\, 345°$

Challenge

28. Solve $\sqrt{\sin x} = \frac{1}{2}\sqrt{2\sqrt{2}}$. $45°, 135°$

CHAPTERS 1–16   Cumulative Review

1–2   Evaluate each expression for $a = -2$, $c = 7$.

1. $|a - 2c| - |2a - c| - ac$ 19   **2.** $-5|a^2 + ac| - 3|2ac - 1|$ −137

1–5   Simplify.

3. $11x - [x + (4x - 6) + 4x] - 2$ **4.** $[(4 - 7x)x + 5x^2]x$ **5.** $\dfrac{-56x^{-3}y}{49x^{-4}y^2}$

2x + 4   4x² − 2x³ $-\frac{8}{7}x^{-1}y^{-1}$ or $-\frac{8}{7xy}$

2–2   Solve.

6. $4x - 3[4(x + 6) + 1] = 2x - 5$ −7   **7.** $\frac{2}{3}x + \frac{3}{4} = 2(x - 11) + \frac{7}{4}$ 30

2–5

8. $4a + 3 < 9a - 7$ **9.** $-6.1x - 1.1 < 0.8x + 4.2$ 8. $a > -2$ 9. $x < 1$

2–7

10. $-14 < 3x + 1 < 40$ **11.** $|4 - y| \le 10$ 10. $-5 < x < 13$ 11. $-6 \le y \le 14$

3–4

12. Name the x- and y-intercepts of the line containing $\left(-\frac{3}{5}, \frac{4}{5}\right)$
     and $\left(\frac{2}{5} - \frac{16}{5}\right)$. $\left(-\frac{2}{5}, 0\right)$ and $\left(0, -\frac{8}{5}\right)$

3–7

13. Write the slope-intercept form of the line containing $(-3, -1)$
     which is
     a. parallel to the line $2x - 5y = 6$.   **b.** perpendicular to the line $2x - 5y = 6$.

4–1 and 4–7   Solve these systems.   13. a. $y = \frac{2}{5}x + 5$ b. $y = -\frac{5}{2}x - \frac{17}{2}$

14. $5a - b = -11$ **15.** $2x - 3y + 8 = 0$ **16.** $a + b - 4c = -22$
     $4a + 12b = 4$ (−2, 1) $9x + 3y + 3 = 0$ (−1, 2) $-a - 2b + 3c = 13$
                                                $-2a + b + c = 11$ (−1, 3, 6)

5–1 and 5–2   Simplify.

17. $(8x^3 - 6x + 5) - (10x^4 + 4x^2 + 2x)$ **18.** $(4xy + 5y)(x^2 - 2)$ **19.** $(2x - 1)^3$
  −10x⁴ + 8x³ − 4x² − 8x + 5   4x³y + 5x²y − 8xy − 10y   8x³ − 12x² + 6x − 1

5–3, 5–5   Factor.

20. $12x^2 - 132xy + 363y^2$ **21.** $\frac{1}{9}x^6 - 49y^2$ **22.** $2x^3 + 6x^2 - 8x - 24$
  3(2x − 11y)²

726 CHAPTER 16 TRIGONOMETRIC IDENTITIES AND EQUATIONS

5–8   Solve.

23. $6x - x^2 = 0$ **24.** $x^2 - 9x = -8$ 23. (0, 6)   24. (8, 1)

6–1, 6–3   Simplify.   25. $\frac{x + 6}{3(x - 2)}$

25. $\frac{x^2 - 4x - 12}{3x^2 - 12x + 12}$ **26.** $\frac{5a - 2}{a + 3} \div \frac{25a^2 - 4}{a^2 - 9}$ **27.** $\frac{m - 6}{m^2 - 4} + \frac{m - 1}{m - 2} - \frac{m + 1}{m + 2}$

Solve.

26. $\frac{a - 3}{5a + 2}$

28. $\frac{a - 3}{a + 2} = \frac{1}{5}$ $\frac{17}{4}$ **29.** $\frac{15}{m} - \frac{15}{m + 2} = 2$ $-5, 3$

27. $\frac{3}{m + 2}$

7–2 to 7–7   Simplify.

30. $2\sqrt[4]{2}$
31. $3|x|\sqrt{10x}$
32. $30\sqrt{2}$
33. $|x + 3|$

30. $\sqrt[4]{32}$ **31.** $\sqrt{90x^3}$ **32.** $\sqrt{24}\sqrt{75}$ **33.** $\sqrt{x^2 + 6x + 9}$

34. $\frac{\sqrt{40ab^3}}{\sqrt{8a}}$ **35.** $\frac{\sqrt{a^3 + b^3}}{\sqrt{a + b}}$ **36.** $(\sqrt{18a^2b})^3$ **37.** $\frac{\sqrt{63x^5}}{\sqrt{28x^2}}$

34. $|b|\sqrt{5b}$
35. $\sqrt{a^2 - ab + b^2}$
36. $54a^3|b|\sqrt{2b}$
37. $\frac{3}{2}\sqrt{x}$

38. $5\sqrt[3]{32} - 2\sqrt[3]{108} - 5\sqrt[3]{4}$ **39.** $(2\sqrt{7} - 3\sqrt{5})(\sqrt{7} + \sqrt{5})$

38. $-\sqrt[3]{4}$
39. $2\sqrt{35} - 1$
40. $-1 - i$
41. $-40 - 44i + 12$

40. $(5 - 3i) - (6 - 4i)$ **41.** $(8 + 4i)(-5 - 3i)$ **42.** $\frac{2 + i}{3 - 2i}$

42. $\frac{4 + 7i}{13}$

8–1, 8–4   Solve.   43. $\frac{\sqrt{2}}{3}, -\frac{\sqrt{2}}{3}$

43. $9x^2 - 2 = 0$ **44.** $3x^2 = 4x$ $0, \frac{4}{3}$ **45.** $x^2 - 3x - 9 = 0$ $\frac{3 \pm 3\sqrt{5}}{2}$

46. $2x^{\frac{2}{3}} - x^{\frac{1}{3}} + 28 = 0$ 4

8–6

47. Find an equation of variation where y varies inversely as the square of x, and $y = 1.6$ when $x = 4$. $y = \frac{25.6}{x^2}$

9–1   Test the following equations for symmetry with respect to the x-axis and the y-axis.

48. $4y^2 = 2x - 1$ **49.** $5x^2 - 2y^2 = 6$ **50.** $y^3 - x^3 = -7$
x-axis   Both axes   Neither

Determine whether each function is even, odd, or neither.

51. $f(x) = -3x^9$ **52.** $f(x) = x + 2$ **53.** $f(x) = -8$
Odd   Neither   Even

9–5   For each of the following functions, graph the function, find the vertex, the line of symmetry, and the maximum or minimum value.

54. $f(x) = (x + 2)^2 - 4$ **55.** $f(x) = -2(x - 1)^2 + 3$
$(-2, -4), x = -2, \text{min}: -2$ $(1, 3), x = 1, \text{max}: 3$

Chapters 1–16 Cumulative Review **727**

9–7 Find the x-intercepts.

56. $f(x) = x^2 + x - 2$ **57.** $f(x) = 4x^2 + 12x + 9$ **58.** $f(x) = 9x^2 - 12x - 1$

56. $(-2, 0), (1, 0)$

57. $\left(-\dfrac{3}{2}, 0\right)$

10–1 to 10–4 Solve.

58. $\left(\dfrac{2 + \sqrt{5}}{3}, 0\right)\left(\dfrac{2 - \sqrt{5}}{3}, 0\right)$

59. Find the midpoints of the segment with endpoints $(4, 5)$ and $(6, -7)$. $(5, -1)$

60. Find the center and radius of the circle $(x + 1)^2 + (y + 3)^2 = 4$.
Circle with center $(-1, -3)$, radius 2

61. Find the center, vertices, foci, and asymptotes for the hyperbola $\dfrac{(y + 3)^2}{25} - \dfrac{(x + 1)^2}{16} = 1$. Graph the hyperbola.

61. Center: $(-1, -3)$; vertices: $(-1, 2), (-1, 8)$; foci: $(-1, -3 + \sqrt{41})$, $(-1, -3 - \sqrt{41})$; asymptotes: $y + 3 = \dfrac{5}{4}(x + 1)$, $y + 3 = -\dfrac{5}{4}(x + 1)$

11–2 to 11–4 Solve.

62. Use synthetic division to find the quotient and remainder: $(x^3 - 27) \div (x - 3)$. $Q: x^2 + 3x + 9, R\ 0$

63. Suppose a polynomial of degree 5 with rational coefficients has roots $8, 6 - 7i, \frac{1}{2} + \sqrt{11}$. Find the other roots. $6 + 7i, \frac{1}{2} - \sqrt{11}$

64. Find the rational roots of $2x^3 - 3x^2 - x + 1$, if they exist. If possible, find the other roots. $\frac{1}{2}, \frac{1 + \sqrt{5}}{2}, \frac{1 - \sqrt{5}}{2}$

12–1 Write an equation of the inverse relation.

65. $2x + 3y - 7 = 0$ **66.** $y = 2x^2 + 3$ **67.** $f(x) = 2x$ $f(x) = \frac{x}{2}$
$2y + 3x - 7 = 0$ $x = 2y^2 + 3$

12–3 Convert to logarithmic equations.

68. $10^{0.4771} = 3$ **69.** $8^{\log 2} = \log x$ **70.** $x^y = z$
$\log_{10} 3 = 0.4771$ $\log_8 \log x = \log 2$ $\log_x z = y$

12–7 Solve.

71. $4^3 x + 5 = 16$ -1 **72.** $\log(x + 9) - \log x = 1$ 1 **73.** $9^{y^2} \cdot 3^{5y} = 27$ $-3, \frac{1}{2}$

13–1 to 13–4 Solve.

74. State a rule for finding the nth term of $-2, 3, -4, 5, \ldots$. Answers may vary. $(-1)^n(n + 1)$

75. Find the 17th term of the arithmetic sequence $7, 4, 1, \ldots$. -41

76. Find the sum of the infinite geometric series $9 - 3 + 1 - \ldots$. $\frac{27}{4}$

13–5 to 13–7 Evaluate.

77. $9^P 5$ **78.** $5!$ **79.** $7^C 4$ **80.** $\dbinom{8}{4}$ 77. 15,120 78. 120 79. 35 80. 70

13-8

81. Expand $(2a + 3b)^4$. $16a^4 + 96a^3b + 72a^2b^2 + 216ab^3 + 81b^4$

82. $\begin{bmatrix} -3 & 6 & 30 \\ 9 & -12 & 24 \\ 0 & 15 & -3 \end{bmatrix}$

14-1 Let $A = \begin{bmatrix} -1 & 2 & 10 \\ 3 & -4 & 8 \\ 0 & 5 & -1 \end{bmatrix}$ and $B = \begin{bmatrix} 2 & 1 \\ -5 & -3 \\ 4 & 0 \end{bmatrix}$.

83. $\begin{bmatrix} 28 & -7 \\ 58 & 15 \\ -29 & -15 \end{bmatrix}$

82. Find $3A$.   **83.** Find AB.   **84.** Find A^{-1}.

84. $\begin{bmatrix} -\frac{3}{16} & \frac{13}{48} & \frac{7}{24} \\ \frac{1}{64} & \frac{1}{192} & \frac{19}{96} \\ \frac{5}{64} & \frac{5}{192} & -\frac{1}{96} \end{bmatrix}$

15-1

85. In triangle ABC, $\angle C$ is a right angle, $m \angle B = 45°$, $a = 10$ cm. What is the length of side c? $10\sqrt{2}$

86. If $\cos \theta = \dfrac{\sqrt{2}}{3}$, find the other five trigonometric function values.

86. $\sin \theta = \dfrac{\sqrt{7}}{3}$, $\tan \theta = \dfrac{\sqrt{14}}{2}$, $\sec \theta = \dfrac{3\sqrt{2}}{2}$, $\cot \theta = \dfrac{\sqrt{14}}{7}$, $\csc \theta = \dfrac{3\sqrt{7}}{7}$

15-2 In which quadrant does the terminal side of each angle lie?

87. $-45°$ **88.** $240°$ **89.** $-120°$ **90.** $460°$

87. Fourth
88. Third
89. Third
90. Second

91. Give the signs of the six trigonometric function values for a rotation of $-420°$. Cosine and secant are positive; the other four function values are negative.

15-7

92. Factor and simplify: $1 = \cos^4 x$. $(1 + \cos^2 x)(1 + \cos x)(1 - \cos x)$

93. Solve $\cos x - 2 \sin^2 x + 1 = 0$ for $\cos x$. $(2 \cos x - 1)(\cos x + 1)$

16-5 Solve, finding all solutions from 0 to 2π.

94. $\cos^2 x - 1 = 2 \sin x$ **95.** $2 \tan x = 1 - \tan^2 x$

94. $0, \pi, 2\pi$

95. $\dfrac{3\pi}{8}, \dfrac{5\pi}{8}, \dfrac{11\pi}{8}, \dfrac{13\pi}{8}$

16-6 Solve the triangles. Angle C is a right angle.

96. $a = 9.2$, $c = 10.1$ $m \angle A = 65°40', m \angle B = 24°20', b = 4.16$

16-10 Do the following calculations, where $\mathbf{u} = (1, -2)$, $\mathbf{v} = (2, 5)$, $m = 3$, and $n = -1$.

97. $\mathbf{u} + \mathbf{v}$ **98.** $m\mathbf{u} + n\mathbf{v}$ **99.** $|n\mathbf{u} - m\mathbf{v}|$ **100.** $|\mathbf{u}| + m|\mathbf{v}|$

(3, 3)   (1, -11) $3\sqrt{35}$ $\sqrt{5} + 3\sqrt{29}$

16-11 Find trigonometric notation.

101. $-\sqrt{3} - i$ **102.** $-1 - i$ **103.** $\dfrac{1}{2} + \dfrac{\sqrt{3}}{2}i$

101. $2 \operatorname{cis} \dfrac{7\pi}{6}$

102. $\sqrt{2} \operatorname{cis} \dfrac{5\pi}{4}$

103. $1 \operatorname{cis} \dfrac{2\pi}{3}$

16-11 Compute.

104. $10 \operatorname{cis} 60° \div 5 \operatorname{cis} 45°$ $2 \operatorname{cis} 15°$ **105.** $(1 - i)^8$ 16 **106.** $\left(-\dfrac{\sqrt{3}}{2} + \dfrac{1}{2}i \right)^3$ i

COMPUTER APPENDIX

Expressions and Numbers in BASIC
BASIC Programs
INPUT and IF . . . THEN Statements
READ and DATA Statements
FOR . . . NEXT Statements
Programs for Quadratic Equations
Programs for Sequences and Series

COMPUTER ACTIVITIES

Expressions and Numbers in BASIC

In order to use a computer, we must use a computer language. One of the most common computer languages is called BASIC. There are different versions of BASIC, so minor changes may be necessary for a particular computer.

To represent numbers in BASIC we use signs and decimal points, but not commas. We do not use fractional notation.

$$-125 \quad 25.692 \quad 49321 \quad .333333334$$

BASIC uses a type of exponential notation for very large or small numbers.

$1.23456789E+05$: The "$E+05$" means "times 10^5" so, $1.23456789E+05$ means 123456.789

$7.9872E-06$: The "$E-06$" means "times 10^{-6}" so, $7.9872E-06$ means $.0000079872$

To represent variables we use a single letter, or a single letter followed by a single digit.

$$X \quad T \quad T5 \quad N1 \quad A2$$

There are five arithmetic operations in BASIC. The order in which the computer performs these operations is the same as in algebra.

Operation	BASIC symbol	Example
Exponentiation	^	$Y ^\wedge 2$ means Y^2
Multiplication	*	$6 * T$ means $6T$
Division	/	$P/3$ means $P \div 3$
Addition	+	$R + S$ means $R + S$
Subtraction	–	$5 - Q$ means $5 - Q$

1. Operations within parentheses first.
2. Exponentiations in order from left to right.
3. Multiplication and division from left to right.
4. Addition and subtraction from left to right.

When $Y = 2$: $Y ^\wedge 3 + 3 * Y - 5$ means $Y^3 + 3Y - 5$ or $2^3 + (3 \cdot 2) - 5$ or $8 + 6 - 5 = 9$

When $X = 5$: $X ^\wedge 2 + 2 * X - (X + 4)/3$ means $X^2 + 2X - \dfrac{X + 4}{3}$ or $5^2 + 2(5) - \dfrac{5 + 4}{3} = 25 + 10 - 3 = 32$

Exercises

Represent these numbers in BASIC.

1. $-8,128$ 2. $\frac{1}{3}$ 3. $5\frac{1}{2}$ 5.5   4. 10^9 5. 10^{-9} 1E − 09

−8128   .333333333   1E + 09

Determine whether these are acceptable variables in BASIC. If not, tell why not.

6. Q Yes   7. A33 No; letter and three digits   8. XYZ No; three letters   9. RS8 No; two letters and digit   10. Y2 Yes

Write each expression in BASIC.

11. $B^2 - 4AC$ 12. $Y + 9$ 13. $3X^2 - 5X + 15$

11. B ^ 2 − 4 * A * C
12. Y + 9
13. 3 * X ^ 2 − 5 * X + 15

14. $15 + (X - 2)$ 15. $16T \div (4 - 3)$

15 + (X − 2)   16 * T / (4 − 3)

Evaluate each BASIC expression.

16. $45 * (3 + 2)$ 225   17. $161 / (29 - 6)$ 7   18. $2 \wedge 4 + (-3) \wedge 3$ −11

19. $4 - 16 / 4 * 8$ −28   20. $((3 + 5) / 4) \wedge 2$ 4

Evaluate each BASIC expression using the values given.

21. $5 * R \wedge 3 + 6$ for $R = 2$ 46   22. $X \wedge 2 / 4$ for $X = 10$ 25

23. $5 * (Y - 3) / 5$ for $Y = 6$ 3   24. $T3 - 49 + 38$ for $T3 = 11$ 0

25. $100 - P1 * (25 / 5)$ for $P1 = 19$ 5

BASIC Programs

We can use the computer to help us solve problems in algebra. We need to know how to program a computer. A computer program in BASIC consists of a series of numbered statements. The numbers specify the order in which we want the computer to consider the statements. We usually number by tens so that additional statements can be inserted later if necessary. Here is a program.

```
10  LET X = 5 ^ 2 + 3          The LET statement assigns a value to a variable.
20  LET Y = 64 / 4 - (3 + 6)
30  LET Z = X + Y              Z is assigned the value that is computed on
                              right of the equals sign.
40  PRINT X, Y, Z             The PRINT statement tells the computer what
                              to write.
50  END                       The END statement (not required on all
                              computers) ends the program.

    OUTPUT:   28   7   35
```

The PRINT statement, as in line 40 above, can be written in different ways to provide different outputs.

Statement	Output
PRINT 354	354 The computer prints the number.
PRINT 3,5,4	3 5 4 Commas give wide spacing.
PRINT 3;5;4	3 5 4 Semicolons close in the spacing or eliminate it on some computers).
PRINT 7 - 5	2 The computer prints the difference.
PRINT 6 / 12	.5 The computer prints the quotient in decimal notation.
PRINT	The computer leaves a blank line.
PRINT "R + S"	R + S The computer prints exactly what is
PRINT "7 - 5"	7 - 5 enclosed in quotation marks.
PRINT "ALGEBRA IS EASY."	ALGEBRA IS EASY.

In order to run a program, we must use system commands correctly. System commands are executed immediately. They do not need line numbers because they are not part of the BASIC program. Here are some examples.

NEW Deletes all previous statements.
LIST Lists the program currently in memory.
RUN Starts execution of the program currently in memory.

To enter and run a program, we type the following.

NEW This will clear out any statements in memory.
Program Steps These must be numbered.
RUN This will start the execution of the program.

We press RETURN at the end of each line. If we want to see the program steps listed, we type LIST; for example if we have made an error and need to correct it.

Exercises

1. If you have a computer, enter and run the program in this section. Remember, you must type it exactly as shown and you must use system commands correctly.

2. Revise the program in Exercise 1 so that $Z = X \div Y$. 30 LET Z = X / Y

Determine the output for each program. If you have a computer, enter and run the program.

3. 10 LET P1 = 3.14159 CIRCUMFERENCE FOR THE CIRCLE IS 37.69908
                          AREA OF THE CIRCLE IS 113.09724
   20 LET R = 6
   30 LET C = 2 * P1 * R
   40 LET A = P1 * R ^ 2
   50 PRINT "CIRCUMFERENCE OF THE CIRCLE IS "; C
   60 PRINT "AREA OF THE CIRCLE IS "; A
   70 END

4. ```
   10  LET X = 1000
   20  PRINT "X =" X, "X ^ 2 =" X ^ 2, "X ^ 3 =" X ^ 3, "X ^ 4 =" X ^ 4
   30  END
   ```

5. Write a program using the LET and PRINT statements that will print the Celsius temperature for 77° Fahrenheit. Use $C = \frac{5}{9}(F - 32)$.

6. Write a program using the LET and PRINT statements that will print the value (V) of the expression $\frac{1}{3}\pi R^2 H$ when $R = 6$ and $H = 10$. Use 3.14159 for π.

INPUT and IF . . . THEN Statements

In BASIC one way to assign values to variables and expressions is the LET statement. Another way is the INPUT statement. We use an INPUT statement if we want to assign the values when the program is run. This allows us to use the same program over and over with different values assigned to the variable(s).

This program computes the slope of a line using an INPUT statement.

```
10  PRINT "INPUT X1, Y1, X2, Y2"
```
After RUN the computer prints: INPUT X1, Y1, X2, Y2.

```
20  INPUT X1, Y1, X2, Y2
```
The computer prints: ? (We type in the values separated by commas.)

```
30  IF X1 = X2 THEN 70
```
If X1 = X2, the computer goes to line 70. If not, the computer continues to the next line (line 40).

```
40  LET M = {Y2 - Y1} / {X1 - X2}
```
M is assigned the value computed on the right.
```
50  PRINT "THE SLOPE = "; M
60  GO TO 80
```
The computer is instructed where to go next.
```
70  PRINT "THERE IS NO SLOPE"
80  END
```

The IF . . . THEN statement in line 30 makes a decision. Its usual form is:

IF (relationship) THEN (line number)

When the statement following the IF is true, the computer goes to the line named after THEN. When it is not true, the computer goes on to the next line. Without the IF . . . THEN statement in the above program, the computer would print DIVISION BY ZERO ERROR IN LINE 40 when X1 = X2.

The IF . . . THEN statement may use relational symbols other than the = sign. Some of the BASIC symbols are different from algebra.

= equals   < = is less than or equal to
< is less than   > = is greater than or equal to
> is greater than   <> is not equal to
```

Here is another example using INPUT and IF...THEN statements. This program determines whether an ordered pair is a solution of the equation $Y = 3X - 1$.

```
10 PRINT "INPUT X, Y"
20 INPUT X, Y
30 IF Y <> 3 * X - 1 THEN 60
40 PRINT " {"'X'", "'Y'"} IS A SOLUTION"
50 GO TO 70
60 PRINT "{"'X'", "'Y'"} IS NOT A SOLUTION"
70 END
```

Exercises

1. If you have a computer, type and run the program for finding slope of a line given two points. Use these pairs of inputs.
   a. (2, 3) (1, −4) 7   b. (1, −1) (3, −4) −1.5 c. (1, 2) (3, 6) 2
   d. (8, 2) (−4, −3) .416666667   e. (9, 1) (−7, 1) 0   f. (5, 2) (5, 7) No slope

2. If you have a computer, type and run the program that determines whether an ordered pair is a solution to $Y = 3X - 1$. Test these ordered pairs.
   a. (−3, −10) Yes b. (2, 4) No c. (0, −1) Yes d. (−5, −16) Yes

Revise the program that determines whether an ordered pair is a solution to an equation to test these ordered pairs in these equations.

3. $XY = 12$ (−3, −4) (0, 12) (12, 1) (2.5, 4) 30 IF X * Y <> 12 THEN 60

4. $Y = -4X + 1$ (−2, 9) (−2, 7) (5, 2) (−5, 21) 30 IF Y <> −4 * X + 1 THEN 60

5. $2X - 3Y = 6$ (10.5, 5) (20, 2.5) (3, 0) (−2, −3) 30 IF 2 * X − 3 * Y <> 6 THEN 60

6. If $F(X) = 2X + 1$ and $G(X) = X^2 + 2$, write a program using INPUT that will compute the composition $H(X)$, for entered values of X, where $H(X) = F(G(X))$.

READ and DATA Statements

We can use the computer to find the solution (X, Y) of a system of two linear equations in two variables using Cramer's Rule. For a system

$$A_1X + B_1Y = C_1$$
$$A_2X + B_2Y = C_2$$

the solution is

$$\frac{C_1B_2 - C_2B_1}{A_1B_2 - A_2B_1}, \frac{A_1C_2 - A_2C_1}{A_1B_2 - A_2B_1}$$

where $A_1B_2 - A_2B_1 \neq 0$.

Here is a program for using Cramer's Rule to find solutions.

```
10  PRINT "INPUT A1, B1, C1, A2, B2, C2"
20  INPUT A1, B1, C1, A2, B2, C2
30  IF A1 * B2 - A2 * B1 = 0 THEN 80
40  LET X = {C1 * B2 - B1 * C2} / {A1 * B2 - B1 * A2}
50  LET Y = {A1 * C2 - C1 * A2} / {A1 * B2 - B1 * A2}
60  PRINT "THE SOLUTION IS {": X; ", ; Y; "}"
70  GO TO 90
80  PRINT "NO UNIQUE SOLUTION"
90  END
```

If the values are entered from the system

$$2X + 5Y = 7$$
$$5X - 2Y = -3$$

then the computer prints the following output.

```
THE SOLUTION IS {-.0344827586, 1.4137931}
```

Another way of assigning values to variables is by using READ/DATA statements. READ tells the computer to go to the DATA statement and read the value listed there. If the READ statement has six variables, then DATA given must be in groups of six.

We can rewrite the above program using READ/DATA statements. The following systems provide the data for lines 90, 100, 110, and 120.

$$2X + Y = 4 \quad 4X + 3Y = 7 \quad 3X + 4Y = 2 \quad 4X + 6Y = 16$$
$$3X + Y = 7 \quad 2X - 7Y = 5 \quad -X + 6Y = 3 \quad 2X + 3Y = 7$$

```
10   READ A1, B1, C1, A2, B2, C2
20   IF A1 * B2 - A2 * B1 = 0 THEN 70
30   LET X = {C1 * B2 - B1 * C2} / {A1 * B2 - B1 * A2}
40   LET Y = {A1 * C2 - C1 * A2} / {A1 * B2 - B1 * A2}
50   PRINT "THE SOLUTION IS {"; X; ","; Y; "}"
60   GO TO 10
70   PRINT "NO UNIQUE SOLUTION"
80   GO TO 10
90   DATA 2, 1, 4, 3, 1, 7
100  DATA 4, 3, 7, 2, -7, 5
110  DATA 3, 4, 2, -1, 6, 3
120  DATA 4, 6, 16, 2, 3, 7
130  END
```

When the computer runs out of data it will print OUT OF DATA ERROR IN 10.

Exercises

1. If you have a computer, enter and run the second program in this section.

2. Determine the output for this program to compute gross pay at different hourly rates and time-and-a-half for overtime. If you have a computer, enter and run the program. Note how the computer returns to the DATA statement, reading the next values until they run out.

```
10  READ H, R
20  IF H > 40 THEN 50
30  LET P = H * R
40  GO TO 60
50  LET P = 40 * R + (H - 40) * 1.5 * R
60  PRINT "GROSS PAY = $"; P
70  GO TO 10
80  DATA 46,8.40,40,9.00,32,7.20,52,3.75
90  END
```

3. Write a program using READ/DATA statements which will compute simple interest, I, at the rate, R, of 12% for two years (T = 2) for each of these principal amounts.

$600 $1000 $2500 $10,000 $50,000

If you have a computer, enter and run your program.

FOR ... NEXT Statements

The compound interest formula in this chapter can easily be used on a computer.

$$A = P\left(1 + \frac{R}{N}\right)^{NT}$$

Suppose $100 is invested at 12% compounded quarterly. How much will be in the account at the end of five years?

```
10  LET P = 100
20  LET R = .12
30  LET N = 4
40  LET T = 5
50  LET A = P * (1 + R / N) ^ (N * T)
60  PRINT "$"; P; INVESTED FOR 5 YEARS GROWS TO $"; A
70  END
```

To determine the amount after five years for many different principal amounts, we must tell the computer to repeat the instructions over and over. We use a loop to do this. FOR ... NEXT statements are helpful in constructing loops. The FOR statement starts the loop, the NEXT ends the loop.

The following program uses the information from the preceding problem to compute compound interest on the amounts from $100 to $125 using a FOR...NEXT loop.

```
10 LET R = .12
20 LET N = 4
30 LET T = 5
40 FOR P = 100 TO 125
50 LET A = P * (1 + R / N) ^ (N * T)
60 PRINT "$"; P INVESTED FOR 5
   YEARS GROWS TO $"; A
70 NEXT P
80 END
```

Values are assigned to the variables R, N, and T.

The first time through the loop, P is assigned the value 100.

When NEXT is encountered, one is added to P and the loop is repeated with P as 101

The process of adding one to P and executing lines 50 and 60 continues through P = 125. The range of values for P may be any values needed.

Exercises

1. If you have a computer, enter and run the two programs in this section. Try different values for the variables.

2. Revise the compound interest program with the loop to determine A for these values.

R	N	T	P
a. .15	4	10	10,000–10,025
b. .18	12	25	500–515

3. Write a program using a FOR...NEXT loop that will print X, X^2, and X^3 for X = 1 to 10.

4. Write a program using a FOR...NEXT loop to evaluate $2X^2 + 8X + 10$ using positive integers less than 10 as the range of values for X.

5. Write a program using a FOR...NEXT loop that will add the integers from 1 to 25 and print their sum.

2–5. Answers may vary.

```
2.a. 10  LET  R = .15
     20  LET N = 4
     30  LET T = 10
     40  FOR P = 1000 TO
         10025
          ⋮
   b. 10  LET R = .18
      20  LET N = 12
      30  LET T = 25
      40  FOR P = 500 TO
          515
           ⋮
3. 10  FOR × = 1 TO 10
   20  PRINT X, X ^ 2, × ^ 3
   30  NEXT X
   40  END
4. 10  FOR X = 1 TO 9
   20  LET Y = 2 * X ^ 2 + 8
       * X + 10
   30  PRINT X, Y
   40  NEXT X
   50  END
5. 10  LET S = 0
   20  FOR N = 1 TO 25
   30  LET S = S + N
   40  NEXT N
   50  PRINT "THE SUM IS"; S
   60  END
```

Programs for Solving Quadratic Equations

Quadratic equations can be solved with the help of the computer. To solve equations of the form $AX^2 + BX + C = 0$, $A \neq 0$, we have used the quadratic formula.

$$X = \frac{-B \pm \sqrt{B^2 - 4AC}}{2A}$$

738 Computer Activities

The following BASIC program uses READ/DATA statements to assign values from these equations.

$$X^2 + 5X + 6 = 0, \; X^2 + X + 0.25 = 0, \; X^2 - 2X + 4 = 0$$

The REM statement in line 10 is a REMARK. Although REM statements are printed in the listing of the program, they are ignored during execution of the program.

```
10   REM SOLVE BY QUADRATIC FORMULA
20   READ A, B, C
30   LET D = B ^ 2 - 4 * A * C
40   IF D = 0 THEN 100
50   IF D < 0 THEN 120
60   LET X1 = {-B + SQR{D}} / {2 * A}
70   LET X2 = {-B - SQR{D}} / {2 * A}
80   PRINT "THE SOLUTIONS ARE ";X1; " AND "; X2
90   GO TO 20
100  PRINT "THE ONE SOLUTION IS"; -B / {2 * A}
110  GO TO 20
120  PRINT "NO REAL-NUMBER SOLUTIONS"
130  GO TO 20
140  DATA 1,5,6,1,1,.25,1,-2,4
150  END
```

The computer has a built-in function for square root.

The computer has built-in functions other than the square root function. Here are some common built-in, or library functions.

Function	Definition
INT{X}	Greatest integer less than or equal to X
ABS{X}	Absolute value of X
SQR{X}	Square root of X
RND{X}	Random value between 0.0 and 1.0
SGN{X}	Sign of X ($+1$ if positive, -1 if negative, 0 if zero)

Exercises

1. If you have a computer, enter and run the program in this section. Compare the solutions printed by the computer with those that you calculate.

2. Revise the DATA statement in the program in this section to solve these equations.

$$2X^2 + 8X + 8 = 0, \; 2X^2 + 3X + 3 = 0, \; 6X^2 - X - 2 = 0$$

3. Write a program using INPUT and the SQR function that will compute the hypotenuse, C, of a right triangle given the lengths of the sides A and B. Use these pairs of values.

$$A = 1, B = 1 \qquad A = 3, B = 4 \qquad A = 16, B = 25 \qquad A = 20, B = 30$$

4. Write a program using a FOR...NEXT loop and built-in functions that will print the integers between -11 and 11, their signs, and their absolute values. Use a REM statement for clarification.

5. Write a program using a FOR...NEXT loop and the SQR function that will compute $V = 3.5\sqrt{H}$. (At a height of H meters you can see V kilometers to the horizon.) Use the first ten positive integers for H.

```
4. 10  REM NUMBERS, SIGNS,
       ABSOLUTE VALUES
   20  FOR X = -10 TO 10
   30  PRINT X, SGN(X),
       ABS(X)
   40  NEXT X
   50  END
   Output:
   -10  -1  10
    -9  -1   9
     :
```

Programs for Sequences and Series

Up to now, we have been using only simple BASIC variables such as X, N1, and so on, to assign values. If we wanted to assign many numbers, say 100, we would need 100 variables. There is another way of doing this using a list called a one-dimensional array. A one-dimensional array may be thought of as a row (or column) of compartments, each having a unique address and each capable of holding a piece of data. This is a picture of an array named Y.

```
5. 10  REM DISTANCE (KM)
       YOU CAN SEE
   20  FOR H = 1 TO 10
   30  LET V = 3.5 * SQR(H)
   40  PRINT "WHEN H = ";
       H; "V = "; V
   50  NEXT H
   60  END
   Output:
   When H = 1   V = 3.5
   When H = 2   V =
                .94974747
   When H = 3   V =
                6.06217783
   When H = 4   V = 7
   When H = 5   V =
                7.82623792
   When H = 6   V =
                8.57321411
   When H = 7   V =
                9.26012959
   When H = 8   V =
                9.89949495
   When H = 9   V = 10.5
   When H = 10  V =
                11.0079718
```

Y | 1 | 2 | 3 | 4 | 5 |

Each location is named by the variable Y and a number in parentheses called the subscript. The first location is named Y(1) and is read "Y sub one." (Some computers start numbering with zero.) The next is Y(2), and so on.

To tell the computer how many locations are needed, a DIMension statement is used. The statement DIM Y(5) tells the computer to reserve five locations for the list named Y.

We can use a one-dimensional array in a program that will generate the first 25 terms of the Fibonacci sequence. The sequence begins 1, 1, ... and each term thereafter is the sum of the two preceding terms.

```
10  REM FIBONACCI SEQUENCE
20  DIM S(25)
30  LET S(1) = 1
40  LET S(2) = 1
50  FOR X = 3 TO 25
60  LET S(X) = S(X - 1) + S(X - 2)
70  NEXT X
80  PRINT "FIBONACCI SEQUENCE"
90  FOR X = 1 TO 25
```

DIM reserves 25 locations for S.
S(1) is assigned a value.
S(2) is assigned a value.

S(3) and so on are assigned values equal to the sum of the preceding two terms.

```
100  PRINT S{X}
110  NEXT X
120  END
```

The computer prints the value in each location.

Note how a FOR ... NEXT loop generates and stores the terms and another FOR ... NEXT loop prints the terms.

Exercises

1. If you have a computer, enter and run the Fibonacci sequence program. Revise the program to print the first 40 terms.

2. Write a program that will read eight test scores, enter them into an array, and print their average. You will need two loops, one to read the data, and one to compute the average.

3. Write a short program using INPUT that will print the sum,

$$S_N = \frac{A_1 - A_1 R^N}{1 - R}$$

of each of these geometric series.

a. $\left(\frac{1}{2}\right)^2 + \left(\frac{1}{2}\right)^3 + \left(\frac{1}{2}\right)^4 + \left(\frac{1}{2}\right)^5 + \left(\frac{1}{2}\right)^6$

b. $16 - 8 + 4 - 2 + 1 - \frac{1}{2}$

c. $5 + 10 + 20 + 40 + 80 + 160 + 320 + 640$

1. 20 DIM S(40)
      ⋮
   50 FOR X = 3 TO 40
      ⋮
   90 FOR X = 1 TO 40

2. Answers may vary. In line 50 any test scores may be used.
   10   REM FIND AVERAGE
   20   DIM Y(8)
   30   FOR I = 1 TO 8
   40   READ Y(I)
   50   DATA 0, 0, 0, 0, 0, 0, 0, 0
   60   NEXT I
   70   LET S = 0
   80   FOR I = 1 TO 8
   90   LET S = S + Y(I)
   100 NEXT I
   110 PRINT "THE AVERAGE IS"; S/8
   120 END

3. Answers may vary.
   10   REM SUM OF GEO-METRIC SERIES
   20   PRINT "INPUT A, R, N"
   30   INPUT A, R, N
   40   LET S = (A − A * R ˆ N)/(1 − R)
   50   PRINT "SUM IS"; S
   60   END
   a. Output: SUM IS .484375
   b. Output: SUM IS 10.5
   c. Output: SUM IS 1275

TABLE 1 Squares and Square Roots

N	N^2	$\sqrt{N}$	N	N^2	$\sqrt{N}$
1	1	1	51	2,601	7.141
2	4	1.414	52	2,704	7.211
3	9	1.732	53	2,809	7.280
4	16	2	54	2,916	7.348
5	25	2.236	55	3,025	7.416
6	36	2.449	56	3,136	7.483
7	49	2.646	57	3,249	7.550
8	64	2.828	58	3,364	7.616
9	81	3	59	3,481	7.681
10	100	3.162	60	3,600	7.746
11	121	3.317	61	3,721	7.810
12	144	3.464	62	3,844	7.874
13	169	3.606	63	3,969	7.937
14	196	3.742	64	4,096	8
15	225	3.873	65	4,225	8.062
16	256	4	66	4,356	8.124
17	289	4.123	67	4,489	8.185
18	324	4.243	68	4,624	8.246
19	361	4.359	69	4,761	8.307
20	400	4.472	70	4,900	8.367
21	441	4.583	71	5,041	8.426
22	484	4.690	72	5,184	8.485
23	529	4.796	73	5,329	8.544
24	576	4.899	74	5,476	8.602
25	625	5	75	5,625	8.660
26	676	5.099	76	5,776	8.718
27	729	5.196	77	5,929	8.775
28	784	5.292	78	6,084	8.832
29	841	5.385	79	6,241	8.888
30	900	5.477	80	6,400	8.944
31	961	5.568	81	6,561	9
32	1,024	5.657	82	6,724	9.055
33	1,089	5.745	83	6,889	9.110
34	1,156	5.831	84	7,056	9.165
35	1,225	5.916	85	7,225	9.220
36	1,296	6	86	7,396	9.274
37	1,369	6.083	87	7,569	9.327
38	1,444	6.164	88	7,744	9.381
39	1,521	6.245	89	7,921	9.434
40	1,600	6.325	90	8,100	9.487
41	1,681	6.403	91	8,281	9.539
42	1,764	6.481	92	8,464	9.592
43	1,849	6.557	93	8,649	9.644
44	1,936	6.633	94	8,836	9.695
45	2,025	6.708	95	9,025	9.747
46	2,166	6.782	96	9,216	9.798
47	2,209	6.856	97	9,409	9.849
48	2,304	6.928	98	9,604	9.899
49	2,401	7	99	9,801	9.950
50	2,500	7.071	100	10,000	10

TABLE 2 Common Logarithms

x	0	1	2	3	4	5	6	7	8	9
1.0	.0000	.0043	.0086	.0128	.0170	.0212	.0253	.0294	.0334	.0374
1.1	.0414	.0453	.0492	.0531	.0569	.0607	.0645	.0682	.0719	.0755
1.2	.0792	.0828	.0864	.0899	.0934	.0969	.1004	.1038	.1072	.1106
1.3	.1139	.1173	.1206	.1239	.1271	.1303	.1335	.1367	.1399	.1430
1.4	.1461	.1492	.1523	.1553	.1584	.1614	.1644	.1673	.1703	.1732
1.5	.1761	.1790	.1818	.1847	.1875	.1903	.1931	.1959	.1987	.2014
1.6	.2041	.2068	.2095	.2122	.2148	.2175	.2201	.2227	.2253	.2279
1.7	.2304	.2330	.2355	.2380	.2405	.2430	.2455	.2480	.2504	.2529
1.8	.2553	.2577	.2601	.2625	.2648	.2672	.2695	.2718	.2742	.2765
1.9	.2788	.2810	.2833	.2856	.2878	.2900	.2923	.2945	.2967	.2989
2.0	.3010	.3032	.3054	.3075	.3096	.3118	.3139	.3160	.3181	.3201
2.1	.3222	.3243	.3263	.3284	.3304	.3324	.3345	.3365	.3385	.3404
2.2	.3424	.3444	.3464	.3483	.3502	.3522	.3541	.3560	.3579	.3598
2.3	.3617	.3636	.3655	.3674	.3692	.3711	.3729	.3747	.3766	.3784
2.4	.3802	.3820	.3838	.3856	.3874	.3892	.3909	.3927	.3945	.3962
2.5	.3979	.3997	.4014	.4031	.4048	.4065	.4082	.4099	.4116	.4133
2.6	.4150	.4166	.4183	.4200	.4216	.4232	.4249	.4265	.4281	.4298
2.7	.4314	.4330	.4346	.4362	.4378	.4393	.4409	.4425	.4440	.4456
2.8	.4472	.4487	.4502	.4518	.4533	.4548	.4564	.4579	.4594	.4609
2.9	.4624	.4639	.4654	.4669	.4683	.4698	.4713	.4728	.4742	.4757
3.0	.4771	.4786	.4800	.4814	.4829	.4843	.4857	.4871	.4886	.4900
3.1	.4914	.4928	.4942	.4955	.4969	.4983	.4997	.5011	.5024	.5038
3.2	.5051	.5065	.5079	.5092	.5105	.5119	.5132	.5145	.5159	.5172
3.3	.5185	.5198	.5211	.5224	.5237	.5250	.5263	.5276	.5289	.5307
3.4	.5315	.5328	.5340	.5353	.5366	.5378	.5391	.5403	.5416	.5428
3.5	.5441	.5453	.5465	.5478	.5490	.5502	.5514	.5527	.5539	.5551
3.6	.5563	.5575	.5587	.5599	.5611	.5623	.5635	.5647	.5658	.5670
3.7	.5682	.5694	.5705	.5717	.5729	.5740	.5752	.5763	.5775	.5786
3.8	.5798	.5809	.5821	.5832	.5843	.5855	.5866	.5877	.5888	.5899
3.9	.5911	.5922	.5933	.5944	.5955	.5966	.5977	.5988	.5999	.6010
4.0	.6021	.6031	.6042	.6053	.6064	.6075	.6085	.6096	.6107	.6117
4.1	.6128	.6138	.6149	.6160	.6170	.6180	.6191	.6201	.6212	.6222
4.2	.6232	.6243	.6253	.6263	.6274	.6284	.6294	.6304	.6314	.6325
4.3	.6335	.6345	.6355	.6365	.6375	.6385	.6395	.6405	.6415	.6425
4.4	.6435	.6444	.6454	.6464	.6474	.6484	.6493	.6503	.6513	.6522
4.5	.6532	.6542	.6551	.6561	.6571	.6580	.6590	.6599	.6609	.6618
4.6	.6628	.6637	.6646	.6656	.6665	.6675	.6684	.6693	.6702	.6712
4.7	.6721	.6730	.6739	.6749	.6758	.6767	.6776	.6785	.6794	.6803
4.8	.6812	.6821	.6830	.6839	.6848	.6857	.6866	.6875	.6884	.6893
4.9	.6902	.6911	.6920	.6928	.6937	.6946	.6955	.6964	.6972	.6981
5.0	.6990	.6998	.7007	.7016	.7024	.7033	.7042	.7050	.7059	.7067
5.1	.7076	.7084	.7093	.7101	.7110	.7118	.7126	.7135	.7143	.7152
5.2	.7160	.7168	.7177	.7185	.7193	.7202	.7210	.7218	.7226	.7235
5.3	.7243	.7251	.7259	.7267	.7275	.7284	.7292	.7300	.7308	.7316
5.4	.7324	.7332	.7340	.7348	.7356	.7364	.7372	.7380	.7388	.7396

x	0	1	2	3	4	5	6	7	8	9
5.5	.7404	.7412	.7419	.7427	.7435	.7443	.7451	.7459	.7466	.7474
5.6	.7482	.7490	.7497	.7505	.7513	.7520	.7528	.7536	.7543	.7551
5.7	.7559	.7566	.7574	.7582	.7589	.7597	.7604	.7612	.7619	.7627
5.8	.7634	.7642	.7649	.7657	.7664	.7672	.7679	.7686	.7694	.7701
5.9	.7709	.7716	.7723	.7731	.7738	.7745	.7752	.7760	.7767	.7774
6.0	.7782	.7789	.7796	.7803	.7810	.7818	.7825	.7832	.7839	.7846
6.1	.7853	.7860	.7868	.7875	.7882	.7889	.7896	.7903	.7910	.7917
6.2	.7924	.7931	.7938	.7945	.7952	.7959	.7966	.7973	.7980	.7987
6.3	.7993	.8000	.8007	.8014	.8021	.8028	.8035	.8041	.8048	.8055
6.4	.8062	.8069	.8075	.8082	.8089	.8096	.8102	.8109	.8116	.8122
6.5	.8129	.8136	.8142	.8149	.8156	.8162	.8169	.8176	.8182	.8189
6.6	.8195	.8202	.8209	.8215	.8222	.8228	.8235	.8241	.8248	.8254
6.7	.8261	.8267	.8274	.8280	.8287	.8293	.8299	.8306	.8312	.8319
6.8	.8325	.8331	.8338	.8344	.8351	.8357	.8363	.8370	.8376	.8382
6.9	.8388	.8395	.8401	.8407	.8414	.8420	.8426	.8432	.8439	.8445
7.0	.8451	.8457	.8463	.8470	.8476	.8482	.8488	.8494	.8500	.8506
7.1	.8513	.8519	.8525	.8531	.8537	8543	.8549	.8555	.8561	.8567
7.2	.8573	.8579	.8585	.8591	.8597	.8603	.8609	.8615	.8621	.8627
7.3	.8633	.8639	.8645	.8651	.8657	.8663	.8669	.8675	.8681	.8686
7.4	.8692	.8698	.8704	.8710	.8716	.8722	.8727	.8733	.8739	.8745
7.5	.8751	.8756	.8762	.8768	.8774	.8779	.8785	.8791	.8797	.8802
7.6	.8808	.8814	.8820	.8825	.8831	.8837	.8842	.8848	.8854	.8859
7.7	.8865	.8871	.8876	.8882	.8887	.8893	.8899	.8904	.8910	.8915
7.8	.8921	.8927	.8932	.8938	.8943	.8949	.8954	.8960	.8965	.8971
7.9	.8976	.8982	.8987	.8993	.8998	.9004	.9009	.9015	.9020	.9025
8.0	.9031	.9036	.9042	.9047	.9053	.9058	.9063	.9069	.9074	.9079
8.1	.9085	.9090	.9096	.9101	.9106	.9112	.9117	.9122	.9128	.9133
8.2	.9138	.9143	.9149	.9154	.9159	.9165	.9170	.9175	.9180	.9186
8.3	.9191	.9196	.9201	.9206	.9212	.9217	.9222	.9227	.9232	.9238
8.4	.9243	.9248	.9253	.9258	.9263	.9269	.9274	.9279	.9284	.9289
8.5	.9294	.9299	.9304	.9309	.9315	.9320	.9325	.9330	.9335	.9340
8.6	.9345	.9350	.9555	.9360	.9365	.9370	.9375	.9380	.9385	.9390
8.7	.9395	.9400	.9405	.9410	.9415	.9420	.9425	.9430	.9435	.9440
8.8	.9445	.9450	.9455	.9460	.9465	.9469	.9474	.9479	.9484	.9489
8.9	.9494	.9499	.9504	.9509	.9513	.9518	.9523	.9528	.9533	.9538
9.0	.9542	.9547	.9552	.9557	.9562	.9566	.9571	.9576	.9581	.9586
9.1	.9590	.9595	.9600	.9605	.9609	.9614	.9619	.9624	.9628	.9633
9.2	.9638	.9643	.9647	.9652	.9657	.9661	.9666	.9671	.9675	.9680
9.3	.9685	.9689	.9694	.9699	.9703	.9708	.9713	.9717	.9722	.9727
9.4	.9731	.9736	.9741	.9745	.9750	.9754	.9759	.9763	.9768	.9773
9.5	.9777	.9782	.9786	.9791	.9795	.9800	.9805	.9809	.9914	.9818
9.6	.9823	.9827	.9832	.9836	.9841	.9845	.9850	.9854	.9859	.9863
9.7	.9868	.9872	.9877	.9881	.9886	.9890	.9894	.9899	.9903	.9908
9.8	.9912	.9917	.9921	.9926	.9930	.9934	.9939	.9943	.9948	.9952
9.9	.9956	.9961	.9965	.9969	.9974	.9978	.9983	.9987	.9991	.9996

TABLE 3 Values of Trigonometric Functions

Degrees	Radians	Sin	Cos	Tan	Cot	Sec	Csc		
0° 00′	0.0000	0.0000	1.0000	0.0000	—	1.000	—	1.5708	90° 00′
10	029	029	000	029	343.8	000	343.8	679	50
20	058	058	000	058	171.9	000	171.9	650	40
30	0.0087	0.0087	1.0000	0.0087	114.6	1.000	114.6	1.5621	30
40	116	116	0.9999	116	85.94	000	85.95	592	20
50	145	145	999	145	68.75	000	68.76	563	10
1° 00′	0.0175	0.0175	0.9998	0.0175	57.29	1.000	57.30	1.5533	89° 00′
10	204	204	998	204	49.10	000	49.11	504	50
20	233	233	997	233	42.96	000	42.98	475	40
30	0.0262	0.0262	0.9997	0.0262	38.19	1.000	38.20	1.5446	30
40	291	291	996	291	34.37	000	34.38	417	20
50	320	320	995	320	31.24	001	31.26	388	10
2° 00′	0.0349	0.0349	0.9994	0.0349	28.64	1.001	28.65	1.5359	88°00′
10	378	378	993	378	26.43	001	26.45	330	50
20	407	407	992	407	24.54	001	24.56	301	40
30	0.0436	0.0436	0.9990	0.0437	22.90	1.001	22.93	1.5272	30
40	465	465	989	466	21.47	001	21.49	243	20
50	495	494	988	495	20.21	001	20.23	213	10
3° 00′	0.0524	0.0523	0.9986	0.0524	19.08	1.001	19.11	1.5184	87° 00′
10	553	552	985	553	18.07	002	18.10	155	50
20	582	581	983	582	17.17	002	17.20	126	40
30	0.0611	0.0610	0.9981	0.0612	16.35	1.002	16.38	1.5097	30
40	640	640	980	641	15.60	002	15.64	068	20
50	669	669	978	670	14.92	002	14.96	039	10
4° 00′	0.0698	0.0698	0.9976	0.0699	14.30	1.002	14.34	1.5010	86° 00′
10	727	727	974	729	13.73	003	13.76	981	50
20	756	756	971	758	13.20	003	13.23	952	40
30	0.0785	0.7785	0.9969	0.0787	12.71	1.003	12.75	1.4923	30
40	814	814	967	816	12.25	003	12.29	893	20
50	844	843	964	846	11.83	004	11.87	864	10
5° 00′	0.0873	0.0872	0.9962	0.0875	11.43	1.004	11.47	1.4835	85° 00′
10	902	901	959	904	11.06	004	11.10	806	50
20	931	929	957	934	10.71	004	10.76	777	40
30	0.0960	0.0958	0.9954	0.0963	10.39	1.005	10.43	1.4748	30
40	989	987	951	992	10.08	005	10.13	719	20
50	0.1018	0.1016	948	0.1022	9.788	005	9.839	690	10
6° 00′	0.1047	0.1045	0.9945	0.1051	95.14	1.006	9.567	1.4661	84° 00′
10	076	074	942	080	9.255	006	9.309	632	50
20	105	103	939	110	9.010	006	9.065	603	40
30	0.1134	0.1132	0.9936	0.1139	8.777	1.006	8.834	1.4573	30
40	164	161	932	169	8.556	007	8.614	544	20
50	193	190	929	198	8.345	007	8.405	515	10
7° 00′	0.1222	0.1219	0.9925	0.1228	8.144	1.008	8.206	1.4486	83° 00′
10	251	248	922	257	7.953	008	8.016	457	50
20	280	276	918	287	7.770	008	7.834	428	40
30	0.1309	0.1305	0.9914	0.1317	7.596	1.009	7.661	1.4399	30
40	338	334	911	346	7.429	009	7.496	370	20
50	367	363	907	376	7.269	009	7.337	341	10
8° 00′	0.1396	0.1392	0.9903	0.1405	7.115	1.010	7.185	1.4312	82° 00′
10	425	421	899	435	6.968	010	7.040	283	50
20	454	449	894	465	6.827	011	6.900	254	40
30	0.1484	0.1478	0.9890	0.1495	6.691	1.011	6.765	1.4224	30
40	513	507	886	524	6.561	012	6.363	195	20
50	542	536	881	554	6.435	012	6.512	166	10
9° 00′	0.1571	0.1564	0.9877	0.1584	6.314	1.012	6.392	1.4137	81° 00′
		Cos	Sin	Cot	Tan	Csc	Sec	Radians	Degrees

Degrees	Radians	Sin	Cos	Tan	Cot	Sec	Csc		
9° 00'	0.1571	0.1564	0.9877	0.1584	6.314	1.012	6.392	1.4137	81° 00'
10	600	593	872	614	197	013	277	108	50
20	629	622	868	644	084	013	166	079	40
30	0.1658	0.1650	0.9863	0.1673	5.976	1.014	6.059	1.4050	30
40	687	679	858	703	871	014	5.955	1.4021	20
50	716	708	853	733	769	015	855	992	10
10° 00'	0.1745	0.1736	0.9848	0.1763	5.671	1.015	5.759	1.3963	80° 00'
10	774	765	843	793	576	016	665	934	50
20	804	794	838	823	485	016	575	904	40
30	0.1833	0.1822	0.9833	0.1853	5.396	1.017	5.487	1.3875	30
40	862	851	827	883	309	018	403	846	20
50	891	880	822	914	226	018	320	817	10
11° 00'	0.1920	0.1908	0.9816	0.1944	5.145	1.019	5.241	1.3788	79° 00'
10	949	937	811	974	066	019	164	759	50
20	978	965	805	0.2004	4.989	020	089	730	40
30	0.2007	0.1994	0.9799	0.2035	4.915	1.020	5.016	1.3701	30
40	036	0.2022	793	065	843	021	4.945	672	20
50	065	051	787	095	773	022	876	643	10
12° 00'	0.2094	0.2079	0.9781	0.2126	4.705	1.022	4.810	1.3614	78° 00'
10	123	108	775	156	638	023	745	584	50
20	153	136	769	186	574	024	682	555	40
30	0.2182	0.2164	0.9763	0.2217	4.511	1.024	4.620	1.3526	30
40	211	193	757	247	449	025	560	497	20
50	240	221	750	278	390	026	502	468	10
13° 00'	0.2269	0.2250	0.9744	0.2309	4.331	1.026	4.445	1.3439	77° 00'
10	298	278	737	339	275	027	390	410	50
20	327	306	730	370	219	028	336	381	40
30	0.2356	0.2334	0.9724	0.2401	4.165	1.028	4.284	1.3352	30
40	385	363	717	432	113	029	232	323	20
50	414	391	710	462	061	030	182	294	10
14° 00'	0.2443	0.2419	0.9703	0.2493	4.011	1.031	4.134	1.3265	76° 00'
10	473	447	696	524	3.962	031	086	235	50
20	502	476	689	555	914	032	039	206	40
30	0.2531	0.2504	0.9681	0.2586	3.867	1.033	3.994	1.3177	30
40	560	532	674	617	821	034	950	148	20
50	589	560	667	648	776	034	906	119	10
15° 00'	0.2618	0.2588	0.9659	0.2679	3.732	1.035	3.864	1.3090	75° 00'
10	647	616	652	711	689	036	822	061	50
20	676	644	644	742	647	037	782	032	40
30	0.2705	0.2672	0.9636	0.2773	3.606	1.038	3.742	1.3003	30
40	734	700	628	805	566	039	703	974	20
50	763	728	621	836	526	039	665	945	10
16° 00'	0.2793	0.2756	0.9613	0.2867	3.487	1.040	3.628	1.2915	74° 00'
10	822	784	605	899	450	041	592	886	50
20	851	812	596	931	412	042	556	857	40
30	0.2880	0.2840	0.9588	0.2962	3.376	1.043	3.521	1.2828	30
40	909	868	580	994	340	044	487	799	20
50	938	896	572	0.3026	305	045	453	770	10
17° 00'	0.2967	0.2924	0.9563	0.3057	3.271	1.046	3.420	1.2741	73° 00'
10	996	952	555	089	237	047	388	712	50
20	0.3025	979	546	121	204	048	356	683	40
30	0.3054	0.3007	0.9537	0.3153	3.172	1.049	3.326	1.2654	30
40	083	035	528	185	140	049	295	625	20
50	113	062	520	217	108	050	265	595	10
18° 00'	0.3142	0.3090	0.9511	0.3249	3.078	1.051	3.236	1.2566	72° 00'
		Cos	Sin	Cot	Tan	Csc	Sec	Radians	Degrees

Degrees	Radians	Sin	Cos	Tan	Cot	Sec	Csc		
18° 00′	0.3142	0.3090	0.9511	0.3249	3.078	1.051	3.236	1.2566	72° 00′
10	171	118	502	281	047	052	207	537	50
20	200	145	492	314	018	053	179	508	40
30	0.3229	0.3173	0.9483	0.3346	2.989	1.054	3.152	1.2479	30
40	258	201	474	378	960	056	124	450	20
50	287	228	465	411	932	057	098	421	10
19° 00′	0.3316	0.3256	0.9455	0.3443	2.904	1.058	3.072	1.2392	71° 00′
10	345	283	446	476	877	059	046	363	50
20	374	311	436	508	850	060	021	334	40
30	0.3403	0.3338	0.9426	0.3541	2.824	1.061	2.996	1.2305	30
40	432	365	417	574	798	062	971	275	20
50	462	393	407	607	773	063	947	246	10
20° 00′	0.3491	0.3420	0.9397	0.3640	2.747	1.064	2.924	1.2217	70° 00′
10	520	448	387	673	723	065	901	188	50
20	549	475	377	706	699	066	878	159	40
30	0.3578	0.3502	0.9367	0.3739	2.675	1.068	2.855	1.2130	30
40	607	529	356	772	651	069	833	101	20
50	636	557	346	805	628	070	812	072	10
21° 00′	0.3665	0.3584	0.9336	0.3839	2.605	1.071	2.790	1.2043	69° 00′
10	694	611	325	872	583	072	769	1.2014	50
20	723	638	315	906	560	074	749	985	40
30	0.3752	0.3665	0.9304	0.3939	2.539	1.075	2.729	1.1956	30
40	782	692	293	973	517	076	709	926	20
50	811	719	283	0.4006	496	077	689	897	10
22° 00′	0.3840	0.3746	0.9272	0.4040	2.475	1.079	2.669	1.1868	68° 00′
10	869	773	261	074	455	080	650	839	50
20	898	800	250	108	434	081	632	810	40
30	0.3927	0.3827	0.9239	0.4142	2.414	1.082	2.613	1.1781	30
40	956	854	228	176	394	084	595	752	20
50	985	881	216	210	375	085	577	723	10
23° 00′	0.4014	0.3907	0.9205	0.4245	2.356	1.086	2.559	1.1694	67° 00′
10	043	934	194	279	337	088	542	665	50
20	072	961	182	314	318	089	525	636	40
30	0.4102	0.3987	0.9171	0.4348	2.300	1.090	2.508	1.1606	30
40	131	0.4014	159	383	282	092	491	577	20
50	160	041	147	417	264	093	475	548	10
24° 00′	0.4189	0.4067	0.9135	0.4452	2.246	1.095	2.459	1.1519	66° 00′
10	218	094	124	487	229	096	443	490	50
20	247	120	112	552	211	097	427	461	40
30	0.4276	0.4147	0.9100	0.4557	2.194	1.099	2.411	1.1432	30
40	305	173	088	592	177	100	396	403	20
50	334	200	075	628	161	102	381	374	10
25° 00′	0.4363	0.4226	0.9063	0.4663	2.145	1.103	2.366	1.1345	65° 00′
10	392	253	051	699	128	105	352	316	50
20	422	279	038	734	112	106	337	286	40
30	0.4451	0.4305	0.9026	0.4770	2.097	1.108	2.323	1.1257	30
40	480	331	013	806	081	109	309	228	20
50	509	358	001	841	066	111	295	199	10
26° 00′	0.4538	0.4384	0.8988	0.4877	2.050	1.113	2.281	1.1170	64° 00′
10	567	410	975	913	035	114	268	141	50
20	596	436	962	950	020	116	254	112	40
30	0.4625	0.4462	0.8949	0.4986	2.006	1.117	2.241	1.1083	30
40	654	488	936	0.5022	1.991	119	228	054	20
50	683	514	923	059	977	121	215	1.1025	10
27° 00′	0.4712	0.4540	0.8910	0.5095	1.963	1.122	2.203	1.0996	63° 00′
		Cos	Sin	Cot	Tan	Csc	Sec	Radians	Degrees

Degrees	Radians	Sin	Cos	Tan	Cot	Sec	Csc		
27° 00′	0.4712	0.4540	0.8910	0.5095	1.963	1.122	2.203	1.0966	63° 00′
10	741	566	897	132	949	124	190	966	50
20	771	592	884	169	935	126	178	937	40
30	0.4800	0.4617	0.8870	0.5206	1.921	1.127	2.166	1.0908	30
40	829	643	857	243	907	129	154	879	20
50	858	669	843	280	894	131	142	850	10
28° 00′	0.4887	0.4695	0.8829	0.5317	1.881	1.133	2.130	1.0821	62° 00′
10	916	720	816	354	868	134	118	792	50
20	945	746	802	392	855	136	107	763	40
30	0.4974	0.4772	0.8788	0.5430	1.842	1.138	2.096	1.0734	30
40	0.5003	797	774	467	829	140	085	705	20
50	032	823	760	505	816	142	074	676	10
29° 00′	0.5061	0.4848	0.8746	0.5543	1.804	1.1143	2.063	1.0647	61° 00′
10	091	874	732	581	792	145	052	617	50
20	120	899	718	619	780	147	041	588	40
30	0.5149	0.4924	0.8704	0.5658	1.767	1.149	2.031	1.0559	30
40	178	950	689	696	756	151	020	530	20
50	207	975	675	735	744	153	010	501	10
30° 00′	0.5236	0.5000	0.8660	0.5774	1.732	1.155	2.000	1.0472	60° 00′
10	265	025	646	812	720	157	1.990	443	50
20	294	050	631	851	709	159	980	414	40
30	0.5323	0.5075	0.8616	0.5890	1.698	1.161	1.970	1.0385	30
40	352	100	601	930	868	163	961	356	20
50	381	125	587	969	675	165	951	327	10
31° 00′	0.5411	0.5150	0.8572	0.6009	1.664	1.167	1.942	1.0297	59° 00′
10	440	175	557	048	653	169	932	268	50
20	469	200	542	088	643	171	923	239	40
30	0.5498	0.5225	0.8526	0.6128	1.632	1.173	1.914	1.0210	30
40	527	250	511	168	621	175	905	181	20
50	556	275	496	208	611	177	896	152	10
32° 00′	0.5585	0.5299	0.8480	0.6249	1.600	1.179	1.887	1.0123	58° 00′
10	614	324	465	289	590	181	878	094	50
20	643	348	450	330	580	184	870	065	40
30	0.5672	0.5373	0.8434	0.6371	1.570	1.186	1.861	1.0036	30
40	701	398	418	412	560	188	853	1.007	20
50	730	422	403	453	550	190	844	977	10
33° 00′	0.5760	0.5446	0.8387	0.6494	1.540	1.192	1.836	0.9948	57° 00′
10	789	471	371	536	530	195	828	919	50
20	818	495	355	577	520	197	820	890	40
30	0.5847	0.5519	0.8339	0.6619	1.511	1.199	1.812	0.9861	30
40	876	544	323	661	501	202	804	832	20
50	905	568	307	703	1.492	204	796	803	10
34° 00′	0.5934	0.5592	0.8290	0.6745	1.483	1.206	1.788	0.9774	56° 00′
10	963	616	274	787	473	209	781	745	50
20	992	640	258	830	464	211	773	716	40
30	0.6021	0.5664	0.8241	0.6873	1.455	1.213	1.766	0.9687	30
40	050	688	225	916	446	216	758	657	20
50	080	712	208	959	437	218	751	628	10
35° 00′	0.6109	0.5736	0.8192	0.7002	1.428	1.221	1.743	0.9599	55° 10′
10	138	760	175	046	419	223	736	570	50
20	167	783	158	089	411	226	729	541	40
30	0.6196	0.5807	0.8141	0.7133	1.402	1.228	1.722	0.9512	30
40	225	831	124	177	393	231	715	483	20
50	254	854	107	221	385	233	708	454	10
36° 00′	0.6283	0.5878	0.8090	0.7265	1.376	1.236	1.701	0.9425	54° 00′
		Cos	Sin	Cot	Tan	Csc	Sec	Radians	Degrees

Degrees	Radians	Sin	Cos	Tan	Cot	Sec	Csc		
36° 00′	0.6283	0.5878	0.8090	0.7265	1.376	1.236	1.701	0.9425	54° 00′
10	312	901	073	310	368	239	695	396	50
20	341	925	056	355	360	241	688	367	40
30	0.6370	0.5948	0.8039	0.7400	1.351	1.244	1.681	0.9338	30
40	400	972	021	445	343	247	675	308	20
50	429	995	004	490	335	249	668	279	10
37° 00′	0.6458	0.6018	0.7986	0.7536	1.327	1.252	1.662	0.9250	53° 00′
10	487	041	969	581	319	255	655	221	50
20	516	065	951	627	311	258	649	192	40
30	0.6545	0.6088	0.7934	0.7673	1.303	1.260	1.643	0.9163	30
40	574	111	916	720	295	263	636	134	20
50	603	134	898	766	288	266	630	105	10
38° 00′	0.6632	0.6157	0.7880	0.7813	1.280	1.269	1.624	0.9076	52° 00′
10	661	180	862	860	272	272	618	047	50
20	690	202	844	907	265	275	612	0.9018	40
30	0.6720	0.6225	0.7826	0.7954	1.257	1.278	1.606	0.8988	30
40	749	248	808	0.8002	250	281	601	959	20
50	778	271	790	050	242	284	595	930	10
39° 00′	0.6807	0.6293	0.7771	0.8098	1.235	1.287	1.589	0.8901	51° 00′
10	836	316	753	146	228	290	583	872	50
20	865	338	735	195	220	293	578	843	40
30	0.6894	0.6361	0.7716	0.8243	1.213	1.296	1.572	0.8814	30
40	923	383	698	292	206	299	567	785	20
50	952	406	679	342	199	302	561	756	10
40° 00′	0.6981	0.6428	0.7660	0.8391	1.192	1.305	1.556	0.8727	50° 00′
10	0.7010	450	642	441	185	309	550	698	50
20	039	472	623	491	178	312	545	668	40
30	0.7069	0.6494	0.7604	0.8541	1.171	1.315	1.540	0.8639	30
40	098	517	585	591	164	318	535	610	20
50	127	539	566	642	157	322	529	581	10
41 00′	0.7156	0.6561	0.7547	0.8693	1.150	1.325	1.524	0.8552	49° 00′
10	185	583	528	744	144	328	519	523	50
20	214	604	509	796	137	332	514	494	40
30	0.7243	0.6626	0.7490	0.8847	1.130	1.335	1.509	0.8465	30
40	272	648	470	899	124	339	504	436	20
50	301	670	451	952	117	342	499	407	10
42° 00′	0.7330	0.6691	0.7431	0.9004	1.111	1.346	1.494	0.8378	48° 00′
10	359	713	412	057	104	349	490	348	50
20	389	734	392	110	098	353	485	319	40
30	0.7418	0.6756	0.7373	0.9163	1.091	1.356	1.480	0.8290	30
40	447	777	353	217	085	360	476	261	20
50	476	799	333	271	079	364	471	232	10
43° 00′	0.7505	0.6820	0.7314	0.9325	1.072	1.367	1.466	0.8203	47° 00′
10	534	841	294	380	066	371	462	174	50
20	563	862	274	435	060	375	457	145	40
30	0.7592	0.6884	0.7254	0.9490	1.054	1.379	1.453	0.8116	30
40	621	905	234	545	048	382	448	087	20
50	650	926	214	601	042	386	444	058	10
44° 00′	0.7679	0.6947	0.7193	0.9657	1.036	1.390	1.440	0.8029	46° 00′
10	709	967	173	713	030	394	435	999	50
20	738	988	153	770	024	398	431	970	40
30	0.7767	0.7009	0.7133	0.9827	1.018	1.402	1.427	0.7941	30
40	796	030	112	884	012	406	423	912	20
50	825	050	092	942	006	410	418	883	10
45° 00′	0.7854	0.7071	0.7071	1.000	1.000	1.414	1.414	0.7854	45° 00′
		Cos	Sin	Cot	Tan	Csc	Sec	Radians	Degrees

TABLE 4 Function Values for e^x and e^{-x}

x	e^x	e^{-x}	x	e^x	e^{-x}	x	e^x	e^{-x}
0.00	1.0000	1.0000	0.55	1.7333	0.5769	3.6	36.598	0.0273
0.01	1.0101	0.9900	0.60	1.8221	0.5488	3.7	40.447	0.0247
0.02	1.0202	0.9802	0.65	1.9155	0.5220	3.8	44.701	0.0224
0.03	1.0305	0.9704	0.70	2.0138	0.4966	3.9	49.402	0.0202
0.04	1.0408	0.9608	0.75	2.1170	0.4724	4.0	54.598	0.0183
0.05	1.0513	0.9512	0.80	2.2255	0.4493	4.1	60.340	0.0166
0.06	1.0618	0.9418	0.85	2.3396	0.4274	4.2	66.686	0.0150
0.07	1.0725	0.9324	0.90	2.4596	0.4066	4.3	73.700	0.0136
0.08	1.0833	0.9231	0.95	2.5857	0.3867	4.4	81.451	0.0123
0.09	1.0942	0.9139	1.0	2.7183	0.3679	4.5	90.017	0.0111
0.10	1.1052	0.9048	1.1	3.0042	0.3329	4.6	99.484	0.0101
0.11	1.1163	0.8958	1.2	3.3201	0.3012	4.7	109.95	0.0091
0.12	1.1275	0.8869	1.3	3.6693	0.2725	4.8	121.51	0.0082
0.13	1.1388	0.8781	1.4	4.0552	0.2466	4.9	134.29	0.0074
0.14	1.1503	0.8694	1.5	4.4817	0.2231	5	148.41	0.0067
0.15	1.1618	0.8607	1.6	4.9530	0.2019	6	403.43	0.0025
0.16	1.1735	0.8521	1.7	5.4739	0.1827	7	1096.6	0.0009
0.17	1.1853	0.8437	1.8	6.0496	0.1653	8	2981.0	0.0003
0.18	1.1972	0.8353	1.9	6.6859	0.1496	9	8103.1	0.0001
0.19	1.2092	0.8270	2.0	7.3891	0.1353	10	22026	0.00005
0.20	1.2214	0.8187	2.1	8.1662	0.1225	11	59874	0.00002
0.21	1.2337	0.8106	2.2	9.0250	0.1108	12	162,754	0.000006
0.22	1.2461	0.8025	2.3	9.9742	0.1003	13	442,413	0.000002
0.23	1.2586	0.7945	2.4	11.023	0.0907	14	1,202,604	0.0000008
0.24	1.2712	0.7866	2.5	12.182	0.0821	15	3,269,017	0.0000003
0.25	1.2840	0.7788	2.6	13.464	0.0743			
0.26	1.2969	0.7711	2.7	14.880	0.0672			
0.27	1.3100	0.7634	2.8	16.445	0.0608			
0.28	1.3231	0.7558	2.9	18.174	0.0550			
0.29	1.3364	0.7483	3.0	20.086	0.0498			
0.30	1.3499	0.7408	3.1	22.198	0.0450			
0.35	1.4191	0.7047	3.2	24.533	0.0408			
0.40	1.4918	0.6703	3.3	27.113	0.0369			
0.45	1.5683	0.6376	3.4	29.964	0.0334			
0.50	1.6487	0.6065	3.5	33.115	0.0302			

TABLE 5 Natural Logarithms (ln x)

x	0.00	0.01	0.02	0.03	0.04	0.05	0.06	0.07	0.08	0.09
1.0	0.0000	0.0100	0.0198	0.0296	0.0392	0.0488	0.0583	0.0677	0.0770	0.0862
1.1	0.0953	0.1044	0.1133	0.1222	0.1310	0.1398	0.1484	0.1570	0.1655	0.1740
1.2	0.1823	0.1906	0.1989	0.2070	0.2151	0.2231	0.2311	0.2390	0.2469	0.2546
1.3	0.2624	0.2700	0.2776	0.2852	0.2927	0.3001	0.3075	0.3148	0.3221	0.3293
1.4	0.3365	0.3436	0.3507	0.3577	0.3646	0.3716	0.3784	0.3853	0.3920	0.3988
1.5	0.4055	0.4121	0.4187	0.4253	0.4318	0.4383	0.4447	0.4511	0.4574	0.4637
1.6	0.4700	0.4762	0.4824	0.4886	0.4947	0.5008	0.5068	0.5128	0.5188	0.5247
1.7	0.5306	0.5365	0.5423	0.5481	0.5539	0.5596	0.5653	0.5710	0.5766	0.5822
1.8	0.5878	0.5933	0.5988	0.6043	0.6098	0.6152	0.6206	0.6259	0.6313	0.6366
1.9	0.6419	0.6471	0.6523	0.6575	0.6627	0.6678	0.6729	0.6780	0.6831	0.6881
2.0	0.6931	0.6981	0.7031	0.7080	0.7130	0.7178	0.7227	0.7275	0.7324	0.7372
2.1	0.7419	0.7467	0.7514	0.7561	0.7608	0.7655	0.7701	0.7747	0.7793	0.7839
2.2	0.7885	0.7930	0.7975	0.8020	0.8065	0.8109	0.8154	0.8198	0.8242	0.8286
2.3	0.8329	0.8372	0.8416	0.8459	0.8502	0.8544	0.8587	0.8629	0.8671	0.8713
2.4	0.8755	0.8796	0.8838	0.8879	0.8920	0.8961	0.9002	0.9042	0.9083	0.9123
2.5	0.9163	0.9203	0.9243	0.9282	0.9322	0.9361	0.9400	0.9439	0.9478	0.9517
2.6	0.9555	0.9594	0.9632	0.9670	0.9708	0.9746	0.9783	0.9821	0.9858	0.9895
2.7	0.9933	0.9969	1.0006	1.0043	1.0080	1.0116	1.0152	0.0188	1.0225	1.0260
2.8	1.0296	1.0332	1.0367	1.0403	1.0438	1.0473	1.0508	1.0543	1.0578	1.0613
2.9	1.0647	1.0682	1.0716	1.0750	1.0784	1.0818	1.0852	1.0886	1.0919	1.0953
3.0	1.0986	1.1019	1.1053	1.1086	1.1119	1.1151	1.1184	1.1217	1.1249	1.1282
3.1	1.1314	1.1346	1.1378	1.1410	1.1442	1.1474	1.1506	1.1537	1.1569	1.1600
3.2	1.1632	1.1663	1.1694	1.1725	1.1756	1.1787	1.1817	1.1848	1.1878	1.1909
3.3	1.1939	1.1970	1.2000	1.2030	1.2060	1.2090	1.2119	1.2149	1.2179	1.2208
3.4	1.2238	1.2267	1.2296	1.2326	1.2355	1.2384	1.2413	1.2442	1.2470	1.2499
3.5	1.2528	1.2556	1.2585	1.2613	1.2641	1.2669	1.2698	1.2726	1.2754	1.2782
3.6	1.2809	1.2837	1.2865	1.2892	1.2920	1.2947	1.2975	1.3002	1.3029	1.3056
3.7	1.3083	1.3110	1.3137	1.3164	1.3191	1.3218	1.3244	1.3271	1.3297	1.3324
3.8	1.3350	1.3376	1.3403	1.3429	1.3455	1.3481	1.3507	1.3533	1.3558	1.3584
3.9	1.3610	1.3635	1.3661	1.3686	1.3712	1.3737	1.3762	1.3788	1.3813	1.3838
4.0	1.3863	1.3888	1.3913	1.3938	1.3962	1.3987	1.4012	1.4036	1.4061	1.4085
4.1	1.4110	1.4134	1.4159	1.4183	1.4207	1.4231	1.4255	1.4279	1.4303	1.4327
4.2	1.4351	1.4375	1.4398	1.4422	1.4446	1.4469	1.4493	1.4516	1.4540	1.4563
4.3	1.4586	1.4609	1.4633	1.4656	1.4679	1.4702	1.4725	1.4748	1.4770	1.4793
4.4	1.4816	1.4839	1.4861	1.4884	1.4907	1.4929	1.4952	1.4974	1.4996	1.5019
4.5	1.5041	1.5063	1.5085	1.5107	1.5129	1.5151	1.5173	1.5195	1.5217	1.5239
4.6	1.5261	1.5282	1.5304	1.5326	1.5347	1.5369	1.5390	1.5412	1.5433	1.5454
4.7	1.5476	1.5497	1.5518	1.5539	1.5560	1.5581	1.5602	1.5623	1.5644	1.5665
4.8	1.5686	1.5707	1.5728	1.5748	1.5769	1.5790	1.5810	1.5831	1.5851	1.5872
4.9	1.5892	1.5913	1.5933	1.5953	1.5974	1.5994	1.6014	1.6034	1.6054	1.6074
5.0	1.6094	1.6114	1.6134	1.6154	1.6174	1.6194	1.6214	1.6233	1.6253	1.6273
5.1	1.6292	1.6312	1.6332	1.6351	1.6371	1.6390	1.6409	1.6429	1.6448	1.6467
5.2	1.6487	1.6506	1.6525	1.6544	1.6563	1.6582	1.6601	1.6620	1.6639	1.6658
5.3	1.6677	1.6696	1.6715	1.6734	1.6752	1.6771	1.6790	1.6808	1.6827	1.6845
5.4	1.6864	1.6882	1.6901	1.6919	1.6938	1.6956	1.6974	1.6993	1.7001	1.7029

x	0.00	0.01	0.02	0.03	0.04	0.05	0.06	0.07	0.08	0.09
5.5	1.7047	1.7066	1.7084	1.7102	1.7120	1.7138	1.7156	1.7174	1.7192	1.7210
5.6	1.7228	1.7246	1.7263	1.7281	1.7299	1.7317	1.7334	1.7352	1.7370	1.7387
5.7	1.7405	1.7422	1.7440	1.7457	1.7475	1.7492	1.7509	1.7527	1.7544	1.7561
5.8	1.7579	1.7596	1.7613	1.7630	1.7647	1.7664	1.7682	1.7699	1.7716	1.7733
5.9	1.7750	1.7766	1.7783	1.7800	1.7817	1.7834	1.7851	1.7867	1.7884	1.7901
6.0	1.7918	1.7934	1.7951	1.7967	1.7984	1.8001	1.8017	1.8034	1.8050	1.8066
6.1	1.8083	1.8099	1.8116	1.8132	1.8148	1.8165	1.8181	1.8197	1.8213	1.8229
6.2	1.8245	1.8262	1.8278	1.8294	1.8310	1.8326	1.8342	1.8358	1.8374	1.8390
6.3	1.8406	1.8421	1.8437	1.8453	1.8469	1.8485	1.8500	1.8516	1.8532	1.8547
6.4	1.8563	1.8579	1.8594	1.8610	1.8625	1.8641	1.8656	1.8672	1.8687	1.8703
6.5	1.8718	1.8733	1.8749	1.8764	1.8779	1.8795	1.8810	1.8825	1.8840	1.8856
6.6	1.8871	1.8886	1.8901	1.8916	1.8931	1.8946	1.8961	1.8976	1.8991	1.9006
6.7	1.9021	1.9036	1.9051	1.9066	1.9081	1.9095	1.9110	1.9125	1.9140	1.9155
6.8	1.9169	1.9184	1.9199	1.9213	1.9228	1.9242	1.9257	1.9272	1.9286	1.9301
6.9	1.9315	1.9330	1.9344	1.9359	1.9373	1.9387	1.9402	1.9416	1.9430	1.9445
7.0	1.9459	1.9473	1.9488	1.9502	1.9516	1.9530	1.9544	1.9559	1.9573	1.9587
7.1	1.9601	1.9615	1.9629	1.9643	1.9657	1.9671	1.9685	1.9699	1.9713	1.9727
7.2	1.9741	1.9755	1.9769	1.9782	1.9796	1.9810	1.9824	1.9838	1.9851	1.9865
7.3	1.9879	1.9892	1.9906	1.9920	1.9933	1.9947	1.9961	1.9974	1.9988	2.0001
7.4	2.0015	2.0028	2.0042	2.0055	2.0069	2.0082	2.0096	2.0109	2.0122	2.0136
7.5	2.0149	2.0162	2.0176	2.0189	2.0202	2.0215	2.0229	2.0242	2.0255	2.0268
7.6	2.0282	2.0295	2.0308	2.0321	2.0334	2.0347	2.0360	2.0373	2.0386	2.0399
7.7	2.0412	2.0425	2.0438	2.0451	2.0464	2.0477	2.0490	2.0503	2.0516	2.0528
7.8	2.0541	2.0554	2.0567	2.0580	2.0592	2.0605	2.0618	2.0631	2.0643	2.0665
7.9	2.0669	2.0681	2.0694	2.0707	2.0719	2.0732	2.0744	2.0757	2.0769	2.0782
8.0	2.0794	2.0807	2.0819	2.0832	2.0844	2.0857	2.0869	2.0882	2.0894	2.0906
8.1	2.0919	2.0931	2.0943	2.0956	2.0968	2.0980	2.0992	2.1005	2.1017	2.1029
8.2	2.1041	2.1054	2.1066	2.1078	2.1090	2.1102	2.1114	2.1126	2.1138	2.1150
8.3	2.1163	2.1175	2.1187	2.1199	2.1211	2.1223	2.1235	2.1247	2.1258	2.1270
8.4	2.1282	2.1294	2.1306	2.1318	2.1330	2.1342	2.1353	2.1365	2.1377	2.1389
8.5	2.1401	2.1412	2.1424	2.1436	2.1448	2.1459	2.1471	2.1483	2.1494	2.1506
8.6	2.1518	2.1529	2.1541	2.1552	2.1564	2.1576	2.1587	2.1599	2.1610	2.1622
8.7	2.1633	2.1645	2.1656	2.1668	2.1679	2.1691	2.1702	2.1713	2.1725	2.1736
8.8	2.1748	2.1759	2.1770	2.1782	2.1793	2.1804	2.1815	2.1827	2.1838	2.1849
8.9	2.1861	2.1872	2.1883	2.1894	2.1905	2.1917	2.1928	2.1939	2.1950	2.1961
9.0	2.1972	2.1983	2.1994	2.2006	2.2017	2.2028	2.2039	2.2050	2.2061	2.2072
9.1	2.2083	2.2094	2.2105	2.2116	2.2127	2.2138	2.2148	2.2159	2.2170	2.2181
9.2	2.2192	2.2203	2.2214	2.2225	2.2235	2.2246	2.2257	2.2268	2.2279	2.2289
9.3	2.2300	2.2311	2.2322	2.2332	2.2343	2.2354	2.2364	2.2375	2.2386	2.2396
9.4	2.2407	2.2418	2.2428	2.2439	2.2450	2.2460	2.2471	2.2481	2.2492	2.2502
9.5	2.2513	2.2523	2.2534	2.2544	2.2555	2.2565	2.2576	2.2586	2.2597	2.2607
9.6	2.2618	2.2628	2.2638	2.2649	2.2659	2.2670	2.2680	2.2690	2.2701	2.2711
9.7	2.2721	2.2732	2.2742	2.2752	2.2762	2.2773	2.2783	2.2793	2.2803	2.2814
9.8	2.2824	2.2834	2.2844	2.2854	2.2865	2.2875	2.2885	2.2895	2.2905	2.2915
9.9	2.2925	2.2935	2.2946	2.2956	2.2966	2.2976	2.2986	2.2996	2.3006	2.3016

TABLE 6 Symbols

$<$	is less than	$\sqrt{}$	principal square root
$>$	is greater than	$\approx$	is approximately equal to
$\|n\|$	absolute value of n	$\sqrt[n]{a}$	nth root of a
$-n$	additive inverse of n	i	$\sqrt{-1}$
a^n	nth power of a	$\bar{z}$	conjugate
$\therefore$	therefore	$\pm$	plus or minus
π	pi, approximately 3.14	$f^{-1}(x)$	the inverse of a function f
$\leq$	is less than or equal to	$\log_a x$	the log, base, a, of x
$\geq$	is greater than or equal to	$\ln x$	the log, base e, of x
$\{\ \}$	set braces	$_nP_r$	number of permutations of n objects, taken r at a time
$\{x \mid x > 3\}$	the set of all real numbers x such that $x > 3$	$_nC_r$	number of combinations of n objects, taken r at a time
$\cap$	the intersection of	$n!$	n factorial
$\cup$	the union of	$\sum\limits_{k=1}^{n} 2k$	the sum, as k goes from 1 to n, of $2k$
$\subset$	is a subset of	$\sin A$	the sine of A
$\emptyset$	the empty set	$\cos A$	the cosine of A
(x, y)	ordered pair	$\tan A$	the tangent of A
$f(x)$	f of x, the value of f at x		
$\begin{bmatrix} a & b \\ c & d \end{bmatrix}$	matrix	$\mathbf{v}$	vector
$\begin{vmatrix} a_1 & b_1 \\ a_2 & b_2 \end{vmatrix}$	determinant	$\|\mathbf{v}\|$	length of $\mathbf{v}$

GLOSSARY

Absolute value The absolute value of a number is its distance from 0 on the number line.

Addition principle For equations: If an equation $a = b$ is true, then $a + c = b + c$ is true for any number c. For inequalities: If any number is added on both sides of a true inequality we get another true inequality.

Additive identity Zero is the additive identity for addition.

Additive inverse If the sum of two numbers is 0, they are addditive inverses of each other.

Additive property of zero For any real number a, $a + 0 = a$.

Amplitude In the graph of a periodic function, the amplitude is the maximum displacement from a central position.

Angle of depression The angle from the horizontal downward to a line of sight.

Angle of elevation The angle from the horizontal upward to a line of sight.

Antecedent *See* If, then statement.

Antilogarithm As a function, the inverse of a logarithm function. $\text{Antilog}_b x = b^x$

Arithmetic means Numbers $m_1, m_2, m_3, \ldots$ are arithmetic means between a and b if $a, m_1, m_2, m_3 \ldots, b$ forms an arithmetic sequence.

Arithmetic sequence A sequence in which a constant d can be added to each term to get the next term. The constant d is called the common difference.

Arithmetic series A series associated with an arithmetic sequence.

Associative laws Addition: For any numbers $a, b,$ and $c, a + (b + c) = (a + b) + c$. Multiplication: $(a \cdot b) \cdot c = a \cdot (b \cdot c)$.

Asymptote A line is an asymptote to a curve if the curve gets very close to the line as the distance from the origin increases.

Axiom A property assumed or accepted without proof.

Base In exponential notation n^x, n is the base. In logarithmic notation, $\log_b x$, b is the base.

Binomial coefficient The binomial coefficient $\binom{n}{a}$ means $\dfrac{n!}{a!(n-a)!}$.

Binomial theorem A theorem that tells how to expand a power of a binomial.

Cartesian coordinates When axes are placed on a plane at right angles so that ordered pairs of numbers are matched with the points of the plane we say we have a cartesian coordinate system.

Cartesian product (of sets) The cartesian product of sets A and B, denoted $A \times B$, is the set of all ordered pairs with first member from A and second member from B.

Characteristic (of logarithm) The integer part of a base 10 logarithm.

Circle The set of all points in a plane that are at a fixed distance from a fixed point in that plane.

Coefficient In any term, the coefficient is the number that is multiplied by the variable.

Combination A combination of r objects of a set is a subset containing r objects.

Common logarithm A base 10 logarithm.

Commutative laws Addition: For any numbers a and b, $a + b = b + a$. Multiplication: $a \cdot b = b \cdot a$.

Completing the square Adding one or more terms to an expression to make it the square of a binomial.

Complex fractional expression A fractional expression that has fractional expressions within it.

Complex number The sum of a real and an imaginary number.

Composition of functions If f and g are functions, the composition of f and g is given by $f(g(x))$.

Compound event An event that is considered to be made up of two or more events.

Conditional sentence An if-then sentence.

Conic section The nonempty intersection of any plane with a cone.

Conjugate The conjugate of the complex number $a + bi$ is $a - bi$.

Conjunction An expression formed by connecting two or more sentences with the word *and*.

Consequent *See* If, then statement.

Consistent system A system of equations or inequalities having a solution.

Constant term A term with no variable.

Constant of variation Whenever a situation gives rise to a relation $y = kx$, where x and y are variables, k is the constant of variation.

Converse The converse of a sentence "if a, then b," is "if b, then a."

Coordinates The numbers associated with a point on a number line or in a plane.

Cosine ratio In a right triangle, the ratio of the length of the adjacent side to the length of the hypotenuse.

Cramer's rule A rule for solving systems of equations using determinants.

Degree The degree of a term is its exponent (or the number of times a variable occurs as a factor). The degree of a polynomial is the greatest degree of any of its terms.

Dependent system A system of n equations is dependent if it is equivalent to a system of fewer than n of them.

Determinant A number assigned to a square array of numbers.

Direct variation A relation between variables x and y in which their relationship can be expressed by an equation $y = kx$, where k is a constant.

Discriminant For a quadratic equation $ax^2 + bx + c = 0$, the expression $b^2 - 4ac$ is called the discriminant.

Disjunction An expression formed by connecting two or more sentences with the word *or*.

Distance formula A formula giving the distance between any two points.

Distributive laws Multiplication over addition: For any numbers a, b, and c, $(a + b) \cdot c = a \cdot c + b \cdot c$. Multiplication over subtraction: For any numbers a, b, and c, $(a - b) \cdot c = a \cdot c - b \cdot c$.

Domain *See* function.

Ellipse A set of all points P in a plane such that the sum of the distances from P to two fixed points F_1 and F_2 is constant.

Equivalent expressions Expressions that represent the same number for all sensible replacements of the variables.

Even function If $f(a) = f(-a)$ for all a in the domain of a function, then that function is even.

Exponent In exponential notation n^x, x is the exponent.

Factor When two or more numbers (or expressions) are multiplied, each of the numbers is a factor of the product.

Factor theorem If a number a, when substituted into a polynomial, makes the expression zero, then $x - a$ is a factor of the polynomial.

Focus Ellipses, hyperbolas, and parabolas have associated with them a point called a focus or points called *foci* (plural).

Fractional equation An equation containing at least one fractional expression.

Fractional expression A quotient of polynomials.

Function A correspondence or rule that assigns to each member of one set (called the *domain*) exactly one member of some set (called the *range*).

Fundamental counting principle If an event can occur in n_1 ways, another in n_2 ways, then the combined event can occur in $n_1 \cdot n_2$ ways.

Fundamental theorem of algebra Any polynomial of degree n greater than 1, with complex number coefficients, can be factored into n linear factors.

Geometric means Numbers $m_1, m_2, m_3, \ldots$ are geometric means of a and b if $a, m_1, m_2, m_3, \ldots, b$ forms a geometric sequence.

Geometric sequence A sequence in which a constant r can be multiplied by each term to get the next term. The constant r is called the common ratio.

Geometric series A series associated with a geometric sequence.

Hyperbola A set of all points P in a plane such that the absolute value of the difference of the distances from P to two fixed points F_1 and F_2 is constant.

Identity An equation which is true for all sensible replacements of the variables.

If, then statement A conditional statement made up of two parts: If . . . , then . . . . The "if" part is called the *antecedent*. The "then" part is called the *consequent*.

Image Under a transformation, the point corresponding to a given point.

Imaginary number The square root of a negative number.

Inconsistent system A system of equations or inequalities having no solution.

Inequality A sentence formed by placing $>$, $<$, $\geq$, or $\leq$ between two expressions.

Integer Any natural number, the additive inverse of a natural number, or zero.

Intercept In the graph of an equation in two variables, the point where the graph crosses an axis.

Interpolation A process by which function values can be determined between other values in a table.

Inverse of a function The relation obtained by interchanging the first and second members of all ordered pairs in the relation.

Inverse variation A relation between two variables, x and y, in which $y = \frac{k}{x}$, $x \neq 0$, and k is a constant.

Irrational number A number that cannot be named by fractional notation $\frac{a}{b}$, where a and b are integers.

Line of symmetry In any figure, a line that divides the figure so that if it is folded on the line the two halves will match.

Linear equation An equation in which the variables occur to the first power only.

Linear function A function that can be described by a linear equation.

Linear programming A kind of mathematics in which maximum and minimum values of certain functions can be found.

Logarithmic function The inverse of an exponential function.

Mantissa The portion of a base 10 logarithm between 0 and 1.

Matrix A rectangular array.

Monomial A polynomial with just one term.

Multiplication principle For equations: If an equation $a = b$ is true, then $a \cdot c = b \cdot c$ is true for any number c. For inequalities: If we multiply on both sides of a true inequality by a positive number, we get another true inequality. If we multiply by a negative number, the inequality sign must be reversed to get another true inequality.

Multiplicative identity The number 1 is the multiplicative identity.

Multiplicative inverse *See* reciprocal.

Multiplicative property of one For any real number a, $a \cdot 1 = a$.

Multiplicative property of zero For any real number a, $a \cdot 0 = 0$.

Nonsensible replacement A replacement for a variable for which an expression does not name any number.

Odd function If $f(a) = -f(-a)$ for all a in the domain of a function, then that function is odd.

Parabola A set of all points in a plane equidistant from a fixed line and a fixed point.

Period The smallest horizontal distance needed for a graph to complete a cycle.

Permutation A permutation of a set is an ordered arrangement of that set, without repetition.

Polynomial An expression $a_n x^n + a_{n-1} x^{n-1} + \cdots a_1 x + a_0$.

Polynomial function A function given by a polynomial.

Principle of zero products An equation with 0 on one side and with a factorization on the other can be solved by finding those numbers that make the factors 0.

Probability If an event E can occur m ways out of n possible equally likely outcomes of sample space S, the probability of that event is given by $P(E) = \dfrac{m}{n}$.

Quadratic equation An equation in which the term of highest degree has degree two.

Quadratic formula A formula for finding the solutions of a quadratic equation.

Quadratic function A function that can be described by a quadratic equation.

Radian A measure of angles. There are 2π radians in a circle.

Radical The symbol $\sqrt{\ }$ is called a radical.

Radicand The expression under a radical.

Rational number Any number of ordinary arithmetic or the additive inverse of any number of ordinary arithmetic.

Real number There is a real number for every point of the number line.

Reciprocal Two expressions are reciprocals if their product is 1. A reciprocal is also called a *multiplicative inverse*.

Reference angle The smallest angle that the terminal side of an angle makes with the x-axis.

Reflection A transformation in which points are reflected across a line.

Relation Any set of ordered pairs.

Root of a polynomial Any number which makes the polynomial zero.

Scientific notation A number expressed as the product of a number between 1 and 10 and a power of 10 is in scientific notation.

Sequence An ordered set of numbers.

Series A sum of terms of a sequence.

Sine ratio In a right triangle, the ratio of the length of the opposite side to the length of the hypotenuse.

Slope of a line A number that tells how steeply the line slants.

Solution set The set of all replacements that make a sentence true.

Statement A sentence that is either true or false.

Synthetic division A method of division of a polynomial by a binomial $x - a$, in which the variables are not written.

Tangent ratio In a right triangle, the ratio of the length of the opposite side to the length of the adjacent side.

Theorem A property that can be proved.

Transformation A function from a set to itself.

Translation A geometric transformation in which all points are moved in the same direction, the same distance.

Trigonometric function A function that uses one of the six trigonometric ratios to assign values to the measures of the acute angles of a right triangle.

Vector A quantity having a direction and a magnitude

Zero (of a polynomial) A number, which when substituted into a polynomial, makes it zero.

SELECTED ANSWERS

Chapter 1

Section 1-1 TRY THIS

1. 1, 12, 17   **2.** 0, 1, 12, 17   **3.** −5, 0, 1, 12, 17
4. $\frac{-3}{7}, \frac{3}{-7}$ **5.** $\frac{-13}{1}, \frac{26}{-2}$ **6.** $\frac{93}{10}, \frac{-93}{-10}$ **7.** $\frac{4}{5}, \frac{-8}{-10}$
8. 0.875   **9.** $0.\overline{63}$ **10.** $-1.1\overline{3}$ **11.** $\frac{53}{10}$ **12.** $\frac{-367}{1000}$
13. $\frac{19,032}{10,000}$ **14.** Rational   **15.** Rational
16. Rational   **17.** Irrational   **18.** Rational
19. Irrational   **20.** <   **21.** <   **22.** <

Exercise Set 1-1

1. 2, 14   **3.** All the numbers are rational.
5-11. Answers may vary.   **5.** $\frac{28}{2}, \frac{14}{1}$ **7.** $\frac{26}{10}, \frac{-26}{-10}$
9. $\frac{8}{1}, \frac{24}{3}$ **11.** $\frac{415}{100}, \frac{-830}{-200}$ **13.** 0.375   **15.** $1.\overline{6}$
17. 0.4285 . . .   **19.** 0.5625   **21.** $\frac{27}{10}$ **23.** $\frac{-145}{1000}$
25. $\frac{-23}{100}$ **27.** $\frac{11,235}{1000}$ **29.** $\frac{3}{17}, -\sqrt{25}, -12.33 \ldots$
31. >   **33.** <   **35.** <   **37.** >   **39-41.** Answers
may vary.   **39.** $\frac{4}{2}, \sqrt{4}, \frac{39}{18}, \sqrt[3]{8}, (\sqrt{2})^2$ **41.** $\frac{5}{10}$,
$\frac{50}{100}, \frac{10}{20}, \frac{2.5}{5}, \frac{-25}{-50}$ **43.** $0.\overline{076923}, 0.\overline{153846}$,
$0.\overline{230769}, \ldots, 0.\overline{923076}$; The repeating portion of
$\frac{2}{13}$ is two times the repeating portion of $\frac{1}{13}$ and the
repeating portion of $\frac{3}{13}$ is three times the repeating
portion of $\frac{1}{13}$ and so on.   **45.** Answers may vary.
Example: 0.909900999000 . . .

Section 1-2 TRY THIS

1. 45   **2.** 148   **3.** $-x = -10; -(-x) = 10$
4. $-x = -(-x) = 0$ **5.** $-x = 8; -(-x) = -8$
6. 8   **7.** 4

Exercise Set 1-2

1. 54   **3.** 91   **5.** 103   **7.** −4   **9.** −17   **11.** −6
13. −15   **15.** 4   **17.** 9   **19.** $\frac{2}{3}$ **21.** 0   **23.** 18
25. 30   **27.** 12   **29.** $5 + |x|$ **31.** $|x - y|$
33. $|x + y|$ **35.** $|x - y| > 5$ **37.** $3|x| = 8$
39. The sum of the absolute value of two numbers is
equal to the absolute value of their sum when the two
numbers have the same sign or one of them is zero.

Section 1-3 TRY THIS

1. −17   **2.** −18.6   **3.** $-\frac{35}{10} = -\frac{7}{2}$ **4.** −14
5. 3.3   **6.** $-\frac{11}{24}$ **7.** 17   **8.** 17.8   **9.** $\frac{59}{48}$

10. $-5x + (-3y)$ **11.** $3x - 2y$ **12.** $-6p - (-5t)$
13. $4x + 5y$; commutative   **14.** $(3m + 2n) + 4$;
associative   **15.** $(2z + 6x) + 5y$; commutative and
associative

Exercise Set 1-3

1. −28   **3.** −16   **5.** 5   **7.** 4   **9.** −7   **11.** −24
13. 1.2   **15.** −8.86   **17.** $\frac{1}{7}$ **19.** $-\frac{16}{12} = -\frac{4}{3}$
21. $\frac{1}{10}$ **23.** −2   **25.** −12   **27.** 5   **29.** 15
31. −11.6   **33.** −29.25   **35.** $-\frac{14}{4} = -\frac{7}{2}$ **37.** $-\frac{5}{12}$
39-49. Answers may vary.   **39.** $-3x + (-4y)$, Thm.
1−1   **41.** $3m - n$, Thm. 1−1   **43.** $3b + 5a$, commutative law   **45.** $3x$, additive property of 0
47. $(3x + 4y) + 5$, associative law   **49.** $(4x + 7z) +$
$5y$, associative and commutative laws   **51.** 2
53. 19   **55.** −43   **57.** 0   **59.** −19.45   **61.** No
63b. No   **63c.** No   **65.** −102.816

Section 1-4 TRY THIS

1. −24   **2.** 28.35   **3.** $\frac{8}{15}$ **4.** 42.77   **5.** 0   **6.** $\frac{3}{4}$
7. $\frac{17}{25}$ **8.** −3   **9.** −2   **10.** $\frac{1}{4} = 0.25$ **11.** $\frac{8}{3}$
12. $-\frac{1}{27}$ **13.** $-\frac{234}{112}$ **14.** $\frac{10}{56}$ **15.** $-\frac{6}{7}$ **16.** $\frac{36}{7}$
17. Possible   **18.** Not possible   **19.** Not possible
20. Not possible   **21.** Equivalent; commutative law
22. Equivalent; commutative law   **23.** Not equivalent; subtraction is not commutative   **24.** Equivalent; Theorem 1−2 and commutative law
25. Equivalent; The multiplicative property of 1

Exercise Set 1-4

1. −21   **3.** −8   **5.** 16   **7.** 126   **9.** 34.2
11. 26.46   **13.** 2   **15.** 60   **17.** 24   **19.** $-\frac{12}{35}$
21. 1   **23.** $-\frac{8}{27}$ **25.** −2   **27.** −7   **29.** 7
31. 0.3   **33.** −6   **35.** 5   **37.** $\frac{4}{3}$ **39.** $\frac{1}{26}$
41. $-\frac{6}{77}$ **43.** 25   **45.** Not possible   **47.** 0
49. Equivalent. Commutative law   **51.** Not equivalent.   **53.** Equivalent. Associative law   **55.** Equivalent. Theorem 1−2   **61.** $-11\frac{5}{8}$ **63.** Never true
65. All real values   **67.** −0.00168012

Section 1-5 TRY THIS

1. $5x + 45$ **2.** $8y - 80$ **3.** $ax + ay - az$
4. $2(l + w)$ **5.** $a(c - y)$ **6.** $6(x - 2)$
7. $5(-5y + 3w + 1)$ **8.** $20x$ **9.** $-7x$
10. $23.4x + 3.9$ **11.** $0.92P$ **12.** $-9x$ **13.** $24t$
14. $-7 + y$ **15.** $-x + y$ **16.** $-9x - 6y - 11$
17. $3x + 2y - 1$ **18.** $2x + 5z - 24$ **19.** $-\frac{1}{4}t -$
$41w + 5d - 23$ **20.** $-5x, -7y, 67t, -\frac{4}{5}$ **21.** $-9a$,

$-4b, 1.7c, -24$ **22.** $3x + 8$ **23.** $-2x - 9y - 6$
24. $-x - 2y$ **25.** $23x - 10y$ **26.** $23x + 52$
27. $12a + 12$

Exercise Set 1−5

1. $3a + 3$ **3.** $4x - 4y$ **5.** $-10a - 15b$ **7.** $2ab -$
$2ac + 2ad$ **9.** $2\pi rh + 2\pi r$ **11.** $\frac{1}{2}ha + \frac{1}{2}hb$
13. $8(x + y)$ **15.** $9(p - 1)$ **17.** $7(x - 3)$
19. $x(y + 1)$ **21.** $2(x - y + z)$ **23.** $3(x + 2y - 1)$
25. $a(b + c - d)$ **27.** $\pi r(r + s)$ **29.** $9a$ **31.** $-3b$
33. $15y$ **35.** $11a$ **37.** $-8t$ **39.** $10x$ **41.** $8x -$
$8y$ **43.** $2c + 10d$ **45.** $22x + 18$ **47.** $2x - 33y$
49. $4b$ **51.** $-a - 2$ **53.** $-b + 3$ **55.** $-t + y$
57. $-a - b - c$ **59.** $-8x + 6y - 13$ **61.** $2c -$
$5d + 3e - 4f$ **63.** $4a, -5b, 6$ **65.** $2x, -3y, -2z$
67. $-a - 5$ **69.** $m + 1$ **71.** $5d - 12$ **73.** $-7x +$
14 **75.** $-9x + 21$ **77.** $44a - 22$ **79.** -190
81. $-12y - 145$ **83.** $17x + 14y + 129$
85. $-42x - 360y - 276$ **87.** $-490,990a +$
$855,484b$ **89.** $0.008733x - 0.000784y$ **91.** -10
93. $4x + 12y$ **95.** $-31a$ **97.** $\$134.40$

Section 1−6 TRY THIS

1. 8^4 **2.** m^3 **3.** $(4y)^5$ **4.** $25y^2$ **5.** $-8x^3$
6. 8 **7.** -31 **8.** 1 **9.** 1 **10.** 1 **11.** $\frac{1}{10^4}$
12. $\frac{1}{(-4)^3}$, or $\frac{1}{-64}$ **13.** $\frac{1}{5y^3}$ **14.** 4^{-3}
15. $(-5)^{-4}$ **16.** $(2x)^{-6}$

Exercise Set 1−6

1. 4^6 **3.** y^6 **5.** $(3a)^4$ **7.** $(-4x)^3$ **9.** $5^2x^3y^4$
11. $81yyyy$ **13.** $-5bbb$ **15.** $1, p \neq 0$ **17.** $\frac{1}{8^4}$
19. $\frac{1}{16^2}$ **21.** $\frac{1}{(-4)^3}$ **23.** $\frac{1}{(-5y)^2}$ **25.** $\frac{1}{(-3m)^3}$
27. $\frac{2a^2}{b^5}$ **29.** $\frac{a^2c^4}{b^3d^5}$ **31.** $\frac{a^2y^2}{x^3b^3}$ **33.** 9^{-2}
35. $(-8)^{-6}$ **37.** $(5x)^{-5}$ **39.** $\frac{b^{-3}}{4}$ **41.** $\frac{a^{-2}d^{-4}}{x^{-3}b^{-3}}$
43. $\frac{x^{-3}b^{-3}}{a^{-2}y^{-2}}$ **45.** 71 **47.** 544 **49.** $\frac{5}{3}$
51. $\frac{984}{9}$, or $\frac{328}{3}$

Section 1−7 TRY THIS

1. 8^4 **2.** y^5 **3.** $-18x^{11}$ **4.** $-75x^{-14} = \frac{-75}{x^{14}}$
5. $-10x^{-12}y^2 = \frac{-10y^2}{x^{12}}$ **6.** 5^6 **7.** 10^6
8. $-2y^{10}x^{-4} = \frac{-2y^{10}}{x^4}$ **9.** $\frac{3a^{-2}b^2}{2} = \frac{3b^2}{2a^2}$ **10.** 3^{42}

11. x^{-14} **12.** t^6 **13.** $8x^3y^3$ **14.** $\frac{x^4}{16y^{14}}$
15. $-32x^{20}y^{10}$ **16.** $\frac{1000y^{21}}{x^{12}z^6}$ **17.** x^9y^{12}
18. $\frac{9x^4}{4y^{16}}$ **19.** 16 **20.** 24 **21.** 20

Exercise Set 1−7

1. 5^9 **3.** 8^{-4} **5.** 8^{-6} **7.** b^{-3} **9.** a^3 **11.** $6x^5$
13. $-28m^5n^5$ **15.** $-14x^{-11}$ **17.** 6^5 **19.** 4^5
21. 10^{-9} **23.** 9^2 **25.** a^5 **27.** 1 **29.** $\frac{-4x^9}{3y^2}$
31. $\frac{3x^3}{2y^2}$ **33.** 4^6 **35.** 8^{-12} **37.** 6^{12}
39. $3^3x^6y^6$ or $27x^6y^6$ **41.** $(-2)^{-2}x^{-6}y^8$ or $\frac{1}{4}x^{-6}y^8$
43. $(-6)^{-2}a^4b^{-6}c^{-2}$ or $\frac{1}{36}a^4b^{-6}c^{-2}$ **45.** $\frac{1}{4^9 \cdot 3^{12}}$
47. $\frac{8x^9y^3}{27}$ **49.** 10 **51.** 24 **53.** 2^{21} **55.** $\frac{2^4x^4}{(-3)^6y^{62}}$
57. $64x^{22}y^2$ **59.** x^{9y} **61.** a^{6b}
63. $x^{ca+cb}y^{ca+cb}$ **65.** $4x^{2a}y^{2b}$

Section 1−8 TRY THIS

1. 4.6×10^{11} **2.** 1.5×10^8 **3.** 1.235×10^{-8}
4. 1.7×10^{-24} **5.** 7.462×10^{-13} **6.** 5.6×10^{-15}
7. 2×10^3 **8.** 5.5×10^2

Exercise Set 1−8

1. 4.7×10^{10} **3.** 8.63×10^{17} **5.** 1.6×10^{-8}
7. 7×10^{-11} **9.** 0.0004 **11.** $673,000,000$
13. 0.0000000008923 **15.** 9.11×10^{-28}
17. 4.8×10^{-10} **19.** 9.66×10^{-5}
21. 1.3338×10^{-11} **23.** 8.34×10^{10}
25. 2.5×10^3 **27.** 5×10^{-4} **29.** 3×10^{11}
31. 4.5×10^2 **33.** 1.1×10^{11} **35.** 6.5×10

Section 1−9 TRY THIS

1. Axiom 2 (Associative law)   **2.** None. We need a
theorem.   **3.** Axiom 4 (Additive property of zero)
4. Axiom 7 (Property of reciprocals)   **5.** 1. Axiom 2
(Associative law of addition), 3. Axiom 4 (Additive
property of zero)

Exercise Set 1−9

1. Axiom 3   **3.** Axiom 5   **5.** None   **7.** None
9. Symmetric property of equality   **11.** Axiom 1
13. None   **15.** Axiom 1   **17.** 1. Axiom 1 and
Axiom 2, repeated use. 2. Axiom 5, 3. Axiom 4,
4. Axiom 5

Chapter 2

Section 2−1 TRY THIS

1. -7 2. 38   3. -1 4. 140.3   5. $\frac{5}{4}$ 6. -16
7. $\frac{2}{7}$ 8. -3 9. $\frac{4}{3}$ 10. 4   11. -2

Exercise Set 2−1

1. -3 3. 40   5. -15 7. -14 9. 39   11. 7
13. -9 15. -9 17. 36   19. 18   21. 5
23. 24   25. 7   27. 8   29. 21   31. 2   33. 2
35. $\frac{18}{5}$ 37. 0   39. $\frac{4}{5}$ 41. $\frac{17}{6}$ 43. $\frac{155}{8}$ 45. 1
47. -8 49. 0.214022   51. All real numbers
53. No   55. No   57. Yes

Section 2−2 TRY THIS

1. $\frac{2}{5}$ 2. 2   3. $-\frac{19}{8}$ 4. 19, -5 5. 0, $\frac{17}{3}$ 6. $-\frac{2}{9}$, $\frac{1}{2}$

Exercise Set 2−2

1. $\frac{4}{3}$ 3. $\frac{37}{5}$ 5. 13   7. 2   9. 2   11. 7   13. 5
15. $-\frac{51}{31}$ 17. 5   19. 2   21. -2, 5   23. 8, 9
25. $\frac{3}{2}$, $\frac{2}{3}$ 27. 0, 8   29. 0, 1, -2 31. -6
33. $-\frac{16}{3}$ 35. $\frac{c-3}{8}$ 37. $\frac{5a-3h}{c}$ 39. $\frac{12}{a-b}$
41. 1, -1 43. 0, 2

Section 2−3 TRY THIS

1. 8 ft, 24 ft   2. $\frac{1}{2}$ 3. 1.5925 min   4. $1.92
5. $124   6. $725   7. 17, 19

Exercise Set 2−3

1. 8 cm; 4 cm   3. $1\frac{3}{5}$ m; $2\frac{2}{5}$ m   5. $14.75   7. 5
9. $45   11. $650   13. 32°, 96°, 52°   15. Length
is 31 m; width is 17 m   17. 11, 13, 15   19. $8000
21. $1644   23. 98%   25. 84   27. 143 gallons
29. 20 cm and 32 cm

Section 2−4 TRY THIS

1. $b = \frac{2A}{h}$ 2. $c = \frac{5}{3}P - 10$ 3. $m = \frac{H - 2r}{3}$
4. $Q = \frac{T}{1 + iy}$

Exercise Set 2−4

1. $l = \frac{A}{w}$ 3. $I = \frac{W}{E}$ 5. $m = \frac{F}{a}$ 7. $t = \frac{I}{Pr}$
9. $m = \frac{E}{c^2}$ 11. $l = \frac{P - 2w}{2}$ 13. $a^2 = c^2 - b^2$
15. $r^2 = \frac{A}{\pi}$ 17. $F = \frac{9}{5}C + 32$ 19. $r^3 = \frac{3V}{4\pi}$
21. $h = \frac{2A}{(a + b)}$ 23. $m = \frac{rF}{v^2}$ 25. $a = \frac{2s - 2v_i t}{t^2}$

27. 0.4 yr   29. Take the square root of both sides.
31. $V_1 = \frac{T_1 P_2 V_2}{P_1 T_2}$

Section 2−5 TRY THIS

1. Yes   2. No   3. Yes   7. $\left\{x \mid x > 3\right\}$
8. $\left\{x \mid x \le 3\right\}$ 9. $\left\{x \mid x \ge -2\right\}$ 10. $\left\{y \mid y \le \frac{3}{10}\right\}$
11. $\left\{y \mid y < -\frac{5}{12}\right\}$ 12. $\left\{x \mid x \ge 12\right\}$ 13. $\left\{y \mid y \ge 36\right\}$
14. $\left\{y \mid \frac{1}{5} \ge y\right\}$ 15. $\left\{x \mid x < \frac{1}{2}\right\}$ 16. $\left\{y \mid \frac{22}{13} \le y\right\}$

Exercise Set 2−5

5. $x > -5$ 7. $y < 6$ 9. $a \le -21$ 11. $t \ge -5$
13. $y > -6$ 15. $x \le 9$ 17. $x \ge 3$ 19. $x < -60$
21. $x \le 0.9$ 23. $x \le \frac{5}{6}$ 25. $x < 6$ 27. $y \le -3$
29. $y > \frac{2}{3}$ 31. $x \ge 11.25$ 33. $x \le \frac{1}{2}$
35. $y \le -8\frac{5}{6}$ 37. $x > -\frac{2}{17}$ 39. $m > \frac{7}{3}$
41. $-3 < y < 3$ 43. $\left\{x \mid x \le -3 \text{ or } x > 3\right\}$
45a. True   45b. False, because $-3 < -2$, but $9 > 4$.

Section 2−6 TRY THIS

1. 71 or higher   2. $n < 100$

Exercise Set 2−6

1. Less than 620 miles   3. $20,000   5. $2
7. 100 hours or less

Section 2−7 TRY THIS

3. $\left\{x \mid -2 < x < 1\right\}$ 6. $\left\{x \mid x < 1 \text{ or } x \ge 7\right\}$
7. $\left\{x \mid x \ge -\frac{7}{2} \text{ or } x < -2\right\}$

Exercise Set 2−7

5. $-4 < x < 6$ 7. $-2 < y \le 2$ 9. $-\frac{5}{3} \le x \le \frac{4}{3}$
17. $x < -9 \text{ or } x > -5$ 19. $x \le \frac{5}{2} \text{ or } x \ge 11$
21. $x < \frac{4}{3} \text{ or } x > 15$ 23. $-\frac{3}{2} \le a \le 1$
25. $-4 < x \le 1$ 27. $\frac{2}{5} \le x \le \frac{4}{5}$ 29. $-\frac{1}{8} < x < 2$
31. T   33. F   35. F   37. $-\frac{2}{5} \le x \le 2$

Section 2−8 TRY THIS

1. $7|x|$ 2. x^8 3. $5a^2 |b|$ 4. $\frac{7|a|}{b^2}$ 5. $9|x|$
6. 29   7. 5   8. 20   9. $\left\{6, -6\right\}$ 10. $\left\{-\frac{1}{2}, \frac{1}{2}\right\}$
11. $\left\{x \mid -5 < x < 5\right\}$ 12. $\left\{x \mid -6.5 < x < 6.5\right\}$
13. $\left\{y \mid y \le -8 \text{ or } y \ge 8\right\}$ 14. $\left\{x \mid x > \frac{1}{2} \text{ or } x < -\frac{1}{2}\right\}$
15. $\left\{\frac{5}{3}, -\frac{13}{3}\right\}$ 16. $\left\{x \mid -2 < x < 5\right\}$
17. $\left\{x \mid x > \frac{11}{2} \text{ or } x < -\frac{3}{2}\right\}$

Exercise Set 2−8

1. $3|x|$ 3. y^8 5. $9x^2 y^2 |y|$ 7. $\frac{a^2}{|b|}$ 9. $16|m|$

11. $t^2|t|$ **13.** $b^8|b|$ **15.** $x^2y^2|x|$ **17.** 34   **19.** 11
21. 33   **23.** 5   **25.** $-3, 3$ **27.** $-3 < x < 3$
29. $x \le -2$ or $x \ge 2$ **31.** $t < -5.5$ or $t \ge 5.5$
33. $-9, 15$ **35.** $-\frac{1}{2} \le x \le \frac{7}{2}$ **37.** $y < -\frac{3}{2}$ or $y > \frac{17}{2}$
39. $x \le -\frac{5}{4}$ or $x \ge \frac{23}{4}$ **41.** $x > -\frac{3}{5}$ or $x < -1$
43. $x \le -1$ or $x \ge \frac{7}{3}$ **45.** $x \le 0.1396$ or $x \ge 0.1417$
47. $t \le 6$ or $t \ge 8$ **49.** 0, 7   **51.** No solution
53. $-33 < x < -31$ **55.** $3 \le x \le 6$ or $-4 \le x \le -1$
57. No solution

Section 2−9 TRY THIS

2. If $x < 17$, then $x < 12$.   **3.** If $x = 9$, then
$3x + 7 = 37$.   **5.** $\{x \mid x > 5\}$ **6.** 12   **7.** Yes
8. No   **9.** No   **10.** Yes   **11.** No   **12.** No

Exercise Set 2−9

5. If $6y = 10$, then $3y = 5$.   **7.** If $2x + 5 = 14$, then
$5x + 3 = 17$.   **9.** If $x = 7$, then $7x - 12 = 37$.
11. If $x \ge \frac{16}{17}$, then $15x - 5 \ge 11 - 2x$.
13. $\{x \mid -\frac{9}{2} < x\}$ **15.** $-\frac{4}{7}$ **17.** $-\frac{17}{2}$ **19.** $-\frac{5}{3}$
21. Yes   **23.** Yes   **25.** No   **27.** Yes   **29.** $\frac{1}{7}$
41. Answers may vary.

Chapter 3

Section 3−1 TRY THIS

1. $(d, 1)$ $(e, 1)$ $(d, 2)$ $(e, 2)$ **2.** (x, x) (y, x) (z, x)
(x, y) (y, y) (z, y) (x, z) (y, z) (z, z)
3. $\{(2, 2)$ $(3, 3)$ $(4, 4)$ $(5, 5)\}$ **4.** Domain: $\{2, 3, 4, 5\}$;
range: $\{2, 3, 4, 5\}$ **5.** Domain: $\{1, 2\}$; range: $\{1, 2, 3\}$
6. $\{6\}$ **7.** $\{(3, 4), (3, 5), (4, 4), (4, 5), (5, 4), (5, 5)\}$

Exercise Set 3−1

1. $\{(0, a), (0, b), (0, c), (2, a), (2, b), (2, c), (4, a),$
$(4, b), (4, c), (5, a), (5, b), (5, c)\}$ **3.** $\{(x, 1), (x, 2),$
$(y, 1), (y, 2), (z, 1), (z, 2)\}$ **5.** $\{(5, 5), (5, 6), (5, 7),$
$(5, 8), (6, 5), (6, 6), (6, 7), (6, 8), (7, 5), (7, 6),$
$(7, 7), (7, 8), (8, 5), (8, 6), (8, 7), (8, 8)\}$
7. $\{(-1, 0), (-1, 1), (-1, 2), (0, 1), (0, 2), (1, 2)\}$
9. $\{(-1, -1), (-1, 0), (-1, 1), (-1, 2), (0, 0), (0, 1),$
$(0, 2), (1, 1), (1, 2), (2, 2)\}$ **11.** $\{(-1, -1), (0, 0),$
$(1, 1), (2, 2)\}$ **13.** Domain: $\{5, 6, 8\}$; range: $\{2, 4, 6\}$
15. Domain: $\{6, 7, 8\}$; range: $\{0, 5\}$ **17.** Domain:
$\{8, 5\}$; range: $\{1\}$ **19.** Domain: $\{5\}$; range: $\{6\}$
21a. $\{(-1, -1)$ $(0, -1)$ $(1, -1)$ $(2, -1)$ $(-1, 0)$ $(0, 0)$
$(1, 0)$ $(2, 0)$ $(-1, 1)$ $(0, 1)$ $(1, 1)$ $(2, 1)$ $(-1, 2)$ $(0, 2)$
$(1, 2)$ $(2, 2)\}$ **21b.** $\{(-1, -1), (0, 0), (1, 1), (2, 2)\}$
21c. Domain: $\{-1, 0, 1, 2\}$; range: $\{-1, 0, 1, 2\}$
23. $\{8, 10, 12\}$ **25.** $\{4, 6, 8\}$ **27.** $\{(2, 2), (2, 3)\}$
29. $\{(2, 3), (3, 3)\}$ **31.** $\{(3, 2)\}$

Section 3−2 TRY THIS

1d. $\{3, -5, -4\}$ **1e.** $\{2, -2, 3\}$ **2.** Yes   **3.** No
4. No   **7.** The shapes are the same, but this curve
opens to the right instead of up.

Exercise Set 3−2

9. Yes   **11.** No   **13.** Yes   **15.** Yes   **17.** Yes
19. No   **37b.** $\{x \mid 2 \le x \le 6\}$ **37c.** $\{y \mid 1 \le y \le 5\}$

Section 3−3 TRY THIS

1a. Yes   **1b.** Yes   **1c.** Yes   **1d.** No   **2a.** -2
2b. -1 **2c.** 0   **3a.** -4 **3b.** -7 **3c.** 3   **3d.** $-\frac{7}{2}$
4a. 0   **4b.** 6   **4c.** 20   **4d.** 20   **5a.** $-\frac{1}{2}$ **5b.** $\frac{1}{4}$
5c. $\frac{1}{3}$ **5d.** -3 **6a.** 1   **6b.** 4   **6c.** 4
6d. $12a^2 + 1$ **7.** They are not possible.
$\{x \mid x \ne 1$ and $x \ne -3\}$

Exercise Set 3−3

1. Yes   **3.** No   **5.** Yes   **7a.** 1   **7b.** -3 **7c.** -6
7d. 9   **9a.** 0   **9b.** 1   **9c.** 57   **9d.** $5t^2 + 4t$
11a. 15   **11b.** 32   **11c.** 20   **11d.** 4   **13a.** $\frac{2}{3}$
13b. $\frac{10}{9}$ **13c.** 0   **13d.** Not possible   **15a.** 3.14977
15b. 55.73147   **15c.** 3178.20675   **15d.** 1166.70323
17. R **19.** $\{x \mid x \ne 0\}$ **21.** $\{x \mid x \ne -\frac{8}{5}\}$
23. $\{x \mid x \ne 0, x \ne -2,$ and $x \ne 1\}$ **25.** Yes   **27.** Yes
29. Yes   **31.** Yes   **33.** No   **37.** -9 **39.** -15 **43.** No
45. $h(x) = 3|x| - 4$ **47.** $h(x) = 2\left(\frac{x - 3}{2}\right) + 3 = x$

Section 3−4 TRY THIS

1. Yes   **2.** Yes   **3.** No   **4.** No   **5.** No   **6.** Yes
7. $-5x + 5y - \frac{1}{2} = 0$ **8.** $0x + 3y - 10 = 0$
13. The graph of $y = 2x + 1$ is moved up 1 unit from
the graph of $y = 2x$.   **14.** The graph of $y = 2x - 4$
is moved down 4 units from the graph of $y = 2x$.

Exercise Set 3−4

1. Yes   **3.** No, second degree term   **5.** Yes   **7.** Yes
9. Yes   **11.** $4x - y - 8 = 0$ **13.** $-2x + y - 3 = 0$
15. $-4x + y - 4 = 0$ **17.** $x + 0y - 6 = 0$
19. $-3x + \sqrt{2}y + 0 = 0$ **21.** Line through $(4, 0)$
and $(0, 2)$ **23.** Line through $(-8, 0)$ and $(0, 2)$
25. Line through $(2, 0)$ and $(0, 8)$ **27.** Line through
$(1, 3)$ and $(-1, -1)$ **29.** Line through $(-\frac{8}{5}, 0)$ and
$(0, -4)$ **31.** Line through $(6, 0)$ and $(0, 3)$
33-41. Each graph is a line through the intercepts
given in the answers.   **33.** $(0, -2), (2, 0)$
35. $(0, -1), (\frac{1}{3}, 0)$ **37.** $(0, -5), (4, 0)$ **39.** $(0, -5),$
$(-1, 0)$ **41.** $(0, 2), (7, 0)$ **43.** Vertical line through
$(2, 0)$ **45.** Horizontal line through $(0, -6)$
47. Vertical line through $(-5, 0)$ **49.** Horizontal

line through (0, 7)   **51.** Horizontal line through
(0, 3)   **53.** Vertical line through (5, 0)   **55.** $(0, -\frac{2}{3})$,
$(\frac{10}{3}, 0)$ **57.** (0, −0.1), (10, 0)   **59.** (10, −3.07),
(0.6239837, 0)   **61.** The horizontal lines.
63. $y = -\frac{A}{B}x - \frac{C}{B}$

Section 3−5 TRY THIS

1. $\frac{13}{11}$ **2.** 1   **3.** 0   **4.** No slope   **5.** $y = -3x - 2$
6. $y = \frac{1}{4}x - 9$ **7.** $y = -\frac{1}{2}x + \frac{5}{2}$

Exercise Set 3−5

1. 8   **3.** −1   **5.** $-\frac{1}{2}$ **7.** 2   **9.** $\frac{3}{7}$ **11.** $\frac{1}{2}$ **13.** $\frac{2}{5}$
15. No slope   **17.** No slope   **19.** 0   **21.** No slope
23. 0   **25.** No slope   **27.** 0   **29.** 0   **31.** No slope
33. $y = 4x - 10$ **35.** $y = -x - 7$ **37.** $y = \frac{1}{2}x + 7$
39. $y = -7$ **41.** 1.7441860   **43.** $y = 3.516x -$
13.1602   **45.** Yes   **47.** $\frac{5}{8}$ **49.** Answers may vary.
(1, −25), (2, −50), (3, −75), (−1, 25)   **51.** $m = -\frac{3}{5}$
53. Figure *EFGH* is a rhombus and its diagonals are
perpendicular.

Section 3−6 TRY THIS

1. $y = -3x + 7$ **2.** $y = -\frac{10}{3}x + 4$ **3a.** $y = \frac{2}{3}x + 2$
3b. $m = \frac{2}{3}, b = 2$

Exercise Set 3−6

1. $y = \frac{1}{2}x + \frac{1}{2}$ **3.** $y = x$ **5.** $y = \frac{5}{2}x + 5$
7. $y = \frac{1}{4}x + \frac{17}{4}$ **9.** $y = \frac{2}{5}x$ **11.** $y = 3x + 5$
13. $m = 2, b = 3$ **15.** $m = -4, b = 9$ **17.** $m = -1$,
$b = 6$ **19.** $m = -3, b = 5$ **21.** $m = \frac{3}{4}, b = -3$
23. $m = -3, b = 4$ **25.** $m = -\frac{7}{3}, b = -3$
27. $m = 0, b = 7$ **29.** $m = 0, b = -\frac{10}{3}$
31. $m = 1.9833212, b = -4.4118926$ **33.** $y =$
$-4x + 3$ **35.** $y = 75x - 18$ **37.** $y = 2x + 1.1$
39. $y = -\frac{3}{4}x - \frac{3}{2}$ **41.** $y = \frac{2}{15}x + \frac{2}{5}$ **45.** $m = \frac{3}{2}$

Section 3−7 TRY THIS

1. Yes   **2.** No   **3.** No   **4.** $y = -4x - 12$ **5a.** Yes
5b. No   **6.** $y = -\frac{8}{7}x + \frac{6}{7}$ **7.** $y = \frac{1}{2}x + \frac{5}{2}$

Exercise Set 3−7

1. Yes   **3.** No   **5.** Yes   **7.** $y = -\frac{1}{2}x + \frac{17}{2}$
9. $y = \frac{5}{7}x - \frac{17}{7}$ **11.** $y = \frac{1}{3}x + 4$ **13.** Yes   **15.** No
17. $y = \frac{1}{2}x + 4$ **19.** $y = \frac{4}{3}x - 6$ **21.** $y = \frac{5}{2}x + 9$
23. $y = -\frac{7}{3}x + \frac{22}{3}$ **27.** $y = 2x + \frac{5}{7}$ **29.** 2

Section 3−8 TRY THIS

1. $R = -0.01t + 10.43$ **2.** 9.73 seconds;

9.23 seconds   **3.** 2063

Exercise Set 3−8

1a. $E = \frac{3}{20}t + 72$ **1b.** 77.9 years; 78.3 years
3a. $D = \frac{1}{5}t + 20$ **3b.** 27.4 quadrillion joules; 30
quadrillion joules   **5a.** $R = -0.075t + 46.8$
5b. 42.3 seconds; 41.6 seconds   **5c.** 2021
7a. $C = 0.15m + 15$ **7b.** \$45.00   **9.** 21.1°C
11. 100.03916 cm; 99.96796 cm   **13a.** Plan A:
$E = 600 + 0.04x$; Plan B: $E = 100 + 0.06x$
13b. $x \geq 25,000$

Chapter 4

Section 4−1 TRY THIS

1. Yes   **2.** No   **3.** (4, 7)   **4.** (4, −2)   **5.** (−2, 5)
6. (−3, 2)   **7.** $(-\frac{1}{3}, \frac{1}{2})$ **8.** (2, −1)

Exercise Set 4−1

1. No   **3.** No   **5.** Yes   **7.** No   **9.** (3, 1)
11. (3, 2)   **13.** (1, −5)   **15.** (2, 1)   **17.** $(\frac{5}{2}, -2)$
19. (3, −2)   **21.** (−4, 3)   **23.** (−3, −15)
25. (2, −2)   **27.** (−2, 1)   **29.** (1, 2)   **31.** (3, 0)
33. (−1, 2)   **35.** (−3, 2)   **37.** (6, 2)   **39.** (3, −3)
41. $(\frac{1}{2}, -\frac{1}{2})$ **43.** $(-\frac{4}{3}, -\frac{19}{3})$ **45.** (90.91, −90.91)
47. (−12, 0)   **49.** No solution   **51.** $(-\frac{1}{4}, -\frac{1}{2})$
53. $\{(5, 3), (-5, 3), (5, -3), (-5, -3)\}$
55. $y = 0 \cdot x^2 + 3$ or $y = 3$

Section 4−2 TRY THIS

1. 35, 140   **2.** 30 liters of 5% and 70 liters of 15%
3. 280 km

Exercise Set 4−2

1. 5, −47   **3.** 24, 8   **5.** 150 lb soybean meal; 200
lb corn meal   **7.** 5 L of each   **9.** \$4100 at 14%,
\$4700 at 16%   **11.** \$725 at 12%, \$425 at 11%
13. 375 km   **15.** $1\frac{3}{4}$ **17.** 8 white, 22 yellow
19. 13 at \$9.75; 32 at \$8.50   **21.** Maria 20, Carlos
28   **23.** $l = 160$ m; $w = 154$ m   **25.** $l = 31$ cm;
$w = 12$ cm   **27.** Joan, 14 yrs, James, 32 years
29. 82   **31.** 137°   **33.** $4\frac{4}{7}$ L

Section 4−3 TRY THIS

1. No   **2.** Yes   **3.** (1, −2, 3)   **4.** (5, −1, 2)
5. $(2, \frac{1}{2}, -2)$

Exercise Set 4−3

1. Yes   **3.** (1, 2, 3)   **5.** (−1, 5, −2)   **7.** (3, 1, 2)

9. $(-3, -4, 2)$ **11.** $(2, 4, 1)$ **13.** $(-3, 0, 4)$
15. $(2, 2, 4)$ **17.** $(\frac{1}{2}, 4, -6)$ **19.** $(\frac{1}{2}, \frac{1}{3}, \frac{1}{6})$
21. $(\frac{1}{2}, \frac{2}{3}, -\frac{5}{6})$ **23.** $(1, -1, 2)$ **25.** $(1, -2, 4, -1)$
27. $(-1, \frac{1}{5}, -\frac{1}{2})$ **29.** $a = 2$; $b = -1$; $c = 3$
31. $z = 8 - 2x - 4y$

Section 4−4 TRY THIS

1. A−112, B−90, C−85

Exercise Set 4−4

1. 17, 9, 79   **3.** 4, 2, −1   **5.** $A = 34°, B = 104°$,
$C = 42°$ **7.** $A = 25°, B = 50°, C = 105°$ **9.** \$21
on Thur., \$18 on Fri., \$27 on Sat.   **11.** first score is
74.5, second score is 68.5, third score is 82   **13.** A−
1500, B−1900, C−2300   **15.** A−900 gal/hr; B−
1300 gal/hr; C−1500 gal/hr   **17.** 20   **19.** 35

Section 4−5 TRY THIS

1. Inconsistent   **2.** Consistent   **3.** Inconsistent
4. Consistent   **5.** Dependent   **6.** Independent
7. Dependent   **8.** Independent

Exercise Set 4−5

1. Inconsistent   **3.** Consistent   **5.** Consistent
7. Inconsistent   **9.** Consistent   **11.** Dependent
13. Independent   **15.** Dependent   **17.** Independent
19. $(0, -5), (1, -2), (-1, -8)$ **21.** No solution
23. No solution   **25.** Dependent: 19, 23; consistent:
19   **27.** 2   **29.** $\left(\frac{1 - 3y}{2}, y\right)$

Section 4−6 TRY THIS

1. $(-8, 2)$ **2.** $(-1, 2, 3)$

Exercise Set 4−6

1. $(\frac{3}{2}, \frac{5}{2})$ **3.** $(\frac{1}{2}, \frac{3}{2})$ **5.** $(3, -2)$ **7.** $(-1, 2, -2)$
9. $(\frac{3}{2}, -4, 3)$ **11.** $(-3, 0)$ **13.** $(1, -3, -2, -1)$

Section 4−7 TRY THIS

1. 14   **2.** −2   **3.** $-2x + 12$ **4.** $(3, 1)$
5. $(-\frac{10}{41}, -\frac{13}{41})$ **6.** 93   **7.** 60   **8.** $x^3 - x^2$
9. $(1, 3, -2)$

Exercise Set 4−7

1. 3   **3.** 36   **5.** −10.3   **7.** 0   **9.** $(2, 0)$
11. $(-4, -5)$ **13.** $(\frac{1}{3}, -\frac{2}{3})$ **15.** −10   **17.** −30
19. 93   **21.** $(2, -1, 4)$ **23.** $(1, 2, 3)$ **25.** $(\frac{3}{2}, \frac{13}{14}, \frac{33}{14})$
27. $x^3 - 4x$ **29.** $z + 3z^2$ **31.** 2, −2
33. $\left(\frac{15 - 4\pi}{-3\sqrt{3} - \pi^2}, \frac{4\sqrt{3} + 5\pi}{-3\sqrt{3} - \pi^2}\right)$ **35.** $\begin{vmatrix} a & b \\ -b & a \end{vmatrix}$

Section 4−8 TRY THIS

1. No   **9.** Vertices: $(0, 0), (4, 0), (4, \frac{5}{3}), (0, 3), (\frac{12}{5}, 3)$

Exercise Set 4−8

1. Yes   **3.** No   **41.** $(0, 1), (2, -5), (2, 5)$
43. $(0, 0), (0, 6), (4, 4), (6, 0)$
45. $(0, 0), (0, 4), (\frac{40}{11}, \frac{24}{11}), (5, 0)$

Section 4−9 TRY THIS

1. The snack bar will make a maximum profit of
\$23.70 by selling 40 hamburgers and 50 hot dogs.

Exercise Set 4−9

1. 8 of A and 10 of B to maximize score at 102.
3. \$7000 at Bank X and \$15,000 at Bank Y to maximize income at \$1395.   **5.** Maximum \$192, 2 knits;
4 worsteds   **7.** 30 P-1 airplanes and 10 P-2 airplanes
to minimize cost at \$460,000.

Chapter 5

Section 5−1 TRY THIS

1. 1, 0, 1, 7, 3; 7   **2.** $7xy^4 - 2xy^3 - 8xy^2 + 3xy$
3. $-4 + 5xy^2 + 4x^2yz + 5x^3yz^2$ **4.** $3x^2 + 2x^4$
5. $9x^3y^2 - 2x^2y^3$ **6.** $7xy^2 - 2x^2y$ **7.** $-4x^3 +$
$2x^2 - 4x - \frac{3}{2}$ **8.** $5p^2q^4 + p^2q^2 - 6pq^2 - 3q + 5$
9. $-5x^2t^2 + 4xy^2t + 3xt - 6x + 5$ **10.** $3x^2y -$
$5xy + 7x - 4y - 2$ **11.** $8xy^4 - 9xy^2 + 4x^2 +$
$2y - 7$ **12.** $7x^2y - 9x^3y^2 + 5x^2y^3 - x^2y^2 + 9y$

Exercise Set 5−1

1. 4, 3, 2, 1, 0; 4   **3.** 3, 6, 6, 0; 6   **5.** 5, 6, 2, 1, 0;
6   **7.** $3x^2y - 5xy^2 + 7xy + 2$ **9.** $3x + 2y - 2z - 3$
11. $9.46y^4 + 2.50y^3 - 11.8y - 3.1$ **13.** $-5x^3 +$
$7x^2 - 3x + 6$ **15.** $-2x^2 + 6x - 2$ **17.** $-4a^2 +$
$8ab - 5b^2$ **19.** $0.06y^4 + 0.032y^3 - 0.94y^2 + 0.93$
21. $-1.047p^2q - 2.479pq^2 + 8.879pq - 104.144$
23. 28; 190   **25.** $55x^5 - 59x^4 + 14x^3 + 12x^2 +$
$18x + 175$ **27.** $29x^5 - 15x^4 + 86x^3 - 68x^2 +$
$50x + 25$ **29.** $x^2 + 4xh$ **31.** $8x^{2a} + 7x^a + 7$
33. $x^{6a} - 5x^{5a} - 4x^{4a} + x^{3a} - 2x^{2a} + 8$

Section 5−2 TRY THIS

1. $3x^3y^2 + 4x^2y^2 - xy^2 + 6y^2$ **2.** $2p^4q^2 + 3p^3q^2 +$
$3p^2q^2 + 2q^2$ **3.** $2x^3y - 4xy + 3x^3 - 6x$
4. $15x^2 - xy - 6y^2$ **5.** $6xy - 40x + 60y - 400$
6. $16x^2 - 40xy + 25y^2$ **7.** $4y^4 + 24x^2y^3 + 36x^4y^2$
8. $16x^2 - 49$ **9.** $25x^4y^2 - 4y^2$ **10.** $4x^2 + 12x +$
$9 - 25y^2$ **11.** $25t^2 - 4x^6y^4$ **12.** $x^3 + 3x^2 +$
$3x + 1$ **13.** $x^3 - 3x^2 + 3x - 1$ **14.** $t^6 - 9t^4b +$
$27t^2b^2 - 27b^3$ **15.** $8a^9 - 60a^6b^2 + 150a^3b^4 -$
$125b^6$

Exercise Set 5-2

1. $6x^3 + 4x^2 + 32x - 64$ 3. $4a^3b^2 - 10a^2b^2 + 3ab^3 + 4ab^2 - 6b^3 + 4a^2b - 2ab + 3b^2$ 5. $a^3 - b^3$
7. $4x^2 + 8xy + 3y^2$ 9. $12x^3 + x^2y - \frac{3}{2}xy - \frac{1}{8}y^2$
11. $4x^3 - 4x^2y - 2xy^2 + 2y^3$ 13. $4x^2 + 12xy + 9y^2$ 15. $4x^4 - 12x^2y + 9y^2$ 17. $4x^6 + 12x^3y^2 + 9y^4$ 19. $9x^2 - 4y^2$ 21. $x^4 - y^2z^2$ 23. $9x^4 - 4$
25. $y^3 + 15y^2 + 75y + 125$ 27. $m^6 - 6m^4n + 12m^2n^2 - 8n^3$ 29. $0.002601x^2 + 0.00408xy + 0.0016y^2$ 31. $2462.0358x^2 - 945.0214x - 38.908$
33. $\frac{1}{4}x^4 - \frac{3}{5}x^2y + \frac{9}{25}y^2$ 35. $0.25x^2 + 0.70xy^2 + 0.49y^4$ 37. $4x^2 + 12xy + 9y^2 - 16$ 39. $x^4 - 1$
41. $16x^4 - y^4$ 43. $16x^4 - 16x^3 + 4x^2$ 45. $x^6 - 1$
47. $y^{3+3n}z^{n+3} - 4y^4z^{3n}$ 49. $x^2 + 2$
51. $x^3 - 3x^2 + 3x - 1$

Section 5-3 TRY THIS

1. $3x(x - 2)$ 2. $P(1 + rt)$ 3. $3y^2(3y^2 - 5y + 1)$
4. $3x^2y(2 - 7xy + y^2)$ 5. $(y + 2)(y - 2)$
6. $(7x^2 + 5y^5)(7x^2 - 5y^5)$
7. $(6x^2 + 4y^3)(6x^2 - 4y^3)$ 8. Yes   9. Yes
10. No   11. Yes   12. No   13. No   14. No
15. No   16. $(x + 7)^2$ 17. $(3y - 5)^2$
18. $(9y + 4x)^2$ 19. $(4x^2 - 5y^3)^2$
20. $-2(2a - 3b)^2$ 21. $-3y^2(2x^2 - 5y^3)^2$

Exercise Set 5-3

1. $y(y - 5)$ 3. $2a(2a + 1)$ 5. $y^2(y + 9)$
7. $3(y^2 - y - 3)$ 9. $3x^2(2 - x^2)$
11. $2a(2b - 3c + 6d)$ 13. $4xy(x - 3y)$
15. $x^2(x^4 + x^3 - x + 1)$ 17. $12x(2x^2 - 3x + 6)$
19. $(x + 4)(x - 4)$ 21. $(3x + 5)(3x - 5)$
23. $(2x + 5)(2x - 5)$ 25. $6(x + y)(x - y)$
27. $3(x^4 + y^4)(x^2 + y^2)(x + y)(x - y)$
29. $4x(y^2 + z^2)(y + z)(y - z)$ 31. $(y - 3)^2$
33. $(x + 7)^2$ 35. $(x + 1)^2$ 37. $(a + 2)^2$
39. $(y - 6)^2$ 41. $y(y - 9)^2$ 43. $3(2a + 3)^2$
45. $2(x - 10)^2$ 47. $(1 - 4d)^2$
49. $\frac{1}{7}x(4x^5 - 6x^3 + x - 3)$ 51. $(0.5 + y)(0.5 - y)$
53. $(xy + 2)^2(xy - 2)^2$ 55. $(3y^4 + 2)^2$
57. $(0.5x + 0.3)^2$ 59. $9x(x + 6)$
61. $(y^{16} + 1)(y^8 + 1)(y^4 + 1)(y^2 + 1)(y + 1)(y - 1)$
63. $(x^{2a} - y^b)(x^{2a} + y^b)$ 65. $(y^a - 3)(y^a - 3)$

Section 5-4 TRY THIS

1. $(x + 7)(x - 2)$ 2. $(x - 7)(x - 3)$
3. $(y - 2)(y + 1)$ 4. $(3x + 2)(x + 1)$
5. $(2x + 3)(2x - 1)$ 6. $2(4y - 1)(3y - 5)$
7. $(2x^2y^3 + 5)(x^2y^3 - 4)$

Exercise Set 5-4

1. $(x + 5)(x + 4)$ 3. $(y - 4)^2$ 5. $(x - 9)(x + 3)$
7. $(m - 7)(m + 4)$ 9. $(x + 9)(x + 5)$
11. $(y + 9)(y - 7)$ 13. $(t - 7)(t - 4)$
15. $(x + 5)(x - 2)$ 17. $(x + 2)(x + 3)$
19. $(8 - y)(4 + y)$ 21. $(t + 5)(t + 3)$
23. $(3x + 1)(3x + 4)$ 25. $(3a - 4)(a + 1)$
27. $(12z + 1)(z - 3)$ 29. $(2t + 5)(2t - 3)$
31. $(3x + 5)(2x - 5)$ 33. $(5y + 4)(2y - 3)$
35. $(4a - 1)(3a - 1)$ 37. $(3a + 2)(3a + 4)$
39. $(5x + 3)(3x - 1)$ 41. $6(3x - 4)(x + 1)$
43. $y(6y - 5)(3y + 2)$ 45. $(5y + 2)(3y - 5)$
47. $(5y + 4)(2y + 3)$ 49. $(6y + 5)(4y - 3)$
51. $(4a - 3)(5a - 2)$ 53. $(y^2 + 12)(y^2 - 7)$
55. $(y + \frac{4}{7})(y - \frac{2}{7})$ 57. $(t + 0.9)(t - 0.3)$
59. $(2m + 5n)(m - 2n)$ 61. $(2t + s)(t - 4s)$
63. $(9xy - 4)(xy + 1)$ 65. $x(x - 15)(x + 15)$
67. $3x(y - 25)^2$ 69. $12(x - 3y)^2$
71. $6x(x + 9)(x + 4)$ 73. $(x + a)(x + b)$
75. $(bx + a)(dx + c)$ 77. $\frac{1}{3}(\frac{2}{3}r + \frac{1}{2}s)^2$

Section 5-5 TRY THIS

1. $(x + 4)(x + 5)$ 2. $(y + 2)(5y + 2)$
3. $(p - q)(x + y)$ 4. $(x + 1 - p)(x + 1 + p)$
5. $(4 - x)(12 + x)$ 6. $x^2 + 14x + 49$ 7. $y^2 - 10by + 25b^2$ 8. $x^2 - \frac{2}{5}x + \frac{1}{25}$ 9. $x^2 + 4.2x + 4.41$ 10. $(x + 20)(x + 6)$
11. $2(x - 3)(x - 21)$ 12. $(x + 2.2)(x + 6.2)$

Exercise Set 5-5

1. $(a + c)(b - 2)$ 3. $(x - 2)(2x + 13)$
5. $2a^2(x - y)$ 7. $(a + b)(c + d)$
9. $(b^2 + 2)(b - 1)$ 11. $(y - 1)(y - 8)$
13. $(2y^2 + 5)(y^2 + 3)$ 15. $(a + b + 3)(a + b - 3)$
17. $(r - 1 - 2s)(r - 1 + 2s)$
19. $2(m + n - 5b)(m + n + 5b)$
21. $(3 - a - b)(3 + a + b)$
23. $(5y - x - 4)(5y + x + 4)$ 25. $y^2 - 24y + 144$
27. $y^2 + 3.6y + 3.24$ 29. $(x - 21)(x - 5)$
31. $2(x - 12a)(x - 4a)$ 33. $3(x - 1)(x - 13)$
35. $5(a + 6)(a - 14)$ 37. $(x + 5.766)(x - 1.284)$
39. $5.72(x + 18.6)(x - 12.4)$ 41. $y^2 + \frac{3}{4}ay + \frac{9}{64}a^2$
43. $(x - \frac{9}{2})(x - \frac{1}{2})$ 45. $(x - 2.6)(x - 0.6)$
47. $(x - \frac{9}{4})(x - \frac{5}{4})$
49. $(5y^a - x^b + 1)(5y^a + x^b + 1)$
51. $(x - 3a)(x + a)$

Section 5-6 TRY THIS

1. $(x - 2)(x^2 + 2x + 4)$ 2. $(y - 3)(y^2 + 3y + 9)$
3. $(3x + y)(9x^2 - 3xy + y^2)$
4. $(2y + z)(4y^2 - 2yz + z^2)$
5. $2xy(2x^2 + 3y^2)(4x^4 - 6x^2y^2 + 9y^4)$

6. $(9x^2 - 4y^2)(81x^4 + 36x^2y^2 + 16y^4)$
7. $(x - 0.3)(x^2 + 0.3x + 0.09)$

Exercise Set 5-6

1. $(x + 2)(x^2 - 2x + 4)$ **3.** $(y - 4)(y^2 + 4y + 16)$
5. $(w + 1)(w^2 - w + 1)$ **7.** $(2a + 1)(4a^2 - 2a + 1)$
9. $(y - 2)(y^2 + 2y + 4)$
11. $(2 - 3b)(4 + 6b + 9b^2)$
13. $(4y + 1)(16y^2 - 4y + 1)$
15. $(2x + 3)(4x^2 - 6x + 9)$
17. $(a - b)(a^2 + ab + b^2)$
19. $(a + \frac{1}{2})(a^2 - \frac{1}{2}a + \frac{1}{4})$
21. $(2x - 3y)(4x^2 + 6xy + 9y^2)$
23. $a(b + 5)(b^2 - 5b + 25)$
25. $2(y - 3z)(y^2 + 3yz + 9z^2)$
27. $(y + 0.5)(y^2 - 0.5y + 0.25)$
29. $(5c^2 - 2d^2)(25c^4 + 10c^2d^2 + 4d^4)$
31. $(ax - by)(a^2x^2 + axby + b^2y^2)$
33. $(\frac{2}{3}x + \frac{1}{4}y)(\frac{4}{9}x^2 - \frac{1}{6}xy + \frac{1}{16}y^2)$
35. $\frac{1}{2}(\frac{1}{2}x^a + y^{2a}z^{3b})(\frac{1}{4}x^{2a} - \frac{1}{2}x^a y^{2a}z^{3b} + y^{4a}z^{6b})$

Section 5-7 TRY THIS

1. $2(1 + 4x^2)(1 + 2x)(1 - 2x)$
2. $7(a + 1)(a^2 - a + 1)(a - 1)(a^2 + a + 1)$
3. $(3 + x)(4 + x)$ **4.** $(c - d + t + 4)(c - d - t - 4)$

Exercise Set 5-7

1. $(x + 12)(x - 12)$ **3.** $3(x^2 + 2)(x^2 - 2)$
5. $(a + 5)^2$ **7.** $2(x - 11)(x + 6)$
9. $(3x + 5y)(3x - 5y)$ **11.** $(2c - d)^2$
13. $(x^2 + 2)(2x - 7)$ **15.** $(4x - 15)(x - 3)$
17. $(m^3 + 10)(m^3 - 2)$ **19.** $(c - b)(a + d)$
21. $(m + 1)(m^2 - m + 1)(m - 1)(m^2 + m + 1)$
23. $(x + y + 3)(x - y + 3)$ **25.** $(6y - 5)(6y + 7)$
27. $(a^4 + b^4)(a^2 + b^2)(a + b)(a - b)$
29. $(2p + 3q)(4p^2 - 6pq + 9q^2)$
31. $(4p - 1)(16p^2 + 4p + 1)$
33. $ab(a + 4b)(a - 4b)$ **35.** $(4xy - 3)(5xy - 2)$
37. $2(x + 2)(x - 2)(x + 3)$
39. $2(5x - 4y)(25x^2 + 20xy + 16y^2)$
41. $2(2x + 3y)(4x^2 - 6xy + 9y^2)$ **43.** $x(x - 2p)$
45. $5(c^{10} - 4d^{10})(c^{10} + 4d^{10})$ **47.** $8(a - 7)^2$
49. $(x - 1)^3(x^2 + 1)(x + 1)$ **51.** $y(y - 1)^2(y - 2)$
53. $c(c^w + 1)^2$

Section 5-8 TRY THIS

1. $4, 2$ **2.** $\frac{1}{2}, -3$ **3.** $0, 2$ **4.** -5 **5.** $-\frac{3}{2}, \frac{3}{2}$

Exercise Set 5-8

1. $-7, 4$ **3.** 4 **5.** 6 **7.** $-5, -4$ **9.** $0, -8$

11. $-3, 3$ **13.** $-6, 6$ **15.** $-5, -9$ **17.** $-9, 7$
19. $7, 4$ **21.** $8, -4$ **23.** $-\frac{2}{3}, -2$ **25.** $\frac{3}{4}, \frac{1}{2}$
27. $0, 6$ **29.** $-\frac{3}{4}, \frac{2}{3}$ **31.** $-2, 2$ **33.** $\frac{1}{2}, 7$
35. $-\frac{5}{7}, \frac{2}{3}$ **37.** $0, \frac{1}{5}$ **39.** $-\frac{9}{10}, \frac{9}{10}$ **41.** $-\frac{1}{8}, \frac{1}{8}$
43. $-5, 4$ **45.** $-3, 15$ **47.** $-\frac{1}{4}, \frac{2}{3}, -\frac{11}{8}$
49. $\frac{1}{3}, -\frac{1}{3}, 0$ **51.** 1

Section 5-9 TRY THIS

1. $8, -6$ **2.** Length is 8 cm; width is 3 cm

Exercise Set 5-9

1. $\frac{7}{2}, -\frac{3}{2}$ **3.** $-12, 11$ **5.** Length is 12 cm; width
is 5 cm   **7.** Length is 100 m; width is 75 m   **9.** 9
and 11   **11.** 3 cm   **13.** Height is 7 cm; base is
16 cm   **15.** 2   **17.** $-10, -8$, and -6; 6, 8, 10
19. 11, 12, and 13; $-2, -1$, and 0   **21.** 3, 14
23. $x = \dfrac{14 - 2b}{5}$ **25.** Width is 30 in.; length is
40 in.; depth is 20 in.   **27.** 54 cm^2

Chapter 6

Section 6-1 TRY THIS

1. $\dfrac{(x - 2)(x + 2)}{5(x + 4)}$ **2.** $\dfrac{(x + y)(x + y)}{(x + 3)(x - 3)}$
3. $\dfrac{(3x + 2y)x}{(5x + 4y)x}$ **4.** $\dfrac{(2x^2 - y)(3x + 2)}{(3x + 4)(3x + 2)}$ **5.** $\dfrac{-1 \cdot (2a - 5)}{-1 \cdot (a - b)}$
6. $7x$ **7.** $2a + 3$ **8.** $\dfrac{3x + 2}{x + 2}$ **9.** $\dfrac{y + 2}{y - 1}$
10. $\dfrac{3(x - y)}{x + y}$ **11.** $a - b$ **12.** $\dfrac{x - 5}{x + 3}$ **13.** $\dfrac{1}{x + 7}$
14. $y^3 - 9$ **15.** $\dfrac{(x + 5)}{2(x - 5)}$ **16.** $\dfrac{2ab(a + b)}{(a - b)}$

Exercise Set 6-1

1. $\dfrac{3x(x + 1)}{3x(x + 3)}$ **3.** $\dfrac{(t - 3)(t + 3)}{(t + 2)(t + 3)}$ **5.** $\dfrac{3y}{5}$ **7.** $a - 2$
9. $\dfrac{x + 2}{x - 2}$ **11.** $\dfrac{p - 5}{p + 5}$ **13.** $\dfrac{y + 6}{3(y - 2)}$
15. $\dfrac{a^2 + ab + b^2}{a + b}$ **17.** $\dfrac{(x + 4)(x - 4)}{x(x + 3)}$ **19.** $\dfrac{y + 4}{2}$
21. $\dfrac{(x + 5)(2x + 3)}{7x}$ **23.** $c - 2$ **25.** $\dfrac{1}{x + y}$ **27.** 3
29. $\dfrac{(y - 3)(y + 2)}{y}$ **31.** $\dfrac{2a + 1}{a + 2}$ **33.** $\dfrac{(x + 4)(x + 2)}{3(x - 5)}$
35. $\dfrac{y(y^2 + 3)}{(y + 3)(y - 2)}$ **37.** $\dfrac{x^2 + 4x + 16}{(x + 4)^2}$
39. $\dfrac{21,934.2x^2}{y^2 - 182,499.84}$ **41.** $\dfrac{246,636}{x^2 - 8811.5769}$
43. $\dfrac{2s}{r + 2s}$ **45.** $\dfrac{x - 3}{(x + 1)(x + 3)}$ **47.** $\dfrac{m - t}{m + t + 1}$

49. $\dfrac{x^2 + xy + y^2 + x + y}{x - y}$ **51.** $\dfrac{-2x}{x - 1}$ **53.** $3x^2 +$ $3xh + h^2$ **55.** $3x^2 + 3xh + h^2 - 2x - h$

Section 6−2 TRY THIS

1. 90 **2.** 72 **3.** $5a^3b^2$ **4.** $(y + 4)^2(y + 3)$
5. $2x^2(x - 3)(x + 3)(x + 2)$ **6.** $2(a - b)(a + b)$

Exercise Set 6−2

1. $2^2 \cdot 3^2$ **3.** $2^4 \cdot 3^2$ **5.** $2^3 \cdot 3^2$ **7.** $3^2 \cdot 5$
9. 504 **11.** $24x^3$ **13.** $12x^2y$ **15.** $30a^3b^2$
17. $(a + b)(a - b)$ **19.** $6(y - 2)$ or $6(2 - y)$
21. $3(y + 3)(y - 3)$ **23.** $5(y - 3)(y - 3)$
25. $(a + 1)(a - 1)(a - 1)$ **27.** $(x + 2)(x - 2)$ or
$(x + 2)(2 - x)$ **29.** $(x + 5)(x + 5)(x - 3)$
31. $(2r + 3)(r - 4)(3r - 1)$
33. $(2x + 1)(x - 3)(x - 3)(x - 1)$
35. $x^4(x^2 + 1)(x^2 - 1)(x^2 + x + 1)(x^2 - x + 1)$

Section 6−3 TRY THIS

1. $\dfrac{12 + y}{y}$ **2.** $3x + 1$ **3.** $\dfrac{a - b}{b + 2}$ **4.** $\dfrac{y + 12}{x^2 + y^2}$
5. $\dfrac{2x^2 + 11}{x - 5}$ **6.** $\dfrac{11x^2}{2x - y}$ **7.** $\dfrac{9x^2 + 28y}{21x}$ **8.** $\dfrac{3}{x + y}$
9. $\dfrac{3y^2 + 12y + 3}{(y - 4)(y - 3)(y + 5)}$ **10.** $\dfrac{a + 12}{a(a + 3)}$

Exercise Set 6−3

1. 2 **3.** $\dfrac{3y + 5}{y - 2}$ **5.** $a + b$ **7.** $\dfrac{11}{x}$ **9.** $\dfrac{1}{x + 5}$
11. $\dfrac{2y^2 + 22}{y^2 - y - 20}$ **13.** $\dfrac{x + y}{x - y}$ **15.** $\dfrac{3x - 4}{x^2 - 3x + 2}$
17. $\dfrac{8x + 1}{x^2 - 1}$ **19.** $\dfrac{2x - 14}{15x + 75}$ **21.** $\dfrac{-a^2 + 7ab - b^2}{a^2 - b^2}$
23. $\dfrac{y}{(y - 2)(y - 3)}$ **25.** $\dfrac{3y - 10}{y^2 - y - 20}$
27. $\dfrac{3y^2 - 3y - 29}{(y - 3)(y + 8)(y - 4)}$ **29.** $\dfrac{2x^2 - 13x + 7}{(x + 3)(x - 1)(x - 3)}$
31. 0 **33.** $\dfrac{-3x^2 - 3x - 4}{x^2 - 1}$ **35.** $\dfrac{2y^2 + 3 - 7x^3y}{x^2y^2}$
37. $\dfrac{5y + 23}{5 - 2y}$ **39.** $\dfrac{x - y + x^2 + xy}{x + y - x^2 + xy}$ **41.** $\dfrac{x + 4}{x + 5}$

Section 6−4 TRY THIS

1. $\dfrac{14y + 7}{14y - 2}$ **2.** $\dfrac{x}{x + 1}$

Exercise Set 6−4

1. $\dfrac{1 + 4x}{1 - 3x}$ **3.** $\dfrac{x^2 - 1}{x^2 + 1}$ **5.** $\dfrac{3y + 4x}{4y - 3x}$ **7.** $\dfrac{x + y}{x}$
9. $\dfrac{a^2(b - 3)}{b^2(a - 1)}$ **11.** $\dfrac{1}{a - b}$ **13.** $\dfrac{1 + x^2}{x}$ **15.** $\dfrac{y - 3}{y + 5}$

17. $\dfrac{1 + x}{1 - x}$ **19.** $\dfrac{3}{4}$ **21.** $\dfrac{6x - 2}{5x + 6}$ **23.** $\dfrac{x}{x + 1}$ **25.** a
27. $\dfrac{5x + 3}{3x + 2}$ **29.** $\dfrac{x - 1}{x}$; x **31.** $\dfrac{-5}{x(x + h)}$
33. $\dfrac{1}{(1 + x)(1 + x + h)}$

Section 6−5 TRY THIS

1. $\frac{1}{2}x^2 + 8x + 3$ **2.** $4x^2 + x + 2$ **3.** $2x^6 + \frac{3}{2}x^5 +$
$3x^4 + 6x^3 + x^2 + \frac{1}{2}x + 1$ **4.** $5y^3 - 2y^2 + 6y$
5. $\frac{1}{2}x^2 + 5x + 8$ **6.** $4y^3 + y^2 + \frac{1}{2}y$ **7.** $x + 5$
8. $3y^3 - 2y^2 + 6y - 4$ **9.** $y^2 - 8y - 24$, R -66
10. $y - 11 + \dfrac{3y - 27}{y^2 - 3}$

Exercise Set 6−5

1. $6x^4 - 3x^2 + 8$ **3.** $-2a^2 + 4a - 3$ **5.** $y^3 -$
$2y^2 + 3y$ **7.** $-6x^5 + 3x^3 + 2x$ **9.** $1 - ab^2 - a^3b$
11. $-2pq + 3p - 4q$ **13.** $x + 7$ **15.** $a - 12$, R 32
17. $y - 5$ **19.** $y^2 - 2y - 1$, R -8 **21.** $a^2 + 4a +$
15, R 72 **23.** $4x^2 - 6x + 9$ **25.** $x^2 + 6$
27. $x^3 + x^2 - 1$, R 1 **29.** $2y^2 + 2y - 1 + \dfrac{8}{5y - 2}$
31. $2x^2 - x - 9 + \dfrac{3x + 12}{x^2 + 2}$ **33.** $x^2 + 2y$
35. $x^3 + x^2y + xy^2 + y^3$ **37.** $\frac{14}{3}$

Section 6−6 TRY THIS

1. $\frac{2}{3}$ **2.** $y = 57$ **3.** No solution **4.** 3 **5.** $x = 4$,
$x = -3$ **6.** $x = 7$ **7.** $x = -13$

Exercise Set 6−6

1. $\frac{51}{2}$ **3.** $\frac{40}{9}$ **5.** $-5, -1$ **7.** -1 **9.** $\frac{17}{4}$ **11.** No
solution **13.** 2 **15.** $\frac{3}{5}$ **17.** 6 **19.** -145
21. $-\frac{10}{3}$ **23.** -3 **25.** $-6, 5$ **27.** No solution
29. 0.947 **31.** All real numbers except -2
33. Yes **35.** $-\frac{7}{2}$

Section 6−7 TRY THIS

1. $2\frac{2}{5}$ hours **2.** A, 32 hours, B, 96 hours
3. 35.5 mi/h

Exercise Set 6−7

1. $\frac{35}{12}$ **3.** $-3, -2$ **5.** $\frac{7}{4}$ **7.** 7 km/h **9.** Train A
46 km/h, Train B 58 km/h **11.** 9 km/h **13.** 2 km
15. $3\frac{3}{14}$ hours **17.** $2\frac{2}{9}$ hours **19.** 30 hours
21. 50 km/h and 75 km/h **23.** $3\frac{3}{14}$ hours
25. 53 mi/h **27.** $51\frac{3}{7}$ mi/h **29.** 10:35
31a. $1447\frac{7}{8}$ miles from Los Angeles **31b.** Return
to Los Angeles

Section 6−8 TRY THIS

1. $T = \frac{PV}{k}$ 2. $R = \frac{r_1 r_2}{r_1 + r_2}$

Exercise Set 6−8

1. $d_1 = \frac{d_2 W_1}{W_2}$ 3. $t = \frac{2S}{v_1 + v_2}$ 5. $r_2 = \frac{Rr_1}{r_1 - R}$

7. $s = \frac{Rg}{g - R}$ 9. $r = \frac{2V - IR}{2I}$ 11. $f = \frac{pq}{q + p}$

13. $r = \frac{nE - IR}{In}$ 15. $H = m(t_1 - t_2)S$

17. $E = \frac{Er}{R + r}$ 19. $a = \frac{S - Sr}{1 - r^n}$ 21a. $t = \frac{ab}{b + a}$

21b. $a = \frac{tb}{b - t}$ 21c. $b = \frac{ta}{a - t}$

Section 6−9 TRY THIS

1. $y = 0.4x$ 2. 50 volts   3. $y = \frac{0.6}{x}$ 4. $7\frac{1}{2}$ hr

Exercise Set 6−9

1. $y = 8x$ 3. $y = -6x$ 5. $y = 5x$ 7. $y = \frac{15}{4}x$
9. $y = \frac{8}{5}x$ 11. 6 amperes   13. 125,000
15. 532,500 tons   17. 40 kg   19. $y = \frac{60}{x}$

21. $y = \frac{12}{x}$ 23. $y = \frac{36}{x}$ 25. $y = \frac{9}{x}$ 27. $\frac{2}{9}$ ampere

29. 160 cm^3 31. $6\frac{2}{3}$ hours   33. 10 cents per ounce
35. 2074

Chapter 7

Section 7−1 TRY THIS

1. $3, -3$ 2. $6, -6$ 3. $11, -11$ 4. 1   5. -6
6. $\frac{9}{10}$ 7. -0.08 8. 24   9. $5|y|$ 10. $4|y|$
11. $|x + 7|$ 12. -4 13. $3y$ 14. $-\frac{7}{4}$ 15. 3
16. -3 17. -3 18. 2   19. $-2x$ 20. $3x + 2$
21. 3   22. -3 23. Does not exist   24. $2|x - 2|$
25. $|x|$ 26. $|x + 3|$

Exercise Set 7−1

1. $4, -4$ 3. $12, -12$ 5. $20, -20$ 7. $-\frac{7}{6}$ 9. 14
11. $-\frac{4}{9}$ 13. 0.3   15. -0.07 17. $4|x|$ 19. $7|c|$
21. $|a + 1|$ 23. $|x - 2|$ 25. $|2x + 7|$ 27. -4
29. $-5y$ 31. 10   33. $0.7(x + 1)$ 35. 5   37. -1
39. $-\frac{2}{3}$ 41. $|x|$ 43. $5|a|$ 45. 6   47. $|a + b|$
49. y 51. $x - 2$ 53a. 12.5   53b. 15   53c. 17.5
53d. 20   55. All real numbers   57. $\{x \mid x \le \frac{4}{3}\}$
59. All real numbers
61. $\{x \mid x \ge -3 \text{ and } x \ne 2 \text{ and } x \ne -1\}$

Section 7−2 TRY THIS

1. $\sqrt{133}$ 2. $\sqrt{x^2 - 4y^2}$ 3. $\sqrt[4]{2821}$
4. $\sqrt[3]{8x^5 + 40x}$ 5. $4\sqrt{2}$ 6. $2\sqrt[3]{10}$ 7. $10\sqrt{3}$
8. $(x + 2)\sqrt{3}$ 9. $2bc\sqrt{3ab}$ 10. $2\sqrt[3]{2}$ 11. $3xy^2$
12. $(a + b)\sqrt[3]{a + b}$ 13. $3\sqrt{2}$ 14. $6y\sqrt{7}$
15. $3x\sqrt[3]{4y}$ 16. $7\sqrt{3ab}$ 17. 12.6   18. 18.5
19. -2.3

Exercise Set 7−2

1. $\sqrt{6}$ 3. $\sqrt[3]{10}$ 5. $\sqrt[4]{72}$ 7. $\sqrt{30ab}$ 9. $\sqrt[5]{18t^3}$
11. $\sqrt{x^2 - a^2}$ 13. $\sqrt[3]{0.06x^2}$ 15. $\sqrt[4]{x^3 - 1}$
17. $\sqrt{\frac{6y}{5x}}$ 19. $2\sqrt{2}$ 21. $2\sqrt{6}$ 23. $6x^2\sqrt{5}$
25. $3x^2\sqrt[3]{2x^2}$ 27. $2x^2\sqrt[3]{10x^2}$ 29. $2\sqrt[4]{2}$
31. $3cd\sqrt[4]{2d^2}$ 33. $(x + y)\sqrt[3]{x + y}$ 35. $5\sqrt{2}$
37. 8   39. $6\sqrt{7}$ 41. $30\sqrt{3}$ 43. $2x^2y\sqrt{6}$
45. $25t^3\sqrt[3]{t}$ 47. $(x + y)^2\sqrt[3]{(x + y)^2}$ 49. 13.4
51. 14.0   53. 3.6   55a. $-3.3°C$ 55b. $-16.6°C$
55c. $-25.5°C$ 55d. $-54.0°C$

Section 7−3 TRY THIS

1. $\frac{5}{6}$ 2. $\frac{10}{3}$ 3. $\frac{x}{10}$ 4. $\frac{2a\sqrt{a}}{b^2}$ 5. 5   6. $56\sqrt{xy}$

7. $5a$ 8. $\frac{20}{7}$ 9. $\frac{2ab}{3}$ 10. $5\sqrt[3]{2}$

Exercise Set 7−3

1. $\frac{4}{5}$ 3. $\frac{4}{3}$ 5. $\frac{7}{y}$ 7. $\frac{5y\sqrt{y}}{x^2}$ 9. $\frac{2x\sqrt[3]{x^2}}{3y}$ 11. $\sqrt{7}$
13. 3   15. $y\sqrt{5y}$ 17. $2\sqrt[3]{a^2b}$ 19. $3\sqrt{xy}$
21. $\sqrt{x^2 + xy + y^2}$ 23a. 1.62 sec   23b. 1.99 sec
23c. 2.20 sec

Section 7−4 TRY THIS

1. $13\sqrt{2}$ 2. $10\sqrt[4]{5x} - \sqrt{7}$ 3. $19\sqrt{5}$
4. $(3y + 4)\sqrt[3]{y^2} + 2y^2$ 5. $2\sqrt{x - 1}$ 6. $5\sqrt{6} +$
$3\sqrt{14}$ 7. $3\sqrt{ab} + 6\sqrt{3b} - 4\sqrt{3a} - 24$ 8. $20 -$
$4y\sqrt{5} + y^2$ 9. $\frac{\sqrt{6}}{3}$ 10. $\frac{\sqrt{70}}{7}$ 11. $\frac{\sqrt[3]{4}}{2}$
12. $\frac{2\sqrt{3ab}}{3|b|}$ 13. $\frac{2x^2\sqrt{3xy}}{3y^2}$ 14. $\frac{\sqrt[3]{28}}{2}$
15. $\frac{\sqrt[7]{192y^6x^5}}{2y}$ 16. $\frac{1 + \sqrt{2}}{1 + \sqrt{2}}, -5(1 + \sqrt{2})$
17. $\frac{\sqrt{2} - \sqrt{3}}{\sqrt{2} - \sqrt{3}}, -\sqrt{2} + \sqrt{3}$ 18. $\frac{\sqrt{3} + 1}{\sqrt{3} + 1},$
$\frac{\sqrt{15} + \sqrt{3} + \sqrt{5} + 1}{2}$

Exercise Set 7−4

1. $8\sqrt{3}$ 3. $3\sqrt[3]{5}$ 5. $13\sqrt[3]{y}$ 7. $7\sqrt{2}$ 9. $6\sqrt[3]{5}$

11. $23\sqrt{2}$ **13.** $21\sqrt{3}$ **15.** $38\sqrt{5}$ **17.** $122\sqrt{2}$
19. $9\sqrt[3]{2}$ **21.** $4\sqrt[3]{4}$ **23.** $29\sqrt{2}$ **25.** $(1+6a)\sqrt{5a}$
27. $(2-x)\sqrt[3]{3x}$ **29.** $10(a-1)\sqrt[3]{a}$ **31.** $3\sqrt{2y-2}$
33. $(x+3)\sqrt{x-1}$ **35.** $2\sqrt{6}-18$ **37.** $\sqrt{6}-\sqrt{10}$
39. $2\sqrt{15}-6\sqrt{3}$ **41.** -6 **43.** $3a\sqrt[3]{2}$ **45.** 1
47. -12 **49.** $a-b$ **51.** $1+\sqrt{5}$ **53.** $7+3\sqrt{3}$
55. -6 **57.** $a+\sqrt{3a}+\sqrt{2a}+\sqrt{6}$ **59.** $2\sqrt[3]{9}-$
$3\sqrt[3]{6}-2\sqrt[3]{4}$ **61.** $7+4\sqrt{3}$ **63.** $21-6\sqrt{6}$
65. $\frac{\sqrt{30}}{5}$ **67.** $\frac{\sqrt{70}}{7}$ **69.** $\frac{2\sqrt{15}}{5}$ **71.** $\frac{2\sqrt[3]{6}}{3}$
73. $\frac{\sqrt[3]{75ac^2}}{5c}$ **75.** $\frac{y\sqrt[3]{9yx^2}}{3x^2}$ **77.** $\frac{\sqrt[3]{x^2y^2}}{xy}$
79. $\frac{5(8+\sqrt{6})}{58}$ **81.** $-2\sqrt{7}(\sqrt{5}+\sqrt{3})$
83. $-\frac{\sqrt{15}+20-6\sqrt{2}-8\sqrt{30}}{77}$
85. $\frac{|x|-2\sqrt{xy}+|y|}{|x|-|y|}$ **87.** $\frac{3\sqrt{6}+4}{2}$ **89.** $\frac{7}{\sqrt{21}}$
91. $\frac{52}{3\sqrt{91}}$ **93.** $\frac{7|x|}{\sqrt{21xy}}$ **95.** $\frac{-11}{4(\sqrt{3}-5)}$
97. $\frac{3}{\sqrt{10}+2+\sqrt{15}+\sqrt{6}}$ **99.** $x-6$
101. $\frac{x}{\sqrt{x}(\sqrt{x+1}-1)}$

Section 7−5 TRY THIS

1. $(\sqrt[3]{125})^2=25, \sqrt[3]{125^2}=25$ **2.** $(\sqrt{6y})^3=6y\sqrt{6y}$,
$\sqrt{(6y)^3}=6y\sqrt{6y}$ **3.** $\sqrt[4]{y}$ **4.** $\sqrt{3a}$ **5.** $\sqrt[4]{16}$ or 2
6. $\sqrt[3]{125}$ or 5 **7.** $\sqrt[5]{a^3b^2c}$ **8.** $19^{1/3}$ **9.** $(abc)^{1/2}$
10. $\left(\frac{x^2y}{16}\right)^{1/5}$ **11.** $x\sqrt{x}$ **12.** 4 **13.** 32
14. $(7abc)^{4/3}$ **15.** $6^{7/5}$ **16.** $x^{1/2}y^{3/4}$ **17.** $\frac{1}{5^{1/4}}$
18. $\frac{1}{(3xy)^{7/8}}$ **19.** $7^{14/15}$ **20.** $5^{1/3}$ **21.** $9^{2/5}$
22. $\sqrt{a}$ **23.** x **24.** $\sqrt{2}$ **25.** ab^2 **26.** xy^3
27. $x^{1/4}y^{1/2}$ **28.** $\sqrt[4]{63}$ **29.** $\sqrt[4]{a-b}$ **30.** $\sqrt[6]{x^4y^3z^5}$
31. $\sqrt[4]{ab}$

Exercise Set 7−5

1. $6a\sqrt{6a}$ **3.** $4b\sqrt[3]{4b}$ **5.** $54a^3b\sqrt{2b}$ **7.** $2c\sqrt[3]{18cd^2}$
9. $\sqrt[4]{x}$ **11.** 2 **13.** $\sqrt[5]{a^2b^2}$ **15.** $\sqrt[3]{a^2}$ **17.** 8
19. $20^{1/3}$ **21.** $17^{1/2}$ **23.** $(cd)^{1/4}$ **25.** $(xy^2z)^{1/5}$
27. $(3mn)^{3/2}$ **29.** $(8x^2y)^{5/7}$ **31.** $\frac{1}{x^{1/3}}$ **33.** $\frac{1}{(2rs)^{3/4}}$
35. $10^{2/3}$ **37.** $x^{2/3}$ **39.** $5^{7/8}$ **41.** $7^{1/4}$
43. $8.3^{7/20}$ **45.** $10^{6/25}$ **47.** $\sqrt[3]{a^2}$ **49.** $2y^2$
51. $2c^2d^3$ **53.** $\frac{m^2n^4}{2}$ **55.** $\sqrt[4]{r^2s}$ **57.** $\sqrt{2ts}$
59. $\sqrt[6]{x^5-4x^4+4x^3}$ **61.** $\sqrt[6]{a+b}$ **63.** $\sqrt[12]{a^8b^9}$
65. $\sqrt[4]{st^4}$ **67a.** 27.4 m **67b.** 45.9 m
67c. 21.9 m **67d.** 79.4 m

Section 7−6 TRY THIS

1. 100 **2.** No solution **3.** 4 **4.** 9 **5.** 5

Exercise Set 7−6

1. 2 **3.** 168 **5.** 3 **7.** 19 **9.** $\frac{80}{3}$ **11.** 4
13. -27 **15.** 397 **17.** No solution **19.** $\frac{1}{64}$
21. -6 **23.** 5 **25.** $-\frac{1}{4}$ **27.** 3 **29.** 9 **31.** 7
33. $\frac{80}{9}$ **35.** -1 **37.** 6, 2 **39.** No solution
41. 208 mi **43.** 8 **45.** $5\pm2\sqrt{2}$ **47.** $-\frac{8}{9}$
49. 2 **51.** $\frac{-5+\sqrt{61}}{18}$

Section 7−7 TRY THIS

1. $i\sqrt{7}$ **2.** $-6i$ **3.** $4i\sqrt{10}$ **4.** -18 **5.** $-3\sqrt{3}$
6. $-3\sqrt{2}$ **7.** $7i$ **8.** $4+7i$ **9.** $-2-5i$ **10.** 0
11. $-i$ **12.** $-3+5i$ **13.** $-2+7i$ **14.** $-6-9i$

Exercise Set 7−7

1. $i\sqrt{2}$ **3.** $6i$ **5.** $-3i$ **7.** $8i\sqrt{2}$ **9.** $\frac{3}{4}i$
11. $-4i\sqrt{5}$ **13.** $92i$ **15.** $-4\sqrt{3}$ **17.** $-\sqrt{6}$
19. 6 **21.** $-3\sqrt{5}$ **23.** -10 **25.** $9i$ **27.** $-6i$
29. $8-2i$ **31.** $8+i$ **33.** $9-5i$ **35.** $-17i$
37. i **39.** $-5+5i$ **41.** $-9+5i$ **43.** $-3+2i$
45. $4-7i$ **47.** $-830.6607+7322.7624i$ **49.** 1
51. $-i$ **53.** $-2i$

Section 7−8 TRY THIS

1. $x=-1, y=2$ **2.** -30 **3.** -100 **4.** $3-28i$
5. $6-3i$ **6.** $-9+5i$ **7.** $7i$ **8.** -8 **9.** 53
10. 10 **11.** p^2+q^2 **12.** $2i$ **13.** $\frac{10}{17}-\frac{11}{17}i$
14. $\frac{3}{25}-\frac{4}{25}i$

Exercise Set 7−8

1. $x=-\frac{3}{2}, y=7$ **3.** $x=-2, y=-8$ **5.** $x=2$,
$y=3$ **7.** -63 **9.** -81 **11.** -9 **13.** $1+5i$
15. $38+9i$ **17.** $21-20i$ **19.** $-4-8i$
21. $6+5i$ **23.** $\sqrt{2}+\frac{1}{2}i$ **25.** $r+ti$ **27.** 2
29. $\frac{5}{4}$ **31.** 4 **33.** i **35.** $-\frac{37}{53}-\frac{50}{53}i$
37. $\frac{1}{3}+\frac{2}{3}\sqrt{2}i$ **39.** $2-3i$ **41.** $-i$ **43.** $\frac{1}{10}+\frac{2}{5}i$
45. $-\frac{4}{65}-\frac{7}{65}i$ **47.** i **49.** $-\frac{1}{2}-\frac{1}{2}i$
51. $\frac{a}{a^2+b^2}-\frac{b}{a^2+b^2}i$

Section 7−9 TRY THIS

1. $(1+i)^2-2(1+i)+2=1+2i+i^2-2-2i+$
$2=0$ **2.** $(1-i)^2+2(1-i)+1=1-2i+i^2+$
$2-2i+1=3-4i$; Therefore $(1-i)$ is not a solution of $x^2+2x+1=0$. **3.** $x^2-2ix-x+i-1=$
0 **4.** $x^3-2x^2+x-2=0$ **5.** $2+5i$
6. $(x+2i)(x-2i)=x^2+2ix-2ix-4i^2=x^2+4$
7. $(-1+i)^2=1-2i+i^2=1-2i-1=-2i, 1-i$

Exercise Set 7−9

1. Yes, yes **3.** No, yes **5.** Yes, yes **7.** $x^2 + 25$
9. $x^2 - 2x + 2$ **11.** $x^2 - 4x + 13$ **13.** $x^2 - ix - 3x + 3i$ **15.** $x^3 - x^2 + 9x - 9$ **17.** $x^3 - 2ix^2 - 3x^2 + 5ix + x - 2i + 2$ **19.** $\frac{2}{5} + \frac{6}{5}i$ **21.** $\frac{8}{5} - \frac{9}{5}i$
23. $2 - i$ **25.** $\frac{11}{25} + \frac{2}{25}i$

Section 7−10 TRY THIS

2. 5 **3.** 13 **4.** $\sqrt{2}$

Exercise Set 7−10

7. 5 **9.** 17 **11.** $\sqrt{10}$ **13.** 3 **15.** $\sqrt{c^2 + d^2}$
17. $2\sqrt{4c^2 + 1}$

Section 7−11 TRY THIS

1. $\overline{(3 + 2i) + (4 - 5i)} = \overline{(7 - 3i)} = 7 + 3i$, $\overline{(3 + 2i)} + \overline{(4 - 5i)} = (3 - 2i) + (4 + 5i) = 7 + 3i$
2. $\overline{(2 + 5i)(1 + 3i)} = \overline{(-13 + 11i)} = -13 - 11i$, $\overline{(2 + 5i)} \cdot \overline{(1 + 3i)} = (2 - 5i)(1 - 3i) = -13 - 11i$
3. $\overline{z^3} = \overline{z \cdot z \cdot z} = \bar{z} \cdot \bar{z} \cdot \bar{z} = \bar{z}^3$ **4.** $5\bar{z}^3 + 4\bar{z}^2 - 2\bar{z} + 1$ **5.** $7\bar{z}^5 - 3\bar{z}^3 + 8\bar{z}^2 + \bar{z}$

Exercise Set 7−11

1. $\bar{z}^2 - 3\bar{z} + 5$ **3.** $3\bar{z}^5 - 4\bar{z}^2 + 3\bar{z} - 5$
5. $7\bar{z}^4 + 5\bar{z}^3 - 12\bar{z}$ **7.** $5\bar{z}^{10} - 7\bar{z}^8 + 13\bar{z}^2 - 4$
9. $7\bar{z}^{100} - 15\bar{z}^{89} + \bar{z}^2$ **11.** $z = 1$ **13.** a

Chapter 8

Section 8−1 TRY THIS

1. $\frac{3}{5}, 1$ **2.** 3, 8 **3.** $\pm\sqrt{3}$ **4.** 0 **5.** $\pm\frac{i\sqrt{2}}{2}$
6. $0, \frac{3}{4}$ **7.** 2 cm **8.** A: 4 km/h; B: 3 km/h

Exercise Set 8−1

1. 5, 1 **3.** 5, −1 **5.** −5, −3 **7.** $\frac{2}{3}, -\frac{1}{2}$
9. $-\frac{4}{3}, -\frac{1}{3}$ **11.** $-\frac{5}{3}, 1$ **13.** $-\frac{1}{4}, \frac{3}{2}$ **15.** 10, −3
17. −2, −1 **19.** $\pm\sqrt{5}$ **21.** 0 **23.** $\pm\frac{\sqrt{6}}{2}$
25. $\pm\frac{\sqrt{15}}{3}$ **27.** $\pm\frac{2}{5}i$ **29.** $\pm\frac{i\sqrt{3}}{3}$ **31.** $\pm i\sqrt{5}$
33. $\pm i\sqrt{7}$ **35.** $\pm\frac{3}{2}$ **37.** 0, 5 **39.** 0, −2
41. $0, \frac{2}{3}$ **43.** $0, -\frac{9}{14}$ **45.** 0, 5 **47.** 3 cm
49. Length is 8 m; width is 3 m **51.** Length is 26 m; width is 13 m **53.** 12 m and 5 m **55.** 24 km and 7 km **57.** 4, 5, and 6 **59.** A: 350 km/h; B: 400 km/h **61.** $-8, -\frac{10}{3}, 0 \frac{7}{2}$ **63.** $\pm\sqrt{\frac{b}{a}}$

Section 8−2 TRY THIS

1. $\frac{-1 \pm \sqrt{22}}{3}$ **2.** $\frac{1 \pm i\sqrt{7}}{2}$ **3.** 1.2, −1.9

Exercise Set 8−2

1. $-3 \pm \sqrt{5}$ **3.** 1, −5 **5.** 3, −10 **7.** $2, -\frac{1}{2}$
9. $-1, -\frac{5}{3}$ **11.** $\frac{1 \pm i\sqrt{3}}{2}$ **13.** $-1 \pm 2i$ **15.** $1 \pm 2i$
17. $2 \pm 3i$ **19.** $\pm i\sqrt{5}$ **21.** $\frac{-3 \pm \sqrt{41}}{2}$ **23.** $\pm\frac{\sqrt{10}}{2}$
25. 0, −1 **27.** $\frac{-1 \pm 2i}{5}$ **29.** $\frac{3}{4}, -2$ **31.** $\frac{1 \pm 3i}{2}$
33. $\frac{3}{2}, \frac{2}{3}$ **35.** 1.3, −5.3 **37.** 5.2, 0.8 **39.** 2.8, −1.3 **41.** 0.4567764, −0.6567764 **43.** 1.1753905, −0.4253905 **45.** $\frac{-1 \pm \sqrt{1 + 4\sqrt{2}}}{2}$
47. $\frac{-\sqrt{5} \pm \sqrt{5 + 4\sqrt{3}}}{2}$ **49.** $\frac{-3 \pm \sqrt{9 - 4i}}{2}$
51. 4.8 km/h **53.** $\frac{1}{2}$

Section 8−3 TRY THIS

1. Two real **2.** One real **3.** Two nonreal
4. Sum = 4; product = $\frac{4}{3}$ **5.** Sum = $-\sqrt{2}$; product = −4 **6.** $4x^2 - 12x - 1 = 0$ **7.** $3x^2 + 7x - 20 = 0$ **8.** $x^2 - x - 56 = 0$ **9.** $x^2 - (m + n)x + mn = 0$ **10.** $x^2 + x - 72 = 0$ **11.** $x^2 - 6x + 7 = 0$
12. $4x^2 - 8x - 1 = 0$

Exercise Set 8−3

1. One real **3.** Two nonreal **5.** Two real **7.** One real **9.** Two nonreal **11.** Two real **13.** Two real
15. One real **17.** Sum = 2; product = 10
19. Sum = −1; product = −1 **21.** Sum = $-\frac{1}{2}$; product = 2 **23.** Sum = 0; product = −49
25. Sum = $\frac{12}{25}$; product = $\frac{2}{25}$ **27.** Sum = −4; product = −2 **29.** $4x^2 + 4\pi x + 1 = 0$ **31.** $x^2 - 5x - \sqrt{2} = 0$ **33.** $x^2 - 16 = 0$ **35.** $x^2 + 10x + 25 = 0$
37. $8x^2 + 6x + 1 = 0$ **39.** $12x^2 - (4k + 3m)x + km = 0$ **41.** $x^2 - \sqrt{3}x - 6 = 0$ **43.** $x^2 - \pi x - 12\pi^2 = 0$ **45.** $x^2 - 11x + 30 = 0$ **47.** $4x^2 + 23x - 6 = 0$ **49.** $x^2 - 4x + 1 = 0$ **51.** $x^2 - x - 3 = 0$ **53.** $ghx^2 - (g^2 - h^2)x - gh = 0$ **55.** $x^2 - 8x + 25 = 0$ **57a.** $k < \frac{1}{4}$ **57b.** $k = \frac{1}{4}$ **57c.** $k > \frac{1}{4}$
59a. $k < 1$ **59b.** $k = 1$ **59c.** $k > 1$ **61a.** $k > \frac{11}{3}$
61b. $k = \frac{11}{3}$ **61c.** $k < \frac{11}{3}$ **63.** $-\frac{1}{3}, k = -\frac{3}{5}$
65. −1 **67a.** Two rational solutions **67b.** Two real (not rational) solutions **71.** $\frac{-q(r - p)}{p(q - r)} - 2$ or $\frac{r(p - q)}{2p(q - r)}$

Section 8−4 TRY THIS

1. $\pm 3, \pm 1$ **2.** 4 **3.** 4, 2, −1, −3 **4.** 125, −8

Exercise Set 8−4

1. 81, 1 **3.** $\pm\sqrt{5}$ **5.** $-27, 8$ **7.** 16 **9.** 7, -1, 5, 1 **11.** 4, 1, 6, -1 **13.** $\pm\sqrt{2+\sqrt{6}}, \pm\sqrt{2-\sqrt{6}}$
15. $\frac{1}{3}, -\frac{1}{2}$ **17.** 2, -1 **19.** 28.5 **21.** $1 \pm \sqrt{2}$
23. $\frac{5 \pm \sqrt{21}}{2}, \frac{3 \pm \sqrt{5}}{2}$ **25.** $\frac{1}{3}$ **27.** 1, 4 **29.** 19
31. $\frac{2}{51 + 7\sqrt{61}}$ or $\frac{7\sqrt{61} - 51}{194}$

Section 8−5 TRY THIS

1. $w_2 = \frac{w_1}{A^2}$ **2.** $r = \sqrt{\frac{V}{\pi h}}$ **3.** $s = \frac{R \pm \sqrt{R^2 + 4LC}}{2L}$
4a. 4.33 s **4b.** 1.87 s **4c.** 44.9 m

Exercise Set 8−5

1. $s = \frac{\sqrt{P}}{2}$ **3.** $r = \sqrt{\frac{Gm_1 m_2}{F}}$ **5.** $L = \frac{gT^2}{16\pi^2}$
7. $r = \sqrt{x^2 + y^2}$ **9.** $z = \sqrt{d^2 - x^2 - y^2}$
11. $t = \frac{v_0 \pm \sqrt{v_0^2 - 64h}}{32}$ **13.** $t = \sqrt{\frac{2S}{g}}$
15. $r = \frac{-\pi h + \sqrt{\pi^2 h^2 + 2\pi A}}{2\pi}$
17. $t = \frac{\pi \pm \sqrt{\pi^2 - 12k\sqrt{2}}}{2\sqrt{2}}$ **19a.** 3.91 s **19b.** 1.91 s
19c. 79.6 m **21a.** 18.75% **21b.** 10% **21c.** 11%
21d. 12.75% **23.** 7 ft **25.** $90\sqrt{2} \approx 127.28$ ft
27. A: 24 km/h; B: 10 km/h **29.** 2.2199 cm;
8.0101 cm **31.** $a = \frac{b}{\sqrt{T^2 - 1}}$ **33.** 2, $\frac{1}{1 - k}$
35a. $4y, -y$ **35b.** $-x, \frac{x}{4}$ **37.** 7 **39.** 3 cm × 4 cm

Section 8−6 TRY THIS

1. $y = 7x^2$ **2.** $y = \frac{9}{x^2}$ **3.** $y = \frac{1}{2}xz$ **4.** $y = \frac{5xz^2}{w}$
5. 490 m **6.** Division by zero is undefined.

Exercise Set 8−6

1. $y = \frac{3}{2}x$ **3.** $y = 15x^2$ **5.** $y = \frac{0.0015}{x^2}$ **7.** $y = xz$
9. $y = \frac{3}{10}xz^2$ **11.** $y = \frac{1xz}{5wp}$ **13.** 180 m
15. 94.03 kg **17.** 97 **19.** 68.56 m **21.** y is multiplied by $\frac{1}{3}$. **23.** y is multiplied by n^2 **27.** t varies directly as $\sqrt{P}$.

Chapter 9

Section 9−1 TRY THIS

2. Symmetric with respect to y-axis **3.** Symmetric with respect to both axes **5.** Yes **6.** Yes **7.** No
8. No **9.** Even **10.** Neither **11.** Odd

Exercise Set 9−1

1. Yes; no **3.** No; no **5.** Yes; yes **11.** y-axis
13. Both axes **15.** Neither axis **17.** y-axis
19. Both axes **21.** Neither axis **27.** Yes **29.** Yes
31. Yes **33.** Yes **35.** No **37.** No **39.** Neither
41. Even **43.** Even **45.** Odd **47.** Neither
49. Even **51.** Even **53.** Even **55.** Odd **57.** Odd
63. Both axes **65.** y-axis **67.** Both axes

Section 9−2 TRY THIS

1-4. Each graph passes through the points given.
1. $(2, 1), (0, -1), (-2, 1)$ **2.** $(2, 6), (0, 4), (-2, 6)$
3. $(0, 3), (-3, 0), (-6, 3)$ **4.** $(4, 3), (1, 0), (-2, 3)$

Exercise Set 9−2

1-19. Each graph passes through the points given.
1. $(2, 4), (0, 2), (-2, 4)$ **3.** $(2, 0), (0, -2), (-2, 0)$
5. $(2, 7), (0, 5), (-2, 7)$ **7.** $(4, 0), (0, -4), (-4, 0)$
9. $(3, \frac{7}{2}), (0, \frac{1}{2}), (-3, \frac{7}{2})$ **11.** $(6, 3), (3, 0), (0, 3)$
13. $(1, 3), (-2, 0), (-5, 3)$ **15.** $(7, 3), (4, 0), (1, 3)$
17. $(-2, 3), (-5, 0), (-8, 3)$ **19.** $(\frac{7}{2}, 3), (\frac{1}{2}, 0)$,
$(-\frac{5}{2}, 3)$ **21.** $(2, -3)$

Section 9−3 TRY THIS

1-6. Graphs consist of segments with endpoints given.
1. $(-6, 0), (-4, 6), (-2, 0), (0, 6), (2, 0), (4, 6), (6, 0)$
2. $(-6, 0), (-4, 1), (-2, 0), (0, 1), (2, 0), (4, 1), (6, 0)$
3. $(-6, 0), (-4, -1), (-2, 0), (-1, -1), (2, 0), (4, -1)$,
$(6, 0)$ **4.** $(-2, 0), (-\frac{3}{2}, 2), (-\frac{1}{2}, -2), (\frac{1}{2}, 2), (\frac{3}{2}, -2)$,
$(2, 0)$ **5.** $(-8, 0), (-6, 2), (-2, -2), (2, 2), (6, -2)$,
$(8, 0)$ **6.** $(-8, 0), (-6, -2), (-2, 2), (2, -2), (6, 2)$,
$(8, 0)$

Exercise Set 9−3

1-9. Each graph passes through the points given.
1. $(2, 8), (0, 0), (-2, 8)$ **3.** $(2, 10), (0, 0), (-2, 10)$
5. $(4, 1), (0, 0), (-4, 1)$ **7.** $(2, -6), (0, 0), (-2, -6)$
9. $(4, -1), (0, 0), (-4, -1)$ **11-17.** Graphs consist of
segments with endpoints given. **11.** $(-4, 0), (0, 8)$,
$(2, -8), (3, 0)$ **13.** $(-4, 0), (0, -12), (2, 12), (3, 0)$
15. $(-4, 0), (0, 20), (2, -20), (3, 0)$ **17.** $(-4, 0)$,
$(0, \frac{4}{3}), (2, -\frac{4}{3}), (3, 0)$ **19.** Ray from $(0, 0)$ through
$(4, 8)$; ray from $(0, 0)$ through $(-4, 8)$ **21.** Ray from
$(0, 0)$ through $(4, 2)$; ray from $(0, 0)$ through $(-4, 2)$
23-27. Graphs of segments with endpoints given.
23. $(-2, 0), (0, 4), (1, -4), (\frac{3}{2}, 0)$ **25.** $(-12, 0)$,
$(0, 4), (6, -4), (9, 0)$ **27.** $(-1, 0), (-\frac{2}{3}, -4), (0, 4)$,
$(\frac{4}{3}, 0)$

Section 9-4 TRY THIS

1a. Parabola through $(-1, 3), (0, 0), (1, 3)$ **1b.** Upward **1c.** y-axis $(x = 0)$ **1d.** $(0, 0)$ **2a.** Parabola through $(-4, -4), (0, 0), (4, -4)$ **2b.** Downward **2c.** y-axis $(x = 0)$ **2d.** $(0, 0)$ **3a.** Parabola through $(-1, 3), (0, 0), (1, 3)$ **3b.** Parabola through $(1, 3), (2, 0), (3, 3)$ **3c.** $(2, 0)$ **3d.** $x = 2$ **3e.** Upward **3f.** To the right **4a.** Parabola through $(-1, -3), (0, 0), (1, -3)$ **4b.** Parabola through $(-3, -3), (-2, 0), (-1, -3)$ **4c.** $(-2, 0)$ **4d.** $x = -2$ **4e.** Downward **4f.** To the left

Exercise Set 9-4

1-17. Each graph is a parabola through the first three points given. **1.** $(-2, 4), (0, 0), (2, 4); (0, 0); x = 0$ **3.** $(-1, -4), (0, 0), (1, -4); (0, 0); x = 0$ **5.** $(1, 4), (3, 0), (5, 4); (3, 0); x = 3$ **7.** $(-5, -1), (-4, 0), (-3, -1); (-4, 0); x = -4$ **9.** $(2, 2), (3, 0), (4, 2); (3, 0); x = 3$ **11.** $(-10, -2), (-9, 0), (-8, -2); (-9, 0); x = -9$ **13.** $(0, 3), (1, 0), (2, 3); (1, 0); x = 1$ **15.** $(0, -\frac{3}{4}), (\frac{1}{2}, 0), (1, -\frac{3}{4}); (\frac{1}{2}, 0); x = 0$ **17.** $(-2, \frac{1}{2}), (-1, 0), (0, \frac{1}{2}); (-1, 0); x = -1$

Section 9-5 TRY THIS

1a. Parabola through $(1, 7), (2, 4), (3, 7)$ **1b.** $(2, 4)$ **1c.** $x = 2$ **1d.** Yes, 4 **1e.** No **2a.** Parabola through $(-3, -4), (-2, -1), (-1, -4)$ **2b.** $(-2, -1)$ **2c.** $x = -2$ **2d.** No **2e.** Yes, -1 **3a.** $(5, 40)$ **3b.** $x = 5$ **3c.** Yes, 40 **3d.** No **4a.** $(5, 0)$ **4b.** $x = 5$ **4c.** No **4d.** Yes, 0 **5a.** $(-\frac{3}{4}, -6)$ **5b.** $x = -\frac{3}{4}$ **5c.** Yes, -6 **5d.** No **6a.** $(-9, 3)$ **6b.** $x = -9$ **6c.** No **6d.** Yes, 3

Exercise Set 9-5

1. Parabola through $(1, 5), (3, 1), (5, 5); (3, 1); x = 3; \min. = 1$ **3.** Parabola through $(-3, 2), (-1, -2), (1, 2); (-1, -2); x = -1; \min. = -2$ **5.** Parabola through $(0, -1), (1, -3), (2, -1); (1, -3); x = 1; \min. = -3$ **7.** Parabola through $(-5, -2), (-4, 1), (-3, -2); (-4, 1); x = -4; \max. = 1$ **9.** $(9, 5); x = 9; \text{Min.} = 5$ **11.** $(-\frac{1}{4}, -13); x = -\frac{1}{4}; \text{Min.} = -13$ **13.** $(10, -20); x = 10; \text{Max.} = -20$ **15.** $(-4.58, 65\pi); x = -4.58; \text{Min.} = 65\pi$ **17.** $f(x) = -2x^2 + 4$ **19.** $f(x) = 2(x - 6)^2$ **21.** $f(x) = -2(x - 3)^2 + 8$ **23.** $f(x) = 2(x + 3)^2 + 6$ **25.** $f(x) = 2(x - 2)^2 - 3$ **27.** $y = -\frac{1}{2}(x - 1)^2 - 6$

Section 9-6 TRY THIS

1a. $f(x) = (x - 2)^2 + 3$ **1b.** $(2, 3), x = 2, \text{Min.} = 3$ **2a.** $f(x) = -4(x - \frac{3}{2})^2 + 4$ **2b.** $(\frac{3}{2}, 4), x = \frac{3}{2}, \text{Max.} = 4$ **3.** 225 **4.** 25 m by 25 m

Exercise Set 9-6

1. $f(x) = (x - 1)^2 - 4; (1, -4), x = 1, \min. = -4$ **3.** $f(x) = -(x - 2)^2 + 10; (2, 10), x = 2, \max. = 10$ **5.** $f(x) = (x + \frac{3}{2})^2 - \frac{49}{4}; (-\frac{3}{2}, -\frac{49}{4}), x = -\frac{3}{2}, \min. = -\frac{49}{4}$ **7.** $f(x) = (x - \frac{9}{2})^2 - \frac{81}{4}; (\frac{9}{2}, -\frac{81}{4}), x = \frac{9}{2}, \min. = -\frac{81}{4}$ **9.** $f(x) = 3(x - 4)^2 + 2; (4, 2), x = 4, \min. = 2$ **11.** $f(x) = \frac{3}{4}(x + 6)^2 - 27; (-6, -27), x = -6, \min. = -27$ **13.** 19 m by 19 m; 361 m^2 **15.** 121; 11 and 11 **17.** -4; 2 and -2 **19.** $-\frac{25}{4}$; $\frac{5}{2}$ and $-\frac{5}{2}$ **21.** $f(x) = a\left[x - \left(-\frac{b}{2a}\right)\right]^2 + \frac{4ac - b^2}{4a}$ **25.** Min, -6.95 **27.** Minimum, -6.081; ± 2.466 **29.** 30 **31.** 6 cm by 4.5 cm; 27 cm^2 **33.** 19 cm by 19 cm; 180.5 cm^2

Section 9-7 TRY THIS

1. $(1 + \sqrt{6}, 0), (1 - \sqrt{6}, 0)$ **2.** $(3, 0), (-1, 0)$ **3.** $(-4, 0)$ **4.** None

Exercise Set 9-7

1. $(2 + \sqrt{3}, 0), (2 - \sqrt{3}, 0)$ **3.** $(3, 0), (-1, 0)$ **5.** $(4, 0), (-1, 0)$ **7.** $(4, 0), (-1, 0)$ **9.** $\left(\frac{-2 + \sqrt{6}}{2}, 0\right), \left(\frac{-2 - \sqrt{6}}{2}, 0\right)$ **11.** None **13.** None **15.** $\left(\frac{3 + \sqrt{6}}{3}, 0\right), \left(\frac{3 - \sqrt{6}}{3}, 0\right)$ **17.** $(1.5571557, 0), (-4.042996, 0)$ **19.** $(1.27200, 0), (-0.72575, 0)$ **21.** Answers may vary. **21a.** $1, -3$ **21b.** $2.5, -4.5$ **21c.** $3.5, -5.5$

Section 9-8 TRY THIS

1. $f(x) = x^2 - 2x + 1$ **2a.** $f(x) = 0.1875x^2 - 16.25x + 500$ **2b.** 288 **3a.** Max. height $= 12.4$ m in 0.286 s **3b.** 1.876 s

Exercise Set 9-8

1. $f(x) = 2x^2 + 3x - 1$ **3.** $f(x) = -3x^2 + 13x - 5$ **5a.** $f(x) = -4x^2 + 40x + 2$ **5b.** \$98 **7a.** $f(x) = 0.05x^2 - 10.5x + 650$ **7b.** 250 **9a.** Max. height $= 1102.5$ m in 15 s **9b.** 30 s **11.** $f(x) = 0.0499218x^2 - 2.7573651x + 29.571379$ **13.** 300 m^2 **15.** $\frac{p + q}{2}$

Chapter 10

Section 10-1 TRY THIS

1. $\sqrt{149}$ **2.** $6\sqrt{2}$ **3.** $(\frac{3}{2}, -\frac{5}{2})$ **4.** $(9, -5)$

Exercise Set 10−1

1. 5 **3.** $3\sqrt{2}$ **5.** 5 **7.** 8 **9.** $\sqrt{a^2 + 64}$
11. $\sqrt{a^2 + b^2}$ **13.** $2\sqrt{a}$ **15.** 18.8061
17. $(-\frac{1}{2}, -1)$ **19.** $(-\frac{7}{2}, -\frac{15}{2})$ **21.** (4, 4)
23. $(a, 0)$ **25.** Yes **31.** (0, 4)

Section 10−2 TRY THIS

1. $(x + 3)^2 + (y - 7)^2 = 25$ **2.** $(x - 5)^2 +$
$(y + 2)^2 = 3$ **3.** $(x + 2)^2 + (y + 6)^2 = 7$
4. (−1, 3), 2 **5.** (7, −2), 8 **6.** (6, 4), 5

Exercise Set 10−2

1. $x^2 + y^2 = 49$ **3.** $(x + 2)^2 + (y - 7)^2 = 5$
5. (−1, −3), 2 **7.** (8, −3), $2\sqrt{10}$ **9.** (0, 0), $\sqrt{2}$
11. (5, 0), $\frac{1}{2}$ **13.** (−4, 3), $2\sqrt{10}$ **15.** (4, −1), 2
17. (2, 0), 2 **19.** $x^2 + y^2 = 25$ **21.** $(x - 2)^2 +$
$(y - 4)^2 = 16$ **23.** $(x - 1)^2 + (y - 2)^2 = 41$
25. Yes **27.** No **29.** $a_1 = 20 - 10\sqrt{3}$ ft,
$a_2 = 20 + 10\sqrt{3}$ ft

Section 10−3 TRY THIS

1. Vertices: (−3, 0), (3, 0), (0, 1), (0, −1); Foci:
$(-2\sqrt{2}, 0), (2\sqrt{2}, 0)$ **2.** Vertices: (−5, 0), (5, 0),
(0, −3), (0, 3); Foci: (−4, 0), (4, 0) **3.** Vertices:
(−2, 0), (2, 0), (0, $-\sqrt{2}$), (0, $\sqrt{2}$); Foci: $(-\sqrt{2}, 0)$,
$(\sqrt{2}, 0)$ **4.** Center: (0, 0); Vertices: (−1, 0), (1, 0),
(0, −3), (0, 3); Foci: (0, $-2\sqrt{2}$), (0, $2\sqrt{2}$) **5.** Center: (0, 0); Vertices: (−3, 0), (3, 0), (0, −5), (0, 5);
Foci: (0, −4), (0, 4) **6.** Center: (0, 0); Vertices:
$(-\sqrt{2}, 0), (\sqrt{2}, 0)$, (0, −2), (0, 2); Foci: (0, $-\sqrt{2}$),
(0, $\sqrt{2}$) **7.** Center: (0, 0); Vertices: $(-4\sqrt{3}, 0)$,
$(4\sqrt{3}, 0)$, (0, 4), (0, −4); Foci: (0, $4\sqrt{2}$), (0, $-4\sqrt{2}$)
8. Center: (−3, 2); Vertices: $(-3\frac{1}{5}, 2), (-3, 2\frac{1}{3})$,
$(-3, 1\frac{2}{3}), (-2\frac{4}{5}, 2)$; Foci: $(-3, 2\frac{4}{15}), (-3, 1\frac{11}{15})$
9. Center: (2, −3); Vertices: $(2\frac{1}{3}, -3), (2, -3\frac{1}{5})$,
$(2, -2\frac{4}{5}), (1\frac{2}{3}, -3)$; Foci: $(2\frac{4}{15}, -3), (1\frac{11}{15}, -3)$

Exercise Set 10−3

1. Vertices: (−2, 0), (2, 0), (0, −1), (0, 1); Foci:
$(-\sqrt{3}, 0), (\sqrt{3}, 0)$ **3.** Vertices: (−3, 0), (3, 0),
(0, −4), (0, 4); Foci: (0, $-\sqrt{7}$), (0, $\sqrt{7}$) **5.** Vertices: $(-\sqrt{3}, 0), (\sqrt{3}, 0)$, (0, $-\sqrt{2}$), (0, $\sqrt{2}$); Foci:
(−1, 0), (1, 0) **7.** Vertices: $(-\frac{1}{2}, 0), (\frac{1}{2}, 0)$,
$(0, -\frac{1}{3}), (0, \frac{1}{3})$; Foci: $\left(-\frac{\sqrt{5}}{6}, 0\right), \left(\frac{\sqrt{5}}{6}, 0\right)$
9. Center: (1, 2); Vertices: (−1, 2), (3, 2), (1, 1),
(1, 3); Foci: (1 $-\sqrt{3}$, 2), (1 $+\sqrt{3}$, 2) **11.** Center:
(−3, 2); Vertices: (−8, 2), (2, 2), (−3, −2), (−3, 6);
Foci: (−6, 2), (0, 2) **13.** Center: (−2, 1); Vertices:

(−10, 1), (6, 1), $(-2, 1 - 4\sqrt{3})$, $(-2, 1 + 4\sqrt{3})$;
Foci: (−6, 1), (2, 1) **15.** Center: (2, −1); Vertices:
(−1, −1), (5, −1), (2, −3), (2, 1); Foci:
$(2 - \sqrt{5}, -1), (2 + \sqrt{5}, -1)$ **17.** Center: (1, 1);
Vertices: (0, 1), (2, 1), (1, −1), (1, 3); Foci:
$(1, 1 - \sqrt{3}), (1, 1 + \sqrt{3})$ **19.** Center:
(2.003125, −1.00513); Vertices:
(5.0234302, −1.00515), (−1.0171802, −1.00515),
(2.003125, −3.0186868), (2.003125, 1.0083868)
21. $\frac{x^2}{4} + \frac{y^2}{9} = 1$ **23.** $\frac{(x - 3)^2}{4} + \frac{(y - 1)^2}{25} = 1$
25. $(x + 2)^2 + \frac{(y - 3)^2}{16} = 1$ **27a.** No **27b.** $y =$
$\pm 3\sqrt{1 - x^2}$ **27c.** This is a graph of a function;
Domain $\{x \mid -1 \le x \le 1\}$; Range $\{y \mid 0 \le y \le 3\}$
27d. This is a graph of a function; Domain
$\{x \mid -1 \le x \le 1\}$; Range $\{y \mid -3 \le y \le 0\}$

Section 10−4 TRY THIS

1. Vertices: (−3, 0), (3, 0); Foci: $(-\sqrt{13}, 0)$,
$(\sqrt{13}, 0)$; Asymptotes: $y = -\frac{2}{3}x, y = \frac{2}{3}x$ **2.** Vertices: (−4, 0), (4, 0); Foci: $(-4\sqrt{2}, 0), (4\sqrt{2}, 0)$;
Asymptotes: $y = x, y = -x$ **3.** Vertices: (0, −5),
(0, 5); Foci: (0, $-\sqrt{34}$), (0, $\sqrt{34}$); Asymptotes: $y =$
$-\frac{5}{3}x, y = \frac{5}{3}x$ **4.** Vertices: (0, 5), (0, −5); Foci:
(0, $-5\sqrt{2}$), (0, $5\sqrt{2}$); Asymptotes: $y = x, y = -x$
5. Center: (1, −2); Vertices: (−4, −2), (6, −2);
Foci: $(1 - \sqrt{29}, -2), (1 + \sqrt{29}, -2)$; Asymptotes:
$y + 2 = -\frac{2}{5}(x - 1), y + 2 = \frac{2}{5}(x - 1)$ **6.** Center:
(−1, 2); Vertices: (−1, −1), (−1, 5); Foci:
(−1, −3), (−1, 7); Asymptotes: $y - 2 = -\frac{3}{4}(x + 1)$,
$y - 2 = \frac{3}{4}(x + 1)$

Exercise Set 10−4

1. Center: (0, 0); Vertices: (−3, 0), (3, 0); Foci:
$(-\sqrt{10}, 0), (\sqrt{10}, 0)$; Asym: $y = -\frac{1}{3}x, y = \frac{1}{3}x$
3. Center: (2, −5); Vertices: (−1, −5), (5, −5);
Foci: $(2 - \sqrt{10}, -5), (2 + \sqrt{10}, -5)$; Asym:
$y + 5 = -\frac{1}{3}(x - 2), y + 5 = \frac{1}{3}(x - 2)$ **5.** Center:
(−1, −3); Vertices: (−1, −5), (−1, −1); Foci:
$(-1, -3 - 2\sqrt{5}), (-1, -3 + 2\sqrt{5})$; Asym: $y + 3 =$
$-\frac{1}{2}(x + 1), y + 3 = \frac{1}{2}(x + 1)$ **7.** Center: (0, 0);
Vertices: (−2, 0), (2, 0); Foci: $(-\sqrt{5}, 0), (\sqrt{5}, 0)$;
Asym: $y = -\frac{1}{2}x, y = \frac{1}{2}x$ **9.** Center: (0, 0); Vertices: (0, −1), (0, 1); Foci: (0, $-\sqrt{5}$), (0, $\sqrt{5}$);
Asym: $y = -\frac{1}{2}x, y = \frac{1}{2}x$ **11.** Center: (0, 0); Vertices: $(-\sqrt{2}, 0), (\sqrt{2}, 0)$; Foci: (−2, 0), (2, 0);
Asym: $y = -x, y = x$ **13.** Center: (1, −2); Vertices: (0, −2), (2, −2); Foci: $(1 - \sqrt{2}, -2)$,

$(1 + \sqrt{2}, -2)$; Asym: $y + 2 = -(x - 1)$, $y + 2 = (x - 1)$ **15.** Center: $(\frac{1}{3}, 3)$; Vertices: $(-\frac{2}{3}, 3)$, $(\frac{4}{3}, 3)$; Foci: $(\frac{1}{3} - \sqrt{37}, 3)$, $(\frac{1}{3} + \sqrt{37}, 3)$; Asym: $y - 3 = -6(x - \frac{1}{3})$, $y - 3 = 6(x - \frac{1}{3})$ **21.** Center: $(1.023, -2.044)$; Vertices: $(2.07, -2.044)$, $(-0.024, -2.044)$; Asym: $y + 2.044 = -(x - 1.023)$, $y + 2.044 = x - 1.023$ **23.** $\frac{x^2}{4} - \frac{y^2}{9} = 1$ **25.** Hyperbola, axis $\overline{AB}$

Section 10−5 TRY THIS

1. Vertex: $(0, 0)$; Focus: $(0, 2)$; Directrix: $y = -2$
2. Vertex: $(0, 0)$; Focus: $(0, \frac{1}{8})$; Directrix: $y = -\frac{1}{8}$
3. Vertex: $(0, 0)$; Focus: $(-\frac{3}{2}, 0)$; Directrix: $x = \frac{3}{2}$
4. $y^2 = 12x$ **5.** $x^2 = 2y$ **6.** $y^2 = -24x$ **7.** $x^2 = -4y$ **8.** Vertex: $(-1, -\frac{1}{2})$; Focus: $(-1, \frac{3}{2})$; Directrix: $y = -\frac{5}{2}$ **9.** Vertex: $(2, -1)$; Focus: $(1, -1)$; Directrix: $x = 3$

Exercise Set 10−5

1. Vertex: $(0, 0)$; Focus: $(0, 2)$; Directrix: $y = -2$
3. Vertex: $(0, 0)$; Focus: $(-\frac{3}{2}, 0)$; Directrix: $x = \frac{3}{2}$
5. Vertex: $(0, 0)$; Focus: $(0, 1)$; Directrix: $y = -1$
7. Vertex: $(0, 0)$; Focus: $(0, \frac{1}{8})$; Directrix: $y = -\frac{1}{8}$
9. $y^2 = 16x$ **11.** $y^2 = -4\sqrt{2}x$ **13.** $(y - 2)^2 = 14(x + \frac{1}{2})$ **15.** Vertex: $(-2, 1)$; Focus: $(-2, -\frac{1}{2})$; Directrix: $y = \frac{5}{2}$ **17.** Vertex: $(-1, -3)$; Focus: $(-1, -\frac{7}{2})$; Directrix: $y = -\frac{5}{2}$ **19.** Vertex: $(0, -2)$; Focus: $(0, -\frac{7}{4})$; Directrix: $y = -\frac{9}{4}$ **21.** Vertex: $(-2, -1)$; Focus: $(-2, -\frac{3}{4})$; Directrix: $y = -\frac{5}{4}$ **23.** Vertex: $(\frac{23}{4}, \frac{1}{2})$; Focus: $(6, \frac{1}{2})$; Directrix: $x = \frac{11}{2}$ **25.** Vertex: $(0, 0)$; Focus: $(0, 2014.0625)$; Directrix: $y = -2014.0625$ **29.** $(x + 1)^2 = -4(y - 2)$ **31.** 10 ft, 11.6 ft, 16.4 ft, 24.4 ft, 35.6 ft, 50 ft

Section 10−6 TRY THIS

1. $(4, 3)$, $(-3, -4)$ **2.** $(4, 7)$, $(-1, 2)$ **3.** $(2, 1)$, $(-4, 4)$ **4.** $(-3, -4)$, $(4, 3)$ **5.** $(4, 7)$, $(-1, 2)$ **6.** $(2, 1)$, $(-4, 4)$ **7.** $(1, -2)$, $(-\frac{5}{7}, \frac{22}{7})$ **8.** 11 and 7 **9.** $l = 12$, $w = 5$

Exercise Set 10−6

1. $(-4, -3)$, $(3, 4)$ **3.** $(4, 5)$, $(0, -3)$ **5.** $(0, 2)$, $(3, 0)$ **7.** $(-2, 1)$ **9.** $(3, 2)$, $(4, \frac{2}{3})$ **11.** $(\frac{7}{3}, \frac{1}{3})$, $(1, -1)$ **13.** $(1, 4)$, $(\frac{11}{4}, -\frac{5}{4})$ **15.** $5, 9$ **17.** 6 cm, 8 cm **19.** 4 in., 5 in. **21.** $\left(\frac{-1 + \sqrt{5}}{2}, \frac{1 + \sqrt{5}}{2}\right)$, $\left(\frac{-1 - \sqrt{5}}{2}, \frac{1 - \sqrt{5}}{2}\right)$ **23.** $(0.965, 4402.33)$, $(-0.965, -4402.33)$

27. $(x - 2)^2 + (y - 3)^2 = 1$ **29.** $l = \sqrt{2 + \sqrt{3}}$, $w = \sqrt{2 - \sqrt{3}}$

Section 10−7 TRY THIS

1. $(-2, 0)$, $(2, 0)$ **2.** $(-4, 0)$, $(4, 0)$ **3.** $(0, -4)$, $(0, 4)$ **4.** $(-2, -3)$, $(-2, 3)$, $(2, -3)$, $(2, 3)$ **5.** $(-3, -2)$, $(-2, -3)$, $(3, 2)$, $(2, 3)$ **6.** $l = 1$ ft, $w = 2$ ft

Exercise Set 10−7

1. $(4, -3)$, $(4, 3)$, $(-5, 0)$ **3.** $(-3, 0)$, $(3, 0)$ **5.** $(-4, -3)$, $(-3, -4)$, $(3, 4)$, $(4, 3)$ **7.** No solution **9.** $(-\sqrt{2}, -\sqrt{14})$, $(-\sqrt{2}, \sqrt{14})$, $(\sqrt{2}, -\sqrt{14})$, $(\sqrt{2}, \sqrt{14})$ **11.** $(-2, -1)$, $(-1, -2)$, $(1, 2)$, $(2, 1)$ **13.** $(-3, -2)$, $(-2, -3)$, $(2, 3)$, $(3, 2)$ **15.** $\left(\frac{5 - 9\sqrt{15}}{20}, \frac{-45 + 3\sqrt{15}}{20}\right)$, $\left(\frac{5 + 9\sqrt{15}}{20}, \frac{-45 - 3\sqrt{15}}{20}\right)$ **17.** $(8.53, 2.53)$, $(8.53, -2.53)$, $(-8.53, 2.53)$, $(-8.53, -2.53)$ **19.** 12, 13 and -12, -13 **21.** $l = \sqrt{3}$ m, $w = 1$ m **23.** 16 ft, 24 ft **25.** $(x + \frac{5}{13})^2 + (y - \frac{32}{13})^2 = \frac{5365}{169}$

Chapter 11

Section 11−1 TRY THIS

1a. Yes **1b.** No **1c.** Yes **2a.** Yes **2b.** Yes **2c.** No **2d.** No **3a.** No **3b.** Yes **3c.** No **4.** $x^3 + 2x^2 - 5x - 6 = (x - 3)(x^2 + 5x + 10) + 24$

Exercise Set 11−1

1. Yes, no, no **3.** Yes, no, yes, yes **5a.** Yes **5b.** No **5c.** No **7a.** Yes **7b.** Yes **7c.** No **9a.** $x^3 + 6x^2 - x - 30 = (x - 2)(x^2 + 8x + 15) + 0$ **9b.** $x^3 + 6x^2 - x - 30 = (x - 3)(x^2 + 9x + 26) + 48$ **11.** $x^3 - 8 = (x + 2)(x^2 - 2x + 4) + (-16)$ **13.** $x^4 + 9x^2 + 20 = (x^2 + 4)(x^2 + 5) + 0$ **15.** $5x^7 - 3x^4 + 2x^2 - 3 = (2x^2 - x + 1)(\frac{5}{2}x^5 + \frac{5}{4}x^4 - \frac{5}{8}x^3 - \frac{39}{16}x^2 - \frac{29}{32}x + \frac{113}{64}) + \frac{171x - 305}{64}$ **17a.** -32 **17b.** -32 **17c.** -65 **17d.** -65 **19a.** -2 **19b.** -2 **21.** All exponents even; yes

Section 11−2 TRY THIS

1. Q: $x^2 + 8x + 15$, R: 0 **2.** Q: $y^2 - y + 1$, R: 0 **3.** 73,120; $-37,292$ **4.** Yes **5.** No **6.** Yes **7.** No **8.** Yes **9a.** Yes **9b.** $x^2 + 8x + 15$ **9c.** $(x - 2)(x + 5)(x + 3)$ **9d.** $2, -5, -3$

Exercise Set 11–2

1. $Q(x) = 2x^3 + x^2 - 3x + 10, R(x) = -42$
3. $Q(x) = x^2 - 4x + 8, R(x) = -24$ **5.** $Q(x) = x^3 + x^2 + x + 1, R(x) = 0$ **7.** $Q(x) = 2x^3 + x^2 + \frac{7}{2}x + \frac{7}{4}, R(x) = -\frac{1}{8}$ **9.** $Q(x) = x^3 + x^2y + xy^2 + y^3, R(x) = 0$ **11.** $P(1) = 0; P(-2) = -60; P(3) = 0$
13. $P(20) = 5,935,988; P(-3) = -772$ **15.** Yes; no
17. No; no **19.** No **21.** Yes **23.** Yes **25a.** Yes
25b. $x^2 + 3x + 2$ **25c.** $(x - 1)(x + 2)(x + 1)$
25d. $1, -2, -1$ **27.** $P(x) = (x - 1)(x + 2)(x + 3);$
$1, -2, -3$ **29.** $P(x) = (x - 2)(x - 5)(x + 1); 2, 5, -1$ **31.** $P(x) = (x - 2)(x - 3)(x + 4); 2, 3, -4$
33. $P(x) = (x - 1)(x - 2)(x - 3)(x + 5); 1, 2, 3, -5$
35. $-5 < x < 1$ or $x > 2$ **37.** 4 **39.** None
41a. -485.1587 **41b.** -485.1588

Section 11–3 TRY THIS

1. -7 (multiplicity 2), 3 (multiplicity 1) **2.** 4 (multiplicity 2), 3 (multiplicity 2) **3.** 1 (multiplicity 1), -1 (multiplicity 1) **4.** $(x + 1)(x - 2)(x - 5) = x^3 - 6x^2 + 3x + 10$ **5.** $x^2(x + 2)^3 = x^5 + 6x^4 + 12x^3 + 8x^2$ **6.** $7 + 2i, 3 - \sqrt{5}$ **7.** $x^4 - 6x^3 + 11x^2 - 10x + 2$ **8.** $x^3 - 2x^2 + 4x - 8$ **9.** $-i, -2, 1$

Exercise Set 11–3

1. -3 (multiplicity 2); 1 (multiplicity 1) **3.** 3 (multiplicity 2); -4 (multiplicity 3); 0 (multiplicity 4)
5. 2 (multiplicity 2); 3 (multiplicity 2) **7.** $x^3 - 6x^2 - x + 30$ **9.** $x^3 - 2x^2 + x - 2$ **11.** $x^3 - 7x^2 + 17x - 15$ **13.** $x^3 - \sqrt{3}x^2 - 2x + 2\sqrt{3}$, No
15. $x^4 - 10x^3 + 25x^2$ **17.** $x^4 - 3x^3 - 7x^2 + 15x + 18$ **19.** $5 - i, 2i$ **21.** $-3 - 4i, 4 + \sqrt{5}$ **23.** $1 + i$
25. $x^3 - 4x^2 + 6x - 4$ **27.** $x^3 + 2x^2 + 9x + 18$
29. $x^4 - 6x^3 + 11x^2 - 10x + 2$ **31.** $x^4 + 4x^2 - 45$
33. $x^4 - 4x^3 + 9x^2 + 8x - 22$ **35.** $i, 3, 2$
37. $-2i, 2, -2$ **39.** $2 + i, 2 - i$ **41.** $-1 + i\sqrt{3}, -1 - i\sqrt{3}$ **43.** $\sqrt{3}, 1 + 3i, 1 - 3i$ **45.** $4, i, -i$
47. $i, -i, 1 + \sqrt{2}, 1 - \sqrt{2}$

Section 11–4 TRY THIS

1. $-1, 3, -3$ **2.** $1, -1, 2, -2$ **3.** $1, -1, \frac{1}{2}, -\frac{1}{2}, 3, -3, \frac{3}{2}, -\frac{3}{2}$ **4.** $-3, \frac{1}{2}$ **5.** $3 + \sqrt{10}, 3 - \sqrt{10}$
6. $1, -1, 2, -2, 4, -4, 7, -7, 14, -14, 28, -28$
7. $1, -1$ **8.** $1, -1, 2, -2, 4, -4, 7, -7, 14, -14, 28, -28$ **9.** All coefficients of $P(x)$ are positive. When any positive number is substituted in $P(x)$, we get a positive value, never 0. **10.** -7 **11.** $2i, -2i$
12a. All coefficients of $P(x)$ are positive. **12b.** None
13a. None **13b.** $\dfrac{-3 + i\sqrt{3}}{2}, \dfrac{-3 - i\sqrt{3}}{2}$, Since $x^2 + 3x + 3$ is quadratic, the quadratic formula can be used.

Exercise Set 11–4

1. $1, -1$ **3.** $\pm(1, \frac{1}{3}, \frac{1}{5}, \frac{1}{15}, 2, \frac{2}{3}, \frac{2}{5}, \frac{2}{15})$ **5.** $-3, \sqrt{2}, -\sqrt{2}$ **7.** $1, -\frac{1}{5}, 2i, -2i$ **9.** $-1, -2, 3 + \sqrt{13}, 3 - \sqrt{13}$ **11.** $1, -1, -3$ **13.** $-2, 1 + i\sqrt{3}, 1 - i\sqrt{3}$ **15.** $\frac{3}{4}, i, -i$ **17.** $1, 2, -2$ **19.** No rational **21.** No rational **23.** No rational **25a.** 2 (multiplicity 2), -3 (multiplicity 1) **25b.** $1, -1, \frac{2}{3}, -\frac{1}{2}$ **25c.** $\frac{1}{2}$ **25d.** $\frac{3}{4}$ **27.** 5 cm **29.** 5 cm

Section 11–5 TRY THIS

1. 1 **2.** 5, 3, or 1 **3.** 2 or 0 **4.** 2 or 0 **5.** 1
6. 0 **7-8.** Answers may vary. **7.** 2 or 3 **8.** 75
9. -4 **10.** -2

Exercise Set 11–5

1. 3 or 1 **3.** 0 **5.** 2 or 0 **7.** 0 **9.** 3 or 1
11. 2 or 0 **13-19.** Answers may vary. **13.** 3
15. 4 **17.** -1 **19.** -3 **21.** 3 or 1 positive; 1 negative; upper bound 2; lower bound -3 **23.** 1 positive; 1 negative; 2 nonreal; upper bound 2; lower bound -2 **25.** 2 or 0 positive; 2 or 0 negative; upper bound 4; lower bound -3 **27.** 0 positive; 0 negative; 4 nonreal

Section 11–6 TRY THIS

2b. $0.7, -0.5, 2.9$

Exercise Set 11–6

7. $-1, 2$ **9.** 2.2 **11.** No real solution **13.** $\pm 1.4, \pm 2$ **15.** $1, \pm 1.4$ **17.** 0.75 **19.** -1.27

Chapter 12

Section 12–1 TRY THIS

1. $\{(1, 0), (5, -2), (-2, 5)\}$ **2.** $x = y^2 + 4$ **3.** Yes
4. No **5.** $g^{-1}(x) = x - 2$ **6.** $g^{-1}(x) = \frac{1}{5}(x - 2)$
7. $f^{-1}(x) = x^2 - 1$ **8.** $f^{-1}(f(579)) = 579,$
$f(f^{-1}(-83,479)) = -83,479$

Exercise Set 12–1

1. $\{(1, 0), (6, 5), (-4, -2)\}$ **3.** $\{(-1, -1), (-4, -3)\}$
5. $x = 3y + 5$ **7.** $x = 5y^2 - 4$ **9.** $2y^2 + 5x^2 = 4$
11. $y \cdot x = -5$ **13.** No **15.** Yes **17.** Yes
19. Yes **21.** Yes **23.** No **25.** $f^{-1}(x) = x + 1$
27. $f^{-1}(x) = x - 4$ **29.** $f^{-1}(x) = x - 8$
31. $f^{-1}(x) = \frac{x - 5}{2}$ **33.** $f^{-1}(x) = \frac{x + 1}{3}$
35. $f^{-1}(x) = 2(x - 2)$ **37.** $f^{-1}(x) = x^2 + 1$

39. $f^{-1}(x) = x^2 - 2$ **41.** $5, -12$ **43.** 489,
$-17,422$ **49.** x, x **51.** $x^2 + 6x + 9$; $x^2 + 3$
53. $12x^2 - 12x + 5$; $6x^2 + 3$ **55.** $x^4 - 2x^2$; $x^4 - 2x^2$

Section 12–2 TRY THIS

1a. R **1b.** $\{x \mid x > 0\}$ **1c.** 1 **1d.** 3.3 **4.** Domain:
$\{x \mid x > 0\}$; range: R **5.** Domain: $\{x \mid x > 0\}$; range: R

Exercise Set 12–2

9. R **11.** 1 **29.** $\{x \mid x > 0\}$ **31.** $\{x \mid x > 0\}$
33. $\{x \mid x \neq 0\}$ **35.** π^5

Section 12–3 TRY THIS

1. $\log_6 1 = 0$ **2.** $\log_{10} 0.001 = -3$ **3.** $\log_{16} 2 = \frac{1}{4}$
4. $\log_{6/5} \frac{25}{36} = -2$ **5.** $2^5 = 32$ **6.** $10^3 = 1000$
7. $10^{-2} = 0.01$ **8.** $(\sqrt{5})^2 = 5$ **9.** 10,000 **10.** 3
11. 4 **12.** -2 **13.** 3 **14.** 42 **15.** 37 **16.** 3.2

Exercise Set 12–3

1. $3 = \log_{10} 1000$ **3.** $\frac{1}{3} = \log_8 2$ **5.** $-3 = \log_5 \frac{1}{125}$
7. $0.3010 = \log_{10} 2$ **9.** $-b = \log_a c$ **11.** $7^h = 10$
13. $6^1 = 6$ **15.** $10^{-2} = 0.01$ **17.** $10^{0.4771} = 3$
19. 9 **21.** 4 **23.** $\frac{1}{2}$ **25.** 2 **27.** 3 **29.** 3
31. 4 **33.** 4 **35.** 1 **37.** 4 **39.** 9
41. $\{x \mid x \geq 0\}$ **43.** $\{x \mid x < 1\}$ **45.** $\emptyset$

Section 12–4 TRY THIS

1a. $\log_a M + \log_a N$ **1b.** $\log_5 25 + \log_5 5$
2a. $\log_3 35$ **2b.** $\log_a CABIN$ **3.** $5 \log_7 4$
4. $\frac{1}{2} \log_a 5$ **5a.** $\log_a M - \log_a N$ **5b.** $\log_c 1 -$
$\log_c 4$ **6.** $\log_{10} 4 + \log_{10} \pi - \frac{1}{2} \log_{10} 23$
7. $\frac{1}{2}[3 \log_a z - \log_a x - \log_a y]$ **8.** $\log_a \frac{x^5 \sqrt[4]{z}}{y}$
9a. 0.954 **9b.** 0.1505 **9c.** 0.1003 **9d.** 0.176
9e. 1.585 **10.** 1 **11.** 0 **12.** 1

Exercise Set 12–4

1. $\log_2 32 + \log_2 8$ **3.** $\log_4 64 + \log_4 16$
5. $\log_c B + \log_c x$ **7.** $\log_a (6 \cdot 70)$ **9.** $\log_c (k \cdot y)$
11. $5 \log_b t$ **13.** $\log_a 67 - \log_a 5$ **15.** $\log_b 3 -$
$\log_b 4$ **17.** $\log_a 5 + \log_a x + 4 \log_a y + 3 \log_a z$
19. $\log_a \frac{\sqrt[3]{x^2}\sqrt{y}}{y}$ **21.** $\log_a \frac{2x^4}{y^3}$ **23.** $\log_a \frac{\sqrt{a}}{x}$
25. 0.602 **27.** 1.699 **29.** 1.778 **31.** -0.088
33. 1.954 **35.** -0.602 **37.** False **39.** False
41. False **43.** $\frac{1}{2}$ **45.** $\sqrt{7}$ **47.** $-2, 0$ **49.** -2

Section 12–5 TRY THIS

1. 16 **2.** 8 **3.** 5 **4.** 2 **5.** 9 **6a.** 0.4969
6b. 0.9996 **6c.** 0.6021 **7a.** 5.74 **7b.** 1.00

7c. 3.62 **8.** $0.4609 + 2$ **9.** $0.4609 + (-4)$
10. 4.8312 **11.** 5.9504 **12.** 1.6618 **13.** 64,100
14. 64,100 **15.** 8560 **16.** 0.000425 **17.** 0.0105

Exercise Set 12–5

1. 0.3909 **3.** 0.7251 **5.** 0.5705 **7.** 0.0294
9. 0.8007 **11.** 2.24 **13.** 1.38 **15.** 8.30
17. 6.34 **19.** 9.14 **21.** 7.34 **23.** 3.9405
25. 1.3139 **27.** 1.9657 **29.** 5.7952
31. $8.8463 - 10$ **33.** $6.3345 - 10$
35. $7.5403 - 10$ **37.** 2330 **39.** 18 **41.** 0.613
43. 25.2 **45.** 0.00973 **47.** 0.000613 **49.** 6.34
51. 0.613 **53.** 2.5378 **55.** 4.754264
57. -0.321371 **59.** 78,397,100 **61.** 0.000583

Section 12–6 TRY THIS

1. 3.6592 **2.** $8.3779 - 10$ **3.** 2856 **4.** 0.0005956

Exercise Set 12–6

1. 1.6194 **3.** 0.4689 **5.** 2.8130 **7.** $9.1538 - 10$
9. $7.6291 - 10$ **11.** $9.2494 - 10$ **13.** 2.7786
15. 2.9032 **17.** 224.5 **19.** 14.53 **21.** 70,030
23. 0.09245 **25.** 0.5343 **27.** 0.007295
29. $9.8445 - 10$ **31.** 773.2

Section 12–7 TRY THIS

1. 2.8076 **2.** 2.9999 **3.** 3 **4.** 125 **5.** 8.75
6. 2 **7.** 10 years **8.** 34 decibels **9.** 60 decibels
10. 8.4

Exercise Set 12–7

1. 3 **3.** 3.3223 **5.** $\frac{5}{2}$ **7.** $-3, -1$ **9.** 1.4036
11. 2.7093 **13.** 3.6064 **15.** 5.6467 **17.** 1
19. 1 **21.** $\sqrt{41}$ **23.** $1, 10^{16}$ **25.** $\pm\frac{\sqrt{2}}{4}$
27. 22.5 **29.** 64 decibels **31.** 120 decibels
33. 8.25 **35.** 10^7 times I_0 **37.** 7.8 **39.** $\pm 2\sqrt{6}$
41. $25, \frac{1}{25}$ **43.** $100, \frac{1}{100}$ **45.** $-\frac{1}{2}$ **47.** $t =$
$\dfrac{\log_b y - \log_b k}{a}$ **49.** $n = \log_v c - \log_v P$, or $\log_v \frac{c}{P}$
51. $y = xa^{2x}$ **53.** $100, \frac{1}{10}$ **55.** $\{x \mid x \geq 1\}$ for bases
a such that $a > 1$ **57.** 2^{10} **59.** 88 **61.** $(0, \frac{3}{2})$

Section 12–8 TRY THIS

3. 0.693147 **4.** 4.605170 **5.** -2.599375
6. -0.000100 **7a.** 0.08 **7b.** 275,580
8. 3.5 grams **9.** 3 **10.** 4.7385 **11.** 0.4343
12. 6.937 **13.** -0.783 **14.** 2.8076

Exercise Set 12–8

7. 0.6313 **9.** -3.9739 **11.** 0.7561 **13.** -1.5465
15. 8.4119 **17.** -7.4875 **19.** -2.5258

21. 13.7953   **23.** $k = 0.0065$; $P = 616,040$
25. 125 grams   **27.** 248,000 years   **29a.** 1850 years
29b. 3600 years   **31.** 2.1610   **33.** -0.1544

35. 2.4849   **37.** $t = \dfrac{\ln P - \ln P_0}{k}$ **41.** e^{π}

45. $N = N_0 2^{-\frac{t}{H}}$

Chapter 13

Section 13-1 TRY THIS

1a. 1, 3, 5   **1b.** 67   **2.** $-1, 4, -9, 16$ **3-6.** Answers may vary.   **3.** $2n$ **4.** n **5.** n^3 **6.** 2^{n-1}
7. $S_1 = \frac{1}{2}$, $S_2 = \frac{3}{4}$, $S_3 = \frac{7}{8}$, $S_4 = \frac{15}{16}$ **8.** $3 + 2\frac{1}{2} + 2\frac{1}{3}$
9. $5^0 + 5^1 + 5^2 + 5^3 + 5^4$ **10-11.** Answers may vary.   **10.** $\displaystyle\sum_{k=1}^{5} 2k$ **11.** $\displaystyle\sum_{k=1}^{n} (-1)^{k+1}(k+1)$

Exercise Set 13-1

1. 4, 7, 10, 13; 31; 46   **3.** $\frac{1}{2}, \frac{2}{3}, \frac{3}{4}, \frac{4}{5}; \frac{10}{11}; \frac{15}{16}$
5. $-1, 0, 3, 8; 80; 195$ **7.** $2, 2\frac{1}{2}, 3\frac{1}{3}, 4\frac{1}{4}; 10\frac{1}{10}; 15\frac{1}{15}$ **9-15.** Answers may vary.   **9.** $2n - 1$
11. $\frac{n+1}{n+2}$ **13.** $3^{n/2}$ **15.** $-(3n - 2)$ **17.** $\frac{1}{2} + \frac{1}{4} + \frac{1}{6} + \frac{1}{8} + \frac{1}{10}$ **19.** $2^0 + 2^1 + 2^2 + 2^3 + 2^4 + 2^5$
21. $\log 7 + \log 8 + \log 9 + \log 10$ **23-27.** Answers may vary.   **23.** $\displaystyle\sum_{k=1}^{6} \frac{k}{k+1}$ **25.** $\displaystyle\sum_{k=1}^{6} (-1)^k 2^k$
27. $\displaystyle\sum_{k=2}^{n} (-1)^k k^2$ **29.** $\frac{3}{2}, \frac{3}{2}, \frac{3}{2}, \frac{3}{2}, \frac{3}{2}$ **31.** 0, 0.693, 1.792, 3.178, 4.787   **33.** 1.645751

Section 13-2 TRY THIS

1. $a_1 = 2, d = 1$ **2.** $a_1 = 1, d = 3$ **3.** $a_1 = 19, d = -5$ **4.** $a_1 = 10, d = -\frac{1}{2}$ **5.** 50   **6.** 75th
7. 17   **8.** 13   **9.** $a_1 = 7, d = 12$; 7, 19, 31, 43, ...
10. 3, 10, 17, 24   **11.** 20,100   **12.** 225   **13.** 455

Exercise Set 13-2

1. $a_1 = 2, d = 5$ **3.** $a_1 = 7, d = -4$ **5.** $a_1 = \frac{3}{2}, d = \frac{3}{4}$ **7.** 46   **9.** -41 **11.** 27th   **13.** 102nd
15. 101   **17.** 5   **19.** 28   **21.** 8, 5, 2, $-1, -4$
23. 2, 7, 12, 17, 22   **25.** 670   **27.** 2550   **29.** 990
31. 432   **33.** 855   **35.** 465   **37.** n^2 **39.** 16 means, $d = \frac{49}{17}$ **41.** $a_1 = p - 5q, d = 3p + 2q$
43. 51,679.65

Section 13-3 TRY THIS

1. 5   **2.** -3 **3.** $-\frac{1}{4}$ **4.** $\frac{1}{3}$ **5.** -9375 **6.** 10 or -10 **7.** \$547.05   **8.** 11,718   **9.** $\frac{341}{256}$ **10.** 363

Exercise Set 13-3

1. 2   **3.** -1 **5.** $\frac{1}{x}$ **7.** 243   **9.** 1250   **11.** 3, 12, 48   **13.** \$1113.92   **15.** 762   **17.** $\frac{547}{18}$ **19.** $\frac{1-x^8}{1-x}$
21. $\frac{63}{32}$ **23.** 21,844   **25.** $\frac{1}{256}$ ft   **27a.** \$5866.60
27b. \$1296.05   **29.** $\frac{1-x^n}{1-x}$ **33.** \$1,529,908.60

Section 13-4 TRY THIS

1. $1, \frac{1}{2}, \frac{3}{4}, \frac{5}{8}, \frac{11}{16}$ **2.** $\frac{2}{3}$ **3.** No   **4.** No   **5.** Yes
6. $\frac{3}{2}$ **7.** $\frac{16}{5}$

Exercise Set 13-4

1. 2, No   **3.** $\frac{1}{3}$, Yes   **5.** 0.1, Yes   **7.** $-\frac{1}{5}$, Yes
9. 8   **11.** 2   **13.** $\frac{160}{9}$ **15.** $\frac{7}{9}$ **17.** $\frac{7}{33}$ **19.** $\frac{170}{33}$
21. 24 m   **23.** $2\frac{3}{4}$

Section 13-5 TRY THIS

1. 6, 27   **2.** 120   **3.** 6   **4.** 120   **5.** 720   **6.** 720
7. 362,880   **8.** 18!   **9.** $10 \cdot 9!$ **10.** $11 \cdot 10 \cdot 9 \cdot 8!$

Exercise Set 13-5

1. 24, 256   **3.** 720   **5.** 336   **7.** 720   **9.** 24
11. 5040   **13.** 720   **15.** 40,320   **17.** 120   **19.** 1
21. $9 \cdot 8!$ **23.** $a \cdot (a - 1)!$
25. $27 \cdot 26 \cdot 25 \cdot 24 \cdot 23 \cdot 22!$
27. $9 \cdot 9 \cdot 8 \cdot 7 \cdot 6 \cdot 5 \cdot 4$, or 544,320

Section 13-6 TRY THIS

1. 210   **2.** 5040   **3.** 56   **4.** 55,440   **5.** 151,200
6. 144   **7.** 26^5 **8a.** 2652   **8b.** 2704

Exercise Set 13-6

1. 24   **3.** 604,800   **5.** 380   **7.** 336   **9.** 120, 60
11. 360   **13.** 20,160   **15.** 1296, 360   **17.** 11,880
19. 648, 180   **21.** 648, 180   **23.** $80 \cdot 26 \cdot 9999 = 20,797,920$ **25.** 11   **27.** 9   **29.** $n - 1$

Section 13-7 TRY THIS

1a. 1   **1b.** 4   **1c.** 6   **1d.** 4   **1e.** 1   **2.** 45
3. 45   **4.** 21   **5.** 21   **6.** 792   **7.** 6160
8. $\binom{9}{0} + \binom{9}{1} + \binom{9}{2} + \cdots + \binom{9}{9}$ or 512

Exercise Set 13-7

1. 126   **3.** 1225   **5.** 495   **7.** $\frac{n(n-1)(n-2)}{6}$
9. 8855   **11.** 72   **13.** 28, 56   **15.** 1200

17. $\binom{58}{6} \cdot \binom{42}{4}$ 19. 56   21. 4   23. $\frac{n(n-1)}{2}$;
$\frac{n(n-3)}{2}$

Section 13-8 TRY THIS
1. $-1512x^5$ 2. $8064y^{10}$ 3. $x^{10} - 5x^8 +$
$10x^6 - 10x^4 + 5x^2 - 1$ 4. $16x^4 + 32\frac{x^3}{y} +$
$24\frac{x^2}{y^2} + 8\frac{x}{y^3} + \frac{1}{y^4}$ 5. 2^{50}

Exercise Set 13-8
1. $15a^4b^2$ 3. $-745,472a^3$ 5. $-1,959,552u^5v^{10}$
7. $m^5 + 5m^4n + 10m^3n^2 + 10m^2n^3 + 5mn^4 + n^5$
9. $x^{10} - 15x^8y + 90x^6y^2 - 270x^4y^3 + 405x^2y^4 -$
$243y^5$ 11. $\binom{n}{0} - \binom{n}{1} + \binom{n}{2} - \binom{n}{3} + \cdots +$
$\binom{n}{n}(-1)^n$ 13. $99 + 70\sqrt{2}$ 15. 128   17. 2^{26}
19. $-7 - 4\sqrt{2}i$ 21. $\sum_{r=0}^{n} \binom{n}{r}(-1)^r a^{n-r} b^r$
23. -3 25. 5

Section 13-9 TRY THIS
1. $\frac{1}{2}$ 2. $\frac{11}{850}$ 3. $\frac{1}{6}$

Exercise Set 13-9
1. $\frac{1}{4}$ 3. $\frac{1}{13}$ 5. $\frac{1}{2}$ 7. $\frac{2}{13}$ 9. $\frac{2}{7}$ 11. 0
13. $\frac{11}{4165}$ 15. $\frac{28}{65}$ 17. $\frac{1}{18}$ 19. $\frac{30}{323}$
21a. $13 \cdot 48 = 624$ 21b. $\frac{624}{2,598,950}$

Chapter 14

Section 14-1 TRY THIS
1. 3×2 2. 2×2 3. 3×3 4. 1×2 5. 2×1
6. 1×1 7a. $\begin{bmatrix} -2 & -6 \\ 13 & 0 \end{bmatrix}$ 7b. $\begin{bmatrix} -2 & -6 \\ 13 & 0 \end{bmatrix}$
8. $\mathbf{A} + \mathbf{O} = \begin{bmatrix} 4 & -3 \\ 5 & 8 \end{bmatrix} = \mathbf{O} + \mathbf{A} = \mathbf{A}$ 9. $\begin{bmatrix} -1 & 4 & -7 \\ -2 & -4 & 8 \end{bmatrix}$
10. $\begin{bmatrix} -6 & 6 \\ 1 & -4 \\ -7 & 5 \end{bmatrix}$ 11. $\begin{bmatrix} -2 & 1 & -5 \\ -6 & -4 & 3 \end{bmatrix}$ 12. $\begin{bmatrix} 0 & 0 & 0 \\ 0 & 0 & 0 \end{bmatrix}$
13. $\begin{bmatrix} -1 & 4 & -7 \\ -2 & -4 & 8 \end{bmatrix}$

Section 14-2 TRY THIS
1. $\begin{bmatrix} 5 & -10 & 5x \\ 20 & 5y & 5 \\ 0 & -25 & 5x^2 \end{bmatrix}$ 2. $\begin{bmatrix} t & -t & 4t & xt \\ yt & 3t & -2t & yt \\ t & 4t & -5t & yt \end{bmatrix}$

3. $[-13]$ 4. $[-2x + y]$ 5. $\begin{bmatrix} 12 \\ 13 \\ 5 \\ 16 \end{bmatrix}$ 6. $\begin{bmatrix} 0 & 26 \\ -8 & 3 \\ -13 & 33 \\ -7 & 32 \end{bmatrix}$
7. $[8 \ 5 \ 4]$ 8. $\mathbf{AB} = \begin{bmatrix} 2 & 8 & 6 \\ -29 & -34 & -7 \end{bmatrix}$; $\mathbf{BA}$ not
possible   9. $\mathbf{AB} = \begin{bmatrix} -2 & 32 \\ 4 & 16 \end{bmatrix}$; $\mathbf{BA} = \begin{bmatrix} 8 & -13 \\ -16 & 6 \end{bmatrix}$
10. $\begin{bmatrix} 3 & 4 & -2 \\ 2 & -2 & 5 \\ 6 & 7 & -1 \end{bmatrix} \begin{bmatrix} x \\ y \\ z \end{bmatrix} = \begin{bmatrix} 5 \\ 3 \\ 0 \end{bmatrix}$

Section 14-3 TRY THIS
1a. $\begin{bmatrix} 1 & 0 & 0 \\ 0 & 1 & 0 \\ 0 & 0 & 1 \end{bmatrix} = \mathbf{I}$ 1b. $\mathbf{I}$ 1c. Both equal $\mathbf{I}$
2. $\mathbf{A}^{-1} = \begin{bmatrix} -\frac{1}{2} & \frac{1}{2} & \frac{1}{2} \\ 1 & 0 & -1 \\ \frac{3}{2} & -\frac{1}{2} & -\frac{1}{2} \end{bmatrix}$ 3. $\mathbf{A}^{-1} = \begin{bmatrix} 2 & -\frac{5}{2} \\ -1 & \frac{3}{2} \end{bmatrix}$
4a. $\begin{bmatrix} 4 & -2 \\ 1 & 5 \end{bmatrix} \begin{bmatrix} x \\ y \end{bmatrix} = \begin{bmatrix} -1 \\ 1 \end{bmatrix}$ 4b. $\mathbf{A} = \begin{bmatrix} 4 & -2 \\ 1 & 5 \end{bmatrix}$
4c. $\mathbf{A}^{-1} = \frac{1}{22} \begin{bmatrix} 5 & 2 \\ -1 & 4 \end{bmatrix}$ 4d. $x = -\frac{3}{22}, y = \frac{5}{22}$

Chapter 15

Section 15-1 TRY THIS
1. $\frac{4}{5}, \frac{3}{5}, \frac{4}{3}$ 2. $12\sqrt{2}$ 3. 1.33, 1.25, 1.67   4. $\sin \theta = \frac{15}{17}$, $\tan \theta = \frac{15}{8}$, $\csc \theta = \frac{17}{15}$, $\sec \theta = \frac{17}{8}$, $\cot \theta = \frac{8}{15}$

Exercise Set 15-1
1. $\frac{7}{25}, \frac{24}{25}, \frac{7}{24}$ 3. $\frac{8}{17}, \frac{15}{17}, \frac{8}{15}$ 5. $a = 3$ 7. $b = 9\sqrt{3}$
9. 3.43, 1.04, 3.57   11. 1.88, 1.13, 2.13
13. $\sin \theta = \frac{\sqrt{3}}{2}$, $\cos \theta = \frac{1}{2}$, $\cot \theta = \frac{\sqrt{3}}{3}$, $\sec \theta = 2$, $\csc \theta = \frac{2\sqrt{3}}{3}$ 15. $\cos \theta = \frac{\sqrt{3}}{2}$, $\tan \theta = \frac{\sqrt{3}}{3}$, $\cot \theta = \sqrt{3}$, $\sec \theta = \frac{2\sqrt{3}}{3}$, $\csc \theta = 2$ 17. $\sin \theta = \frac{1}{2}$, $\cos \theta = \frac{\sqrt{3}}{2}$, $\tan \theta = \frac{\sqrt{3}}{3}$, $\cot \theta = \sqrt{3}$, $\sec \theta = \frac{2\sqrt{3}}{3}$, $\csc \theta = 2$
19. $\sin \theta = \frac{\sqrt{2}}{2}$, $\cos \theta = \frac{\sqrt{2}}{2}$, $\tan \theta = 1$, $\cot \theta = 1$, $\sec \theta = \sqrt{2}$, $\csc \theta = \sqrt{2}$ 21. $60°$ 23. $5\sqrt{3}$

Section 15-2 TRY THIS
1. First   2. Third   3. Fourth   4. Third   5. First

6. First **7.** $-\frac{1}{2}, \frac{\sqrt{3}}{2}, -\frac{\sqrt{3}}{3}$ **8.** Cosine and secant values are positive, the other four function values are negative. **9.** $\sin 180° = 0$, $\cos 180° = -1$, $\tan 180° = 0$, $\sin 270° = -1$, $\cos 270° = 0$, $\tan 270°$ is undefined
10. $30°$ **11.** $30°$ **12.** $\sin -765° = -\frac{\sqrt{2}}{2}$, $\cos -765° = \frac{\sqrt{2}}{2}$, $\tan -765° = -1$

Exercise Set 15-2

1. First **3.** Third **5.** First **7.** Second **9.** Second
11. Fourth **13.** $-\frac{3}{5}, -\frac{4}{5}, \frac{3}{4}$ **15.** $-\frac{3}{5}, \frac{4}{5}, -\frac{3}{4}$
17. $\frac{\sqrt{3}}{2}, -\frac{1}{2}, -\sqrt{3}$ **19.** All function values are positive. **21.** The cosine and secant function values are positive, the other four are negative. **23.** All function values are positive. **27.** $30°$ **29.** $45°$ **31.** $45°$
33. 0 **35.** Undefined **37.** Undefined **39.** $-\frac{\sqrt{2}}{2}$
41. $-\frac{\sqrt{3}}{2}$ **43.** $\frac{\sqrt{3}}{3}$ **45.** $-\sqrt{2}$ **47.** 1 **49.** $-\frac{\sqrt{3}}{2}$
51. $\sqrt{3}$ **53.** $\frac{\sqrt{2}}{2}$ **55.** $-\sqrt{3}$ **57.** $\sin 60° = 0.866$, $\cos 60° = 0.500$, $\tan 60° = 1.732$, $\csc 60° = 1.155$, $\sec 60° = 2.000$, $\cot 60° = 0.577$ **59.** $\sin 225° = -0.707$, $\cos 225° = -0.707$, $\tan 225° = 1.000$, $\csc 225° = -1.414$, $\sec 225° = -1.414$, $\cot 225° = 1.000$ **61.** $\sin \theta = \frac{4}{7}$, $\cos \theta = -\frac{\sqrt{33}}{7}$, $\tan \theta = -\frac{4\sqrt{33}}{33}$, $\csc \theta = \frac{7}{4}$, $\sec \theta = -\frac{7\sqrt{33}}{33}$, $\cot \theta = -\frac{\sqrt{33}}{4}$
63. $-\frac{2}{3}$ **65.** $\frac{\sqrt{5}}{2}$ **67.** $-\frac{3}{2}$

Section 15-3 TRY THIS

1. $\frac{5}{4}\pi$ **2.** $\frac{5}{3}\pi$ **3.** $-\frac{7}{4}\pi$ **4.** $240°$ **5.** $450°$
6. $-144°$ **7.** 2 **8.** $\sqrt{3}$ **9.** $\sqrt{2}$ **10.** 0.2644
11. 0.4699 **12.** 0.6383 **13.** 0.6264 **14.** 1.900
15. $21°15'$ **16.** $31°47'$

Exercise Set 15-3

1. $\frac{\pi}{6} \approx 0.52$ **3.** $\frac{5\pi}{9} \approx 1.74$ **5.** $\frac{5\pi}{12} \approx 1.31$ **7.** $\frac{2\pi}{3} \approx 2.10$ **9.** $-\frac{16\pi}{9} \approx -5.58$ **11.** $-\frac{17\pi}{36} \approx -1.48$
13. $57.3°$ **15.** $1440°$ **17.** $135°$ **19.** $\sqrt{3}$
21. $\frac{2\sqrt{3}}{3}$ **23.** 1 **25.** $\frac{\sqrt{3}}{3}$ **27.** 0 **29.** 0.6648
31. 0.3118 **33.** 1.550 **35.** 1.063 **37.** -0.3987
39. -0.1161 **41.** 0.5977 **43.** 0.1642
45. 0.7186 **47.** $22°44'$ **49.** $69°17'$ **51.** $14°34'$
53. 0.0707222π **55.** 0.4103888π **57.** $134.54140°$
59. $401.56050°$ **61.** $-2543.4°$ **63.** $-216.9°$
65. 0.8441 **67.** 0.5812 **69.** 0.1407 **71.** 0.6255
73. $\frac{15\pi}{9} \approx 5.233$ **75.** Third **77.** Fourth **79.** $\frac{\pi}{6}$

81. $\frac{\pi}{3}$ **83.** 0.3420 **85.** 2.747 **87.** $\frac{\sqrt{3}}{3}$ **89.** $\sqrt{3}$

Section 15-4 TRY THIS

1. R **2.** $\{y \mid -1 \le y \le 1\}$ **3.** 1 **4.** Odd **5.** 2π
6. $\{x \mid x \ge 1 \text{ or } x \le -1\}$

Exercise Set 15-4

5. R **7.** 2π **9.** Yes **11.** 4 **13.** 1 **19.** The set of all real numbers except πk, k an integer **21.** Yes, π
23. The set of all real numbers except $k\pi$, k an integer
25. Yes, 2π **33a.** $\{x \mid x = \frac{\pi}{2} + 2k\pi, k \text{ an integer}\}$
33b. $\{x \mid x = \frac{3\pi}{2} + 2k\pi, k \text{ an integer}\}$
35. $\{x \mid x = k\pi, k \text{ an integer}\}$ **39.** The sine and tangent functions; the cosine and cotangent functions.
41. $\{x \mid -\frac{\pi}{2} + 2k\pi < x < \frac{\pi}{2} + 2\pi k, k \text{ an integer}\}$

Section 15-5 TRY THIS

1. $\cos \theta = \cot \theta \cdot \sin \theta$ **2.** $\sin^2 \theta \equiv 1 - \cos^2 \theta$
3. $\sin \theta \equiv \pm\sqrt{1 - \cos^2 \theta}$ **4.** $\sec^2 \theta - \tan^2 \theta \equiv 1$; $\tan^2 \theta \equiv \sec^2 \theta - 1$ **5.** $\cos\left(0 - \frac{\pi}{2}\right) = \cos -\frac{\pi}{2} = 0 = \sin 0$ **6.** $\cot\left(\theta + \frac{\pi}{2}\right) \equiv -\tan \theta$

Exercise Set 15-5

1. $\sin^2 \theta$ **3.** $\cos \theta \equiv \frac{\sin \theta}{\tan \theta}$ **5.** $\csc \theta \equiv \pm\sqrt{1 + \cot^2 \theta}$
7. $\cot \theta \equiv \pm\sqrt{\csc^2 \theta - 1}$ **13.** $\sin 25° = 0.4226$, $\cos 25° = 0.9063$, $\tan 25° = 0.4663$, $\cot 25° = 2.145$, $\sec 25° = 1.103$, $\csc 25° = 2.366$ **15.** $\sin 38° = 0.6157$, $\cos 38° = 0.7880$, $\tan 38° = 0.7813$, $\cot 38° = 1.280$, $\sec 38° = 1.269$, $\csc 38° = 1.624$
17. $\tan\left(\theta - \frac{\pi}{2}\right) \equiv -\cot \theta$ **19.** $\sec\left(\frac{\pi}{2} - \theta\right) \equiv \csc \theta$
21. $\sin \theta \equiv \cos\left(\frac{\pi}{2} - \theta\right)$, $\cos \theta \equiv \sin\left(\frac{\pi}{2} - \theta\right)$, $\tan \theta \equiv \cot\left(\frac{\pi}{2} - \theta\right)$, $\cot \theta \equiv \tan\left(\frac{\pi}{2} - \theta\right)$, $\sec \theta \equiv \csc\left(\frac{\pi}{2} - \theta\right)$, $\csc \theta \equiv \sec\left(\frac{\pi}{2} - \theta\right)$ **23.** $-\sin \theta$
25. $-\cos \theta$ **27.** $\cos \theta$ **29.** $-\cos \theta$ **31.** 0.92388
33. 0.92388 **35.** 0.38268 **37-39.** Answers may vary.

Section 15-6 TRY THIS

1. 2 **2.** π **3.** $A = 3$, period $= \pi$

Exercise Set 15-6

1. $A = \frac{1}{2}$ **3.** $A = 3$ **5.** $A = \frac{1}{3}$ **7.** $A = 4$
9. $A = 2$ **11.** $\frac{2\pi}{3}$ **13.** 4π **15.** 6π **17.** π
19. $A = 2$, period $= \pi$ **21.** $A = \frac{1}{2}$, period $= \pi$
23. $A = 2$, period $= 4\pi$ **25.** $A = \frac{1}{2}$, period $= \pi$
27. $A = \frac{1}{2}$, period $= \pi$ **31.** $A = 2$, period $= \pi$

Section 15−7 TRY THIS

1. $\cos x + 1$ 2. $\sin \theta$ 3. $\cos x (\csc x - 1)$
4. $\cot x = -4$ or $\cot x = 3$

Exercise Set 15−7

1. $\sin^2 x - \cos^2 x$ 3. $\sin x - \sec x$ 5. $\sin \theta + \cos \theta$
7. $\cot x - \tan x$ 9. $1 - 2 \sin y \cos y$ 11. $\sec^2 \theta +$
$2 \tan \theta$ 13. $\cos x (\sin x + \cos x)$
15. $(\sin y - \cos y)(\sin y + \cos y)$ 17. $\tan x + \sin x$
19. $\sin^2 \theta - \cos^2 \theta$ 21. $3(\cot y + 1)^2$
23. $(\csc^2 \theta + 5)(\cot^2 \theta)$ 25. $\tan x$ 27. $\frac{2}{9} \cos \theta \cot \theta$
29. $\cos x - 1$ 31. $\cos x + 1$ 33. $\tan x = -7$ or
$\tan x = 3$ 35. $\sin \theta = \frac{3}{4}$ or $\sin \theta = -\frac{1}{2}$
37. $\cot x = -10$ or $\cot x = 1$ 39. $\sin \theta = 3$ or
$\sin \theta = -2$ 41. $\tan \theta = 3 \pm \sqrt{13}$

Chapter 16

Section 16−1 TRY THIS

1. $\frac{1}{2}$ 2. $\frac{\sqrt{2} - \sqrt{6}}{4}$ 3. $\frac{\sqrt{6} - \sqrt{2}}{4}$ 4. $\frac{\sqrt{2} + \sqrt{6}}{4}$
5. $-2 - \sqrt{3}$

Exercise Set 16−1

1. $\cos A \cos B + \sin A \sin B$ 3. $\frac{\sqrt{6} - \sqrt{2}}{4}$
5. $\frac{\sqrt{2} - \sqrt{6}}{4}$ 7. $\frac{\sqrt{2} - \sqrt{6}}{4}$ 9. $\frac{-\sqrt{2} - \sqrt{6}}{4}$
11. $-\frac{\sqrt{2}}{2}$ 13. $\sin P \cos Q + \cos P \sin Q$
15. $\frac{\tan P - \tan Q}{1 + \tan P \tan Q}$ 17. $\frac{\sqrt{2} + \sqrt{6}}{4}$ 19. $2 + \sqrt{3}$
21. $\sin (P + Q)$ 23. $\frac{\sqrt{6} - \sqrt{2}}{4}$ 25. $\frac{\sqrt{2}}{2}$
27. $2 + \sqrt{3}$ 29. $\cos \pi = -1$ 31. $\cos (A - B)$
33. $2 \cos \alpha \cos \beta$ 35. $\tan (A - B)$ 37. $\tan 52° =$
1.280 39. $2 \sin \alpha \cos \beta$ 41. $-\frac{\sqrt{3}}{2}$
43. $2 \sin \theta \cos \theta$ 45. $\frac{\cot \alpha \cot \beta - 1}{\cot \beta + \cot \alpha}$
47. $\sin \frac{\pi}{2} \cos x - \cos \frac{\pi}{2} \sin x = 1 \cdot \cos x - 0 \cdot \sin x =$
$\cos x$ 49. $\cos \frac{\pi}{2} \cos x + \sin \frac{\pi}{2} \sin x = 0 + \sin x =$
$\sin x$ 53. 0.8448 55. $\sin (\sin x) \cos (\sin y) +$
$\cos (\sin x) \sin (\sin y)$ 57. $\sin x \cos y \cos z +$
$\cos x \sin y \cos z + \cos x \cos y \sin z - \sin x \sin y \cos z$

Section 16−2 TRY THIS

1. $\frac{24}{25}$ 2. $\sin 2\theta = \frac{120}{169}$, $\cos 2\theta = -\frac{119}{169}$, $\tan 2\theta =$
$-\frac{120}{119}$, second quadrant   3. $\cos^3 \theta - 3 \sin^2 \theta \cos \theta$,
$\cos \theta - 4 \sin^2 \theta \cos \theta$ or $2 \cos^3 \theta - \cos \theta -$

$2 \sin^2 \theta \cos \theta$ 4. $\frac{\sqrt{2 - \sqrt{3}}}{2}$ 5. 1

Exercise Set 16−2

1. $\frac{24}{25}, -\frac{7}{25}, -\frac{24}{7},$ II   3. $\frac{24}{25}, \frac{7}{25}, \frac{24}{7},$ I   5. $\frac{24}{25}, -\frac{7}{25},$
$-\frac{24}{7},$ II   7. $\frac{\sqrt{2 + \sqrt{3}}}{2}$ 9. $2 + \sqrt{3}$ 11. $\frac{\sqrt{2 + \sqrt{2}}}{2}$
13. $\frac{\sqrt{2 + \sqrt{2}}}{2}$ 15. $\frac{\sqrt{2 + \sqrt{3}}}{2}$ 17. $8 \sin \theta \cos^3 \theta -$
$4 \sin \theta \cos \theta$, or $4 \sin \theta \cos^3 \theta - 4 \sin^3 \theta \cos \theta$, or
$4 \sin \theta \cos \theta - 8 \sin^3 \theta \cos \theta$
19. $\frac{1}{8}(3 - 4 \cos 2\theta + \cos 4\theta)$ 21. Use Theorem
16−1 using θ for both α and β.   23. $\cos x$
25. $\sin 4x$ 27. 1   29. 1   31. 8   33. $\sin 2x$

Section 16−4 TRY THIS

1. Not a function
2. $\left\{ x \mid x = \frac{\pi}{6} + 2k\pi \text{ or } x = \frac{5\pi}{6} + 2k\pi, k \text{ an integer} \right\}$
3. $\frac{\pi}{3}$ 4. $\frac{3\pi}{4}$ 5. $\frac{3\pi}{4}$ 6. $-\frac{\pi}{4}$

Exercise Set 16−4

1. $\frac{\pi}{4} + 2k\pi, \frac{3\pi}{4} + 2k\pi$ 3. $\frac{\pi}{4} + 2k\pi, \frac{7\pi}{4} + 2k\pi$
5. $\frac{\pi}{4} + k\pi$ 7. $\frac{5\pi}{4} + 2k\pi, \frac{7\pi}{4} + 2k\pi$ 9. $\frac{3\pi}{4} + 2k\pi,$
$\frac{5\pi}{4} + 2k\pi$ 11. $\frac{\pi}{4} + k\pi$ 13. $\frac{\pi}{4} + k\pi$ 15. $\frac{5\pi}{6} + k\pi$
17. $\frac{5\pi}{6}$ 19. $\frac{\pi}{3}$ 21. $-\frac{\pi}{3}$ 23. $-\frac{\pi}{6}$ 25. $\frac{2\pi}{3}$
27. $74° + k360°, 106° + k360°$ 29. $61° + k360°,$
$199° + k360°$ 31. $22°6' + k360°, 337°54' + k360°$
33. $74°8' + k360°, 285°52' + k360°$ 35. $47°30' +$
$k180°$ 37. $64°30' + k180°$ 39. $46° + k360°,$
$314° + k360°$ 41. $\frac{3\pi}{4} + k\pi$ 43. $2k\pi$ 45. $\frac{\pi}{2} +$
$2k\pi$ 51. $13°30'$ 53. $-39°30'$ 55. $152°50'$
57. $-22°10'$ 59. $169°30'$

Section 16−5 TRY THIS

1. $\frac{\pi}{6}, \frac{5\pi}{6}, \frac{7\pi}{6}, \frac{11\pi}{6}$ plus $2k\pi$ 2. $\frac{\pi}{6}, \frac{5\pi}{6}, \frac{7\pi}{6}, \frac{11\pi}{6}$
3. $75°31', 284°29', 120°, 240°$ 4. $\frac{\pi}{2}, \frac{3\pi}{2}, \frac{2\pi}{3}, \frac{4\pi}{3}$

Exercise Set 16−5

1. $\frac{4\pi}{3}, \frac{5\pi}{3}$ 3. $123°41', 303°41'$ 5. $\frac{\pi}{6}, \frac{5\pi}{6}, \frac{7\pi}{6}, \frac{11\pi}{6}$
7. $\frac{\pi}{6}, \frac{5\pi}{6}, \frac{3\pi}{2}$ 9. 0   11. $\frac{\pi}{6}, \frac{5\pi}{6}$ 13. $109°28', 120°,$
$240°, 250°32'$ 15. $0, \frac{\pi}{2}, \pi, \frac{3\pi}{2}$ 17. $0, \pi$ 19. $\frac{3\pi}{4},$
$\frac{7\pi}{4}$ 21. $\frac{\pi}{4}, \frac{\pi}{2}, \frac{3\pi}{4}, \frac{5\pi}{4}, \frac{3\pi}{2}, \frac{7\pi}{4}$ 23. $0, \frac{\pi}{2}, \pi, \frac{3\pi}{2}$
25. 0   27. $\frac{\pi}{6}, \frac{5\pi}{6}, \pi$ 29. $\frac{\pi}{6}, \frac{5\pi}{6}, \frac{7\pi}{6}, \frac{11\pi}{6}$

31. $63°26', 243°26', 101°19', 281°19'$ **33.** $\frac{2\pi}{3}, \frac{4\pi}{3}$
35. $\frac{\pi}{12}, \frac{5\pi}{12}$ **37.** $\frac{\pi}{6}, \frac{3\pi}{2}$ **39.** $60°, 120°, 240°, 300°$
41. $60°, 240°$ **43.** $30°$

Section 16−6 TRY THIS

1. $a = 38.43, b = 54.89$ **2.** $m\angle A = 56°19',$
$m\angle B = 33°41', c = 7.211$ **3.** 11.9 m **4.** 26 km

Exercise Set 16−6

1. $m\angle B = 53°50', b = 37.2, c = 46.1$ **3.** $m\angle A = 77°20', a = 436.5, c = 447.4$ **5.** $m\angle B = 72°40',$
$a = 4.2, c = 14.2$ **7.** $m\angle A = 66°50', b = 0.0148,$
$c = 0.0375$ **9.** $m\angle A = 42°30', a = 35.6, b = 32.6$
11. $m\angle A = 7°40', a = 0.131, b = 0.973$ **13.** $c = 21.6, m\angle A = 33°40', m\angle B = 56°20'$ **15.** $b = 12.0,$
$m\angle A = 53°10', m\angle B = 36°50'$ **17.** $a = 3.57,$
$m\angle A = 63°20', m\angle B = 26°40'$ **19.** 15.9 m
21. $1°40'$ **23.** $32°50'$ **25.** 6203 m **27.** 109 km
29. 23.9 km **31.** 7.92 km **33.** 3.45 km
35. 121.1 ft **39.** $y = 5.2180$

Section 16−7 TRY THIS

1. $m\angle B = 87°, b = 9.94, c = 7.84$ **2.** $m\angle A = 42°50', m\angle C = 140°10', c = 35.6$ or $m\angle A = 137°10',$
$m\angle C = 9°50', c = 6.27$ **3.** 8.452

Exercise Set 16−7

1. $m\angle C = 50°, a = 18.4, c = 16.3$ **3.** $m\angle C = 96°,$
$b = 15.2, c = 20.3$ **5.** $m\angle C = 17°, a = 26.3, c = 10.5$ **7.** $m\angle A = 121°, a = 33.4, c = 14.0$
9. $m\angle B = 68°50', a = 32.3, b = 32.3$ **11.** $m\angle A = 12°20', m\angle C = 17°40', c = 4.25$ **13.** $m\angle A = 20°20', m\angle A = 99°40', b = 34.1$ **15.** $m\angle B = 56°20', m\angle C = 87°40', c = 40.8$ or $m\angle B = 123°40',$
$m\angle C = 20°20', c = 14.2$ **17.** $m\angle C = 44°40',$
$m\angle B = 19°, b = 6.25$ **19.** $m\angle B = 44°20', m\angle A = 74°30', a = 33.3$ **21.** 30 **23.** 76.3 m **25.** 50.8 ft
27. 1467 km **29.** 10.6 km

Section 16−8 TRY THIS

1. $a = 40.5, m\angle B = 22°10', m\angle C = 35°50'$
2. $m\angle A = 108°10', m\angle B = 22°20', m\angle C = 49°30'$

Exercise Set 16−8

1. $c = 12.0, m\angle A = 20°40', m\angle B = 24°20'$ **3.** $a = 14.9, m\angle B = 23°40', m\angle C = 126°20'$ **5.** $a = 24.8,$
$m\angle B = 20°40', m\angle C = 26°20'$ **7.** $b = 74.8,$
$m\angle A = 95°30', m\angle C = 11°50'$ **9.** $m\angle A = 29°,$
$m\angle B = 46°30', m\angle C = 104°30'$ **11.** $m\angle A = 34°50', m\angle B = 58°50', m\angle C = 86°20'$ **13.** $m\angle A = 36°10', m\angle B = 43°30', m\angle C = 100°20'$
15. $m\angle A = 73°40', m\angle B = 51°50', m\angle C = 54°30'$
17. $m\angle A = 25°40', m\angle B = 126°, m\angle C = 28°20'$

19. 3.7 nautical miles **21.** 59.4 ft **23.** $68°, 68°,$
$44°$ **25.** 42.6 ft **27a.** 15.73 ft **27b.** 118.2 ft²
29. 3424 yd² **31.** Area $= \frac{1}{2}a^2 \sin \theta$; $\theta = 90°$

Section 16−9 TRY THIS

1. 14.9 kg, $19°40'$ **2.** 171 km/hr, $75°$

Exercise Set 16−9

1. $57, 38°$ **3.** $18.4, 37°$ **5.** $20.9, 58°$ **7.** $68.3,$
$18°$ **9.** 13 kg, $67°$ **11.** 655 kg, $21°$
13. 21.6 ft/sec, $34°$ **15.** 726 lb, $47°$ **17.** 174
nautical mi, $516°E$ **19.** An angle of $11°$ upstream

Section 16−10 TRY THIS

1. E, $50\sqrt{2}$; S, $50\sqrt{2}$ **2.** $(12, -8)$ **3.** $(12, 4)$
4. $(1, 7)$ **5.** $(7, -3)$ **6.** $(-23, 21)$ **7.** 19.03

Exercise Set 16−10

1. h, 92.3; v, 118 **3.** S, 192 km/hr; W, 161 km/hr
5. $(5, 16)$ **7.** $(4.8, 13.7)$ **9.** $(-662, -426)$
11. $(19, 36)$ **13.** $(14, 8)$ **15.** 18 **17.** 17.89
19. 35.78 **21.** 28.84 **23.** 0

Section 16−11 TRY THIS

1. $1 - i$ **2.** $\sqrt{2}(\cos 315° + i \sin 315°)$ **3.** 20 cis 55°
4. 2 cis $\frac{\pi}{4}$ **5.** 32 cis 270° **6.** 16 cis 120°
7. $\sqrt{2}$ cis 45° and $\sqrt{2}$ cis 225° or $1 + i$ and $1 - i$

Exercise Set 16−11

1. $\frac{3\sqrt{3}}{2} + \frac{3}{2}i$ **3.** $-2\sqrt{2} + 2i\sqrt{2}$ **5.** $-10i$
7. $\frac{5\sqrt{2}}{2} - \frac{5\sqrt{2}}{2}i$ **9.** $2 + 2i$ **11.** $2\sqrt{3} + 2i$
13. $-2 - 2i$ **15.** $\sqrt{2}$ cis $\frac{7\pi}{4}$ or $\sqrt{2}$ cis 315°
17. 2 cis $\frac{\pi}{6}$ or 2 cis 30° **19.** 20 cis $\frac{11\pi}{6}$ or 20 cis 330°
21. 2 cis $\frac{\pi}{2}$ or 2 cis 90° **23.** 5 cis π or 5 cis 180°
25. 4 cis $\frac{3\pi}{2}$ or 4 cis 270° **27.** 4 cis 0 **29.** 40 cis 0
31. 8 cis $\frac{2\pi}{3}$ **33.** cis $\frac{\pi}{2}$ **35.** $\frac{\sqrt{2}}{2}$ cis $\frac{7\pi}{12}$ **37.** 2 cis $\frac{3\pi}{2}$
39. 8 cis π or 8 cis 180° **41.** 64 cis π or 64 cis 180°
43. 8 cis $\frac{3\pi}{2}$ or 8 cis 270° **45.** $-8 - 8i\sqrt{3}$
47. $-8 - 8i\sqrt{3}$ **49.** i **51.** 1 **53.** $\sqrt{2}$ cis 60° and
$\sqrt{2}$ cis 240° or $\sqrt{2}$ cis $\frac{\pi}{3}$ and $\sqrt{2}$ cis $\frac{4\pi}{3}$ **55.** cis 30°,
cis 150°, and cis 270° or cis $\frac{\pi}{6}$, cis $\frac{5\pi}{6}$, and cis $\frac{3\pi}{2}$
57. 2 cis 0°, 2 cis 90°, 2 cis 180°, and 2 cis 270° or
2 cis 0, 2 cis $\frac{\pi}{2}$, 2 cis π, and 2 cis $\frac{3\pi}{2}$ **61.** cis 90°,
cis 180°, cis 270°, cis 0° or $\pm 1, \pm i$ **65.** $\sqrt[3]{456.86}$,
$\sqrt[3]{456.86}$ cis 120°, $\sqrt[3]{456.86}$ cis 240°

INDEX

Absolute value, 8–9, 84
  of a complex number,
    333–334
Addition
  of fractional expressions, 255
  of matrices, 601
  of polynomials, 208–209
  principle for equations, 55
  principle for inequalities, 74
  of radical terms, 304
  of real numbers, rules for, 11
Addition method
  for solving systems of linear
    equations, 160
  for solving systems of second
    degree equations, 455
Additive inverse, 5, 7, 25
  of an expression, 26
  of a matrix, 603
  of a polynomial, 210
Additive property of zero, 5, 14
Amplitude, 647–649
Angle(s)
  radian measure for, 638
  reference, 634
Antilogarithm, 525, 528, 533
Applications. See also Formulas,
    Solving problems.
  aerial navigation, 695
  anthropology, 150
  area of a cube, 375
  cloud height, 693
  cricket chirps and tempera-
    ture, 146
  compound interest, 512, 537
  consumer price index, 548
  distance, 272–273
  earned run average, 272
  earthquake magnitude, 539
  force, 716
  gravity, 366
  horizon, 320
  investment, 25, 30
  life expectancy, 148
  loudness of sound, 538
  maximizing area, 414
  maximizing yield, 407
  mixture, 165
  motion, 166, 272–273
  Ohm's law, 280
  pendulum, 303
  percent, 66, 68
  population growth, 543

predicting earnings, 413
radioactive decay, 544
road grade, 135
sales commission, 150
snow melt, 279
speed of a skidding car,
  300, 375
straight line depreciation, 566
surveying, 708
unit price, 284
volume, 284
volume of a gas, 375
wavelength, 284
wind chill temperature, 300
wind friction, 147
work, 271–272
Arccosine (arccos), 686–687
Arccotangent (arccot), 686–687
Arcsine (arcsin), 686–687
Arctangent (arctan), 686–687
Arithmetic sequence, 559
Arithmetic series, 562
Associative law(s), 5, 13, 17
Asymptotes, 437, 440
Axioms, 5, 44. See also
    Properties.
Axis(es)
  conjugate, 437
  imaginary, 333
  major and minor, 429
  transverse, 437

Base, 31
Binomial(s), 207–215
Binomial coefficient, 585
Binomial expansion, 590
Binomial theorem, 589

Calculator, Using a
  algebraic logic, 251
  evaluating polynomials, 495
  power and log keys, 508
  power and memory keys, 139
  solving equations, 69
  square root key, 296
  what's stored in the mem-
    ory, 453
Careers
  aerial surveying, 666
  astronomy, 496
  clothing manufacturing, 98
  communications, 415

engineering, 596
forestry, 49
oceanography, 339
railroad traffic control, 240
stress analysis, 618
Cartesian coordinate system, 107
Cartesian products, 103
Circle(s), 424–428
Circular functions, 638, 653
Closure, 48
Coefficient(s), 465, 476–477
Cofunctions, 639, 656
  identities, 639, 656–657, 676
  relations, 640
Combinations, 576, 585
Common difference, 559
Common logarithms, 524
Common ratio, 566
Commutative law(s), 5, 13, 17
Completing the square, 226,
    404, 427, 445
  factoring by, 227
Complex fractional expres-
    sions, 260
Complex number(s), 322
  absolute value of, 333–334
  addition of, 322
  conjugate of, 326, 335
  divison of, 327
  equality for, 325
  graphic representation of, 333
  imaginary part, 322
  imaginary unit, 322
  multiplication of, 325–326
  powers of, 324
  real part, 322
  roots of, 119
  as solutions of equations, 329
  solving equations in, 330
  square root of, 331
  subtraction of, 322–323
Composition of functions,
    121, 676
Computer activities, 730–741
Conditional, 90
Conic sections, 424
  identifying, 480
Conjugate(s), 326
  axis, 437
  complex, 476
  of polynomials, 335, 338
  of powers, 337
  of a product, 336

Conjunction, 80
  of sentences, 157
  of two inequalities, 194
Constants, 7, 70
Constraints, 199
Consumer applications
  buying a new car, 151
  filing income tax returns, 722
  financing a home, 454
  finding a job, 549
  understanding life insur-
    ance, 285
Converses, 91
Coordinates, 85, 107
Cosecant function, 627
  complement of, 639
Cosine function, 625
  graph of, 647
  identity, 671–672
  period of, 648
Cotangent function, 627
  complement of, 639
Cramer's rule, 187–188, 190
Cube(s)
  sums or differences of, 229
Cube roots, 293

Decimal(s), 2, 3
De Moivre's theorem, 718
Dense set of numbers, 6
Descarte's rule of signs, 486
Determinant(s), 187, 189
Directrix of a parabola, 443
Discriminant, 357
Disjunctions, 82
Distance between two
    points, 421
Division, 17–18
  of complex numbers, 327
  definition of, 18
  with exponential notation, 36
  of fractional expressions,
    248–249
  of polynomials, 263–264
  of real numbers, rules for, 18
  in scientific notation, 42
  synthetic, 469
  theorem, 19, 46
  by zero, 20
Domain
  of a function, 114, 118
  of a relation, 104, 111
Double-angle identities, 677

Ellipse, 429–431
Empty set, 80

Equality, 44
  for complex numbers, 325
Equation(s), 55
  with absolute value, 85–86
  addition principle for, 55
  for circles, 424–426
  complex numbers as solutions
    of, 329
  dependent, 188
  for ellipses, 429, 431
  equivalent, 94
  exponential, 535
  first-degree, 122–127
  fractional, 267
  for hyperbolas, 436, 438
  of the inverse relation, 503
  linear, 122. See also Linear
    equations.
  logarithmic, 536
  methods of solving, 61
  multiplication principle for, 55
  for parabolas, 443, 445
  of parallel lines, 142
  of perpendicular lines,
    142–144
  point-slope, 132
  polynomial, 493
  quadratic, 347–349, 362
  radical, 317
  slope intercept, 137
  solving, 55, 60, 93, 234,
    267, 330
  trigonometric, 664, 689
  of variation, 370
Equivalent statements, 94
Even functions, 385
Events, 576
Exponent(s), 31–32
  multiplying, 37
  negative rational, 312
  properties of, 35
  rational, 310
Exponential equations, 515, 535
Exponential functions, 509, 525
  base e, 524
  graphs of, 510–511
  inverses of, 516
Exponential notation, 31
Expressions
  algebraic, 7
  complex fractional, 260
  equivalent, 13
  evaluating, 7
  factoring, 218
  fractional, 245
  and number properties, 13, 20

powers of, 37
radical, 292
trigonometric, 663
values of, 7

Factor, largest common, 24
Factorial notation, 578
Factoring, 24, 218
  by completing the square, 227
  difference of squares, 218, 225
  general strategy, 232
  by grouping, 225
  polynomials, 218
  polynomial equations, 234
  sum or difference of two
    cubes, 229
  trinomials, 222–223
  trinomial squares, 219
Field, 5
Focus
  of an ellipse, 429
  of a hyperbola, 436
  of a parabola, 443
Formula(s), 70, 365
  area of a triangle, 71
  compound interest, 512
  distance, 421
  gravity, 366
  interest, 72
  midpoint, 422
  Ohm's law, 280
  solving, 70, 276
Fractional equation(s), 267
Fractional expressions
  adding, 255
  complex, 260
  dividing, 248–249
  multiplying, 245
  simplifying, 246, 260–261
  subtracting, 255
Function(s), 114–115
  absolute value, 118
  composition of, 121, 676
  constant, 117
  domain of, 114, 118
  even, 385
  exponential, 509, 525
  graphs of, 114
  greatest integer, 119
  inverse, 505
  linear, 146
  logarithmic, 512
  notation for, 115
  add, 386
  periodic, 647–648
  polynomial, 212

quadratic, 398
range of, 114
reciprocal, 627
trigonometric, 625
values, 117, 401, 470
Fundamental counting principle, 576
Fundamental theorem of algebra, 330, 475

Geometric means, 567
Geometric sequence, 566
Geometric series, 568–569, 572
Graph(s)
    of complex numbers, 333
    of cosine function, 647
    of ellipses, 429
    of equations, 108–109
    of functions, 114–121
    of hyperbolas, 436–441
    of inequalities in one variable, 73–88
    of inequalities in two variables, 193
    of linear equations, 122
    of ordered pairs, 107
    of parabolas, 444–447
    of parallel lines, 140
    of points on a number line, 84
    of quadratic functions, 398–401
    of secant function, 650
    of sine function, 646
    of systems of linear equations, 158
    of tangent function, 649
    using, to solve second degree equations, 454

Half angle identities, 679–680
Half planes, 193
Hyperbola, 436
Hypothesis, 90

Identity(ies), 59, 270
    cofunction, 656–657, 676
    cosine, 672
    double angle, 677
    half angle, 679–680
    proving, 682
    Pythagorean, 654–655
    sum and difference, 671, 673–674
Identity matrix, 602
If and only if, 62
IF-THEN statements, 90
Images, 381, 383

Imaginary axis, 333
Imaginary numbers, 321–324
Independent events, 576
Inequality(ies), 73
    with absolute value, 85–86
    addition principle for, 74
    compound, 80
    and disjunctions, 82
    equivalent, 94
    graphs of, 73–88
    linear, 73–74
    multiplication principle for, 75
    solving, 73, 78, 93
    symbols, 73
    systems of, 195
    in two variables, 193
Integer(s), 1
Intercept(s), 123, 125, 126, 137
Interpolation, 531, 642
Intersection, 80
Inverse(s)
    additive, 5, 7
    additive, of a matrix, 603
    of functions, 505
    of an inverse, 7
    multiplicative, 16
    multiplicative, of a matrix, 612–613
    operations, 12
    of products, 47
    of relations, 503
    of a sum, 25
    and symmetry, 504
    of trigonometric functions, 685
Inverse of a sum property, 26
Inverse variation, 280
Irrational numbers, 3

Law of cosines, 704
Law of sines, 698
Least common multiple (LCM), 252
Like terms, 24, 208, 304
Line of reflection, 831
Linear combination, 160
Linear equation(s)
    consistent, 179
    dependent, 180–181
    graphs of, 122–123, 140
    inconsistent, 179
    independent, 180–181
    of parallel lines, 142
    of perpendicular lines, 142–144
    point slope, 132

procedure for graphing, 127
    slope-intercept, 137
    standard form of, 122
    systems of, 159
    triangularization algorithm for solving, 172
    using, to solve problems, 237
Linear function(s), 146
Linear inequality, 73–74
Logarithm(s), 524
    changing bases, 545
    common, 524
    natural, 542
Logarithmic equation(s), 515, 536
    simplifying, 516
    solving, 515–516, 536
    writing, in exponential form, 515–516
    using, to solve problems, 537–539
Logarithmic function(s), 512
    graphs of, 513
    inverse of, 516
    properties of, 518, 522
Lower bounds, 489

Mantissa, 527
Matrix (matrices), 184
    addition of, 601
    additive identity, 602
    additive inverse of, 603
    column, 606
    determinants of, 187
    dimensions of, 601
    inverses of, 612–613
    multiplication of, 605
    multiplicative identity, 612
    row, 606
    row equivalent, 184
    square, properties of, 609
    subtraction of, 602–603
    using, to solve systems of linear equations, 184, 615
    zero, 602
Maximum function value, 401
Midpoint formula, 422
Minimum function value, 401
Monomial(s), 207
Multiplication
    of complex numbers, 325
    with exponential notation, 35
    of exponents, 37
    of fractional expressions, 245
    of matrices, 605
    of polynomials, 213

principle for equations, 55
principle for inequalities, 75
in scientific notation, 42
Multiplicative identity, 16
Multiplicative property(ies), 5, 16, 25, 46

Natural logarithms, 542
Natural numbers, 1
Negative exponents, 32, 312
Numbers
  complex, 322
  consecutive, 67
  imaginary, 321
  irrational, 3
  natural, 1
  rational, 2
  real, 1
  whole, 1
Number line, 4
  distance on, 84

Odd function, 386
Opposites, 7
Order
  on a number line, 4
  of operations, 13, 17, 28, 39
Ordered pair(s), 103, 157
Ordered triple, 170
Ordinate, 107
Origin, 107
Outcome(s), 576
  equally likely, 593

Parabola, 398–447
Period, 647–648
  change of, 660–661
Permutations, 577–582
Points
  coordinates of, 107
  ordered pairs, 103, 157
  symmetric, 381–382
Point-slope equation of a
  line, 132
Polar notation, 714
Polynomial(s), 207–208
  addition of, 208–209
  additive inverse of, 210
  complex roots of, 476
  conjugates of, 335, 338
  degree of, 207
  dividing by a monomial, 263
  dividing by a binomial,
    264–265
  dividing by a polynomial, 466
  as factors, 466
  factors of, 472

function values for, 470
graphing, 492
multiplication of, 213
roots of, 465, 475
solving equations, 493
specified roots of, 476
subtraction of, 210
synthetic division, 469
zero of, 465
Polynomial function(s), 212, 465
  graphs of, 491
Power(s), 37
Principal square root, 291
Principal values, 686–687
Principle of powers, 317
Probability, 593
Problem solving. See Solving
  problems.
Proof(s), 45, 90, 133
Property(ies)
  of absolute value, 84
  additive inverse, 5
  additive property of zero,
    5, 14
  associative laws, 5, 13
  commutative laws, 5, 13
  of determinants, 187–189
  distributive law, 5
  of exponents, 35
  inverse of a sum, 26
  of logarithmic functions,
    518–522
  of -1, 25
  multiplicative, of one, 5, 16
  multiplicative, of zero, 16
  of reciprocals, 5
  reflexive, 44
  of square matrices, 609
  symmetric, 44
  transitive, 44
Proportion(s), 279, 281
Pythagorean identities,
  654 – 655
Pythagorean theorem, 625

Quadrant, 107
Quadratic equations, 347–349
  applications of, 349
  completing the square, 404
  discriminant of, 357
  quadratic formula, 353
  standard form of, 347, 404
  solutions of, 357
  sum and product solu-
    tions, 358
  writing, from solutions, 359

Quadratic form of equa-
  tions, 362
Quadratic formula, 353
Quadratic function(s), 398–401
  applications of, 410
Quadratic variation, 370
Quotient(s)
  power of, 38
  roots of, 301
Quotient identities, 654

Radian, 638
Radical equations, 317–318
Radical expressions, 291–292
  adding, 304
  dividing, 302
  factoring, 297–298
  multiplying, 297–298, 305
  simplifying, 297–298, 302,
    313, 315
  subtracting, 304
Radical sign, 292
Radicand, 292
Range
  of a function, 114, 118
  of a relation, 104, 111
Rational coefficients, 476–477
Rational exponents, 310–311
  negative, 312
Rational expressions. See
  Fractional expressions.
Rational number(s), 2
  decimal notation for, 2–3
  as exponents, 310
  fractional notation for, 2
Rational root theorem, 481
Rationalizing denominators, 305
Real coefficients, 476–477
Real numbers, 1
  axioms for, 5
  division of, 17
  rules for addition of, 11
  rules for multiplication of, 16
  subsets of, 1
  subtraction of, 12
Reciprocals
  and complex numbers, 327
  definition of, 18
  and exponential notation, 33
  multiplication by, 19
  property of, 5
Reciprocal functions, 627
Reference angles, 634, 641
Reflexive property of
  equality, 44

Relation(s), 104
  domain of, 104, 111
  graphs of, 107
  inverse of, 503
  range of, 104, 111
  symmetry of, 383
Replacement set, 55
Resultant of vectors, 708
Review(s)
  Chapter, 50, 99, 152, 202,
    241, 286, 340, 377, 416,
    461, 497, 550, 597, 619,
    667, 723
  Cumulative, 204, 342, 498,
    620, 726,
Roots, 291
  complex, 476
  cube, 293
  even, 294
  finding by factoring, 475
  of multiplicity, 475
  negative, 487
  odd, 294
  of quotients, 301
  rational, 481
  positive real, 486
  square, 291
  upper, lower bounds on, 488
Rotations, 631

Sample space, 593
Scalar, 714
Scientific notation, 41
Secant function, 627
  complement of, 639
  graph of, 650
Sequences, 555–566
Series, 556
  arithmetic, 562
  convergent, 572
  geometric, 568
  infinite, 572
Set(s)
  dense, 6
  empty, 80
  replacement, 55
  solution, 55, 62, 73
Shrinking, 393
Sigma notation, 557
Similar terms, 24
Simultaneous equations, 164
Sine function, 625
  complement of, 639
  graph of, 646
  reciprocal of, 627
  period of, 648

Slope-intercept equation of a
  line, 137
Slope of a line, 129–132
Solution(s), 55
  complex numbers as, 329
  of conjunctions, 157
  of systems of linear equations,
    160, 164
  of systems of equations in
    three variables, 170–172
Solution set(s), 55, 62, 73
  intersection of, 157
Solving problems
  drawing a picture, 64
  direct variation, 279
  with equations of varia-
    tion, 372
  with inequalities, 78
  using matrices, 184, 615
  maximum and minimum, 405
  steps for, 64
  with quadratic equations, 350
  with quadratic functions, 411
  with sequences and series,
    565, 568, 570–571, 578
  with three equations, 176
  by translating to equa-
    tions, 237
Square matrix, 609
Square root(s), 291
  approximating, 299
  of complex numbers, 331
Squares of binomials, 214
Standard form
  for the equation of a
    circle, 427
  for the equation of an ellipse,
    429, 431
  for the equation of a
    hyperbola, 436, 438
  of linear equations, 122
  for the equation of a parabola,
    443, 445
  of quadratic equations,
    347, 404
Statements, 45
Stretching(s), 393
Subset, 91, 591
Substitution method, 159,
    450, 456
Subtraction
  of complex numbers, 322–323
  distributive law of
    multiplication over, 23, 47
  of fractional expressions, 255
  of matrices, 602–603

of polynomials, 210
of radical terms, 304
of real numbers, 12
theorem, 12, 46
Symbols
  grouping, 28
  inequality, 73
  radical, 292
  set, 91
Symmetric points, 381–382
Symmetric property of
  equality, 44
Symmetry, 381–384
  of relations and their in-
    verses, 504
Synthetic division, 469
Systems of linear equations, 159
  consistent, 179
  dependent, 180–181
  graphing, 158
  inconsistent, 179
  independent, 180–181
  solving, using linear
    combinations, 160
  solving, using matrices, 184
  of three equations in three
    variables, 170–172
Systems of second degree
  equations, 454
  solving algebraically, 450–1,
    455–6
  solving graphically, 449, 454

Tangent, 428
Tangent function, 625
  complement of, 639
  graph of, 649
  reciprocal of, 627
Term(s)
  of an expression, 27
  like (similar), 24
Tests
  Chapter, 52, 100, 154, 203,
    242, 287, 341, 378, 417,
    462, 498, 552, 598, 619,
    668, 724
Theorem(s), 5, 12, 44–45
  addition principle for
    equations, 55
  distributive law for three
    addends, 45
  division, 19
  division with exponential
    notation, 36
  inverse products, 47

inverse of sums, 25, 46
multiplication with
    exponential notation, 35
multiplication principle for
    equations, 55
multiplicative property of
    minus one, 25, 46
multiplicative property of zero,
    16, 46
power of an expression, 37
power of a power, 37
power of a quotient, 38
products of inverses, 47
properties of absolute
    value, 84
subtraction, 12, 46
zero products, 61, 234
Transformations, 389
Transitive property of
    equality, 44
Translation(s), 389–391
Transverse axis, 437
Triangle(s)
    area of, 701
    solving right, 692, 697
    solving oblique, 698–701,
        701–705
Triangularization algorithm, 172
Trigonometric equations,
    664, 689
    solving, 689–690
    standard form, 690
Trigonometric functions, 625
    amplitude of, 648
    computing with, 663
    cosecant, 627

cosine, 625
cotangent, 627
    graphs of, 646
    inverses of, 685
    period of, 648
    radian measure and, 638
    reciprocal functions, 627
    and rotations, 632
    secant, 627
    simplifying, 663
    sine, 625
    solving equations, 664
    tangent, 625
    values of, 633
Trigonometric identities,
    654–655, 656–657, 672,
    676, 677, 679–680, 682
Trinomial(s), 207
    Factoring, 219, 222–223
Trinomial squares, 219

Union, 82
Unit circle, 428
Unit price, 284
Upper bounds, 488

Value(s)
    of an algebraic expression, 7
    of a function, 115
    maximum function, 401
    minimum function, 401
Variable(s), 7
Variation, 278
    direct, 278, 370
    inverse, 280, 371
    joint, 371
    quadratic, 370–371

Vector(s), 708
    analytic representation of, 714
    components of, 712, 714
    inner product of, 716
    polar notation, 714
    properties of, 714
    resultant of, 708
    standard position of, 714
    sum of, 708, 713
    symbols for, 709
Vertex, 195
    of a parabola, 398

Whole numbers, 1

x-axis, 107
    symmetry with respect to, 382
x-coordinate, 107
x-intercept
    of a line, 126
    of a graph of quadratic
        function, 408

y-axis, 107
    symmetry with respect to, 382
y-coordinate, 107
y-intercept, 125

Zero, 1
    division by, 20
    as exponent, 32
    matrix, 602
    multiplication property of,
        16, 46
Zero matrix, 602
Zero polynomial, 465
Zero products, principle of,
    61, 234